....

The Oxford Spanish Language Programme

The inauguration of the Oxford Spanish Language Programme marked the start of a new age of Spanish dictionaries. The Programme has produced, with unrivalled clarity and authority, the only dictionaries to present the full wealth of Spanish from both sides of the Atlantic and across 24 different Spanish-speaking countries and regions.

● The Bank of Spanish

Drawing on The Bank of Spanish, a vast electronic databank of up-to-date, authentic language in use, these dictionaries provide a more accurate and complete picture of _real_ language than has ever been possible before. The Bank shapes every dictionary entry and translation to meet the needs of today's users, highlighting important constructions, illustrating difficult meanings, and focusing attention on common usage.

● The richest choice of words

In-depth coverage of over 24 different regional varieties of Spanish with special emphasis on modern idioms and colloquial usage are distinctive elements of the Oxford Spanish Language Programme. Words and phrases restricted to particular areas of the Spanish-speaking world are precisely labelled for country or wider region, from Spain to Chile to Mexico, from Central America to the River Plate. In addition, variant pronunciations and the register of words, from formal right through to taboo, are signalled throughout.

● The Spanish Literary Heritage

A wide range of vocabulary and usage found in the literary heritage of the Spanish-speaking world has been analysed and described by the editors of the Programme to assist readers and students of Spanish literature.

● The British National Corpus

Each English entry is shaped by di̶̶̶̶̶̶ ̶̶̶̶̶ ̶̶onal Corpus, an unrivalled l̶̶̶̶̶ ̶̶̶̶̶̶ ̶̶text representing every kind

Total Language Accessibility

Oxford's unparalleled reputation in the field of dictionary publishing is founded on more than 150 years of experience. Each dictionary in the range bears the Oxford hallmarks of integrity and authority. The Oxford Spanish dictionaries are an integral part of this tradition and offer an unequalled range of carefully-designed benefits to ensure maximum language accessibility.

● Rapid access design

Oxford's new quick-access page designs and typography have been specially created to ensure exceptional clarity and accessibility. Entries are written in clear, jargon-free language without confusing abbreviations.

● Unrivalled practical help

Extended treatment of the core vocabulary offers the user step-by-step guidance on how to translate a given word correctly. Unrivalled practical grammatical help has been built into every dictionary within the range. Thousands of examples, drawn from the evidence of the Bank of Spanish, are carefully chosen to illustrate the many different nuances of meaning and context.

● Supplementary Information

All the dictionaries in the Oxford range offer valuable additional help and information, including verb tables, thematic vocabulary boxes, political and cultural information, guides to effective communication (how to write letters, CVs, book holidays, or take minutes), pronunciation guidance, and colour texts for easy access.

● The best range in the world

Oxford provides Spanish dictionaries for all levels of user, from advanced to beginner. In addition, Oxford also publishes a wealth of Spanish reference titles, including guides to Spanish grammar, usage, verbs, correspondence and core vocabulary. Whatever type of dictionary — whether for children, native speakers, university students or learners; on paper or CD-ROM; in English, French, Spanish, German, Italian, Russian, Japanese, Latin, Greek, Arabic, Turkish, Portuguese, Hungarian, Hindi, Gujarati or Chinese — Oxford offers the most trusted range available anywhere in the world today.

The Oxford
Quick Reference
Spanish
Dictionary

SPANISH–ENGLISH
ENGLISH–SPANISH

ESPAÑOL–INGLÉS
INGLÉS–ESPAÑOL

Christine Lea

Spanish in Context
*prepared by Michael Britton
and Carol Styles*

OXFORD UNIVERSITY PRESS
1998

Oxford University Press, Great Clarendon Street, Oxford OX2 6DP

Oxford New York

Athens Auckland Bangkok Bogota Bombay
Buenos Aires Calcutta Cape Town Dar es Salaam
Delhi Florence Hong Kong Istanbul Karachi
Kuala Lumpur Madras Madrid Melbourne
Mexico City Nairobi Paris Singapore
Taipei Tokyo Toronto Warsaw

and associated companies in
Berlin Ibadan

Oxford is a trade mark of Oxford University Press

British Library Cataloguing in Publication Data

Data available

Library of Congress Cataloging-in-Publication Data

Lea, Christine. [Oxford paperback Spanish dictionary]
The Oxford quick reference Spanish dictionary : Spanish–English,
English–Spanish = español–inglés, inglés–español / Christine Lea.
Originally published as: The Oxford paperback Spanish dictionary.
Oxford [England] ; New York : Oxford University Press, 1994.
1. Spanish language—Dictionaries—English. 2. English language–
Dictionaries—Spanish. I. Title.
PC4640.L44 1998 463'.21—dc21 97–40950

ISBN 0–19–860185–9

10 9 8 7 6 5 4 3 2 1

Printed in Great Britain by
Mackays of Chatham plc
Chatham, Kent

Contents · Índice

Preface to *The Oxford Quick Reference Spanish Dictionary*

The Oxford Quick Reference Spanish Dictionary is the latest addition to the Oxford Spanish Dictionary range. It is specifically designed for beginners of Spanish as an affordable, accessible dictionary with valuable additional help provided by the unique *Spanish in Context* supplement in the middle of the book. *Spanish in Context* is designed to help you build your knowledge of grammar and vocabulary, and provides valuable practice in dealing with everyday situations and conversations.

Foreword

This dictionary has been written with speakers of both English and Spanish in mind and contains the most useful words and expressions of the English and Spanish languages of today. Wide coverage of culinary and motoring terms has been included to help the tourist.

Common abbreviations, names of countries, and other useful geographical names are included.

English pronunciation is given by means of the International Phonetic Alphabet. It is shown for all headwords and for those derived words whose pronunciation is not easily deduced from that of a headword. The rules for pronunciation of Spanish are given on page x.

I should like to thank particularly Mary-Carmen Beaven, whose comments have been invaluable. I would also like to acknowledge the help given to me unwittingly by Dr M. Janes and Mrs J. Andrews, whose French and Italian Minidictionaries have served as models for the present work.

C. A. L

Prólogo

Este diccionario de Oxford se escribió tanto para los hispano-hablantes como para los angloparlantes y contiene las palabras y frases más corrientes de ambas lenguas de hoy. Se incluyen muchos términos culinarios y de movilismo que pueden servir al turista.

Las abreviaturas más corrientes, los nombres de países, y otros términos geográficos figuran en este diccionario.

La pronunciación inglesa sigue el Alfabeto Fonético Internacional. Se incluye para cada palabra clave y todas las derivadas cuya pronunciación no es fácil de deducir a partir de la palabra clave. Las reglas de la pronunciación española se encuentran en la página x.

Quisiera reconocer la ayuda de Mary-Carmen Beaven cuyas observaciones me han sido muy valiosas. También quiero agradecerles al Dr. M. Janes y a la Sra. J. Andrews cuyos minidiccionarios del francés y del italiano me han servido de modelo para el presente.

C. A. L

Introduction

The swung dash (~) is used to replace a headword or that part
of a headword preceding the vertical bar (|). In both English
and Spanish only irregular plurals are given. Normally Spanish
nouns and adjectives ending in an unstressed vowel form the
plural by adding s (e.g. *libro, libros*). Nouns and adjectives ending
in a stressed vowel or a consonant add *es* (e.g. *rubí, rubíes; pared,
paredes*). An accent on the final syllable is not required when *es*
is added (e.g. *nación, naciones*). Final *z* becomes *ces* (e.g. *vez, veces*).
Spanish nouns and adjectives ending in *o* form the feminine by
changing the final *o* to *a* (e.g. *hermano, hermana*). Most Spanish
nouns and adjectives ending in anything other than final *o* do
not have a separate feminine form with the exception of those
denoting nationality etc.; these add *a* to the masculine singular
form (e.g. *español, española*). An accent on the final syllable is
then not required (e.g. *inglés, inglesa*). Adjectives ending in *án*,
ón, or *or* behave like those denoting nationality with the following exceptions: *inferior, mayor, mejor, menor, peor, superior*, where
the feminine has the same form as the masculine. Spanish verb
tables will be found in the appendix.

The Spanish alphabet

In Spanish *ch, ll* and *ñ* are considered separate letters and in the
Spanish–English section, therefore, they will be found after *cu,
luî* and *ny* respectively.

Introducción

La tilde (~) se emplea para sustituir a la palabra cabeza de artículo o aquella parte de tal palabra que precede a la barra vertical (|). Tanto en inglés como en español se dan los plurales solamente si son irregulares. Para formar el plural regular en inglés se añade la letra *s* al sustantivo singular, pero se añade *es* cuando se trata de una palabra que termina en *ch, sh, s, ss, us, x, o, z* (p.ej. *sash, sashes*). En el caso de una palabra que termine en *y* precedida por una consonante, la *y* se cambia en *ies* (p.ej. *baby, babies*). Para formar el tiempo pasado y el participio pasado se añade *ed* al infinitivo de los verbos regulares ingleses (p.ej. *last, lasted*). En el caso de los verbos ingleses que terminan en *e* muda se añade sólo la *d* (p.ej. *move, moved*). En el caso de los verbos ingleses que terminan en *y* hay que cambiar la *y* por *ied* (p.ej. *carry, carried*). Los verbos irregulares se encuentran en el diccionario por orden alfabético remitidos al infinitivo, y también en la lista en el apéndice.

Pronunciation of Spanish

Vowels

a between pronunciation of *a* in English *cat* and *arm*

e like *e* in English *bed*

i like *ee* in English *see* but a little shorter

o like *o* in English *hot* but a little longer

u like *oo* in English *too*

y when a vowel, like Spanish **i**

Consonants

b (1) in initial position or after nasal consonant, like English *b*
(2) in other positions, between English *b* and English *v*

c (1) before **e** or **i**, like *th* in English *thin*
(2) in other positions, like *c* in English *cat*

ch like *ch* in English *chip*

d (1) in initial position, after nasal consonants and after **l**,
like English **d**
(2) in other positions, like *th* in English *this*

f like English *f*

g (1) before **e** or **i**, like *ch* in Scottish *loch*
(2) in initial position, like *g* in English *get*
(3) in other positions, like (**2**) but a little softer

h silent in Spanish but see also **ch**

j like *ch* in Scottish *loch*

k like English *k*

l like English *l* but see also **ll**

ll like *lli* in English *million*

m like English *m*

n like English *n*

ñ like *ni* in English *opinion*

p   like English *p*

q   like English *k*

r   rolled or trilled

s   like *s* in English *sit*

t   like English *t*

v   (1) in initial position or after nasal consonant, like English *b*
     (2) in other positions, between English *b* and English *v*

w   like Spanish **b** or **v**

x   like English *x*

y   like English *y*

z   like *th* in English *thin*

Pronunciación Inglesa

Símbolos fonéticos

Vocales y diptongos

i:	see	ɔ:	saw	eɪ	page	ɔɪ	join
ɪ	sit	ʊ	put	əʊ	home	ɪə	near
e	ten	u:	too	aɪ	five	eə	hair
æ	hat	ʌ	cup	aɪə	fire	ʊə	poor
ɑ	arm	ɜ:	fur	aʊ	now		
ɒ	got	ə	ago	aʊə	flour		

Consonantes

p	pen	tʃ	chin	s	so	n	no
b	bad	dʒ	June	z	zoo	ŋ	sing
t	tea	f	fall	ʃ	she	l	leg
d	dip	v	voice	ʒ	measure	r	red
k	cat	θ	thin	h	how	j	yes
g	got	ð	then	m	man	w	wet

Abbreviations / Abreviaturas

adjective	*a*	adjetivo
abbreviation	*abbr /abrev*	abreviatura
administration	*admin*	administración
adverb	*adv*	adverbio
American	*Amer*	americano
anatomy	*anat*	anatomía
architecture	*archit /arquit*	arquitectura
definite article	*art def*	artículo definido
indefinite article	*art indef*	artículo indefinido
astrology	*astr*	astrología
motoring	*auto*	automóvil
auxiliary	*aux*	auxiliar
aviation	*aviat /aviac*	aviación
biology	*biol*	biología
botany	*bot*	botánica
commerce	*com*	comercio
conjunction	*conj*	conjunción
cooking	*culin*	cocina
electricity	*elec*	electricidad
school	*escol*	enseñanza
Spain	*Esp*	España
feminine	*f*	femenino
familiar	*fam*	familiar
figurative	*fig*	figurado
philosophy	*fil*	filosofía
photography	*foto*	fotografía
geography	*geog*	geografía
geology	*geol*	geología
grammar	*gram*	gramática
humorous	*hum*	humorístico
interjection	*int*	interjección
interrogative	*inter*	interrogativo
invariable	*invar*	invariable
legal, law	*jurid*	jurídico
Latin American	*LAm*	latinoamericano
language	*lang*	lengua(je)
masculine	*m*	masculino
mathematics	*mat(h)*	matemáticas
mechanics	*mec*	mecánica
medicine	*med*	medicina

military	mil	militar
music	mus	música
mythology	myth	mitología
noun	n	nombre
nautical	naut	náutica
oneself	o. s.	uno mismo, se
proprietary term	P	marca registrada
pejorative	pej	peyorativo
philosophy	phil	filosofía
photography	photo	fotografía
plural	pl	plural
politics	pol	política
possessive	poss	posesivo
past participle	pp	participio pasado
prefix	pref	prefijo
preposition	prep	preposición
present participle	pres p	participio de presente
pronoun	pron	pronombre
psychology	psych	psicología
past tense	pt	tiempo pasado
railroad	rail	ferrocarril
relative	rel	relativo
religion	relig	religión
school	schol	enseñanza
singular	sing	singular
slang	sl	argot
someone	s. o.	alguien
something	sth	algo
technical	tec	técnico
television	TV	televisión
university	univ	universidad
auxiliary verb	v aux	verbo auxiliar
verb	vb	verbo
intransitive verb	vi	verbo intransitivo
pronominal verb	vpr	verbo pronominal
transitive verb	vt	verbo transitivo
transitive & intransitive verb	vti	verbo transitivo e intransitivo

A

a *prep* in, at; (*dirección*) to; (*tiempo*) at; (*hasta*) to, until; (*fecha*) on; (*más tarde*) later; (*medio*) by; (*precio*) for, at. ~ **5 km** 5 km away. ¿~ **cuántos estamos?** what's the date? ~**l día siguiente** the next day. ~ **la francesa** in the French fashion. ~ **las 2** at 2 o'clock. ~ **los 25 años** (*edad*) at the age of 25; (*después de*) after 25 years. ~ **no ser por** but for. ~ **que** I bet. ~ **28 de febrero** on the 28th of February

ábaco *m* abacus

abad *m* abbot

abadejo *m* (*pez*) cod

abad|esa *f* abbess. ~**ía** *f* abbey

abajo *adv* (down) below; (*dirección*) down(wards); (*en casa*) downstairs. ● *int* down with. **calle** ~ down the street. **el** ~ **firmante** the undersigned. **escaleras** ~ downstairs. **la parte de** ~ the bottom part. **los de** ~ those at the bottom. **más** ~ below.

abalanzarse [10] *vpr* rush towards

abalorio *m* glass bead

abanderado *m* standard-bearer

abandon|ado *adj* abandoned; (*descuidado*) neglected; (*personas*) untidy. ~**ar** *vt* leave ‹*un lugar*›; abandon ‹*personas, cosas*›. ● *vi* give up. ~**arse** *vpr* give in; (*descuidarse*) let o.s. go. ~**o** *m* abandonment; (*estado*) abandon

abani|car [7] *vt* fan. ~**co** *m* fan. ~**queo** *m* fanning

abarata|miento *m* reduction in price. ~**r** *vt* reduce. ~**rse** *vpr* (*precios*) come down

abarca *f* sandal

abarcar [7] *vt* put one's arms around, embrace; (*comprender*) embrace; (*LAm*, *acaparar*) monopolize

abarquillar *vt* warp. ~**se** *vpr* warp

abarrotar *vt* overfill, pack full

abarrotes *mpl* (*LAm*) groceries

abast|ecer [11] *vt* supply. ~**ecimiento** *m* supply; (*acción*) supplying. ~**o** *m* supply. **dar** ~**o a** supply

abati|do *a* depressed. ~**miento** *m* depression. ~**r** *vt* knock down, demolish; (*fig*, *humillar*) humiliate. ~**rse** *vpr* swoop (**sobre** on); (*ponerse abatido*) get depressed

abdica|ción *f* abdication. ~**r** [7] *vt* give up. ● *vi* abdicate

abdom|en *m* abdomen. ~**inal** *a* abdominal

abec|é *m* (*fam*) alphabet, ABC. ~**edario** *m* alphabet

abedul *m* birch (tree)

abej|a *f* bee. ~**arrón** *m* bumble-bee. ~**ón** *m* drone. ~**orro** *m* bumble-bee; (*insecto coleóptero*) cockchafer

aberración *f* aberration

abertura *f* opening

abet|al *m* fir wood. ~**o** *m* fir (tree)

abierto *pp véase* **abrir**. ● *a* open

abigarra|do *a* multi-coloured; (*fig*, *mezclado*) mixed. ~**miento** *m* variegation

abigeato *m* (*Mex*) rustling

abism|al *a* abysmal; (*profundo*) deep. ~**ar** *vt* throw into an abyss; (*fig*, *abatir*) humble. ~**arse** *vpr* be absorbed (**en** in), be lost (**en** in). ~**o** *m* abyss; (*fig*, *diferencia*) world of difference

abizcochado *a* spongy

abjura|ción *f* abjuration. ~**r** *vt* forswear. ● *vi*. ~**r de** forswear

ablanda|miento *m* softening. ~**r** *vt* soften. ~**rse** *vpr* soften

ablución *f* ablution

abnega|ción *f* self-sacrifice. ~**do** *a* self-sacrificing

aboba|do *a* silly. ~**miento** *m* silliness

aboca|do *a* ‹*vino*› medium. ~**r** [7] *vt* pour out

abocetar *vt* sketch

abocinado *a* trumpet-shaped

abochornar *vt* suffocate; *(fig, avergonzar)* embarrass. **~se** *vpr* feel embarrassed; *(plantas)* wilt

abofetear *vt* slap

aboga|cía *f* legal profession. **~do** *m* lawyer; *(notario)* solicitor; *(en el tribunal)* barrister, attorney *(Amer)*. **~r** [12] *vi* plead

abolengo *m* ancestry

aboli|ción *f* abolition. **~cionismo** *m* abolitionism. **~cionista** *m & f* abolitionist. **~r** [24] *vt* abolish

abolsado *a* baggy

abolla|dura *f* dent. **~r** *vt* dent

abomba|do *a* convex; *(Arg, borracho)* drunk. **~r** *vt* make convex. **~rse** *vpr* *(LAm, corromperse)* start to rot, go bad

abomina|ble *a* abominable. **~ción** *f* abomination. **~r** *vt* detest. ● *vi.* **~r de** detest

abona|ble *a* payable. **~do** *a* paid. ● *m* subscriber

abonanzar *vi* *(tormenta)* abate; *(tiempo)* improve

abon|ar *vt* pay; *(en agricultura)* fertilize. **~aré** *m* promissory note. **~arse** *vpr* subscribe. **~o** *m* payment; *(estiércol)* fertilizer; *(a un periódico)* subscription

aborda|ble *a* reasonable; *(persona)* approachable. **~je** *m* boarding. **~r** *vt* tackle *(un asunto)*; approach *(una persona)*; *(naut)* come alongside

aborigen *a & m* native

aborrascarse [7] *vpr* get stormy

aborrec|er [11] *vt* hate; *(exasperar)* annoy. **~ible** *a* loathsome. **~ido** *a* hated. **~imiento** *m* hatred

aborregado *a* *(cielo)* mackerel

abort|ar *vi* have a miscarriage. **~ivo** *a* abortive. **~o** *m* miscarriage; *(voluntario)* abortion; *(fig, monstruo)* abortion. **hacerse ~ar** have an abortion

abotaga|miento *m* swelling. **~rse** [12] *vpr* swell up

abotonar *vt* button (up)

aboveda|do *a* vaulted. **~r** *vt* vault

abra *f* cove

abracadabra *m* abracadabra

abrasa|dor *a* burning. **~r** *vt* burn; *(fig, consumir)* consume. **~rse** *vpr* burn

abrasi|ón *f* abrasion; *(geología)* erosion. **~vo** *a* abrasive

abraz|adera *f* bracket. **~ar** *vt* [10] embrace; *(encerrar)* enclose. **~arse**
vpr embrace. **~o** *m* hug. **un fuerte ~o de** *(en una carta)* with best wishes from

abrecartas *m* paper-knife

ábrego *m* south wind

abrelatas *m invar* tin opener *(Brit)*, can opener

abreva|dero *m* watering place. **~r** *vt* water *(animales)*. **~rse** *vpr* *(animales)* drink

abrevia|ción *f* abbreviation; *(texto abreviado)* abridged text. **~do** *a* brief; *(texto)* abridged. **~r** *vt* abbreviate; abridge *(texto)*; cut short *(viaje etc)*. ● *vi* be brief. **~tura** *f* abbreviation

abrig|ada *f* shelter. **~adero** *m* shelter. **~ado** *a* *(lugar)* sheltered; *(personas)* well wrapped up. **~ar** [12] *vt* shelter; cherish *(esperanza)*; harbour *(duda, sospecha)*. **~arse** *vpr* (take) shelter; *(con ropa)* wrap up. **~o** *m* (over)coat; *(lugar)* shelter

abril *m* April. **~eño** *a* April

abrillantar *vt* polish

abrir [*pp* **abierto**] *vt/i* open. **~se** *vpr* open; *(extenderse)* open out; *(el tiempo)* clear

abrocha|dor *m* buttonhook. **~r** *vt* do up; *(con botones)* button up

abrojo *m* thistle

abroncar [7] *vt* *(fam)* tell off; *(abuchear)* boo; *(avergonzar)* shame. **~se** *vpr* be ashamed; *(enfadarse)* get annoyed

abroquelarse *vpr* shield o.s.

abruma|dor *a* overwhelming. **~r** *vt* overwhelm

abrupto *a* steep; *(áspero)* harsh

abrutado *a* brutish

absceso *m* abscess

absentismo *m* absenteeism

ábside *m* apse

absintio *m* absinthe

absolución *f* *(relig)* absolution; *(jurid)* acquittal

absolut|amente *adv* absolutely, completely. **~ismo** *m* absolutism. **~ista** *a & m & f* absolutist. **~o** *a* absolute. **~orio** *a* of acquittal. **en ~o** *(de manera absoluta)* absolutely; *(con sentido negativo)* (not) at all

absolver [2, *pp* **absuelto**] *vt* *(relig)* absolve; *(jurid)* acquit

absor|bente *a* absorbent; *(fig, interesante)* absorbing. **~ber** *vt* absorb. **~ción** *f* absorption. **~to** *a* absorbed

abstemio *a* teetotal. ● *m* teetotaller

absten|ción *f* abstention. **~erse** [40] *vpr* abstain, refrain (**de** from)

abstinen|cia *f* abstinence. **~te** *a* abstinent

abstra|cción *f* abstraction. **~cto** *a* abstract. **~er** [41] *vt* abstract. **~erse** *vpr* be lost in thought. **~ído** *a* absent-minded

abstruso *a* abstruse

absuelto *a* (*relig*) absolved; (*jurid*) acquitted

absurdo *a* absurd. ● *m* absurd thing

abuche|ar *vt* boo. **~o** *m* booing

abuel|a *f* grandmother. **~o** *m* grandfather. **~os** *mpl* grandparents

ab|ulia *f* lack of willpower. **~úlico** *a* weak-willed

abulta|do *a* bulky. **~miento** *m* bulkiness. **~r** *vt* enlarge; (*hinchar*) swell; (*fig, exagerar*) exaggerate. ● *vi* be bulky

abunda|ncia *f* abundance. **~nte** *a* abundant, plentiful. **~r** *vi* be plentiful. **nadar en la ~ncia** be rolling in money

aburguesa|miento *m* conversion to a middle-class way of life. **~rse** *vpr* become middle-class

aburri|do *a* (*con estar*) bored; (*con ser*) boring. **~miento** *m* boredom; (*cosa pesada*) bore. **~r** *vt* bore. **~rse** *vpr* be bored, get bored

abus|ar *vi* take advantage. **~ar de la bebida** drink too much. **~ivo** *a* excessive. **~o** *m* abuse. **~ón** *a* (*fam*) selfish

abyec|ción *f* wretchedness. **~to** *a* abject

acá *adv* here; (*hasta ahora*) until now. **~ y allá** here and there. **de ~ para allá** to and fro. **de ayer ~** since yesterday

acaba|do *a* finished; (*perfecto*) perfect; (*agotado*) worn out. ● *m* finish. **~miento** *m* finishing; (*fin*) end. **~r** *vt/i* finish. **~rse** *vpr* finish; (*agotarse*) run out; (*morirse*) die. **~r con** put an end to. **~r de** (+ *infinitivo*) háve just (+ *pp*). **~ de llegar** he has just arrived. **~r por** (+ *infinitivo*) end up (+ *gerundio*). **¡se acabó!** that's it!

acabóse *m*. **ser el ~** be the end, be the limit

acacia *f* acacia

acad|emia *f* academy. **~émico** *a* academic

acaec|er [11] *vi* happen. **~imiento** *m* occurrence

acalora|damente *adv* heatedly. **~do** *a* heated. **~miento** *m* heat. **~r** *vt* warm up; (*fig, excitar*) excite. **~rse** *vpr* get hot; (*fig, excitarse*) get excited

acallar *vt* silence

acampanado *a* bell-shaped

acampar *vi* camp

acanala|do *a* grooved. **~dura** *f* groove. **~r** *vt* groove

acantilado *a* steep. ● *m* cliff

acanto *m* acanthus

acapara|r *vt* hoard; (*monopolizar*) monopolize. **~miento** *m* hoarding; (*monopolio*) monopolizing

acaracolado *a* spiral

acaricia|dor *a* caressing. **~r** *vt* caress; (*rozar*) brush; ⟨*proyectos etc*⟩ have in mind

ácaro *m* mite

acarre|ar *vt* transport; ⟨*desgracias etc*⟩ cause. **~o** *m* transport

acartona|do *a* ⟨*persona*⟩ wizened. **~rse** *vpr* (*ponerse rígido*) go stiff; ⟨*persona*⟩ become wizened

acaso *adv* maybe, perhaps. ● *m* chance. **~ llueva mañana** perhaps it will rain tomorrow. **al ~** at random. **por si ~** in case

acata|miento *m* respect (**a** for). **~r** *vt* respect

acatarrarse *vpr* catch a cold, get a cold

acaudalado *a* well off

acaudillar *vt* lead

acceder *vi* agree; (*tener acceso*) have access

acces|ibilidad *f* accessibility. **~ible** *a* accessible; ⟨*persona*⟩ approachable. **~o** *m* access, entry; (*med, ataque*) attack; (*llegada*) approach

accesorio *a* & *m* accessory

accidentado *a* ⟨*terreno*⟩ uneven; (*agitado*) troubled; ⟨*persona*⟩ injured

accident|al *a* accidental. **~arse** *vpr* have an accident. **~e** *m* accident

acci|ón *f* (*incl jurid*) action; (*hecho*) deed. **~onar** *vt* work. ● *vi* gesticulate. **~onista** *m* & *f* shareholder

acebo *m* holly (tree)

acebuche *m* wild olive tree

acecinar *vt* cure ⟨*carne*⟩. **~se** *vpr* become wizened

acech|ar *vt* spy on; (*aguardar*) lie in wait for. **~o** *m* spying. **al ~o** on the look-out

acedera *f* sorrel

acedía *f* (*pez*) plaice; (*acidez*) heartburn

aceit|ar *vt* oil; (*culin*) add oil to. **~e** *m* oil; (*de oliva*) olive oil. **~era** *f* oil bottle; (*para engrasar*) oilcan. **~ero** *a* oil. **~oso** *a* oily

aceitun|a *f* olive. **~ado** *a* olive. **~o** *m* olive tree

acelera|ción *f* acceleration. **~damente** *adv* quickly. **~dor** *m* accelerator. **~r** *vt* accelerate; (*fig*) speed up, quicken

acelga *f* chard

ac|émila *f* mule; (*como insulto*) ass (*fam*). **~emilero** *m* muleteer

acendra|do *a* pure. **~r** *vt* purify; refine ‹*metales*›

acensuar *vt* tax

acent|o *m* accent; (*énfasis*) stress. **~uación** *f* accentuation. **~uar** [21] *vt* stress; (*fig*) emphasize. **~uarse** *vpr* become noticeable

aceña *f* water-mill

acepción *f* meaning, sense

acepta|ble *a* acceptable. **~ción** *f* acceptance; (*aprobación*) approval. **~r** *vt* accept

acequia *f* irrigation channel

acera *f* pavement (*Brit*), sidewalk (*Amer*)

acerado *a* steel; (*fig, mordaz*) sharp

acerca de *prep* about

acerca|miento *m* approach; (*fig*) reconciliation. **~r** [7] *vt* bring near. **~rse** *vpr* approach

acería *f* steelworks

acerico *m* pincushion

acero *m* steel. **~ inoxidable** stainless steel

acérrimo *a* (*fig*) staunch

acert|ado *a* right, correct; (*apropiado*) appropriate. **~ar** [1] *vt* hit ‹*el blanco*›; (*adivinar*) get right, guess. ● *vi* get right. **~ar a** happen to. **~ar con** hit on. **~ijo** *m* riddle

acervo *m* pile; (*bienes*) common property

acetato *m* acetate

acético *a* acetic

acetileno *m* acetylene

acetona *f* acetone

aciago *a* unlucky

aciano *m* cornflower

ac|íbar *m* aloes; (*planta*) aloe; (*fig, amargura*) bitterness. **~ibarar** *vt* add aloes to; (*fig, amargar*) embitter

acicala|do *a* dressed up, overdressed. **~r** *vt* dress up. **~rse** *vpr* get dressed up

acicate *m* spur

acid|ez *f* acidity. **~ificar** [7] *vt* acidify. **~ificarse** *vpr* acidify

ácido *a* sour. ● *m* acid

acierto *m* success; (*idea*) good idea; (*habilidad*) skill

aclama|ción *f* acclaim; (*aplausos*) applause. **~r** *vt* acclaim; (*aplaudir*) applaud

aclara|ción *f* explanation. **~r** *vt* lighten ‹*colores*›; (*explicar*) clarify; (*enjuagar*) rinse. ● *vi* ‹*el tiempo*› brighten up. **~rse** *vpr* become clear. **~torio** *a* explanatory

aclimata|ción *f* acclimatization, acclimation (*Amer*). **~r** *vt* acclimatize, acclimate (*Amer*). **~rse** *vpr* become acclimatized, become acclimated (*Amer*)

acné *m* acne

acobardar *vt* intimidate. **~se** *vpr* get frightened

acocil *m* (*Mex*) freshwater shrimp

acod|ado *a* bent. **~ar** *vt* (*doblar*) bend; (*agricultura*) layer. **~arse** *vpr* lean on (**en** on). **~o** *m* layer

acog|edor *a* welcoming; ‹*ambiente*› friendly. **~er** [14] *vt* welcome; (*proteger*) shelter; (*recibir*) receive. **~erse** *vpr* take refuge. **~ida** *f* welcome; (*refugio*) refuge

acogollar *vi* bud. **~se** *vpr* bud

acolcha|do *a* quilted. **~r** *vt* quilt, pad

acólito *m* acolyte; (*monaguillo*) altar boy

acomet|edor *a* aggressive; (*emprendedor*) enterprising. **~er** *vt* attack; (*emprender*) undertake; (*llenar*) fill. **~ida** *f* attack. **~ividad** *f* aggression; (*iniciativa*) enterprise

acomod|able *a* adaptable. **~adizo** *a* accommodating. **~ado** *a* well off. **~ador** *m* usher. **~adora** *f* usherette. **~amiento** *m* suitability. **~ar** *vt* arrange; (*adaptar*) adjust. ● *vi* be suitable. **~arse** *vpr* settle down; (*adaptarse*) conform. **~aticio** *a* accommodating. **~o** *m* position

acompaña|do *a* accompanied; (*concurrido*) busy. **~miento** *m* accompaniment. **~nta** *f* companion. **~nte** *m* companion; (*mus*) accompanist. **~r** *vt* accompany; (*adjuntar*) enclose. **~rse** *vpr* (*mus*) accompany o.s.

acompasa|do *a* rhythmic. **~r** *vt* keep in time; (*fig*, *ajustar*) adjust

acondiciona|do *a* equipped. **~miento** *m* conditioning. **~r** *vt* fit out; (*preparar*) prepare

acongojar *vt* distress. **~se** *vpr* get upset

acónito *m* aconite

aconseja|ble *a* advisable. **~do** *a* advised. **~r** *vt* advise. **~rse** *vpr* take advice. **~rse con** consult

aconsonantar *vt/i* rhyme

acontec|er [11] *vi* happen. **~imiento** *m* event

acopi|ar *vt* collect. **~o** *m* store

acopla|do *a* coordinated. **~miento** *m* coupling; (*elec*) connection. **~r** *vt* fit; (*elec*) connect; (*rail*) couple

acoquina|miento *m* intimidation. **~r** *vt* intimidate. **~rse** *vpr* be intimidated

acoraza|do *a* armour-plated. ● *m* battleship. **~r** [10] *vt* armour

acorazonado *a* heart-shaped

acorcha|do *a* spongy. **~rse** *vpr* go spongy; (*parte del cuerpo*) go to sleep

acord|ado *a* agreed. **~ar** [2] *vt* agree (upon); (*decidir*) decide; (*recordar*) remind. **~e** *a* in agreement; (*mus*) harmonious. ● *m* chord

acorde|ón *m* accordion. **~onista** *m* & *f* accordionist

acordona|do *a* (*lugar*) cordoned off. **~miento** *m* cordoning off. **~r** *vt* tie, lace; (*rodear*) surround, cordon off

acorrala|miento *m* (*de animales*) rounding up; (*de personas*) cornering. **~r** *vt* round up (*animales*); corner (*personas*)

acorta|miento *m* shortening. **~r** *vt* shorten; (*fig*) cut down

acos|ar *vt* hound; (*fig*) pester. **~o** *m* pursuit; (*fig*) pestering

acostar [2] *vt* put to bed; (*naut*) bring alongside. ● *vi* (*naut*) reach land. **~se** *vpr* go to bed; (*echarse*) lie down; (*Mex*, *parir*) give birth

acostumbra|do *a* (*habitual*) usual. **~do a** used to, accustomed to. **~r** *vt* get used to. **me ha acostumbrado a levantarme por la noche** he's got me used to getting up at night. ● *vi*. **~r (a)** be accustomed to. **acostumbro comer a la una** I usually have lunch at one o'clock. **~rse** *vpr* become accustomed, get used

acota|ción *f* (*nota*) marginal note; (*en el teatro*) stage direction; (*cota*) elevation mark. **~do** *a* enclosed. **~r** *vt* mark out (*terreno*); (*anotar*) annotate

ácrata *a* anarchistic. ● *m* & *f* anarchist

acre *m* acre. ● *a* (*olor*) pungent; (*sabor*) sharp, bitter

acrecenta|miento *m* increase. **~r** [1] *vt* increase. **~rse** *vpr* increase

acrec|er [11] *vt* increase. **~imiento** *m* increase

acredita|do *a* reputable; (*pol*) accredited. **~r** *vt* prove; accredit (*representante diplomático*); (*garantizar*) guarantee; (*autorizar*) authorize. **~rse** *vpr* make one's name

acreedor *a* worthy (**a** of). ● *m* creditor

acribillar *vt* (*a balazos*) riddle (**a** with); (*a picotazos*) cover (**a** with); (*fig*, *a preguntas etc*) pester (**a** with)

acrimonia *f* (*de sabor*) sharpness; (*de olor*) pungency; (*fig*) bitterness

acrisola|do *a* pure; (*fig*) proven. **~r** *vt* purify; (*confirmar*) prove

acritud *f* (*de sabor*) sharpness; (*de olor*) pungency; (*fig*) bitterness

acr|obacia *f* acrobatics. **~obacias aéreas** aerobatics. **~óbata** *m* & *f* acrobat. **~obático** *a* acrobatic. **~obatismo** *m* acrobatics

acrónimo *m* acronym

acróstico *a* & *m* acrostic

acta *f* minutes; (*certificado*) certificate

actinia *f* sea anemone

actitud *f* posture, position; (*fig*) attitude, position

activ|ación *f* speed-up. **~amente** *adv* actively. **~ar** *vt* activate; (*acelerar*) speed up. **~idad** *f* activity. **~o** *a* active. ● *m* assets

acto *m* act; (*ceremonia*) ceremony. **en el ~** immediately

act|or *m* actor. **~riz** *f* actress

actuación *f* action; (*conducta*) behaviour; (*theat*) performance

actual *a* present; (*asunto*) topical. **~idad** *f* present. **~idades** *fpl* current affairs. **~ización** *f* modernization. **~izar** [10] *vt* modernize. **~mente** *adv* now, at the present time. **en la ~idad** nowadays

actuar [21] *vt* work. ● *vi* act. **~ como**, **~ de** act as

actuario *m* clerk of the court. ~ **(de seguros)** actuary

acuarel|a *f* watercolour. ~**ista** *m* & *f* watercolourist

acuario *m* aquarium. **A**~ Aquarius

acuartela|do *a* quartered. ~**miento** *m* quartering. ~**r** *vt* quarter, billet; *(mantener en cuartel)* confine to barracks

acuático *a* aquatic

acuci|ador pressing. ~**ar** *vt* urge on; *(dar prisa a)* hasten. ~**oso** *a* keen

acuclillarse *vpr* crouch down, squat down

acuchilla|do *a* slashed; *⟨persona⟩* stabbed. ~**r** *vt* slash; stab *⟨persona⟩*; *(alisar)* smooth

acudir *vi*. ~ **a** go to, attend; keep *⟨una cita⟩*; *(en auxilio)* go to help

acueducto *m* aqueduct

acuerdo *m* agreement. ● *vb véase* **acordar**. **¡de ~!** OK! **de ~ con** in accordance with. **estar de ~** agree. **ponerse de ~** agree

acuesto *vb véase* **acostar**

acuidad *f* acuity, sharpness

acumula|ción *f* accumulation. ~**dor** *a* accumulative. ● *m* accumulator. ~**r** *vt* accumulate. ~**rse** *vpr* accumulate

acunar *vt* rock

acuña|ción *f* minting, coining. ~**r** *vt* mint, coin

acuos|idad *f* wateriness. ~**o** *a* watery

acupuntura *f* acupuncture

acurrucarse [7] *vpr* curl up

acusa|ción *f* accusation. ~**do** *a* accused; *(destacado)* marked. ● *m* accused. ~**dor** *a* accusing. ● *m* accuser. ~**r** *vt* accuse; *(mostrar)* show; *(denunciar)* denounce. ~**rse** *vpr* confess; *(notarse)* become marked. ~**torio** *a* accusatory

acuse *m*. ~ **de recibo** acknowledgement of receipt

acus|ica *m* & *f (fam)* telltale. ~**ón** *a* & *m* telltale

acústic|a *f* acoustics. ~**o** *a* acoustic

achacar [7] *vt* attribute

achacoso *a* sickly

achaflanar *vt* bevel

achantar *vt (fam)* intimidate. ~**se** *vpr* hide; *(fig)* back down

achaparrado *a* stocky

achaque *m* ailment

achares *mpl (fam)*. **dar** ~ make jealous

achata|miento *m* flattening. ~**r** *vt* flatten

achica|do *a* childish. ~**r** [7] *vt* make smaller; *(fig, empequeñecer, fam)* belittle; *(naut)* bale out. ~**rse** *vpr* become smaller; *(humillarse)* be humiliated

achicopalado *a (Mex)* depressed

achicoria *f* chicory

achicharra|dero *m* inferno. ~**nte** *a* sweltering. ~**r** *vt* burn; *(fig)* pester. ~**rse** *vpr* burn

achispa|do *a* tipsy. ~**rse** *vpr* get tipsy

achocolatado *a* (chocolate-)brown

achuch|ado *a (fam)* hard. ~**ar** *vt* jostle, push. ~**ón** *m* shove, push

achulado *a* cocky

adagio *m* adage, proverb; *(mus)* adagio

adalid *m* leader

adamascado *a* damask

adapta|ble *a* adaptable. ~**ción** *f* adaptation. ~**dor** *m* adapter. ~**r** *vt* adapt; *(ajustar)* fit. ~**rse** *vpr* adapt o.s.

adecentar *vt* clean up. ~**se** *vpr* tidy o.s. up

adecua|ción *f* suitability. ~**damente** *adv* suitably. ~**do** *a* suitable. ~**r** *vt* adapt, make suitable

adelant|ado *a* advanced; *⟨niño⟩* precocious; *⟨reloj⟩* fast. ~**amiento** *m* advance(ment); *(auto)* overtaking. ~**ar** *vt* advance, move forward; *(acelerar)* speed up; put forward *⟨reloj⟩*; *(auto)* overtake. ● *vi* advance, go forward; *⟨reloj⟩* gain, be fast. ~**arse** *vpr* advance, move forward; *⟨reloj⟩* gain; *(auto)* overtake. ~**e** *adv* forward. ● *int* come in!; *(¡siga!)* carry on! ~**o** *m* advance; *(progreso)* progress. **más** ~**e** *(lugar)* further on; *(tiempo)* later on. **pagar por** ~**ado** pay in advance.

adelfa *f* oleander

adelgaza|dor *a* slimming. ~**miento** *m* slimming. ~**r** [10] *vt* make thin. ● *vi* lose weight; *(adrede)* slim. ~**rse** *vpr* lose weight; *(adrede)* slim

ademán *m* gesture. **ademanes** *mpl (modales)* manners. **en** ~ **de** as if to

además *adv* besides; *(también)* also. ~ **de** besides

adentr|arse *vpr*. ~ **en** penetrate into; study thoroughly *⟨tema etc⟩*. ~**o** *adv* in(side). **mar** ~**o** out at sea. **tierra** ~**o** inland

adepto *m* supporter

aderez|ar [10] *vt* flavour ⟨*bebidas*⟩; (*condimentar*) season; dress ⟨*ensalada*⟩. **~o** *m* flavouring; (*con condimentos*) seasoning; (*para ensalada*) dressing

adeud|ar *vt* owe. **~o** *m* debit

adhe|rencia *f* adhesion; (*fig*) adherence. **~rente** *a* adherent. **~rir** [4] *vt* stick on. ● *vi* stick. **~rirse** *vpr* stick; (*fig*) follow. **~sión** *f* adhesion; (*fig*) support. **~sivo** *a* & *m* adhesive

adici|ón *f* addition. **~onal** *a* additional. **~onar** *vt* add

adicto *a* devoted. ● *m* follower

adiestra|do *a* trained. **~miento** *m* training. **~r** *vt* train. **~rse** *vpr* practise

adinerado *a* wealthy

adiós *int* goodbye!; (*al cruzarse con alguien*) hello!

adit|amento *m* addition; (*accesorio*) accessory. **~ivo** *m* additive

adivin|ación *f* divination; (*por conjeturas*) guessing. **~ador** *m* fortune-teller. **~anza** *f* riddle. **~ar** *vt* foretell; (*acertar*) guess. **~o** *m* fortune-teller

adjetivo *a* adjectival. ● *m* adjective

adjudica|ción *f* award. **~r** [7] *vt* award. **~rse** *vpr* appropriate. **~tario** *m* winner of an award

adjunt|ar *vt* enclose. **~o** *a* enclosed; (*auxiliar*) assistant. ● *m* assistant

adminículo *m* thing, gadget

administra|ción *f* administration; (*gestión*) management. **~dor** *m* administrator; (*gerente*) manager. **~dora** *f* administrator; manageress. **~r** *vt* administer. **~tivo** *a* administrative

admira|ble *a* admirable. **~ción** *f* admiration. **~dor** *m* admirer. **~r** *vt* admire; (*asombrar*) astonish. **~rse** *vpr* be astonished. **~tivo** *a* admiring

admi|sibilidad *f* admissibility. **~sible** *a* acceptable. **~sión** *f* admission; (*aceptación*) acceptance. **~tir** *vt* admit; (*aceptar*) accept

adobar *vt* (*culin*) pickle; (*fig*) twist

adobe *m* sun-dried brick. **~ra** *f* mould for making (sun-dried) bricks

adobo *m* pickle

adocena|do *a* common. **~rse** *vpr* become common

adoctrinamiento *m* indoctrination

adolecer [11] *vi* be ill. **~ de** suffer with

adolescen|cia *f* adolescent. **~te** *a* & *m* & *f* adolescent

adonde *conj* where

adónde *adv* where?

adop|ción *f* adoption. **~tar** *vt* adopt. **~tivo** *a* adoptive; ⟨*patria*⟩ of adoption

adoqu|ín *m* paving stone; (*imbécil*) idiot. **~inado** *m* paving. **~inar** *vt* pave

adora|ble *a* adorable. **~ción** *f* adoration. **~dor** *a* adoring. ● *n* worshipper. **~r** *vt* adore

adormec|edor *a* soporific; ⟨*droga*⟩ sedative. **~er** [11] *vt* send to sleep; (*fig, calmar*) calm, soothe. **~erse** *vpr* fall asleep; (*un miembro*) go to sleep. **~ido** *a* sleepy; ⟨*un miembro*⟩ numb. **~imiento** *m* sleepiness; (*de un miembro*) numbness

adormidera *f* opium poppy

adormilarse *vpr* doze

adorn|ar *vt* adorn (**con, de** with). **~o** *m* decoration

adosar *vt* lean (**a** against)

adqui|rido *a* acquired. **~rir** [4] *vt* acquire; (*comprar*) buy. **~sición** *f* acquisition; (*compra*) purchase. **~sitivo** *a* acquisitive. **poder** *m* **~sitivo** purchasing power

adrede *adv* on purpose

adrenalina *f* adrenalin

adscribir [*pp* **adscrito**] *vt* appoint

aduan|a *f* customs. **~ero** *a* customs. ● *m* customs officer

aducir [47] *vt* allege

adueñarse *vpr* take possession

adul|ación *f* flattery. **~ador** *a* flattering. ● *m* flatterer. **~ar** *vt* flatter

ad|ulteración *f* adulteration. **~ulterar** *vt* adulterate. ● *vi* commit adultery. **~ulterino** *a* adulterous. **~ulterio** *m* adultery. **~últera** *f* adulteress. **~últero** *a* adulterous. ● *m* adulterer

adulto *a* & *m* adult, grown-up

adusto *a* severe, harsh

advenedizo *a* & *m* upstart

advenimiento *m* advent, arrival; (*subida al trono*) accession

adventicio *a* accidental

adverbi|al *a* adverbial. **~o** *m* adverb

advers|ario *m* adversary. **~idad** *f* adversity. **~o** *a* adverse, unfavourable

advert|encia *f* warning; (*prólogo*) foreword. **~ido** *a* informed. **~ir** [4] *vt* warn; (*notar*) notice

adviento *m* Advent

advocación *f* dedication

adyacente *a* adjacent

aéreo *a* air; (*photo*) aerial; ‹*ferrocarril*› overhead; (*fig*) flimsy

aeróbica *f* aerobics

aerodeslizador *m* hovercraft

aerodinámic|a *f* aerodynamics. **~o** *a* aerodynamic

aeródromo *m* aerodrome, airdrome (*Amer*)

aero|espacial *a* aerospace. **~faro** *m* beacon. **~lito** *m* meteorite. **~nauta** *m* & *f* aeronaut. **~náutica** *f* aeronautics. **~náutico** *a* aeronautical. **~nave** *f* airship. **~puerto** *m* airport. **~sol** *m* aerosol

afab|ilidad *f* affability. **~le** *a* affable

afamado *a* famous

af|án *m* hard work; (*deseo*) desire. **~anar** *vt* (*fam*) pinch. **~anarse** *vpr* strive (**en, por** to). **~anoso** *a* laborious

afea|miento *m* disfigurement. **~r** *vt* disfigure, make ugly; (*censurar*) censure

afección *f* disease

afecta|ción *f* affectation. **~do** *a* affected. **~r** *vt* affect

afect|ísimo *a* affectionate. **~ísimo amigo** (*en cartas*) my dear friend. **~ividad** *f* emotional nature. **~ivo** *a* sensitive. **~o** *m* (*cariño*) affection. ● *a*. **~o** *a* attached to. **~uosidad** *f* affection. **~uoso** *a* affectionate. **con un ~uoso saludo** (*en cartas*) with kind regards. **suyo ~ísimo** (*en cartas*) yours sincerely

afeita|do *m* shave. **~dora** *f* electric razor. **~r** *vt* shave. **~rse** *vpr* (have a) shave

afelpado *a* velvety

afemina|do *a* effeminate. ● *m* effeminate person. **~miento** *m* effeminacy. **~rse** *vpr* become effeminate

aferrar [1] *vt* grasp

afgano *a* & *m* Afghan

afianza|miento *m* (*reforzar*) strengthening; (*garantía*) guarantee. **~rse** [10] *vpr* become established

afici|ón *f* liking; (*conjunto de aficionados*) fans. **~onado** *a* keen (a on), fond (a of). ● *m* fan. **~onar** *vt* make fond. **~onarse** *vpr* take a liking to. **por ~ón** as a hobby

afila|do *a* sharp. **~dor** *m* knifegrinder. **~dura** *f* sharpening. **~r** *vt* sharpen. **~rse** *vpr* get sharp; (*ponerse flaco*) grow thin

afilia|ción *f* affiliation. **~do** *a* affiliated. **~rse** *vpr* become a member (a of)

afiligranado *a* filigreed; (*fig*) delicate

afín *a* similar; (*próximo*) adjacent; ‹*personas*› related

afina|ción *f* refining; (*auto, mus*) tuning. **~do** *a* finished; (*mus*) in tune. **~r** *vt* refine; (*afilar*) sharpen; (*acabar*) finish; (*auto, mus*) tune. ● *vi* be in tune. **~rse** *vpr* become more refined

afincarse [7] *vpr* settle

afinidad *f* affinity; (*parentesco*) relationship

afirma|ción *f* affirmation. **~r** *vt* make firm; (*asentir*) affirm. **~rse** *vpr* steady o.s.; (*confirmar*) confirm. **~tivo** *a* affirmative

aflic|ción *f* affliction. **~tivo** *a* distressing

afligi|do *a* distressed. ● *m* afflicted. **~r** [14] *vt* distress. **~rse** *vpr* grieve

afloja|miento *m* loosening. **~r** *vt* loosen; (*relajar*) ease. ● *vi* let up

aflora|miento *m* outcrop. **~r** *vi* appear on the surface

aflu|encia *f* flow. **~ente** *a* flowing. ● *m* tributary. **~ir** [17] *vi* flow (a into)

af|onía *f* hoarseness. **~ónico** *a* hoarse

aforismo *m* aphorism

aforo *m* capacity

afortunado *a* fortunate, lucky

afrancesado *a* francophile

afrent|a *f* insult; (*vergüenza*) disgrace. **~ar** *vt* insult. **~oso** *a* insulting

África *f* Africa. **~ del Sur** South Africa

africano *a* & *m* African

afrodisíaco *a* & *m*, **afrodisiaco** *a* & *m* aphrodisiac

afrontar *vt* bring face to face; (*enfrentar*) face, confront

afuera *adv* out(side). **¡~!** out of the way! **~s** *fpl* outskirts

agachar *vt* lower. **~se** *vpr* bend over

agalla *f* (*de los peces*) gill. **~s** *fpl* (*fig*) guts

agarrada *f* row

agarrader|a *f* (*LAm*) handle. **~o** *m* handle. **tener ~as** (*LAm*), **tener ~os** have influence

agarr|ado a (fig, fam) mean. **∼ador** a (Arg) ⟨bebida⟩ strong. **∼ar** vt grasp; (esp LAm) take, catch. ● vi ⟨plantas⟩ take root. **∼arse** vpr hold on; (reñirse, fam) fight. **∼ón** m tug; (LAm, riña) row

agarrota|miento m tightening; (auto) seizing up. **∼r** vt tie tightly; ⟨el frío⟩ stiffen; garotte ⟨un reo⟩. **∼rse** vpr go stiff; (auto) seize up

agasaj|ado m guest of honour. **∼ar** vt look after well. **∼o** m good treatment

ágata f agate

agavilla|dora f (máquina) binder. **∼r** vt bind

agazaparse vpr hide

agencia f agency. **∼ de viajes** travel agency. **∼ inmobiliaria** estate agency (Brit), real estate agency (Amer). **∼r** vt find. **∼rse** vpr find (out) for o.s.

agenda f notebook

agente m agent; (de policía) policeman. **∼ de aduanas** customs officer. **∼ de bolsa** stockbroker

ágil a agile

agilidad f agility

agita|ción f waving; (de un líquido) stirring; (intranquilidad) agitation. **∼do** a ⟨el mar⟩ rough; (fig) agitated. **∼dor** m (pol) agitator

agitanado a gypsy-like

agitar vt wave; shake ⟨botellas etc⟩; stir ⟨líquidos⟩; (fig) stir up. **∼se** vpr wave; ⟨el mar⟩ get rough; (fig) get excited

aglomera|ción f agglomeration; (de tráfico) traffic jam. **∼r** vt amass. **∼rse** vpr form a crowd

agn|osticismo m agnosticism. **∼óstico** a & m agnostic

agobi|ador a ⟨trabajo⟩ exhausting; ⟨calor⟩ oppressive. **∼ante** a ⟨trabajo⟩ exhausting; ⟨calor⟩ oppressive. **∼ar** vt weigh down; (fig, abrumar) overwhelm. **∼o** m weight; (cansancio) exhaustion; (opresión) oppression

agolpa|miento m (de gente) crowd; (de cosas) pile. **∼rse** vpr crowd together

agon|ía f death throes; (fig) agony. **∼izante** a dying; ⟨luz⟩ failing. **∼izar** [10] vi be dying

agor|ar [16] vt prophesy. **∼ero** a of ill omen. ● m soothsayer

agostar vt wither

agosto m August. **hacer su ∼** feather one's nest

agota|do a exhausted; ⟨libro⟩ out of print. **∼dor** a exhausting. **∼miento** m exhaustion. **∼r** vt exhaust. **∼rse** vpr be exhausted; ⟨libro⟩ go out of print

agracia|do a attractive; (que tiene suerte) lucky. **∼r** make attractive

agrada|ble a pleasant, nice. **∼r** vi please. **esto me ∼** I like this

agradec|er [11] vt thank ⟨persona⟩; be grateful for ⟨cosa⟩. **∼ido** a grateful. **∼imiento** m gratitude. **¡muy ∼ido!** thanks a lot!

agrado m pleasure; (amabilidad) friendliness

agrandar vt enlarge; (fig) exaggerate. **∼se** vpr get bigger

agrario a agrarian, land; ⟨política⟩ agricultural

agrava|miento m worsening. **∼nte** a aggravating. ● f additional problem. **∼r** vt aggravate; (aumentar el peso) make heavier. **∼rse** vpr get worse

agravi|ar vt offend; (perjudicar) wrong. **∼arse** vpr be offended. **∼o** m offence

agraz m. **en ∼** prematurely

agredir [24] vt attack. **∼ de palabra** insult

agrega|do m aggregate; (funcionario diplomático) attaché. **∼r** [12] vt add; (unir) join; appoint ⟨persona⟩

agremiar vt form into a union. **∼se** vpr form a union

agres|ión f aggression; (ataque) attack. **∼ividad** f aggressiveness. **∼ivo** aggressive. **∼or** m aggressor

agreste a country

agria|do a (fig) embittered. **∼r** [regular, o raramente 20] vt sour. **∼rse** vpr turn sour; (fig) become embittered

agr|ícola a agricultural. **∼icultor** a agricultural. ● m farmer. **∼icultura** f agriculture, farming

agridulce a bitter-sweet; (culin) sweet-and-sour

agriera f (LAm) heartburn

agrietar vt crack. **∼se** vpr crack; ⟨piel⟩ chap

agrimens|or m surveyor. **∼ura** f surveying

agrio a sour; (fig) sharp. **∼s** mpl citrus fruits

agronomía f agronomy

agropecuario *a* farming

agrupa|ción *f* group; *(acción)* grouping. **~r** *vt* group. **~rse** *vpr* form a group

agua *f* water; *(lluvia)* rain; *(marea)* tide; *(vertiente del tejado)* slope. **~ abajo** downstream. **~ arriba** upstream. **~ bendita** holy water. **~ caliente** hot water. **estar entre dos ~s** sit on the fence. **hacer ~** *(naut)* leak. **nadar entre dos ~s** sit on the fence

aguacate *m* avocado pear; *(árbol)* avocado pear tree

aguacero *m* downpour, heavy shower

agua f corriente running water

aguachinarse *vpr (Mex)* ⟨cultivos⟩ be flooded

aguada *f* watering place; *(naut)* drinking water; *(acuarela)* water-colour

agua f de colonia eau-de-Cologne

aguad|o *a* watery. **~ucho** *m* refreshment kiosk

agua: ~ dulce fresh water. **~fiestas** *m & f invar* spoil-sport, wet blanket. **~ fría** cold water. **~fuerte** *m* etching

aguaje *m* spring tide

agua: ~mala f, ~mar m jellyfish

aguamarina *f* aquamarine

agua: ~miel f mead. **~ mineral con gas** fizzy mineral water. **~ mineral sin gas** still mineral water. **~nieve f** sleet

aguanoso *a* watery; ⟨tierra⟩ waterlogged

aguant|able *a* bearable. **~aderas** *fpl* patience. **~ar** *vt* put up with, bear; *(sostener)* support. ● *vi* hold out. **~arse** *vpr* restrain o.s. **~e** *m* patience; *(resistencia)* endurance

agua: ~pié *m* watery wine. **~ potable** drinking water. **~r** [15] *vt* water down. **~ salada** salt water.

aguardar *vt* wait for. ● *vi* wait

agua: ~rdiente *m* (cheap) brandy. **~rrás** *m* turpentine, turps *(fam)*. **~turma** *f* Jerusalem artichoke. **~zal** *m* puddle

agud|eza *f* sharpness; *(fig, perspicacia)* insight; *(fig, ingenio)* wit. **~izar** [10] *vt* sharpen. **~izarse** *vpr* ⟨enfermedad⟩ get worse. **~o** *a* sharp; ⟨ángulo, enfermedad⟩ acute; ⟨voz⟩ high-pitched

agüero *m* omen. **ser de buen ~** augur well

aguij|ada *f* goad. **~ar** *vt (incl fig)* goad. **~ón** *m* point of a goad. **~onazo** *m* prick. **~onear** *vt* goad

águila *f* eagle; *(persona perspicaz)* astute person

aguileña *f* columbine

aguil|eño *a* aquiline. **~ucho** *m* eaglet

aguinaldo *m* Christmas box

aguja *f* needle; *(del reloj)* hand; *(arquit)* steeple. **~s fpl** *(rail)* points

agujer|ear *vt* make holes in. **~o** *m* hole

agujetas *fpl* stiffness. **tener ~** be stiff

agujón *m* hairpin

agusanado *a* full of maggots

agutí *m (LAm)* guinea pig

aguza|do *a* sharp. **~miento** *m* sharpening. **~r** [10] *vt* sharpen

ah *int* ah!, oh!

aherrojar *vt (fig)* oppress

ahí *adv* there. **de ~ que** so that. **por ~** over there; *(aproximadamente)* thereabouts

ahija|da *f* god-daughter, godchild. **~do** *m* godson, godchild. **~r** *vt* adopt

ahínco *m* enthusiasm; *(empeño)* insistence

ahíto *a* full up

ahog|ado *a (en el agua)* drowned; *(asfixiado)* suffocated. **~ar** [12] *vt (en el agua)* drown; *(asfixiar)* suffocate; put out ⟨fuego⟩. **~arse** *vpr (en el agua)* drown; *(asfixiarse)* suffocate. **~o** *m* breathlessness; *(fig, angustia)* distress; *(apuro)* financial trouble

ahondar *vt* deepen. ● *vi* go deep. **~ en** *(fig)* examine in depth. **~se** *vpr* get deeper

ahora *adv* now; *(hace muy poco)* just now; *(dentro de poco)* very soon. **~ bien** but. **~ mismo** right now. **de ~ en adelante** from now on, in future. **por ~** for the time being

ahorca|dura *f* hanging. **~r** [7] *vt* hang. **~rse** *vpr* hang o.s.

ahorita *adv (fam)* now. **~ mismo** right now

ahorquillar *vt* shape like a fork

ahorr|ador *a* thrifty. **~ar** *vt* save. **~arse** *vpr* save o.s. **~o** *m* saving; *(cantidad ahorrada)* savings. **~os** *mpl* savings

ahuecar [7] *vt* hollow; fluff up ⟨colchón⟩; deepen ⟨la voz⟩; *(marcharse, fam)* clear off *(fam)*

ahuizote *m* (*Mex*) bore

ahulado *m* (*LAm*) oilskin

ahuma|do *a* (*culin*) smoked; (*de colores*) smoky. ~**r** *vt* (*culin*) smoke; (*llenar de humo*) fill with smoke. • *vi* smoke. ~**rse** *vpr* become smoky; ‹*comida*› acquire a smoky taste; (*emborracharse, fam*) get drunk

ahusa|do *a* tapering. ~**rse** *vpr* taper

ahuyentar *vt* drive away; banish ‹*pensamientos etc*›

airado *a* annoyed

aire *m* air; (*viento*) breeze; (*corriente*) draught; (*aspecto*) appearance; (*mus*) tune, air. ~**ación** *f* ventilation. ~ **acondicionado** air-conditioned. ~**ar** *vt* air; (*ventilar*) ventilate; (*fig, publicar*) make public. ~**arse** *vpr*. salir para ~**arse** go out for some fresh air. al ~ libre in the open air. darse ~**s** give o.s. airs

airón *m* heron

airos|amente *adv* gracefully. ~**o** *a* draughty; (*fig*) elegant

aisla|do *a* isolated; (*elec*) insulated. ~**dor** *a* (*elec*) insulating. • *m* (*elec*) insulator. ~**miento** *m* isolation; (*elec*) insulation. ~**nte** *a* insulating. ~**r** [23] *vt* isolate; (*elec*) insulate

ajajá *int* good! splendid!

ajar *vt* crumple; (*estropear*) spoil

ajedre|cista *m & f* chess-player. ~**z** *m* chess. ~**zado** *a* chequered, checked

ajenjo *m* absinthe

ajeno *a* (*de otro*) someone else's; (*de otros*) other people's; (*extraño*) alien

ajetre|arse *vpr* be busy. ~**o** *m* bustle

ají *m* (*LAm*) chilli; (*salsa*) chilli sauce

aj|iaceite *m* garlic sauce. ~**ilimójili** *m* piquant garlic sauce. ~**illo** *m* garlic. al ~**illo** cooked with garlic. ~**o** *m* garlic. ~**o-a-rriero** *m* cod in garlic sauce

ajorca *f* bracelet

ajuar *m* furnishings; (*de novia*) trousseau

ajuma|do *a* (*fam*) drunk. ~**rse** *vpr* (*fam*) get drunk

ajust|ado *a* right; ‹*vestido*› tight. ~**ador** *m* fitter. ~**amiento** *m* fitting; (*adaptación*) adjustment; (*acuerdo*) agreement; (*de una cuenta*) settlement. ~**ar** *vt* fit; (*adaptar*) adapt; (*acordar*) agree; settle ‹*una cuenta*›;

(*apretar*) tighten. • *vi* fit. ~**arse** *vpr* fit; (*adaptarse*) adapt o.s.; (*acordarse*) come to an agreement. ~**e** *m* fitting; (*adaptación*) *f* adjustment; (*acuerdo*) agreement; (*de una cuenta*) settlement

ajusticiar *vt* execute

al = a; **el**

ala *f* wing; (*de sombrero*) brim; (*deportes*) winger

alaba|ncioso *a* boastful. ~**nza** *f* praise. ~**r** *vt* praise. ~**rse** *vpr* boast

alabastro *m* alabaster

álabe *m* (*paleta*) paddle; (*diente*) cog

alabe|ar *vt* warp. ~**arse** *vpr* warp. ~**o** *m* warping

alacena *f* cupboard (*Brit*), closet (*Amer*)

alacrán *m* scorpion

alacridad *f* alacrity

alado *a* winged

alambi|cado *a* distilled; (*fig*) subtle. ~**camiento** *m* distillation; (*fig*) subtlety. ~**car** [7] *vt* distil. ~**que** *m* still

alambr|ada *f* wire fence; (*de alambre de espinas*) barbed wire fence. ~**ar** *vt* fence. ~**e** *m* wire. ~**e de espinas** barbed wire. ~**era** *f* fireguard

alameda *f* avenue; (*plantío de álamos*) poplar grove

álamo *m* poplar. ~ **temblón** aspen

alano *m* mastiff

alarde *m* show. ~**ar** *vi* boast

alarga|dera *f* extension. ~**do** *a* long. ~**dor** *m* extension. ~**miento** *m* lengthening. ~**r** [12] *vt* lengthen; stretch out ‹*mano etc*›; (*dar*) give, pass. ~**rse** *vpr* lengthen, get longer

alarido *m* shriek

alarm|a *f* alarm. ~**ante** *a* alarming. ~**ar** *vt* alarm, frighten. ~**arse** *vpr* be alarmed. ~**ista** *m & f* alarmist

alba *f* dawn

albacea *m* executor. • *f* executrix

albacora (*culin*) tuna(-fish)

albahaca *f* basil

albanés *a & m* Albanian

Albania *f* Albania

albañal *m* sewer, drain

albañil *m* bricklayer. ~**ería** *f* (*arte*) bricklaying

albarán *m* delivery note

albarda *f* packsaddle; (*Mex*) saddle. ~**r** *vt* saddle

albaricoque *m* apricot. ~**ro** *m* apricot tree

albatros *m* albatross

albedrío *m* will. **libre** ~ free will

albéitar *m* veterinary surgeon (*Brit*), veterinarian (*Amer*), vet (*fam*)

alberca *f* tank, reservoir

alberg|ar [12] *vt* (*alojar*) put up; ⟨*viviendas*⟩ house; (*dar asilo*) shelter. ~**arse** *vpr* stay; (*refugiarse*) shelter. ~**ue** *m* accommodation; (*refugio*) shelter. ~**ue de juventud** youth hostel

albóndiga *f* meatball, rissole

albor *m* dawn. ~**ada** *f* dawn; (*mus*) dawn song. ~**ear** *vi* dawn

albornoz *m* (*de los moros*) burnous; (*para el baño*) bathrobe

alborot|adizo *a* excitable. ~**ado** *a* excited; (*aturdido*) hasty. ~**ador** *a* rowdy. ● *m* trouble-maker. ~**ar** *vt* disturb, upset. ● *vi* make a racket. ~**arse** *vpr* get excited; ⟨*el mar*⟩ get rough. ~**o** *m* row, uproar

alboroz|ado *a* overjoyed. ~**ar** [10] *vt* make laugh; (*regocijar*) make happy. ~**arse** *vpr* be overjoyed. ~**o** *m* joy

albufera *f* lagoon

álbum *m* (*pl* ~**es** *o* ~**s**) album

alcachofa *f* artichoke

alcald|e *m* mayor. ~**esa** *f* mayoress. ~**ía** *f* mayoralty; (*oficina*) mayor's office

álcali *m* alkali

alcalino *a* alkaline

alcance *m* reach; (*de arma, telescopio etc*) range; (*déficit*) deficit

alcancía *f* money-box

alcantarilla *f* sewer; (*boca*) drain

alcanzar [10] *vt* (*llegar a*) catch up; (*coger*) reach; catch ⟨*un autobús*⟩; ⟨*bala etc*⟩ strike, hit. ● *vi* reach; (*ser suficiente*) be enough. ~ **a** manage

alcaparra *f* caper

alcaucil *m* artichoke

alcayata *f* hook

alcazaba *f* fortress

alcázar *m* fortress

alcoba *f* bedroom

alcoh|ol *m* alcohol. ~**ol desnaturalizado** methylated spirits, meths (*fam*). ~**ólico** *a* & *m* alcoholic. ~**olímetro** *m* breathalyser (*Brit*). ~**olismo** *m* alcoholism. ~**olizarse** [10] *vpr* become an alcoholic

Alcorán *m* Koran

alcornoque *m* cork-oak; (*persona torpe*) idiot

alcuza *f* (olive) oil bottle

aldaba *f* door-knocker. ~**da** *f* knock at the door

alde|a *f* village. ~**ano** *a* village; (*campesino*) rustic, country. ~**huela** *f* hamlet

alea|ción *f* alloy. ~**r** *vt* alloy

aleatorio *a* uncertain

alecciona|dor *a* instructive. ~**miento** *m* instruction. ~**r** *vt* instruct

aledaños *mpl* outskirts

alega|ción *f* allegation; (*Arg, Mex, disputa*) argument. ~**r** [12] *vt* claim; (*jurid*) allege. ● *vi* (*LAm*) argue. ~**to** *m* plea

aleg|oría *f* allegory. ~**órico** *a* allegorical

alegr|ar *vt* make happy; (*avivar*) brighten up. ~**arse** *vpr* be happy; (*emborracharse*) get merry. ~**e** *a* happy; (*achispado*) merry, tight. ~**emente** *adv* happily. ~**ía** *f* happiness. ~**ón** *m* sudden joy, great happiness

aleja|do *a* distant. ~**miento** *m* removal; (*entre personas*) estrangement; (*distancia*) distance. ~**r** *vt* remove; (*ahuyentar*) get rid of; (*fig, apartar*) separate. ~**rse** *vpr* move away

alela|do *a* stupid. ~**r** *vt* stupefy. ~**rse** *vpr* be stupefied

aleluya *m* & *f* alleluia

alemán *a* & *m* German

Alemania *f* Germany. ~ **Occidental** (*historia*) West Germany. ~ **Oriental** (*historia*) East Germany

alenta|dor *a* encouraging. ~**r** [1] *vt* encourage. ● *vi* breathe

alerce *m* larch

al|ergia *f* allergy. ~**érgico** *a* allergic

alero *m* (*del tejado*) eaves

alerón *m* aileron

alerta *adv* alert, on the alert. ¡~! look out! ~**r** *vt* alert

aleta *f* wing; (*de pez*) fin

aletarga|do *a* lethargic. ~**miento** *m* lethargy. ~**r** [12] *vt* make lethargic. ~**rse** *vpr* become lethargic

alet|azo *m* (*de un ave*) flap of the wings; (*de un pez*) flick of the fin. ~**ear** *vi* flap its wings, flutter. ~**eo** *m* flapping (of the wings)

aleve *a* treacherous

alevín *m* young fish

alevos|ía *f* treachery. ~**o** *a* treacherous

alfab|ético *a* alphabetical. ~**etizar** [10] *vt* alphabetize; teach to read

and write ⟨*a uno*⟩. **~eto** *m* alphabet.
~eto Morse Morse code
alfalfa *f* lucerne (*Brit*), alfalfa
(*Amer*)
alfar *m* pottery. **~ería** *f* pottery.
~ero *m* potter
alféizar *m* window-sill
alferecía *f* epilepsy
alférez *m* second lieutenant
alfil *m* (*en ajedrez*) bishop
alfile|r *m* pin. **~razo** *m* pinprick.
~tero *m* pin-case
alfombr|a *f* (*grande*) carpet;
(*pequeña*) rug, mat. **~ar** *vt* carpet.
~illa *f* rug, mat; (*med*) German
measles
alforja *f* saddle-bag
algas *fpl* seaweed
algarabía *f* (*fig, fam*) gibberish,
nonsense
algarada *f* uproar
algarrob|a *f* carob bean. **~o** *m* carob
tree
algazara *f* uproar
álgebra *f* algebra
algebraico *a* algebraic
álgido *a* (*fig*) decisive
algo *pron* something; (*en frases
interrogativas*) anything. ● *adv*
rather. ¿**~ más?** is there anything
else? ¿**quieres tomar algo?** (*de beber*)
would you like a drink?; (*de comer*)
would you like something to eat?
algod|ón *m* cotton. **~ón de azúcar**
candy floss (*Brit*), cotton candy
(*Amer*). **~onero** *a* cotton. ● *m* cotton plant. **~ón hidrófilo** cotton
wool
alguacil *m* bailiff
alguien *pron* someone, somebody;
(*en frases interrogativas*) anyone,
anybody
alguno *a* (*delante de nombres mas-
culinos en singular* **algún**) some; (*en
frases interrogativas*) any; (*pospuesto al nombre en frases negativas*) at all. **no tiene idea alguna** he
hasn't any idea at all. ● *pron* one;
(*en plural*) some; (*alguien*)
someone. **alguna que otra vez** from
time to time. **algunas veces, alguna
vez** sometimes
alhaja *f* piece of jewellery; (*fig*) treasure. **~r** *vt* deck with jewels; (*amueblar*) furnish
alharaca *f* fuss
alhelí *m* wallflower
alheña *f* privet
alhucema *f* lavender

alia|do *a* allied. ● *m* ally. **~nza** *f* alli-
ance; (*anillo*) wedding ring. **~r** [20]
vt combine. **~rse** *vpr* be combined;
(*formar una alianza*) form an
alliance
alias *adv* & *m* alias
alicaído *a* (*fig, débil*) weak; (*fig, abatido*) depressed
alicates *mpl* pliers
aliciente *m* incentive; (*de un lugar*)
attraction
alien|ado *a* mentally ill. **~ista** *m* & *f*
psychiatrist
aliento *m* breath; (*ánimo*) courage
aligera|miento *m* lightening; (*ali-
vio*) alleviation. **~r** *vt* make lighter;
(*aliviar*) alleviate, ease; (*apresurar*)
quicken
alij|ar *vt* (*descargar*) unload;
smuggle ⟨*contrabando*⟩. **~o** *m*
unloading; (*contrabando*) contraband
alimaña *f* vicious animal
aliment|ación *f* food; (*acción*) feed-
ing. **~ar** *vt* feed; (*nutrir*) nourish.
● *vi* be nourishing. **~arse** *vpr* feed
(**con, de** on). **~icio** *a* nourishing.
~o *m* food. **~os** *mpl* (*jurid*)
alimony. **productos** *mpl* **~icios**
foodstuffs
alimón. al ~ *adv* jointly
alinea|ción *f* alignment; (*en
deportes*) line-up. **~r** *vt* align, line
up
aliñ|ar *vt* (*culin*) season. **~o** *m*
seasoning
alioli *m* garlic sauce
alisar *vt* smooth
alisios *apl.* **vientos** *mpl* **~** trade
winds
aliso *m* alder (tree)
alista|miento *m* enrolment. **~r** *vt*
put on a list; (*mil*) enlist. **~rse** *vpr*
enrol; (*mil*) enlist
aliteración *f* alliteration
alivi|ador *a* comforting. **~ar** *vt*
lighten; relieve ⟨*dolor, etc*⟩; (*hurtar,
fam*) steal, pinch (*fam*). **~arse** *vpr*
⟨*dolor*⟩ diminish; ⟨*persona*⟩ get
better. **~o** *m* relief
aljibe *m* tank
alma *f* soul; (*habitante*) inhabitant
almac|én *m* warehouse; (*LAm,
tienda*) grocer's shop; (*de un arma*)
magazine. **~enes** *mpl* department
store. **~enaje** *m* storage; (*derechos*)
storage charges. **~enamiento** *m*
storage; (*mercancías almacenadas*)
stock. **~enar** *vt* store; stock up with

⟨provisiones⟩. **~enero** m (Arg)
shopkeeper. **~enista** m & f shopkeeper
almádena f sledge-hammer
almanaque m almanac
almeja f clam
almendr|a f almond. **~ado** a
almond-shaped. **~o** m almond tree
almiar m haystack
alm|íbar m syrup. **~ibarado** a
syrupy. **~ibarar** vt cover in syrup
almid|ón m starch. **~onado** a
starched; (fig, estirado) starchy
alminar m minaret
almirant|azgo m admiralty. **~e** m
admiral
almirez m mortar
almizcle m musk
almohad|a f cushion; (de la cama)
pillow; (funda) pillowcase. **~illa** f
small cushion; (acerico) pincushion. **~ón** m large pillow, bolster.
consultar con la **~a** sleep on it
almorranas fpl haemorrhoids, piles
alm|orzar [2 & 10] vt (a mediodía)
have for lunch; (desayunar) have
for breakfast. ● vi (a mediodía) have
lunch; (desayunar) have breakfast.
~uerzo m (a mediodía) lunch;
(desayuno) breakfast
alocado a scatter-brained
alocución f address, speech
aloja|do m (Mex) lodger, guest. **~mi-
ento** m accommodation. **~r** vt put
up. **~rse** vpr stay
alondra f lark
alpaca f alpaca
alpargat|a f canvas shoe, espadrille.
~ería f shoe shop
Alpes mpl Alps
alpin|ismo m mountaineering,
climbing. **~ista** m & f mountaineer,
climber. **~o** a Alpine
alpiste m birdseed
alquil|ar vt (tomar en alquiler) hire
⟨vehículo⟩, rent ⟨piso, casa⟩; (dar en
alquiler) hire (out) ⟨vehículo⟩, rent
(out) ⟨piso, casa⟩. **~arse** vpr ⟨casa⟩
be let; ⟨vehículo⟩ be on hire. se
alquila to let (Brit), for rent (Amer).
~er m (acción de alquilar un piso
etc) renting; (acción de alquilar un
vehículo) hiring; (precio por el que se
alquila un piso etc) rent; (precio por
el que se alquila un vehículo) hire
charge. de **~er** for hire
alquimi|a f alchemy. **~sta** m al-
chemist
alquitara f still. **~r** vt distil

alquitr|án m tar. **~anar** vt tar
alrededor adv around. **~ de**
around; (con números) about. **~es**
mpl surroundings; (de una ciudad)
outskirts
alta f discharge
altamente adv highly
altaner|ía f (orgullo) pride. **~o** a
proud, haughty
altar m altar
altavoz m loudspeaker
altera|bilidad f changeability. **~ble**
a changeable. **~ción** f change,
alteration. **~do** a changed, altered;
(perturbado) disturbed. **~r** vt
change, alter; (perturbar) disturb;
(enfadar) anger, irritate. **~rse** vpr
change, alter; (agitarse) get upset;
(enfadarse) get angry; ⟨comida⟩ go
off
alterca|do m argument. **~r** [7] vi
argue
altern|ado a alternate. **~ador** m
alternator. **~ante** a alternating.
~ar vt/i alternate. **~arse** vpr take
turns. **~ativa** f alternative. **~ativo**
a alternating. **~o** a alternate
alteza f height. **A~** (título) Highness
altibajos mpl (de terreno) unevenness; (fig) ups and downs
altiplanicie f high plateau
altísimo a very high. ● m. el **A~** the
Almighty
altisonánte a, **altísono** a pompous
altitud f height; (aviat, geog)
altitude
altiv|ez f arrogance. **~o** a arrogant
alto a high; ⟨persona⟩ tall; ⟨voz⟩
loud; (fig, elevado) lofty; (mus) ⟨no-
ta⟩ high(-pitched); (mus) ⟨voz,
instrumento⟩ alto; ⟨horas⟩ early.
tiene 3 metros de **~** it is 3 metres
high. ● adv high; (de sonidos)
loud(ly). ● m height; (de un edificio)
high floor; (viola) viola; (voz) alto;
(parada) stop. ● int halt!, stop! en lo
~ de on the top of
altoparlante m (esp LAm)
loudspeaker
altruis|mo m altruism. **~ta** a altru-
istic. ● m & f altruist
altura f height; (altitud) altitude; (de
agua) depth; (fig, cielo) sky. a estas
~s at this stage. tiene 3 metros de
~ it is 3 metres high
alubia f French bean
alucinación f hallucination
alud m avalanche

aludi|do *a* in question. **darse por ~do** take it personally. **no darse por ~do** turn a deaf ear. **~r** *vi* mention

alumbra|do *a* lit; *(achispado, fam)* tipsy. ● *m* lighting. **~miento** *m* lighting; *(parto)* childbirth. **~r** *vt* light. ● *vi* give birth. **~rse** *vpr* *(emborracharse)* get tipsy

aluminio *m* aluminium *(Brit)*, aluminum *(Amer)*

alumno *m* pupil; *(univ)* student

aluniza|je *m* landing on the moon. **~r** [10] *vi* land on the moon

alusi|ón *f* allusion. **~vo** *a* allusive

alverja *f* vetch; *(LAm, guisante)* pea

alza *f* rise. **~cuello** *m* clerical collar, dog-collar *(fam)*. **~da** *f* *(de caballo)* height; *(jurid)* appeal. **~do** *a* raised; *(persona)* fraudulently bankrupt; *(Mex, soberbio)* vain; *(precio)* fixed. **~miento** *m* raising; *(aumento)* rise, increase; *(pol)* revolt. **~r** [10] *vt* raise, lift (up); raise *(precios)*. **~rse** *vpr* rise; *(ponerse en pie)* stand up; *(pol)* revolt; *(quebrar)* go fraudulently bankrupt; *(apelar)* appeal

allá *adv* there. ¡**~ él!** that's his business. **~ fuera** out there. **~ por el 1970** around about 1970. **el más ~** the beyond. **más ~** further on. **más ~ de** beyond. **por ~** over there

allana|miento *m* levelling; *(de obstáculos)* removal. **~miento de morada** burglary. **~r** *vt* level; remove *(obstáculos)*; *(fig)* iron out *(dificultades etc)*; burgle *(una casa)*. **~rse** *vpr* level off; *(hundirse)* fall down; *(ceder)* submit (**a** to)

allega|do *a* close. ● *m* relation. **~r** [12] *vt* collect

allí *adv* there; *(tiempo)* then. **~ donde** wherever. **~ fuera** out there. **por ~** over there

ama *f* lady of the house. **~ de casa** housewife. **~ de cría** wet-nurse. **~ de llaves** housekeeper

amab|ilidad *f* kindness. **~le** *a* kind; *(simpático)* nice

amado *a* dear. **~r** *m* lover

amaestra|do *a* trained; *(en circo)* performing. **~miento** *m* training. **~r** *vt* train

amag|ar [12] *vt* *(amenazar)* threaten; *(mostrar intención de)* show signs of. ● *vi* threaten; *(algo bueno)* be in the offing. **~o** *m* threat; *(señal)* sign; *(med)* sympton

amalgama *f* amalgam. **~r** *vt* amalgamate

amamantar *vt* breast-feed

amancebarse *vpr* live together

amanecer *m* dawn. ● *vi* dawn; *(persona)* wake up. **al ~** at dawn, at daybreak

amanera|do *a* affected. **~miento** *m* affectation. **~rse** *vpr* become affected

amanezca *f* *(Mex)* dawn

amansa|dor *m* tamer. **~miento** *m* taming. **~r** *vt* tame; break in *(un caballo)*; soothe *(dolor etc)*. **~rse** *vpr* calm down

amante *a* fond. ● *m & f* lover

amañ|ar *vt* arrange. **~o** *m* scheme

amapola *f* poppy

amar *vt* love

amara|je *m* landing on the sea; *(de astronave)* splash-down. **~r** *vt* land on the sea; *(astronave)* splash down

amarg|ado *a* embittered. **~ar** [12] *vt* make bitter; embitter *(persona)*. **~arse** *vpr* get bitter. **~o** *a* bitter. ● *m* bitterness. **~ura** *f* bitterness

amariconado *a* effeminate

amarill|ear *vi* go yellow. **~ento** *a* yellowish; *(tez)* sallow. **~ez** *f* yellow; *(de una persona)* paleness. **~o** *a & m* yellow

amarra *f* mooring rope. **~s** *fpl* *(fig, fam)* influence. **~do** *a* *(LAm)* mean. **~r** *vt* moor; *(atar)* tie. ● *vi* *(empollar, fam)* study hard, swot *(fam)*

amartillar *vt* cock *(arma de fuego)*

amas|ar *vt* knead; *(fig, tramar, fam)* concoct, cook up *(fam)*. **~ijo** *m* dough; *(acción)* kneading; *(fig, mezcla, fam)* hotchpotch

amate *m* *(Mex)* fig tree

amateur *a & m & f* amateur

amatista *f* amethyst

amazona *f* Amazon; *(mujer varonil)* mannish woman; *(que monta a caballo)* horsewoman

Amazonas *m*. **el río ~** the Amazon

ambages *mpl* circumlocutions. **sin ~** in plain language

ámbar *m* amber

ambarino *a* amber

ambici|ón *f* ambition. **~onar** *vt* strive after. **~onar ser** have an ambition to be. **~oso** *a* ambitious. ● *m* ambitious person

ambidextro *a* ambidextrous. ● *m* ambidextrous person

ambient|ar *vt* give an atmosphere to. **~arse** *vpr* adapt o.s. **~e** *m* atmosphere; *(medio)* environment

ambig|uamente *adv* ambiguously. **~üedad** *f* ambiguity. **~uo** *a* ambiguous; (*fig, afeminado, fam*) effeminate

ámbito *m* ambit

ambos *a* & *pron* both. **~ a dos** both (of them)

ambulancia *f* ambulance; (*hospital móvil*) field hospital

ambulante *a* travelling

ambulatorio *m* out-patients' department

amedrentar *vt* frighten, scare. **~se** *vpr* be frightened

amén *m* amen. ● *int* amen! **en un decir ~** in an instant

amenaza *f* threat. **~dor** *a*, **~nte** *a* threatening. **~r** [10] *vt* threaten

amen|idad *f* pleasantness. **~izar** [10] *vt* brighten up. **~o** *a* pleasant

América *f* America. **~ Central** Central America. **~ del Norte** North America. **~ del Sur** South America. **~ Latina** Latin America

american|a *f* jacket. **~ismo** *m* Americanism. **~ista** *m* & *f* Americanist. **~o** *a* American

amerindio *a* & *m* & *f* Amerindian, American Indian

ameriza|je *m* landing on the sea; (*de astronave*) splash-down. **~r** [10] *vt* land on the sea; ⟨astronave⟩ splash down

ametralla|dora *f* machine-gun. **~r** *vt* machine-gun

amianto *m* asbestos

amig|a *f* friend; (*novia*) girl-friend; (*amante*) lover. **~able** *a* friendly. **~ablemente** *adv* amicably. **~rse** [12] *vpr* live together

am|ígdala *f* tonsil. **~igdalitis** *f* tonsillitis

amigo *a* friendly. ● *m* friend; (*novio*) boy-friend; (*amante*) lover. **ser ~ de** be fond of. **ser muy ~s** be good friends

amilanar *vt* frighten, scare. **~se** *vpr* be frightened

aminorar *vt* lessen; slow down ⟨velocidad⟩

amist|ad *f* friendship. **~ades** *mpl* friends. **~osamente** *adv* amicably. **~oso** *a* friendly

amnesia *f* amnesia

amnist|ía *f* amnesty. **~iar** [20] *vt* grant an amnesty to

amo *m* master; (*dueño*) owner; (*jefe*) boss; (*cabeza de familia*) head of the family

amodorra|miento *m* sleepiness. **~rse** *vpr* get sleepy

amojonar *vt* mark out

amola|dor *m* knife-grinder. **~r** [2] *vt* sharpen; (*molestar, fam*) annoy

amoldar *vt* mould; (*acomodar*) fit

amonedar *vt* coin, mint

amonesta|ción *f* rebuke, reprimand; (*de una boda*) banns. **~r** *vt* rebuke, reprimand; (*anunciar la boda*) publish the banns

amoníaco *m*, **amoníaco** *m* ammonia

amontillado *m* Amontillado, pale dry sherry

amontona|damente *adv* in a heap. **~miento** *m* piling up. **~r** *vt* pile up; (*fig, acumular*) accumulate. **~rse** *vpr* pile up; ⟨gente⟩ crowd together; (*amancebarse, fam*) live together

amor *m* love. **~es** *mpl* (*relaciones amorosas*) love affairs. **con mil ~es, de mil ~es** with (the greatest of) pleasure. **hacer el ~** make love. **por (el) ~ de Dios** for God's sake

amorata|do *a* purple; (*de frío*) blue. **~rse** *vpr* go black and blue

amorcillo *m* Cupid

amordazar [10] *vt* gag; (*fig*) silence

amorfo *a* amorphous, shapeless

amor: ~ío *m* affair. **~oso** *a* loving; ⟨cartas⟩ love

amortajar *vt* shroud

amortigua|dor *a* deadening. ● *m* (*auto*) shock absorber. **~miento** *m* deadening; (*de la luz*) dimming. **~r** [15] *vt* deaden ⟨ruido⟩; dim ⟨luz⟩; cushion ⟨golpe⟩; tone down ⟨color⟩

amortiza|ble *a* redeemable. **~ción** *f* (*de una deuda*) repayment; (*recuperación*) redemption. **~r** [10] *vt* repay ⟨una deuda⟩

amoscarse [7] *vpr* (*fam*) get cross, get irritated

amostazarse [10] *vpr* get cross

amotina|do *a* & *m* insurgent, rebellious. **~miento** *m* riot; (*mil*) mutiny. **~r** *vt* incite to riot. **~rse** *vpr* rebel; (*mil*) mutiny

ampar|ar *vt* help; (*proteger*) protect. **~arse** *vpr* seek protection; (*de la lluvia*) shelter. **~o** *m* protection; (*de la lluvia*) shelter. **al ~o de** under the protection of

amperio *m* ampere, amp (*fam*)

amplia|ción *f* extension; (*photo*) enlargement. **~r** [20] *vt* enlarge, extend; (*photo*) enlarge

amplifica|ción *f* amplification. **~dor** *m* amplifier. **~r** [7] amplify

ampli|o *a* wide; (*espacioso*) spacious; ⟨*ropa*⟩ loose-fitting. **~tud** *f* extent; (*espaciosidad*) spaciousness; (*espacio*) space

ampolla *f* (*med*) blister; (*frasco*) flask; (*de medicamento*) ampoule, phial

ampuloso *a* pompous

amputa|ción *f* amputation; (*fig*) deletion. **~r** *vt* amputate; (*fig*) delete

amueblar *vt* furnish

amuinar *vt* (*Mex*) annoy

amuralla|do *a* walled. **~r** *vt* build a wall around

anacardo *m* (*fruto*) cashew nut

anaconda *f* anaconda

anacr|ónico *a* anachronistic. **~onismo** *m* anachronism

ánade *m & f* duck

anagrama *m* anagram

anales *mpl* annals

analfabet|ismo *m* illiteracy. **~o** *a & m* illiterate

analgésico *a & m* analgesic, pain-killer

an|álisis *m invar* analysis. **~álisis de sangre** blood test. **~alista** *m & f* analyst. **~alítico** *a* analytical. **~alizar** [10] *vt* analyze

an|alogía *f* analogy. **~álogo** *a* analogous

ananás *m* pineapple

anaquel *m* shelf

anaranjado *a* orange

an|arquía *f* anarchy. **~árquico** *a* anarchic. **~arquismo** *m* anarchism. **~arquista** *a* anarchistic. **●** *m & f* anarchist

anatema *m* anathema

anat|omía *f* anatomy. **~ómico** *a* anatomical

anca *f* haunch; (*parte superior*) rump; (*nalgas, fam*) bottom. **~s fpl de rana** frogs' legs

ancestral *a* ancestral

anciano *a* elderly, old. **●** *m* elderly man, old man; (*relig*) elder. **los ~s** old people

ancla *f* anchor. **~dero** *m* anchorage. **~r** *vi* anchor, drop anchor. **echar ~s** anchor. **levar ~s** weigh anchor

áncora *f* anchor; (*fig*) refuge

ancho *a* wide; ⟨*ropa*⟩ loose-fitting; (*fig*) relieved; (*demasiado grande*) too big; (*ufano*) smug. **●** *m* width; (*rail*) gauge. **a mis anchas, a sus**

anchas etc comfortable, relaxed. **quedarse tan ancho** behave as if nothing has happened. **tiene 3 metros de ~** it is 3 metres wide

anchoa *f* anchovy

anchura *f* width; (*medida*) measurement

andaderas *fpl* baby-walker

andad|or *a* good at walking. **●** *m* baby-walker. **~ura** *f* walking; (*manera de andar*) walk

Andalucía *f* Andalusia

andaluz *a & m* Andalusian

andamio *m* platform. **~s** *mpl* scaffolding

andar [25] *vt* (*recorrer*) cover, go. **●** *vi* walk; ⟨*máquina*⟩ go, work; (*estar*) be; (*moverse*) move. **●** *m* walk. **¡anda!** go on! come on! **~iego** *a* fond of walking; (*itinerante*) wandering. **~ por** be about. **~se** *vpr* (*marcharse*) go away

andén *m* platform; (*de un muelle*) quayside; (*LAm, acera*) pavement (*Brit*), sidewalk (*Amer*)

Andes *mpl* Andes

andino *a* Andean

Andorra *f* Andorra

andrajo *m* rag. **~so** *a* ragged

andurriales *mpl* (*fam*) out-of-the-way place

anduve *vb véase* **andar**

anécdota *f* anecdote

anega|dizo *a* subject to flooding. **~r** [12] *vt* flood. **~rse** *vpr* be flooded, flood

anejo *a* attached. **●** *m* annexe; (*de libro etc*) appendix

an|emia *f* anaemia. **~émico** *a* anaemic

anest|esia *f* anaesthesia. **~ésico** *a & m* anaesthetic. **~esista** *m & f* anaesthetist

anex|ión *f* annexation. **~ionar** *vt* annex. **~o** *a* attached. **●** *m* annexe

anfibio *a* amphibious. **●** *m* amphibian

anfiteatro *m* amphitheatre; (*en un teatro*) upper circle

anfitri|ón *m* host. **~ona** *f* hostess

ángel *m* angel; (*encanto*) charm

angelical *a*, **angélico** *a* angelic

angina *f*. **~ de pecho** angina (pectoris). **tener ~s** have tonsillitis

anglicano *a & m* Anglican

anglicismo *m* Anglicism

anglófilo *a & m* Anglophile

anglo|hispánico *a* Anglo-Spanish. **~sajón** *a & m* Anglo-Saxon

angosto *a* narrow

anguila *f* eel

angula *f* elver, baby eel

angular *a* angular

ángulo *m* angle; (*rincón, esquina*) corner; (*curva*) bend

anguloso *a* angular

angusti|a *f* anguish. **~ar** *vt* distress; (*inquietar*) worry. **~arse** *vpr* get distressed; (*inquietarse*) get worried. **~oso** *a* anguished; (*que causa angustia*) distressing

anhel|ante *a* panting; (*deseoso*) longing. **~ar** *vt* (+ *nombre*) long for; (+ *verbo*) long to. ● *vi* pant. **~o** *m* (*fig*) yearning. **~oso** *a* panting; (*fig*) eager

anidar *vi* nest

anill|a *f* ring. **~o** *m* ring. **~o de boda** wedding ring

ánima *f* soul

anima|ción *f* (*de personas*) life; (*de cosas*) liveliness; (*bullicio*) bustle; (*en el cine*) animation. **~do** *a* lively; (*sitio etc*) busy. **~dor** *m* compère, host

animadversión *f* ill will

animal *a* animal; (*fig, torpe, fam*) stupid. ● *m* animal; (*fig, idiota, fam*) idiot; (*fig, bruto, fam*) brute

animar *vt* give life to; (*dar ánimo*) encourage; (*dar vivacidad*) liven up. **~se** *vpr* (*decidirse*) decide; (*ponerse alegre*) cheer up. **¿te animas a venir al cine?** do you fancy coming to the cinema?

ánimo *m* soul; (*mente*) mind; (*valor*) courage; (*intención*) intention. **¡~!** come on!, cheer up! **dar ~s** encourage

animosidad *f* animosity

animoso *a* brave; (*resuelto*) determined

aniquila|ción *f* annihilation. **~miento** *m* annihilation. **~r** *vt* annihilate; (*acabar con*) ruin. **~rse** *vpr* deteriorate

anís *m* aniseed; (*licor*) anisette

aniversario *m* anniversary

ano *m* anus

anoche *adv* last night, yesterday evening

anochecer [11] *vi* get dark; (*persona*) be at dusk. **anochecí en Madrid** I was in Madrid at dusk. ● *m* nightfall, dusk. **al ~** at nightfall

anodino *a* indifferent

an|omalía *f* anomaly. **~ómalo** *a* anomalous

an|onimato *m* anonymity. **~ónimo** *a* anonymous; (*sociedad*) limited. ● *m* anonymity; (*carta*) anonymous letter

anormal *a* abnormal; (*fam*) stupid, silly. **~idad** *f* abnormality

anota|ción *f* noting; (*acción de poner notas*) annotation; (*nota*) note. **~r** *vt* (*poner nota*) annotate; (*apuntar*) make a note of

anquilosa|miento *m* paralysis. **~r** *vt* paralyze. **~rse** *vpr* become paralyzed

ansi|a *f* anxiety, worry; (*anhelo*) yearning. **~ar** [20 *o regular*] *vt* long for. **~edad** *f* anxiety. **~oso** *a* anxious; (*deseoso*) eager

antag|ónico *a* antagonistic. **~onismo** *m* antagonism. **~onista** *m & f* antagonist

antaño *adv* in days gone by

antártico *a & m* Antarctic

ante *prep* in front of, before; (*en comparación con*) compared with; (*frente a peligro, enemigo*) in the face of; (*en vista de*) in view of. ● *m* (*piel*) suede. **~anoche** *adv* the night before last. **~ayer** *adv* the day before yesterday. **~brazo** *m* forearm

ante... *pref* ante...

antece|dente *a* previous. ● *m* antecedent. **~dentes** *mpl* history, background. **~dentes penales** criminal record. **~der** *vt* precede. **~sor** *m* predecessor; (*antepasado*) ancestor

antedicho *a* aforesaid

antelación *f* advance. **con ~** in advance

antemano *adv*. **de ~** beforehand

antena *f* antenna; (*radio, TV*) aerial

anteojeras *fpl* blinkers

anteojo *m* telescope. **~s** *mpl* (*gemelos*) opera glasses; (*prismáticos*) binoculars; (*LAm, gafas*) glasses, spectacles

ante: **~pasados** *mpl* forebears, ancestors. **~pecho** *m* rail; (*de ventana*) sill. **~poner** [34] *vt* put in front (**a** of); (*fig*) put before, prefer. **~proyecto** *m* preliminary sketch; (*fig*) blueprint. **~puesto** *a* put before

anterior *a* previous; (*delantero*) front, fore. **~idad** *f*. **con ~idad** previously. **~mente** *adv* previously

antes *adv* before; (*antiguamente*) in days gone by; (*mejor*) rather; (*primero*) first. **~ de** before. **~ de ayer**

the day before yesterday. ~ **de que** + *subj* before. ~ **de que llegue** before he arrives. **cuanto** ~**, lo** ~ **posible** as soon as possible

antesala *f* anteroom; (*sala de espera*) waiting-room. **hacer** ~ wait (to be received)

anti... *pref* anti...

anti: ~**aéreo** *a* anti-aircraft. ~**biótico** *a* & *m* antibiotic. ~**ciclón** *m* anticyclone

anticip|ación *f* anticipation. **con** ~**ación** in advance. **con media hora de** ~**ación** half an hour early. ~**adamente** *adv* in advance. ~**ado** *a*. **por** ~**ado** in advance. ~**ar** *vt* bring forward; advance (*dinero*). ~**arse** *vpr* be early. ~**o** *m* (*dinero*) advance; (*fig*) foretaste

anti: ~**concepcional** *a* & *m* contraceptive. ~**conceptivo** *a* & *m* contraceptive. ~**congelante** *m* antifreeze

anticua|do *a* old-fashioned. ~**rio** *m* antique dealer. ~**rse** *vpr* go out of date

anticuerpo *m* antibody

antídoto *m* antidote

anti: ~**estético** *a* ugly. ~**faz** *m* mask. ~**gás** *a invar*. **careta** ~**gás** gas mask

antig|ualla *f* old relic. ~**uamente** *adv* formerly; (*hace mucho tiempo*) long ago. ~**üedad** *f* antiquity; (*objeto*) antique; (*en un empleo*) length of service. ~**uo** *a* old, ancient. **chapado a la** ~**ua** old-fashioned

antílope *m* antelope

Antillas *fpl* West Indies

antinatural *a* unnatural

antip|atía *f* dislike; (*cualidad de antipático*) unpleasantness. ~**ático** *a* unpleasant, unfriendly

anti: ~**semita** *m* & *f* anti-Semite. ~**semítico** *a* anti-Semitic. ~**semitismo** *m* anti-Semitism. ~**séptico** *a* & *m* antiseptic. ~**social** *a* antisocial

antítesis *f invar* antithesis

antoj|adizo *a* capricious. ~**arse** *vpr* fancy. **se le** ~**a un caramelo** he fancies a sweet. ~**o** *m* whim; (*de embarazada*) craving

antología *f* anthology

antorcha *f* torch

antro *m* cavern; (*fig*) dump, hole. ~ **de perversión** den of iniquity

antropófago *m* cannibal

antrop|ología *f* anthropology. ~**ólogo** *m* & *f* anthropologist

anua|l *a* annual. ~**lidad** *f* annuity. ~**lmente** *adv* yearly. ~**rio** *m* yearbook

anudar *vt* tie, knot; (*fig, iniciar*) begin; (*fig, continuar*) resume. ~**se** *vpr* get into knots. ~**se la voz** get a lump in one's throat

anula|ción *f* annulment, cancellation. ~**r** *vt* annul, cancel. ● *a* (*dedo*) ring. ● *m* ring finger

Anunciación *f* Annunciation

anunci|ante *m* & *f* advertiser. ~**ar** *vt* announce; advertise (*producto comercial*); (*presagiar*) be a sign of. ~**arse** *vpr* promise to be. ~**o** *m* announcement; (*para vender algo*) advertisement, advert (*fam*); (*cartel*) poster

anzuelo *m* (fish)hook; (*fig*) bait. **tragar el** ~ be taken in, fall for it

añadi|do *a* added. ~**dura** *f* addition. ~**r** *vt* add. **por** ~**dura** besides

añejo *a* (*vino*) mature; (*jamón etc*) cured

añicos *mpl* bits. **hacer** ~ (*romper*) smash (to pieces); (*dejar cansado*) wear out

añil *m* indigo

año *m* year. ~ **bisiesto** leap year. ~ **nuevo** new year. **al** ~ per year, a year. **¿cuántos** ~**s tiene? tiene 5** ~**s** how old is he? he's 5 (years old). **el** ~ **pasado** last year. **el** ~ **que viene** next year. **entrado en** ~**s** elderly. **los** ~**s 60** the sixties

añora|nza *f* nostalgia. ~**r** *vt* miss. ● *vi* pine

apabullar *vt* crush; (*fig*) intimidate

apacentar [1] *vt* graze. ~**se** *vpr* graze

apacib|ilidad *f* gentleness; (*calma*) peacefulness. ~**le** *a* gentle; (*tiempo*) mild

apacigua|dor *a* pacifying. ~**miento** *m* appeasement. ~**r** [15] *vt* pacify; (*calmar*) calm; relieve (*dolor etc*). ~**rse** *vpr* calm down

apadrina|miento *m* sponsorship. ~**r** *vt* sponsor; be godfather to (*a un niño*); (*en una boda*) be best man for

apaga|dizo *a* slow to burn. ~**do** *a* extinguished; (*color*) dull; (*aparato eléctrico*) off; (*persona*) lifeless; (*sonido*) muffled. ~**r** [12] *vt* put out (*fuego, incendio*); turn off, switch off (*aparato eléctrico*); quench (*sed*); muffle (*sonido*). ~**rse** *vpr* (*fuego*) go out; ⟨luz⟩ go out; ⟨sonido⟩ die away; (fig) pass away

apagón m blackout

apalabrar vt make a verbal agreement; (contratar) engage. ~se vpr come to a verbal agreement

apalanca|miento m leverage. ~r [7] vt (levantar) lever up; (abrir) lever open

apalea|miento m (de grano) winnowing; (de alfombras, frutos, personas) beating. ~r vt winnow ⟨grano⟩; beat ⟨alfombras, frutos, personas⟩; (fig) be rolling in ⟨dinero⟩

apantallado a (Mex) stupid

apañ|ado a handy. ~ar vt (arreglar) fix; (remendar) mend; (agarrar) grasp, take hold of. ~arse vpr get along, manage. ¡estoy ~ado! that's all I need!

aparador m sideboard

aparato m apparatus; (máquina) machine; (teléfono) telephone; (rad, TV) set; (ostentación) show, pomp. ~samente adv ostentatiously; (impresionante) spectacularly. ~sidad f ostentation. ~so a showy, ostentatious; ⟨caída⟩ spectacular

aparca|miento m car park (Brit), parking lot (Amer). ~r [7] vt/i park

aparea|miento m pairing off. ~r vt pair off; mate ⟨animales⟩. ~rse vpr match; ⟨animales⟩ mate

aparecer [11] vi appear. ~se vpr appear

aparej|ado a ready; (adecuado) fitting. llevar ~ado, traer ~ado mean, entail. ~o m preparation; (avíos) equipment

aparent|ar vt (afectar) feign; (parecer) look. ● vi show off. ~a 20 años she looks like she's 20. ~e a apparent; (adecuado, fam) suitable

apari|ción f appearance; (visión) apparition. ~encia f appearance; (fig) show. cubrir las ~encias keep up appearances

apartad|ero m lay-by; (rail) siding. ~o a separated; (aislado) isolated. ● m (de un texto) section. ~o (de correos) post-office box, PO box

apartamento m flat (Brit), apartment

apart|amiento m separation; (LAm, piso) flat (Brit), apartment; (aislamiento) seclusion. ~ar vt separate; (quitar) remove. ~arse vpr leave; abandon ⟨creencia⟩; (quitarse

de en medio) get out of the way; (aislarse) cut o.s. off. ~e adv apart; (por separado) separately; (además) besides. ● m aside; (párrafo) new paragraph. ~e de apart from. dejar ~e leave aside. eso ~e apart from that

apasiona|do a passionate; (entusiasta) enthusiastic; (falto de objetividad) biassed. ● m lover (de of). ~miento m passion. ~r vt excite. ~rse vpr get excited (de, por about), be mad (de, por about); (ser parcial) become biassed

ap|atía f apathy. ~ático a apathetic

apea|dero m (rail) halt. ~r vt fell ⟨árbol⟩; (disuadir) dissuade; overcome ⟨dificultad⟩; sort out ⟨problema⟩. ~rse vpr (de un vehículo) get off

apechugar [12] vi push (with one's chest). ~ con put up with

apedrear vt stone

apeg|ado a attached. ~o m (fam) affection. tener ~o a be fond of

apela|ción f appeal. ~r appeal; (recurrir) resort (a to)

apelmazar [10] vt compress

apellid|ar vt call. ~arse vpr be called. ¿cómo te apellidas? what's your surname? ~o m surname

apenar vt pain. ~se vpr grieve

apenas adv hardly, scarcely; (enseguida que) as soon as. ~ si (fam) hardly

ap|éndice m (med) appendix; (fig) appendage; (de un libro) appendix. ~endicitis f appendicitis

apercibi|miento m warning. ~r vt warn (de of, about); (amenazar) threaten. ~rse vpr prepare; (percatarse) provide o.s. (de with)

apergaminado a ⟨piel⟩ wrinkled

aperitivo m (bebida) aperitif; (comida) appetizer

aperos mpl agricultural equipment

apertura f opening

apesadumbrar vt upset. ~se vpr be upset

apestar vt stink out; (fastidiar) pester. ● vi stink (a of)

apet|ecer [11] vt long for; (interesar) appeal to. ¿te ~ece una copa? do you fancy a drink? do you feel like a drink?. ● vi be welcome. ~ecible a attractive. ~ito m appetite; (fig) desire. ~itoso a tempting

apiadarse vpr feel sorry (de for)

ápice *m* (*nada, en frases negativas*) anything. **no ceder un** ~ not give an inch

apicult|or *m* bee-keeper. ~**ura** *f* bee-keeping

apilar *vt* pile up

apiñar *vt* pack in. ~**se** *vpr* ⟨*personas*⟩ crowd together; ⟨*cosas*⟩ be packed tight

apio *m* celery

apisonadora *f* steamroller

aplacar [7] *vt* placate; relieve ⟨*dolor*⟩

aplanar *vt* smooth. ~**se** *vpr* become smooth; ⟨*persona*⟩ lose heart

aplasta|nte *a* overwhelming. ~**r** *vt* crush. ~**rse** *vpr* flatten o.s.

aplatanarse *vpr* become lethargic

aplau|dir *vt* clap, applaud; (*fig*) applaud. ~**so** *m* applause; (*fig*) praise

aplaza|miento *m* postponement. ~**r** [10] *vt* postpone; defer ⟨*pago*⟩

aplebeyarse *vpr* lower o.s.

aplica|ble *a* applicable. ~**ción** *f* application. ~**do** *a* ⟨*persona*⟩ diligent. ~**r** [7] *vt* apply; (*fijar*) attach. ~**rse** *vpr* apply o.s.

aplom|ado *a* self-confident; (*vertical*) vertical. ~**o** *m* (self-) confidence, aplomb; (*verticalidad*) verticality

apocado *a* timid

Apocalipsis *f* Apocalypse

apocalíptico *a* apocalyptic

apoca|miento *m* diffidence. ~**r** [7] *vt* belittle ⟨*persona*⟩. ~**rse** *vpr* feel small

apodar *vt* nickname

apodera|do *m* representative. ~**r** *vt* authorize. ~**rse** *vpr* seize

apodo *m* nickname

apogeo *m* (*fig*) height

apolilla|do *a* moth-eaten. ~**rse** *vpr* get moth-eaten

apolítico *a* non-political

apología *f* defence

apoltronarse *vpr* get lazy

apoplejía *f* stroke

apoquinar *vt/i* (*fam*) fork out

aporrear *vt* hit, thump; beat up ⟨*persona*⟩

aporta|ción *f* contribution. ~**r** *vt* contribute

aposent|ar *vt* put up, lodge. ~**o** *m* room, lodgings

apósito *m* dressing

aposta *adv* on purpose

apostar[1] [2] *vt/i* bet

apostar[2] *vt* station. ~**se** *vpr* station o.s.

apostilla *f* note. ~**r** *vt* add notes to

apóstol *m* apostle

apóstrofo *m* apostrophe

apoy|ar *vt* lean (**en** against); (*descansar*) rest; (*asentar*) base; (*reforzar*) support. ~**arse** *vpr* lean, rest. ~**o** *m* support

apreci|able *a* appreciable; (*digno de estima*) worthy. ~**ación** *f* appreciation; (*valoración*) appraisal. ~**ar** *vt* value; (*estimar*) appreciate. ~**ativo** *a* appreciative. ~**o** *m* appraisal; (*fig*) esteem

aprehensión *f* capture

apremi|ante *a* urgent, pressing. ~**ar** *vt* urge; (*obligar*) compel; (*dar prisa a*) hurry up. ● *vi* be urgent. ~**o** *m* urgency; (*obligación*) obligation

aprender *vt/i* learn. ~**se** *vpr* learn (by heart)

aprendiz *m* apprentice. ~**aje** *m* apprenticeship

aprensi|ón *f* apprehension; (*miedo*) fear. ~**vo** *a* apprehensive, fearful

apresa|dor *m* captor. ~**miento** *m* capture. ~**r** *vt* seize; (*prender*) capture

aprestar *vt* prepare. ~**se** *vpr* prepare

apresura|damente *adv* hurriedly, in a hurry. ~**do** *a* in a hurry; (*hecho con prisa*) hurried. ~**miento** *m* hurry. ~**r** *vt* hurry. ~**rse** *vpr* hurry

apret|ado *a* tight; (*difícil*) difficult; (*tacaño*) stingy, mean. ~**ar** [1] *vt* tighten; press ⟨*botón*⟩; squeeze ⟨*persona*⟩; (*comprimir*) press down. ● *vi* be too tight. ~**arse** *vpr* crowd together. ~**ón** *m* squeeze. ~**ón de manos** handshake

aprieto *m* difficulty. **verse en un** ~ be in a tight spot

aprisa *adv* quickly

aprisionar *vt* imprison

aproba|ción *f* approval. ~**r** [2] *vt* approve (of); pass ⟨*examen*⟩. ● *vi* pass

apropia|do *a* appropriate. ~**rse** *vpr*. ~**rse de** appropriate, take

aprovecha|ble *a* usable. ~**do** *a* (*aplicado*) diligent; (*ingenioso*) resourceful; (*egoísta*) selfish; (*económico*) thrifty. ~**miento** *m* advantage; (*uso*) use. ~**r** *vt* make use of; (*utilizar*) make use of. ● *vi* be useful. ~**rse** *vpr* make the most of it. **~rse de** take advantage of. **¡que aproveche!** enjoy your meal!

aprovisionar *vt* supply (**con, de** with)

aproxima|ción *f* approximation; (*proximidad*) closeness; (*en la lotería*) consolation prize. **~damente** *adv* roughly, approximately. **~do** *a* approximate, rough. **~r** *vt* bring near; (*fig*) bring together ⟨*personas*⟩. **~rse** *vpr* come closer, approach

apt|itud *f* suitability; (*capacidad*) ability. **~o** *a* (*capaz*) capable; (*adecuado*) suitable

apuesta *f* bet

apuesto *m* smart. ● *vb véase* **apostar**

apunta|ción *f* note. **~do** *a* sharp. **~dor** *m* prompter

apuntalar *vt* shore up

apunt|amiento *m* aiming; (*nota*) note. **~ar** *vt* aim ⟨*arma*⟩; (*señalar*) point at; (*anotar*) make a note of, note down; (*sacar punta*) sharpen; (*en el teatro*) prompt. **~arse** *vpr* put one's name down; score ⟨*triunfo, tanto etc*⟩. **~e** *m* note; (*bosquejo*) sketch. **tomar ~s** take notes

apuñalar *vt* stab

apur|adamente *adv* with difficulty. **~ado** *a* difficult; (*sin dinero*) hard up; (*agotado*) exhausted; (*exacto*) precise, carefully done. **~ar** *vt* exhaust; (*acabar*) finish; drain ⟨*vaso etc*⟩; (*fastidiar*) annoy; (*causar vergüenza*) embarrass. **~arse** *vpr* worry; (*esp LAm, apresurarse*) hurry up. **~o** *m* tight spot, difficult situation; (*vergüenza*) embarrassment; (*estrechez*) hardship, want; (*esp LAm, prisa*) hurry

aquejar *vt* trouble

aquel *a* (*f* **aquella**, *mpl* **aquellos**, *fpl* **aquellas**) that; (*en plural*) those; (*primero de dos*) former

aquél *pron* (*f* **aquélla**, *mpl* **aquéllos**, *fpl* **aquéllas**) that one; (*en plural*) those; (*primero de dos*) the former

aquello *pron* that; (*asunto*) that business

aquí *adv* here. **de ~** from here. **de ~ a 15 días** in a fortnight's time. **de ~ para allí** to and fro. **de ~ que** so that. **hasta ~** until now. **por ~** around here

aquiescencia *f* acquiescence

aquietar *vt* calm (down)

aquí: ~ fuera out here. **~ mismo** right here

árabe *a* & *m* & *f* Arab; (*lengua*) Arabic

Arabia *f* Arabia. **~ saudita, ~ saudí** Saudi Arabia

arábigo *a* Arabic

arado *m* plough. **~r** *m* ploughman

Aragón *m* Aragon

aragonés *a* & *m* Aragonese

arancel *m* tariff. **~ario** *a* tariff

arandela *f* washer

araña *f* spider; (*lámpara*) chandelier

arañar *vt* scratch

arar *vt* plough

arbitra|je *m* arbitration; (*en deportes*) refereeing. **~r** *vt/i* arbitrate; (*en fútbol etc*) referee; (*en tenis etc*) umpire

arbitr|ariedad *f* arbitrariness. **~ario** *a* arbitrary. **~io** *m* (free) will; (*jurid*) decision, judgement

árbitro *m* arbitrator; (*en fútbol etc*) referee; (*en tenis etc*) umpire

árbol *m* tree; (*eje*) axle; (*palo*) mast

arbol|ado *m* trees. **~adura** *f* rigging. **~eda** *f* wood

árbol: ~ genealógico family tree. **~ de navidad** Christmas tree

arbusto *m* bush

arca *f* (*caja*) chest. **~ de Noé** Noah's ark

arcada *f* arcade; (*de un puente*) arches; (*náuseas*) retching

arca|ico *a* archaic. **~ísmo** *m* archaism

arcángel *m* archangel

arcano *m* mystery. ● *a* mysterious, secret

arce *m* maple (tree)

arcén *m* (*de autopista*) hard shoulder; (*de carretera*) verge

arcilla *f* clay

arco *m* arch; (*de curva*) arc; (*arma, mus*) bow. **~ iris** *m* rainbow

archipiélago *m* archipelago

archiv|ador *m* filing cabinet. **~ar** *vt* file (away). **~o** *m* file; (*de documentos históricos*) archives

arder *vt/i* burn; (*fig, de ira*) seethe. **~se** *vpr* burn (up). **estar que arde** be very tense. **y va que arde** and that's enough

ardid *m* trick, scheme

ardiente *a* burning. **~mente** *adv* passionately

ardilla *f* squirrel

ardor *m* heat; *(fig)* ardour. ~ **del estómago** *m* heartburn. ~**oso** *a* burning

arduo *a* arduous

área *f* area

arena *f* sand; *(en deportes)* arena; *(en los toros)* (bull)ring. ~**l** *m* sandy area

arenga *f* harangue. ~**r** [12] *vt* harangue

aren|isca *f* sandstone. ~**isco** *a*, ~**oso** *a* sandy

arenque *m* herring. ~ **ahumado** kipper

argamasa *f* mortar

Argel *m* Algiers. ~**ia** *f* Algeria

argelino *a* & *m* Algerian

argentado *a* silver-plated

Argentina *f*. **la** ~ Argentina

argentin|ismo *m* Argentinism. ~**o** *a* silvery; *(de la Argentina)* Argentinian, Argentine. ● *m* Argentinian

argolla *f* ring

argot *m* slang

argucia *f* sophism

argüir [19] *vt (deducir)* deduce; *(probar)* prove, show; *(argumentar)* argue; *(echar en cara)* reproach. ● *vi* argue

argument|ación *f* argument. ~**ador** *a* argumentative. ~**ar** *vt/i* argue. ~**o** *m* argument; *(de libro, película etc)* story, plot; *(resumen)* synopsis

aria *f* aria

aridez *f* aridity, dryness

árido *a* arid, dry. ● *m*. ~**s** *mpl* dry goods

Aries *m* Aries

arisco *a* ⟨persona⟩ unsociable; ⟨animal⟩ vicious

arist|ocracia *f* aristocracy. ~**ócrata** *m* & *f* aristocrat. ~**ocrático** *a* aristocratic

aritmética *f* arithmetic

arma *f* arm, weapon; *(sección)* section. ~**da** *f* navy; *(flota)* fleet. ~ **de fuego** firearm. ~**do** *a* armed (**de** with). ~**dura** *f* armour; *(de gafas etc)* frame; *(tec)* framework. ~**mento** *m* arms, armaments; *(acción de armar)* armament. ~**r** *vt* arm (**de** with); *(montar)* put together. ~**r un lío** kick up a fuss. **La A**~**da Invencible** the Armada

armario *m* cupboard; *(para ropa)* wardrobe. ~ **ropero** wardrobe

armatoste *m* monstrosity, hulk *(fam)*

armazón *m* & *f* frame(work)

armer|ía *f* gunsmith's shop; *(museo)* war museum. ~**o** *m* gunsmith

armiño *m* ermine

armisticio *m* armistice

armonía *f* harmony

armónica *f* harmonica, mouth organ

armoni|oso harmonious. ~**zación** *f* harmonizing. ~**zar** [10] *vt* harmonize. ● *vi* harmonize; *(personas)* get on well (**con** with); ⟨colores⟩ go well (**con** with)

arnés *m* armour. **arneses** *mpl* harness

aro *m* ring, hoop; *(Arg, pendiente)* ear-ring

arom|a *m* aroma; *(de vino)* bouquet. ~**ático** *a* aromatic. ~**atizar** [10] *vt* perfume; *(culin)* flavour

arpa *f* harp

arpado *a* serrated

arpía *f* harpy; *(fig)* hag

arpillera *f* sackcloth, sacking

arpista *m* & *f* harpist

arp|ón *m* harpoon. ~**onar** *vt*, ~**onear** *vt* harpoon

arque|ar *vt* arch, bend. ~**arse** *vpr* arch, bend. ~**o** *m* arching, bending

arque|ología *f* archaeology. ~**ológico** *a* archaeological. ~**ólogo** *m* archaeologist

arquería *f* arcade

arquero *m* archer; *(com)* cashier

arqueta *f* chest

arquetipo *m* archetype; *(prototipo)* prototype

arquitect|o *m* architect. ~**ónico** *a* architectural. ~**ura** *f* architecture

arrabal *m* suburb; *(LAm, tugurio)* slum. ~**es** *mpl* outskirts. ~**ero** *a* suburban; *(de modales groseros)* common .

arracima|do *a* in a bunch; *(apiñado)* bunched together. ~**rse** *vpr* bunch together

arraiga|damente *adv* firmly. ~**r** [12] *vi* take root. ~**rse** *vpr* take root; *(fig)* settle

arran|cada *f* sudden start. ~**car** [7] *vt* pull up ⟨planta⟩; extract ⟨diente⟩; *(arrebatar)* snatch; *(auto)* start. ● *vi* start. ~**carse** *vpr* start. ~**que** *m* sudden start; *(auto)* start; *(de emoción)* outburst

arras *fpl* security

arrasa|dor *a* overwhelming, devastating. ~**r** *vt* level, smooth; raze to the ground ⟨edificio etc⟩; *(llenar)* fill to the brim. ● *vi* ⟨el cielo⟩ clear.

~rse *vpr* ‹*el cielo*› clear; ‹*los ojos*› fill with tears; (*triunfar*) triumph

arrastr|ado *a* (*penoso*) wretched. **~ar** *vt* pull; (*rozar contra el suelo*) drag (along); (*give rise to* ‹*consecuencias*›. ● *vi* trail on the ground. **~arse** *vpr* crawl; (*humillarse*) grovel. **~e** *m* dragging; (*transporte*) haulage. **estar para el ~e** (*fam*) have had it, be worn out. **ir ~ado** be hard up

arrayán *m* myrtle

arre *int* gee up! **~ar** *vt* urge on; give ‹*golpe*›

arrebañar *vt* scrape together; scrape clean ‹*plato etc*›

arrebat|ado *a* enraged; (*irreflexivo*) impetuous; ‹*cara*› flushed. **~ar** *vt* snatch (away); ‹*el viento*› blow away; (*fig*) win (over); captivate ‹*corazón etc*›. **~arse** *vpr* get carried away. **~o** *m* (*de cólera etc*) fit; (*éxtasis*) extasy

arrebol *m* red glow

arreciar *vi* get worse, increase

arrecife *m* reef

arregl|ado *a* neat; (*bien vestido*) well-dressed; (*moderado*) moderate. **~ar** *vt* arrange; (*poner en orden*) tidy up; sort out ‹*asunto, problema etc*›; (*reparar*) mend. **~arse** *vpr* (*ponerse bien*) improve; (*prepararse*) get ready; (*apañarse*) manage, make do; (*ponerse de acuerdo*) come to an agreement. **~árselas** manage, get by. **~o** *m* (*incl mus*) arrangement; (*acción de reparar*) repair; (*acuerdo*) agreement; (*orden*) order. **con ~o a** according to

arrellanarse *vpr* lounge, sit back

arremangar [12] *vt* roll up ‹*mangas*›; tuck up ‹*falda*›. **~se** *vpr* roll up one's sleeves

arremet|er *vt/i* attack. **~ida** *f* attack

arremolinarse *vpr* mill about

arrenda|dor *m* (*que da en alquiler*) landlord; (*que toma en alquiler*) tenant. **~miento** *m* renting; (*contrato*) lease; (*precio*) rent. **~r** [1] *vt* (*dar casa en alquiler*) let; (*dar cosa en alquiler*) hire out; (*tomar en alquiler*) rent. **~tario** *m* tenant

arreos *mpl* harness

arrepenti|miento *m* repentance, regret. **~rse** [4] *vpr*. **~rse de** be sorry, regret; repent ‹*pecados*›

arrest|ar *vt* arrest, detain; (*encarcelar*) imprison. **~o** *m* arrest; (*encarcelamiento*) imprisonment

arriar [20] *vt* lower ‹*bandera, vela*›; (*aflojar*) loosen; (*inundar*) flood. **~se** *vpr* be flooded

arriba *adv* (up) above; (*dirección*) up(wards); (*en casa*) upstairs. ● *int* up with; (*¡levántate!*) up you get!; (*¡ánimo!*) come on! **¡~ España!** long live Spain! **~ mencionado** aforementioned. **calle ~** up the street. **de ~ abajo** from top to bottom. **de 100 pesetas para ~** more than 100 pesetas. **escaleras ~** upstairs. **la parte de ~** the top part. **los de ~** those at the top. **más ~** above

arribar *vi* ‹*barco*› reach port; (*esp LAm, llegar*) arrive

arribista *m & f* self-seeking person, arriviste

arribo *m* (*esp LAm*) arrival

arriero *m* muleteer

arriesga|do *a* risky. **~r** [12] *vt* risk; (*aventurar*) venture. **~rse** *vpr* take a risk

arrim|ar *vt* bring close(r); (*apartar*) move out of the way ‹*cosa*›; (*apartar*) push aside ‹*persona*›. **~arse** *vpr* come closer, approach; (*apoyarse*) lean (**a** on). **~o** *m* support. **al ~o de** with the support of

arrincona|do *a* forgotten. **~rse** *vt* put in a corner; (*perseguir*) corner; (*arrumbar*) put aside; (*apartar a uno*) leave out, ignore. **~rse** *vpr* become a recluse

arriscado *a* ‹*terreno*› uneven

arrobar *vt* entrance. **~se** *vpr* be enraptured

arrocero *a* rice

arrodillarse *vpr* kneel (down)

arrogan|cia *f* arrogance; (*orgullo*) pride. **~te** *a* arrogant; (*orgulloso*) proud

arrogarse [12] *vpr* assume

arroj|ado *a* brave. **~ar** *vt* throw; (*dejar caer*) drop; (*emitir*) give off, throw out; (*producir*) produce. ● *vi* (*esp LAm, vomitar*) be sick. **~arse** *vpr* throw o.s. **~o** *m* courage

arrolla|dor *a* overwhelming. **~r** *vt* roll (up); (*atropellar*) run over; ‹*ejército*› crush; ‹*agua*› sweep away; (*tratar sin respeto*) have no respect for

arropar *vt* wrap up; (*en la cama*) tuck up; (*fig, amparar*) protect. **~se** *vpr* wrap (o.s.) up

arroy|o *m* stream; (*de una calle*) gutter; (*fig, de lágrimas*) flood; (*fig, de sangre*) pool. **poner en el ~o** throw into the street. **~uelo** *m* small stream

arroz *m* rice. **~al** *m* rice field. **~ con leche** rice pudding

arruga *f* (*en la piel*) wrinkle, line; (*en tela*) crease. **~r** [12] *vt* wrinkle; crumple ‹*papel*›; crease ‹*tela*›. **~rse** *vpr* ‹*la piel*› wrinkle, get wrinkled; ‹*tela*› crease, get creased

arruinar *vt* ruin; (*destruir*) destroy. **~se** *vpr* ‹*persona*› be ruined; ‹*edificio*› fall into ruins

arrullar *vt* lull to sleep. ● *vi* ‹*palomas*› coo. **~se** *vpr* bill and coo

arrumaco *m* caress; (*zalamería*) flattery

arrumbar *vt* put aside

arsenal *m* (*astillero*) shipyard; (*de armas*) arsenal; (*fig*) store

arsénico *m* arsenic

arte *m en singular, f en plural* art; (*habilidad*) skill; (*astucia*) cunning. **bellas ~s** fine arts. **con ~** skilfully. **malas ~s** trickery. **por amor al ~** for nothing, for love

artefacto *m* device

arter|amente *adv* artfully. **~ía** *f* cunning

arteria *f* artery; (*fig, calle*) main road

artero *a* cunning

artesan|al *a* craft. **~ía** *f* handicrafts. **~o** *m* artisan, craftsman. **objeto** *m* **de ~ía** hand-made article

ártico *a & m* Arctic

articula|ción *f* joint; (*pronunciación*) articulation. **~damente** *adv* articulately. **~do** *a* articulated; ‹*lenguaje*› articulate. **~r** *vt* articulate

articulista *m & f* columnist

artículo *m* article. **~s** *mpl* (*géneros*) goods. **~ de exportación** export commodity. **~ de fondo** editorial, leader

artificial *a* artificial

artificiero *m* bomb-disposal expert

artificio *m* (*habilidad*) skill; (*dispositivo*) device; (*engaño*) trick. **~so** *a* clever; (*astuto*) artful

artilugio *m* gadget

artiller|ía *f* artillery. **~o** *m* artilleryman, gunner

artimaña *f* trap

art|ista *m & f* artist; (*en espectáculos*) artiste. **~ísticamente** *adv* artistically. **~ístico** *a* artistic

artr|ítico *a* arthritic. **~itis** *f* arthritis

arveja *f* vetch; (*LAm, guisante*) pea

arzobispo *m* archbishop

as *m* ace

asa *f* handle

asad|o *a* roast(ed). ● *m* roast (meat), joint. **~o a la parrilla** grilled. **~o al horno** (*sin grasa*) baked; (*con grasa*) roast. **~or** *m* spit. **~ura** *f* offal

asalariado *a* salaried. ● *m* employee

asalt|ante *m* attacker; (*de un banco*) robber. **~ar** *vt* storm ‹*fortaleza*›; attack ‹*persona*›; raid ‹*banco etc*›; (*fig*) ‹*duda*› assail; (*fig*) ‹*idea etc*› cross one's mind. **~o** *m* attack; (*en boxeo*) round

asamble|a *f* assembly; (*reunión*) meeting; (*congreso*) conference. **~ísta** *m & f* member of an assembly

asapán *m* (*Mex*) flying squirrel

asar *vt* roast; (*fig, acosar*) pester (a with). **~se** *vpr* be very hot. **~ a la parrilla** grill. **~ al horno** (*sin grasa*) bake; (*con grasa*) roast

asbesto *m* asbestos

ascendencia *f* descent

ascend|ente *a* ascending. **~er** [1] *vt* promote. ● *vi* go up, ascend; ‹*cuenta etc*› come to, amount to; (*ser ascendido*) be promoted. **~iente** *m & f* ancestor; (*influencia*) influence

ascens|ión *f* ascent; (*de grado*) promotion. **~ional** *a* upward. **~o** *m* ascent; (*de grado*) promotion. **día** *m* **de la A~ión** Ascension Day

ascensor *m* lift (*Brit*), elevator (*Amer*). **~ista** *m & f* lift attendant (*Brit*), elevator operator (*Amer*)

asc|eta *m & f* ascetic. **~ético** *a* ascetic

asco *m* disgust. **dar ~** be disgusting; (*fig, causar enfado*) be infuriating. **estar hecho un ~** be disgusting. **hacer ~s de algo** turn up one's nose at sth. **me da ~ el ajo** I can't stand garlic. **¡qué ~!** how disgusting! **ser un ~** be a disgrace

ascua *f* ember. **estar en ~s** be on tenterhooks

asea|damente *adv* cleanly. **~do** *a* clean; (*arreglado*) neat. **~r** *vt* (*lavar*) wash; (*limpiar*) clean; (*arreglar*) tidy up

asedi|ar *vt* besiege; (*fig*) pester. **~o** *m* siege

asegura|do *a & m* insured. **~dor** *m* insurer. **~r** *vt* secure, make safe; (*decir*) assure; (*concertar un seguro*)

insure; (*preservar*) safeguard. ~**rse** *vpr* make sure
asemejarse *vpr* be alike
asenta|da *f*. **de una** ~**da** at a sitting. ~**do** *a* situated; (*arraigado*) established. ~**r** [1] *vt* place; (*asegurar*) settle; (*anotar*) note down. ● *vi* be suitable. ~**rse** *vpr* settle; (*estar situado*) be situated
asenti|miento *m* consent. ~**r** [4] *vi* agree (**a** to). ~**r con la cabeza** nod
aseo *m* cleanliness. ~**s** *mpl* toilets
asequible *a* obtainable; (*precio*) reasonable; (*persona*) approachable
asesin|ar *vt* murder; (*pol*) assassinate. ~**ato** *m* murder; (*pol*) assassination. ~**o** *m* murderer; (*pol*) assassin
asesor *m* adviser, consultant. ~**amiento** *m* advice. ~**ar** *vt* advise. ~**arse** *vpr*. ~**arse con/de** consult. ~**ía** *f* consultancy; (*oficina*) consultant's office
asestar *vt* aim (*arma*); strike (*golpe etc*); (*disparar*) fire
asevera|ción *f* assertion. ~**r** *vt* assert
asfalt|ado *a* asphalt. ~**ar** *vt* asphalt. ~**o** *m* asphalt
asfixia *f* suffocation. ~**nte** *a* suffocating. ~**r** *vt* suffocate. ~**rse** *vpr* suffocate
así *adv* so; (*de esta manera*) like this, like that. ● *a* such. ~ ~, ~ **asá**, ~ **asado** so-so. ~ **como** just as. ~... **como** both... and. ~ **pues** so. ~ **que** so; (*enseguida*) as soon as. ~ **sea** so be it. ~ **y todo** even so. **aun** ~ even so. **¿no es** ~? isn't that right? **y** ~ **(sucesivamente)** and so on
Asia *f* Asia
asiático *a* & *m* Asian
asidero *m* handle; (*fig, pretexto*) excuse
asidu|amente *adv* regularly. ~**idad** *f* regularity. ~**o** *a* & *m* regular
asiento *m* seat; (*situación*) site. ~ **delantero** front seat. ~ **trasero** back seat. **tome Vd** ~ please take a seat
asigna|ción *f* assignment; (*sueldo*) salary. ~**r** *vt* assign; allot (*porción, tiempo etc*)
asignatura *f* subject. ~ **pendiente** (*escol*) failed subject; (*fig*) matter still to be resolved
asil|ado *m* inmate. ~**ado político** refugee. ~**o** *m* asylum; (*fig*) shelter;

(*de ancianos etc*) home. ~**o de huérfanos** orphanage. **pedir** ~**o político** ask for political asylum
asimétrico *a* asymmetrical
asimila|ción *f* assimilation. ~**r** *vt* assimilate. ~**rse** *vpr* be assimilated. ~**rse a** resemble
asimismo *adv* in the same way, likewise
asir [45] *vt* grasp. ~**se** *vpr* grab hold (**a, de** of)
asist|encia *f* attendance; (*gente*) people (present); (*en un teatro etc*) audience; (*ayuda*) assistance. ~**encia médica** medical care. ~**enta** *f* assistant; (*mujer de la limpieza*) charwoman. ~**ente** *m* assistant. ~**ente social** social worker. ~**ido** *a* assisted. ~**ir** *vt* assist, help; (*un médico*) treat. ● *vi*. ~**ir a** attend, be present at
asm|a *f* asthma. ~**ático** *a* & *m* asthmatic
asn|ada *f* (*fig*) silly thing. ~**o** *m* donkey; (*fig*) ass
asocia|ción *f* association; (*com*) partnership. ~**do** *a* associated; (*miembro etc*) associate. ● *m* associate. ~**r** *vt* associate; (*com*) take into partnership. ~**rse** *vpr* associate; (*com*) become a partner
asolador *a* destructive
asolar[1] [1] *vt* destroy. ~**se** *vpr* be destroyed
asolar[2] *vt* dry up (*plantas*)
asoma|da *f* brief appearance. ~**r** *vt* show. ● *vi* appear, show. ~**rse** *vpr* (*persona*) lean out (**a, por** of); (*cosa*) appear
asombr|adizo *a* easily frightened. ~**ar** *vt* (*pasmar*) amaze; (*sorprender*) surprise. ~**arse** *vpr* be amazed; (*sorprenderse*) be surprised. ~**o** *m* amazement, surprise. ~**osamente** *adv* amazingly. ~**oso** *a* amazing, astonishing
asomo *m* sign. **ni por** ~ by no means
asonada *f* mob; (*motín*) riot
aspa *f* cross, X-shape; (*de molino*) (windmill) sail. ~**do** *a* X-shaped
aspaviento *m* show, fuss. ~**s** *mpl* gestures. **hacer** ~**s** make a big fuss
aspecto *m* look, appearance; (*fig*) aspect
aspereza *f* roughness; (*de sabor etc*) sourness
áspero *a* rough; (*sabor etc*) bitter
aspersión *f* sprinkling

aspiración *f* breath; (*deseo*) ambition

aspirador *a* suction. ~a *f* vacuum cleaner

aspira|nte *m* candidate. ~r *vt* breathe in; ‹*máquina*› suck up. ● *vi* breathe in; ‹*máquina*› suck. ~r a aspire to

aspirina *f* aspirin

asquear *vt* sicken. ● *vi* be sickening. ~se *vpr* be disgusted

asqueros|amente *adv* disgustingly. ~idad *f* filthiness. ~o *a* disgusting

asta *f* spear; (*de la bandera*) flagpole; (*mango*) handle; (*cuerno*) horn. a media ~ at half-mast. ~do *a* horned

asterisco *m* asterisk

astilla *f* splinter. ~s *fpl* firewood. ~r *vt* splinter. hacer ~s smash. hacerse ~s shatter

astillero *m* shipyard

astringente *a & m* astringent

astro *m* star

astr|ología *f* astrology. ~ólogo *m* astrologer

astrona|uta *m & f* astronaut. ~ve *f* spaceship

astr|onomía *f* astronomy. ~onómico *a* astronomical. ~ónomo *a* astronomer

astu|cia *f* cleverness; (*ardid*) cunning. ~to *a* astute; (*taimado*) cunning

asturiano *a & m* Asturian

Asturias *fpl* Asturias

asueto *m* time off, holiday

asumir *vt* assume

asunción *f* assumption. A~ Assumption

asunto *m* subject; (*cuestión*) matter; (*de una novela*) plot; (*negocio*) business. ~s *mpl* exteriores foreign affairs. el ~ es que the fact is that

asusta|dizo *a* easily frightened. ~r *vt* frighten. ~rse *vpr* be frightened

ataca|nte *m & f* attacker. ~r [7] *vt* attack

atad|ero *m* rope; (*cierre*) fastening; (*gancho*) hook. ~ijo *m* bundle. ~o *a* tied; (*fig*) timid. ● *m* bundle. ~ura *f* tying; (*cuerda*) string

ataj|ar *vi* take a short cut. ~o *m* short cut; (*grupo*) bunch. echar por el ~o take the easy way out

atalaya *f* watch-tower; (*fig*) vantage point

atañer [22] *vt* concern

ataque *m* attack; (*med*) fit, attack. ~ al corazón heart attack. ~ de nervios hysterics

atar *vt* tie (up). ~se *vpr* get tied up

atardecer [11] *vi* get dark. ● *m* dusk. al ~ at dusk

atarea|do *a* busy. ~rse *vpr* work hard

atasc|adero *m* (*fig*) stumbling block. ~ar [7] *vt* block; (*fig*) hinder. ~arse *vpr* get stuck; ‹*tubo etc*› block. ~o *m* obstruction; (*auto*) traffic jam

ataúd *m* coffin

atav|iar [20] *vt* dress up. ~iarse *vpr* dress up, get dressed up. ~ío *m* dress, attire

atemorizar [10] *vt* frighten. ~se *vpr* be frightened

Atenas *fpl* Athens

atenazar [10] *vt* (*fig*) torture; ‹*duda, miedo*› grip

atención *f* attention; (*cortesía*) courtesy, kindness; (*interés*) interest. ¡~! look out! ~ a beware of. llamar la ~ attract attention, catch the eye. prestar ~ pay attention

atender [1] *vt* attend to; heed ‹*consejo etc*›; (*cuidar*) look after. ● *vi* pay attention

atenerse [40] *vpr* abide (a by)

atentado *m* offence; (*ataque*) attack. ~ contra la vida de uno attempt on s.o.'s life

atentamente *adv* attentively; (*con cortesía*) politely; (*con amabilidad*) kindly. le saluda ~ (*en cartas*) yours faithfully

atentar *vi* commit an offence. ~ contra la vida de uno make an attempt on s.o.'s life

atento *a* attentive; (*cortés*) polite; (*amable*) kind

atenua|nte *a* extenuating. ● *f* extenuating circumstance. ~r [21] *vt* attenuate; (*hacer menor*) diminish, lessen. ~rse *vpr* weaken

ateo *a* atheistic. ● *m* atheist

aterciopelado *a* velvety

aterido *a* frozen (stiff), numb (with cold)

aterra|dor *a* terrifying. ~r *vt* terrify. ~rse *vpr* be terrified

aterriza|je *m* landing. ~je forzoso emergency landing. ~r [10] *vt* land

aterrorizar [10] *vt* terrify

atesorar *vt* hoard

atesta|do *a* packed, full up. ● *m* sworn statement. ~r *vt* fill up, pack; (*jurid*) testify

atestiguar [15] *vt* testify to; (*fig*) prove

atiborrar *vt* fill, stuff. **~se** *vpr* stuff o.s.

ático *m* attic

atilda|do *a* elegant, neat. **~r** *vt* put a tilde over; (*arreglar*) tidy up. **~rse** *vpr* smarten o.s. up

atina|damente *adv* rightly. **~do** *a* right; (*juicioso*) wise, sensible. **~r** *vt/i* hit upon; (*acertar*) guess right

atípico *a* exceptional

atiplado *a* high-pitched

atirantar *vt* tighten

atisb|ar *vt* spy on; (*vislumbrar*) make out. **~o** *m* spying; (*indicio*) hint, sign

atizar [10] *vt* poke; give (*golpe*); (*fig*) stir up; arouse, excite (*pasión etc*)

atlántico *a* Atlantic. **el (océano) A~** the Atlantic (Ocean)

atlas *m* atlas

atl|eta *m* & *f* athlete. **~ético** *a* athletic. **~etismo** *m* athletics

atm|ósfera *f* atmosphere. **~osférico** *a* atmospheric

atolondra|do *a* scatter-brained; (*aturdido*) bewildered. **~miento** *m* bewilderment; (*irreflexión*) thoughtlessness. **~r** *vt* bewilder; (*pasmar*) stun. **~rse** *vpr* be bewildered

atolladero *m* bog; (*fig*) tight corner

at|ómico *a* atomic. **~omizador** *m* atomizer. **~omizar** [10] *vt* atomize

átomo *m* atom

atónito *m* amazed

atonta|do *a* bewildered; (*tonto*) stupid. **~r** *vt* stun. **~rse** *vpr* get confused

atormenta|dor *a* tormenting. **●** *m* tormentor. **~r** *vt* torture. **~rse** *vpr* worry, torment o.s.

atornillar *vt* screw on

atosigar [12] *vt* pester

atracadero *m* quay

atracador *m* bandit

atracar [7] *vt* (*amarrar*) tie up; (*arrimar*) bring alongside; rob (*banco, persona*). **●** *vi* (*barco*) tie up; (*astronave*) dock. **~se** *vpr* stuff o.s. (**de** with)

atracci|ón *f* attraction. **~ones** *fpl* entertainment, amusements

atrac|o *m* hold-up, robbery. **~ón** *m*. **darse un ~ón** stuff o.s.

atractivo *a* attractive. **●** *m* attraction; (*encanto*) charm

atraer [41] *vt* attract

atragantarse *vpr* choke (**con** on). **la historia se me atraganta** I can't stand history

atranc|ar [7] *vt* bolt (*puerta*); block up (*tubo etc*). **~arse** *vpr* get stuck; (*tubo*) get blocked. **~o** *m* difficulty

atrapar *vt* trap; (*fig*) land (*empleo etc*); catch (*resfriado*)

atrás *adv* behind; (*dirección*) backwards; (*tiempo*) previously, before. **●** *int* back! **dar un paso ~** step backwards. **hacia ~, para ~** backwards

atras|ado *a* behind; (*reloj*) slow; (*con deudas*) in arrears; (*país*) backward. **llegar ~ado** arrive late. **~ar** *vt* slow down; (*retrasar*) put back; (*demorar*) delay, postpone. **●** *vi* (*reloj*) be slow. **~arse** *vpr* be late; (*reloj*) be slow; (*quedarse atrás*) be behind. **~o** *m* delay; (*de un reloj*) slowness; (*de un país*) backwardness. **~os** *mpl* arrears

atravesa|do *a* lying across; (*bizco*) cross-eyed; (*fig, malo*) wicked. **~r** [1] *vt* cross; (*traspasar*) go through; (*poner transversalmente*) lay across. **~rse** *vpr* lie across; (*en la garganta*) get stuck, stick; (*entrometerse*) interfere

atrayente *a* attractive

atrev|erse *vpr* dare. **~erse con** tackle. **~ido** *a* daring, bold; (*insolente*) insolent. **~imiento** *m* daring, boldness; (*descaro*) insolence

atribución *f* attribution. **atribuciones** *fpl* authority

atribuir [17] *vt* attribute; confer (*función*). **~se** *vpr* take the credit for

atribular *vt* afflict. **~se** *vpr* be distressed

atribut|ivo *a* attributive. **~o** *m* attribute; (*símbolo*) symbol

atril *m* lectern; (*mus*) music stand

atrincherar *vt* fortify with trenches. **~se** *vpr* entrench (o.s.)

atrocidad *f* atrocity. **decir ~es** make silly remarks. **¡qué ~!** how terrible!

atrochar *vi* take a short cut

atrojarse *vpr* (*Mex*) be cornered

atrona|dor *a* deafening. **~r** [2] *vt* deafen

atropell|adamente *adv* hurriedly. **~ado** *a* hasty. **~ar** *vt* knock down, run over; (*empujar*) push aside; (*maltratar*) bully; (*fig*) outrage, insult. **~arse** *vpr* rush. **~o** *m* (*auto*) accident; (*fig*) outrage

atroz *a* atrocious; (*fam*) huge. ∼**mente** *adv* atrociously, awfully

atuendo *m* dress, attire

atufar *vt* choke; (*fig*) irritate. ∼**se** *vpr* be overcome; (*enfadarse*) get cross

atún *m* tuna (fish)

aturdi|do *a* bewildered; (*irreflexivo*) thoughtless. ∼**r** *vt* bewilder, stun; ⟨*ruido*⟩ deafen. ∼**rse** *vpr* be stunned; (*intentar olvidar*) try to forget

atur(r)ullar *vt* bewilder

atusar *vt* smooth; trim ⟨*pelo*⟩

auda|cia *f* boldness, audacity. ∼**z** *a* bold

audib|ilidad *f* audibility. ∼**le** *a* audible

audición *f* hearing; (*concierto*) concert

audiencia *f* audience; (*tribunal*) court

auditor *m* judge-advocate; (*de cuentas*) auditor

auditorio *m* audience; (*sala*) auditorium

auge *m* peak; (*com*) boom

augur|ar *vt* predict; ⟨*cosas*⟩ augur. ∼**io** *m* omen. ∼**ios** *mpl.* con nuestros ∼**ios para** with our best wishes for

augusto *a* august

aula *f* class-room; (*univ*) lecture room

aulaga *f* gorse

aull|ar [23] *vi* howl. ∼**ido** *m* howl

aument|ar *vt* increase; put up ⟨*precios*⟩; magnify ⟨*imagen*⟩; step up ⟨*producción, voltaje*⟩. ● *vi* increase. ∼**arse** *vpr* increase. ∼**ativo** *a & m* augmentative. ∼**o** *m* increase; (*de sueldo*) rise

aun *adv* even. ∼ **así** even so. ∼ **cuando** although. **más** ∼ even more. **ni** ∼ not even

aún *adv* still, yet. ∼ **no ha llegado** it still hasn't arrived, it hasn't arrived yet

aunar [23] *vt* join. ∼**se** *vpr* join together

aunque *conj* although, (even) though

aúpa *int* up! **de** ∼ wonderful

aureola *f* halo

auricular *m* (*de teléfono*) receiver. ∼**es** *mpl* headphones

aurora *f* dawn

ausen|cia *f* absence. ∼**tarse** *vpr* leave. ∼**te** *a* absent. ● *m & f*

absentee; (*jurid*) missing person. **en** ∼ **de** in the absence of

auspicio *m* omen. **bajo los** ∼**s de** sponsored by

auster|idad *f* austerity. ∼**o** *a* austere

austral *a* southern. ● *m* (*unidad monetaria argentina*) austral

Australia *m* Australia

australiano *a & m* Australian

Austria *f* Austria

austriaco, austríaco *a & m* Austrian

aut|enticar [7] authenticate. ∼**enticidad** *f* authenticity. ∼**éntico** *a* authentic

auto *m* sentence; (*auto, fam*) car. ∼**s** *mpl* proceedings

auto... *pref* auto...

auto|ayuda *f* self-help. ∼**biografía** *f* autobiography. ∼**biográfico** *a* autobiographical. ∼**bombo** *m* self-glorification

autobús *m* bus. **en** ∼ by bus

autocar *m* coach (*Brit*), (long-distance) bus (*Amer*)

aut|ocracia *f* autocracy. ∼**ócrata** *m & f* autocrat. ∼**ocrático** *a* autocratic

autóctono *a* autochthonous

auto: ∼**determinación** *f* self-determination. ∼**defensa** *f* self-defence. ∼**didacto** *a* self-taught. ● *m* autodidact. ∼**escuela** *f* driving school. ∼**giro** *m* autogiro

autógrafo *m* autograph

automación *f* automation

autómata *m* robot

autom|ático *a* automatic. ● *m* press-stud. ∼**atización** *f* automation. ∼**atizar** [10] *vt* automate

automotor *a* (*f* **automotriz**) self-propelled. ● *m* diesel train

autom|óvil *a* self-propelled. ● *m* car. ∼**ovilismo** *m* motoring. ∼**ovilista** *m & f* driver, motorist

aut|onomía *f* autonomy. ∼**onómico** *a*, ∼**ónomo** *a* autonomous

autopista *f* motorway (*Brit*), freeway (*Amer*)

autopsia *f* autopsy

autor *m* author. ∼**a** *f* author(ess)

autori|dad *f* authority. ∼**tario** *a* authoritarian. ∼**tarismo** *m* authoritarianism

autoriza|ción *f* authorization. ∼**damente** *adv* officially, ∼**do** *a* authorized, offical; ⟨*opinión etc*⟩ authoritative. ∼**r** [10] *vt* authorize

auto: ∼**rretrato** *m* self-portrait. ∼**servicio** *m* self-service restaurant. ∼**stop** *m* hitch-hiking. **hacer** ∼**stop** hitch-hike

autosuficien|cia *f* self-sufficiency. ∼**te** *a* self-sufficient

autovía *f* dual carriageway

auxili|ar *a* assistant; ⟨*servicios*⟩ auxiliary. ● *m* assistant. ● *vt* help. ∼**o** *m* help. ¡∼**o!** help! ∼**os espirituales** last rites. **en** ∼**o de** in aid of. **pedir** ∼**o** shout for help. **primeros** ∼**os** first aid

Av. *abrev* (*Avenida*) Ave, Avenue

aval *m* guarantee

avalancha *f* avalanche

avalar *vt* guarantee

avalorar *vt* enhance; (*fig*) encourage

avance *m* advance; (*en el cine*) trailer; (*balance*) balance; (*de noticias*) early news bulletin. ∼ **informativo** publicity hand-out

avante *adv* (*esp LAm*) forward

avanza|do *a* advanced. ∼**r** [10] *vt* move forward. ● *vi* advance

avar|icia *f* avarice. ∼**icioso** *a*, ∼**iento** *a* greedy; (*tacaño*) miserly. ∼**o** *a* miserly. ● *m* miser

avasalla|dor *a* overwhelming. ∼**r** *vt* dominate

Avda. *abrev* (*Avenida*) Ave, Avenue

ave *f* bird. ∼ **de paso** (*incl fig*) bird of passage. ∼ **de presa**, ∼ **de rapiña** bird of prey

avecinarse *vpr* approach

avecindarse *vpr* settle

avejentarse *vpr* age

avellan|a *f* hazel-nut. ∼**o** *m* hazel (tree)

avemaría *f* Hail Mary. **al** ∼ at dusk

avena *f* oats

avenar *vt* drain

avenida *f* (*calle*) avenue; (*de río*) flood

avenir [53] *vt* reconcile. ∼**se** *vpr* come to an agreement

aventaja|do *a* outstanding. ∼**r** *vt* surpass

aventar [1] *vt* fan; winnow ⟨*grano etc*⟩; ⟨*viento*⟩ blow away

aventur|a *f* adventure; (*riesgo*) risk. ∼**a amorosa** love affair. ∼**ado** *a* risky. ∼**ar** *vt* risk. ∼**arse** *vpr* dare. ∼**a sentimental** love affair. ∼**ero** *a* adventurous. ● *m* adventurer

avergonza|do *a* ashamed; (*embarazado*) embarrassed. ∼**r** [10 & 16] *vt* shame; (*embarazar*) embar-

rass. ∼**rse** *vpr* be ashamed; (*embarazarse*) be embarrassed

aver|ía *f* (*auto*) breakdown; (*daño*) damage. ∼**iado** *a* broken down; (*fruta*) damaged, spoilt. ∼**iar** [20] *vt* damage. ∼**iarse** *vpr* get damaged; ⟨*coche*⟩ break down

averigua|ble *a* verifiable. ∼**ción** *f* verification; (*investigación*) investigation; (*Mex, disputa*) argument. ∼**dor** *m* investigator. ∼**r** [15] *vt* verify; (*enterarse de*) find out; (*investigar*) investigate. ● *vi* (*Mex*) quarrel

aversión *f* aversion (**a, hacia, por** for)

avestruz *m* ostrich

aviación *f* aviation; (*mil*) air force

aviado *a* (*Arg*) well off. **estar** ∼ be in a mess

aviador *m* (*aviat*) member of the crew; (*piloto*) pilot; (*Arg, prestamista*) money-lender; (*Arg, de minas*) mining speculator

aviar [20] *vt* get ready, prepare; (*arreglar*) tidy; (*reparar*) repair; (*LAm, prestar dinero*) lend money; (*dar prisa*) hurry up. ∼**se** *vpr* get ready. ¡**avíate!** hurry up!

av|ícula *a* poultry. ∼**icultor** *m* poultry farmer. ∼**icultura** *f* poultry farming

avidez *f* eagerness, greed

ávido *a* eager, greedy

avieso *a* (*maligno*) wicked

avinagra|do *a* sour. ∼**r** *vt* sour; (*fig*) embitter. ∼**rse** *vpr* go sour; (*fig*) become embittered

avío *m* preparation. ∼**s** *mpl* provisions; (*utensilios*) equipment

avi|ón *m* aeroplane (*Brit*), airplane (*Amer*). ∼**oneta** *f* light aircraft

avis|ado *a* wise. ∼**ar** *vt* warn; (*informar*) notify, inform; call ⟨*médico etc*⟩. ∼**o** *m* warning; (*anuncio*) notice. **estar sobre** ∼**o** be on the alert. **mal** ∼**ado** ill-advised. **sin previo** ∼**o** without notice

avisp|a *f* wasp. ∼**ado** *a* sharp. ∼**ero** *m* wasps' nest; (*fig*) mess. ∼**ón** *m* hornet

avistar *vt* catch sight of

avitualla|miento *m* supplying. ∼**r** *vt* provision

avivar *vt* stoke up ⟨*fuego*⟩; brighten up ⟨*color*⟩; arouse ⟨*interés, pasión*⟩; intensify ⟨*dolor*⟩. ∼**se** *vpr* revive; (*animarse*) cheer up

axila *f* axilla, armpit

axiom|a *m* axiom. **~ático** *a* axiomatic

ay *int* (*de dolor*) ouch!; (*de susto*) oh!; (*de pena*) oh dear! **~ de** poor. **¡~ de tí!** poor you!

aya *f* governess, child's nurse

ayer *adv* yesterday. ● *m* past. **antes de ~** the day before yesterday. **~ por la mañana** yesterday morning. **~ (por la) noche** last night

ayo *m* tutor

ayote *m* (*Mex*) pumpkin

ayuda *f* help, aid. **~ de cámara** valet. **~nta** *f*, **~nte** *m* assistant; (*mil*) adjutant. **~nte técnico sanitario (ATS)** nurse. **~r** *vt* help

ayun|ar *vi* fast. **~as** *fpl.* **estar en ~as** have had no breakfast; (*fig, fam*) be in the dark. **~o** *m* fasting

ayuntamiento *m* town council, city council; (*edificio*) town hall

azabache *m* jet

azad|a *f* hoe. **~ón** *m* (large) hoe

azafata *f* air hostess

azafrán *m* saffron

azahar *m* orange blossom

azar *m* chance; (*desgracia*) misfortune. **al ~** at random. **por ~** by chance

azararse *vpr* go wrong; (*fig*) get flustered

azaros|amente *adv* hazardously. **~o** *a* hazardous, risky; (*persona*) unlucky

azoga|do *a* restless. **~rse** [12] *vpr* be restless

azolve *m* (*Mex*) obstruction

azora|do *a* flustered, excited, alarmed. **~miento** *m* confusion, embarrassment. **~r** *vt* embarrass; (*aturdir*) alarm. **~rse** *vpr* get flustered, be alarmed

Azores *fpl* Azores

azot|aina *f* beating. **~ar** *vt* whip, beat. **~e** *m* whip; (*golpe*) smack; (*fig, calamidad*) calamity

azotea *f* flat roof. **estar mal de la ~** be mad

azteca *a* & *m* & *f* Aztec

az|úcar *m* & *f* sugar. **~ucarado** *a* sweet. **~ucarar** *vt* sweeten. **~ucarero** *m* sugar bowl

azucena *f* (white) lily

azufre *m* sulphur

azul *a* & *m* blue. **~ado** *a* bluish. **~ de lavar** (washing) blue. **~ marino** navy blue

azulejo *m* tile

azuzar *vt* urge on, incite

B

bab|a *f* spittle. **~ear** *vi* drool, slobber; (*niño*) dribble. **caerse la ~a** be delighted

babel *f* bedlam

babe|o *m* drooling; (*de un niño*) dribbling. **~ro** *m* bib

Babia *f.* **estar en ~** have one's head in the clouds

babieca *a* stupid. ● *m* & *f* simpleton

babor *m* port. **a ~** to port, on the port side

babosa *f* slug

babosada *f* (*Mex*) silly remark

babos|ear *vt* slobber over; (*niño*) dribble over. **~eo** *m* drooling; (*de niño*) dribbling. **~o** *a* slimy; (*LAm, tonto*) silly

babucha *f* slipper

babuino *m* baboon

baca *f* luggage rack

bacaladilla *f* small cod

bacalao *m* cod

bacon *m* bacon

bacteria *f* bacterium

bache *m* hole; (*fig*) bad patch

bachillerato *m* school-leaving examination

badaj|azo *m* stroke (of a bell). **~o** *m* clapper; (*persona*) chatterbox

bagaje *m* baggage; (*animal*) beast of burden; (*fig*) knowledge

bagatela *f* trifle

Bahamas *fpl* Bahamas

bahía *f* bay

bail|able *a* dance. **~ador** *a* dancing. ● *m* dancer. **~aor** *m* Flamenco dancer. **~ar** *vt/i* dance. **~arín** dancer. **~arina** *f* dancer; (*de baile clásico*) ballerina. **~e** *m* dance. **~e de etiqueta** ball. **ir a ~ar** go dancing

baja *f* drop, fall; (*mil*) casualty. **~ por maternidad** maternity leave. **~da** *f* slope; (*acto de bajar*) descent. **~mar** *m* low tide. **~r** *vt* lower; (*llevar abajo*) get down; bow (*la cabeza*). **~r la escalera** go downstairs. ● *vi* go down; (*temperatura, precio*) fall. **~rse** *vpr* bend down. **~r(se) de** get out of (*coche*); get off (*autobús, caballo, tren, bicicleta*). **dar(se) de ~** take sick leave

bajeza *f* vile deed

bajío *m* sandbank

bajo *a* low; (*de estatura*) short, small; ⟨*cabeza, ojos*⟩ lowered; (*humilde*) humble, low; (*vil*) vile, low; ⟨*color*⟩ pale; ⟨*voz*⟩ low; (*mus*) deep. ● *m* lowland; (*bajío*) sandbank; (*mus*) bass. ● *adv* quietly; ⟨*volar*⟩ low. ● *prep* under; (*temperatura*) below. ∼ **la lluvia** in the rain. **los** ∼**s fondos** the low district. **por lo** ∼ under one's breath; (*fig*) in secret
bajón *m* drop; (*de salud*) decline; (*com*) slump
bala *f* bullet; (*de algodón etc*) bale. ∼ **perdida** stray bullet. **como una** ∼ like a shot
balada *f* ballad
baladí *a* trivial
baladrón *a* boastful
baladron|ada *f* boast. ∼**ear** *vi* boast
balan|ce *m* swinging; (*de una cuenta*) balance; (*documento*) balance sheet. ∼**cear** *vt* balance. ● *vi* hesitate. ∼**cearse** *vpr* swing; (*vacilar*) hesitate. ∼**ceo** *m* swinging. ∼**za** *f* scales; (*com*) balance
balar *vi* bleat
balaustrada *f* balustrade, railing(s); (*de escalera*) banisters
balay *m* (*LAm*) wicker basket
balazo *m* (*disparo*) shot; (*herida*) bullet wound
balboa *f* (*unidad monetaria panameña*) balboa
balbuc|ear *vt/i* stammer; ⟨*niño*⟩ babble. ∼**eo** *m* stammering; (*de niño*) babbling. ∼**iente** *a* stammering; ⟨*niño*⟩ babbling. ∼**ir** [24] *vt/i* stammer; ⟨*niño*⟩ babble
balc|ón *m* balcony. ∼**onada** *f* row of balconies. ∼**onaje** *m* row of balconies
balda *f* shelf
baldado *a* disabled, crippled; (*rendido*) shattered. ● *m* disabled person, cripple
baldaquín *m*, **baldaquino** *m* canopy
baldar *vt* cripple
balde *m* bucket. **de** ∼ free (of charge). **en** ∼ in vain. ∼**ar** *vt* wash down
baldío *a* ⟨*terreno*⟩ waste; (*fig*) useless
baldosa *f* (floor) tile; (*losa*) flagstone
balduque *m* (*incl fig*) red tape
balear *a* Balearic. ● *m* native of the Balearic Islands. **las Islas** *fpl* **B**∼**es** the Balearics, the Balearic Islands

baleo *m* (*LAm, tiroteo*) shooting; (*Mex, abanico*) fan
balido *m* bleat; (*varios sonidos*) bleating
bal|ín *m* small bullet. ∼**ines** *mpl* shot
balística *f* ballistics
baliza *f* (*naut*) buoy; (*aviat*) beacon
balneario *m* spa; (*con playa*) seaside resort. ● *a*. **estación** *f* **balnearia** spa; (*con playa*) seaside resort
balompié *m* football (*Brit*), soccer
bal|ón *m* ball, football. ∼**oncesto** *m* basketball. ∼**onmano** *m* handball. ∼**volea** *m* volleyball
balotaje *m* (*LAm*) voting
balsa *f* (*de agua*) pool; (*plataforma flotante*) raft
bálsamo *m* balsam; (*fig*) balm
balsón *m* (*Mex*) stagnant water
baluarte *m* (*incl fig*) bastion
balumba *f* mass, mountain
ballena *f* whale
ballesta *f* crossbow
ballet /ba'le/ (*pl* **ballets** uba'le/) *m* ballet
bambole|ar *vi* sway; ⟨*mesa etc*⟩ wobble. ∼**arse** *vpr* sway; ⟨*mesa etc*⟩ wobble. ∼**o** *m* swaying; (*de mesa etc*) wobbling
bambú *m* (*pl* **bambúes**) bamboo
banal *a* banal. ∼**idad** *f* banality
banan|a *f* (*esp LAm*) banana. ∼**o** *m* (*LAm*) banana tree
banast|a *f* large basket. ∼**o** *m* large round basket
banc|a *f* banking; (*en juegos*) bank; (*LAm, asiento*) bench. ∼**ario** *a* bank, banking. ∼**arrota** *f* bankruptcy. ∼**o** *m* (*asiento*) bench; (*com*) bank; (*bajío*) sandbank. **hacer** ∼**arrota, ir a la** ∼**arrota** go bankrupt
banda *f* (*incl mus, radio*) band; (*grupo*) gang, group; (*lado*) side. ∼**da** *f* (*de aves*) flock; (*de peces*) shoal. ∼ **de sonido,** ∼ **sonora** sound-track
bandeja *f* tray; (*LAm, plato*) serving dish. **servir algo en** ∼ **a uno** hand sth to s.o. on a plate
bandera *f* flag; (*estandarte*) banner, standard
banderill|a *f* banderilla. ∼**ear** *vt* stick the banderillas in. ∼**ero** *m* banderillero
banderín *m* pennant, small flag, banner
bandido *m* bandit

bando *m* edict, proclamation; (*partido*) faction. **~s** *mpl* banns. **pasarse al otro ~** go over to the other side

bandolero *m* bandit

bandolina *f* mandolin

bandoneón *m* large accordion

banjo *m* banjo

banquero *m* banker

banqueta *f* stool; (*LAm, acera*) pavement (*Brit*), sidewalk (*Amer*)

banquete *m* banquet; (*de boda*) wedding reception. **~ar** *vt/i* banquet

banquillo *m* bench; (*jurid*) dock; (*taburete*) footstool

bañ|ado *m* (*LAm*) swamp. **~ador** *m* (*de mujer*) swimming costume; (*de hombre*) swimming trunks. **~ar** *vt* bathe, immerse; bath (*niño*); (*culin, recubrir*) coat. **~arse** *vpr* go swimming, have a swim; (*en casa*) have a bath. **~era** *f* bath, bath-tub. **~ero** *m* life-guard. **~ista** *m & f* bather. **~o** *m* bath; (*en piscina, mar etc*) swim; (*bañera*) bath, bath-tub; (*capa*) coat(ing)

baptisterio *m* baptistery; (*pila*) font

baquet|a *f* (*de fusil*) ramrod; (*de tambor*) drumstick. **~ear** *vt* bother. **~eo** *m* nuisance, bore

bar *m* bar

barahúnda *f* uproar

baraja *f* pack of cards. **~r** *vt* shuffle; juggle, massage ‹*cifras etc*›. ● *vi* argue (**con** with); (*enemistarse*) fall out (**con** with). **~s** *fpl* argument. **jugar a la ~** play cards. **jugar a dos ~s, jugar con dos ~s** be deceitful, indulge in double-dealing

baranda *f*, **barandal** *m*, **barandilla** *f* handrail; (*de escalera*) banisters

barat|a *f* (*Mex*) sale. **~ija** *f* trinket. **~illo** *m* junk shop; (*géneros*) cheap goods. **~o** *a* cheap. ● *m* sale. ● *adv* cheap(ly). **~ura** *f* cheapness

baraúnda *f* uproar

barba *f* chin; (*pelo*) beard. **~do** *a* bearded

barbacoa *f* barbecue; (*Mex, carne*) barbecued meat

bárbaramente *adv* savagely; (*fig*) tremendously

barbari|dad *f* barbarity; (*fig*) outrage; (*mucho, fam*) awful lot (*fam*). **¡qué ~dad!** how awful! **~e** *f* barbarity; (*fig*) ignorance. **~smo** *m* barbarism

bárbaro *a* barbaric, cruel; (*bruto*) uncouth; (*estupendo, fam*) terrific (*fam*). ● *m* barbarian. **¡qué ~!** how marvellous!

barbear *vt* (*afeitar*) shave; (*Mex, lisonjear*) fawn on

barbecho *m* fallow

barber|ía *f* barber's (shop). **~o** *m* barber; (*Mex, adulador*) flatterer

barbi|lampiño *a* beardless; (*fig*) inexperienced, green. **~lindo** *m* dandy

barbilla *f* chin

barbitúrico *m* barbiturate

barbo *m* barbel. **~ de mar** red mullet

barbot|ar *vt/i* mumble. **~ear** *vt/i* mumble. **~eo** *m* mumbling

barbudo *a* bearded

barbullar *vi* jabber

barca *f* (small) boat. **~ de pasaje** ferry. **~je** *m* fare. **~za** *f* barge

Barcelona *f* Barcelona

barcelonés *a* of Barcelona, from Barcelona. ● *m* native of Barcelona

barco *m* boat; (*navío*) ship. **~ cisterna** tanker. **~ de vapor** steamer. **~ de vela** sailing boat. **ir en ~** go by boat

bario *m* barium

barítono *m* baritone

barman *m* (*pl* **barmans**) barman

barniz *m* varnish; (*para loza etc*) glaze; (*fig*) veneer. **~ar** [10] *vt* varnish; glaze ‹*loza etc*›

bar|ométrico *a* barometric. **~ómetro** *m* barometer

bar|ón *m* baron. **~onesa** *f* baroness

barquero *m* boatman

barra *f* bar; (*pan*) French bread; (*de oro o plata*) ingot; (*palanca*) lever. **~ de labios** lipstick. **no pararse en ~s** stop at nothing

barrabasada *f* mischief, prank

barraca *f* hut; (*vivienda pobre*) shack, shanty

barranco *m* ravine, gully; (*despeñadero*) cliff, precipice

barre|dera *f* road-sweeper. **~dura** *f* rubbish. **~minas** *m* *invar* mine-sweeper

barren|a *f* drill, bit. **~ar** *vt* drill. **~o** *m* large (mechanical) drill. **entrar en ~a** ‹*avión*› go into a spin

barrer *vt* sweep; (*quitar*) sweep aside

barrera *f* barrier. **~ del sonido** sound barrier

barriada *f* district

barrica f barrel
barricada f barricade
barrido m sweeping
barrig|a f (pot-)belly. **~ón** a, **~udo** a pot-bellied
barril m barrel. **~ete** m keg, small barrel
barrio m district, area. **~bajero** a vulgar, common. **~s bajos** poor quarter, poor area. **el otro ~** (fig, fam) the other world
barro m mud; (arcilla) clay; (arcilla cocida) earthenware
barroco a Baroque. ● m Baroque style
barrote m heavy bar
barrunt|ar vt sense, have a feeling. **~e** m, **~o** m sign; (presentimiento) feeling
bartola f. **tenderse a la ~, tumbarse a la ~** take it easy
bártulos mpl things. **liar los ~** pack one's bags
barullo m uproar; (confusión) confusion. **a ~** galore
basa f, **basamento** m base; (fig) basis
basar vt base. **~se** vpr. **~se en** be based on
basc|a f crowd. **~as** fpl nausea. **~osidad** f filth. **la ~a** the gang
báscula f scales
bascular vi tilt
base f base; (fig) basis, foundation. **a ~ de** thanks to; (mediante) by means of; (en una receta) as the basic ingredient(s). **a ~ de bien** very well. **partiendo de la ~ de**, **tomando como ~** on the basis of
básico a basic
basílica f basilica
basilisco m basilisk. **hecho un ~** furious
basta f tack, tacking stitch
bastante a enough; (varios) quite a few, quite a lot of. ● adv rather, fairly; (mucho tiempo) long enough; (suficiente) enough; (Mex, muy) very
bastar vi be enough. **¡basta!** that's enough! **basta decir que** suffice it to say that. **basta y sobra** that's more than enough
bastardilla f italics. **poner en ~** italicize
bastardo m bastard; (fig, vil) mean, base
bastidor m frame; (auto) chassis. **~es** mpl (en el teatro) wings. **entre ~es** behind the scenes

bastión f (incl fig) bastion
basto a coarse. **~s** mpl (naipes) clubs
bast|ón m walking stick. **empuñar el ~ón** take command. **~onazo** m blow with a stick
basur|a f rubbish, garbage (Amer); (en la calle) litter. **~ero** m dustman (Brit), garbage collector (Amer); (sitio) rubbish dump; (recipiente) dustbin (Brit), garbage can (Amer). **cubo** m **de la ~a** dustbin (Brit), garbage can (Amer)
bata f dressing-gown; (de médico etc) white coat. **~ de cola** Flamenco dress
batall|a f battle. **~a campal** pitched battle. **~ador** a fighting. ● m fighter. **~ar** vi battle, fight. **~ón** m battalion. ● a. **cuestión** f **batallona** vexed question. **de ~a** everyday
batata f sweet potato
bate m bat. **~ador** m batter; (cricket) batsman
batería f battery; (mus) percussion. **~ de cocina** kitchen utensils, pots and pans
batido a beaten; (nata) whipped. ● m batter; (bebida) milk shake. **~ra** f beater. **~ra eléctrica** mixer
batín m dressing-gown
batir vt beat; (martillar) hammer; mint (monedas); whip (nata); (derribar) knock down. **~ el récord** break the record. **~ palmas** clap. **~se** vpr fight
batuta f baton. **llevar la ~** be in command, be the boss
baúl m trunk; (LAm, auto) boot (Brit), trunk (Amer)
bauti|smal a baptismal. **~smo** m baptism, christening. **~sta** a & m & f Baptist. **~zar** [10] vt baptize, christen
baya f berry
bayeta f (floor-)cloth
bayoneta f bayonet. **~zo** m (golpe) bayonet thrust; (herida) bayonet wound
baza f (naipes) trick; (fig) advantage. **meter ~** interfere
bazar m bazaar
bazofia f leftovers; (basura) rubbish
beat|itud f (fig) bliss. **~o** a blessed; (de religiosidad afectada) sanctimonious
bebé m baby
beb|edero m drinking trough; (sitio) watering place. **~edizo** a

drinkable. ● *m* potion; (*veneno*)
poison. **~edor** *a* drinking. ● *m*
heavy drinker. **~er** *vt/i* drink. **dar
de ~er a uno** give s.o. a drink. **~ida**
f drink. **~ido** *a* tipsy, drunk
beca *f* grant, scholarship. **~rio** *m*
scholarship holder, scholar
becerro *m* calf
befa *f* jeer, taunt. **~r** *vt* scoff at. **~rse**
vpr. **~rse de** scoff at. **hacer ~ de**
scoff at
beige /beis, bes/ *a & m* beige
béisbol *m* baseball
beldad *f* beauty
belén *m* crib, nativity scene;
(*barullo*) confusion
belga *a & m & f* Belgian
Bélgica *f* Belgium
bélico *a*, **belicoso** *a* warlike
beligerante *a* belligerent
bella|co *a* wicked. ● *m* rogue.
~quear *vi* cheat. **~quería** *f* dirty
trick
bell|eza *f* beauty. **~o** *a* beautiful.
~as artes *fpl* fine arts
bellota *f* acorn
bemol *m* flat. **tener (muchos) ~es** be
difficult
bencina *f* (*Arg, gasolina*) petrol
(*Brit*), gasoline (*Amer*)
bend|ecir [46 *pero imperativo* **bend-
ice**, *futuro, condicional y pp regulares*] *vt* bless. **~ición** *f* blessing.
~ito *a* blessed, holy; (*que tiene
suerte*) lucky; (*feliz*) happy
benefactor *m* benefactor. **~a** *f*
benefactress
benefic|encia *f* (*organización pú-
blica*) charity. **~iar** *vt* benefit. **~iarse**
vpr benefit. **~iario** *m* beneficiary;
(*de un cheque etc*) payee. **~io** *m*
benefit; (*ventaja*) advantage; (*ganancia*) profit, gain. **~ioso** *a* beneficial, advantageous
benéfico *a* beneficial; (*de bene-
ficencia*) charitable
benemérito *a* worthy
beneplácito *m* approval
ben|evolencia *f* benevolence. **~év-
olo** *a* benevolent
bengala *f* flare. **luz** *f* **de B~** flare
benign|idad *f* kindness; (*falta de
gravedad*) mildness. **~o** *a* kind;
(*moderado*) gentle, mild; (*tumor*)
benign
beodo *a* drunk
berberecho *m* cockle
berenjena *f* aubergine (*Brit*), egg-
plant. **~l** *m* (*fig*) mess

bermejo *a* red
berr|ear *vi* (*animales*) low, bellow;
(*niño*) howl; (*cantar mal*) screech.
~ido *m* bellow; (*de niño*) howl; (*de
cantante*) screech
berrinche *m* temper; (*de un niño*)
tantrum
berro *m* watercress
berza *f* cabbage
besamel(a) *f* white sauce
bes|ar *vt* kiss; (*rozar*) brush against.
~arse *vpr* kiss (each other);
(*tocarse*) touch each other. **~o** *m*
kiss
bestia *f* beast; (*bruto*) brute; (*idiota*)
idiot. **~ de carga** beast of burden.
~l *a* bestial, animal; (*fig, fam*) terrific. **~lidad** *f* bestiality; (*acción
brutal*) horrid thing
besugo *m* sea-bream. **ser un ~** be
stupid
besuquear *vt* cover with kisses
betún *m* bitumen; (*para el calzado*)
shoe polish
biberón *m* feeding-bottle
Biblia *f* Bible
bíblico *a* biblical
bibliografía *f* bibliography
biblioteca *f* library; (*librería*) bookcase. **~ de consulta** reference
library. **~ de préstamo** lending library. **~rio** *m* librarian
bicarbonato *m* bicarbonate. **~
sódico** bicarbonate of soda
bici *f* (*fam*) bicycle, bike (*fam*).
~cleta *f* bicycle. **ir en ~cleta** go by
bicycle, cycle. **montar en ~cleta**
ride a bicycle
bicolor *a* two-colour
bicultural *a* bicultural
bicho *m* (*animal*) small animal,
creature; (*insecto*) insect. **~ raro**
odd sort. **cualquier ~ viviente, todo
~ viviente** everyone
bidé *m*, **bidet** *m* bidet
bidón *m* drum, can
bien *adv* (**mejor**) well; (*muy*) very,
quite; (*correctamente*) right; (*de
buena gana*) willingly. ● *m* good;
(*efectos*) property; (*provecho*)
advantage, benefit. ¡**~!** fine!, OK!,
good! **~... (o)** either... or. **~ que**
although. ¡**está ~!** fine! alright! **más
~** rather. ¡**muy ~!** good! **no ~** as
soon as. ¡**qué ~!** marvellous!, great!
(*fam*). **si ~** although
bienal *a* biennial
bien|aventurado *a* fortunate. **~es-
tar** *m* well-being. **~hablado** *a* well-
spoken. **~hechor** *m* benefactor.

~hechora f benefactress. ~intencionado a well-meaning

bienio m two years, two year-period

bien: ~quistar vt reconcile. ~quistarse vpr become reconciled. ~quisto a well-liked

bienvenid|a f welcome. ~o a welcome. ¡~o! welcome! dar la ~a a uno welcome s.o.

bife m (Arg), biftek m steak

bifurca|ción f fork, junction. ~rse [7] vpr fork

b|igamia f bigamy. ~ígamo a bigamous. ● m & f bigamist

bigot|e m moustache. ~udo a with a big moustache

bikini m bikini; (culin) toasted cheese and ham sandwich

bilingüe a bilingual

billar m billiards

billete m ticket; (de banco) note (Brit), bill (Amer). ~ de banco banknote. ~ de ida y vuelta return ticket (Brit), round-trip ticket (Amer). ~ sencillo single ticket (Brit), one-way ticket (Amer). ~ro m, ~ra f wallet, billfold (Amer)

billón m billion (Brit), trillion (Amer)

bimbalete m (Mex) swing

bi|mensual a fortnightly, twice-monthly. ~mestral a two-monthly. ~motor a twin-engined. ● m twin-engined plane

binocular a binocular. ~es mpl binoculars

biodegradable a biodegradable

bi|ografía f biography. ~ográfico a biographical. ~ógrafo m biographer

bi|ología f biology. ~ológico a biological. ~ólogo m biologist

biombo m folding screen

biopsia f biopsy

bioquímic|a f biochemistry; (persona) biochemist. ~o m biochemist

bípedo m biped

biplano m biplane

biquini m bikini

birlar vt (fam) steal, pinch (fam)

birlibirloque m. por arte de ~ (as if) by magic

Birmania f Burma

birmano a & m Burmese

biromen m (Arg) ball-point pen

bis m encore. ● adv twice. ¡~! encore! vivo en el 3 ~ I live at 3A

bisabuel|a f great-grandmother. ~o m great-grandfather. ~os mpl great-grandparents

bisagra f hinge

bisar vt encore

bisbise|ar vt whisper. ~o m whisper(ing)

bisemanal a twice-weekly

bisiesto a leap. año m ~ leap year

bisniet|a f great-granddaughter. ~o m great-grandson. ~os mpl great-grandchildren

bisonte m bison

bisté m, bistec m steak

bisturí m scalpel

bisutería f imitation jewellery, costume jewellery

bizco a cross-eyed. quedarse ~ be dumbfounded

bizcocho m sponge (cake); (Mex, galleta) biscuit

bizquear vi squint

blanc|a f white woman; (mus) minim. ~o a white; ⟨tez⟩ fair. ● m white; (persona) white man; (intervalo) interval; (espacio) blank; (objetivo) target. ~o de huevo white of egg, egg-white. dar en el ~o hit the mark. dejar en ~o leave blank. pasar la noche en ~o have a sleepless night. ~o y negro black and white. ~ura f whiteness. ~uzco a whitish

blandir [24] vt brandish

bland|o a soft; ⟨carácter⟩ weak; (cobarde) cowardly; ⟨palabras⟩ gentle, tender. ~ura f softness. ~uzco a softish

blanque|ar vt whiten; white-wash ⟨paredes⟩; bleach ⟨tela⟩. ● vi turn white; (presentarse blanco) look white. ~cino a whitish. ~o m whitening

blasfem|ador a blasphemous. ● m blasphemer. ~ar vi blaspheme. ~ia f blasphemy. ~o a blasphemous. ● m blasphemer

blas|ón m coat of arms; (fig,) honour, glory. ~onar vt emblazon. ● vi boast (de of, about)

bledo m nothing. me importa un ~, no se me da un ~ I couldn't care less

blinda|je m armour. ~r vt armour

bloc m (pl blocs) pad

bloque m block; (pol) bloc. ~ar vt block; (mil) blockade; (com) freeze. ~o m blockade; (com) freezing. en ~ en bloc

blusa f blouse

boato m show, ostentation

bob|ada f silly thing. **~alicón** a stupid. **~ería** f silly thing. **decir ~adas** talk nonsense

bobina f bobbin, reel; (foto) spool; (elec) coil

bobo a silly, stupid. ● m idiot, fool

boca f mouth; (fig, entrada) entrance; (de cañón) muzzle; (agujero) hole. **~ abajo** face down. **~ arriba** face up. **a ~ de jarro** point-blank. **con la ~ abierta** dumbfounded

bocacalle f junction. **la primera ~ a la derecha** the first turning on the right

bocad|illo m sandwich; (comida ligera, fam) snack. **~o** m mouthful; (mordisco) bite; (de caballo) bit

boca: ~jarro. a ~jarro point-blank. **~manga** f cuff

bocanada f puff; (de vino etc) mouthful

bocaza f invar, **bocazas** f invar big-mouth

boceto m outline, sketch

bocina f horn. **~zo** m toot, blast. **tocar la ~** sound one's horn

bock m beer mug

bocha f bowl. **~s** fpl bowls

bochinche m uproar

bochorno m sultry weather; (fig, vergüenza) embarrassment. **~so** a oppressive; (fig) embarrassing. **¡qué ~!** how embarrassing!

boda f marriage; (ceremonia) wedding

bodeg|a f cellar; (de vino) wine cellar; (almacén) warehouse; (de un barco) hold. **~ón** m cheap restaurant; (pintura) still life

bodoque m pellet; (tonto, fam) thickhead

bofes mpl lights. **echar los ~** slog away

bofet|ada f slap; (fig) blow. **dar una ~ada a uno** slap s.o. in the face. **darse de ~adas** clash. **~ón** m punch

boga m & f rower; (hombre) oarsman; (mujer) oarswoman; (moda) fashion. **estar en ~** be in fashion, be in vogue. **~da** f stroke (of the oar). **~dor** rower, oarsman. **~r** [12] vt row. **~vante** m (crustáceo) lobster

Bogotá f Bogotá

bogotano a from Bogotá. ● m native of Bogotá

bohemio a & m Bohemian

bohío m (LAm) hut

boicot m (pl **boicots**) boycott. **~ear** vt boycott. **~eo** m boycott. **hacer el ~** boycott

boina f beret

boîte /bwat/ m night-club

bola f ball; (canica) marble; (naipes) slam; (betún) shoe polish; (mentira) fib; (Mex, reunión desordenada) rowdy party. **~ del mundo** (fam) globe. **contar ~s** tell fibs. **dejar que ruede la ~** let things take their course. **meter ~s** tell fibs

bolas fpl (LAm) bolas

boleada f (Mex) polishing of shoes

boleadoras (LAm) fpl bolas

bolera f bowling alley

bolero m (baile, chaquetilla) bolero; (fig, mentiroso, fam) liar; (Mex, limpiabotas) bootblack

boletín m bulletin; (publicación periódica) journal; (escolar) report. **~ de noticias** news bulletin. **~ de precios** price list. **~ informativo** news bulletin. **~ meteorológico** weather forecast

boleto m (esp LAm) ticket

boli m (fam) Biro (P), ball-point pen

boliche m (juego) bowls; (bolera) bowling alley

bolígrafo m Biro (P), ball-point pen

bolillo m bobbin; (Mex, panecillo) (bread) roll

bolívar m (unidad monetaria venezolana) bolívar

Bolivia f Bolivia

boliviano a Bolivian. ● m Bolivian; (unidad monetaria de Bolivia) boliviano

bolo m skittle

bolsa f bag; (monedero) purse; (LAm, bolsillo) pocket; (com) stock exchange; (cavidad) cavity. **~ de agua caliente** hot-water bottle

bolsillo m pocket; (monedero) purse. **de ~** pocket

bolsista m & f stockbroker

bolso m (de mujer) handbag

boll|ería f baker's shop. **~ero** m baker. **~o** m roll; (con azúcar) bun; (abolladura) dent; (chichón) lump; (fig, jaleo, fam) fuss

bomba f bomb; (máquina) pump; (noticia) bombshell. **~ de aceite** (auto) oil pump. **~ de agua** (auto) water pump. **~ de incendios** fire-engine. **pasarlo ~** have a marvellous time

bombach|as fpl (LAm) knickers, pants. **~o** m (esp Mex) baggy trousers, baggy pants (Amer)

bombarde|ar vt bombard; (mil) bomb. **~o** m bombardment; (mil) bombing. **~ro** m (avión) bomber

bombazo m explosion

bombear vt pump; (mil) bomb

bombero m fireman. **cuerpo** m **de ~s** fire brigade (Brit), fire department (Amer)

bombilla f (light) bulb; (LAm, para maté) pipe for drinking maté; (Mex, cucharón) ladle

bombín m pump; (sombrero, fam) bowler (hat) (Brit), derby (Amer)

bombo m (tambor) bass drum. **a ~ y platillos** with a lot of fuss

bomb|ón m chocolate. **ser un ~ón** be a peach. **~ona** f container. **~onera** f chocolate box

bonachón a easygoing; (bueno) good-natured

bonaerense a from Buenos Aires. ● m native of Buenos Aires

bonanza f (naut) fair weather; (prosperidad) prosperity. **ir en ~** (naut) have fair weather; (fig) go well

bondad f goodness; (amabilidad) kindness. **tenga la ~ de** would you be kind enough to. **~osamente** adv kindly. **~oso** a kind

bongo m (LAm) canoe

boniato m sweet potato

bonito a nice; (mono) pretty. **¡muy ~!, ¡qué ~!** that's nice!, very nice!. ● m bonito

bono m voucher; (título) bond. **~ del Tesoro** government bond

boñiga f dung

boqueada f gasp. **dar las ~s** be dying

boquerón m anchovy

boquete m hole; (brecha) breach

boquiabierto a open-mouthed; (fig) amazed, dumbfounded. **quedarse ~** be amazed

boquilla f mouthpiece; (para cigarillos) cigarette-holder; (filtro de cigarillo) tip

borboll|ar vi bubble. **~ón** m bubble. **hablar a ~ones** gabble. **salir a ~ones** gush out

borbot|ar vt bubble. **~ón** m bubble. **hablar a ~ones** gabble. **salir a ~ones** gush out

bordado a embroidered. ● m embroidery. **quedar ~, salir ~** come out very well

bordante m (Mex) lodger

bordar vt embroider; (fig, fam) do very well

bord|e m edge; (de carretera) side; (de plato etc) rim; (de un vestido) hem. **~ear** vt go round the edge of; (fig) border on. **~illo** m kerb. **al ~ de** on the edge of; (fig) on the brink of

bordo m board. **a ~** on board

borinqueño a & m Puerto Rican

borla f tassel

borra f flock; (pelusa) fluff; (sedimento) sediment

borrach|era f drunkenness. **~ín** m drunkard. **~o** a drunk. ● m drunkard; (temporalmente) drunk. **estar ~o** be drunk. **ni ~o** never in a million years. **ser ~o** be a drunkard

borrador m rough copy; (libro) rough notebook

borradura f crossing-out

borrajear vt/i scribble

borrar vt rub out; (tachar) cross out

borrasc|a f storm. **~oso** a stormy

borreg|o m year-old lamb; (fig) simpleton; (Mex, noticia falsa) hoax. **~uil** a meek

borric|ada f silly thing. **~o** m donkey; (fig, fam) ass

borrón m smudge; (fig, imperfección) blemish; (de una pintura) sketch. **~ y cuenta nueva** let's forget about it!

borroso a blurred; (fig) vague

bos|caje m thicket. **~coso** a wooded. **~que** m wood, forest. **~quecillo** m copse

bosquej|ar vt sketch. **~o** m sketch

bosta f dung

bostez|ar [10] vi yawn. **~o** m yawn

bota f boot; (recipiente) leather wine bottle

botadero m (Mex) ford

botánic|a f botany. **~o** a botanical. ● m botanist

botar vt launch. ● vi bounce. **estar que bota** be hopping mad

botarat|ada f silly thing. **~e** m idiot

bote m bounce; (golpe) blow; (salto) jump; (sacudida) jolt; (lata) tin, can; (vasija) jar; (en un bar) jar for tips; (barca) boat. **~ salvavidas** lifeboat. **de ~ en ~** packed

botell|a f bottle. **~ita** f small bottle

botica f chemist's (shop) (Brit), drugstore (Amer). **~rio** m chemist (Brit), druggist (Amer)

botija f, **botijo** m earthenware jug

botín m half boot; (despojos) booty; (LAm, calcetín) sock

botiquín *m* medicine chest; (*de primeros auxilios*) first aid kit

bot|ón *m* button; (*yema*) bud. ~on**adura** *f* buttons. ~**ón de oro** buttercup. ~**ones** *m invar* bellboy (*Brit*), bellhop (*Amer*)

botulismo *m* botulism

boutique /bu'tik/ *m* boutique

bóveda *f* vault

boxe|ador *m* boxer. ~**ar** *vi* box. ~**o** *m* boxing

boya *f* buoy; (*corcho*) float. ~**nte** *a* buoyant

bozal *m* (*de perro etc*) muzzle; (*de caballo*) halter

bracear *vi* wave one's arms; (*nadar*) swim, crawl

bracero *m* labourer. **de** ~ (*fam*) arm in arm

braga *f* underpants, knickers; (*cuerda*) rope. ~**dura** *f* crotch. ~**s** *fpl* knickers, pants. ~**zas** *m invar* (*fam*) henpecked man

bragueta *f* flies

braille /breil/ *m* Braille

bram|ar *vi* roar; (*vaca*) moo; (*viento*) howl. ~**ido** *m* roar

branquia *f* gill

bras|a *f* hot coal. **a la** ~**a** grilled. ~**ero** *m* brazier; (*LAm, hogar*) hearth

Brasil *m*. **el** ~ Brazil

brasile|ño *a & m* Brazilian. ~**ro** *a & m* (*LAm*) Brazilian

bravata *f* boast

bravío *a* wild; (*persona*) coarse, uncouth

brav|o *a* brave; (*animales*) wild; (*mar*) rough. ¡~! *int* well done! bravo! ~**ura** *f* ferocity; (*valor*) courage

braz|a *f* fathom. **nadar a** ~**a** do the breast-stroke. ~**ada** *f* waving of the arms; (*en natación*) stroke; (*cantidad*) armful. ~**ado** *m* armful. ~**al** *m* arm-band. ~**alete** *m* bracelet; (*brazal*) arm-band. ~**o** *m* arm; (*de animales*) foreleg; (*rama*) branch. ~**o derecho** right-hand man. **a** ~**o** by hand. **del** ~**o** arm in arm

brea *f* tar, pitch

brear *vt* ill-treat

brécol *m* broccoli

brecha *f* gap; (*mil*) breach; (*med*) gash. **estar en la** ~ be in the thick of it

brega *f* struggle. ~**r** [12] *vi* struggle; (*trabajar mucho*) work hard, slog away. **andar a la** ~ work hard

breña *f*, **breñal** *m* scrub

Bretaña *f* Brittany. **Gran** ~ Great Britain

breve *a* short. ~**dad** *f* shortness. **en** ~ soon, shortly. **en** ~**s momentos** soon

brez|al *m* moor. ~**o** *m* heather

brib|ón *m* rogue, rascal. ~**onada** *f*, ~**onería** *f* dirty trick

brida *f* bridle. **a toda** ~ at full speed

bridge /britʃ/ *m* bridge

brigada *f* squad; (*mil*) brigade. **general de** ~ brigadier (*Brit*), brigadier-general (*Amer*)

brill|ante *a* brilliant. ● *m* diamond. ~**antez** *f* brilliance. ~**ar** *vi* shine; (*centellear*) sparkle. ~**o** *m* shine; (*brillantez*) brilliance; (*centelleo*) sparkle. **dar** ~**o, sacar** ~**o** polish

brinc|ar [7] *vi* jump up and down. ~**o** *m* jump. **dar un** ~**o** jump. **estar que brinca** be hopping mad. **pegar un** ~**o** jump

brind|ar *vt* offer. ● *vi*. ~**ar por** toast, drink a toast to. ~**is** *m* toast

br|ío *m* energy; (*decisión*) determination. ~**ioso** *a* spirited; (*garboso*) elegant

brisa *f* breeze

británico *a* British. ● *m* Briton, British person

brocado *m* brocade

bróculi *m* broccoli

brocha *f* paintbrush; (*para afeitarse*) shaving-brush

broche *m* clasp, fastener; (*joya*) brooch; (*Arg, sujetapapeles*) paperclip

brocheta *f* skewer

brom|a *f* joke. ~**a pesada** practical joke. ~**ear** *vi* joke. ~**ista** *a* funloving. ● *m & f* joker. **de** ~**a, en** ~**a** in fun. **ni de** ~**a** never in a million years

bronca *f* row; (*represión*) telling-off

bronce *m* bronze. ~**ado** *a* bronze; (*por el sol*) tanned, sunburnt. ~**ar** *vt* tan (*piel*). ~**arse** *vpr* get a suntan

bronco *a* rough

bronquitis *f* bronchitis

broqueta *f* skewer

brot|ar *vi* (*plantas*) bud, sprout; (*med*) break out; (*líquido*) gush forth; (*lágrimas*) well up. ~**e** *m* bud, shoot; (*med*) outbreak; (*de líquido*) gushing; (*de lágrimas*) welling-up

bruces *mpl*. **de** ~ face down(wards). **caer de** ~ fall flat on one's face

bruj|a f witch. ● a (Mex) penniless. **~ear** vi practise witchcraft. **~ería** f witchcraft. **~o** m wizard, magician; (LAm) medicine man

brújula f compass

brum|a f mist; (fig) confusion. **~oso** a misty, foggy

bruñi|do m polish. **~r** [22] vt polish

brusco a (repentino) sudden; (persona) brusque

Bruselas fpl Brussels

brusquedad f abruptness

brut|al a brutal. **~alidad** f brutality; (estupidez) stupidity. **~o** a (estúpido) stupid; (tosco) rough, uncouth; ⟨peso, sueldo⟩ gross

bucal a oral

buce|ar vi dive; (fig) explore. **~o** m diving

bucle m curl

budín m pudding

budis|mo m Buddhism. **~ta** m & f Buddhist

buen véase **bueno**

buenamente adv easily; (voluntariamente) willingly

buenaventura f good luck; (adivinación) fortune. **decir la ~ a uno, echar la ~ a uno** tell s.o.'s fortune

bueno a (delante de nombre masculino en singular **buen**) good; (apropiado) fit; (amable) kind; (tiempo) fine. ● int well!; (de acuerdo) OK!, very well! **¡buena la has hecho!** you've gone and done it now! **¡buenas noches!** good night! **¡buenas tardes!** (antes del atardecer) good afternoon!; (después del atardecer) good evening! **¡~s días!** good morning! **estar de buenas** be in a good mood. **por las buenas** willingly

Buenos Aires m Buenos Aires

buey m ox

búfalo m buffalo

bufanda f scarf

bufar vi snort. **estar que bufa** be hopping mad

bufete m (mesa) writing-desk; (despacho) lawyer's office

bufido m snort; (de ira) outburst

buf|o a comic. **~ón** a comical. ● m buffoon. **~onada** f joke

bugle m bugle

buharda f, **buhardilla** f attic; (ventana) dormer window

búho m owl

buhoner|ía f pedlar's wares. **~o** m pedlar

buitre m vulture

bujía f candle; (auto) spark(ing)-plug

bula f bull

bulbo m bulb

bulevar m avenue, boulevard

Bulgaria f Bulgaria

búlgaro a & m Bulgarian

bulo m hoax

bulto m (volumen) volume; (tamaño) size; (forma) shape; (paquete) package; (protuberancia) lump. **a ~** roughly

bulla f uproar; (muchedumbre) crowd

bullicio m hubbub; (movimiento) bustle. **~so** a bustling; (ruidoso) noisy

bullir [22] vt stir, move. ● vi boil; (burbujear) bubble; (fig) bustle

buñuelo m doughnut; (fig) mess

BUP abrev (Bachillerato Unificado Polivalente) secondary school education

buque m ship, boat

burbuj|a f bubble. **~ear** vi bubble; ⟨vino⟩ sparkle. **~eo** m bubbling

burdel m brothel

burdo a rough, coarse; ⟨excusa⟩ clumsy

burgu|és a middle-class, bourgeois. ● m middle-class person. **~esía** f middle class, bourgeoisie

burla f taunt; (broma) joke; (engaño) trick. **~dor** a mocking. ● m seducer. **~r** vt trick, deceive; (seducir) seduce. **~rse** vpr. **~rse de** mock, make fun of

burlesco a funny

burlón a mocking

bur|ocracia f civil service. **~ócrata** m & f civil servant. **~ocrático** a bureaucratic

burro m donkey; (fig) ass

bursátil a stock-exchange

bus m (fam) bus

busca f search. **a la ~ de** in search of. **en ~ de** in search of

busca: ~pié m feeler. **~pleitos** m invar (LAm) trouble-maker

buscar [7] vt look for. ● vi look. **buscársela** ask for it. **ir a ~ a uno** fetch s.o.

buscarruidos m invar trouble-maker

buscona f prostitute

busilis m snag

búsqueda f search

busto m bust

butaca f armchair; (*en el teatro etc*) seat

butano m butane

buzo m diver

buzón m postbox (*Brit*), mailbox (*Amer*)

C

Cu *abrev* (*Calle*) St, Street, Rd, Road

cabal a exact; (*completo*) complete. **no estar en sus ~es** not be in one's right mind

cabalga|dura f mount, horse. **~r** [12] *vt* ride. ● *vi* ride, go riding. **~ta** f ride; (*desfile*) procession

cabalmente adv completely; (*exactamente*) exactly

caballa f mackerel

caballada f (*LAm*) stupid thing

caballeresco a gentlemanly. **literatura** f **caballeresca** books of chivalry

caballer|ía f mount, horse. **~iza** f stable. **~izo** m groom

caballero m gentleman; (*de orden de caballería*) knight; (*tratamiento*) sir. **~samente** adv like a gentleman. **~so** a gentlemanly

caballete m (*del tejado*) ridge; (*de la nariz*) bridge; (*de pintor*) easel

caballito m pony. **~ del diablo** dragonfly. **~ de mar** sea-horse. **los ~s** (*tiovivo*) merry-go-round

caballo m horse; (*del ajedrez*) knight; (*de la baraja española*) queen. **~ de vapor** horsepower. **a ~** on horseback

cabaña f hut

cabaret /kaba're/ m (*pl* **cabarets** /kaba're/) night-club

cabece|ar *vi* nod; (*para negar*) shake one's head. **~o** m nodding, nod; (*acción de negar*) shake of the head

cabecera f (*de la cama, de la mesa*) head; (*en un impreso*) heading

cabecilla m leader

cabell|o m hair. **~os** mpl hair. **~udo** a hairy

caber [28] *vi* fit (**en** into). **los libros no caben en la caja** the books won't fit into the box. **no cabe duda** there's no doubt

cabestr|illo m sling. **~o** m halter

cabeza f head; (*fig, inteligencia*) intelligence. **~da** f butt; (*golpe recibido*) blow; (*saludo, al dormirse*)

nod. **~zo** m butt; (*en fútbol*) header. **andar de ~** have a lot to do. **dar una ~da** nod off

cabida f capacity; (*extensión*) area. **dar ~ a** leave room for, leave space for

cabina f (*de avión*) cabin, cockpit; (*electoral*) booth; (*de camión*) cab. **~ telefónica** telephone box (*Brit*), telephone booth (*Amer*)

cabizbajo a crestfallen

cable m cable

cabo m end; (*trozo*) bit; (*mil*) corporal; (*mango*) handle; (*geog*) cape; (*naut*) rope. **al ~** eventually. **al ~ de una hora** after an hour. **de ~ a rabo** from beginning to end. **llevar(se) a ~** carry out

cabr|a f goat. **~a montesa** f mountain goat. **~iola** f jump, skip. **~itilla** f kid. **~ito** m kid

cabrón m cuckold

cabuya f (*LAm*) pita, agave

cacahuate m (*Mex*), **cacahuete** m peanut

cacao m (*planta y semillas*) cacao; (*polvo*) cocoa; (*fig*) confusion

cacare|ar *vt* boast about. ● *vi* 〈*gallo*〉 crow; 〈*gallina*〉 cluck. **~o** m (*incl fig*) crowing; (*de gallina*) clucking

cacería f hunt

cacerola f casserole, saucepan

caciqu|e m cacique, Indian chief; (*pol*) cacique, local political boss. **~il** a despotic. **~ismo** m caciquism, despotism

caco m pickpocket, thief

cacof|onía f cacophony. **~ónico** a cacophonous

cacto m cactus

cacumen m acumen

cacharro m earthenware pot; (*para flores*) vase; (*coche estropeado*) wreck; (*cosa inútil*) piece of junk; (*chisme*) thing. **~s** mpl pots and pans

cachear *vt* frisk

cachemir m, **cachemira** f cashmere

cacheo m frisking

cachetada f (*LAm*), **cachete** m slap

cachimba f pipe

cachiporra f club, truncheon. **~zo** m blow with a club

cachivache m thing, piece of junk

cacho m bit, piece; (*LAm, cuerno*) horn; (*miga*) crumb

cachondeo m (*fam*) joking, joke

cachorro m (*perrito*) puppy; (*de otros animales*) young

cada *a invar* each, every. ∼ **uno** each one, everyone. **uno de** ∼ **cinco** one in five

cadalso *m* scaffold

cadáver *m* corpse. **ingresar** ∼ be dead on arrival

cadena *f* chain; (*TV*) channel. ∼ **de fabricación** production line. ∼ **de montañas** mountain range. ∼ **perpetua** life imprisonment

cadencia *f* cadence, rhythm

cadera *f* hip

cadete *m* cadet

caduc|ar [7] *vi* expire. ∼**idad** *f*. **fecha** *f* **de** ∼**idad** sell-by date. ∼**o** *a* decrepit

cae|dizo *a* unsteady. ∼**r** [29] *vi* fall. ∼**rse** *vpr* fall (over). **dejar** ∼**r** drop. **estar al** ∼**r** be about to happen. **este vestido no me** ∼ **bien** this dress doesn't suit me. **hacer** ∼**r** knock over. **Juan me** ∼ **bien** I get on well with Juan. **su cumpleaños cayó en Martes** his birthday fell on a Tuesday

café *m* coffee; (*cafetería*) café. ● *a*. **color** ∼ coffee-coloured. ∼ **con leche** white coffee. ∼ **cortado** coffee with a little milk. ∼ **(solo)** black coffee

cafe|ína *f* caffeine. ∼**tal** *m* coffee plantation. ∼**tera** *f* coffee-pot. ∼**tería** *f* café. ∼**tero** *a* coffee

caíd|a *f* fall; (*disminución*) drop; (*pendiente*) slope. ∼**o** *a* fallen; (*abatido*) dejected. ● *m* fallen

caigo *vb véase* **caer**

caimán *m* cayman, alligator

caj|a *f* box; (*grande*) case; (*de caudales*) safe; (*donde se efectúan los pagos*) cash desk; (*en supermercado*) check-out. ∼**a de ahorros** savings bank. ∼**a de caudales**, ∼**a fuerte** safe. ∼**a postal de ahorros** post office savings bank. ∼**a registradora** till. ∼**ero** *m* cashier. ∼**etilla** *f* packet. ∼**ita** *f* small box. ∼**ón** *m* large box; (*de mueble*) drawer; (*puesto de mercado*) stall. **ser de** ∼**ón** be a matter of course

cal *m* lime

cala *f* cove

calaba|cín *m* marrow; (*fig, idiota, fam*) idiot. ∼**za** *f* pumpkin; (*fig, idiota, fam*) idiot

calabozo *m* prison; (*celda*) cell

calado *a* soaked. ● *m* (*naut*) draught. **estar** ∼ **hasta los huesos** be soaked to the skin

calamar *m* squid

calambre *m* cramp

calami|dad *f* calamity, disaster. ∼**toso** *a* calamitous, disastrous

calar *vt* soak; (*penetrar*) pierce; (*fig, penetrar*) see through; sample (*fruta*). ∼**se** *vpr* get soaked; (*zapatos*) leak; (*auto*) stall

calavera *f* skull

calcar [7] *vt* trace; (*fig*) copy

calceta *f*. **hacer** ∼ knit

calcetín *m* sock

calcinar *vt* burn

calcio *m* calcium

calco *m* tracing. ∼**manía** *f* transfer. **papel** *m* **de** ∼ tracing-paper

calcula|dor *a* calculating. ∼**dora** *f* calculator. ∼**dora de bolsillo** pocket calculator. ∼**r** *vt* calculate; (*suponer*) reckon, think

cálculo *m* calculation; (*fig*) reckoning

caldea|miento *m* heating. ∼**r** *vt* heat, warm. ∼**rse** *vpr* get hot

calder|a *f* boiler; (*Arg, para café*) coffee-pot; (*Arg, para té*) teapot. ∼**eta** *f* small boiler

calderilla *f* small change, coppers

calder|o *m* small boiler. ∼**ón** *m* large boiler

caldo *m* stock; (*sopa*) soup, broth. **poner a** ∼ **a uno** give s.o. a dressing-down

calefacción *f* heating. ∼ **central** central heating

caleidoscopio *m* kaleidoscope

calendario *m* calendar

caléndula *f* marigold

calenta|dor *m* heater. ∼**miento** *m* heating; (*en deportes*) warm-up. ∼**r** [1] *vt* heat, warm. ∼**rse** *vpr* get hot, warm up

calentur|a *f* fever, (high) temperature. ∼**iento** *a* feverish

calibr|ar *vt* calibrate; (*fig*) measure. ∼**e** *m* calibre; (*diámetro*) diameter; (*fig*) importance

calidad *f* quality; (*función*) capacity. **en** ∼ **de** as

cálido *a* warm

calidoscopio *m* kaleidoscope

caliente *a* hot, warm; (*fig, enfadado*) angry

califica|ción *f* qualification; (*evaluación*) assessment; (*nota*) mark. ∼**r** [7] *vt* qualify; (*evaluar*) assess; mark (*examen etc*). ∼**r de** describe as, label. ∼**tivo** *a* qualifying. ● *m* epithet

caliz|a f limestone. **~o** a lime

calm|a f calm. ¡**~a!** calm down! **~ante** a & m sedative. **~ar** vt calm, soothe. ● vi ⟨viento⟩ abate. **~arse** vpr calm down; ⟨viento⟩ abate. **~oso** a calm; ⟨flemático, fam⟩ phlegmatic. **en ~a** calm. **perder la ~a** lose one's composure

calor m heat, warmth. **hace ~** it's hot. **tener ~** be hot

caloría f calorie

calorífero m heater

calumni|a f calumny; ⟨oral⟩ slander; ⟨escrita⟩ libel. **~ar** vt slander; ⟨por escrito⟩ libel. **~oso** a slanderous; ⟨cosa escrita⟩ libellous

caluros|amente adv warmly. **~o** a warm

calv|a f bald patch. **~ero** m clearing. **~icie** f baldness. **~o** a bald; ⟨terreno⟩ barren

calza f (fam) stocking; ⟨cuña⟩ wedge

calzada f road

calza|do a wearing shoes. ● m footwear, shoe. **~dor** m shoehorn. **~r** [10] vt put shoes on; ⟨llevar⟩ wear. ● vi wear shoes. ● vpr put on. **¿qué número calza Vd?** what size shoe do you take?

calz|ón m shorts; ⟨ropa interior⟩ knickers, pants. **~ones** mpl shorts. **~oncillos** mpl underpants

calla|do a quiet. **~r** vt silence; keep ⟨secreto⟩; hush up ⟨asunto⟩. ● vi be quiet, keep quiet, shut up (fam). **~rse** vpr be quiet, keep quiet, shut up (fam). **¡cállate!** be quiet! shut up! (fam)

calle f street, road; ⟨en deportes, en autopista⟩ lane. **~ de dirección única** one-way street. **~ mayor** high street, main street. **abrir ~** make way

callej|a f narrow street. **~ear** vi wander about the streets. **~ero** a street. ● m street plan. **~ón** m alley. **~uela** f back street, side street. **~ón sin salida** cul-de-sac

call|ista m & f chiropodist. **~o** m corn, callus. **~os** mpl tripe. **~oso** a hard, rough

cama f bed. **~ de matrimonio** double bed. **~ individual** single bed. **caer en la ~** fall ill. **guardar ~** be confined to bed

camada f litter; ⟨fig, de ladrones⟩ gang

camafeo m cameo

camaleón m chameleon

cámara f room; ⟨de reyes⟩ royal chamber; ⟨fotográfica⟩ camera; ⟨de armas, pol⟩ chamber. **~ fotográfica** camera. **a ~ lenta** in slow motion

camarada f colleague; ⟨amigo⟩ companion

camarer|a f chambermaid; ⟨de restaurante etc⟩ waitress; ⟨en casa⟩ maid. **~o** m waiter

camarín m dressing-room; (naut) cabin

camarón m shrimp

camarote m cabin

cambi|able a changeable; ⟨com etc⟩ exchangeable. **~ante** a variable. **~ar** vt change; ⟨trocar⟩ exchange. ● vi change. **~ar de idea** change one's mind. **~arse** vpr change. **~o** m change; ⟨com⟩ exchange rate; ⟨moneda menuda⟩ (small) change. **~sta** m & f money-changer. **en ~o** on the other hand

camelia f camellia

camello m camel

camilla f stretcher; ⟨sofá⟩ couch

camina|nte m traveller. **~r** vt cover. ● vi travel; ⟨andar⟩ walk; ⟨río, astros etc⟩ move. **~ta** f long walk

camino m road; ⟨sendero⟩ path, track; ⟨dirección, medio⟩ way. **~ de** towards, on the way to. **abrir ~** make way. **a medio ~, a la mitad del ~** half-way. **de ~** on the way. **ponerse en ~** set out

cami|ón m lorry; ⟨Mex, autobús⟩ bus. **~onero** m lorry-driver. **~oneta** f van

camis|a f shirt; ⟨de un fruto⟩ skin. **~a de dormir** nightdress. **~a de fuerza** strait-jacket. **~ería** f shirt shop. **~eta** f T-shirt; ⟨ropa interior⟩ vest. **~ón** m nightdress

camorra f (fam) row. **buscar ~** look for trouble, pick a quarrel

camote m (LAm) sweet potato

campamento m camp

campan|a f bell. **~ada** f stroke of a bell; ⟨de reloj⟩ striking. **~ario** m bell tower, belfry. **~eo** m peal of bells. **~illa** f bell. **~udo** a bell-shaped; ⟨estilo⟩ bombastic

campaña f countryside; ⟨mil, pol⟩ campaign. **de ~** ⟨mil⟩ field

campe|ón a & m champion. **~onato** m championship

campes|ino a country. ● m peasant. **~tre** a country

camping /'kampin/ m (pl **campings** /'kampin/) camping; ⟨lugar⟩ campsite. **hacer ~** go camping

campiña *f* countryside

campo *m* country; (*agricultura*, *fig*) field; (*de tenis*) court; (*de fútbol*) pitch; (*de golf*) course. **~santo** *m* cemetery

camufla|do *a* camouflaged. **~je** *m* camouflage. **~r** *vt* camouflage

cana *f* grey hair, white hair. **echar una ~ al aire** have a fling. **peinar ~s** be getting old

Canadá *m*. **el ~** Canada

canadiense *a* & *m* Canadian

canal *m* (*incl TV*) channel; (*artificial*) canal; (*del tejado*) gutter. **~ de la Mancha** English Channel. **~ de Panamá** Panama Canal. **~ón** *m* (*horizontal*) gutter; (*vertical*) drain-pipe

canalla *f* rabble. ● *m* (*fig, fam*) swine. **~da** *f* dirty trick

canapé *m* sofa, couch; (*culin*) canapé

Canarias *fpl*. **(las islas) ~** the Canary Islands, the Canaries

canario *a* of the Canary Islands. ● *m* native of the Canary Islands; (*pájaro*) canary

canast|a *f* (large) basket. **~illa** *f* small basket; (*para un bebé*) layette. **~illo** *m* small basket. **~o** *m* (large) basket

cancela *f* gate

cancela|ción *f* cancellation . **~r** *vt* cancel; write off (*deuda*); (*fig*) forget

cáncer *m* cancer. **C~** Cancer

canciller *m* chancellor; (*LAm, ministro de asuntos exteriores*) Minister of Foreign Affairs

canci|ón *f* song. **~ón de cuna** lullaby. **~onero** *m* song-book. **¡siempre la misma ~ón!** always the same old story!

cancha *f* (*de fútbol*) pitch, ground; (*de tenis*) court

candado *m* padlock

candel|a *f* candle. **~ero** *m* candlestick. **~illa** *f* candle

candente *a* (*rojo*) red-hot; (*blanco*) white-hot; (*fig*) burning

candidato *m* candidate

candidez *f* innocence; (*ingenuidad*) naïvety

cándido *a* naïve

candil *m* oil-lamp; (*Mex, araña*) chandelier. **~ejas** *fpl* footlights

candinga *m* (*Mex*) devil

candor *m* innocence; (*ingenuidad*) naïvety. **~oso** *a* innocent; (*ingenuo*) naïve

canela *f* cinnamon. **ser ~** be beautiful

cangrejo *m* crab. **~ de río** crayfish

canguro *m* kangaroo; (*persona*) baby-sitter

can|íbal *a* & *m* cannibal. **~ibalismo** *m* cannibalism

canica *f* marble

canijo *m* weak

canino *a* canine. ● *m* canine (tooth)

canje *m* exchange. **~ar** *vt* exchange

cano *a* grey-haired

canoa *f* canoe; (*con motor*) motor boat

canon *m* canon

can|ónigo *m* canon. **~onizar** [10] *vt* canonize

canoso *a* grey-haired

cansa|do *a* tired. **~ncio** *m* tiredness. **~r** *vt* tire; (*aburrir*) bore. ● *vi* be tiring; (*aburrir*) get boring. **~rse** *vpr* get tired

cantábrico *a* Cantabrian. **el mar ~** the Bay of Biscay

canta|nte *a* singing. ● *m* singer; (*en óperas*) opera singer. **~or** *m* Flamenco singer. **~r** *vt/i* sing. ● *m* singing; (*canción*) song; (*poema*) poem. **~rlas claras** speak frankly

cántar|a *f* pitcher. **~o** *m* pitcher. **llover a ~os** pour down

cante *m* folk song. **~ flamenco, ~ jondo** Flamenco singing

cantera *f* quarry

cantidad *f* quantity; (*número*) number; (*de dinero*) sum. **una ~ de** lots of

cantilena *f*, **cantinela** *f* song

cantimplora *f* water-bottle

cantina *f* canteen; (*rail*) buffet

canto *m* singing; (*canción*) song; (*borde*) edge; (*de un cuchillo*) blunt edge; (*esquina*) corner; (*piedra*) pebble. **~ rodado** boulder. **de ~** on edge

cantonés *a* Cantonese

cantor *a* singing. ● *m* singer

canturre|ar *vt/i* hum. **~o** *m* humming

canuto *m* tube

caña *f* stalk, stem; (*planta*) reed; (*vaso*) glass; (*de la pierna*) shin. **~ de azúcar** sugar-cane. **~ de pescar** fishing-rod

cañada *f* ravine; (*camino*) track

cáñamo *m* hemp. **~ índio** cannabis

cañ|ería *f* pipe; (*tubería*) piping. **~o** *m* pipe, tube; (*de fuente*) jet. **~ón** *m* pipe, tube; (*de órgano*) pipe; (*de *chimenea*) flue; (*arma de fuego*) cannon; (*desfiladero*) canyon. **~onazo** *m* gunshot. **~onera** *f* gunboat

caoba *f* mahogany

ca|os *m* chaos. **~ótico** *a* chaotic

capa *f* cloak; (*de pintura*) coat; (*culin*) coating; (*geol*) stratum, layer

capacidad *f* capacity; (*fig*) ability

capacitar *vt* qualify, enable; (*instruir*) train

caparazón *m* shell

capataz *m* foreman

capaz *a* capable, able; (*espacioso*) roomy. **~ para** which holds, with a capacity of

capazo *m* large basket

capcioso *a* sly, insidious

capellán *m* chaplain

caperuza *f* hood; (*de pluma*) cap

capilla *f* chapel; (*mus*) choir

capita *f* small cloak, cape

capital *a* capital, very important. ● *m* (*dinero*) capital. ● *f* (*ciudad*) capital; (*LAm, letra*) capital (letter). **~ de provincia** county town

capitali|smo *m* capitalism. **~sta** *a & m & f* capitalist. **~zar** [10] *vt* capitalize

capit|án *m* captain. **~anear** *vt* lead, command; (*un equipo*) captain

capitel *m* (*arquit*) capital

capitulaci|ón *f* surrender; (*acuerdo*) agreement. **~ones** *fpl* marriage contract

capítulo *m* chapter. **~s matrimoniales** marriage contract

capó *m* bonnet (*Brit*), hood (*Amer*)

capón *m* (*pollo*) capon

caporal *m* chief, leader

capota *f* (*de mujer*) bonnet; (*auto*) folding top, sliding roof

capote *m* cape

Capricornio *m* Capricorn

capricho *m* whim. **~so** *a* capricious, whimsical. **a ~** capriciously

cápsula *f* capsule

captar *vt* harness ‹agua›; grasp ‹sentido›; hold ‹atención›; win ‹confianza›; (*radio*) pick up

captura *f* capture. **~r** *vt* capture

capucha *f* hood

capullo *m* bud; (*de insecto*) cocoon

caqui *m* khaki

cara *f* face; (*de una moneda*) obverse; (*de un objeto*) side; (*aspecto*) look, appearance; (*descaro*) cheek. **~ a** towards; (*frente a*) facing. **~ a ~** face to face. **~ o cruz** heads or tails.

dar la ~ face up to. **hacer ~ a** face. **no volver la ~ atrás** not look back. **tener ~ de** look, seem to be. **tener ~ para** have the face to. **tener mala ~** look ill. **volver la ~** look the other way

carabela *f* caravel, small light ship

carabina *f* rifle; (*fig, señora, fam*) chaperone

Caracas *m* Caracas

caracol *m* snail; (*de pelo*) curl. **¡~es!** Good Heavens! **escalera** *f* **de ~** spiral staircase

carácter *m* (*pl* **caracteres**) character. **con ~ de, por su ~ de** as

característic|a *f* characteristic; (*LAm, teléfonos*) dialling code. **~o** *a* characteristic, typical

caracteriza|do *a* characterized; (*prestigioso*) distinguished. **~r** [10] *vt* characterize

cara: ~ dura cheek, nerve. **~dura** *m & f* cheeky person, rotter (*fam*)

caramba *int* good heavens!, goodness me!

carámbano *m* icicle

caramelo *m* sweet (*Brit*), candy (*Amer*); (*azúcar fundido*) caramel

carancho *m* (*Arg*) vulture

carapacho *m* shell

caraqueño *a* from Caracas. ● *m* native of Caracas

carátula *f* mask; (*fig, teatro*) theatre; (*Mex, esfera del reloj*) face

caravana *f* caravan; (*fig, grupo*) group; (*auto*) long line, traffic jam

caray *int* (*fam*) good heavens!, goodness me!

carb|ón *m* coal; (*papel*) carbon (paper); (*para dibujar*) charcoal. **~oncillo** *m* charcoal. **~onero** *a* coal. ● *m* coal-merchant. **~onizar** [10] *vt* (*fig*) burn (to a cinder). **~ono** *m* carbon

carburador *m* carburettor

carcajada *f* burst of laughter. **reírse a ~s** roar with laughter. **soltar una ~** burst out laughing

cárcel *m* prison, jail; (*en carpintería*) clamp

carcel|ario *a* prison. **~ero** *a* prison. ● *m* prison officer

carcom|a *f* woodworm. **~er** *vt* eat away; (*fig*) undermine. **~erse** *vpr* be eaten away; (*fig*) waste away

cardenal *m* cardinal; (*contusión*) bruise

cárdeno *a* purple

cardiaco, cardíaco a cardiac, heart. ● m heart patient

cardinal a cardinal

cardiólogo m cardiologist, heart specialist

cardo m thistle

carear vt bring face to face ‹personas›; compare ‹cosas›

carecer [11] vi. ~ de lack. ~ de sentido not to make sense

caren|cia f lack. ~te a lacking

carero a expensive

carestía f (precio elevado) high price; (escasez) shortage

careta f mask

carey m tortoiseshell

carga f load; (fig) burden; (acción) loading; (de barco) cargo; (obligación) obligation. ~do a loaded; (fig) burdened; ‹tiempo› heavy; ‹hilo› live; ‹pila› charged. ~mento m load; (acción) loading; (de un barco) cargo. ~nte a demanding. ~r [12] vt load; (fig) burden; (mil, elec) charge; fill ‹pluma etc›; (fig, molestar, fam) annoy. ● vi load. ~r con pick up. ~rse vpr (llenarse) fill; ‹cielo› become overcast; (enfadarse, fam) get cross. **llevar la ~ de algo** be responsible for sth

cargo m load; (fig) burden; (puesto) post; (acusación) accusation, charge; (responsabilidad) charge. **a ~ de** in the charge of. **hacerse ~ de** take responsibility for. **tener a su ~** be in charge of

carguero m (Arg) beast of burden; (naut) cargo ship

cari m (LAm) grey

cariacontecido a crestfallen

caria|do a decayed. ~rse vpr decay

caribe a Caribbean. **el mar m C~** the Caribbean (Sea)

caricatura f caricature

caricia f caress

caridad f charity. **¡por ~!** for goodness sake!

caries f invar (dental) decay

carilampiño a clean-shaven

cariño m affection; (caricia) caress. **~ mío** my darling. **~samente** adv tenderly, lovingly; (en carta) with love from. **~so** a affectionate. **con mucho ~** (en carta) with love from. **tener ~ a** be fond of. **tomar ~ a** take a liking to. **un ~** (en carta) with love from

carism|a m charisma. **~ático** a charismatic

caritativo a charitable

cariz m look

carlinga f cockpit

carmesí a & m crimson

carmín m (de labios) lipstick; (color) red

carnal a carnal; ‹pariente› blood, full. **primo ~** first cousin

carnaval m carnival. **~esco** a carnival. **martes** m **de ~** Shrove Tuesday

carne f (incl de frutos) flesh; (para comer) meat. **~ de cerdo** pork. **~ de cordero** lamb. **~ de gallina** gooseflesh. **~ picada** mince. **~ de ternera** veal. **~ de vaca** beef. **me pone la ~ de gallina** it gives me the creeps. **ser de ~ y hueso** be only human

carné m card; (cuaderno) notebook. **~ de conducir** driving licence (Brit), driver's license (Amer). **~ de identidad** identity card.

carnero m sheep; (culin) lamb

carnet /kar'ne/ m card; (cuaderno) notebook. **~ de conducir** driving licence (Brit), driver's license (Amer). **~ de identidad** identity card

carnicer|ía f butcher's (shop); (fig) massacre. **~o** a carnivorous; (fig, cruel) cruel, savage. ● m butcher; (animal) carnivore

carnívoro a carnivorous. ● m carnivore

carnoso a fleshy

caro a dear. ● adv dear, dearly. **costar ~ a uno** cost s.o. dear

carpa f carp; (tienda) tent

carpeta f file, folder. **~zo** m. **dar ~zo a** shelve, put on one side

carpinter|ía f carpentry. **~o** m carpenter, joiner

carraspe|ar vi clear one's throat. **~ra** f. **tener ~ra** have a frog in one's throat

carrera f run; (prisa) rush; (concurso) race; (recorrido, estudios) course; (profesión) profession, career

carreta f cart. **~da** f cart-load

carrete m reel; (película) 35mm film

carretera f road. **~ de circunvalación** bypass, ring road. **~ nacional** A road (Brit), highway (Amer). **~ secundaria** B road (Brit), secondary road (Amer)

carret|illa f trolley; (de una rueda) wheelbarrow; (de bebé) baby-walker. **~ón** m small cart

carril m rut; (*rail*) rail; (*de autopista etc*) lane

carrillo m cheek; (*polea*) pulley

carrizo m reed

carro m cart; (*LAm, coche*) car. ~ **de asalto**, ~ **de combate** tank

carrocería f (*auto*) bodywork; (*taller*) car repairer's

carroña f carrion

carroza f coach, carriage; (*en desfile de fiesta*) float

carruaje m carriage

carrusel m merry-go-round

carta f letter; (*documento*) document; (*lista de platos*) menu; (*lista de vinos*) list; (*geog*) map; (*naipe*) card. ~ **blanca** free hand. ~ **de crédito** credit card

cartearse vpr correspond

cartel m poster; (*de escuela etc*) wall-chart. ~**era** f hoarding; (*en periódico*) entertainments. ~**ito** m notice. **de** ~ celebrated. **tener** ~ be a hit, be successful

cartera f wallet; (*de colegial*) satchel; (*para documentos*) briefcase

cartería f sorting office

carterista m & f pickpocket

cartero m postman, mailman (*Amer*)

cartílago m cartilage

cartilla f first reading book. ~ **de ahorros** savings book. **leerle la** ~ **a uno** tell s.o. off

cartón m cardboard

cartucho m cartridge

cartulina f thin cardboard

casa f house; (*hogar*) home; (*empresa*) firm; (*edificio*) building. ~ **de correos** post office. ~ **de huéspedes** boarding-house. ~ **de socorro** first aid post. **amigo** m **de la** ~ family friend. **ir a** ~ go home. **salir de** ~ go out

casad|a f married woman. ~**o** a married. ● m married man. **los recién** ~**os** the newly-weds

casamentero m matchmaker

casa|miento m marriage; (*ceremonia*) wedding. ~**r** vt marry. ● vi get married. ~**rse** vpr get married

cascabel m small bell. ~**eo** m jingling

cascada f waterfall

cascado a broken; (*voz*) harsh

cascanueces m invar nutcrackers

cascar [7] vt break; crack (*frutos secos*); (*pegar*) beat. ● vi (*fig, fam*) chatter, natter (*fam*). ~**se** vpr crack

cáscara f (*de huevo, frutos secos*) shell; (*de naranja*) peel; (*de plátano*) skin

casco m helmet; (*de cerámica etc*) piece, fragment; (*cabeza*) head; (*de barco*) hull; (*envase*) empty bottle; (*de caballo*) hoof; (*de una ciudad*) part, area

cascote m rubble

caserío m country house; (*conjunto de casas*) hamlet

casero a home-made; (*doméstico*) domestic, household; (*amante del hogar*) home-loving; ‹reunión› family. ● m owner; (*vigilante*) caretaker

caseta f small house, cottage. ~ **de baño** bathing hut

caset(t)e m & f cassette

casi adv almost, nearly; (*en frases negativas*) hardly. ~ ~ very nearly. ~ **nada** hardly any. ¡~ **nada!** is that all! ~ **nunca** hardly ever

casilla f small house; (*cabaña*) hut; (*de mercado*) stall; (*en ajedrez etc*) square; (*departamento de casillero*) pigeon-hole

casillero m pigeon-holes

casimir m cashmere

casino m casino; (*sociedad*) club

caso m case; (*atención*) notice. ~ **perdido** hopeless case. ~ **urgente** emergency. **darse el** ~ **(de) que** happen. **el** ~ **es que** the fact is that. **en** ~ **de** in the event of. **en cualquier** ~ in any case, whatever happens. **en ese** ~ in that case. **en todo** ~ in any case. **en último** ~ as a last resort. **hacer** ~ **de** take notice of. **poner por** ~ suppose

caspa f dandruff

cáspita int good heavens!, goodness me!

casquivano a scatter-brained

cassette m & f cassette

casta f (*de animal*) breed; (*de persona*) descent

castaña f chestnut

castañet|a f click of the fingers. ~**ear** vi ‹dientes› chatter

castaño a chestnut, brown. ● m chestnut (tree)

castañuela f castanet

castellano a Castilian. ● m (*persona*) Castilian; (*lengua*) Castilian, Spanish. ~**parlante** a Castilian-speaking, Spanish-speaking. ¿**habla Vd** ~? do you speak Spanish?

castidad f chastity

castig|ar [12] vt punish; (en deportes) penalize. ~o m punishment; (en deportes) penalty

Castilla f Castille. ~ la Nueva New Castille. ~ la Vieja Old Castille

castillo m castle

cast|izo a true; (lengua) pure. ~o a pure

castor m beaver

castra|ción f castration. ~r vt castrate

castrense m military

casual a chance, accidental. ~idad f chance, coincidence. ~mente adv by chance. dar la ~idad happen. de ~idad, por ~idad by chance. ¡qué ~idad! what a coincidence!

cataclismo m cataclysm

catador m taster; (fig) connoisseur

catalán a & m Catalan

catalejo m telescope

catalizador m catalyst

cat|alogar [12] vt catalogue; (fig) classify. ~álogo m catalogue

Cataluña f Catalonia

catamarán m catamaran

cataplúm int crash! bang!

catapulta f catapult

catar vt taste, try

catarata f waterfall, falls; (med) cataract

catarro m cold

cat|ástrofe m catastrophe. ~astrófico a catastrophic

catecismo m catechism

catedral f cathedral

catedrático m professor; (de instituto) teacher, head of department

categ|oría f category; (clase) class. ~órico a categorical. de ~oría important. de primera ~oría first-class

catinga f (LAm) bad smell

catita f (Arg) parrot

catoche m (Mex) bad mood

cat|olicismo m catholicism. ~ólico a (Roman) Catholic. ● m (Roman) Catholic

catorce a & m fourteen

cauce m river bed; (fig, artificial) channel

caución f caution; (jurid) guarantee

caucho m rubber

caudal m (de río) flow; (riqueza) wealth. ~oso a (río) large

caudillo m leader, caudillo

causa f cause; (motivo) reason; (jurid) lawsuit. ~r vt cause. a ~ de, por ~ de because of

cáustico a caustic

cautel|a f caution. ~arse vpr guard against. ~osamente adv warily, cautiously. ~oso a cautious, wary

cauterizar [10] vt cauterize; (fig) apply drastic measures to

cautiv|ar vt capture; (fig, fascinar) captivate. ~erio m, ~idad f captivity. ~o a & m captive

cauto a cautious

cavar vt/i dig

caverna f cave, cavern

caviar m caviare

cavidad f cavity

cavil|ar vi ponder, consider. ~oso a worried

cayado m (de pastor) crook; (de obispo) crozier

caza f hunting; (una expedición) hunt; (animales) game. ● m fighter. ~dor m hunter. ~dora f jacket. ~ mayor big game hunting. ~ menor small game hunting. ~r [10] vt hunt; (fig) track down; (obtener) catch, get. andar a (la) ~ de be in search of. dar ~ chase, go after

cazo m saucepan; (cucharón) ladle. ~leta f (small) saucepan

cazuela f casserole

cebada f barley

ceb|ar vt fatten (up); (con trampa) bait; prime (arma de fuego). ~o m bait; (de arma de fuego) charge

ceboll|a f onion. ~ana f chive. ~eta f spring onion. ~ino m chive

cebra f zebra

cece|ar vi lisp. ~o m lisp

cedazo m sieve

ceder vt give up. ● vi give in; (disminuir) ease off; (fallar) give way, collapse. ceda el paso give way

cedilla f cedilla

cedro m cedar

cédula f document; (ficha) index card

CE(E) abrev (Comunidad (Económica) Europea) E(E)C, European (Economic) Community

cefalea f severe headache

ceg|ador a blinding. ~ar [1 & 12] vt blind; (tapar) block up. ~arse vpr be blinded (de by). ~ato a short-sighted. ~uera f blindness

ceja f eyebrow

cejar vi move back; (fig) give way

celada f ambush; (fig) trap

cela|dor m (de niños) monitor; (de cárcel) prison warder; (de museo etc) attendant. ~r vt watch

celda f cell

celebra|ción f celebration. ~**r** vt celebrate; (*alabar*) praise. ~**rse** vpr take place

célebre a famous; (*fig, gracioso*) funny

celebridad f fame; (*persona*) celebrity

celeridad f speed

celest|e a heavenly. ~**ial** a heavenly. **azul** ~**e** sky-blue

celibato m celibacy

célibe a celibate

celo m zeal. ~**s** mpl jealousy. **dar** ~**s** make jealous. **papel** m ~ adhesive tape, Sellotape (P). **tener** ~**s** be jealous

celofán m cellophane

celoso a enthusiastic; (*que tiene celos*) jealous

celta a Celtic. ● m & f Celt

céltico a Celtic

célula f cell

celular a cellular

celuloide m celluloid

celulosa f cellulose

cellisca f sleetstorm

cementerio m cemetery

cemento m cement; (*hormigón*) concrete; (*LAm, cola*) glue

cena f dinner; (*comida ligera*) supper. ~**duría** f (*Mex*) restaurant

cenag|al m marsh, bog; (*fig*) tight spot. ~**oso** a muddy

cenar vt have for dinner; (*en cena ligera*) have for supper. ● vi have dinner; (*tomar cena ligera*) have supper

cenicero m ashtray

cenit m zenith

ceniz|a f ash. ~**o** a ashen. ● m jinx

censo m census. ~ **electoral** electoral roll

censura f censure; (*de prensa etc*) censorship. ~**r** vt censure; censor ⟨*prensa etc*⟩

centavo a & m hundredth; (*moneda*) centavo

centell|a f flash; (*chispa*) spark. ~**ar** vi, ~**ear** vi sparkle. ~**eo** m sparkle, sparkling

centena f hundred. ~**r** m hundred. **a** ~**res** by the hundred

centenario a centenary; ⟨*persona*⟩ centenarian. ● m centenary; (*persona*) centenarian

centeno m rye

centésim|a f hundredth. ~**o** a hundredth; (*moneda*) centésimo

cent|ígrado a centigrade, Celsius. ~**ígramo** m centigram. ~**ilitro** m centilitre. ~**ímetro** m centimetre

céntimo a hundredth. ● m cent

centinela f sentry

centolla f, **centollo** m spider crab

central a central. ● f head office. ~ **de correos** general post office. ~ **eléctrica** power station. ~ **nuclear** nuclear power station. ~ **telefónica** telephone exchange. ~**ismo** m centralism. ~**ita** f switchboard

centraliza|ción f centralization. ~**r** [10] vt centralize

centrar vt centre

céntrico a central

centrífugo a centrifugal

centro m centre. ~ **comercial** shopping centre

Centroamérica f Central America

centroamericano a & m Central American

centuplicar [7] vt increase a hundredfold

ceñi|do a tight. ~**r** [5 & 22] vt surround, encircle; ⟨*vestido*⟩ be a tight fit. ~**rse** vpr limit o.s. (**a** to)

ceñ|o m frown. ~**udo** a frowning. **fruncir el** ~**o** frown

cepill|ar vt brush; (*en carpintería*) plane. ~**o** m brush; (*en carpintería*) plane. ~**o de dientes** toothbrush

cera f wax

cerámic|a f ceramics; (*materia*) pottery; (*objeto*) piece of pottery. ~**o** a ceramic

cerca f fence. ● adv near, close. ~**s** mpl foreground. ~ **de** prep near; (*con números, con tiempo*) nearly. **de** ~ from close up, closely

cercado m enclosure

cercan|ía f nearness, proximity. ~**ías** fpl outskirts. **tren** m **de** ~**ías** local train. ~**o** a near, close. **C**~**o Oriente** m Near East

cercar [7] vt fence in, enclose; ⟨*gente*⟩ surround, crowd round; (*asediar*) besiege

cerciorar vt convince. ~**se** vpr make sure, find out

cerco m (*grupo*) circle; (*cercado*) enclosure; (*asedio*) siege

Cerdeña f Sardinia

cerdo m pig; (*carne*) pork

cereal m cereal

cerebr|al a cerebral. ~**o** m brain; (*fig, inteligencia*) intelligence, brains

ceremoni|a f ceremony. **~al** a ceremonial. **~oso** a ceremonious, stiff

céreo a wax

cerez|a f cherry. **~o** cherry tree

cerill|a f match. **~o** m (Mex) match

cern|er [1] vt sieve. **~erse** vpr hover; (fig, amenazar) hang over. **~idor** m sieve

cero m nought, zero; (fútbol) nil (Brit), zero (Amer); (tenis) love; (persona) nonentity. **partir de ~** start from scratch

cerquillo m (LAm, flequillo) fringe

cerquita adv very near

cerra|do a shut, closed; (espacio) shut in, enclosed; (cielo) overcast; (curva) sharp. **~dura** f lock; (acción de cerrar) shutting, closing. **~jero** m locksmith. **~r** [1] vt shut, close; (con llave) lock; (con cerrojo) bolt; (cercar) enclose; turn off (grifo); block up (agujero etc). ● vi shut, close. **~rse** vpr shut, close; (herida) heal. **~r con llave** lock

cerro m hill. **irse por los ~s de Úbeda** ramble on

cerrojo m bolt. **echar el ~** bolt

certamen m competition, contest

certero a accurate

certeza f, **certidumbre** f certainty

certifica|do a (carta etc) registered. ● m certificate; (carta) registered letter. **~r** [7] vt certify; register (carta etc)

certitud f certainty

cervato m fawn

cerve|cería f beerhouse, bar; (fábrica) brewery. **~za** f beer. **~za de barril** draught beer. **~za de botella** bottled beer

cesa|ción f cessation, suspension. **~nte** a out of work. **~r** vt stop, cease; (dejar un empleo) give up. **sin ~r** incessantly

cesárea f Caesarian. **operación** f **cesárea** Caesarian section

cese m cessation; (de un empleo) dismissal

césped m grass, lawn

cest|a f basket. **~ada** f basketful. **~o** m basket. **~o de los papeles** wastepaper basket

cetro m sceptre; (fig) power

cianuro m cyanide

ciática f sciatica

cibernética f cibernetics

cicatriz f scar. **~ación** f healing. **~ar** [10] vt/i heal. **~arse** vpr heal

ciclamino m cyclamen

cíclico a cyclic(al)

ciclis|mo m cycling. **~ta** m & f cyclist

ciclo m cycle; (LAm, curso) course

ciclomotor m moped

ciclón m cyclone

ciclostilo m cyclostyle, duplicating machine

ciego a blind. ● m blind man, blind person. **a ciegas** in the dark

cielo m sky; (relig) heaven; (persona) darling. **¡~s!** good heavens!, goodness me!

ciempiés m invar centipede

cien a a hundred. **~ por ~** (fam) completely, one hundred per cent. **me pone a ~** it drives me mad

ciénaga f bog, swamp

ciencia f science; (fig) knowledge. **~s** fpl (univ etc) science. **~s empresariales** business studies. **saber a ~ cierta** know for a fact, know for certain

cieno m mud

científico a scientific. ● m scientist

ciento a & m (delante de nombres, y numerales a los que multiplica **cien**) a hundred, one hundred. **por ~** per cent

cierne m blossoming. **en ~** in blossom; (fig) in its infancy

cierre m fastener; (acción de cerrar) shutting, closing. **~ de cremallera** zip, zipper (Amer)

cierro vb véase **cerrar**

cierto a certain; (verdad) true. **estar en lo ~** be right. **lo ~ es que** the fact is that. **no es ~** that's not true. **¿no es ~?** right? **por ~** certainly, by the way. **si bien es ~ que** although

ciervo m deer

cifra f figure, number; (cantidad) sum. **~do** a coded. **~r** vt code; (resumir) summarize. **en ~** code, in code

cigala f (Norway) lobster

cigarra f cicada

cigarr|illo m cigarette. **~o** m (cigarillo) cigarette; (puro) cigar

cigüeña f stork

cil|índrico a cylindrical. **~indro** m cylinder; (Mex, organillo) barrel organ

cima f top; (fig) summit

címbalo m cymbal

cimbrear vt shake. **~se** vpr sway

cimentar [1] vt lay the foundations of; (fig, reforzar) strengthen

cimer|a f crest. **~o** a highest

cimiento *m* foundations; (*fig*) source. **desde los ~s** from the very beginning

cinc *m* zinc

cincel *m* chisel. **~ar** *vt* chisel

cinco *a* & *m* five

cincuent|a *a* & *m* fifty; (*quincuagésimo*) fiftieth. **~ón** *a* about fifty

cine *m* cinema. **~matografiar** [20] *vt* film

cinético *a* kinetic

cínico *a* cynical; (*desvergonzado*) shameless. ● *m* cynic

cinismo *m* cynicism; (*desvergüenza*) shamelessness

cinta *f* band; (*adorno de pelo etc*) ribbon; (*película*) film; (*magnética*) tape; (*de máquina de escribir etc*) ribbon. **~ aisladora**, **~ aislante** insulating tape. **~ magnetofónica** magnetic tape. **~ métrica** tape measure

cintur|a *f* waist. **~ón** *m* belt. **~ón de seguridad** safety belt. **~ón salvavidas** lifebelt

ciprés *m* cypress (tree)

circo *m* circus

circuito *m* circuit; (*viaje*) tour. **~ cerrado** closed circuit. **corto ~** short circuit

circula|ción *f* circulation; (*vehículos*) traffic. **~r** *a* circular. ● *vt* circulate. ● *vi* circulate; ‹*líquidos*› flow; (*conducir*) drive; ‹*autobús etc*› run

círculo *m* circle. **~ vicioso** vicious circle. **en ~** in a circle

circunci|dar *vt* circumcise. **~sión** *f* circumcision

circunda|nte *a* surrounding. **~r** *vt* surround

circunferencia *f* circumference

circunflejo *m* circumflex

circunscri|bir [*pp* **circunscrito**] *vt* confine. **~pción** *f* (*distrito*) district. **~pción electoral** constituency

circunspecto *a* wary, circumspect

circunstan|cia *f* circumstance. **~te** *a* surrounding. ● *m* bystander. **los ~tes** those present

circunvalación *f*. **carretera** *f* **de ~** bypass, ring road

cirio *m* candle

ciruela *f* plum. **~ claudia** greengage. **~ damascena** damson

ciru|gía *f* surgery. **~jano** *m* surgeon

cisne *m* swan

cisterna *f* tank, cistern

cita *f* appointment; (*entre chico y chica*) date; (*referencia*) quotation. **~ción** *f* quotation; (*jurid*) summons. **~do** *a* aforementioned. **~r** *vt* make an appointment with; (*mencionar*) quote; (*jurid*) summons. **~rse** *vpr* arrange to meet

cítara *f* zither

ciudad *f* town; (*grande*) city. **~anía** *f* citizenship; (*habitantes*) citizens. **~ano** *a* civic ● *m* citizen, inhabitant; (*habitante de ciudad*) city dweller

cívico *a* civic

civil *a* civil. ● *m* civil guard. **~idad** *f* politeness

civiliza|ción *f* civilization. **~r** [10] *vt* civilize. **~rse** *vpr* become civilized

civismo *m* community spirit

cizaña *f* (*fig*) discord

clam|ar *vi* cry out, clamour. **~or** *m* cry; (*griterío*) noise, clamour; (*protesta*) outcry. **~oroso** *a* noisy

clandestin|idad *f* secrecy. **~o** *a* clandestine, secret

clara *f* (*de huevo*) egg white

claraboya *f* skylight

clarear *vi* dawn; (*aclarar*) brighten up. **~se** *vpr* be transparent

clarete *m* rosé

claridad *f* clarity; (*luz*) light

clarifica|ción *f* clarification. **~r** [7] *vt* clarify

clarín *m* bugle

clarinet|e *m* clarinet; (*músico*) clarinettist. **~ista** *m* & *f* clarinettist

clarividen|cia *f* clairvoyance; (*fig*) far-sightedness. **~te** *a* clairvoyant; (*fig*) far-sighted

claro *a* (*con mucha luz*) bright; (*transparente, evidente*) clear; ‹*colores*› light; ‹*líquido*› thin. ● *m* (*en bosque etc*) clearing; (*espacio*) gap. ● *adv* clearly. ● *int* of course! **~ de luna** moonlight. **¡~ que sí!** yes of course! **¡~ que no!** of course not!

clase *f* class; (*aula*) classroom. **~ media** middle class. **~ obrera** working class. **~ social** social class. **dar ~s** teach. **toda ~ de** all sorts of

clásico *a* classical; (*fig*) classic. ● *m* classic

clasifica|ción *f* classification; (*deportes*) league. **~r** [7] *vt* classify; (*seleccionar*) sort

claudia *f* greengage

claudicar [7] (*ceder*) give in; (*cojear*) limp

claustro *m* cloister; (*univ*) staff
claustrof|obia *f* claustrophobia. **~óbico** *a* claustrophobic
cláusula *f* clause
clausura *f* closure; (*ceremonia*) closing ceremony. **~r** *vt* close
clava|do *a* fixed; (*con clavo*) nailed. **~r** *vt* knock in ⟨*clavo*⟩; (*introducir a mano*) stick; (*fijar*) fix; (*juntar*) nail together. **es ~do a su padre** he's the spitting image of his father
clave *f* key; (*mus*) clef; (*clavicémbalo*) harpsichord
clavel *m* carnation
clavicémbalo *m* harpsichord
clavícula *f* collar bone, clavicle
clavija *f* peg; (*elec*) plug
clavo *m* nail; (*culin*) clove
claxon *m* (*pl* **claxons** /ˈklakson/) horn
clemen|cia *f* clemency, mercy. **~te** *a* clement, merciful
clementina *f* tangerine
cleptómano *m* kleptomaniac
cler|ecía *f* priesthood. **~ical** *a* clerical
clérigo *m* priest
clero *m* clergy
cliché *m* cliché; (*foto*) negative
cliente *m* & *f* client, customer; (*de médico*) patient. **~la** *f* clientele, customers; (*de médico*) patients, practice
clim|a *m* climate. **~ático** *a* climatic. **~atizado** *a* air-conditioned. **~atológico** *a* climatological
clínic|a *f* clinic. **~o** *a* clinical. ● *m* clinician
clip *m* (*pl* **clips**) clip
clo *m* cluck. **hacer ~ ~** cluck
cloaca *f* drain, sewer
cloque|ar *vi* cluck. **~o** *m* clucking
cloro *m* chlorine
club *m* (*pl* **clubs** *o* **clubes**) club
coacci|ón *f* coercion, compulsion. **~onar** *vt* coerce, compel
coagular *vt* coagulate; clot ⟨*sangre*⟩; curdle ⟨*leche*⟩. **~se** *vpr* coagulate; ⟨*sangre*⟩ clot; ⟨*leche*⟩ curdle
coalición *f* coalition
coartada *f* alibi
coartar *vt* hinder; restrict ⟨*libertad etc*⟩
cobard|e *a* cowardly. ● *m* coward. **~ía** *f* cowardice
cobaya *f*, **cobayo** *m* guinea pig
cobert|era *f* (*tapadera*) lid. **~izo** *m* lean-to, shelter. **~or** *m* bedspread; (*manta*) blanket. **~ura** *f* covering

cobij|a *f* (*LAm, ropa de cama*) bedclothes; (*Mex, manta*) blanket. **~ar** *vt* shelter. **~arse** *vpr* shelter, take shelter. **~o** *m* shelter
cobra *f* cobra
cobra|dor *m* conductor. **~dora** *f* conductress. **~r** *vt* collect; (*ganar*) earn; charge ⟨*precio*⟩; cash ⟨*cheque*⟩; (*recuperar*) recover. ● *vi* be paid. **~rse** *vpr* recover
cobre *m* copper; (*mus*) brass (instruments)
cobro *m* collection; (*de cheque*) cashing; (*pago*) payment. **ponerse en ~** go into hiding. **presentar al ~** cash
cocada *f* (*LAm*) sweet coconut
cocaína *f* cocaine
cocción *f* cooking; (*tec*) baking, firing
cocear *vt/i* kick
coc|er [2 & 9] *vt/i* cook; (*hervir*) boil; (*en horno*) bake. **~ido** *a* cooked. ● *m* stew
cociente *m* quotient. **~ intelectual** intelligence quotient, IQ
cocin|a *f* kitchen; (*arte de cocinar*) cookery, cuisine; (*aparato*) cooker. **~a de gas** gas cooker. **~a eléctrica** electric cooker. **~ar** *vt/i* cook. **~ero** *m* cook
coco *m* coconut; (*árbol*) coconut palm; (*cabeza*) head; (*duende*) bogeyman. **comerse el ~** think hard
cocodrilo *m* crocodile
cocotero *m* coconut palm
cóctel *m* (*pl* **cócteles** *o* **cócteles**) cocktail; (*reunión*) cocktail party
coche *m* car (*Brit*), motor car (*Brit*), automobile (*Amer*); (*de tren*) coach, carriage. **~-cama** sleeper. **~-fúnebre** hearse. **~ra** *f* garage; (*de autobuses*) depot. **~ restaurante** dining-car. **~s de choque** dodgems
cochin|ada *f* dirty thing. **~o** *a* dirty, filthy. ● *m* pig
cod|azo *m* nudge (with one's elbow); (*Mex, aviso secreto*) tip-off. **~ear** *vt/i* elbow, nudge
codici|a *f* greed. **~ado** *a* coveted, sought after. **~ar** *vt* covet. **~oso** *a* greedy (**de** for)
código *m* code. **~ de la circulación** Highway Code
codo *m* elbow; (*dobladura*) bend. **hablar por los ~s** talk too much. **hasta los ~s** up to one's neck
codorniz *m* quail
coeducación *f* coeducation

coerción f coercion
coetáneo a & m contemporary
coexist|encia f coexistence. **~ir** vi coexist
cofradía f brotherhood
cofre m chest
coger [14] vt (España) take; catch ‹tren, autobús, pelota, catarro›; (agarrar) take hold of; (del suelo) pick up; pick ‹frutos etc›. ● vi (caber) fit. **~se** vpr trap, catch
cogollo m (de lechuga etc) heart; (fig, lo mejor) cream; (fig, núcleo) centre
cogote m back of the neck
cohech|ar vt bribe. **~o** m bribery
coherente a coherent
cohesión f cohesion
cohete m rocket; (Mex, pistola) pistol
cohibi|ción f inhibition. **~r** vt restrict; inhibit ‹persona›. **~rse** vpr feel inhibited; (contenerse) restrain o.s.
coincid|encia f coincidence. **~ente** a coincidental. **~ir** vt coincide. **dar la ~encia** happen
coje|ar vt limp; ‹mueble› wobble. **~ra** f lameness
coj|ín m cushion. **~inete** m small cushion. **~inete de bolas** ball bearing
cojo a lame; ‹mueble› wobbly. ● m lame person
col f cabbage. **~es de Bruselas** Brussel sprouts
cola f tail; (fila) queue; (para pegar) glue. **a la ~** at the end. **hacer ~** queue (up). **tener ~, traer ~** have serious consequences
colabora|ción f collaboration. **~dor** m collaborator. **~r** vi collaborate
colada f washing. **hacer la ~** do the washing
colador m strainer
colapso m collapse; (fig) stoppage
colar [2] vt strain ‹líquidos›; (lavar) wash; pass ‹moneda falsa etc›. ● vi ‹líquido› seep through; (fig) be believed, wash (fam). **~se** vpr slip; (no hacer caso de la cola) jump the queue; (en fiesta) gatecrash; (meter la pata) put one's foot in it
colch|a f bedspread. **~ón** m mattress. **~oneta** f mattress
colear vi wag its tail; ‹asunto› not be resolved. **vivito y coleando** alive and kicking
colecci|ón f collection; (fig, gran número de) a lot of. **~onar** vt collect. **~onista** m & f collector

colecta f collection
colectiv|idad f community. **~o** a collective. ● m (Arg) minibus
colector m (en las alcantarillas) main sewer
colega m & f colleague
colegi|al m schoolboy. **~ala** f schoolgirl. **~o** m private school; (de ciertas profesiones) college. **~o mayor** hall of residence
colegir [5 & 14] vt gather
cólera f cholera; (ira) anger, fury. **descargar su ~** vent one's anger. **montar en ~** fly into a rage
colérico a furious, irate
colesterol m cholesterol
coleta f pigtail
colga|nte a hanging. ● m pendant. **~r** [2 & 12] vt hang; hang out ‹colada›; hang up ‹abrigo etc›. ● vi hang; (teléfono) hang up, ring off. **~rse** vpr hang o.s. **dejar a uno ~do** let s.o. down
cólico m colic
coliflor m cauliflower
colilla f cigarette end
colina f hill
colinda|nte a adjacent. **~r** vt border (con on)
colisión f collision, crash; (fig) clash
colmar vt fill to overflowing; (fig) fulfill. **~ a uno de amabilidad** overwhelm s.o. with kindness
colmena f beehive, hive
colmillo m eye tooth, canine (tooth); (de elefante) tusk; (de otros animales) fang
colmo m height. **ser el ~** be the limit, be the last straw
coloca|ción f positioning; (empleo) job, position. **~r** [7] vt put, place; (buscar empleo) find work for. **~rse** vpr find a job
Colombia f Colombia
colombiano a & m Colombian
colon m colon
colón m (unidad monetaria de Costa Rica y El Salvador) colón
Colonia f Cologne
coloni|a f colony; (agua de colonia) eau-de-Cologne; (LAm, barrio) suburb. **~a de verano** holiday camp. **~al** a colonial. **~ales** mpl imported foodstuffs; (comestibles en general) groceries. **~alista** m & f colonialist. **~zación** f colonization. **~zar** [10] colonize
coloqui|al a colloquial. **~o** m conversation; (congreso) conference

color *m* colour. **~ado** *a* (*rojo*) red.
~ante *m* colouring. **~ar** *vt* colour.
~ear *vt/i* colour. **~ete** *m* rouge.
~ido *m* colour. **de ~** colour. **en ~**
(*fotos, película*) colour

colosal *a* colossal; (*fig, magnífico,
fam*) terrific

columna *f* column; (*fig, apoyo*)
support

columpi|ar *vt* swing. **~arse** *vpr*
swing. **~o** *m* swing

collar *m* necklace; (*de perro etc*)
collar

coma *f* comma. ● *m* (*med*) coma

comadre *f* midwife; (*madrina*) godmother; (*vecina*) neighbour. **~ar** *vi*
gossip

comadreja *f* weasel

comadrona *f* midwife

comand|ancia *f* command. **~ante** *m*
commander. **~o** *m* command; (*soldado*) commando

comarca *f* area, region

comba *f* bend; (*juguete*) skipping-
rope. **~r** *vt* bend. **~rse** *vpr* bend.
saltar a la ~ skip

combat|e *m* fight; (*fig*) struggle.
~iente *m* fighter. **~ir** *vt/i* fight

combina|ción *f* combination;
(*bebida*) cocktail; (*arreglo*) plan,
scheme; (*prenda*) slip. **~r** *vt* combine; (*arreglar*) arrange; (*armonizar*) match, go well with. **~rse** *vpr*
combine; (*ponerse de acuerdo*) agree
(**para**) to

combustible *m* fuel

comedia *f* comedy; (*cualquier obra
de teatro*) play. **hacer la ~** pretend

comedi|do *a* reserved. **~rse** [5] *vpr*
be restrained

comedor *m* dining-room; (*restaurante*) restaurant; (*persona*)
glutton. **ser buen ~** have a good
appetite

comensal *m* companion at table, fellow diner

comentar *vt* comment on; (*anotar*)
annotate. **~io** *m* commentary;
(*observación*) comment; (*fam*)
gossip. **~ista** *m & f* commentator

comenzar [1 & 10] *vt/i* begin, start

comer *vt* eat; (*a mediodía*) have for
lunch; (*corroer*) eat away; (*en ajedrez*) take. ● *vi* eat; (*a mediodía*) have
lunch. **~se** *vpr* eat (up). **dar de ~ a**
feed

comerci|al *a* commercial. **~ante** *m*
trader; (*de tienda*) shopkeeper. **~ar**

vt trade (**con, en** in); (*con otra persona*) do business. **~o** *m* commerce;
(*actividad*) trade; (*tienda*) shop;
(*negocio*) business

comestible *a* edible. **~s** *mpl* food.
tienda de ~s grocer's (shop) (*Brit*),
grocery (*Amer*)

cometa *m* comet. ● *f* kite

comet|er *vt* commit; make (*falta*).
~ido *m* task

comezón *m* itch

comicastro *m* poor actor, ham (*fam*)

comicios *mpl* elections

cómico *a* comic(al). ● *m* comic actor;
(*cualquier actor*) actor

comida *f* food; (*a mediodía*) lunch.
hacer la ~ prepare the meals

comidilla *f* topic of conversation. **ser
la ~ del pueblo** be the talk of the
town

comienzo *m* beginning, start. **a ~s
de** at the beginning of

comil|ón *a* greedy. **~ona** *f* feast

comillas *fpl* inverted commas

comino *m* cumin. **(no) me importa
un ~** I couldn't care less

comisar|ía *f* police station. **~io** *m*
commissioner; (*deportes*) steward.
~io de policía police superintendent

comisión *f* assignment; (*comité*)
commission, committee; (*com*)
commission

comisura *f* corner. **~ de los labios**
corner of the mouth

comité *m* committee

como *adv* like, as. ● *conj* as; (*en
cuanto*) as soon as. **~ quieras** as you
like. **~ sabes** as you know. **~ si** as if

cómo *a* how? **¿~?** I beg your pardon?
¿~ está Vd? how are you? **¡~ no!** (*esp
LAm*) of course! **¿~ son?** what are
they like? **¿~ te llamas?** what's your
name? **¡y ~!** and how!

cómoda *f* chest of drawers

comodidad *f* comfort. **a su ~** at your
convenience

cómodo *a* comfortable; (*útil*) handy

comoquiera *conj.* **~ que** since. **~
que sea** however it may be

compacto *a* compact; (*denso*) dense;
(*líneas etc*) close

compadecer [11] *vt* feel sorry for.
~se *vpr.* **~se de** feel sorry for

compadre *m* godfather; (*amigo*)
friend

compañ|ero *m* companion; (*de tra-
bajo*) colleague; (*amigo*) friend. **~ía**
f company. **en ~ía de** with

compara|ble *a* comparable. **~ción** *f* comparison. **~r** *vt* compare. **~tivo** *a* & *m* comparative. **en ~ción con** in comparison with, compared with

comparecer [11] *vi* appear

comparsa *f* group; *(en el teatro)* extra

compartimiento *m* compartment

compartir *vt* share

compás *m* *(instrumento)* (pair of) compasses; *(ritmo)* rhythm; *(división)* bar *(Brit)*, measure *(Amer)*; *(naut)* compass. **a ~** in time

compasi|ón *f* compassion, pity. **tener ~ón de** feel sorry for. **~vo** *a* compassionate

compatib|ilidad *f* compatibility. **~le** *a* compatible

compatriota *m* & *f* compatriot

compeler *vt* compel, force

compendi|ar *vt* summarize. **~o** *m* summary

compenetración *f* mutual understanding

compensa|ción *f* compensation. **~ción por despido** redundancy payment. **~r** *vt* compensate

competen|cia *f* competition; *(capacidad)* competence; *(terreno)* field, scope. **~te** *a* competent; *(apropiado)* appropriate, suitable

competi|ción *f* competition. **~dor** *m* competitor. **~r** [5] *vi* compete

compilar *vt* compile

compinche *m* accomplice; *(amigo, fam)* friend, mate *(fam)*

complac|encia *f* pleasure; *(indulgencia)* indulgence. **~er** [32] *vt* please; *(prestar servicio)* help. **~erse** *vpr* have pleasure, be pleased. **~iente** *a* helpful; ‹*marido*› complaisant

complej|idad *f* complexity. **~o** *a* & *m* complex

complement|ario *a* complementary. **~o** *m* complement; *(gram)* object, complement

complet|ar *vt* complete. **~o** *a* complete; *(lleno)* full; *(perfecto)* perfect

complexión *f* disposition; *(constitución)* constitution

complica|ción *f* complication. **~r** [7] *vt* complicate; involve ‹*persona*›. **~rse** *vpr* become complicated

cómplice *m* accomplice

complot *m* (*pl* **complots**) plot

compon|ente *a* component. ● *m* component; *(culin)* ingredient; *(miembro)* member. **~er** [34] *vt*

make up; *(mus, literatura etc)* write, compose; *(reparar)* mend; *(culin)* prepare; *(arreglar)* restore; settle ‹*estómago*›; reconcile ‹*diferencias*›. **~erse** *vpr* be made up; *(arreglarse)* get ready. **~érselas** manage

comporta|miento *m* behaviour. **~r** *vt* involve. **~rse** *vpr* behave. **~rse como es debido** behave properly. **~rse mal** misbehave

composi|ción *f* composition. **~tor** *m* composer

compostelano *a* from Santiago de Compostela. ● *m* native of Santiago de Compostela

compostura *f* composition; *(arreglo)* repair; *(culin)* condiment; *(comedimiento)* composure

compota *f* stewed fruit

compra *f* purchase. **~ a plazos** hire purchase. **~dor** *m* buyer; *(en una tienda)* customer. **~r** *vt* buy. **~venta** *f* dealing. **hacer la ~, ir a la ~, ir de ~s** do the shopping, go shopping. **negocio** *m* **de ~venta** second-hand shop

compren|der *vt* understand; *(incluir)* include. **~sible** *a* understandable. **~sión** *f* understanding. **~sivo** *a* understanding; *(que incluye)* comprehensive

compresa *f* compress; *(de mujer)* sanitary towel

compr|esión *f* compression. **~imido** *a* compressed. ● *m* pill, tablet. **~imir** *vt* compress; keep back ‹*lágrimas*›; *(fig)* restrain

comproba|nte *m* *(recibo)* receipt. **~r** *vt* check; *(confirmar)* confirm

comprometer *vt* compromise; *(arriesgar)* endager. **~erse** *vpr* compromise o.s.; *(obligarse)* agree to. **~ido** *a* ‹*situación*› awkward, embarrassing

compromiso *m* obligation; *(apuro)* predicament; *(cita)* appointment; *(acuerdo)* agreement. **sin ~** without obligation

compuesto *a* compound; ‹*persona*› smart. ● *m* compound

compungido *a* sad, sorry

computador *m*, **computadora** *f* computer

computar *vt* calculate

cómputo *m* calculation

comulgar [12] *vi* take Communion

común *a* common. ● *m* community. **en ~** in common. **por lo ~** generally

comunal *a* municipal, communal
comunica|ción *f* communication.
~**do** *m* communiqué. ~**do a la pren-**
sa press release. ~**r** [7] *vt/i* com-
municate; pass on ‹*enfermedad*,
información›. ~**rse** *vpr* com-
municate; ‹*enfermedad*› spread.
~**tivo** *a* communicative. **está** ~**ndo**
(*al teléfono*) it's engaged, the line's
engaged
comunidad *f* community. ~ **de ve-**
cinos residents' association. **C~**
(Económica) Europea European
(Economic) Community. **en** ~
together
comunión *f* communion; (*relig*)
(Holy) Communion
comunis|mo *m* communism. ~**ta** *a*
& *m* & *f* communist
comúnmente *adv* generally,
usually
con *prep* with; (*a pesar de*) in spite
of; (+ *infinitivo*) by. ~ **decir la ver-**
dad by telling the truth. ~ **que** so.
~ **tal que** as long as
conato *m* attempt
concatenación *f* chain, linking
cóncavo *a* concave
concebir [5] *vt/i* conceive
conceder *vt* concede, grant; award
‹*premio*›; (*admitir*) admit
concej|al *m* councillor. ~**o** *m* town
council
concentra|ción *f* concentration.
~**do** *m* concentrated. ~**r** *vt* concentrate. ~**rse** *vpr* concentrate
concep|ción *f* conception. ~**to** *m*
concept; (*opinión*) opinion. **bajo**
ningún ~**to** in no way. **en mi** ~**to** in
my view. **por ningún** ~**to** in no way
concerniente *a* concerning. **en lo** ~
a with regard to
concertar [1] *vt* (*mus*) harmonize;
(*coordinar*) coordinate; (*poner de*
acuerdo) agree. ● *vi* be in tune; (*fig*)
agree. ~**se** *vpr* agree
concertina *f* concertina
concesión *f* concession
conciencia *f* conscience; (*con-*
ocimiento) consciousness. ~**ción** *f*
awareness. ~ **limpia** clear conscience. ~ **sucia** guilty conscience.
a ~ **de que** fully aware that. **en** ~
honestly. **tener** ~ **de** be aware of.
tomar ~ **de** become aware of
concienzudo *a* conscientious
concierto *m* concert; (*acuerdo*)
agreement; (*mus, composición*)
concerto

concilia|ble *a* reconcilable. ~**ción** *f*
reconciliation. ~**r** *vt* reconcile. ~**r**
el sueño get to sleep. ~**rse** *vpr* gain
concilio *m* council
conciso *m* concise
conciudadano *m* fellow citizen
conclu|ir [17] *vt* finish; (*deducir*) con-
clude. ● *vi* finish, end. ~**irse** *vpr*
finish, end. ~**sión** *f* conclusion.
~**yente** *a* conclusive
concord|ancia *f* agreement. ~**ar** [2]
vt reconcile. ● *vi* agree. ~**e** *a* in
agreement. ~**ia** *f* harmony
concret|amente *adv* specifically, to
be exact. ~**ar** *vt* make specific.
~**arse** *vpr* become definite; (*limi-*
tarse) confine o.s. ~**o** *a* concrete;
(*determinado*) specific, particular.
● *m* (*LAm, hormigón*) concrete. **en**
~**o** definite; (*concretamente*) to be
exact; (*en resumen*) in short
concurr|encia *f* coincidence; (*re-*
unión) crowd, audience. ~**ido** *a*
crowded, busy. ~**ir** *vi* meet; (*asistir*)
attend; (*coincidir*) coincide; (*con-*
tribuir) contribute; (*en concurso*)
compete
concurs|ante *m* & *f* competitor, con-
testant. ~**ar** *vi* compete, take part.
~**o** *m* competition; (*concurrencia*)
crowd; (*ayuda*) help
concha *f* shell; (*carey*) tortoiseshell
condado *m* county
conde *m* earl, count
condena *f* sentence. ~**ción** *f* con-
demnation. ~**do** *m* convict. ~**r** *vt*
condemn; (*jurid*) convict
condensa|ción *f* condensation. ~**r**
vt condense. ~**rse** *vpr* condense
condesa *f* countess
condescende|ncia *f* condescension;
(*tolerancia*) indulgence. ~**r** [1] *vi*
agree; (*dignarse*) condescend
condici|ón *f* condition; (*naturaleza*)
nature. ~**onado** *a*, ~**onal** *a* con-
ditional. ~**onar** *vt* condition. **a** ~**ón**
de (que) on the condition that
condiment|ar *vt* season. ~**o** *m*
condiment
condolencia *f* condolence
condominio *m* joint ownership
condón *m* condom
condonar *vt* (*perdonar*) reprieve;
cancel ‹*deuda*›
conducir [47] *vt* drive ‹*vehículo*›;
carry ‹*electricidad, gas, agua etc*›.
● *vi* drive; (*fig, llevar*) lead. ~**se** *vpr*
behave. **¿a qué conduce?** what's the
point?

conducta f behaviour
conducto m pipe, tube; (*anat*) duct.
por ~ de through
conductor m driver; (*jefe*) leader;
(*elec*) conductor
conduzco vb véase **conducir**
conectar vt/i connect; (*enchufar*)
plug in
conejo m rabbit
conexión f connection
confabularse vpr plot
confecci|ón f making; (*prenda*)
ready-made garment. **~ones** fpl
clothing, clothes. **~onado** a ready-
made. **~onar** vt make
confederación f confederation
conferencia f conference; (*al teléfono*) long-distance call; (*univ etc*)
lecture. **~ cumbre, ~ en la cima, ~
en la cumbre** summit conference.
~nte m & f lecturer
conferir [4] vt confer; award
⟨*premio*⟩
confes|ar [1] vt/i confess. **~arse** vpr
confess. **~ión** f confession. **~ional**
a confessional. **~ionario** m confessional. **~or** m confessor
confeti m confetti
confia|do a trusting; (*seguro de sí
mismo*) confident. **~nza** f trust; (*en
sí mismo*) confidence; (*intimidad*)
familiarity. **~r** [20] vt entrust. ● vi
trust. **~rse** vpr put one's trust in
confiden|cia f confidence, secret.
~cial a confidential. **~te** m & f close
friend; (*de policía*) informer
configuración f configuration,
shape
conf|ín m border. **~inar** vt confine;
(*desterrar*) banish. ● vi border (**con**
on). **~ines** mpl outermost parts
confirma|ción f confirmation. **~r** vt
confirm
confiscar [7] vt confiscate
confit|ería f sweet-shop (*Brit*),
candy store (*Amer*). **~ura** f jam
conflagración f conflagration
conflicto m conflict
confluencia f confluence
conforma|ción f conformation,
shape. **~r** vt (*acomodar*) adjust. ● vi
agree. **~rse** vpr conform
conform|e a in agreement; (*con-
tento*) happy, satisfied; (*según*)
according (**con** to). ● conj as. ● int
OK! **~e** a in accordance with,
according to. **~idad** f agreement;
(*tolerancia*) resignation. **~ista** m &
f conformist

conforta|ble a comfortable. **~nte** a
comforting. **~r** vt comfort
confronta|ción f confrontation;
(*comparación*) comparison. **~r** vt
confront; (*comparar*) compare
confu|ndir vt blur; (*equivocar*) mis-
take, confuse; (*perder*) lose; (*mezclar*) mix up, confuse. **~ndirse** vpr
become confused; (*equivocarse*)
make a mistake. **~sión** f confusion;
(*vergüenza*) embarrassment. **~so** a
confused; (*avergonzado*) embarrassed
congela|do a frozen. **~dor** m
freezer. **~r** vt freeze
congeniar vi get on
congesti|ón f congestion. **~onado** a
congested. **~onar** vt congest. **~on-
arse** vpr become congested
congoja f distress
congraciar vt win over. **~se** vpr
ingratiate o.s.
congratular vt congratulate
congrega|ción f gathering; (*relig*)
congregation. **~rse** [12] vpr gather,
assemble
congres|ista m & f delegate, mem-
ber of a congress. **~o** m congress,
conference. **C~o de los Diputados**
House of Commons
cónico a conical
conífer|a f conifer. **~o** a coniferous
conjetura f conjecture, guess. **~r** vt
conjecture, guess
conjuga|ción f conjugation. **~r** [12]
vt conjugate
conjunción f conjunction
conjunto a joint. ● m collection;
(*mus*) band; (*ropa*) suit, outfit. **en ~**
altogether
conjura f, **conjuración** f conspiracy
conjurar vt plot, conspire
conmemora|ción f commem-
oration. **~r** vt commemorate.
~tivo a commemorative
conmigo pron with me
conminar vt threaten; (*avisar*) warn
conmiseración f commiseration
conmo|ción f shock; (*tumulto*)
upheaval; (*terremoto*) earthquake.
~cionar vt shock. **~ cerebral** concussion. **~ver** [2] vt shake;
(*emocionar*) move
conmuta|dor m switch. **~r** vt
exchange
connivencia f connivance
connota|ción f connotation. **~r** vt
connote
cono m cone

conoc|edor *a* & *m* expert. **~er** [11] *vt* know; (*por primera vez*) meet; (*reconocer*) recognize, know. **~erse** *vpr* know o.s.; ‹*dos personas*› know each other; (*notarse*) be obvious. **dar a ~er** make known. **darse a ~er** make o.s. known. **~ido** *a* well-known. ● *m* acquaintance. **~imiento** *m* knowledge; (*sentido*) consciousness; (*conocido*) acquaintance. **perder el ~imiento** faint. **se ~e que** apparently. **tener ~imiento de** know about

conozco *vb véase* **conocer**

conque *conj* so

conquense *a* from Cuenca. ● *m* native of Cuenca

conquista *f* conquest. **~dor** *a* conquering. ● *m* conqueror; (*de América*) conquistador; (*fig*) lady-killer. **~r** *vt* conquer, win

consabido *a* well-known

consagra|ción *f* consecration. **~r** *vt* consecrate; (*fig*) devote. **~rse** *vpr* devote o.s.

consanguíneo *m* blood relation

consciente *a* conscious

consecución *f* acquisition; (*de un deseo*) realization

consecuen|cia *f* consequence; (*firmeza*) consistency. **~te** *a* consistent. **a ~cia de** as a result of. **en ~cia, por ~cia** consequently

consecutivo *a* consecutive

conseguir [5 & 13] *vt* get, obtain; (*lograr*) manage; achieve ‹*objetivo*›

conseja *f* story, fable

consej|ero *m* adviser; (*miembro de consejo*) member. **~o** *m* advice; (*pol*) council. **~o de ministros** cabinet

consenso *m* assent, consent

consenti|do *a* ‹*niño*› spoilt. **~miento** *m* consent. **~r** [4] *vt* allow. ● *vi* consent. **~rse** *vpr* break

conserje *m* porter, caretaker. **~ría** *f* porter's office

conserva *f* preserves; (*mermelada*) jam, preserve; (*en lata*) tinned food. **~ción** *f* conservation; (*de alimentos*) preservation; (*de edificio*) maintenance. **en ~** preserved

conservador *a* & *m* (*pol*) conservative

conservar *vt* keep; preserve ‹*alimentos*›. **~se** *vpr* keep; ‹*costumbre etc*› survive

conservatorio *m* conservatory

considera|ble *a* considerable. **~ción** *f* consideration; (*respeto*) respect. **~do** *a* considered; (*amable*) considerate; (*respetado*) respected. **~r** *vt* consider; (*respetar*) respect. **de ~ción** considerable. **de su ~ción** (*en cartas*) yours faithfully. **tomar en ~ción** take into consideration

consigna *f* order; (*rail*) left luggage office (*Brit*), baggage room (*Amer*); (*eslogan*) slogan

consigo *pron* (*él*) with him; (*ella*) with her; (*Ud, Uds*) with you; (*uno mismo*) with o.s.

consiguiente *a* consequent. **por ~** consequently

consist|encia *f* consistency. **~ente** *a* consisting (**en** of); (*firme*) solid. **~ir** *vi* consist (**en** of); (*deberse*) be due (**en** to)

consola|ción *f* consolation. **~r** [2] *vt* console, comfort

consolidar *vt* consolidate. **~se** *vpr* consolidate

consomé *m* clear soup, consommé

consonan|cia *f* consonance. **~te** *a* consonant. ● *f* consonant

consorcio *m* consortium

consorte *m* & *f* consort

conspicuo *a* eminent; (*visible*) visible

conspira|ción *f* conspiracy. **~dor** *m* conspirator. **~r** *vi* conspire

constan|cia *f* constancy. **~te** *a* constant

constar *vi* be clear; (*figurar*) appear, figure; (*componerse*) consist. **hacer ~** point out. **me consta que** I'm sure that. **que conste que** believe me

constatar *vt* check; (*confirmar*) confirm

constelación *f* constellation

consternación *f* consternation

constipa|do *m* cold. ● *a.* **estar ~do** have a cold. **~rse** *vpr* catch a cold

constitu|ción *f* constitution; (*establecimiento*) setting up. **~cional** *a* constitutional. **~ir** [17] *vt* constitute; (*formar*) form; (*crear*) set up, establish. **~irse** *vpr* set o.s. up (**en** as); (*presentarse*) appear. **~tivo** *a*, **~yente** *a* constituent

constreñir [5 & 22] *vt* force, oblige; (*restringir*) restrain

constricción *f* constriction

constru|cción *f* construction. **~ctor** *m* builder. **~ir** [17] *vt* construct; build ‹*edificio*›

consuelo *m* consolation, comfort

consuetudinario *a* customary

cónsul *m* consul

consula|do *m* consulate. **~r** *a* consular

consult|a *f* consultation. **~ar** *vt* consult. **~orio** *m* surgery. **~orio sentimental** problem page. **horas** *fpl* de **~a** surgery hours. **obra** *f* de **~a** reference book

consumar *vt* complete; commit ⟨*crimen*⟩; consummate ⟨*matrimonio*⟩

consum|ición *f* consumption; (*bebida*) drink; (*comida*) food. **~ido** *a* ⟨*persona*⟩ skinny, wasted; ⟨*frutas*⟩ shrivelled. **~idor** *m* consumer. **~ir** *vt* consume. **~irse** *vpr* ⟨*persona*⟩ waste away; ⟨*cosa*⟩ wear out; (*quedarse seco*) dry up. **~ismo** *m* consumerism. **~o** *m* consumption

contab|ilidad *f* book-keeping; (*profesión*) accountancy. **~le** *m & f* accountant

contacto *m* contact. **ponerse en ~ con** get in touch with

contado *a* counted. **~s** *apl* few. **~r** *m* meter; (*LAm, contable*) accountant. **al ~** cash

contagi|ar *vt* infect ⟨*persona*⟩; pass on ⟨*enfermedd*⟩; (*fig*) contaminate. **~o** *m* infection. **~oso** *a* infectious

contamina|ción *f* contamination, pollution. **~r** *vt* contaminate, pollute

contante *a*. **dinero** *m* **~** cash

contar [2] *vt* count; tell ⟨*relato*⟩. ● *vi* count. **~ con** rely on, count on. **~se** *vpr* be included (**entre** among); (*decirse*) be said

contempla|ción *f* contemplation. **~r** *vt* look at; (*fig*) contemplate. **sin ~ciones** unceremoniously

contemporáneo *a & m* contemporary

contend|er [1] *vi* compete. **~iente** *m & f* competitor

conten|er [40] *vt* contain; (*restringir*) restrain. **~erse** *vpr* restrain o.s. **~ido** *a* contained. ● *m* contents

content|ar *vt* please. **~arse** *vpr*. **~arse de** be satisfied with, be pleased with. **~o** *a* (*alegre*) happy; (*satisfecho*) pleased

contesta|ción *f* answer. **~dor** *m*. **~ automático** answering machine. **~r** *vt/i* answer; (*replicar*) answer back

contexto *m* context

contienda *f* struggle

contigo *pron* with you

contiguo *a* adjacent

continen|cia *f* continence. **~tal** *a* continental. **~te** *m* continent

contingen|cia *f* contingency. **~te** *a* contingent; ● *m* contingent; (*cuota*) quota

continu|ación *f* continuation. **~ar** [21] *vt* continue, resume. ● *vi* continue. **~ará** (*en revista, TV etc*) to be continued. **~idad** *f* continuity. **~o** *a* continuous; (*muy frecuente*) continual. **a ~ación** immediately after. **corriente** *f* **~a** direct current

contorno *m* outline; (*geog*) contour. **~s** *mpl* surrounding area

contorsión *f* contortion

contra *adv & prep* against. ● *m* cons. **en ~** against

contraalmirante *m* rear-admiral

contraata|car [7] *vt/i* counter-attack. **~que** *m* counter-attack

contrabajo *m* double-bass; (*persona*) double-bass player

contrabalancear *vt* counterbalance

contraband|ista *m & f* smuggler. **~o** *m* contraband

contracción *f* contraction

contrachapado *m* plywood

contrad|ecir [46] *vt* contradict. **~icción** *f* contradiction. **~ictorio** *a* contradictory

contraer [41] *vt* contract. **~ matrimonio** marry. **~se** *vpr* contract; (*limitarse*) limit o.s.

contrafuerte *m* buttress

contragolpe *m* backlash

contrahecho *a* fake; ⟨*moneda*⟩ counterfeit; ⟨*persona*⟩ hunch-backed

contraindicación *f* contraindication

contralto *m* alto. ● *f* contralto

contramano. **a ~** in the wrong direction

contrapartida *f* compensation

contrapelo. **a ~** the wrong way

contrapes|ar *vt* counterbalance. **~o** *m* counterbalance

contraponer [34] oppose; (*comparar*) compare

contraproducente *a* counter-productive

contrari|ar [20] *vt* oppose; (*molestar*) annoy. **~edad** *f* obstacle; (*disgusto*) annoyance. **~o** *a* contrary; ⟨*dirección*⟩ opposite; ⟨*persona*⟩ opposed. **al ~o** on the contrary. **al**

~o **de** contrary to. **de lo** ~o otherwise. **en** ~o against. **llevar la** ~**a** contradict. **por el** ~o on the contrary

contrarrestar *vt* counteract

contrasentido *m* contradiction

contraseña *f* secret mark; (*palabra*) password

contrast|ar *vt* check, verify. ● *vi* contrast. ~**e** *m* contrast; (*en oro, plata etc*) hallmark

contratar *vt* sign a contract for; engage (*empleados*)

contratiempo *m* setback; (*accidente*) accident

contrat|ista *m & f* contractor. ~**o** *m* contract

contraven|ción *f* contravention. ~**ir** [53] *vi*. ~**ir a** contravene

contraventana *f* shutter

contribu|ción *f* contribution; (*tributo*) tax. ~**ir** [17] *vt/i* contribute. ~**yente** *m & f* contributor; (*que paga impuestos*) taxpayer

contrincante *m* rival, opponent

contrito *a* contrite

control *m* control; (*inspección*) check. ~**ar** *vt* control; (*examinar*) check

controversia *f* controversy

contundente *a* (*arma*) blunt; (*argumento etc*) convincing

conturbar *vt* perturb

contusión *f* bruise

convalec|encia *f* convalescence. ~**er** [11] *vi* convalesce. ~**iente** *a & m & f* convalescent

convalidar *vt* confirm; recognize (*título*)

convenc|er [9] *vt* convince. ~**imiento** *m* conviction

convenci|ón *f* convention. ~**onal** *a* conventional

conveni|encia *f* convenience; (*aptitud*) suitability. ~**encias (sociales)** conventions. ~**ente** *a* suitable; (*aconsejable*) advisable; (*provechoso*) useful, advantageous. ~**o** *m* agreement. ~**r** [53] *vt* agree. ● *vi* agree; (*ser conveniente*) be convenient for, suit; (*ser aconsejable*) be advisable

convento *m* (*de monjes*) monastery; (*de monjas*) convent

convergente *a* converging

converger [14] *vi*, **convergir** [14] *vi* converge

conversa|ción *f* conversation. ~**r** *vi* converse, talk

conver|sión *f* conversion. ~**so** *a* converted. ● *m* convert. ~**tible** *a* convertible. ~**tir** [4] *vt* convert. ~**tirse** *vpr* be converted

convexo *a* convex

convic|ción *f* conviction. ~**to** *a* convicted

convida|do *m* guest. ~**r** *vt* invite. **te convido a un helado** I'll treat you to an ice-cream

convincente *a* convincing

convite *m* invitation; (*banquete*) banquet

conviv|encia *f* coexistence. ~**ir** *vi* live together

convocar [7] *vt* convene (*reunión*); summon (*personas*)

convoy *m* convoy; (*rail*) train; (*vinagrera*) cruet

convulsión *f* convulsion; (*fig*) upheaval

conyugal *a* conjugal; (*vida*) married

cónyuge *m* spouse. ~**s** *mpl* (married) couple

coñac *m* (*pl* **coñacs**) brandy

coopera|ción *f* co-operation. ~**r** *vi* co-operate. ~**tiva** *f* co-operative. ~**tivo** *a* co-operative

coord|enada *f* coordinate. ~**inación** *f* co-ordination. ~**inar** *vt* co-ordinate

copa *f* glass; (*deportes, fig*) cup. ~**s** *fpl* (*naipes*) hearts. **tomar una** ~ have a drink

copia *f* copy. ~ **en limpio** fair copy. ~**r** *vt* copy. **sacar una** ~ make a copy

copioso *a* copious; (*lluvia, nevada etc*) heavy

copla *f* verse; (*canción*) song

copo *m* flake. ~ **de nieve** snowflake. ~**s de maíz** cornflakes

coquet|a *f* flirt; (*mueble*) dressing-table. ~**ear** *vi* flirt. ~**eo** *m* flirtation. ~**o** *a* flirtatious

coraje *m* courage; (*rabia*) anger. **dar** ~ make mad, make furious

coral *a* choral. ● *m* (*materia, animal*) coral

Corán *m* Koran

coraza *f* (*naut*) armour-plating; (*de tortuga*) shell

coraz|ón *m* heart; (*persona*) darling. ~**onada** *f* hunch; (*impulso*) impulse. **sin** ~**ón** heartless. **tener buen** ~**ón** be good-hearted

corbata *f* tie, necktie (*esp Amer*). ~ **de lazo** bow tie

corcova f hump. **~do** a hunch-backed

corchea f quaver

corchete m fastener, hook and eye; (*gancho*) hook; (*paréntesis*) square bracket

corcho m cork

cordel m cord, thin rope

cordero m lamb

cordial a cordial, friendly. ● m tonic. **~idad** f cordiality, warmth

cordillera f mountain range

córdoba m (*unidad monetaria de Nicaragua*) córdoba

Córdoba f Cordova

cordón m string; (*de zapatos*) lace; (*cable*) flex; (*fig*) cordon. **~ umbilical** umbilical cord

corear vt chant

coreografía f choreography

corista m & f member of the chorus. ● f (*bailarina*) chorus girl

cornet|a f bugle. **~ín** m cornet

Cornualles m Cornwall

cornucopia f cornucopia

cornudo a horned. ● m cuckold

coro m chorus; (*relig*) choir

corona f crown; (*de flores*) wreath, garland. **~ción** f coronation. **~r** vt crown

coronel m colonel

coronilla f crown. **estar hasta la ~** be fed up

corporación f corporation

corporal a corporal

corpulento a stout

corpúsculo m corpuscle

corral m pen. **aves** fpl **de ~** poultry

correa f strap; (*de perro*) lead; (*cinturón*) belt

correc|ción f correction; (*reprensión*) rebuke; (*cortesía*) good manners. **~to** a correct; (*cortés*) polite

corre|dizo a running. **nudo ~dizo** slip knot. **puerta** f **~diza** sliding door. **~dor** m runner; (*pasillo*) corridor; (*agente*) agent, broker. **~dor automovilista** racing driver

corregir [5 & 14] vt correct; (*reprender*) rebuke

correlaci|ón f correlation. **~onar** vt correlate

correo m courier; (*correos*) post, mail; (*tren*) mail train. **~s** mpl post office. **echar al ~** post

correr vt run; (*viajar*) travel; draw (*cortinas*). ● vi run; (*agua, electricidad etc*) flow; (*tiempo*) pass. **~se** vpr (*apartarse*) move along;

(*pasarse*) go too far; (*colores*) run. **~se una juerga** have a ball

correspond|encia f correspondence. **~er** vi correspond; (*ser adecuado*) be fitting; (*contestar*) reply; (*pertenecer*) belong; (*incumbir*) fall to. **~erse** vpr (*amarse*) love one another. **~iente** a corresponding

corresponsal m correspondent

corrid|a f run. **~a de toros** bullfight. **~o** a (*peso*) good; (*continuo*) continuous; (*avergonzado*) embarrassed. **de ~a** from memory

corriente a (*agua*) running; (*monedas, publicación, cuenta, año etc*) current; (*ordinario*) ordinary. ● f current; (*de aire*) draught; (*fig*) tendency. ● m current month. **al ~** (*al día*) up-to-date; (*enterado*) aware

corr|illo m small group, circle. **~o** m circle

corroborar vt corroborate

corroer [24 & 37] vt corrode; (*geol*) erode; (*fig*) eat away. **~se** vpr corrode

corromper vt rot (*madera*); turn bad (*alimentos*); (*fig*) corrupt. ● vi (*fam*) stink. **~se** vpr (*madera*) rot; (*alimentos*) go bad; (*fig*) be corrupted

corrosi|ón f corrosion. **~vo** a corrosive

corrupción f (*de madera etc*) rot; (*soborno*) bribery; (*fig*) corruption

corsé m corset

cortacésped m invar lawn-mower

cortad|o a cut; (*leche*) sour; (*avergonzado*) embarrassed; (*confuso*) confused. ● m coffee with a little milk. **~ura** f cut

corta|nte a sharp; (*viento*) biting; (*frío*) bitter. **~r** vt cut; (*recortar*) cut out; (*aislar, detener*) cut off; (*interrumpir*) cut in. ● vi cut. **~rse** vpr cut o.s.; (*leche etc*) curdle; (*al teléfono*) be cut off; (*fig*) be embarrassed, become tongue-tied. **~rse el pelo** have one's hair cut. **~rse las uñas** cut one's nails

cortauñas m invar nail-clippers

corte m cutting; (*de instrumento cortante*) cutting edge; (*de corriente*) cut; (*de prendas de vestir*) cut; (*de tela*) length. ● f court. **~ de luz** power cut. **~ y confección** dressmaking. **hacer la ~** court. **las C~s** the Spanish parliament

cortej|ar vt court. **~o** m (de rey etc) entourage. **~o fúnebre** cortège, funeral procession. **~o nupcial** wedding procession

cortés a polite

cortesan|a f courtesan. **~o** m courtier

cortesía f courtesy

corteza f bark; (de naranja etc) peel, rind; (de pan) crust

cortijo m farm; (casa) farmhouse

cortina f curtain

corto a short; (escaso) scanty; (apocado) shy. **~circuito** m short circuit. **~ de alcances** dim, thick. **~ de oído** hard of hearing. **~ de vista** short-sighted. **a la corta o a la larga** sooner or later. **quedarse ~** fall short; (miscalcular) under-estimate

Coruña f. **La ~** Corunna

corvo a bent

cosa ·f thing; (asunto) business; (idea) idea. **~ de** about. **como si tal ~** just like that; (como si no hubiera pasado nada) as if nothing had happened. **decirle a uno cuatro ~s** tell s.o. a thing or two. **lo que son las ~s** much to my surprise

cosaco a & m Cossack

cosech|a f harvest; (de vino) vintage. **~ar** vt harvest. **~ero** m harvester

coser vt/i sew. **~se** vpr stick to s.o. **eso es ~ y cantar** it's as easy as pie

cosmético a & m cosmetic

cósmico a cosmic

cosmonauta m & f cosmonaut

cosmopolita a & m & f cosmopolita

cosmos m cosmos

cosquillas fpl ticklishness. **buscar a uno las ~** provoke s.o. **hacer ~** tickle. **tener ~** be ticklish

costa f coast. **a ~ de** at the expense of. **a toda ~** at any cost

costado m side

costal m sack

costar [2] vt/i cost. **~ caro** be expensive. **cueste lo que cueste** at any cost

Costa Rica f Costa Rica

costarricense a & m, **costarriqueño** a & m Costa Rican

coste m cost. **~ar** vt pay for; (naut) sail along the coast

costero a coastal

costilla f rib; (chuleta) chop

costo m cost. **~so** a expensive

costumbre f custom, habit. **de ~** a usual. ● adv usually

costur|a f sewing; (línea) seam; (confección) dressmaking. **~era** f dressmaker. **~ero** m sewing box

cotejar vt compare

cotidiano a daily

cotille|ar vt gossip. **~o** m gossip

cotiza|ción f quotation, price. **~r** [10] vt (en la bolsa) quote. ● vi pay one's subscription. **~rse** vpr fetch; (en la bolsa) stand at; (fig) be valued

coto m enclosure; (de caza) preserve. **~ de caza** game preserve

cotorr|a f parrot; (urraca) magpie; (fig) chatterbox. **~ear** vi chatter

coyuntura f joint; (oportunidad) opportunity; (situación) situation; (circunstancia) occasion, juncture

coz f kick

cráneo m skull

cráter m crater

crea|ción f creation. **~dor** a creative. ● m creator. **~r** vt create

crec|er [11] vi grow; (aumentar) increase. **~ida** f (de río) flood. **~ido** a (persona) grown-up; (número) large, considerable; (plantas) fully-grown. **~iente** a growing; (luna) crescent. **~imiento** m growth

credencial a credential. **~es** fpl credentials

credibilidad f credibility

crédito m credit. **digno de ~** reliable, trustworthy

credo m creed. **en un ~** in a flash

crédulo a credulous

cre|encia f belief. **~er** [18] believe; (pensar) think. **~o que no** I don't think so, I think not. **~o que sí** I think so. ● vi believe. **~erse** vpr consider o.s. **no me lo ~o** I don't believe it. **~íble** a credible. **¡ya lo ~o!** I should think so!

crema f cream; (culin) custard. **~ bronceadora** sun-tan cream

cremación f cremation; (de basura) incineration

cremallera f zip, zipper (Amer)

crematorio m crematorium; (de basura) incinerator

crepitar vi crackle

crepúsculo m twilight

crescendo m crescendo

cresp|o a frizzy. **~ón** m crêpe

cresta f crest; (tupé) toupee; (geog) ridge

Creta f Crete

cretino m cretin

creyente m believer

cría *f* breeding; *(animal)* baby animal

cria|da *f* maid, servant. **~dero** *m* nursery. **~do** *a* brought up. ● *m* servant. **~dor** *m* breeder. **~nza** *f* breeding. **~r** [20] *vt* suckle; grow ‹plantas›; breed ‹animales›; *(educar)* bring up. **~rse** *vpr* grow up

criatura *f* creature; *(niño)* baby

crim|en *m* crime. **~inal** *a* & *m* & *f* criminal

crin *m* mane; *(relleno)* horsehair

crinolina *f* crinoline

crío *m* child

criollo *a* & *m* Creole

cripta *f* crypt

crisantemo *m* chrysanthemum

crisis *f* crisis

crisol *m* melting-pot

crispar *vt* twitch; *(irritar, fam)* annoy. **~ los nervios a uno** get on s.o.'s nerves

cristal *m* crystal; *(vidrio)* glass; *(de una ventana)* pane of glass. **~ de aumento** magnifying glass. **~ino** *a* crystalline; *(fig)* crystal-clear. **~izar** [10] crystallize. **limpiar los ~es** clean the windows

cristian|amente *adv* in a Christian way. **~dad** *f* Christianity. **~ismo** *m* Christianity. **~o** *a* & *m* Christian

Cristo *m* Christ

cristo *m* crucifix

criterio *m* criterion; *(opinión)* opinion

crí|tica *f* criticism; *(reseña)* review. **~iticar** [7] *vt* criticize. **~ítico** *a* critical. ● *m* critic

croar *vi* croak

crom|ado *a* chromium-plated. **~o** *m* chromium, chrome

cromosoma *m* chromosome

crónic|a *f* chronicle; *(de periódico)* news. **~o** *a* chronic

cronista *m* & *f* reporter

cronol|ogía *f* chronology. **~ógico** *a* chronological

cron|ometraje *m* timing. **~ometrar** *vt* time. **~ómetro** *m* chronometer; *(en deportes)* stop-watch

croquet /'kroket/ *m* croquet

croqueta *f* croquette

cruce *m* crossing; *(de calles, de carreteras)* crossroads; *(de peatones)* (pedestrian) crossing

crucial *a* cross-shaped; *(fig)* crucial

crucifi|car [7] *vt* crucify. **~jo** *m* crucifix. **~xión** *f* crucifixion

crucigrama *m* crossword (puzzle)

crudo *a* raw; *(fig)* crude. **petróleo** *m* **~** crude oil

cruel *a* cruel. **~dad** *f* cruelty

cruji|do *m* *(de seda, de hojas secas etc)* rustle; *(de muebles etc)* creak. **~r** *vi* ‹seda, hojas secas etc› rustle; ‹muebles etc› creak

cruz *f* cross; *(de moneda)* tails. **~ gamada** swastika. **la C~ Roja** the Red Cross

cruzada *f* crusade

cruzar [10] *vt* cross; *(poner de un lado a otro)* lay across. **~se** *vpr* cross; *(pasar en la calle)* pass

cuaderno *m* exercise book; *(para apuntes)* notebook

cuadra *f* *(caballeriza)* stable; *(LAm, manzana)* block

cuadrado *a* & *m* square

cuadragésimo *a* fortieth

cuadr|ar *vt* square. ● *vi* suit; *(estar de acuerdo)* agree. **~arse** *vpr* *(mil)* stand to attention; *(fig)* dig one's heels in. **~ilátero** *a* quadrilateral. ● *m* quadrilateral; *(boxeo)* ring

cuadrilla *f* group; *(pandilla)* gang

cuadro *m* square; *(pintura)* painting; *(de obra de teatro, escena)* scene; *(de jardín)* bed; *(de números)* table; *(de mando etc)* panel; *(conjunto del personal)* staff. **~ de distribución** switchboard. **a ~s, de ~s** check. **en ~** in a square. **¡qué ~!**, **¡vaya un ~!** what a sight!

cuadrúpedo *m* quadruped

cuádruple *a* & *m* quadruple

cuajar *vt* thicken; clot ‹sangre›; curdle ‹leche›; *(llenar)* fill up. ● *vi* ‹nieve› settle; *(fig, fam)* work out. **cuajado de** full of. **~se** *vpr* coagulate; ‹sangre› clot; ‹leche› curdle. **~ón** *m* clot

cual *pron*. **el ~, la ~** etc *(animales y cosas)* that, which; *(personas, sujeto)* who, that; *(personas, objeto)* whom. ● *adv* as, like. ● *a* such as. **~ si** as if. **~... tal** like... like. **cada ~** everyone. **por lo ~** because of which

cuál *pron* which

cualidad *f* quality; *(propiedad)* property

cualquiera *a* *(delante de nombres cualquier, pl cualesquiera)* any. ● *pron* *(pl cualesquiera)* anyone, anybody; *(cosas)* whatever, whichever. **un ~** a nobody

cuando *adv* when. ● *conj* when; *(aunque)* even if. **~ más** at the most.

~ **menos** at the least. ~ **no** if not.
aun ~ even if. **de** ~ **en** ~ from time
to time

cuándo *adv & conj* when. ¿**de** ~ **acá?**,
¿**desde** ~**?** since when?

cuant|ía *f* quantity; (*extensión*)
extent. ~**ioso** *a* abundant

cuanto *a* as much... as, as many...
as. ● *pron* as much as, as many as.
● *adv* as much as. ~ **más, mejor** the
more the merrier. **en** ~ as soon as.
en ~ **a** as for. **por** ~ since. **unos** ~**s**
a few, some

cuánto *a* (*interrogativo*) how
much?; (*interrogativo en plural*)
how many?; (*exclamativo*) what a
lot of! ● *pron* how much?; (*en
plural*) how many? ● *adv* how
much. ¿~ **tiempo?** how long? **¡**~
tiempo sin verte! it's been a long
time! ¿**a** ~**?** how much? ¿**a** ~**s estamos?** what's the date today? **un Sr.
no sé** ~**s** Mr So-and-So

cuáquero *m* Quaker

cuarent|a *a & m* forty; (*cua-
dragésimo*) fortieth. ~**ena** *f* (about)
forty; (*med*) quarantine. ~**ón** *a*
about forty

cuaresma *f* Lent

cuarta *f* (*palmo*) span

cuartear *vt* quarter, divide into four;
(*zigzaguear*) zigzag. ~**se** *vpr* crack

cuartel *m* (*mil*) barracks. ~ **general**
headquarters. **no dar** ~ show no
mercy

cuarteto *m* quartet

cuarto *a* fourth. ● *m* quarter; (*habitación*) room. ~ **de baño** bathroom.
~ **de estar** living room. ~ **de hora**
quarter of an hour. **estar sin un** ~
be broke. **menos** ~ (a) quarter to. **y**
~ (a) quarter past

cuarzo *m* quartz

cuatro *a & m* four. ~**cientos** *a & m*
four hundred

Cuba *f* Cuba

cuba: ~**libre** *m* rum and Coke (P).
~**no** *a & m* Cuban

cúbico *a* cubic

cubículo *m* cubicle

cubiert|a *f* cover, covering; (*de la
cama*) bedspread; (*techo*) roof; (*neumático*) tyre; (*naut*) deck. ~**o** *a*
covered; (*cielo*) overcast. ● *m* place
setting, cutlery; (*comida*) meal. **a**
~**o** under cover. **a** ~**o de** safe from

cubis|mo *m* cubism. ~**ta** *a & m & f*
cubist

cubil *m* den, lair. ~**ete** *m* bowl;
(*molde*) mould; (*para echar los
dados*) cup

cubo *m* bucket; (*en geometría y matemáticas*) cube

cubrecama *m* bedspread

cubrir *vt* [*pp* **cubierto**] cover; (*sonido*) drown; fill (*vacante*). ~**se** *vpr*
cover o.s.; (*ponerse el sombrero*) put
on one's hat; (*el cielo*) cloud over,
become overcast

cucaracha *f* cockroach

cuclillas. en ~ *adv* squatting

cuclillo *m* cuckoo

cuco *a* shrewd; (*mono*) pretty, nice.
● *m* cuckoo; (*insecto*) grub

cucurucho *m* cornet

cuchar|a *f* spoon. ~**ada** *f* spoonful.
~**adita** *f* teaspoonful. ~**illa** *f*, ~**ita** *f*
teaspoon. ~**ón** *m* ladle

cuchiche|ar *vi* whisper. ~**o** *m*
whispering

cuchill|a *f* large knife; (*de carnicero*)
cleaver; (*hoja de afeitar*) razor
blade. ~**ada** *f* slash; (*herida*) knife
wound. ~**o** *m* knife

cuchitril *m* pigsty; (*fig*) hovel

cuello *m* neck; (*de camisa*) collar.
cortar el ~ **a uno** cut s.o.'s throat

cuenc|a *f* hollow; (*del ojo*) (eye)
socket; (*geog*) basin. ~**o** *m* hollow;
(*vasija*) bowl

cuenta *f* count; (*acción de contar*)
counting; (*factura*) bill; (*en banco,
relato*) account; (*asunto*) affair; (*de
collar etc*) bead. ~ **corriente** current
account, checking account (*Amer*).
ajustar las ~**s** settle accounts. **caer
en la** ~ **de que** realize that. **darse**
~ **de** realize. **en resumidas** ~**s** in
short. **por mi** ~ for myself. **tener en**
~, **tomar en** ~ bear in mind

cuentakilómetros *m invar*
milometer

cuent|ista *m & f* story-writer; (*de
mentiras*) fibber. ~**o** *m* story; (*mentira*) fib, tall story. ● *vb véase* **contar**

cuerda *f* rope; (*más fina*) string;
(*mus*) string. ~ **floja** tightrope. **dar**
~ **a** wind up (*un reloj*)

cuerdo *a* (*persona*) sane; (*acción*)
sensible

cuern|a *f* horns. ~**o** *m* horn

cuero *m* leather; (*piel*) skin; (*del
grifo*) washer. ~ **cabelludo** scalp.
en ~**s** (*vivos*) stark naked

cuerpo *m* body

cuervo *m* crow

cuesta f slope, hill. ～ **abajo** downhill. ～ **arriba** uphill. **a** ～**s** on one's back

cuesti|ón f matter; (*altercado*) quarrel; (*dificultad*) trouble. ～**onario** m questionnaire

cueva f cave; (*sótano*) cellar

cuida|do m care; (*preocupación*) worry; (*asunto*) affair. ¡～**do!** (be) careful! ～**doso** a careful. ～**dosamente** adv carefully. ～**r** vt look after. ● vi. ～**r de** look after. ～**rse** vpr look after o.s. ～**rse de** be careful to. **tener** ～**do** be careful

culata f (*de arma de fuego*) butt; (*auto*) cylinder head. ～**zo** m recoil

culebra f snake

culebrón m (*LAm*) soap opera

culinario a culinary

culmina|ción f culmination. ～**r** vi culminate

culo m (*fam*) bottom. **ir de** ～ go downhill

culpa f fault; (*jurid*) guilt. ～**bilidad** f guilt. ～**ble** a guilty. ● m culprit. ～**r** vt blame (**de** for). **echar la** ～ blame. **por** ～ **de** because of. **tener la** ～ **de** be to blame for

cultiv|ar vt farm; grow 〈*plantas*〉; (*fig*) cultivate. ～**o** m farming; (*de plantas*) growing

cult|o a 〈*tierra etc*〉 cultivated; 〈*persona*〉 educated. ● m cult; (*homenaje*) worship. ～**ura** f culture. ～**ural** a cultural

culturismo m body-building

cumbre f summit; (*fig*) height

cumpleaños m invar birthday

cumplido a perfect; (*grande*) large; (*cortés*) polite. ● m compliment. ～**r** a reliable. **de** ～ courtesy. **por** ～ out of politeness

cumplim|entar vt carry out; (*saludar*) pay a courtesy call to; (*felicitar*) congratulate. ～**iento** m carrying out, execution

cumplir vt carry out; observe 〈*ley*〉; serve 〈*condena*〉; reach 〈*años*〉; keep 〈*promesa*〉. ● vi do one's duty. ～**se** vpr expire; (*realizarse*) be fulfilled. **hoy cumple 3 años** he's 3 (years old) today. **por** ～ as a mere formality

cumulativo a cumulative

cúmulo m pile, heap

cuna f cradle; (*fig, nacimiento*) birthplace

cundir vi spread; (*rendir*) go a long way

cuneta f gutter

cuña f wedge

cuñad|a f sister-in-law. ～**o** m brother-in-law

cuño m stamp. **de nuevo** ～ new

cuota f quota; (*de sociedad etc*) subscription, fees

cupe vb véase **caber**

cupé m coupé

Cupido m Cupid

cupo m cuota

cupón m coupon

cúpula f dome

cura f cure; (*tratamiento*) treatment. ● m priest. ～**ble** a curable. ～**ción** f healing. ～**ndero** m faith-healer. ～**r** vt (*incl culin*) cure; dress 〈*herida*〉; (*tratar*) treat; (*fig*) remedy; tan 〈*pieles*〉. ● vi 〈*persona*〉 get better; 〈*herida*〉 heal; (*fig*) be cured. ～**rse** vpr get better

curios|ear vi pry; (*mirar*) browse. ～**idad** f curiosity; (*limpieza*) cleanliness. ～**o** a curious; (*raro*) odd, unusual; (*limpio*) clean

curriculum vitae m curriculum vitae

cursar vt send; (*estudiar*) study

cursi a pretentious, showy. ● m affected person

cursillo m short course

cursiva f italics

curso m course; (*univ etc*) year. **en** ～ under way; (*año etc*) current

curtir vt tan; (*fig*) harden. ～**se** vpr become tanned; (*fig*) become hardened

curv|a f curve; (*de carretera*) bend. ～**o** a curved

cúspide f peak

custodi|a f care, safe-keeping. ～**ar** vt take care of. ～**o** a & m guardian

cutáneo a skin. **enfermedad** f **cutánea** skin disease

cutícula f cuticle

cutis m skin, complexion

cuyo pron (*de persona*) whose, of whom; (*de cosa*) whose, of which. **en** ～ **caso** in which case

CH

chabacano a common; 〈*chiste etc*〉 vulgar. ● m (*Mex, albaricoque*) apricot

chabola f shack. ～**s** fpl shanty town

chacal m jackal

chacota f fun. **echar a** ～ make fun of

chacra f (LAm) farm

cháchara f chatter

chacharear vt (Mex) sell. ● vi chatter

chafar vt crush. **quedar chafado** be nonplussed

chal m shawl

chalado a (fam) crazy

chalé m house (with a garden), villa

chaleco m waistcoat, vest (Amer). ~ **salvavidas** life-jacket

chalequear vt (Arg, Mex) trick

chalet m (pl **chalets**) house (with a garden), villa

chalón m (LAm) shawl

chalote m shallot

chalupa f boat

chamac|a f (esp Mex) girl. ~**o** m (esp Mex) boy

chamagoso a (Mex) filthy

chamarr|a f sheepskin jacket. ~**o** m (LAm) coarse blanket

chamba f (fam) fluke; (Mex, empleo) job. **por** ~ by fluke

champán m, **champaña** m champagne

champiñón m mushroom

champú m (pl **champúes** o **champús**) shampoo

chamuscar [7] vt scorch; (Mex, vender) sell cheaply

chance m (esp LAm) chance

chanclo m clog; (de caucho) rubber overshoe

chancho m (LAm) pig

chanchullo m swindle, fiddle (fam)

chandal m tracksuit

chanquete m whitebait

chantaj|e m blackmail. ~**ista** m & f blackmailer

chanza f joke

chapa f plate, sheet; (de madera) plywood; (de botella) metal top. ~**do** a plated. ~**do a la antigua** old-fashioned. ~**do de oro** gold-plated

chaparrón m downpour. **llover a chaparrones** pour (down), rain cats and dogs

chapotear vi splash

chapuce|ar vt botch; (Mex, engañar) deceive. ~**ro** a (persona) careless; (cosas) shoddy. ● m careless worker

chapurrar vt, **chapurrear** vt speak badly, speak a little; mix (licores)

chapuza f botched job, mess; (de poca importancia) odd job

chaqueta f jacket. **cambiar la** ~ change sides

chaquetero m turncoat

charada f charade

charc|a f pond, pool. ~**o** m puddle, pool. **cruzar el** ~**o** cross the water; (ir a América) cross the Atlantic

charla f chat; (conferencia) talk. ~**dor** a talkative. ~**r** vi (fam) chat

charlatán a talkative. ● m chatterbox; (curandero) charlatan

charol m varnish; (cuero) patent leather

chárter a charter

chascar [7] vt crack ‹látigo›; click ‹lengua›; snap ‹dedos›. ● vi ‹látigo› crack; (con la lengua) click one's tongue; (los dedos) snap

chascarrillo m joke, funny story

chasco m disappointment; (broma) joke; (engaño) trick

chasis m (auto) chassis

chasqu|ear vt crack ‹látigo›; click ‹lengua›; snap ‹dedos›. ● vi ‹látigo› crack; (con la lengua) click one's tongue; ‹los dedos› snap. ~**ido** m crack; (de la lengua) click; (de los dedos) snap

chatarra f scrap iron; (fig) scrap

chato a ‹nariz› snub; ‹persona› snub-nosed; ‹objetos› flat. ● m wine glass; (niño, mujer, fam) dear, darling; (hombre, fam) mate (fam)

chaval m (fam) boy, lad. ~**a** f girl, lass

che int (Arg) listen!, hey!

checo a & m Czech. **la república** f **Checa** the Czech Republic

checoslovaco a & m (history) Czechoslovak

Checoslovaquia f (history) Czechoslovakia

chelín m shilling

chelo a (Mex, rubio) fair

cheque m cheque. ~ **de viaje** traveller's cheque. ~**ra** f cheque-book

chica f girl; (criada) maid, servant

chicano a & m Chicano, Mexican-American

chicle m chewing-gum

chico a (fam) small. ● m boy. ~**s** mpl children

chicoleo m compliment

chicoria f chicory

chicharra f cicada; (fig) chatterbox

chicharrón m (de cerdo) crackling; (fig) sunburnt person

chichón m bump, lump

chifla|do a (fam) crazy, daft. ~**r** vt (fam) drive crazy. ~**rse** vpr be mad (**por** about). **le chifla el chocolate**

he's mad about chocolate. **le tiene chiflado esa chica** he's crazy about that girl

Chile *m* Chile

chile *m* chilli

chileno *a & m* Chilean

chill|ar *vi* scream, shriek; ⟨*gato*⟩ howl; ⟨*ratón*⟩ squeak; ⟨*cerdo*⟩ squeal. **~ido** *m* scream, screech; (*de gato etc*) howl. **~ón** *a* noisy; ⟨*colores*⟩ loud; ⟨*sonido*⟩ shrill

chimenea *f* chimney; (*hogar*) fireplace

chimpancé *m* chimpanzee

China *f* China

chinch|ar *vt* (*fam*) annoy, pester. **~e** *m* drawing-pin (*Brit*), thumbtack (*Amer*); (*insecto*) bedbug; (*fig*) nuisance. **~eta** *f* drawing-pin (*Brit*), thumbtack (*Amer*)

chinela *f* slipper

chino *a & m* Chinese

Chipre *m* Cyprus

chipriota *a & m & f* Cypriot

chiquillo *a* childish. ● *m* child, kid (*fam*)

chiquito *a* small, tiny. ● *m* child, kid (*fam*)

chiribita *f* spark. **estar que echa ~s** be furious

chirimoya *f* custard apple

chiripa *f* fluke. **por ~** by fluke

chirivía *f* parsnip

chirri|ar *vi* creak; ⟨*pájaro*⟩ chirp. **~do** *m* creaking; (*al freír*) sizzling; (*de pájaros*) chirping

chis *int* sh!, hush!; (*para llamar a uno, fam*) hey!, psst!

chism|e *m* gadget, thingumajig (*fam*); (*chismorreo*) piece of gossip. **~es** *mpl* things, bits and pieces. **~orreo** *m* gossip. **~oso** *a* gossipy. ● *m* gossip

chispa *f* spark; (*gota*) drop; (*gracia*) wit; (*fig*) sparkle. **estar que echa ~(s)** be furious

chispea|nte *a* sparkling. **~r** *vi* spark; (*lloviznar*) drizzle; (*fig*) sparkle

chisporrotear *vt* throw out sparks; ⟨*fuego*⟩ crackle; ⟨*aceite*⟩ sizzle

chistar *vi* speak. **sin ~** without saying a word

chiste *m* joke, funny story. **hacer ~ de** make fun of. **tener ~** be funny

chistera *f* (*fam*) top hat, topper (*fam*)

chistoso *a* funny

chiva|r *vi* inform ⟨*policía*⟩; ⟨*niño*⟩ tell. **~tazo** *m* tip-off. **~to** *m* informer; (*niño*) telltale

chivo *m* kid, young goat

choca|nte *a* surprising; ⟨*persona*⟩ odd. **~r** [7] *vt* clink ⟨*vasos*⟩; shake ⟨*la mano*⟩. ● *vi* collide, hit. **~r con**, **~r contra** crash into. **lo ~nte es que** the surprising thing is that

chocolate *m* chocolate. **tableta** *f* **de ~** bar of chocolate

choch|ear *vi* be senile. **~o** *a* senile; (*fig*) soft

chófer *m* chauffeur; (*conductor*) driver

cholo *a & m* (*LAm*) half-breed

chopo *m* poplar

choque *m* collision; (*fig*) clash; (*eléctrico*) shock; (*auto, rail etc*) crash, accident; (*sacudida*) jolt

chorizo *m* salami

chorr|ear *vi* gush forth; (*fig*) be dripping. **~o** *m* jet, stream; (*caudal pequeño*) trickle; (*fig*) stream. **a ~os** (*fig*) in abundance. **hablar a ~os** jabber

chovinis|mo *m* chauvinism. **~ta** *a* chauvinistic. ● *m & f* chauvinist

choza *f* hut

chubas|co *m* squall, heavy shower; (*fig*) bad patch. **~quero** *m* raincoat, anorak

chuchería *f* trinket; (*culin*) sweet

chufa *f* tiger nut

chuleta *f* chop

chulo *a* insolent; (*vistoso*) showy. ● *m* ruffian; (*rufián*) pimp

chumbo *m* prickly pear; (*fam*) bump. **higo** *m* **~** prickly pear

chup|ada *f* suck; (*al cigarro etc*) puff. **~ado** *a* skinny; (*fácil, fam*) very easy. **~ar** *vt* suck, lick; puff at ⟨*cigarro etc*⟩; (*absorber*) absorb. **~arse** *vpr* lose weight. **~ete** *m* dummy (*Brit*), pacifier (*Amer*)

churro *m* fritter; (*fam*) mess. **me salió un ~** I made a mess of it

chusco *a* funny

chusma *f* riff-raff

chutar *vi* shoot. **¡va que chuta!** it's going well!

D

dactilógrafo *m* typist

dado *m* dice. ● *a* given; ⟨*hora*⟩ gone. **~ que** since, given that

dalia *f* dahlia

daltoniano *a* colour-blind

dama *f* lady; (*en la corte*) lady-in-waiting. **∼s** *fpl* draughts (*Brit*), checkers (*Amer*)

damasco *m* damask

danés *a* Danish. ● *m* Dane; (*idioma*) Danish

danza *f* dance; (*acción*) dancing; (*enredo*) affair. **∼r** [10] *vt/i* dance

dañ|ado *a* damaged. **∼ar** *vt* damage; harm ⟨*persona*⟩. **∼ino** *a* harmful. **∼o** *m* damage; (*a una persona*) harm. **∼oso** *a* harmful. **∼os y perjuicios** damages. **hacer ∼o a** harm; hurt ⟨*persona*⟩. **hacerse ∼o** hurt o.s.

dar [26] *vt* give; (*producir*) yield; strike ⟨*la hora*⟩. ● *vi* give. **da igual** it doesn't matter. **¡dale!** go on! **da lo mismo** it doesn't matter. **∼ a** ⟨*ventana*⟩ look on to; ⟨*edificio*⟩ face. **∼ a luz** give birth. **∼ con** meet ⟨*persona*⟩; find ⟨*cosa*⟩. **∼ de cabeza** fall flat on one's face. **∼ por** assume; (+ *infinitivo*) decide. **∼se** *vpr* give o.s. up; (*suceder*) happen. **dárselas de** make o.s. out to be. **∼se por** consider o.s. **¿qué más da?** it doesn't matter!

dardo *m* dart

dársena *f* dock

datar *vt* date. ● *vi*. **∼ de** date from

dátil *m* date

dato *m* fact. **∼s** *mpl* data, information

de *prep* of; (*procedencia*) from; (*suposición*) if. **∼ día** by day. **∼ dos en dos** two by two. **∼ haberlo sabido** if I (you, he etc) had known. **∼ niño** as a child. **el libro ∼ mi amigo** my friend's book. **las 2 ∼ la madrugada** 2 (o'clock) in the morning. **un puente ∼ hierro** an iron bridge. **soy ∼ Loughborough** I'm from Loughborough

deambular *vi* stroll

debajo *adv* underneath. **∼ de** underneath, under. **el de ∼** the one underneath. **por ∼** underneath. **por ∼ de** below

debat|e *m* debate. **∼ir** *vt* debate

deber *vt* owe. ● *vi* have to, must. ● *m* duty. **∼es** *mpl* homework. **∼se** *vpr*. **∼se a** be due to. **debo marcharme** I must go, I have to go

debido *a* due; (*correcto*) proper. **∼ a** due to. **como es ∼** as is proper. **con el respeto** ∼ with due respect

débil *a* weak; ⟨*ruido*⟩ faint; ⟨*luz*⟩ dim

debili|dad *f* weakness. **∼tar** *vt* weaken. **∼tarse** *vpr* weaken, get weak

débito *m* debit; (*deuda*) debt

debutar *vi* make one's debut

década *f* decade

deca|dencia *f* decline. **∼dente** *a* decadent. **∼er** [29] *vi* decline; (*debilitarse*) weaken. **∼ído** *a* depressed. **∼imiento** *m* decline, weakening

decano *m* dean; (*miembro más antiguo*) senior member

decantar *vt* decant ⟨*vino etc*⟩

decapitar *vt* behead

decena *f* ten; (*aproximadamente*) about ten

decencia *f* decency, honesty

decenio *m* decade

decente *a* ⟨*persona*⟩ respectable, honest; ⟨*cosas*⟩ modest; (*limpio*) clean, tidy

decepci|ón *f* disappointment. **∼onar** *vt* disappoint

decibelio *m* decibel

decidi|do *a* decided; ⟨*persona*⟩ determined, resolute. **∼r** *vt* decide; settle ⟨*cuestión etc*⟩. ● *vi* decide. **∼rse** *vpr* make up one's mind

decimal *a & m* decimal

décimo *a & m* tenth. ● *m* (*de lotería*) tenth part of a lottery ticket

decimo: ∼ctavo *a & m* eighteenth. **∼cuarto** *a & m* fourteenth. **∼nono** *a & m*, **∼noveno** *a & m* nineteenth. **∼quinto** *a & m* fifteenth. **∼séptimo** *a & m* seventeenth. **∼sexto** *a & m* sixteenth. **∼tercero** *a & m*, **∼tercio** *a & m* thirteenth

decir [46] *vt* say; (*contar*) tell. ● *m* saying. **∼se** *vpr* be said. **∼ que no** say no. **∼ que sí** say yes. **dicho de otro modo** in other words. **dicho y hecho** no sooner said than done. **¿dígame?** can I help you? **¡dígame!** (*al teléfono*) hello! **digamos** let's say. **es ∼** that is to say. **mejor dicho** rather. **¡no me digas!** you don't say!, really! **por así ∼, por ∼lo así** so to speak, as it were. **querer ∼** mean. **se dice que** it is said that, they say that

decisi|ón *f* decision. **∼vo** *a* decisive

declamar *vt* declaim

declara|ción *f* statement. **∼ción de renta** income tax return. **∼r** *vt/i* declare. **∼rse** *vpr* declare o.s.; (*epidemia etc*) break out

declina|ción *f* (*gram*) declension. **∼r** *vt/i* decline; ⟨*salud*⟩ deteriorate

declive *m* slope; (*fig*) decline. **en** ~ sloping

decolorar *vt* discolour, fade. ~**se** *vpr* become discoloured, fade

decora|ción *f* decoration. ~**do** *m* (*en el teatro*) set. ~**dor** *m* decorator. ~**r** *vt* decorate. ~**tivo** *a* decorative

decoro *m* decorum; (*respeto*) respect. ~**so** *a* proper; (*modesto*) modest; (*profesión*) honourable

decrecer [11] *vi* decrease, diminish; (*aguas*) subside

decrépito *a* decrepit

decret|ar *vt* decree. ~**o** *m* decree

dedal *m* thimble

dedica|ción *f* dedication. ~**r** [7] *vt* dedicate; devote (*tiempo*). ~**toria** *f* dedication, inscription

ded|il *m* finger-stall. ~**illo** *m*. **al** ~**illo** at one's fingertips. ~**o** *m* finger; (*del pie*) toe. ~**o anular** ring finger. ~**o corazón** middle finger. ~**o gordo** thumb. ~**o índice** index finger. ~**o meñique** little finger. ~**o pulgar** thumb

deduc|ción *f* deduction. ~**ir** [47] *vt* deduce; (*descontar*) deduct

defect|o *m* fault, defect. ~**uoso** *a* defective

defen|der [1] *vt* defend. ~**sa** *f* defence. ~**sivo** *a* defensive. ~**sor** *m* defender. **abogado** *m* ~**sor** defence counsel

deferen|cia *f* deference. ~**te** *a* deferential

deficien|cia *f* deficiency. ~**cia mental** mental handicap. ~**te** *a* deficient; (*imperfecto*) defective. ~**te mental** mentally handicapped

déficit *m invar* deficit

defini|ción *f* definition. ~**do** *a* defined. ~**r** *vt* define; (*aclarar*) clarify. ~**tivo** *a* definitive. **en** ~**tiva** (*en resumen*) in short

deflación *f* deflation

deform|ación *f* deformation; (*TV etc*) distortion. ~**ar** *vt* deform; (*TV etc*) distort. ~**arse** *vpr* go out of shape. ~**e** *a* deformed; (*feo*) ugly

defraudar *vt* cheat; (*decepcionar*) disappoint; evade (*impuestos etc*)

defunción *f* death

degenera|ción *f* degeneration; (*moral*) degeneracy. ~**do** *a* degenerate. ~**r** *vi* degenerate

deglutir *vt/i* swallow

degollar [16] *vt* cut s.o.'s throat; (*fig, arruinar*) ruin

degradar *vt* degrade. ~**se** *vpr* lower o.s.

degusta|ción *f* tasting. ~**r** *vt* taste

dehesa *f* pasture

dei|dad *f* deity. ~**ficar** [7] *vt* deify

deja|ción *f* surrender. ~**dez** *f* abandon; (*pereza*) laziness. ~**do** *a* negligent. ~**r** *vt* leave; (*abandonar*) abandon; (*prestar*) lend; (*permitir*) let. ~**r aparte**, ~**r a un lado** leave aside. ~**r de** stop. **no** ~**r de** not fail to

dejo *m* aftertaste; (*tonillo*) accent

del = **de|el**

delantal *m* apron

delante *adv* in front; (*enfrente*) opposite. ~ **de** in front of. **de** ~ front

delanter|a *f* front; (*de teatro etc*) front row; (*ventaja*) advantage. **coger la** ~**a** get ahead. ~**o** *a* front. ● *m* forward. **llevar la** ~**a** be ahead

delat|ar *vt* denounce. ~**or** *m* informer

delega|ción *f* delegation; (*sucursal*) branch. ~**do** *m* delegate; (*com*) agent, representative. ~**r** [12] *vt* delegate

deleit|ar *vt* delight. ~**e** *m* delight

deletéreo *a* deleterious

deletre|ar *vt* spell (out). ~**o** *m* spelling

deleznable *a* brittle, crumbly; (*argumento etc*) weak

delfín *m* dolphin

delgad|ez *f* thinness. ~**o** *a* thin; (*esbelto*) slim. ~**ucho** *a* skinny

delibera|ción *f* deliberation. ~**r** *vt* discuss, decide. ● *vi* deliberate

delicad|eza *f* delicacy; (*fragilidad*) frailty; (*tacto*) tact. ~**o** *a* delicate; (*sensible*) sensitive; (*discreto*) tactful, discreet. **falta de** ~**eza** tactlessness

delici|a *f* delight. ~**oso** *a* delightful; (*sabor etc*) delicious; (*gracioso, fam*) funny

delimitar *vt* delimit

delincuen|cia *f* delinquency. ~**te** *a* & *m* delinquent

delinea|nte *m* draughtsman. ~**r** *vt* outline; (*dibujar*) draw

delinquir [8] *vi* commit an offence

delir|ante *a* delirious. ~**ar** *vi* be delirious; (*fig*) talk nonsense. ~**io** *m* delirium; (*fig*) frenzy

delito *m* crime, offence

delta *f* delta

demacrado *a* emaciated

demagogo *m* demagogue

demanda *f.* **en ∼ de** asking for; (*en busca de*) in search of. **∼nte** *m & f* (*jurid*) plaintiff. **∼r** *vt* (*jurid*) bring an action against

demarca|ción *f* demarcation. **∼r** [7] *vt* demarcate

demás *a* rest of the, other. ● *pron* rest, others. **lo ∼** the rest. **por ∼** useless; (*muy*) very. **por lo ∼** otherwise

demasía *f* excess; (*abuso*) outrage; (*atrevimiento*) insolence. **en ∼** too much

demasiado *a* too much; (*en plural*) too many. ● *adv* too much; (*con adjetivo*) too

demen|cia *f* madness. **∼te** *a* demented, mad

dem|ocracia *f* democracy. **∼ócrata** *m & f* democrat. **∼ocrático** *a* democratic

demol|er [2] *vt* demolish. **∼ición** *f* demolition

demonio *m* devil, demon. **¡∼s!** hell! **¿cómo ∼s?** how the hell? **¡qué ∼s!** what the hell!

demora *f* delay. **∼r** *vt* delay. ● *vi* stay on. **∼rse** *vpr* be a long time

demostra|ción *f* demonstration, show. **∼r** [2] *vt* demonstrate; (*mostrar*) show; (*probar*) prove. **∼tivo** *a* demonstrative

denegar [1 & 12] *vt* refuse

deng|oso *a* affected, finicky. **∼ue** *m* affectation

denigrar *vt* denigrate

denomina|ción *f* denomination. **∼do** *a* called. **∼dor** *m* denominator. **∼r** *vt* name

denotar *vt* denote

dens|idad *f* density. **∼o** *a* dense, thick

denta|dura *f* teeth. **∼dura postiza** denture, false teeth. **∼l** *a* dental

dentera *f.* **dar ∼ a uno** set s.o.'s teeth on edge; (*dar envidia*) make s.o. green with envy

dentífrico *m* toothpaste

dentista *m & f* dentist

dentro *adv* inside; (*de un edificio*) indoors. **∼ de** in. **∼ de poco** soon. **por ∼** inside

denuncia *f* report; (*acusación*) accusation. **∼r** *vt* report (a crime); (*periódico etc*) denounce; (*indicar*) indicate

departamento *m* department; (*Arg, piso*) flat (*Brit*), apartment (*Amer*)

dependencia *f* dependence; (*sección*) section; (*sucursal*) branch

depender *vi* depend (**de** on)

dependient|a *f* shop assistant. **∼e** *a* dependent (**de** on). ● *m* employee; (*de oficina*) clerk; (*de tienda*) shop assistant

depila|ción *f* depilation. **∼r** *vt* depilate. **∼torio** *a* depilatory

deplora|ble *a* deplorable. **∼r** *vt* deplore, regret

deponer [34] *vt* remove from office. ● *vi* give evidence

deporta|ción *f* deportation. **∼r** *vt* deport

deport|e *m* sport. **∼ista** *m* sportsman. ● *f* sportswoman. **∼ivo** *a* sports. ● *m* sports car. **hacer ∼e** take part in sports

deposición *f* deposition; (*de un empleo*) removal from office

dep|ositador *m* depositor. **∼ositante** *m & f* depositor. **∼ositar** *vt* deposit; (*poner*) put, place. **∼ósito** *m* deposit; (*conjunto de cosas*) store; (*almacén*) warehouse; (*mil*) depot; (*de líquidos*) tank

deprava|ción *f* depravity. **∼do** *a* depraved. **∼r** *vt* deprave. **∼rse** *vpr* become depraved

deprecia|ción *f* depreciation. **∼r** *vt* depreciate. **∼rse** *vpr* depreciate

depresión *f* depression

deprim|ente *a* depressing. **∼ido** *a* depressed. **∼ir** *vt* depress. **∼irse** *vpr* get depressed

depura|ción *f* purification; (*pol*) purging. **∼r** *vt* purify; (*pol*) purge

derech|a *f* (*mano*) right hand; (*lado*) right. **∼ista** *a* right-wing. ● *m & f* right-winger. **∼o** *a* right; (*vertical*) upright; (*recto*) straight. ● *adv* straight. ● *m* right; (*ley*) law; (*lado*) right side. **∼os** *mpl* dues. **∼os de autor** royalties. **la ∼a** on the right; (*hacia el lado derecho*) to the right. **todo ∼o** straight on

deriva *f* drift. **a la ∼** drifting, adrift

deriva|ción *f* derivation; (*cambio*) diversion. **∼do** *a* derived. ● *m* derivative, by-product. **∼r** *vt* derive; (*cambiar la dirección de*) divert. ● *vi*. **∼r de** derive from, be derived from. **∼rse** *vpr* be derived

derram|amiento *m* spilling. **∼amiento de sangre** bloodshed. **∼ar** *vt* spill; (*verter*) pour; shed ‹*lágrimas*›. **∼arse** *vpr* spill. **∼e** *m* spilling; (*pérdida*) leakage; (*cantidad perdida*) spillage; (*med*) discharge; (*med, de sangre*) haemorrhage

derretir [5] vt melt. ~**se** vpr melt; (*enamorarse*) fall in love (**por** with)

derriba|do a fallen down. ~**r** vt knock down; bring down, overthrow ‹*gobierno etc*›. ~**rse** vpr fall down

derrocar [7] vt bring down, overthrow ‹*gobierno etc*›

derroch|ar vt squander. ~**e** m waste

derrot|a f defeat; (*rumbo*) course. ~**ar** vt defeat. ~**ado** a defeated; ‹*vestido*› shabby. ~**ero** m course

derrumba|miento m collapse. ~**r** vt (*derribar*) knock down. ~**rse** vpr collapse

desaborido a tasteless; ‹*persona*› dull

desabotonar vt unbutton, undo. ● vi bloom. ~**se** vpr come undone

desabrido a tasteless; ‹*tiempo*› unpleasant; ‹*persona*› surly

desabrochar vt undo. ~**se** vpr come undone

desacat|ar vt have no respect for. ~**o** m disrespect

desac|ertado a ill-advised; (*erróneo*) wrong. ~**ertar** [1] vt be wrong. ~**ierto** m mistake

desaconseja|ble a inadvisable. ~**do** a unwise, ill-advised. ~**r** vt advise against, dissuade

desacorde a discordant

desacostumbra|do a unusual. ~**r** vt give up

desacreditar vt discredit

desactivar vt defuse

desacuerdo m disagreement

desafiar [20] vt challenge; (*afrontar*) defy

desafilado a blunt

desafina|do a out of tune. ~**r** vi be out of tune. ~**rse** vpr go out of tune

desafío m challenge; (*combate*) duel

desaforado a ‹*comportamiento*› outrageous; (*desmedido*) excessive; ‹*sonido*› huge; (*enorme*) huge

desafortunad|amente adv unfortunately. ~**o** a unfortunate

desagrada|ble a unpleasant. ~**r** vt displease. ● vi be unpleasant. **me** ~ **el sabor** I don't like the taste

desagradecido a ungrateful

desagrado m displeasure. **con** ~ unwillingly

desagravi|ar vt make amends to. ~**o** m amends; (*expiación*) atonement

desagregar [12] vt break up. ~**se** vpr disintegrate

desagüe m drain; (*acción*) drainage. **tubo** m **de** ~ drain-pipe

desaguisado a illegal. ● m offence; (*fam*) disaster

desahog|ado a roomy; (*adinerado*) well-off; (*fig, descarado, fam*) impudent. ~**ar** [12] vt relieve; vent ‹*ira*›. ~**arse** vpr (*desfogarse*) let off steam. ~**o** m comfort; (*alivio*) relief

desahuci|ar vt deprive of hope; give up hope for ‹*enfermo*›; evict ‹*inquilino*›. ~**o** m eviction

desair|ado a humiliating; ‹*persona*› humiliated, spurned. ~**ar** vt snub ‹*persona*›; disregard ‹*cosa*›. ~**e** m rebuff

desajuste m maladjustment; (*avería*) breakdown

desal|entador a disheartening. ~**entar** [1] vt (*fig*) discourage. ~**iento** m discouragement

desaliño m untidiness, scruffiness

desalmado a wicked

desalojar vt eject ‹*persona*›; evacuate ‹*sitio*›. ● vi move (house)

desampar|ado a helpless; (*abandonado*) abandoned. ~**ar** vt abandon. ~**o** m helplessness; (*abandono*) abandonment

desangelado a insipid, dull

desangrar vt bleed. ~**se** vpr bleed

desanima|do a down-hearted. ~**r** vt discourage. ~**rse** vpr lose heart

desánimo m discouragement

desanudar vt untie

desapacible a unpleasant; ‹*sonido*› harsh

desapar|ecer [11] vi disappear; ‹*efecto*› wear off. ~**ecido** a disappeared. ● m missing person. ~**ecidos** mpl missing. ~**ición** f disappearance

desapasionado a dispassionate

desapego m indifference

desapercibido a unnoticed

desaplicado a lazy

desaprensi|ón f unscrupulousness. ~**vo** a unscrupulous

desaproba|ción f disapproval. ~**r** [2] vt disapprove of; (*rechazar*) reject

desaprovecha|do a wasted; ‹*alumno*› lazy. ~**r** vt waste

desarm|ar vt disarm; (*desmontar*) take to pieces. ~**e** m disarmament

desarraig|ado a rootless. ~**ar** [12] vt uproot; (*fig, erradicar*) wipe out. ~**o** m uprooting; (*fig*) eradication

desarregl|ado *a* untidy; (*desordenado*) disorderly. **~ar** *vt* mess up; (*deshacer el orden*) make untidy. **~o** *m* disorder; (*de persona*) untidiness

desarroll|ado *a* (well-) developed. **~ar** *vt* develop; (*desenrollar*) unroll, unfold. **~arse** *vpr* (*incl foto*) develop; (*desenrollarse*) unroll; (*suceso*) take place. **~o** *m* development

desarrugar [12] *vt* smooth out

desarticular *vt* dislocate (*hueso*); (*fig*) break up

desaseado *a* dirty; (*desordenado*) untidy

desasirse [45] *vpr* let go (**de** of)

desasos|egar [1 & 12] *vt* disturb. **~egarse** *vpr* be uneasy. **~iego** *m* anxiety; (*intranquilidad*) restlessness

desastr|ado *a* scruffy. **~e** *m* disaster. **~oso** *a* disastrous

desata|do *a* untied; (*fig*) wild. **~r** *vt* untie; (*fig, soltar*) unleash. **~rse** *vpr* come undone

desatascar [7] *vt* pull out of the mud; unblock (*tubo etc*)

desaten|ción *f* inattention; (*descortesía*) discourtesy. **~der** [1] *vt* not pay attention to; neglect (*deber etc*). **~to** *a* inattentive; (*descortés*) discourteous

desatin|ado *a* silly. **~o** *m* silliness; (*error*) mistake

desatornillar *vt* unscrew

desatracar [7] *vt/i* cast off

desautorizar [10] *vt* declare unauthorized; (*desmentir*) deny

desavenencia *f* disagreement

desayun|ar *vt* have for breakfast. ● *vi* have breakfast. **~o** *m* breakfast

desazón *m* (*fig*) anxiety

desbandarse *vpr* (*mil*) disband; (*dispersarse*) disperse

desbarajust|ar *vt* throw into confusion. **~e** *m* confusion

desbaratar *vt* spoil

desbloquear *vt* unfreeze

desbocado *a* (*vasija etc*) chipped; (*caballo*) runaway; (*persona*) foul-mouthed

desborda|nte *a* overflowing. **~r** *vt* go beyond; (*exceder*) exceed. ● *vi* overflow. **~rse** *vpr* overflow

descabalgar [12] *vi* dismount

descabellado *a* crazy

descabezar [10] *vt* behead

descafeinado *a* decaffeinated. ● *m* decaffeinated coffee

descalabr|ar *vt* injure in the head; (*fig*) damage. **~o** *m* disaster

descalificar [7] *vt* disqualify; (*desacreditar*) discredit

descalz|ar [10] *vt* take off (*zapato*). **~o** *a* barefoot

descaminar *vt* misdirect; (*fig*) lead astray

descamisado *a* shirtless; (*fig*) shabby

descampado *a* open. ● *m* open ground

descans|ado *a* rested; (*trabajo*) easy. **~apiés** *m* footrest. **~ar** *vt/i* rest. **~illo** *m* landing. **~o** *m* rest; (*descansillo*) landing; (*en deportes*) half-time; (*en el teatro etc*) interval

descapotable *a* convertible

descarado *a* insolent, cheeky; (*sin vergüenza*) shameless

descarg|a *f* unloading; (*mil, elec*) discharge. **~ar** [12] *vt* unload; (*mil, elec*) discharge, shock; deal (*golpe etc*). ● *vi* flow into. **~o** *m* unloading; (*recibo*) receipt; (*jurid*) evidence

descarnado *a* scrawny, lean; (*fig*) bare

descaro *m* insolence, cheek; (*cinismo*) nerve, effrontery

descarriar [20] *vt* misdirect; (*fig*) lead astray. **~se** *vpr* go the wrong way; (*res*) stray; (*fig*) go astray

descarrila|miento *m* derailment. **~r** *vi* be derailed. **~se** *vpr* be derailed

descartar *vt* discard; (*rechazar*) reject. **~se** *vpr* discard

descascarar *vt* shell

descen|dencia *f* descent; (*personas*) descendants. **~dente** *a* descending. **~der** [1] *vt* lower, get down; go down (*escalera etc*). ● *vi* go down; (*provenir*) be descended (**de** from). **~diente** *m* & *f* descendent. **~so** *m* descent; (*de temperatura, fiebre etc*) fall, drop

descentralizar [10] *vt* decentralize

descifrar *vt* decipher; decode (*clave*)

descolgar [2 & 12] *vt* take down; pick up (*el teléfono*). **~se** *vpr* let o.s. down; (*fig, fam*) turn up

descolorar *vt* discolour, fade

descolori|do *a* discoloured, faded; (*persona*) pale. **~r** *vt* discolour, fade

descomedido *a* rude; (*excesivo*) excessive, extreme

descomp|ás m disproportion. **~asado** a disproportionate

descomp|oner [34] vt break down; decompose ‹substancia›; distort ‹rasgos›; (estropear) break; (desarreglar) disturb, spoil. **~onerse** vpr decompose; (persona) lose one's temper. **~osición** f decomposition; (med) diarrhoea. **~ostura** f breaking; (de un motor) breakdown; (desorden) disorder. **~uesto** a broken; (podrido) decomposed; (encolerizado) angry. **estar ~uesto** have diarrhoea

descomunal a (fam) enormous

desconc|ertante a disconcerting. **~ertar** [1] vt disconcert; (dejar perplejo) puzzle. **~ertarse** vpr be put out, be disconcerted; ‹mecanismo› break down. **~ierto** m confusion

desconectar vt disconnect

desconfia|do a distrustful. **~nza** f distrust, suspicion. **~r** [20] vi. **~r de** not trust; (no creer) doubt

descongelar vt defrost; (com) unfreeze

desconoc|er [11] vt not know, not recognize. **~ido** a unknown; (cambiado) unrecognizable. • m stranger. **~imiento** m ignorance

desconsidera|ción f lack of consideration. **~do** a inconsiderate

descons|olado a distressed. **~olar** [2] vt distress. **~olarse** vpr despair. **~uelo** m distress; (tristeza) sadness

desconta|do a. **dar por ~do** take for granted. **por ~do** of course. **~r** [2] vt discount

descontent|adizo a hard to please. **~ar** vt displease. **~o** a unhappy (**de** about), discontented (**de** with). • m discontent

descontrolado a uncontrolled

descorazonar vt discourage. **~se** vpr lose heart

descorchar vt uncork

descorrer vt draw ‹cortina›. **~ el cerrojo** unbolt the door

descort|és a rude, discourteous. **~esía** f rudeness

descos|er vt unpick. **~erse** vpr come undone. **~ido** a unstitched; (fig) disjointed. **como un ~ido** a lot

descoyuntar vt dislocate

descrédito m disrepute. **ir en ~ de** damage the reputation of

descreído a unbelieving

descremar vt skim

descri|bir [pp descrito] vt describe. **~pción** f description. **~ptivo** a descriptive

descuartizar [10] vt cut up

descubierto a discovered; (no cubierto) uncovered; (expuesto) exposed; ‹cielo› clear; (sin sombrero) bareheaded. • m overdraft; (déficit) deficit. **poner al ~** expose

descubri|miento m discovery. **~r** [pp descubierto] vt discover; (quitar lo que cubre) uncover; (revelar) reveal; unveil ‹estatua›. **~rse** vpr be discovered; ‹cielo› clear; (quitarse el sombrero) take off one's hat

descuento m discount

descuid|ado a careless; ‹aspecto etc› untidy; (desprevenido) unprepared. **~ar** vt neglect. • vi not worry. **~arse** vpr be careless; (no preocuparse) not worry. **¡~a!** don't worry! **~o** m carelessness; (negligencia) negligence. **al ~o** nonchalantly. **estar ~ado** not worry, rest assured

desde prep (lugar etc) from; (tiempo) since, from. **~ hace poco** for a short time. **~ hace un mes** for a month. **~ luego** of course. **~ Madrid hasta Barcelona** from Madrid to Barcelona. **~ niño** since childhood

desdecir [46, pero imperativo desdice, futuro y condicional regulares] vi. **~ de** be unworthy of; (no armonizar) not match. **~se** vpr. **~ de** take back ‹palabras etc›; go back on ‹promesa›

desd|én m scorn. **~eñable** a contemptible. **~eñar** vt scorn. **~eñoso** a scornful

desdicha f misfortune. **~do** a unfortunate. **por ~** unfortunately

desdoblar vt straighten; (desplegar) unfold

desea|ble a desirable. **~r** vt want; wish ‹algo a uno›. **de ~r** desirable. **le deseo un buen viaje** I hope you have a good journey. **¿qué desea Vd?** can I help you?

desecar [7] vt dry up

desech|ar vt throw out. **~o** m rubbish

desembalar vt unpack

desembarazar [10] vt clear. **~se** vpr free o.s.

desembarca|dero m landing stage. **~r** [7] vt unload. • vi disembark

desemboca|dura f (de río) mouth; (de calle) opening. **~r** [7] vi. **~r en**

⟨río⟩ flow into; ⟨calle⟩ join; (fig) lead to, end in

desembols|ar vt pay. **~o** m payment

desembragar [12] vi declutch

desembrollar vt unravel

desembuchar vi tell, reveal a secret

desemejan|te a unlike, dissimilar. **~za** f dissimilarity

desempapelar vt unwrap

desempaquetar vt unpack, unwrap

desempat|ar vi break a tie. **~e** m tie-breaker

desempeñ|ar vt redeem; play ⟨papel⟩; hold ⟨cargo⟩; perform, carry out ⟨deber etc⟩. **~arse** vpr get out of debt. **~o** m redemption; (de un papel, de un cargo) performance

desemple|ado a unemployed. • m unemployed person. **~o** m unemployment. **los ~ados** mpl the unemployed

desempolvar vt dust; (fig) unearth

desencadenar vt unchain; (fig) unleash. **~se** vpr break loose; ⟨guerra etc⟩ break out

desencajar vt dislocate; (desconectar) disconnect. **~se** vpr become distorted

desencant|ar vt disillusion. **~o** m disillusionment

desenchufar vt unplug

desenfad|ado a uninhibited. **~ar** vt calm down. **~arse** vpr calm down. **~o** m openness; (desenvoltura) assurance

desenfocado a out of focus

desenfren|ado a unrestrained. **~arse** vpr rage. **~o** m licentiousness

desenganchar vt unhook

desengañ|ar vt disillusion. **~arse** vpr be disillusioned; (darse cuenta) realize. **~o** m disillusionment, disappointment

desengrasar vt remove the grease from. • vi lose weight

desenla|ce m outcome. **~zar** [10] vt undo; solve ⟨problema⟩

desenmarañar vt unravel

desenmascarar vt unmask

desenojar vt calm down. **~se** vpr calm down

desenred|ar vt unravel. **~arse** vpr extricate o.s. **~o** m denoument

desenrollar vt unroll, unwind

desenroscar [7] vt unscrew

desentenderse [1] vpr want nothing to do with; (afectar ignorancia)

pretend not to know. **hacerse el desentendido** (fingir no oir) pretend not to hear

desenterrar [1] vt exhume; (fig) unearth

desenton|ar vi be out of tune; ⟨colores⟩ clash. **~o** m rudeness

desentrañar vt work out

desenvoltura f ease; (falta de timidez) confidence; (descaro) insolence

desenvolver [2, pp **desenvuelto**] vt unwrap; expound ⟨idea etc⟩. **~se** vpr act with confidence

deseo m wish, desire. **~so** a desirous. **arder en ~s de** long for. **buen ~** good intentions. **estar ~so de** be eager to

desequilibr|ado a unbalanced. **~io** m imbalance

des|erción f desertion; (pol) defection. **~ertar** vt desert. **~értico** a desert-like. **~ertor** m deserter

desespera|ción f despair. **~do** a desperate. **~nte** a infuriating. **~r** vt drive to despair. • vi despair (**de** of). **~rse** vpr despair

desestimar vt (rechazar) reject

desfachat|ado a brazen, impudent. **~ez** f impudence

desfalc|ar [7] vt embezzle. **~o** m embezzlement

desfallec|er [11] vt weaken. • vi get weak; (desmayarse) faint. **~imiento** m weakness

desfas|ado a ⟨persona⟩ out of place, out of step; ⟨máquina etc⟩ out of phase. **~e** m jet-lag. **estar ~ado** have jet-lag

desfavor|able a unfavourable. **~ecer** [11] vt ⟨ropa⟩ not suit

desfigurar vt disfigure; (desdibujar) blur; (fig) distort

desfiladero m pass

desfil|ar vi march (past). **~e** m procession, parade. **~e de modelos** fashion show

desfogar [12] vt vent (**en, con** on). **~se** vpr let off steam

desgajar vt tear off; (fig) uproot ⟨persona⟩. **~se** vpr come off

desgana f (falta de apetito) lack of appetite; (med) weakness, faintness; (fig) unwillingness

desgarr|ador a heart-rending. **~ar** vt tear; (fig) break ⟨corazón⟩. **~o** m tear, rip; (descaro) insolence. **~ón** m tear

desgast|ar *vt* wear away; wear out ⟨*ropa*⟩. **~arse** *vpr* wear away; ⟨*ropa*⟩ be worn out; ⟨*persona*⟩ wear o.s. out. **~e** *m* wear

desgracia *f* misfortune; (*accidente*) accident; (*mala suerte*) bad luck. **~damente** *adv* unfortunately. **~do** *a* unlucky; (*pobre*) poor; (*desagradable*) unpleasant. ● *m* unfortunate person, poor devil (*fam*). **~r** *vt* spoil. **caer en ~** fall from favour. **estar en ~** be unfortunate. **por ~** unfortunately. **¡qué ~!** what a shame!

desgranar *vt* shell ⟨*guisantes etc*⟩

desgreñado *a* ruffled, dishevelled

desgua|ce *m* scrapyard. **~zar** [10] *vt* scrap

deshabitado *a* uninhabited

deshabituarse [21] *vpr* get out of the habit

deshacer [31] *vt* undo; strip ⟨*cama*⟩; unpack ⟨*maleta*⟩; (*desmontar*) take to pieces; break ⟨*trato*⟩; (*derretir*) melt; (*en agua*) dissolve; (*destruir*) destroy; (*estropear*) spoil; (*derrotar*) defeat. **~se** *vpr* come undone; (*descomponerse*) fall to pieces; (*derretirse*) melt. **~se de algo** get rid of sth. **~se en lágrimas** burst into tears. **~se por hacer algo** go out of one's way to do sth

deshelar [1] *vt* thaw. **~se** *vpr* thaw

desheredar *vt* disinherit

deshidratar *vt* dehydrate. **~se** *vpr* become dehydrated

deshielo *m* thaw

deshilachado *a* frayed

deshincha|do *a* ⟨*neumático*⟩ flat. **~r** *vt* deflate. **~rse** *vpr* go down

deshollina|dor *m* (chimney-)sweep. **~r** *vt* sweep ⟨*chimenea*⟩

deshon|esto *a* dishonest; (*obsceno*) indecent. **~or** *m*, **~ra** *f* disgrace. **~rar** *vt* dishonour

deshora *f*. **a ~** (*a hora desacostumbrada*) at an unusual time; (*a hora inoportuna*) at an inconvenient time; (*a hora avanzada*) very late

deshuesar *vt* bone ⟨*carne*⟩; stone ⟨*fruta*⟩

desidia *f* laziness

desierto *a* deserted. ● *m* desert

designa|ción *f* designation. **~r** *vt* designate; (*fijar*) fix

desigual *a* unequal; ⟨*terreno*⟩ uneven; (*distinto*) different. **~dad** *f* inequality

desilusi|ón *f* disappointment; (*pérdida de ilusiones*) disillusionment. **~onar** *vt* disappoint; (*quitar las ilusiones*) disillusion. **~onarse** *vpr* become disillusioned

desinfecta|nte *m* disinfectant. **~r** *vt* disinfect

desinfestar *vt* decontaminate

desinflar *vt* deflate. **~se** *vpr* go down

desinhibido *a* uninhibited

desintegra|ción *f* disintegration. **~r** *vt* disintegrate. **~rse** *vpr* disintegrate

desinter|és *m* impartiality; (*generosidad*) generosity. **~esado** *a* impartial; (*liberal*) generous

desistir *vi*. **~ de** give up

desleal *a* disloyal. **~tad** *f* disloyalty

desleír [51] *vt* thin down, dilute

deslenguado *a* foul-mouthed

desligar [12] *vt* untie; (*separar*) separate; (*fig, librar*) free. **~se** *vpr* break away; (*de un compromiso*) free o.s.

deslizar [10] *vt* slide, slip. **~se** *vpr* slide, slip; ⟨*tiempo*⟩ slide by, pass; (*fluir*) flow

deslucido *a* tarnished; (*gastado*) worn out; (*fig*) undistinguished

deslumbrar *vt* dazzle

deslustrar *vt* tarnish

desmadr|ado *a* unruly. **~arse** *vpr* get out of control. **~e** *m* excess

desmán *m* outrage

desmandarse *vpr* get out of control

desmantelar *vt* dismantle; (*despojar*) strip

desmañado *a* clumsy

desmaquillador *m* make-up remover

desmay|ado *a* unconscious. **~ar** *vi* lose heart. **~arse** *vpr* faint. **~o** *m* faint; (*estado*) unconsciousness; (*fig*) depression

desmedido *a* excessive

desmedrarse *vpr* waste away

desmejorarse *vpr* deteriorate

desmelenado *a* dishevelled

desmembrar *vt* (*fig*) divide up

desmemoriado *a* forgetful

desmentir [4] *vt* deny. **~se** *vpr* contradict o.s.; (*desdecirse*) go back on one's word

desmenuzar [10] *vt* crumble; chop ⟨*carne etc*⟩

desmerecer [11] *vt* be unworthy of. ● *vi* deteriorate

desmesurado *a* excessive; (*enorme*) enormous

desmigajar *vt*, **desmigar** [12] *vt* crumble

desmonta|ble *a* collapsible. **~r** *vt* (*quitar*) remove; (*desarmar*) take to pieces; (*derribar*) knock down; (*allanar*) level. ● *vi* dismount

desmoralizar [10] *vt* demoralize

desmoronar *vt* wear away; (*fig*) make inroads into. **~se** *vpr* crumble

desmovilizar [10] *vt/i* demobilize

desnatar *vt* skim

desnivel *m* unevenness; (*fig*) difference, inequality

desnud|ar *vt* strip; undress, strip (*persona*). **~arse** *vpr* get undressed. **~ez** *f* nudity. **~o** *a* naked; (*fig*) bare. ● *m* nude

desnutri|ción *f* malnutrition. **~do** *a* undernourished

desobed|ecer [11] *vt* disobey. **~iencia** *f* disobedience. **~iente** *a* disobedient

desocupa|do *a* (*asiento etc*) vacant, free; (*sin trabajo*) unemployed; (*ocioso*) idle. **~r** *vt* vacate

desodorante *m* deodorant

desoír [50] *vt* take no notice of

desola|ción *f* desolation; (*fig*) distress. **~do** *a* desolate; (*persona*) sorry, sad. **~r** *vt* ruin; (*desconsolar*) distress

desollar *vt* skin; (*fig, criticar*) criticize; (*fig, hacer pagar demasiado, fam*) fleece

desorbitante *a* excessive

desorden *m* disorder, untidiness; (*confusión*) confusion. **~ado** *a* untidy. **~ar** *vt* disarrange, make a mess of

desorganizar [10] *vt* disorganize; (*trastornar*) disturb

desorienta|do *a* confused. **~r** *vt* disorientate. **~rse** *vpr* lose one's bearings

desovar *vi* (*pez*) spawn; (*insecto*) lay eggs

despabila|do *a* wide awake; (*listo*) quick. **~r** *vt* (*despertar*) wake up; (*avivar*) brighten up. **~rse** *vpr* wake up; (*avivarse*) brighten up. ¡**despabílate**! get a move on!

despaci|o *adv* slowly. ● *int* easy does it! **~to** *adv* slowly

despach|ar *vt* finish; (*tratar con*) deal with; (*vender*) sell; (*enviar*) send; (*despedir*) send away; issue (*billete*). ● *vi* hurry up. **~arse** *vpr* get rid; (*terminar*) finish. **~o** *m* dispatch; (*oficina*) office; (*venta*) sale; (*del teatro*) box office

despampanante *a* stunning

desparejado *a* odd

desparpajo *m* confidence; (*descaro*) impudence

desparramar *vt* scatter; spill (*líquidos*); squander (*fortuna*)

despavorido *a* terrified

despectivo *a* disparaging; (*sentido etc*) pejorative

despecho *m* spite. **a ~ de** in spite of. **por ~** out of spite

despedazar [10] *vt* tear to pieces

despedi|da *f* goodbye, farewell. **~da de soltero** stag-party. **~r** [5] *vt* say goodbye, see off; dismiss (*empleado*); evict (*inquilino*); (*arrojar*) throw; give off (*olor etc*). **~rse** *vpr*. **~rse de** say goodbye to

despeg|ado *a* cold, indifferent. **~ar** [12] *vt* unstick. ● *vi* (*avión*) take off. **~o** *m* indifference. **~ue** *m* take-off

despeinar *vt* ruffle the hair of

despeja|do *a* clear; (*persona*) wide awake. **~r** *vt* clear; (*aclarar*) clarify. ● *vi* clear. **~rse** *vpr* (*aclararse*) become clear; (*cielo*) clear; (*tiempo*) clear up; (*persona*) liven up

despellejar *vt* skin

despensa *f* pantry, larder

despeñadero *m* cliff

desperdici|ar *vt* waste. **~o** *m* waste. **~os** *mpl* rubbish. **no tener ~o** be good all the way through

desperezarse [10] *vpr* stretch

desperfecto *m* flaw

desperta|dor *m* alarm clock. **~r** [1] *vt* wake up; (*fig*) awaken. **~rse** *vpr* wake up

despiadado *a* merciless

despido *m* dismissal

despierto *a* awake; (*listo*) bright

despilfarr|ar *vt* waste. **~o** *m* squandering; (*gasto innecesario*) extravagance

despista|do *a* (*con estar*) confused; (*con ser*) absent-minded. **~r** *vt* throw off the scent; (*fig*) mislead. **~rse** *vpr* go wrong; (*fig*) get confused

despiste *m* swerve; (*error*) mistake; (*confusión*) muddle

desplaza|do *a* out of place. **~miento** *m* displacement; (*de opinión etc*) swing, shift. **~r** [10] *vt* displace. **~rse** *vpr* travel

despl|egar [1 & 12] vt open out; spread ⟨alas⟩; ⟨fig⟩ show. **~iegue** m opening; ⟨fig⟩ show

desplomarse vpr lean; ⟨caerse⟩ collapse

desplumar vt pluck; ⟨fig, fam⟩ fleece

despobla|do m deserted area. **~r** [2] vt depopulate

despoj|ar vt deprive ⟨persona⟩; strip ⟨cosa⟩. **~o** m plundering; ⟨botín⟩ booty. **~os** mpl left-overs; ⟨de res⟩ offal; ⟨de ave⟩ giblets

desposado a & m newly-wed

déspota m & f despot

despreci|able a despicable; ⟨cantidad⟩ negligible. **~ar** vt despise; ⟨rechazar⟩ scorn. **~o** m contempt

desprend|er vt remove; give off ⟨olor⟩. **~erse** vpr fall off; ⟨fig⟩ part with; ⟨deducirse⟩ follow. **~imiento** m loosening; ⟨generosidad⟩ generosity

despreocupa|ción f carelessness. **~do** a unconcerned; ⟨descuidado⟩ careless. **~rse** vpr not worry

desprestigiar vt discredit

desprevenido a unprepared. **coger a uno ~** catch s.o. unawares

desproporci|ón f disproportion. **~onado** a disproportionate

despropósito m irrelevant remark

desprovisto a. **~ de** lacking, without

después adv after, afterwards; ⟨más tarde⟩ later; ⟨a continuación⟩ then. **~ de** after. **~ de comer** after eating. **~ de todo** after all. **~ que** after. **poco ~** soon after. **una semana ~** a week later

desquiciar vt ⟨fig⟩ disturb

desquit|ar vt compensate. **~arse** vpr make up for; ⟨vengarse⟩ take revenge. **~e** m compensation; ⟨venganza⟩ revenge

destaca|do a outstanding. **~r** [7] vt emphasize. ● vi stand out. **~rse** vpr stand out

destajo m piece-work. **hablar a ~** talk nineteen to the dozen

destap|ar vt uncover; open ⟨botella⟩. **~e** m ⟨fig⟩ permissiveness

destartalado a ⟨habitación⟩ untidy; ⟨casa⟩ rambling

destell|ar vi sparkle. **~o** m sparkle; ⟨de estrella⟩ twinkle; ⟨fig⟩ glimmer

destemplado a out of tune; ⟨agrio⟩ harsh; ⟨tiempo⟩ unsettled; ⟨persona⟩ out of sorts

desteñir [5 & 22] vt fade; ⟨manchar⟩ discolour. ● vi fade. **~se** vpr fade; ⟨color⟩ run

desterra|do m exile. **~r** [1] vt banish

destetar vt wean

destiempo m. **a ~** at the wrong moment

destierro m exile

destil|ación f distillation. **~ar** vt distil. **~ería** f distillery

destin|ar vt destine; ⟨nombrar⟩ appoint. **~atario** m addressee. **~o** m ⟨uso⟩ use, function; ⟨lugar⟩ destination; ⟨empleo⟩ position; ⟨suerte⟩ destiny. **con ~o a** going to, bound for. **dar ~o a** find a use for

destitu|ción f dismissal. **~ir** [17] vt dismiss

destornilla|dor m screwdriver. **~r** vt unscrew

destreza f skill

destripar vt rip open

destroz|ar [10] vt ruin; ⟨fig⟩ shatter. **~o** m destruction. **causar ~os, hacer ~os** ruin

destru|cción f destruction. **~ctivo** a destructive. **~ir** [17] vt destroy; demolish ⟨edificio⟩

desunir vt separate

desus|ado a old-fashioned; ⟨insólito⟩ unusual. **~o** m disuse. **caer en ~o** become obsolete

desvaído a pale; ⟨borroso⟩ blurred; ⟨persona⟩ dull

desvalido a needy, destitute

desvalijar vt rob; burgle ⟨casa⟩

desvalorizar [10] vt devalue

desván m loft

desvanec|er [11] vt make disappear; tone down ⟨colores⟩; ⟨borrar⟩ blur; ⟨fig⟩ dispel. **~erse** vpr disappear; ⟨desmayarse⟩ faint. **~imiento** m ⟨med⟩ fainting fit

desvariar [20] vi be delirious; ⟨fig⟩ talk nonsense

desvel|ar vt keep awake. **~arse** vpr stay awake, have a sleepless night. **~o** m insomnia, sleeplessness

desvencijar vt break; ⟨agotar⟩ exhaust

desventaja f disadvantage

desventura f misfortune. **~do** a unfortunate

desverg|onzado a impudent, cheeky. **~üenza** f impudence, cheek

desvestirse [5] vpr undress

desv|iación f deviation; ⟨auto⟩ diversion. **~iar** [20] vt deflect, turn aside.

~**iarse** *vpr* be deflected; (*del camino*) make a detour; (*del tema*) stray. ~**ío** *m* diversion; (*frialdad*) *f* indifference

desvivirse *vpr* long (**por** for); (*afanarse*) strive, do one's utmost

detall|ar *vt* relate in detail. ~**e** *m* detail; (*fig*) gesture. ~**ista** *m & f* retailer. **al** ~**e** in detail; (*al por menor*) retail. **con todo** ~**e** in great detail. **en** ~**es** in detail. **¡qué** ~**e!** how thoughtful!

detect|ar *vt* detect. ~**ive** *m* detective

deten|ción *f* stopping; (*jurid*) arrest; (*en la cárcel*) detention. ~**er** [40] *vt* stop; (*jurid*) arrest; (*encarcelar*) detain; (*retrasar*) delay. ~**erse** *vpr* stop; (*entretenerse*) spend a lot of time. ~**idamente** *adv* carefully. ~**ido** *a* (*jurid*) under arrest; (*minucioso*) detailed. ● *m* prisoner

detergente *a & m* detergent

deterior|ar *vt* damage, spoil. ~**arse** *vpr* deteriorate. ~**o** *m* damage

determina|ción *f* determination; (*decisión*) decison. ~**nte** *a* decisive. ~**r** *vt* determine; (*decidir*) decide; (*fijar*) fix. **tomar una** ~**ción** make a decision

detestar *vt* detest

detonar *vi* explode

detrás *adv* behind; (*en la parte posterior*) on the back. ~ **de** behind. **por** ~ on the back; (*detrás de*) behind

detrimento *m* detriment. **en** ~ **de** to the detriment of

detrito *m* debris

deud|a *f* debt. ~**or** *m* debtor

devalua|ción *f* devaluation. ~**r** [21] *vt* devalue

devanar *vt* wind

devasta|dor *a* devastating. ~**r** *vt* devastate

devoción *f* devotion

devol|ución *f* return; (*com*) repayment, refund. ~**ver** [5] (*pp* **devuelto**) *vt* return; (*com*) repay, refund; restore ‹*edificio etc*›. ● *vi* be sick

devorar *vt* devour

devoto *a* devout; ‹*amigo etc*› devoted. ● *m* enthusiast

di *vb véase* **dar**

día *m* day. ~ **de fiesta** (public) holiday. ~ **del santo** saint's day. ~ **festivo** (public) holiday. ~ **hábil**, ~ **laborable** working day. **al** ~ up to

date. **al** ~ **siguiente** (on) the following day. **¡buenos** ~**s!** good morning! **dar los buenos** ~**s** say good morning. **de** ~ by day. **el** ~ **de hoy** today. **el** ~ **de mañana** tomorrow. **en pleno** ~ in broad daylight. **en su** ~ in due course. **todo el santo** ~ all day long. **un** ~ **de estos** one of these days. **un** ~ **sí y otro no** every other day. **vivir al** ~ live from hand to mouth

diab|etes *f* diabetes. ~**ético** *a* diabetic

diab|lo *m* devil. ~**lura** *f* mischief. ~**ólico** *a* diabolical

diácono *m* deacon

diadema *f* diadem

diáfano *a* diaphanous

diafragma *m* diaphragm

diagn|osis *f* diagnosis. ~**osticar** [7] *vt* diagnose. ~**óstico** *a* diagnostic

diagonal *a & f* diagonal

diagrama *m* diagram

dialecto *m* dialect

diálisis *f* dialysis

di|alogar [12] *vi* talk. ~**álogo** *m* dialogue

diamante *m* diamond

diámetro *m* diameter

diana *f* reveille; (*blanco*) bull's-eye

diapasón *m* (*para afinar*) tuning fork

diapositiva *f* slide, transparency

diari|amente *adv* every day. ~**o** *a* daily. ● *m* newspaper; (*libro*) diary. **a** ~**o** daily. ~**o hablado** (*en la radio*) news bulletin. **de** ~**o** everyday, ordinary

diarrea *f* diarrhoea

diatriba *f* diatribe

dibuj|ar *vt* draw. ~**o** *m* drawing. ~**os animados** cartoon (film)

diccionario *m* dictionary

diciembre *m* December

dictado *m* dictation

dictad|or *m* dictator. ~**ura** *f* dictatorship

dictamen *m* opinion; (*informe*) report

dictar *vt* dictate; pronounce ‹*sentencia etc*›

dich|a *f* happiness. ~**o** *a* said; (*susodicho*) aforementioned. ● *m* saying. ~**oso** *a* happy; (*afortunado*) fortunate. ~**o y hecho** no sooner said than done. **mejor** ~**o** rather. **por** ~**a** fortunately

didáctico *a* didactic

dieci|nueve *a & m* nineteen. **~ocho** *a & m* eighteen. **~séis** *a & m* sixteen. **~siete** *a & m* seventeen

diente *m* tooth; (*de tenedor*) prong; (*de ajo*) clove. **~ de león** dandelion. **hablar entre ~s** mumble

diesel /'disel/ *a* diesel

diestr|a *f* right hand. **~o** *a* (*derecho*) right; (*hábil*) skillful

dieta *f* diet

diez *a & m* ten

diezmar *vt* decimate

difama|ción *f* (*con palabras*) slander; (*por escrito*) libel. **~r** *vt* (*hablando*) slander; (*por escrito*) libel

diferen|cia *f* difference; (*desacuerdo*) disagreement. **~ciar** *vt* differentiate between. ● *vi* differ. **~ciarse** *vpr* differ. **~te** *a* different

difer|ido *a* (*TV etc*) recorded. **~ir** [4] *vt* postpone, defer. ● *vi* differ

dif|ícil *a* difficult. **~icultad** *f* difficulty; (*problema*) problem. **~icultar** *vt* make difficult

difteria *f* diphtheria

difundir *vt* spread; (*TV etc*) broadcast. **~se** *vpr* spread

difunto *a* late, deceased. ● *m* deceased

difusión *f* spreading

dige|rir [4] *vt* digest. **~stión** *f* digestion. **~stivo** *a* digestive

digital *a* digital; (*de los dedos*) finger

dignarse *vpr* deign. **dígnese Vd** be so kind as

dign|atario *m* dignitary. **~idad** *f* dignity; (*empleo*) office. **~o** *a* worthy; (*apropiado*) appropriate

digo *vb véase* **decir**

digresión *f* digression

dije *vb véase* **decir**

dila|ción *f* delay. **~tación** *f* dilation, expansion. **~tado** *a* extensive; (*tiempo*) long. **~tar** *vt* expand; (*med*) dilate; (*prolongar*) prolong. **~tarse** *vpr* expand; (*med*) dilate; (*extenderse*) extend. **sin ~ción** immediately

dilema *m* dilemma

diligen|cia *f* diligence; (*gestión*) job; (*historia*) stagecoach. **~te** *a* diligent

dilucidar *vt* explain; solve (*misterio*)

diluir [17] *vt* dilute

diluvio *m* flood

dimensión *f* dimension; (*tamaño*) size

diminut|ivo *a & m* diminutive. **~o** *a* minute

dimi|sión *f* resignation. **~tir** *vt/i* resign

Dinamarca *f* Denmark

dinamarqués *a* Danish. ● *m* Dane

din|ámica *f* dynamics. **~ámico** *a* dynamic. **~amismo** *m* dynamism

dinamita *f* dynamite

dínamo *m*, **dinamo** *m* dynamo

dinastía *f* dynasty

dineral *m* fortune

dinero *m* money. **~ efectivo** cash. **~ suelto** change

dinosaurio *m* dinosaur

diócesis *f* diocese

dios *m* god. **~a** *f* goddess. **¡D~ mío!** good heavens! **¡gracias a D~!** thank God! **¡válgame D~!** bless my soul!

diploma *m* diploma

diplomacia *f* diplomacy

diplomado *a* qualified

diplomático *a* diplomatic. ● *m* diplomat

diptongo *m* diphthong

diputa|ción *f* delegation. **~ción provincial** county council. **~do** *m* delegate; (*pol, en España*) member of the Cortes; (*pol, en Inglaterra*) Member of Parliament; (*pol, en Estados Unidos*) congressman

dique *m* dike

direc|ción *f* direction; (*señas*) address; (*los que dirigen*) management; (*pol*) leadership. **~ción prohibida** no entry. **~ción única** one-way. **~ta** *f* (*auto*) top gear. **~tiva** *f* directive, guideline. **~tivo** *m* executive. **~to** *a* direct; (*línea*) straight; (*tren*) through. **~tor** *m* director; (*mus*) conductor; (*de escuela etc*) headmaster; (*de periódico*) editor; (*gerente*) manager. **~tora** *f* (*de escuela etc*) headmistress. **en ~to** (*TV etc*) live. **llevar la ~ción de** direct

dirig|ente *a* ruling. ● *m & f* leader; (*de empresa*) manager. **~ible** *a & m* dirigible. **~ir** [14] *vt* direct; (*mus*) conduct; run (*empresa etc*); address (*carta etc*). **~irse** *vpr* make one's way; (*hablar*) address

discernir [1] *vt* distinguish

disciplina *f* discipline. **~r** *vt* discipline. **~rio** *a* disciplinary

discípulo *m* disciple; (*alumno*) pupil

disco *m* disc; (*mus*) record; (*deportes*) discus; (*de teléfono*) dial; (*auto*) lights; (*rail*) signal

disconforme *a* not in agreement

discontinuo *a* discontinuous

discord|ante a discordant. **~e** a discordant. **~ia** f discord

discoteca f discothèque, disco (fam); (colección de discos) record library

discreción f discretion

discrepa|ncia f discrepancy; (desacuerdo) disagreement. **~r** vi differ

discreto a discreet; (moderado) moderate; ⟨color⟩ subdued

discrimina|ción f discrimination. **~r** vt (distinguir) discriminate between; (tratar injustamente) discriminate against

disculpa f apology; (excusa) excuse. **~r** vt excuse, forgive. **~rse** vpr apologize. **dar ~s** make excuses. **pedir ~s** apologize

discurrir vt think up. ● vi think (en about); ⟨tiempo⟩ pass

discurs|ante m speaker. **~ar** vi speak (sobre about). **~o** m speech

discusión f discussion; (riña) argument. **eso no admite ~** there can be no argument about that

discuti|ble a debatable. **~r** vt discuss; (argumentar) argue about; (contradecir) contradict. ● vi discuss; (argumentar) argue

disec|ar [7] vt dissect; stuff ⟨animal muerto⟩. **~ción** f dissection

disemina|ción f dissemination. **~r** vt disseminate, spread

disentería f dysentery

disenti|miento m dissent, disagreement. **~r** [4] vi disagree (de with) (en on)

diseñ|ador m designer. **~ar** vt design. **~o** m design; (fig) sketch

disertación f dissertation

disfraz m disguise; (vestido) fancy dress. **~ar** [10] vt disguise. **~arse** vpr. **~arse de** disguise o.s. as

disfrutar vt enjoy. ● vi enjoy o.s. **~ de** enjoy

disgregar [12] vt disintegrate

disgust|ar vt displease; (molestar) annoy. **~arse** vpr get annoyed, get upset; ⟨dos personas⟩ fall out. **~o** m annoyance; (problema) trouble; (repugnancia) disgust; (riña) quarrel; (dolor) sorrow, grief

disiden|cia f disagreement, dissent. **~te** a & m & f dissident

disímil a (LAm) dissimilar

disimular vt conceal. ● vi pretend

disipa|ción f dissipation; (de dinero) squandering. **~r** vt dissipate; (derrochar) squander

diskette m floppy disk

dislocarse [7] vpr dislocate

disminu|ción f decrease. **~ir** [17] vi diminish

disociar vt dissociate

disolver [2, pp **disuelto**] vt dissolve. **~se** vpr dissolve

disonante a dissonant

dispar a different

disparar vt fire. ● vi shoot (contra at)

disparat|ado a absurd. **~ar** vi talk nonsense. **~e** m silly thing; (error) mistake. **decir ~es** talk nonsense. ¡qué **~e!** how ridiculous! **un ~e** (mucho, fam) a lot, an awful lot (fam)

disparidad f disparity

disparo m (acción) firing; (tiro) shot

dispensar vt distribute; (disculpar) excuse. ¡**Vd dispense!** forgive me

dispers|ar vt scatter, disperse. **~arse** vpr scatter, disperse. **~ión** f dispersion. **~o** a scattered

dispon|er [34] vt arrange; (preparar) prepare. ● vi. **~er de** have; (vender etc) dispose of. **~erse** vpr get ready. **~ibilidad** f availability. **~ible** a available

disposición f arrangement; (aptitud) talent; (disponibilidad) disposal; (jurid) order, decree. **~ de ánimo** frame of mind. **a la ~ de** at the disposal of. **a su ~** at your service

dispositivo m device

dispuesto a ready; (hábil) clever; (inclinado) disposed; (servicial) helpful

disputa f dispute. **~r** vt dispute. ● vi. **~r por** argue about; (competir para) compete for. **sin ~** undoubtedly

distan|cia f distance. **~ciar** vt space out; (en deportes) outdistance. **~ciarse** vpr ⟨dos personas⟩ fall out. **~te** a distant. **a ~cia** from a distance. **guardar las ~cias** keep one's distance

distar vi be away; (fig) be far. **dista 5 kilómetros** it's 5 kilometres away

distin|ción f distinction. **~guido** a distinguished; (en cartas) Honoured. **~guir** [13] vt/i distinguish. **~guirse** vpr distinguish o.s.; (diferenciarse) differ; (verse) be visible. **~tivo** a distinctive. ● m badge. **~to** a different; (claro) distinct

distorsión f distortion; (med) sprain

distra|cción f amusement; (descuido) absent-mindedness, inattention. **~er** [41] vt distract; (divertir)

amuse; embezzle ⟨*fondos*⟩. ● *vi* be
entertaining. **~erse** *vpr* amuse o.s.;
(*descuidarse*) not pay attention.
~ido *a* amusing; (*desatento*)
absent-minded

distribu|ción *f* distribution. **~idor**
m distributor, agent. **~idor automático** vending machine. **~ir** [17] *vt*
distribute

distrito *m* district

disturbio *m* disturbance

disuadir *vt* dissuade

diurético *a* & *m* diuretic

diurno *a* daytime

divagar [12] *vi* (*al hablar*) digress

diván *m* settee, sofa

diverg|encia *f* divergence. **~ente** *a*
divergent. **~ir** [14] *vi* diverge

diversidad *f* diversity

diversificar [7] *vt* diversify

diversión *f* amusement, enter-
tainment; (*pasatiempo*) pastime

diverso *a* different

diverti|do *a* amusing; (*que tiene gra-
cia*) funny; (*agradable*) enjoyable.
~r [4] *vt* amuse, entertain. **~rse** *vpr*
enjoy o.s.

dividir *vt* divide; (*repartir*) share out

divin|idad *f* divinity. **~o** *a* divine

divisa *f* emblem. **~s** *fpl* foreign
exchange

divisar *vt* make out

divis|ión *f* division. **~or** *m* divisor.
~orio *a* dividing

divorci|ado *a* divorced. ● *m* divor-
cee. **~ar** *vt* divorce. **~arse** *vpr* get
divorced. **~o** *m* divorce

divulgar [12] *vt* divulge; (*propagar*)
spread. **~se** *vpr* become known

do *m* C; (*solfa*) doh

dobl|adillo *m* hem; (*de pantalón*)
turn-up (*Brit*), cuff (*Amer*). **~ado** *a*
double; (*plegado*) folded; ⟨*película*⟩
dubbed. **~ar** *vt* double; (*plegar*)
fold; (*torcer*) bend; turn ⟨*esquina*⟩;
dub ⟨*película*⟩. ● *vi* turn; ⟨*campana*⟩
toll. **~arse** *vpr* double; (*encorvarse*)
bend; (*ceder*) give in. **~e** *a* double.
● *m* double; (*pliegue*) fold. **~egar**
[12] *vt* (*fig*) force to give in. **~egarse**
vpr give in. **el ~e** twice as much

doce *a* & *m* twelve. **~na** *f* dozen.
~no *a* twelfth

docente *a* teaching. ● *m* & *f* teacher

dócil *a* obedient

doct|o *a* learned. **~or** *m* doctor. **~or-
ado** *m* doctorate. **~rina** *f* doctrine

document|ación *f* documentation;
papers. **~al** *a* & *m* documentary.
~ar *vt* document. **~arse** *vpr* gather
information. **~o** *m* document. **D~o
Nacional de Identidad** national
identity card

dogm|a *m* dogma. **~ático** *a*
dogmatic

dólar *m* dollar

dol|er [2] *vi* hurt, ache; (*fig*) grieve.
me duele la cabeza my head hurts.
le duele el estómago he has a pain
in his stomach. **~erse** *vpr* regret;
(*quejarse*) complain. **~or** *m* pain;
(*sordo*) ache; (*fig*) sorrow. **~oroso** *a*
painful. **~or de cabeza** headache.
~or de muelas toothache

domar *vt* tame; break in ⟨*caballo*⟩

dom|esticar [7] *vt* domesticate. **~és-
tico** *a* domestic. ● *m* servant

domicilio *m* home. **a ~** at home. **servicio a ~** home delivery service

domina|ción *f* domination. **~nte** *a*
dominant; ⟨*persona*⟩ domineering.
~r *vt* dominate; (*contener*) control;
(*conocer*) have a good knowledge of.
● *vi* dominate; (*destacarse*) stand
out. **~rse** *vpr* control o.s.

domin|go *m* Sunday. **~guero** *a*
Sunday. **~ical** *a* Sunday

dominio *m* authority; (*territorio*)
domain; (*fig*) good knowledge

dominó *m* (*juego*) dominoes

don *m* talent, gift; (*en un sobre*) Mr.
~ Pedro Pedro. **tener ~ de lenguas**
have a gift for languages. **tener ~
de gentes** have a way with people

donación *f* donation

donaire *m* grace, charm

dona|nte *m* (*de sangre*) donor. **~r** *vt*
donate

doncella *f* (*criada*) maid

donde *adv* where

dónde *adv* where? **¿hasta ~?** how
far? **¿por ~?** whereabouts?; (*¿por qué
camino?*) which way? **¿a ~ vas?**
where are you going? **¿de ~ eres?**
where are you from?

dondequiera *adv* anywhere; (*en
todas partes*) everywhere. **~ que**
wherever. **por ~** everywhere

doña *f* (*en un sobre*) Mrs. **~ María**
María

dora|do *a* golden; (*cubierto de oro*)
gilt. **~dura** *f* gilding. **~r** *vt* gilt;
(*culin*) brown

dormi|lón *m* sleepyhead. ● *a* lazy.
~r [6] *vt* send to sleep. ● *vi* sleep.
~rse *vpr* go to sleep. **~tar** *vi* doze.
~torio *m* bedroom. **~r la siesta**

have an afternoon nap, have a siesta. **echarse a dormir** go to bed

dors|al *a* back. ● *m* (*en deportes*) number. ~**o** *m* back

dos *a* & *m* two. ~**cientos** *a* & *m* two hundred. **cada** ~ **por tres** every five minutes. **de** ~ **en** ~ in twos, in pairs. **en un** ~ **por tres** in no time. **los dos, las dos** both (of them)

dosi|ficar [7] *vt* dose; (*fig*) measure out. ~**s** *f* dose

dot|ado *a* gifted. ~**ar** *vt* give a dowry; (*proveer*) endow (**de** with). ~**e** *m* dowry

doy *vb véase* **dar**

dragar [12] *vt* dredge

drago *m* dragon tree

dragón *m* dragon

dram|a *m* drama; (*obra de teatro*) play. ~**ático** *a* dramatic. ~**atizar** [10] *vt* dramatize. ~**aturgo** *m* playwright

drástico *a* drastic

droga *f* drug. ~**dicto** *m* drug addict. ~**do** *a* drugged. ~**r** [12] *vt* drug. ~**rse** *vpr* take drugs. ~**ta** *m* & *f* (*fam*) drug addict

droguería *f* hardware shop (*Brit*), hardware store (*Amer*)

dromedario *m* dromedary

ducha *f* shower. ~**rse** *vpr* have a shower

dud|a *f* doubt. ~**ar** *vt/i* doubt. ~**oso** *a* doubtful; (*sospechoso*) dubious. **poner en** ~**a** question. **sin** ~**a** (**alguna**) without a doubt

duelo *m* duel; (*luto*) mourning

duende *m* imp

dueñ|a *f* owner, proprietress; (*de una pensión*) landlady. ~**o** *m* owner, proprietor; (*de una pensión*) landlord

duermo *vb véase* **dormir**

dul|ce *a* sweet; (*agua*) fresh; (*suave*) soft, gentle. ● *m* sweet. ~**zura** *f* sweetness; (*fig*) gentleness

duna *f* dune

dúo *m* duet, duo

duodécimo *a* & *m* twelfth

duplica|do *a* in duplicate. ● *m* duplicate. ~**r** [7] *vt* duplicate. ~**rse** *vpr* double

duque *m* duke. ~**sa** *f* duchess

dura|ción *f* duration, length. ~**dero** *a* lasting

durante *prep* during, in; (*medida de tiempo*) for. ~ **todo el año** all year round

durar *vi* last

durazno *m* (*LAm, fruta*) peach

dureza *f* hardness, toughness; (*med*) hard patch

durmiente *a* sleeping

duro *a* hard; (*culin*) tough; (*fig*) harsh. ● *adv* hard. ● *m* five-peseta coin. **ser** ~ **de oído** be hard of hearing

E

e *conj* and

ebanista *m* & *f* cabinet-maker

ébano *m* ebony

ebri|edad *f* drunkenness. ~**o** *a* drunk

ebullición *f* boiling

eccema *m* eczema

eclesiástico *a* ecclesiastical. ● *m* clergyman

eclipse *m* eclipse

eco *m* echo. **hacer(se)** ~ echo

ecolog|ía *f* ecology. ~**ista** *m* & *f* ecologist

economato *m* cooperative store

econ|omía *f* economy; (*ciencia*) economics. ~**ómicamente** *adv* economically. ~**ómico** *a* economic(al); (*no caro*) inexpensive. ~**omista** *m* & *f* economist. ~**omizar** [10] *vt/i* economize

ecuación *f* equation

ecuador *m* equator. **el E**~ Ecuador

ecuánime *a* level-headed; (*imparcial*) impartial

ecuanimidad *f* equanimity

ecuatoriano *a* & *m* Ecuadorian

ecuestre *a* equestrian

echar *vt* throw; post ‹*carta*›; give off ‹*olor*›; pour ‹*líquido*›; sprout ‹*hojas etc*›; (*despedir*) throw out; dismiss ‹*empleado*›; (*poner*) put on; put out ‹*raíces*›; show ‹*película*›. ~**se** *vpr* throw o.s.; (*tumbarse*) lie down. ~ **a** start. ~ **a perder** spoil. ~ **de menos** miss. ~**se atrás** (*fig*) back down. **echárselas de** feign

edad *f* age. ~ **avanzada** old age. **E**~ **de Piedra** Stone Age. **E**~ **Media** Middle Ages. **¿qué** ~ **tiene?** how old is he?

edición *f* edition; (*publicación*) publication

edicto *m* edict

edific|ación *f* building. ~**ante** *a* edifying. ~**ar** [7] *vt* build; (*fig*) edify. ~**io** *m* building; (*fig*) structure

Edimburgo *m* Edinburgh

edit|ar *vt* publish. **~or** *a* publishing. ● *m* publisher. **~orial** *a* editorial. ● *m* leading article. ● *f* publishing house

edredón *m* eiderdown

educa|ción *f* upbringing; (*modales*) (good) manners; (*enseñanza*) education. **~do** *a* polite. **~dor** *m* teacher. **~r** [7] *vt* bring up; (*enseñar*) educate. **~tivo** *a* educational. **bien ~do** polite. **falta de ~ción** rudeness, bad manners. **mal ~do** rude

edulcorante *m* sweetener

EE.UU. *abrev* (*Estados Unidos*) USA, United States (of America)

efect|ivamente *adv* really; (*por supuesto*) indeed. **~ivo** *a* effective; (*auténtico*) real; (*empleo*) permanent. ● *m* cash. **~o** *m* effect; (*impresión*) impression. **~os** *mpl* belongings; (*com*) goods. **~uar** [21] *vt* carry out, effect; make (*viaje, compras etc*). **en ~o** in fact; (*por supuesto*) indeed

efervescen|cia *f* effervescence; (*bebidas*) fizzy

efica|cia *f* effectiveness; (*de persona*) efficiency. **~z** *a* effective; (*persona*) efficient

eficien|cia *f* efficiency. **~te** *a* efficient

efigie *f* effigy

efímero *a* ephemeral

efluvio *m* outflow

efusi|ón *n* effusion. **~vo** *a* effusive; (*gracias*) warm

Egeo *m*. **mar ~** Aegean Sea

égida *f* aegis

egipcio *a & m* Egyptian

Egipto *m* Egypt

ego|céntrico *a* egocentric. ● *m* egocentric person. **~ísmo** *m* selfishness. **~ísta** *a* selfish. ● *m* selfish person

egregio *a* eminent

egresar *vi* (*LAm*) leave; (*univ*) graduate

eje *m* axis; (*tec*) axle

ejecu|ción *f* execution; (*mus etc*) performance. **~tante** *m & f* executor; (*mus etc*) performer. **~tar** *vt* carry out; (*mus etc*) perform; (*matar*) execute

ejecutivo *m* director, manager

ejempl|ar *a* exemplary. ● *m* (*ejemplo*) example, specimen; (*libro*) copy; (*revista*) issue, number. **~ificar** [7] *vt* exemplify. **~o** *m* example.

dar ~o set an example. **por ~o** for example. **sin ~** unprecedented

ejerc|er [9] *vt* exercise; practise (*profesión*); exert (*influencia*). ● *vi* practise. **~icio** *m* exercise; (*de una profesión*) practice. **~itar** *vt* exercise. **~itarse** *vpr* exercise. **hacer ~icios** take exercise

ejército *m* army

el *art def m* (*pl* **los**) the. ● *pron* (*pl* **los**) the one. **~ de Antonio** Antonio's. **~ que** whoever, the one

él *pron* (*persona*) he; (*persona con prep*) him; (*cosa*) it. **el libro de ~** his book

elabora|ción *f* processing; (*fabricación*) manufacture. **~r** *vt* process; manufacture (*producto*); (*producir*) produce

el|asticidad *f* elasticity. **~ástico** *a & m* elastic

elec|ción *f* choice; (*de político etc*) election. **~ciones** *fpl* (*pol*) election. **~tor** *m* voter. **~torado** *m* electorate. **~toral** *a* electoral

electri|dad *f* electricity. **~sta** *m & f* electrician

eléctrico *a* electric; (*de la electricidad*) electrical

electrificar [7] *vt*, **electrizar** [10] *vt* electrify

electrocutar *vt* electrocute

electrodo *m* electrode

electrodoméstico *a* electrical household. **~s** *mpl* electrical household appliances

electrólisis *f* electrolysis

electrón *m* electron

electrónic|a *f* electronics. **~o** *a* electronic

elefante *m* elephant

elegan|cia *f* elegance. **~te** *a* elegant

elegía *f* elegy

elegi|ble *a* eligible. **~do** *a* chosen. **~r** [5 & 14] *vt* choose; (*por votación*) elect

element|al *a* elementary. **~o** *m* element; (*persona*) person, bloke (*fam*). **~os** *mpl* (*nociones*) basic principles

elenco *m* (*en el teatro*) cast

eleva|ción *f* elevation; (*de precios*) rise, increase; (*acción*) raising. **~dor** *m* (*LAm*) lift. **~r** *vt* raise; (*promover*) promote

elimina|ción *f* elimination. **~r** *vt* eliminate. **~toria** *f* preliminary heat

el|ipse *f* ellipse. **~íptico** *a* elliptical

élite /e'lit, e'lite/ *f* elite

elixir *m* elixir

elocución *f* elocution

elocuen|cia *f* eloquence. **~te** *a* eloquent

elogi|ar *vt* praise. **~o** *m* praise

elote *m* (*Mex*) corn on the cob

eludir *vt* avoid, elude

ella *pron* (*persona*) she; (*persona con prep*) her; (*cosa*) it. **~s** *pron pl* they; (*con prep*) them. **el libro de ~** her book. **el libro de ~s** their book

ello *pron* it

ellos *pron pl* they; (*con prep*) them. **el libro de ~** their book

emaciado *a* emaciated

emana|ción *f* emanation. **~r** *vi* emanate (**de** from); (*originarse*) originate (**de** from, in)

emancipa|ción *f* emancipation. **~do** *a* emancipated. **~r** *vt* emancipate. **~rse** *vpr* become emancipated

embadurnar *vt* smear

embajad|a *f* embassy. **~or** *m* ambassador

embalar *vt* pack

embaldosar *vt* tile

embalsamar *vt* embalm

embalse *m* dam; (*pantano*) reservoir

embaraz|ada *a* pregnant. ● *f* pregnant woman. **~ar** [10] *vt* hinder. **~o** *m* hindrance; (*de mujer*) pregnancy. **~oso** *a* awkward, embarrassing

embar|cación *f* boat. **~cadero** *m* jetty, pier. **~car** [7] *vt* embark (*personas*); ship (*mercancías*). **~carse** *vpr* embark. **~carse en** (*fig*) embark upon

embargo *m* embargo; (*jurid*) seizure. **sin ~** however

embarque *m* loading

embarullar *vt* muddle

embaucar [7] *vt* deceive

embeber *vt* absorb; (*empapar*) soak. ● *vi* shrink. **~se** *vpr* be absorbed

embelesar *vt* delight. **~se** *vpr* be delighted

embellecer [11] *vt* embellish

embesti|da *f* attack. **~r** [5] *vt/i* attack

emblema *m* emblem

embobar *vt* amaze

embobecer [11] *vt* make silly. **~se** *vpr* get silly

embocadura *f* (*de un río*) mouth

emboquillado *a* tipped

embolsar *vt* pocket

emborrachar *vt* get drunk. **~se** *vpr* get drunk

emborrascarse [7] *vpr* get stormy

emborronar *vt* blot

embosca|da *f* ambush. **~rse** [7] *vpr* lie in wait

embotar *vt* blunt; (*fig*) dull

embotella|miento *m* (*de vehículos*) traffic jam. **~r** *vt* bottle

embrague *m* clutch

embriag|ar [12] *vt* get drunk; (*fig*) intoxicate; (*fig, enajenar*) enrapture. **~arse** *vpr* get drunk. **~uez** *f* drunkenness; (*fig*) intoxication

embrión *m* embryo

embroll|ar *vt* mix up; involve (*personas*). **~arse** *vpr* get into a muddle; *en un asunto*) get involved. **~o** *m* tangle; (*fig*) muddle. **~ón** *m* troublemaker

embromar *vt* make fun of; (*engañar*) fool

embruja|do *a* bewitched; (*casa etc*) haunted. **~r** *vt* bewitch

embrutecer [11] *vt* brutalize

embuchar *vt* wolf (*comida*)

embudo *m* funnel

embuste *m* lie. **~ro** *a* deceitful. ● *m* liar

embuti|do *m* (*culin*) sausage. **~r** *vt* stuff

emergencia *f* emergency; (*acción de emerger*) emergence. **en caso de ~** in case of emergency

emerger [14] *vi* appear, emerge; (*submarino*) surface

emigra|ción *f* emigration. **~nte** *m* & *f* emigrant. **~r** *vi* emigrate

eminen|cia *f* eminence. **~te** *a* eminent

emisario *m* emissary

emis|ión *f* emission; (*de dinero*) issue; (*TV etc*) broadcast. **~or** *a* issuing; (*TV etc*) broadcasting. **~ora** *f* radio station

emitir *vt* emit; let out (*grito*); (*TV etc*) broadcast; (*expresar*) express; (*poner en circulación*) issue

emoci|ón *f* emotion; (*excitación*) excitement. **~onado** *a* moved. **~onante** *a* exciting; (*conmovedor*) moving. **~onar** *vt* excite; (*conmover*) move. **~onarse** *vpr* get excited; (*conmoverse*) be moved. **¡qué ~ón!** how exciting!

emotivo *a* emotional; (*conmovedor*) moving

empacar [7] *vt* (*LAm*) pack

empacho *m* indigestion; (*vergüenza*) embarrassment

empadronar *vt* register. ~**se** *vpr* register

empalagoso *a* sickly; (*demasiado amable*) ingratiating; (*demasiado sentimental*) mawkish

empalizada *f* fence

empalm|ar *vt* connect, join. ● *vi* meet. ~**e** *m* junction; (*de trenes*) connection

empanad|a *f* (savoury) pie. ~**illa** *f* (small) pie. ~**o** *a* fried in breadcrumbs

empanizado *a* (*Mex*) fried in breadcrumbs

empantanar *vt* flood. ~**se** *vpr* become flooded; (*fig*) get bogged down

empañar *vt* mist; dull ⟨*metales etc*⟩; (*fig*) tarnish. ~**se** *vpr* ⟨*cristales*⟩ steam up

empapar *vt* soak; (*absorber*) soak up. ~**se** *vpr* be soaked

empapela|do *m* wallpaper. ~**r** *vt* paper; (*envolver*) wrap (in paper)

empaquetar *vt* package; pack together ⟨*personas*⟩

emparedado *m* sandwich

emparejar *vt* match; (*nivelar*) make level. ~**se** *vpr* pair off

empast|ar *vt* fill ⟨*muela*⟩. ~**e** *m* filling

empat|ar *vi* draw. ~**e** *m* draw

empedernido *a* inveterate; (*insensible*) hard

empedrar [1] *vt* pave

empeine *m* instep

empeñ|ado *a* in debt; (*decidido*) determined; (*acalorado*) heated. ~**ar** *vt* pawn; pledge ⟨*palabras*⟩; (*principiar*) start. ~**arse** *vpr* (*endeudarse*) get into debt; (*meterse*) get involved; (*estar decidido a*) insist (*en* on). ~**o** *m* pledge; (*resolución*) determination. **casa de** ~**s** pawnshop

empeorar *vt* make worse. ● *vi* worse. ~**se** *vpr* get worse

empequeñecer [11] *vt* dwarf; (*fig*) belittle

empera|dor *m* emperor. ~**triz** *f* empress

empezar [1 & 10] *vt/i* start, begin. **para** ~ to begin with

empina|do *a* upright; ⟨*cuesta*⟩ steep. ~**r** *vt* raise. ~**rse** *vpr* ⟨*persona*⟩ stand on tiptoe; ⟨*animal*⟩ rear

empírico *a* empirical

emplasto *m* plaster

emplaza|miento *m* (*jurid*) summons; (*lugar*) site. ~**r** [10] *vt* summon; (*situar*) site

emple|ado *m* employee. ~**ar** *vt* use; employ ⟨*persona*⟩; spend ⟨*tiempo*⟩. ~**arse** *vpr* be used; ⟨*persona*⟩ be employed. ~**o** *m* use; (*trabajo*) employment; (*puesto*) job

empobrecer [11] *vt* impoverish. ~**se** *vpr* become poor

empolvar *vt* powder

empoll|ar *vt* incubate ⟨*huevos*⟩; (*estudiar, fam*) swot up (*Brit*), grind away at (*Amer*). ● *vi* ⟨*ave*⟩ sit; ⟨*estudiante*⟩ swot (*Brit*), grind away (*Amer*). ~**ón** *m* swot

emponzoñar *vt* poison

emporio *m* emporium; (*LAm, almacén*) department store

empotra|do *a* built-in, fitted. ~**r** *vt* fit

emprendedor *a* enterprising

emprender *vt* undertake; set out on ⟨*viaje etc*⟩. ~**la con uno** pick a fight with s.o.

empresa *f* undertaking; (*com*) company, firm. ~**rio** *m* impresario; (*com*) contractor

empréstito *m* loan

empuj|ar *vt* push; press ⟨*botón*⟩. ~**e** *m* push, shove; (*fig*) drive. ~**ón** *m* push, shove

empuñar *vt* grasp; take up ⟨*pluma, espada*⟩

emular *vt* emulate

emulsión *f* emulsion

en *prep* in; (*sobre*) on; (*dentro*) inside, in; (*con dirección*) into; (*medio de transporte*) by. ~ **casa** at home. ~ **coche** by car. ~ **10 días** in 10 days. **de pueblo** ~ **pueblo** from town to town

enagua *f* petticoat

enajena|ción *f* alienation; (*éxtasis*) rapture. ~**r** *vt* alienate; (*volver loco*) drive mad; (*fig, extasiar*) enrapture. ~**ción mental** insanity

enamora|do *a* in love. ● *m* lover. ~**r** *vt* win the love of. ~**rse** *vpr* fall in love (**de** with)

enan|ito *m* dwarf. ~**o** *a & m* dwarf

enardecer [11] *vt* inflame. ~**se** *vpr* get excited (**por** about)

encabeza|miento *m* heading; (*de periódico*) headline. ~**r** [10] *vt* introduce ⟨*escrito*⟩; (*poner título a*) entitle; head ⟨*una lista*⟩; lead ⟨*revolución etc*⟩; (*empadronar*) register

encadenar *vt* chain; (*fig*) tie down

encaj|ar *vt* fit; fit together ‹*varias piezas*›. • *vi* fit; (*estar de acuerdo*) tally. **~arse** *vpr* squeeze into. **~e** *m* lace; (*acción de encajar*) fitting

encajonar *vt* box; (*en sitio estrecho*) squeeze in

encalar *vt* whitewash

encallar *vt* run aground; (*fig*) get bogged down

encaminar *vt* direct. **~se** *vpr* make one's way

encandilar *vt* (*pasmar*) bewilder; (*estimular*) stimulate

encanecer [11] *vi* go grey

encant|ado *a* enchanted; (*hechizado*) bewitched; ‹*casa etc*› haunted. **~ador** *a* charming. • *m* magician. **~amiento** *m* magic. **~ar** *vt* bewitch; (*fig*) charm, delight. **~o** *m* magic; (*fig*) delight. ¡**~ado!** pleased to meet you! **me ~a la leche** I love milk

encapotado *a* ‹*cielo*› overcast

encapricharse *vpr*. **~ con** take a fancy to

encarar *vt* face. **~se** *vpr*. **~se con** face

encarcelar *vt* imprison

encarecer [11] *vt* put up the price of; (*alabar*) praise. • *vi* go up

encarg|ado *a* in charge. • *m* manager, attendant, person in charge. **~ar** [12] *vt* entrust; (*pedir*) order. **~arse** *vpr* take charge (de of). **~o** *m* job; (*com*) order; (*recado*) errand. **hecho de ~o** made to measure

encariñarse *vpr*. **~ con** take to, become fond of

encarna|ción *f* incarnation. **~do** *a* incarnate; (*rojo*) red. • *m* red

encarnizado *a* bitter

encarpetar *vt* file; (*LAm, dar carpetazo*) shelve

encarrilar *vt* put back on the rails; (*fig*) direct, put on the right road

encasillar *vt* pigeonhole

encastillarse *vpr*. **~ en** (*fig*) stick to

encauzar [10] *vt* channel

encend|edor *m* lighter. **~er** [1] *vt* light; (*pegar fuego a*) set fire to; switch on, turn on ‹*aparato eléctrico*›; (*fig*) arouse. **~erse** *vpr* light; (*prender fuego*) catch fire; (*excitarse*) get excited; (*ruborizarse*) blush. **~ido** *a* lit; ‹*aparato eléctrico*› on; (*rojo*) bright red. • *m* (*auto*) ignition

encera|do *a* waxed. • *m* (*pizarra*) blackboard. **~r** *vt* wax

encerr|ar [1] *vt* shut in; (*con llave*) lock up; (*fig, contener*) contain. **~ona** *f* trap

encía *f* gum

encíclica *f* encyclical

enciclop|edia *f* encyclopaedia. **~édico** *a* encyclopaedic

encierro *m* confinement; (*cárcel*) prison

encima *adv* on top; (*arriba*) above. **~ de** on, on top of; (*sobre*) over; (*además de*) besides, as well as. **por ~** on top; (*a la ligera*) superficially. **por ~ de todo** above all

encina *f* holm oak

encinta *a* pregnant

enclave *m* enclave

enclenque *a* weak; (*enfermizo*) sickly

encog|er [14] *vt* shrink; (*contraer*) contract. **~erse** *vpr* shrink. **~erse de hombros** shrug one's shoulders. **~ido** *a* shrunk; (*fig, tímido*) timid

encolar *vt* glue; (*pegar*) stick

encolerizar [10] *vt* make angry. **~se** *vpr* get angry, lose one's temper

encomendar [1] *vt* entrust

encomi|ar *vt* praise. **~o** *m* praise

encono *m* bitterness, ill will

encontra|do *a* contrary, conflicting. **~r** [2] *vt* find; (*tropezar con*) meet. **~rse** *vpr* meet; (*hallarse*) be. **no ~rse** feel uncomfortable

encorvar *vt* bend, curve. **~se** *vpr* stoop

encrespado *a* ‹*pelo*› curly; ‹*mar*› rough

encrucijada *f* crossroads

encuaderna|ción *f* binding. **~dor** *m* bookbinder. **~r** *vt* bind

encuadrar *vt* frame

encub|ierto *a* hidden. **~rir** [*pp* encubierto] *vt* hide, conceal; shelter ‹*delincuente*›

encuentro *m* meeting; (*colisión*) crash; (*en deportes*) match; (*mil*) skirmish

encuesta *f* survey; (*investigación*) inquiry

encumbra|do *a* eminent. **~r** *vt* (*fig, elevar*) exalt. **~rse** *vpr* rise

encurtidos *mpl* pickles

encharcar [7] *vt* flood. **~se** *vpr* be flooded

enchuf|ado *a* switched on. **~ar** *vt* plug in; fit together ‹*tubos etc*›. **~e** *m* socket; (*clavija*) plug; (*de tubos* *etc*) joint; (*fig, empleo, fam*) cushy job; (*influencia, fam*) influence. **tener** ~**e** have friends in the right places

endeble *a* weak

endemoniado *a* possessed; (*malo*) wicked

enderezar [10] *vt* straighten out; (*poner vertical*) put upright (again); (*fig, arreglar*) put right, sort out; (*dirigir*) direct. ~**se** *vpr* straighten out

endeudarse *vpr* get into debt

endiablado *a* possessed; (*malo*) wicked

endomingarse [12] *vpr* dress up

endosar *vt* endorse ‹*cheque etc*›; (*fig, fam*) lumber

endrogarse [12] *vpr* (*Mex*) get into debt

endulzar [10] *vt* sweeten; (*fig*) soften

endurecer [11] *vt* harden. ~**se** *vpr* harden; (*fig*) become hardened

enema *m* enema

enemi|go *a* hostile. ● *m* enemy. ~**stad** *f* enmity. ~**star** *vt* make an enemy of. ~**starse** *vpr* fall out (con with)

en|ergía *f* energy. ~**érgico** *a* ‹*persona*› lively; ‹*decisión*› forceful

energúmeno *m* madman

enero *m* January

enervar *vt* enervate

enésimo *a* nth, umpteenth (*fam*)

enfad|adizo *a* irritable. ~**ado** *a* cross, angry. ~**ar** *vt* make cross, anger; (*molestar*) annoy. ~**arse** *vpr* get cross. ~**o** *m* anger; (*molestia*) annoyance

énfasis *m invar* emphasis, stress. **poner** ~ stress, emphasize

enfático *a* emphatic

enferm|ar *vi* fall ill. ~**edad** *f* illness. ~**era** *f* nurse. ~**ería** *f* sick bay. ~**ero** *m* (male) nurse. ~**izo** *a* sickly. ~**o** *a* ill. ● *m* patient

enflaquecer [11] *vt* make thin. ● *vi* lose weight

enfo|car [7] *vt* shine on; focus ‹*lente etc*›; (*fig*) consider. ~**que** *m* focus; (*fig*) point of view

enfrascarse [7] *vpr* (*fig*) be absorbed

enfrentar *vt* face, confront; (*poner frente a frente*) bring face to face. ~**se** *vpr*. ~**se con** confront; (*en deportes*) meet

enfrente *adv* opposite. ~ **de** opposite. **de** ~ opposite

enfria|miento *m* cooling; (*catarro*) cold. ~**r** [20] *vt* cool (down); (*fig*) cool down. ~**rse** *vpr* go cold; (*fig*) cool off

enfurecer [11] *vt* infuriate. ~**se** *vpr* lose one's temper; ‹*mar*› get rough

enfurruñarse *vpr* sulk

engalanar *vt* adorn. ~**se** *vpr* dress up

enganchar *vt* hook; hang up ‹*ropa*›. ~**se** *vpr* get caught; (*mil*) enlist

engañ|ar *vt* deceive, trick; (*ser infiel*) be unfaithful. ~**arse** *vpr* be wrong, be mistaken; (*no admitir la verdad*) deceive o.s. ~**o** *m* deceit, trickery; (*error*) mistake. ~**oso** *a* deceptive; ‹*persona*› deceitful

engarzar [10] *vt* string ‹*cuentas*›; set ‹*joyas*›; (*fig*) link

engatusar *vt* (*fam*) coax

engendr|ar *vt* breed; (*fig*) produce. ~**o** *m* (*monstruo*) monster; (*fig*) brainchild

englobar *vt* include

engomar *vt* glue

engordar *vt* fatten. ● *vi* get fatter, put on weight

engorro *m* nuisance

engranaje *m* (*auto*) gear

engrandecer [11] *vt* (*enaltecer*) exalt, raise

engrasar *vt* grease; (*con aceite*) oil; (*ensuciar*) make greasy

engreído *a* arrogant

engrosar [2] *vt* swell. ● *vi* ‹*persona*› get fatter; ‹*río*› swell

engullir [22] *vt* gulp down

enharinar *vt* sprinkle with flour

enhebrar *vt* thread

enhorabuena *f* congratulations. **dar la** ~ congratulate

enigm|a *m* enigma. ~**ático** *a* enigmatic

enjabonar *vt* soap; (*fig, fam*) butter up

enjalbegar [12] *vt* whitewash

enjambre *m* swarm

enjaular *vt* put in a cage

enjuag|ar [12] *vt* rinse (out). ~**atorio** *m* mouthwash. ~**ue** *m* rinsing; (*para la boca*) mouthwash

enjugar [12] *vt* dry; (*limpiar*) wipe; cancel ‹*deuda*›

enjuiciar *vt* pass judgement on

enjuto *a* ‹*persona*› skinny

enlace *m* connection; (*matrimonial*) wedding

enlatar *vt* tin, can

enlazar [10] *vt* tie together; (*fig*) relate, connect

enlodar *vt*, **enlodazar** [10] *vt* cover in mud

enloquecer [11] *vt* drive mad. ● *vi* go mad. **~se** *vpr* go mad

enlosar *vt* (*con losas*) pave; (*con baldosas*) tile

enlucir [11] *vt* plaster

enluta|do *a* in mourning. **~r** *vt* dress in mourning; (*fig*) sadden

enmarañar *vt* tangle (up), entangle; (*confundir*) confuse. **~se** *vpr* get into a tangle; (*confundirse*) get confused

enmarcar [7] *vt* frame

enmascarar *vt* mask. **~se de** masquerade as

enm|endar *vt* correct. **~endarse** *vpr* mend one's way. **~ienda** *f* correction; (*de ley etc*) amendment

enmohecerse [11] *vpr* (*con óxido*) go rusty; (*con hongos*) go mouldy

enmudecer [11] *vi* be dumbstruck; (*callar*) say nothing

ennegrecer [11] *vt* blacken

ennoblecer [11] *vt* ennoble; (*fig*) add style to

enoj|adizo *a* irritable. **~ado** *a* angry, cross. **~ar** *vt* make cross, anger; (*molestar*) annoy. **~arse** *vpr* get cross. **~o** *m* anger; (*molestia*) annoyance. **~oso** *a* annoying

enorgullecerse [11] *vpr* be proud

enorm|e *a* enormous; (*malo*) wicked. **~emente** *adv* enormously. **~idad** *f* immensity; (*atrocidad*) enormity. **me gusta una ~idad** I like it enormously

enrabiar *vt* infuriate

enraizar [10 & 20] *vi* take root

enrarecido *a* rarefied

enrasar *vt* make level

enred|adera *f* creeper. **~adero** *a* climbing. **~ar** *vt* tangle (up), entangle; (*confundir*) confuse; (*comprometer a uno*) involve, implicate; (*sembrar la discordia*) cause trouble between. ● *vi* get up to mischief. **~ar con** fiddle with, play with. **~arse** *vpr* get into a tangle; (*confundirse*) get confused; (*persona*) get involved. **~o** *m* tangle; (*fig*) muddle, mess

enrejado *m* bars

enrevesado *a* complicated

enriquecer [11] *vt* make rich; (*fig*) enrich. **~se** *vpr* get rich

enrojecer [11] *vt* turn red, redden. **~se** *vpr* (*persona*) go red, blush

enrolar *vt* enlist

enrollar *vt* roll (up); wind (*hilo etc*)

enroscar [7] *vt* coil; (*atornillar*) screw in

ensalad|a *f* salad. **~era** *f* salad bowl. **~illa** *f* Russian salad. **armar una ~a** make a mess

ensalzar [10] *vt* praise; (*enaltecer*) exalt

ensambladura *f*, **ensamblaje** *m* (*acción*) assembling; (*efecto*) joint

ensamblar *vt* join

ensanch|ar *vt* widen; (*agrandar*) enlarge. **~arse** *vpr* get wider. **~e** *m* widening; (*de ciudad*) new district

ensangrentar [1] *vt* stain with blood

ensañarse *vpr*. **~ con** treat cruelly

ensartar *vt* string (*cuentas etc*)

ensay|ar *vt* test; rehearse (*obra de teatro etc*). **~arse** *vpr* rehearse. **~o** *m* test, trial; (*composición literaria*) essay

ensenada *f* inlet, cove

enseña|nza *f* education; (*acción de enseñar*) teaching. **~nza media** secondary education. **~r** *vt* teach; (*mostrar*) show

enseñorearse *vpr* take over

enseres *mpl* equipment

ensillar *vt* saddle

ensimismarse *vpr* be lost in thought

ensoberbecerse [11] *vpr* become conceited

ensombrecer [11] *vt* darken

ensordecer [11] *vt* deafen. ● *vi* go deaf

ensortijar *vt* curl (*pelo etc*)

ensuciar *vt* dirty. **~se** *vpr* get dirty

ensueño *m* dream

entablar *vt* (*empezar*) start

entablillar *vt* put in a splint

entalegar [12] *vt* put into a bag; (*fig*) hoard

entallar *vt* fit (*un vestido*). ● *vi* fit

entarimado *m* parquet

ente *m* entity, being; (*persona rara, fam*) odd person; (*com*) firm, company

entend|er [1] *vt* understand; (*opinar*) believe, think; (*querer decir*) mean. ● *vi* understand. **~erse** *vpr* make o.s. understood; (*comprenderse*) be understood. **~er de** know all about. **~erse con** get on with. **~ido** *a* understood; (*enterado*) well-informed. ● *interj* agreed!, OK! (*fam*). **~imiento** *m* understanding.

a mi ~er in my opinion. **dar a ~er** hint. **no darse por ~ido** pretend not to understand, turn a deaf ear

entenebrecer [11] *vt* darken. **~se** *vpr* get dark

enterado *a* well-informed; (*que sabe*) aware. **no darse por ~** pretend not to understand, turn a deaf ear

enteramente *adv* entirely, completely

enterar *vt* inform. **~se** *vpr*. **~se de** find out about, hear of. **¡entérate!** listen! **¿te enteras?** do you understand?

entereza *f* (*carácter*) strength of character

enternecer [11] *vt* (*fig*) move, touch. **~se** *vpr* be moved, be touched

entero *a* entire, whole; (*firme*) firm. **por ~** entirely, completely

enterra|dor *m* gravedigger. **~r** [1] *vt* bury

entibiar *vt* cool. **~se** *vpr* cool down; (*fig*) cool off

entidad *f* entity; (*organización*) organization; (*com*) company

entierro *m* burial; (*ceremonia*) funeral

entona|ción *f* intonation; (*fig*) arrogance. **~r** *vt* intone. ● *vi* (*mus*) be in tune; (*colores*) match. **~rse** *vpr* (*fortalecerse*) tone o.s. up; (*engreírse*) be arrogant

entonces *adv* then. **en aquel ~, por aquel ~** at that time, then

entontecer [11] *vt* make silly. **~se** *vpr* get silly

entornar *vt* half close; leave ajar (*puerta*)

entorpecer [11] *vt* (*frío etc*) numb; (*dificultar*) hinder

entra|da *f* entrance; (*acceso*) admission, entry; (*billete*) ticket; (*de datos, tec*) input. **~do** *a*. **~do en años** elderly. **ya ~da la noche** late at night. **~nte** *a* next, coming. **dar ~da a** (*admitir*) admit. **de ~da** right away.

entraña *f* (*fig*) heart. **~s** *fpl* entrails; (*fig*) heart. **~ble** *a* (*cariño etc*) deep; (*amigo*) close. **~r** *vt* involve

entrar *vt* put; (*traer*) bring. ● *vi* go in, enter; (*venir*) come in, enter; (*empezar*) start, begin. **no ~ ni salir en** have nothing to do with

entre *prep* (*de dos personas o cosas*) between; (*más de dos*) among(st)

entreab|ierto *a* half-open. **~rir** [*pp* **entreabierto**] *vt* half open

entreacto *m* interval

entrecano *a* (*pelo*) greying; (*persona*) who is going grey

entrecejo *m* forehead. **arrugar el ~, fruncir el ~** frown

entrecerrar [1] *vt* (*Amer*) half close

entrecortado *a* (*voz*) faltering; (*respiración*) laboured

entrecruzar [10] *vt* intertwine

entrega *f* handing over; (*de mercancías etc*) delivery; (*de novela etc*) instalment; (*dedicación*) commitment. **~r** [12] *vt* hand over, deliver, give. **~rse** *vpr* surrender, give o.s. up; (*dedicarse*) devote o.s. (*a* to)

entrelazar [10] *vt* intertwine

entremés *m* hors-d'oeuvre; (*en el teatro*) short comedy

entremet|er *vt* insert. **~erse** *vpr* interfere. **~ido** *a* interfering

entremezclar *vt* mix

entrena|dor *m* trainer. **~miento** *m* training. **~r** *vt* train. **~rse** *vpr* train

entrepierna *f* crotch

entresacar [7] *vt* pick out

entresuelo *m* mezzanine

entretanto *adv* meanwhile

entretejer *vt* interweave

entreten|er [40] *vt* entertain, amuse; (*detener*) delay, keep; (*mantener*) keep alive, keep going. **~erse** *vpr* amuse o.s.; (*tardar*) delay, linger. **~ido** *a* entertaining. **~imiento** *m* entertainment; (*mantenimiento*) upkeep

entrever [43] *vt* make out, glimpse

entrevista *f* interview; (*reunión*) meeting. **~rse** *vpr* have an interview

entristecer [11] *vt* sadden, make sad. **~se** *vpr* be sad

entromet|erse *vpr* interfere. **~ido** *a* interfering

entroncar [7] *vi* be related

entruchada *f*, **entruchado** *m* (*fam*) plot

entumec|erse [11] *vpr* go numb. **~ido** *a* numb

enturbiar *vt* cloud

entusi|asmar *vt* fill with enthusiasm; (*gustar mucho*) delight. **~asmarse** *vpr*. **~asmarse con** get enthusiastic about; (*ser aficionado a*) be mad about, love. **~asmo** *m* enthusiasm. **~asta** *a* enthusiastic.

● *m* & *f* enthusiast. ~**ástico** *a* enthusiastic

enumera|ción *f* count, reckoning. ~**r** *vt* enumerate

enuncia|ción *f* enunciation. ~**r** *vt* enunciate

envainar *vt* sheathe

envalentonar *vt* encourage. ~**se** *vpr* be brave, pluck up courage

envanecer [11] *vt* make conceited. ~**se** *vpr* be conceited

envas|ado *a* tinned. ● *m* packaging. ~**ar** *vt* package; (*en latas*) tin, can; (*en botellas*) bottle. ~**e** *m* packing; (*lata*) tin, can; (*botella*) bottle

envejec|er [11] *vt* make old. ● *vi* get old, grow old. ~**erse** *vpr* get old, grow old. ~**ido** *a* aged, old

envenenar *vt* poison

envergadura *f* (*alcance*) scope

envés *m* wrong side

envia|do *a* sent. ● *m* representative; (*de la prensa*) correspondent. ~**r** *vt* send

enviciar *vt* corrupt

envidi|a *f* envy; (*celos*) jealousy. ~**able** *a* enviable. ~**ar** *vt* envy, be envious of. ~**oso** *a* envious. **tener** ~**a a** envy

envilecer [11] *vt* degrade

envío *m* sending, dispatch; (*de mercancías*) consignment; (*de dinero*) remittance. ~ **contra reembolso** cash on delivery. **gastos** *mpl* **de envío** postage and packing (costs)

enviudar *vi* ⟨*mujer*⟩ become a widow, be widowed; ⟨*hombre*⟩ become a widower, be widowed

env|oltura *f* wrapping. ~**olver** [2, *pp* **envuelto**] *vt* wrap; (*cubrir*) cover; (*fig, acorralar*) corner; (*fig, enredar*) involve; (*mil*) surround. ~**olvimiento** *m* involvement. ~**uelto** *a* wrapped (up)

enyesar *vt* plaster; (*med*) put in plaster

enzima *f* enzyme

épica *f* epic

epicentro *m* epicentre

épico *a* epic

epid|emia *f* epidemic. ~**émico** *a* epidemic

epil|epsia *f* epilepsy. ~**éptico** *a* epileptic

epílogo *m* epilogue

episodio *m* episode

epístola *f* epistle

epitafio *m* epitaph

epíteto *m* epithet

epítome *m* epitome

época *f* age; (*período*) period. **hacer** ~ make history, be epoch-making

equidad *f* equity

equilátero *a* equilateral

equilibr|ar *vt* balance. ~**io** *m* balance; (*de balanza*) equilibrium. ~**ista** *m* & *f* tightrope walker

equino *a* horse, equine

equinoccio *m* equinox

equipaje *m* luggage (*esp Brit*), baggage (*esp Amer*); (*de barco*) crew

equipar *vt* equip; (*de ropa*) fit out

equiparar *vt* make equal; (*comparar*) compare

equipo *m* equipment; (*en deportes*) team

equitación *f* riding

equivale|ncia *f* equivalence. ~**nte** *a* equivalent. ~**r** [42] *vi* be equivalent; (*significar*) mean

equivoca|ción *f* mistake, error. ~**do** *a* wrong. ~**r** [7] *vt* mistake. ~**rse** *vpr* be mistaken, be wrong, make a mistake. ~**rse de** be wrong about. ~**rse de número** dial the wrong number. ~**rse si no me equivoco** if I'm not mistaken

equívoco *a* equivocal; (*sospechoso*) suspicious. ● *m* ambiguity; (*juego de palabras*) pun; (*doble sentido*) double meaning

era *f* era. ● *vb véase* **ser**

erario *m* treasury

erección *f* erection; (*fig*) establishment

eremita *m* hermit

eres *vb véase* **ser**

erguir [48] *vt* raise. ~ **la cabeza** hold one's head high. ~**se** *vpr* straighten up

erigir [14] *vt* erect. ~**se** *vpr* set o.s. up (**en** as)

eriza|do *a* prickly. ~**rse** [10] *vpr* stand on end

erizo *m* hedgehog; (*de mar*) sea urchin. ~ **de mar,** ~ **marino** sea urchin

ermita *f* hermitage. ~**ño** *m* hermit

erosi|ón *f* erosion. ~**onar** *vt* erode

er|ótico *a* erotic. ~**otismo** *m* eroticism

errar [1, *la* **i** *inicial se escribe* **y**] *vt* miss. ● *vi* wander; (*equivocarse*) make a mistake, be wrong

errata *f* misprint

erróneo *a* erroneous, wrong

error *m* error, mistake. **estar en un** ~ be wrong, be mistaken

eructar *vi* belch

erudi|ción *f* learning, erudition. ~to *a* learned

erupción *f* eruption; (*med*) rash

es *vb véase* **ser**

esa *a véase* **ese**

ésa *pron véase* **ése**

esbelto *a* slender, slim

esboz|ar [10] *vt* sketch, outline. ~o *m* sketch, outline

escabeche *m* pickle. **en ~** pickled

escabroso *a* ‹*terreno*› rough; ‹*asunto*› difficult; ‹*atrevido*› crude

escabullirse [22] *vpr* slip away

escafandra *f*, **escafandro** *m* diving-suit

escala *f* scale; (*escalera de mano*) ladder; (*de avión*) stopover. ~da *f* climbing; (*pol*) escalation. ~r *vt* scale; break into ‹*una casa*›. ● *vi* (*pol*) escalate. **hacer ~ en** stop at. **vuelo sin ~s** non-stop flight

escaldar *vt* scald

escalera *f* staircase, stairs; (*de mano*) ladder. **~ de caracol** spiral staircase. **~ de incendios** fire escape. **~ mecánica** escalator. **~ plegable** step-ladder

escalfa|do *a* poached. ~r *vt* poach

escalinata *f* flight of steps

escalofrío *m* shiver

escal|ón *m* step; (*de escalera interior*) stair; (*de escala*) rung. ~onar *vt* spread out

escalope *m* escalope

escam|a *f* scale; (*de jabón*) flake; (*fig*) suspicion. ~oso *a* scaly

escamotear *vt* make disappear; (*robar*) steal, pinch (*fam*); disregard ‹*dificultad*›

escampar *vi* stop raining

esc|andalizar [10] *vt* scandalize, shock. ~andalizarse *vpr* be shocked. ~ándalo *m* scandal; (*alboroto*) uproar. ~andaloso *a* scandalous; (*alborotador*) noisy

Escandinavia *f* Scandinavia

escandinavo *a & m* Scandinavian

escaño *m* bench; (*pol*) seat

escapa|da *f* escape; (*visita*) flying visit. ~do *a* in a hurry. ~r *vi* escape. ~rse *vpr* escape; ‹*líquido, gas*› leak. **dejar ~r** let out

escaparate *m* (shop) window. **ir de ~s** go window-shopping

escapatoria *f* (*fig, fam*) way out

escape *m* (*de gas, de líquido*) leak; (*fuga*) escape; (*auto*) exhaust

escarabajo *m* beetle

escaramuza *f* skirmish

escarbar *vt* scratch; pick ‹*dientes, herida etc*›; (*fig, escudriñar*) delve (**en** into)

escarcha *f* frost. ~do *a* ‹*fruta*› crystallized

escarlat|a *a invar* scarlet. ~ina *f* scarlet fever

escarm|entar [1] *vt* punish severely. ● *vi* learn one's lesson. ~iento *m* punishment; (*lección*) lesson

escarn|ecer [11] *vt* mock. ~io *m* ridicule

escarola *f* endive

escarpa *f* slope. ~do *a* steep

escas|ear *vi* be scarce. ~ez *f* scarcity, shortage; (*pobreza*) poverty. ~o *a* scarce; (*poco*) little; (*insuficiente*) short; (*muy justo*) barely

escatimar *vt* be sparing with

escayola *f* plaster. ~r *vt* put in plaster

escena *f* scene; (*escenario*) stage. ~rio *m* stage; (*en el cine*) scenario; (*fig*) scene

escénico *a* scenic

escenografía *f* scenery

esc|epticismo *m* scepticism. ~éptico *a* sceptical. ● *m* sceptic

esclarecer [11] *vt* (*fig*) throw light on, clarify

esclavina *f* cape

esclav|itud *f* slavery. ~izar [10] *vt* enslave. ~o *m* slave

esclerosis *f* sclerosis

esclusa *f* lock

escoba *f* broom

escocer [2 & 9] *vt* hurt. ● *vi* sting

escocés *a* Scottish. ● *m* Scotsman

Escocia *f* Scotland

escog|er [14] *vt* choose, select. ~ido *a* chosen; (*de buena calidad*) choice

escolar *a* school. ● *m* schoolboy. ● *f* schoolgirl. ~idad *f* schooling

escolta *f* escort

escombros *mpl* rubble

escond|er *vt* hide. ~erse *vpr* hide. ~idas. a ~idas** secretly. ~ite *m* hiding place; (*juego*) hide-and-seek. ~rijo *m* hiding place

escopeta *f* shotgun. ~zo *m* shot

escoplo *m* chisel

escoria *f* slag; (*fig*) dregs

Escorpión *m* Scorpio

escorpión *m* scorpion

escot|ado *a* low-cut. ~adura *f* low neckline. ~ar *vt* cut out. ● *vi* pay one's share. **~e** *m* low neckline. **ir a ~e, pagar a ~e** share the expenses

escozor *m* pain

escri|bano *m* clerk. **~biente** *m* clerk. **~bir** [*pp* escrito] *vt/i* write. **~bir a máquina** type. **~birse** *vpr* write to each other; (*deletrearse*) be spelt. **~to** *a* written. • *m* writing; (*documento*) document. **~tor** *m* writer. **~torio** *m* desk; (*oficina*) office. **~tura** *f* (hand)writing; (*documento*) document; (*jurid*) deed. **¿cómo se escribe...?** how do you spell...? **poner por ~to** put into writing

escr|úpulo *m* scruple; (*escrupulosidad*) care, scrupulousness. **~uloso** *a* scrupulous

escrut|ar *vt* scrutinize; count (*votos*). **~inio** *m* count. **hacer el ~inio** count the votes

escuadr|a *f* (*instrumento*) square; (*mil*) squad; (*naut*) fleet. **~ón** *m* squadron

escuálido *a* skinny; (*sucio*) squalid

escuchar *vt* listen to. • *vi* listen

escudilla *f* bowl

escudo *m* shield. **~ de armas** coat of arms

escudriñar *vt* examine

escuela *f* school. **~ normal** teachers' training college

escueto *a* simple

escuincle *m* (*Mex, perro*) stray dog; (*Mex, muchacho, fam*) child, kid (*fam*)

escul|pir *vt* sculpture. **~tor** *m* sculptor. **~tora** *f* sculptress. **~tura** *f* sculpture; (*en madera*) carving

escupir *vt/i* spit

escurr|eplatos *m invar* plate-rack. **~idizo** *a* slippery. **~ir** *vt* drain; wring out (*ropa*). • *vi* drip; (*ser resbaladizo*) be slippery. **~irse** *vpr* slip

ese *a* (*f* esa, *mpl* esos, *fpl* esas) that; (*en plural*) those

ése *pron* (*f* ésa, *mpl* ésos, *fpl* ésas) that one; (*en plural*) those; (*primero de dos*) the former. **ni por ésas** on no account

esencia *f* essence. **~l** *a* essential. **lo ~l** the main thing

esf|era *f* sphere; (*de reloj*) face. **~érico** *a* spherical

esfinge *f* sphinx

esf|orzarse [2 & 10] *vpr* make an effort. **~uerzo** *m* effort

esfumarse *vpr* fade away; (*persona*) vanish

esgrim|a *f* fencing. **~ir** *vt* brandish; (*fig*) use

esguince *m* swerve; (*med*) sprain

eslab|ón *m* link. **~onar** *vt* link (together)

eslavo *a* Slav, Slavonic

eslogan *m* slogan

esmalt|ar *vt* enamel; varnish (*uñas*); (*fig*) adorn. **~e** *m* enamel. **~ de uñas, ~e para las uñas** nail varnish (*Brit*), nail polish (*Amer*)

esmerado *a* careful

esmeralda *f* emerald

esmerarse *vpr* take care (**en** over)

esmeril *m* emery

esmero *m* care

esmoquin *m* dinner jacket, tuxedo (*Amer*)

esnob *a invar* snobbish. • *m & f* (*pl* esnobs) snob. **~ismo** *m* snobbery

esnórkel *m* snorkel

eso *pron* that. **¡~ es!** that's it! **~ mismo** exactly. **¡~ no!** certainly not! **¡~ sí!** of course. **a ~ de** about. **en ~** at that moment. **¿no es ~?** isn't that right? **por ~** therefore. **y ~ que** although

esos *a pl véase* ese

ésos *pron pl véase* ése

espabila|do *a* bright. **~r** *vt* snuff (*vela*); (*avivar*) brighten up; (*despertar*) wake up. **~rse** *vpr* wake up; (*apresurarse*) hurry up

espaci|al *a* space. **~ar** *vt* space out. **~o** *m* space. **~oso** *a* spacious

espada *f* sword. **~s** *fpl* (*en naipes*) spades

espagueti *m* spaghetti

espald|a *f* back. **~illa** *f* shoulder-blade. **a ~as de uno** behind s.o.'s back. **a las ~as** on one's back. **tener las ~as anchas** be broad-shouldered. **volver la ~a a uno, volver las ~as a uno** give s.o. the cold shoulder

espant|ada *f* stampede. **~adizo** *a* timid, timorous. **~ajo** *m*, **~apájaros** *m inv* scarecrow. **~ar** *vt* frighten; (*ahuyentar*) frighten away. **~arse** *vpr* be frightened; (*ahuyentarse*) be frightened away. **~o** *m* terror; (*horror*) horror. **~oso** *a* frightening; (*muy grande*) terrible. **¡qué ~ajo!** what a sight!

España *f* Spain

español *a* Spanish. • *m* (*persona*) Spaniard; (*lengua*) Spanish. **los**

~es the Spanish. **~izado** *a* Hispanicized

esparadrapo *m* sticking-plaster, plaster (*Brit*)

esparci|do *a* scattered; (*fig*) widespread. **~r** [9] *vt* scatter; (*difundir*) spread. **~rse** *vpr* be scattered; (*difundirse*) spread; (*divertirse*) enjoy o.s.

espárrago *m* asparagus

esparto *m* esparto (grass)

espasm|o *m* spasm. **~ódico** *a* spasmodic

espátula *f* spatula; (*en pintura*) palette knife

especia *f* spice

especial *a* special. **~idad** *f* speciality (*Brit*), specialty (*Amer*). **~ista** *a & m & f* specialist. **~ización** *f* specialization. **~izar** [10] *vt* specialize. **~izarse** *vpr* specialize. **~mente** *adv* especially. **en ~** especially

especie *f* kind, sort; (*en biología*) species; (*noticia*) piece of news. **en ~** in kind

especifica|ción *f* specification. **~r** [7] *vt* specify

específico *a* specific

espect|áculo *m* sight; (*diversión*) entertainment, show. **~ador** *m & f* spectator. **~acular** *a* spectacular

espectro *m* spectre; (*en física*) spectrum

especula|ción *f* speculation. **~dor** *m* speculator. **~r** *vi* speculate. **~tivo** *a* speculative

espej|ismo *m* mirage. **~o** *m* mirror. **~o retrovisor** (*auto*) rear-view mirror

espeleólogo *m* potholer

espeluznante *a* horrifying

espera *f* wait. **sala f de ~** waiting room

espera|nza *f* hope. **~r** *vt* hope; (*aguardar*) wait for; (*creer*) expect. • *vi* hope; (*aguardar*) wait. **~r en uno** trust in s.o. **en ~ de** awaiting. **espero que no** I hope not. **espero que sí** I hope so

esperma *f* sperm

esperpento *m* fright; (*disparate*) nonsense

espes|ar *vt* thicken. **~arse** *vpr* thicken. **~o** *a* thick; (*pasta etc*) stiff. **~or** *m*, **~ura** *f* thickness; (*bot*) thicket

espetón *m* spit

esp|ía *f* spy. **~iar** [20] *vt* spy on. • *vi* spy

espiga *f* (*de trigo etc*) ear

espina *f* thorn; (*de pez*) bone; (*dorsal*) spine; (*astilla*) splinter; (*fig, dificultad*) difficulty. **~ dorsal** spine

espinaca *f* spinach

espinazo *m* spine

espinilla *f* shin; (*med*) blackhead

espino *m* hawthorn. **~ artificial** barbed wire. **~so** *a* thorny; (*pez*) bony; (*fig*) difficult

espionaje *m* espionage

espiral *a & f* spiral

espirar *vt/i* breathe out

esp|iritismo *m* spiritualism. **~iritoso** *a* spirited. **~iritista** *m & f* spiritualist. **~íritu** *m* spirit; (*mente*) mind; (*inteligencia*) intelligence. **~iritual** *a* spiritual. **~iritualismo** *m* spiritualism

espita *f* tap, faucet (*Amer*)

espl|éndido *a* splendid; (*persona*) generous. **~endor** *m* splendour

espliego *m* lavender

espolear *vt* (*fig*) spur on

espoleta *f* fuse

espolvorear *vt* sprinkle

esponj|a *f* sponge; (*tejido*) towelling. **~oso** *a* spongy. **pasar la ~a** forget about it

espont|aneidad *f* spontaneity. **~áneo** *a* spontaneous

esporádico *a* sporadic

espos|a *f* wife. **~as** *fpl* handcuffs. **~ar** *vt* handcuff. **~o** *m* husband. **los ~os** the couple

espuela *f* spur; (*fig*) incentive. **dar de ~s** spur on

espum|a *f* foam; (*en bebidas*) froth; (*de jabón*) lather. **~ar** *vt* skim. • *vi* foam; (*bebidas*) froth; (*jabón*) lather. **~oso** *a* (*vino*) sparkling. **echar ~a** foam, froth

esqueleto *m* skeleton

esquem|a *m* outline. **~ático** *a* sketchy

esqu|í *m* (*pl* **esquís**) ski; (*el deporte*) skiing. **~iador** *m* skier. **~iar** [20] *vi* ski

esquilar *vt* shear

esquimal *a & m* Eskimo

esquina *f* corner

esquirol *m* blackleg

esquiv|ar *vt* avoid. **~o** *a* aloof

esquizofrénico *a & m* schizophrenic

esta *a* véase **este**

ésta *pron* véase **éste**

estab|ilidad *f* stability. **~ilizador** *m* stabilizer. **~ilizar** [10] *vt* stabilize. **~le** *a* stable

establec|er [11] *vt* establish. **~erse**
vpr settle; (*com*) start a business.
~imiento *m* establishment

establo *m* cowshed

estaca *f* stake; (*para apalear*) stick.
~da *f* (*cerca*) fence

estación *f* station; (*del año*) season;
(*de vacaciones*) resort. **~ de servicio**
service station

estaciona|miento *m* parking. **~r** *vt*
station; (*auto*) park. **~rio** *a*
stationary

estadio *m* stadium; (*fase*) stage

estadista *m* statesman. **●** *f*
stateswoman

estadístic|a *f* statistics. **~o** *a*
statistical

estado *m* state. **~ civil** marital
status. **~ de ánimo** frame of mind.
~ de cuenta bank statement. **~
mayor** (*mil*) staff. **en buen ~** in
good condition. **en ~ (interesante)**
pregnant

Estados Unidos *mpl* United States

estadounidense *a* American,
United States. **●** *m & f* American

estafa *f* swindle. **~r** *vt* swindle

estafeta *f* (*oficina de correos*) (sub-)
post office

estala|ctita *f* stalactite. **~gmita** *f*
stalagmite

estall|ar *vi* explode; ⟨*olas*⟩ break;
⟨*guerra, epidemia etc*⟩ break out;
(*fig*) burst. **~ar en llanto** burst into
tears. **~ar de risa** burst out laughing. **~ido** *m* explosion; (*de guerra,
epidemia etc*) outbreak; (*de risa etc*)
outburst

estamp|a *f* print; (*aspecto*) appear-
ance. **~ado** *a* printed. **●** *m* printing;
(*tela*) cotton print. **~ar** *vt* stamp;
(*imprimir*) print. **dar a la ~a** (*imprimir*) print; (*publicar*) publish. **la
viva ~a** the image

estampía. de ~ía suddenly

estampido *m* explosion

estampilla *f* stamp; (*Mex*) (postage)
stamp

estanca|do *a* stagnant. **~miento** *m*
stagnation. **~r** [7] *vt* stem; (*com*)
turn into a monopoly

estanci|a *f* stay; (*Arg, finca*) ranch,
farm; (*cuarto*) room. **~ero** *m* (*Arg*)
farmer

estanco *a* watertight. **●** *m* tobacconist's (shop)

estandarte *m* standard, banner

estanque *m* lake; (*depósito de agua*)
reservoir

estanquero *m* tobacconist

estante *m* shelf. **~ría** *f* shelves;
(*para libros*) bookcase

estañ|o *m* tin. **~adura** *f* tin-plating

estar [27] *vi* be; (*quedarse*) stay;
(*estar en casa*) be in. **¿estamos?**
alright? **estamos a 29 de noviembre**
it's the 29th of November. **~ para**
be about to. **~ por** remain to be;
(*con ganas de*) be tempted to; (*ser
partidario de*) be in favour of. **~se**
vpr stay. **¿cómo está Vd?, ¿cómo
estás?** how are you?

estarcir [9] *vt* stencil

estatal *a* state

estático *a* static; (*pasmado*) dumbfounded

estatua *f* statue

estatura *f* height

estatut|ario *a* statutory. **~o** *m*
statute

este *m* east; (*viento*) east wind. **●** *a* (*f
esta, mpl estos, fpl estas*) this; (*en
plural*) these. **●** *int* (*LAm*) well, er

éste *pron* (*f ésta, mpl éstos, fpl
éstas*) this one, (*en plural*) these;
(*segundo de dos*) the latter

estela *f* wake; (*arquit*) carved stone

estera *f* mat; (*tejido*) matting

est|éreo *a* stereo. **~ereofónico** *a*
stereo, stereophonic

esterilla *f* mat

estereotip|ado *a* stereotyped. **~o** *m*
stereotype

est|éril *a* sterile; ⟨*mujer*⟩ infertile;
⟨*terreno*⟩ barren. **~erilidad** *f* ster-
ility; (*de mujer*) infertility; (*de
terreno*) barrenness

esterlina *a* sterling. **libra** *f* **~** pound
sterling

estético *a* aesthetic

estevado *a* bow-legged

estiércol *m* dung; (*abono*) manure

estigma *m* stigma. **~s** *mpl* (*relig*)
stigmata

estilarse *vpr* be used

estil|ista *m & f* stylist. **~izar** [10] *vt*
stylize. **~o** *m* style. **por el ~o** of
that sort

estilográfica *f* fountain pen

estima *f* esteem. **~do** *a* esteemed.
~do señor (*en cartas*) Dear Sir. **~r**
vt esteem; have great respect for
⟨*persona*⟩; (*valorar*) value; (*juzgar*)
think

est|imulante *a* stimulating. **●** *m*
stimulant. **~imular** *vt* stimulate;
(*incitar*) incite. **~ímulo** *m* stimulus

estipular *vt* stipulate

estir|ado _a_ stretched; ⟨persona⟩ haughty. **∼ar** _vt_ stretch; (_fig_) stretch out. **∼ón** _m_ pull, tug; (_crecimiento_) sudden growth

estirpe _m_ stock

estival _a_ summer

esto _pron neutro_ this; (_este asunto_) this business. **en ∼** at this point. **en ∼ de** in this business of. **por ∼** therefore

estofa _f_ class. **de baja ∼** ⟨gente⟩ low-class

estofa|do _a_ stewed. ● _m_ stew. **∼r** _vt_ stew

estoic|ismo _m_ stoicism. **∼o** _a_ stoical. ● _m_ stoic

estómago _m_ stomach. **dolor _m_ de ∼** stomach-ache

estorb|ar _vt_ hinder, obstruct; (_molestar_) bother, annoy. ● _vi_ be in the way. **∼o** _m_ hindrance; (_molestia_) nuisance

estornino _m_ starling

estornud|ar _vi_ sneeze. **∼o** _m_ sneeze

estos _a mpl véase_ **este**

éstos _pron mpl véase_ **éste**

estoy _vb véase_ **estar**

estrabismo _m_ squint

estrado _m_ stage; (_mus_) bandstand

estrafalario _a_ outlandish

estrag|ar [12] _vt_ devastate. **∼o** _m_ devastation. **hacer ∼os** devastate

estragón _m_ tarragon

estrambótico _a_ outlandish

estrangula|ción _f_ strangulation. **∼dor** _m_ strangler; (_auto_) choke. **∼miento** _m_ blockage; (_auto_) bottleneck. **∼r** _vt_ strangle

estraperlo _m_ black market. **comprar algo de ∼** buy sth on the black market

estratagema _f_ stratagem

estrateg|a _m & f_ strategist. **∼ia** _f_ strategy

estratégic|amente _adv_ strategically. **∼o** _a_ strategic

estrato _m_ stratum

estratosfera _f_ stratosphere

estrech|ar _vt_ make narrower; take in ⟨vestido⟩; (_apretar_) squeeze; hug ⟨persona⟩. **∼ar la mano a uno** shake hands with s.o. **∼arse** _vpr_ become narrower; (_apretarse_) squeeze up. **∼ez** _f_ narrowness; (_apuro_) tight spot; (_falta de dinero_) want. **∼o** _a_ narrow; ⟨vestido etc⟩ tight; (_fig, íntimo_) close. ● _m_ straits. **∼o de miras, de miras ∼as** narrow-minded

estregar [1 & 12] _vt_ rub

estrella _f_ star. **∼ de mar, ∼mar** _m_ starfish

estrellar _vt_ smash; fry ⟨huevos⟩. **∼se** _vpr_ smash; (_fracasar_) fail. **∼se contra** crash into

estremec|er [11] _vt_ shake. **∼erse** _vpr_ tremble (**de** with). **∼imiento** _m_ shaking

estren|ar _vt_ use for the first time; wear for the first time ⟨vestido etc⟩; show for the first time ⟨película⟩. **∼arse** _vpr_ make one's début; ⟨película⟩ have its première; ⟨obra de teatro⟩ open. **∼o** _m_ first use; (_de película_) première; (_de obra de teatro_) first night

estreñi|do _a_ constipated. **∼miento** _m_ constipation

estr|épito _m_ din. **∼epitoso** _a_ noisy; (_fig_) resounding

estreptomicina _f_ streptomycin

estrés _m_ stress

estría _f_ groove

estribar _vt_ rest (**en** on); (_consistir_) lie (**en** in)

estribillo _m_ refrain; (_muletilla_) catchphrase

estribo _m_ stirrup; (_de vehículo_) step; (_contrafuerte_) buttress. **perder los ∼s** lose one's temper

estribor _m_ starboard

estricto _a_ strict

estridente _a_ strident, raucous

estrofa _f_ strophe

estropajo _m_ scourer. **∼so** _a_ ⟨carne etc⟩ tough; ⟨persona⟩ slovenly

estropear _vt_ spoil; (_romper_) break. **∼se** _vpr_ be damaged; ⟨fruta etc⟩ go bad; (_fracasar_) fail

estructura _f_ structure. **∼l** _a_ structural

estruendo _m_ din; (_de mucha gente_) uproar. **∼so** _a_ deafening

estrujar _vt_ squeeze; (_fig_) drain

estuario _m_ estuary

estuco _m_ stucco

estuche _m_ case

estudi|ante _m & f_ student. **∼antil** _a_ student. **∼ar** _vt_ study. **∼o** _m_ study; (_de artista_) studio. **∼oso** _a_ studious

estufa _f_ heater; (_LAm_) cooker

estupefac|ción _f_ astonishment. **∼iente** _a_ astonishing. ● _m_ narcotic. **∼to** _a_ astonished

estupendo _a_ marvellous; (_hermoso_) beautiful

est|upidez _f_ stupidity; (_acto_) stupid thing. **∼úpido** _a_ stupid

estupor *m* amazement

esturión *m* sturgeon

estuve *vb véase* **estar**

etapa *f* stage. **hacer ~ en** break the journey at. **por ~s** in stages

etc *abrev* (*etcétera*) etc

etcétera *adv* et cetera

éter *m* ether

etéreo *a* ethereal

etern|amente *adv* eternally. **~idad** *f* eternity. **~izar** [10] *vt* drag out. **~izarse** *vpr* be interminable. **~o** *a* eternal

étic|a *f* ethics. **~o** *a* ethical

etimología *f* etymology

etiqueta *f* ticket, tag; (*ceremonial*) etiquette. **de ~** formal

étnico *a* ethnic

eucalipto *m* eucalyptus

eufemismo *m* euphemism

euforia *f* euphoria

Europa *f* Europe

europe|o *a & m* European. **~izar** [10] *vt* Europeanize

eutanasia *f* euthanasia

evacua|ción *f* evacuation. **~r** [21 *o regular*] *vt* evacuate

evadir *vt* avoid. **~se** *vpr* escape

evaluar [21] *vt* evaluate

evang|élico *a* evangelical. **~elio** *m* gospel. **~elista** *m & f* evangelist

evapora|ción *f* evaporation. **~r** *vi* evaporate. **~rse** *vpr* evaporate; (*fig*) disappear

evasi|ón *f* evasion; (*fuga*) escape. **~vo** *a* evasive

evento *m* event. **a todo ~** at all events

eventual *a* possible. **~idad** *f* eventuality

eviden|cia *f* evidence. **~ciar** *vt* show. **~ciarse** *vpr* be obvious. **~te** *a* obvious. **~temente** *adv* obviously. **poner en ~cia** show; (*fig*) make a fool of

evitar *vt* avoid; (*ahorrar*) spare

evocar [7] *vt* evoke

evoluci|ón *f* evolution. **~onado** *a* fully-developed. **~onar** *vi* evolve; (*mil*) manoeuvre

ex *pref* ex-, former

exacerbar *vt* exacerbate

exact|amente *adv* exactly. **~itud** *f* exactness. **~o** *a* exact; (*preciso*) accurate; (*puntual*) punctual. **¡~!** exactly!. **con ~itud** exactly

exagera|ción *f* exaggeration. **~do** *a* exaggerated. **~r** *vt/i* exaggerate

exalta|do *a* exalted; (*fanático*) fanatical. **~r** *vt* exalt. **~rse** *vpr* get excited

exam|en *m* examination; (*escol, univ*) exam(ination). **~inador** *m* examiner. **~inar** *vt* examine. **~inarse** *vpr* take an exam

exánime *a* lifeless

exaspera|ción *f* exasperation. **~r** *vt* exasperate. **~rse** *vpr* get exasperated

excava|ción *f* excavation. **~dora** *f* digger. **~r** *vt* excavate

excede|ncia *f* leave of absence. **~nte** *a & m* surplus. **~r** *vi* exceed. **~rse** *vpr* go too far. **~rse a sí mismo** excel o.s.

excelen|cia *f* excellence; (*tratamiento*) Excellency. **~te** *a* excellent

exc|entricidad *f* eccentricity. **~éntrico** *a & m* eccentric

excepci|ón *f* exception. **~onal** *a* exceptional. **a ~ón de, con ~ón de** except (for)

except|o *prep* except (for). **~uar** [21] *vt* except

exces|ivo *a* excessive. **~o** *m* excess. **~o de equipaje** excess luggage (*esp Brit*), excess baggage (*esp Amer*)

excita|ble *a* excitable. **~ción** *f* excitement. **~nte** *a* exciting. ● *m* stimulant. **~r** *vt* excite; (*incitar*) incite. **~rse** *vpr* get excited

exclama|ción *f* exclamation. **~r** *vi* exclaim

exclu|ir [17] *vt* exclude. **~sión** *f* exclusion. **~siva** *f* sole right; (*en la prensa* exclusive (story). **~sive** *adv* exclusive; (*exclusivamente*) exclusively. **~sivo** *a* exclusive

excomu|lgar [12] *vt* excommunicate. **~nión** *f* excommunication

excremento *m* excrement

exculpar *vt* exonerate; (*jurid*) acquit

excursi|ón *f* excursion, trip. **~onista** *m & f* day-tripper. **ir de ~ón** go on an excursion

excusa *f* excuse; (*disculpa*) apology. **~r** *vt* excuse. **presentar sus ~s** apologize

execra|ble *a* loathsome. **~r** *vt* loathe

exento *a* exempt; (*libre*) free

exequias *fpl* funeral rites

exhala|ción *f* shooting star. **~r** *vt* exhale, breath out; give off (*color etc*). **~rse** *vpr* hurry. **como una ~ción** at top speed

exhaust|ivo *a* exhaustive. **~o** *a* exhausted

exhibi|ción *f* exhibition. **~cionista** *m & f* exhibitionist. **~r** *vt* exhibit

exhortar *vt* exhort (**a** to)

exhumar *vt* exhume; (*fig*) dig up

exig|encia *f* demand. **~ente** *a* demanding. **~ir** [14] *vt* demand. **tener muchas ~encias** be very demanding

exiguo *a* meagre

exil|(i)ado *a* exiled. ● *m* exile. **~(i)arse** *vpr* go into exile. **~io** *m* exile

eximio *a* distinguished

eximir *vt* exempt; (*liberar*) free

existencia *f* existence. **~s** *fpl* stock

existencial *a* existential. **~ismo** *m* existentialism

exist|ente *a* existing. **~ir** *vi* exist

éxito *m* success. **no tener ~** fail. **tener ~** be successful

exitoso *a* successful

éxodo *m* exodus

exonerar *vt* (*de un empleo*) dismiss; (*de un honor etc*) strip

exorbitante *a* exorbitant

exorci|smo *m* exorcism. **~zar** [10] *vt* exorcise

exótico *a* exotic

expan|dir *vt* expand; (*fig*) spread. **~dirse** *vpr* expand. **~sión** *f* expansion. **~sivo** *a* expansive

expatria|do *a & m* expatriate. **~r** *vt* banish. **~rse** *vpr* emigrate; (*exiliarse*) go into exile

expectativa *f*. **estar a la ~** be on the lookout

expedición *f* dispatch; (*cosa expedida*) shipment; (*mil, científico etc*) expedition

expediente *m* expedient; (*jurid*) proceedings; (*documentos*) record, file

expedi|r [5] *vt* dispatch, send; issue ‹*documento*›. **~to** *a* clear

expeler *vt* expel

expende|dor *m* dealer. **~dor automático** vending machine. **~duría** *f* shop; (*de billetes*) ticket office. **~r** *vt* sell

expensas *fpl*. **a ~ de** at the expense of. **a mis ~** at my expense

experiencia *f* experience

experiment|al *a* experimental. **~ar** *vt* test, experiment with; (*sentir*) experience. **~o** *m* experiment

experto *a & m* expert

expiar [20] *vt* atone for

expirar *vi* expire; (*morir*) die

explana|da *f* levelled area; (*paseo*) esplanade. **~r** *vt* level

explayar *vt* extend. **~se** *vpr* spread out, extend; (*hablar*) be long-winded; (*confiarse*) confide (**a** in)

expletivo *m* expletive

explica|ción *f* explanation. **~r** [7] *vt* explain. **~rse** *vpr* understand; (*hacerse comprender*) explain o.s. **no me lo explico** I can't understand it

explícito *a* explicit

explora|ción *f* exploration. **~dor** *m* explorer; (*muchacho*) boy scout. **~r** *vt* explore. **~torio** *a* exploratory

explosi|ón *f* explosion; (*fig*) outburst. **~onar** *vt* blow up. **~vo** *a & m* explosive

explota|ción *f* working; (*abuso*) exploitation. **~r** *vt* work ‹*mina*›; farm ‹*tierra*›; (*abusar*) exploit. ● *vi* explode

expone|nte *m* exponent. **~r** [34] *vt* expose; display ‹*mercancías*›; (*explicar*) expound; exhibit ‹*cuadros etc*›; (*arriesgar*) risk. ● *vi* hold an exhibition. **~rse** *vpr* run the risk (**a** of)

exporta|ción *f* export. **~dor** *m* exporter. **~r** *vt* export

exposición *f* exposure; (*de cuadros etc*) exhibition; (*en escaparate etc*) display; (*explicación*) exposition, explanation

expresamente *adv* specifically

expres|ar *vt* express. **~arse** *vpr* express o.s. **~ión** *f* expression. **~ivo** *a* expressive; (*cariñoso*) affectionate

expreso *a* express. ● *m* express messenger; (*tren*) express

exprimi|dor *m* squeezer. **~r** *vt* squeeze; (*explotar*) exploit

expropiar *vt* expropriate

expuesto *a* on display; ‹*lugar etc*› exposed; (*peligroso*) dangerous. **estar ~ a** be liable to

expuls|ar *vt* expel; throw out ‹*persona*›; send off ‹*jugador*›. **~ión** *f* expulsion

expurgar [12] *vt* expurgate

exquisit|o *a* exquisite. **~amente** *adv* exquisitely

extasiar [20] *vt* enrapture

éxtasis *m invar* ecstasy

extático *a* ecstatic

extend|er [1] *vt* spread (out); draw up ‹*documento*›. **~erse** *vpr* spread;

⟨*paisaje etc*⟩ extend, stretch; (*tenderse*) stretch out. ~**ido** *a* spread out; (*generalizado*) widespread; ⟨*brazos*⟩ outstretched

extens|amente *adv* widely; (*detalladamente*) in full. ~**ión** *f* extension; (*amplitud*) expanse; (*mus*) range. ~**o** *a* extensive

extenuar [21] *vt* exhaust

exterior *a* external, exterior; (*del extranjero*) foreign; ⟨*aspecto etc*⟩ outward. ● *m* exterior; (*países extranjeros*) abroad. ~**izar** [10] *vt* show

extermin|ación *f* extermination. ~**ar** *vt* exterminate. ~**io** *m* extermination

externo *a* external; ⟨*signo etc*⟩ outward. ● *m* day pupil

extin|ción *f* extinction. ~**guir** [13] *vt* extinguish. ~**guirse** *vpr* die out; ⟨*fuego*⟩ go out. ~**to** *a* extinguished; ⟨*raza etc*⟩ extinct. ~**tor** *m* fire extinguisher

extirpa|r *vt* uproot; extract ⟨*muela etc*⟩; remove ⟨*tumor*⟩. ~**ción** *f* (*fig*) eradication

extorsi|ón *f* (*fig*) inconvenience. ~**onar** *vt* inconvenience

extra *a invar* extra; (*de buena calidad*) good-quality; ⟨*huevos*⟩ large. **paga** *f* ~ bonus

extrac|ción *f* extraction; (*de lotería*) draw. ~**to** *m* extract

extradición *f* extradition

extraer [41] *vt* extract

extranjero *a* foreign. ● *m* foreigner; (*países*) foreign countries. **del** ~ from abroad. **en el** ~, **por el** ~ abroad

extrañ|ar *vt* surprise; (*encontrar extraño*) find strange; (*LAm*, *echar de menos*) miss; (*desterrar*) banish. ~**arse** *vpr* be surprised (**de** at); ⟨*2 personas*⟩ grow apart. ~**eza** *f* strangeness; (*asombro*) surprise. ~**o** *a* strange. ● *m* stranger

extraoficial *a* unofficial

extraordinario *a* extraordinary. ● *m* (*correo*) special delivery; (*plato*) extra dish; (*de periódico etc*) special edition. **horas** *fpl* **extraordinarias** overtime

extrarradio *m* suburbs

extrasensible *a* extra-sensory

extraterrestre *a* extraterrestrial. ● *m* alien

extravagan|cia *f* oddness, eccentricity. ~**te** *a* odd, eccentric

extravertido *a & m* extrovert

extrav|iado *a* lost; ⟨*lugar*⟩ isolated. ~**iar** [20] *vt* lose. ~**iarse** *vpr* get lost; ⟨*objetos*⟩ be missing. ~**ío** *m* loss

extremar *vt* overdo. ~**se** *vpr* make every effort

extremeño *a* from Extremadura. ● *m* person from Extremadura

extrem|idad *f* extremity. ~**idades** *fpl* extremities. ~**ista** *a & m & f* extremist. ~**o** *a* extreme. ● *m* end; (*colmo*) extreme. **en** ~**o** extremely. **en último** ~**o** as a last resort

extrovertido *a & m* extrovert

exuberan|cia *f* exuberance. ~**te** *a* exuberant

exulta|ción *f* exultation. ~**r** *vi* exult

eyacular *vt/i* ejaculate

F

fa *m* F; (*solfa*) fah

fabada *f* Asturian stew

fábrica *f* factory. **marca** *f* **de** ~ trade mark

fabrica|ción *f* manufacture. ~**ción en serie** mass production. ~**nte** *m & f* manufacturer. ~**r** [7] *vt* manufacture; (*inventar*) fabricate

fábula *f* fable; (*mentira*) story, lie; (*chisme*) gossip

fabuloso *a* fabulous

facci|ón *f* faction. ~**ones** *fpl* (*de la cara*) features

faceta *f* facet

fácil *a* easy; (*probable*) likely; ⟨*persona*⟩ easygoing

facili|dad *f* ease; (*disposición*) aptitude. ~**dades** *fpl* facilities. ~**tar** *vt* facilitate; (*proporcionar*) provide

fácilmente *adv* easily

facistol *m* lectern

facón *m* (*Arg*) gaucho knife

facsímil(e) *m* facsimile

factible *a* feasible

factor *m* factor

factoría *f* agency; (*esp LAm*, *fábrica*) factory

factura *f* bill, invoice; (*hechura*) manufacture. ~**r** *vt* (*hacer la factura*) invoice; (*cobrar*) charge; (*en ferrocarril*) register (*Brit*), check (*Amer*)

faculta|d *f* faculty; (*capacidad*) ability; (*poder*) power. ~**tivo** *a* optional

facha *f* (*aspecto*, *fam*) look

fachada *f* façade; (*fig, apariencia*) show

faena *f* job. **~s domésticas** housework

fagot *m* bassoon; (*músico*) bassoonist

faisán *m* pheasant

faja *f* (*de tierra*) strip; (*corsé*) corset; (*mil etc*) sash

fajo *m* bundle; (*de billetes*) wad

falang|e *f* (*política española*) Falange. **~ista** *m & f* Falangist

falda *f* skirt; (*de montaña*) side

fálico *a* phallic

fals|ear *vt* falsify, distort. **~edad** *f* falseness; (*mentira*) lie, falsehood. **~ificación** *f* forgery. **~ificador** *m* forger. **~ificar** [7] *vt* forge. **~o** *a* false; (*equivocado*) wrong; (*falsificado*) fake

falt|a *f* lack; (*ausencia*) absence; (*escasez*) shortage; (*defecto*) fault, defect; (*culpa*) fault; (*error*) mistake; (*en fútbol etc*) foul; (*en tenis*) fault. **~ar** *vi* be lacking; (*estar ausente*) be absent. **~o** *a* lacking (de in). **a ~a de** for lack of. **echar en ~a** miss. **hacer ~a** be necessary. **me hace ~a** I need. **¡no ~aba más!** don't mention it! (*naturalmente*) of course! **sacar ~as** find fault

falla *f* (*incl geol*) fault. **~r** *vi* fail; (*romperse*) break, give way; (*motor, tiro etc*) miss. **sin ~r** without fail

fallec|er [11] *vi* die. **~ido** *a* late. ● *m* deceased

fallido *a* vain; (*fracasado*) unsuccessful

fallo *m* failure; (*defecto*) fault; (*jurid*) sentence

fama *f* fame; (*reputación*) reputation. **de mala ~** of ill repute. **tener ~ de** have the reputation of

famélico *a* starving

familia *f* family. **~ numerosa** large family. **~r** *a* familiar; (*de la familia*) family; (*sin ceremonia*) informal. **~ridad** *f* familiarity. **~rizarse** [10] *vpr* become familiar (con with)

famoso *a* famous

fanático *a* fanatical. ● *m* fanatic

fanfarr|ón *a* boastful. ● *m* braggart. **~onada** *f* boasting; (*dicho*) boast. **~onear** *vi* show off

fango *m* mud. **~so** *a* muddy

fantas|ear *vi* daydream; (*imaginar*) fantasize. **~ía** *f* fantasy. **de ~** fancy

fantasma *m* ghost

fantástico *a* fantastic

fantoche *m* puppet

faringe *f* pharynx

fardo *m* bundle

farfullar *vi* jabber, gabble

farmac|éutico *a* pharmaceutical. ● *m* chemist (*Brit*), pharmacist, druggist (*Amer*). **~ia** *f* (*ciencia*) pharmacy; (*tienda*) chemist's (shop) (*Brit*), pharmacy, drugstore (*Amer*)

faro *m* lighthouse; (*aviac*) beacon; (*auto*) headlight

farol *m* lantern; (*de la calle*) street lamp. **~a** *f* street lamp. **~ita** *f* small street lamp

farsa *f* farce

fas *adv*. **por ~ o por nefas** rightly or wrongly

fascículo *m* instalment

fascina|ción *f* fascination. **~r** *vt* fascinate

fascis|mo *m* fascism. **~ta** *a & m & f* fascist

fase *f* phase

fastidi|ar *vt* annoy; (*estropear*) spoil. **~arse** *vpr* (*aguantarse*) put up with it; (*hacerse daño*) hurt o.s. **~o** *m* nuisance; (*aburrimiento*) boredom. **~oso** *a* annoying. **¡para que te ~es!** so there! **¡qué ~o!** what a nuisance!

fatal *a* fateful; (*mortal*) fatal; (*pésimo, fam*) terrible. **~idad** *f* fate; (*desgracia*) misfortune. **~ista** *m & f* fatalist

fatig|a *f* fatigue. **~as** *fpl* troubles. **~ar** [12] *vt* tire. **~arse** *vpr* get tired. **~oso** *a* tiring

fatuo *a* fatuous

fauna *f* fauna

fausto *a* lucky

favor *m* favour. **~able** *a* favourable. **a ~ de, en ~ de** in favour of. **haga el ~ de** would you be so kind as to, please. **por ~** please

favorec|edor *a* flattering. **~er** [11] *vt* favour; (*vestido, peinado etc*) suit. **~ido** *a* favoured

favorit|ismo *m* favouritism. **~o** *a & m* favourite

faz *f* face

fe *f* faith. **dar ~ de** certify. **de buena ~** in good faith

fealdad *f* ugliness

febrero *m* February

febril *a* feverish

fecund|ación *f* fertilization. **~ación artificial** artificial insemination. **~ar** *vt* fertilize. **~o** *a* fertile; (*fig*) prolific

fecha f date. ~**r** vt date. **a estas** ~**s** now; (*todavía*) still. **hasta la** ~ so far. **poner la** ~ date

fechoría f misdeed

federa|ción f federation. ~**l** a federal

feísimo a hideous

felici|dad f happiness. ~**dades** fpl best wishes; (*congratulaciones*) congratulations. ~**tación** f congratulation. ~**tar** vt congratulate. ~**tarse** vpr be glad

feligr|és m parishioner. ~**esía** f parish

felino a & m feline

feliz a happy; (*afortunado*) lucky. **¡Felices Pascuas!** Happy Christmas! **¡F~ Año Nuevo!** Happy New Year!

felpudo a plush. ● m doormat

femeni|l a feminine. ~**no** a feminine; (*biol, bot*) female. ● m feminine. ~**nidad** f femininity. ~**sta** a & m & f feminist

fen|omenal a phenomenal. ~**ómeno** m phenomenon; (*monstruo*) freak

feo a ugly; (*desagradable*) nasty; (*malo*) bad

féretro m coffin

feria f fair; (*verbena*) carnival; (*descanso*) holiday; (*Mex, cambio*) change. ~**do** a. **día** ~**do** holiday

ferment|ación f fermentation. ~**ar** vt/i ferment. ~**o** m ferment

fero|cidad f ferocity. ~**z** a fierce; (*persona*) savage

férreo a iron. **vía férrea** railway (*Brit*), railroad (*Amer*)

ferreter|ía f ironmonger's (shop) (*Brit*), hardware store (*Amer*). ~**o** m ironmonger (*Brit*), hardware dealer (*Amer*)

ferro|bús m local train. ~**carril** m railway (*Brit*), railroad (*Amer*). ~**viario** a rail. ● m railwayman (*Brit*), railroad worker (*Amer*)

fértil a fertile

fertili|dad f fertility. ~**zante** m fertilizer. ~**zar** [10] vt fertilize

férvido a fervent

ferv|iente a fervent. ~**or** m fervour

festej|ar vt celebrate; entertain (*persona*); court (*novia etc*); (*Mex, golpear*) beat. ~**o** m entertainment; (*celebración*) celebration

festiv|al m festival. ~**idad** f festivity. ~**o** a festive; (*humorístico*) humorous. **día** ~**o** feast day, holiday

festonear vt festoon

fétido a stinking

feto m foetus

feudal a feudal

fiado m. **al** ~ on credit. ~**r** m fastener; (*jurid*) guarantor

fiambre m cold meat

fianza f (*dinero*) deposit; (*objeto*) surety. **bajo** ~ on bail. **dar** ~ pay a deposit

fiar [20] vt guarantee; (*vender*) sell on credit; (*confiar*) confide. ● vi trust. ~**se** vpr. ~**se de** trust

fiasco m fiasco

fibra f fibre; (*fig*) energy. ~ **de vidrio** fibreglass

fic|ción f fiction. ~**ticio** a fictitious; (*falso*) false

fich|a f token; (*tarjeta*) index card; (*en los juegos*) counter. ~**ar** vt file. ~**ero** m card index. **estar** ~**ado** have a (police) record

fidedigno a reliable

fidelidad f faithfulness. **alta** ~ hi-fi (*fam*), high fidelity

fideos mpl noodles

fiebre f fever. ~ **del heno** hay fever. **tener** ~ have a temperature

fiel a faithful; (*memoria, relato etc*) reliable. ● m believer; (*de balanza*) needle. **los** ~**es** the faithful

fieltro m felt

fier|a f wild animal; (*persona*) brute. ~**o** a fierce; (*cruel*) cruel. **estar hecho una** ~**a** be furious

fierro m (*LAm*) iron

fiesta f party; (*día festivo*) holiday. ~**s** fpl celebrations. ~ **nacional** bank holiday (*Brit*), national holiday

figura f figure; (*forma*) shape; (*en obra de teatro*) character; (*en naipes*) court-card. ~**r** vt feign; (*representar*) represent. ● vi figure; (*ser importante*) be important. ~**rse** vpr imagine. **¡figúrate!** just imagine! ~**tivo** a figurative

fij|ación f fixing. ~**ar** vt fix; stick (*sello*); post (*cartel*). ~**arse** vpr settle; (*fig, poner atención*) notice. **¡fíjate!** just imagine! ~**o** a fixed; (*firme*) stable; (*persona*) settled. **de** ~**o** certainly

fila f line; (*de soldados etc*) file; (*en el teatro, cine etc*) row; (*cola*) queue. **ponerse en** ~ line up

filamento m filament

fil|antropía f philanthropy. ~**antrópico** a philanthropic. ~**ántropo** m philanthropist

filarmónico *a* philharmonic
filat|elia *f* stamp collecting, philately. **~élico** *a* philatelic. **●** *m* stamp collector, philatelist
filete *m* fillet
filfa *f* (*fam*) hoax
filial *a* filial. **●** *f* subsidiary
filigrana *f* filigree (work); (*en papel*) watermark
Filipinas *fpl.* **las (islas) ~** the Philippines
filipino *a* Philippine, Filipino
filmar *vt* film
filo *m* edge; (*de hoja*) cutting edge; (*Mex, hambre*) hunger. **al ~ de las doce** at exactly twelve o'clock. **dar ~ a, sacar ~ a** sharpen
filología *f* philology
filón *m* vein; (*fig*) gold-mine
fil|osofía *f* philosophy. **~osófico** *a* philosophical. **~ósofo** *m* philosopher
filtr|ar *vt* filter. **~arse** *vpr* filter; (*dinero*) disappear. **~o** *m* filter; (*bebida*) philtre
fin *m* end; (*objetivo*) aim. **~ de semana** weekend. **a ~ de** in order to. **a ~ de cuentas** all things considered. **a ~ de que** in order that. **a ~es de** at the end of. **al ~** finally. **al ~ y al cabo** after all. **dar ~ a** end. **en ~** in short. **poner ~ a** end. **por ~** finally. **sin ~** endless
final *a* final, last. **●** *m* end. **●** *f* final. **~idad** *f* aim. **~ista** *m* & *f* finalist. **~izar** [10] *vt/i* end. **~mente** *adv* finally
financi|ar *vt* finance. **~ero** *a* financial. **●** *m* financier
finca *f* property; (*tierras*) estate; (*LAm, granja*) farm
finés *a* Finnish. **●** *m* Finn; (*lengua*) Finnish
fingi|do *a* false. **~r** [14] *vt* feign; (*simular*) simulate. **●** *vi* pretend. **~rse** *vpr* pretend to be
finito *a* finite
finlandés *a* Finnish. **●** *m* (*persona*) Finn; (*lengua*) Finnish
Finlandia *f* Finland
fin|o *a* fine; (*delgado*) slender; (*astuto*) shrewd; (*sentido*) keen; (*cortés*) polite; (*jerez*) dry. **~ura** *f* fineness; (*astucia*) shrewdness; (*de sentido*) keenness; (*cortesía*) politeness
fiordo *m* fiord
firma *f* signature; (*empresa*) firm
firmamento *m* firmament

firmar *vt* sign
firme *a* firm; (*estable*) stable, steady; (*persona*) steadfast. **●** *m* (*pavimento*) (road) surface. **●** *adv* hard. **~za** *f* firmness. **de ~** hard. **en ~** firm, definite
fisc|al *a* fiscal. **●** *m* & *f* public prosecutor. **~o** *m* treasury
fisg|ar [12] *vt* pry into ‹*asunto*›; spy on ‹*persona*›. **●** *vi* pry. **~ón** *a* prying. **●** *m* busybody
físic|a *f* physics. **~o** *a* physical. **●** *m* physique; (*persona*) physicist
fisi|ología *f* physiology. **~ológico** *a* physiological. **~ólogo** *m* physiologist
fisioterap|euta *m* & *f* physiotherapist. **~ia** *f* physiotherapy. **~ista** *m* & *f* (*fam*) physiotherapist
fisonom|ía *f* physiognomy, face. **~ista** *m* & *f*. **ser buen ~ista** be good at remembering faces
fisura *f* (*Med*) fracture
fláccido *a* flabby
flaco *a* thin, skinny; (*débil*) weak
flagelo *m* scourge
flagrante *a* flagrant. **en ~** red-handed
flamante *a* splendid; (*nuevo*) brand-new
flamenco *a* flamenco; (*de Flandes*) Flemish. **●** *m* (*música etc*) flamenco
flan *m* crème caramel
flaqueza *f* thinness; (*debilidad*) weakness
flash *m* flash
flato *m*, **flatulencia** *f* flatulence
flaut|a *f* flute. **●** *m* & *f* (*músico*) flautist, flutist (*Amer*). **~ín** *m* piccolo. **~ista** *m* & *f* flautist, flutist (*Amer*)
fleco *m* fringe
flecha *f* arrow
flem|a *f* phlegm. **~ático** *a* phlegmatic
flequillo *m* fringe
fletar *vt* charter
flexib|ilidad *f* flexibility. **~le** *a* flexible. **●** *m* flex, cable
flirte|ar *vi* flirt. **~o** *m* flirting
floj|ear *vi* ease up. **~o** *a* loose; (*poco fuerte*) weak; (*viento*) light; (*perezoso*) lazy
flor *f* flower; (*fig*) cream. **~a** *f* flora. **~al** *a* floral. **~ecer** [11] *vi* flower, bloom; (*fig*) flourish. **~eciente** *a* (*fig*) flourishing. **~ero** *m* flower vase. **~ido** *a* flowery; (*selecto*) select; (*lenguaje*) florid. **~ista** *m* & *f* florist

flota f fleet
flot|ador m float. ~**ar** vi float. ~**e** m.
   a ~**e** afloat
flotilla f flotilla
fluctua|ción f fluctuation. ~**r** [21] vi
   fluctuate
flu|idez f fluidity; (fig) fluency. ~**ido**
   a fluid; (fig) fluent. ● m fluid. ~**ir**
   [17] vi flow. ~**jo** m flow. ~**o y reflujo**
   ebb and flow
fluorescente a fluorescent
fluoruro m fluoride
fluvial a river
fobia f phobia
foca f seal
foc|al a focal. ~**o** m focus; (lámpara)
   floodlight; (LAm, bombilla) light
   bulb
fogón m (cocina) cooker
fogoso a spirited
folio m leaf
folk|lore m folklore. ~**órico** a folk
follaje m foliage
follet|ín m newspaper serial. ~**o** m
   pamphlet
follón m (lío) mess; (alboroto) row
fomentar vt foment, stir up
fonda f (pensión) boarding-house
fondo m bottom; (parte más lejana)
   bottom, end; (de escenario, pintura
   etc) background; (profundidad)
   depth. ~**s** mpl funds, money. **a** ~
   thoroughly. **en el** ~ deep down
fonétic|a f phonetics. ~**o** a phonetic
fono m (LAm, del teléfono) earpiece
fontaner|ía plumbing. ~**o** m
   plumber
footing /'futin/ m jogging
forastero a alien. ● m stranger
forceje|ar vi struggle. ~**o** m
   struggle
fórceps m invar forceps
forense a forensic
forjar vt forge
forma f form, shape; (horma)
   mould; (modo) way; (de zapatero)
   last. ~**s** fpl conventions. ~**ción** f
   formation; (educación) training.
   dar ~ **a** shape; (expresar) formulate. **de** ~ **que** so (that). **de todas**
   ~**s** anyway. **estar en** ~ be in good
   form. **guardar** ~**s** keep up
   appearances
formal a formal; (de fiar) reliable;
   (serio) serious. ~**idad** f formality;
   (fiabilidad) reliability; (seriedad)
   seriousness
formar vt form; (hacer) make;
   (enseñar) train. ~**se** vpr form;
   (desarrollarse) develop

formato m format
formidable a formidable; (muy
   grande) enormous; (muy bueno,
   fam) marvellous
fórmula f formula; (receta) recipe
formular vt formulate; make ‹queja
   etc›; (expresar) express
fornido a well-built
forraje m fodder. ~**ar** vt/i forage
forr|ar vt (en el interior) line; (en el
   exterior) cover. ~**o** m lining; (cubierta) cover. ~**o del freno** brake
   lining
fortale|cer [11] vt strengthen. ~**za** f
   strength; (mil) fortress; (fuerza
   moral) fortitude
fortificar [7] vt fortify
fortuito a fortuitous. **encuentro** m
   ~ chance meeting
fortuna f fortune; (suerte) luck. **por**
   ~ fortunately
forz|ado a hard. ~**ar** [2 & 10] vt
   force. ~**osamente** adv necessarily.
   ~**oso** a inevitable; (necesario)
   necessary
fosa f grave
fosfato m phosphate
fósforo m phosphorus; (cerilla)
   match
fósil a & m fossil
fosilizarse [10] vpr fossilize
foso m ditch
foto f photo, photograph. **sacar** ~**s**
   take photographs
fotocopia f photocopy. ~**dora** f pho-
   tocopier. ~**r** vt photocopy
fotogénico a photogenic
fot|ografía f photography; (foto)
   photograph. ~**ografiar** [20] vt photograph. ~**ográfico** a photo-
   graphic. ~**ógrafo** m photographer.
   sacar ~**ografías** take photographs
foyer m foyer
frac m (pl **fraques** o **fracs**) tails
fracas|ar vi fail. ~**o** m failure
fracción f fraction; (pol) faction
fractura f fracture. ~**r** vt fracture,
   break. ~**rse** vpr fracture, break
fragan|cia f fragrance. ~**te** a
   fragrant
fragata f frigate
fr|ágil a fragile; (débil) weak. ~**ag-
   ilidad** f fragility; (debilidad) weakness
fragment|ario a fragmentary. ~**o**
   m fragment
fragor m din
fragoso a rough

fragua f forge. **~r** [15] vt forge; (fig) concoct. ● vi harden

fraile m friar; (monje) monk

frambuesa f raspberry

francés a French. ● m (persona) Frenchman; (lengua) French

Francia f France

franco a frank; (com) free. ● m (moneda) franc

francotirador m sniper

franela f flannel

franja f border; (fleco) fringe

franque|ar vt clear; stamp ⟨carta⟩; overcome ⟨obstáculo⟩. **~o** m stamping; (cantidad) postage

franqueza f frankness; (familiaridad) familiarity

franquis|mo m General Franco's regime; (política) Franco's policy. **~ta** a pro-Franco

frasco m small bottle

frase f phrase; (oración) sentence. **~ hecha** set phrase

fratern|al a fraternal. **~idad** f fraternity

fraud|e m fraud. **~ulento** a fraudulent

fray m brother, friar

frecuen|cia f frequency. **~tar** vt frequent. **~te** a frequent. **con ~cia** frequently

frega|dero m sink. **~r** [1 & 12] vt scrub; wash up ⟨los platos⟩; mop ⟨el suelo⟩; (LAm, fig, molestar, fam) annoy

freír [51, pp **frito**] vt fry; (fig, molestar, fam) annoy. **~se** vpr fry; (persona) be very hot, be boiling (fam)

frenar vt brake; (fig) check

fren|esí m frenzy. **~ético** a frenzied

freno m (de caballería) bit; (auto) brake; (fig) check

frente m front. ● f forehead. **~ a** opposite; (en contra de) opposed to. **~ por ~** opposite; (en un choque) head-on. **al ~** at the head; (hacia delante) forward. **arrugar la ~** frown. **de ~** forward. **hacer ~ a** ⟨cosa⟩; stand up to ⟨persona⟩

fresa f strawberry

fresc|a f fresh air. **~o** a (frío) cool; (nuevo) fresh; (descarado) cheeky. ● m fresh air; (frescor) coolness; (mural) fresco; (persona) impudent person. **~or** m coolness. **~ura** f freshness; (frío) coolness; (descaro) cheek. **al ~o** in the open air. **hacer**

~o be cool. **tomar el ~o** get some fresh air

fresno m ash (tree)

friable a friable

frialdad f coldness; (fig) indifference

fricci|ón f rubbing; (fig, tec) friction; (masaje) massage. **~onar** vt rub

frigidez f coldness; (fig) frigidity

frígido a frigid

frigorífico m refrigerator, fridge (fam)

fríjol m bean. **~es refritos** (Mex) purée of black beans

frío a & m cold. **coger ~** catch cold. **hacer ~** be cold

frisar vi. **~ en** be getting on for, be about

frito a fried; (exasperado) exasperated. **me tiene ~** I'm sick of him

fr|ivolidad f frivolity. **~ívolo** a frivolous

fronda f foliage

fronter|a f frontier; (fig) limit. **~izo** a frontier. **~o** a opposite

frontón m pelota court

frotar vt rub; strike ⟨cerilla⟩

fructífero a fruitful

frugal a frugal

fruncir [9] vt gather ⟨tela⟩; wrinkle ⟨piel⟩

fruslería f trifle

frustra|ción f frustration. **~r** vt frustrate. **~rse** vpr (fracasar) fail. **quedar ~do** be disappointed

frut|a f fruit. **~ería** f fruit shop. **~ero** a fruit. ● m fruiterer; (recipiente) fruit bowl. **~icultura** f fruit-growing. **~illa** f (LAm) strawberry. **~o** m fruit

fucsia f fuchsia

fuego m fire. **~s artificiales** fireworks. **a ~ lento** on a low heat. **tener ~** have a light

fuente f fountain; (manantial) spring; (plato) serving dish; (fig) source

fuera adv out; (al exterior) outside; (en otra parte) away; (en el extranjero) abroad. ● vb véase **ir** y **ser**. **~ de** outside; (excepto) except for, besides. **por ~** on the outside

fuerte a strong; ⟨color⟩ bright; ⟨sonido⟩ loud; ⟨dolor⟩ severe; (duro) hard; (grande) large; ⟨lluvia, nevada⟩ heavy. ● m fort; (fig) strong point. ● adv hard; (con hablar etc) loudly; (mucho) a lot

fuerza f strength; (poder) power; (en física) force; (mil) forces. **~ de**

voluntad will-power. **a ~ de** by dint of, by means of. **a la ~** by necessity. **por ~** by force; (*por necesidad*) by necessity. **tener ~s para** have the strength to

fuese *vb véase* **ir** *y* **ser**

fug|a *f* flight, escape; (*de gas etc*) leak; (*mus*) fugue. **~arse** [12] *vpr* flee, escape. **~az** *a* fleeting. **~itivo** *a & m* fugitive. **ponerse en ~a** take to flight

fui *vb véase* **ir** *y* **ser**

fulano *m* so-and-so. **~, mengano y zutano** Tom, Dick and Harry

fulgor *m* brilliance; (*fig*) splendour

fulminar *vt* strike by lightning; (*fig, mirar*) look daggers at

fuma|dor *a* smoking. ● *m* smoker. **~r** *vt/i* smoke. **~rse** *vpr* smoke; (*fig, gastar*) squander. **~rada** *f* puff of smoke. **~r en pipa** smoke a pipe. **prohibido ~r** no smoking

funámbulo *m* tightrope walker

funci|ón *f* function; (*de un cargo etc*) duties; (*de teatro*) show, performance. **~onal** *a* functional. **~onar** *vi* work, function. **~onario** *m* civil servant. **no ~ona** out of order

funda *f* cover. **~ de almohada** pillowcase

funda|ción *f* foundation. **~mental** *a* fundamental. **~mentar** *vt* lay the foundations of; (*fig*) base. **~mento** *m* foundation. **~r** *vt* found; (*fig*) base. **~rse** *vpr* be based

fundi|ción *f* melting; (*de metales*) smelting; (*taller*) foundry. **~r** *vt* melt; smelt ⟨*metales*⟩; cast ⟨*objeto*⟩; blend ⟨*colores*⟩; (*fusionar*) merge. **~rse** *vpr* melt; (*unirse*) unite

fúnebre *a* funeral; (*sombrío*) gloomy

funeral *a* funeral. ● *m* funeral. **~es** *mpl* funeral

funicular *a & m* funicular

furg|ón *m* van. **~oneta** *f* van

fur|ia *f* fury; (*violencia*) violence. **~ibundo** *a* furious. **~ioso** *a* furious. **~or** *m* fury

furtivo *a* furtive

furúnculo *m* boil

fuselaje *m* fuselage

fusible *m* fuse

fusil *m* gun. **~ar** *vt* shoot

fusión *f* melting; (*unión*) fusion; (*com*) merger

fútbol *m* football

futbolista *m* footballer

fútil *a* futile

futur|ista *a* futuristic. ● *m & f* futurist. **~o** *a & m* future

G

gabán *m* overcoat

garbardina *f* raincoat; (*tela*) gabardine

gabinete *m* (*pol*) cabinet; (*en museo etc*) room; (*de dentista, médico etc*) consulting room

gacela *f* gazelle

gaceta *f* gazette

gachas *fpl* porridge

gacho *a* drooping

gaélico *a* Gaelic

gafa *f* hook. **~s** *fpl* glasses, spectacles. **~s de sol** sun-glasses

gaf|ar *vt* hook; (*fam*) bring bad luck to. **~e** *m* jinx

gaita *f* bagpipes

gajo *m* (*de naranja, nuez etc*) segment

gala|s *fpl* finery, best clothes. **estar de ~** be dressed up. **hacer ~ de** show off

galán *m* (*en el teatro*) male lead; (*enamorado*) lover

galante *m* gallant. **~ar** *vt* court. **~ría** *f* gallantry

galápago *m* turtle

galardón *m* reward

galaxia *f* galaxy

galeón *m* galleon

galera *f* galley

galería *f* gallery

Gales *m* Wales. **país de ~** Wales

gal|és *a* Welsh. ● *m* Welshman; (*lengua*) Welsh. **~esa** *f* Welshwoman

galgo *m* greyhound

Galicia *f* Galicia

galimatías *m invar* (*fam*) gibberish

galón *m* gallon; (*cinta*) braid; (*mil*) stripe

galop|ar *vi* gallop. **~e** *m* gallop

galvanizar [10] *vt* galvanize

gallard|ía *f* elegance. **~o** *a* elegant

gallego *a & m* Galician

galleta *f* biscuit (*Brit*), cookie (*Amer*)

gall|ina *f* hen, chicken; (*fig, fam*) coward. **~o** *m* cock

gama *f* scale; (*fig*) range

gamba *f* prawn (*Brit*), shrimp (*Amer*)

gamberro *m* hooligan

gamuza *f* (*piel*) chamois leather

gana f wish, desire; (*apetito*) appetite. **de buena ∼** willingly. **de mala ∼** reluctantly. **no me da la ∼** I don't feel like it. **tener ∼s de** (+ *infinitivo*) feel like (+ *gerundio*)

ganad|ería f cattle raising; (*ganado*) livestock. **∼o** m livestock. **∼o de cerda** pigs. **∼o lanar** sheep. **∼o vacuno** cattle

ganar vt earn; (*en concurso, juego etc*) win; (*alcanzar*) reach; (*aventajar*) beat. ● vi (*vencer*) win; (*mejorar*) improve. **∼se la vida** earn a living. **salir ganando** come out better off

ganch|illo m crochet. **∼o** m hook. **∼oso** a, **∼udo** a hooked. **echar ∼o a** hook. **hacer ∼illo** crochet. **tener ∼o** be very attractive

gandul a & m & f good-for-nothing

ganga f bargain; (*buena situación*) easy job, cushy job (*fam*)

gangrena f gangrene

gans|ada f silly thing. **∼o** m goose

gañi|do m yelping. **∼r** [22] vi yelp

garabat|ear vt/i (*garrapatear*) scribble. **∼o** m (*garrapato*) scribble

garaj|e m garage. **∼ista** m & f garage attendant

garant|e m & f guarantor. **∼ía** f guarantee. **∼ir** [24] vt (*esp LAm*), **∼izar** [10] vt guarantee

garapiñado a. **almendras** fpl **garapiñadas** sugared almonds

garbanzo m chick-pea

garbo m poise; (*de escrito*) style. **∼so** a elegant

garfio m hook

garganta f throat; (*desfiladero*) gorge; (*de botella*) neck

gárgaras fpl. **hacer ∼** gargle

gargarismo m gargle

gárgola f gargoyle

garita f hut; (*de centinela*) sentry box

garito m gambling den

garra f (*de animal*) claw; (*de ave*) talon

garrafa f carafe

garrapata f tick

garrapat|ear vi scribble. **∼o** m scribble

garrote m club, cudgel; (*tormento*) garrotte

gárrulo a garrulous

garúa f (*LAm*) drizzle

garza f heron

gas m gas. **con ∼** fizzy. **sin ∼** still

gasa f gauze

gaseosa f lemonade

gasfitero m (*Arg*) plumber

gas|óleo m diesel. **∼olina** f petrol (*Brit*), gasoline (*Amer*), gas (*Amer*). **∼olinera** f petrol station (*Brit*), gas station (*Amer*); (*lancha*) motor boat. **∼ómetro** m gasometer

gast|ado a spent; (*vestido etc*) worn out. **∼ador** m spendthrift. **∼ar** vt spend; (*consumir*) use; (*malgastar*) waste; wear (*vestido etc*); crack (*broma*). ● vi spend. **∼arse** vpr wear out. **∼o** m expense; (*acción de gastar*) spending

gástrico a gastric

gastronomía f gastronomy

gat|a f cat. **a ∼as** on all fours. **∼ear** vi crawl

gatillo m trigger; (*de dentista*) (dental) forceps

gat|ito m kitten. **∼o** m cat. **dar ∼o por liebre** take s.o. in

gaucho a & m Gaucho

gaveta f drawer

gavilla f sheaf; (*de personas*) band, gang

gaviota f seagull

gazpacho m gazpacho, cold soup

géiser m geyser

gelatina f gelatine; (*jalea*) jelly

gelignita f gelignite

gema f gem

gemelo m twin. **∼s** mpl (*anteojos*) binoculars; (*de camisa*) cuff-links. **G∼s** Gemini

gemido m groan

Géminis mpl Gemini

gemir [5] vi groan; ⟨*animal*⟩ whine, howl

gen m, **gene** m gene

geneal|ogía f genealogy. **∼ógico** a genealogical. **árbol** m **∼ógico** family tree

generación f generation

general a general; (*corriente*) common. ● m general. **∼ísimo** m generalissimo, supreme commander. **∼ización** f generalization. **∼izar** [10] vt/i generalize. **∼mente** adv generally. **en ∼** in general. **por lo ∼** generally

generar vt generate

género m type, sort; (*biol*) genus; (*gram*) gender; (*producto*) product. **∼s de punto** knitwear. **∼ humano** mankind

generos|idad f generosity. **∼o** a generous; ⟨*vino*⟩ full-bodied

génesis m genesis

genétic|a f genetics. **∼o** a genetic

genial *a* brilliant; *(agradable)* pleasant

genio *m* temper; *(carácter)* nature; *(talento, persona)* genius

genital *a* genital. **~es** *mpl* genitals

gente *f* people; *(nación)* nation; *(familia, fam)* family; *(Mex, persona)* person

gentil *a* charming; *(pagano)* pagan. **~eza** *f* elegance; *(encanto)* charm; *(amabilidad)* kindness

gentío *m* crowd

genuflexión *f* genuflection

genuino *a* genuine

ge|ografía *f* geography. **~ográfico** *a* geographical. **~ógrafo** *m* geographer

ge|ología *f* geology. **~ólogo** *m* geologist

geom|etría *f* geometry. **~étrico** *a* geometrical

geranio *m* geranium

geren|cia *f* management. **~te** *m* manager

geriatría *f* geriatrics

germánico *a* & *m* Germanic

germen *m* germ

germicida *f* germicide

germinar *vi* germinate

gestación *f* gestation

gesticula|ción *f* gesticulation. **~r** *vi* gesticulate; *(hacer muecas)* grimace

gesti|ón *f* step; *(administración)* management. **~onar** *vt* take steps to arrange; *(dirigir)* manage

gesto *m* expression; *(ademán)* gesture; *(mueca)* grimace

Gibraltar *m* Gibraltar

gibraltareño *a* & *m* Gibraltarian

gigante *a* gigantic. ● *m* giant. **~sco** *a* gigantic

gimn|asia *f* gymnastics. **~asio** *m* gymnasium, gym *(fam)*. **~asta** *m* & *f* gymnast. **~ástica** *f* gymnastics

gimotear *vi* whine

ginebra *f* gin

Ginebra *f* Geneva

ginec|ología *f* gynaecology. **~ólogo** *m* gynaecologist

gira *f* excursion; *(a varios sitios)* tour

girar *vt* spin; *(por giro postal)* transfer. ● *vi* rotate, go round; *(camino etc)* turn

girasol *m* sunflower

gir|atorio *a* revolving. **~o** *m* turn; *(com)* draft; *(locución)* expression. **~o postal** postal order

giroscopio *m* gyroscope

gis *m* chalk

gitano *a* & *m* gypsy

glacia|l *a* icy. **~r** *m* glacier

gladiador *m* gladiator

glándula *f* gland

glasear *vt* glaze; *(culin)* ice

glicerina *f* glycerine

glicina *f* wisteria

glob|al *a* global; *(fig)* overall. **~o** *m* globe; *(aeróstato, juguete)* balloon

glóbulo *m* globule; *(med)* corpuscle

gloria *f* glory. **~rse** *vpr* boast *(de* about)

glorieta *f* bower; *(auto)* roundabout *(Brit)*, *(traffic)* circle *(Amer)*

glorificar [7] *vt* glorify

glorioso *a* glorious

glosario *m* glossary

glot|ón *a* gluttonous. ● *m* glutton. **~onería** *f* gluttony

glucosa *f* glucose

gnomo /'nomo/ *m* gnome

gob|ernación *f* government. **~ernador** *a* governing. ● *m* governor. **~ernante** *a* governing. **~ernar** [1] *vt* govern; *(dirigir)* manage, direct. **~ierno** *m* government; *(dirección)* management, direction. **~ierno de la casa** housekeeping. **Ministerio** *m* **de la G~ernación** Home Office *(Brit)*, Department of the Interior *(Amer)*

goce *m* enjoyment

gol *m* goal

golf *m* golf

golfo *m* gulf; *(niño)* urchin; *(holgazán)* layabout

golondrina *f* swallow

golos|ina *f* titbit; *(dulce)* sweet. **~o** *a* fond of sweets

golpe *m* blow; *(puñetazo)* punch; *(choque)* bump; *(de emoción)* shock; *(acceso)* fit; *(en fútbol)* shot; *(en golf, en tenis, de remo)* stroke. **~ar** *vt* hit; *(dar varios golpes)* beat; *(con mucho ruido)* bang; *(con el puño)* punch. ● *vi* knock. **~ de estado** coup d'etat. **~ de fortuna** stroke of luck. **~ de mano** raid. **~ de vista** glance. **~ militar** military coup. **de ~** suddenly. **de un ~** at one go

gom|a *f* rubber; *(para pegar)* glue; *(anillo)* rubber band; *(elástico)* elastic. **~a de borrar** rubber. **~a de pegar** glue. **~a espuma** foam rubber. **~ita** *f* rubber band

gongo *m* gong

gord|a *f* *(Mex)* thick tortilla. **~iflón** *m* *(fam)*, **~inflón** *m* *(fam)* fatty. **~o** *a* *(persona)* fat; *(carne)* fatty;

(*grande*) large, big. ● *m* first prize.
~**ura** *f* fatness; (*grasa*) fat
gorila *f* gorilla
gorje|ar *vi* chirp. ~**o** *m* chirping
gorra *f* cap
gorrión *m* sparrow
gorro *m* cap; (*de niño*) bonnet
got|a *f* drop; (*med*) gout. ~**ear**
vi drip. ~**eo** *m* dripping. ~**era** *f* leak.
ni ~**a** nothing
gótico *a* Gothic
gozar [10] *vt* enjoy. ● *vi.* ~ **de** enjoy.
~**se** *vpr* enjoy
gozne *m* hinge
gozo *m* pleasure; (*alegría*) joy. ~**so**
a delighted
graba|ción *f* recording. ~**do** *m*
engraving, print; (*en libro*) illus-
tration. ~**r** *vt* engrave; record ⟨*discos etc*⟩
gracejo *m* wit
graci|a *f* grace; (*favor*) favour;
(*humor*) wit. ~**as** *fpl* thanks. ¡~**as!**
thank you!, thanks! ~**oso** *a* funny.
● *m* fool, comic character. **dar las**
~**as** thank. **hacer** ~**a** amuse; (*gustar*) please. ¡**muchas** ~**as!** thank
you very much! **tener** ~**a** be funny
grad|a *f* step; (*línea*) row; (*de anfi-
teatro*) tier. ~**ación** *f* gradation. ~**o**
m degree; (*escol*) year (*Brit*), grade
(*Amer*); (*voluntad*) willingness
gradua|ción *f* graduation; (*de alco-
hol*) proof. ~**do** *m* graduate. ~**l** *a*
gradual. ~**r** [21] *vt* graduate;
(*medir*) measure; (*univ*) confer a
degree on. ~**rse** *vpr* graduate
gráfic|a *f* graph. ~**o** *a* graphic. ● *m*
graph
grajo *m* rook
gram|ática *f* grammar. ~**atical** *a*
grammatical
gramo *m* gram, gramme (*Brit*)
gramófono *m* record-player,
gramophone (*Brit*), phonograph
(*Amer*)
gran *a* véase **grande**
grana *f* (*color*) scarlet
granada *f* pomegranate; (*mil*)
grenade
granate *m* garnet
Gran Bretaña *f* Great Britain
grande *a* (*delante de nombre en singular* **gran**) big, large; (*alto*) tall;
(*fig*) great. ● *m* grandee. ~**za** *f*
greatness
grandioso *a* magnificent
granel *m.* **a** ~ in bulk; (*suelto*) loose;
(*fig*) in abundance

granero *m* barn
granito *m* granite; (*grano*) small
grain
graniz|ado *m* iced drink. ~**ar** [10] *vi*
hail. ~**o** *m* hail
granj|a *f* farm. ~**ero** *m* farmer
grano *m* grain; (*semilla*) seed; (*de
café*) bean; (*med*) spot. ~**s** *mpl*
cereals
granuja *m* & *f* rogue
gránulo *m* granule
grapa *f* staple
gras|a *f* grease; (*culin*) fat. ~**iento** *a*
greasy
gratifica|ción *f* (*propina*) tip; (*de
sueldo*) bonus. ~**r** [7] *vt* (*dar propina*) tip
gratis *adv* free
gratitud *f* gratitude
grato *a* pleasant; (*bienvenido*)
welcome
gratuito *a* free; (*fig*) uncalled for
grava *f* gravel
grava|men *m* obligation. ~**r** *vt* tax;
(*cargar*) burden
grave *a* serious; (*pesado*) heavy;
⟨*sonido*⟩ low; ⟨*acento*⟩ grave. ~**dad**
f gravity
gravilla *f* gravel
gravita|ción *f* gravitation. ~**r** *vi*
gravitate; (*apoyarse*) rest (**sobre**
on); (*fig, pesar*) weigh (**sobre** on)
gravoso *a* onerous; (*costoso*)
expensive
graznar *vi* ⟨*cuervo*⟩ caw; ⟨*pato*⟩
quack
Grecia *f* Greece
gregario *a* gregarious
greguería *f* uproar
gremio *m* union
greñ|a *f* mop of hair. ~**udo** *a*
unkempt
gresca *f* uproar; (*riña*) quarrel
griego *a* & *m* Greek
grieta *f* crack
grifo *m* tap, faucet (*Amer*); (*animal
fantástico*) griffin
grilletes *mpl* shackles
grillo *m* cricket; (*bot*) shoot. ~**s** *mpl*
shackles
grima *f.* **dar** ~ annoy
gringo *m* (*LAm*) Yankee (*fam*),
American
gripe *f* flu (*fam*), influenza
gris *a* grey. ● *m* grey; (*policía, fam*)
policeman
grit|ar *vt* shout (for); (*como protesta*)
boo. ● *vi* shout. ~**ería** *f*, ~**erío** *m*

uproar. **~o** *m* shout; (*de dolor, sorpresa*) cry; (*chillido*) scream. **dar ~s** shout

grosella *f* redcurrant. **~ negra** blackcurrant

groser|ía *f* coarseness; (*palabras etc*) coarse remark. **~o** *a* coarse; (*descortés*) rude

grosor *m* thickness

grotesco *a* grotesque

grúa *f* crane

grues|a *f* gross. **~o** *a* thick; (*persona*) fat, stout. ● *m* thickness; (*fig*) main body

grulla *f* crane

grumo *m* clot; (*de leche*) curd

gruñi|do *m* grunt; (*fig*) grumble. **~r** [22] *vi* grunt; (*perro*) growl; (*refunfuñar*) grumble

grupa *f* hindquarters

grupo *m* group

gruta *f* grotto

guacamole *m* (*Mex*) avocado purée

guadaña *f* scythe

guagua *f* trifle; (*esp LAm, autobús, fam*) bus

guante *m* glove

guapo *a* good-looking; (*chica*) pretty; (*elegante*) smart

guarapo *m* (*LAm*) sugar cane liquor

guarda *m & f* guard; (*de parque etc*) keeper. ● *f* protection. **~barros** *m invar* mudguard. **~bosque** *m* gamekeeper. **~costas** *m invar* coastguard vessel. **~dor** *a* careful. ● *m* keeper. **~espaldas** *m invar* bodyguard. **~meta** *m invar* goalkeeper. **~r** *vt* keep; (*vigilar*) guard; (*proteger*) protect; (*reservar*) save, keep. **~rse** *vpr* be on one's guard. **~rse de** (+ *infinitivo*) avoid (+ *gerundio*). **~rropa** *m* wardrobe; (*en local público*) cloakroom. **~vallas** *m invar* (*LAm*) goalkeeper

guardería *f* nursery

guardia *f* guard; (*custodia*) care. ● *f* guard. **G~ Civil** Civil Guard. **~ municipal** policeman. **~ de tráfico** traffic policeman. **estar de ~** be on duty. **estar en ~** be on one's guard. **montar la ~** mount guard

guardián *m* guardian; (*de parque etc*) keeper; (*de edificio*) caretaker

guardilla *f* attic

guar|ecer [11] (*albergar*) give shelter to. **~ecerse** *vpr* take shelter. **~ida** *f* den, lair; (*de personas*) hideout

guarn|ecer [11] *vt* provide; (*adornar*) decorate; (*culin*) garnish. **~ición** *m* decoration; (*de caballo*) harness; (*culin*) garnish; (*mil*) garrison; (*de piedra preciosa*) setting

guarro *m* pig

guasa *f* joke; (*ironía*) irony

guaso *a* (*Arg*) coarse

guasón *a* humorous. ● *m* joker

Guatemala *f* Guatemala

guatemalteco *a* from Guatemala. ● *m* person from Guatemala

guateque *m* party

guayaba *f* guava; (*dulce*) guava jelly

guayabera *f* (*Mex*) shirt

gubernamental *a*, **gubernativo** *a* governmental

güero *a* (*Mex*) fair

guerr|a *f* war; (*método*) warfare. **~a civil** civil war. **~ear** *vi* wage war. **~ero** *a* war; (*belicoso*) fighting. ● *m* warrior. **~illa** *f* band of guerillas. **~illero** *m* guerilla. **dar ~a** annoy

guía *m & f* guide. ● *f* guidebook; (*de teléfonos*) directory; (*de ferrocarriles*) timetable

guiar [20] *vt* guide; (*llevar*) lead; (*auto*) drive. **~se** *vpr* be guided (*por* by)

guij|arro *m* pebble. **~o** *m* gravel

guillotina *f* guillotine

guind|a *f* morello cherry. **~illa** *f* chilli

guiñapo *m* rag; (*fig, persona*) reprobate

guiñ|ar *vt/i* wink. **~o** *m* wink. **hacer ~os** wink

gui|ón *m* hyphen, dash; (*de película etc*) script. **~onista** *m & f* scriptwriter

guirnalda *f* garland

güiro *m* (*LAm*) gourd

guisa *f* manner, way. **a ~ de** as. **de tal ~** in such a way

guisado *m* stew

guisante *m* pea. **~ de olor** sweet pea

guis|ar *vt/i* cook. **~o** *m* dish

güisqui *m* whisky

guitarr|a *f* guitar. **~ista** *m & f* guitarist

gula *f* gluttony

gusano *m* worm; (*larva de mosca*) maggot

gustar *vt* taste. ● *vi* please. **¿te gusta?** do you like it? **me gusta el vino** I like wine

gusto *m* taste; (*placer*) pleasure. **~so** *a* tasty; (*agradable*) pleasant. **a ~** comfortable. **a mi ~** to my liking.

buen ∼ (good) taste. **con mucho ∼** with pleasure. **dar ∼** please. **mucho ∼** pleased to meet you

gutural a guttural

H

ha vb véase **haber**

haba f broad bean; (de café etc) bean

Habana f. **la ∼** Havana

haban|era f habanera, Cuban dance. **∼ero** a from Havana. ● m person from Havana. **∼o** m (puro) Havana

haber v aux [30] have. ● v impersonal (presente s & pl **hay**, imperfecto s & pl **había**, pretérito s & pl **hubo**) be. **hay 5 bancos en la plaza** there are 5 banks in the square. **hay que hacerlo** it must be done, you have to do it. **he aquí** here is, here are. **no hay de qué** don't mention it, not at all. **¿qué hay?** (¿qué pasa?) what's the matter?; (¿qué tal?) how are you?

habichuela f bean

hábil a skilful; (listo) clever; (adecuado) suitable

habilidad f skill; (astucia) cleverness

habilita|ción f qualification. **∼r** vt qualify

habita|ble a habitable. **∼ción** f room; (casa etc) dwelling; (cuarto de dormir) bedroom; (en biología) habitat. **∼ción de matrimonio, ∼ción doble** double room. **∼ción individual** , **∼ción sencilla** single room. **∼do** a inhabited. **∼nte** m inhabitant. **∼r** vt live in. ● vi live

hábito m habit

habitual a usual, habitual; ‹cliente› regular. **∼mente** adv usually

habituar [21] vt accustom. **∼se** vpr. **∼se a** get used to

habla f speech; (idioma) language; (dialecto) dialect. **al ∼** (al teléfono) speaking. **ponerse al ∼ con** get in touch with. **∼dor** a talkative. ● m chatterbox. **∼duría** f rumour. **∼durías** fpl gossip. **∼nte** a speaking. ● m & f speaker. **∼r** vt speak. ● vi speak, talk (con to). **∼rse** vpr speak. **¡ni ∼r!** out of the question! **se ∼ español** Spanish spoken

hacedor m creator, maker

hacendado m landowner; (LAm) farmer

hacendoso a hard-working

hacer [31] vt do; (fabricar, producir etc) make; (en matemáticas) make, be. ● v impersonal (con expresiones meteorológicas) be; (con determinado periodo de tiempo) ago. **∼se** vpr become; (acostumbrarse) get used (a to); (estar hecho) be made. **∼ a** act as. **∼se a la mar** put to sea. **∼se el sordo** pretend to be deaf. **hace buen tiempo** it's fine weather. **hace calor** it's hot. **hace frío** it's cold. **hace poco** recently. **hace 7 años** 7 years ago. **hace sol** it's sunny. **hace viento** it's windy. **¿qué le vamos a ∼?** what are we going to do?

hacia prep towards; (cerca de) near; (con tiempo) at about. **∼ abajo** down(wards). **∼ arriba** up(wards). **∼ las dos** at about two o'clock

hacienda f country estate; (en LAm) ranch; (LAm, ganado) livestock; (pública) treasury. **Ministerio de H∼** Ministry of Finance; (en Gran Bretaña) Exchequer; (en Estados Unidos) Treasury. **ministro de H∼** Minister of Finance; (en Gran Bretaña) Chancellor of the Exchequer; (en Estados Unidos) Secretary of the Treasury

hacinar vt stack

hacha f axe; (antorcha) torch

hachís m hashish

hada f fairy. **cuento m de ∼s** fairy tale

hado m fate

hago vb véase **hacer**

Haití m Haiti

halag|ar [12] vt flatter. **∼üeño** a flattering

halcón m falcon

hálito m breath

halo m halo

hall /xol/ m hall

halla|r vt find; (descubrir) discover. **∼rse** vpr be. **∼zgo** m discovery

hamaca f hammock; (asiento) deck-chair

hambr|e f hunger; (de muchos) famine. **∼iento** a starving. **tener ∼e** be hungry

Hamburgo m Hamburg

hamburguesa f hamburger

hamp|a f underworld. **∼ón** m thug

handicap /'xandikap/ m handicap

hangar m hangar

haragán *a* lazy, idle. ● *m* layabout

harap|iento *a* in rags. **~o** *m* rag

harina *f* flour

harpa *f* harp

hart|ar *vt* satisfy; (*fastidiar*) annoy. **~arse** *vpr* (*comer*) eat one's fill; (*cansarse*) get fed up (**de** with). **~azgo** *m* surfeit. **~o** *a* full; (*cansado*) tired; (*fastidiado*) fed up (**de** with). ● *adv* enough; (*muy*) very. **~ura** *f* surfeit; (*abundancia*) plenty; (*de deseo*) satisfaction

hasta *prep* as far as; (*con tiempo*) until, till; (*Mex*) not until. ● *adv* even. ¡**~ la vista!** goodbye!, see you! (*fam*). ¡**~ luego!** see you later! ¡**~ mañana!** see you tomorrow! ¡**~ pronto!** see you soon!

hast|iar [20] *vt* annoy; (*cansar*) weary, tire; (*aburrir*) bore. **~iarse** *vpr* get fed up (**de** with). **~ío** *m* weariness; (*aburrimiento*) boredom; (*asco*) disgust

hat|illo *m* bundle (of belongings); (*ganado*) small flock. **~o** *m* belongings; (*ganado*) flock, herd

haya *f* beech (tree). ● *vb véase* **haber**

Haya *f*. **la ~** the Hague

haz *m* bundle; (*de trigo*) sheaf; (*de rayos*) beam

hazaña *f* exploit

hazmerreír *m* laughing-stock

he *vb véase* **haber**

hebdomadario *a* weekly

hebilla *f* buckle

hebra *f* thread; (*fibra*) fibre

hebreo *a* Hebrew; (*actualmente*) Jewish. ● *m* Hebrew; (*actualmente*) Jew; (*lengua*) Hebrew

hecatombe *m* (*fig*) disaster

hechi|cera *f* witch. **~cería** *f* witchcraft. **~cero** *a* magic. ● *m* wizard. **~zar** [10] *vt* cast a spell on; (*fig*) fascinate. **~zo** *m* witchcraft; (*un acto de brujería*) spell; (*fig*) fascination

hech|o *pp de* **hacer**. ● *a* mature; (*terminado*) finished; ⟨*vestidos etc*⟩ ready-made; (*culin*) done. ● *m* fact; (*acto*) deed; (*cuestión*) matter; (*suceso*) event. **~ura** *f* making; (*forma*) form; (*del cuerpo*) build; (*calidad de fabricación*) workmanship. **de ~o** in fact

hed|er [1] *vi* stink. **~iondez** *f* stench. **~iondo** *a* stinking, smelly. **~or** *m* stench

hela|da *f* freeze; (*escarcha*) frost. **~dera** *f* (*LAm*) refrigerator, fridge (*Brit*, *fam*). **~dería** *f* ice-cream

shop. **~do** *a* frozen; (*muy frío*) very cold. ● *m* ice-cream. **~dora** *f* freezer. **~r** [1] *vt* freeze. **~rse** *vpr* freeze

helecho *m* fern

hélice *f* spiral; (*propulsor*) propeller

heli|cóptero *m* helicopter. **~puerto** *m* heliport

hembra *f* female; (*mujer*) woman

hemisferio *m* hemisphere

hemorragia *f* haemorrhage

hemorroides *fpl* haemorrhoids, piles

henchir [5] *vt* fill. **~se** *vpr* stuff o.s.

hend|er [1] *vt* split. **~idura** *f* crack, split; (*geol*) fissure

heno *m* hay

heráldica *f* heraldry

herb|áceo *a* herbaceous. **~olario** *m* herbalist. **~oso** *a* grassy

hered|ad *f* country estate. **~ar** *vt/i* inherit. **~era** *f* heiress. **~ero** *m* heir. **~itario** *a* hereditary

herej|e *m* heretic. **~ía** *f* heresy

herencia *f* inheritance; (*fig*) heritage

heri|da *f* injury. **~do** *a* injured, wounded. ● *m* injured person. **~r** [4] *vt* injure, wound; (*fig*) hurt. **~rse** *vpr* hurt o.s. **los ~dos** the injured; (*cantidad*) the number of injured

herman|a *f* sister. **~a política** sister-in-law. **~astra** *f* stepsister. **~astro** *m* stepbrother. **~dad** *f* brotherhood. **~o** *m* brother. **~o político** brother-in-law. **~os gemelos** twins

hermético *a* hermetic; (*fig*) watertight

hermos|o *a* beautiful; (*espléndido*) splendid; ⟨*hombre*⟩ handsome. **~ura** *f* beauty

hernia *f* hernia

héroe *m* hero

hero|ico *a* heroic. **~ína** *f* heroine; (*droga*) heroin. **~ismo** *m* heroism

herr|adura *f* horseshoe. **~amienta** *f* tool. **~ería** *f* smithy. **~ero** *m* blacksmith. **~umbre** *f* rust

herv|idero *m* (*manantial*) spring; (*fig*) hotbed; (*multitud*) throng. **~ir** [4] *vt/i* boil. **~or** *m* boiling; (*fig*) ardour

heterogéneo *a* heterogeneous

heterosexual *a* & *m* & *f* heterosexual

hex|agonal *a* hexagonal. **~ágono** *m* hexagon

hiato *m* hiatus

hiberna|ción *f* hibernation. **~r** *vi* hibernate

hibisco *m* hibiscus

híbrido *a & m* hybrid

hice *vb véase* **hacer**

hidalgo *m* nobleman

hidrata|nte *a* moisturizing. **~r** *vt* hydrate; ⟨*crema etc*⟩ moisturize. **crema** *f* **~nte** moisturizing cream

hidráulico *a* hydraulic

hidroavión *m* seaplane

hidroeléctrico *a* hydroelectric

hidrófilo *a* absorbent

hidr|ofobia *f* rabies. **~ófobo** *a* rabid

hidrógeno *m* hydrogen

hidroplano *m* seaplane

hiedra *f* ivy

hiel *f* (*fig*) bitterness

hielo *m* ice; (*escarcha*) frost; (*fig*) coldness

hiena *f* hyena; (*fig*) brute

hierba *f* grass; (*culin, med*) herb. **~buena** *f* mint. **mala ~** weed; (*gente*) bad people, evil people

hierro *m* iron

hígado *m* liver

higi|ene *f* hygiene. **~énico** *a* hygienic

hig|o *m* fig. **~uera** *f* fig tree

hij|a *f* daughter. **~a política** daughter-in-law. **~astra** *f* step-daughter. **~astro** *m* stepson. **~o** *m* son. **~o político** son-in-law. **~s** *mpl* sons; (*chicos y chicas*) children

hilar *vt* spin. **~ delgado** split hairs

hilaridad *f* laughter, hilarity

hilera *f* row; (*mil*) file

hilo *m* thread; (*elec*) wire; (*de líquido*) trickle; (*lino*) linen

hilv|án *m* tacking. **~anar** *vt* tack; (*fig, bosquejar*) outline

himno *m* hymn. **~ nacional** anthem

hincapié *m*. **hacer ~ en** stress, insist on

hincar [7] *vt* drive in. **~se** *vpr* sink into. **~se de rodillas** kneel down

hincha *f* (*fam*) grudge; (*aficionado, fam*) fan

hincha|do *a* inflated; (*med*) swollen; ⟨*persona*⟩ arrogant. **~r** *vt* inflate, blow up. **~rse** *vpr* swell up; (*fig, comer mucho, fam*) gorge o.s. **~zón** *f* swelling; (*fig*) arrogance

hindi *m* Hindi

hindú *a* Hindu

hiniesta *f* (*bot*) broom

hinojo *m* fennel

hiper... *pref* hyper...

hiper|mercado *m* hypermarket. **~sensible** *a* hypersensitive. **~tensión** *f* high blood pressure

hípico *a* horse

hipn|osis *f* hypnosis. **~ótico** *a* hypnotic. **~otismo** *m* hypnotism. **~otizador** *m* hypnotist. **~otizar** [10] *vt* hypnotize

hipo *m* hiccup. **tener ~** have hiccups

hipocondríaco *a & m* hypochondriac

hip|ocresía *f* hypocrisy. **~ócrita** *a* hypocritical. ● *m & f* hypocrite

hipodérmico *a* hypodermic

hipódromo *m* racecourse

hipopótamo *m* hippopotamus

hipoteca *f* mortgage. **~r** [7] *vt* mortgage

hip|ótesis *f invar* hypothesis. **~otético** *a* hypothetical

hiriente *a* offensive, wounding

hirsuto *a* shaggy

hirviente *a* boiling

hispánico *a* Hispanic

hispano... *pref* Spanish

Hispanoamérica *f* Spanish America

hispano|americano *a* Spanish American. **~hablante** *a*, **~parlante** *a* Spanish-speaking

hist|eria *f* hysteria. **~érico** *a* hysterical. **~erismo** *m* hysteria

hist|oria *f* history; (*cuento*) story. **~oriador** *m* historian. **~órico** *a* historical. **~orieta** *f* tale; (*con dibujos*) strip cartoon. **pasar a la ~oria** go down in history

hito *m* milestone

hizo *vb véase* **hacer**

hocico *m* snout; (*fig, de enfado*) grimace

hockey *m* hockey. **~ sobre hielo** ice hockey

hogar *m* hearth; (*fig*) home. **~eño** *a* home; ⟨*persona*⟩ home-loving

hogaza *f* large loaf

hoguera *f* bonfire

hoja *f* leaf; (*de papel, metal etc*) sheet; (*de cuchillo, espada etc*) blade. **~ de afeitar** razor blade. **~lata** *f* tin. **~latería** *f* tinware. **~latero** *m* tinsmith

hojaldre *m* puff pastry, flaky pastry

hojear *vt* leaf through; (*leer superficialmente*) glance through

hola *int* hello!

Holanda *f* Holland

holand|és *a* Dutch. ● *m* Dutchman; (*lengua*) Dutch. **~esa** *f* Dutchwoman

holg|ado *a* loose; (*fig*) comfortable. **~ar** [2 & 12] *vt* (*no trabajar*) not work, have a day off; (*sobrar*) be unnecessary. **~azán** *a* lazy. ● *m* idler. **~ura** *f* looseness; (*fig*) comfort; (*en mecánica*) play. **huelga decir que** needless to say
holocausto *m* holocaust
hollín *m* soot
hombre *m* man; (*especie humana*) man(kind). ● *int* Good Heavens!; (*de duda*) well. **~ de estado** statesman. **~ de negocios** businessman. **~ rana** frogman. **el ~ de la calle** the man in the street
hombr|era *f* epaulette; (*almohadilla*) shoulder pad. **~o** *m* shoulder
hombruno *a* masculine
homenaje *m* homage; (*fig*) tribute. **rendir ~** a pay tribute to
home|ópata *m* homoeopath. **~opatía** *f* homoeopathy. **~opático** *a* homoeopathic
homicid|a *a* murderous. ● *m & f* murderer. **~io** *m* murder
homogéneo *a* homogeneous
homosexual *a & m & f* homosexual. **~idad** *f* homosexuality
hond|o *a* deep. **~onada** *f* hollow. **~ura** *f* depth
Honduras *fpl* Honduras
hondureño *a & m* Honduran
honest|idad *f* decency. **~o** *a* proper
hongo *m* fungus; (*culin*) mushroom; (*venenoso*) toadstool
hon|or *m* honour. **~orable** *a* honourable. **~orario** *a* honorary. **~orarios** *mpl* fees. **~ra** *f* honour; (*buena fama*) good name. **~radez** *f* honesty. **~rado** *a* honest. **~rar** *vt* honour. **~rarse** *vpr* be honoured
hora *f* hour; (*momento determinado, momento oportuno*) time. **~ avanzada** late hour. **~ punta** rush hour. **~s** *fpl* **de trabajo** working hours. **~s** *fpl* **extraordinarias** overtime. **a estas ~s** now. **¿a qué ~?** at what time? when? **de ~ en ~** hourly. **de última ~** last-minute. **en buena ~** at the right time. **media ~** half an hour. **¿qué ~ es?** what time is it? **¿tiene Vd ~?** can you tell me the time? **horario** *a* time; (*cada hora*) hourly. ● *m* timetable. **a ~** (*LAm*) on time
horca *f* gallows
horcajadas, a ~ astride
horchata *f* tiger-nut milk
horda *f* horde

horizont|al *a & f* horizontal. **~e** *m* horizon
horma *f* mould; (*para fabricar calzado*) last; (*para conservar forma del calzado*) shoe-tree
hormiga *f* ant
hormigón *m* concrete
hormigue|ar *vt* tingle; (*bullir*) swarm. **me ~a la mano** I've got pins and needles in my hand. **~o** *m* tingling; (*fig*) anxiety
hormiguero *m* anthill; (*de gente*) swarm
hormona *f* hormone
horn|ada *f* batch. **~ero** *m* baker. **~illo** *m* cooker. **~o** *m* oven; (*para ladrillos, cerámica etc*) kiln; (*tec*) furnace
horóscopo *m* horoscope
horquilla *f* pitchfork; (*para el pelo*) hairpin
horr|endo *a* awful. **~ible** *a* horrible. **~ipilante** *a* terrifying. **~or** *m* horror; (*atrocidad*) atrocity. **~orizar** [10] *vt* horrify. **~orizarse** *vpr* be horrified. **~oroso** *a* horrifying. **¡qué ~or!** how awful!
hort|aliza *f* vegetable. **~elano** *m* market gardener. **~icultura** *f* horticulture
hosco *a* surly; ⟨*lugar*⟩ gloomy
hospeda|je *m* lodging. **~r** *vt* put up. **~rse** *vpr* lodge
hospital *m* hospital
hospital|ario *m* hospitable. **~idad** *f* hospitality
hostal *m* boarding-house
hostería *f* inn
hostia *f* (*relig*) host; (*golpe, fam*) punch
hostigar [12] *vt* whip; (*fig, excitar*) urge; (*fig, molestar*) pester
hostil *a* hostile. **~idad** *f* hostility
hotel *m* hotel. **~ero** *a* hotel. ● *m* hotelier
hoy *adv* today. **~ (en) día** nowadays. **~ mismo** this very day. **~ por ~** for the time being. **de ~ en adelante** from now on
hoy|a *f* hole; (*sepultura*) grave. **~o** *m* hole; (*sepultura*) grave. **~uelo** *m* dimple
hoz *f* sickle; (*desfiladero*) pass
hube *vb véase* **haber**
hucha *f* money box
hueco *a* hollow; (*vacío*) empty; (*esponjoso*) spongy; (*resonante*) resonant. ● *m* hollow

huelg|a f strike. **~a de brazos caídos** sit-down strike. **~a de celo** work-to-rule. **~a de hambre** hunger strike. **~uista** m & f striker. **declarar la ~a, declararse en ~a** come out on strike

huelo vb véase **oler**

huella f footprint; (de animal, vehículo etc) track. **~ dactilar, ~ digital** fingerprint

huérfano a orphaned. ● m orphan. **~ de** without

huero a empty

huert|a f market garden (Brit), truck farm (Amer); (terreno de regadío) irrigated plain. **~o** m vegetable garden; (de árboles frutales) orchard

huesa f grave

hueso m bone; (de fruta) stone. **~so** a bony

huésped m guest; (que paga) lodger; (animal) host

huesudo a bony

huev|a f roe. **~era** f eggcup. **~o** m egg. **~o duro** hard-boiled egg. **~o escalfado** poached egg. **~o estrellado, ~o frito** fried egg. **~o pasado por agua** boiled egg. **~os revueltos** scrambled eggs

hui|da f flight, escape. **~dizo** a (tímido) shy; (fugaz) fleeting. **~r** [17] vt/i flee, run away; (evitar) avoid

huipil m (Mex) embroidered smock

huitlacoche m (Mex) edible black fungus

hule m oilcloth, oilskin

human|idad f mankind; (fig) humanity. **~idades** fpl humanities. **~ismo** m humanism. **~ista** m & f humanist. **~itario** a humanitarian. **~o** a human; (benévolo) humane. ● m human (being)

hum|areda f cloud of smoke. **~ear** vi smoke; (echar vapor) steam

humed|ad f dampness (en meteorología) humidity. **~ecer** [11] vt moisten. **~ecerse** vpr become moist

húmedo a damp; (clima) humid; (mojado) wet

humi|ldad f humility. **~lde** a humble. **~llación** f humiliation. **~llar** vt humiliate. **~llarse** vpr humble o.s.

humo m smoke; (vapor) steam; (gas nocivo) fumes. **~s** mpl conceit

humor m mood, temper; (gracia) humour. **~ismo** m humour. **~ista** m & f humorist. **~ístico** a humorous. **estar de mal ~** be in a bad mood

hundi|do a sunken. **~miento** m sinking. **~r** vt sink; destroy (edificio). **~rse** vpr sink; (edificio) collapse

húngaro a & m Hungarian

Hungría f Hungary

huracán m hurricane

huraño a unsociable

hurg|ar [12] vt poke; (fig) stir up. **~ón** m poker

hurón m ferret. ● a unsociable

hurra int hurray!

hurraca f magpie

hurtadillas. a ~ stealthily

hurt|ar vt steal. **~o** m theft; (cosa robada) stolen object

husmear vt sniff out; (fig) pry into

huyo vb véase **huir**

I

Iberia f Iberia

ibérico a Iberian

ibero a & m Iberian

íbice m ibex, mountain goat

Ibiza f Ibiza

iceberg /iθ'ber/ m iceberg

icono m icon

ictericia f jaundice

ida f outward journey; (salida) departure. **de ~ y vuelta** return (Brit), round-trip (Amer)

idea f idea; (opinión) opinion. **cambiar de ~** change one's mind. **no tener la más remota ~, no tener la menor ~** not have the slightest idea, not have a clue (fam)

ideal a ideal; (imaginario) imaginary. ● m ideal. **~ista** m & f idealist. **~izar** [10] vt idealize

idear vt think up, conceive; (inventar) invent

ídem pron & adv the same

idéntico a identical

identi|dad f identity. **~ficación** f identification. **~ficar** [7] vt identify. **~ficarse** vpr. **~ficarse con** identify with

ideol|ogía f ideology. **~ógico** a ideological

idílico a idyllic

idilio m idyll

idiom|a m language. **~ático** a idiomatic

idiosincrasia f idiosyncrasy
idiot|a a idiotic. ● m & f idiot. ~**ez** f idiocy
idiotismo m idiom
idolatrar vt worship; (fig) idolize
ídolo m idol
idóneo a suitable (**para** for)
iglesia f church
iglú m igloo
ignición f ignition
ignomini|a f ignominy, disgrace. ~**oso** a ignominious
ignora|ncia f ignorance. ~**nte** a ignorant. ● m ignoramus. ~**r** vt not know, be unaware of
igual a equal; (mismo) the same; (similar) like; (llano) even; (liso) smooth. ● adv easily. ● m equal. ~ **que** (the same) as. **al** ~ **que** the same as. **da** ~, **es** ~ it doesn't matter
igual|ar vt make equal; (ser igual) equal; (allanar) level. ~**arse** vpr be equal. ~**dad** f equality. ~**mente** adv equally; (también) also, likewise; (respuesta de cortesía) the same to you
ijada f flank
ilegal a illegal
ilegible a illegible
ilegítimo a illegitimate
ileso a unhurt
ilícito a illicit
ilimitado a unlimited
ilógico a illogical
ilumina|ción f illumination; (alumbrado) lighting; (fig) enlightenment. ~**r** vt light (up); (fig) enlighten. ~**rse** vpr light up
ilusi|ón f illusion; (sueño) dream; (alegría) joy. ~**onado** a excited. ~**onar** vt give false hope. ~**onarse** vpr have false hopes. **hacerse** ~**ones** build up one's hopes. **me hace** ~**ón** I'm thrilled; I'm looking forward to ⟨algo en el futuro⟩
ilusionis|mo m conjuring. ~**ta** m & f conjurer
iluso a easily deceived. ● m dreamer. ~**rio** a illusory
ilustra|ción f learning; (dibujo) illustration. ~**do** a learned; (con dibujos) illustrated. ~**r** vt explain; (instruir) instruct; (añadir dibujos etc) illustrate. ~**rse** vpr acquire knowledge. ~**tivo** a illustrative
ilustre a illustrious
imagen f image; (TV etc) picture

imagina|ble a imaginable. ~**ción** f imagination. ~**r** vt imagine. ~**rse** vpr imagine. ~**rio** m imaginary. ~**tivo** a imaginative
imán m magnet
imantar vt magnetize
imbécil a stupid. ● m & f imbecile, idiot
imborrable a indelible; ⟨recuerdo etc⟩ unforgettable
imbuir [17] vt imbue (**de** with)
imita|ción f imitation. ~**r** vt imitate
impacien|cia f impatience. ~**tarse** vpr lose one's patience. ~**te** a impatient; (intranquilo) anxious
impacto m impact
impar a odd
imparcial a impartial. ~**idad** f impartiality
impartir vt impart
impasible a impassive
impávido a fearless; (impasible) impassive
impecable a impeccable
impedi|do a disabled. ~**menta** f (esp mil) baggage. ~**mento** m hindrance. ~**r** [5] vt prevent; (obstruir) hinder
impeler vt drive
impenetrable a impenetrable
impenitente a unrepentant
impensa|ble a unthinkable. ~**do** a unexpected
imperar vi reign
imperativo a imperative; ⟨persona⟩ imperious
imperceptible a imperceptible
imperdible m safety pin
imperdonable a unforgivable
imperfec|ción f imperfection. ~**to** a imperfect
imperial a imperial. ● f upper deck. ~**ismo** m imperialism
imperio m empire; (poder) rule; (fig) pride. ~**so** a imperious
impermeable a waterproof. ● m raincoat
impersonal a impersonal
impertérrito a undaunted
impertinen|cia f impertinence. ~**te** a impertinent
imperturbable a imperturbable
ímpetu m impetus; (impulso) impulse; (impetuosidad) impetuosity
impetuos|idad f impetuosity; (violencia) violence. ~**o** a impetuous; (violento) violent

impío *a* ungodly; *(acción)* irreverent

implacable *a* implacable

implantar *vt* introduce

implica|ción *f* implication. ∼**r** [7] *vt* implicate; *(significar)* imply

implícito *a* implicit

implora|ción *f* entreaty. ∼**r** *vt* implore

imponderable *a* imponderable; *(inapreciable)* invaluable

impon|ente *a* imposing; *(fam)* terrific. ∼**er** [34] *vt* impose; *(requerir)* demand; deposit *(dinero)*. ∼**erse** *vpr* be imposed; *(hacerse obedecer)* assert o.s.; *(hacerse respetar)* command respect. ∼**ible** *a* taxable

impopular *a* unpopular. ∼**idad** *f* unpopularity

importa|ción *f* import; *(artículo)* import. ∼**dor** *a* importing. ● *m* importer

importa|ncia *f* importance; *(tamaño)* size. ∼**nte** *a* important; *(en cantidad)* considerable. ∼**r** *vt* import; *(valer)* cost. ● *vi* be important, matter. ¡**le importa...?** would you mind...? **no** ∼ it doesn't matter

importe *m* price; *(total)* amount

importun|ar *vt* bother. ∼**o** *a* troublesome; *(inoportuno)* inopportune

imposib|ilidad *f* impossibility. ∼**le** *a* impossible. **hacer lo** ∼**le** do all one can

imposición *f* imposition; *(impuesto)* tax

impostor *m & f* impostor

impotable *a* undrinkable

impoten|cia *f* impotence. ∼**te** *a* powerless, impotent

impracticable *a* impracticable; *(intransitable)* unpassable

impreca|ción *f* curse. ∼**r** [7] *vt* curse

imprecis|ión *f* vagueness. ∼**o** *a* imprecise

impregnar *vt* impregnate; *(empapar)* soak; *(fig)* cover

imprenta *f* printing; *(taller)* printing house, printer's

imprescindible *a* indispensable, essential

impresi|ón *f* impression; *(acción de imprimir)* printing; *(tirada)* edition; *(huella)* imprint. ∼**onable** *a* impressionable. ∼**onante** *a* impressive; *(espantoso)* frightening. ∼**onar** *vt* impress; *(conmover)* move; *(foto)* expose. ∼**onarse**

vpr be impressed; *(conmover)* be moved

impresionis|mo *m* impressionism. ∼**ta** *a & m & f* impressionist

impreso *a* printed. ● *m* printed paper, printed matter. ∼**ra** *f* printer

imprevis|ible *a* unforeseeable. ∼**to** *a* unforeseen

imprimir [*pp* **impreso**] *vt* impress; print *(libro etc)*

improbab|ilidad *f* improbability. ∼**le** *a* unlikely, improbable

improcedente *a* unsuitable

improductivo *a* unproductive

improperio *m* insult. ∼**s** *mpl* abuse

impropio *a* improper

improvis|ación *f* improvisation. ∼**adamente** *adv* suddenly. ∼**ado** *a* improvised. ∼**ar** *vt* improvise. ∼**o** *a.* **de** ∼**o** suddenly

impruden|cia *f* imprudence. ∼**te** *a* imprudent

impuden|cia *f* impudence. ∼**te** *a* impudent

imp|údico *a* immodest; *(desvergonzado)* shameless. ∼**udor** *m* immodesty; *(desvergüenza)* shamelessness

impuesto *a* imposed. ● *m* tax. ∼ **sobre el valor añadido** VAT, value added tax

impugnar *vt* contest; *(refutar)* refute

impulsar *vt* impel

impuls|ividad *f* impulsiveness. ∼**ivo** *a* impulsive. ∼**o** *m* impulse

impun|e *a* unpunished. ∼**idad** *f* impunity

impur|eza *f* impurity. ∼**o** *a* impure

imputa|ción *f* charge. ∼**r** *vt* attribute; *(acusar)* charge

inacabable *a* interminable

inaccesible *a* inaccessible

inaceptable *a* unacceptable

inacostumbrado *a* unaccustomed

inactiv|idad *f* inactivity. ∼**o** *a* inactive

inadaptado *a* maladjusted

inadecuado *a* inadequate; *(inapropiado)* unsuitable

inadmisible *a* inadmissible; *(intolerable)* intolerable

inadvert|ido *a* unnoticed. ∼**encia** *f* inadvertence

inagotable *a* inexhaustible

inaguantable *a* unbearable; *(persona)* insufferable

inaltera|ble *a* unchangeable; *(color)* fast; *(carácter)* calm. ∼**do** *a* unchanged

inanimado *a* inanimate
inaplicable *a* inapplicable
inapreciable *a* imperceptible
inapropiado *a* inappropriate
inarticulado *a* inarticulate
inasequible *a* out of reach
inaudito *a* unheard-of
inaugura|ción *f* inauguration. ~l *a* inaugural. ~r *vt* inaugurate
inca *a* Incan. ● *m & f* Inca. ~ico *a* Incan
incalculable *a* incalculable
incandescen|cia *f* incandescence. ~te *a* incandescent
incansable *a* tireless
incapa|cidad *f* incapacity. ~citar *vt* incapacitate. ~z *a* incapable
incauto *a* unwary; (*fácil de engañar*) gullible
incendi|ar *vt* set fire to. ~arse *vpr* catch fire. ~ario *a* incendiary. ● *m* arsonist. ~o *m* fire
incentivo *m* incentive
incertidumbre *f* uncertainty
incesante *a* incessant
incest|o *m* incest. ~uoso *a* incestuous
inciden|cia *f* incidence; (*incidente*) incident. ~tal *a* incidental. ~te *m* incident
incidir *vi* fall; (*influir*) influence
incienso *m* incense
incierto *a* uncertain
incinera|ción *f* incineration; (*de cadáveres*) cremation. ~dor *m* incinerator. ~r *vt* incinerate; cremate ⟨*cadáver*⟩
incipiente *a* incipient
incisión *f* incision
incisivo *a* incisive. ● *m* incisor
incitar *vt* incite
incivil *a* rude
inclemen|cia *f* harshness. ~te *a* harsh
inclina|ción *f* slope; (*de la cabeza*) nod; (*fig*) inclination. ~r *vt* incline. ~rse *vpr* lean; (*encorvarse*) stoop; (*en saludo*) bow; (*fig*) be inclined. ~rse a (*parecerse*) resemble
inclu|ido *a* included; ⟨*precio*⟩ inclusive; (*en cartas*) enclosed. ~ir [17] *vt* include; (*en cartas*) enclose. ~sión *f* inclusion. ~sive *adv* inclusive. **hasta el lunes** ~sive up to and including Monday. ~so *a* included; (*en cartas*) enclosed. ● *adv* including; (*hasta*) even
incógnito *a* unknown. **de** ~ incognito

incoheren|cia *f* incoherence. ~te *a* incoherent
incoloro *a* colourless
incólume *a* unharmed
incomestible *a*, **incomible** *a* uneatable, inedible
incomodar *vt* inconvenience; (*molestar*) bother. ~se *vpr* trouble o.s.; (*enfadarse*) get angry
incómodo *a* uncomfortable; (*inoportuno*) inconvenient
incomparable *a* imcomparable
incompatib|ilidad *f* incompatibility. ~le *a* incompatible
incompeten|cia *f* incompetence. ~te *a* incompetent
incompleto *a* incomplete
incompren|dido *a* misunderstood. ~sible *a* incomprehensible. ~sión *f* incomprehension
incomunicado *a* isolated; ⟨*preso*⟩ in solitary confinement
inconcebible *a* inconceivable
inconciliable *a* irreconcilable
inconcluso *a* unfinished
incondicional *a* unconditional
inconfundible *a* unmistakable
incongruente *a* incongruous
inconmensurable *a* (*fam*) enormous
inconscien|cia *f* unconsciousness; (*irreflexión*) recklessness. ~te *a* unconscious; (*irreflexivo*) reckless
inconsecuente *a* inconsistent
inconsiderado *a* inconsiderate
inconsistente *a* insubstantial
inconsolable *a* unconsolable
inconstan|cia *f* inconstancy. ~te *a* changeable; ⟨*persona*⟩ fickle
incontable *a* countless
incontaminado *a* uncontaminated
incontenible *a* irrepressible
incontestable *a* indisputable
incontinen|cia *f* incontinence. ~te *a* incontinent
inconvenien|cia *f* disadvantage. ~te *a* inconvenient; (*inapropiado*) inappropriate; (*incorrecto*) improper. ● *m* difficulty; (*desventaja*) drawback
incorpora|ción *f* incorporation. ~r *vt* incorporate; (*culin*) mix. ~rse *vpr* sit up; join ⟨*sociedad, regimiento etc*⟩
incorrecto *a* incorrect; ⟨*acción*⟩ improper; (*descortés*) discourteous
incorregible *a* incorrigible
incorruptible *a* incorruptible
incrédulo *a* incredulous

increíble *a* incredible

increment|ar *vt* increase. **∼o** *m* increase

incriminar *vt* incriminate

incrustar *vt* encrust

incuba|ción *f* incubation. **∼dora** *f* incubator. **∼r** *vt* incubate; (*fig*) hatch

incuestionable *a* unquestionable

inculcar [7] *vt* inculcate

inculpar *vt* accuse; (*culpar*) blame

inculto *a* uncultivated; ⟨*persona*⟩ uneducated

incumplimiento *m* non-fulfilment; (*de un contrato*) breach

incurable *a* incurable

incurrir *vi*. **∼ en** incur; fall into ⟨*error*⟩; commit ⟨*crimen*⟩

incursión *f* raid

indaga|ción *f* investigation. **∼r** [12] *vt* investigate

indebido *a* undue

indecen|cia *f* indecency. **∼te** *a* indecent

indecible *a* inexpressible

indecis|ión *f* indecision. **∼o** *a* undecided

indefenso *a* defenceless

indefini|ble *a* indefinable. **∼do** *a* indefinite

indeleble *a* indelible

indelicad|eza *f* indelicacy. **∼o** *a* indelicate; (*falto de escrúpulo*) unscrupulous

indemn|e *a* undamaged; ⟨*persona*⟩ unhurt. **∼idad** *f* indemnity. **∼izar** [10] *vt* indemnify, compensate

independ|encia *f* independence. **∼iente** *a* independent

independizarse [10] *vpr* become independent

indescifrable *a* indecipherable, incomprehensible

indescriptible *a* indescribable

indeseable *a* undesirable

indestructible *a* indestructible

indetermina|ble *a* indeterminable. **∼do** *a* indeterminate

India *f.* **la ∼** India. **las ∼s** *fpl* the Indies

indica|ción *f* indication; (*sugerencia*) suggestion. **∼ciones** *fpl* directions. **∼dor** *m* indicator; (*tec*) gauge. **∼r** [7] *vt* show, indicate; (*apuntar*) point at; (*hacer saber*) point out; (*aconsejar*) advise. **∼tivo** *a* indicative. ● *m* indicative; (*al teléfono*) dialling code

índice *m* indication; (*dedo*) index finger; (*de libro*) index; (*catálogo*) catalogue; (*aguja*) pointer

indicio *m* indication, sign; (*vestigio*) trace

indiferen|cia *f* indifference. **∼te** *a* indifferent. **me es ∼te** it's all the same to me

indígena *a* indigenous. ● *m & f* native

indigen|cia *f* poverty. **∼te** *a* needy

indigest|ión *f* indigestion. **∼o** *a* undigested; (*difícil de digerir*) indigestible

indign|ación *f* indignation. **∼ado** *a* indignant. **∼ar** *vt* make indignant. **∼arse** *vpr* be indignant. **∼o** *a* unworthy; (*despreciable*) contemptible

indio *a & m* Indian

indirect|a *f* hint. **∼o** *a* indirect

indisciplina *f* lack of discipline. **∼do** *a* undisciplined

indiscre|ción *f* indiscretion. **∼to** *a* indiscreet

indiscutible *a* unquestionable

indisoluble *a* indissoluble

indispensable *a* indispensable

indispon|er [34] *vt* (*enemistar*) set against. **∼onerse** *vpr* fall out; (*ponerse enfermo*) fall ill. **∼osición** *f* indisposition. **∼uesto** *a* indisposed

indistinto *a* indistinct

individu|al *a* individual; ⟨*cama*⟩ single. **∼alidad** *f* individuality. **∼alista** *m & f* individualist. **∼alizar** [10] *vt* individualize. **∼o** *a & m* individual

índole *f* nature; (*clase*) type

indolen|cia *f* indolence. **∼te** *a* indolent

indoloro *a* painless

indomable *a* untameable

indómito *a* indomitable

Indonesia *f* Indonesia

inducir [47] *vt* induce; (*deducir*) infer

indudable *a* undoubted. **∼mente** *adv* undoubtedly

indulgen|cia *f* indulgence. **∼te** *a* indulgent

indult|ar *vt* pardon; exempt (*de un pago etc*). **∼o** *m* pardon

industria *f* industry. **∼l** *a* industrial. ● *m* industrialist. **∼lización** *f* industrialization. **∼lizar** [10] *vt* industrialize

industriarse *vpr* do one's best

industrioso *a* industrious

inédito *a* unpublished; (*fig*) unknown

ineducado *a* impolite

inefable *a* inexpressible

ineficaz *a* ineffective

ineficiente *a* inefficient

inelegible *a* ineligible

ineludible *a* inescapable, unavoidable

inept|itud *f* ineptitude. ~o *a* inept

inequívoco *a* unequivocal

iner|cia *f* inertia

inerme *a* unarmed; (*fig*) defenceless

inerte *a* inert

inesperado *a* unexpected

inestable *a* unstable

inestimable *a* inestimable

inevitable *a* inevitable

inexacto *a* inaccurate; (*incorrecto*) incorrect; (*falso*) untrue

inexistente *a* non-existent

inexorable *a* inexorable

inexper|iencia *f* inexperience. ~to *a* inexperienced

inexplicable *a* inexplicable

infalible *a* infallible

infam|ar *vt* defame. ~atorio *a* defamatory. ~e *a* infamous; (*fig*, *muy malo*, *fam*) awful. ~ia *f* infamy

infancia *f* infancy

infant|a *f* infanta, princess. ~e *m* infante, prince; (*mil*) infantryman. ~ería *f* infantry. ~il *a* (*de niño*) child's; (*como un niño*) infantile

infarto *m* coronary (thrombosis)

infatigable *a* untiring

infatua|ción *f* conceit. ~rse *vpr* get conceited

infausto *a* unlucky

infec|ción *f* infection. ~cioso *a* infectious. ~tar *vt* infect. ~tarse *vpr* become infected. ~to *a* infected; (*fam*) disgusting

infecundo *a* infertile

infeli|cidad *f* unhappiness. ~z *a* unhappy

inferior *a* inferior. ● *m* & *f* inferior. ~idad *f* lower; (*calidad*) inferiority

inferir [4] *vt* infer; (*causar*) cause

infernal *a* infernal, hellish

infestar *vt* infest; (*fig*) inundate

infi|delidad *f* unfaithfulness. ~el *a* unfaithful

infierno *m* hell

infiltra|ción *f* infiltration. ~rse *vpr* infiltrate

ínfimo *a* lowest

infini|dad *f* infinity. ~tivo *m* infinitive. ~to *a* infinite. ● *m* infinite; (*en matemáticas*) infinity. una ~dad de countless

inflación *f* inflation; (*fig*) conceit

inflama|ble *a* (in)flammable. ~ción *f* inflammation. ~r *vt* set on fire; (*fig*, *med*) inflame. ~rse *vpr* catch fire; (*med*) become inflamed

inflar *vt* inflate; (*fig*, *exagerar*) exaggerate

inflexi|ble *a* inflexible. ~ón *f* inflexion

infligir [14] *vt* inflict

influ|encia *f* influence. ~enza *f* flu (*fam*), influenza. ~ir [17] *vt/i* influence. ~jo *m* influence. ~yente *a* influential

informa|ción *f* information. ~ciones *fpl* (*noticias*) news; (*de teléfonos*) directory enquiries. ~dor *m* informant

informal *a* informal; (*incorrecto*) incorrect

inform|ante *m* & *f* informant. ~ar *vt/i* inform. ~arse *vpr* find out. ~ática *f* information technology. ~ativo *a* informative

informe *a* shapeless. ● *m* report; (*información*) information

infortun|ado *a* unfortunate. ~io *m* misfortune

infracción *f* infringement

infraestructura *f* infrastructure

infranqueable *a* impassable; (*fig*) insuperable

infrarrojo *a* infrared

infrecuente *a* infrequent

infringir [14] *vt* infringe

infructuoso *a* fruitless

infundado *a* unfounded

infu|ndir *vt* instil. ~sión *f* infusion

ingeniar *vt* invent

ingenier|ía *f* engineering. ~o *m* engineer

ingenio *m* ingenuity; (*agudeza*) wit; (*LAm*, *de azúcar*) refinery. ~so *a* ingenious

ingenu|idad *f* ingenuousness. ~o *a* ingenuous

ingerir [4] *vt* swallow

Inglaterra *f* England

ingle *f* groin

ingl|és *a* English. ● *m* Englishman; (*lengua*) English. ~esa *f* Englishwoman

ingrat|itud *f* ingratitude. ~o *a* ungrateful; (*desagradable*) thankless

ingrediente *m* ingredient

ingres|ar *vt* deposit. ● *vi*. ~**ar en** come in, enter; join ⟨*sociedad*⟩. ~**o** *m* entry; (*en sociedad, hospital etc*) admission. ~**os** *mpl* income
inh|ábil *a* unskillful; (*no apto*) unfit. ~**abilidad** *f* unskillfulness
inhabitable *a* uninhabitable
inhala|ción *f* inhalation. ~**dor** *m* inhaler. ~**r** *vt* inhale
inherente *a* inherent
inhibi|ción *f* inhibition. ~**r** *vt* inhibit
inhospitalario *a*, **inhóspito** *a* inhospitable
inhumano *a* inhuman
inicia|ción *f* beginning. ~**l** *a & f* initial. ~**r** *vt* initiate; (*comenzar*) begin, start. ~**tiva** *f* initiative
inicio *m* beginning
inicuo *a* iniquitous
inigualado *a* unequalled
ininterrumpido *a* continuous
injer|encia *f* interference. ~**ir** [4] *vt* insert. ~**irse** *vpr* interfere
injert|ar *vt* graft. ~**to** *m* graft
injuri|a *f* insult; (*ofensa*) offence. ~**ar** *vt* insult. ~**oso** *a* offensive
injust|icia *f* injustice. ~**o** *a* unjust
inmaculado *a* immaculate
inmaduro *a* unripe; ⟨*persona*⟩ immature
inmediaciones *fpl* neighbourhood
inmediat|amente *adv* immediately. ~**o** *a* immediate; (*contiguo*) next
inmejorable *a* excellent
inmemorable *a* immemorial
inmens|idad *f* immensity. ~**o** *a* immense
inmerecido *a* undeserved
inmersión *f* immersion
inmigra|ción *f* immigration. ~**nte** *a & m* immigrant. ~**r** *vt* immigrate
inminen|cia *f* imminence. ~**te** *a* imminent
inmiscuirse [17] *vpr* interfere
inmobiliario *a* property
inmoderado *a* immoderate
inmodesto *a* immodest
inmolar *vt* sacrifice
inmoral *a* immoral. ~**idad** *f* immorality
inmortal *a* immortal. ~**izar** [10] *vt* immortalize
inmóvil *a* immobile
inmueble *a*. **bienes** ~**s** property
inmund|icia *f* filth. ~**icias** *fpl* rubbish. ~**o** *a* filthy
inmun|e *a* immune. ~**idad** *f* immunity. ~**ización** *f* immunization. ~**izar** [10] *vt* immunize

inmuta|ble *a* unchangeable. ~**rse** *vpr* turn pale
innato *a* innate
innecesario *a* unnecessary
innegable *a* undeniable
innoble *a* ignoble
innova|ción *f* innovation. ~**r** *vt/i* innovate
innumerable *a* innumerable
inocen|cia *f* innocence. ~**tada** *f* practical joke. ~**te** *a* innocent. ~**tón** *a* naïve
inocuo *a* innocuous
inodoro *a* odourless. ● *m* toilet
inofensivo *a* inoffensive
inolvidable *a* unforgettable
inoperable *a* inoperable
inopinado *a* unexpected
inoportuno *a* untimely; (*incómodo*) inconvenient
inorgánico *a* inorganic
inoxidable *a* stainless
inquebrantable *a* unbreakable
inquiet|ar *vt* worry. ~**arse** *vpr* get worried. ~**o** *a* worried; (*agitado*) restless. ~**ud** *f* anxiety
inquilino *m* tenant
inquirir [4] *vt* enquire into, investigate
insaciable *a* insatiable
insalubre *a* unhealthy
insanable *a* incurable
insatisfecho *a* unsatisfied; (*descontento*) dissatisfied
inscri|bir [*pp* **inscrito**] *vt* inscribe; (*en registro etc*) enrol, register. ~**birse** *vpr* register. ~**pción** *f* inscription; (*registro*) registration
insect|icida *m* insecticide. ~**o** *m* insect
insegur|idad *f* insecurity. ~**o** *a* insecure; (*dudoso*) uncertain
insemina|ción *f* insemination. ~**r** *vt* inseminate
insensato *a* senseless
insensible *a* insensitive; (*med*) insensible; (*imperceptible*) imperceptible
inseparable *a* inseparable
insertar *vt* insert
insidi|a *f* trap. ~**oso** *a* insidious
insigne *a* famous
insignia *f* badge; (*bandera*) flag
insignificante *a* insignificant
insincero *a* insincere
insinua|ción *f* insinuation. ~**nte** *a* insinuating. ~**r** [21] *vt* insinuate. ~**rse** *vpr* ingratiate o.s. ~**rse en** creep into

insípido *a* insipid

insist|encia *f* insistence. **~ente** *a* insistent. **~ir** *vi* insist; (*hacer hincapié*) stress

insolación *f* sunstroke

insolen|cia *f* rudeness, insolence. **~te** *a* rude, insolent

insólito *a* unusual

insoluble *a* insoluble

insolven|cia *f* insolvency. **~te** *a* & *m* & *f* insolvent

insomn|e *a* sleepless. **~io** *m* insomnia

insondable *a* unfathomable

insoportable *a* unbearable

insospechado *a* unexpected

insostenible *a* untenable

inspec|ción *f* inspection. **~cionar** *vt* inspect. **~tor** *m* inspector

inspira|ción *f* inspiration. **~r** *vt* inspire. **~rse** *vpr* be inspired

instala|ción *f* installation. **~r** *vt* install. **~rse** *vpr* settle

instancia *f* request

instant|ánea *f* snapshot. **~áneo** *a* instantaneous; (*café etc*) instant. **~e** *m* instant. **a cada ~e** constantly. **al ~e** immediately

instar *vt* urge

instaura|ción *f* establishment. **~r** *vt* establish

instiga|ción *f* instigation. **~dor** *m* instigator. **~r** [12] *vt* instigate; (*incitar*) incite

instint|ivo *a* instinctive. **~o** *m* instinct

institu|ción *f* institution. **~cional** *a* institutional. **~ir** [17] *vt* establish. **~to** *m* institute; (*escol*) (secondary) school. **~triz** *f* governess

instru|cción *f* instruction. **~ctivo** *a* instructive. **~ctor** *m* instructor. **~ir** [17] *vt* instruct; (*enseñar*) teach

instrument|ación *f* instrumentation. **~al** *a* instrumental. **~o** *m* instrument; (*herramienta*) tool

insubordina|ción *f* insubordination. **~r** *vt* stir up. **~rse** *vpr* rebel

insuficien|cia *f* insufficiency; (*inadecuación*) inadequacy. **~te** *a* insufficient

insufrible *a* insufferable

insular *a* insular

insulina *f* insulin

insulso *a* tasteless; (*fig*) insipid

insult|ar *vt* insult. **~o** *m* insult

insuperable *a* insuperable; (*excelente*) excellent

insurgente *a* insurgent

insurrec|ción *f* insurrection. **~to** *a* insurgent

intacto *a* intact

intachable *a* irreproachable

intangible *a* intangible

integra|ción *f* integration. **~l** *a* integral; (*completo*) complete; ⟨pan⟩ wholemeal (*Brit*), wholewheat (*Amer*). **~r** *vt* make up

integridad *f* integrity; (*entereza*) wholeness

íntegro *a* complete; (*fig*) upright

intelect|o *m* intellect. **~ual** *a* & *m* & *f* intellectual

inteligen|cia *f* intelligence. **~te** *a* intelligent

inteligible *a* intelligible

intemperancia *f* intemperance

intemperie *f* bad weather. **a la ~** in the open

intempestivo *a* untimely

intenci|ón *f* intention. **~onado** *a* deliberate. **~onal** *a* intentional. **bien ~onado** well-meaning. **mal ~onado** malicious. **segunda ~ón** duplicity

intens|idad *f* intensity. **~ificar** [7] *vt* intensify. **~ivo** *a* intensive. **~o** *a* intense

intent|ar *vt* try. **~o** *m* intent; (*tentativa*) attempt. **de ~o** intentionally

intercalar *vt* insert

intercambio *m* exchange

interceder *vt* intercede

interceptar *vt* intercept

intercesión *f* intercession

interdicto *m* ban

inter|és *m* interest; (*egoísmo*) self-interest. **~esado** *a* interested; (*parcial*) biassed; (*egoísta*) selfish. **~esante** *a* interesting. **~esar** *vt* interest; (*afectar*) concern. ● *vi* be of interest. **~esarse** *vpr* take an interest (**por** in)

interfer|encia *f* interference. **~ir** [4] *vi* interfere

interino *a* temporary; ⟨persona⟩ acting. ● *m* stand-in; (*médico*) locum

interior *a* interior. ● *m* inside. **Ministerio** *m* **del I~** Home Office (*Brit*), Department of the Interior (*Amer*)

interjección *f* interjection

interlocutor *m* speaker

interludio *m* interlude

intermediario *a* & *m* intermediary

intermedio *a* intermediate. ● *m* interval

interminable *a* interminable
intermitente *a* intermittent. ● *m* indicator
internacional *a* international
intern|ado *m* (*escol*) boarding-school. ~**ar** *vt* intern; (*en manicomio*) commit. ~**arse** *vpr* penetrate. ~**o** *a* internal; (*escol*) boarding. ● *m* (*escol*) boarder
interpelar *vt* appeal
interponer [34] *vt* interpose. ~**se** *vpr* intervene
int|erpretación *f* interpretation. ~**erpretar** *vt* interpret. ~**érprete** *m* interpreter; (*mus*) performer
interroga|ción *f* question; (*acción*) interrogation; (*signo*) question mark. ~**r** [12] *vt* question. ~**tivo** *a* interrogative
interru|mpir *vt* interrupt; (*suspender*) stop. ~**pción** *f* interruption. ~**ptor** *m* switch
intersección *f* intersection
interurbano *a* inter-city; (*conferencia*) long-distance
intervalo *m* interval; (*espacio*) space. **a ~s** at intervals
interven|ir [53] *vt* control; (*med*) operate on. ● *vi* intervene; (*participar*) take part. ~**tor** *m* inspector; (*com*) auditor
intestino *m* intestine
intim|ar *vi* become friendly. ~**idad** *f* intimacy
intimidar *vt* intimidate
íntimo *a* intimate. ● *m* close friend
intitular *vt* entitle
intolera|ble *a* intolerable. ~**nte** *a* intolerant
intoxicar [7] *vt* poison
intranquil|izar [10] *vt* worry. ~**o** *a* worried
intransigente *a* intransigent
intransitable *a* impassable
intransitivo *a* intransitive
intratable *a* intractable
intrépido *a* intrepid
intriga *f* intrigue. ~**nte** *a* intriguing. ~**r** [12] *vt/i* intrigue
intrincado *a* intricate
intrínseco *a* intrinsic
introduc|ción *f* introduction. ~**ir** [47] *vt* introduce; (*meter*) insert. ~**irse** *vpr* get into; (*entrometerse*) interfere
intromisión *f* interference
introvertido *a* & *m* introvert
intrus|ión *f* intrusion. ~**o** *a* intrusive. ● *m* intruder

intui|ción *f* intuition. ~**r** [17] *vt* sense. ~**tivo** *a* intuitive
inunda|ción *f* flooding. ~**r** *vt* flood
inusitado *a* unusual
in|útil *a* useless; (*vano*) futile. ~**utilidad** *f* uselessness
invadir *vt* invade
inv|alidez *f* invalidity; (*med*) disability. ~**álido** *a* & *m* invalid
invaria|ble *a* invariable. ~**do** *a* unchanged
invas|ión *f* invasion. ~**or** *a* invading. ● *m* invader
invectiva *f* invective
invencible *a* invincible
inven|ción *f* invention. ~**tar** *vt* invent
inventario *m* inventory
invent|iva *f* inventiveness. ~**ivo** *a* inventive. ~**or** *m* inventor
invernadero *m* greenhouse
invernal *a* winter
inverosímil *a* improbable
inversión *f* inversion; (*com*) investment
inverso *a* inverse; (*contrario*) opposite. **a la inversa** the other way round
invertebrado *a* & *m* invertebrate
inverti|do *a* inverted; (*homosexual*) homosexual. ● *m* homosexual. ~**r** [4] *vt* reverse; (*volcar*) turn upside down; (*com*) invest; spend ⟨*tiempo*⟩
investidura *f* investiture
investiga|ción *f* investigation; (*univ*) research. ~**dor** *m* investigator. ~**r** [12] *vt* investigate
investir [5] *vt* invest
inveterado *a* inveterate
invicto *a* unbeaten
invierno *m* winter
inviolable *a* inviolate
invisib|ilidad *f* invisibility. ~**le** *a* invisible
invita|ción *f* invitation. ~**do** *m* guest. ~**r** *vt* invite. **te invito a una copa** I'll buy you a drink
invoca|ción *f* invocation. ~**r** [7] *vt* invoke
involuntario *a* involuntary
invulnerable *a* invulnerable
inyec|ción *f* injection. ~**tar** *vt* inject
ion *m* ion
ir [49] *vi* go; ⟨*ropa*⟩ (*convenir*) suit. ● *m* going. ~**se** *vpr* go away. ~ **a hacer** be going to do. ~ **a pie** walk. ~ **de paseo** go for a walk. ~ **en coche** go by car. **no me va ni me viene** it's all the same to me. **no**

vaya a ser que in case. **¡qué va!** nonsense! **va mejorando** it's gradually getting better. **¡vamos!, ¡vámonos!** come on! let's go! **¡vaya!** fancy that! **¡vete a saber!** who knows? **¡ya voy!** I'm coming!

ira f anger. **~cundo** a irascible

Irak m Iraq

Irán m Iran

iraní a & m & f Iranian

iraquí a & m & f Iraqi

iris m (anat) iris; (arco iris) rainbow

Irlanda f Ireland

irland|és a Irish. • m Irishman; (lengua) Irish. **~esa** f Irishwoman

ir|onía f irony. **~ónico** a ironic

irracional a irrational

irradiar vt/i radiate

irrazonable a unreasonable

irreal a unreal. **~idad** f unreality

irrealizable a unattainable

irreconciliable a irreconcilable

irreconocible a unrecognizable

irrecuperable a irretrievable

irreducible a irreducible

irreflexión f impetuosity

irrefutable a irrefutable

irregular a irregular. **~idad** f irregularity

irreparable a irreparable

irreprimible a irrepressible

irreprochable a irreproachable

irresistible a irresistible

irresoluto a irresolute

irrespetuoso a disrespectful

irresponsable a irresponsible

irrevocable a irrevocable

irriga|ción f irrigation. **~r** [12] vt irrigate

irrisorio a derisive; (insignificante) ridiculous

irrita|ble a irritable. **~ción** f irritation. **~r** vt irritate. **~rse** vpr get annoyed

irrumpir vi burst (**en** in)

irrupción f irruption

isla f island. **las I~s Británicas** the British Isles

Islam m Islam

islámico a Islamic

islandés a Icelandic. • m Icelander; (lengua) Icelandic

Islandia f Iceland

isleño a island. • m islander

Israel m Israel

israelí a & m Israeli

istmo /'ismo/ m isthmus

Italia f Italy

italiano a & m Italian

itinerario a itinerary

IVA abrev (impuesto sobre el valor añadido) VAT, value added tax

izar [10] vt hoist

izquierd|a f left(-hand); (pol) left (-wing). **~ista** m & f leftist. **~o** a left. **a la ~a** on the left; (con movimiento) to the left

J

ja int ha!

jabalí m wild boar

jabalina f javelin

jab|ón m soap. **~onar** vt soap. **~onoso** a soapy

jaca f pony

jacinto m hyacinth

jacta|ncia f boastfulness; (acción) boasting. **~rse** vpr boast

jadea|nte a panting. **~r** vi pant

jaez m harness

jaguar m jaguar

jalea f jelly

jaleo m row, uproar. **armar un ~** kick up a fuss

jalón m (LAm, tirón) pull; (Mex, trago) drink

Jamaica f Jamaica

jamás adv never; (en frases afirmativas) ever

jamelgo m nag

jamón m ham. **~ de York** boiled ham. **~ serrano** cured ham

Japón m. **el ~** Japan

japonés a & m Japanese

jaque m check. **~ mate** checkmate

jaqueca f migraine. **dar ~** bother

jarabe m syrup

jardín m garden. **~ de la infancia** kindergarten, nursery school

jardiner|ía f gardening. **~o** m gardener

jarocho a (Mex) from Veracruz

jarr|a f jug. **~o** m jug. **echar un ~o de agua fría a** throw cold water on. **en ~as** with hands on hips

jaula f cage

jauría f pack of hounds

jazmín m jasmine

jef|a f boss. **~atura** f leadership; (sede) headquarters. **~e** m boss; (pol etc) leader. **~e de camareros** head waiter. **~e de estación** stationmaster. **~e de ventas** sales manager

jengibre m ginger

jeque *m* sheikh
jer|arquía *f* hierarchy. **~árquico** *a* hierarchical
jerez *m* sherry. **al ~** with sherry
jerga *f* coarse cloth; (*argot*) jargon
jerigonza *f* jargon; (*galimatías*) gibberish
jeringa *f* syringe; (*LAm, molestia*) nuisance. **~r** [12] *vt* (*fig, molestar, fam*) annoy
jeroglífico *m* hieroglyph(ic)
jersey *m* (*pl* **jerseys**) jersey
Jerusalén *m* Jerusalem
Jesucristo *m* Jesus Christ. **antes de ~** BC, before Christ
jesuita *a* & *m* & *f* Jesuit
Jesús *m* Jesus. ● *int* good heavens!; (*al estornudar*) bless you!
jícara *f* small cup
jilguero *m* goldfinch
jinete *m* rider, horseman
jipijapa *f* straw hat
jirafa *f* giraffe
jirón *m* shred, tatter
jitomate *m* (*Mex*) tomato
jocoso *a* funny, humorous
jorna|da *f* working day; (*viaje*) journey; (*etapa*) stage. **~l** *m* day's wage; (*trabajo*) day's work. **~lero** *m* day labourer
joroba *f* hump. **~do** *a* hunchbacked. ● *m* hunchback. **~r** *vt* annoy
jota *f* letter J; (*danza*) jota, popular dance; (*fig*) iota. **ni ~** nothing
joven (*pl* **jóvenes**) *a* young. ● *m* young man, youth. ● *f* young woman, girl
jovial *a* jovial
joy|a *f* jewel. **~as** *fpl* jewellery. **~ería** *f* jeweller's (shop). **~ero** *m* jeweller; (*estuche*) jewellery box
juanete *m* bunion
jubil|ación *f* retirement. **~ado** *a* retired. **~ar** *vt* pension off. **~arse** *vpr* retire. **~eo** *m* jubilee
júbilo *m* joy
jubiloso *a* jubilant
judaísmo *m* Judaism
judía *f* Jewish woman; (*alubia*) bean. **~ blanca** haricot bean. **~ escarlata** runner bean. **~ verde** French bean
judicial *a* judicial
judío *a* Jewish. ● *m* Jewish man
judo *m* judo

juego *m* game; (*de niños, tec*) play; (*de azar*) gambling; (*conjunto*) set. ● *vb véase* **jugar**. **estar en ~** be at stake. **estar fuera de ~** be offside. **hacer ~** match
juerga *f* spree
jueves *m* Thursday
juez *m* judge. **~ de instrucción** examining magistrate. **~ de línea** linesman
juga|dor *m* player; (*en juegos de azar*) gambler. **~r** [3] *vt* play. ● *vi* play; (*a juegos de azar*) gamble; (*apostar*) bet. **~rse** *vpr* risk. **~r al fútbol** play football
juglar *m* minstrel
jugo *m* juice; (*de carne*) gravy; (*fig*) substance. **~so** *a* juicy; (*fig*) substantial
juguet|e *m* toy. **~ear** *vi* play. **~ón** *a* playful
juicio *m* judgement; (*opinión*) opinion; (*razón*) reason. **~so** *a* wise. **a mi ~** in my opinion
juliana *f* vegetable soup
julio *m* July
junco *m* rush, reed
jungla *f* jungle
junio *m* June
junt|a *f* meeting; (*consejo*) board, committee; (*pol*) junta; (*tec*) joint. **~ar** *vt* join; (*reunir*) collect. **~arse** *vpr* join; (*gente*) meet. **~o** *a* joined; (*en plural*) together. **~o a** next to. **~ura** *f* joint. **por ~o** all together
jura|do *a* sworn. ● *m* jury; (*miembro de jurado*) juror. **~mento** *m* oath. **~r** *vt*/*i* swear. **~r en falso** commit perjury. **jurárselas a uno** have it in for s.o. **prestar ~mento** take the oath
jurel *m* (type of) mackerel
jurídico *a* legal
juris|dicción *f* jurisdiction. **~prudencia** *f* jurisprudence
justamente *a* exactly; (*con justicia*) fairly
justicia *f* justice
justifica|ción *f* justification. **~r** [7] *vt* justify
justo *a* fair, just; (*exacto*) exact; (*ropa*) tight. ● *adv* just. **~ a tiempo** just in time
juven|il *a* youthful. **~tud** *f* youth; (*gente joven*) young people
juzga|do *m* (*tribunal*) court. **~r** [12] *vt* judge. **a ~r por** judging by

K

kilo *m*, **kilogramo** *m* kilo, kilogram
kil|ometraje *m* distance in kilometres, mileage. **~ométrico** *a* (*fam*) endless. **~ómetro** *m* kilometre.
~ómetro cuadrado square kilometre
kilovatio *m* kilowatt
kiosco *m* kiosk

L

la *m* A; (*solfa*) lah. ● *art def f* the. ● *pron* (*ella*) her; (*Vd*) you; (*ello*) it. **~ de** the one. **~ de Vd** your one, yours. **~ que** whoever, the one
laberinto *m* labyrinth, maze
labia *f* glibness
labio *m* lip
labor *f* work; (*tarea*) job. **~able** *a* working. **~ar** *vi* work. **~es** *fpl de aguja* needlework. **~es** *fpl de ganchillo* crochet. **~es** *fpl de punto* knitting. **~es** *fpl* **domésticas** housework
laboratorio *m* laboratory
laborioso *a* laborious
laborista *a* Labour. ● *m & f* member of the Labour Party
labra|do *a* worked; ⟨*madera*⟩ carved; ⟨*metal*⟩ wrought; ⟨*tierra*⟩ ploughed. **~dor** *m* farmer; (*obrero*) labourer. **~nza** *f* farming. **~r** *vt* work; carve ⟨*madera*⟩; cut ⟨*piedra*⟩; till ⟨*la tierra*⟩; (*fig, causar*) cause
labriego *m* peasant
laca *f* lacquer
lacayo *m* lackey
lacerar *vt* lacerate
lacero *m* lassoer; (*cazador*) poacher
lacio *a* straight; (*flojo*) limp
lacón *m* shoulder of pork
lacónico *a* laconic
lacra *f* scar
lacr|ar *vt* seal. **~e** *m* sealing wax
lactante *a* breast-fed
lácteo *a* milky. **productos** *mpl* **~s** dairy products
ladear *vt/i* tilt. **~se** *vpr* lean
ladera *f* slope
ladino *a* astute
lado *m* side. **al ~** near. **al ~ de** at the side of, beside. **los de al ~** the next

door neighbours. **por otro ~** on the other hand. **por todos ~s** on all sides. **por un ~** on the one hand
ladr|ar *vi* bark. **~ido** *m* bark
ladrillo *m* brick; (*de chocolate*) block
ladrón *a* thieving. ● *m* thief
lagart|ija *f* (small) lizard. **~o** *m* lizard
lago *m* lake
lágrima *f* tear
lagrimoso *a* tearful
laguna *f* small lake; (*fig, omisión*) gap
laico *a* lay
lamé *m* lamé
lamedura *f* lick
lament|able *a* lamentable, pitiful. **~ar** *vt* be sorry about. **~arse** *vpr* lament; (*quejarse*) complain. **~o** *m* moan
lamer *vt* lick; ⟨*olas etc*⟩ lap
lámina *f* sheet; (*foto*) plate; (*dibujo*) picture
lamina|do *a* laminated. **~r** *vt* laminate
lámpara *f* lamp; (*bombilla*) bulb; (*lamparón*) grease stain. **~ de pie** standard lamp
lamparón *m* grease stain
lampiño *a* clean-shaven, beardless
lana *f* wool. **~r** *a*. **ganado** *m* **~r** sheep. **de ~** wool(len)
lanceta *f* lancet
lancha *f* boat. **~ motora** *f* motor boat. **~ salvavidas** lifeboat
lanero *a* wool(len)
langost|a *f* ⟨*crustáceo marino*⟩ lobster; (*insecto*) locust. **~ino** *m* prawn
languide|cer [11] *vi* languish. **~z** *f* languor
lánguido *a* languid; (*decaído*) listless
lanilla *f* nap; (*tela fina*) flannel
lanudo *a* woolly
lanza *f* lance, spear
lanza|llamas *m invar* flame-thrower. **~miento** *m* throw; (*acción de lanzar*) throwing; (*de proyectil, de producto*) launch. **~r** [10] *vt* throw; (*de un avión*) drop; launch ⟨*proyectil, producto*⟩. **~rse** *vpr* fling o.s.
lapicero *m* (propelling) pencil
lápida *f* memorial tablet. **~ sepulcral** tombstone
lapidar *vt* stone
lápiz *m* pencil; (*grafito*) lead. **~ de labios** lipstick
Laponia *f* Lapland

lapso *m* lapse

larg|a *f*. **a la ~a** in the long run. **dar ~as** put off. **~ar** [12] *vt* slacken; (*dar, fam*) give; (*fam*) deal ⟨*bofetada etc*⟩. **~arse** *vpr* (*fam*) go away, clear off (*fam*). **~o** *a* long; (*demasiado*) too long. ● *m* length. ¡**~o!** go away! **~ueza** *f* generosity. **a lo ~o** lengthwise. **a lo ~o de** along. **tener 100 metros de ~o** be 100 metres long

laring|e *f* larynx. **~itis** *f* laryngitis

larva *f* larva

las *art def fpl* the. ● *pron* them. **~ de** those, the ones. **~ de Vd** your ones, yours. **~ que** whoever, the ones

lascivo *a* lascivious

láser *m* laser

lástima *f* pity; (*queja*) complaint. **dar ~** be pitiful. **ella me da ~** I feel sorry for her. ¡**qué ~!** what a pity!

lastim|ado *a* hurt. **~ar** *vt* hurt. **~arse** *vpr* hurt o.s. **~ero** *a* doleful. **~oso** *a* pitiful

lastre *m* ballast

lata *f* tinplate; (*envase*) tin (*esp Brit*), can; (*molestia, fam*) nuisance. **dar la ~** be a nuisance. ¡**qué ~!** what a nuisance!

latente *a* latent

lateral *a* side, lateral

latido *m* beating; (*cada golpe*) beat

latifundio *m* large estate

latigazo *m* (*golpe*) lash; (*chasquido*) crack

látigo *m* whip

latín *m* Latin. **saber ~** (*fam*) not be stupid

latino *a* Latin. **L~américa** *f* Latin America. **~americano** *a* & *m* Latin American

latir *vi* beat; ⟨*herida*⟩ throb

latitud *f* latitude

latón *m* brass

latoso *a* annoying; (*pesado*) boring

laucha *f* (*Arg*) mouse

laúd *m* lute

laudable *a* laudable

laureado *a* honoured; (*premiado*) prize-winning

laurel *m* laurel; (*culin*) bay

lava *f* lava

lava|ble *a* washable. **~bo** *m* washbasin; (*retrete*) toilet. **~dero** *m* sink, wash-basin. **~do** *m* washing. **~do de cerebro** brainwashing. **~do en seco** dry-cleaning. **~dora** *f* washing machine. **~ndería** *f* laundry. **~ndería automática** launderette, laundromat (*esp Amer*). **~parabrisas** *m*

invar windscreen washer (*Brit*), windshield washer (*Amer*). **~platos** *m* & *f invar* dishwasher; (*Mex, fregadero*) sink. **~r** *vt* wash. **~r en seco** dry-clean. **~rse** *vpr* have a wash. **~rse las manos** (*incl fig*) wash one's hands. **~tiva** *f* enema. **~vajillas** *m* & *f inv* dishwasher

lax|ante *a* & *m* laxative. **~o** *a* loose

laz|ada *f* bow. **~o** *m* knot; (*lazada*) bow; (*fig, vínculo*) tie; (*cuerda con nudo corredizo*) lasso; (*trampa*) trap

le *pron* (*acusativo, él*) him; (*acusativo, Vd*) you; (*dativo, él*) (to) him; (*dativo, ella*) (to) her; (*dativo, ello*) (to) it; (*dativo, Vd*) (to) you

leal *a* loyal; (*fiel*) faithful. **~tad** *f* loyalty; (*fidelidad*) faithfulness

lebrel *m* greyhound

lección *f* lesson; (*univ*) lecture

lect|or *m* reader; (*univ*) language assistant. **~ura** *f* reading

leche *f* milk; (*golpe*) bash. **~ condensada** condensed milk. **~ desnatada** skimmed milk. **~ en polvo** powdered milk. **~ra** *f* (*vasija*) milk jug. **~ría** *f* dairy. **~ro** *a* milk, dairy. ● *m* milkman. **~ sin desnatar** whole milk. **tener mala ~** be spiteful

lecho *m* bed

lechoso *a* milky

lechuga *f* lettuce

lechuza *f* owl

leer [18] *vt/i* read

legación *f* legation

legado *m* legacy; (*enviado*) legate

legajo *m* bundle, file

legal *a* legal. **~idad** *f* legality. **~izar** [10] *vt* legalize; (*certificar*) authenticate. **~mente** *adv* legally

legar [12] *vt* bequeath

legendario *a* legendary

legible *a* legible

legi|ón *f* legion. **~onario** *m* legionary

legisla|ción *f* legislation. **~dor** *m* legislator. **~r** *vi* legislate. **~tura** *f* legislature

leg|itimidad *f* legitimacy. **~ítimo** *a* legitimate; (*verdadero*) real

lego *a* lay; (*ignorante*) ignorant. ● *m* layman

legua *f* league

legumbre *f* vegetable

lejan|ía *f* distance. **~o** *a* distant

lejía *f* bleach

lejos *adv* far. **~ de** far from. **a lo ~** in the distance. **desde ~** from a distance, from afar

lelo *a* stupid

lema *m* motto

lencería *f* linen; (*de mujer*) lingerie

lengua *f* tongue; (*idioma*) language. **irse de la** ~ talk too much. **morderse la** ~ hold one's tongue. **tener mala** ~ have a vicious tongue

lenguado *m* sole

lenguaje *m* language

lengüeta *f* (*de zapato*) tongue

lengüetada *f*, **lengüetazo** *m* lick

lente *f* lens. ~**s** *mpl* glasses. ~**s de contacto** contact lenses

lentej|a *f* lentil. ~**uela** *f* sequin

lentilla *f* contact lens

lent|itud *f* slowness. ~**o** *a* slow

leñ|a *f* firewood. ~**ador** *m* woodcutter. ~**o** *m* log

Leo *m* Leo

le|ón *m* lion. **León** Leo. ~**ona** *f* lioness

leopardo *m* leopard

leotardo *m* thick tights

lepr|a *f* leprosy. ~**oso** *m* leper

lerdo *a* dim; (*torpe*) clumsy

les *pron* (*acusativo*) them; (*acusativo, Vds*) you; (*dativo*) (to) them; (*dativo, Vds*) (to) you

lesbia(na) *f* lesbian

lesbiano *a*, **lesbio** *a* lesbian

lesi|ón *f* wound. ~**onado** *a* injured. ~**onar** *vt* injure; (*dañar*) damage

letal *a* lethal

letanía *f* litany

let|árgico *a* lethargic. ~**argo** *m* lethargy

letr|a *f* letter; (*escritura*) handwriting; (*de una canción*) words, lyrics. ~**a de cambio** bill of exchange. ~**a de imprenta** print. ~**ado** *a* learned. ~**ero** *m* notice; (*cartel*) poster

letrina *f* latrine

leucemia *f* leukaemia

levadizo *a*. **puente** *m* ~ drawbridge

levadura *f* yeast. ~ **en polvo** baking powder

levanta|miento *m* lifting; (*sublevación*) uprising. ~**r** *vt* raise, lift; (*construir*) build; (*recoger*) pick up; (*separar*) take off. ~**rse** *vpr* get up; (*ponerse de pie*) stand up; (*erguirse, sublevarse*) rise up

levante *m* east; (*viento*) east wind. **L**~ Levant

levar *vt* weigh (*ancla*). ● *vi* set sail

leve *a* light; (*enfermedad etc*) slight; (*de poca importancia*) trivial. ~**dad** *f* lightness; (*fig*) slightness

léxico *m* vocabulary

lexicografía *f* lexicography

ley *f* law; (*parlamentaria*) act. **plata** *f* **de** ~ sterling silver

leyenda *f* legend

liar [20] *vt* tie; (*envolver*) wrap up; roll (*cigarillo*); (*fig, confundir*) confuse; (*fig, enredar*) involve. ~**se** *vpr* get involved

libanés *a* & *m* Lebanese

Líbano *m*. **el** ~ Lebanon

libel|ista *m* & *f* satirist. ~**o** *m* satire

libélula *f* dragonfly

libera|ción *f* liberation. ~**dor** *a* liberating. ● *m* liberator

liberal *a* & *m* & *f* liberal. ~**idad** *f* liberality. ~**mente** *adv* liberally

liber|ar *vt* free. ~**tad** *f* freedom. ~**tad de cultos** freedom of worship. ~**tad de imprenta** freedom of the press. ~**tad provisional** bail. ~**tar** *vt* free. **en** ~**tad** free

libertino *m* libertine

Libia *f* Libya

libido *m* libido

libio *a* & *m* Libyan

libra *f* pound. ~ **esterlina** pound sterling

Libra *f* Libra

libra|dor *m* (*com*) drawer. ~**r** *vt* free; (*de un peligro*) rescue. ~**rse** *vpr* free o.s. ~**rse de** get rid of

libre *a* free; (*aire*) open; (*en natación*) freestyle. ~ **de impuestos** tax-free. ● *m* (*Mex*) taxi

librea *f* livery

libr|ería *f* bookshop (*Brit*), bookstore (*Amer*); (*mueble*) bookcase. ~**ero** *m* bookseller. ~**eta** *f* notebook. ~**o** *m* book. ~**o de a bordo** logbook. ~**o de bolsillo** paperback. ~**o de ejercicios** exercise book. ~**o de reclamaciones** complaints book

licencia *f* permission; (*documento*) licence. ~**do** *m* graduate. ~ **para manejar** (*LAm*) driving licence. ~**r** *vt* (*mil*) discharge; (*echar*) dismiss. ~**tura** *f* degree

licencioso *a* licentious

liceo *m* (*esp LAm*) (secondary) school

licita|dor *m* bidder. ~**r** *vt* bid for

lícito *a* legal; (*permisible*) permissible

licor *m* liquid; (*alcohólico*) liqueur

licua|dora *f* liquidizer. ~**r** [21] liquefy

lid *f* fight. **en buena** ~ by fair means

líder *m* leader

liderato *m*, **liderazgo** *m* leadership

lidia *f* bullfighting; (*lucha*) fight; (*LAm, molestia*) nuisance. **~r** *vt/i* fight

liebre *f* hare

lienzo *m* linen; (*del pintor*) canvas; (*muro, pared*) wall

liga *f* garter; (*alianza*) league; (*mezcla*) mixture. **~dura** *f* bond; (*mus*) slur; (*med*) ligature. **~mento** *m* ligament. **~r** [12] *vt* tie; (*fig*) join; (*mus*) slur. ● *vi* mix. **~r con** (*fig*) pick up. **~rse** *vpr* (*fig*) commit o.s.

liger|eza *f* lightness; (*agilidad*) agility; (*rapidez*) swiftness; (*de carácter*) fickleness. **~o** *a* light; (*rápido*) quick; (*ágil*) agile; (*superficial*) superficial; (*de poca importancia*) slight. ● *adv* quickly. **a la ~a** lightly, superficially

liguero *m* suspender belt

lija *f* dogfish; (*papel de lija*) sandpaper. **~r** *vt* sand

lila *f* lilac

Lima *f* Lima

lima *f* file; (*fruta*) lime. **~duras** *fpl* filings. **~r** *vt* file (down)

limbo *m* limbo

limita|ción *f* limitation. **~do** *a* limited. **~r** *vt* limit. **~r con** border on. **~tivo** *a* limiting

límite *m* limit. **~ de velocidad** speed limit

limítrofe *a* bordering

limo *m* mud

lim|ón *m* lemon. **~onada** *f* lemonade

limosn|a *f* alms. **~ear** *vi* beg. **pedir ~a** beg

limpia *f* cleaning. **~botas** *m invar* bootblack. **~parabrisas** *m invar* windscreen wiper (*Brit*), windshield wiper (*Amer*). **~pipas** *m invar* pipe-cleaner. **~r** *vt* clean; (*enjugar*) wipe

limpi|eza *f* cleanliness; (*acción de limpiar*) cleaning. **~eza en seco** dry-cleaning. **~o** *a* clean; (*cielo*) clear; (*fig, honrado*) honest. ● *adv* fairly. **en ~o** (*com*) net. **jugar ~o** play fair

linaje *m* lineage; (*fig, clase*) kind

lince *m* lynx

linchar *vt* lynch

lind|ante *a* bordering (**con** on). **~ar** *vi* border (**con** on). **~e** *f* boundary. **~ero** *m* border

lindo *a* pretty, lovely. **de lo ~** (*fam*) a lot

línea *f* line. **en ~s generales** in broad outline. **guardar la ~** watch one's figure

lingote *m* ingot

lingü|ista *m & f* linguist. **~ística** *f* linguistics. **~ístico** *a* linguistic

lino *m* flax; (*tela*) linen

linóleo *m*, **linóeum** *m* lino, linoleum

linterna *f* lantern; (*de bolsillo*) torch, flashlight (*Amer*)

lío *m* bundle; (*jaleo*) fuss; (*embrollo*) muddle; (*amorío*) affair

liquen *m* lichen

liquida|ción *f* liquidation; (*venta especial*) (clearance) sale. **~r** *vt* liquify; (*com*) liquidate; settle ⟨*cuenta*⟩

líquido *a* liquid; (*com*) net. ● *m* liquid

lira *f* lyre; (*moneda italiana*) lira

líric|a *f* lyric poetry. **~o** *a* lyric(al)

lirio *m* iris. **~ de los valles** lily of the valley

lirón *m* dormouse; (*fig*) sleepyhead. **dormir como un ~** sleep like a log

Lisboa *f* Lisbon

lisia|do *a* disabled. **~r** *vt* disable; (*herir*) injure

liso *a* smooth; ⟨*pelo*⟩ straight; ⟨*tierra*⟩ flat; (*sencillo*) plain

lisonj|a *f* flattery. **~eador** *a* flattering. ● *m* flatterer. **~ear** *vt* flatter. **~ero** *a* flattering

lista *f* stripe; (*enumeración*) list; (*de platos*) menu. **~ de correos** poste restante. **~do** *a* striped. **a ~s** striped

listo *a* clever; (*preparado*) ready

listón *m* ribbon; (*de madera*) strip

lisura *f* smoothness

litera *f* (*en barco*) berth; (*en tren*) sleeper; (*en habitación*) bunk bed

literal *a* literal

litera|rio *a* literary. **~tura** *f* literature

litig|ar [12] *vi* dispute; (*jurid*) litigate. **~io** *m* dispute; (*jurid*) litigation

litografía *f* (*arte*) lithography; (*cuadro*) lithograph

litoral *a* coastal. ● *m* coast

litro *m* litre

lituano *a & m* Lithuanian

liturgia *f* liturgy

liviano *a* fickle, inconstant

lívido *a* livid

lizo *m* warp thread

lo *art def neutro*. ~ **importante** what is important, the important thing. ● *pron* (*él*) him; (*ello*) it. ~ **que** what(ever), that which

loa *f* praise. ~**ble** *a* praiseworthy. ~**r** *vt* praise

lobo *m* wolf

lóbrego *a* gloomy

lóbulo *m* lobe

local *a* local. ● *m* premises; (*lugar*) place. ~**idad** *f* locality; (*de un espectáculo*) seat; (*entrada*) ticket. ~**izar** [10] *vt* localize; (*encontrar*) find, locate

loción *f* lotion

loco *a* mad; (*fig*) foolish. ● *m* lunatic. ~ **de alegría** mad with joy. **estar ~ por** be crazy about. **volverse ~** go mad

locomo|ción *f* locomotion. ~**tora** *f* locomotive

locuaz *a* talkative

locución *f* expression

locura *f* madness; (*acto*) crazy thing. **con ~** madly

locutor *m* announcer

locutorio *m* (*de teléfono*) telephone booth

lod|azal *m* quagmire. ~**o** *m* mud

logaritmo *m* logarithm, log

lógic|a *f* logic. ~**o** *a* logical

logística *f* logistics

logr|ar *vt* get; win (*premio*). ~ **hacer** manage to do. ~**o** *m* achievement; (*de premio*) winning; (*éxito*) success

loma *f* small hill

lombriz *f* worm

lomo *m* back; (*de libro*) spine; (*doblez*) fold. ~ **de cerdo** loin of pork

lona *f* canvas

loncha *f* slice; (*de tocino*) rasher

londinense *a* from London. ● *m* Londoner

Londres *m* London

loneta *f* thin canvas

longánimo *a* magnanimous

longaniza *f* sausage

longev|idad *f* longevity. ~**o** *a* long-lived

longitud *f* length; (*geog*) longitude

lonja *f* slice; (*de tocino*) rasher; (*com*) market

lord *m* (*pl* **lores**) lord

loro *m* parrot

los *art def mpl* the. ● *pron* them. ~ **de Antonio** Antonio's. ~ **que** whoever, the ones

losa *f* slab; (*baldosa*) flagstone. ~ **sepulcral** tombstone

lote *m* share

lotería *f* lottery

loto *m* lotus

loza *f* crockery

lozano *a* fresh; (*vegetación*) lush; (*persona*) lively

lubri(fi)ca|nte *a* lubricating. ● *m* lubricant. ~**r** [7] *vt* lubricate

lucero *m* (*estrella*) bright star; (*planeta*) Venus

lucid|ez *f* lucidity. ~**o** *a* splendid

lúcido *a* lucid

luciérnaga *f* glow-worm

lucimiento *m* brilliance

lucir [11] *vt* (*fig*) show off. ● *vi* shine; (*lámpara*) give off light; (*joya*) sparkle. ~**se** *vpr* (*fig*) shine, excel

lucr|ativo *a* lucrative. ~**o** *m* gain

lucha *f* fight. ~**dor** *m* fighter. ~**r** *vi* fight

luego *adv* then; (*más tarde*) later. ● *conj* therefore. ~ **que** as soon as. **desde ~** of course

lugar *m* place. ~ **común** cliché. ~**eño** *a* village. **dar ~ a** give rise to. **en ~ de** instead of. **en primer ~** in the first place. **hacer ~** make room. **tener ~** take place

lugarteniente *m* deputy

lúgubre *a* gloomy

lujo *m* luxury. ~**so** *a* luxurious. **de ~** de luxe

lujuria *f* lust

lumbago *m* lumbago

lumbre *f* fire; (*luz*) light. **¿tienes ~?** have you got a light?

luminoso *a* luminous; (*fig*) brilliant

luna *f* moon; (*de escaparate*) window; (*espejo*) mirror. ~ **de miel** honeymoon. ~**r** *a* lunar. ● *m* mole. **claro de ~** moonlight. **estar en la ~** be miles away

lunes *m* Monday. **cada ~ y cada martes** day in, day out

lupa *f* magnifying glass

lúpulo *m* hop

lustr|abotas *m inv* (*LAm*) bootblack. ~**ar** *vt* shine, polish. ~**e** *m* shine; (*fig*, *esplendor*) splendour. ~**oso** *a* shining. **dar ~e a, sacar ~e a** polish

luto *m* mourning. **estar de ~** be in mourning

luxación *f* dislocation

Luxemburgo *m* Luxemburg

luz *f* light; (*electricidad*) electricity. **luces** *fpl* intelligence. ~ **antiniebla**

(*auto*) fog light. **a la ~ de** in the light of. **a todas luces** obviously. **dar a ~** give birth. **hacer la ~ sobre** shed light on. **sacar a la ~** bring to light

llov|er [2] *vi* rain. **~izna** *f* drizzle. **~iznar** *vi* drizzle
llueve *vb véase* **llover**
lluvi|a *f* rain; (*fig*) shower. **~oso** *a* rainy; ‹*clima*› wet

LL

llaga *f* wound; (*úlcera*) ulcer
llama *f* flame; (*animal*) llama
llamada *f* call; (*golpe*) knock; (*señal*) sign
llama|do *a* known as. **~miento** *m* call. **~r** *vt* call; (*por teléfono*) ring (up). ● *vi* call; (*golpear en la puerta*) knock; (*tocar el timbre*) ring. **~rse** *vpr* be called. **~r por teléfono** ring (up), telephone. **¿cómo te ~s?** what's your name?
llamarada *f* blaze; (*fig*) blush; (*fig, de pasión etc*) outburst
llamativo *a* loud, gaudy
llamear *vi* blaze
llan|eza *f* simplicity. **~o** *a* flat, level; ‹*persona*› natural; (*sencillo*) plain. ● *m* plain
llanta *f* (*auto*) (wheel) rim; (*LAm, neumático*) tyre
llanto *m* weeping
llanura *f* plain
llave *f* key; (*para tuercas*) spanner; (*grifo*) tap (*Brit*), faucet (*Amer*); (*elec*) switch. **~ inglesa** monkey wrench. **~ro** *m* key-ring. **cerrar con ~** lock. **echar la ~** lock up
llega|da *f* arrival. **~r** [12] *vi* arrive, come; (*alcanzar*) reach; (*bastar*) be enough. **~rse** *vpr* come near; (*ir*) go (round). **~r a** (*conseguir*) manage to. **~r a saber** find out. **~r a ser** become
llen|ar *vt* fill (up); (*rellenar*) fill in. **~o** *a* full. ● *m* (*en el teatro etc*) full house. **de ~** completely
lleva|dero *a* tolerable. **~r** *vt* carry; (*inducir, conducir*) lead; (*acompañar*) take; wear ‹*ropa*›; (*traer*) bring. **~rse** *vpr* run off with ‹*cosa*›. **~rse bien** get on well together. **¿cuánto tiempo ~s aquí?** how long have you been here? **llevo 3 años estudiando inglés** I've been studying English for 3 years
llor|ar *vi* cry; ‹*ojos*› water. **~iquear** *vi* whine. **~iqueo** *m* whining. **~o** *m* crying. **~ón** *a* whining. ● *m* crybaby. **~oso** *a* tearful

M

maca *f* defect; (*en fruta*) bruise
macabro *a* macabre
macaco *a* (*LAm*) ugly. ● *m* macaque (monkey)
macadam *m*, **macadán** *m* Tarmac (P)
macanudo *a* (*fam*) great
macarrón *m* macaroon. **~es** *mpl* macaroni
macerar *vt* macerate
maceta *f* mallet; (*tiesto*) flowerpot
macilento *a* wan
macizo *a* solid. ● *m* mass; (*de plantas*) bed
macrobiótico *a* macrobiotic
mácula *f* stain
macuto *m* knapsack
mach /mak/ *m*. **(número de) ~** Mach (number)
machac|ar [7] *vt* crush. ● *vi* go on (**en** about). **~ón** *a* boring. ● *m* bore
machamartillo. a ~ *adv* firmly
machaqueo *m* crushing
machet|azo *m* blow with a machete; (*herida*) wound from a machete. **~e** *m* machete
mach|ista *m* male chauvinist. **~o** *a* male; (*varonil*) macho
machón *m* buttress
machucar [7] *vt* crush; (*estropear*) damage
madeja *f* skein
madera *m* (*vino*) Madeira. ● *f* wood; (*naturaleza*) nature. **~ble** *a* yielding timber. **~je** *m*, **~men** *m* woodwork
madero *m* log; (*de construcción*) timber
madona *f* Madonna
madr|astra *f* stepmother. **~e** *f* mother. **~eperla** *f* mother-of-pearl. **~eselva** *f* honeysuckle
madrigal *m* madrigal
madriguera *f* den; (*de liebre*) burrow
madrileño *a* of Madrid. ● *m* person from Madrid
madrina *f* godmother; (*en una boda*) chief bridesmaid
madroño *m* strawberry-tree

madrug|ada f dawn. **~ador** a who gets up early. ● m early riser. **~ar** [12] vi get up early. **~ón** m. **darse un ~ón** get up very early

madur|ación f maturing; (de fruta) ripening. **~ar** vt/i mature; ⟨fruta⟩ ripen. **~ez** f maturity; (de fruta) ripeness. **~o** a mature; ⟨fruta⟩ ripe

maestr|a f teacher. **~ía** f skill. **~o** m master. **~a**, **~o** (de escuela) schoolteacher

mafia f Mafia

magdalena f madeleine, small sponge cake

magia f magic

mágico a magic; (maravilloso) magical

magín m (fam) imagination

magisterio m teaching (profession); (conjunto de maestros) teachers

magistrado m magistrate; (juez) judge

magistral a teaching; (bien hecho) masterly; ⟨lenguaje⟩ pedantic

magistratura f magistracy

magn|animidad f magnanimity. **~ánimo** a magnanimous

magnate m magnate

magnesia f magnesia. **~ efervescente** milk of magnesia

magnético a magnetic

magneti|smo m magnetism. **~zar** [10] vt magnetize

magnetofón m, **magnetófono** m tape recorder

magnificencia f magnificence

magnífico a magnificent

magnitud f magnitude

magnolia f magnolia

mago m magician. **los (tres) reyes ~s** the Magi

magr|a f slice of ham. **~o** a lean; ⟨tierra⟩ poor; ⟨persona⟩ thin

magulla|dura f bruise. **~r** vt bruise

mahometano a & m Muhammadan

maíz m maize, corn (Amer)

majada f sheepfold; (estiércol) manure; (LAm) flock of sheep

majader|ía f silly thing. **~o** m idiot; (mano del mortero) pestle. ● a stupid

majador m crusher

majagranzas m idiot

majar vt crush; (molestar) bother

majest|ad f majesty. **~uoso** a majestic

majo a nice

mal adv badly; (poco) poorly; (difícilmente) hardly; (equivocadamente) wrongly. ● a see

malo. ● m evil; (daño) harm; (enfermedad) illness. **~ que bien** somehow (or other). **de ~ en peor** worse and worse. **hacer ~ en** be wrong to. **¡menos ~!** thank goodness!

malabar a. **juegos ~es** juggling. **~ismo** m juggling. **~ista** m & f juggler

malaconsejado a ill-advised

malacostumbrado a with bad habits

malagueño a of Málaga. ● m person from Málaga

malamente adv badly; (fam) hardly enough

malandanza f misfortune

malapata m & f nuisance

malaria f malaria

Malasia f Malaysia

malasombra m & f clumsy person

malavenido a incompatible

malaventura f misfortune. **~do** a unfortunate

malayo a Malay(an)

malbaratar vt sell off cheap; (malgastar) squander

malcarado a ugly

malcasado a unhappily married; (infiel) unfaithful

malcomer vi eat poorly

malcriad|eza f (LAm) bad manners. **~o** a ⟨niño⟩ spoilt

maldad f evil; (acción) wicked thing

maldecir [46 pero imperativo **maldice**, futuro y condicional regulares, pp **maldecido** o **maldito**] vt curse. ● vi speak ill (de of); (quejarse) complain (de about)

maldici|ente a backbiting; (que blasfema) foul-mouthed. **~ón** f curse

maldit|a f tongue. **¡~a sea!** damn it! **~o** a damned. ● m (en el teatro) extra

maleab|ilidad f malleability. **~le** a malleable

malea|nte a wicked. ● m vagrant. **~r** vt damage; (pervertir) corrupt. **~rse** vpr be spoilt; (pervertirse) be corrupted

malecón m breakwater; (rail) embankment; (para atracar) jetty

maledicencia f slander

maleficio m curse

maléfico a evil

malestar m indisposition; (fig) uneasiness

malet|a f (suit)case; (auto) boot, trunk (Amer); (LAm, lío de ropa)

malevolencia

131

manchón

bundle; (*LAm, de bicicleta*) saddle-bag. **hacer la ~a** pack one's bags. ● *m & f* (*fam*) bungler. **~ero** *m* porter; (*auto*) boot, trunk (*Amer*). **~ín** *m* small case

malevolencia *f* malevolence

malévolo *a* malevolent

maleza *f* weeds; (*matorral*) undergrowth

malgasta|dor *a* wasteful. ● *m* spendthrift. **~r** *vt* waste

malgeniado *a* (*LAm*) bad-tempered

malhablado *a* foul-mouthed

malhadado *a* unfortunate

malhechor *m* criminal

malhumorado *a* bad-tempered

malici|a *f* malice. **~arse** *vpr* suspect. **~as** *fpl* (*fam*) suspicions. **~oso** *a* malicious

malign|idad *f* malice; (*med*) malignancy. **~o** *a* malignant; ⟨*persona*⟩ malicious

malintencionado *a* malicious

malmandado *a* disobedient

malmirado *a* (*con estar*) disliked; (*con ser*) inconsiderate

malo *a* (*delante de nombre masculino en singular* **mal**) bad; (*enfermo*) ill. **~ de** difficult. **estar de malas** be out of luck; (*malhumorado*) be in a bad mood. **lo ~ es que** the trouble is that. **ponerse a malas con uno** fall out with s.o. **por las malas** by force

malogr|ar *vt* waste; (*estropear*) spoil. **~arse** *vpr* fall through. **~o** *m* failure

maloliente *a* smelly

malparto *m* miscarriage

malpensado *a* nasty, malicious

malquerencia *f* dislike

malquist|ar *vt* set against. **~arse** *vpr* fall out. **~o** *a* disliked

malsano *a* unhealthy; (*enfermizo*) sickly

malsonante *a* ill-sounding; (*grosero*) offensive

malta *f* malt; (*cerveza*) beer

maltés *a & m* Maltese

maltratar *vt* ill-treat

maltrecho *a* battered

malucho *a* (*fam*) poorly

malva *f* mallow. **(color de) ~** *a invar* mauve

malvado *a* wicked

malvavisco *m* marshmallow

malvender *vt* sell off cheap

malversa|ción *f* embezzlement. **~dor** *a* embezzling. ● *m* embezzler. **~r** *vt* embezzle

Malvinas *fpl*. **las islas ~** the Falkland Islands

malla *f* mesh. **cota de ~** coat of mail

mallo *m* mallet

Mallor|ca *f* Majorca. **~quín** *a & m* Majorcan

mama *f* teat; (*de mujer*) breast

mamá *f* mum(my)

mama|da *f* sucking. **~r** *vt* suck; (*fig*) grow up with; (*engullir*) gobble

mamario *a* mammary

mamarrach|adas *fpl* nonsense. **~o** *m* clown; (*cosa ridícula*) (ridiculous) sight

mameluco *a* Brazilian half-breed; (*necio*) idiot

mamífero *a* mammalian. ● *m* mammal

mamola *f*. **hacer la ~** chuck (under the chin); (*fig*) make fun of

mamotreto *m* notebook; (*libro voluminoso*) big book

mampara *f* screen

mamporro *m* blow

mampostería *f* masonry

mamut *m* mammoth

maná *f* manna

manada *f* herd; (*de lobos*) pack. **en ~** in crowds

manager /ˈmanaʒer/ *m* manager

mana|ntial *m* spring; (*fig*) source. **~r** *vi* flow; (*fig*) abound. ● *vt* run with

manaza *f* big hand; (*sucia*) dirty hand. **ser un ~s** be clumsy

manceb|a *f* concubine. **~ía** *f* brothel. **~o** *m* youth; (*soltero*) bachelor

mancera *f* plough handle

mancilla *f* stain. **~r** *vt* stain

manco *a* (*de una mano*) one-handed; (*de las dos manos*) handless; (*de un brazo*) one-armed; (*de los dos brazos*) armless

mancomún *adv.* **de ~** jointly

mancomun|adamente *adv* jointly. **~ar** *vt* unite; (*jurid*) make jointly liable. **~arse** *vpr* unite. **~idad** *f* union

mancha *f* stain

Mancha *f*. **la ~** la Mancha (region of Spain). **el canal de la ~** the English Channel

mancha|do *a* dirty; ⟨*animal*⟩ spotted. **~r** *vt* stain. **~rse** *vpr* get dirty

manchego *a* of la Mancha. ● *m* person from la Mancha

manchón *m* large stain

manda *f* legacy

manda|dero *m* messenger. **~miento** *m* order; (*relig*) commandment. **~r** *vt* order; (*enviar*) send; (*gobernar*) rule. • *vi* be in command. **¿mande?** (*esp LAm*) pardon?

mandarín *m* mandarin

mandarin|a *f* (*naranja*) mandarin; (*lengua*) Mandarin. **~o** *m* mandarin tree

mandat|ario *m* attorney. **~o** *m* order; (*jurid*) power of attorney

mandíbula *f* jaw

mandil *m* apron

mandioca *f* cassava

mando *m* command; (*pol*) term of office. **~ a distancia** remote control. **los ~s** the leaders

mandolina *f* mandolin

mandón *a* bossy

manducar [7] *vt* (*fam*) stuff oneself with

manecilla *f* needle; (*de reloj*) hand

manej|able *a* manageable. **~ar** *vt* handle; (*fig*) manage; (*LAm, conducir*) drive. **~arse** *vpr* behave. **~o** *m* handling; (*intriga*) intrigue

manera *f* way. **~s** *fpl* manners. **de ~ que** so (that). **de ninguna ~** not at all. **de otra ~** otherwise. **de todas ~s** anyway

manga *f* sleeve; (*tubo de goma*) hose-(pipe); (*red*) net; (*para colar*) filter

mangante *m* beggar; (*fam*) scrounger

mangle *m* mangrove

mango *m* handle; (*fruta*) mango

mangonear *vt* boss about. • *vi* (*entrometerse*) interfere

manguera *f* hose(pipe)

manguito *m* muff

manía *f* mania; (*antipatía*) dislike

maniaco *a*, **maníaco** *a* maniac(al). • *m* maniac

maniatar *vt* tie s.o.'s hands

maniático *a* maniac(al); (*fig*) crazy

manicomio *m* lunatic asylum

manicura *f* manicure; (*mujer*) manicurist

manido *a* stale; (*carne*) high

manifesta|ción *f* manifestation; (*pol*) demonstration. **~nte** *m* demonstrator. **~r** [1] *vi* manifest; (*pol*) state. **~rse** *vpr* show; (*pol*) demonstrate

manifiesto *a* clear; (*error*) obvious; (*verdad*) manifest. • *m* manifesto

manilargo *a* light-fingered

manilla *f* bracelet; (*de hierro*) handcuffs

manillar *m* handlebar(s)

maniobra *f* manoeuvring; (*rail*) shunting; (*fig*) manoeuvre. **~r** *vt* operate; (*rail*) shunt. • *vi* manoeuvre. **~s** *fpl* (*mil*) manoeuvres

manipula|ción *f* manipulation. **~r** *vt* manipulate

maniquí *m* dummy. • *f* model

manirroto *a* extravagant. • *m* spendthrift

manita *f* little hand

manivela *f* crank

manjar *m* (*special*) dish

mano *f* hand; (*de animales*) front foot; (*de perros, gatos*) front paw. **~ de obra** work force. **¡~s arriba!** hands up! **a ~** by hand; (*próximo*) handy. **de segunda ~** second hand. **echar una ~** lend a hand. **tener buena ~ para** be good at

manojo *m* bunch

manose|ar *vt* handle; (*fig*) overwork. **~o** *m* handling

manotada *f*, **manotazo** *m* slap

manote|ar *vi* gesticulate. **~o** *m* gesticulation

mansalva. a ~ *adv* without risk

mansarda *f* attic

mansedumbre *f* gentleness; (*de animal*) tameness

mansión *f* stately home

manso *a* gentle; ‹*animal*› tame

manta *f* blanket. **~ eléctrica** electric blanket. **a ~ (de Dios)** a lot

mantec|a *f* fat; (*LAm*) butter. **~ado** *m* bun; (*helado*) ice-cream. **~oso** *a* greasy

mantel *m* tablecloth; (*del altar*) altar cloth. **~ería** *f* table linen

manten|er [40] *vt* support; (*conservar*) keep; (*sostener*) maintain. **~erse** *vpr* remain. **~ de/con** live off. **~imiento** *m* maintenance

mantequ|era *f* butter churn. **~ería** *f* dairy. **~illa** *f* butter

mantilla *f* mantilla

manto *m* cloak

mantón *m* shawl

manual *a* & *m* manual

manubrio *m* crank

manufactura *f* manufacture; (*fábrica*) factory

manuscrito *a* handwritten. • *m* manuscript

manutención *f* maintenance

manzana f apple. ~r m (apple) orchard

manzanilla f camomile tea; (vino) manzanilla, pale dry sherry

manzano m apple tree

maña f skill. ~s fpl cunning

mañan|a f morning; (el día siguiente) tomorrow. ● m future. ● adv tomorrow. ~ero a who gets up early. ● m early riser. ~a por la ~a tomorrow morning. **pasado** ~a the day after tomorrow. **por la** ~a in the morning

mañoso a clever; (astuto) crafty

mapa m map. ~**mundi** m map of the world

mapache m racoon

mapurite m skunk

maqueta f scale model

maquiavélico a machiavellian

maquilla|je m make-up. ~r vt make up. ~**rse** vpr make up

máquina f machine; (rail) engine. ~ **de escribir** typewriter. ~ **fotográfica** camera

maquin|ación f machination. ~**al** a mechanical. ~**aria** f machinery. ~**ista** m & f operator; (rail) engine driver

mar m & f sea. **alta** ~ high seas. **la** ~ **de** (fam) lots of

maraña f thicket; (enredo) tangle; (embrollo) muddle

maravedí m (pl **maravedís, maravedises**) maravedi, old Spanish coin

maravill|a f wonder. ~**ar** vt astonish. ~**arse** vpr be astonished (**con** at). ~**oso** a marvellous, wonderful. **a** ~**a, a las mil** ~**as** marvellously. **contar/decir** ~**as de** speak wonderfully of. **hacer** ~**as** work wonders

marbete m label

marca f mark; (de fábrica) trademark; (deportes) record. ~**do** a marked. ~**dor** m marker; (deportes) scoreboard. ~**r** [7] vt mark; (señalar) show; (anotar) note down; score ‹un gol›; dial ‹número de teléfono›. ● vi score. **de** ~ brand name; (fig) excellent. **de** ~ **mayor** (fam) first-class

marcial a martial

marciano a & m Martian

marco m frame; (moneda alemana) mark; (deportes) goal-posts

marcha f (incl mus) march; (auto) gear; (curso) course. **a toda** ~ at full speed. **dar/hacer** ~ **atrás** put into

reverse. **poner en** ~ start; (fig) set in motion

marchante m (f **marchanta**) dealer; (LAm, parroquiano) client

marchar vi go; (funcionar) work, go. ~**se** vpr go away, leave

marchit|ar vt wither. ~**arse** vpr wither. ~**o** a withered

marea f tide. ~**do** a sick; (en el mar) seasick; (aturdido) dizzy; (borracho) drunk. ~**r** vt sail, navigate; (baquetear) annoy. ~**rse** vpr feel sick; (en un barco) be seasick; (estar aturdido) feel dizzy; (irse la cabeza) feel faint; (emborracharse) get slightly drunk

marejada f swell; (fig) wave

maremagno m (de cosas) sea; (de gente) (noisy) crowd

mareo m sickness; (en el mar) seasickness; (aturdimiento) dizziness; (fig, molestia) nuisance

marfil m ivory. ~**eño** a ivory. **torre** f **de** ~ ivory tower

margarina f margarine

margarita f pearl; (bot) daisy

marg|en m margin; (borde) edge, border; (de un río) bank; (de un camino) side; (nota marginal) marginal note. ~**inado** a on the edge. ● m outcast. ~**inal** a marginal. ~**inar** vt (excluir) exclude; (dejar márgenes) leave margins; (poner notas) write notes in the margin. **al** ~**en** (fig) outside

mariachi (Mex) m (música popular de Jalisco) Mariachi; (conjunto popular) Mariachi band

mariano a Marian

marica f (hombre afeminado) sissy; (urraca) magpie

maricón m homosexual, queer (sl)

marid|aje m married life; (fig) harmony. ~**o** m husband

mariguana f, **marihuana** f marijuana

marimacho m mannish woman

marimandona f bossy woman

marimba f (type of) drum; (LAm, especie de xilofón) marimba

marimorena f (fam) row

marin|a f coast; (cuadro) seascape; (conjunto de barcos) navy; (arte de navegar) seamanship; (conjunto de marineros) crew. ~**era** f seamanship. ~**ero** a marine; ‹barco› seaworthy. ● m sailor. ~**o** a marine. ~**a de guerra** navy. ~**a mercante** merchant navy. **a la** ~**era** in tomato and garlic sauce. **azul** ~**o** navy blue

marioneta _f_ puppet. ~**s** _fpl_ puppet show

maripos|a _f_ butterfly. ~**ear** _vi_ be fickle; (_galantear_) flirt. ~**n** _m_ flirt. ~**a nocturna** moth

mariquita _f_ ladybird, ladybug (_Amer_)

marisabidilla _f_ know-all

mariscador _m_ shell-fisher

mariscal _m_ marshal

maris|co _m_ seafood, shellfish. ~**quero** _m_ (_persona que pesca mariscos_) seafood fisherman; (_persona que vende mariscos_) seafood seller

marital _a_ marital

marítimo _a_ maritime; ⟨_ciudad etc_⟩ coastal, seaside

maritornes _f_ uncouth servant

marmit|a _f_ pot. ~**ón** _m_ kitchen boy

mármol _m_ marble

marmol|era _f_ marblework, marbles. ~**ista** _a & f_ marble worker

marmóreo _a_ marble

marmota _f_ marmot

maroma _f_ rope; (_LAm, función de volatines_) tightrope walking

marqu|és _m_ marquess. ~**esa** _f_ marchioness. ~**esina** _f_ glass canopy

marquetería _f_ marquetry

marrajo _a_ ⟨_toro_⟩ vicious; ⟨_persona_⟩ cunning. ● _m_ shark

marran|a _f_ sow. ~**ada** _f_ filthy thing; (_cochinada_) dirty trick. ~**o** _a_ filthy. ● _m_ hog

marrar _vt_ (_errar_) miss; (_fallar_) fail

marrón _a & m_ brown

marroquí _a & m & f_ Moroccan. ● _m_ (_tafilete_) morocco

marrubio _m_ (_bot_) horehound

Marruecos _m_ Morocco

marruller|ía _f_ cajolery. ~**o** _a_ cajoling. ● _m_ cajoler

marsopa _f_ porpoise

marsupial _a & m_ marsupial

marta _f_ marten

martajar _vt_ (_Mex_) grind ⟨_maíz_⟩

Marte _m_ Mars

martes _m_ Tuesday

martill|ada _f_ blow with a hammer. ~**ar** _vt_ hammer. ~**azo** _m_ blow with a hammer. ~**ear** _vt_ hammer. ~**eo** _m_ hammering. ~**o** _m_ hammer

martín _m_ **pescador** kingfisher

martinete _m_ (_macillo del piano_) hammer; (_mazo_) drop hammer

martingala _f_ (_ardid_) trick

mártir _m & f_ martyr

martir|io _m_ martyrdom. ~**izar** [10] _vt_ martyr; (_fig_) torment, torture. ~**ologio** _m_ martyrology

marxis|mo _m_ Marxism. ~**ta** _a & m & f_ Marxist

marzo _m_ March

más _adv & a_ (_comparativo_) more; (_superlativo_) most. ~ **caro** dearer. ~ **curioso** more curious. **el** ~ **caro** the dearest; (_de dos_) the dearer. **el** ~ **curioso** the most curious; (_de dos_) the more curious. ● _conj_ and, plus. ● _m_ plus (sign). ~ **bien** rather. ~ **de** (_cantidad indeterminada_) more than. ~ **o menos** more or less. ~ **que** more than. ~ **y** ~ more and more. **a lo** ~ at (the) most. **de** ~ too many. **es** ~ moreover. **no** ~ no more

masa _f_ dough; (_cantidad_) mass; (_física_) mass. **en** ~ en masse

masacre _f_ massacre

masaj|e _m_ massage. ~**ista** _m_ masseur. ● _f_ masseuse

masca|da _f_ (_LAm_) plug of tobacco. ~**dura** _f_ chewing. ~**r** [7] _vt_ chew

máscara _f_ mask; (_persona_) masked figure/person

mascar|ada _f_ masquerade. ~**illa** _f_ mask. ~**ón** _m_ (large) mask

mascota _f_ mascot

masculin|idad _f_ masculinity. ~**o** _a_ masculine; ⟨_sexo_⟩ male. ● _m_ masculine

mascullar [3] _vt_ mumble

masilla _f_ putty

masivo _a_ massive, large-scale

mas|ón _m_ (free)mason. ~**onería** _f_ (free)masonry. ~**ónico** _a_ masonic

masoquis|mo _m_ masochism. ~**ta** _a_ masochistic. ● _m & f_ masochist

mastate _m_ (_Mex_) loincloth

mastelero _m_ topmast

mastica|ción _f_ chewing. ~**r** [7] _vt_ chew; (_fig_) chew over

mástil _m_ mast; (_palo_) pole; (_en instrumentos de cuerda_) neck

mastín _m_ mastiff

mastitis _f_ mastitis

mastodonte _m_ mastodon

mastoides _a & f_ mastoid

mastuerzo _m_ cress

masturba|ción _f_ masturbation. ~**rse** _vpr_ masturbate

mata _f_ grove; (_arbusto_) bush

matad|ero _m_ slaughterhouse. ~**or** _a_ killing. ● _m_ killer; (_torero_) matador

matadura _f_ sore

matamoscas *m invar* fly swatter

mata|nza *f* killing. **~r** *vt* kill ‹*personas*›; slaughter ‹*reses*›. **~rife** *m* butcher. **~rse** *vpr* commit suicide; (*en un acidente*) be killed. **estar a ~r con uno** be deadly enemies with s.o.

matarratas *m invar* cheap liquor

matasanos *m invar* quack

matasellos *m invar* postmark

match *m* match

mate *a* matt, dull; ‹*sonido*› dull. ● *m* (*ajedrez*) (check)mate; (*LAm*, *bebida*) maté

matemátic|as *fpl* mathematics, maths (*fam*), math (*Amer*, *fam*). **~o** *a* mathematical. ● *m* mathematician

materia *f* matter; (*material*) material. **~ prima** raw material. **en ~ de** on the question of

material *a & m* material. **~idad** *f* material nature. **~ismo** *m* materialism. **~ista** *a* materialistic. ● *m & f* materialist. **~izar** [10] *vt* materialize. **~izarse** *vpr* materialize. **~mente** *adv* materially; (*absolutamente*) absolutely

matern|al *a* maternal; (*como de madre*) motherly. **~idad** *f* motherhood; (*casa de maternidad*) maternity home. **~o** *a* motherly; ‹*lengua*› mother

matin|al *a* morning. **~ée** *m* matinée

matiz *m* shade. **~ación** *f* combination of colours. **~ar** [10] *vt* blend ‹*colores*›; (*introducir variedad*) vary; (*teñir*) tinge (**de** with)

matojo *m* bush

mat|ón *m* bully. **~onismo** *m* bullying

matorral *m* scrub; (*conjunto de matas*) thicket

matra|ca *f* rattle. **~quear** *vt* rattle; (*dar matraca*) pester. **dar ~ca** pester. **ser un(a) ~ca** be a nuisance

matraz *m* flask

matriarca|do *m* matriarchy. **~l** *a* matriarchal

matr|ícula *f* (*lista*) register, list; (*acto de matricularse*) registration; (*auto*) registration number. **~icular** *vt* register. **~icularse** *vpr* enrol, register

matrimoni|al *a* matrimonial. **~o** *m* marriage; (*pareja*) married couple

matritense *a* from Madrid

matriz *f* matrix; (*anat*) womb, uterus

matrona *f* matron; (*partera*) midwife

Matusalén *m* Methuselah. **más viejo que ~** as old as Methuselah

matute *m* smuggling. **~ro** *m* smuggler

matutino *a* morning

maula *f* piece of junk

maull|ar *vi* miaow. **~ido** *m* miaow

mauritano *a & m* Mauritanian

mausoleo *m* mausoleum

maxilar *a* maxillary. **hueso ~** jaw(bone)

máxima *f* maxim

máxime *adv* especially

máximo *a* maximum; (*más alto*) highest. ● *m* maximum

maya *f* daisy; (*persona*) Maya Indian

mayestático *a* majestic

mayo *m* May; (*palo*) maypole

mayólica *f* majolica

mayonesa *f* mayonnaise

mayor *a* (*más grande, comparativo*) bigger; (*más grande, superlativo*) biggest; (*de edad, comparativo*) older; (*de edad, superlativo*) oldest; (*adulto*) grown-up; (*principal*) main, major; (*mus*) major. ● *m & f* boss; (*adulto*) adult. **~al** *m* foreman; (*pastor*) head shepherd. **~azgo** *m* entailed estate. **al por ~** wholesale

mayordomo *m* butler

mayor|ía *f* majority. **~ista** *m & f* wholesaler. **~mente** *adv* especially

mayúscul|a *f* capital (letter). **~o** *a* capital; (*fig, grande*) big

maza *f* mace

mazacote *m* hard mass

mazapán *m* marzipan

mazmorra *f* dungeon

mazo *m* mallet; (*manojo*) bunch

mazorca *f.* **~ de maíz** corn on the cob

me *pron* (*acusativo*) me; (*dativo*) (to) me; (*reflexivo*) (to) myself

meandro *m* meander

mecánic|a *f* mechanics. **~o** *a* mechanical. ● *m* mechanic

mecani|smo *m* mechanism. **~zación** *f* mechanization. **~zar** [10] *vt* mechanize

mecanograf|ía *f* typing. **~iado** *a* typed, typewritten. **~iar** [20] *vt* type

mecanógrafo *m* typist

mecate *m* (*LAm*) (*pita*) rope

mecedora *f* rocking chair

mecenazgo *m* patronage

mecer [9] *vt* rock; swing ‹*columpio*›. **∼se** *vpr* rock; (*en un columpio*) swing

mecha *f* (*de vela*) wick; (*de mina*) fuse

mechar *vt* stuff, lard

mechero *m* (cigarette) lighter

mechón *m* (*de pelo*) lock

medall|a *f* medal. **∼ón** *m* medallion; (*relicario*) locket

media *f* stocking; (*promedio*) average

mediación *f* mediation

mediado *a* half full; ‹*trabajo etc*› halfway through. **a ∼s de marzo** in the middle of March

mediador *m* mediator

medialuna *f* croissant

median|amente *adv* fairly. **∼era** *f* party wall. **∼ero** *a* ‹*muro*› party. **∼a** *f* average circumstances. **∼o** *a* average, medium; (*mediocre*) mediocre

medianoche *f* midnight; (*culin*) small sandwich

mediante *prep* through, by means of

mediar *vi* mediate; (*llegar a la mitad*) be halfway (**en** through)

mediatizar [10] *vt* annex

medic|ación *f* medication. **∼amento** *m* medicine. **∼ina** *f* medicine. **∼inal** *a* medicinal. **∼inar** *vt* administer medicine

medición *f* measurement

médico *a* medical. ● *m* doctor. **∼ de cabecera** GP, general practitioner

medid|a *f* measurement; (*unidad*) measure; (*disposición*) measure, step; (*prudencia*) moderation. **∼or** *m* (*LAm*) meter. **a la ∼a** made to measure. **a ∼a que** as. **en cierta ∼a** to a certain point

mediero *m* share-cropper

medieval *a* medieval. **∼ista** *m & f* medievalist

medio *a* half (a); (*mediano*) average. **∼ litro** half a litre. ● *m* middle; (*manera*) means; (*en deportes*) half(-back). **en ∼** in the middle (de of). **por ∼ de** through

mediocr|e *a* (*mediano*) average; (*de escaso mérito*) mediocre. **∼idad** *f* mediocrity

mediodía *m* midday, noon; (*sur*) south

medioevo *m* Middle Ages

Medio Oriente *m* Middle East

medir [5] *vt* medir; weigh up ‹*palabras etc*›. ● *vi* measure, be. **∼se** *vpr* (*moderarse*) be moderate

medita|bundo *a* thoughtful. **∼ción** *f* meditation. **∼r** *vt* think about. ● *vi* meditate

Mediterráneo *m* Mediterranean

mediterráneo *a* Mediterranean

médium *m & f* medium

medrar *vi* thrive

medroso *a* (*con estar*) frightened; (*con ser*) fearful

médula *f* marrow

medusa *f* jellyfish

mefítico *a* noxious

mega... *pref* mega...

megáfono *m* megaphone

megal|ítico *a* megalithic. **∼ito** *m* megalith

megal|omanía *f* megalomania. **∼ómano** *m* megalomaniac

mejicano *a & m* Mexican

Méjico *m* Mexico

mejido *a* ‹*huevo*› beaten

mejilla *f* cheek

mejillón *m* mussel

mejor *a & adv* (*comparativo*) better; (*superlativo*) best. **∼a** *f* improvement. **∼able** *a* improvable. **∼amiento** *m* improvement. **∼ dicho** rather. **a lo ∼** perhaps. **tanto ∼** so much the better

mejorana *f* marjoram

mejorar *vt* improve, better. ● *vi* get better

mejunje *m* mixture

melanc|olía *f* melancholy. **∼ólico** *a* melancholic

melaza *f* molasses, treacle (*Amer*)

melen|a *f* long hair; (*de león*) mane. **∼udo** *a* long-haired

melifluo *a* mellifluous

melillense *a* of/from Melilla. ● *m* person from Melilla

melindr|e *m* (*mazapán*) sugared marzipan cake; (*masa frita con miel*) honey fritter. **∼oso** *a* affected

melocot|ón *m* peach. **∼onero** *m* peach tree

mel|odía *f* melody. **∼ódico** *a* melodic. **∼odioso** *a* melodious

melodram|a *m* melodrama. **∼áticamente** *adv* melodramatically. **∼ático** *a* melodramatic

melómano *m* music lover

mel|ón *m* melon; (*bobo*) fool. **∼onada** *f* something stupid

meloncillo *m* (*animal*) mongoose

melos|idad *f* sweetness. **∼o** *a* sweet

mella f notch. ~**do** a jagged. ~**r** vt notch

mellizo a & m twin

membran|a f membrane. ~**oso** a membranous

membrete m letterhead

membrill|ero m quince tree. ~**o** m quince

membrudo a burly

memez f something silly

memo a stupid. ● m idiot

memorable a memorable

memorando m, **memorándum** m notebook; (nota) memorandum

memoria f memory; (informe) report; (tesis) thesis. ~**s** fpl (recuerdos personales) memoirs. **de** ~ from memory

memorial m memorial. ~**ista** m amanuensis

memor|ión m good memory. ~**ista** a having a good memory. ~**ístico** a memory

mena f fore

menaje m furnishings

menci|ón f mention. ~**onado** a aforementioned. ~**onar** vt mention

menda|cidad f mendacity. ~**z** a lying

mendi|cante a & m mendicant. ~**cidad** f begging. ~**gar** [12] vt beg (for). ● vi beg. ~**go** m beggar

mendrugo m (pan) hard crust; (zoquete) blockhead

mene|ar vt move, shake. ~**arse** vpr move, shake. ~**o** m movement, shake

menester m need. ~**oso** a needy. **ser** ~ be necessary

menestra f stew

menestral m artesan

mengano m so-and-so

mengua f decrease; (falta) lack; (descrédito) discredit. ~**do** a miserable; (falto de carácter) spineless. ~**nte** a decreasing; (luna) waning; (marea) ebb. ● f (del mar) ebb tide; (de un río) low water. ~**r** [15] vt/i decrease, diminish

meningitis f meningitis

menisco m meniscus

menjurje m mixture

menopausia f menopause

menor a (más pequeño, comparativo) smaller; (más pequeño, superlativo) smallest; (más joven, comparativo) younger; (más joven) youngest; (mus) minor. ● m & f

(menor de edad) minor. **al por** ~ retail

Menorca f Minorca

menorquín a & m Minorcan

menos a (comparativo) less; (comparativo, con plural) fewer; (superlativo) least; (superlativo, con plural) fewest. ● adv (comparativo) less; (superlativo) least. ● prep except. ~**cabar** vt lessen; (fig, estropear) damage. ~**cabo** m lessening. ~**preciable** a contemptible. ~**preciar** vt despise. ~**precio** m contempt. **a** ~ **que** unless. **al** ~ at least. **ni mucho** ~ far from it. **por lo** ~ at least

mensaje m message. ~**ro** m messenger

menso a (Mex) stupid

menstru|ación f menstruation. ~**al** a menstrual. ~**ar** [21] vi menstruate. ~**o** m menstruation

mensual a monthly. ~**idad** f monthly pay

ménsula f bracket

mensurable a measurable

menta f mint

mental a mental. ~**idad** f mentality. ~**mente** adv mentally

mentar [1] vt mention, name

mente f mind

mentecato a stupid. ● m idiot

mentir [4] vi lie. ~**a** f lie. ~**oso** a lying. ● m liar. **de** ~**ijillas** for a joke

mentís m invar denial

mentol m menthol

mentor m mentor

menú m menu

menudear vi happen frequently

menudencia f trifle

menudeo m retail trade

menudillos mpl giblets

menudo a tiny; (lluvia) fine; (insignificante) insignificant. ~**s** mpl giblets. **a** ~ often

meñique a (dedo) little. ● m little finger

meollo m brain; (médula) marrow; (parte blanda) soft part; (fig, inteligencia) brains

meramente adv merely

mercachifle m hawker; (fig) profiteer

mercader m (LAm) merchant

mercado m market. **M**~ **Común** Common Market. ~ **negro** black market

mercan|cía f article. ~**cías** fpl goods, merchandise. ~**te** a & m merchant. ~til *a* mercantile, commercial. ~tilismo *m* mercantilism

mercar [7] *vt* buy

merced *f* favour. su/vuestra ~ your honour

mercenario *a* & *m* mercenary

mercer|ía *f* haberdashery, notions (*Amer*). ~o *m* haberdasher

mercurial *a* mercurial

Mercurio *m* Mercury

mercurio *m* mercury

merec|edor *a* deserving. ~er [11] *vt* deserve. ● *vi* be deserving. ~idamente *adv* deservedly. ~ido *a* well deserved. ~imiento *m* (*mérito*) merit

merend|ar [1] vt have as an afternoon snack. ● *vi* have an afternoon snack. ~ero *m* snack bar; (*lugar*) picnic area

merengue *m* meringue

meretriz *f* prostitute

mergo *m* cormorant

meridian|a *f* (*diván*) couch. ~o *a* midday; (*fig*) dazzling. ● *m* meridian

meridional *a* southern. ● *m* southerner

merienda *f* afternoon snack

merino *a* merino

mérito *m* merit; (*valor*) worth

meritorio *a* meritorious. ● *m* unpaid trainee

merlo *m* black wrasse

merluza *f* hake

merma *f* decrease. ~r *vt/i* decrease, reduce

mermelada *f* jam

mero *a* mere; (*Mex, verdadero*) real. ● *adv* (*Mex, precisamente*) exactly; (*Mex, verdaderamente*) really. ● *m* grouper

merode|ador *a* marauding. ● *m* marauder. ~ar *vi* maraud. ~o *m* marauding

merovingio *a* & *m* Merovingian

mes *m* month; (*mensualidad*) monthly pay

mesa *f* table; (*para escribir o estudiar*) desk. poner la ~ lay the table

mesana *f* (*palo*) mizen-mast

mesarse *vpr* tear at one's hair

mesenterio *m* mesentery

meseta *f* plateau; (*descansillo*) landing

mesiánico *a* Messianic

Mesías *m* Messiah

mesilla *f* small table. ~ de noche bedside table

mesón *m* inn

mesoner|a *f* landlady. ~o *m* landlord

mestiz|aje *m* crossbreeding. ~o *a* ⟨*persona*⟩ half-caste; ⟨*animal*⟩ cross-bred. ● *m* (*persona*) half-caste; (*animal*) cross-breed

mesura *f* moderation. ~do *a* moderate

meta *f* goal; (*de una carrera*) finish

metabolismo *m* metabolism

metacarpiano *m* metacarpal

metafísic|a *f* metaphysics. ~o *a* metaphysical

met|áfora *f* metaphor. ~afórico *a* metaphorical

met|al *m* metal; (*instrumentos de latón*) brass; (*de la voz*) timbre. ~álico *a* ⟨*objeto*⟩ metal; ⟨*sonido*⟩ metallic. ~alizarse [10] *vpr* (*fig*) become mercenary

metal|urgia *f* metallurgy. ~úrgico *a* metallurgical

metam|órfico *a* metamorphic. ~orfosear *vt* transform. ~orfosis *f* metamorphosis

metano *m* methane

metatarsiano *m* metatarsal

metátesis *f invar* metathesis

metedura *f*. ~ de pata blunder

mete|órico *a* meteoric. ~orito *m* meteorite. ~oro *m* meteor. ~orología *f* meteorology. ~orológico meteorological. ~orólogo *m* meteorologist

meter *vt* put, place; (*ingresar*) deposit; score ⟨*un gol*⟩; (*enredar*) involve; (*causar*) make. ~se *vpr* get; (*entrometerse*) meddle. ~se con uno pick a quarrel with s.o.

meticulos|idad *f* meticulousness. ~o *a* meticulous

metido *m* reprimand. ● *a*. ~ en años getting on. estar muy ~ con uno be well in with s.o.

metilo *m* methyl

metódico *a* methodical

metodis|mo *m* Methodism. ~ta *a* & *m* & *f* Methodist

método *m* method

metodología *f* methodology

metomentodo *m* busybody

metraje *m* length. de largo ~ ⟨*película*⟩ feature

metrall|a *f* shrapnel. ~eta *f* submachine gun

métric|a *f* metrics. ~o *a* metric; ⟨*verso*⟩ metrical

metro _m_ metre; _(tren)_ underground, subway _(Amer)._ ~ **cuadrado** cubic metre

metrónomo _m_ metronome

metr|ópoli _f_ metropolis. ~**opolitano** _a_ metropolitan. ● _m_ metropolitan; _(tren)_ underground, subway _(Amer)_

mexicano _a_ & _m (LAm)_ Mexican

México _m (LAm)_ Mexico. ~ **D. F.** Mexico City

mezcal _m (Mex)_ (type of) brandy

mezc|la _f (acción)_ mixing; _(substancia)_ mixture; _(argamasa)_ mortar. ~**lador** _m_ mixer. ~**lar** _vt_ mix; shuffle ⟨los naipes⟩. ~**larse** _vpr_ mix; _(intervenir)_ interfere. ~**olanza** _f_ mixture

mezquin|dad _f_ meanness. ~**o** _a_ mean; _(escaso)_ meagre. ● _m_ mean person

mezquita _f_ mosque

mi _a_ my. ● _m (mus)_ E; _(solfa)_ mi

mí _pron_ me

miaja _f_ crumb

miasma _m_ miasma

miau _m_ miaow

mica _f (silicato)_ mica; _(Mex, embriaguez)_ drunkenness

mico _m_ (long-tailed) monkey

micro... _pref_ micro...

microbio _m_ microbe

micro: ~**biología** _f_ microbiology. ~**cosmo** _m_ microcosm. ~**film(e)** _m_ microfilm

micrófono _m_ microphone

micrómetro _m_ micrometer

microonda _f_ microwave. **horno** _m_ **de** ~**s** microwave oven

microordenador _m_ microcomputer

microsc|ópico _a_ microscopic. ~**opio** _m_ microscope

micro: ~**surco** _m_ long-playing record. ~**taxi** _m_ minicab

miedo _m_ fear. ~**so** _a_ fearful. **dar** ~ frighten. **morirse de** ~ be scared to death. **tener** ~ be frightened

miel _f_ honey

mielga _f_ lucerne, alfalfa _(Amer)_

miembro _m_ limb; _(persona)_ member

mientras _conj_ while. ● _adv_ meanwhile. ~ **que** whereas. ~ **tanto** in the meantime

miércoles _m_ Wednesday. ~ **de ceniza** Ash Wednesday

mierda _f (vulgar)_ shit

mies _f_ corn, grain _(Amer)_

miga _f_ crumb; _(fig, meollo)_ essence. ~**jas** _fpl_ crumbs. ~**r** [12] _vt_ crumble

migra|ción _f_ migration. ~**torio** _a_ migratory

mijo _m_ millet

mil _a_ & _m_ a/one thousand. ~**es de** thousands of. ~ **novecientos noventa y dos** nineteen ninety-two. ~ **pesetas** a thousand pesetas

milagro _m_ miracle. ~**so** _a_ miraculous

milano _m_ kite

mildeu _m_, **mildiu** _m_ mildew

milen|ario _a_ millenial. ~**io** _m_ millennium

milenrama _f_ milfoil

milésimo _a_ & _m_ thousandth

mili _f (fam)_ military service

milicia _f_ soldiering; _(gente armada)_ militia

mili|gramo _m_ milligram. ~**litro** _m_ millilitre

milímetro _m_ millimetre

militante _a_ militant

militar _a_ military. ● _m_ soldier. ~**ismo** _m_ militarism. ~**ista** _a_ militaristic. ● _m_ & _f_ militarist. ~**izar** [10] _vt_ militarize

milonga _f (Arg, canción)_ popular song; _(Arg, baile)_ popular dance

milord _m_. **vivir como un** ~ live like a lord

milpies _m invar_ woodlouse

milla _f_ mile

millar _m_ thousand. **a** ~**es** by the thousand

mill|ón _m_ million. ~**onada** _f_ fortune. ~**onario** _m_ millionaire. ~**onésimo** _a_ & _m_ millionth. **un** ~**n de libros** a million books

mimar _vt_ spoil

mimbre _m_ & _f_ wicker. ~**arse** _vpr_ sway. ~**ra** _f_ osier. ~**ral** _m_ osier-bed

mimetismo _m_ mimicry

mímic|a _f_ mime. ~**o** _a_ mimic

mimo _m_ mime; _(a un niño)_ spoiling; _(caricia)_ caress

mimosa _f_ mimosa

mina _f_ mine. ~**r** _vt_ mine; _(fig)_ undermine

minarete _m_ minaret

mineral _m_ mineral; _(mena)_ ore. ~**ogía** _f_ mineralogy. ~**ogista** _m_ & _f_ mineralogist

miner|ía _f_ mining. ~**o** _a_ mining. ● _m_ miner

mini... _pref_ mini...

miniar _vt_ paint in miniature

miniatura _f_ miniature

minifundio _m_ smallholding

minimizar [10] _vt_ minimize

mínim|o *a & m* minimum. **~um** *m* minimum

minino *m* (*fam*) cat, puss (*fam*)

minio *m* red lead

minist|erial *a* ministerial. **~erio** *m* ministry. **~ro** *m* minister

minor|ación *f* diminution. **~a** *f* minority. **~idad** *f* minority. **~ista** *m & f* retailer

minuci|a *f* trifle. **~osidad** *f* thoroughness; (*con muchos detalles*) detailed

minué *m* minuet

minúscul|a *f* small letter, lower case letter. **~o** *a* tiny

minuta *f* draft; (*menú*) menu

minut|ero *m* minute hand. **~o** *m* minute

mío *a & pron* mine. **un amigo ~** a friend of mine

miop|e *a* short-sighted. **●** *m & f* short-sighted person. **~ía** *f* short-sightedness

mira *f* sight; (*fig, intención*) aim. **~da** *f* look. **~do** *a* thought of; (*comedido*) considerate; (*cirunspecto*) circumspect. **~dor** *m* windowed balcony; (*lugar*) viewpoint. **~miento** *m* consideration. **~r** *vt* look at; (*observar*) watch; (*considerar*) consider. **~r fijamente a** stare at. **●** *vi* look; (*edificio etc*) face. **~rse** *vpr* (*personas*) look at each other. **a la ~** on the lookout. **con ~s a** with a view to. **echar una ~da a** a glance at

mirilla *f* peephole

miriñaque *m* crinoline

mirlo *m* blackbird

mirón *a* nosey. **●** *m* nosey-parker; (*espectador*) onlooker

mirra *f* myrrh

mirto *m* myrtle

misa *f* mass

misal *m* missal

mis|antropía *f* misanthropy. **~antrópico** *a* misanthropic. **~ántropo** *m* misanthropist

miscelánea *f* miscellany; (*Mex, tienda*) corner shop

miser|able *a* very poor; (*lastimoso*) miserable; (*tacaño*) mean. **~ia** *f* extreme poverty; (*suciedad*) squalor

misericordi|a *f* pity; (*piedad*) mercy. **~oso** *a* merciful

mísero *a* very poor; (*lastimoso*) miserable; (*tacaño*) mean

misil *m* missile

misi|ón *f* mission. **~onal** *a* missionary. **~onero** *m* missionary

misiva *f* missive

mism|amente *adv* just. **~ísimo** *a* very same. **~o** *a* same; (*después de pronombre personal*) myself, yourself, himself, herself, itself, ourselves, yourselves, themselves; (*enfático*) very. **●** *adv* right. **ahora ~** right now. **aquí ~** right here

mis|oginia *f* misogyny. **~ógino** *m* misogynist

misterio *m* mystery. **~so** *a* mysterious

mística *f* mysticism. **~o** *a* mystical

mistifica|ción *f* falsification; (*engaño*) trick. **~r** [7] *vt* falsify; (*engañar*) deceive

mitad *f* half; (*centro*) middle

mítico *a* mythical

mitiga|ción *f* mitigation. **~r** [12] *vt* mitigate; quench ⟨*sed*⟩; relieve ⟨*dolor etc*⟩

mitin *m* meeting

mito *m* myth. **~logía** *f* mythology. **~lógico** *a* mythological

mitón *m* mitten

mitote *m* (*LAm*) Indian dance

mitra *f* mitre. **~do** *m* prelate

mixteca *f* (*Mex*) southern Mexico

mixt|o *a* mixed. **●** *m* passenger and goods train; (*cerilla*) match. **~ura** *f* mixture

mnemotécnic|a *f* mnemonics. **~o** *a* mnemonic

moaré *m* moiré

mobiliario *m* furniture

moblaje *m* furniture

moca *m* mocha

moce|dad *f* youth. **~ro** *m* young people. **~tón** *m* strapping lad

moción *f* motion

moco *m* mucus

mochales *a invar.* **estar ~** be round the bend

mochila *f* rucksack

mocho *a* blunt. **●** *m* butt end

mochuelo *m* little owl

moda *f* fashion. **~l** *a* modal. **~les** *mpl* manners. **~lidad** *f* kind. **de ~** in fashion

model|ado *m* modelling. **~ador** *m* modeller. **~ar** *vt* model; (*fig, configurar*) form. **~o** *m* model

modera|ción *f* moderation. **~do** *a* moderate. **~r** *vt* moderate; reduce ⟨*velocidad*⟩. **~rse** *vpr* control oneself

modern|amente *adv* recently.
~idad *f* modernity. **~ismo** *m* modernism. **~ista** *m* & *f* modernist.
~izar [10] *vt* modernize. **~o** *a*
modern

modest|ia *f* modesty. **~o** *a* modest

modicidad *f* reasonableness

módico *a* moderate

modifica|ción *f* modification. **~r** [7]
vt modify

modismo *m* idiom

modist|a *f* dressmaker. **~o** *m* & *f*
designer

modo *m* manner, way; (*gram*)
mood; (*mus*) mode. **~ de ser** character. **de ~ que** so that. **de ningún
~** certainly not. **de todos ~s**
anyhow

modorr|a *f* drowsiness. **~o** *a*
drowsy

modoso *a* well-behaved

modula|ción *f* modulation. **~dor** *m*
modulator. **~r** *vt* modulate

módulo *m* module

mofa *f* mockery. **~rse** *vpr*. **~rse de**
make fun of

mofeta *f* skunk

moflet|e *m* chubby cheek. **~udo** *a*
with chubby cheeks

mogol *m* Mongol. **el Gran M~** the
Great Mogul

moh|ín *m* grimace. **~ino** *a* sulky.
hacer un ~ín pull a face

moho *m* mould; (*óxido*) rust. **~so** *a*
mouldy; ‹*metales*› rusty

moisés *m* Moses basket

mojado *a* damp, wet

mojama *f* salted tuna

mojar *vt* wet; (*empapar*) soak;
(*humedecer*) moisten, dampen. ● *vi*.
~ en get involved in

mojicón *m* blow in the face; (*bizcocho*) sponge cake

mojiganga *f* masked ball; (*en el teatro*) farce

mojigat|ería *f* hypocrisy. **~o** *a*
hypocrite

mojón *m* boundary post; (*señal*)
signpost

molar *m* molar

mold|e *m* mould; (*aguja*) knitting
needle. **~ear** *vt* mould, shape; (*fig*)
form. **~ura** *f* moulding

mole *f* mass, bulk. ● *m* (*Mex, guisado*) (Mexican) stew with chili
sauce

mol|écula *f* molecule. **~ecular** *a*
molecular

mole|dor *a* grinding. ● *m* grinder;
(*persona*) bore. **~r** [2] grind; (*hacer
polvo*) pulverize

molest|ar *vt* annoy; (*incomodar*)
bother. **¿le ~a que fume?** do you
mind if I smoke? **no ~ar** do not disturb. ● *vi* be a nuisance. **~arse** *vpr*
bother; (*ofenderse*) take offence.
~ia *f* bother, nuisance; (*inconveniente*) inconvenience; (*incomodidad*) discomfort. **~o** *a*
annoying; (*inconveniente*) inconvenient; (*ofendido*) offended

molicie *f* softness; (*excesiva comodidad*) easy life

molido *a* ground; (*fig, muy cansado*)
worn out

molienda *f* grinding

molin|ero *m* miller. **~ete** *m* toy
windmill. **~illo** *m* mill; (*juguete*) toy
windmill. **~o** *m* (water) mill. **~o de
viento** windmill

molusco *m* mollusc

mollar *a* soft

molleja *f* gizzard

mollera *f* (*de la cabeza*) crown; (*fig,
sesera*) brains

moment|áneamente *adv* momentarily; (*por el momento*) right
now. **~áneo** *a* momentary. **~o** *m*
moment; (*mecánica*) momentum

momi|a *f* mummy. **~ficación** *f*
mummification. **~ficar** [7] *vt* mummify. **~ficarse** *vpr* become
mummified

momio *a* lean. ● *m* bargain; (*trabajo*) cushy job

monaca|l *a* monastic. **~to** *m*
monasticism

monada *f* beautiful thing; (*de un
niño*) charming way; (*acción tonta*)
silliness

monaguillo *m* altar boy

mon|arca *m* & *f* monarch. **~arquía** *f*
monarchy. **~árquico** *a* monarchic(al). **~arquismo** *m* monarchism

mon|asterio *m* monastery. **~ástico**
a monastic

monda *f* pruning; (*peladura*) peel

mond|adientes *m invar* toothpick.
~adura *f* pruning; (*peladura*) peel.
~ar *vt* peel ‹*fruta etc*›; dredge ‹*un
río*›. **~o** *a* (*sin pelo*) bald; (*sin
dinero*) broke; (*sencillo*) plain

mondongo *m* innards

moned|a *f* coin; (*de un país*)
currency. **~ero** *m* minter; (*portamonedas*) purse

monetario *a* monetary

mongol *a* & *m* Mongolian

mongolismo *m* Down's syndrome

monigote *m* weak character; (*muñeca*) rag doll; (*dibujo*) doodle

monises *mpl* money, dough (*fam*)

monitor *m* monitor

monj|a *f* nun. **~e** *m* monk. **~il** *a* nun's; (*como de monja*) like a nun

mono *m* monkey; (*sobretodo*) overalls. ● *a* pretty

mono... *pref* mono...

monocromo *a* & *m* monochrome

monóculo *m* monocle

mon|ogamia *f* monogamy. **~ógamo** *a* monogamous

monografía *f* monograph

monograma *m* monogram

monol|ítico *a* monolithic. **~ito** *m* monolith

mon|ologar [12] *vi* soliloquize. **~ólogo** *m* monologue

monoman|ía *f* monomania. **~iaco** *m* monomaniac

monoplano *m* monoplane

monopoli|o *m* monopoly. **~zar** [10] *vt* monopolize

monos|ilábico *a* monosyllabic. **~ílabo** *m* monosyllable

monoteís|mo *m* monotheism. **~ta** *a* monotheistic. ● *m* & *f* monotheist

mon|otonía *f* monotony. **~ótono** *a* monotonous

monseñor *m* monsignor

monserga *f* boring talk

monstruo *m* monster. **~sidad** *f* monstrosity. **~so** *a* monstrous

monta *f* mounting; (*valor*) value

montacargas *m invar* service lift

monta|do *a* mounted. **~dor** *m* fitter. **~je** *m* assembly; (*cine*) montage; (*teatro*) staging, production

montañ|a *f* mountain. **~ero** *a* mountaineer. **~és** *a* mountain. ● *m* highlander. **~ismo** *m* mountaineering. **~oso** *a* mountainous. **~a rusa** big dipper

montaplatos *m invar* service lift

montar *vt* ride; (*subirse*) get on; (*ensamblar*) assemble; cock ⟨*arma*⟩; set up ⟨*una casa, un negocio*⟩. ● *vi* ride; (*subirse a*) mount. **~ a caballo** ride a horse

montaraz *a* ⟨*animales*⟩ wild; ⟨*personas*⟩ mountain

monte *m* (*montaña*) mountain; (*terreno inculto*) scrub; (*bosque*) forest. **~ de piedad** pawn-shop. **ingeniero** *m* **de ~s** forestry expert

montepío *m* charitable fund for dependents

monter|a *f* cloth cap. **~o** *m* hunter

montés *a* wild

Montevideo *m* Montevideo

montevideano *a* & *m* Montevidean

montículo *m* hillock

montón *m* heap, pile. **a montones** in abundance, lots of

montuoso *a* hilly

montura *f* mount; (*silla*) saddle

monument|al *a* monumental; (*fig, muy grande*) enormous. **~o** *m* monument

monzón *m* & *f* monsoon

moñ|a *f* hair ribbon. **~o** *m* bun

moque|o *m* runny nose. **~ro** *m* handkerchief

moqueta *f* fitted carpet

moquillo *m* distemper

mora *f* mulberry; (*zarzamora*) blackberry

morada *f* dwelling

morado *a* purple

morador *m* inhabitant

moral *m* mulberry tree. ● *f* morals. ● *a* moral. **~eja** *f* moral. **~idad** *f* morality. **~ista** *m* & *f* moralist. **~izador** *a* moralizing. ● *m* moralist. **~izar** [10] *vt* moralize

morapio *m* (*fam*) cheap red wine

morar *vi* live

moratoria *f* moratorium

morbidez *f* softness

mórbido *a* soft; (*malsano*) morbid

morbo *m* illness. **~sidad** *f* morbidity. **~so** *a* unhealthy

morcilla *f* black pudding

morda|cidad *f* bite. **~z** *a* biting

mordaza *f* gag

mordazmente *adv* bitingly

morde|dura *f* bite. **~r** [2] *vt* bite; (*fig, quitar porciones a*) eat into; (*denigrar*) gossip about. ● *vi* bite

mordis|car [7] *vt* nibble (at). ● *vi* nibble. **~co** *m* bite. **~quear** *vt* nibble (at)

morelense *a* (*Mex*) from Morelos. ● *m* & *f* person from Morelos

morena *f* (*geol*) moraine

moreno *a* dark; (*de pelo obscuro*) dark-haired; (*de raza negra*) negro

morera *f* mulberry tree

morería *f* Moorish lands; (*barrio*) Moorish quarter

moretón *m* bruise

morfema *m* morpheme

morfin|a *f* morphine. **~ómano** *a* morphine. ● *m* morphine addict

morfol|ogía f morphology. **~ógico** a morphological

moribundo a moribund

morillo m andiron

morir [6] (pp **muerto**) vi die; (fig, extinguirse) die away; (fig, terminar) end. **~se** vpr die. **~se de hambre** starve to death; (fig) be starving. **se muere por una flauta** she's dying to have a flute

moris|co a Moorish. ● m Moor. **~ma** f Moors

morm|ón m & f Mormon. **~ónico** a Mormon. **~onismo** m Mormonism

moro a Moorish. ● m Moor

moros|idad f dilatoriness. **~o** a dilatory

morrada f butt; (puñetazo) punch

morral m (mochila) rucksack; (del cazador) gamebag; (para caballos) nosebag

morralla f rubbish

morrillo m nape of the neck

morriña f homesickness

morro m snout

morrocotudo a (esp Mex) (fam) terrific (fam)

morsa f walrus

mortaja f shroud

mortal a & m & f mortal. **~idad** f mortality. **~mente** adv mortally

mortandad f death toll

mortecino a failing; (color) faded

mortero m mortar

mortífero a deadly

mortifica|ción f mortification. **~r** [7] vt (med) damage; (atormentar) plague; (humillar) humiliate. **~rse** vpr (Mex) feel embarrassed

mortuorio a death

morueco m ram

moruno a Moorish

mosaico a of Moses, Mosaic. ● m mosaic

mosca f fly. **~rda** f blowfly. **~rdón** m botfly; (mosca de cuerpo azul) bluebottle

moscatel a muscatel

moscón m botfly; (mosca de cuerpo azul) bluebottle

moscovita a & m & f Muscovite

Moscú m Moscow

mosque|arse vpr get cross. **~o** m resentment

mosquete m musket. **~ro** m musketeer

mosquit|ero m mosquito net. **~o** m mosquito; (mosca pequeña) fly, gnat

mostacho m moustache

mostachón m macaroon

mostaza f mustard

mosto m must

mostrador m counter

mostrar [2] vt show. **~se** vpr (show oneself to) be. **se mostró muy amable** he was very kind

mostrenco a ownerless; (animal) stray; (torpe) thick; (gordo) fat

mota f spot, speck

mote m nickname; (lema) motto

motea|do a speckled. **~r** vt speckle

motejar vt call

motel m motel

motete m motet

motín m riot; (rebelión) uprising; (de tropas) mutiny

motiv|ación f motivation. **~ar** vt motivate; (explicar) explain. **~o** m reason. **con ~o de** because of

motocicl|eta f motor cycle, motor bike (fam). **~ista** m & f motorcyclist

motón m pulley

motonave f motor boat

motor a motor. ● m motor, engine. **~a** f motor boat. **~ de arranque** starter motor

motoris|mo m motorcycling. **~ta** m & f motorist; (de una moto) motorcyclist

motorizar [10] vt motorize

motriz a f motive, driving

move|dizo a movable; (poco firme) unstable; (persona) fickle. **~r** [2] vt move; shake (la cabeza); (provocar) cause. **~rse** vpr move; (darse prisa) hurry up. **arenas** fpl **~dizas** quicksand

movi|ble a movable. **~do** a moved; (foto) blurred; (inquieto) fidgety

móvil a movable. ● m motive

movili|dad f mobility. **~zación** f mobilization. **~zar** [10] vt mobilize

movimiento m movement, motion; (agitación) bustle

moza f girl; (sirvienta) servant, maid. **~lbete** m young lad

mozárabe a Mozarabic. ● m & f Mozarab

moz|o m boy, lad. **~uela** f young girl. **~uelo** m young boy/lad

muaré m moiré

mucam|a f (Arg) servant. **~o** m (Arg) servant

mucos|idad f mucus. **~o** a mucous

muchach|a f girl; (sirvienta) servant, maid. **~o** m boy, lad; (criado) servant

muchedumbre *f* crowd

muchísimo *a* very much. ● *adv* a lot

mucho *a* much (*pl* **many**), a lot of. ● *pron* a lot; (*personas*) many (people). ● *adv* a lot, very much; (*de tiempo*) long, a long time. **ni** ~ **menos** by no means. **por** ~ **que** however much

muda *f* change of clothing; (*de animales*) moult. ~**ble** *a* changeable; ⟨*personas*⟩ fickle. ~**nza** *f* change; (*de casa*) removal. ~**r** *vt/i* change. ~**rse** (*de ropa*) change one's clothes; (*de casa*) move (house)

mudéjar *a & m & f* Mudéjar

mud|ez *f* dumbness. ~**o** *a* dumb; (*callado*) silent

mueble *a* movable. ● *m* piece of furniture

mueca *f* grimace, face. **hacer una** ~ pull a face

muela *f* (*diente*) tooth; (*diente molar*) molar; (*piedra de afilar*) grindstone; (*piedra de molino*) millstone

muelle *a* soft. ● *m* spring; (*naut*) wharf; (*malecón*) jetty

muérdago *m* mistletoe

muero *vb véase* **morir**

muert|e *f* death; (*homicidio*) murder. ~**o** *a* dead; (*matado, fam*) killed; (*colores*) pale. ● *m* dead person; (*cadáver*) body, corpse

muesca *f* nick; (*ranura*) slot

muestra *f* sample; (*prueba*) proof; (*modelo*) model; (*seal*) sign. ~**rio** *m* collection of samples

muestro *vb véase* **mostrar**

muevo *vb véase* **mover**

mugi|do *m* moo. ~**r** [14] *vi* moo; (*fig*) roar

mugr|e *m* dirt. ~**iento** *a* dirty, filthy

mugrón *m* sucker

muguete *m* lily of the valley

mujer *f* woman; (*esposa*) wife. ● *int* my dear! ~**iego** *a* ⟨*hombre*⟩ fond of the women. ~**il** *a* womanly. ~**ío** *m* (crowd of) women. ~**zuela** *f* prostitute

mújol *m* mullet

mula *f* mule; (*Mex*) unsaleable goods. ~**da** *f* drove of mules

mulato *a & m* mulatto

mulero *m* muleteer

mulet|a *f* crutch; (*fig*) support; (*toreo*) stick with a red flag

mulo *m* mule

multa *f* fine. ~**r** *vt* fine

multi... *pref* multi...

multicolor *a* multicolour(ed)

multicopista *m* copying machine

multiforme *a* multiform

multilateral *a* multilateral

multilingüe *a* multilingual

multimillonario *m* multimillionaire

múltiple *a* multiple

multiplic|ación *f* multiplication. ~**ar** [7] *vt* multiply. ~**arse** *vpr* multiply; (*fig*) go out of one's way. ~**idad** *f* multiplicity

múltiplo *a & m* multiple

multitud *f* multitude, crowd. ~**inario** *a* multitudinous

mulli|do *a* soft. ● *m* stuffing. ~**r** [22] *vt* soften

mund|ano *a* wordly; (*de la sociedad elegante*) society. ● *m* socialite. ~**ial** *a* world-wide. **la segunda guerra** ~**ial** the Second World War. ~**illo** *m* world, circles. ~**o** *m* world. ~**ología** *f* worldly wisdom. **todo el** ~**o** everybody

munición *f* ammunition; (*provisiones*) supplies

municip|al *a* municipal. ~**alidad** *f* municipality. ~**io** *m* municipality; (*ayuntamiento*) town council

mun|ificencia *f* munificence. ~**ífico** *a* munificent

muñe|ca *f* (*anat*) wrist; (*juguete*) doll; (*maniquí*) dummy. ~**co** *m* boy doll. ~**quera** *f* wristband

muñón *m* stump

mura|l *a* mural, wall. ● *m* mural. ~**lla** *f* (city) wall. ~**r** *vt* wall

murciélago *m* bat

murga *f* street band; (*lata*) bore, nuisance. **dar la** ~ bother, be a pain (*fam*)

murmullo *m* (*de personas*) whisper(ing), murmur(ing); (*del agua*) rippling; (*del viento*) sighing, rustle

murmura|ción *f* gossip. ~**dor** *a* gossiping. ● *m* gossip. ~**r** *vi* murmur; (*hablar en voz baja*) whisper; (*quejarse en voz baja*) mutter; (*criticar*) gossip

muro *m* wall

murri|a *f* depression. ~**o** *a* depressed

mus *m* card game

musa *f* muse

musaraña *f* shrew

muscula|r *a* muscular. ~**tura** *f* muscles

músculo *m* muscle

musculoso *a* muscular

muselina *f* muslin

museo *m* museum. **~ de arte** art gallery

musgaño *m* shrew

musgo *m* moss. **~so** *a* mossy

música *f* music

musical *a & m* musical

músico *a* musical. ● *m* musician

music|ología *f* musicology. **~ólogo** *m* musicologist

musitar *vt/i* mumble

muslímico *a* Muslim

muslo *m* thigh

mustela *a* weasel

musti|arse *vpr* wither, wilt. **~o** *a* ⟨*plantas*⟩ withered; ⟨*cosas*⟩ faded; ⟨*personas*⟩ gloomy; (*Mex, hipócrita*) hypocritical

musulmán *a & m* Muslim

muta|bilidad *f* mutability. **~ción** *f* change; (*en biología*) mutation

mutila|ción *f* mutilation. **~do** *a* crippled. ● *m* cripple. **~r** *vt* mutilate; cripple, maim ⟨*persona*⟩

mutis *m* (*en el teatro*) exit. **~mo** *m* silence

mutu|alidad *f* mutuality; (*asociación*) friendly society. **~amente** *adv* mutually. **~o** *a* mutual

muy *adv* very; (*demasiado*) too

N

nab|a *f* swede. **~o** *m* turnip

nácar *m* mother-of-pearl

nac|er [11] *vi* be born; ⟨*huevo*⟩ hatch; ⟨*planta*⟩ sprout. **~ido** *a* born. **~iente** *a* ⟨*sol*⟩ rising. **~imiento** *m* birth; (*de río*) source; (*belén*) crib. **dar ~imiento a** give rise to. **lugar** *m* **de ~imiento** place of birth. **recien ~ido** newborn. **volver a ~er** have a narrow escape

naci|ón *f* nation. **~onal** *a* national. **~onalidad** *f* nationality. **~onalismo** *m* nationalism. **~onalista** *a & f* nationalist. **~onalizar** [10] *vt* nationalize. **~onalizarse** *vpr* become naturalized

nada *pron* nothing, not anything. ● *adv* not at all. **¡~ de eso!** nothing of the sort! **antes de ~** first of all. **¡de ~!** (*después de 'gracias'*) don't mention it! **para ~** (not) at all. **por ~ del mundo** not for anything in the world

nada|dor *m* swimmer. **~r** *vi* swim

nadería *f* trifle

nadie *pron* no one, nobody

nado *adv*. **a ~** swimming

nafta *f* (*LAm, gasolina*) petrol, (*Brit*), gas (*Amer*)

nailon *m* nylon

naipe *m* (playing) card. **juegos** *mpl* **de ~s** card games

nalga *f* buttock. **~s** *fpl* bottom

nana *f* lullaby

Nápoles *m* Naples

naranj|a *f* orange. **~ada** *f* orangeade. **~al** *m* orange grove. **~o** *m* orange tree

narcótico *a & m* narcotic

nariz *f* nose; (*orificio de la nariz*) nostril. **¡narices!** rubbish!

narra|ción *f* narration. **~dor** *m* narrator. **~r** *vt* tell. **~tivo** *a* narrative

nasal *a* nasal

nata *f* cream

natación *f* swimming

natal *a* birth; ⟨*pueblo etc*⟩ home. **~idad** *f* birth rate

natillas *fpl* custard

natividad *f* nativity

nativo *a & m* native

nato *a* born

natural *a* natural. ● *m* native. **~eza** *f* nature; (*nacionalidad*) nationality; (*ciudadanía*) naturalization. **~eza muerta** still life. **~idad** *f* naturalness. **~ista** *m & f* naturalist. **~izar** [10] *vt* naturalize. **~izarse** *vpr* become naturalized. **~mente** *adv* naturally. ● *int* of course!

naufrag|ar [12] *vi* ⟨*barco*⟩ sink; ⟨*persona*⟩ be shipwrecked; (*fig*) fail. **~io** *m* shipwreck

náufrago *a* shipwrecked. ● *m* shipwrecked person

náusea *f* nausea. **dar ~s a uno** make s.o. feel sick. **sentir ~s** feel sick

nauseabundo *a* sickening

náutico *a* nautical

navaja *f* penknife; (*de afeitar*) razor. **~zo** *m* slash

naval *a* naval

Navarra *f* Navarre

nave *f* ship; (*de iglesia*) nave. **~ espacial** spaceship. **quemar las ~s** burn one's boats

navega|ble *a* navigable; ⟨*barco*⟩ seaworthy. **~ción** *f* navigation. **~nte** *m & f* navigator. **~r** [12] *vi* sail; ⟨*avión*⟩ fly

Navid|ad *f* Christmas. **~eño** *a* Christmas. **en ~ades** at Christmas. **¡feliz ~ad!** Happy Christmas! **por ~ad** at Christmas

navío *m* ship

nazi *a* & *m* & *f* Nazi

neblina *f* mist

nebuloso *a* misty; (*fig*) vague

necedad *f* foolishness. **decir ~es** talk nonsense. **hacer una ~** do sth stupid

necesari|amente *adv* necessarily. **~o** *a* necessary

necesi|dad *f* necessity; (*pobreza*) poverty. **~dades** *fpl* hardships. **por ~dad** (out) of necessity. **~tado** *a* in need (**de** of); (*pobre*) needy. **~tar** *vt* need. ● *vi*. **~tar de** need

necio *a* silly. ● *m* idiot

necrología *f* obituary column

néctar *m* nectar

nectarina *f* nectarine

nefasto *a* unfortunate, ominous

nega|ción *f* negation; (*desmentimiento*) denial; (*gram*) negative. **~do** *a* incompetent. **~r** [1 & 12] *vt* deny; (*rehusar*) refuse. **~rse** *vpr*. **~rse a** refuse. **~tiva** *f* negative; (*acción*) denial; (*acción de rehusar*) refusal. **~tivo** *a* & *m* negative

negligen|cia *f* negligence. **~te** *a* negligent

negoci|able *a* negotiable. **~ación** *f* negotiation. **~ante** *m* & *f* dealer. **~ar** *vt/i* negotiate. **~ar en** trade in. **~o** *m* business; (*com, trato*) deal. **~os** *mpl* business. **hombre** *m* **de ~os** businessman

negr|a *f* Negress; (*mus*) crotchet. **~o** *a* black; ⟨*persona*⟩ Negro. ● *m* (*color*) black; (*persona*) Negro. **~ura** *f* blackness. **~uzco** *a* blackish

nene *m* & *f* baby, child

nenúfar *m* water lily

neo... *pref* neo...

neocelandés *a* from New Zealand. ● *m* New Zealander

neolítico *a* Neolithic

neón *m* neon

nepotismo *m* nepotism

nervio *m* nerve; (*tendón*) sinew; (*bot*) vein. **~sidad** *f*, **~sismo** *m* nervousness; (*impaciencia*) impatience. **~so** *a* nervous; (*de temperamento*) highly-strung. **crispar los ~s a uno** (*fam*) get on s.o.'s nerves. **ponerse ~so** get excited

neto *a* clear; ⟨*verdad*⟩ simple; (*com*) net

neumático *a* pneumatic. ● *m* tyre

neumonía *f* pneumonia

neuralgia *f* neuralgia

neur|ología *f* neurolgy. **~ólogo** *m* neurologist

neur|osis *f* neurosis. **~ótico** *a* neurotic

neutr|al *a* neutral. **~alidad** *f* neutrality. **~alizar** [10] *vt* neutralize. **~o** *a* neutral; (*gram*) neuter

neutrón *m* neutron

neva|da *f* snowfall. **~r** [1] *vi* snow. **~sca** *f* blizzard

nevera *f* fridge (*Brit, fam*), refrigerator

nevisca *f* light snowfall. **~r** [7] *vi* snow lightly

nexo *m* link

ni *conj* nor, neither; (*ni siquiera*) not even. **~... ~** neither... nor. **~ que** as if. **~ siquiera** not even

Nicaragua *f* Nicaragua

nicaragüense *a* & *m* & *f* Nicaraguan

nicotina *f* nicotine

nicho *m* niche

nido *m* nest; (*de ladrones*) den; (*escondrijo*) hiding-place

niebla *f* fog; (*neblina*) mist. **hay ~** it's foggy

niet|a *f* granddaughter. **~o** *m* grandson. **~os** *mpl* grandchildren

nieve *f* snow; (*LAm, helado*) ice-cream

Nigeria *f* Nigeria. **~no** *a* Nigerian

niki *m* T-shirt

nilón *m* nylon

nimbo *m* halo

nimi|edad *f* triviality. **~o** *a* insignificant

ninfa *f* nymph

ninfea *f* water lily

ningún *véase* **ninguno**

ninguno *a* (*delante de nombre masculino en singular* **ningún**) no, not any. ● *pron* none; (*persona*) no-one, nobody; (*de dos*) neither. **de ninguna manera**, **de ningún modo** by no means. **en ninguna parte** nowhere

niñ|a *f* (little) girl. **~ada** *f* childish thing. **~era** *f* nanny. **~ería** *f* childish thing. **~ez** *f* childhood. **~o** *a* childish. ● *m* (little) boy. **de ~o** as a child. **desde ~o** from childhood

níquel *m* nickel

níspero *m* medlar

nitidez *f* clearness

nítido *a* clear; (*foto*) sharp

nitrato *m* nitrate

nítrico *a* nitric

nitrógeno *m* nitrogen

nivel *m* level; (*fig*) standard. **∼ar** *vt* level. **∼arse** *vpr* become level. **∼ de vida** standard of living

no *adv* not; (*como respuesta*) no. ¿**∼**? isn't it? **∼ más** only. **¡a que ∼!** I bet you don't! **¡cómo ∼!** of course! **Felipe ∼ tiene hijos** Felipe has no children. **¡que ∼!** certainly not!

nob|iliario *a* noble. **∼le** *a & m & f* noble. **∼leza** *f* nobility

noción *f* notion. **nociones** *fpl* rudiments

nocivo *a* harmful

nocturno *a* nocturnal; (*clase*) evening; (*tren etc*) night. ● *m* nocturne

noche *f* night. **∼ vieja** New Year's Eve. **de ∼** at night. **hacer ∼** spend the night. **media ∼** midnight. **por la ∼** at night

Nochebuena *f* Christmas Eve

nodo *m* (*Esp, película*) newsreel

nodriza *f* nanny

nódulo *m* nodule

nogal *m* walnut(-tree)

nómada *a* nomadic. ● *m & f* nomad

nombr|adía *f* fame. **∼ado** *a* famous; (*susodicho*) aforementioned. **∼amiento** *m* appointment. **∼ar** *vt* appoint; (*citar*) mention. **∼e** *m* name; (*gram*) noun; (*fama*) renown. **∼e de pila** Christian name. **en ∼e de** in the name of. **no tener ∼e** be unspeakable. **poner de ∼e** call

nomeolvides *m invar* forget-me-not

nómina *f* payroll

nomina|l *a* nominal. **∼tivo** *a & m* nominative. **∼tivo a** (*cheque etc*) made out to

non *a* odd. ● *m* odd number

nonada *f* trifle

nono *a* ninth

nordeste *a* (*región*) north-eastern; (*viento*) north-easterly. ● *m* north-east

nórdico *a* northern. ● *m* northerner

noria *f* water-wheel; (*en una feria*) ferris wheel

norma *f* rule

normal *a* normal. ● *f* teachers' training college. **∼idad** *f* normality (*Brit*), normalcy (*Amer*). **∼izar** [10] *vt* normalize. **∼mente** *adv* normally, usually

Normandía *f* Normandy

noroeste *a* (*región*) north-western; (*viento*) north-westerly. ● *m* north-west

norte *m* north; (*viento*) north wind; (*fig, meta*) aim

Norteamérica *f* (North) America

norteamericano *a & m* (North) American

norteño *a* northern. ● *m* northerner

Noruega *f* Norway

noruego *a & m* Norwegian

nos *pron* (*acusativo*) us; (*dativo*) (to) us; (*reflexivo*) (to) ourselves; (*recíproco*) (to) each other

nosotros *pron* we; (*con prep*) us

nost|algia *f* nostalgia; (*de casa, de patria*) homesickness. **∼álgico** *a* nostalgic

nota *f* note; (*de examen etc*) mark. **∼ble** *a* notable. **∼ción** *f* notation. **∼r** *vt* notice; (*apuntar*) note down. **de mala ∼** notorious. **de ∼** famous. **digno de ∼** notable. **es de ∼r** it should be noted. **hacerse ∼r** stand out

notario *m* notary

notici|a *f* (piece of) news. **∼as** *fpl* news. **∼ario** *m* news. **∼ero** *a* news. **atrasado de ∼as** behind the times. **tener ∼as de** hear from

notifica|ción *f* notification. **∼r** [7] *vt* notify

notori|edad *f* notoriety. **∼o** *a* well-known; (*evidente*) obvious

novato *m* novice

novecientos *a & m* nine hundred

noved|ad *f* newness; (*noticia*) news; (*cambio*) change; (*moda*) latest fashion. **∼oso** *a* (*LAm*) novel. **sin ∼ad** no news

novel|a *f* novel. **∼ista** *m & f* novelist

noveno *a* ninth

novent|a *a & m* ninety; (*nonagésimo*) ninetieth. **∼ón** *a & m* ninety-year-old

novia *f* girlfriend; (*prometida*) fiancée; (*en boda*) bride. **∼zgo** *m* engagement

novicio *m* novice

noviembre *m* November

novilunio *m* new moon

novill|a *f* heifer. **∼o** *m* bullock. **hacer ∼os** play truant

novio *m* boyfriend; (*prometido*) fiancé; (*en boda*) bridegroom. **los ∼s** the bride and groom

novísimo *a* very new

nub|arrón *m* large dark cloud. **∼e** *f* cloud; (*de insectos etc*) swarm. **∼lado** *a* cloudy, overcast. ● *m*

cloud. **∼lar** *vt* cloud. **∼larse** *vpr*
become cloudy. **∼loso** *a* cloudy
nuca *f* back of the neck
nuclear *a* nuclear
núcleo *m* nucleus
nudillo *m* knuckle
nudis|mo *m* nudism. **∼ta** *m & f*
nudist
nudo *m* knot; (*de asunto etc*) crux.
∼so *a* knotty. **tener un ∼ en la gar-**
ganta have a lump in one's throat
nuera *f* daughter-in-law
nuestro *a* our; (*pospuesto al sus-*
tantivo) of ours. ● *pron* ours. **∼**
coche our car. **un coche ∼** a car of
ours
nueva *f* (piece of) news. **∼s** *fpl* news.
∼mente *adv* newly; (*de nuevo*)
again
Nueva York *f* New York
Nueva Zelanda *f*, **Nueva Zelandia** *f*
(*LAm*) New Zealand
nueve *a & m* nine
nuevo *a* new. **de ∼** again
nuez *f* nut; (*del nogal*) walnut; (*anat*)
Adam's apple. **∼ de Adán** Adam's
apple. **∼ moscada** nutmeg
nul|idad *f* incompetence; (*persona,*
fam) nonentity. **∼o** *a* useless;
(*jurid*) null and void
num|eración *f* numbering. **∼eral** *a*
& m numeral. **∼erar** *vt* number.
∼érico *a* numerical
número *m* number; (*arábigo,*
romano) numeral; (*de zapatos etc*)
size. **sin ∼** countless
numeroso *a* numerous
nunca *adv* never, not ever. **∼**
(ja)más never again. **casi ∼** hardly
ever. **más que ∼** more than ever
nupcia|l *a* nuptial. **∼s** *fpl* wedding.
banquete ∼l wedding breakfast
nutria *f* otter
nutri|ción *f* nutrition. **∼do** *a* nour-
ished, fed; (*fig*) large; (*aplausos*)
loud; (*fuego*) heavy. **∼r** *vt* nourish,
feed; (*fig*) feed. **∼tivo** *a* nutritious.
valor *m* **∼tivo** nutritional value
nylon *m* nylon

Ñ

ña *f* (*LAm, fam*) Mrs
ñacanina *f* (*Arg*) poisonous snake
ñame *m* yam
ñapindá *m* (*Arg*) mimosa
ñato (*LAm*) snub-nosed

ño *m* (*LAm, fam*) Mr
ñoñ|ería *f*, **∼ez** *f* insipidity. **∼o** *a*
insipid; (*tímido*) bashful; (*quis-*
quilloso) prudish
ñu *m* gnu

O

o *conj* or. **∼ bien** rather. **∼... ∼**
either... or. **∼ sea** in other words
oasis *m invar* oasis
obcecar [7] *vt* blind
obed|ecer [11] *vt/i* obey. **∼iencia** *f*
obedience. **∼iente** *a* obedient
obelisco *m* obelisk
obertura *f* overture
obes|idad *f* obesity. **∼o** *a* obese
obispo *m* bishop
obje|ción *f* objection. **∼tar** *vt/i*
object
objetiv|idad *f* objectivity. **∼o** *a*
objective. ● *m* objective; (*foto etc*)
lens
objeto *m* object
objetor *m* objector. **∼ de conciencia**
conscientious objector
oblicuo *a* oblique; (*mirada*) side-
long
obliga|ción *f* obligation; (*com*) bond.
∼do *a* obliged; (*forzoso*) obligatory;
∼r [12] *vt* force, oblige. **∼rse** *vpr*.
∼rse a undertake to. **∼torio** *a*
obligatory
oboe *m* oboe; (*músico*) oboist
obra *f* work; (*de teatro*) play; (*cons-*
trucción) building. **∼ maestra**
masterpiece. **en ∼s** under con-
struction. **por ∼ de** thanks to. **∼r** *vt*
do; (*construir*) build
obrero *a* labour; (*clase*) working.
● *m* workman; (*en fábrica*) worker
obscen|idad *f* obscenity. **∼o** *a*
obscene
obscu... *véase* **oscu...**
obsequi|ar *vt* lavish attention on.
∼ar con give, present with. **∼o** *m*
gift, present; (*agasajo*) attention.
∼oso *a* obliging. **en ∼o de** in honour of
observa|ción *f* observation; (*obje-*
ción) objection. **∼dor** *m* observer.
∼ncia *f* observance. **∼nte** *a* observ-
ant. **∼r** *vt* observe; (*notar*) notice.
∼rse *vpr* be noted. **∼torio** *m* observatory. **hacer una ∼ción** make a
remark

obses|ión *f* obsession. **~ionar** *vt* obsess. **~ivo** *a* obsessive. **~o** *a* obsessed

obst|aculizar [10] *vt* hinder. **~áculo** *m* obstacle

obstante. no ~ *adv* however, nevertheless. ● *prep* in spite of

obstar *vi*. **~ para** prevent

obstétrico *a* obstetric

obstina|ción *f* obstinacy. **~do** *a* obstinate. **~rse** *vpr* be obstinate. **~rse en** (+ *infinitivo*) persist in (+ *gerundio*)

obstru|cción *f* obstruction. **~ir** [17] *vt* obstruct

obtener [40] *vt* get, obtain

obtura|dor *m* (*foto*) shutter. **~r** *vt* plug; fill ⟨*muela etc*⟩

obtuso *a* obtuse

obviar *vt* remove

obvio *a* obvious

oca *f* goose

ocasi|ón *f* occasion; (*oportunidad*) opportunity; (*motivo*) cause. **~onal** *a* chance. **~onar** *vt* cause. **aprovechar la ~ón** take the opportunity. **con ~ón de** on the occasion of. **de ~ón** bargain; (*usado*) second-hand. **en ~ones** sometimes. **perder una ~ón** miss a chance

ocaso *m* sunset; (*fig*) decline

occident|al *a* western. ● *m & f* westerner. **~e** *m* west

océano *m* ocean

ocio *m* idleness; (*tiempo libre*) leisure time. **~sidad** *f* idleness. **~so** *a* idle; (*inútil*) pointless

oclusión *f* occlusion

octano *m* octane. **índice** *m* **de ~** octane number, octane rating

octav|a *f* octave. **~o** *a* & *m* eighth

octogenario *a* & *m* octogenarian, eighty-year-old

oct|ogonal *a* octagonal. **~ógono** *m* octagon

octubre *m* October

oculista *m & f* oculist, optician

ocular *a* eye

ocult|ar *vt* hide. **~arse** *vpr* hide. **~o** *a* hidden; (*secreto*) secret

ocupa|ción *f* occupation. **~do** *a* occupied; ⟨*persona*⟩ busy. **~nte** *m* occupant. **~r** *vt* occupy. **~rse** *vpr* look after

ocurr|encia *f* occurrence, event; (*idea*) idea; (*que tiene gracia*) witty remark. **~irse** *vpr* occur. **¿qué ~e?** what's the matter? **se me ~e que** it occurs to me that

ochent|a *a* & *m* eighty. **~ón** *a* & *m* eighty-year-old

ocho *a* & *m* eight. **~cientos** *a* & *m* eight hundred

oda *f* ode

odi|ar *vt* hate. **~o** *m* hatred. **~oso** *a* hateful

odisea *f* odyssey

oeste *m* west; (*viento*) west wind

ofen|der *vt* offend; (*insultar*) insult. **~derse** *vpr* take offence. **~sa** *f* offence. **~siva** *f* offensive. **~sivo** *a* offensive

oferta *f* offer; (*en subasta*) bid; (*regalo*) gift. **~s de empleo** situations vacant. **en ~** on (special) offer

oficial *a* official. ● *m* skilled worker; (*funcionario*) civil servant; (*mil*) officer. **~a** *f* skilled (woman) worker

oficin|a *f* office. **~a de colocación** employment office. **~a de Estado** government office. **~a de turismo** tourist office. **~ista** *m & f* office worker. **horas** *fpl* **de ~a** business hours

oficio *m* job; (*profesión*) profession; (*puesto*) post. **~so** *a* (*no oficial*) unofficial

ofrec|er [11] *vt* offer; give ⟨*fiesta, banquete etc*⟩; (*prometer*) promise. **~erse** *vpr* ⟨*persona*⟩ volunteer; ⟨*cosa*⟩ occur. **~imiento** *m* offer

ofrenda *f* offering. **~r** *vt* offer

ofusca|ción *f* blindness; (*confusión*) confusion. **~r** [7] *vt* blind; (*confundir*) confuse. **~rse** *vpr* be dazzled

ogro *m* ogre

oí|ble *a* audible. **~da** *f* hearing. **~do** *m* hearing; (*anat*) ear. **al ~do** in one's ear. **de ~das** by hearsay. **de ~do** by ear. **duro de ~do** hard of hearing

oigo *vb véase* **oír**

oír [50] *vt* hear. **~ misa** go to mass. **¡oiga!** listen!; (*al teléfono*) hello!

ojal *m* buttonhole

ojalá *int* I hope so! ● *conj* if only

ojea|da *f* glance. **~r** *vt* eye; (*para inspeccionar*) see; (*ahuyentar*) scare away. **dar una ~da a, echar una ~da a** glance at

ojeras *fpl* (*del ojo*) bags

ojeriza *f* ill will. **tener ~ a** have a grudge against

ojete *m* eyelet

ojo *m* eye; (*de cerradura*) keyhole; (*de un puente*) span. ¡~! careful!

ola *f* wave

olé *int* bravo!

olea|da *f* wave. **~je** *m* swell

óleo *m* oil; (*cuadro*) oil painting

oleoducto *m* oil pipeline

oler [2, *las formas que empezarían por* **ue** *se escriben* **hue**] *vt* smell; (*curiosear*) pry into; (*descubrir*) discover. ● *vi* smell (**a** of)

olfat|ear *vt* smell, sniff; (*fig*) sniff out. **~o** *m* (sense of) smell; (*fig*) intuition

olimpiada *f*, **olimpíada** *f* Olympic games, Olympics

olímpico *a* (*juegos*) Olympic

oliv|a *f* olive; (*olivo*) olive tree. **~ar** *m* olive grove. **~o** *m* olive tree

olmo *m* elm (tree)

olor *m* smell. **~oso** *a* sweet-smelling

olvid|adizo *a* forgetful. **~ar** *vt* forget. **~arse** *vpr* forget; (*estar olvidado*) be forgotten. **~o** *m* oblivion; (*acción de olvidar*) forgetfulness. **se me ~ó** I forgot

olla *f* pot, casserole; (*guisado*) stew. **~ a/de presión, ~ exprés** pressure cooker. **~ podrida** Spanish stew

ombligo *m* navel

ominoso *a* awful, abominable

omi|sión *f* omission; (*olvido*) forgetfulness. **~tir** *vt* omit

ómnibus *a* omnibus

omnipotente *a* omnipotent

omóplato *m*, **omoplato** *m* shoulder blade

once *a & m* eleven

ond|a *f* wave. **~a corta** short wave. **~a larga** long wave. **~ear** *vi* wave; (*agua*) ripple. **~ulación** *f* undulation; (*del pelo*) wave. **~ular** *vi* wave. **longitud** *f* **de ~a** wavelength

oneroso *a* onerous

ónice *m* onyx

onomástico *a*. **día ~, fiesta onomástica** name-day

ONU *abrev* (*Organización de las Naciones Unidas*) UN, United Nations

onza *f* ounce

opa *a* (*LAm*) stupid

opaco *a* opaque; (*fig*) dull

ópalo *m* opal

opción *f* option

ópera *f* opera

opera|ción *f* operation; (*com*) transaction. **~dor** *m* operator; (*cirujano*) surgeon; (*TV*) cameraman. **~r** *vt* operate on; work (*milagro etc*). ● *vi* operate; (*com*) deal. **~rse** *vpr* occur; (*med*) have an operation. **~torio** *a* operative

opereta *f* operetta

opin|ar *vi* think. **~ión** *f* opinion. **la ~ión pública** public opinion

opio *m* opium

opone|nte *a* opposing. ● *m & f* opponent. **~r** *vt* oppose; offer (*resistencia*); raise (*objeción*). **~rse** *vpr* be opposed; (*dos personas*) oppose each other

oporto *m* port (wine)

oportun|idad *f* opportunity; (*cualidad de oportuno*) timeliness. **~ista** *m & f* opportunist. **~o** *a* opportune; (*apropiado*) suitable

oposi|ción *f* opposition. **~ciones** *fpl* competition, public examination. **~tor** *m* candidate

opres|ión *f* oppression; (*ahogo*) difficulty in breathing. **~ivo** *a* oppressive. **~o** *a* oppressed. **~or** *m* oppressor

oprimir *vt* squeeze; press (*botón etc*); (*ropa*) be too tight for; (*fig*) oppress

oprobio *m* disgrace

optar *vi* choose. **~ por** opt for

óptic|a *f* optics; (*tienda*) optician's (shop). **~o** *a* optic(al). ● *m* optician

optimis|mo *m* optimism. **~ta** *a* optimisitic. ● *m & f* optimist

opuesto *a* opposite; (*enemigo*) opposed

opulen|cia *f* opulence. **~to** *a* opulent

oración *f* prayer; (*discurso*) speech; (*gram*) sentence

oráculo *m* oracle

orador *m* speaker

oral *a* oral

orar *vi* pray

oratori|a *f* oratory. **~o** *a* oratorical. ● *m* (*mus*) oratorio

orbe *m* orb

órbita *f* orbit

orden *m & f* order; (*Mex, porción*) portion. **~ado** *a* tidy. **~ del día** agenda. **órdenes** *fpl* **sagradas** Holy Orders. **a sus órdenes** (*esp Mex*) can I help you? **en ~** in order. **por ~** in turn

ordenador *m* computer

ordena|nza *f* order. ● *m* (*mil*) orderly. **~r** *vt* put in order; (*mandar*) order; (*relig*) ordain

ordeñar *vt* milk

ordinal *a & m* ordinal

ordinario *a* ordinary; (*grosero*) common

orear *vt* air

orégano *m* oregano

oreja *f* ear

orfanato *m* orphanage

orfebre *m* goldsmith, silversmith

orfeón *m* choral society

orgánico *a* organic

organigrama *m* flow chart

organillo *m* barrel-organ

organismo *m* organism

organista *m* & *f* organist

organiza|ción *f* organization. ∼**dor** *m* organizer. ∼**r** [10] *vt* organize. ∼**rse** *vpr* get organized

órgano *m* organ

orgasmo *m* orgasm

orgía *f* orgy

orgullo *m* pride. ∼**so** *a* proud

orientación *f* direction

oriental *a* & *m* & *f* oriental

orientar *vt* position. ∼**se** *vpr* point; ⟨*persona*⟩ find one's bearings

oriente *m* east. **O**∼ **Medio** Middle East

orificio *m* hole

orig|en *m* origin. ∼**inal** *a* original; (*excéntrico*) odd. ∼**inalidad** *f* originality. ∼**inar** *vt* give rise to. ∼**inario** *a* original; (*nativo*) native. **dar** ∼**en a** give rise to. **ser** ∼**inario de** come from

orilla *f* (*del mar*) shore; (*de río*) bank; (*borde*) edge

orín *m* rust

orina *f* urine. ∼**l** *m* chamber-pot. ∼**r** *vi* urinate

oriundo *a*. ∼ **de** ⟨*persona*⟩ (originating) from; ⟨*animal etc*⟩ native to

orla *f* border

ornamental *a* ornamental

ornitología *f* ornithology

oro *m* gold. ∼**s** *mpl* Spanish card suit. ∼ **de ley** 9 carat gold. **hacerse de** ∼ make a fortune. **prometer el** ∼ **y el moro** promise the moon

oropel *m* tinsel

orquesta *f* orchestra. ∼**l** *a* orchestral. ∼**r** *vt* orchestrate

orquídea *f* orchid

ortiga *f* nettle

ortodox|ia *f* orthodoxy. ∼**o** *a* orthodox

ortografía *f* spelling

ortop|edia *f* orthopaedics. ∼**édico** *a* orthopaedic

oruga *f* caterpillar

orzuelo *m* sty

os *pron* (*acusativo*) you; (*dativo*) (to) you; (*reflexivo*) (to) yourselves; (*recíproco*) (to) each other

osad|ía *f* boldness. ∼**o** *a* bold

oscila|ción *f* swinging; (*de precios*) fluctuation; (*tec*) oscillation. ∼**r** *vi* swing; ⟨*precio*⟩ fluctuate; (*tec*) oscillate; (*fig, vacilar*) hesitate

oscur|ecer [11] *vi* darken; (*fig*) obscure. ∼**ecerse** *vpr* grow dark; (*nublarse*) cloud over. ∼**idad** *f* darkness; (*fig*) obscurity. ∼**o** *a* dark; (*fig*) obscure. **a** ∼**as** in the dark

óseo *a* bony

oso *m* bear. ∼ **de felpa**, ∼ **de peluche** teddy bear

ostensible *a* obvious

ostent|ación *f* ostentation. ∼**ar** *vt* show off; (*mostrar*) show. ∼**oso** *a* ostentatious

osteoartritis *f* osteoarthritis

oste|ópata *m* & *f* osteopath. ∼**opatía** *f* osteopathy

ostión *m* (*esp Mex*) oyster

ostra *f* oyster

ostracismo *m* ostracism

Otan *abrev* (*Organización del Tratado del Atlántico Norte*) NATO, North Atlantic Treaty Organization

otear *vt* observe; (*escudriñar*) scan, survey

otitis *f* inflammation of the ear

otoño *m* autumn (*Brit*), fall (*Amer*)

otorga|miento *m* granting; (*documento*) authorization. ∼**r** [12] *vt* give; (*jurid*) draw up

otorrinolaringólogo *m* ear, nose and throat specialist

otro *a* other; (*uno más*) another. ● *pron* another (one); (*en plural*) others; (*otra persona*) someone else. **el** ∼ the other. **el uno al** ∼ one another, each other

ovación *f* ovation

oval *a* oval

óvalo *m* oval

ovario *m* ovary

oveja *f* sheep; (*hembra*) ewe

overol *m* (*LAm*) overalls

ovino *a* sheep

ovillo *m* ball. **hacerse un** ∼ curl up

OVNI *abrev* (*objeto volante no identificado*) UFO, unidentified flying object

ovulación *f* ovulation

oxida|ción *f* rusting. **~r** *vi* rust.
~rse *vpr* go rusty
óxido *m* oxide
oxígeno *m* oxygen
oye *vb véase* **oír**
oyente *a* listening. ● *m & f* listener
ozono *m* ozone

P

pabellón *m* bell tent; (*edificio*) building; (*de instrumento*) bell; (*bandera*) flag
pabilo *m* wick
paceño *a* from La Paz. ● *m* person from La Paz
pacer [11] *vi* graze
pacien|cia *f* patience. **~te** *a & m & f* patient
pacificar [7] *vt* pacify; reconcile ⟨*dos personas*⟩. **~se** *vpr* calm down
pacífico *a* peaceful. **el (Océano** *m* **) P~** the Pacific (Ocean)
pacifis|mo *m* pacifism. **~ta** *a & m & f* pacifist
pact|ar *vi* agree, make a pact. **~o** *m* pact, agreement
pachucho *a* ⟨*fruta*⟩ overripe; ⟨*persona*⟩ poorly
padec|er [11] *vt/i* suffer (**de** from); (*soportar*) bear. **~imiento** *m* suffering; (*enfermedad*) ailment
padrastro *m* stepfather
padre *a* (*fam*) great. ● *m* father. **~s** *mpl* parents
padrino *m* godfather; (*en boda*) best man
padrón *m* census
paella *f* paella
paga *f* pay, wages. **~ble** *a*, **~dero** *a* payable
pagano *a & m* pagan
pagar [12] *vt* pay; pay for ⟨*compras*⟩. ● *vi* pay. **~é** *m* IOU
página *f* page
pago *m* payment
pagoda *f* pagoda
país *m* country; (*región*) region. **~ natal** native land. **el P~ Vasco** the Basque Country. **los P~es Bajos** the Low Countries
paisa|je *m* countryside. **~no** *a* of the same country. ● *m* compatriot
paja *f* straw; (*fig*) nonsense
pajarera *f* aviary
pájaro *m* bird. **~ carpintero** woodpecker

paje *m* page
Pakistán *m*. **el ~** Pakistan
pala *f* shovel; (*laya*) spade; (*en deportes*) bat; (*de tenis*) racquet
palabr|a *f* word; (*habla*) speech. **~ota** *f* swear-word. **decir ~otas** swear. **pedir la ~a** ask to speak. **soltar ~otas** swear. **tomar la ~a** (begin) to speak
palacio *m* palace; (*casa grande*) mansion
paladar *m* palate
paladino *a* clear; (*público*) public
palanca *f* lever; (*fig*) influence. **~ de cambio (de velocidades)** gear lever (*Brit*), gear shift (*Amer*)
palangana *f* wash-basin
palco *m* (*en el teatro*) box
Palestina *f* Palestine
palestino *a & m* Palestinian
palestra *f* (*fig*) arena
paleta *f* (*de pintor*) palette; (*de albañil*) trowel
paleto *m* yokel
paliativo *a & m* palliative
palide|cer [11] *vi* turn pale. **~z** *f* paleness
pálido *a* pale
palillo *m* small stick; (*de dientes*) toothpick
palique *m*. **estar de ~** be chatting
paliza *f* beating
palizada *f* fence; (*recinto*) enclosure
palma *f* (*de la mano*) palm; (*árbol*) palm (tree); (*de dátiles*) date palm. **~s** *fpl* applause. **~da** *f* slap. **~das** *fpl* applause. **dar ~(da)s** clap. **tocar las ~s** clap
palmera *f* date palm
palmo *m* span; (*fig, pequeña cantidad*) small amount. **~ a ~** inch by inch
palmote|ar *vi* clap, applaud. **~o** *m* clapping, applause
palo *m* stick; (*del teléfono etc*) pole; (*mango*) handle; (*de golf*) club; (*golpe*) blow; (*de naipes*) suit; (*mástil*) mast
paloma *f* pigeon, dove
palomitas *fpl* popcorn
palpa|ble *a* palpable. **~r** *vt* feel
palpita|ción *f* palpitation. **~nte** *a* throbbing. **~r** *vi* throb; (*latir*) beat
palta *f* (*LAm*) avocado pear
pal|údico *a* marshy; (*de paludismo*) malarial. **~udismo** *m* malaria
pamp|a *f* pampas. **~ear** *vi* (*LAm*) travel across the pampas. **~ero** *a* of the pampas

pan *m* bread; (*barra*) loaf. ~ **integral** wholemeal bread (*Brit*), whole-wheat bread (*Amer*). ~ **tostado** toast. ~ **rallado** breadcrumbs. **ganarse el** ~ earn one's living

pana *f* corduroy

panacea *f* panacea

panader|ía *f* bakery; (*tienda*) baker's (shop). ~**o** *m* baker

panal *m* honeycomb

Panamá *f* Panama

panameño *a & m* Panamanian

pancarta *f* placard

panda *m* panda; (*pandilla*) gang

pander|eta *f* (small) tambourine. ~**o** *m* tambourine

pandilla *f* gang

panecillo *m* (bread) roll

panel *m* panel

panfleto *m* pamphlet

pánico *m* panic

panor|ama *m* panorama. ~**ámico** *a* panoramic

panqué *m* (*LAm*) pancake

pantaletas *fpl* (*LAm*) underpants, knickers

pantal|ón *m* trousers. ~**ones** *mpl* trousers. ~**ón corto** shorts. ~**ón tejano**, ~**ón vaquero** jeans

pantalla *f* screen; (*de lámpara*) (lamp)shade

pantano *m* marsh; (*embalse*) reservoir. ~**so** *a* boggy

pantera *f* panther

pantomima *f* pantomime

pantorrilla *f* calf

pantufla *f* slipper

panucho *m* (*Mex*) stuffed tortilla

panz|a *f* belly. ~**ada** *f* (*hartazgo*, *fam*) bellyful; (*golpe*, *fam*) blow in the belly. ~**udo** *a* fat, pot-bellied

pañal *m* nappy (*Brit*), diaper (*Amer*)

pañ|ería *f* draper's (shop). ~**o** *m* material; (*de lana*) woollen cloth; (*trapo*) cloth. ~**o de cocina** dish-cloth; (*para secar*) tea towel. ~**o higiénico** sanitary towel. **en** ~**os menores** in one's underclothes

pañuelo *m* handkerchief; (*de cabeza*) scarf

papa *m* pope. ● *f* (*esp LAm*) potato. ~**s francesas** (*LAm*) chips

papá *m* dad(dy). ~**s** *mpl* parents. **P~ Noel** Father Christmas

papada *f* (*de persona*) double chin

papado *m* papacy

papagayo *m* parrot

papal *a* papal

papanatas *m inv* simpleton

paparrucha *f* (*tontería*) silly thing

papaya *f* pawpaw

papel *m* paper; (*en el teatro etc*) role. ~ **carbón** carbon paper. ~ **celofán** celophane paper. ~ **de calcar** carbon paper. ~ **de embalar**, ~ **de envolver** wrapping paper. ~ **de plata** silver paper. ~ **de seda** tissue paper. ~**era** *f* waste-paper basket. ~**ería** *f* stationer's (shop). ~**eta** *f* ticket; (*para votar*) paper. ~ **higiénico** toilet paper. ~ **pintado** wallpaper. ~ **secante** blotting paper. **blanco como el** ~ as white as a sheet. **desempeñar un** ~, **hacer un** ~ play a role

paperas *fpl* mumps

paquebote *m* packet (boat)

paquete *m* packet; (*paquebote*) packet (boat); (*Mex, asunto difícil*) difficult job. ~ **postal** parcel

paquistaní *a & m* Pakistani

par *a* equal; (*número*) even. ● *m* couple; (*dos cosas iguales*) pair; (*igual*) equal; (*título*) peer. **a la** ~ at the same time; (*monedas*) at par. **al** ~ **que** at the same time. **a** ~**es** two by two. **de** ~ **en** ~ wide open. **sin** ~ without equal

para *prep* for; (*hacia*) towards; (*antes del infinitivo*) (in order) to. ~ **con** to(wards). **¿~ qué?** why? ~ **que** so that

parabienes *mpl* congratulations

parábola *f* (*narración*) parable

parabrisas *m inv* windscreen (*Brit*), windshield (*Amer*)

paraca *f* (*LAm*) strong wind (from the Pacific)

paraca|ídas *m inv* parachute. ~**idista** *m & f* parachutist; (*mil*) paratrooper

parachoques *m inv* bumper (*Brit*), fender (*Amer*); (*rail*) buffer

parad|a *f* (*acción*) stopping; (*sitio*) stop; (*de taxis*) rank; (*mil*) parade. ~**ero** *m* whereabouts; (*alojamiento*) lodging. ~**o** *a* stationary; (*obrero*) unemployed; (*lento*) slow. **dejar** ~**o** confuse. **tener mal** ~**ero** come to a sticky end

paradoja *f* paradox

parador *m* state-owned hotel

parafina *f* paraffin

par|afrasear *vt* paraphrase. ~**áfrasis** *f inv* paraphrase

paraguas *m inv* umbrella

Paraguay *m* Paraguay

paraguayo *a & m* Paraguayan

paraíso *m* paradise; (*en el teatro*) gallery

paralel|a *f* parallel (line). **∼as** *fpl* parallel bars. **∼o** *a* & *m* parallel

par|álisis *f inv* paralysis. **∼alítico** *a* paralytic. **∼alizar** [10] *vt* paralyse

paramilitar *a* paramilitary

páramo *m* barren plain

parang|ón *m* comparison. **∼onar** *vt* compare

paraninfo *m* hall

paranoi|a *f* paranoia. **∼co** *a* paranoiac

parapeto *m* parapet; (*fig*) barricade

parapléjico *a* & *m* paraplegic

parar *vt/i* stop. **∼se** *vpr* stop. **sin ∼** continuously

pararrayos *m inv* lightning conductor

parásito *a* parasitic. ● *m* parasite

parasol *m* parasol

parcela *f* plot. **∼r** *vt* divide into plots

parcial *a* partial. **∼idad** *f* prejudice; (*pol*) faction. **a tiempo ∼** part-time

parco *a* sparing, frugal

parche *m* patch

pardo *a* brown

parear *vt* pair off

parec|er *m* opinion; (*aspecto*) appearance. ● *vi* [11] seem; (*asemejarse*) look like; (*aparecer*) appear. **∼erse** *vpr* resemble, look like. **∼ido** *a* similar. ● *m* similarity. **al ∼er** apparently. **a mi ∼er** in my opinion. **bien ∼ido** good-looking. **me ∼e** I think. **¿qué te parece?** what do you think? **según ∼e** apparently

pared *f* wall. **∼ón** *m* thick wall; (*de ruinas*) standing wall. **∼ por medio** next door. **llevar al ∼ón** shoot

parej|a *f* pair; (*hombre y mujer*) couple; (*la otra persona*) partner. **∼o** *a* alike, the same; (*liso*) smooth

parent|ela *f* relations. **∼sco** *m* relationship

paréntesis *m inv* parenthesis; (*signo ortográfico*) bracket. **entre ∼** (*fig*) by the way

paria *m* & *f* outcast

paridad *f* equality

pariente *m* & *f* relation, relative

parihuela *f*, **parihuelas** *fpl* stretcher

parir *vt* give birth to. ● *vi* have a baby, give birth

París *m* Paris

parisiense *a* & *m* & *f*, **parisino** *a* & *m* Parisian

parking /'parkin/ *m* car park (*Brit*), parking lot (*Amer*)

parlament|ar *vi* discuss. **∼ario** *a* parliamentary. ● *m* member of parliament (*Brit*), congressman (*Amer*). **∼o** *m* parliament

parlanchín *a* talkative. ● *m* chatterbox

parmesano *a* Parmesan

paro *m* stoppage; (*desempleo*) unemployment; (*pájaro*) tit

parodia *f* parody. **∼r** *vt* parody

parpadear *vi* blink; (*luz*) flicker; (*estrella*) twinkle

párpado *m* eyelid

parque *m* park. **∼ de atracciones** funfair. **∼ infantil** children's playground. **∼ zoológico** zoo, zoological gardens

parqué *m* parquet

parquedad *f* frugality; (*moderación*) moderation

parra *f* grapevine

párrafo *m* paragraph

parrilla *f* grill; (*LAm, auto*) radiator grill. **∼da** *f* grill. **a la ∼** grilled

párroco *m* parish priest

parroquia *f* parish; (*iglesia*) parish church. **∼no** *m* parishioner; (*cliente*) customer

parsimoni|a *f* thrift. **∼oso** *a* thrifty

parte *m* message; (*informe*) report. ● *f* part; (*porción*) share; (*lado*) side; (*jurid*) party. **dar ∼** report. **de mi ∼** for me. **de ∼ de** from. **¿de ∼ de quién?** (*al teléfono*) who's speaking? **en cualquier ∼** anywhere. **en gran ∼** largely. **en ∼** partly. **en todas ∼s** everywhere. **la mayor ∼** the majority. **ninguna ∼** nowhere. **por otra ∼** on the other hand. **por todas ∼s** everywhere

partera *f* midwife

partición *f* sharing out

participa|ción *f* participation; (*noticia*) notice; (*de lotería*) lottery ticket. **∼nte** *a* participating. ● *m* & *f* participant. **∼r** *vt* notify. ● *vi* take part

participio *m* participle

partícula *f* particle

particular *a* particular; (*clase*) private. ● *m* matter. **∼idad** *f* peculiarity. **∼izar** [10] *vt* distinguish; (*detallar*) give details about. **en ∼** in particular. **nada de ∼** nothing special

partida *f* departure; (*en registro*) entry; (*documento*) certificate; (*juego*) game; (*de gente*) group. **mala ∼** dirty trick

partidario *a & m* partisan. **~ de** keen on

parti|do *a* divided. ● *m* (*pol*) party; (*encuentro*) match, game; (*equipo*) team. **~r** *vt* divide; (*romper*) break; (*repartir*) share; crack ⟨*nueces*⟩. ● *vi* leave; (*empezar*) start. **~rse** *vpr* (*romperse*) break; (*dividirse*) split. **a ~r de** (starting) from

partitura *f* (*mus*) score

parto *m* birth; (*fig*) creation. **estar de ~** be in labour

párvulo *m*. **colegio de ~s** nursery school

pasa *f* raisin. **~ de Corinto** currant. **~ de Esmirna** sultana

pasa|ble *a* passable. **~da** *f* passing; (*de puntos*) row. **~dero** *a* passable. **~dizo** *m* passage. **~do** *a* past; ⟨*día, mes etc*⟩ last; (*anticuado*) old-fashioned; ⟨*comida*⟩ bad, off. **~do mañana** the day after tomorrow. **~dor** *m* bolt; (*de pelo*) hair-slide; (*culin*) strainer. **de ~da** in passing. **el lunes ~do** last Monday

pasaje *m* passage; (*naut*) crossing; (*viajeros*) passengers. **~ro** *a* passing. ● *m* passenger

pasamano(s) *m* handrail; (*barandilla de escalera*) banister(s)

pasamontañas *m inv* Balaclava (helmet)

pasaporte *m* passport

pasar *vt* pass; (*poner*) put; (*filtrar*) strain; spend ⟨*tiempo*⟩; (*tragar*) swallow; show ⟨*película*⟩; (*tolerar*) tolerate, overlook; give ⟨*mensaje, enfermedad*⟩. ● *vi* pass; (*suceder*) happen; (*ir*) go; (*venir*) come; ⟨*tiempo*⟩ go by. **~ de** have no interest in. **~se** *vpr* pass; (*terminarse*) be over; ⟨*flores*⟩ wither; ⟨*comida*⟩ go bad; spend ⟨*tiempo*⟩; (*excederse*) go too far. **~lo bien** have a good time. **~ por alto** leave out. **como si no hubiese pasado nada** as if nothing had happened. **lo que pasa es que** the fact is that. **pase lo que pase** whatever happens. **¡pase Vd!** come in!, go in! **¡que lo pases bien!** have a good time! **¿qué pasa?** what's the matter?, what's happening?

pasarela *f* footbridge; (*naut*) gangway

pasatiempo *m* hobby, pastime

pascua *f* (*fiesta de los hebreos*) Passover; (*de Resurrección*) Easter; (*Navidad*) Christmas. **~s** *fpl* Christmas. **hacer la ~ a uno** mess

things up for s.o. **¡y santas ~s!** and that's that!

pase *m* pass

pase|ante *m & f* passer-by. **~ar** *vt* take for a walk; (*exhibir*) show off. ● *vi* go for a walk; (*en coche etc*) go for a ride. **~arse** *vpr* go for a walk; (*en coche etc*) go for a ride. **~o** *m* walk; (*en coche etc*) ride; (*calle*) avenue. **~o marítimo** promenade. **dar un ~o** go for a walk. **¡vete a ~o!** (*fam*) go away!, get lost! (*fam*)

pasillo *m* passage

pasión *f* passion

pasiv|idad *f* passiveness. **~o** *a* passive

pasm|ar *vt* astonish. **~arse** *vpr* be astonished. **~o** *m* astonishment. **~oso** *a* astonishing

paso *a* ⟨*fruta*⟩ dried ● *m* step; (*acción de pasar*) passing; (*huella*) footprint; (*manera de andar*) walk; (*camino*) way through; (*entre montañas*) pass; (*estrecho*) strait(s). **~ a nivel** level crossing (*Brit*), grade crossing (*Amer*). **~ de cebra** Zebra crossing. **~ de peatones** pedestrian crossing. **~ elevado** flyover. **a cada ~** at every turn. **a dos ~s** very near. **al ~ que** at the same time as. **a ~ lento** slowly. **ceda el ~** give way. **de ~** in passing. **de ~ por** on the way through. **prohibido el ~** no entry

pasodoble *m* (*baile*) pasodoble

pasota *m & f* drop-out

pasta *f* paste; (*masa*) dough; (*dinero, fam*) money. **~s** *fpl* pasta; (*pasteles*) pastries. **~ de dientes**, **~ dentífrica** toothpaste

pastar *vt/i* graze

pastel *m* cake; (*empanada*) pie; (*lápiz*) pastel. **~ería** *f* cakes; (*tienda*) cake shop, confectioner's

paste(u)rizar [10] *vt* pasteurize

pastiche *m* pastiche

pastilla *f* pastille; (*de jabón*) bar; (*de chocolate*) piece

pastinaca *f* parsnip

pasto *m* pasture; (*hierba*) grass; (*Mex, césped*) lawn. **~r** *m* shepherd; (*relig*) minister. **~ral** *a* pastoral

pata *f* leg; (*pie*) paw, foot. **~s arriba** upside down. **a cuatro ~s** on all fours. **meter la ~** put one's foot in it. **tener mala ~** have bad luck

pataca *f* Jerusalem artichoke

pata|da *f* kick. **~lear** *vt* stamp; ⟨*niño pequeño*⟩ kick

pataplum *int* crash!

patata *f* potato. **~s fritas** chips (*Brit*), French fries (*Amer*). **~s fritas (a la inglesa)** (potato) crisps (*Brit*), potato chips (*Amer*)

patent|ar *vt* patent. **~e** *a* obvious. ● *f* licence. **~e de invención** patent

patern|al *a* paternal; ⟨cariño etc⟩ fatherly. **~idad** *f* paternity. **~o** *a* paternal; ⟨cariño etc⟩ fatherly

patético *a* moving

patillas *fpl* sideburns

patín *m* skate; (*juguete*) scooter

pátina *f* patina

patina|dero *m* skating rink. **~dor** *m* skater. **~je** *m* skating. **~r** *vi* skate; (*deslizarse*) slide. **~zo** *m* skid; (*fig*, *fam*) blunder

patio *m* patio. **~ de butacas** stalls (*Brit*), orchestra (*Amer*)

pato *m* duck

patol|ogía *f* pathology. **~ógico** *a* pathological

patoso *a* clumsy

patraña *f* hoax

patria *f* native land

patriarca *m* patriarch

patrimonio *m* inheritance; (*fig*) heritage

patri|ota *a* patriotic. ● *m & f* patriot. **~ótico** *a* patriotic. **~otismo** *m* patriotism

patrocin|ar *vt* sponsor. **~io** *m* sponsorship

patr|ón *m* patron; (*jefe*) boss; (*de pensión etc*) landlord; (*modelo*) pattern. **~onato** *m* patronage; (*fundación*) trust, foundation

patrulla *f* patrol; (*fig*, *cuadrilla*) group. **~r** *vt/i* patrol

paulatinamente *adv* slowly

pausa *f* pause. **~do** *a* slow

pauta *f* guideline

paviment|ar *vt* pave. **~o** *m* pavement

pavo *m* turkey. **~ real** peacock

pavor *m* terror. **~oso** *a* terrifying

payas|ada *f* buffoonery. **~o** *m* clown

paz *f* peace. **La P~** La Paz

peaje *m* toll

peatón *m* pedestrian

pebet|a *f* (*LAm*) little girl. **~e** *m* little boy

peca *f* freckle

peca|do *m* sin; (*defecto*) fault. **~dor** *m* sinner. **~minoso** *a* sinful. **~r** [7] *vi* sin

pecoso *a* freckled

pectoral *a* pectoral; (*para la tos*) cough

peculiar *a* peculiar, particular. **~idad** *f* peculiarity

pech|era *f* front. **~ero** *m* bib. **~o** *m* chest; (*de mujer*) breast; (*fig*, *corazón*) heart. **~uga** *f* breast. **dar el ~o** breast-feed ⟨a un niño⟩; (*afrontar*) confront. **tomar a ~o** take to heart

pedagogo *m* teacher

pedal *m* pedal. **~ear** *vi* pedal

pedante *a* pedantic

pedazo *m* piece, bit. **a ~s** in pieces. **hacer ~s** break to pieces. **hacerse ~s** fall to pieces

pedernal *m* flint

pedestal *m* pedestal

pedestre *a* pedestrian

pediatra *m & f* paediatrician

pedicuro *m* chiropodist

pedi|do *m* order. **~r** [5] *vt* ask (for); (*com, en restaurante*) order. ● *vi* ask. **~r prestado** borrow

pegadizo *a* sticky; (*mus*) catchy

pegajoso *a* sticky

pega|r [12] *vt* stick (on); (*coser*) sew on; give ⟨enfermedad etc⟩; (*juntar*) join; (*golpear*) hit; (*dar*) give. ● *vi* stick. **~rse** *vpr* stick; (*pelearse*) hit each other. **~r fuego a** set fire to. **~tina** *f* sticker

pein|ado *m* hairstyle. **~ar** *vt* comb. **~arse** *vpr* comb one's hair. **~e** *m* comb. **~eta** *f* ornamental comb

p.ej. *abrev* (*por ejemplo*) e.g., for example

pela|do *a* ⟨fruta⟩ peeled; ⟨cabeza⟩ bald; (*número*) exactly; ⟨terreno⟩ barren. ● *m* bare patch. **~dura** *f* (*acción*) peeling; (*mondadura*) peelings

pela|je *m* (*de animal*) fur; (*fig*, *aspecto*) appearance. **~mbre** *m* (*de animal*) fur; (*de persona*) thick hair

pelar *vt* cut the hair; (*mondar*) peel; (*quitar el pellejo*) skin

peldaño *m* step; (*de escalera de mano*) rung

pelea *f* fight; (*discusión*) quarrel. **~r** *vi* fight. **~rse** *vpr* fight

peletería *f* fur shop

peliagudo *a* difficult, tricky

pelícano *m*, **pelicano** *m* pelican

película *f* film (*esp Brit*), movie (*Amer*). **~ de dibujos (animados)** cartoon (film). **~ en colores** colour film

peligro *m* danger; (*riesgo*) risk. **~so** *a* dangerous. **poner en ~** endanger

pelirrojo *a* red-haired

pelma *m & f*, **pelmazo** *m* bore, nuisance

pel|o *m* hair; (*de barba o bigote*) whisker. **~ón** *a* bald; (*rapado*) with very short hair. **no tener ~os en la lengua** be outspoken. **tomar el ~o a uno** pull s.o.'s leg

pelota *f* ball; (*juego vasco*) pelota. **~ vasca** pelota. **en ~(s)** naked

pelotera *f* squabble

pelotilla *f*. **hacer la ~ a** ingratiate o.s. with

peluca *f* wig

peludo *a* hairy

peluquer|ía *f* (*de mujer*) hairdresser's; (*de hombre*) barber's. **~o** *m* (*de mujer*) hairdresser; (*de hombre*) barber

pelusa *f* down; (*celos, fam*) jealousy

pelvis *f* pelvis

pella *f* lump

pelleja *f*, **pellejo** *m* skin

pellizc|ar [7] *vt* pinch. **~o** *m* pinch

pena *f* sadness; (*dificultad*) difficulty. **~ de muerte** death penalty. **a duras ~s** with difficulty. **da ~ que** it's a pity that. **me da ~ que** I'm sorry that. **merecer la ~** be worthwhile. **¡qué ~!** what a pity! **valer la ~** be worthwhile

penacho *m* tuft; (*fig*) plume

penal *a* penal; (*criminal*) criminal. ● *m* prison. **~idad** *f* suffering; (*jurid*) penalty. **~izar** [10] *vt* penalize

penalty *m* penalty

penar *vt* punish. ● *vi* suffer. **~ por** long for

pend|er *vi* hang. **~iente** *a* hanging; ‹*terreno*› sloping; ‹*cuenta*› outstanding; (*fig*) ‹*asunto etc*› pending. ● *m* earring. ● *f* slope

pendón *m* banner

péndulo *a* hanging. ● *m* pendulum

pene *m* penis

penetra|nte *a* penetrating; ‹*sonido*› piercing; ‹*herida*› deep. **~r** *vt* penetrate; (*fig*) pierce; (*entender*) understand. ● *vi* penetrate; (*entrar*) go into

penicilina *f* penicillin

pen|ínsula *f* peninsula. **península Ibérica** Iberian Peninsula. **~insular** *a* peninsular

penique *m* penny

peniten|cia *f* penitence; (*castigo*) penance. **~te** *a & m & f* penitent

penoso *a* painful; (*difícil*) difficult

pensa|do *a* thought. **~dor** *m* thinker. **~miento** *m* thought. **~r** [1] *vt* think; (*considerar*) consider. ● *vi* think. **~r en** think about. **~tivo** *a* thoughtful. **bien ~do** all things considered. **cuando menos se piensa** when least expected. **menos ~do** least expected. **¡ni ~rlo!** certainly not! **pienso que sí** I think so

pensi|ón *f* pension; (*casa de huéspedes*) guest-house. **~ón completa** full board. **~onista** *m & f* pensioner; (*huésped*) lodger; (*escol*) boarder

pentágono *m* pentagon

pentagrama *m* stave

Pentecostés *m* Whitsun; (*fiesta judía*) Pentecost

penúltimo *a & m* penultimate, last but one

penumbra *f* half-light

penuria *f* shortage

peñ|a *f* rock; (*de amigos*) group; (*club*) club. **~ón** *m* rock. **el peñón de Gibraltar** The Rock (of Gibraltar)

peón *m* labourer; (*en ajedrez*) pawn; (*en damas*) piece; (*juguete*) (spinning) top

peonía *f* peony

peonza *f* (spinning) top

peor *a* (*comparativo*) worse; (*superlativo*) worst. ● *adv* worse. **~ que** ~ worse and worse. **lo ~** the worst thing. **tanto ~** so much the worse

pepin|illo *m* gherkin. **~o** *m* cucumber. **(no) me importa un ~o** I couldn't care less

pepita *f* pip

pepitoria *f* fricassee

pequeñ|ez *f* smallness; (*minucia*) trifle. **~ito** *a* very small, tiny. **~o** *a* small, little. **de ~o** as a child. **en ~o** in miniature

pequinés *m* (*perro*) Pekingese

pera *f* (*fruta*) pear. **~l** *m* pear (tree)

percance *m* setback

percatarse *vpr*. **~ de** notice

perc|epción *f* perception. **~eptible** *a* perceptible. **~eptivo** *a* perceptive. **~ibir** *vt* perceive; earn ‹*dinero*›

percusión *f* percussion

percutir *vt* tap

percha *f* hanger; (*de aves*) perch. **de ~** off the peg

perde|dor *a* losing. ● *m* loser. **~r** [1] *vt* lose; (*malgastar*) waste; miss ‹*tren etc*›. ● *vi* lose; ‹*tela*› fade. **~rse** *vpr* get lost; (*desaparecer*) disappear;

(*desperdiciarse*) be wasted; (*estropearse*) be spoilt. **echar(se) a** ∼**r** spoil

pérdida *f* loss; (*de líquido*) leak; (*de tiempo*) waste

perdido *a* lost

perdiz *f* partridge

perd|ón *m* pardon, forgiveness. ● *int* sorry! ∼**onar** *vt* excuse, forgive; (*jurid*) pardon. ¡∼**one (Vd)!** sorry! **pedir** ∼**ón** apologize

perdura|ble *a* lasting. ∼**r** *vi* last

perece|dero *a* perishable. ∼**r** [11] *vi* perish

peregrin|ación *f* pilgrimage. ∼**ar** *vi* go on a pilgrimage; (*fig, fam*) travel. ∼**o** *a* strange. ● *m* pilgrim

perejil *m* parsley

perengano *m* so-and-so

perenne *a* everlasting; (*bot*) perennial

perentorio *a* peremptory

perez|a *f* laziness. ∼**oso** *a* lazy

perfec|ción *f* perfection. ∼**cionamiento** *m* perfection; (*mejora*) improvement. ∼**cionar** *vt* perfect; (*mejorar*) improve. ∼**cionista** *m & f* perfectionist. ∼**tamente** *adv* perfectly. ● *int* of course! ∼**to** *a* perfect; (*completo*) complete. **a la** ∼**ción** perfectly, to perfection

perfidia *f* treachery

pérfido *a* treacherous

perfil *m* profile; (*contorno*) outline; ∼**es** *mpl* (*fig, rasgos*) features. ∼**ado** *a* (*bien terminado*) well-finished. ∼**ar** *vt* draw in profile; (*fig*) put the finishing touches to

perfora|ción *f* perforation. ∼**do** *m* perforation. ∼**dora** *f* punch. ∼**r** *vt* pierce, perforate; punch (*papel, tarjeta etc*)

perfum|ar *vt* perfume. ∼**arse** *vpr* put perfume on. ∼**e** *m* perfume, scent. ∼**ería** *f* perfumery

pergamino *m* parchment

pericia *f* expertise

pericón *m* popular Argentinian dance

perif|eria *f* (*de población*) outskirts. ∼**érico** *a* peripheral

perilla *f* (*barba*) goatee

perímetro *m* perimeter

periódico *a* periodic(al). ● *m* newspaper

periodis|mo *m* journalism. ∼**ta** *m & f* journalist

período *m*, **periodo** *m* period

periquito *m* budgerigar

periscopio *m* periscope

perito *a & m* expert

perju|dicar [7] *vt* harm; (*desfavorecer*) not suit. ∼**dicial** *a* harmful. ∼**icio** *m* harm. **en** ∼**icio de** to the detriment of

perjur|ar *vi* perjure o.s. ∼**io** *m* perjury

perla *f* pearl. **de** ∼**s** *adv* very well. ● *a* excellent

permane|cer [11] *vi* remain. ∼**ncia** *f* permanence; (*estancia*) stay. ∼**nte** *a* permanent. ● *f* perm

permeable *a* permeable

permi|sible *a* permissible. ∼**sivo** *a* permissive. ∼**so** *m* permission; (*documento*) licence; (*mil etc*) leave. ∼**so de conducción**, ∼**so de conducir** driving licence (*Brit*), driver's license (*Amer*). ∼**tir** *vt* allow, permit. ∼**tirse** *vpr* be allowed. **con** ∼**so** excuse me. ¿**me** ∼**te?** may I?

permutación *f* exchange; (*math*) permutation

pernicioso *a* pernicious; (*persona*) wicked

pernio *m* hinge

perno *m* bolt

pero *conj* but. ● *m* fault; (*objeción*) objection

perogrullada *f* platitude

perol *m* pan

peronista *m & f* follower of Juan Perón

perorar *vi* make a speech

perpendicular *a & f* perpendicular

perpetrar *vt* perpetrate

perpetu|ar [21] *vt* perpetuate. ∼**o** *a* perpetual

perplej|idad *f* perplexity. ∼**o** *a* perplexed

perr|a *f* (*animal*) bitch; (*moneda*) coin, penny (*Brit*), cent (*Amer*); (*rabieta*) tantrum. ∼**era** *f* kennel. ∼**ería** *f* (*mala jugada*) dirty trick; (*palabra*) harsh word. ∼**o** *a* awful ● *m* dog. ∼**o corredor** hound. ∼**o de aguas** spaniel. ∼**o del hortelano** dog in the manger. ∼**o galgo** greyhound. **de** ∼**os** awful. **estar sin una** ∼**a** be broke

persa *a & m & f* Persian

perse|cución *f* pursuit; (*tormento*) persecution. ∼**guir** [5 & 13] *vt* pursue; (*atormentar*) persecute

persevera|ncia *f* perseverance. ∼**nte** *a* persevering. ∼**r** *vi* persevere

persiana *f* (Venetian) blind

persist|encia f persistence. **~ente** a persistent. **~ir** vi persist
person|a f person. **~as** fpl people. **~aje** m (persona importante) important person; (de obra literaria) character. **~al** a personal; (para una persona) single. ● m staff. **~alidad** f personality. **~arse** vpr appear in person. **~ificar** [7] vt personify. **~ificación** f personification
perspectiva f perspective
perspica|cia f shrewdness; (de vista) keen eye-sight. **~z** a shrewd; ⟨vista⟩ keen
persua|dir vt persuade. **~sión** f persuasion. **~sivo** a persuasive
pertenecer [11] vi belong
pertinaz a persistent
pertinente a relevant
perturba|ción f disturbance. **~r** vt perturb
Perú m. **el ~** Peru
peruano a & m Peruvian
perver|sión f perversion. **~so** a perverse. ● m pervert. **~tir** [4] vt pervert
pervivir vi live on
pesa f weight. **~dez** f weight; (de cabeza etc) heaviness; (lentitud) sluggishness; (cualidad de fastidioso) tediousness; (cosa fastidiosa) bore, nuisance
pesadilla f nightmare
pesad|o a heavy; (lento) slow; (duro) hard; (aburrido) boring, tedious. **~umbre** f (pena) sorrow
pésame m sympathy, condolences
pesar vt/i weigh. ● m sorrow; (remordimiento) regret. **a ~ de (que)** in spite of. **me pesa que** I'm sorry that. **pese a (que)** in spite of
pesario m pessary
pesca f fishing; (peces) fish; (pescado) catch. **~da** f hake. **~dería** f fish shop. **~dilla** f whiting. **~do** m fish. **~dor** a fishing. ● m fisherman. **~r** [7] vt catch. ● vi fish. **ir de ~** go fishing
pescuezo m neck
pesebre m manger
pesero m (Mex) minibus taxi
peseta f peseta; (Mex) twenty-five centavos
pesimis|mo m pessimism. **~ta** a pessimistic. ● m & f pessimist
pésimo a very bad, awful
peso m weight; (moneda) peso. **~ bruto** gross weight. **~ neto** net

weight. **a ~** by weight. **de ~** influential
pesquero a fishing
pesquisa f inquiry
pestañ|a f eyelash. **~ear** vi blink. **sin ~ear** without batting an eyelid
peste f plague; (hedor) stench. **~icida** m pesticide. **~ilencia** f pestilence; (hedor) stench
pestillo m bolt
pestiño m pancake with honey
petaca f tobacco case; (LAm, maleta) suitcase
pétalo m petal
petardo m firework
petición f request; (escrito) petition. **a ~ de** at the request of
petirrojo m robin
petrificar [7] vt petrify
petr|óleo m oil. **~olero** a oil. ● m oil tanker. **~olífero** a oil-bearing
petulante a arrogant
peyorativo a pejorative
pez f fish; (substancia negruzca) pitch. **~ espada** swordfish
pezón m nipple; (bot) stalk
pezuña f hoof
piada f chirp
piadoso a compassionate; (devoto) devout
pian|ista m & f pianist. **~o** m piano. **~o de cola** grand piano
piar [20] vi chirp
pib|a f (LAm) little girl. **~e** m (LAm) little boy
picad|illo m mince; (guiso) stew. **~o** a perforated; ⟨carne⟩ minced; (ofendido) offended; ⟨mar⟩ choppy; ⟨diente⟩ bad. **~ura** f bite, sting; (de polilla) moth hole
picante a hot; ⟨palabras etc⟩ cutting
picaporte m door-handle; (aldaba) knocker
picar [7] vt prick, pierce; ⟨ave⟩ peck; ⟨insecto, pez⟩ bite; ⟨avispa⟩ sting; (comer poco) pick at; mince ⟨carne⟩. ● vi prick; ⟨ave⟩ peck; ⟨insecto, pez⟩ bite; ⟨sol⟩ scorch; ⟨sabor fuerte⟩ be hot. **~ alto** aim high
picard|ear vt corrupt. **~ía** f wickedness; (travesura) naughty thing
picaresco a roguish; ⟨literatura⟩ picaresque
pícaro a villainous; ⟨niño⟩ mischievous. ● m rogue
picatoste m toast; (frito) fried bread
picazón f itch
pico m beak; (punta) corner; (herramienta) pickaxe; (cima) peak.

∼**tear** vt peck; (comer, fam) pick at.
y ∼ (con tiempo) a little after; (con
cantidad) a little more than
picudo a pointed
pich|ona f (fig) darling; ∼**ón** m
pigeon
pido vb véase **pedir**
pie m foot; (bot, de vaso) stem. ∼ **cuadrado** square foot. **a cuatro** ∼**s** on
all fours. **al** ∼ **de la letra** literally. **a**
∼ on foot. **a** ∼(**s) juntillas** (fig)
firmly. **buscarle tres** ∼**s al gato** split
hairs. **de** ∼ standing (up). **de** ∼**s a
cabeza** from head to foot. **en** ∼
standing (up). **ponerse de/en** ∼
stand up
piedad f pity; (relig) piety
piedra f stone; (de mechero) flint;
(granizo) hailstone
piel f skin; (cuero) leather. **artículos
de** ∼ leather goods
pienso vb véase **pensar**
pierdo vb véase **perder**
pierna f leg. **estirar las** ∼**s** stretch
one's legs
pieza f piece; (parte) part; (obra
teatral) play; (moneda) coin; (habitación) room. ∼ **de recambio** spare
part
pífano m fife
pigment|ación f pigmentation. ∼**o**
m pigment
pigmeo a & m pygmy
pijama m pyjamas
pila f (montón) pile; (recipiente)
basin; (eléctrica) battery. ∼ **bautismal** font
píldora f pill
pilot|ar vt pilot. ∼**o** m pilot
pilla|je m pillage. ∼**r** vt pillage;
(alcanzar, agarrar) catch; (atropellar) run over
pillo a wicked. ● m rogue
pim|entero m (vasija) pepper-pot.
∼**entón** m paprika, cayenne
pepper. ∼**ienta** f pepper. ∼**iento** m
pepper. **grano** m **de** ∼**ienta**
peppercorn
pináculo m pinnacle
pinar m pine forest
pincel m paintbrush. ∼**ada** f brush-
stroke. **la última** ∼**ada** (fig) the finishing touch
pinch|ar vt pierce, prick; puncture
(neumático); (fig, incitar) push;
(med, fam) give an injection to.
∼**azo** m prick; (en neumático) puncture. ∼**itos** mpl kebab(s); (tapas)
savoury snacks. ∼**o** m point

ping|ajo m rag. ∼**o** m rag
ping-pong m table tennis, ping-
pong
pingüino m penguin
pino m pine (tree)
pint|a f spot; (fig, aspecto) appear-
ance. ∼**ada** f graffiti. ∼**ar** vt paint.
∼**arse** vpr put on make-up. ∼**or** m
painter. ∼**or de brocha gorda**
painter and decorator. ∼**oresco** a
picturesque. ∼**ura** f painting. **no**
∼**a nada** (fig) it doesn't count. **tener**
∼**a de** look like
pinza f (clothes-)peg (Brit), (clothes-)
pin (Amer); (de cangrejo etc) claw.
∼**s** fpl tweezers
pinzón m chaffinch
piñ|a f pine cone; (ananás) pine-
apple; (fig, grupo) group. ∼**ón** m
(semilla) pine nut
pío a pious; (caballo) piebald. ● m
chirp. **no decir (ni)** ∼ not say a word
piocha f pickaxe
piojo m louse
pionero m pioneer
pipa f pipe; (semilla) seed; (de girasol) sunflower seed
pipián m (LAm) stew
pique m resentment; (rivalidad)
rivalry. **irse a** ∼ sink
piqueta f pickaxe
piquete m picket
piragua f canoe
pirámide f pyramid
pirata m & f pirate
Pirineos mpl Pyrenees
piropo m (fam) compliment
piruet|a f pirouette. ∼**ear** vi
pirouette
pirulí m lollipop
pisa|da f footstep; (huella) footprint.
∼**papeles** m invar paperweight. ∼**r**
vt tread on; (apretar) press; (fig)
walk over. ● vi tread. **no** ∼**r el
césped** keep off the grass
piscina f swimming pool; (para
peces) fish-pond
Piscis m Pisces
piso m floor; (vivienda) flat (Brit),
apartment (Amer); (de zapato) sole
pisotear vt trample (on)
pista f track; (fig, indicio) clue. ∼ **de
aterrizaje** runway. ∼ **de baile** dance
floor. ∼ **de hielo** skating-rink. ∼ **de
tenis** tennis court
pistacho m pistachio (nut)
pisto m fried vegetables
pistol|a f pistol. ∼**era** f holster. ∼**ero**
m gunman

pistón m piston

pit|ar vt whistle at. ● vi blow a whistle; (auto) sound one's horn. ~ido m whistle

pitill|era f cigarette case. ~o m cigarette

pito m whistle; (auto) horn

pitón m python

pitorre|arse vpr. ~arse de make fun of. ~o m teasing

pitorro m spout

pivote m pivot

pizarr|a f slate; (encerrado) blackboard. ~ón m (LAm) blackboard

pizca f (fam) tiny piece; (de sal) pinch. **ni** ~ not at all

pizz|a f pizza. ~ería f pizzeria

placa f plate; (conmemorativa) plaque; (distintivo) badge

pláceme m congratulations

place|ntero a pleasant. ~r [32] vt please. **me** ~ I like. ● m pleasure

plácido a placid

plaga f plague; (fig, calamidad) disaster; (fig, abundancia) glut. ~r [12] vt fill

plagi|ar vt plagiarize. ~o m plagiarism

plan m plan; (med) course of treatment. **a todo** ~ on a grand scale. **en** ~ **de** as

plana f (llanura) plain; (página) page. **en primera** ~ on the front page

plancha f iron; (lámina) sheet. ~do m ironing. ~r vt/i iron. **a la** ~ grilled. **tirarse una** ~ put one's foot in it

planeador m glider

planear vt plan. ● vi glide

planeta m planet. ~rio a planetary. ● m planetarium

planicie f plain

planifica|ción f planning. ~r [7] vt plan

planilla f (LAm) list

plano a flat. ● m plane; (de ciudad) plan. **primer** ~ foreground; (foto) close-up

planta f (anat) sole; (bot, fábrica) plant; (plano) ground plan; (piso) floor. ~ **baja** ground floor (Brit), first floor (Amer)

planta|ción f plantation. ~do a planted. ~r vt plant; deal (golpe). ~r **en la calle** throw out. ~rse vpr stand; (fig) stand firm. **bien** ~do good-looking

plantear vt (exponer) expound; (causar) create; raise ‹cuestión›

plantilla f insole; (modelo) pattern; (personal) personnel

plaqué m plate

plasma m plasma

plástico a & m plastic

plata f silver; (fig, dinero, fam) money. ~ **de ley** sterling silver. ~ **alemana** nickel silver

plataforma f platform

plátano m plane (tree); (fruta) banana; (platanero) banana tree

platea f stalls (Brit), orchestra (Amer)

plateado a silver-plated; (color de plata) silver

pl|ática f chat, talk. ~aticar [7] vi chat, talk

platija f plaice

platillo m saucer; (mus) cymbal. ~ **volante** flying saucer

platino m platinum. ~s mpl (auto) points

plato m plate; (comida) dish; (parte de una comida) course

platónico a platonic

plausible a plausible; (loable) praiseworthy

playa f beach; (fig) seaside

plaza f square; (mercado) market; (sitio) place; (empleo) job. ~ **de toros** bullring

plazco vb véase **placer**

plazo m period; (pago) instalment; (fecha) date. **comprar a** ~s buy on hire purchase (Brit), buy on the installment plan (Amer)

plazuela f little square

pleamar f high tide

plebe f common people. ~yo a & m plebeian

plebiscito m plebiscite

plectro m plectrum

plega|ble a pliable; ‹silla etc› folding. ~r [1 & 12] vt fold. ~rse vpr bend; (fig) give way

pleito m (court) case; (fig) dispute

plenilunio m full moon

plen|itud f fullness; (fig) height. ~o a full. **en** ~o **día** in broad daylight. **en** ~o **verano** at the height of the summer

pleuresía f pleurisy

plieg|o m sheet. ~ue m fold; (en ropa) pleat

plinto m plinth

plisar vt pleat

plom|ero m (esp LAm) plumber. **~o** m lead; (elec) fuse. **de ~o** lead

pluma f feather; (para escribir) pen. **~ estilográfica** fountain pen. **~je** m plumage

plúmbeo a leaden

plum|ero m feather duster; (para plumas, lapices etc) pencil-case. **~ón** m down

plural a & m plural. **~idad** f plurality; (mayoría) majority. **en ~** in the plural

pluriempleo m having more than one job

plus m bonus

pluscuamperfecto m pluperfect

plusvalía f appreciation

plut|ocracia f plutocracy. **~ócrata** m & f plutocrat. **~ocrático** a plutocratic

plutonio m plutonium

pluvial a rain

pobla|ción f population; (ciudad) city, town; (pueblo) village. **~do** a populated. ● m village. **~r** [2] vt populate; (habitar) inhabit. **~rse** vpr get crowded

pobre a poor. ● m & f poor person; (fig) poor thing. ¡**~cito!** poor (little) thing! ¡**~ de mí!** poor (old) me! **~za** f poverty

pocilga f pigsty

poción f potion

poco a not much, little; (en plural) few; (unos) a few. ● m (a) little. ● adv little, not much; (con adjetivo) not very; (poco tiempo) not long. **a ~** little by little, gradually. **a ~ de** soon after. **dentro de ~** soon. **hace ~** not long ago. **poca cosa** nothing much. **por ~** (fam) nearly

podar vt prune

poder [33] vi be able. **no pudo venir** he couldn't come. ¿**puedo hacer algo?** can I do anything? ¿**puedo pasar?** may I come in? ● m power. **~es** mpl **públicos** authorities. **~oso** a powerful. **en el ~** in power. **no ~ con** not be able to cope with; (no aguantar) not be able to stand. **no ~ más** be exhausted; (estar harto de algo) not be able to manage any more. **no ~ menos que** not be able to help. **puede que** it is possible that. **puede ser** it is possible. ¿**se puede ...?** may I ...?

podrido a rotten

po|ema m poem. **~esía** f poetry; (poema) poem. **~eta** m poet. **~ético** a poetic

polaco a Polish. ● m Pole; (lengua) Polish

polar a polar. **estrella ~** polestar

polarizar [10] vt polarize

polca f polka

polea f pulley

pol|émica f controversy. **~émico** a polemic(al). **~emizar** [10] vi argue

polen m pollen

policía f police (force); (persona) policewoman. ● m policeman. **~co** a police; (novela etc) detective

policlínica f clinic, hospital

policromo, polícromo a polychrome

polideportivo m sports centre

poliéster m polyester

poliestireno m polystyrene

polietileno m polythene

pol|igamia f polygamy. **~ígamo** a polygamous

polígloto m & f polyglot

polígono m polygon

polilla f moth

polio(mielitis) f polio(myelitis)

pólipo m polyp

politécnic|a f polytechnic. **~o** a polytechnic

polític|a f politics. **~o** a political; (pariente) -in-law. ● m politician. **padre** m **~o** father-in-law

póliza f document; (de seguros) policy

polo m pole; (helado) ice lolly (Brit); (juego) polo. **~ helado** ice lolly (Brit). **~ norte** North Pole

Polonia f Poland

poltrona f armchair

polución f (contaminación) pollution

polv|areda f cloud of dust; (fig, escándalo) scandal. **~era** f compact. **~o** m powder; (suciedad) dust. **~os** mpl powder. **en ~o** powdered. **estar hecho ~o** be exhausted. **quitar el ~o** dust

pólvora f gunpowder; (fuegos artificiales) fireworks

polvor|iento a dusty. **~ón** m Spanish Christmas shortcake

poll|ada f brood. **~era** f (para niños) baby-walker; (LAm, falda) skirt. **~ería** f poultry shop. **~o** m chicken; (gallo joven) chick

pomada f ointment

pomelo m grapefruit

pómez a. **piedra f ~** pumice stone

pomp|a f bubble; (esplendor) pomp. **~as fúnebres** funeral. **~oso** a pompous; (espléndido) splendid

pómulo *m* cheek; (*hueso*) cheekbone

poncha|do *a* (*Mex*) punctured, flat. **∼r** *vt* (*Mex*) puncture

ponche *m* punch

poncho *m* poncho

ponderar *vt* (*alabar*) speak highly of

poner [34] *vt* put; put on ⟨*ropa, obra de teatro, TV etc*⟩; (*suponer*) suppose; lay ⟨*la mesa, un huevo*⟩; (*hacer*) make; (*contribuir*) contribute; give ⟨*nombre*⟩; show ⟨*película, interés*⟩; open ⟨*una tienda*⟩; equip ⟨*una casa*⟩. ● *vi* lay. **∼se** *vpr* put o.s.; (*volverse*) get; put on ⟨*ropa*⟩; ⟨*sol*⟩ set. **∼ con** (*al teléfono*) put through to. **∼ en claro** clarify. **∼ por escrito** put into writing. **∼ una multa** fine. **∼se a** start to. **∼se a mal con uno** fall out with s.o. **pongamos** let's suppose

pongo *vb véase* **poner**

poniente *m* west; (*viento*) west wind

pont|ificado *m* pontificate. **∼ifical** *a* pontifical. **∼ificar** [7] *vi* pontificate. **∼ífice** *m* pontiff

pontón *m* pontoon

popa *f* stern

popelín *m* poplin

popul|acho *m* masses. **∼ar** *a* popular; ⟨*lenguaje*⟩ colloquial. **∼aridad** *f* popularity. **∼arizar** [10] *vt* popularize. **∼oso** *a* populous

póquer *m* poker

poquito *m* a little bit. ● *adv* a little

por *prep* for; (*para*) (in order) to; (*a través de*) through; (*a causa de*) because of; (*como agente*) by; (*en matemática*) times; (*como función*) as; (*en lugar de*) instead of. **∼ la calle** along the street. **∼ mi** as for me, for my part. **∼ si** in case. **∼ todo el país** throughout the country. **50 kilómetros ∼ hora** 50 kilometres per hour

porcelana *f* china

porcentaje *m* percentage

porcino *a* pig. ● *m* small pig

porción *f* portion; (*de chocolate*) piece

pordiosero *m* beggar

porf|ía *f* persistence; (*disputa*) dispute. **∼iado** *a* persistent. **∼iar** [20] *vi* insist. **a ∼ía** in competition

pormenor *m* detail

pornogr|afía *f* pornography. **∼áfico** *a* pornographic

poro *m* pore. **∼so** *a* porous

poroto *m* (*LAm, judía*) bean

porque *conj* because; (*para que*) so that

porqué *m* reason

porquería *f* filth; (*basura*) rubbish; (*grosería*) dirty trick

porra *f* club; (*culin*) fritter

porrón *m* wine jug (with a long spout)

portaaviones *m invar* aircraft-carrier

portada *f* façade; (*de libro*) title page

portador *m* bearer

porta|equipaje(s) *m invar* boot (*Brit*), trunk (*Amer*); (*encima del coche*) roof-rack. **∼estandarte** *m* standard-bearer

portal *m* hall; (*puerta principal*) main entrance; (*soportal*) porch

porta|lámparas *m invar* socket. **∼ligas** *m invar* suspender belt. **∼monedas** *m invar* purse

portarse *vpr* behave

portátil *a* portable

portavoz *m* megaphone; (*fig, persona*) spokesman

portazgo *m* toll

portazo *m* bang. **dar un ∼** slam the door

porte *m* transport; (*precio*) carriage. **∼ador** *m* carrier

portento *m* marvel

porteño *a* (*de Buenos Aires*) from Buenos Aires. ● *m* person from Buenos Aires

porter|ía *f* caretaker's lodge, porter's lodge; (*en deportes*) goal. **∼o** *m* caretaker, porter; (*en deportes*) goalkeeper. **∼o automático** intercom (*fam*)

portezuela *f* small door; (*auto*) door

pórtico *m* portico

portill|a *f* gate; (*en barco*) porthole. **∼o** *m* opening

portorriqueño *a* Puerto Rican

Portugal *m* Portugal

portugués *a & m* Portuguese

porvenir *m* future

posada *f* guest house; (*mesón*) inn

posaderas *fpl* (*fam*) bottom

posar *vt* put. ● *vi* ⟨*pájaro*⟩ perch; ⟨*modelo*⟩ sit. **∼se** *vpr* settle

posdata *f* postscript

pose|edor *m* owner. **∼er** [18] *vt* have, own; (*saber*) know well. **∼ído** *a* possessed. **∼sión** *f* possession. **∼sionar** *vt*. **∼sionar de** hand over. **∼sionarse** *vpr*. **∼sionarse de** take possession of. **∼sivo** *a* possessive

posfechar *vt* postdate

posguerra *f* post-war years

posib|ilidad *f* possibility. ∼**le** *a* possible. **de ser** ∼**le** if possible. **en lo** ∼**le** as far as possible. **hacer todo lo** ∼**le para** do everything possible to. **si es** ∼**le** if possible

posición *f* position

positivo *a* positive

poso *m* sediment

posponer [34] *vt* put after; (*diferir*) postpone

posta *f*. **a** ∼ on purpose

postal *a* postal. ● *f* postcard

poste *m* pole

postergar [12] *vt* pass over; (*diferir*) postpone

posteri|dad *f* posterity. ∼**or** *a* back; (*ulterior*) later. ∼**ormente** *adv* later

postigo *m* door; (*contraventana*) shutter

postizo *a* false, artificial. ● *m* hairpiece

postra|do *a* prostrate. ∼**r** *vt* prostrate. ∼**rse** *vpr* prostrate o.s.

postre *m* dessert, sweet (*Brit*). **de** ∼ for dessert

postular *vt* postulate; collect ⟨*dinero*⟩

póstumo *a* posthumous

postura *f* position, stance

potable *a* drinkable; ⟨*agua*⟩ drinking

potaje *m* vegetable stew

potasio *m* potassium

pote *m* jar

poten|cia *f* power. ∼**cial** *a* & *m* potential. ∼**te** *a* powerful. **en** ∼**cia** potential

potingue *m* (*fam*) concoction

potr|a *f* filly. ∼**o** *m* colt; (*en gimnasia*) horse. **tener** ∼**a** be lucky

pozo *m* well; (*hoyo seco*) pit; (*de mina*) shaft

pozole *m* (*Mex*) stew

práctica *f* practice; (*destreza*) skill. **en la** ∼ in practice. **poner en** ∼ put into practice

practica|ble *a* practicable. ∼**nte** *m* & *f* nurse. ∼**r** [7] *vt* practise; play ⟨*deportes*⟩; (*ejecutar*) carry out

práctico *a* practical; (*diestro*) skilled. ● *m* practitioner

prad|era *f* meadow; (*terreno grande*) prairie. ∼**o** *m* meadow

pragmático *a* pragmatic

preámbulo *m* preamble

precario *a* precarious

precaución *f* precaution; (*cautela*) caution. **con** ∼ cautiously

precaver *vt* guard against

precede|ncia *f* precedence; (*prioridad*) priority. ∼**nte** *a* preceding. ● *m* precedent. ∼**r** *vt/i* precede

precepto *m* precept. ∼**r** *m* tutor

precia|do *a* valuable; (*estimado*) esteemed. ∼**rse** *vpr* boast

precinto *m* seal

precio *m* price. ∼ **de venta al público** retail price. **al** ∼ **de** at the cost of. **no tener** ∼ be priceless. **¿qué** ∼ **tiene?** how much is it?

precios|idad *f* value; (*cosa preciosa*) beautiful thing. ∼**o** *a* precious; (*bonito*) beautiful. **¡es una** ∼**idad!** it's beautiful!

precipicio *m* precipice

precipita|ción *f* precipitation. ∼**damente** *adv* hastily. ∼**do** *a* hasty. ∼**r** *vt* hurl; (*acelerar*) accelerate; (*apresurar*) hasten. ∼**rse** *vpr* throw o.s.; (*correr*) rush; (*actuar sin reflexionar*) act rashly

precis|amente *a* exactly. ∼**ar** *vt* require; (*determinar*) determine. ∼**ión** *f* precision; (*necesidad*) need. ∼**o** *a* precise; (*necesario*) necessary

preconcebido *a* preconceived

precoz *a* early; ⟨*niño*⟩ precocious

precursor *m* forerunner

predecesor *m* predecessor

predecir [46]; *o* [46, *pero imperativo* **predice**, *futuro y condicional regulares*] *vt* foretell

predestina|ción *f* predestination. ∼**r** *vt* predestine

prédica *f* sermon

predicamento *m* influence

predicar [7] *vt/i* preach

predicción *f* prediction; (*del tiempo*) forecast

predilec|ción *f* predilection. ∼**to** *a* favourite

predisponer [34] *vt* predispose

predomin|ante *a* predominant. ∼**ar** *vt* dominate. ● *vi* predominate. ∼**io** *m* predominance

preeminente *a* pre-eminent

prefabricado *a* prefabricated

prefacio *m* preface

prefect|o *m* prefect. ∼**ura** *f* prefecture

prefer|encia *f* preference. ∼**ente** *a* preferential. ∼**ible** *a* preferable. ∼**ido** *a* favourite. ∼**ir** [4] *vt* prefer. **de** ∼**encia** preferably

prefigurar *vt* foreshadow

prefij|ar *vt* fix beforehand; (*gram*) prefix. ∼**o** *m* prefix; (*telefónico*) dialling code

preg|ón *m* announcement. **~onar** *vt* announce

pregunta *f* question. **~r** *vt/i* ask. **~rse** *vpr* wonder. **hacer ~s** ask questions

prehistórico *a* prehistoric

preju|icio *m* prejudice. **~zgar** [12] *vt* prejudge

prelado *m* prelate

preliminar *a & m* preliminary

preludio *m* prelude

premarital *a*, **prematrimonial** *a* premarital

prematuro *a* premature

premedita|ción *f* premeditation. **~r** *vt* premeditate

premi|ar *vt* give a prize to; (*recompensar*) reward. **~o** *m* prize; (*recompensa*) reward; (*com*) premium. **~o gordo** first prize

premonición *f* premonition

premura *f* urgency; (*falta*) lack

prenatal *a* antenatal

prenda *f* pledge; (*de vestir*) article of clothing, garment; (*de cama etc*) linen. **~s** *fpl* (*cualidades*) talents; (*juego*) forfeits. **~r** *vt* captivate. **~rse** *vpr* be captivated (**de** by); (*enamorarse*) fall in love (**de** with)

prender *vt* capture; (*sujetar*) fasten. ● *vi* catch; (*arraigar*) take root. **~se** *vpr* (*encenderse*) catch fire

prensa *f* press. **~r** *vt* press

preñado *a* pregnant; (*fig*) full

preocupa|ción *f* worry. **~do** *a* worried. **~r** *vt* worry. **~rse** *vpr* worry. **~rse de** look after. **¡no te preocupes!** don't worry!

prepara|ción *f* preparation. **~do** *a* prepared. ● *m* preparation. **~r** *vt* prepare. **~rse** *vpr* get ready. **~tivo** *a* preparatory. ● *m* preparation. **~torio** *a* preparatory

preponderancia *f* preponderance

preposición *f* preposition

prepotente *a* powerful; (*fig*) presumptuous

prerrogativa *f* prerogative

presa *f* (*acción*) capture; (*cosa*) catch; (*embalse*) dam

presagi|ar *vt* presage. **~o** *m* omen; (*premonición*) premonition

présbita *a* long-sighted

presb|iteriano *a & m* Presbyterian. **~iterio** *m* presbytery. **~ítero** *m* priest

prescindir *vi*. **~ de** do without; (*deshacerse de*) dispense with

prescri|bir (*pp* **prescrito**) *vt* prescribe. **~pción** *f* prescription

presencia *f* presence; (*aspecto*) appearance. **~r** *vt* be present at; (*ver*) witness. **en ~ de** in the presence of

presenta|ble *a* presentable. **~ción** *f* presentation; (*aspecto*) appearance; (*de una persona a otra*) introduction. **~dor** *m* presenter. **~r** *vt* present; (*ofrecer*) offer; (*hacer conocer*) introduce; show (*película*). **~rse** *vpr* present o.s.; (*hacerse conocer*) introduce o.s.; (*aparecer*) turn up

presente *a* present; (*este*) this. ● *m* present. **los ~s** those present. **tener ~** remember

presenti|miento *m* presentiment; (*de algo malo*) foreboding. **~r** [4] *vt* have a presentiment of

preserva|ción *f* preservation. **~r** *vt* preserve. **~tivo** *m* condom

presiden|cia *f* presidency; (*de asamblea*) chairmanship. **~cial** *a* presidential. **~ta** *f* (woman) president. **~te** *m* president; (*de asamblea*) chairman. **~te del gobierno** leader of the government, prime minister

presidi|ario *m* convict. **~o** *m* prison

presidir *vt* preside over

presilla *f* fastener

presi|ón *f* pressure. **~onar** *vt* press; (*fig*) put pressure on. **a ~ón** under pressure. **hacer ~ón** press

preso *a* under arrest; (*fig*) stricken. ● *m* prisoner

presta|do *a* (*a uno*) lent; (*de uno*) borrowed. **~mista** *m & f* moneylender. **pedir ~do** borrow

préstamo *m* loan; (*acción de pedir prestado*) borrowing

prestar *vt* lend; give (*ayuda etc*); pay (*atención*). ● *vi* lend

prestidigita|ción *f* conjuring. **~dor** *m* magician

prestigio *m* prestige. **~so** *a* prestigious

presu|mido *a* presumptuous. **~mir** *vt* presume. ● *vi* be conceited. **~nción** *f* presumption. **~nto** *a* presumed. **~ntuoso** *a* presumptuous

presup|oner [34] *vt* presuppose. **~uesto** *m* budget

presuroso *a* quick

preten|cioso *a* pretentious. **~der** *vt* try to; (*afirmar*) claim; (*solicitar*) apply for; (*cortejar*) court. **~dido** *a* so-called. **~diente** *m* pretender; (*a*

una mujer) suitor. **∿sión** *f* pretension; *(aspiración)* aspiration
pretérito *m* preterite, past
pretexto *m* pretext. **a ∿ de** on the pretext of
prevalec|er [11] *vi* prevail. **∿iente** *a* prevalent
prevalerse [42] *vpr* take advantage
preven|ción *f* prevention; *(prejuicio)* prejudice. **∿ido** *a* ready; *(precavido)* cautious. **∿ir** [53] *vt* prepare; *(proveer)* provide; *(precaver)* prevent; *(advertir)* warn. **∿tivo** *a* preventive
prever [43] *vt* foresee; *(prepararse)* plan
previo *a* previous
previs|ible *a* predictable. **∿ión** *f* forecast; *(prudencia)* prudence. **∿ión de tiempo** weather forecast. **∿to** *a* foreseen
prima *f (pariente)* cousin; *(cantidad)* bonus
primario *a* primary
primate *m* primate; *(fig, persona)* important person
primavera *f* spring. **∿l** *a* spring
primer *a véase* **primero**
primer|a *f (auto)* first (gear); *(en tren etc)* first class. **∿o** *a (delante de nombre masculino en singular* **primer)** first; *(principal)* main; *(anterior)* former; *(mejor)* best. ● *n* (the) first. ● *adv* first. **∿a enseñanza** primary education. **a ∿os de** at the beginning of. **de ∿a** first-class
primitivo *a* primitive
primo *m* cousin; *(fam)* fool. **hacer el ∿** be taken for a ride
primogénito *a & m* first-born, eldest
primor *m* delicacy; *(cosa)* beautiful thing
primordial *a* basic
princesa *f* princess
principado *m* principality
principal *a* principal. ● *m (jefe)* head, boss *(fam)*
príncipe *m* prince
principi|ante *m & f* beginner. **∿ar** *vt/i* begin, start. **∿o** *m* beginning; *(moral, idea)* principle; *(origen)* origin. **al ∿o** at first. **a ∿o(s) de** at the beginning of. **dar ∿o a** a start. **desde el ∿o** from the outset. **en ∿o** in principle. **∿os** *mpl (nociones)* rudiments

pring|oso *a* greasy. **∿ue** *m* dripping; *(mancha)* grease mark
prior *m* prior. **∿ato** *m* priory
prioridad *f* priority
prisa *f* hurry, haste. **a ∿** quickly. **a toda ∿** *(fam)* as quickly as possible. **correr ∿** be urgent. **darse ∿** hurry (up). **de ∿** quickly. **tener ∿** be in a hurry
prisi|ón *f* prison; *(encarcelamiento)* imprisonment. **∿onero** *m* prisoner
prism|a *m* prism. **∿áticos** *mpl* binoculars
priva|ción *f* deprivation. **∿do** *a (particular)* private. **∿r** *vt* deprive **(de** of); *(prohibir)* prevent **(de** from). ● *vi* be popular. **∿tivo** *a* exclusive **(de** to)
privilegi|ado *a* privileged; *(muy bueno)* exceptional. **∿o** *m* privilege
pro *prep* for. ● *m* advantage. ● *pref* pro-. **el ∿ y el contra** the pros and cons. **en ∿ de** on behalf of. **los ∿s y los contras** the pros and cons
proa *f* bows
probab|ilidad *f* probability. **∿le** *a* probable, likely. **∿lemente** *adv* probably
proba|dor *m* fitting-room. **∿r** [2] *vt* try; try on *⟨ropa⟩*; *(demostrar)* prove. ● *vi* try. **∿rse** *vpr* try on
probeta *f* test-tube
problem|a *m* problem. **∿ático** *a* problematic
procaz *a* insolent
proced|encia *f* origin. **∿ente** *a (razonable)* reasonable. **∿ente de** (coming) from. **∿er** *m* conduct. ● *vi* proceed. **∿er contra** start legal proceedings against. **∿er de** come from. **∿imiento** *m* procedure; *(sistema)* process; *(jurid)* proceedings
procesador *m*. **∿ de textos** word processor
procesal *a*. **costas ∿es** legal costs
procesamiento *m* processing. **∿ de textos** word-processing
procesar *vt* prosecute
procesión *f* procession
proceso *m* process; *(jurid)* trial; *(transcurso)* course
proclama *f* proclamation. **∿ción** *f* proclamation. **∿r** *vt* proclaim
procrea|ción *f* procreation. **∿r** *vt* procreate
procura|dor *m* attorney, solicitor. **∿r** *vt* try; *(obtener)* get; *(dar)* give
prodigar [12] *vt* lavish. **∿se** *vpr* do one's best

prodigio *m* prodigy; (*milagro*) miracle. ~**ioso** *a* prodigious
pródigo *a* prodigal
produc|ción *f* production. ~**ir** [47] *vt* produce; (*causar*) cause. ~**irse** *vpr* (*aparecer*) appear; (*suceder*) happen. ~**tivo** *a* productive. ~**to** *m* product. ~**tor** *m* producer. ~**to derivado** by-product. ~**tos agrícolas** farm produce. ~**tos de belleza** cosmetics. ~**tos de consumo** consumer goods
proeza *f* exploit
profan|ación *f* desecration. ~**ar** *vt* desecrate. ~**o** *a* profane
profecía *f* prophecy
proferir [4] *vt* utter; hurl (*insultos etc*)
profes|ar *vt* profess; practise (*profesión*). ~**ión** *f* profession. ~**ional** *a* professional. ~**or** *m* teacher; (*en universidad etc*) lecturer. ~**orado** *m* teaching profession; (*conjunto de profesores*) staff
prof|eta *m* prophet. ~**ético** *a* prophetic. ~**etizar** [10] *vt/i* prophesize
prófugo *a* & *m* fugitive
profund|idad *f* depth. ~**o** *a* deep; (*fig*) profound
profus|ión *f* profusion. ~**o** *a* profuse. **con** ~**ión** profusely
progenie *f* progeny
programa *m* programme; (*de ordenador*) program; (*de estudios*) curriculum. ~**ción** *f* programming; (*TV etc*) programmes; (*en periódico*) TV guide. ~**r** *vt* programme; program (*ordenador*). ~**dor** *m* computer programmer
progres|ar *vi* (make) progress. ~**ión** *f* progression. ~**ista** *a* progressive. ~**ivo** *a* progressive. ~**o** *m* progress. **hacer** ~**os** make progress
prohibi|ción *f* prohibition. ~**do** *a* forbidden. ~**r** *vt* forbid. ~**tivo** *a* prohibitive
prójimo *m* fellow man
prole *f* offspring
proletari|ado *m* proletariat. ~**o** *a* & *m* proletarian
prol|iferación *f* proliferation. ~**iferar** *vi* proliferate. ~**ífico** *a* prolific
prolijo *a* long-winded, extensive
prólogo *m* prologue
prolongar [12] *vt* prolong; (*alargar*) lengthen. ~**se** *vpr* go on
promedio *m* average

prome|sa *f* promise. ~**ter** *vt/i* promise. ~**terse** *vpr* (*novios*) get engaged. ~**térselas muy felices** have high hopes. ~**tida** *f* fiancée. ~**tido** *a* promised; (*novios*) engaged. ● *m* fiancé
prominen|cia *f* prominence. ~**te** *a* prominent
promiscu|idad *f* promiscuity. ~**o** *a* promiscuous
promoción *f* promotion
promontorio *m* promontory
promo|tor *m* promoter. ~**ver** [2] *vt* promote; (*causar*) cause
promulgar [12] *vt* promulgate
pronombre *m* pronoun
pron|osticar [7] *vt* predict. ~**óstico** *m* prediction; (*del tiempo*) forecast; (*med*) prognosis
pront|itud *f* quickness. ~**o** *a* quick; (*preparado*) ready. ● *adv* quickly; (*dentro de poco*) soon; (*temprano*) early. ● *m* urge. **al** ~**o** at first. **de** ~**o** suddenly. **por lo** ~**o** for the time being; (*al menos*) anyway. **tan** ~**o como** as soon as
pronuncia|ción *f* pronunciation. ~**miento** *m* revolt. ~**r** *vt* pronounce; deliver (*discurso*). ~**rse** *vpr* be pronounced; (*declarase*) declare o.s.; (*sublevarse*) rise up
propagación *f* propagation
propaganda *f* propaganda; (*anuncios*) advertising
propagar [12] *vt/i* propagate. ~**se** *vpr* spread
propano *m* propane
propasarse *vpr* go too far
propens|ión *f* inclination. ~**o** *a* inclined
propiamente *adv* exactly
propici|ar *vt* (*provocar*) cause, bring about. ~**o** *a* favourable
propie|dad *f* property; (*posesión*) possession. ~**tario** *m* owner
propina *f* tip
propio *a* own; (*característico*) typical; (*natural*) natural; (*apropiado*) proper. **de** ~ on purpose. **el médico** ~ the doctor himself
proponer [34] *vt* propose. ~**se** *vpr* propose
proporci|ón *f* proportion. ~**onado** *a* proportioned. ~**onal** *a* proportional. ~**onar** *vt* proportion; (*facilitar*) provide
proposición *f* proposition
propósito *m* intention. **a** ~ (*adrede*) on purpose; (*de paso*) incidentally.

a ~ de with regard to. **de ~** on
purpose
propuesta f proposal
propuls|ar vt propel; (fig) promote.
~ión f propulsion. **~ión a chorro**
jet propulsion
prórroga f extension
prorrogar [12] vt extend
prorrumpir vi burst out
prosa f prose. **~ico** a prosaic
proscri|bir (pp proscrito) vt banish;
(prohibido) ban. **~to** a banned. ● m
exile; (persona) outlaw
prosecución f continuation
proseguir [5 & 13] vt/i continue
prospección f prospecting
prospecto m prospectus
prosper|ar vi prosper. **~idad** f pros-
perity; (éxito) success
próspero a prosperous. **¡P~ Año
Nuevo!** Happy New Year!
prostit|ución f prostitution. **~uta** f
prostitute
protagonista m & f protagonist
prote|cción f protection. **~ctor** a
protective. ● m protector; (patrocinador) patron. **~ger** [14] vt
protect. **~gida** f protegée. **~gido** a
protected. ● m protegé
proteína f protein
protesta f protest; (declaración)
protestation
protestante a & m & f (relig)
Protestant
protestar vt/i protest
protocolo m protocol
protuberan|cia f protuberance. **~te**
a protuberant
provecho m benefit. **¡buen ~!** enjoy
your meal! **de ~** useful. **en ~ de** to
the benefit of. **sacar ~ de** benefit
from
proveer [18] (pp proveído y provisto) vt supply, provide
provenir [53] vi come (de from)
proverbi|al a proverbial. **~o** m
proverb
providencia f providence. **~l** a
providential
provincia f province. **~l** a, **~no** a
provincial
provisi|ón f provision; (medida)
measure. **~onal** a provisional
provisto a provided (de with)
provoca|ción f provocation. **~r** [7]
vt provoke; (causar) cause. **~tivo** a
provocative
próximamente adv soon
proximidad f proximity

próximo a next; (cerca) near
proyec|ción f projection. **~tar** vt
hurl; cast ⟨luz⟩; show ⟨película⟩.
~til m missile. **~to** m plan. **~to de
ley** bill. **~tor** m projector. **en ~to**
planned
pruden|cia f prudence. **~nte** a
prudent, sensible
prueba f proof; (examen) test; (de
ropa) fitting. **a ~** on trial. **a ~ de**
proof against. **a ~ de agua** waterproof. **en ~ de** in proof of. **poner a
~** test
pruebo vb véase **probar**
psicoan|álisis f psychoanalysis. **~al-
ista** m & f psychoanalyst. **~alizar**
[10] vt psychoanalyse
psicodélico a psychedelic
psic|ología f psychology. **~ológico**
a psychological. **~ólogo** m psycho-
logist
psicópata m & f psychopath
psicosis f psychosis
psique f psyche
psiqui|atra m & f psychiatrist.
~atría f psychiatry. **~átrico** a
psychiatric
psíquico a psychic
ptas, pts abrev (pesetas) pesetas
púa f sharp point; (bot) thorn; (de
erizo) quill; (de peine) tooth; (mus)
plectrum
pubertad f puberty
publica|ción f publication. **~r** [7] vt
publish; (anunciar) announce
publici|dad f publicity; (com)
advertising. **~tario** a advertising
público a public. ● m public; (de
espectáculo etc) audience. **dar al ~**
publish
puchero m cooking pot; (guisado)
stew. **hacer ~s** (fig, fam) pout
pude vb véase **poder**
púdico a modest
pudiente a rich
pudín m pudding
pudor m modesty. **~oso** a modest
pudrir (pp podrido) vt rot; (fig,
molestar) annoy. **~se** vpr rot
puebl|ecito m small village. **~o** m
town; (aldea) village; (nación)
nation, people
puedo vb véase **poder**
puente m bridge; (fig, fam) long
weekend. **~ colgante** suspension
bridge. **~ levadizo** drawbridge.
hacer ~ (fam) have a long weekend
puerco a filthy; (grosero) coarse.
● m pig. **~ espín** porcupine

pueril *a* childish

puerro *m* leek

puerta *f* door; (*en deportes*) goal; (*de ciudad*) gate. **~ principal** main entrance. **a ~ cerrada** behind closed doors

puerto *m* port; (*fig, refugio*) refuge; (*entre montañas*) pass. **~ franco** free port

Puerto Rico *m* Puerto Rico

puertorriqueño *a & m* Puerto Rican

pues *adv* (*entonces*) then; (*bueno*) well. ● *conj* since

puest|a *f* setting; (*en juegos*) bet. **~a de sol** sunset. **~a en escena** staging. **~a en marcha** starting. **~o** *a* put; (*vestido*) dressed. ● *m* place; (*empleo*) position, job; (*en mercado etc*) stall. ● *conj*. **~o que** since. **~o de socorro** first aid post

pugna *f* fight. **~r** *vt* fight

puja *f* effort; (*en subasta*) bid. **~r** *vt* struggle; (*en subasta*) bid

pulcro *a* neat

pulga *f* flea; (*de juego*) tiddly-wink. **tener malas ~s** be bad-tempered

pulga|da *f* inch. **~r** *m* thumb; (*del pie*) big toe

puli|do *a* neat. **~mentar** *vt* polish. **~mento** *m* polishing; (*substancia*) polish. **~r** *vt* polish; (*suavizar*) smooth

pulm|ón *m* lung. **~onar** *a* pulmonary. **~onía** *f* pneumonia

pulpa *f* pulp

pulpería *f* (*LAm*) grocer's shop (*Brit*), grocery store (*Amer*)

púlpito *m* pulpit

pulpo *m* octopus

pulque *m* (*Mex*) pulque, alcoholic Mexican drink

pulsa|ción *f* pulsation. **~dor** *a* pulsating. ● *m* button. **~r** *vt* (*mus*) play

pulsera *f* bracelet; (*de reloj*) strap

pulso *m* pulse; (*muñeca*) wrist; (*firmeza*) steady hand; (*fuerza*) strength; (*fig, tacto*) tact. **tomar el ~ a uno** take s.o.'s pulse

pulular *vi* teem with

pulveriza|dor *m* (*de perfume*) atomizer. **~r** [10] *vt* pulverize; atomize ⟨*líquido*⟩

pulla *f* cutting remark

pum *int* bang!

puma *m* puma

puna *f* puna, high plateau

punitivo *a* punitive

punta *f* point; (*extremo*) tip; (*clavo*) (small) nail. **estar de ~** be in a bad mood. **estar de ~ con uno** be at odds with s.o. **ponerse de ~ con uno** fall out with s.o.. **sacar ~ a** sharpen; (*fig*) find fault with

puntada *f* stitch

puntal *m* prop, support

puntapié *m* kick

puntear *vt* mark; (*mus*) pluck

puntera *f* toe

puntería *f* aim; (*destreza*) markmanship

puntiagudo *a* sharp, pointed

puntilla *f* (*encaje*) lace. **de ~s** on tiptoe

punto *m* point; (*señal*) dot; (*de examen*) mark; (*lugar*) spot, place; (*de taxis*) stand; (*momento*) moment; (*punto final*) full stop (*Brit*), period (*Amer*); (*puntada*) stitch; (*de tela*) mesh. **~ de admiración** exclamation mark. **~ de arranque** starting point. **~ de exclamación** exclamation mark. **~ de interrogación** question mark. **~ de vista** point of view. **~ final** full stop. **~ muerto** (*auto*) neutral (gear). **~ y aparte** full stop, new paragraph (*Brit*), period, new paragraph (*Amer*). **~ y coma** semicolon. **a ~** on time; (*listo*) ready. **a ~ de** on the point of. **de ~** knitted. **dos ~s** colon. **en ~** exactly. **hacer ~** knit. **hasta cierto ~** to a certain extent

puntuación *f* punctuation; (*en deportes, acción*) scoring; (*en deportes, número de puntos*) score

puntual *a* punctual; (*exacto*) accurate. **~idad** *f* punctuality; (*exactitud*) accuracy

puntuar [21] *vt* punctuate. ● *vi* score

punza|da *f* prick; (*dolor*) pain; (*fig*) pang. **~nte** *a* sharp. **~r** [10] *vt* prick

puñado *m* handful. **a ~s** by the handful

puñal *m* dagger. **~ada** *f* stab

puñ|etazo *m* punch. **~o** *m* fist; (*de ropa*) cuff; (*mango*) handle. **de su ~o (y letra)** in his own handwriting

pupa *f* spot; (*en los labios*) cold sore. **hacer ~** hurt. **hacerse ~** hurt o.s.

pupila *f* pupil

pupitre *m* desk

puquío *m* (*Arg*) spring

puré *m* purée; (*sopa*) thick soup. **~ de patatas** mashed potato

pureza *f* purity

purga *f* purge. **~r** [12] *vt* purge. **~torio** *m* purgatory

purifica|ción f purification. ~**r** [7] vt purify

purista m & f purist

puritano a puritanical. ● m puritan

puro a pure; ⟨cielo⟩ clear; ⟨fig⟩ simple. ● m cigar. **de ~** so. **de pura casualidad** by sheer chance

púrpura f purple

purpúreo a purple

pus m pus

puse vb véase **poner**

pusilánime a cowardly

pústula f spot

puta f whore

putrefacción f putrefaction

pútrido a rotten, putrid

Q

que pron rel ⟨personas, sujeto⟩ who; ⟨personas, complemento⟩ whom; ⟨cosas⟩ which, that. ● conj that. ¡~ **tengan Vds buen viaje!** have a good journey! **¡que venga!** let him come! **~ venga o no venga** whether he comes or not. **a que** I bet. **creo que tiene razón** I think (that) he is right. **de ~** from which. **yo ~ tú** if I were you

qué a ⟨con sustantivo⟩ what; ⟨con a o adv⟩ how. ● pron what. ¡~ **bonito!** how nice. **¿en ~ piensas?** what are you thinking about?

quebra|da f gorge; ⟨paso⟩ pass. ~**dizo** a fragile. ~**do** a broken; ⟨com⟩ bankrupt. ● m ⟨math⟩ fraction. ~**dura** f fracture; ⟨hondonada⟩ gorge. ~**ntar** vt break; ⟨debilitar⟩ weaken. ~**nto** m ⟨pérdida⟩ loss; ⟨daño⟩ damage. ~**r** [1] vt break. ● vi break; ⟨com⟩ go bankrupt. ~**rse** vpr break

quechua a & m & f Quechuan

queda f curfew

quedar vi stay, remain; ⟨estar⟩ be; ⟨faltar, sobrar⟩ be left. **~ bien** come off well. **~se** vpr stay. **~ con** arrange to meet. **~ en** agree to. **~ en nada** come to nothing. **~ por** (+ infinitivo) remain to be (+ pp)

quehacer m job. **~es domésticos** household chores

quej|a f complaint; ⟨de dolor⟩ moan. ~**arse** vpr complain (**de** about); ⟨gemir⟩ moan. ~**ido** m moan. ~**oso** a complaining

quema|do a burnt; ⟨fig, fam⟩ bitter. ~**dor** m burner. ~**dura** f burn. ~**r** vt burn; ⟨prender fuego a⟩ set fire to. ● vi burn. ~**rse** vpr burn o.s.; ⟨consumirse⟩ burn up; ⟨con el sol⟩ get sunburnt. ~**rropa** adv. **a ~rropa** point-blank

quena f Indian flute

quepo vb véase **caber**

queque m ⟨Mex⟩ cake

querella f ⟨riña⟩ quarrel, dispute; ⟨jurid⟩ charge

quer|er [35] vt want; ⟨amar⟩ love; ⟨necesitar⟩ need. ~**er decir** mean. ~**ido** a dear; ⟨amado⟩ loved. ● m darling; ⟨amante⟩ lover. **como quiera que** since; ⟨de cualquier modo⟩ however. **cuando quiera que** whenever. **donde quiera** wherever. **¿quieres darme ese libro?** would you pass me that book? **quiere llover** it's trying to rain. **¿quieres un helado?** would you like an ice-cream? **quisiera ir a la playa** I'd like to go to the beach. **sin ~er** without meaning to

queroseno m kerosene

querubín m cherub

ques|adilla f cheesecake; ⟨Mex, empanadilla⟩ pie. ~**o** m cheese. ~**o de bola** Edam cheese

quiá int never!, surely not!

quicio m frame. **sacar de ~ a uno** infuriate s.o.

quiebra f break; ⟨fig⟩ collapse; ⟨com⟩ bankruptcy

quiebro m dodge

quien pron rel ⟨sujeto⟩ who; ⟨complemento⟩ whom

quién pron interrogativo ⟨sujeto⟩ who; ⟨tras preposición⟩ whom. **¿de ~?** whose. **¿de ~ son estos libros?** whose are these books?

quienquiera pron whoever

quiero vb véase **querer**

quiet|o a still; ⟨inmóvil⟩ motionless; ⟨carácter etc⟩ calm. ~**ud** f stillness

quijada f jaw

quilate m carat

quilla f keel

quimera f ⟨fig⟩ illusion

químic|a f chemistry. ~**o** a chemical. ● m chemist

quincalla f hardware; ⟨de adorno⟩ trinket

quince a & m fifteen. **~ días** a fortnight. ~**na** f fortnight. ~**nal** a fortnightly

quincuagésimo a fiftieth

quiniela *f* pools coupon. **~s** *fpl* (football) pools

quinientos *a & m* five hundred

quinino *m* quinine

quinqué *m* oil-lamp; (*fig, fam*) shrewdness

quinquenio *m* (period of) five years

quinta *f* (*casa*) villa

quintaesencia *f* quintessence

quintal *m* a hundred kilograms

quinteto *m* quintet

quinto *a & m* fifth

quiosco *m* kiosk; (*en jardín*) summerhouse; (*en parque etc*) bandstand

quirúrgico *a* surgical

quise *vb véase* **querer**

quisque *pron.* **cada ~** (*fam*) (absolutely) everybody

quisquill|a *f* trifle; (*camarón*) shrimp. **~oso** *a* irritable; (*chinchorrero*) fussy

quita|manchas *m invar* stain remover. **~nieves** *m invar* snow plough. **~r** *vt* remove, take away; take off ⟨*ropa*⟩; (*robar*) steal. **~ndo** (*a excepción de, fam*) apart from. **~rse** *vpr* be removed; take off ⟨*ropa*⟩. **~rse de** (*no hacerlo más*) stop. **~rse de en medio** get out of the way. **~sol** *m invar* sunshade

Quito *m* Quito

quizá(s) *adv* perhaps

quórum *m* quorum

R

rábano *m* radish. **~ picante** horseradish. **me importa un ~** I couldn't care less

rabi|a *f* rabies; (*fig*) rage. **~ar** *vi* (*de dolor*) be in great pain; (*estar enfadado*) be furious; (*fig, tener ganas, fam*) long. **~ar por algo** long for sth. **~ar por hacer algo** long to do sth. **~eta** *f* tantrum. **dar ~a** infuriate

rabino *m* Rabbi

rabioso *a* rabid; (*furioso*) furious; ⟨*dolor etc*⟩ violent

rabo *m* tail

racial *a* racial

racimo *m* bunch

raciocinio *m* reason; (*razonamiento*) reasoning

ración *f* share, ration; (*de comida*) portion

racional *a* rational. **~izar** [10] *vt* rationalize

racionar *vt* (*limitar*) ration; (*repartir*) ration out

racis|mo *m* racism. **~ta** *a* racist

racha *f* gust of wind; (*fig*) spate

radar *m* radar

radiación *f* radiation

radiactiv|idad *f* radioactivity. **~o** *a* radioactive

radiador *m* radiator

radial *a* radial

radiante *a* radiant

radical *a & m & f* radical

radicar [7] *vi* (*estar*) be. **~ en** (*fig*) lie in

radio *m* radius; (*de rueda*) spoke; (*elemento metálico*) radium. **●** *f* radio

radioactiv|idad *f* radioactivity. **~o** *a* radioactive

radio|difusión *f* broadcasting. **~emisora** *f* radio station. **~escucha** *m & f* listener

radiografía *f* radiography

radi|ología *f* radiology. **~ólogo** *m* radiologist

radioterapia *f* radiotherapy

radioyente *m & f* listener

raer [36] *vt* scrape off

ráfaga *f* (*de viento*) gust; (*de luz*) flash; (*de ametralladora*) burst

rafia *f* raffia

raído *a* threadbare

raigambre *f* roots; (*fig*) tradition

raíz *f* root. **a ~ de** immediately after. **echar raíces** (*fig*) settle

raja *f* split; (*culin*) slice. **~r** *vt* split. **~rse** *vpr* split; (*fig*) back out

rajatabla. a ~ vigorously

ralea *f* sort

ralo *a* sparse

ralla|dor *m* grater. **~r** *vt* grate

rama *f* branch. **~je** *m* branches. **~l** *m* branch. **en ~** raw

rambla *f* gully; (*avenida*) avenue

ramera *f* prostitute

ramifica|ción *f* ramification. **~rse** [7] *vpr* branch out

ramilla *f* twig

ramillete *m* bunch

ramo *m* branch; (*de flores*) bouquet

rampa *f* ramp, slope

ramplón *a* vulgar

rana *f* frog. **ancas** *fpl* **de ~** frogs' legs. **no ser ~** not be stupid

rancio *a* rancid; ⟨*vino*⟩ old; (*fig*) ancient

ranch|ero *m* cook; (*LAm, jefe de rancho*) farmer. **~o** *m* (*LAm*) ranch, farm

rango *m* rank

ranúnculo *m* buttercup

ranura *f* groove; (*para moneda*) slot

rapar *vt* shave; crop (*pelo*)

rapaz *a* rapacious; (*ave*) of prey. ● *m* bird of prey

rapidez *f* speed

rápido *a* fast, quick. ● *adv* quickly. ● *m* (*tren*) express. **~s** *mpl* rapids

rapiña *f* robbery. **ave** *f* **de ~** bird of prey

rapsodia *f* rhapsody

rapt|ar *vt* kidnap. **~o** *m* kidnapping; (*de ira etc*) fit; (*éxtasis*) ecstasy

raqueta *f* racquet

raramente *adv* seldom, rarely

rarefacción *f* rarefaction

rar|eza *f* rarity; (*cosa rara*) oddity. **~o** *a* rare; (*extraño*) odd. **es ~o que** it is strange that. **¡qué ~o!** how strange!

ras *m*. **a ~ de** level with

rasar *vt* level; (*rozar*) graze

rasca|cielos *m* *invar* skyscraper. **~dura** *f* scratch. **~r** [7] *vt* scratch; (*raspar*) scrape

rasgar [12] *vt* tear

rasgo *m* stroke. **~s** *mpl* (*facciones*) features

rasguear *vt* strum; (*fig, escribir*) write

rasguñ|ar *vt* scratch. **~o** *m* scratch

raso *a* (*llano*) flat; (*liso*) smooth; (*cielo*) clear; (*cucharada etc*) level; (*vuelo etc*) low. ● *m* satin. **al ~** in the open air. **soldado** *m* **~** private

raspa *f* (*de pescado*) backbone

raspa|dura *f* scratch; (*acción*) scratching. **~r** *vt* scratch; (*rozar*) scrape

rastr|a *f* rake. **a ~as** dragging. **~ear** *vt* track. **~eo** *m* dragging. **~ero** *a* creeping; (*vuelo*) low. **~illar** *vt* rake. **~illo** *m* rake. **~o** *m* rake; (*huella*) track; (*señal*) sign. **el R~o** the flea market in Madrid. **ni ~o** not a trace

rata *f* rat

rate|ar *vt* steal. **~ría** *f* pilfering. **~ro** *m* petty thief

ratifica|ción *f* ratification. **~r** [7] *vt* ratify

rato *m* moment, short time. **~s libres** spare time. **a ~s** at times. **hace un ~** a moment ago. **¡hasta otro ~!** (*fam*) see you soon! **pasar mal ~** have a rough time

rat|ón *m* mouse. **~onera** *f* mouse-trap; (*madriguera*) mouse hole

raud|al *m* torrent; (*fig*) floods. **~o** *a* swift

raya *f* line; (*lista*) stripe; (*de pelo*) parting. **~r** *vt* rule. ● *vi* border (*con en*). **a ~s** striped. **pasar de la ~** go too far

rayo *m* ray; (*descarga eléctrica*) lightning. **~s X** X-rays

raza *f* race; (*de animal*) breed. **de ~** (*caballo*) thoroughbred; (*perro*) pedigree

raz|ón *f* reason. **a ~ón de** at the rate of. **perder la ~ón** go out of one's mind. **tener ~ón** be right. **~onable** *a* reasonable. **~onamiento** *m* reasoning. **~onar** *vt* reason out. ● *vi* reason

re *m* D; (*solfa*) re

reac|ción *f* reaction. **~cionario** *a* & *m* reactionary. **~ción en cadena** chain reaction. **~tor** *m* reactor; (*avión*) jet

real *a* real; (*de rey etc*) royal. ● *m* real, old Spanish coin

realce *m* relief; (*fig*) splendour

realidad *f* reality; (*verdad*) truth. **en ~** in fact

realis|mo *m* realism. **~ta** *a* realistic. ● *m* & *f* realist; (*monárquico*) royalist

realiza|ción *f* fulfilment. **~r** [10] *vt* carry out; make (*viaje*); achieve (*meta*); (*vender*) sell. **~rse** *vpr* (*plan etc*) be carried out; (*sueño, predicción etc*) come true; (*persona*) fulfil o.s.

realzar [10] *vt* (*fig*) enhance

reanima|ción *f* revival. **~r** *vt* revive. **~rse** *vpr* revive

reanudar *vt* resume; renew (*amistad*)

reaparecer [11] *vi* reappear

rearm|ar *vt* rearm. **~e** *m* rearmament

reavivar *vt* revive

rebaja *f* reduction. **~do** *a* (*precio*) reduced. **~r** *vt* lower. **en ~s** in the sale

rebanada *f* slice

rebaño *m* herd; (*de ovejas*) flock

rebasar *vt* exceed; (*dejar atrás*) leave behind

rebatir *vt* refute

rebel|arse *vpr* rebel. **~de** *a* rebellious. ● *m* rebel. **~día** *f* rebelliousness. **~ión** *f* rebellion

reblandecer [11] *vt* soften

rebosa|nte *a* overflowing. **~r** *vi* overflow; (*abundar*) abound

rebot|ar *vt* bounce; (*rechazar*) repel. ● *vi* bounce; (*bala*) ricochet. **~e** *m* bounce, rebound. **de ~e** on the rebound

rebozar [10] *vt* wrap up; (*culin*) coat in batter

rebullir [22] *vi* stir

rebusca|do *a* affected. **~r** [7] *vt* search thoroughly

rebuznar *vi* bray

recabar *vt* claim

recado *m* errand; (*mensaje*) message. **dejar ~** leave a message

reca|er [29] *vi* fall back; (*med*) relapse; (*fig*) fall. **~ída** *f* relapse

recalcar [7] *vt* squeeze; (*fig*) stress

recalcitrante *a* recalcitrant

recalentar [1] *vt* (*de nuevo*) reheat; (*demasiado*) overheat

recamar *vt* embroider

recámara *f* small room; (*de arma de fuego*) chamber; (*LAm, dormitorio*) bedroom

recambio *m* change; (*de pluma etc*) refill. **~s** *mpl* spare parts. **de ~** spare

recapitula|ción *f* summing up. **~r** *vt* sum up

recarg|ar [12] *vt* overload; (*aumentar*) increase; recharge ‹*batería*›. **~o** *m* increase

recat|ado *a* modest. **~ar** *vt* hide. **~arse** *vpr* hide o.s. away; (*actuar discretamente*) act discreetly. **~o** *m* prudence; (*modestia*) modesty. **sin ~arse, sin ~o** openly

recauda|ción *f* (*cantidad*) takings. **~dor** *m* tax collector. **~r** *vt* collect

recel|ar *vt/i* suspect. **~o** *m* distrust; (*temor*) fear. **~oso** *a* suspicious

recepci|ón *f* reception. **~onista** *m & f* receptionist

receptáculo *m* receptacle

recept|ivo *a* receptive. **~or** *m* receiver

recesión *f* recession

receta *f* recipe; (*med*) prescription

recib|imiento *m* (*acogida*) welcome. **~ir** *vt* receive; (*acoger*) welcome. ● *vi* entertain. **~irse** *vpr* graduate. **~o** *m* receipt. **acusar ~o** acknowledge receipt

reci|én *adv* recently; ‹*casado, nacido etc*› newly. **~ente** *a* recent; (*culin*) fresh

recinto *m* enclosure

recio *a* strong; ‹*voz*› loud. ● *adv* hard; (*en voz alta*) loudly

recipiente *m* (*persona*) recipient; (*cosa*) receptacle

recíproco *a* reciprocal. **a la recíproca** vice versa

recita|l *m* recital; (*de poesías*) reading. **~r** *vt* recite

reclama|ción *f* claim; (*queja*) complaint. **~r** *vt* claim. ● *vi* appeal

reclinar *vi* lean. **~se** *vpr* lean

reclu|ir [17] *vt* shut away. **~sión** *f* seclusion; (*cárcel*) prison. **~so** *m* prisoner

recluta *m* recruit. ● *f* recruitment. **~miento** *m* recruitment; (*conjunto de reclutas*) recruits. **~r** *vt* recruit

recobrar *vt* recover. **~se** *vpr* recover

recodo *m* bend

recog|er [14] *vt* collect; pick up ‹*cosa caída*›; (*cosechar*) harvest; (*dar asilo*) shelter. **~erse** *vpr* withdraw; (*ir a casa*) go home; (*acostarse*) go to bed. **~ida** *f* collection; (*cosecha*) harvest. **~ido** *a* withdrawn; (*pequeño*) small

recolección *f* harvest

recomenda|ción *f* recommendation. **~r** [1] *vt* recommend; (*encomendar*) entrust

recomenzar [1 & 10] *vt/i* start again

recompensa *f* reward. **~r** *vt* reward

recomponer [34] *vt* mend

reconcilia|ción *f* reconciliation. **~r** *vt* reconcile. **~rse** *vpr* be reconciled

recóndito *a* hidden

reconoc|er [11] *vt* recognize; (*admitir*) acknowledge; (*examinar*) examine. **~imiento** *m* recognition; (*admisión*) acknowledgement; (*agradecimiento*) gratitude; (*examen*) examination

reconozco *vb véase* **reconocer**

reconquista *f* reconquest. **~r** *vt* reconquer; (*fig*) win back

reconsiderar *vt* reconsider

reconstitu|ir [17] *vt* reconstitute. **~yente** *m* tonic

reconstru|cción *f* reconstruction. **~ir** [17] *vt* reconstruct

récord /'rekor/ *m* record. **batir un ~** break a record

recordar [2] *vt* remember; (*hacer acordar*) remind; (*Lam, despertar*) wake up. ● *vi* remember. **que yo recuerde** as far as I remember. **si mal no recuerdo** if I remember rightly

recorr|er *vt* tour ‹*país*›; (*pasar por*) travel through; cover ‹*distancia*›; (*registrar*) look over. **∼ido** *m* journey; (*itinerario*) route

recort|ado *a* jagged. **∼ar** *vt* cut (out). **∼e** *m* cutting (out); (*de periódico etc*) cutting

recoser *vt* mend

recostar [2] *vt* lean. **∼se** *vpr* lie back

recoveco *m* bend; (*rincón*) nook

recre|ación *f* recreation. **∼ar** *vt* recreate; (*divertir*) entertain. **∼arse** *vpr* amuse o.s. **∼ativo** *a* recreational. **∼o** *m* recreation; (*escol*) break

recrimina|ción *f* recrimination. **∼r** *vt* reproach

recrudecer [11] *vi* increase, worsen, get worse

recta *f* straight line

rect|angular *a* rectangular; ‹*triángulo*› right-angled. **∼ángulo** *a* rectangular; ‹*triángulo*› right-angled. ● *m* rectangle

rectifica|ción *f* rectification. **∼r** [7] *vt* rectify

rect|itud *f* straightness; (*fig*) honesty. **∼o** *a* straight; (*fig, justo*) fair; (*fig, honrado*) honest. ● *m* rectum. **todo ∼o** straight on

rector *a* governing. ● *m* rector

recuadro *m* (*en periódico*) box

recubrir [*pp* **recubierto**] *vt* cover

recuerdo *m* memory; (*regalo*) souvenir. ● *vb véase* **recordar**. **∼s** *mpl* (*saludos*) regards

recupera|ción *f* recovery. **∼r** *vt* recover. **∼rse** *vpr* recover. **∼r el tiempo perdido** make up for lost time

recur|rir *vi*. **∼rir a** resort to ‹*cosa*›; turn to ‹*persona*›. **∼so** *m* resort; (*medio*) resource; (*jurid*) appeal. **∼sos** *mpl* resources

recusar *vt* refuse

rechaz|ar [10] *vt* repel; reflect ‹*luz*›; (*no aceptar*) refuse; (*negar*) deny. **∼o** *m*. **de ∼o** on the rebound; (*fig*) consequently

rechifla *f* booing; (*burla*) derision

rechinar *vi* squeak; ‹*madera etc*› creak; ‹*dientes*› grind

rechistar *vt* murmur. **sin ∼** without saying a word

rechoncho *a* stout

red *f* network; (*malla*) net; (*para equipaje*) luggage rack; (*fig, engaño*) trap

redac|ción *f* editing; (*conjunto de redactores*) editorial staff; (*oficina*) editorial office; (*escol, univ*) essay. **∼tar** *vt* write. **∼tor** *m* writer; (*de periódico*) editor

redada *f* casting; (*de policía*) raid

redecilla *f* small net; (*para el pelo*) hairnet

rededor *m*. **al ∼**, **en ∼** around

reden|ción *f* redemption. **∼tor** *a* redeeming

redil *f* sheepfold

redimir *vt* redeem

rédito *m* interest

redoblar *vt* redouble; (*doblar*) bend back

redoma *f* flask

redomado *a* sly

redond|a *f* (*de imprenta*) roman (type); (*mus*) semibreve (*Brit*), whole note (*Amer*). **∼amente** *adv* (*categóricamente*) flatly. **∼ear** *vt* round off. **∼el** *m* circle; (*de plaza de toros*) arena. **∼o** *a* round; (*completo*) complete. ● *m* circle. **a la ∼a** around. **en ∼o** round; (*categóricamente*) flatly

reduc|ción *f* reduction. **∼ido** *a* reduced; (*limitado*) limited; (*pequeño*) small; ‹*precio*› low. **∼ir** [47] *vt* reduce. **∼irse** *vpr* be reduced; (*fig*) amount

reduje *vb véase* **reducir**

redundan|cia *f* redundancy. **∼te** *a* redundant

reduplicar [7] *vt* (*aumentar*) redouble

reduzco *vb véase* **reducir**

reedificar [7] *vt* reconstruct

reembols|ar *vt* reimburse. **∼o** *m* repayment. **contra ∼o** cash on delivery

reemplaz|ar [10] *vt* replace. **∼o** *m* replacement

reemprender *vt* start again

reenviar [20] *vt*, **reexpedir** [5] *vt* forward

referencia *f* reference; (*información*) report. **con ∼ a** with reference to. **hacer ∼ a** refer to

referéndum *m* (*pl* **referéndums**) referendum

referir [4] *vt* tell; (*remitir*) refer. **∼se** *vpr* refer. **por lo que se refiere a** as regards

refiero *vb véase* **referir**

refilón. de ∼ obliquely

refin|amiento *m* refinement. **∼ar** *vt* refine. **∼ería** *f* refinery

reflector *m* reflector; (*proyector*) searchlight

reflej|ar *vt* reflect. **~o** *a* reflected; (*med*) reflex. ● *m* reflection; (*med*) reflex; (*en el pelo*) highlights

reflexi|ón *f* reflection. **~onar** *vi* reflect. **~vo** *a* ⟨*persona*⟩ thoughtful; (*gram*) reflexive. **con ~ón** on reflection. **sin ~ón** without thinking

reflujo *m* ebb

reforma *f* reform. **~s** *fpl* (*reparaciones*) repairs. **~r** *vt* reform. **~rse** *vpr* reform

reforzar [2 & 10] *vt* reinforce

refrac|ción *f* refraction. **~tar** *vt* refract. **~tario** *a* heat-resistant

refrán *m* saying

refregar [1 & 12] *vt* rub

refrenar *vt* rein in ⟨*caballo*⟩; (*fig*) restrain

refrendar *vt* endorse

refresc|ar [7] *vt* refresh; (*enfriar*) cool. ● *vi* get cooler. **~arse** *vpr* refresh o.s.; (*salir*) go out for a walk. **~o** *m* cold drink. **~os** *mpl* refreshments

refrigera|ción *f* refrigeration; (*aire acondicionado*) air-conditioning. **~r** *vt* refrigerate. **~dor** *m*, **~dora** *f* refrigerator

refuerzo *m* reinforcement

refugi|ado *m* refugee. **~arse** *vpr* take refuge. **~o** *m* refuge, shelter

refulgir [14] *vi* shine

refundir *vt* (*fig*) revise, rehash

refunfuñar *vi* grumble

refutar *vt* refute

regadera *f* watering-can; (*Mex*, *ducha*) shower

regala|damente *adv* very well. **~do** *a* as a present, free; (*cómodo*) comfortable. **~r** *vt* give; (*agasajar*) treat very well. **~rse** *vpr* indulge o.s.

regaliz *m* liquorice

regalo *m* present, gift; (*placer*) joy; (*comodidad*) comfort

regañ|adientes. a ~adientes reluctantly. **~ar** *vt* scold. ● *vi* moan; (*dos personas*) quarrel. **~o** *m* (*reprensión*) scolding

regar [1 & 12] *vt* water

regata *f* regatta

regate *m* dodge; (*en deportes*) dribbling. **~ar** *vt* haggle over; (*economizar*) economize on. ● *vi* haggle; (*en deportes*) dribble. **~o** *m* haggling; (*en deportes*) dribbling

regazo *m* lap

regencia *f* regency

regenerar *vt* regenerate

regente *m* & *f* regent; (*director*) manager

régimen *m* (*pl* **regímenes**) rule; (*pol*) regime; (*med*) diet. **~ alimenticio** diet

regimiento *m* regiment

regio *a* royal

regi|ón *f* region. **~onal** *a* regional

regir [5 & 14] *vt* rule; govern ⟨*país*⟩; run ⟨*colegio, empresa*⟩. ● *vi* apply, be in force

registr|ado *a* registered. **~ador** *m* recorder; (*persona*) registrar. **~ar** *vt* register; (*grabar*) record; (*examinar*) search. **~arse** *vpr* register; (*darse*) be reported. **~o** *m* (*acción de registrar*) registration; (*libro*) register; (*cosa anotada*) entry; (*inspección*) search. **~o civil** (*oficina*) register office

regla *f* ruler; (*norma*) rule; (*menstruación*) period, menstruation. **~mentación** *f* regulation. **~mentar** *vt* regulate. **~mentario** *a* obligatory. **~mento** *m* regulations. **en ~** in order. **por ~ general** as a rule

regocij|ar *vt* delight. **~arse** *vpr* be delighted. **~o** *m* delight. **~os** *mpl* festivities

regode|arse *vpr* be delighted. **~o** *m* delight

regordete *a* chubby

regres|ar *vi* return. **~ión** *f* regression. **~ivo** *a* a backward. **~o** *m* return

reguer|a *f* irrigation ditch. **~o** *m* irrigation ditch; (*señal*) trail

regula|dor *m* control. **~r** *a* regular; (*mediano*) average; (*no bueno*) so-so. ● *vt* regulate; (*controlar*) control. **~ridad** *f* regularity. **con ~ridad** regularly. **por lo ~r** as a rule

rehabilita|ción *f* rehabilitation; (*en un empleo etc*) reinstatement. **~r** *vt* rehabilitate; (*al empleo etc*) reinstate

rehacer [31] *vt* redo; (*repetir*) repeat; (*reparar*) repair. **~se** *vpr* recover

rehén *m* hostage

rehogar [12] *vt* sauté

rehuir [17] *vt* avoid

rehusar *vt*/*i* refuse

reimpr|esión *f* reprinting. **~imir** (*pp* **reimpreso**) *vt* reprint

reina *f* queen. **~do** *m* reign. **~nte** *a* ruling; (*fig*) prevailing. **~r** *vi* reign; (*fig*) prevail

reincidir *vi* relapse, repeat an offence

reino *m* kingdom. **R∼ Unido** United Kingdom

reinstaurar *vt* restore

reintegr|ar *vt* reinstate ⟨*persona*⟩; refund ⟨*cantidad*⟩. **∼arse** *vpr* return. **∼o** *m* refund

reír [51] *vi* laugh. **∼se** *vpr* laugh. **∼se de** laugh at. **echarse a ∼** burst out laughing

reivindica|ción *f* claim. **∼r** [7] *vt* claim; (*restaurar*) restore

rej|a *f* grille, grating. **∼illa** *f* grille, grating; (*red*) luggage rack; (*de mimbre*) wickerwork. **entre ∼as** behind bars

rejuvenecer [11] *vt/i* rejuvenate. **∼se** *vpr* be rejuvenated

relaci|ón *f* relation(ship); (*relato*) tale; (*lista*) list. **∼onado** *a* concerning. **∼onar** *vt* relate (**con** to). **∼onarse** *vpr* be connected. **bien ∼onado** well-connected. **con ∼ón a, en ∼ón a** in relation to. **hacer ∼ón a** refer to

relaja|ción *f* relaxation; (*aflojamiento*) slackening. **∼do a** loose. **∼r** *vt* relax; (*aflojar*) slacken. **∼rse** *vpr* relax

relamerse *vpr* lick one's lips

relamido *a* overdressed

rel|ámpago *m* (flash of) lightning. **∼ampaguear** *vi* thunder; (*fig*) sparkle

relatar *vt* tell, relate

relativ|idad *f* relativity. **∼o** *a* relative. **en lo ∼o a** in relation to

relato *m* tale; (*informe*) report

relegar [12] *vt* relegate. **∼ al olvido** forget about

relev|ante *a* outstanding. **∼ar** *vt* relieve; (*substituir*) replace. **∼o** *m* relief. **carrera f de ∼os** relay race

relieve *m* relief; (*fig*) importance. **de ∼** important. **poner de ∼** emphasize

religi|ón *f* religion. **∼osa** *f* nun. **∼oso** *a* religious. ● *m* monk

relinch|ar *vi* neigh. **∼o** *m* neigh

reliquia *f* relic

reloj *m* clock; (*de bolsillo o pulsera*) watch. **∼ de caja** grandfather clock. **∼ de pulsera** wrist-watch. **∼ de sol** sundial. **∼ despertador** alarm clock. **∼ería** *f* watchmaker's (shop). **∼ero** *m* watchmaker

reluci|ente *a* shining. **∼r** [11] *vi* shine; (*destellar*) sparkle

relumbrar *vi* shine

rellano *m* landing

rellen|ar *vt* refill; (*culin*) stuff; fill in ⟨*formulario*⟩. **∼o** *a* full up; (*culin*) stuffed. ● *m* filling; (*culin*) stuffing

remach|ar *vt* rivet; (*fig*) drive home. **∼e** *m* rivet

remangar [12] *vt* roll up

remanso *m* pool; (*fig*) haven

remar *vi* row

remat|ado *a* (*total*) complete; ⟨*niño*⟩ very naughty. **∼ar** *vt* finish off; (*agotar*) use up; (*com*) sell off cheap. **∼e** *m* end; (*fig*) finishing touch. **de ∼e** completely

remedar *vt* imitate

remedi|ar *vt* remedy; (*ayudar*) help; (*poner fin a*) put a stop to; (*fig, resolver*) solve. **∼o** *m* remedy; (*fig*) solution. **como último ∼o** as a last resort. **no hay más ∼o** there's no other way. **no tener más ∼o** have no choice

remedo *m* imitation

rem|endar [1] *vt* repair. **∼iendo** *m* patch; (*fig, mejora*) improvement

remilg|ado *a* fussy; (*afectado*) affected. **∼o** *m* fussiness; (*afectación*) affectation

reminiscencia *f* reminiscence

remirar *vt* look again at

remisión *f* sending; (*referencia*) reference; (*perdón*) forgiveness

remiso *a* remiss

remit|e *m* sender's name and address. **∼ente** *m* sender. **∼ir** *vt* send; (*referir*) refer. ● *vi* diminish

remo *m* oar

remoj|ar *vt* soak; (*fig, fam*) celebrate. **∼o** *m* soaking. **poner a ∼o** soak

remolacha *f* beetroot. **∼ azucarera** sugar beet

remolcar [7] *vt* tow

remolino *m* swirl; (*de aire etc*) whirl; (*de gente*) throng

remolque *m* towing; (*cabo*) tow-rope; (*vehículo*) trailer. **a ∼** on tow. **dar ∼ a** tow

remontar *vt* mend. **∼se** *vpr* soar; (*con tiempo*) go back to

rémora *f* (*fig*) hindrance

remord|er [2] *vt* worry. **∼imiento** *m* remorse. **tener ∼imientos** feel remorse

remoto *a* remote

remover [2] *vt* move; stir ⟨*líquido*⟩; turn over ⟨*tierra*⟩; (*quitar*) remove; (*fig, activar*) revive

remozar [10] *vt* rejuvenate ⟨*persona*⟩; renovate ⟨*edificio etc*⟩

remunera|ción *f* remuneration. ~r *vt* remunerate

renac|er [11] *vi* be reborn; (*fig*) revive. ~**imiento** *m* rebirth. **R**~ Renaissance

renacuajo *m* tadpole; (*fig*) tiddler

rencilla *f* quarrel

rencor *m* bitterness. ~**oso** *a* (*estar*) resentful; (*ser*) spiteful. **guardar** ~ **a** have a grudge against

rendi|ción *f* surrender. ~**do** *a* submissive; (*agotado*) exhausted

rendija *f* crack

rendi|miento *m* efficiency; (*com*) yield. ~**r** [5] *vt* yield; (*vencer*) defeat; (*agotar*) exhaust; pay ⟨*homenaje*⟩. ● *vi* pay; (*producir*) produce. ~**rse** *vpr* surrender

renega|do *a* & *m* renegade. ~**r** [1 & 12] *vt* deny. ● *vi* grumble. ~**r de** renounce ⟨*fe etc*⟩; disown ⟨*personas*⟩

RENFE *abrev* (*Red Nacional de los Ferrocarriles Españoles*) Spanish National Railways

renglón *m* line; (*com*) item. **a** ~ **seguido** straight away

reno *m* reindeer

renombr|ado *a* renowned. ~**e** *m* renown

renova|ción *f* renewal; (*de edificio*) renovation; (*de cuarto*) decorating. ~**r** *vt* renew; renovate ⟨*edificio*⟩; decorate ⟨*cuarto*⟩

rent|a *f* income; (*alquiler*) rent; (*deuda*) national debt. ~**able** *a* profitable. ~**ar** *vt* produce, yield; (*LAm, alquilar*) rent, hire. ~**a vitalicia** (life) annuity. ~**ista** *m* & *f* person of independent means

renuncia *f* renunciation. ~**r** *vi*. ~**r a** renounce, give up

reñi|do *a* hard-fought. ~**r** [5 & 22] *vt* tell off. ● *vi* quarrel. **estar** ~**do con** be incompatible with ⟨*cosas*⟩; be on bad terms with ⟨*personas*⟩

reo *m* & *f* culprit; (*jurid*) accused. ~ **de Estado** person accused of treason. ~ **de muerte** prisoner sentenced to death

reojo. mirar de ~ look out of the corner of one's eye at; (*fig*) look askance at

reorganizar [10] *vt* reorganize

repanchigarse [12] *vpr*, **repantigarse** [12] *vpr* sprawl out

repar|ación *f* repair; (*acción*) repairing; (*fig, compensación*) reparation.

~**ar** *vt* repair; (*fig*) make amends for; (*notar*) notice. ● *vi*. ~**ar en** notice; (*hacer caso de*) pay attention to. ~**o** *m* fault; (*objeción*) objection. **poner** ~**os** raise objections

repart|ición *f* division. ~**idor** *m* delivery man. ~**imiento** *m* distribution. ~**ir** *vt* distribute, share out; deliver ⟨*cartas, leche etc*⟩; hand out ⟨*folleto, premio*⟩. ~**o** *m* distribution; (*de cartas, leche etc*) delivery; (*actores*) cast

repas|ar *vt* go over; check ⟨*cuenta*⟩; revise ⟨*texto*⟩; (*leer a la ligera*) glance through; (*coser*) mend. ● *vi* go back. ~**o** *m* revision; (*de ropa*) mending. **dar un** ~**o** look through

repatria|ción *f* repatriation. ~**r** *vt* repatriate

repecho *m* steep slope

repele|nte *a* repulsive. ~**r** *vt* repel

repensar [1] *vt* reconsider

repent|e. de ~ suddenly. ~**ino** *a* sudden

repercu|sión *f* repercussion. ~**tir** *vi* reverberate; (*fig*) have repercussions (**en** on)

repertorio *m* repertoire; (*lista*) index

repeti|ción *f* repetition; (*mus*) repeat. ~**damente** *adv* repeatedly. ~**r** [5] *vt* repeat; (*imitar*) copy; ● *vi*. ~**r de** have a second helping of. **¡que se repita!** encore!

repi|car [7] *vt* ring ⟨*campanas*⟩. ~**que** *m* peal

repisa *f* shelf. ~ **de chimenea** mantlepiece

repito *vb véase* **repetir**

replegarse [1 & 12] *vpr* withdraw

repleto *a* full up

réplica *a* answer; (*copia*) replica

replicar [7] *vi* answer

replie|gue *m* crease; (*mil*) withdrawal

repollo *m* cabbage

reponer [34] *vt* replace; revive ⟨*obra de teatro*⟩; (*contestar*) reply. ~**se** *vpr* recover

report|aje *m* report. ~**ero** *m* reporter

repos|ado *a* quiet; (*sin prisa*) unhurried. ~**ar** *vi* rest. ~**arse** *vpr* settle. ~**o** *m* rest

repost|ar *vt* replenish; refuel ⟨*avión*⟩; fill up ⟨*coche etc*⟩. ~**ería** *f* cake shop

repren|der *vt* reprimand. ~**sible** *a* reprehensible

represalia *f* reprisal. **tomar** ~**s** retaliate

representa|ción *f* representation; (*en el teatro*) performance. **en** ~**ción de** representing. ~**nte** *m* representative; (*actor*) actor. ● *f* representative; (*actriz*) actress. ~**r** *vt* represent; perform ⟨*obra de teatro*⟩; play ⟨*papel*⟩; (*aparentar*) look. ~**rse** *vpr* imagine. ~**tivo** *a* representative

represi|ón *f* repression. ~**vo** *a* repressive

reprimenda *f* reprimand

reprimir *vt* supress. ~**se** *vpr* stop o.s.

reprobar [2] *vt* condemn; reproach ⟨*persona*⟩

réprobo *a* & *m* reprobate

reproch|ar *vt* reproach. ~**e** *m* reproach

reproduc|ción *f* reproduction. ~**ir** [47] *vt* reproduce. ~**tor** *a* reproductive

reptil *m* reptile

rep|ública *f* republic. ~**ublicano** *a* & *m* republican

repudiar *vt* repudiate

repuesto *m* store; (*auto*) spare (part). **de** ~ in reserve

repugna|ncia *f* disgust. ~**nte** *a* repugnant. ~**r** *vt* disgust

repujar *vt* emboss

repuls|a *f* rebuff. ~**ión** *f* repulsion. ~**ivo** *a* repulsive

reputa|ción *f* reputation. ~**do** *a* reputable. ~**r** *vt* consider

requebrar [1] *vt* flatter

requemar *vt* scorch; (*culin*) burn; tan ⟨*piel*⟩

requeri|miento *m* request; (*jurid*) summons. ~**r** [4] *vt* need; (*pedir*) ask

requesón *m* cottage cheese

requete... *pref* extremely

requiebro *m* compliment

réquiem *m* (*pl* **réquiems**) *m* requiem

requis|a *f* inspection; (*mil*) requisition. ~**ar** *vt* requisition. ~**ito** *m* requirement

res *f* animal. ~ **lanar** sheep. ~ **vacuna** (*vaca*) cow; (*toro*) bull; (*buey*) ox. **carne de** ~ (*Mex*) beef

resabido *a* well-known; ⟨*persona*⟩ pedantic

resabio *m* (unpleasant) after-taste; (*vicio*) bad habit

resaca *f* undercurrent; (*después de beber alcohol*) hangover

resaltar *vi* stand out. **hacer** ~ emphasize

resarcir [9] *vt* repay; (*compensar*) compensate. ~**se** *vpr* make up for

resbal|adizo *a* slippery. ~**ar** *vi* slip; (*auto*) skid; ⟨*líquido*⟩ trickle. ~**arse** *vpr* slip; (*auto*) skid; ⟨*líquido*⟩ trickle. ~**ón** *m* slip; (*de vehículo*) skid

rescat|ar *vt* ransom; (*recuperar*) recapture; (*fig*) recover. ~**e** *m* ransom; (*recuperación*) recapture; (*salvamento*) rescue

rescindir *vt* cancel

rescoldo *m* embers

resecar [7] *vt* dry up; (*med*) remove. ~**se** *vpr* dry up

resenti|do *a* resentful. ~**miento** *m* resentment. ~**rse** *vpr* feel the effects; (*debilitarse*) be weakened; (*ofenderse*) take offence (**de** at)

reseña *f* account; (*en periódico*) report, review. ~**r** *vt* describe; (*en periódico*) report on, review

resero *m* (*Arg*) herdsman

reserva *f* reservation; (*provisión*) reserve(s). ~**ción** *f* reservation. ~**do** *a* reserved. ~**r** *vt* reserve; (*guardar*) keep, save. ~**rse** *vpr* save o.s. **a** ~ **de** except for. **a** ~ **de que** unless. **de** ~ in reserve

resfria|do *m* cold; (*enfriamiento*) chill. ~**r** *vt.* ~**r a uno** give s.o. a cold. ~**rse** *vpr* catch a cold; (*fig*) cool off

resguard|ar *vt* protect. ~**arse** *vpr* protect o.s.; (*fig*) take care. ~**o** *m* protection; (*garantía*) guarantee; (*recibo*) receipt

resid|encia *f* residence; (*univ*) hall of residence, dormitory (*Amer*); (*de ancianos etc*) home. ~**encial** *a* residential. ~**ente** *a* & *m* & *f* resident. ~**ir** *vi* reside; (*fig*) lie

residu|al *a* residual. ~**o** *m* remainder. ~**os** *mpl* waste

resigna|ción *f* resignation. ~**damente** *adv* with resignation. ~**r** *vt* resign. ~**rse** *vpr* resign o.s. (**a, con** to)

resina *f* resin

resist|encia *f* resistence. ~**ente** *a* resistent. ~**ir** *vt* resist; (*soportar*) bear. ● *vi* resist. **oponer** ~**encia a** resist

resma *f* ream

resobado *a* trite

resol|ución *f* resolution; (*solución*) solution; (*decisión*) decision. ~**ver**

[2] (*pp* **resuelto**) resolve; solve ⟨*problema etc*⟩. **∼verse** *vpr* be solved; (*resultar bien*) work out; (*decidirse*) make up one's mind

resollar [2] *vi* breathe heavily. **sin ∼** without saying a word

resona|ncia *f* resonance. **∼nte** *a* resonant; (*fig*) resounding. **∼r** [2] *vi* resound. **tener ∼ncia** cause a stir

resopl|ar *vi* puff; (*por enfado*) snort; (*por cansancio*) pant. **∼ido** *m* heavy breathing; (*de enfado*) snort; (*de cansancio*) panting

resorte *m* spring. **tocar (todos los) ∼s** (*fig*) pull strings

respald|ar *vt* back; (*escribir*) endorse. **∼arse** *vpr* lean back. **∼o** *m* back

respect|ar *vi* concern. **∼ivo** *a* respective. **∼o** *m* respect. **al ∼o** on the matter. (**con**) **∼o a** as regards. **en/por lo que ∼a a** as regards

respet|able *a* respectable. ● *m* audience. **∼ar** *vt* respect. **∼o** *m* respect. **∼uoso** *a* respectful. **de ∼o** best. **faltar al ∼o a** be disrespectful to. **hacerse ∼ar** command respect

respingo *m* start

respir|ación *f* breathing; (*med*) respiration; (*ventilación*) ventilation. **∼ador** *a* respiratory. **∼ar** *vi* breathe; (*fig*) breathe a sigh of relief. **no ∼ar** (*no hablar*) not say a word. **∼o** *m* breathing; (*fig*) rest

respland|ecer [11] *vi* shine. **∼eciente** *a* shining. **∼or** *m* brilliance; (*de llamas*) glow

responder *vi* answer; (*replicar*) answer back; (*fig*) reply, respond. **∼ de** answer for

responsab|ilidad *f* responsibility. **∼le** *a* responsible. **hacerse ∼le de** assume responsibilty for

respuesta *f* reply, answer

resquebra|dura *f* crack. **∼jar** *vt* crack. **∼jarse** *vpr* crack

resquemor *m* (*fig*) uneasiness

resquicio *m* crack; (*fig*) possibility

resta *f* subtraction

restablecer [11] *vt* restore. **∼se** *vpr* recover

restallar *vi* crack

restante *a* remaining. **lo ∼** the rest

restar *vt* take away; (*substraer*) subtract. ● *vi* be left

restaura|ción *f* restoration. **∼nte** *m* restaurant. **∼r** *vt* restore

restitu|ción *f* restitution. **∼ir** [17] *vt* return; (*restaurar*) restore

resto *m* rest, remainder; (*en matemática*) remainder. **∼s** *mpl* remains; (*de comida*) leftovers

restorán *m* restaurant

restregar [1 & 12] *vt* rub

restri|cción *f* restriction. **∼ngir** [14] *vt* restrict, limit

resucitar *vt* resuscitate; (*fig*) revive. ● *vi* return to life

resuelto *a* resolute

resuello *m* breath; (*respiración*) breathing

resulta|do *m* result. **∼r** *vi* result; (*salir*) turn out; (*ser*) be; (*ocurrir*) happen; (*costar*) come to

resum|en *m* summary. **∼ir** *vt* summarize; (*recapitular*) sum up; (*abreviar*) abridge. **en ∼en** in short

resur|gir [14] *vi* reappear; (*fig*) revive. **∼gimiento** *m* resurgence. **∼rección** *f* resurrection

retaguardia *f* (*mil*) rearguard

retahíla *f* string

retal *m* remnant

retama *f*, **retamo** *m* (*LAm*) broom

retar *vt* challenge

retardar *vt* slow down; (*demorar*) delay

retazo *m* remnant; (*fig*) piece, bit

retemblar [1] *vi* shake

rete... *pref* extremely

reten|ción *f* retention. **∼er** [40] *vt* keep; (*en la memoria*) retain; (*no dar*) withhold

reticencia *f* insinuation; (*reserva*) reticence, reluctance

retina *f* retina

retintín *m* ringing. **con ∼** (*fig*) sarcastically

retir|ada *f* withdrawal. **∼ado** *a* secluded; (*jubilado*) retired. **∼ar** *vt* move away; (*quitar*) remove; withdraw ⟨*dinero*⟩; (*jubilar*) pension off. **∼arse** *vpr* draw back; (*mil*) withdraw; (*jubilarse*) retire; (*acostarse*) go to bed. **∼o** *m* retirement; (*pensión*) pension; (*lugar apartado*) retreat

reto *m* challenge

retocar [7] *vt* retouch

retoño *m* shoot

retoque *m* (*acción*) retouching; (*efecto*) finishing touch

retorc|er [2 & 9] *vt* twist; wring ⟨*ropa*⟩. **∼erse** *vpr* get twisted up; (*de dolor*) writhe. **∼imiento** *m* twisting; (*de ropa*) wringing

retóric|a *f* rhetoric; (*grandilocuencia*) grandiloquence. **∼o** *m* rhetorical

retorn|ar vt/i return. **~o** m return

retortijón m twist; (de tripas) stomach cramp

retoz|ar [10] vi romp, frolic. **~ón** a playful

retractar vt retract. **~se** vpr retract

retra|er [41] vt retract. **~erse** vpr withdraw. **~ído** a retiring

retransmitir vt relay

retras|ado a behind; ⟨reloj⟩ slow; (poco desarrollado) backward; (anticuado) old-fashioned; (med) mentally retarded. **~ar** vt delay; put back ⟨reloj⟩; (retardar) slow down. ● vi fall behind; ⟨reloj⟩ be slow. **~arse** vpr be behind; ⟨reloj⟩ be slow. **~o** m delay; (poco desarrollo) backwardness; (de reloj) slowness. **~os** mpl arrears. **con 5 minutos de ~o** 5 minutes late. **traer ~o** be late

retrat|ar vt paint a portrait of; (foto) photograph; (fig) protray. **~ista** m & f portrait painter. **~o** m portrait; (fig, descripción) description. **ser el vivo ~o de** be the living image of

retreparse vpr lean back

retreta f retreat

retrete m toilet

retribu|ción f payment. **~ir** [17] vt pay

retroce|der vi move back; (fig) back down. **~so** m backward movement; (de arma de fuego) recoil; (med) relapse

retrógrado a & m (pol) reactionary

retropropulsión f jet propulsion

retrospectivo a retrospective

retrovisor m rear-view mirror

retumbar vt echo; ⟨trueno etc⟩ boom

reuma m, **reúma** m rheumatism

reum|ático a rheumatic. **~atismo** m rheumatism

reuni|ón f meeting; (entre amigos) reunion. **~r** [23] vt join together; (recoger) gather (together). **~rse** vpr join together; ⟨personas⟩ meet

rev|álida f final exam. **~alidar** vt confirm; (escol) take an exam in

revancha f revenge. **tomar la ~** get one's own back

revela|ción f revelation. **~do** m developing. **~dor** a revealing. **~r** vt reveal; (foto) develop

revent|ar [1] vi burst; (tener ganas) be dying to. **~arse** vpr burst. **~ón** m burst; (auto) puncture

reverbera|ción f (de luz) reflection; (de sonido) reverberation. **~r** vi

⟨luz⟩ be reflected; ⟨sonido⟩ reverberate

reveren|cia f reverence; (muestra de respeto) bow; (muestra de respeto de mujer) curtsy. **~ciar** vt revere. **~do** a respected; (relig) reverend. **~te** a reverent

revers|ible a reversible. **~o** m reverse

revertir [4] vi revert

revés m wrong side; (desgracia) misfortune; (en deportes) backhand. **al ~** the other way round; (con lo de arriba abajo) upside down; (con lo de dentro fuera) inside out

revesti|miento m coating. **~r** [5] vt cover; put on ⟨ropa⟩; (fig) take on

revis|ar vt check; overhaul ⟨mecanismo⟩; service ⟨coche etc⟩. **~ión** f check(ing); (inspección) inspection; (de coche etc) service. **~or** m inspector

revist|a f magazine; (inspección) inspection; (artículo) review; (espectáculo) revue. **~ero** m critic; (mueble) magazine rack. **pasar ~a a** inspect

revivir vi come to life again

revocar [7] vt revoke; whitewash ⟨pared⟩

revolcar [2 & 7] vt knock over. **~se** vpr roll

revolotear vi flutter

revoltijo m, **revoltillo** m mess. **~ de huevos** scrambled eggs

revoltoso a rebellious; ⟨niño⟩ naughty

revoluci|ón f revolution. **~onar** vt revolutionize. **~onario** a & m revolutionary

revolver [2, pp **revuelto**] vt mix; stir ⟨líquido⟩; (desordenar) mess up; (pol) stir up. **~se** vpr turn round. **~se contra** turn on

revólver m revolver

revoque m (con cal) whitewashing

revuelo m fluttering; (fig) stir

revuelt|a f turn; (de calle etc) bend; (motín) revolt; (conmoción) disturbance. **~o** a mixed up; ⟨líquido⟩ cloudy; ⟨mar⟩ rough; ⟨tiempo⟩ unsettled; ⟨huevos⟩ scrambled

rey m king. **~es** mpl king and queen

reyerta f quarrel

rezagarse [12] vpr fall behind

rez|ar [10] vt say. ● vi pray; (decir) say. **~o** m praying; (oración) prayer

rezongar [12] vi grumble

rezumar *vt/i* ooze
ría *f* estuary
riachuelo *m* stream
riada *f* flood
ribera *f* bank
ribete *m* border; (*fig*) embellishment
ricino *m*. **aceite de** ~ castor oil
rico *a* rich; (*culin, fam*) delicious. ● *m* rich person
rid|ículo *a* ridiculous. ~**iculizar** [10] *vt* ridicule
riego *m* watering; (*irrigación*) irrigation
riel *m* rail
rienda *f* rein
riesgo *m* risk. **a** ~ **de** at the risk of. **correr (el)** ~ **de** run the risk of
rifa *f* raffle. ~**r** *vt* raffle. ~**rse** *vpr* (*fam*) quarrel over
rifle *m* rifle
rigidez *f* rigidity; (*fig*) inflexibility
rígido *a* rigid; (*fig*) inflexible
rig|or *m* strictness; (*exactitud*) exactness; (*de clima*) severity. ~**uroso** *a* rigorous. **de** ~**or** compulsory. **en** ~**or** strictly speaking
rima *f* rhyme. ~**r** *vt/i* rhyme
rimbombante *a* resounding; (*lenguaje*) pompous; (*fig, ostentoso*) showy
rimel *m* mascara
rincón *m* corner
rinoceronte *m* rhinoceros
riña *f* quarrel; (*pelea*) fight
riñ|ón *m* kidney. ~**onada** *f* loin; (*guiso*) kidney stew
río *m* river; (*fig*) stream. ● *vb véase* **reír.** ~ **abajo** downstream. ~ **arriba** upstream
rioja *m* Rioja wine
riqueza *f* wealth; (*fig*) richness. ~**s** *fpl* riches
riquísimo *a* delicious
risa *f* laugh. **desternillarse de** ~ split one's sides laughing. **la** ~ laughter
risco *m* cliff
ris|ible *a* laughable. ~**otada** *f* guffaw
ristra *f* string
risueño *a* smiling; (*fig*) happy
rítmico *a* rhythmic(al)
ritmo *m* rhythm; (*fig*) rate
rit|o *m* rite; (*fig*) ritual. ~**ual** *a & m* ritual. **de** ~**ual** customary
rival *a & m & f* rival. ~**idad** *f* rivalry. ~**izar** [10] *vi* rival
riz|ado *a* curly. ~**ar** [10] *vt* curl; ripple (*agua*). ~**o** *m* curl; (*en agua*) ripple. ~**oso** *a* curly

róbalo *m* bass
robar *vt* steal (*cosa*); rob (*persona*); (*raptar*) kidnap
roble *m* oak (tree)
roblón *m* rivet
robo *m* theft; (*fig, estafa*) robbery
robot (*pl* **robots**) *m* robot
robust|ez *f* strength. ~**o** *a* strong
roca *f* rock
roce *m* rubbing; (*toque ligero*) touch; (*señal*) mark; (*fig, entre personas*) contact
rociar [20] *vt* spray
rocín *m* nag
rocío *m* dew
rodaballo *m* turbot
rodado *m* (*Arg, vehículo*) vehicle
rodaja *f* disc; (*culin*) slice
roda|je *m* (*de película*) shooting; (*de coche*) running in. ~**r** [2] *vt* shoot (*película*); run in (*coche*); (*recorrer*) travel. ● *vi* roll; (*coche*) run; (*hacer una película*) shoot
rode|ar *vt* surround. ~**arse** *vpr* surround o.s. (**de** with). ~**o** *m* long way round; (*de ganado*) round-up. **andar con** ~**os** beat about the bush. **sin** ~**os** plainly
rodill|a *f* knee. ~**era** *f* knee-pad. **de** ~**as** kneeling
rodillo *m* roller; (*culin*) rolling-pin
rododendro *m* rhododendron
rodrigón *m* stake
roe|dor *m* rodent. ~**r** [37] *vt* gnaw
rogar [2 & 12] *vt/i* ask; (*relig*) pray. **se ruega a los Sres pasajeros...** passengers are requested.... **se ruega no fumar** please do not smoke
roj|ete *m* rouge. ~**ez** *f* redness. ~**izo** *a* reddish. ~**o** *a & m* red. **ponerse** ~**o** blush
roll|izo *a* round; (*persona*) plump. ~**o** *m* roll; (*de cuerda*) coil; (*culin, rodillo*) rolling-pin; (*fig, pesadez, fam*) bore
romance *a* Romance. ● *m* Romance language; (*poema*) romance. **hablar en** ~ speak plainly
rom|ánico *a* Romanesque; (*lengua*) Romance. ~**ano** *a & m* Roman. **a la** ~**ana** (*culin*) (deep-)fried in batter
rom|anticismo *m* romanticism. ~**ántico** *a* romantic
romería *f* pilgrimage
romero *m* rosemary
romo *a* blunt; (*nariz*) snub; (*fig, torpe*) dull
rompe|cabezas *m invar* puzzle; (*con tacos de madera*) jigsaw (puzzle).

~**nueces** *m invar* nutcrackers.
~**olas** *m invar* breakwater

romp|er (*pp* **roto**) *vt* break; break off
⟨*relaciones etc*⟩. ● *vi* break; ⟨*sol*⟩
break through. ~**erse** *vpr* break.
~**er a** burst out. ~**imiento** *m* (*de
relaciones etc*) breaking off

ron *m* rum

ronc|ar [7] *vi* snore. ~**o** *a* hoarse

roncha *f* lump; (*culin*) slice

ronda *f* round; (*patrulla*) patrol;
(*carretera*) ring road. ~**lla** *f* group
of serenaders; (*invención*) story. ~**r**
vt/i patrol

rondón. de ~ unannounced

ronquedad *f*, **ronquera** *f* hoarseness

ronquido *m* snore

ronronear *vi* purr

ronzal *m* halter

roñ|a *f* (*suciedad*) grime. ~**oso** *a*
dirty; (*oxidado*) rusty; (*tacaño*)
mean

rop|a *f* clothes, clothing. ~**a blanca**
linen; (*ropa interior*) underwear.
~**a de cama** bedclothes. ~**a hecha**
ready-made clothes. ~**a interior**
underwear. ~**aje** *m* robes; (*excesivo*) heavy clothing. ~**ero** *m*
wardrobe

ros|a *a invar* pink. ● *f* rose; (*color*)
pink. ~**áceo** *a* pink. ~**ado** *a* rosy.
● *m* (*vino*) rosé. ~**al** *m* rose-bush

rosario *m* rosary; (*fig*) series

rosbif *m* roast beef

rosc|a *f* coil; (*de tornillo*) thread; (*de
pan*) roll. ~**o** *m* roll

rosetón *m* rosette

rosquilla *f* doughnut; (*oruga*) grub

rostro *m* face

rota|ción *f* rotation. ~**tivo** *a* rotary

roto *a* broken

rótula *f* kneecap

rotulador *m* felt-tip pen

rótulo *m* sign; (*etiqueta*) label

rotundo *a* emphatic

rotura *f* break

roturar *vt* plough

roza *f* groove. ~**dura** *f* scratch

rozar [10] *vt* rub against; (*ligeramente*) brush against; (*ensuciar*)
dirty; (*fig*) touch on. ~**se** *vpr* rub;
(*con otras personas*) mix

Rte. *abrev* (*Remite(nte)*) sender

rúa *f* (small) street

rubéola *f* German measles

rubí *m* ruby

rubicundo *a* ruddy

rubio *a* ⟨*pelo*⟩ fair; ⟨*persona*⟩ fair-
haired; ⟨*tabaco*⟩ Virginian

rubor *m* blush; (*fig*) shame. ~**izado**
a blushing; (*fig*) ashamed. ~**izar**
[10] *vt* make blush. ~**izarse** *vpr*
blush

rúbrica *f* red mark; (*de firma*) flourish; (*título*) heading

rudeza *f* roughness

rudiment|al *a* rudimentary. ~**os**
mpl rudiments

rudo *a* rough; (*sencillo*) simple

rueda *f* wheel; (*de mueble*) castor; (*de
personas*) ring; (*culin*) slice. ~ **de
prensa** press conference

ruedo *m* edge; (*redondel*) arena

ruego *m* request; (*súplica*) entreaty.
● *vb véase* **rogar**

rufi|án *m* pimp; (*granuja*) villain.
~**anesco** *a* roguish

rugby *m* Rugby

rugi|do *m* roar. ~**r** [14] *vi* roar

ruibarbo *m* rhubarb

ruido *m* noise; (*alboroto*) din; (*escándalo*) commotion. ~**so** *a* noisy; (*fig*)
sensational

ruin *a* despicable; (*tacaño*) mean

ruina *f* ruin; (*colapso*) collapse

ruindad *f* meanness

ruinoso *a* ruinous

ruiseñor *m* nightingale

ruleta *f* roulette

rulo *m* (*culin*) rolling-pin; (*del pelo*)
curler

Rumania *f* Romania

rumano *a & m* Romanian

rumba *f* rumba

rumbo *m* direction; (*fig*) course; (*fig,
generosidad*) lavishness. ~**so** *a* lavish. **con** ~ **a** in the direction of.
hacer ~ **a** head for

rumia|nte *a & m* ruminant. ~**r** *vt*
chew; (*fig*) chew over. ● *vi* ruminate

rumor *m* rumour; (*ruido*) murmur.
~**earse** *vpr* be rumoured. ~**oso** *a*
murmuring

runr|ún *m* rumour; (*ruido*) murmur.
~**unearse** *vpr* be rumoured

ruptura *f* break; (*de relaciones etc*)
breaking off

rural *a* rural

Rusia *f* Russia

ruso *a & m* Russian

rústico *a* rural; (*de carácter*) coarse.
en rústica paperback

ruta *f* route; (*camino*) road; (*fig*)
course

rutilante *a* shining

rutina *f* routine. ~**rio** *a* routine

S

S.A. *abrev* (*Sociedad Anónima*) Ltd, Limited, plc, Public Limited Company

sábado *m* Saturday

sabana *f* (*esp LAm*) savannah

sábana *f* sheet

sabandija *f* bug

sabañón *m* chilblain

sabático *a* sabbatical

sab|elotodo *m & f invar* know-all (*fam*). ~**er** [38] *vt* know; (*ser capaz de*) be able to, know how to; (*enterarse de*) learn. ● *vi*. ~**er a** taste of. ~**er** *m* knowledge. ~**ido** *a* well-known. ~**iduría** *f* wisdom; (*conocimientos*) knowledge. **a** ~**er si** I wonder if. **¡haberlo** ~**ido!** if only I'd known! **hacer** ~**er** let know. **no sé cuántos** what's-his-name. **para que lo sepas** let me tell you. **¡qué sé yo!** how should I know? **que yo sepa** as far as I know. **¿**~**es nadar?** can you swim? **un no sé qué** a certain sth. **¡yo qué sé!** how should I know?

sabiendas. a ~ knowingly; (*a propósito*) on purpose

sabio *a* learned; (*prudente*) wise

sabor *m* taste, flavour; (*fig*) flavour. ~**ear** *vt* taste; (*fig*) savour

sabot|aje *m* sabotage. ~**eador** *m* saboteur. ~**ear** *vt* sabotage

sabroso *a* tasty; (*fig, substancioso*) meaty

sabueso *m* (*perro*) bloodhound; (*fig, detective*) detective

saca|corchos *m invar* corkscrew. ~**puntas** *m invar* pencil-sharpener

sacar [7] *vt* take out; put out (*parte del cuerpo*); (*quitar*) remove; take (*foto*); win (*premio*); get (*billete, entrada etc*); withdraw (*dinero*); reach (*solución*); draw (*conclusión*); make (*copia*). ~ **adelante** bring up (*niño*); carry on (*negocio*)

sacarina *f* saccharin

sacerdo|cio *m* priesthood. ~**tal** *a* priestly. ~**te** *m* priest

saciar *vt* satisfy

saco *m* bag; (*anat*) sac; (*LAm, chaqueta*) jacket; (*de mentiras*) pack. ~ **de dormir** sleeping-bag

sacramento *m* sacrament

sacrific|ar [7] *vt* sacrifice. ~**arse** *vpr* sacrifice o.s. ~**io** *m* sacrifice

sacr|ilegio *m* sacrilege. ~**ílego** *a* sacrilegious

sacro *a* sacred, holy. ~**santo** *a* sacrosanct

sacudi|da *f* shake; (*movimiento brusco*) jolt, jerk; (*fig*) shock. ~**da eléctrica** electric shock. ~**r** *vt* shake; (*golpear*) beat; (*ahuyentar*) chase away. ~**rse** *vpr* shake off; (*fig*) get rid of

sádico *a* sadistic. ● *m* sadist

sadismo *m* sadism

saeta *f* arrow; (*de reloj*) hand

safari *m* safari

sagaz *a* shrewd

Sagitario *m* Sagittarius

sagrado *a* sacred, holy. ● *m* sanctuary

Sahara *m*, **Sáhara** /ˈsaxara/ *m* Sahara

sainete *m* short comedy

sal *f* salt

sala *f* room; (*en teatro*) house. ~ **de espectáculos** concert hall, auditorium. ~ **de espera** waiting-room. ~ **de estar** living-room. ~ **de fiestas** nightclub

sala|do *a* salty; (*agua del mar*) salt; (*vivo*) lively; (*encantador*) cute; (*fig*) witty. ~**r** *vt* salt

salario *m* wages

salazón *f* (*carne*) salted meat; (*pescado*) salted fish

salchich|a *f* (pork) sausage. ~**ón** *m* salami

sald|ar *vt* pay (*cuenta*); (*vender*) sell off; (*fig*) settle. ~**o** *m* balance; (*venta*) sale; (*lo que queda*) remnant

salero *m* salt-cellar

salgo *vb véase* **salir**

sali|da *f* departure; (*puerta*) exit, way out; (*de gas, de líquido*) leak; (*de astro*) rising; (*com, posibilidad de venta*) opening; (*chiste*) witty remark; (*fig*) way out. ~**da de emergencia** emergency exit. ~**ente** *a* projecting; (*fig*) outstanding. ~**r** [52] *vi* leave; (*de casa etc*) go out; (*revista etc*) be published; (*resultar*) turn out; (*astro*) rise; (*aparecer*) appear. ~**rse** *vpr* leave; (*recipiente, líquido etc*) leak. ~**r adelante** get by. ~**rse con la suya** get one's own way

saliva *f* saliva

salmo *m* psalm

salm|ón *m* salmon. ~**onete** *m* red mullet

salmuera *f* brine

salón *m* lounge, sitting-room. ~ **de actos** assembly hall. ~ **de fiestas** dancehall

salpica|dero m (auto) dashboard. **~dura** f splash; (acción) splashing. **~r** [7] vt splash; (fig) sprinkle

sals|a f sauce; (para carne asada) gravy; (fig) spice. **~a verde** parsley sauce. **~era** f sauce-boat

salt|amontes m invar grasshopper. **~ar** vt jump (over); (fig) miss out. ● vi jump; (romperse) break; ⟨líquido⟩ spurt out; (desprenderse) come off; ⟨pelota⟩ bounce; (estallar) explode. **~eador** m highwayman. **~ear** vt rob; (culin) sauté. ● vi skip through

saltimbanqui m acrobat

salt|o m jump; (al agua) dive. **~o de agua** waterfall. **~ón** a ⟨ojos⟩ bulging. ● m grasshopper. **a ~os by** jumping; (fig) by leaps and bounds. **de un ~o** with one jump

salud f health; (fig) welfare. ● int cheers! **~able** a healthy

salud|ar vt greet, say hello to; (mil) salute. **~o** m greeting; (mil) salute. **~os** mpl best wishes. **le ~a atentamente** (en cartas) yours faithfully

salva f salvo; (de aplausos) thunders

salvación f salvation

salvado m bran

Salvador m. **El ~** El Salvador

salvaguardia f safeguard

salvaje a ⟨planta, animal⟩ wild; (primitivo) savage. ● m & f savage

salvamanteles m invar table-mat

salva|mento m rescue. **~r** vt save, rescue; (atravesar) cross; (recorrer) travel; (fig) overcome. **~rse** vpr save o.s. **~vidas** m invar lifebelt. **chaleco m ~vidas** life-jacket

salvia f sage

salvo a safe. ● adv & prep except (for). **~ que** unless. **~conducto** m safe-conduct. **a ~** out of danger. **poner a ~** put in a safe place

samba f samba

San a Saint, St. **~ Miguel** St Michael

sana|r vt cure. ● vi recover. **~torio** m sanatorium

sanci|ón f sanction. **~onar** vt sanction

sancocho m (LAm) stew

sandalia f sandal

sándalo m sandalwood

sandía f water melon

sandwich /'sambitʃ/ m (pl **sandwichs, sandwiches**) sandwich

sanear vt drain

sangr|ante a bleeding; (fig) flagrant. **~ar** vt/i bleed. **~e** f blood. **a ~e fría** in cold blood

sangría f (bebida) sangria

sangriento a bloody

sangu|ijuela f leech. **~íneo** a blood

san|idad f health. **~itario** a sanitary. **~o** a healthy; (seguro) sound. **~o y salvo** safe and sound. **cortar por lo ~o** settle things once and for all

santiamén m. **en un ~** in an instant

sant|idad f sanctity. **~ificar** [7] vt sanctify. **~iguar** [15] vt make the sign of the cross over. **~iguarse** vpr cross o.s. **~o** a holy; (delante de nombre) Saint, St. ● m saint; (día) saint's day, name day. **~uario** m sanctuary. **~urrón** a sanctimonious, hypocritical

sañ|a f fury; (crueldad) cruelty. **~oso** a, **~udo** a furious

sapo m toad; (bicho, fam) small animal, creature

saque m (en tenis) service; (en fútbol) throw-in; (inicial en fútbol) kick-off

saque|ar vt loot. **~o** m looting

sarampión m measles

sarape m (Mex) blanket

sarc|asmo m sarcasm. **~ástico** a sarcastic

sardana f Catalonian dance

sardina f sardine

sardo a & m Sardinian

sardónico a sardonic

sargento m sergeant

sarmiento m vine shoot

sarpullido m rash

sarta f string

sartén f frying-pan (Brit), fry-pan (Amer)

sastre m tailor. **~ría** f tailoring; (tienda) tailor's (shop)

Satanás m Satan

satánico a satanic

satélite m satellite

satinado a shiny

sátira f satire

satírico a satirical. ● m satirist

satisf|acción f satisfaction. **~acer** [31] vt satisfy; (pagar) pay; (gustar) please; meet ⟨gastos, requisitos⟩. **~acerse** vpr satisfy o.s.; (vengarse) take revenge. **~actorio** a satisfactory. **~echo** a satisfied. **~echo de sí mismo** smug

satura|ción f saturation. **~r** vt saturate

Saturno m Saturn

sauce m willow. **~ llorón** weeping willow

saúco *m* elder
savia *f* sap
sauna *f* sauna
saxofón *m*, **saxófono** *m* saxophone
saz|ón *f* ripeness; (*culin*) seasoning. ~**onado** *a* ripe; (*culin*) seasoned. ~**onar** *vt* ripen; (*culin*) season. **en** ~**ón** in season
se *pron* (*él*) him; (*ella*) her; (*Vd*) you; (*reflexivo*, *él*) himself; (*reflexivo*, *ella*) herself; (*reflexivo*, *ello*) itself; (*reflexivo*, *uno*) oneself; (*reflexivo*, *Vd*) yourself; (*reflexivo*, *ellos*, *ellas*) themselves; (*reflexivo*, *Vds*) yourselves; (*recíproco*) (to) each other. ~ **dice** people say, they say, it is said (que that). ~ **habla español** Spanish spoken
sé *vb véase* **saber** *y* **ser**
sea *vb véase* **ser**
sebo *m* tallow; (*culin*) suet
seca|dor *m* drier; (*de pelo*) hairdrier. ~**nte** *a* drying. ● *m* blotting-paper. ~**r** [7] *vt* dry. ~**rse** *vpr* dry; ⟨*río etc*⟩ dry up; ⟨*persona*⟩ dry o.s.
sección *f* section
seco *a* dry; ⟨*frutos*, *flores*⟩ dried; (*flaco*) thin; ⟨*respuesta*⟩ curt; (*escueto*) plain. **a secas** just. **en** ~ (*bruscamente*) suddenly. **lavar en** ~ dry-clean
secre|ción *f* secretion. ~**tar** *vt* secrete
secretar|ía *f* secretariat. ~**io** *m* secretary
secreto *a* & *m* secret
secta *f* sect. ~**rio** *a* sectarian
sector *m* sector
secuela *f* consequence
secuencia *f* sequence
secuestr|ar *vt* confiscate; kidnap ⟨*persona*⟩; hijack ⟨*avión*⟩. ~**o** *m* seizure; (*de persona*) kidnapping; (*de avión*) hijack(ing)
secular *a* secular
secundar *vt* second, help. ~**io** *a* secondary
sed *f* thirst. ● *vb véase* **ser**. **tener** ~ be thirsty. **tener** ~ **de** (*fig*) be hungry for
seda *f* silk
sedante *a* & *m*, **sedativo** *a* & *m* sedative
sede *f* seat; (*relig*) see
sedentario *a* sedentary
sedici|ón *f* sedition. ~**oso** *a* seditious
sediento *a* thirsty

sediment|ar *vi* deposit. ~**arse** *vpr* settle. ~**o** *m* sediment
seduc|ción *f* seduction. ~**ir** [47] *vt* seduce; (*atraer*) attract. ~**tor** *a* seductive. ● *m* seducer
sega|dor *m* harvester. ~**dora** *f* harvester, mower. ~**r** [1 & 12] *vt* reap
seglar *a* secular. ● *m* layman
segmento *m* segment
segoviano *m* person from Segovia
segrega|ción *f* segregation. ~**r** [12] *vt* segregate
segui|da *f*. **en** ~**da** immediately. ~**do** *a* continuous; (*en plural*) consecutive. ● *adv* straight; (*después*) after. **todo** ~**do** straight ahead. ~**dor** *a* following. ● *m* follower. ~**r** [5 & 13] *vt* follow (*continuar*) continue
según *prep* according to. ● *adv* it depends; (*a medida que*) as
segundo *a* second. ● *m* second; (*culin*) second course
segur|amente *adv* certainly; (*muy probablemente*) surely. ~**idad** *f* safety; (*certeza*) certainty; (*aplomo*) confidence. ~**idad en sí mismo** self-confidence. ~**idad social** social security. ~**o** *a* safe; (*cierto*) certain, sure; (*firme*) secure; (*de fiar*) reliable. ● *adv* for certain. ● *m* insurance; (*dispositivo de seguridad*) safety device. ~**o de sí mismo** self-confident. ~**o de terceros** third-party insurance
seis *a* & *m* six. ~**cientos** *a* & *m* six hundred
seísmo *m* earthquake
selec|ción *f* selection. ~**cionar** *vt* select, choose. ~**tivo** *a* selective. ~**to** *a* selected; (*fig*) choice
selva *f* forest; (*jungla*) jungle
sell|ar *vt* stamp; (*cerrar*) seal. ~**o** *m* stamp; (*en documento oficial*) seal; (*fig*, *distintivo*) hallmark
semáforo *m* semaphore; (*auto*) traffic lights; (*rail*) signal
semana *f* week. ~**l** *a* weekly. ~**rio** *a* & *m* weekly. **S**~ **Santa** Holy Week
semántic|a *f* semantics. ~**o** *a* semantic
semblante *m* face; (*fig*) look
sembrar [1] *vt* sow; (*fig*) scatter
semeja|nte *a* similar; (*tal*) such. ● *m* fellow man; (*cosa*) equal. ~**nza** *f* similarity. ~**r** *vi* seem. ~**rse** *vpr* look alike. **a** ~**nza de** like. **tener** ~**nza con** resemble

semen *m* semen. **∿tal** *a* stud. ● *m* stud animal

semestr|al *a* half-yearly. **∿e** *m* six months

semibreve *m* semibreve (*Brit*), whole note (*Amer*)

semic|ircular *a* semicircular. **∿írculo** *m* semicircle

semicorchea *f* semiquaver (*Brit*), sixteenth note (*Amer*)

semifinal *f* semifinal

semill|a *f* seed. **∿ero** *m* nursery; (*fig*) hotbed

seminario *m* (*univ*) seminar; (*relig*) seminary

sem|ita *a* Semitic. ● *m* Semite. **∿ítico** *a* Semitic

sémola *f* semolina

senado *m* senate; (*fig*) assembly. **∿r** *m* senator

sencill|ez *f* simplicity. **∿o** *a* simple; (*uno solo*) single

senda *f*, **sendero** *m* path

sendos *apl* each

seno *m* bosom. **∿ materno** womb

sensaci|ón *f* sensation. **∿onal** *a* sensational

sensat|ez *f* good sense. **∿o** *a* sensible

sensi|bilidad *f* sensibility. **∿ble** *a* sensitive; (*notable*) notable; (*lamentable*) lamentable. **∿tivo** *a* ⟨*órgano*⟩ sense

sensual *a* sensual. **∿idad** *f* sensuality

senta|do *a* sitting (down). **dar algo por ∿do** take something for granted. **∿r** [1] *vt* place; (*establecer*) establish. ● *vi* suit; (*de medidas*) fit; ⟨*comida*⟩ agree with. **∿rse** *vpr* sit (down); ⟨*sedimento*⟩ settle

sentencia *f* saying; (*jurid*) sentence. **∿r** *vt* sentence

sentido *a* deeply felt; (*sincero*) sincere; (*sensible*) sensitive. ● *m* sense; (*dirección*) direction. **∿ común** common sense. **∿ del humor** sense of humour. **∿ único** one-way. **doble ∿** double meaning. **no tener ∿** not make sense. **perder el ∿** faint. **sin ∿** unconscious; ⟨*cosa*⟩ senseless

sentim|ental *a* sentimental. **∿iento** *m* feeling; (*sentido*) sense; (*pesar*) regret

sentir [4] *vt* feel; (*oír*) hear; (*lamentar*) be sorry for. ● *vi* feel; (*lamentarse*) be sorry. ● *m* (*opinión*) opinion. **∿se** *vpr* feel. **lo siento** I'm sorry

seña *f* sign. **∿s** *fpl* (*dirección*) address; (*descripción*) description

señal *f* sign; (*rail etc*) signal; (*telefónico*) tone; (*com*) deposit. **∿ado** *a* notable. **∿ar** *vt* signal; (*poner señales en*) mark; (*apuntar*) point out; ⟨*manecilla, aguja*⟩ point to; (*determinar*) fix. **∿arse** *vpr* stand out. **dar ∿es de** show signs of. **en ∿ de** as a token of

señero *a* alone; (*sin par*) unique

señor *m* man; (*caballero*) gentleman; (*delante de nombre propio*) Mr; (*tratamiento directo*) sir. **∿a** *f* lady, woman; (*delante de nombre propio*) Mrs; (*esposa*) wife; (*tratamiento directo*) madam. **∿ial** *a* ⟨*casa*⟩ stately. **∿ita** *f* young lady; (*delante de nombre propio*) Miss; (*tratamiento directo*) miss. **∿ito** *m* young gentleman. **el ∿ alcalde** the mayor. **el ∿** Mr. **muy ∿ mío** Dear Sir. **¡no ∿!** certainly not! **ser ∿ de** be master of, control

señuelo *m* lure

sepa *vb véase* **saber**

separa|ción *f* separation. **∿do** *a* separate. **∿r** *vt* separate; (*apartar*) move away; (*de empleo*) dismiss. **∿rse** *vpr* separate; ⟨*amigos*⟩ part. **∿tista** *a* & *m* & *f* separatist. **por ∿do** separately

septentrional *a* north(ern)

séptico *a* septic

septiembre *m* September

séptimo *a* seventh

sepulcro *m* sepulchre

sepult|ar *vt* bury. **∿ura** *f* burial; (*tumba*) grave. **∿urero** *m* gravedigger

sequ|edad *f* dryness. **∿ía** *f* drought

séquito *m* entourage; (*fig*) aftermath

ser [39] *vi* be. ● *m* being. **∿ de** made of; (*provenir de*) come from; (*pertenecer a*) belong to. **∿ humano** human being. **a no ∿ que** unless. **¡así sea!** so be it! **es más** what is more. **lo que sea** anything. **no sea que, no vaya a ∿ que** in case. **o sea** in other words. **sea lo que fuere** be that as it may. **sea... sea** either... or. **siendo así que** since. **soy yo** it's me

seren|ar *vt* calm down. **∿arse** *vpr* calm down; ⟨*tiempo*⟩ clear up. **∿ata** *f* serenade. **∿idad** *f* serenity. **∿o** *a* ⟨*cielo*⟩ clear; ⟨*tiempo*⟩ fine; (*fig*) calm. ● *m* night watchman. **al ∿o** in the open

seri|al *m* serial. ~**e** *f* series. **fuera de**
~**e** (*fig, extraordinario*) special.
producción f en ~ mass production

seri|edad *f* seriousness. ~**o** *a* serious; (*confiable*) reliable. **en** ~**o** seriously. **poco** ~**o** frivolous

sermón *m* sermon

serp|enteante *a* winding. ~**entear**
vi wind. ~**iente** *f* snake. ~**iente de**
cascabel rattlesnake

serrano *a* mountain; ⟨*jamón*⟩ cured

serr|ar [1] *vt* saw. ~**ín** *m* sawdust.
~**ucho** *m* (hand)saw

servi|cial *a* helpful. ~**cio** *m* service;
(*conjunto*) set; (*aseo*) toilet. ~**cio a**
domicilio delivery service. ~**dor** *m*
servant. ~**dumbre** *f* servitude; (*criados*) servants, staff. ~**l** *a* servile.
su (**seguro**) ~**dor** (*en cartas*) yours
faithfully

servilleta *f* serviette, (table) napkin

servir [5] *vt* serve; (*ayudar*) help; (*en*
restaurante) wait on. ● *vi* serve; (*ser*
útil) be of use. ~**se** *vpr* help o.s. ~**se**
de use. **no** ~ **de nada** be useless.
para ~**le** at your service. **sírvase**
sentarse please sit down

sesear *vi* pronounce the Spanish *c*
as an *s*

sesent|a *a & m* sixty. ~**ón** *a & m*
sixty-year-old

seseo *m* pronunciation of the Spanish *c* as an *s*

sesg|ado *a* slanting. ~**o** *m* slant;
(*fig, rumbo*) turn

sesión *f* session; (*en el cine*) showing;
(*en el teatro*) performance

ses|o *m* brain; (*fig*) brains. ~**udo** *a*
inteligent; (*sensato*) sensible

seta *f* mushroom

sete|cientos *a & m* seven hundred.
~**nta** *a & m* seventy. ~**ntón** *a & m*
seventy-year-old

setiembre *m* September

seto *m* fence; (*de plantas*) hedge. ~
vivo hedge

seudo... *pref* pseudo...

seudónimo *m* pseudonym

sever|idad *f* severity. ~**o** *a* severe;
⟨*disciplina, profesor etc*⟩ strict

Sevilla *f* Seville

sevillan|as *fpl* popular dance from
Seville. ~**o** *m* person from Seville

sexo *m* sex

sext|eto *m* sextet. ~**o** *a* sixth

sexual *a* sexual. ~**idad** *f* sexuality

si *m* (*mus*) B; (*solfa*) te. ● *conj* if;
(*dubitativo*) whether. ~ **no** or else.
por ~ (**acaso**) in case

sí *pron reflexivo* (*él*) himself; (*ella*)
herself; (*ello*) itself; (*uno*) oneself;
(*Vd*) yourself; (*ellos, ellas*) themselves; (*Vds*) yourselves; (*recíproco*)
each other

sí *adv* yes. ● *m* consent

Siamés *a & m* Siamese

Sicilia *f* Sicily

sida *m* Aids

siderurgia *f* iron and steel industry

sidra *f* cider

siega *f* harvesting; (*época*) harvest
time

siembra *f* sowing; (*época*) sowing
time

siempre *adv* always. ~ **que** if. **como**
~ as usual. **de** ~ (*acostumbrado*)
usual. **lo de** ~ the same old story.
para ~ for ever

sien *f* temple

siento *vb véase* **sentar** *y* **sentir**

sierra *f* saw; (*cordillera*) mountain
range

siervo *m* slave

siesta *f* siesta

siete *a & m* seven

sífilis *f* syphilis

sifón *m* U-bend; (*de soda*) syphon

sigilo *m* secrecy

sigla *f* initials, abbreviation

siglo *m* century; (*época*) time, age;
(*fig, mucho tiempo, fam*) ages; (*fig,*
mundo) world

significa|ción *f* meaning; (*importancia*) significance. ~**do** *a* (*conocido*) well-known. ● *m* meaning.
~**r** [7] *vt* mean; (*expresar*) express.
~**rse** *vpr* stand out. ~**tivo** *a*
significant

signo *m* sign. ~ **de admiración**
exclamation mark. ~ **de interrogación** question mark

sigo *vb véase* **seguir**

siguiente *a* following, next. **lo** ~ the
following

sílaba *f* syllable

silb|ar *vt/i* whistle. ~**ato** *m*, ~**ido** *m*
whistle

silenci|ador *m* silencer. ~**ar** *vt* hush
up. ~**o** *m* silence. ~**oso** *a* silent

sílfide *f* sylph

silicio *m* silicon

silo *m* silo

silueta *f* silhouette; (*dibujo*) outline

silvestre *a* wild

sill|a *f* chair; (*de montar*) saddle;
(*relig*) see. ~**a de ruedas** wheelchair. ~**ín** *m* saddle. ~**ón** *m*
armchair

simb|ólico *a* symbolic(al). **~olismo** *m* symbolism. **~olizar** [10] *vt* symbolize

símbolo *m* symbol

sim|etría *f* symmetry. **~étrico** *a* symmetric(al)

simiente *f* seed

similar *a* similar

simp|atía *f* liking; (*cariño*) affection; (*fig, amigo*) friend. **~ático** *a* nice, likeable; (*amable*) kind. **~atizante** *m & f* sympathizer. **~atizar** [10] *vi* get on (well together). **me es ~ático** I like

simpl|e *a* simple; (*mero*) mere. **~eza** *f* simplicity; (*tontería*) stupid thing; (*insignificancia*) trifle. **~icidad** *f* simplicity. **~ificar** [7] *vt* simplify. **~ón** *m* simpleton

simposio *m* symposium

simula|ción *f* simulation. **~r** *vt* feign

simultáneo *a* simultaneous

sin *prep* without. **~ que** without

sinagoga *f* synagogue

sincer|idad *f* sincerity. **~o** *a* sincere

síncopa *f* (*mus*) syncopation

sincopar *vt* syncopate

sincronizar [10] *vt* synchronize

sindica|l *a* (trade-)union. **~lista** *m & f* trade-unionist. **~to** *m* trade union

síndrome *m* syndrome

sinfín *m* endless number

sinf|onía *f* symphony. **~ónico** *a* symphonic

singular *a* singular; (*excepcional*) exceptional. **~izar** [10] *vt* single out. **~izarse** *vpr* stand out

siniestro *a* sinister; (*desgraciado*) unlucky. ● *m* disaster

sinnúmero *m* endless number

sino *m* fate. ● *conj* but; (*salvo*) except

sínodo *m* synod

sinónimo *a* synonymous. ● *m* synonym

sinrazón *f* wrong

sintaxis *f* syntax

síntesis *f invar* synthesis

sint|ético *a* synthetic. **~etizar** [10] *vt* synthesize; (*resumir*) summarize

síntoma *f* sympton

sintomático *a* symptomatic

sinton|ía *f* (*en la radio*) signature tune. **~izar** [10] *vt* (*con la radio*) tune (in)

sinuoso *a* winding

sinvergüenza *m & f* scoundrel

sionis|mo *m* Zionism. **~ta** *m & f* Zionist

siquiera *conj* even if. ● *adv* at least. **ni ~** not even

sirena *f* siren

Siria *f* Syria

sirio *a & m* Syrian

siroco *m* sirocco

sirvienta *f*, **sirviente** *m* servant

sirvo *vb véase* **servir**

sise|ar *vt/i* hiss. **~o** *m* hissing

sísmico *a* seismic

sismo *m* earthquake

sistem|a *m* system. **~ático** *a* systematic. **por ~a** as a rule

sitiar *vt* besiege; (*fig*) surround

sitio *m* place; (*espacio*) space; (*mil*) siege. **en cualquier ~** anywhere

situa|ción *f* position. **~r** [21] *vt* situate; (*poner*) put; (*depositar*) deposit. **~rse** *vpr* be successful, establish o.s.

slip /es'lip/ *m* (*pl* **slips** /es'lip/) underpants, briefs

slogan /es'logan/ *m* (*pl* **slogans** /es'logan/) slogan

smoking /es'mokin/ *m* (*pl* **smokings** /es'mokin/) dinner jacket (*Brit*), tuxedo (*Amer*)

sobaco *m* armpit

sobar *vt* handle; knead ‹*masa*›

soberan|ía *f* sovereignty. **~o** *a* sovereign; (*fig*) supreme. ● *m* sovereign

soberbi|a *f* pride; (*altanería*) arrogance. **~o** *a* proud; (*altivo*) arrogant

soborn|ar *vt* bribe. **~o** *m* bribe

sobra *f* surplus. **~s** *fpl* leftovers. **~do** *a* more than enough. **~nte** *a* surplus. **~r** *vi* be left over; (*estorbar*) be in the way. **de ~** more than enough

sobrasada *f* Majorcan sausage

sobre *prep* on; (*encima de*) on top of; (*más o menos*) about; (*por encima de*) above; (*sin tocar*) over; (*además de*) on top of. ● *m* envelope. **~cargar** [12] *vt* overload. **~coger** [14] *vt* startle. **~cogerse** *vpr* be startled. **~cubierta** *f* dust cover. **~dicho** *a* aforementioned. **~entender** [1] *vt* understand, infer. **~entendido** *a* implicit. **~humano** *a* superhuman. **~llevar** *vt* bear. **~mesa** *f*. **de ~mesa** after-dinner. **~natural** *a* supernatural. **~nombre** *m* nickname. **~pasar** *vt* exceed. **~poner** [34] *vt* superimpose; (*fig, anteponer*) put before. **~ponerse** *vpr* overcome. **~pujar** *vt* surpass. **~saliente** *a* (*fig*) outstanding. ● *m* excellent mark. **~salir** [52] *vi* stick out;

(*fig*) stand out. ∼**saltar** *vt* startle.
∼**salto** *m* fright. ∼**sueldo** *m* bonus.
∼**todo** *m* overall; (*abrigo*)
overcoat. ∼ **todo** above all, especially. ∼**venir** [53] *vi* happen. ∼**viviente** *a* surviving. ● *m* & *f*
survivor. ∼**vivir** *vi* survive. ∼**volar**
vt fly over

sobriedad *f* restraint
sobrin|a *f* niece. ∼**o** *m* nephew
sobrio *a* moderate, sober
socarr|ón *a* sarcastic; (*taimado*) sly.
∼**onería** *f* sarcasm
socavar *vt* undermine
soci|able *a* sociable. ∼**al** *a* social.
∼**aldemocracia** *f* social democracy.
∼**aldemócrata** *m* & *f* social democrat. ∼**alismo** *m* socialsim. ∼**alista** *a* & *m* & *f* socialist. ∼**alizar** [10] *vt* nationalize. ∼**edad** *f* society; (*com*)
company. ∼**edad anónima** limited
company. ∼**o** *m* member; (*com*)
partner. ∼**ología** *f* sociology. ∼**ólogo** *m* sociologist
socorr|er *vt* help. ∼**o** *m* help
soda *f* (*bebida*) soda (water)
sodio *m* sodium
sofá *m* sofa, settee
sofistica|ción *f* sophistication. ∼**do**
a sophisticated. ∼**r** [7] *vt* adulterate
sofoca|ción *f* suffocation. ∼**nte** *a*
(*fig*) stifling. ∼**r** [7] *vt* suffocate; (*fig*)
stifle. ∼**rse** *vpr* suffocate; (*ruborizarse*) blush
soga *f* rope
soja *f* soya (bean)
sojuzgar [12] *vt* subdue
sol *m* sun; (*luz solar*) sunlight; (*mus*)
G; (*solfa*) soh. **al** ∼ in the sun. **día** *m*
de ∼ sunny day. **hace** ∼, **hay** ∼ it is
sunny. **tomar el** ∼ sunbathe
solamente *adv* only
solapa *f* lapel; (*de bolsillo etc*) flap.
∼**do** *a* sly. ∼**r** *vt/i* overlap
solar *a* solar. ● *m* plot
solariego *a* (*casa*) ancestral
solaz *m* relaxation
soldado *m* soldier. ∼ **raso** private
solda|dor *m* welder; (*utensilio*) soldering iron. ∼**r** [2] *vt* weld, solder
solea|do *a* sunny. ∼**r** *vt* put in the
sun
soledad *f* solitude; (*aislamiento*)
loneliness
solemn|e *a* solemn. ∼**idad** *f* solemnity; (*ceremonia*) ceremony
soler [2] *vi* be in the habit of. **suele
despertarse a las 6** he usually
wakes up at 6 o'clock

sol|icitar *vt* request; apply for (*empleo*); attract (*atención*). ∼**icito** *a*
solicitous. ∼**icitud** *f* (*atención*) concern; (*petición*) request; (*para un
puesto*) application
solidaridad *f* solidarity
solid|ez *f* solidity; (*de color*) fastness.
∼**ificar** [7] *vt* solidify. ∼**ificarse** *vpr*
solidify
sólido *a* solid; (*color*) fast; (*robusto*)
strong. ● *m* solid
soliloquio *m* soliloquy
solista *m* & *f* soloist
solitario *a* solitary; (*aislado*) lonely.
● *m* recluse; (*juego, diamante*)
solitaire
solo *a* (*sin compañía*) alone; (*aislado*) lonely; (*único*) only; (*mus*)
solo; (*café*) black. ● *m* solo; (*juego*)
solitaire. **a solas** alone
sólo *adv* only. ∼ **que** only. **aunque**
∼ **sea** even if it is only. **con** ∼ **que**
if; (*con tal que*) as long as. **no** ∼...
sino también not only... but also...
tan ∼ only
solomillo *m* sirloin
solsticio *m* solstice
soltar [2] *vt* let go of; (*dejar caer*)
drop; (*dejar salir, decir*) let out; give
(*golpe etc*). ∼**se** *vpr* come undone;
(*librarse*) break loose
solter|a *f* single woman. ∼**o** *a* single.
● *m* bachelor. **apellido** *m* **de** ∼**a**
maiden name
soltura *f* looseness; (*agilidad*) agility; (*en hablar*) ease, fluency
solu|ble *a* soluble. ∼**ción** *f* solution.
∼**cionar** *vt* solve; settle (*huelga,
asunto*)
solvent|ar *vt* resolve; settle (*deuda*).
∼**e** *a* & *m* solvent
sollo *m* sturgeon
solloz|ar [10] *vi* sob. ∼**o** *m* sob
sombr|a *f* shade; (*imagen oscura*)
shadow. ∼**eado** *a* shady. **a la** ∼**a** in
the shade
sombrero *m* hat. ∼ **hongo** bowler
hat
sombrío *a* sombre
somero *a* shallow
someter *vt* subdue; subject (*persona*); (*presentar*) submit. ∼**se** *vpr*
give in
somn|oliento *a* sleepy. ∼**ífero** *m*
sleeping-pill
somos *vb véase* **ser**
son *m* sound. ● *vb véase* **ser**
sonámbulo *m* sleepwalker

sonar [2] *vt* blow; ring ‹*timbre*›. ● *vi* sound; ‹*timbre, teléfono etc*› ring; ‹*reloj*› strike; (*pronunciarse*) be pronounced; (*mus*) play; (*fig, ser conocido*) be familiar. **~se** *vpr* blow one's nose. **~ a** sound like

sonata *f* sonata

sonde|ar *vt* sound; (*fig*) sound out. **~o** *m* sounding; (*fig*) poll

soneto *m* sonnet

sónico *a* sonic

sonido *m* sound

sonoro *a* sonorous; (*ruidoso*) loud

sonr|eír [51] *vi* smile. **~eírse** *vpr* smile. **~iente** *a* smiling. **~isa** *f* smile

sonroj|ar *vt* make blush. **~arse** *vpr* blush. **~o** *m* blush

sonrosado *a* rosy, pink

sonsacar [7] *vt* wheedle out

soñ|ado *a* dream. **~ador** *m* dreamer. **~ar** [2] *vi* dream (**con** of). **¡ni ~arlo!** not likely! (**que) ni ~ado** marvellous

sopa *f* soup

sopesar *vt* (*fig*) weigh up

sopl|ar *vt* blow; blow out ‹*vela*›; blow off ‹*polvo*›; (*inflar*) blow up. ● *vi* blow. **~ete** *m* blowlamp. **~o** *m* puff; (*fig, momento*) moment

soporífero *a* soporific. ● *m* sleeping-pill

soport|al *m* porch. **~ales** *mpl* arcade. **~ar** *vt* support; (*fig*) bear. **~e** *m* support

soprano *f* soprano

sor *f* sister

sorb|er *vt* suck; sip ‹*bebida*›; (*absorber*) absorb. **~ete** *m* sorbet, water-ice. **~o** *m* swallow; (*pequeña cantidad*) sip

sord|amente *adv* silently, dully. **~era** *f* deafness

sórdido *a* squalid; (*tacaño*) mean

sordo *a* deaf; (*silencioso*) quiet. ● *m* deaf person. **~mudo** *a* deaf and dumb. **a la sorda, a sordas** on the quiet. **hacerse el ~** turn a deaf ear

sorna *f* sarcasm. **con ~** sarcastically

soroche *m* (*LAm*) mountain sickness

sorpre|ndente *a* surprising. **~nder** *vt* surprise; (*coger desprevenido*) catch. **~sa** *f* surprise

sorte|ar *vt* draw lots for; (*rifar*) raffle; (*fig*) avoid. ● *vi* draw lots; (*con moneda*) toss up. **~o** *m* draw; (*rifa*) raffle; (*fig*) avoidance

sortija *f* ring; (*de pelo*) ringlet

sortilegio *m* witchcraft; (*fig*) spell

sos|egado *a* calm. **~egar** [1 & 12] *vt* calm. ● *vi* rest. **~iego** *m* calmness. **con ~iego** calmly

soslayo. al ~, de ~ sideways

soso *a* tasteless; (*fig*) dull

sospech|a *f* suspicion. **~ar** *vt/i* suspect. **~oso** *a* suspicious. ● *m* suspect

sost|én *m* support; (*prenda femenina*) bra (*fam*), brassière. **~ener** [40] *vt* support; (*sujetar*) hold; (*mantener*) maintain; (*alimentar*) sustain. **~enerse** *vpr* support o.s.; (*continuar*) remain. **~enido** *a* sustained; (*mus*) sharp. ● *m* (*mus*) sharp

sota *f* (*de naipes*) jack

sótano *m* basement

sotavento *m* lee

soto *m* grove; (*matorral*) thicket

soviético *a* (*historia*) Soviet

soy *vb véase* **ser**

Sr *abrev* (*Señor*) Mr. **~a** *abrev* (*Señora*) Mrs. **~ta** *abrev* (*Señorita*) Miss

su *a* (*de él*) his; (*de ella*) her; (*de ello*) its; (*de uno*) one's; (*de Vd*) your; (*de ellos, de ellas*) their; (*de Vds*) your

suav|e *a* smooth; (*fig*) gentle; ‹*color, sonido*› soft. **~idad** *f* smoothness, softness. **~izar** [10] *vt* smooth, soften

subalimentado *a* underfed

subalterno *a* secondary; ‹*persona*› auxiliary

subarrendar [1] *vt* sublet

subasta *f* auction; (*oferta*) tender. **~r** *vt* auction

sub|campeón *m* runner-up. **~consciencia** *f* subconscious. **~consciente** *a* & *m* subconscious. **~continente** *m* subcontinent. **~desarrollado** *a* under-developed. **~director** *m* assistant manager

súbdito *m* subject

sub|dividir *vt* subdivide. **~estimar** *vt* underestimate. **~gerente** *m* & *f* assistant manager

subi|da *f* ascent; (*aumento*) rise; (*pendiente*) slope. **~do** *a* ‹*precio*› high; ‹*color*› bright; ‹*olor*› strong. **~r** *vt* go up; (*poner*) put; (*llevar*) take up; (*aumentar*) increase. ● *vi* go up. **~r a** get into ‹*coche*›; get on ‹*autobús, avión, barco, tren*›; (*aumentar*) increase. **~rse** *vpr* climb up. **~rse a** get on ‹*tren etc*›

súbito *a* sudden. ● *adv* suddenly. **de ~** suddenly

subjetivo *a* subjective
subjuntivo *a* & *m* subjunctive
subleva|ción *f* uprising. **~r** *vt* incite to rebellion. **~rse** *vpr* rebel
sublim|ar *vt* sublimate. **~e** *a* sublime
submarino *a* underwater. ● *m* submarine
subordinado *a* & *m* subordinate
subrayar *vt* underline
subrepticio *a* surreptitious
subsanar *vt* remedy; overcome ⟨dificultad⟩
subscri|bir *vt* (*pp* **subscrito**) sign. **~birse** *vpr* subscribe. **~pción** *f* subscription
subsidi|ario *a* subsidiary. **~o** *m* subsidy. **~o de paro** unemployment benefit
subsiguiente *a* subsequent
subsist|encia *f* subsistence. **~ir** *vi* subsist; (*perdurar*) survive
substanci|a *f* substance. **~al** *a* important. **~oso** *a* substantial
substantivo *m* noun
substitu|ción *f* substitution. **~ir** [17] *vt/i* substitute. **~to** *a* & *m* substitute
substraer [41] *vt* take away
subterfugio *m* subterfuge
subterráneo *a* underground. ● *m* (*bodega*) cellar; (*conducto*) underground passage
subtítulo *m* subtitle
suburb|ano *a* suburban. ● *m* suburban train. **~io** *m* suburb; (*en barrio pobre*) slum
subvenci|ón *f* grant. **~onar** *vt* subsidize
subver|sión *f* subversion. **~sivo** *a* subversive. **~tir** [4] *vt* subvert
subyugar [12] *vt* subjugate; (*fig*) subdue
succión *f* suction
suce|der *vi* happen; (*seguir*) follow; (*substituir*) succeed. **~dido** *m* event. **lo ~dido** what happened. **~sión** *f* succession. **~sivo** *a* successive; (*consecutivo*) consecutive. **~so** *m* event; (*incidente*) incident. **~sor** *m* successor. **en lo ~sivo** in future. **lo que ~de es que** the trouble is that. **¿qué ~de?** what's the matter?
suciedad *f* dirt; (*estado*) dirtiness
sucinto *a* concise; ⟨prenda⟩ scanty
sucio *a* dirty; (*vil*) mean; ⟨conciencia⟩ guilty. **en ~** in rough

sucre *m* (*unidad monetaria del Ecuador*) sucre
suculento *a* succulent
sucumbir *vi* succumb
sucursal *f* branch (office)
Sudáfrica *m* & *f* South Africa
sudafricano *a* & *m* South African
Sudamérica *f* South America
sudamericano *a* & *m* South American
sudar *vt* work hard for. ● *vi* sweat
sud|este *m* south-east; (*viento*) south-east wind. **~oeste** *m* south-west; (*viento*) south-west wind
sudor *m* sweat
Suecia *f* Sweden
sueco *a* Swedish. ● *m* (*persona*) Swede; (*lengua*) Swedish. **hacerse el ~** pretend not to hear
suegr|a *f* mother-in-law. **~o** *m* father-in-law. **mis ~os** my in-laws
suela *f* sole
sueldo *m* salary
suelo *m* ground; (*dentro de edificio*) floor; (*tierra*) land. *vb véase* **soler**
suelto *a* loose; (*libre*) free; (*sin pareja*) odd; ⟨lenguaje⟩ fluent. ● *m* (*en periódico*) item; (*dinero*) change
sueño *m* sleep; (*ilusión*) dream. **tener ~** be sleepy
suero *m* serum; (*de leche*) whey
suerte *f* luck; (*destino*) fate; (*azar*) chance. **de otra ~** otherwise. **de ~ que** so. **echar ~s** draw lots. **por ~** fortunately. **tener ~** be lucky
suéter *m* jersey
suficien|cia *f* sufficiency; (*presunción*) smugness; (*aptitud*) suitability. **~te** *a* sufficient; (*presumido*) smug. **~temente** *adv* enough
sufijo *m* suffix
sufragio *m* (*voto*) vote
sufri|do *a* ⟨persona⟩ long-suffering; ⟨tela⟩ hard-wearing. **~miento** *m* suffering. **~r** *vt* suffer; (*experimentar*) undergo; (*soportar*) bear. ● *vi* suffer
suge|rencia *f* suggestion. **~rir** [4] *vt* suggest. **~stión** *f* suggestion. **~stionable** *a* impressionable. **~stionar** *vt* influence. **~stivo** *a* (*estimulante*) stimulating; (*atractivo*) attractive
suicid|a *a* suicidal. ● *m* & *f* suicide; (*fig*) maniac. **~arse** *vpr* commit suicide. **~io** *m* suicide
Suiza *f* Switzerland
suizo *a* Swiss. ● *m* Swiss; (*bollo*) bun

suje|ción f subjection. **∼tador** m fastener; (de pelo, papeles etc) clip; (prenda femenina) bra (fam), brassière. **∼tapapeles** m invar paperclip. **∼tar** vt fasten; (agarrar) hold; (fig) restrain. **∼tarse** vr subject o.s.; (ajustarse) conform. **∼to** a fastened; (susceptible) subject. ● m individual

sulfamida f sulpha (drug)

sulfúrico a sulphuric

sult|án m sultan. **∼ana** f sultana

suma f sum; (total) total. **en ∼** in short. **∼mente** adv extremely. **∼r** vt add (up); (fig) gather. ● vi add up. **∼rse** vpr. **∼rse a** join in

sumario a brief. ● m summary; (jurid) indictment

sumergi|ble m submarine. ● a submersible. **∼r** [14] vt submerge

sumidero m drain

suministr|ar vt supply. **∼o** m supply; (acción) supplying

sumir vt sink; (fig) plunge

sumis|ión f submission. **∼o** a submissive

sumo a greatest; (supremo) supreme. **a lo ∼** at the most

suntuoso a sumptuous

supe vb véase **saber**

superar vt surpass; (vencer) overcome; (dejar atrás) get past. **∼se** vpr excel o.s.

superchería f swindle

superestructura f superstructure

superfici|al a superficial. **∼e** f surface; (extensión) area. **de ∼e** surface

superfluo a superfluous

superhombre m superman

superintendente m superintendent

superior a superior; (más alto) higher; (mejor) better; (piso etc) upper. ● m superior. **∼idad** f superiority

superlativo a & m superlative

supermercado m supermarket

supersónico a supersonic

superstici|ón f superstition. **∼oso** a superstitious

supervis|ión f supervision. **∼or** m supervisor

superviviente a surviving. ● m & f survivor

suplantar vt supplant

suplement|ario a supplementary. **∼o** m supplement

suplente a & m & f substitute

súplica f entreaty; (petición) request

suplicar [7] vt beg

suplicio m torture

suplir vt make up for; (reemplazar) replace

supo|ner [34] vt suppose; (significar) mean; (costar) cost. **∼sición** f supposition

supositorio m suppository

suprem|acía f supremacy. **∼o** a supreme; (momento etc) critical

supr|esión f suppression. **∼imir** vt suppress; (omitir) omit

supuesto a supposed. ● m assumption. **∼ que** if. **¡por ∼!** of course!

sur m south; (viento) south wind

surc|ar [7] vt plough. **∼o** m furrow; (de rueda) rut; (en la piel) wrinkle

surgir [14] vi spring up; (elevarse) loom up; (aparecer) appear; (dificultad, oportunidad) arise, crop up

surrealis|mo m surrealism. **∼ta** a & m & f surrealist

surti|do a well-stocked; (variado) assorted. ● m assortment, selection. **∼dor** m (de gasolina) petrol pump (Brit), gas pump (Amer). **∼r** vt supply; have (efecto). **∼rse** vpr provide o.s. (de with)

susceptib|ilidad f susceptibility; (sensibilidad) sensitivity. **∼le** a susceptible; (sensible) sensitive

suscitar vt provoke; arouse (curiosidad, interés, sospechas)

suscr... véase **subscr...**

susodicho a aforementioned

suspen|der vt hang (up); (interrumpir) suspend; (univ etc) fail. **∼derse** vpr stop. **∼sión** f suspension. **∼so** a hanging; (pasmado) amazed; (univ etc) failed. ● m fail. **en ∼so** pending

suspicaz a suspicious

suspir|ar vi (persona) whisper; **∼o** m sigh

sust... véase **subst...**

sustent|ación f support. **∼ar** vt support; (alimentar) sustain; (mantener) maintain. **∼o** m support; (alimento) sustenance

susto m fright. **caerse del ∼** be frightened to death

susurr|ar vi (persona) whisper; (agua) murmur; (hojas) rustle. **∼o** m (de persona) whisper; (de agua) murmur; (de hojas) rustle

sutil a fine; (fig) subtle. **∼eza** f fineness; (fig) subtlety

suyo a & pron (de él) his; (de ella) hers; (de ello) its; (de uno) one's; (de Vd) yours; (de ellos, de ellas) theirs;

(de Vds) yours. **un amigo** ~ a friend of his, a friend of theirs, etc

T

taba *f (anat)* ankle-bone; *(juego)* jacks

tabac|alera *f* (state) tobacconist. **~alero** *a* tobacco. **~o** *m* tobacco; *(cigarillos)* cigarettes; *(rapé)* snuff

tabalear *vi* drum (with one's fingers)

Tabasco *m* Tabasco (**P**)

tabern|a *f* bar. **~ero** *m* barman; *(dueño)* landlord

tabernáculo *m* tabernacle

tabique *m* (thin) wall

tabl|a *f* plank; *(de piedra etc)* slab; *(estante)* shelf; *(de vestido)* pleat; *(lista)* list; *(índice)* index; *(en matemática etc)* table. **~ado** *m* platform; *(en el teatro)* stage. **~ao** *m* place where flamenco shows are held. **~as reales** backgammon. **~ero** *m* board. **~ero de mandos** dashboard. **hacer ~a rasa de** disregard

tableta *f* tablet; *(de chocolate)* bar

tabl|illa *f* small board. **~ón** *m* plank. **~ón de anuncios** notice board *(esp Brit)*, bulletin board *(Amer)*

tabú *m* taboo

tabular *vt* tabulate

taburete *m* stool

tacaño *a* mean

tacita *f* small cup

tácito *a* tacit

taciturno *a* taciturn; *(triste)* miserable

taco *m* plug; *(LAm, tacón)* heel; *(de billar)* cue; *(de billetes)* book; *(de lío, fam)* mess; *(Mex, culin)* filled tortilla

tacógrafo *m* tachograph

tacón *m* heel

táctic|a *f* tactics. **~o** *a* tactical

táctil *a* tactile

tacto *m* touch; *(fig)* tact

tacuara *f (Arg)* bamboo

tacurú *m* (small) ant

tacha *f* fault; *(clavo)* tack. **poner ~s a** find fault with. **sin ~** flawless

tachar *vt (borrar)* rub out; *(con raya)* cross out. **~ de** accuse of

tafia *f (LAm)* rum

tafilete *m* morocco

tahúr *m* card-sharp

Tailandia *f* Thailand

tailandés *a & m* Thai

taimado *a* sly

taj|ada *f* slice. **~ante** *a* sharp. **~o** *m* slash; *(fig, trabajo, fam)* job; *(culin)* chopping block. **sacar ~ada** profit

Tajo *m* Tagus

tal *a* such; *(ante sustantivo en singular)* such a. ● *pron (persona)* someone; *(cosa)* such a thing. ● *adv* so; *(de tal manera)* in such a way. **~ como** the way. **~ cual** *(tal como)* the way; *(regular)* fair. **~ para cual** *(fam)* two of a kind. **con ~ que** as long as. **¿qué ~?** how are you? **un ~** a certain

taladr|ar *vt* drill. **~o** *m* drill; *(agujero)* drill hole

talante *m* mood. **de buen ~** willingly

talar *vt* fell; *(fig)* destroy

talco *m* talcum powder

talcualillo *a (fam)* so so

talega *f,* **talego** *m* sack

talento *m* talent

TALGO *m* high-speed train

talismán *m* talisman

tal|ón *m* heel; *(recibo)* counterfoil; *(cheque)* cheque. **~onario** *m* receipt book; *(de cheques)* cheque book

talla *f* carving; *(grabado)* engraving; *(de piedra preciosa)* cutting; *(estatura)* height; *(medida)* size; *(palo)* measuring stick; *(Arg, charla)* gossip. **~do** *a* carved. ● *m* carving. **~dor** *m* engraver

tallarín *m* noodle

talle *m* waist; *(figura)* figure; *(medida)* size

taller *m* workshop; *(de pintor etc)* studio

tallo *m* stem, stalk

tamal *m (LAm)* tamale

tamaño *a (tan grande)* so big a; *(tan pequeño)* so small a. ● *m* size. **de ~ natural** life-size

tambalearse *vpr* ⟨*persona*⟩ stagger; ⟨*cosa*⟩ wobble

también *adv* also, too

tambor *m* drum. **~ del freno** brake drum. **~ilear** *vi* drum

Támesis *m* Thames

tamiz *m* sieve. **~ar** [10] *vt* sieve

tampoco *adv* nor, neither, not either

tampón *m* tampon; *(para entintar)* ink-pad

tan *adv* so. **tan... ~** as... as

tanda *f* group; (*capa*) layer; (*de obreros*) shift

tangente *a & f* tangent

Tánger *m* Tangier

tangible *a* tangible

tango *m* tango

tanque *m* tank; (*camión, barco*) tanker

tante|ar *vt* estimate; (*ensayar*) test; (*fig*) weigh up. ● *vi* score. ~**o** *m* estimate; (*prueba*) test; (*en deportes*) score

tanto *a* (*en singular*) so much; (*en plural*) so many; (*comparación en singular*) as much; (*comparación en plural*) as many. ● *pron* so much; (*en plural*) so many. ● *adv* so much; (*tiempo*) so long. ● *m* certain amount; (*punto*) point; (*gol*) goal. ~ **como** as well as; (*cantidad*) as much as. ~ **más... cuanto que** all the more... because. ~ **si... como si** whether... or. **a** ~**s de** sometime in. **en** ~, **entre** ~ meanwhile. **en** ~ **que** while. **entre** ~ meanwhile. **estar al** ~ **de** be up to date with. **hasta** ~ **que** until. **no es para** ~ it's not as bad as all that. **otro** ~ the same; (*el doble*) as much again. **por (lo)** ~ so. **un** ~ *adv* somewhat

tañer [22] *vt* play

tapa *f* lid; (*de botella*) top; (*de libro*) cover. ~**s** *fpl* savoury snacks

tapacubos *m invar* hub-cap

tapa|dera *f* cover, lid; (*fig*) cover. ~**r** *vt* cover; (*abrigar*) wrap up; (*obturar*) plug; put the top on ‹*botella*›

taparrabo(s) *m invar* loincloth; (*bañador*) swimming-trunks

tapete *m* (*de mesa*) table cover; (*alfombra*) rug

tapia *f* wall. ~**r** *vt* enclose

tapicería *f* tapestry; (*de muebles*) upholstery

tapioca *f* tapioca

tapiz *m* tapestry. ~**ar** [10] *vt* hang with tapestries; upholster ‹*muebles*›

tap|ón *m* stopper; (*corcho*) cork; (*med*) tampon; (*tec*) plug. ~**onazo** *m* pop

taqui|grafía *f* shorthand. ~**ígrafo** *m* shorthand writer

taquill|a *f* ticket office; (*archivador*) filing cabinet; (*fig, dinero*) takings. ~**ero** *m* clerk, ticket seller. ● *a* box-office

tara *f* (*peso*) tare; (*defecto*) defect

taracea *f* marquetry

tarántula *f* tarantula

tararear *vt/i* hum

tarda|nza *f* delay. ~**r** *vi* take; (*mucho tiempo*) take a long time. **a más** ~**r** at the latest. **sin** ~**r** without delay

tard|e *adv* late. ● *f* (*antes del atardecer*) afternoon; (*después del atardecer*) evening. ~**e o temprano** sooner or later. ~**ío** *a* late. **de** ~**e en** ~**e** from time to time. **por la** ~**e** in the afternoon

tardo *a* (*torpe*) slow

tarea *f* task, job

tarifa *f* rate, tariff

tarima *f* platform

tarjeta *f* card. ~ **de crédito** credit card. ~ **postal** postcard

tarro *m* jar

tarta *f* cake; (*torta*) tart. ~ **helada** ice-cream gateau

tartamud|ear *vi* stammer. ~**o** *a* stammering. ● *m* stammerer. **es** ~**o** he stammers

tártaro *m* tartar

tarugo *m* chunk

tasa *f* valuation; (*precio*) fixed price; (*índice*) rate. ~**r** *vt* fix a price for; (*limitar*) ration; (*evaluar*) value

tasca *f* bar

tatarabuel|a *f* great-great-grandmother. ~**o** *m* great-great-grandfather

tatua|je *m* (*acción*) tattooing; (*dibujo*) tattoo. ~**r** [21] *vt* tattoo

taurino *a* bullfighting

Tauro *m* Taurus

tauromaquia *f* bullfighting

tax|i *m* taxi. ~**ímetro** *m* taxi meter. ~**ista** *m & f* taxi-driver

tayuyá *m* (*Arg*) water melon

taz|a *f* cup. ~**ón** *m* bowl

te *pron* (*acusativo*) you; (*dativo*) (to) you; (*reflexivo*) (to) yourself

té *m* tea. **dar el** ~ bore

tea *f* torch

teatr|al *a* theatre; (*exagerado*) theatrical. ~**alizar** [10] *vt* dramatize. ~**o** *m* theatre; (*literatura*) drama. **obra** *f* ~**al** play

tebeo *m* comic

teca *f* teak

tecla *f* key. ~**do** *m* keyboard. **tocar la** ~, **tocar una** ~ pull strings

técnica *f* technique

tecn|icismo *m* technicality

técnico *a* technical. ● *m* technician

tecnol|ogía *f* technology. ~**ógico** *a* technological

tecolote m (*Mex*) owl

tecomate m (*Mex*) earthenware cup

tech|ado m roof. ~**ar** vt roof. ~**o** m (*interior*) ceiling; (*exterior*) roof. ~**umbre** f roofing. **bajo** ~**ado** indoors

teja f tile. ~**do** m roof. **a toca** ~ cash

teje|dor m weaver. ~**r** vt weave; (*hacer punto*) knit

tejemaneje m (*fam*) fuss; (*intriga*) scheming

tejido m material; (*anat, fig*) tissue. ~**s** mpl textiles

tejón m badger

tela f material; (*de araña*) web; (*en líquido*) skin

telar m loom. ~**es** mpl textile mill

telaraña f spider's web, cobweb

tele f (*fam*) television

tele|comunicación f telecommunication. ~**diario** m television news. ~**dirigido** a remote-controlled. ~**férico** m cable-car; (*tren*) cable-railway

tel|efonear vt/i telephone. ~**efónico** a telephone. ~**efonista** m & f telephonist. ~**éfono** m telephone. **al** ~**éfono** on the phone

tel|egrafía f telegraphy. ~**egrafiar** [20] vt telegraph. ~**egráfico** a telegraphic. ~**égrafo** m telegraph

telegrama m telegram

telenovela f television soap opera

teleobjetivo m telephoto lens

telep|atía f telepathy. ~**ático** a telepathic

telesc|ópico a telescopic. ~**opio** m telescope

telesilla m ski-lift, chair-lift

telespectador m viewer

telesquí m ski-lift

televi|dente m & f viewer. ~**sar** vt televise. ~**sión** f television. ~**sor** m television (set)

télex m telex

telón m curtain. ~ **de acero** (*historia*) Iron Curtain

tema m subject; (*mus*) theme

templ|ar [1] vi shake; (*de miedo*) tremble; (*de frío*) shiver; (*fig*) shudder. ~**or** m shaking; (*de miedo*) trembling; (*de frío*) shivering. ~**or de tierra** earthquake. ~**oroso** a trembling

temer vt be afraid (of). ● vi be afraid. ~**se** vpr be afraid

temerario a reckless

tem|eroso a frightened. ~**ible** a fearsome. ~**or** m fear

témpano m floe

temperamento m temperament

temperatura f temperature

temperie f weather

tempest|ad f storm. ~**uoso** a stormy. **levantar** ~**ades** (*fig*) cause a storm

templ|ado a moderate; (*tibio*) warm; (*clima, tiempo*) mild; (*valiente*) courageous; (*listo*) bright. ~**anza** f moderation; (*de clima o tiempo*) mildness. ~**ar** vt temper; (*calentar*) warm; (*mus*) tune. ~**e** m tempering; (*temperatura*) temperature; (*humor*) mood

templ|ete m niche; (*pabellón*) pavilion. ~**o** m temple

tempora|da f time; (*época*) season. ~**l** a temporary. ● m (*tempestad*) storm; (*período de lluvia*) rainy spell

tempran|ero a (*frutos*) early. ~**o** a & adv early. **ser** ~**ero** be an early riser

tena|cidad f tenacity

tenacillas fpl tongs

tenaz a tenacious

tenaza f, **tenazas** fpl pliers; (*para arrancar clavos*) pincers; (*para el fuego, culin*) tongs

tende|ncia f tendency. ~**nte** a. ~**nte a** aimed at. ~**r** [1] vt spread (out); hang out (*ropa a secar*); (*colocar*) lay. ● vi have a tendency (**a** to). ~**rse** vpr stretch out

tender|ete m stall. ~**o** m shopkeeper

tendido a spread out; (*ropa*) hung out; (*persona*) stretched out. ● m (*en plaza de toros*) front rows. ~**s** mpl (*ropa lavada*) washing

tendón m tendon

tenebroso a gloomy; (*turbio*) shady

tenedor m fork; (*poseedor*) holder

tener [40] vt have (got); (*agarrar*) hold; be (*años, calor, celos, cuidado, frío, ganas, hambre, miedo, razón, sed etc*). **¡ten cuidado!** be careful! **tengo calor** I'm hot. **tiene 3 años** he's 3 (years old). ~**se** vpr stand up; (*considerarse*) consider o.s., think o.s. ~ **al corriente**, ~ **al día** keep up to date. ~ **2 cm de largo** be 2 cms long. ~ **a uno por** consider s.o. ~ **que** have (got) to. **tenemos que comprar pan** we've got to buy some bread. **¡ahí tienes!** there you are! **no** ~ **nada que ver con** have nothing to do with. **¿qué tienes?** what's the matter (with you)? **¡tenga!** here you are!

tengo *vb véase* **tener**

teniente *m* lieutenant. **~ de alcalde** deputy mayor

tenis *m* tennis. **~ta** *m & f* tennis player

tenor *m* sense; (*mus*) tenor. **a este ~** in this fashion

tens|ión *f* tension; (*presión*) pressure; (*arterial*) blood pressure; (*elec*) voltage; (*de persona*) tenseness. **~o** *a* tense

tentación *f* temptation

tentáculo *m* tentacle

tenta|dor *a* tempting. **~r** [1] *vt* feel; (*seducir*) tempt

tentativa *f* attempt

tenue *a* thin; ⟨*luz, voz*⟩ faint

teñi|do *m* dye. **~r** [5 & 22] *vt* dye; (*fig*) tinge (**de** with). **~rse** *vpr* dye one's hair

te|ología *f* theology. **~ológico** *a* theological. **~ólogo** *m* theologian

teorema *m* theorem

te|oría *f* theory. **~órico** *a* theoretical

tepache *m* (*Mex*) (alcoholic) drink

tequila *f* tequila

TER *m* high-speed train

terap|éutico *a* therapeutic. **~ia** *f* therapy

tercer *a véase* **tercero**. **~a** *f* (*auto*) third (gear). **~o** *a* (*delante de nombre masculino en singular* **tercer**) third. ● *m* third party

terceto *m* trio

terciar *vi* mediate. **~ en** join in. **~se** *vpr* occur

tercio *m* third

terciopelo *m* velvet

terco *a* obstinate

tergiversar *vt* distort

terma|l *a* thermal. **~s** *fpl* thermal baths

termes *m invar* termite

térmico *a* thermal

termina|ción *f* ending; (*conclusión*) conclusion. **~l** *a & m* terminal. **~nte** *a* categorical. **~r** *vt* finish, end. **~rse** *vpr* come to an end. **~r por** end up

término *m* end; (*palabra*) term; (*plazo*) period. **~ medio** average. **~ municipal** municipal district. **dar ~ a** finish off. **en último ~** as a last resort. **estar en buenos ~s con** on good terms with. **llevar a ~** carry

out. **poner ~ a** put an end to. **primer ~** foreground

terminología *f* terminology

termita *f* termite

termo *m* Thermos flask (P), flask

termómetro *m* thermometer

termo|nuclear *a* thermonuclear. **~sifón** *m* boiler. **~stato** *m* thermostat

terner|a *f* (*carne*) veal. **~o** *m* calf

ternura *f* tenderness

terquedad *f* stubbornness

terracota *f* terracotta

terrado *m* flat roof

terraplén *m* embankment

terrateniente *m & f* landowner

terraza *f* terrace; (*terrado*) flat roof

terremoto *m* earthquake

terre|no *a* earthly. ● *m* land; (*solar*) plot; (*fig*) field. **~stre** *a* earthly; (*mil*) ground

terr|ible *a* terrible. **~iblemente** *adv* awfully. **~ífico** *a* terrifying

territori|al *a* territorial. **~o** *m* territory

terrón *m* (*de tierra*) clod; (*culin*) lump

terror *m* terror. **~ífico** *a* terrifying. **~ismo** *m* terrorism. **~ista** *m & f* terrorist

terr|oso *a* earthy; (*color*) brown. **~uño** *m* land; (*patria*) native land

terso *a* polished; ⟨*piel*⟩ smooth

tertulia *f* social gathering, get-together (*fam*). **~r** *vi* (*LAm*) get together. **estar de ~** chat. **hacer ~** get together

tesi|na *f* dissertation. **~s** *f inv* thesis; (*opinión*) theory

tesón *m* perseverance

tesor|ería *f* treasury. **~ero** *m* treasurer. **~o** *m* treasure; (*tesorería*) treasury; (*libro*) thesaurus

testa *f* (*fam*) head. **~ferro** *m* figurehead

testa|mento *m* will. **T~mento** (*relig*) Testament. **~r** *vi* make a will

testarudo *a* stubborn

testículo *m* testicle

testi|ficar [7] *vt/i* testify. **~go** *m* witness. **~go de vista**, **~go ocular**, **~go presencial** eyewitness. **~monio** *m* testimony

teta *f* nipple; (*de biberón*) teat

tétanos *m* tetanus

tetera *f* (*para el té*) teapot; (*Mex, biberón*) feeding-bottle

tetilla *f* nipple; (*de biberón*) teat

tétrico *a* gloomy

textil *a & m* textile

text|o *m* text. **~ual** *a* textual

textura *f* texture

teyú *m* (*Arg*) iguana

tez *f* complexion

ti *pron* you

tía *f* aunt; (*fam*) woman

tiara *f* tiara

tibio *a* lukewarm. **ponerle ~ a uno** insult s.o.

tiburón *m* shark

tic *m* tic

tiempo *m* time; (*atmosférico*) weather; (*mus*) tempo; (*gram*) tense; (*en deportes*) half. **a su ~** in due course. **a ~** in time. **¿cuánto ~?** how long? **hace buen ~** the weather is fine. **hace ~** some time ago. **mucho ~** a long time. **perder el ~** waste time. **¿qué ~ hace?** what is the weather like?

tienda *f* shop; (*de campaña*) tent. **~ de comestibles**, **~ de ultramarinos** grocer's (shop) (*Brit*), grocery store (*Amer*)

tiene *vb véase* **tener**

tienta. a ~s gropingly. **andar a ~s** grope one's way

tiento *m* touch; (*de ciego*) blind person's stick; (*fig*) tact

tierno *a* tender; (*joven*) young

tierra *f* land; (*planeta, elec*) earth; (*suelo*) ground; (*geol*) soil, earth. **caer por ~** (*fig*) crumble. **por ~** overland, by land

tieso *a* stiff; (*firme*) firm; (*engreído*) conceited; (*orgulloso*) proud

tiesto *m* flowerpot

tifoideo *a* typhoid

tifón *m* typhoon

tifus *m* typhus; (*fiebre tifoidea*) typhoid (fever); (*en el teatro*) people with complimentary tickets

tigre *m* tiger

tijera *f*, **tijeras** *fpl* scissors; (*de jardín*) shears

tijeret|a *f* (*insecto*) earwig; (*bot*) tendril. **~ear** *vt* snip

tila *f* lime(-tree); (*infusión*) lime tea

tild|ar *vt*. **~ar de** (*fig*) call. **~e** *m* tilde

tilín *m* tinkle. **hacer ~** appeal

tilingo *a* (*Arg, Mex*) silly

tilma *f* (*Mex*) poncho

tilo *m* lime(-tree)

timar *vt* swindle

timbal *m* drum; (*culin*) timbale, meat pie

timbiriche *m* (*Mex*) (alcoholic) drink

timbr|ar *vt* stamp. **~e** *m* (*sello*) stamp; (*elec*) bell; (*sonido*) timbre. **tocar el ~e** ring the bell

timidez *f* shyness

tímido *a* shy

timo *m* swindle

timón *m* rudder; (*fig*) helm

tímpano *m* kettledrum; (*anat*) eardrum. **~s** *mpl* (*mus*) timpani

tina *f* tub. **~ja** *f* large earthenware jar

tinglado *m* (*fig*) intrigue

tinieblas *fpl* darkness; (*fig*) confusion

tino *f* (*habilidad*) skill; (*moderación*) moderation; (*tacto*) tact

tint|a *f* ink. **~e** *m* dyeing; (*color*) dye; (*fig*) tinge. **~ero** *m* ink-well. **de buena ~a** on good authority

tint|ín *m* tinkle; (*de vasos*) chink, clink. **~inear** *vi* tinkle; ⟨vasos⟩ chink, clink

tinto *a* ⟨vino⟩ red

tintorería *f* dyeing; (*tienda*) dry cleaner's

tintura *f* dyeing; (*color*) dye; (*noción superficial*) smattering

tío *m* uncle; (*fam*) man. **~s** *mpl* uncle and aunt

tiovivo *m* merry-go-round

típico *a* typical

tipo *m* type; (*persona, fam*) person; (*figura de mujer*) figure; (*figura de hombre*) build; (*com*) rate

tip|ografía *f* typography. **~ográfico** *a* typographic(al). **~ógrafo** *m* printer

típula *f* crane-fly, daddy-long-legs

tique *m*, **tíquet** *m* ticket

tiquete *m* (*LAm*) ticket

tira *f* strip. **la ~ de** lots of

tirabuzón *m* corkscrew; (*de pelo*) ringlet

tirad|a *f* distance; (*serie*) series; (*de libros etc*) edition. **~o** *a* (*barato*) very cheap; (*fácil, fam*) very easy. **~or** *m* (*asa*) handle; (*juguete*) catapult (*Brit*), slingshot (*Amer*). **de una ~a** at one go

tiran|ía *f* tyranny. **~izar** [10] *vt* tyrannize. **~o** *a* tyrannical. ● *m* tyrant

tirante *a* tight; (*fig*) tense; ⟨relaciones⟩ strained. ● *m* shoulder strap. **~s** *mpl* braces (*esp Brit*), suspenders (*Amer*)

tirar *vt* throw; (*desechar*) throw away; (*derribar*) knock over; give ⟨golpe, coz etc⟩; (*imprimir*) print. ● *vi* (*disparar*) shoot. **~se** *vpr*

throw o.s.; (*tumbarse*) lie down. ∼ **a**
tend to (be); (*parecerse a*) resemble.
∼ **de** pull; (*atraer*) attract. **a todo** ∼
at the most. **ir tirando** get by

tirita *f* sticking-plaster, plaster
(*Brit*)

tirit|ar *vi* shiver. ∼**ón** *m* shiver

tiro *m* throw; (*disparo*) shot; (*alcance*) range. ∼ **a gol** shot at goal.
a ∼ within range. **errar el** ∼ miss.
pegarse un ∼ shoot o.s.

tiroides *m* thyroid (gland)

tirón *m* tug. **de un** ∼ in one go

tirote|ar *vt* shoot at. ∼**o** *m* shooting

tisana *f* herb tea

tisis *f* tuberculosis

tisú *m* (*pl* tisus) tissue

títere *m* puppet. ∼ **de guante** glove
puppet. ∼**s** *mpl* puppet show

titilar *vi* quiver; ⟨*estrella*⟩ twinkle

titiritero *m* puppeteer; (*acróbata*)
acrobat; (*malabarista*) juggler

titube|ante *a* shaky; (*fig*) hesistant.
∼**ar** *vi* stagger; ⟨*cosa*⟩ be unstable;
(*fig*) hesitate. ∼**o** *m* hesitation

titula|do *a* ⟨*libro*⟩ entitled; ⟨*persona*⟩ qualified. ∼**r** *m* headline;
(*persona*) holder. ● *vt* call. ∼**rse** *vpr*
be called

título *m* title; (*persona*) titled person; (*académico*) qualification;
(*univ*) degree; (*de periódico etc*)
headline; (*derecho*) right. **a** ∼ **de** as,
by way of

tiza *f* chalk

tiz|nar *vt* dirty. ∼**ne** *m* soot. ∼**ón** *m*
half-burnt stick; (*fig*) stain

toall|a *f* towel. ∼**ero** *m* towel-rail

tobillo *m* ankle

tobogán *m* slide; (*para la nieve*)
toboggan

tocadiscos *m invar* record-player

toca|do *a* (*con sombrero*) wearing.
● *m* hat. ∼**dor** *m* dressing-table.
∼**dor de señoras** ladies' room.
∼**nte** *a* touching. ∼**r** [7] *vt* touch;
(*mus*) play; ring ⟨*timbre*⟩; (*mencionar*) touch on; ⟨*barco*⟩ stop at.
● *vi* knock; (*corresponder a uno*) be
one's turn. ∼**rse** *vpr* touch each
other; (*cubrir la cabeza*) cover one's
head. **en lo que** ∼ **a**, **en lo** ∼**nte a**
as for. **estar** ∼**do (de la cabeza)** be
mad. **te** ∼ **a ti** it's your turn

tocateja. a ∼ cash

tocayo *m* namesake

tocino *m* bacon

tocólogo *m* obstetrician

todavía *adv* still, yet. ∼ **no** not yet

todo *a* all; (*entero*) the whole; (*cada*)
every. ● *adv* completely, all. ● *m*
whole. ● *pron* everything, all; (*en
plural*) everyone. ∼ **el día** all day.
∼ **el mundo** everyone. ∼ **el que**
anyone who. ∼ **incluido** all in. ∼ **lo
contrario** quite the opposite. ∼ **lo
que** anything which. ∼**s los días**
every day. ∼**s los dos** both (of
them). ∼**s los tres** all three. **ante** ∼
above all. **a** ∼ **esto** meanwhile. **con**
∼ still, however. **del** ∼ completely.
en ∼ **el mundo** anywhere. **estar en**
∼ be on the ball. **es** ∼ **uno** it's all
the same. **nosotros** ∼**s** all of us.
sobre ∼ above all

toldo *m* sunshade

tolera|ncia *f* tolerance. ∼**nte** *a* tolerant. ∼**r** *vt* tolerate

tolondro *m* (*chichón*) lump

toma *f* taking; (*med*) dose; (*de agua*)
outlet; (*elec*) socket; (*elec, clavija*)
plug. ● *int* well!, fancy that! ∼ **de
corriente** power point. ∼**dura** *f*.
∼**dura de pelo** hoax. ∼**r** *vt* take;
catch ⟨*autobús*, *tren etc*⟩; (*beber*)
drink, have; (*comer*) eat, have. ● *vi*
take; (*dirigirse*) go. ∼**rse** *vpr* take;
(*beber*) drink, have; (*comer*) eat,
have. ∼**r a bien** take well. ∼**r a mal**
take badly. ∼**r en serio** take seriously. ∼**rla con uno** pick on s.o. ∼**r
nota** take note. ∼**r por** take for. ∼ **y
daca** give and take. **¿qué va a** ∼**r?**
what would you like?

tomate *m* tomato

tomavistas *m invar* cine-camera

tómbola *f* tombola

tomillo *m* thyme

tomo *m* volume

ton. sin ∼ **ni son** without rhyme or
reason

tonada *f*, **tonadilla** *f* tune

tonel *m* barrel. ∼**ada** *f* ton. ∼**aje** *m*
tonnage

tónic|a *f* tonic water; (*mus*) tonic.
∼**o** *a* tonic; ⟨*sílaba*⟩ stressed. ● *m*
tonic

tonificar [7] *vt* invigorate

tono *m* tone; (*mus*, *modo*) key;
(*color*) shade

tont|ería *f* silliness; (*cosa*) silly
thing; (*dicho*) silly remark. ∼**o** *a*
silly. ● *m* fool, idiot; (*payaso*) clown.
dejarse de ∼**erías** stop wasting
time. **hacer el** ∼**o** act the fool.
hacerse el ∼**o** feign ignorance

topacio *m* topaz

topar vt ‹animal› butt; ‹persona›
bump into; (fig) run into. ● vi. ~ con
run into
tope a maximum. ● m end; (de tren)
buffer. **hasta los ~s** crammed full.
ir a ~ go flat out
tópico a topical. ● m cliché
topo m mole
topogr|afía f topography. **~áfico** a
topographical
toque m touch; (sonido) sound; (de
campana) peal; (de reloj) stroke;
(fig) crux. **~ de queda** curfew.
~tear vt keep fingering, fiddle with.
dar el último ~ put the finishing
touches
toquilla f shawl
tórax m thorax
torbellino m whirlwind; (de polvo)
cloud of dust; (fig) whirl
torcer [2 & 9] vt twist; (doblar) bend;
wring out ‹ropa›. ● vi turn. **~se** vpr
twist; (fig, desviarse) go astray; (fig,
frustrarse) go wrong
tordo a dapple grey. ● m thrush
tore|ar vt fight; (evitar) dodge;
(entretener) put off. ● vi fight (bulls).
~o m bullfighting. **~ro** m
bullfighter
torment|a f storm. **~o** m torture.
~oso a stormy
tornado m tornado
tornar vt return
tornasolado a irridescent
torneo m tournament
tornillo m screw
torniquete m (entrada) turnstile
torno m lathe; (de alfarero) wheel.
en ~ a around
toro m bull. **~s** mpl bullfighting. **ir a
los ~s** go to a bullfight
toronja f grapefruit
torpe a clumsy; (estúpido) stupid
torped|ero m torpedo-boat. **~o** m
torpedo
torpeza f clumsiness; (de inteligencia) slowness
torpor m torpor
torrado m toasted chick-pea
torre f tower; (en ajedrez) castle,
rook
torrefac|ción f roasting. **~to** a
roasted
torren|cial a torrential. **~te** m tor-
rent; (circulatorio) bloodstream;
(fig) flood
tórrido a torrid
torrija f French toast
torsión f twisting

torso m torso
torta f tart; (bollo, fam) cake; (golpe)
slap, punch; (Mex, bocadillo) sandwich. **~zo** m slap, punch. **no entender ni ~** not understand a word of
it. **pegarse un ~zo** have a bad
accident
tortícolis f stiff neck
tortilla f omelette; (Mex, de maíz)
tortilla, maize cake. **~ francesa**
plain omelette
tórtola f turtle-dove
tortuga f tortoise; (de mar) turtle
tortuoso a winding; (fig) devious
tortura f torture. **~r** vt torture
torvo a grim
tos f cough. **~ ferina** whooping
cough
tosco a crude; ‹persona› coarse
toser vi cough
tósigo m poison
tosquedad f crudeness; (de persona)
coarseness
tost|ada f toast. **~ado** a ‹pan›
toasted; ‹café› roasted; ‹persona›
tanned; (marrón) brown. **~ar** vt
toast ‹pan›; roast ‹café›; tan ‹piel›.
~ón m (pan) crouton; (lata) bore
total a total. ● adv after all. ● m
total; (totalidad) whole. **~idad** f
whole. **~itario** a totalitarian. **~izar**
[10] vt total. **~ que** so, to cut a long
story short
tóxico a toxic
toxicómano m drug addict
toxina f toxin
tozudo a stubborn
traba f bond; (fig, obstáculo)
obstacle. **poner ~s a** hinder
trabaj|ador a hard-working. ● m
worker. **~ar** vt work (de as); knead
‹masa›; (estudiar) work at; ‹actor›
act. ● vi work. **~o** m work. **~os** mpl
hardships. **~os forzados** hard
labour. **~oso** a hard. **costar ~o** be
difficult. **¿en qué ~as?** what work do
you do?
trabalenguas m invar tongue-
twister
traba|r vt (sujetar) fasten; (unir)
join; (empezar) start; (culin)
thicken. **~rse** vpr get tangled up.
trabársele la lengua get tongue-
tied. **~zón** f joining; (fig)
connection
trabucar [7] vt mix up
trácala f (Mex) trick
tracción f traction
tractor m tractor

tradici|ón f tradition. **~onal** a traditional. **~onalista** m & f traditionalist

traduc|ción f translation. **~ir** [47] vt translate (**al** into). **~tor** m translator

traer [41] vt bring; (*llevar*) carry; (*atraer*) attract. **traérselas** be difficult

trafica|nte m & f dealer. **~r** [7] vi deal

tráfico m traffic; (*com*) trade

traga|deras fpl (*fam*) throat. **tener buenas ~deras** (*ser crédulo*) swallow anything; (*ser tolerante*) be easygoing. **~luz** m skylight. **~perras** f invar slot-machine. **~r** [12] vt swallow; (*comer mucho*) devour; (*absorber*) absorb; (*fig*) swallow up. **no (poder) ~r** not be able to stand. **~rse** vpr swallow; (*fig*) swallow up

tragedia f tragedy

trágico a tragic. ● m tragedian

trag|o m swallow, gulp; (*pequeña porción*) sip; (*fig, disgusto*) blow. **~ón** a greedy. ● m glutton. **echar(se) un ~o** have a drink

trai|ción f treachery; (*pol*) treason. **~cionar** vt betray. **~cionero** a treacherous. **~dor** a treacherous. ● m traitor

traigo vb véase **traer**

traje m dress; (*de hombre*) suit. ● vb véase **traer**. **~ de baño** swimming-costume. **~ de ceremonia**, **~ de etiqueta**, **~ de noche** evening dress

traj|ín m (*transporte*) haulage; (*jaleo, fam*) bustle. **~inar** vt transport. ● vi bustle about

trama f weft; (*fig*) link; (*fig, argumento*) plot. **~r** vt weave; (*fig*) plot

tramitar vt negotiate

trámite m step. **~s** mpl procedure. **en ~** in hand

tramo m (*parte*) section; (*de escalera*) flight

tramp|a f trap; (*puerta*) trapdoor; (*fig*) trick. **~illa** f trapdoor. **hacer ~a** cheat

trampolín m trampoline; (*fig, de piscina*) springboard

tramposo a cheating. ● m cheat

tranca f stick; (*de puerta*) bar

trance m moment; (*hipnótico etc*) trance. **a todo ~** at all costs

tranco m stride

tranquil|idad f (peace and) quiet; (*de espíritu*) peace of mind. **~izar** [10] vt reassure. **~o** a quiet; (*conciencia*) clear; (*mar*) calm; (*despreocupado*) thoughtless. **estáte ~o** don't worry

trans... pref (véase también **tras...**) trans...

transacción f transaction; (*acuerdo*) compromise

transatlántico a transatlantic. ● m (ocean) liner

transbord|ador m ferry. **~ar** vt transfer. **~arse** vpr change. **~o** m transfer. **hacer ~o** change (**en** at)

transcri|bir (pp **transcrito**) vt transcribe. **~pción** f transcription

transcur|rir vi pass. **~so** m course

transeúnte a temporary. ● m & f passer-by

transfer|encia f transfer. **~ir** [4] vt transfer

transfigurar vt transfigure

transforma|ción f transformation. **~dor** m transformer. **~r** vt transform

transfusión f transfusion. **hacer una ~** give a blood transfusion

transgre|dir vt transgress. **~sión** f transgression

transición f transition

transido a overcome

transigir [14] vi give in, compromise

transistor m transistor; (*radio*) radio

transita|ble a passable. **~r** vi go

transitivo a transitive

tránsito m transit; (*tráfico*) traffic

transitorio a transitory

translúcido a translucent

transmi|sión f transmission; (*radio, TV*) broadcast. **~sor** m transmitter. **~sora** f broadcasting station. **~tir** vt transmit; (*radio, TV*) broadcast; (*fig*) pass on

transparen|cia f transparency. **~tar** vt show. **~te** a transparent

transpira|ción f perspiration. **~r** vi transpire; (*sudar*) sweat

transponer [34] vt move. ● vi disappear round ⟨*esquina etc*⟩; disappear behind ⟨*montaña etc*⟩. **~se** vpr disappear

transport|ar vt transport. **~e** m transport. **empresa** f **de ~es** removals company

transversal a transverse; ⟨*calle*⟩ side

tranvía m tram

trapacería f swindle

trapear vt (*LAm*) mop

trapecio m trapeze; (*math*) trapezium

trapiche m (*para azúcar*) mill; (*para aceitunas*) press

trapicheo m fiddle

trapisonda f (*jaleo, fam*) row; (*enredo, fam*) plot

trapo m rag; (*para limpiar*) cloth. **~s** mpl (*fam*) clothes. **a todo ~** out of control

tráquea f windpipe, trachea

traquete|ar vt bang, rattle. **~o** m banging, rattle

tras prep after; (*detrás*) behind; (*encima de*) as well as

tras... pref (*véase también* **trans...**) trans...

trascende|ncia f importance. **~ntal** a transcendental; (*importante*) important. **~r** [1] vi (*oler*) smell (**a** of); (*saberse*) become known; (*extenderse*) spread

trasegar [1 & 12] vt move around

trasero a back, rear. ● m (*anat*) bottom

trasgo m goblin

traslad|ar vt move; (*aplazar*) postpone; (*traducir*) translate; (*copiar*) copy. **~o** m transfer; (*copia*) copy; (*mudanza*) removal. **dar ~o** send a copy

trasl|úcido a translucent. **~ucirse** [11] vpr be translucent; (*dejarse ver*) show through; (*fig, revelarse*) be revealed. **~uz** m. **al ~uz** against the light

trasmano m. **a ~** out of reach; (*fig*) out of the way

trasnochar vi (*acostarse tarde*) go to bed late; (*no acostarse*) stay up all night; (*no dormir*) be unable to sleep; (*pernoctar*) spend the night

traspas|ar vt pierce; (*transferir*) transfer; (*pasar el límite*) go beyond. **~o** m transfer. **se ~a** for sale

traspié m trip; (*fig*) slip. **dar un ~** stumble; (*fig*) slip up

trasplant|ar vt transplant. **~e** m transplanting; (*med*) transplant

trastada f stupid thing; (*jugada*) dirty trick, practical joke

traste m fret. **dar al ~ con** ruin. **ir al ~** fall through

trastero m storeroom

trastienda f back room; (*fig*) shrewdness

trasto m piece of furniture; (*cosa inútil*) piece of junk; (*persona*) useless person, dead loss (*fam*)

trastorn|ado a mad. **~ar** vt upset; (*volver loco*) drive mad; (*fig, gustar*

mucho, fam) delight. **~arse** vpr get upset; (*volverse loco*) go mad. **~o** m (*incl med*) upset; (*pol*) disturbance; (*fig*) confusion

trastrocar [2 & 7] vt change round

trat|able a friendly. **~ado** m treatise; (*acuerdo*) treaty. **~amiento** m treatment; (*título*) title. **~ante** m & f dealer. **~ar** vt (*incl med*) treat; deal with ‹*asunto etc*›; (*com*) deal; (*manejar*) handle; (*de tú, de Vd*) address (**de** as); (*llamar*) call. ● vi deal (with). **~ar con** have to do with; know ‹*persona*›; (*com*) deal in. **~ar de** be about; (*intentar*) try. **~o** m treatment; (*acuerdo*) agreement; (*título*) title; (*relación*) relationship. **¡~o hecho!** agreed! **~os** mpl dealings. **¿de qué se ~a?** what's it about?

traum|a m trauma. **~ático** a traumatic

través m (*inclinación*) slant. **a ~ de** through; (*de un lado a otro*) across. **de ~** across; (*de lado*) sideways. **mirar de ~** look askance at

travesaño m crosspiece

travesía f crossing; (*calle*) side-street

trav|esura f prank. **~ieso** a ‹*niño*› mischievous, naughty

trayecto m road; (*tramo*) stretch; (*ruta*) route; (*viaje*) journey. **~ria** f trajectory; (*fig*) course

traz|a f plan; (*aspecto*) look, appearance; (*habilidad*) skill. **~ado** a. **bien ~ado** good-looking. **mal ~ado** unattractive. ● m plan. **~ar** [10] vt draw; (*bosquejar*) sketch. **~o** m line

trébol m clover. **~es** mpl (*en naipes*) clubs

trece a & m thirteen

trecho m stretch; (*distancia*) distance; (*tiempo*) while. **a ~s** in places. **de ~ en ~** at intervals

tregua f truce; (*fig*) respite

treinta a & m thirty

tremendo a terrible; (*extraordinario*) terrific

trementina f turpentine

tren m train; (*equipaje*) luggage. **~ de aterrizaje** landing gear. **~ de vida** lifestyle

tren|cilla f braid. **~za** f braid; (*de pelo*) plait. **~zar** [10] vt plait

trepa|dor a climbing. **~r** vt/i climb

tres a & m three. **~cientos** a & m three hundred. **~illo** m three-piece suite; (*mus*) triplet

treta f trick

tri|angular *a* triangular. ~ángulo *m* triangle

trib|al *a* tribal. ~u *f* tribe

tribulación *f* tribulation

tribuna *f* platform; (*de espectadores*) stand

tribunal *m* court; (*de examen etc*) board; (*fig*) tribunal

tribut|ar *vt* pay. ~o *m* tribute; (*impuesto*) tax

triciclo *m* tricycle

tricolor *a* three-coloured

tricornio *a* three-cornered. ● *m* three-cornered hat

tricotar *vt/i* knit

tridimensional *a* three-dimensional

tridente *m* trident

trigésimo *a* thirtieth

trig|al *m* wheat field. ~o *m* wheat

trigonometría *f* trigonometry

trigueño *a* olive-skinned; ⟨pelo⟩ dark blonde

trilogía *f* trilogy

trilla|do *a* (*fig, manoseado*) trite; (*fig, conocido*) well-known. ~r *vt* thresh

trimestr|al *a* quarterly. ~e *m* quarter; (*escol, univ*) term

trin|ar *vi* warble. estar que trina be furious

trinchar *vt* carve

trinchera *f* ditch; (*mil*) trench; (*rail*) cutting; (*abrigo*) trench coat

trineo *m* sledge

trinidad *f* trinity

Trinidad *f* Trinidad

trino *m* warble

trío *m* trio

tripa *f* intestine; (*culin*) tripe; (*fig, vientre*) tummy, belly. ~s *fpl* (*de máquina etc*) parts, workings. me duele la ~ I've got tummy-ache. revolver las ~s turn one's stomach

tripicallos *mpl* tripe

tripl|e *a* triple. ● *m*. el ~e (de) three times as much (as). ~icado *a*. por ~icado in triplicate. ~icar [7] *vt* treble

trípode *m* tripod

tríptico *m* triptych

tripula|ción *f* crew. ~nte *m* & *f* member of the crew. ~r *vt* man

triquitraque *m* (*ruido*) clatter

tris *m* crack; (*de papel etc*) ripping noise. estar en un ~ be on the point of

triste *a* sad; ⟨paisaje, tiempo etc⟩ gloomy; (*fig, insignificante*) miserable. ~za *f* sadness

tritón *m* newt

triturar *vt* crush

triunf|al *a* triumphal. ~ante *a* triumphant. ~ar *vi* triumph (de, sobre over). ~o *m* triumph

triunvirato *m* triumvirate

trivial *a* trivial

triza *f* piece. hacer algo ~s smash sth to pieces

trocar [2 & 7] *vt* (ex)change

trocear *vt* cut up, chop

trocito *m* small piece

trocha *f* narrow path; (*atajo*) short cut

trofeo *m* trophy

tromba *f* waterspout. ~ de agua heavy downpour

trombón *m* trombone; (*músico*) trombonist

trombosis *f* invar thrombosis

trompa *f* horn; (*de orquesta*) French horn; (*de elefante*) trunk; (*hocico*) snout; (*juguete*) (spinning) top; (*anat*) tube. ● *m* horn player. coger una ~ (*fam*) get drunk

trompada *f*, trompazo *m* bump

trompet|a *f* trumpet; (*músico*) trumpeter, trumpet player; (*clarín*) bugle. ~illa *f* ear-trumpet

trompicar [7] *vi* trip

trompo *m* (*juguete*) (spinning) top

trona|da *f* thunder storm. ~r *vt* (*Mex*) shoot. ● *vi* thunder

tronco *m* trunk. dormir como un ~ sleep like a log

tronchar *vt* bring down; (*fig*) cut short. ~se de risa laugh a lot

trono *m* throne

trop|a *f* troops. ~el *m* mob. ser de ~a be in the army

tropero *m* (*Arg, vaquero*) cowboy

tropez|ar [1 & 10] *vi* trip; (*fig*) slip up. ~ar con run into. ~ón *m* stumble; (*fig*) slip

tropical *a* tropical

trópico *a* tropical. ● *m* tropic

tropiezo *m* slip; (*desgracia*) mishap

trot|ar *vi* trot. ~e *m* trot; (*fig*) toing and froing. al ~e trotting; (*de prisa*) in a rush. de mucho ~e hard-wearing

trozo *m* piece, bit. a ~s in bits

truco *m* knack; (*ardid*) trick. coger el ~ get the knack

trucha *f* trout

trueno *m* thunder; (*estampido*) bang

trueque *m* exchange. aun a ~ de even at the expense of

trufa *f* truffle. ~r *vt* stuff with truffles

truhán *m* rogue; (*gracioso*) jester

truncar [7] *vt* truncate; (*fig*) cut short

tu *a* your

tú *pron* you

tuba *f* tuba

tubérculo *m* tuber

tuberculosis *f* tuberculosis

tub|ería *f* pipes; (*oleoducto etc*) pipeline. ~o *m* tube. ~o de ensayo test tube. ~o de escape (*auto*) exhaust (pipe). ~ular *a* tubular

tuerca *f* nut

tuerto *a* one-eyed, blind in one eye. ● *m* one-eyed person

tuétano *m* marrow; (*fig*) heart. hasta los ~s completely

tufo *m* fumes; (*olor*) bad smell

tugurio *m* hovel, slum

tul *m* tulle

tulipán *m* tulip

tulli|do *a* paralysed. ~r [22] *vt* cripple

tumba *f* grave, tomb

tumb|ar *vt* knock down, knock over; (*fig, en examen, fam*) fail; (*pasmar, fam*) overwhelm. ~arse *vpr* lie down. ~o *m* jolt. dar un ~o tumble. ~ona *f* settee; (*sillón*) armchair; (*de lona*) deckchair

tumefacción *f* swelling

tumido *a* swollen

tumor *m* tumour

tumulto *m* turmoil; (*pol*) riot

tuna *f* prickly pear; (*de estudiantes*) student band

tunante *m* & *f* rogue

túnel *m* tunnel

Túnez *m* (*ciudad*) Tunis; (*país*) Tunisia

túnica *f* tunic

Tunicia *f* Tunisia

tupé *m* toupee; (*fig*) nerve

tupido *a* thick

turba *f* peat; (*muchedumbre*) mob

turba|ción *f* disturbance, upset; (*confusión*) confusion. ~do *a* upset

turbante *m* turban

turbar *vt* upset; (*molestar*) disturb. ~se *vpr* be upset

turbina *f* turbine

turbi|o *a* cloudy; (*vista*) blurred; (*asunto etc*) unclear. ~ón *m* squall

turbulen|cia *f* turbulence; (*disturbio*) disturbance. ~te *a* turbulent; (*persona*) restless

turco *a* Turkish. ● *m* Turk; (*lengua*) Turkish

tur|ismo *m* tourism; (*coche*) car. ~ista *m* & *f* tourist. ~ístico *a* tourist. oficina *f* de ~ismo tourist office

turn|arse *vpr* take turns (para to). ~o *m* turn; (*de trabajo*) shift. por ~o in turn

turquesa *f* turquoise

Turquía *f* Turkey

turrón *m* nougat

turulato *a* (*fam*) stunned

tutear *vt* address as *tú*. ~se *vpr* be on familiar terms

tutela *f* (*jurid*) guardianship; (*fig*) protection

tuteo *m* use of the familiar *tú*

tutor *m* guardian; (*escol*) form master

tuve *vb véase* **tener**

tuyo *a* & *pron* yours. un amigo ~ a friend of yours

U

u *conj* or

ubicuidad *f* ubiquity

ubre *f* udder

ucraniano *a* & *m* Ukrainian

Ud *abrev* (*Usted*) you

uf *int* phew!; (*de repugnancia*) ugh!

ufan|arse *vpr* be proud (con, de of); (*jactarse*) boast (con, de about). ~o *a* proud

ujier *m* usher

úlcera *f* ulcer

ulterior *a* later; (*lugar*) further. ~mente *adv* later, subsequently

últimamente *adv* (*recientemente*) recently; (*al final*) finally; (*en último caso*) as a last resort

ultim|ar *vt* complete. ~átum *m* ultimatum

último *a* last; (*más reciente*) latest; (*más lejano*) furthest; (*más alto*) top; (*más bajo*) bottom; (*fig, extremo*) extreme. estar en las últimas be on one's last legs; (*sin dinero*) be down to one's last penny. por ~ finally. ser lo ~ (*muy bueno*) be marvellous; (*muy malo*) be awful. vestido a la última dressed in the latest fashion

ultra *a* ultra, extreme

ultraj|ante *a* outrageous. ~e *m* outrage

ultramar *m* overseas countries. de ~, en ~ overseas

ultramarino *a* overseas. **~s** *mpl*
groceries. **tienda de ~s** grocer's
(shop) (*Brit*), grocery store (*Amer*)
ultranza a ~ (*con decisión*) decis-
ively; (*extremo*) extreme
ultra|sónico *a* ultrasonic. **~violeta**
a invar ultraviolet
ulular *vi* howl; (*búho*) hoot
umbilical *a* umbilical
umbral *m* threshold
umbrío *a*, **umbroso** *a* shady
un *art indef m* (*pl* **unos**) a. ● *a* one.
~os *a pl* some
una *art indef f* a. **la ~** one o'clock
un|ánime *a* unanimous. **~animidad**
f unanimity
undécimo *a* eleventh
ung|ir [14] *vt* anoint. **~üento** *m*
ointment
únic|amente *adv* only. **~o** *a* only;
(*fig, incomparable*) unique
unicornio *m* unicorn
unid|ad *f* unit; (*cualidad*) unity. **~o**
a united
unifica|ción *f* unification. **~r** [7] *vt*
unite, unify
uniform|ar *vt* standardize; (*poner
uniforme a*) put into uniform. **~e** *a*
& *m* uniform. **~idad** *f* uniformity
uni|génito *a* only. **~lateral** *a*
unilateral
uni|ón *f* union; (*cualidad*) unity;
(*tec*) joint. **~r** *vt* join; mix ‹*líquidos*›.
~rse *vpr* join together
unísono *m* unison. **al ~** in unison
unitario *a* unitary
universal *a* universal
universi|dad *f* university. **U~dad a
Distancia** Open University. **~tario**
a university
universo *m* universe
uno *a* one; (*en plural*) some. ● *pron*
one; (*alguien*) someone, somebody.
● *m* one. **~ a otro** each other. **~ y
otro** both. **(los) ~s... (los) otros**
some... others
untar *vt* grease; (*med*) rub; (*fig,
sobornar, fam*) bribe
uña *f* nail; (*de animal*) claw; (*casco*)
hoof
upa *int* up!
uranio *m* uranium
Urano *m* Uranus
urban|idad *f* politeness. **~ismo** *m*
town planning. **~ístico** *a* urban.
~ización *f* development. **~izar** [10]
vt civilize; develop ‹*terreno*›. **~o** *a*
urban
urbe *f* big city

urdimbre *f* warp
urdir *vt* (*fig*) plot
urg|encia *f* urgency; (*emergencia*)
emergency; (*necesidad*) urgent
need. **~ente** *a* urgent. **~ir** [14] *vi* be
urgent. **carta *f* ~ente** express letter
urinario *m* urinal
urna *f* urn; (*pol*) ballot box
urraca *f* magpie
URSS *abrev* (*historia*) (*Unión de
Repúblicas Socialistas Soviéticas*)
USSR, Union of Soviet Socialist
Republics
Uruguay *m*. **el ~** Uruguay
uruguayo *a* & *m* Uruguayan
us|ado *a* used; ‹*ropa etc*› worn.
~anza *f* usage, custom. **~ar** *vt* use;
(*llevar*) wear. **~o** *m* use; (*costumbre*) usage, custom. **al ~o** (*de moda*)
in fashion; (*a la manera de*) in the
style of. **de ~o externo** for external
use
usted *pron* you
usual *a* usual
usuario *a* user
usur|a *f* usury. **~ero** *m* usurer
usurpar *vt* usurp
usuta *f* (*Arg*) sandal
utensilio *m* tool; (*de cocina*) utensil.
~s *mpl* equipment
útero *m* womb
útil *a* useful. **~es** *mpl* implements
utili|dad *f* usefulness. **~tario** *a* util-
itarian; ‹*coche*› utility. **~zación** *f*
use, utilization. **~zar** [10] *vt* use,
utilize
uva *f* grape. **~ pasa** raisin. **mala ~**
bad mood

V

vaca *f* cow; (*carne*) beef
vacaciones *fpl* holiday(s). **estar de
~** be on holiday. **ir de ~** go on
holiday
vaca|nte *a* vacant. ● *f* vacancy. **~r**
[7] *vi* fall vacant
vaci|ar [20] *vt* empty; (*ahuecar*) hol-
low out; (*en molde*) cast; (*afilar*)
sharpen. **~edad** *f* emptiness; (*tontería*) silly thing, frivolity
vacila|ción *f* hesitation. **~nte** *a*
unsteady; (*fig*) hesitant. **~r** *vi* sway;
(*dudar*) hesitate; (*fam*) tease
vacío *a* empty; (*vanidoso*) vain. ● *m*
empty space; (*estado*) emptiness;
(*en física*) vacuum; (*fig*) void

vacuidad *f* emptiness; (*tontería*) silly thing, frivolity

vacuna *f* vaccine. **~ción** *f* vaccination. **~r** *vt* vaccinate

vacuno *a* bovine

vacuo *a* empty

vade *m* folder

vad|ear *vt* ford. **~o** *m* ford

vaga|bundear *vi* wander. **~bundo** *a* vagrant; ⟨*perro*⟩ stray. ● *m* tramp. **~r** [12] *vi* wander (about)

vagina *f* vagina

vago *a* vague; (*holgazán*) idle; ⟨*foto*⟩ blurred. ● *m* idler

vag|ón *m* carriage; (*de mercancías*) truck, wagon. **~ón restaurante** dining-car. **~oneta** *f* truck

vahído *m* dizzy spell

vaho *m* breath; (*vapor*) steam. **~s** *mpl* inhalation

vaina *f* sheath; (*bot*) pod

vainilla *f* vanilla

vaivén *m* swaying; (*de tráfico*) coming and going; (*fig, de suerte*) change. **vaivenes** *mpl* (*fig*) ups and downs

vajilla *f* dishes, crockery. **lavar la ~** wash up

vale *m* voucher; (*pagaré*) IOU. **~dero** *a* valid

valenciano *a* from Valencia

valent|ía *f* courage; (*acción*) brave deed. **~ón** *m* braggart

valer [42] *vt* be worth; (*costar*) cost; (*fig, significar*) mean. ● *vi* be worth; (*costar*) cost; (*servir*) be of use; (*ser valedero*) be valid; (*estar permitido*) be allowed. ● *m* worth. **~ la pena** be worthwhile, be worth it. **¿cuánto vale?** how much is it? **no ~ para nada** be useless. **¡vale!** all right!, OK! (*fam*). **¿vale?** all right?, OK? (*fam*)

valeroso *a* courageous

valgo *vb véase* **valer**

valía *f* worth

validez *f* validity. **dar ~ a** validate

válido *a* valid

valiente *a* brave; (*valentón*) boastful; (*en sentido irónico*) fine. ● *m* brave person; (*valentón*) braggart

valija *f* case; (*de correos*) mailbag. **~ diplomática** diplomatic bag

val|ioso *a* valuable. **~or** *m* value, worth; (*descaro, fam*) nerve. **~ores** *mpl* securities. **~oración** *f* valuation. **~orar** *vt* value. **conceder ~or a** attach importance to. **objetos**

mpl de ~or valuables. **sin ~or** worthless

vals *m invar* waltz

válvula *f* valve

valla *f* fence; (*fig*) barrier

valle *m* valley

vampiro *m* vampire

vanagloriarse [20 *o regular*] *vpr* boast

vanamente *adv* uselessly, in vain

vandalismo *m* vandalism

vándalo *m* vandal

vanguardia *f* vanguard. **de ~** (*en arte, música etc*) avant-garde

vanid|ad *f* vanity. **~oso** *a* vain

vano *a* vain; (*inútil*) useless. **en ~** in vain

vapor *m* steam; (*gas*) vapour; (*naut*) steamer. **~izador** *m* spray. **~izar** [10] vaporize. **al ~** (*culin*) steamed

vaquer|ía *f* dairy. **~o** *m* cow-herd, cowboy. **~os** *mpl* jeans

vara *f* stick; (*de autoridad*) staff; (*medida*) yard

varar *vi* run aground

varia|ble *a & f* variable. **~ción** *f* variation. **~nte** *f* version. **~ntes** *fpl* hors d'oeuvres. **~r** [20] *vt* change; (*dar variedad a*) vary. ● *vi* vary; (*cambiar*) change

varice *f* varicose vein

varicela *f* chickenpox

varicoso *a* having varicose veins

variedad *f* variety

varilla *f* stick; (*de metal*) rod

vario *a* varied; (*en plural*) several

varita *f* wand

variz *f* varicose vein

var|ón *a* male. ● *m* man; (*niño*) boy. **~onil** *a* manly

vasc|o *a & m* Basque. **~ongado** *a* Basque. **~uence** *a & m* Basque. **las V~ongadas** the Basque provinces

vasectomía *f* vasectomy

vaselina *f* Vaseline (P), petroleum jelly

vasija *f* pot, container

vaso *m* glass; (*anat*) vessel

vástago *m* shoot; (*descendiente*) descendant; (*varilla*) rod

vasto *a* vast

Vaticano *m* Vatican

vaticin|ar *vt* prophesy. **~io** *m* prophesy

vatio *m* watt

vaya *vb véase* **ir**

Vd *abrev* (*Usted*) you

vecin|dad *f* neighbourhood, vicinity; (*vecinos*) neighbours. **~dario** *m* inhabitants, neighbourhood. ~o *a* neighbouring; (*de al lado*) next-door. ● *m* neighbour

veda|do *m* preserve. ~**do de caza** game preserve. ~**r** *vt* prohibit

vega *f* fertile plain

vegeta|ción *f* vegetation. ~**l** *a* vegetable. ● *m* plant, vegetable. ~**r** *vi* grow; (*persona*) vegetate. ~**riano** *a & m* vegetarian

vehemente *a* vehement

vehículo *m* vehicle

veinte *a & m* twenty. ~**na** *f* score

veinti|cinco *a & m* twenty-five. ~**cuatro** *a & m* twenty-four. ~**dós** *a & m* twenty-two. ~**nueve** *a & m* twenty-nine; ~**ocho** *a & m* twenty-eight. ~**séis** *a & m* twenty-six. ~**siete** *a & m* twenty-seven. ~**trés** *a & m* twenty-three. ~**ún** *a* twenty-one. ~**uno** *a & m* (*delante de nombre masculino* **veintún**) twenty-one

vejar *vt* humiliate; (*molestar*) vex

vejez *f* old age

vejiga *f* bladder; (*med*) blister

vela *f* (*naut*) sail; (*de cera*) candle; (*falta de sueño*) sleeplessness; (*vigilia*) vigil. **pasar la noche en** ~ have a sleepless night

velada *f* evening party

vela|do *a* veiled; (*foto*) blurred. ~**r** *vt* watch over; (*encubrir*) veil; (*foto*) blur. ● *vi* stay awake, not sleep. ~**r por** look after. ~**rse** *vpr* (*foto*) blur

velero *m* sailing-ship

veleta *f* weather vane

velo *m* veil

veloc|idad *f* speed; (*auto etc*) gear. ~**ímetro** *m* speedometer. ~**ista** *m & f* sprinter. **a toda** ~**idad** at full speed

velódromo *m* cycle-track

veloz *a* fast, quick

vell|o *m* down. ~**ón** *m* fleece. ~**udo** *a* hairy

vena *f* vein; (*en madera*) grain. **estar de/en** ~ be in the mood

venado *m* deer; (*culin*) venison

vencedor *a* winning. ● *m* winner

vencejo *m* (*pájaro*) swift

venc|er [9] *vt* beat; (*superar*) overcome. ● *vi* win; (*plazo*) expire. ~**erse** *vpr* collapse; (*persona*) control o.s. ~**ido** *a* beaten; (*com, atrasado*) in arrears. **darse por** ~**ido** give up. **los** ~**idos** *mpl* (*en deportes etc*) the losers

venda *f* bandage. ~**je** *m* dressing. ~**r** *vt* bandage

vendaval *m* gale

vende|dor *a* selling. ● *m* seller, salesman. ~**dor ambulante** pedlar. ~**r** *vt* sell. ~**rse** *vpr* sell. ~**rse caro** play hard to get. **se** ~ for sale

vendimia *f* grape harvest; (*de vino*) vintage, year

Venecia *f* Venice

veneciano *a* Venetian

veneno *m* poison; (*fig, malevolencia*) spite. ~**so** *a* poisonous

venera *f* scallop shell

venera|ble *a* venerable. ~**ción** *f* reverence. ~**r** *vt* revere

venéreo *a* venereal

venero *m* (*yacimiento*) seam; (*de agua*) spring; (*fig*) source

venezolano *a & m* Venezuelan

Venezuela *f* Venezuela

venga|nza *f* revenge. ~**r** [12] *vt* avenge. ~**rse** *vpr* take revenge (**de**, **por** for) (**de**, **en** on). ~**tivo** *a* vindictive

vengo *vb* *véase* **venir**

venia *f* (*permiso*) permission

venial *a* venial

veni|da *f* arrival; (*vuelta*) return. ~**dero** *a* coming. ~**r** [53] *vi* come; (*estar*, *ser*) be. ~**r a para** come to. ~**r bien** suit. **la semana que viene** next week. **¡venga!** come on!

venta *f* sale; (*posada*) inn. **en** ~ for sale

ventaj|a *f* advantage. ~**oso** *a* advantageous

ventan|a *f* window; (*de la nariz*) nostril. ~**illa** *f* window

ventarrón *m* (*fam*) strong wind

ventear *vt* (*olfatear*) sniff

ventero *m* innkeeper

ventila|ción *f* ventilation. ~**dor** *m* fan. ~**r** *vt* air

vent|isca *f* blizzard. ~**olera** *f* gust of wind. ~**osa** *f* sucker. ~**osidad** *f* wind, flatulence. ~**oso** *a* windy

ventrílocuo *m* ventriloquist

ventrudo *a* pot-bellied

ventur|a *f* happiness; (*suerte*) luck. ~**oso** *a* happy, lucky. **a la** ~**a** at random. **echar la buena** ~**a a uno** tell s.o.'s fortune. **por** ~**a** by chance; (*afortunadamente*) fortunately

Venus *f* Venus

ver [43] *vt* see; watch (*televisión*). ● *vi* see. ~**se** *vpr* see o.s.; (*encontrarse*) find o.s.; (*dos personas*) meet. **a mi (modo de)** ~ in my view. **a** ~ let's see. **de buen** ~ good-looking. **dejarse** ~ show. **¡habráse**

visto! did you ever! **no poder** ～ not be able to stand. **no tener nada que** ～ **con** have nothing to do with. **¡para que veas!** so there! **vamos a** ～ let's see. **ya lo veo** that's obvious. **ya** ～**ás** you'll see. **ya** ～**emos** we'll see
vera f edge; (*de río*) bank
veracruzano a from Veracruz
veran|eante m & f tourist, holiday-maker. ～**ear** vi spend one's holiday. ～**eo** m (summer) holiday. ～**iego** a summer. ～**o** m summer. **casa** f **de** ～**eo** summer-holiday home. **ir de** ～**eo** go on holiday. **lugar** m **de** ～**eo** holiday resort
veras fpl. **de** ～ really
veraz a truthful
verbal a verbal
verbena f (*bot*) verbena; (*fiesta*) fair; (*baile*) dance
verbo m verb. ～**so** a verbose
verdad f truth. **¿**～**?** isn't it?, aren't they?, won't it? etc. ～**eramente** adv really. ～**ero** a true; (*fig*) real. **a decir** ～ to tell the truth. **de** ～ really. **la pura** ～ the plain truth. **si bien es** ～ **que** although
verd|e a green; (*fruta etc*) unripe; (*chiste etc*) dirty, blue. ● m green; (*hierba*) grass. ～**or** m greenness
verdugo m executioner; (*fig*) tyrant
verdu|lería f greengrocer's (shop). ～**lero** m greengrocer. ～**ra** f (green) vegetable(s)
vereda f path; (*LAm, acera*) pavement (*Brit*), sidewalk (*Amer*)
veredicto m verdict
vergel m large garden; (*huerto*) orchard
verg|onzoso a shameful; (*tímido*) shy. ～**üenza** f shame; (*timidez*) shyness. **¡es una** ～**üenza!** it's a disgrace! **me da** ～**üenza** I'm ashamed; (*tímido*) I'm shy about. **tener** ～**üenza** be ashamed; (*tímido*) be shy
verídico a true
verifica|ción f verification. ～**r** [7] vt check. ～**rse** vpr take place; (*resultar verdad*) come true
verja f grating; (*cerca*) railings; (*puerta*) iron gate
vermú m, **vermut** m vermouth
vernáculo a vernacular
verosímil a likely; (*relato etc*) credible
verraco m boar
verruga f wart
versado a versed

versar vi turn. ～ **sobre** be about
versátil a versatile; (*fig*) fickle
versión f version; (*traducción*) translation
verso m verse; (*línea*) line
vértebra f vertebra
verte|dero m rubbish tip; (*desaguadero*) drain. ～**dor** m drain. ～**r** [1] vt pour; (*derramar*) spill. ● vi flow
vertical a & f vertical
vértice f vertex
vertiente f slope
vertiginoso a dizzy
vértigo m dizziness; (*med*) vertigo. **de** ～ (*fam*) amazing
vesania f rage; (*med*) insanity
vesícula f blister. ～ **biliar** gallbladder
vespertino a evening
vestíbulo m hall; (*de hotel, teatro etc*) foyer
vestido m (*de mujer*) dress; (*ropa*) clothes
vestigio m trace. ～**s** mpl remains
vest|imenta f clothing. ～**ir** [5] vt (*ponerse*) put on; (*llevar*) wear; dress (*niño etc*). ● vi dress; (*llevar*) wear. ～**irse** vpr get dressed; (*llevar*) wear. ～**uario** m wardrobe; (*cuarto*) dressing-room
Vesuvio m Vesuvius
vetar vt veto
veterano a veteran
veterinari|a f veterinary science. ～**o** a veterinary. ● m vet (*fam*), veterinary surgeon (*Brit*), veterinarian (*Amer*)
veto m veto. **poner el** ～ **a** veto
vetusto a ancient
vez f time; (*turno*) turn. **a la** ～ at the same time; (*de una vez*) in one go. **alguna que otra** ～ from time to time. **alguna** ～ sometimes; (*en preguntas*) ever. **algunas veces** sometimes. **a su** ～ in (his) turn. **a veces** sometimes. **cada** ～ **más** more and more. **de una** ～ in one go. **de una** ～ **para siempre** once and for all. **de** ～ **en cuando** from time to time. **dos veces** twice. **2 veces 4** 2 times 4. **en** ～ **de** instead of. **érase una** ～, **había una** ～ once upon a time. **muchas veces** often. **otra** ～ again. **pocas veces**, **rara** ～ rarely. **repetidas veces** again and again. **tal** ～ perhaps. **una** ～ **(que)** once
vía f road; (*rail*) line; (*anat*) tract; (*fig*) way. ● prep via. ～ **aérea** by air.

~ **de comunicación** *f* means of communication. ~ **férrea** railway (*Brit*), railroad (*Amer*). ~ **rápida** fast lane. **estar en** ~**s de** be in the process of

viab|ilidad *f* viability. ~**le** *a* viable

viaducto *m* viaduct

viaj|ante *m* & *f* commercial traveller. ~**ar** *vi* travel. ~**e** *m* journey; (*corto*) trip. **e de novios** honeymoon. ~**ero** *m* traveller; (*pasajero*) passenger. **¡buen** ~**e!** have a good journey!

víbora *f* viper

vibra|ción *f* vibration. ~**nte** *a* vibrant. ~**r** *vt/i* vibrate

vicario *m* vicar

vice... *pref* vice-...

viceversa *adv* vice versa

vici|ado *a* corrupt; (*aire*) stale. ~**ar** *vt* corrupt; (*estropear*) spoil. ~**o** *m* vice; (*mala costumbre*) bad habit. ~**oso** *a* dissolute; (*círculo*) vicious

vicisitud *f* vicissitude

víctima *f* victim; (*de un accidente*) casualty

victori|a *f* victory. ~**oso** *a* victorious

vid *f* vine

vida *f* life; (*duración*) lifetime. **¡**~ **mía!** my darling! **de por** ~ for life. **en mi** ~ never (in my life). **en** ~ **de** during the lifetime of. **estar en** ~ be alive

vídeo *m* video recorder

video|cinta *f* videotape. ~**juego** *m* video game

vidriar *vt* glaze

vidri|era *f* stained glass window; (*puerta*) glass door; (*LAm, escaparate*) shop window. ~**ería** *f* glass works. ~**ero** *m* glazier. ~**o** *m* glass. ~**oso** *a* glassy

vieira *f* scallop

viejo *a* old. ● *m* old person

Viena *f* Vienna

viene *vb véase* **venir**

viento *m* wind. **hacer** ~ be windy

vientre *f* belly; (*matriz*) womb; (*intestino*) bowels. **llevar un niño en el** ~ be pregnant

viernes *m* Friday. **V**~ **Santo** Good Friday

viga *f* beam; (*de metal*) girder

vigen|cia *f* validity. ~**te** *a* valid; (*ley*) in force. **entrar en** ~**cia** come into force

vigésimo *a* twentieth

vigía *f* (*torre*) watch-tower; (*persona*) lookout

vigil|ancia *f* vigilance. ~**ante** *a* vigilant. ● *m* watchman, supervisor. ~**ar** *vt* keep an eye on. ● *vi* be vigilant; (*vigía etc*) keep watch. ~**ia** *f* vigil; (*relig*) fasting

vigor *m* vigour; (*vigencia*) force. ~**oso** *a* vigorous. **entrar en** ~ come into force

vil *a* vile. ~**eza** *f* vileness; (*acción*) vile deed

vilipendiar *vt* abuse

vilo. en ~ in the air

villa *f* town; (*casa*) villa. **la V**~ Madrid

villancico *m* (Christmas) carol

villano *a* rustic; (*grosero*) coarse

vinagre *m* vinegar. ~**ra** *f* vinegar bottle. ~**ras** *fpl* cruet. ~**ta** *f* vinaigrette (sauce)

vincular *vt* bind

vínculo *m* bond

vindicar [7] *vt* avenge; (*justificar*) vindicate

vine *vb véase* **venir**

vinicult|or *m* wine-grower. ~**ura** *f* wine growing

vino *m* wine. ~ **de Jerez** sherry. ~ **de la casa** house wine. ~ **de mesa** table wine

viña *f*, **viñedo** *m* vineyard

viola *f* viola; (*músico*) viola player

violación *f* violation; (*de una mujer*) rape

violado *a* & *m* violet

violar *vt* violate; break (*ley*); rape (*mujer*)

violen|cia *f* violence; (*fuerza*) force; (*embarazo*) embarrassment. ~**tar** *vt* force; break into (*casa etc*). ~**tarse** *vpr* force o.s. ~**to** *a* violent; (*fig*) awkward. **hacer** ~**cia a** force

violeta *a invar* & *f* violet

viol|ín *m* violin; (*músico*) violinist. ~**inista** *m* & *f* violinist. ~**ón** *m* double bass; (*músico*) double-bass player. ~**onc(h)elista** *m* & *f* cellist. ~**onc(h)elo** *m* cello

vira|je *m* turn. ~**r** *vt* turn. ● *vi* turn; (*fig*) change direction

virg|en *a* & *f* virgin. ~**inal** *a* virginal. ~**inidad** *f* virginity

Virgo *m* Virgo

viril *a* virile. ~**idad** *f* virility

virtual *a* virtual

virtud *f* virtue; (*capacidad*) ability. **en** ~ **de** by virtue of

virtuoso *a* virtuous. ● *m* virtuoso

viruela *f* smallpox. **picado de ~s** pock-marked

virulé. a la ~ *(fam)* crooked; *(estropeado)* damaged

virulento *a* virulent

virus *m invar* virus

visa|do *m* visa. **~r** *vt* endorse

vísceras *fpl* entrails

viscos|a *f* viscose. **~o** *a* viscous

visera *f* visor; *(de gorra)* peak

visib|ilidad *f* visibility. **~le** *a* visible

visig|odo *a* Visigothic. ● *m* Visigoth. **~ótico** *a* Visigothic

visillo *m (cortina)* net curtain

visi|ón *f* vision; *(vista)* sight. **~onario** *a & m* visionary

visita *f* visit; *(persona)* visitor. **~ de cumplido** courtesy call. **~nte** *m & f* visitor. **~r** *vt* visit. **tener ~** have visitors

vislumbr|ar *vt* glimpse. **~e** *f* glimpse; *(resplandor, fig)* glimmer

viso *m* sheen; *(aspecto)* appearance

visón *m* mink

visor *m* viewfinder

víspera *f* day before, eve

vista *f* sight, vision; *(aspecto, mirada)* look; *(panorama)* view. **apartar la ~** look away; *(fig)* turn a blind eye. **a primera ~, a simple ~** at first sight. **clavar la ~ en** stare at. **con ~s a** with a view to. **en ~ de** in view of, considering. **estar a la ~** be obvious. **hacer la ~ gorda** turn a blind eye. **perder de ~** lose sight of. **tener a la ~** have in front of one. **volver la ~ atrás** look back

vistazo *m* glance. **dar/echar un ~ a** glance at

visto *a* seen; *(corriente)* common; *(considerado)* considered. ● *vb véase* **vestir. ~ bueno** passed. **~ que** since. **bien ~** acceptable. **está ~ que** it's obvious that. **lo nunca ~** an unheard-of thing. **mal ~** unacceptable. **por lo ~** apparently

vistoso *a* colourful, bright

visual *a* visual. ● *f* glance. **echar una ~ a** have a look at

vital *a* vital. **~icio** *a* life. ● *m (life)* annuity. **~idad** *f* vitality

vitamina *f* vitamin

viticult|or *m* wine-grower. **~ura** *f* wine growing

vitorear *vt* cheer

vítreo *a* vitreous

vitrina *f* showcase

vituper|ar *vt* censure. **~io** *m* censure. **~ios** *mpl* abuse

viud|a *f* widow. **~ez** *f* widowhood. **~o** *a* widowed. ● *m* widower

viva *m* cheer

vivacidad *f* liveliness

vivamente *adv* vividly; *(sinceramente)* sincerely

vivaz *a (bot)* perennial; *(vivo)* lively

víveres *mpl* supplies

vivero *m* nursery; *(fig)* hotbed

viveza *f* vividness; *(de inteligencia)* sharpness; *(de carácter)* liveliness

vívido *a* true

vívido *a* vivid

vivienda *f* housing; *(casa)* house; *(piso)* flat

viviente *a* living

vivificar [7] *vt (animar)* enliven

vivir *vt* live through. ● *vi* live. ● *m* life. **~ de** live on. **de mal ~** dissolute. **¡viva!** hurray! **¡viva el rey!** long live the king!

vivisección *f* vivisection

vivo *a* alive; *(viviente)* living; *(color)* bright; *(listo)* clever; *(fig)* lively. **a lo ~, al ~** vividly

Vizcaya *f* Biscay

vizconde *m* viscount. **~sa** *f* viscountess

vocab|lo *m* word. **~ulario** *m* vocabulary

vocación *f* vocation

vocal *a* vocal. ● *f* vowel. ● *m & f* member. **~ista** *m & f* vocalist

voce|ar *vt* call *(mercancías)*; *(fig)* proclaim. ● *vi* shout. **~río** *m* shouting

vociferar *vi* shout

vodka *m & f* vodka

vola|da *f* flight. **~dor** *a* flying. ● *m* rocket. **~ndas. en ~ndas** in the air; *(fig, rápidamente)* very quickly. **~nte** *a* flying. ● *m (auto)* steering-wheel; *(nota)* note; *(rehilete)* shuttlecock; *(tec)* flywheel. **~r** [2] *vt* blow up. ● *vi* fly; *(desaparecer, fam)* disappear

volátil *a* volatile

volcán *m* volcano. **~ico** *a* volcanic

vol|car [2 & 7] *vt* knock over; *(adrede)* empty out. ● *vi* overturn. **~carse** *vpr* fall over; *(vehículo)* overturn; *(fig)* do one's utmost. **~carse en** throw o.s. into

vol(e)ibol *m* volleyball

volquete *m* tipper, dump truck

voltaje *m* voltage

voltear *vt* turn over; *(en el aire)* toss; ring *(campanas)*. **~reta** *f* somersault

voltio m volt
voluble a (fig) fickle
volum|en m volume; (importancia) importance. **~inoso** a voluminous
voluntad f will; (fuerza de voluntad) will-power; (deseo) wish; (intención) intention. **buena ~** goodwill. **mala ~** ill will
voluntario a voluntary. • m volunteer. **~so** a willing; (obstinado) wilful
voluptuoso a voluptuous
volver [2, pp **vuelto**] vt turn; (de arriba a abajo) turn over; (devolver) restore. • vi return; (fig) revert. **~se** vpr turn round; (regresar) return; (hacerse) become. **~ a hacer algo** do sth again. **~ en sí** come round
vomit|ar vt bring up. • vi be sick, vomit. **~ivo** m emetic. • a disgusting
vómito m vomit; (acción) vomiting
vorágine f maelstrom
voraz a voracious
vos pron (LAm) you
vosotros pron you; (reflexivo) yourselves. **el libro de ~** your book
vot|ación f voting; (voto) vote. **~ante** m & f voter. **~ar** vt vote for. • vi vote. **~o** m vote; (relig) vow; (maldición) curse. **hacer ~os por** hope for
voy vb véase **ir**
voz f voice; (grito) shout; (rumor) rumour; (palabra) word. **~ pública** public opinion. **aclarar la ~** clear one's throat. **a media ~** softly. **a una ~** unanimously. **dar voces** shout. **en ~ alta** loudly
vuelco m upset. **el corazón me dio un ~** my heart missed a beat
vuelo m flight; (acción) flying; (de ropa) flare. **al ~** in flight; (fig) in passing
vuelta f turn; (curva) bend; (paseo) walk; (revolución) revolution; (regreso) return; (dinero) change. **a la ~** on one's return; (de página) over the page. **a la ~ de la esquina** round the corner. **dar la ~ al mundo** go round the world. **dar una ~** go for a walk. **estar de ~** be back. **¡hasta la ~!** see you soon!
vuelvo vb véase **volver**
vuestro a your. • pron yours. **un amigo ~** a friend of yours
vulg|ar a vulgar; (persona) common. **~aridad** f ordinariness;

(trivialidad) triviality; (grosería) vulgarity. **~arizar** [10] vt popularize. **~o** m common people
vulnerab|ilidad f vulnerability. **~le** a vulnerable

W

wáter m toilet
whisky /'wiski/ m whisky

X

xenofobia f xenophobia
xilófono m xylophone

Y

y conj and
ya adv already; (ahora) now; (luego) later; (en seguida) immediately; (pronto) soon. • int of course! **~ no** no longer. **~ que** since. **¡~, ~!** oh yes!, all right!
yacaré m (LAm) alligator
yac|er [44] vi lie. **~imiento** m deposit; (de petróleo) oilfield
yanqui m & f American, Yank(ee)
yate m yacht
yegua f mare
yeísmo m pronunciation of the Spanish ll like the Spanish y
yelmo m helmet
yema f (bot) bud; (de huevo) yolk; (golosina) sweet. **~ del dedo** fingertip
yergo vb véase **erguir**
yermo a uninhabited; (no cultivable) barren. • m wasteland
yerno m son-in-law
yerro m mistake. • vb véase **errar**
yerto a stiff
yeso m gypsum; (arquit) plaster. **~ mate** plaster of Paris
yo pron I. • m ego. **~ mismo** I myself. **soy ~** it's me
yodo m iodine
yoga m yoga
yogur m yog(h)urt
York. de ~ ⟨jamón⟩ cooked
yuca f yucca
Yucatán m Yucatán
yugo m yoke

Yugoslavia f Yugoslavia
yugoslavo a & m Yugoslav
yunque m anvil
yunta f yoke
yuxtaponer [34] vt juxtapose
yuyo m (Arg) weed

Z

zafarse vpr escape; get out of ⟨obligación etc⟩
zafarrancho m (confusión) mess; (riña) quarrel
zafio a coarse
zafiro m sapphire
zaga f rear. **no ir en ~** not be inferior
zaguán m hall
zaherir [4] vt hurt one's feelings
zahorí m clairvoyant; (de agua) water diviner
zaino a ⟨caballo⟩ chestnut; ⟨vaca⟩ black
zalamer|ía f flattery. **~o** a flattering. ● m flatterer
zamarra f (piel) sheepskin; (prenda) sheepskin jacket
zamarrear vt shake
zamba f (esp LAm) South American dance; (samba) samba
zambulli|da f dive. **~r** [22] vt plunge. **~rse** vpr dive
zamparse vpr fall; (comer) gobble up
zanahoria f carrot
zancad|a f stride. **~illa** f trip. **echar la ~illa a uno, poner la ~illa a uno** trip s.o. up
zanc|o m stilt. **~udo** a long-legged. ● m (LAm) mosquito
zanganear vi idle
zángano m drone; (persona) idler
zangolotear vt fiddle with. ● vi rattle; ⟨persona⟩ fidget
zanja f ditch. **~r** vt (fig) settle
zapapico m pickaxe

zapat|ear vt/i tap with one's feet. **~ería** f shoe shop; (arte) shoemaking. **~ero** m shoemaker; (el que remienda zapatos) cobbler. **~illa** f slipper. **~illas deportivas** trainers. **~o** m shoe
zaragata f turmoil
Zaragoza f Saragossa
zarand|a f sieve. **~ear** vt sieve; (sacudir) shake
zarcillo m earring
zarpa f claw, paw
zarpar vi weigh anchor
zarza f bramble. **~mora** f blackberry
zarzuela f musical, operetta
zascandil m scatterbrain
zenit m zenith
zigzag m zigzag. **~uear** vi zigzag
zinc m zinc
zipizape m (fam) row
zócalo m skirting-board; (pedestal) plinth
zodiaco m, **zodíaco** m zodiac
zona f zone; (área) area
zoo m zoo. **~logía** f zoology. **~lógico** a zoological
zoólogo m zoologist
zopenco a stupid. ● m idiot
zoquete m (de madera) block; (persona) blockhead
zorr|a f fox; (hembra) vixen. **~o** m fox
zozobra f (fig) anxiety. **~r** vi be shipwrecked; (fig) be ruined
zueco m clog
zulú a & m Zulu
zumb|ar vt (fam) give ⟨golpe etc⟩. ● vi buzz. **~ido** m buzzing
zumo m juice
zurci|do m darning. **~r** [9] vt darn
zurdo a left-handed; ⟨mano⟩ left
zurrar vt (fig, dar golpes, fam) beat up
zurriago m whip
zutano m so-and-so

Spanish in Context

Contents

¿Habla español?

Imagine you are in Spain or any other Spanish-speaking country. Whether you want to travel around, spend a night out, or go shopping, you need to make yourself understood. With what you have learned so far in class or on your own, how well do you think you would cope?

Do you want to find out? The following section is a test-yourself conversation guide, which has been designed precisely to help you practise everyday language. It will help you build up your vocabulary in a fun and relaxed way through role play and model dialogues.

The section includes seven common situations as listed above. For each of them, you will find a variety of role play situations, a reminder of useful structures and vocabulary items, and also a model dialogue.

Jet Set

Role Play

Imagine . . .

1 You want to fly to Madrid/Paris/etc: buy a ticket.
2 You have missed your plane: ask if there is another flight later that day.
3 Your flight is delayed: ask why, and when it will take off.
4 Your flight is cancelled: ask why, and try to find out how you can get to your destination.
5 You are to meet somebody at the airport, but their flight is delayed or cancelled: try to find out the reason for the delay/cancellation and when they are likely to arrive.

Useful vocabulary and structures

el aeropuerto—*the airport*
la terminal—*the terminal*
un billete (Spain), un pasaje (LAm), un boleto (Mex)—*a ticket*
un billete/pasaje de ida y vuelta, un boleto redondo (Mex)
  —*a return ticket*
un billete/pasaje (sólo) de ida, un boleto sencillo (Mex)
  —*a one-way/single ticket*
el mostrador de venta de billetes/pasajes/boletos
  —*the ticket office*
un pasaporte—*a passport*
un visado (Spain),una visa (LAm)
  —*a visa*
el carné de identidad
  —*an identity card*
la facturación de equipajes (Spain), el registro de equipaje (Mex)—*check-in*

el mostrador de facturación
  —*the check-in desk*
ya facturé (Spain) or chequeé (LAm) or registré (Mex) mi equipaje
  —*I've checked in my luggage*
¿cuántos bultos tiene?
  —*how many pieces of luggage do you have?*
el equipaje de mano—*hand luggage*
un asiento junto a la ventanilla
  —*a window seat*
un asiento junto al pasillo
  —*an aisle seat*
una tarjeta de embarque
  —*a boarding card*
un carro or un carrito (para el equipaje)—*a luggage trolley*
la sala de espera
  —*the waiting lounge*

las tiendas libres de impuestos
—*duty free shops*

el duty free—*duty free*

salidas internacionales
—*international departures*

el vuelo procedente de Londres
—*the flight from London*

un vuelo con destino a Roma
—*a flight to Rome*

un vuelo de enlace procedente
de Berlín
—*a connecting flight from Berlín*

el vuelo hace escala en Omán
—*the flight stops (over) in Oman*

el vuelo está retrasado *or*
atrasado (LAm)
—*the flight is delayed*

siempre viaja en clase preferente/
clase económica —*he always
travels business class/tourist class*

los pasajeros con destino a
Praga—*passengers travelling to
Prague*

pasamos por la aduana
—*we went through customs*

no tengo nada que declarar
—*I have nothing to declare*

Model Dialogue

¿En qué vuelo viene?

Una señora = ●
Miembro del personal de tierra = ○

● Buenas tardes, señorita. Perdone que la moleste pero es que he venido a buscar a un amigo que viene de Lisboa y olvidé en casa los datos del vuelo. Sé que llega alrededor de las cuatro pero no sé la hora exacta.

○ Bueno, vamos a ver. ¿Se acuerda del número del vuelo?

● No, pero es el vuelo que hace escala en Lisboa.

○ De acuerdo, pero resulta que hoy hay dos vuelos por la tarde, uno que llega a las cuatro y media y otro a las cinco y veinte.

● ¿De qué líneas aéreas son, por favor?

○ El primero es de Avianca y el segundo de Viasa.

● Tiene que ser el segundo.

○ Por desgracia ese vuelo va a llegar con una hora de retraso, así que tendrá Ud que esperar casi dos horas.

● No importa. Lo bueno es que no se haya ido ya mi amigo. ¿Me dice por favor dónde debo esperar?

○ Claro. La sala de espera para las llegadas internacionales está en la planta baja. Baje por aquella escalera y siga hasta el fondo. Allí verá las puertas automáticas por donde salen los pasajeros.

● Estupendo, pues . . . muchas gracias.

○ No hay de qué. Adiós.

Making Tracks

Role Play

Imagine ...

1 You want 2 tickets, a return and a single, to Alicante, for the following day.
2 You have just arrived by train and need to leave your suitcases in left luggage. Then you want to have some refreshments and use the toilets before leaving the station: you ask a station guard to direct you.
3 You are meeting a friend off a train from Switzerland but the train is not there: ask the guard if the train is delayed and when it is due to arrive.
4 You are about to get on your train when you hear another passenger talking about changing trains during the journey: check with the guard on the platform if this is true and where and when you have to change.

Useful vocabulary and structures

la estación de tren
  —*the train station*
el andén—*the platform*
el mostrador *or* la ventanilla
  de venta de billetes (Spain)
  or boletos (LAm)
  —*the ticket office*
un billete (Spain), un boleto (LAm)
  —*a ticket*
un billete sencillo *or* de ida
  (Spain), un boleto de ida (LAm
  except Mex), un boleto sencillo
  (Mex)—*a single ticket*
un billete/boleto de ida y vuelta,
un boleto (de viaje) redondo (Mex)
  —*a return ticket*
un billete/boleto de primera

clase/segunda (clase)
  —*a first-class/second-class ticket*
un tren expreso/rápido
  —*an express/a fast train*
reservar un asiento
  —*to reserve a seat*
una litera—*a couchette*
el tren para Teruel sale del
  andén 9
  —*the train on platform 9 is
  for Teruel*
un carro, un carrito—*a trolley*
un vagón—*a carriage*
un compartimento de fumadores
  /no fumadores
  —*a smoking/non-smoking
  compartment*

la rejilla (portaequipajes)
—*the luggage rack*

¿este tren tiene coche comedor
or (Mex) carro comedor?
—*does this train have a dining
car?*

el revisor/la revisora
—*the ticket collector* or *inspector*

voy en tren
—*I'm going by train*

cambiar de tren, hacer
transbordo
—*to change trains*

¿dónde está la consigna
—*where is 'left luggage'?*

consigna automática (de
equipajes)
—*(coin-operated) left-luggage
locker*

Model dialogue
El tren no la llegado

Un señor = ●
Empleado = ○

● Oiga, por favor, ¿sabe a qué andén llega el expreso que viene de
Valencia? Debió haber estado aquí a las once y veinticinco pero no
lo encuentro en ningún andén.

○ Lo que pasa es que ese tren viene con retraso.

● ¡Ay no! ¿Se sabe cuándo va a llegar? Es que he venido a buscar a
alguien, y si falta mucho puedo salir y volver luego.

○ Bueno, según nos han informado el tren se ha averiado a unos cuan-
tos kilómetros de aquí y se espera que llegará a eso de la una.

● ¿Pero todavía no se sabe a qué hora exactamente?

○ No. De todos modos, seguro que no llegará antes de las doce y
media. Si quiere llamar por teléfono más tarde, podrán informarle
mejor entonces.

● Pero ya llevo veinte minutos esperando. ¿Por qué no lo anunciaron
por el altavoz antes?

○ Acabamos de enterarnos, señor. Se ruega tener paciencia.

● Sí, por supuesto. ¿Me dice por favor dónde está la cafetería?

○ Al otro lado de la estación, en el fondo.

● Gracias, señor. Adiós.

Time Out

Role play

Imagine ...

1 You want to ask sb out to a concert. You discuss what is on and make arrangements to meet up before.
2 You call the box office of a theatre to book tickets for a play.
3 You call a cinema to find out what is on. Ask if you can book tickets over the phone and check when to pick them up.
4 You call a restaurant to see if they are open on Sundays and book a table for four for that evening.

Useful vocabulary and structures

¿te gustaría ir al cine este fin
de semana?
—*would you like to go to the cinema
at the weekend?*

¿qué tienes ganas de hacer *or*
qué te apetece hacer (Spain)
esta tarde?
—*what do you fancy doing this
afternoon/evening?*

¿estás libre mañana?
—*are you free tomorrow?*

¿tienes algún compromiso
mañana?—*are you doing any-
thing/are you busy tomorrow?*

¿tienes algún plan *or* programa
para esta noche?
—*do you have any plans for
tonight?*

salir/ir a tomar una(s) copa(s)
—*to go (out) for a drink*

vida nocturna—*nightlife*

salir a cenar *or* comer (LAm)
—*to go out for dinner/for a meal*

¿qué dan *or* qué ponen (Spain)
en el Renoir?
—*what's on at the Renoir?*

¿hay que reservar antes?
—*do you have to book in advance?*

la taquilla, la boletería (LAm)
—*the box office/ticket office*

¿a qué hora empieza la película/
la función?
—*what time does the film/
performance start?*

ya se agotaron las localidades
—*it's sold out*

recoger las entradas
—*to pick up/collect the tickets*

¿qué te parece?
—*what do you think (of it)?*

¿te gusta?—*are you enjoying it?*

un concierto al aire libre
—*an open-air concert*

tener una actuación
  —*to do* or *play a gig*
reservar una mesa
  —*to book* or *reserve a table*
¿me trae la carta ?
  —*can I see the menu, please?*
de primer plato *or* de entrada,
  quisiera las espinacas
  —*can I have the spinach to start
  with, please?*

y de segundo, el salmón
  —*and salmon for the main course*
¿me trae una jarra de agua,
  por favor?
  —*could I have a jug of water,
  please?*
(me trae) la cuenta, por favor
  —*can I have the bill, please?*
¿cuánto se deja de propina?
  —*how much tip should I leave?*

Model dialogue

¿Qué hacemos el sábado?

  Ramón = ●
  Eva = ○

● Oye, Eva ¿tienes algún plan para el sábado por la noche?

○ Por el momento no tengo nada planeado, pero iba a llamar a Marichu para quedar con ella*.

● Bueno, pues, vi ayer un cartel de publicidad de 'Los Pachequitos' - van a dar un concierto al aire libre en el Parque del Oeste.

○ ¿Ah, sí? ¿Qué tipo de música tocan?

● ¿No los conoces? Es un grupo cubano que toca son y merengue - seguro que los encontrarás muy buenos. ¿Qué te parece?

○ Me parece bien.

● Estupendo. Entonces iré a sacar las entradas esta tarde. ¿Le compro una a Marichu también?

○ No creo. Que se las arregle como quiera este fin de semana.

● Bueno, entonces nos encontramos en la salida del metro de Moncloa a las ocho, ¿sí? Así podremos ir a tomar una copa antes. De todas maneras te llamo a casa cuando tenga las entradas.

○ De acuerdo. Y primero tengo que hablar con mis padres. Ya sabes como me controlan, ¿eh?

● Claro. Es lo de siempre, ¿no?

○ Bueno, pues nada. Hasta mañana.

● Hasta luego.

* this usage is Peninsular Spanish. In Latin America one would say **'para que nos encontráramos'**.

Hotel Break

Role play

Imagine . . .

1   You call a hotel to book two rooms, a single and a double, for two nights: ask about the price and arrange the dates and arrival time.

2   You arrive at your hotel to find that your room has been double-booked. There is no other hotel nearby and you wish to be given another room also with sea view.

3   When you get up to your room you find that the bathroom is not very clean. You also want something to eat in your room: you call room service.

4   You are going out for the evening and think you may be back quite late: you ask at reception what to do about taking keys with you or ringing the bell.

Useful vocabulary and structures

un hotel de tres/cuatro estrellas
  —*a three/four star hotel*
alojamiento—*accomodation*
un hostal—*a cheap hotel*
una residencia—*a guesthouse
  (usually of category between
  'hotel' and 'pensión')*
una pensión
  —*a guesthouse, rooming house*
una reserva, una reservación
  (LAm)—*a reservation, a booking*
reservar/pagar una habitación
  —*to book/pay for a room*
¿es necesario dejar un depósito?
  —*do you require a deposit?*
una habitación sencilla/
  individual—*a single room*
una habitación doble
  —*a double room*

una habitación con camas
  gemelas—*a twin-bedded room*
una cama de matrimonio or
  de dos plazas (LAm)
  —*a double bed*
una cama individual or de una
  plaza (LAm)—*a single bed*
una habitación con vista al mar
  —*a (room with) sea view*
registrarse—*to check in*
¿podría ver la habitación,
  por favor?
  —*could I see the room, please?*
una caja de seguridad
  —*a safety deposit box*
¿hay un mozo que nos pueda
  subir/bajar las maletas?
  —*is there a porter to take up/
  bring down our suitcases?*

el servicio a las habitaciones
—*room service*

no hay agua caliente
—*there's no hot water*

el televisor/la ducha no
funciona
—*the television/the shower
doesn't work*

¿a qué hora se sirve el desayuno?
—*what time is breakfast?*

¿dónde dejo la llave?
—*where should I leave the key?*

hay servicio de lavandería?
—*is there a laundry service?*

¿me podrían despertar mañana
por la mañana, por favor?
—*could I have a wake-up call in the
morning, please?*

por favor dejen libre la
habitación antes de las once
de la mañana
—*please vacate your room by
11a.m.*

¿a qué hora hay que salir del or
dejar el hotel?
—*what time must I check out by?*

Model dialogue

¡Cámbienme de habitación!

Propietaria = ●
Huésped = ○

● Buenos días, señora. ¿Cómo está? ¿Durmió bien?

○ Pues, la verdad es que no muy bien.

● Lo siento, señora. ¿Y a qué se debió eso?

○ Bueno, primero había mucho ruido en la calle. Parece que todas las motos pasaran por allí. Y la nevera hizo un sonido muy raro - una especie de pitido - durante casi toda la noche.

● ¡Uy, lo siento! En seguida llamo a mi marido para que lo arregle.

○ Además la habitación es muy pequeña y está mal ventilada. Con el calor que hacía me costaba respirar. En fin, quiero que me cambie de habitación.

● Mm... Eso podría ser difícil. Es que todas las habitaciones están ocupadas.

○ No me importa. Hice la reserva hace mucho tiempo y esperaba que la habitación fuera cómoda y tranquila. Debo insistir en que me la cambie.

● Vamos a ver. Ah . . . ahora que veo en el libro, resulta que se van hoy los de la 14, de manera que la puede ocupar Ud esta misma mañana.

○ ¿A qué hora estará disponible entonces?

● Cuanto antes, señora. Nada más terminar la limpieza, le aviso.

Money matters and keeping in touch

Role Play

Imagine ...

1 You go to the post office to send a large parcel to your sister in Austria for her birthday.

2 You want stamps for seven postcards to Scotland, two letters to Italy and an airletter to New Zealand.

3 You are at the counter in the bank. You want to cash a cheque and change some English money into Spanish currency.

4 You want to order 80.000 pesetas worth of travellers cheques in US dollars for a trip to Central America.

5 You want to withdraw some cash: talk to the cashier and find out what you have to do.

Useful vocabulary and structures

voy a la oficina de correos *or*
  voy a Correos (Spain), voy al
  correo (LAm)
  —*I'm going to the post office*
la ventanilla
  —*the counter, the window*
un sello, una estampilla (LAm),
  un timbre (Mexico)—*a stamp*
enviar *or* mandar una carta/
  una postal/un paquete
  —*to send a letter/a postcard/
  a parcel*
mandar algo por avión *or* por
  vía aérea—*to send sth airmail*
un sobre de avión
  —*an airmail envelope*
un aerograma—*an airletter*
póngalo en la balanza
  —*put it on the scales*

hay que rellenar *or* llenar este
  formulario *or* este impreso *or*
  esta forma (Mex)
  —*you have to fill in or fill out this
  form*
abrir una cuenta (bancaria)
  —*to open a bank account*
una cuenta corriente
  —*a current account*
una cuenta de ahorro(s)
  —*a savings/deposit account*
retirar/sacar dinero
  —*to withdraw/take out money*
depositar *or* ingresar (Spain)
  un cheque/dinero
  —*to pay in a cheque/some money*
en efectivo—*in cash*
un cajero automático
  —*a cash dispenser*

hacer cola—*to queue, stand in line*

pase a (la) caja, por favor
—*please go to the cash desk*

cobrar un cheque *or* talón (Spain)
—*to cash a cheque*

el cheque se lo abonarán *or*
cambiarán en (la) caja
—*you can cash the cheque at the
cash desk*

¿puede firmar el dorso del
cheque?
—*can you sign the back of the
cheque?*

quisiera mandar un giro postal
—*I'd like to send a money order*

cheques de viajero
—*traveller's cheques*

una casa de cambio
—*a bureau de change*

divisas, moneda extranjera
—*foreign currency*

la tasa de cambio (Spain), el tipo
de cambio
—*the exchange rate*

¿a cuánto está (el cambio de)
la libra?
—*what's the rate at the moment
for the pound?*

¿me puede dar trescientas
libras en cheques de viajero,
por favor?
—*can I have three hundred pounds
in traveller's cheques, please?*

¿cuánto se paga de comisión?
—*how much commission do you
charge?*

Model Dialogue

En la oficina de correos

Cliente = ●
Empleado de la oficina de correos = ○

● Buenos días. Quisiera mandar este paquete a Grecia. ¿Me dice cuánto puede tardar en llegar, por favor?

○ Entre cuatro y cinco días, señor. ¿Quiere enviarlo por correo aéreo?

● Entonces sí. Quiero que llegue antes del sábado.

○ Póngalo en la balanza, por favor. A ver... así son mil cien pesetas.

● Muy bien. Y querría mandar esta carta a Murcia por correo urgente. ¿Me puede dar también nueve sellos para postales, por favor?

○ ¿Para mandar al extranjero o dentro de España?

● Son todas para Estados Unidos.

○ Bueno, aquí tiene.

● Me han dicho que es mejor mandar las postales en sobre, que llegan más rápido así.

○ No hace falta, señor. Hoy día todas llegan igual. ¡Y le aseguro que los carteros no tienen tiempo para leer la correspondencia ajena!

● ¡Por supuesto que no! Gracias. Adiós.

Where to Find What

Role Play

Imagine ...

1 You want to visit the main museums and galleries in the city: ask what times they are open, whether they are open every day and how much the admission charge is.
2 You would like a map of the city and leaflets about places to visit.
3 You want to find out about good cheap places to eat in the city, and if there are any traditional old cafés to have a drink in.
4 You want some information about visits to the monastery of Montserrat from Barcelona: find out what times the coach trip leaves and returns, how much it costs and what it includes.

Useful vocabulary and structures

un cartel—*a poster*

¿me puedo llevar este folleto?
  —*can I take this leaflet/brochure?*

quisiera informarme sobre...
  —*I'd like to find out about...*

alquiler de coches (Spain) *or* carros (LAm)—*car hire, car rental*

alquilar un coche (Spain) *or* un carro (LAm)—*to hire a car, rent a car*

quisiera averiguar a qué horas está abierto el museo
  —*I'd like to find out what times the museum is open*

¿a qué hora abre/cierra el museo?
  —*what time does the museum open/close?*

¿cuánto cuesta *or* vale la entrada?
  —*how much is admission?*

un museo de arte
  —*an art gallery (museum)*

el casco viejo—*the old quarter*

¿tiene una lista de hoteles económicos?
  —*do you have a list of cheap hotels?*

¿me/nos puede recomendar un buen hotel?
  —*can you recommend a good hotel?*

¿me puede/podría decir cómo llegar a ...?
  —*can you/could you tell me how to get to ...?*

¿me puede decir dónde está *or* queda la estación de tren?
  —*can you tell me where the train station is?*

un plano de la ciudad/del metro
  —*a map of the city/of the underground or subway (US)*

me señaló la ruta en un mapa
—*he showed me the route on a map*

¿cómo es el horario de los bancos?
—*what times are banks open?*

¿dónde se puede cambiar dinero?
—*where can I change money?*

¿hay que pagar por adelantado?
—*do you have to pay in advance?*

¿nos podría sugerir/recomendar alguna excursión interesante?
—*can you suggest/recommend any good day trips?*

ir *or* salir a remar
—*to go rowing*

¿se hacen visitas guiadas del palacio?
—*can one do a guided tour of the palace?*

¿sabe si hay unos servicios (Spain) *or* baños públicos (LAm) por aquí cerca?
—*do you know if there are any public toilets near here?*

Model Dialogue

Dónde alojarse y qué conocer

Empleada de la Oficina de Turismo = ●
Turista = ○

● Buenas tardes. ¿En qué les puedo servir?

○ Buenas tardes. Es que acabamos de llegar a la ciudad y necesitamos encontrar alojamiento. ¿Tiene alguna lista de hoteles económicos?

● Por supuesto. Aquí mismo tengo una, en el mostrador. ¿Quieren quedarse en una zona más bien céntrica?

○ Sí, si es posible.

● Entonces les puedo señalar aquí en este plano algunos buenos hostales y hoteles.

○ Gracias. ¿Nos podría dar un folleto o una guía de los lugares de interés más importantes para visitar? Tenemos poco tiempo aquí y no queremos perdernos nada.

● Claro, aquí tiene. Además, les puedo recomendar una visita organizada de tres horas que sale de la plaza central cada dos horas. Aquí verán la información necesaria.

○ Muy bien. Gracias.

● Tal vez también les interese hacer una excursión por los alrededores de la ciudad?

○ Sí, sería genial. Y por último, ¿nos podría decir cómo llegar al consulado australiano?

● Sin problema - ¡está aquí al lado!

Shop Till You Drop

Role Play

Imagine . . .

1 You go to a clothes shop to buy a jacket: ask to try one on.
2 You are at the local food market. You have come to get some ingredients for a big stew of your choice.
3 You bought a jersey yesterday but have found a hole in it. You bring it back to the shop to change it.
4 You buy a rug in a shop. You want to send it back to Dublin: ask if you can pay by credit card and how much it will cost to send.
5 You want to buy a present for your mother to take back home: go to a department store and ask which floor the different items are on (porcelain, fans, perfume, scarves, CDs and tapes).

Useful vocabulary and structures

unos (grandes) almacenes, una tienda de departamentos (Mex)—*a department store*

un centro comercial
—*a shopping centre*

una tienda de modas
—*a clothes shop*

una tienda de novedades
—*a gift shop*

el dependiente/la dependienta (Spain), el vendedor/la vendedora (LAm)—*the shop assistant*

en la planta baja
—*on the ground floor*

en la primera planta, en el primer piso—*on the first floor*

a precio de ganga
—*at bargain price*

hay que regatear
—*you have to bargain*

¿dónde puedo comprar . . .?
—*where can I get . . .?*

¿lo/la atienden?
—*are you being served?*

estoy mirando solamente
—*I'm just looking, thank you*

¿cuánto vale *or* cuesta esto, por favor?
—*how much is this, please?*

quisiera una chaqueta
—*I'm looking for a jacket*

¿tiene esto en rojo/en otros colores?—*do you have this in red/ in other colours?*

¿me puedo probar esto?
—*can I try this on?*

¿me lo/la puedo probar?
—*can I try it on?*

¿dónde está el probador?
—*where is the fitting room?*

¿qué talla tiene or usa?
—*what size do you take? [clothes]*

calzo el numero 44
—*I take size 10 shoes*

me llevo éste/ésta, por favor
—*I'll take this (one), please*

quisiera cambiar éste/ésta por
otro/otra
—*I'd like to change this for
another one*

¿dónde se paga?—*where do I pay?*

¿puedo pagar con cheque?
—*can I pay by cheque?*

¿aceptan tarjetas de crédito?
—*do you take credit cards?*

¿cuánto cobran por el envío
(a domicilio)?
—*how much is the delivery charge?*

¿se puede enviar/mandar por
barco a . . . ?
—*is it possible to have it shipped
to . . . ?*

¿puedo pedir que se me devuelva
el impuesto?
—*can I claim tax back on it?*

¿a cuánto están los tomates?
—*how much are the tomatoes?*

¿me da or me pone (Spain)
medio kilo de queso, por
favor?—*can I have half a kilo
of cheese, please?*

¿quién es la última?*
—*who's last in the queue or line?*

Model dialogue

Compras de última hora

    Dependiente = ●

    Cliente = ○

● Buenos días, señor. ¿Qué desea?

○ Me da una caja de aspirinas, por favor.

● Sí, señor. ¿Quiere algo más?

○ ¿Tiene repelente para mosquitos?

● ¿Prefiere loción o en espray?

○ En espray, por favor. Y me hace falta también una crema bronceadora. ¿Cuánto vale la de esta marca?

● Pues, cuesta mil trescientas pesetas.

○ ¿Y me puede dar un jarabe para la tos, para niños?

● Muy bien. Aquí tiene. ¿Algo más?

○ Nada más, gracias. ¿Cuánto es, por favor?

● Vamos a ver. Son . . . 2.900 pesetas en total.

○ Tenga Ud.

● Gracias, aquí tiene la vuelta.

ENGLISH-SPANISH
INGLÉS-ESPAÑOL

A

a /ə, eɪ/ *indef art* (*before vowel* **an**) un *m*; una *f*

aback /ə'bæk/ *adv.* **be taken** ~ quedar desconcertado

abacus /'æbəkəs/ *n* ábaco *m*

abandon /ə'bændən/ *vt* abandonar. ● *n* abandono *m*, desenfado *m*. ~**ed** *a* abandonado; ⟨*behaviour*⟩ perdido. ~**ment** *n* abandono *m*

abase /ə'beɪs/ *vt* degradar. ~**ment** *n* degradación *f*

abashed /ə'bæʃt/ *a* confuso

abate /ə'beɪt/ *vt* disminuir. ● *vi* disminuir; ⟨*storm etc*⟩ calmarse. ~**ment** *n* disminución *f*

abattoir /'æbətwɑː(r)/ *n* matadero *m*

abbess /'æbis/ *n* abadesa *f*

abbey /'æbɪ/ *n* abadía *f*

abbot /'æbət/ *n* abad *m*

abbreviat|e /ə'briːvɪeɪt/ *vt* abreviar. ~**ion** /-'eɪʃn/ *n* abreviatura *f*; (*act*) abreviación *f*

ABC /'eɪbiː'siː/ *n* abecé *m*, abecedario *m*

abdicat|e /'æbdɪkeɪt/ *vt/i* abdicar. ~**ion** /-'eɪʃn/ *n* abdicación *f*

abdom|en /'æbdəmən/ *n* abdomen *m*. ~**inal** /-'dɒmɪnl/ *a* abdominal

abduct /æb'dʌkt/ *vt* secuestrar. ~**ion** /-ʃn/ *n* secuestro *m*. ~**or** *n* secuestrador *m*

aberration /æbə'reɪʃn/ *n* aberración *f*

abet /ə'bet/ *vt* (*pt* **abetted**) (*jurid*) ser cómplice de

abeyance /ə'beɪəns/ *n*. **in** ~ en suspenso

abhor /əb'hɔː(r)/ *vt* (*pt* **abhorred**) aborrecer. ~**rence** /-'hɒrəns/ *n* aborrecimiento *m*; (*thing*) abominación *f*. ~**rent** /-'hɒrənt/ *a* aborrecible

abide /ə'baɪd/ *vt* (*pt* **abided**) soportar. ● *vi* (*old use, pt* **abode**) morar. ~ **by** atenerse a; cumplir ⟨*promise*⟩

abiding /ə'baɪdɪŋ/ *a* duradero, permanente

ability /ə'bɪlətɪ/ *n* capacidad *f*; (*cleverness*) habilidad *f*

abject /'æbdʒekt/ *a* (*wretched*) miserable; (*vile*) abyecto

ablaze /ə'bleɪz/ *a* en llamas

able /'eɪbl/ *a* (**-er, -est**) capaz. **be** ~ poder; (*know how to*) saber

ablutions /ə'bluːʃnz/ *npl* ablución *f*

ably /'eɪblɪ/ *adv* hábilmente

abnormal /æb'nɔːml/ *a* anormal. ~**ity** /-'mælətɪ/ *n* anormalidad *f*

aboard /ə'bɔːd/ *adv* a bordo. ● *prep* a bordo de

abode /ə'bəʊd/ *see* **abide**. ● *n* (*old use*) domicilio *m*

abolish /ə'bɒlɪʃ/ *vt* suprimir, abolir

abolition /æbə'lɪʃn/ *n* supresión *f*, abolición *f*

abominable /ə'bɒmɪnəbl/ *a* abominable

abominat|e /ə'bɒmɪneɪt/ *vt* abominar. ~**ion** /-'neɪʃn/ *n* abominación *f*

aborigin|al /æbə'rɪdʒənl/ *a & n* aborigen (*m & f*), indígena (*m & f*). ~**es** /-iːz/ *npl* aborígenes *mpl*

abort /ə'bɔːt/ *vt* hacer abortar. ● *vi* abortar. ~**ion** /-ʃn/ *n* aborto *m* provocado; (*fig*) aborto *m*. ~**ionist** *n* abortista *m & f*. ~**ive** *a* abortivo; (*fig*) fracasado

abound /ə'baʊnd/ *vi* abundar (**in** de, en)

about /ə'baʊt/ *adv* (*approximately*) alrededor de; (*here and there*) por todas partes; (*in existence*) por aquí. ~ **here** por aquí. **be** ~ **to** estar a punto de. **be up and** ~ estar levantado. ● *prep* sobre; (*around*) alrededor de; (*somewhere in*) en. **talk** ~ hablar de. ~**-face** *n* (*fig*) cambio *m* rotundo. ~**-turn** *n* (*fig*) cambio *m* rotundo

above /ə'bʌv/ *adv* arriba. ● *prep* encima de; (*more than*) más de. ~ **all** sobre todo. ~**-board** *a* honrado.

● *adv* abiertamente. **∼mentioned** *a* susodicho

abrasi|on /ə'breɪʒn/ *n* abrasión *f*. **∼ve** /ə'breɪsɪv/ *a* & *n* abrasivo (*m*); (*fig*) agresivo, brusco

abreast /ə'brest/ *adv* de frente. **keep ∼ of** mantenerse al corriente de

abridge /ə'brɪdʒ/ *vt* abreviar. **∼ment** *n* abreviación *f*; (*abstract*) resumen *m*

abroad /ə'brɔːd/ *adv* (*be*) en el extranjero; (*go*) al extranjero; (*far and wide*) por todas partes

abrupt /ə'brʌpt/ *a* brusco. **∼ly** *adv* (*suddenly*) repentinamente; (*curtly*) bruscamente. **∼ness** *n* brusquedad *f*

abscess /'æbsɪs/ *n* absceso *m*

abscond /əb'skɒnd/ *vi* fugarse

absen|ce /'æbsəns/ *n* ausencia *f*; (*lack*) falta *f*. **∼t** /'æbsənt/ *a* ausente. /æb'sent/ *vr*. **∼ o.s.** ausentarse. **∼tly** *adv* distraídamente. **∼t-minded** *a* distraído. **∼t-mindedness** *n* distracción *f*, despiste *m*

absentee /æbsən'tiː/ *n* ausente *m* & *f*. **∼ism** *n* absentismo *m*

absinthe /'æbsɪnθ/ *n* ajenjo *m*

absolute /'æbsəluːt/ *a* absoluto. **∼ly** *adv* absolutamente

absolution /æbsə'luːʃn/ *n* absolución *f*

absolve /əb'zɒlv/ *vt* (*from sin*) absolver; (*from obligation*) liberar

absor|b /əb'zɔːb/ *vt* absorber. **∼bent** *a* absorbente. **∼ption** *n* absorción *f*

abstain /əb'steɪn/ *vi* abstenerse (**from** de)

abstemious /əb'stiːmɪəs/ *a* abstemio

abstention /əb'stenʃn/ *n* abstención *f*

abstinen|ce /'æbstɪnəns/ *n* abstinencia *f*. **∼t** *a* abstinente

abstract /'æbstrækt/ *a* abstracto. ● *n* (*quality*) abstracto *m*; (*summary*) resumen *m*. /əb'strækt/ *vt* extraer; (*summarize*) resumir. **∼ion** /-ʃn/ *n* abstracción *f*

abstruse /əb'struːs/ *a* abstruso

absurd /əb'sɜːd/ *a* absurdo. **∼ity** *n* absurdo *m*, disparate *m*

abundan|ce /ə'bʌndəns/ *n* abundancia *f*. **∼t** *a* abundante

abuse /ə'bjuːz/ *vt* (*misuse*) abusar de; (*ill-treat*) maltratar; (*insult*) insultar. /ə'bjuːs/ *n* abuso *m*; (*insults*) insultos *mpl*

abusive /ə'bjuːsɪv/ *a* injurioso

abut /ə'bʌt/ *vi* (*pt* **abutted**) confinar (**on** con)

abysmal /ə'bɪzməl/ *a* abismal; (*bad*, *fam*) pésimo; (*fig*) profundo

abyss /ə'bɪs/ *n* abismo *m*

acacia /ə'keɪʃə/ *n* acacia *f*

academic /ækə'demɪk/ *a* académico; (*pej*) teórico. ● *n* universitario *m*, catedrático *m*. **∼ian** /-də'mɪʃn/ *n* académico *m*

academy /ə'kædəmɪ/ *n* academia *f*. **∼ of music** conservatorio *m*

accede /ək'siːd/ *vi*. **∼ to** acceder a (*request*); tomar posesión de (*office*). **∼ to the throne** subir al trono

accelerat|e /ək'seləreɪt/ *vt* acelerar. **∼ion** /-'reɪʃn/ *n* aceleración *f*. **∼or** *n* acelerador *m*

accent /'æksənt/ *n* acento *m*. /æk'sent/ *vt* acentuar

accentuate /ək'sentʃʊeɪt/ *vt* acentuar

accept /ək'sept/ *vt* aceptar. **∼able** *a* aceptable. **∼ance** *n* aceptación *f*; (*approval*) aprobación *f*

access /'ækses/ *n* accceso *m*. **∼ibility** /-ɪ'bɪlətɪ/ *n* accesibilidad *f*. **∼ible** /ək'sesəbl/ *a* accesible; (*person*) tratable

accession /æk'seʃn/ *n* (*to power*, *throne etc*) ascenso *m*; (*thing added*) adquisición *f*

accessory /ək'sesərɪ/ *a* accesorio. ● *n* accesorio *m*, complemento *m*; (*jurid*) cómplice *m* & *f*

accident /'æksɪdənt/ *n* accidente *m*; (*chance*) casualidad *f*. **by ∼** por accidente, por descuido, sin querer; (*by chance*) por casualidad. **∼al** /-'dentl/ *a* accidental, fortuito. **∼ally** /-'dentəlɪ/ *adv* por accidente, por descuido, sin querer; (*by chance*) por casualidad

acclaim /ə'kleɪm/ *vt* aclamar. ● *n* aclamación *f*

acclimatiz|ation /əklaɪmətaɪ'zeɪʃn/ *n* aclimatación *f*. **∼e** /ə'klaɪmətaɪz/ *vt* aclimatar. ● *vi* aclimatarse

accolade /'ækəleɪd/ *n* (*of knight*) acolada *f*, (*praise*) encomio *m*

accommodat|e /ə'kɒmədeɪt/ *vt* (*give hospitality to*) alojar; (*adapt*) acomodar; (*supply*) proveer; (*oblige*) complacer. **∼ing** *a* complaciente. **∼ion** /-'deɪʃn/ *n* alojamiento *m*; (*rooms*) habitaciones *fpl*

accompan|iment /ə'kʌmpənɪmənt/ *n* acompañamiento *m*. **∼ist** *n* acompañante *m* & *f*. **∼y** /ə'kʌmpənɪ/ *vt* acompañar

accomplice /əˈkʌmplɪs/ *n* cómplice *m & f*

accomplish /əˈkʌmplɪʃ/ *vt* (*complete*) acabar; (*achieve*) realizar; (*carry out*) llevar a cabo. **~ed** *a* consumado. **~ment** *n* realización *f*; (*ability*) talento *m*; (*thing achieved*) triunfo *m*, logro *m*

accord /əˈkɔːd/ *vi* concordar. ● *vt* conceder. ● *n* acuerdo *m*; (*harmony*) armonía *f*. **of one's own ~** espontáneamente. **~ance** *n*. **in ~ance with** de acuerdo con

according /əˈkɔːdɪŋ/ *adv*. **~ to** según. **~ly** *adv* en conformidad; (*therefore*) por consiguiente

accordion /əˈkɔːdɪən/ *n* acordeón *m*

accost /əˈkɒst/ *vt* abordar

account /əˈkaʊnt/ *n* cuenta *f*; (*description*) relato *m*; (*importance*) importancia *f*. **on ~ of** a causa de. **on no ~** de ninguna manera. **on this ~** por eso. **take into ~** tener en cuenta. ● *vt* considerar. **~ for** dar cuenta de, explicar

accountab|ility /əkaʊntəˈbɪlətɪ/ *n* responsabilidad *f*. **~le** *a* responsable (**for** de)

accountan|cy /əˈkaʊntənsɪ/ *n* contabilidad *f*. **~t** *n* contable *m & f*

accoutrements /əˈkuːtrəmənts/ *npl* equipo *m*

accredited /əˈkredɪtɪd/ *a* acreditado; (*authorized*) autorizado

accrue /əˈkruː/ *vi* acumularse

accumulat|e /əˈkjuːmjʊleɪt/ *vt* acumular. ● *vi* acumularse. **~ion** /-ˈleɪʃn/ *n* acumulación *f*. **~or** *n* (*elec*) acumulador *m*

accura|cy /ˈækjərəsɪ/ *n* exactitud *f*, precisión *f*. **~te** *a* exacto, preciso

accus|ation /ækjuːˈzeɪʃn/ *n* acusación *f*. **~e** *vt* acusar

accustom /əˈkʌstəm/ *vt* acostumbrar. **~ed** *a* acostumbrado. **get ~ed (to)** acostumbrarse (a)

ace /eɪs/ *n* as *m*

acetate /ˈæsɪteɪt/ *n* acetato *m*

ache /eɪk/ *n* dolor *m*. ● *vi* doler. **my leg ~s** me duele la pierna

achieve /əˈtʃiːv/ *vt* realizar; lograr ‹*success*›. **~ment** *n* realización *f*; (*feat*) éxito *m*; (*thing achieved*) proeza *f*, logro *m*

acid /ˈæsɪd/ *a & n* ácido (*m*). **~ity** /əˈsɪdətɪ/ *n* acidez *f*

acknowledge /əkˈnɒlɪdʒ/ *vt* reconocer. **~ receipt of** acusar recibo de.

~ment *n* reconocimiento *m*; (*com*) acuse *m* de recibo

acme /ˈækmɪ/ *n* cima *f*

acne /ˈæknɪ/ *n* acné *m*

acorn /ˈeɪkɔːn/ *n* bellota *f*

acoustic /əˈkuːstɪk/ *a* acústico. **~s** *npl* acústica *f*

acquaint /əˈkweɪnt/ *vt*. **~ s.o. with** poner a uno al corriente de. **be ~ed with** conocer ‹*person*›; saber ‹*fact*›. **~ance** *n* conocimiento *m*; (*person*) conocido *m*

acquiesce /ækwɪˈes/ *vi* consentir (**in** en). **~nce** *n* aquiescencia *f*, consentimiento *m*

acqui|re /əˈkwaɪə(r)/ *vt* adquirir; aprender ‹*language*›. **~re a taste for** tomar gusto a. **~sition** /ækwɪˈzɪʃn/ *n* adquisición *f*. **~sitive** /-ˈkwɪzətɪv/ *a* codicioso

acquit /əˈkwɪt/ *vt* (*pt* **acquitted**) absolver; **~ o.s. well** defenderse bien, tener éxito. **~tal** *n* absolución *f*

acre /ˈeɪkə(r)/ *n* acre *m*. **~age** *n* superficie *f* (en acres)

acrid /ˈækrɪd/ *a* acre

acrimon|ious /ækrɪˈməʊnɪəs/ *a* cáustico, mordaz. **~y** /ˈækrɪmənɪ/ *n* acrimonia *f*, acritud *f*

acrobat /ˈækrəbæt/ *n* acróbata *m & f*. **~ic** /-ˈbætɪk/ *a* acrobático. **~ics** /-ˈbætɪks/ *npl* acrobacia *f*

acronym /ˈækrənɪm/ *n* acrónimo *m*, siglas *fpl*

across /əˈkrɒs/ *adv & prep* (*side to side*) de un lado al otro; (*on other side*) del otro lado de; (*crosswise*) a través. **go** *or* **walk ~** atravesar

act /ækt/ *n* acto *m*; (*action*) acción *f*; (*in variety show*) número *m*; (*decree*) decreto *m*. ● *vt* hacer ‹*part, role*›. ● *vi* actuar; (*pretend*) fingir; (*function*) funcionar. **~ as** actuar de. **~ for** representar. **~ing** *a* interino. ● *n* (*of play*) representación *f*; (*by actor*) interpretación *f*; (*profession*) profesión *f* de actor

action /ˈækʃn/ *n* acción *f*; (*jurid*) demanda *f*; (*plot*) argumento *m*. **out of ~** (*on sign*) no funciona. **put out of ~** inutilizar. **take ~** tomar medidas

activate /ˈæktɪveɪt/ *vt* activar

activ|e /ˈæktɪv/ *a* activo; (*energetic*) enérgico; ‹*volcano*› en actividad. **~ity** /-ˈtɪvətɪ/ *n* actividad *f*

act|or /ˈæktə(r)/ *n* actor *m*. **~ress** *n* actriz *f*

actual /'æktʃʊəl/ *a* verdadero. ~**ity** /-'ælətɪ/ *n* realidad *f*. ~**ly** *adv* en realidad, efectivamente; (*even*) incluso

actuary /'æktʃʊərɪ/ *n* actuario *m*

actuate /'æktjʊeɪt/ *vt* accionar, impulsar

acumen /'ækjʊmen/ *n* perspicacia *f*

acupunctur|e /'ækjʊpʌŋktʃə(r)/ *n* acupuntura *f*. ~**ist** *n* acupunturista *m & f*

acute /ə'kjuːt/ *a* agudo. ~**ly** *adv* agudamente. ~**ness** *n* agudeza *f*

ad /æd/ *n* (*fam*) anuncio *m*

AD /eɪ'diː/ *abbr* (*Anno Domini*) d.J.C.

adamant /'ædəmənt/ *a* inflexible

Adam's apple /'ædəmz'æpl/ *n* nuez *f* (de Adán)

adapt /ə'dæpt/ *vt* adaptar. ● *vi* adaptarse

adaptab|ility /ədæptə'bɪlətɪ/ *n* adaptabilidad *f*. ~**le** /ə'dæptəbl/ *a* adaptable

adaptation /ædæp'teɪʃn/ *n* adaptación *f*; (*of book etc*) versión *f*

adaptor /ə'dæptə(r)/ *n* (*elec*) adaptador *m*

add /æd/ *vt* añadir. ● *vi* sumar. ~ **up** sumar; (*fig*) tener sentido. ~ **up to** equivaler a

adder /'ædə(r)/ *n* víbora *f*

addict /'ædɪkt/ *n* adicto *m*; (*fig*) entusiasta *m & f*. ~**ed** /ə'dɪktɪd/ *a*. ~**ed to** adicto a; (*fig*) fanático de. ~**ion** /-ʃn/ *n* (*med*) dependencia *f*; (*fig*) afición *f*. ~**ive** *a* que crea dependencia

adding machine /'ædɪŋməʃiːn/ *n* máquina *f* de sumar, sumadora *f*

addition /ə'dɪʃn/ *n* suma *f*. **in** ~ además. ~**al** /-ʃənl/ *a* suplementario

additive /'ædɪtɪv/ *a & n* aditivo (*m*)

address /ə'dres/ *n* señas *fpl*, dirección *f*; (*speech*) discurso *m*. ● *vt* poner la dirección; (*speak to*) dirigirse a. ~**ee** /ædre'siː/ *n* destinatario *m*

adenoids /'ædɪnɔɪdz/ *npl* vegetaciones *fpl* adenoideas

adept /'ædept/ *a & n* experto (*m*)

adequa|cy /'ædɪkwəsɪ/ *n* suficiencia *f*. ~**te** *a* suficiente, adecuado. ~**tely** *adv* suficientemente, adecuadamente

adhere /əd'hɪə(r)/ *vi* adherirse (**to** a); observar (*rule*). ~**nce** /-rəns/ *n* adhesión *f*; (*to rules*) observancia *f*

adhesion /əd'hiːʒn/ *n* adherencia *f*

adhesive /əd'hiːsɪv/ *a & n* adhesivo (*m*)

ad infinitum /ædɪnfɪ'naɪtəm/ *adv* hasta el infinito

adjacent /ə'dʒeɪsnt/ *a* contiguo

adjective /'ædʒɪktɪv/ *n* adjetivo *m*

adjoin /ə'dʒɔɪn/ *vt* lindar con. ~**ing** *a* contiguo

adjourn /ə'dʒɜːn/ *vt* aplazar; suspender (*meeting etc*). ● *vi* suspenderse. ~ **to** trasladarse a

adjudicate /ə'dʒuːdɪkeɪt/ *vt* juzgar. ● *vi* actuar como juez

adjust /ə'dʒʌst/ *vt* ajustar (*machine*); (*arrange*) arreglar. ● *vi*. ~ (**to**) adaptarse (a). ~**able** *a* ajustable. ~**ment** *n* adaptación *f*; (*tec*) ajuste *m*

ad lib /æd'lɪb/ *a* improvisado. ● *vi* (*pt* -**libbed**) (*fam*) improvisar

administer /əd'mɪnɪstə(r)/ *vt* administrar, dar, proporcionar

administrat|ion /ədmɪnɪ'streɪʃn/ *n* administración *f*. ~**or** *n* administrador *m*

admirable /'ædmərəbl/ *a* admirable

admiral /'ædmərəl/ *n* almirante *m*

admiration /ædmə'reɪʃn/ *n* admiración *f*

admire /əd'maɪə(r)/ *vt* admirar. ~**r** /-'maɪərə(r)/ *n* admirador *m*; (*suitor*) enamorado *m*

admissible /əd'mɪsəbl/ *a* admisible

admission /əd'mɪʃn/ *n* admisión *f*; (*entry*) entrada *f*

admit /əd'mɪt/ *vt* (*pt* **admitted**) dejar entrar; (*acknowledge*) admitir, reconocer. ~ **to** confesar. **be** ~**ted** (*to hospital etc*) ingresar. ~**tance** *n* entrada *f*. ~**tedly** *adv* es verdad que

admoni|sh /əd'mɒnɪʃ/ *vt* reprender; (*advise*) aconsejar. ~**tion** /-'nɪʃn/ *n* represión *f*

ado /ə'duː/ *n* alboroto *m*; (*trouble*) dificultad *f*. **without more** ~ en seguida, sin más

adolescen|ce /ædə'lesns/ *n* adolescencia *f*. ~**t** *a & n* adolescente (*m & f*)

adopt /ə'dɒpt/ *vt* adoptar. ~**ed** (*child*) adoptivo. ~**ion** /-ʃn/ *n* adopción *f*. ~**ive** *a* adoptivo

ador|able /ə'dɔːrəbl/ *a* adorable. ~**ation** /ædə'reɪʃn/ *n* adoración *f*. ~**e** /ə'dɔː(r)/ *vt* adorar

adorn /ə'dɔːn/ *vt* adornar. ~**ment** *n* adorno *m*

adrenalin /ə'drenəlɪn/ n adrenalina f

adrift /ə'drɪft/ a & adv a la deriva

adroit /ə'drɔɪt/ a diestro

adulation /ædjʊ'leɪʃn/ n adulación f

adult /'ædʌlt/ a & n adulto (m)

adulterat|ion /ədʌltə'reɪʃn/ n adulteración f. **~e** /ə'dʌltəreɪt/ vt adulterar

adulter|er /ə'dʌltərə(r)/ n adúltero m. **~ess** n adúltera f. **~ous** a adúltero. **~y** n adulterio m

advance /əd'vɑ:ns/ vt adelantar. ● vi adelantarse. ● n adelanto m. **in ~** con anticipación, por adelantado. **~d** a avanzado; ⟨studies⟩ superior. **~ment** n adelanto m; (in job) promoción f

advantage /əd'vɑ:ntɪdʒ/ n ventaja f. **take ~ of** aprovecharse de; abusar de ⟨person⟩. **~ous** /ædvən'teɪdʒəs/ a ventajoso

advent /'ædvənt/ n venida f. **A~** n adviento m

adventur|e /əd'ventʃə(r)/ n aventura f. **~er** n aventurero m. **~ous** a ⟨persona⟩ aventurero; ⟨cosa⟩ arriesgado; (fig, bold) llamativo

adverb /'ædvɜ:b/ n adverbio m

adversary /'ædvəsərɪ/ n adversario m

advers|e /'ædvɜ:s/ a adverso, contrario, desfavorable. **~ity** /əd'vɜ:sətɪ/ n infortunio m

advert /'ædvɜ:t/ n (fam) anuncio m. **~ise** /'ædvətaɪz/ vt anunciar. ● vi hacer publicidad; (seek, sell) poner un anuncio. **~isement** /əd'vɜ:tɪsmənt/ n anuncio m. **~iser** /-ə(r)/ n anunciante m & f

advice /əd'vaɪs/ n consejo m; (report) informe m

advis|able /əd'vaɪzəbl/ a aconsejable. **~e** vt aconsejar; (inform) avisar. **~e against** aconsejar en contra de. **~er** n consejero m; (consultant) asesor m. **~ory** a consultivo

advocate /'ædvəkət/ n defensor m; (jurid) abogado m. /'ædvəkeɪt/ vt recomendar

aegis /'i:dʒɪs/ n égida f. **under the ~ of** bajo la tutela de, patrocinado por

aeon /'i:ən/ n eternidad f

aerial /'eərɪəl/ a aéreo. ● n antena f

aerobatics /eərə'bætɪks/ npl acrobacia f aérea

aerobics /eə'rɒbɪks/ npl aeróbica f

aerodrome /'eərədrəʊm/ n aeródromo m

aerodynamic /eərəʊdaɪ'næmɪk/ a aerodinámico

aeroplane /'eərəpleɪn/ n avión m

aerosol /'eərəsɒl/ n aerosol m

aesthetic /i:s'θetɪk/ a estético

afar /ə'fa:(r)/ adv lejos

affable /'æfəbl/ a afable

affair /ə'feə(r)/ n asunto m. **(love) ~** aventura f, amorío m. **~s** npl (business) negocios mpl

affect /ə'fekt/ vt afectar; (pretend) fingir

affect|ation /æfek'teɪʃn/ n afectación f. **~ed** a afectado, amanerado

affection /ə'fekʃn/ n cariño m; (disease) afección f. **~ate** /-ʃənət/ a cariñoso

affiliat|e /ə'fɪlɪeɪt/ vt afiliar. **~ion** /-'eɪʃn/ n afiliación f

affinity /ə'fɪnətɪ/ n afinidad f

affirm /ə'fɜ:m/ vt afirmar. **~ation** /æfə'meɪʃn/ n afirmación f

affirmative /ə'fɜ:mətɪv/ a afirmativo. ● n respuesta f afirmativa

affix /ə'fɪks/ vt sujetar; añadir ⟨signature⟩; pegar ⟨stamp⟩

afflict /ə'flɪkt/ vt afligir. **~ion** /-ʃn/ n aflicción f, pena f

affluen|ce /'æfluəns/ n riqueza f. **~t** a rico. ● n (geog) afluente m

afford /ə'fɔ:d/ vt permitirse; (provide) dar

affray /ə'freɪ/ n reyerta f

affront /ə'frʌnt/ n afrenta f, ofensa f. ● vt afrentar, ofender

afield /ə'fi:ld/ adv. **far ~** muy lejos

aflame /ə'fleɪm/ adv & a en llamas

afloat /ə'fləʊt/ adv a flote

afoot /ə'fʊt/ adv. **sth is ~** se está tramando algo

aforesaid /ə'fɔ:sed/ a susodicho

afraid /ə'freɪd/ a. **be ~** tener miedo **(of** a); (be sorry) sentir, lamentar

afresh /ə'freʃ/ adv de nuevo

Africa /'æfrɪkə/ n África f. **~n** a & n africano (m)

after /'ɑ:ftə(r)/ adv después; (behind) detrás. ● prep después de; (behind) detrás de. **be ~** (seek) buscar, andar en busca de. ● conj después de que. ● a posterior

afterbirth /'ɑ:ftəbɜ:θ/ n placenta f

after-effect /'ɑ:ftərɪfekt/ n consecuencia f, efecto m secundario

aftermath /'ɑ:ftəmæθ/ n secuelas fpl

afternoon /ɑ:ftə'nu:n/ n tarde f

aftershave /'ɑ:ftəʃeɪv/ n loción f para después del afeitado

afterthought /'ɑːftəθɔːt/ n ocurrencia f tardía

afterwards /'ɑːftəwədz/ adv después

again /ə'gen/ adv otra vez; (besides) además. ~ **and** ~ una y otra vez

against /ə'genst/ prep contra, en contra de

age /eɪdʒ/ n edad f. **of** ~ mayor de edad. **under** ~ menor de edad. ● vt/i (pres p **ageing**) envejecer. ~**d** /'eɪdʒd/ a de ... años. ~**d 10** de 10 años, que tiene 10 años. ~**d** /'eɪdʒɪd/ a viejo, anciano. ~**less** a siempre joven; (eternal) eterno, inmemorial. ~**s** (fam) siglos mpl

agency /'eɪdʒənsɪ/ n agencia f, organismo m, oficina f; (means) mediación f

agenda /ə'dʒendə/ npl orden m del día

agent /'eɪdʒənt/ n agente m & f; (representative) representante m & f

agglomeration /əɡlɒmə'reɪʃn/ n aglomeración f

aggravat|e /'æɡrəveɪt/ vt agravar; (irritate, fam) irritar. ~**ion** /-'veɪʃn/ n agravación f; (irritation, fam) irritación f

aggregate /'æɡrɪɡət/ a total. ● n conjunto m. /'æɡrɪɡeɪt/ vt agregar. ● vi ascender a

aggress|ion /ə'ɡreʃn/ n agresión f. ~**ive** a agresivo. ~**iveness** n agresividad f. ~**or** n agresor m

aggrieved /ə'ɡriːvd/ a apenado, ofendido

aghast /ə'ɡɑːst/ a horrorizado

agil|e /'ædʒaɪl/ a ágil. ~**ity** /ə'dʒɪlətɪ/ n agilidad f

agitat|e /'ædʒɪteɪt/ vt agitar. ~**ion** /-'teɪʃn/ n agitación f, excitación f. ~**or** n agitador m

agnostic /æɡ'nɒstɪk/ a & n agnóstico (m). ~**ism** /-sɪzəm/ n agnosticismo m

ago /ə'ɡəʊ/ adv hace. **a long time** ~ hace mucho tiempo. **3 days** ~ hace 3 días

agog /ə'ɡɒɡ/ a ansioso

agon|ize /'æɡənaɪz/ vi atormentarse. ~**izing** a atroz, angustioso, doloroso. ~**y** n dolor m (agudo); (mental) angustia f

agree /ə'ɡriː/ vt acordar. ● vi estar de acuerdo; (of figures) concordar; (get on) entenderse. ~ **with** (of food etc) sentar bien a. ~**able** /ə'ɡriːəbl/ a agradable. **be** ~**able** (willing) estar

de acuerdo. ~**d** a (time, place) convenido. ~**ment** /ə'ɡriːmənt/ n acuerdo m. **in** ~**ment** de acuerdo

agricultur|al /æɡrɪ'kʌltʃərəl/ a agrícola. ~**e** /'æɡrɪkʌltʃə(r)/ n agricultura f

aground /ə'ɡraʊnd/ adv. **run** ~ (of ship) varar, encallar

ahead /ə'hed/ adv delante; (of time) antes de. **be** ~ ir delante

aid /eɪd/ vt ayudar. ● n ayuda f. **in** ~ **of** a beneficio de

aide /eɪd/ n (Amer) ayudante m & f

AIDS /eɪdz/ n (med) SIDA m

ail /eɪl/ vt afligir. ~**ing** a enfermo. ~**ment** n enfermedad f

aim /eɪm/ vt apuntar; (fig) dirigir. ● vi apuntar; (fig) pretender. ● n puntería f; (fig) propósito m. ~**less** a, ~**lessly** adv sin objeto, sin rumbo

air /eə(r)/ n aire m. **be on the** ~ estar en el aire. **put on** ~**s** darse aires. ● vt airear. ● a (base etc) aéreo. ~**borne** a en el aire; (mil) aerotransportado. ~**conditioned** a climatizado, con aire acondicionado. ~**craft** /'eəkrɑːft/ n (pl invar) avión m. ~**field** /'eəfiːld/ n aeródromo m. **A**~ **Force** fuerzas fpl aéreas. ~**gun** /'eəɡʌn/ n escopeta f de aire comprimido. ~**lift** /'eəlɪft/ n puente m aéreo. ~**line** /'eəlaɪn/ n línea f aérea. ~**lock** /'eəlɒk/ n (in pipe) burbuja f de aire; (chamber) esclusa f de aire. ~ **mail** n correo m aéreo. ~**man** /'eəmən/ (pl **-men**) n aviador m. ~**port** /'eəpɔːt/ n aeropuerto m. ~**tight** /'eətaɪt/ a hermético. ~**worthy** /'eəwɜːðɪ/ a en condiciones de vuelo. ~**y** /'eərɪ/ a (**-ier, -iest**) aireado; (manner) ligero

aisle /aɪl/ n nave f lateral; (gangway) pasillo m

ajar /ə'dʒɑː(r)/ adv & a entreabierto

akin /ə'kɪn/ a semejante (**a** to)

alabaster /'æləbɑːstə(r)/ n alabastro m

alacrity /ə'lækrətɪ/ n prontitud f

alarm /ə'lɑːm/ n alarma f; (clock) despertador m. ● vt asustar. ~**ist** n alarmista m & f

alas /ə'læs/ int ¡ay!, ¡ay de mí!

albatross /'ælbətrɒs/ n albatros m

albino /æl'biːnəʊ/ a & n albino (m)

album /'ælbəm/ n álbum m

alchem|ist /'ælkəmɪst/ n alquimista m & f. ~**y** n alquimia f

alcohol /'ælkəhɒl/ n alcohol m. ~**ic** /-'hɒlɪk/ a & n alcohólico (m). ~**ism** n alcoholismo m

alcove /'ælkəʊv/ n nicho m
ale /eɪl/ n cerveza f
alert /ə'lɜːt/ a vivo; (watchful) vigilante. ● n alerta f. **on the ~** alerta. ● vt avisar. **~ness** n vigilancia f
algebra /'ældʒɪbrə/ n álgebra f
Algeria /æl'dʒɪərɪə/ n Argelia f. **~n** a & n argelino (m)
alias /'eɪlɪəs/ n (pl **-ases**) alias m invar. ● adv alias
alibi /'ælɪbaɪ/ (pl **-is**) coartada f
alien /'eɪlɪən/ n extranjero m. ● a ajeno
alienat|e /'eɪlɪəneɪt/ vt enajenar. **~ion** /-'neɪʃn/ n enajenación f
alight[1] /ə'laɪt/ vi bajar; ⟨bird⟩ posarse
alight[2] /ə'laɪt/ a ardiendo; ⟨light⟩ encendido
align /ə'laɪn/ vt alinear. **~ment** n alineación f
alike /ə'laɪk/ a parecido, semejante. **look** or **be ~** parecerse. ● adv de la misma manera
alimony /'ælɪmənɪ/ n pensión f alimenticia
alive /ə'laɪv/ a vivo. **~ to** sensible a. **~ with** lleno de
alkali /'ælkəlaɪ/ n (pl **-is**) álcali m. **~ne** a alcalino
all /ɔːl/ a & pron todo. **~ but one** todos excepto uno. **~ of it** todo. ● adv completamente. **~ but** casi. **~ in** (fam) rendido. **~ of a sudden** de pronto. **~ over** (finished) acabado; (everywhere) por todas partes. **~ right!** ¡vale! **be ~ for** estar a favor de. **not at ~** de ninguna manera; (after thanks!) ¡no hay de qué!
allay /ə'leɪ/ vt aliviar ⟨pain⟩; aquietar ⟨fears etc⟩
all-clear /ɔːl'klɪə(r)/ n fin m de (la) alarma
allegation /ælɪ'geɪʃn/ n alegato m
allege /ə'ledʒ/ vt alegar. **~dly** /-ɪdlɪ/ adv según se dice, supuestamente
allegiance /ə'liːdʒəns/ n lealtad f
allegor|ical /ælɪ'gɒrɪkl/ a alegórico. **~y** /'ælɪgərɪ/ n alegoría f
allerg|ic /ə'lɜːdʒɪk/ a alérgico. **~y** /'ælədʒɪ/ n alergia f
alleviat|e /ə'liːvɪeɪt/ vt aliviar. **~ion** /-'eɪʃn/ n alivio m
alley /'ælɪ/ (pl **-eys**) n callejuela f; (for bowling) bolera f
alliance /ə'laɪəns/ n alianza f
allied /'ælaɪd/ a aliado
alligator /'ælɪgeɪtə(r)/ n caimán m

allocat|e /'æləkeɪt/ vt asignar; (share out) repartir. **~ion** /-'keɪʃn/ n asignación f; (share) ración f; (distribution) reparto m
allot /ə'lɒt/ vt (pt **allotted**) asignar. **~ment** n asignación f; (share) ración f; (land) parcela f
all-out /ɔːl'aʊt/ a máximo
allow /ə'laʊ/ vt permitir; (grant) conceder; (reckon on) prever; (agree) admitir. **~ for** tener en cuenta. **~ance** /ə'laʊəns/ n concesión f; (pension) pensión f; (com) rebaja f. **make ~ances for** ser indulgente con; (take into account) tener en cuenta
alloy /'ælɔɪ/ n aleación f. /ə'lɔɪ/ vt alear
all-round /ɔːl'raʊnd/ a completo
allude /ə'luːd/ vi aludir
allure /ə'lʊə(r)/ vt atraer. ● n atractivo m
allusion /ə'luːʒn/ n alusión f
ally /'ælaɪ/ n aliado m. /ə'laɪ/ vt aliarse
almanac /'ɔːlmənæk/ n almanaque m
almighty /ɔːl'maɪtɪ/ a todopoderoso; (big, fam) enorme. ● n. **the A~** el Todopoderoso m
almond /'ɑːmənd/ n almendra f; (tree) almendro m
almost /'ɔːlməʊst/ adv casi
alms /ɑːmz/ n limosna f
alone /ə'ləʊn/ a solo. ● adv sólo, solamente
along /ə'lɒŋ/ prep por, a lo largo de. ● adv. **~ with** junto con. **all ~** todo el tiempo. **come ~** venga
alongside /əlɒŋ'saɪd/ adv (naut) al costado. ● prep al lado de
aloof /ə'luːf/ adv apartado. ● a reservado. **~ness** n reserva f
aloud /ə'laʊd/ adv en voz alta
alphabet /'ælfəbet/ n alfabeto m. **~ical** /-'betɪkl/ a alfabético
alpine /'ælpaɪn/ a alpino
Alps /ælps/ npl. **the ~** los Alpes mpl
already /ɔːl'redɪ/ adv ya
Alsatian /æl'seɪʃn/ n (geog) alsaciano m; (dog) pastor m alemán
also /'ɔːlsəʊ/ adv también; (moreover) además
altar /'ɔːltə(r)/ n altar m
alter /'ɔːltə(r)/ vt cambiar. ● vi cambiarse. **~ation** /-'reɪʃn/ n modificación f; (to garment) arreglo m
alternate /ɔːl'tɜːnət/ a alterno. /'ɔːltəneɪt/ vt/i alternar. **~ly** adv alternativamente

alternative /ɔːlˈtɜːnətɪv/ *a* alternativo. ● *n* alternativa *f*. **~ly** *adv* en cambio, por otra parte

although /ɔːlˈðəʊ/ *conj* aunque

altitude /ˈæltɪtjuːd/ *n* altitud *f*

altogether /ɔːltəˈgeðə(r)/ *adv* completamente; (*on the whole*) en total

altruis|m /ˈæltruːɪzəm/ *n* altruismo *m*. **~t** /ˈæltruːɪst/ *n* altruista *m & f*. **~tic** /-ˈɪstɪk/ *a* altruista

aluminium /æljʊˈmɪnɪəm/ *n* aluminio *m*

always /ˈɔːlweɪz/ *adv* siempre

am /æm/ *see* be

a.m. /ˈeɪem/ *abbr* (*ante meridiem*) de la mañana

amalgamate /əˈmælgəmeɪt/ *vt* amalgamar. ● *vi* amalgamarse

amass /əˈmæs/ *vt* amontonar

amateur /ˈæmətə(r)/ *n* aficionado *m*. ● *a* no profesional; (*in sports*) amateur. **~ish** *a* (*pej*) chapucero

amaz|e /əˈmeɪz/ *vt* asombrar. **~ed** *a* asombrado, estupefacto. **be ~ed at** quedarse asombrado de, asombrarse de. **~ement** *n* asombro *m*. **~ingly** *adv* extraordinariamente

ambassador /æmˈbæsədə(r)/ *n* embajador *m*

amber /ˈæmbə(r)/ *n* ámbar *m*; (*auto*) luz *f* amarilla

ambidextrous /æmbɪˈdekstrəs/ *a* ambidextro

ambience /ˈæmbɪəns/ *n* ambiente *m*

ambigu|ity /æmbɪˈgjuːətɪ/ *n* ambigüedad *f*. **~ous** /æmˈbɪgjʊəs/ *a* ambiguo

ambit /ˈæmbɪt/ *n* ámbito *m*

ambiti|on /æmˈbɪʃn/ *n* ambición *f*. **~ous** *a* ambicioso

ambivalen|ce /æmˈbɪvələns/ *n* ambivalencia *f*. **~t** *a* ambivalente

amble /ˈæmbl/ *vi* andar despacio, andar sin prisa

ambulance /ˈæmbjʊləns/ *n* ambulancia *f*

ambush /ˈæmbʊʃ/ *n* emboscada *f*. ● *vt* tender una emboscada a

amen /ɑːˈmen/ *int* amén

amenable /əˈmiːnəbl/ *a*. **~ to** (*responsive*) sensible a, flexible a

amend /əˈmend/ *vt* enmendar. **~ment** *n* enmienda *f*. **~s** *npl*. **make ~s** reparar

amenities /əˈmiːnətɪz/ *npl* atractivos *mpl*, comodidades *fpl*, instalaciones *fpl*

America /əˈmerɪkə/ *n* América; (*North America*) Estados *mpl*

Unidos. **~n** *a & n* americano (*m*); (*North American*) estadounidense (*m & f*). **~nism** *n* americanismo *m*. **~nize** *vt* americanizar

amethyst /ˈæmɪθɪst/ *n* amatista *f*

amiable /ˈeɪmɪəbl/ *a* simpático

amicabl|e /ˈæmɪkəbl/ *a* amistoso. **~y** *adv* amistosamente

amid(st) /əˈmɪd(st)/ *prep* entre, en medio de

amiss /əˈmɪs/ *a* malo. ● *adv* mal. **sth ~** algo que no va bien. **take sth ~** llevar algo a mal

ammonia /əˈməʊnɪə/ *n* amoníaco *m*, amoniaco *m*

ammunition /æmjʊˈnɪʃn/ *n* municiones *fpl*

amnesia /æmˈniːzɪə/ *n* amnesia *f*

amnesty /ˈæmnəstɪ/ *n* amnistía *f*

amok /əˈmɒk/ *adv*. **run ~** volverse loco

among(st) /əˈmʌŋ(st)/ *prep* entre

amoral /eɪˈmɒrəl/ *a* amoral

amorous /ˈæmərəs/ *a* amoroso

amorphous /əˈmɔːfəs/ *a* amorfo

amount /əˈmaʊnt/ *n* cantidad *f*; (*total*) total *m*, suma *f*. ● *vi*. **~ to** sumar; (*fig*) equivaler a, significar

amp(ere) /ˈæmp(eə(r))/ *n* amperio *m*

amphibi|an /æmˈfɪbɪən/ *n* anfibio *m*. **~ous** *a* anfibio

amphitheatre /ˈæmfɪθɪətə(r)/ *n* anfiteatro *m*

ampl|e /ˈæmpl/ *a* (**-er, -est**) amplio; (*enough*) suficiente; (*plentiful*) abundante. **~y** *adv* ampliamente, bastante

amplif|ier /ˈæmplɪfaɪə(r)/ *n* amplificador *m*. **~y** *vt* amplificar

amputat|e /ˈæmpjʊteɪt/ *vt* amputar. **~ion** /-ˈteɪʃn/ *n* amputación *f*

amuse /əˈmjuːz/ *vt* divertir. **~ement** *n* diversión *f*. **~ing** *a* divertido

an /ən, æn/ *see* a

anachronism /əˈnækrənɪzəm/ *n* anacronismo *m*

anaemi|a /əˈniːmɪə/ *n* anemia *f*. **~c** *a* anémico

anaesthe|sia /ænɪsˈθiːzɪə/ *n* anestesia *f*. **~tic** /ænɪsˈθetɪk/ *n* anestésico *m*. **~tist** /əˈniːsθətɪst/ *n* anestesista *m & f*

anagram /ˈænəgræm/ *n* anagrama *m*

analogy /əˈnælədʒɪ/ *n* analogía *f*

analys|e /ˈænəlaɪz/ *vt* analizar. **~is** /əˈnæləsɪs/ *n* (*pl* **-yses** /-siːz/) *n* análisis *m*. **~t** /ˈænəlɪst/ *n* analista *m & f*

analytic(al) /ænə'lɪtɪk(əl)/ a analítico

anarch|ist /'ænəkɪst/ n anarquista m & f. **~y** n anarquía f

anathema /ə'næθəmə/ n anatema m

anatom|ical /ænə'tɒmɪkl/ a anatómico. **~y** /ə'nætəmɪ/ n anatomía f

ancest|or /'ænsestə(r)/ n antepasado m. **~ral** /-'sestrəl/ a ancestral. **~ry** /'ænsestrɪ/ n ascendencia f

anchor /'æŋkə(r)/ n ancla f. ● vt anclar; (fig) sujetar. ● vi anclar

anchovy /'æntʃəvɪ/ n (fresh) boquerón m; (tinned) anchoa f

ancient /'eɪnʃənt/ a antiguo, viejo

ancillary /æn'sɪlərɪ/ a auxiliar

and /ənd, ænd/ conj y; (before i- and hi-) e. **go ~ see him** vete a verle. **more ~ more** siempre más, cada vez más. **try ~ come** ven si puedes, trata de venir

Andalusia /ændə'lu:zjə/ f Andalucía f

anecdote /'ænɪkdəʊt/ n anécdota f

anew /ə'nju:/ adv de nuevo

angel /'eɪndʒl/ n ángel m. **~ic** /æn'dʒelɪk/ a angélico

anger /'æŋgə(r)/ n ira f. ● vt enojar

angle¹ /'æŋgl/ n ángulo m; (fig) punto m de vista

angle² /'æŋgl/ vi pescar con caña. **~ for** (fig) buscar. **~r** /-ə(r)/ n pescador m

Anglican /'æŋglɪkən/ a & n anglicano (m)

Anglo-... /'æŋgləʊ/ pref anglo...

Anglo-Saxon /'æŋgləʊ'sæksn/ a & n anglosajón (m)

angr|ily /'æŋgrɪlɪ/ adv con enojo. **~y** /'æŋgrɪ/ a (-ier, -iest) enojado. **get ~y** enfadarse

anguish /'æŋgwɪʃ/ n angustia f

angular /'æŋgjʊlə(r)/ a angular; (face) anguloso

animal /'ænɪməl/ a & n animal (m)

animat|e /'ænɪmət/ a vivo. /'ænɪmeɪt/ vt animar. **~ion** /-'meɪʃn/ n animación f

animosity /ænɪ'mɒsətɪ/ n animosidad f

aniseed /'ænɪsi:d/ n anís m

ankle /'æŋkl/ n tobillo m. **~ sock** escarpín m, calcetín m

annals /'ænlz/ npl anales mpl

annex /ə'neks/ vt anexionar. **~ation** /ænek'seɪʃn/ n anexión f

annexe /'æneks/ n anexo m, dependencia f

annihilat|e /ə'naɪəleɪt/ vt aniquilar. **~ion** /-'leɪʃn/ n aniquilación f

anniversary /ænɪ'vɜ:sərɪ/ n aniversario m

annotat|e /'ænəteɪt/ vt anotar. **~ion** /-'teɪʃn/ n anotación f

announce /ə'naʊns/ vt anunciar, comunicar. **~ment** n anuncio m, aviso m, declaración f. **~r** /-e(r)/ n (radio, TV) locutor m

annoy /ə'nɔɪ/ vt molestar. **~ance** n disgusto m. **~ed** a enfadado. **~ing** a molesto

annual /'ænjʊəl/ a anual. ● n anuario m. **~ly** adv cada año

annuity /ə'nju:ətɪ/ n anualidad f. **life ~** renta f vitalicia

annul /ə'nʌl/ vt (pt annulled) anular. **~ment** n anulación f

anoint /ə'nɔɪnt/ vt ungir

anomal|ous /ə'nɒmələs/ a anómalo. **~y** n anomalía f

anon /ə'nɒn/ adv (old use) dentro de poco

anonymous /ə'nɒnɪməs/ a anónimo

anorak /'ænəræk/ n anorac m

another /ə'nʌðə(r)/ a & pron otro (m). **~ 10 minutes** 10 minutos más. **in ~ way** de otra manera. **one ~** unos a otros

answer /'ɑ:nsə(r)/ n respuesta f; (solution) solución f. ● vt contestar a; escuchar, oír (prayer). **~ the door** abrir la puerta. ● vi contestar. **~ back** replicar. **~ for** ser responsable de. **~able** a responsable. **~ing-machine** n contestador m automático

ant /ænt/ n hormiga f

antagoni|sm /æn'tægənɪzəm/ n antagonismo m. **~stic** /-'nɪstɪk/ a antagónico, opuesto. **~ze** /æn'tægənaɪz/ vt provocar la enemistad de

Antarctic /æn'tɑ:ktɪk/ a antártico. ● n Antártico m

ante-... /'æntɪ/ pref ante...

antecedent /æntɪ'si:dnt/ n antecedente m

antelope /'æntɪləʊp/ n antílope m

antenatal /'æntɪneɪtl/ a prenatal

antenna /æn'tenə/ n antena f

anthem /'ænθəm/ n himno m

anthill /'ænthɪl/ n hormiguero m

anthology /æn'θɒlədʒɪ/ n antología f

anthropolog|ist /ænθrə'pɒlədʒɪst/ n antropólogo m. **~y** n antropología f

anti-... /'æntɪ/ pref anti... **~aircraft** a antiaéreo

antibiotic /ˌæntɪbaɪˈɒtɪk/ *a & n* antibiótico (*m*)

antibody /ˈæntɪbɒdɪ/ *n* anticuerpo *m*

antic /ˈæntɪk/ *n* payasada *f*, travesura *f*

anticipat|e /ænˈtɪsɪpeɪt/ *vt* anticiparse a; (*foresee*) prever; (*forestall*) prevenir. ∼**ion** /-ˈpeɪʃn/ *n* anticipación *f*; (*expectation*) esperanza *f*

anticlimax /æntɪˈklaɪmæks/ *n* decepción *f*

anticlockwise /æntɪˈklɒkwaɪz/ *adv & a* en sentido contrario al de las agujas del reloj, hacia la izquierda

anticyclone /æntɪˈsaɪkləʊn/ *n* anticiclón *m*

antidote /ˈæntɪdəʊt/ *m* antídoto *m*

antifreeze /ˈæntɪfriːz/ *n* anticongelante *m*

antipathy /ænˈtɪpəθɪ/ *n* antipatía *f*

antiquarian /æntɪˈkweərɪən/ *a & n* anticuario (*m*)

antiquated /ˈæntɪkweɪtɪd/ *a* anticuado

antique /ænˈtiːk/ *a* antiguo. ● *n* antigüedad *f*. ∼ **dealer** anticuario *m*. ∼ **shop** tienda *f* de antigüedades

antiquity /ænˈtɪkwətɪ/ *n* antigüedad *f*

anti-Semitic /æntɪsɪˈmɪtɪk/ *a* antisemítico

antiseptic /æntɪˈseptɪk/ *a & n* antiséptico (*m*)

antisocial /æntɪˈsəʊʃl/ *a* antisocial

antithesis /ænˈtɪθəsɪs/ *n* (*pl* -eses /-siːz/) antítesis *f*

antler /ˈæntlər/ *n* cornamenta *f*

anus /ˈeɪnəs/ *n* ano *m*

anvil /ˈænvɪl/ *n* yunque *m*

anxiety /æŋˈzaɪətɪ/ *n* ansiedad *f*; (*worry*) inquietud *f*; (*eagerness*) anhelo *m*

anxious /ˈæŋkʃəs/ *a* inquieto; (*eager*) deseoso. ∼**ly** *adv* con inquietud; (*eagerly*) con impaciencia

any /ˈenɪ/ *a* algún *m*; (*negative*) ningún *m*; (*whatever*) cualquier; (*every*) todo. **at** ∼ **moment** en cualquier momento. **have you** ∼ **wine?** ¿tienes vino? ● *pron* alguno; (*negative*) ninguno. **have we** ∼**?** ¿tenemos algunos? **not** ∼ *adv* (*a little*) un poco, algo. **is it** ∼ **better?** ¿está algo mejor? **it isn't** ∼ **good** no sirve para nada

anybody /ˈenɪbɒdɪ/ *pron* alguien; (*after negative*) nadie. ∼ **can do it** cualquiera sabe hacerlo, cualquiera puede hacerlo

anyhow /ˈenɪhaʊ/ *adv* de todas formas; (*in spite of all*) a pesar de todo; (*badly*) de cualquier modo

anyone /ˈenɪwʌn/ *pron* alguien; (*after negative*) nadie

anything /ˈenɪθɪŋ/ *pron* algo; (*whatever*) cualquier cosa; (*after negative*) nada. ∼ **but** todo menos

anyway /ˈenɪweɪ/ *adv* de todas formas

anywhere /ˈenɪweə(r)/ *adv* en cualquier parte; (*after negative*) en ningún sitio; (*everywhere*) en todas partes. ∼ **else** en cualquier otro lugar. ∼ **you go** dondequiera que vayas

apace /əˈpeɪs/ *adv* rápidamente

apart /əˈpɑːt/ *adv* aparte; (*separated*) apartado, separado. ∼ **from** aparte de. **come** ∼ romperse. **take** ∼ desmontar

apartheid /əˈpɑːtheɪt/ *n* segregación *f* racial, apartheid *m*

apartment /əˈpɑːtmənt/ *n* (*Amer*) apartamento *m*

apath|etic /æpəˈθetɪk/ *a* apático, indiferente. ∼**y** /ˈæpəθɪ/ *n* apatía *f*

ape /eɪp/ *n* mono *m*. ● *vt* imitar

aperient /əˈpɪərɪənt/ *a & n* laxante (*m*)

aperitif /əˈperətɪf/ *n* aperitivo *m*

aperture /ˈæpətʃʊə(r)/ *n* abertura *f*

apex /ˈeɪpeks/ *n* ápice *m*

aphorism /ˈæfərɪzəm/ *n* aforismo *m*

aphrodisiac /æfrəˈdɪzɪæk/ *a & n* afrodisíaco (*m*), afrodisiaco (*m*)

apiece /əˈpiːs/ *adv* cada uno

aplomb /əˈplɒm/ *n* aplomo *m*

apolog|etic /əpɒləˈdʒetɪk/ *a* lleno de disculpas. **be** ∼**etic** disculparse. ∼**ize** /əˈpɒlədʒaɪz/ *vi* disculparse (**for** de). ∼**y** /əˈpɒlədʒɪ/ *n* disculpa *f*; (*poor specimen*) birria *f*

apople|ctic /æpəˈplektɪk/ *a* apoplético. ∼**xy** /ˈæpəpleksɪ/ *n* apoplejía *f*

apostle /əˈpɒsl/ *n* apóstol *m*

apostrophe /əˈpɒstrəfɪ/ *n* (*punctuation mark*) apóstrofo *m*

appal /əˈpɔːl/ *vt* (*pt* **appalled**) horrorizar. ∼**ling** *a* espantoso

apparatus /æpəˈreɪtəs/ *n* aparato *m*

apparel /əˈpærəl/ *n* ropa *f*, indumentaria *f*

apparent /əˈpærənt/ *a* aparente; (*clear*) evidente. ∼**ly** *adv* por lo visto

apparition /æpəˈrɪʃn/ *n* aparición *f*

appeal /ə'pi:l/ *vi* apelar; (*attract*) atraer. ● *n* llamamiento *m*; (*attraction*) apelación *f*. ~ing *a* atrayente

appear /ə'pɪə(r)/ *vi* aparecer; (*arrive*) llegar; (*seem*) parecer; (*on stage*) actuar. ~ance *n* aparición *f*; (*aspect*) aspecto *m*

appease /ə'pi:z/ *vt* aplacar; (*pacify*) apaciguar

append /ə'pend/ *vt* adjuntar. ~age /ə'pendɪdʒ/ *n* añadidura *f*

appendicitis /əpendɪ'saɪtɪs/ *n* apendicitis *f*

appendix /ə'pendɪks/ *n* (*pl* -ices /-si:z/) (*of book*) apéndice *m*. (*pl* -ixes) (*anat*) apéndice *m*

appertain /æpə'teɪn/ *vi* relacionarse (**to** con)

appetite /'æpɪtaɪt/ *n* apetito *m*

appetiz|er /'æpɪtaɪzə(r)/ *n* aperitivo *m*. ~ing *a* apetitoso

applau|d /ə'plɔ:d/ *vt/i* aplaudir. ~se *n* aplausos *mpl*

apple /'æpl/ *n* manzana *f*. ~tree *n* manzano *m*

appliance /ə'plaɪəns/ *n* aparato *m*. **electrical** ~ electrodoméstico *m*

applicable /'æplɪkəbl/ *a* aplicable; (*relevant*) pertinente

applicant /'æplɪkənt/ *n* candidato *m*, solicitante *m & f*

application /æplɪ'keɪʃn/ *n* aplicación *f*; (*request*) solicitud *f*. ~ **form** formulario *m* (de solicitud)

appl|ied /ə'plaɪd/ *a* aplicado. ~y /ə'plaɪ/ *vt* aplicar. ● *vi* aplicarse; (*ask*) dirigirse. ~y **for** solicitar (*job etc*)

appoint /ə'pɔɪnt/ *vt* nombrar; (*fix*) señalar. ~ment *n* cita *f*; (*job*) empleo *m*

apportion /ə'pɔ:ʃn/ *vt* repartir

apposite /'æpəzɪt/ *a* apropiado

apprais|al /ə'preɪzl/ *n* evaluación *f*. ~e *vt* evaluar

appreciable /ə'pri:ʃəbl/ *a* sensible; (*considerable*) considerable

appreciat|e /ə'pri:ʃɪeɪt/ *vt* apreciar; (*understand*) comprender; (*be grateful for*) agradecer. ● *vi* (*increase value*) aumentar en valor. ~ion /-'eɪʃn/ *n* aprecio *m*; (*gratitude*) agradecimiento *m*. ~ive /ə'pri:ʃɪətɪv/ *a* (*grateful*) agradecido

apprehen|d /æprɪ'hend/ *vt* detener; (*understand*) comprender. ~sion /-ʃn/ *n* detención *f*; (*fear*) recelo *m*

apprehensive /æprɪ'hensɪv/ *a* aprensivo

apprentice /ə'prentɪs/ *n* aprendiz *m*. ● *vt* poner de aprendiz. ~ship *n* aprendizaje *m*

approach /ə'prəʊtʃ/ *vt* acercarse a. ● *vi* acercarse. ● *n* acercamiento *m*; (*to problem*) enfoque *m*; (*access*) acceso *m*. **make** ~es **to** dirigirse a. ~able *a* accesible

approbation /æprə'beɪʃn/ *n* aprobación *f*

appropriate /ə'prəʊprɪət/ *a* apropiado. /ə'prəʊprɪeɪt/ *vt* apropiarse de. ~ly *adv* apropiadamente

approval /ə'pru:vl/ *n* aprobación *f*. **on** ~ a prueba

approv|e /ə'pru:v/ *vt/i* aprobar. ~ingly *adv* con aprobación

approximat|e /ə'prɒksɪmət/ *a* aproximado. /ə'prɒksɪmeɪt/ *vt* aproximarse a. ~ely *adv* aproximadamente. ~ion /-'meɪʃn/ *n* aproximación *f*

apricot /'eɪprɪkɒt/ *n* albaricoque *m*, chabacano *m* (*Mex*). ~tree *n* albaricoquero *m*, chabacano *m* (*Mex*)

April /'eɪprəl/ *n* abril *m*. ~ **fool!** ¡inocentón!

apron /'eɪprən/ *n* delantal *m*

apropos /'æprəpəʊ/ *adv* a propósito

apse /æps/ *n* ábside *m*

apt /æpt/ *a* apropiado; (*pupil*) listo. **be** ~ **to** tener tendencia a

aptitude /'æptɪtju:d/ *n* aptitud *f*

aptly /'æptlɪ/ *adv* acertadamente

aqualung /'ækwəlʌŋ/ *n* pulmón *m* acuático

aquarium /ə'kweərɪəm/ *n* (*pl* -ums) acuario *m*

Aquarius /ə'kweərɪəs/ *n* Acuario *m*

aquatic /ə'kwætɪk/ *a* acuático

aqueduct /'ækwɪdʌkt/ *n* acueducto *m*

aquiline /'ækwɪlaɪn/ *a* aquilino

Arab /'ærəb/ *a & n* árabe *m*. ~ian /ə'reɪbɪən/ *a* árabe. ~ic /'ærəbɪk/ *a & n* árabe (*m*). ~ic **numerals** números *mpl* arábigos

arable /'ærəbl/ *a* cultivable

arbiter /'ɑ:bɪtə(r)/ *n* árbitro *m*

arbitrary /'ɑ:bɪtrərɪ/ *a* arbitrario

arbitrat|e /'ɑ:bɪtreɪt/ *vi* arbitrar. ~ion /-'treɪʃn/ *n* arbitraje *m*. ~or *n* árbitro *m*

arc /ɑ:k/ *n* arco *m*

arcade /ɑ:'keɪd/ *n* arcada *f*; (*around square*) soportales *mpl*; (*shops*) galería f. **amusement** ~ galería f de atracciones

arcane /ɑ:'keɪn/ a misterioso

arch[1] /ɑ:tʃ/ n arco m. ● vt arquear. ● vi arquearse

arch[2] /ɑ:tʃ/ a malicioso

archaeolog|ical /ɑ:kɪə'lɒdʒɪkl/ a arqueológico. ~ist /ɑ:kɪ'ɒlədʒɪst/ n arqueólogo m. ~y /ɑ:kɪ'ɒlədʒɪ/ n arqueología f

archaic /ɑ:'keɪɪk/ a arcaico

archbishop /ɑ:tʃ'bɪʃəp/ n arzobispo m

arch-enemy /ɑ:tʃ'enəmɪ/ n enemigo m jurado

archer /ɑ:tʃə(r)/ n arquero m. ~y tiro m al arco

archetype /ɑ:kɪtaɪp/ n arquetipo m

archipelago /ɑ:kɪ'peləgəʊ/ n (pl -os) archipiélago m

architect /ɑ:kɪtekt/ n arquitecto m. ~ure /ɑ:kɪtektʃə(r)/ n arquitectura f. ~ural /-'tektʃərəl/ a arquitectónico

archiv|es /ɑ:kaɪvz/ npl archivo m. ~ist /-ɪvɪst/ n archivero m

archway /ɑ:tʃweɪ/ n arco m

Arctic /ɑ:ktɪk/ a ártico. ● n Ártico m

arctic /ɑ:ktɪk/ a glacial

ardent /ɑ:dənt/ a ardiente, fervoroso, apasionado. ~ly adv ardientemente

ardour /ɑ:də(r)/ n ardor m, fervor m, pasión f

arduous /ɑ:djʊəs/ a arduo

are /ɑ:(r)/ see be

area /'eərɪə/ n (surface) superficie f; (region) zona f; (fig) campo m

arena /ə'ri:nə/ n arena f; (in circus) pista f; (in bullring) ruedo m

aren't /ɑ:nt/ = are not

Argentin|a /ɑ:dʒən'ti:nə/ n Argentina f. ~ian /-'tɪnɪən/ a & n argentino (m)

arguable /ɑ:gjʊəbl/ a discutible

argue /ɑ:gju:/ vi discutir; (reason) razonar

argument /ɑ:gjʊmənt/ n disputa f; (reasoning) argumento m. ~ative /-'mentətɪv/ a discutidor

arid /ærɪd/ a árido

Aries /'eəri:z/ n Aries m

arise /ə'raɪz/ vi (pt arose, pp arisen) levantarse; (fig) surgir. ~ from resultar de

aristocra|cy /ærɪ'stɒkrəsɪ/ n aristocracia f. ~t /'ærɪstəkræt/ n aristócrata m & f. ~tic /-'krætɪk/ a aristocrático

arithmetic /ə'rɪθmətɪk/ n aritmética f

ark /ɑ:k/ n (relig) arca f

arm[1] /ɑ:m/ n brazo m. ~ in ~ cogidos del brazo

arm[2] /ɑ:m/ n. ~s npl armas fpl. ● vt armar

armada /ɑ:'mɑ:də/ n armada f

armament /'ɑ:məmənt/ n armamento m

armchair /'ɑ:mtʃeə(r)/ n sillón m

armed robbery /ɑ:md'rɒbərɪ/ n robo m a mano armada

armful /'ɑ:mfʊl/ n brazada f

armistice /'ɑ:mɪstɪs/ n armisticio m

armlet /'ɑ:mlɪt/ n brazalete m

armour /'ɑ:mə(r)/ n armadura f. ~ed a blindado

armoury /'ɑ:mərɪ/ n arsenal m

armpit /'ɑ:mpɪt/ n sobaco m, axila f

army /'ɑ:mɪ/ n ejército m

aroma /ə'rəʊmə/ n aroma m. ~tic /ærə'mætɪk/ a aromático

arose /ə'rəʊz/ see arise

around /ə'raʊnd/ adv alrededor; (near) cerca. all ~ por todas partes. ● prep alrededor de; (with time) a eso de

arouse /ə'raʊz/ vt despertar

arpeggio /ɑ:'pedʒɪəʊ/ n arpegio m

arrange /ə'reɪndʒ/ vt arreglar; (fix) fijar. ~ment n arreglo m; (agreement) acuerdo m; (pl, plans) preparativos mpl

array /ə'reɪ/ vt (dress) ataviar; (mil) formar. ● n atavío m; (mil) orden m; (fig) colección f, conjunto m

arrears /ə'rɪəz/ npl atrasos mpl. in ~ atrasado en pagos

arrest /ə'rest/ vt detener; llamar (attention). ● n detención f. under ~ detenido

arriv|al /ə'raɪvl/ n llegada f. new ~al recien llegado m. ~e /ə'raɪv/ vi llegar

arrogan|ce /'ærəgəns/ n arrogancia f. ~t a arrogante. ~tly adv con arrogancia

arrow /'ærəʊ/ n flecha f

arsenal /'ɑ:sənl/ n arsenal m

arsenic /'ɑ:snɪk/ n arsénico m

arson /'ɑ:sn/ n incendio m provocado. ~ist n incendiario m

art[1] /ɑ:t/ n arte m. A~s npl (Univ) Filosofía y Letras fpl. fine ~s bellas artes fpl

art[2] /ɑ:t/ (old use, with thou) = are

artefact /'ɑ:tɪfækt/ n artefacto m

arterial /ɑ:'tɪərɪəl/ a arterial. ~ road n carretera f nacional

artery /'ɑ:tərɪ/ n arteria f

artesian /ɑːˈtiːzjən/ a. ~ **well** pozo m artesiano

artful /ˈɑːtfʊl/ a astuto. ~**ness** n astucia f

art gallery /ˈɑːtgælərɪ/ n museo m de pinturas, pinacoteca f, galería f de arte

arthriti|c /ɑːˈθrɪtɪk/ a artrítico. ~**s** /ɑːˈθraɪtɪs/ n artritis f

artichoke /ˈɑːtɪtʃəʊk/ n alcachofa f. **Jerusalem** ~ pataca f

article /ˈɑːtɪkl/ n artículo m. ~ **of clothing** prenda f de vestir. **leading** ~ artículo de fondo

articulat|e /ɑːˈtɪkjʊlət/ a articulado; ⟨person⟩ elocuente. /ɑːˈtɪkjʊleɪt/ vt/i articular. ~**ed lorry** n camión m con remolque. ~**ion** /-ˈleɪʃn/ n articulación f

artifice /ˈɑːtɪfɪs/ n artificio m

artificial /ɑːtɪˈfɪʃl/ a artificial; ⟨hair etc⟩ postizo

artillery /ɑːˈtɪlərɪ/ n artillería f

artisan /ɑːtɪˈzæn/ n artesano m

artist /ˈɑːtɪst/ n artista m & f

artiste /ɑːˈtiːst/ n (in theatre) artista m & f

artist|ic /ɑːˈtɪstɪk/ a artístico. ~**ry** n arte m, habilidad f

artless /ˈɑːtlɪs/ a ingenuo

arty /ˈɑːtɪ/ a (fam) que se las da de artista

as /æz, əz/ adv & conj como; (since) ya que; (while) mientras. ~ **big** ~ tan grande como. ~ **far** ~ (distance) hasta; (qualitative) en cuanto a. ~ **far** ~ **I know** que yo sepa. ~ **if** como si. ~ **long** ~ mientras. ~ **much** ~ tanto como. ~ **soon** ~ tan pronto como. ~ **well** también

asbestos /æzˈbestɒs/ n amianto m, asbesto m

ascen|d /əˈsend/ vt/i subir. ~**t** /əˈsent/ n subida f

ascertain /æsəˈteɪn/ vt averiguar

ascetic /əˈsetɪk/ a ascético. ● n asceta m & f

ascribe /əˈskraɪb/ vt atribuir

ash¹ /æʃ/ n ceniza f

ash² /æʃ/ n. ~**(-tree)** fresno m

ashamed /əˈʃeɪmd/ a avergonzado. **be** ~ avergonzarse

ashen /ˈæʃn/ a ceniciento

ashore /əˈʃɔː(r)/ adv a tierra. **go** ~ desembarcar

ash: ~**tray** /ˈæʃtreɪ/ n cenicero m. **A**~ **Wednesday** n Miércoles m de Ceniza

Asia /ˈeɪʃə/ n Asia f. ~**n** a & n asiático (m). ~**tic** /-ˈætɪk/ a asiático

aside /əˈsaɪd/ adv a un lado. ● n (in theatre) aparte m

asinine /ˈæsɪnaɪn/ a estúpido

ask /ɑːsk/ vt pedir; preguntar ⟨question⟩; (invite) invitar. ~ **about** enterarse de. ~ **after** pedir noticias de. ~ **for help** pedir ayuda. ~ **for trouble** buscarse problemas. ~ **s.o. in** invitar a uno a pasar

askance /əˈskæns/ adv. **look** ~ **at** mirar de soslayo

askew /əˈskjuː/ adv & a ladeado

asleep /əˈsliːp/ adv & a dormido. **fall** ~ dormirse, quedar dormido

asparagus /əˈspærəgəs/ n espárrago m

aspect /ˈæspekt/ n aspecto m; (of house etc) orientación f

aspersions /əˈspɜːʃnz/ npl. **cast** ~ **on** difamar

asphalt /ˈæsfælt/ n asfalto m. ● vt asfaltar

asphyxia /æsˈfɪksɪə/ n asfixia f. ~**te** /əsˈfɪksɪeɪt/ vt asfixiar. ~**tion** /-ˈeɪʃn/ n asfixia f

aspic /ˈæspɪk/ n gelatina f

aspir|ation /æspəˈreɪʃn/ n aspiración f. ~**e** /əsˈpaɪə(r)/ vi aspirar

aspirin /ˈæsprɪn/ n aspirina f

ass /æs/ n asno m; (fig, fam) imbécil m

assail /əˈseɪl/ vt asaltar. ~**ant** n asaltador m

assassin /əˈsæsɪn/ n asesino m. ~**ate** /əˈsæsɪneɪt/ vt asesinar. ~**ation** /-ˈeɪʃn/ n asesinato m

assault /əˈsɔːlt/ n (mil) ataque m; (jurid) atentado m. ● vt asaltar

assemblage /əˈsemblɪdʒ/ n (of things) colección f; (of people) reunión f; (mec) montaje m

assemble /əˈsembl/ vt reunir; (mec) montar. ● vi reunirse

assembly /əˈsemblɪ/ n reunión f; (pol etc) asamblea f. ~ **line** n línea f de montaje

assent /əˈsent/ n asentimiento m. ● vi asentir

assert /əˈsɜːt/ vt afirmar; hacer valer ⟨one's rights⟩. ~**ion** /-ʃn/ n afirmación f. ~**ive** a positivo, firme

assess /əˈses/ vt valorar; (determine) determinar; fijar ⟨tax etc⟩. ~**ment** n valoración f

asset /ˈæset/ n (advantage) ventaja f; (pl, com) bienes mpl

assiduous /əˈsɪdjʊəs/ a asiduo

assign /ə'saɪn/ vt asignar; (appoint) nombrar

assignation /æsɪg'neɪʃn/ n asignación f; (meeting) cita f

assignment /ə'saɪnmənt/ n asignación f, misión f; (task) tarea f

assimilat|e /ə'sɪmɪleɪt/ vt asimilar. ● vi asimilarse. ~ion /-'eɪʃn/ n asimilación f

assist /ə'sɪst/ vt/i ayudar. ~ance n ayuda f. ~ant /ə'sɪstənt/ n ayudante m & f; (shop) dependienta f, dependiente m. ● a auxiliar, adjunto

associat|e /ə'səʊʃɪeɪt/ vt asociar. ● vi asociarse. /ə'səʊʃɪət/ a asociado. ● n colega m & f; (com) socio m. ~ion /-'eɪʃn/ n asociación f. A~ion football n fútbol m

assort|ed /ə'sɔːtɪd/ a surtido. ~ment n surtido m

assume /ə'sjuːm/ vt suponer; tomar ⟨power, attitude⟩; asumir ⟨role, burden⟩

assumption /ə'sʌmpʃn/ n suposición f. the A~ la Asunción f

assur|ance /ə'ʃʊərəns/ n seguridad f; (insurance) seguro m. ~e /ə'ʃʊə(r)/ vt asegurar. ~ed a seguro. ~edly /-rɪdlɪ/ adv seguramente

asterisk /'æstərɪsk/ n asterisco m

astern /ə'stɜːn/ adv a popa

asthma /'æsmə/ n asma f. ~tic /-'mætɪk/ a & n asmático (m)

astonish /ə'stɒnɪʃ/ vt asombrar. ~ing a asombroso. ~ment n asombro m

astound /ə'staʊnd/ vt asombrar

astray /ə'streɪ/ adv & a. go ~ extraviarse. lead ~ llevar por mal camino

astride /ə'straɪd/ adv a horcajadas. ● prep a horcajadas sobre

astringent /ə'strɪndʒənt/ a astringente; (fig) austero. ● n astringente m

astrolog|er /ə'strɒlədʒə(r)/ n astrólogo m. ~y n astrología f

astronaut /'æstrənɔːt/ n astronauta m & f

astronom|er /ə'strɒnəmə(r)/ n astrónomo m. ~ical /æstrə'nɒmɪkl/ a astronómico. ~y /ə'strɒnəmɪ/ n astronomía f

astute /ə'stjuːt/ a astuto. ~ness n astucia f

asunder /ə'sʌndə(r)/ adv en pedazos; (in two) en dos

asylum /ə'saɪləm/ n asilo m. **lunatic** ~ manicomio m

at /ət, æt/ prep a. ~ **home** en casa. ~ **night** por la noche. ~ **Robert's** en casa de Roberto. ~ **once** en seguida; (simultaneously) a la vez. ~ **sea** en el mar. ~ **the station** en la estación. ~ **times** a veces. **not** ~ **all** nada; (after thanks) ¡de nada!

ate /et/ see **eat**

atheis|m /'eɪθɪzəm/ n ateísmo m. ~t /'eɪθɪɪst/ n ateo m

athlet|e /'æθliːt/ n atleta m & f. ~ic /-'letɪk/ a atlético. ~ics /-'letɪks/ npl atletismo m

Atlantic /ət'læntɪk/ a & n atlántico (m). ● n. ~ **(Ocean)** (Océano m) Atlántico m

atlas /'ætləs/ n atlas m

atmospher|e /'ætməsfɪə(r)/ n atmósfera f; (fig) ambiente m. ~ic /-'ferɪk/ a atmosférico. ~ics /-'ferɪks/ npl parásitos mpl

atom /'ætəm/ n átomo m. ~ic /ə'tɒmɪk/ a atómico

atomize /'ætəmaɪz/ vt atomizar. ~r /'ætəmaɪzə(r)/ n atomizador m

atone /ə'təʊn/ vi. ~ **for** expiar. ~ment n expiación f

atroci|ous /ə'trəʊʃəs/ a atroz. ~ty /ə'trɒsətɪ/ n atrocidad f

atrophy /'ætrəfɪ/ n atrofia f

attach /ə'tætʃ/ vt sujetar; adjuntar ⟨document etc⟩. **be ~ed to** (be fond of) tener cariño a

attaché /ə'tæʃeɪ/ n agregado m. ~ **case** maletín m

attachment /ə'tætʃmənt/ n (affection) cariño m; (tool) accesorio m

attack /ə'tæk/ n ataque m. ● vt/i atacar. ~er n agresor m

attain /ə'teɪn/ vt conseguir. ~able a alcanzable. ~ment n logro m. ~ments npl conocimientos mpl, talento m

attempt /ə'tempt/ vt intentar. ● n tentativa f; (attack) atentado m

attend /ə'tend/ vt asistir a; (escort) acompañar. ● vi prestar atención. ~ **to** (look after) ocuparse de. ~ance n asistencia f; (people present) concurrencia f. ~ant /ə'tendənt/ a concomitante. ● n encargado m; (servant) sirviente m

attention /ə'tenʃn/ n atención f. ~! (mil) ¡firmes! **pay** ~ prestar atención

attentive /ə'tentɪv/ a atento. ~ness n atención f

attenuate /ə'tenjʊeɪt/ vt atenuar

attest /ə'test/ *vt* atestiguar. ● *vi* dar testimonio. **∼ation** /æteˈsteɪʃn/ *n* testimonio *m*

attic /'ætɪk/ *n* desván *m*

attire /ə'taɪə(r)/ *n* atavío *m*. ● *vt* vestir

attitude /'ætɪtjuːd/ *n* postura *f*

attorney /ə'tɜːnɪ/ *n* (*pl* **-eys**) apoderado *m*; (*Amer*) abogado *m*

attract /ə'trækt/ *vt* atraer. **∼ion** /-ʃn/ *n* atracción *f*; (*charm*) atractivo *m*

attractive /ə'træktɪv/ *a* atractivo; (*interesting*) atrayente. **∼ness** *n* atractivo *m*

attribute /ə'trɪbjuːt/ *vt* atribuir. /'ætrɪbjuːt/ *n* atributo *m*

attrition /ə'trɪʃn/ *n* desgaste *m*

aubergine /'əʊbəʒiːn/ *n* berenjena *f*

auburn /'ɔːbən/ *a* castaño

auction /'ɔːkʃn/ *n* subasta *f*. ● *vt* subastar. **∼eer** /-ə'nɪə(r)/ *n* subastador *m*

audaci|ous /ɔː'deɪʃəs/ *a* audaz. **∼ty** /-æsətɪ/ *n* audacia *f*

audible /'ɔːdəbl/ *a* audible

audience /'ɔːdɪəns/ *n* (*interview*) audiencia *f*; (*teatro, radio*) público *m*

audio-visual /ɔːdɪəʊ'vɪʒʊəl/ *a* audio-visual

audit /'ɔːdɪt/ *n* revisión *f* de cuentas. ● *vt* revisar

audition /ɔː'dɪʃn/ *n* audición *f*. ● *vt* dar audición a

auditor /'ɔːdɪtə(r)/ *n* interventor *m* de cuentas

auditorium /ɔːdɪ'tɔːrɪəm/ *n* sala *f*, auditorio *m*

augment /ɔːg'ment/ *vt* aumentar

augur /'ɔːgə(r)/ *vt* augurar. **it ∼s well** es de buen agüero

august /ɔː'gʌst/ *a* augusto

August /'ɔːgəst/ *n* agosto *m*

aunt /ɑːnt/ *n* tía *f*

au pair /əʊ'peə(r)/ *n* chica *f* au pair

aura /'ɔːrə/ *n* atmósfera *f*, halo *m*

auspices /'ɔːspɪsɪz/ *npl* auspicios *mpl*

auspicious /ɔː'spɪʃəs/ *a* propicio

auster|e /ɔː'stɪə(r)/ *a* austero. **∼ity** /-erətɪ/ *n* austeridad *f*

Australia /ɒ'streɪlɪə/ *n* Australia *f*. **∼n** *a & n* australiano (*m*)

Austria /'ɒstrɪə/ *n* Austria *f*. **∼n** *a & n* austríaco (*m*)

authentic /ɔː'θentɪk/ *a* auténtico. **∼ate** /ɔː'θentɪkeɪt/ *vt* autenticar. **∼ity** /-ən'tɪsətɪ/ *n* autenticidad *f*

author /'ɔːθə(r)/ *n* autor *m*. **∼ess** *n* autora *f*

authoritarian /ɔːθɒrɪ'teərɪən/ *a* autoritario

authoritative /ɔː'θɒrɪtətɪv/ *a* autorizado; (*manner*) autoritario

authority /ɔː'θɒrətɪ/ *n* autoridad *f*; (*permission*) autorización *f*

authoriz|ation /ɔːθəraɪ'zeɪʃn/ *n* autorización *f*. **∼e** /'ɔːθəraɪz/ *vt* autorizar

authorship /'ɔːθəʃɪp/ *n* profesión *f* de autor; (*origin*) paternidad *f* literaria

autistic /ɔː'tɪstɪk/ *a* autista

autobiography /ɔːtəʊbaɪ'ɒgrəfɪ/ *n* autobiografía *f*

autocra|cy /ɔː'tɒkrəsɪ/ *n* autocracia *f*. **∼t** /'ɔːtəkræt/ *n* autócrata *m & f*. **∼tic** /-'krætɪk/ *a* autocrático

autograph /'ɔːtəgrɑːf/ *n* autógrafo *m*. ● *vt* firmar

automat|e /'ɔːtəmeɪt/ *vt* automatizar. **∼ic** /ɔː'tə'mætɪk/ *a* automático. **∼ion** /-'meɪʃn/ *n* automatización *f*. **∼on** /ɔː'tɒmətən/ *n* autómata *m*

automobile /'ɔːtəməbiːl/ *n* (*Amer*) coche *m*, automóvil *m*

autonom|ous /ɔː'tɒnəməs/ *a* autónomo. **∼y** *n* autonomía *f*

autopsy /'ɔːtɒpsɪ/ *n* autopsia *f*

autumn /'ɔːtəm/ *n* otoño *m*. **∼al** /-'tʌmnəl/ *a* de otoño, otoñal

auxiliary /ɔːg'zɪlɪərɪ/ *a* auxiliar. ● *n* asistente *m*; (*verb*) verbo *m* auxiliar; (*pl, troops*) tropas *fpl* auxiliares

avail /ə'veɪl/ *vt/i* servir. **∼ o.s. of** aprovecharse de. ● *n* ventaja *f*. **to no ∼** inútil

availab|ility /əveɪlə'bɪlətɪ/ *n* disponibilidad *f*. **∼le** /ə'veɪləbl/ *a* disponible

avalanche /'ævəlɑːnʃ/ *n* avalancha *f*

avaric|e /'ævərɪs/ *n* avaricia *f*. **∼ious** /-'rɪʃəs/ *a* avaro

avenge /ə'vendʒ/ *vt* vengar

avenue /'ævənjuː/ *n* avenida *f*; (*fig*) vía *f*

average /'ævərɪdʒ/ *n* promedio *m*. **on ∼** por término medio. ● *a* medio. ● *vt* calcular el promedio de. ● *vi* alcanzar un promedio de

avers|e /ə'vɜːs/ *a* enemigo (**to** de). **be ∼e to** sentir repugnancia por, no gustarle. **∼ion** /-ʃn/ *n* repugnancia *f*

avert /ə'vɜːt/ vt (turn away) apartar; (ward off) desviar

aviary /'eɪvɪərɪ/ n pajarera f

aviation /eɪvɪ'eɪʃn/ n aviación f

aviator /'eɪvɪeɪtə(r)/ n (old use) aviador m

avid /'ævɪd/ a ávido. **~ity** /-'vɪdətɪ/ n avidez f

avocado /ævə'kɑːdəʊ/ n (pl -os) aguacate m

avoid /ə'vɔɪd/ vt evitar. **~able** a evitable. **~ance** n el evitar m

avuncular /ə'vʌŋkjʊlə(r)/ a de tío

await /ə'weɪt/ vt esperar

awake /ə'weɪk/ vt/i (pt awoke, pp awoken) despertar. ● a despierto. **wide ~** completamente despierto; (fig) despabilado. **~n** /ə'weɪkən/ vt/i despertar. **~ning** n el despertar m

award /ə'wɔːd/ vt otorgar; (jurid) adjudicar. ● n premio m; (jurid) adjudicación f; (scholarship) beca f

aware /ə'weə(r)/ a consciente. **are you ~ that?** ¿te das cuenta de que? **~ness** n conciencia f

awash /ə'wɒʃ/ a inundado

away /ə'weɪ/ adv (absent) fuera; (far) lejos; (persistently) sin parar. ● a & n. **~ (match)** partido m fuera de casa

awe /ɔː/ n temor m. **~some** a imponente. **~struck** a atemorizado

awful /'ɔːfʊl/ a terrible, malísimo. **~ly** adv terriblemente

awhile /ə'waɪl/ adv un rato

awkward /'ɔːkwəd/ a difícil; (inconvenient) inoportuno; (clumsy) desmañado; (embarrassed) incómodo. **~ly** adv con dificultad; (clumsily) de manera torpe. **~ness** n dificultad f; (discomfort) molestia f; (clumsiness) torpeza f

awning /'ɔːnɪŋ/ n toldo m

awoke, awoken /ə'wəʊk, ə'wəʊkən/ see **awake**

awry /ə'raɪ/ adv & a ladeado. **go ~** salir mal

axe /æks/ n hacha f. ● vt (pres p axing) cortar con hacha; (fig) recortar

axiom /'æksɪəm/ n axioma m

axis /'æksɪs/ n (pl axes /-iːz/) eje m

axle /'æksl/ n eje m

ay(e) /aɪ/ adv & n sí (m)

B

BA abbr see **bachelor**

babble /'bæbl/ vi balbucir; (chatter) parlotear; (of stream) murmullar. ● n balbuceo m; (chatter) parloteo m; (of stream) murmullo m

baboon /bə'buːn/ n mandril m

baby /'beɪbɪ/ n niño m, bebé m; (Amer, sl) chica f. **~ish** /'beɪbɪɪʃ/ a infantil. **~sit** vi cuidar a los niños, hacer de canguro. **~sitter** n persona f que cuida a los niños, canguro m

bachelor /'bætʃələ(r)/ n soltero m. **B~ of Arts (BA)** licenciado m en filosofía y letras. **B~ of Science (BSc)** licenciado m en ciencias

back /bæk/ n espalda f; (of car) parte f trasera; (of chair) respaldo m; (of cloth) revés m; (of house) parte f de atrás; (of animal, book) lomo m; (of hand, document) dorso m; (football) defensa m & f. **~ of beyond** en el quinto pino. ● a trasero; (taxes) atrasado. ● adv atrás; (returned) de vuelta. ● vt apoyar; (betting) apostar a; dar marcha atrás a (car). ● vi retroceder; (car) dar marcha atrás. **~ down** vi volverse atrás. **~ out** vi retirarse. **~ up** vi (auto) retroceder. **~ache** /'bækeɪk/ n dolor m de espalda. **~bencher** n (pol) diputado m sin poder ministerial. **~biting** /'bækbaɪtɪŋ/ n maledicencia f. **~bone** /'bækbəʊn/ n columna f vertebral; (fig) pilar m. **~chat** /'bæktʃæt/ n impertinencias fpl. **~date** /bæk'deɪt/ vt antedatar. **~er** /'bækə(r)/ n partidario m; (com) financiador m. **~fire** /bæk'faɪə(r)/ vi (auto) petardear; (fig) fallar, salir el tiro por la culata. **~gammon** /bæk'gæmən/ n backgamon m. **~ground** /'bækgraʊnd/ n fondo m; (environment) antecedentes mpl. **~hand** /'bækhænd/ n (sport) revés m. **~handed** a dado con el dorso de la mano; (fig) equívoco, ambiguo. **~hander** n (sport) revés m; (fig) ataque m indirecto; (bribe, sl) soborno m. **~ing** /'bækɪŋ/ n apoyo m. **~lash** /'bæklæʃ/ n reacción f. **~log** /'bæklɒg/ n atrasos mpl. **~side** /bæk'saɪd/ n (fam) trasero m. **~stage** /bæk'steɪdʒ/ a de bastidores. ● adv entre bastidores. **~stroke** /'bækstrəʊk/ n (tennis etc) revés m; (swimming) braza f de espaldas. **~up** n apoyo m. **~ward** /'bækwəd/ a (step etc) hacia atrás;

(*retarded*) atrasado. **~wards**
/'bækwədz/ *adv* hacia atrás; (*fall*) de
espaldas; (*back to front*) al revés. **go
~wards and forwards** ir de acá
para allá. **~water** /'bækwɔːtə(r)/ *n*
agua *f* estancada; (*fig*) lugar *m*
apartado

bacon /'beɪkən/ *n* tocino *m*

bacteria /bæk'tɪərɪə/ *npl* bacterias
fpl. **~l** *a* bacteriano

bad /bæd/ *a* (**worse, worst**) malo;
(*serious*) grave; (*harmful*) nocivo;
(*language*) indecente. **feel ~** sentirse mal

bade /beɪd/ *see* **bid**

badge /bædʒ/ *n* distintivo *m*, chapa *f*

badger /'bædʒə(r)/ *n* tejón *m*. ● *vt*
acosar

bad: ~ly *adv* mal. **want ~ly** desear
muchísimo. **~ly off** mal de dinero.
~mannered *a* mal educado

badminton /'bædmɪntən/ *n* bád-
minton *m*

bad-tempered /bæd'tempəd/ *a*
(*always*) de mal genio; (*tem-
porarily*) de mal humor

baffle /'bæfl/ *vt* desconcertar

bag /bæg/ *n* bolsa *f*; (*handbag*) bolso
m. ● *vt* (*pt* **bagged**) ensacar; (*take*)
coger (*not LAm*), agarrar (*LAm*). **~s**
npl (*luggage*) equipaje *m*. **~s of**
(*fam*) montones de

baggage /'bægɪdʒ/ *n* equipaje *m*

baggy /'bægɪ/ *a* (*clothes*) holgado

bagpipes /'bægpaɪps/ *npl* gaita *f*

Bahamas /bə'hɑːməz/ *npl*. **the ~** las
Bahamas *fpl*

bail[1] /beɪl/ *n* caución *f*, fianza *f*. ● *vt*
poner en libertad bajo fianza. **~ s.o.
out** obtener la libertad de uno bajo
fianza

bail[2] /beɪl/ *n* (*cricket*) travesaño *m*

bail[3] /beɪl/ *vt* (*naut*) achicar

bailiff /'beɪlɪf/ *n* alguacil *m*; (*estate*)
administrador *m*

bait /beɪt/ *n* cebo *m*. ● *vt* cebar; (*torment*) atormentar

bak|e /beɪk/ *vt* cocer al horno. ● *vi*
cocerse. **~er** *n* panadero *m*. **~ery**
/'beɪkərɪ/ *n* panadería *f*. **~ing** *n*
cocción *f*; (*batch*) hornada *f*. **~ing-
powder** *n* levadura *f* en polvo

balance /'bæləns/ *n* equilibrio *m*;
(*com*) balance *m*; (*sum*) saldo *m*;
(*scales*) balanza *f*; (*remainder*) resto
m. ● *vt* equilibrar; (*com*) saldar; nivelar (*budget*). ● *vi* equilibrarse;
(*com*) saldarse. **~d** *a* equilibrado

balcony /'bælkənɪ/ *n* balcón *m*

bald /bɔːld/ *a* (**-er, -est**) calvo; (*tyre*)
desgastado

balderdash /'bɔːldədæʃ/ *n* tonterías
fpl

bald: ~ly *adv* escuetamente. **~ness**
n calvicie *f*

bale /beɪl/ *n* bala *f*, fardo *m*. ● *vi*. **~
out** lanzarse en paracaídas

Balearic /bælɪ'ærɪk/ *a*. **~ Islands**
Islas *fpl* Baleares

baleful /'beɪlfʊl/ *a* funesto

balk /bɔːk/ *vt* frustrar. ● *vi*. **~ (at)**
resistirse (a)

ball[1] /bɔːl/ *n* bola *f*; (*tennis etc*) pelota
f; (*football etc*) balón *m*; (*of yarn*)
ovillo *m*

ball[2] /bɔːl/ (*dance*) baile *m*

ballad /'bæləd/ *n* balada *f*

ballast /'bæləst/ *n* lastre *m*

ball: ~-bearing *n* cojinete *m* de
bolas. **~cock** *n* llave *f* de bola

ballerina /bælə'riːnə/ *f* bailarina *f*

ballet /'bæleɪ/ *n* ballet *m*

ballistic /bə'lɪstɪk/ *a* balístico. **~s** *n*
balística *f*

balloon /bə'luːn/ *n* globo *m*

balloonist /bə'luːnɪst/ *n* aeronauta
m & f

ballot /'bælət/ *n* votación *f*. **~
(-paper)** *n* papeleta *f*. **~-box** *n* urna
f

ball-point /'bɔːlpɔɪnt/ *n*. **~ (pen)**
bolígrafo *m*

ballroom /'bɔːlruːm/ *n* salón *m* de
baile

ballyhoo /bælɪ'huː/ *n* (*publicity*)
publicidad *f* sensacionalista;
(*uproar*) jaleo *m*

balm /bɑːm/ *n* bálsamo *m*. **~y** *a*
(*mild*) suave; (*sl*) chiflado

baloney /bə'ləʊnɪ/ *n* (*sl*) tonterías *fpl*

balsam /'bɔːlsəm/ *n* bálsamo *m*

balustrade /bælə'streɪd/ *n* barandilla *f*

bamboo /bæm'buː/ *n* bambú *m*

bamboozle /bæm'buːzl/ *vt*
engatusar

ban /bæn/ *vt* (*pt* **banned**) prohibir. **~
from** excluir de. ● *n* prohibición *f*

banal /bə'nɑːl/ *a* banal. **~ity** /-ælətɪ/ *n*
banalidad *f*

banana /bə'nɑːnə/ *n* plátano *m*,
banana *f* (*LAm*). **~tree** plátano *m*,
banano *m*

band[1] /bænd/ *n* banda *f*

band[2] /bænd/ *n* (*mus*) orquesta *f*;
(*military, brass*) banda *f*. ● *vi*. **~
together** juntarse

bandage /'bændɪdʒ/ n venda f. ● vt vendar

b & b abbr (bed and breakfast) cama f y desayuno

bandit /'bændɪt/ n bandido m

bandstand /'bændstænd/ n quiosco m de música

bandwagon /'bændwægən/ n. **jump on the ~** (fig) subirse al carro

bandy[1] /'bændɪ/ a (-ier, -iest) patizambo

bandy[2] /'bændɪ/ vt. **~ about** repetir. **be bandied about** estar en boca de todos

bandy-legged /'bændɪlegd/ a patizambo

bane /beɪn/ n (fig) perdición f. **~ful** a funesto

bang /bæŋ/ n (noise) ruido m; (blow) golpe m; (of gun) estampido m; (of door) golpe m. ● vt/i golpear. ● adv exactamente. ● int ¡pum!

banger /'bæŋə(r)/ n petardo m; (culin, sl) salchicha f

bangle /'bæŋgl/ n brazalete m

banish /'bænɪʃ/ vt desterrar

banisters /'bænɪstəz/ npl barandilla f

banjo /'bændʒəʊ/ n (pl -os) banjo m

bank[1] /bæŋk/ n (of river) orilla f. ● vt cubrir (fire). ● vi (aviat) ladearse

bank[2] /bæŋk/ n banco m. ● vt depositar. **~ on** vt contar con. **~ with** tener una cuenta con. **~er** n banquero m. **~ holiday** n día m festivo, fiesta f. **~ing** n (com) banca f. **~note** /'bæŋknəʊt/ n billete m de banco

bankrupt /'bæŋkrʌpt/ a & n quebrado (m). ● vt hacer quebrar. **~cy** n bancarrota f, quiebra f

banner /'bænə(r)/ n bandera f; (in demonstration) pancarta f

banns /bænz/ npl amonestaciones fpl

banquet /'bæŋkwɪt/ n banquete m

bantamweight /'bæntəmweɪt/ n peso m gallo

banter /'bæntə(r)/ n chanza f. ● vi chancearse

bap /bæp/ n panecillo m blando

baptism /'bæptɪzəm/ n bautismo m; (act) bautizo m

Baptist /'bæptɪst/ n bautista m & f

baptize /bæp'taɪz/ vt bautizar

bar /bɑː(r)/ n barra f; (on window) reja f; (of chocolate) tableta f; (of soap) pastilla f; (pub) bar m; (mus) compás m; (jurid) abogacía f; (fig) obstáculo m. ● vt (pt **barred**) atrancar (door); (exclude) excluir; (prohibit) prohibir. ● prep excepto

barbar|ian /bɑː'beərɪən/ a & n bárbaro (m). **~ic** /bɑː'bærɪk/ a bárbaro. **~ity** /-ətɪ/ n barbaridad f. **~ous** a /'bɑːbərəs/ a bárbaro

barbecue /'bɑːbɪkjuː/ n barbacoa f. ● vt asar a la parilla

barbed /bɑːbd/ a. **~ wire** alambre m de espinas

barber /'bɑːbə(r)/ n peluquero m, barbero m

barbiturate /bɑː'bɪtjʊrət/ n barbitúrico m

bare /beə(r)/ a (-er, -est) desnudo; (room) con pocos muebles; (mere) simple; (empty) vacío. ● vt desnudar; (uncover) descubrir. **~ one's teeth** mostrar los dientes. **~back** /'beəbæk/ adv a pelo. **~faced** /'beəfeɪst/ a descarado. **~foot** a descalzo. **~headed** /'beəhedɪd/ a descubierto. **~ly** adv apenas. **~ness** n desnudez f

bargain /'bɑːgɪn/ n (agreement) pacto m; (good buy) ganga f. ● vi negociar; (haggle) regatear. **~ for** esperar, contar con

barge /bɑːdʒ/ n barcaza f. ● vi. **~ in** irrumpir

baritone /'bærɪtəʊn/ n barítono m

barium /'beərɪəm/ n bario m

bark[1] /bɑːk/ n (of dog) ladrido m. ● vi ladrar

bark[2] /bɑːk/ n (of tree) corteza f

barley /'bɑːlɪ/ n cebada f. **~water** n hordiate m

bar: ~maid /'bɑːmeɪd/ n camarera f. **~man** /'bɑːmən/ n (pl -men) camarero m

barmy /'bɑːmɪ/ a (sl) chiflado

barn /bɑːn/ n granero m

barometer /bə'rɒmɪtə(r)/ n barómetro m

baron /'bærən/ n barón m. **~ess** n baronesa f

baroque /bə'rɒk/ a & n barroco (m)

barracks /'bærəks/ npl cuartel m

barrage /'bærɑːʒ/ n (mil) barrera f; (dam) presa f; (of questions) bombardeo m

barrel /'bærəl/ n tonel m; (of gun) cañón m. **~organ** n organillo m

barren /'bærən/ a estéril. **~ness** n esterilidad f, aridez f

barricade /bærɪ'keɪd/ n barricada f. ● vt cerrar con barricadas

barrier /'bærɪə(r)/ n barrera f

barring /'bɑːrɪŋ/ *prep* salvo

barrister /'bærɪstə(r)/ *n* abogado *m*

barrow /'bærəu/ *n* carro *m*; (*wheelbarrow*) carretilla *f*

barter /'bɑːtə(r)/ *n* trueque *m*. ● *vt* trocar

base /beɪs/ *n* base *f*. ● *vt* basar. ● *a* vil

baseball /'beɪsbɔːl/ *n* béisbol *m*

baseless /'beɪslɪs/ *a* infundado

basement /'beɪsmənt/ *n* sótano *m*

bash /bæʃ/ *vt* golpear. ● *n* golpe *m*. **have a ∼** (*sl*) probar

bashful /'bæʃfl/ *a* tímido

basic /'beɪsɪk/ *a* básico, fundamental. **∼ally** *adv* fundamentalmente

basil /'bæzl/ *n* albahaca *f*

basilica /bə'zɪlɪkə/ *n* basílica *f*

basin /'beɪsn/ *n* (*for washing*) palangana *f*; (*for food*) cuenco *m*; (*geog*) cuenca *f*

basis /'beɪsɪs/ *n* (*pl* **bases** /-siːz/) base *f*

bask /bɑːsk/ *vi* asolearse; (*fig*) gozar (**in** de)

basket /'bɑːskɪt/ *n* cesta *f*; (*big*) cesto *m*. **∼ball** /'bɑːskɪtbɔːl/ *n* baloncesto *m*

Basque /bɑːsk/ *a & n* vasco (*m*). **∼ Country** *n* País *m* Vasco. **∼ Provinces** *npl* Vascongadas *fpl*

bass[1] /beɪs/ *a* bajo. ● *n* (*mus*) bajo *m*

bass[2] /bæs/ *n* (*marine fish*) róbalo *m*; (*freshwater fish*) perca *f*

bassoon /bə'suːn/ *n* fagot *m*

bastard /'bɑːstəd/ *a & n* bastardo *m*. **you ∼!** (*fam*) ¡cabrón!

baste /beɪst/ *vt* (*sew*) hilvanar; (*culin*) lard(e)ar

bastion /'bæstɪən/ *n* baluarte *m*

bat[1] /bæt/ *n* bate *m*; (*for table tennis*) raqueta *f*. **off one's own ∼** por sí solo. ● *vt* (*pt* **batted**) golpear. ● *vi* batear

bat[2] /bæt/ *n* (*mammal*) murciélago *m*

bat[3] /bæt/ *vt*. **without ∼ting an eyelid** sin pestañear

batch /bætʃ/ *n* (*of people*) grupo *m*; (*of papers*) lío *m*; (*of goods*) remesa *f*; (*of bread*) hornada *f*

bated /'beɪtɪd/ *a*. **with ∼ breath** con aliento entrecortado

bath /bɑːθ/ *n* (*pl* **-s** /bɑːðz/) baño *m*; (*tub*) bañera *f*; (*pl, swimming pool*) piscina *f*. ● *vt* bañar. ● *vi* bañarse

bathe /beɪð/ *vt* bañar. ● *vi* bañarse. ● *n* baño *m*. **∼r** /-ə(r)/ *n* bañista *m & f*

bathing /'beɪðɪŋ/ *n* baños *mpl*. **∼costume** *n* traje *m* de baño

bathroom /'bɑːθrʊm/ *n* cuarto *m* de baño

batman /'bætmən/ *n* (*pl* **-men**) (*mil*) ordenanza *f*

baton /'bætən/ *n* (*mil*) bastón *m*; (*mus*) batuta *f*

batsman /'bætsmən/ *n* (*pl* **-men**) bateador *m*

battalion /bə'tælɪən/ *n* batallón *m*

batter[1] /'bætə(r)/ *vt* apalear

batter[2] /'bætə(r)/ *n* batido *m* para rebozar, albardilla *f*

batter: **∼ed** *a* (*car etc*) estropeado; (*wife etc*) golpeado. **∼ing** *n* (*fam*) bombardeo *m*

battery /'bætərɪ/ *n* (*mil, auto*) batería *f*; (*of torch, radio*) pila *f*

battle /'bætl/ *n* batalla *f*; (*fig*) lucha *f*. ● *vi* luchar. **∼axe** /'bætlæks/ *n* (*woman, fam*) arpía *f*. **∼field** /'bætlfiːld/ *n* campo *m* de batalla. **∼ments** /'bætlmənts/ *npl* almenas *fpl*. **∼ship** /'bætlʃɪp/ *n* acorazado *m*

batty /'bætɪ/ *a* (*sl*) chiflado

baulk /bɔːlk/ *vt* frustrar. ● *vi*. **∼ (at)** resistirse (a)

bawd /iness /'bɔːdɪnəs/ *n* obscenidad *f*. **∼y** /'bɔːdɪ/ *a* (**-ier, -iest**) obsceno, verde

bawl /bɔːl/ *vt/i* gritar

bay[1] /beɪ/ *n* (*geog*) bahía *f*

bay[2] /beɪ/ *n* (*bot*) laurel *m*

bay[3] /beɪ/ *n* (*of dog*) ladrido *m*. **keep at ∼** mantener a raya. ● *vi* ladrar

bayonet /'beɪənet/ *n* bayoneta *f*

bay window /beɪ'wɪndəʊ/ *n* ventana *f* saledizada

bazaar /bə'zɑː(r)/ *n* bazar *m*

BC /biː'siː/ *abbr* (*before Christ*) a. de C., antes de Cristo

be /biː/ *vi* (*pres* **am, are, is**; *pt* **was, were**; *pp* **been**) (*position or temporary*) estar; (*permanent*) ser. **∼ cold/hot, etc** tener frío/calor, etc. **∼ reading/singing, etc** (*aux*) leer/cantar, etc. **∼ that as it may** sea como fuere. **he is 30** (*age*) tiene 30 años. **he is to come** (*must*) tiene que venir. **how are you?** ¿cómo estás? **how much is it?** ¿cuánto vale?, ¿cuánto es? **have been to** haber estado en. **it is cold/hot, etc** (*weather*) hace frío/calor, etc

beach /biːtʃ/ *n* playa *f*

beachcomber /'biːtʃkəʊmə(r)/ *n* raquero *m*

beacon /'biːkən/ *n* faro *m*

bead /biːd/ n cuenta f; (of glass) abalorio m

beak /biːk/ n pico m

beaker /'biːkə(r)/ n jarra f, vaso m

beam /biːm/ n viga f; (of light) rayo m; (naut) bao m. ● vt emitir. ● vi irradiar; (smile) sonreír. **∼-ends** npl. **be on one's ∼-ends** no tener más dinero. **∼ing** a radiante

bean /biːn/ n judía; (broad bean) haba f; (of coffee) grano m

beano /'biːnəʊ/ n (pl -os) (fam) juerga f

bear[1] /beə(r)/ vt (pt bore, pp borne) llevar; parir ⟨niño⟩; (endure) soportar. **∼ right** torcer a la derecha. **∼ in mind** tener en cuenta. **∼ with** tener paciencia con

bear[2] /beə(r)/ n oso m

bearable /'beərəbl/ a soportable

beard /bɪəd/ n barba f. **∼ed** a barbudo

bearer /'beərə(r)/ n portador m; (of passport) poseedor m

bearing /'beərɪŋ/ n comportamiento m; (relevance) relación f; (mec) cojinete m. **get one's ∼s** orientarse

beast /biːst/ n bestia f; (person) bruto m. **∼ly** /'biːstlɪ/ a (-ier, -iest) bestial; (fam) horrible

beat /biːt/ vt (pt beat, pp beaten) golpear; (culin) batir; (defeat) derrotar; (better) sobrepasar; (baffle) dejar perplejo. **∼ a retreat** (mil) batirse en retirada. **∼ it** (sl) largarse. ● vi ⟨heart⟩ latir. ● n latido m; (mus) ritmo m; (of policeman) ronda f. **∼ up** dar una paliza a; (culin) batir. **∼er** n batidor m. **∼ing** n paliza f

beautician /bjuː'tɪʃn/ n esteticista m & f

beautiful /'bjuːtɪfl/ a hermoso. **∼ly** adv maravillosamente

beautify /'bjuːtɪfaɪ/ vt embellecer

beauty /'bjuːtɪ/ n belleza f. **∼ parlour** n salón m de belleza. **∼ spot** (on face) lunar m; (site) lugar m pintoresco

beaver /'biːvə(r)/ n castor m

became /bɪ'keɪm/ see become

because /bɪ'kɒz/ conj porque. ● adv. **∼ of** a causa de

beck /bek/ n. **be at the ∼ and call of** estar a disposición de

beckon /'bekən/ vt/i. **∼ (to)** hacer señas (a)

become /bɪ'kʌm/ vt (pt became, pp become) ⟨clothes⟩ sentar bien. ● vi

hacerse, llegar a ser, volverse, convertirse en. **what has ∼ of her?** ¿qué es de ella?

becoming /bɪ'kʌmɪŋ/ a ⟨clothes⟩ favorecedor

bed /bed/ n cama f; (layer) estrato m; (of sea, river) fondo m; (of flowers) macizo m. ● vi (pt bedded). **∼ down** acostarse. **∼ and breakfast (b & b)** cama y desayuno. **∼bug** /'bedbʌg/ n chinche f. **∼clothes** /'bedkləʊðz/ npl, **∼ding** n ropa f de cama

bedevil /bɪ'devl/ vt (pt bedevilled) (torment) atormentar

bedlam /'bedləm/ n confusión f, manicomio m

bed: ∼pan /'bedpæn/ n orinal m de cama. **∼post** /'bedpəʊst/ n columna f de la cama

bedraggled /bɪ'drægld/ a sucio

bed: ∼ridden /'bedrɪdn/ a encamado. **∼room** /'bedrʊm/ n dormitorio m, habitación f. **∼side** /'bedsaɪd/ n cabecera f. **∼sitting-room** /bed'sɪtɪŋruːm/ n salón m con cama, estudio m. **∼spread** /'bedspred/ n colcha f. **∼time** /'bedtaɪm/ n hora f de acostarse

bee /biː/ n abeja f. **make a ∼-line for** ir en línea recta hacia

beech /biːtʃ/ n haya f

beef /biːf/ n carne f de vaca, carne f de res (LAm). ● vi (sl) quejarse. **∼burger** /'biːfbɜːgə(r)/ n hamburguesa f

beefeater /'biːfiːtə(r)/ n alabardero m de la torre de Londres

beefsteak /biːf'steɪk/ n filete m, bistec m, bife m (Arg)

beefy /'biːfɪ/ a (-ier, -iest) musculoso

beehive /'biːhaɪv/ n colmena f

been /biːn/ see be

beer /bɪə(r)/ n cerveza f

beet /biːt/ n remolacha f

beetle /'biːtl/ n escarabajo m

beetroot /'biːtruːt/ n invar remolacha f

befall /bɪ'fɔːl/ vt (pt befell, pp befallen) acontecer a. ● vi acontecer

befit /bɪ'fɪt/ vt (pt befitted) convenir a

before /bɪ'fɔː(r)/ prep (time) antes de; (place) delante de. **∼ leaving** antes de marcharse. ● adv (place) delante; (time) antes. **a week ∼** una semana antes. **the week ∼** la semana anterior. ● conj (time) antes de que. **∼ he leaves** antes de que se vaya. **~hand** /bɪˈfɔːhænd/ *adv* de antemano

befriend /bɪˈfrend/ *vt* ofrecer amistad a

beg /beg/ *vt/i* (*pt* **begged**) mendigar; (*entreat*) suplicar; (*ask*) pedir. **~ s.o.'s pardon** pedir perdón a uno. **I ~ your pardon!** ¡perdone Vd! **I ~ your pardon?** ¿cómo? **it's going ~ging** no lo quiere nadie

began /bɪˈgæn/ *see* **begin**

beget /bɪˈget/ *vt* (*pt* **begot**, *pp* **begotten**, *pres p* **begetting**) engendrar

beggar /ˈbegə(r)/ *n* mendigo *m*; (*sl*) individuo *m*, tío *m* (*fam*)

begin /bɪˈgɪn/ *vt/i* (*pt* **began**, *pp* **begun**, *pres p* **beginning**) comenzar, empezar. **~ner** *n* principiante *m* & *f*. **~ning** *n* principio *m*

begot, **begotten** /bɪˈgɒt, bɪˈgɒtn/ *see* **beget**

begrudge /bɪˈgrʌdʒ/ *vt* envidiar; (*give*) dar de mala gana

beguile /bɪˈgaɪl/ *vt* engañar, seducir; (*entertain*) entretener

begun /bɪˈgʌn/ *see* **begin**

behalf /bɪˈhɑːf/ *n*. **on ~ of** de parte de, en nombre de

behav|e /bɪˈheɪv/ *vi* comportarse, portarse. **~ (o.s.)** portarse bien. **~iour** /bɪˈheɪvjə(r)/ *n* comportamiento *m*

behead /bɪˈhed/ *vt* decapitar

beheld /bɪˈheld/ *see* **behold**

behind /bɪˈhaɪnd/ *prep* detrás de. **•** *adv* detrás; (*late*) atrasado. **•** *n* (*fam*) trasero *m*

behold /bɪˈhəʊld/ *vt* (*pt* **beheld**) (*old use*) mirar, contemplar

beholden /bɪˈhəʊldən/ *a* agradecido

being /ˈbiːɪŋ/ *n* ser *m*. **come into ~** nacer

belated /bɪˈleɪtɪd/ *a* tardío

belch /beltʃ/ *vi* eructar. **•** *vt*. **~ out** arrojar ‹*smoke*›

belfry /ˈbelfrɪ/ *n* campanario *m*

Belgi|an /ˈbeldʒən/ *a* & *n* belga (*m* & *f*). **~um** /ˈbeldʒəm/ *n* Bélgica *f*

belie /bɪˈlaɪ/ *vt* desmentir

belie|f /bɪˈliːf/ *n* (*trust*) fe *f*; (*opinion*) creencia *f*. **~ve** /bɪˈliːv/ *vt/i* creer. **make ~ve** fingir. **~ver** /-ə(r)/ *n* creyente *m* & *f*; (*supporter*) partidario *m*

belittle /bɪˈlɪtl/ *vt* empequeñecer; (*fig*) despreciar

bell /bel/ *n* campana *f*; (*on door*) timbre *m*

belligerent /bɪˈlɪdʒərənt/ *a* & *n* beligerante (*m* & *f*)

bellow /ˈbeləʊ/ *vt* gritar. **•** *vi* bramar

bellows /ˈbeləʊz/ *npl* fuelle *m*

belly /ˈbelɪ/ *n* vientre *m*. **~ful** /ˈbelɪfʊl/ *n* panzada *f*. **have a ~ful of** (*sl*) estar harto de

belong /bɪˈlɒŋ/ *vi* pertenecer; (*club*) ser socio (**to** de)

belongings /bɪˈlɒŋɪŋz/ *npl* pertenencias *fpl*. **personal ~** efectos *mpl* personales

beloved /bɪˈlʌvɪd/ *a* & *n* querido (*m*)

below /bɪˈləʊ/ *prep* debajo de; (*fig*) inferior a. **•** *adv* abajo

belt /belt/ *n* cinturón *m*; (*area*) zona *f*. **•** *vt* (*fig*) rodear; (*sl*) pegar

bemused /bɪˈmjuːzd/ *a* perplejo

bench /bentʃ/ *n* banco *m*. **the B~** (*jurid*) la magistratura *f*

bend /bend/ *vt* (*pt* & *pp* **bent**) doblar; torcer ‹*arm, leg*›. **•** *vi* doblarse; ‹*road*› torcerse. **•** *n* curva *f*. **~ down/over** inclinarse

beneath /bɪˈniːθ/ *prep* debajo de; (*fig*) inferior a. **•** *adv* abajo

benediction /benɪˈdɪkʃn/ *n* bendición *f*

benefactor /ˈbenɪfæktə(r)/ *n* bienhechor *m*, benefactor *m*

beneficial /benɪˈfɪʃl/ *a* provechoso

beneficiary /benɪˈfɪʃərɪ/ *a* & *n* beneficiario (*m*)

benefit /ˈbenɪfɪt/ *n* provecho *m*, ventaja *f*; (*allowance*) subsidio *m*; (*financial gain*) beneficio *m*. **•** *vt* (*pt* **benefited**, *pres p* **benefiting**) aprovechar. **•** *vi* aprovecharse

benevolen|ce /bɪˈnevələns/ *n* benevolencia *f*. **~t** *a* benévolo

benign /bɪˈnaɪn/ *a* benigno

bent /bent/ *see* **bend**. **•** *n* inclinación *f*. **•** *a* encorvado; (*sl*) corrompido

bequeath /bɪˈkwiːð/ *vt* legar

bequest /bɪˈkwest/ *n* legado *m*

bereave|d /bɪˈriːvd/ *n*. **the ~d** la familia *f* del difunto. **~ment** *n* pérdida *f*; (*mourning*) luto *m*

bereft /bɪˈreft/ *a*. **~ of** privado de

beret /ˈbereɪ/ *n* boina *f*

Bermuda /bəˈmjuːdə/ *n* Islas *fpl* Bermudas

berry /ˈberɪ/ *n* baya *f*

berserk /bəˈsɜːk/ *a*. **go ~** volverse loco, perder los estribos

berth /bɜːθ/ *n* litera *f*; (*anchorage*) amarradero *m*. **give a wide ~ to** evitar. **•** *vi* atracar

beseech /bɪ'siːtʃ/ vt (pt **besought**) suplicar

beset /bɪ'set/ vt (pt **beset**, pres p **besetting**) acosar

beside /bɪ'saɪd/ prep al lado de. **be ~ o.s.** estar fuera de sí

besides /bɪ'saɪdz/ prep además de; (except) excepto. ● adv además

besiege /bɪ'siːdʒ/ vt asediar; (fig) acosar

besought /bɪ'sɔːt/ see **beseech**

bespoke /bɪ'spəʊk/ a ⟨tailor⟩ que confecciona a la medida

best /best/ a (el) mejor. **the ~ thing is to...** lo mejor es... ● adv (lo) mejor. **like ~** preferir. ● n lo mejor. **at ~** a lo más. **do one's ~** hacer todo lo posible. **make the ~ of** contentarse con. **~ man** n padrino m (de boda)

bestow /bɪ'stəʊ/ vt conceder

bestseller /best'selə(r)/ n éxito m de librería, bestseller m

bet /bet/ n apuesta f. ● vt/i (pt **bet** or **betted**) apostar

betray /bɪ'treɪ/ vt traicionar. **~al** n traición f

betroth|al /bɪ'trəʊðəl/ n esponsales mpl. **~ed** a prometido

better /'betə(r)/ a & adv mejor. **~ off** en mejores condiciones; (richer) más rico. **get ~** mejorar. **all the ~** tanto mejor. **I'd ~** más vale que. **the ~ part of** la mayor parte de. **the sooner the ~** cuanto antes mejor. ● vt mejorar; (beat) sobrepasar. ● n superior m. **get the ~ of** vencer a. **one's ~s** sus superiores mpl

between /bɪ'twiːn/ prep entre. ● adv en medio

beverage /'bevərɪdʒ/ n bebida f

bevy /bevɪ/ n grupo m

beware /bɪ'weə(r)/ vi tener cuidado. ● int ¡cuidado!

bewilder /bɪ'wɪldə(r)/ vt desconcertar. **~ment** n aturdimiento m

bewitch /bɪ'wɪtʃ/ vt hechizar

beyond /bɪ'jɒnd/ prep más allá de; (fig) fuera de. **~ doubt** sin lugar a duda. **~ reason** irrazonable. ● adv más allá

bias /'baɪəs/ n predisposición f; (prejudice) prejuicio m; (sewing) sesgo m. ● vt (pt **biased**) influir en. **~ed** a parcial

bib /bɪb/ n babero m

Bible /'baɪbl/ n Biblia f

biblical /'bɪblɪkl/ a bíblico

bibliography /bɪblɪ'ɒɡrəfɪ/ n bibliografía f

biceps /'baɪseps/ n bíceps m

bicker /'bɪkə(r)/ vi altercar

bicycle /'baɪsɪkl/ n bicicleta f. ● vi ir en bicicleta

bid /bɪd/ n (offer) oferta f; (attempt) tentativa f. ● vi hacer una oferta. ● vt (pt **bid**, pres p **bidding**) ofrecer; (pt **bid**, pp **bidden**, pres p **bidding**) mandar; dar ⟨welcome, good-day etc⟩. **~der** n postor m. **~ding** n (at auction) ofertas fpl; (order) mandato m

bide /baɪd/ vt. **~ one's time** esperar el momento oportuno

biennial /baɪ'enɪəl/ a bienal. ● n (event) bienal f; (bot) planta f bienal

bifocals /baɪ'fəʊklz/ npl gafas fpl bifocales, anteojos mpl bifocales (LAm)

big /bɪɡ/ a (**bigger**, **biggest**) grande; (generous, sl) generoso. ● adv. **talk ~** fanfarronear

bigam|ist /'bɪɡəmɪst/ n bígamo m. **~ous** a bígamo. **~y** n bigamia f

big-headed /bɪɡ'hedɪd/ a engreído

bigot /'bɪɡət/ n fanático m. **~ed** a fanático. **~ry** n fanatismo m

bigwig /'bɪɡwɪɡ/ n (fam) pez m gordo

bike /baɪk/ n (fam) bicicleta f, bici f (fam)

bikini /bɪ'kiːnɪ/ n (pl **-is**) biquini m, bikini m

bilberry /'bɪlbərɪ/ n arándano m

bile /baɪl/ n bilis f

bilingual /baɪ'lɪŋɡwəl/ a bilingüe

bilious /'bɪlɪəs/ a (med) bilioso

bill¹ /bɪl/ n cuenta f; (invoice) factura f; (notice) cartel m; (Amer, banknote) billete m; (pol) proyecto m de ley. ● vt pasar la factura; (in theatre) anunciar

bill² /bɪl/ n (of bird) pico m

billet /'bɪlɪt/ n (mil) alojamiento m. ● vt alojar

billiards /'bɪlɪədz/ n billar m

billion /'bɪlɪən/ n billón m; (Amer) mil millones mpl

billy-goat /'bɪlɪɡəʊt/ n macho m cabrío

bin /bɪn/ n recipiente m; (for rubbish) cubo m; (for waste paper) papelera f

bind /baɪnd/ vt (pt **bound**) atar; encuadernar ⟨book⟩; (jurid) obligar. ● n (sl) lata f. **~ing**

/'baɪndɪŋ/ n (of books) encuadernación f; (braid) ribete m

binge /bɪndʒ/ n (sl) (of food) comilona f; (of drink) borrachera f. **go on a ~** ir de juerga

bingo /'bɪŋgəʊ/ n bingo m

binoculars /bɪ'nɒkjʊləz/ npl prismáticos mpl

biochemistry /baɪəʊ'kemɪstrɪ/ n bioquímica f

biograph|er /baɪ'ɒgrəfə(r)/ n biógrafo m. **~y** n biografía f

biolog|ical /baɪə'lɒdʒɪkl/ a biológíco. **~ist** n biólogo m. **~** /baɪ'ɒlədʒɪ/ n biología f

biped /'baɪped/ n bípedo m

birch /bɜːtʃ/ n (tree) abedul m; (whip) férula f

bird /bɜːd/ n ave f; (small) pájaro m; (fam) tipo m; (girl, sl) chica f

Biro /'baɪərəʊ/ n (pl -os) (P) bolígrafo m, biromen m (Arg)

birth /bɜːθ/ n nacimiento m. **~certificate** n partida f de nacimiento. **~control** n control m de la natalidad. **~day** /'bɜːθdeɪ/ n cumpleaños m invar. **~mark** /'bɜːθmɑːk/ n marca f de nacimiento. **~rate** n natalidad f. **~right** /'bɜːθraɪt/ n derechos mpl de nacimiento

biscuit /'bɪskɪt/ n galleta f

bisect /baɪ'sekt/ vt bisecar

bishop /'bɪʃəp/ n obispo m

bit[1] /bɪt/ n trozo m; (quantity) poco m

bit[2] /bɪt/ see **bite**

bit[3] /bɪt/ n (of horse) bocado m; (mec) broca f

bitch /bɪtʃ/ n perra f; (woman, fam) mujer f maligna, bruja f (fam). ● vi (fam) quejarse (**about** de). **~y** a malintencionado

bit|e /baɪt/ vt/i (pt **bit**, pp **bitten**) morder. **~e one's nails** morderse las uñas. ● n mordisco m; (mouthful) bocado m; (of insect etc) picadura f. **~ing** /'baɪtɪŋ/ a mordaz

bitter /'bɪtə(r)/ a amargo; (of weather) glacial. **to the ~ end** hasta el final. ● n cerveza f amarga. **~ly** adv amargamente. **it's ~ly cold** hace un frío glacial. **~ness** n amargor m; (resentment) amargura f

bizarre /bɪ'zɑː(r)/ a extraño

blab /blæb/ vi (pt **blabbed**) chismear

black /blæk/ a (-er, -est) negro. **~ and blue** amoratado. ● n negro m. ● vt ennegrecer; limpiar ‹shoes›. **~**

blackball /'blækbɔːl/ vt votar en contra de

blackberry /'blækbərɪ/ n zarzamora f

blackbird /'blækbɜːd/ n mirlo m

blackboard /'blækbɔːd/ n pizarra f

blackcurrant /blæk'kʌrənt/ n casis f

blacken /'blækən/ vt ennegrecer. ● vi ennegrecerse

blackguard /'blægɑːd/ n canalla m

blackleg /'blækleg/ n esquirol m

blacklist /'blæklɪst/ vt poner en la lista negra

blackmail /'blækmeɪl/ n chantaje m. ● vt chantajear. **~er** n chantajista m & f

black-out /'blækaʊt/ n apagón m; (med) desmayo m; (of news) censura f

blacksmith /'blæksmɪθ/ n herrero m

bladder /'blædə(r)/ n vejiga f

blade /bleɪd/ n hoja f; (razor-blade) cuchilla f. **~ of grass** brizna f de hierba

blame /bleɪm/ vt echar la culpa a. **be to ~** tener la culpa. ● n culpa f. **~less** a inocente

bland /blænd/ a (-er, -est) suave

blandishments /'blændɪʃmənts/ npl halagos mpl

blank /blæŋk/ a en blanco; ‹cartridge› sin bala; (fig) vacío. **~ verse** n verso m suelto. ● n blanco m

blanket /'blæŋkɪt/ n manta f; (fig) capa f. ● vt (pt **blanketed**) (fig) cubrir (**in, with** de)

blare /bleə(r)/ vi sonar muy fuerte. ● n estrépito m

blarney /'blɑːnɪ/ n coba f. ● vt dar coba

blasé /'blɑːzeɪ/ a hastiado

blasphem|e /blæs'fiːm/ vt/i blasfemar. **~er** n blasfemador m. **~ous** /'blæsfəməs/ a blasfemo. **~y** /'blæsfəmɪ/ n blasfemia f

blast /blɑːst/ n explosión f; (gust) ráfaga f; (sound) toque m. ● vt volar. **~ed** a maldito. **~furnace** n alto horno m. **~off** n (of missile) despegue m

blatant /'bleɪtnt/ a patente; (shameless) descarado

blaze /bleɪz/ n llamarada f; (of light) resplandor m; (fig) arranque m. ● vi arder en llamas; (fig) brillar. **~ a trail** abrir un camino

blazer /'bleɪzə(r)/ n chaqueta f

bleach /bliːtʃ/ n lejía f; (*for hair*) decolorante m. ● vt blanquear; decolorar ⟨*hair*⟩. ● vi blanquearse

bleak /bliːk/ a (**-er, -est**) desolado; (*fig*) sombrío

bleary /ˈblɪərɪ/ a ⟨*eyes*⟩ nublado; (*indistinct*) indistinto

bleat /bliːt/ n balido m. ● vi balar

bleed /bliːd/ vt/i (*pt* **bled**) sangrar

bleep /bliːp/ n pitido m. ~**er** n busca m, buscapersonas m

blemish /ˈblemɪʃ/ n tacha f

blend /blend/ n mezcla f. ● vt mezclar. ● vi combinarse

bless /bles/ vt bendecir. ~ **you!** (*on sneezing*) ¡Jesús! ~**ed** a bendito. **be ~ed with** estar dotado de. ~**ing** n bendición f; (*advantage*) ventaja f

blew /bluː/ *see* **blow**[1]

blight /blaɪt/ n añublo m, tizón m; (*fig*) plaga f. ● vt añublar, atizonar; (*fig*) destrozar

blighter /ˈblaɪtə(r)/ n (*sl*) tío m (*fam*), sinvergüenza m

blind /blaɪnd/ a ciego. ~ **alley** n callejón m sin salida. ● n persiana f; (*fig*) pretexto m. ● vt cegar. ~**fold** /ˈblaɪndfəʊld/ a & adv con los ojos vendados. ● n venda f. ● vt vendar los ojos. ~**ly** adv a ciegas. ~**ness** n ceguera f

blink /blɪŋk/ vi parpadear; (*of light*) centellear

blinkers /ˈblɪŋkəz/ npl anteojeras fpl; (*auto*) intermitente m

bliss /blɪs/ n felicidad f. ~**ful** a feliz. ~**fully** adv felizmente; (*completely*) completamente

blister /ˈblɪstə(r)/ n ampolla f. ● vi formarse ampollas

blithe /blaɪð/ a alegre

blitz /blɪts/ n bombardeo m aéreo. ● vt bombardear

blizzard /ˈblɪzəd/ n ventisca f

bloated /ˈbləʊtɪd/ a hinchado (**with** de)

bloater /ˈbləʊtə(r)/ n arenque m ahumado

blob /blɒb/ n gota f; (*stain*) mancha f

bloc /blɒk/ n (*pol*) bloque m

block /blɒk/ n bloque m; (*of wood*) zoquete m; (*of buildings*) manzana f, cuadra f (*LAm*); (*in pipe*) obstrucción f. **in ~ letters** en letra de imprenta. **traffic ~** embotellamiento m. ● vt obstruir. ~**ade** /blɒˈkeɪd/ n bloqueo m. ● vt bloquear. ~**age** n obstrucción f

blockhead /ˈblɒkhed/ n (*fam*) zopenco m

bloke /bləʊk/ n (*fam*) tío m (*fam*), tipo m

blond /blɒnd/ a & n rubio (m). ~**e** a & n rubia (f)

blood /blʌd/ n sangre f. ~ **count** n recuento m sanguíneo. ~**curdling** a horripilante

bloodhound /ˈblʌdhaʊnd/ n sabueso m

blood: ~ **pressure** n tensión f arterial. **high ~ pressure** hipertensión f. ~**shed** /ˈblʌdʃed/ n efusión f de sangre, derramamiento m de sangre, matanza f. ~**shot** /ˈblʌdʃɒt/ a sanguinolento; ⟨*eye*⟩ inyectado de sangre. ~**stream** /ˈblʌdstriːm/ n sangre f

bloodthirsty /ˈblʌdθɜːstɪ/ a sanguinario

bloody /ˈblʌdɪ/ a (**-ier, -iest**) sangriento; (*stained*) ensangrentado; (*sl*) maldito. ~**y-minded** a (*fam*) terco

bloom /bluːm/ n flor f. ● vi florecer

bloomer /ˈbluːmə(r)/ n (*sl*) metedura f de pata

blooming a floreciente; (*fam*) maldito

blossom /ˈblɒsəm/ n flor f. ● vi florecer. ~ **out (into)** (*fig*) llegar a ser

blot /blɒt/ n borrón m. ● vt (*pt* **blotted**) manchar; (*dry*) secar. ~ **out** oscurecer

blotch /blɒtʃ/ n mancha f. ~**y** a lleno de manchas

blotter /ˈblɒtə(r)/ n, **blotting-paper** /ˈblɒtɪŋpeɪpə(r)/ n papel m secante

blouse /blaʊz/ n blusa f

blow[1] /bləʊ/ vt (*pt* **blew**, *pp* **blown**) soplar; fundir ⟨*fuse*⟩; tocar ⟨*trumpet*⟩. ● vi soplar; ⟨*fuse*⟩ fundirse; (*sound*) sonar. ● n (*puff*) soplo m. ~ **down** vt derribar. ~ **out** apagar ⟨*candle*⟩. ~ **over** pasar. ~ **up** vt inflar; (*explode*) volar; (*photo*) ampliar. ● vi (*explode*) estallar; (*burst*) reventar

blow[2] /bləʊ/ n (*incl fig*) golpe m

blow-dry /ˈbləʊdraɪ/ vt secar con secador

blowlamp /ˈbləʊlæmp/ n soplete m

blow: ~**out** n (*of tyre*) reventón m. ~**up** n (*photo*) ampliación f

blowzy /ˈblaʊzɪ/ a desaliñado

blubber /ˈblʌbə(r)/ n grasa f de ballena

bludgeon /'blʌdʒən/ n cachiporra f.
● vt aporrear

blue /blu:/ a (-er, -est) azul; ⟨joke⟩
verde. ● n azul m. out of the ~
totalmente inesperado. ~s npl.
have the ~s tener tristeza

bluebell /'blu:bel/ n campanilla f

bluebottle /'blu:bɒtl/ n moscarda f

blueprint /'blu:prɪnt/ n ferro-
prusiato m; (fig, plan) anteproyecto
m

bluff /blʌf/ a ⟨person⟩ brusco. ● n
(poker) farol m. ● vt engañar. ● vi
(poker) tirarse un farol

blunder /'blʌndə(r)/ vi cometer un
error. ● n metedura f de pata

blunt /blʌnt/ a desafilado; ⟨person⟩
directo, abrupto. ● vt desafilar. ~ly
adv francamente. ~ness n embot-
adura f; (fig) franqueza f, brusquedad f

blur /blɜ:(r)/ n impresión f indis-
tinta. ● vt (pt blurred) hacer
borroso

blurb /blɜ:b/ n resumen m
publicitario

blurt /blɜ:t/ vt. ~ out dejar escapar

blush /blʌʃ/ vi ruborizarse. ● n
sonrojo m

bluster /'blʌstə(r)/ vi ⟨weather⟩ bramar; ⟨person⟩ fanfarronear. ~y a
tempestuoso

boar /bɔ:(r)/ n verraco m

board /bɔ:d/ n tabla f, tablero m; (for
notices) tablón m; (food) pensión f;
(admin) junta f. ~ and lodging casa
y comida. above ~ correcto. full ~
pensión f completa. go by the ~ ser
abandonado. ● vt alojar; (naut)
embarcar en. ● vi alojarse (with en
casa de); (at school) ser interno. ~er
n huésped m; (schol) interno m.
~ing-house n casa f de huéspedes,
pensión f. ~ing-school n internado
m

boast /bəʊst/ vt enorgullecerse de.
● vi jactarse. ● n jactancia f. ~er n
jactancioso m. ~ful a jactancioso

boat /bəʊt/ n barco m; (large) navío
m; (small) barca f

boater /'bəʊtə(r)/ n (hat) canotié m

boatswain /'bəʊsn/ n con-
tramaestre m

bob[1] /bɒb/ vi (pt bobbed) menearse,
subir y bajar. ~ up presentarse
súbitamente

bob[2] /bɒb/ n invar (sl) chelín m

bobbin /'bɒbɪn/ n carrete m; (in sewing machine) canilla f

bobby /'bɒbɪ/ n (fam) policía m, poli
m (fam)

bobsleigh /'bɒbsleɪ/ n bob(sleigh) m

bode /bəʊd/ vi presagiar. ~ well/ill
ser de buen/mal agüero

bodice /'bɒdɪs/ n corpiño m

bodily /'bɒdɪlɪ/ a físico, corporal.
● adv físicamente; (in person) en
persona

body /'bɒdɪ/ n cuerpo m. ~guard
/'bɒdɪgɑ:d/ n guardaespaldas m
invar. ~work n carrocería f

boffin /'bɒfɪn/ n (sl) científico m

bog /bɒg/ n ciénaga f. ● vt (pt
bogged). get ~ged down
empantanarse

bogey /'bəʊgɪ/ n duende m; (nuisance) pesadilla f

boggle /'bɒgl/ vi sobresaltarse. the
mind ~s ¡no es posible!

bogus /'bəʊgəs/ a falso

bogy /'bəʊgɪ/ n duende m; (nuisance) pesadilla f

boil[1] /bɔɪl/ vt/i hervir. be ~ing hot
estar ardiendo; ⟨weather⟩ hacer
mucho calor. ~ away evaporarse.
~ down to reducirse a. ~ over
rebosar

boil[2] /bɔɪl/ n furúnculo m

boiled /bɔɪld/ a hervido; ⟨egg⟩ pasado por agua

boiler /'bɔɪlə(r)/ n caldera f. ~ suit n
mono m

boisterous /'bɔɪstərəs/ a ruidoso,
bullicioso

bold /bəʊld/ a (-er, -est) audaz.
~ness n audacia f

Bolivia /bə'lɪvɪə/ n Bolivia f. ~n a &
n boliviano (m)

bollard /'bɒləd/ n (naut) noray m;
(Brit, auto) poste m

bolster /'bəʊlstə(r)/ n cabezal m.
● vt. ~ up sostener

bolt /bəʊlt/ n cerrojo m; (for nut)
perno m; (lightning) rayo m; (leap)
fuga f. ● vt echar el cerrojo a ⟨door⟩;
engullir ⟨food⟩. ● vi fugarse. ● adv.
~ upright rígido

bomb /bɒm/ n bomba f. ● vt bombardear. ~ard /bɒm'bɑ:d/ vt
bombardear

bombastic /bɒm'bæstɪk/ a ampuloso

bomb: ~er /'bɒmə(r)/ n bom-
bardero m. ~ing n bombardeo m.
~shell n bomba f

bonanza /bə'nænzə/ n bonanza f

bond /bɒnd/ n (agreement) obligación f; (link) lazo m; (com) bono m

bondage /'bɒndɪdʒ/ n esclavitud f
bone /bəʊn/ n hueso m; (of fish)
espina f. ● vt deshuesar. ~**dry** a
completamente seco. ~ **idle** a
holgazán
bonfire /'bɒnfaɪə(r)/ n hoguera f
bonnet /'bɒnɪt/ n gorra f; (auto)
capó m, tapa f del motor (Mex)
bonny /'bɒnɪ/ a (-ier, -iest) bonito
bonus /'bəʊnəs/ n prima f; (fig) plus
m
bony /'bəʊnɪ/ a (-ier, -iest) huesudo;
⟨fish⟩ lleno de espinas
boo /buː/ int ¡bu! ● vt/i abuchear
boob /buːb/ n (mistake, sl) metedura f de pata. ● vi (sl) meter la pata
booby /'buːbɪ/ n bobo m. ~ **trap**
trampa f, (mil) trampa f explosiva
book /bʊk/ n libro m; (of cheques etc)
talonario m; (notebook) libreta f;
(exercise book) cuaderno m; (pl,
com) cuentas fpl. ● vt (enter) registrar; (reserve) reservar. ● vi reservar. ~**able** a que se puede reservar.
~**case** /'bʊkkeɪs/ n estantería f,
librería f. ~**ing-office** (in theatre)
taquilla f; (rail) despacho m de
billetes. ~**let** /'bʊklɪt/ n folleto m
bookkeeping /'bʊkiːpɪŋ/ n con-
tabilidad f
bookmaker /'bʊkmeɪkə(r)/ n corredor m de apuestas
book: ~**mark** /'bʊkmɑː(r)k/ n señal f.
~**seller** /'bʊkselə(r)/ n librero m.
~**shop** /'bʊkʃɒp/ n librería f. ~**stall**
/'bʊkstɔːl/ n quiosco m de libros.
~**worm** /'bʊkwɜːm/ n (fig) ratón m
de biblioteca
boom /buːm/ vi retumbar; (fig)
prosperar. ● n estampido m; (com)
auge m
boon /buːn/ n beneficio m
boor /bʊə(r)/ n patán m. ~**ish** a
grosero
boost /buːst/ vt estimular; reforzar
⟨morale⟩; aumentar ⟨price⟩; (publicize) hacer publicidad por. ● n
empuje m. ~**er** n (med) reva-
cunación f
boot /buːt/ n bota f; (auto) maletero
m, baúl m (LAm). **get the** ~ (sl) ser
despedido
booth /buːð/ n cabina f; (at fair) puesto m
booty /'buːtɪ/ n botín m
booze /buːz/ vi (fam) beber mucho.
● n (fam) alcohol m; (spree) borrachera f

border /'bɔːdə(r)/ n borde m; (frontier) frontera f; (in garden) arriate
m. ● vi. ~ **on** lindar con
borderline /'bɔːdəlaɪn/ n línea f
divisoria. ~ **case** n caso m dudoso
bore[1] /bɔː(r)/ vt (tec) taladrar. ● vi
taladrar
bore[2] /bɔː(r)/ vt (annoy) aburrir. ● n
(person) pelmazo m; (thing) lata f
bore[3] /bɔː(r)/ see **bear**[1]
boredom /'bɔːdəm/ n aburrimiento
m
boring /'bɔːrɪŋ/ a aburrido, pesado
born /bɔːn/ a nato. **be** ~ nacer
borne /bɔːn/ see **bear**[1]
borough /'bʌrə/ n municipio m
borrow /'bɒrəʊ/ vt pedir prestado
Borstal /'bɔːstl/ n reformatorio m
bosh /bɒʃ/ int & n (sl) tonterías (fpl)
bosom /'bʊzəm/ n seno m. ~ **friend**
n amigo m íntimo
boss /bɒs/ n (fam) jefe m. ● vt. ~
(**about**) dar órdenes a. ~**y**
/'bɒsɪ/ a mandón
botan|**ical** /bə'tænɪkl/ a botánico.
~**ist** /'bɒtənɪst/ n botánico m. ~**y**
/'bɒtənɪ/ n botánica f
botch /bɒtʃ/ vt chapucear. ● n
chapuza f
both /bəʊθ/ a & pron ambos (mpl),
los dos (mpl). ● adv al mismo
tiempo, a la vez
bother /'bɒðə(r)/ vt molestar;
(worry) preocupar. ~ **it!** int ¡caramba! ● vi molestarse. ~ **about**
preocuparse de. ~ **doing** tenerse la
molestia de hacer. ● n molestia f
bottle /'bɒtl/ n botella f; (for baby)
biberón m. ● vt embotellar. ~ **up**
(fig) reprimir. ~**neck** /'bɒtlnek/ n
(traffic jam) embotellamiento m.
~**opener** n destapador m, abrebotellas m invar; (corkscrew) sacacorchos m invar
bottom /'bɒtəm/ n fondo m; (of hill)
pie m; (buttocks) trasero m. ● a
último, inferior. ~**less** a sin fondo
bough /baʊ/ n rama f
bought /bɔːt/ see **buy**
boulder /'bəʊldə(r)/ n canto m
boulevard /'buːləvɑːd/ n bulevar m
bounc|**e** /baʊns/ vt hacer rebotar.
● vi rebotar; ⟨person⟩ saltar;
⟨cheque, sl⟩ ser rechazado. ● n
rebote m. ~**ing** /'baʊnsɪŋ/ a robusto
bound[1] /baʊnd/ vi saltar. ● n salto
m
bound[2] /baʊnd/ n. **out of** ~**s** zona f
prohibida

bound³ /baʊnd/ *a*. be ~ for dirigirse a

bound⁴ /baʊnd/ *see* **bind**. ~ to obligado a; (*certain*) seguro de

boundary /'baʊndərɪ/ *n* límite *m*

boundless /'baʊndləs/ *a* ilimitado

bountiful /'baʊntɪfl/ *a* abundante

bouquet /bʊ'keɪ/ *n* ramo *m*; (*perfume*) aroma *m*; (*of wine*) buqué *m*, nariz *f*

bout /baʊt/ *n* período *m*; (*med*) ataque *m*; (*sport*) encuentro *m*

bow¹ /bəʊ/ *n* (*weapon, mus*) arco *m*; (*knot*) lazo *m*

bow² /baʊ/ *n* reverencia *f*. ● *vi* inclinarse. ● *vt* inclinar

bow³ /baʊ/ *n* (*naut*) proa *f*

bowels /'baʊəlz/ *npl* intestinos *mpl*; (*fig*) entrañas *fpl*

bowl¹ /bəʊl/ *n* cuenco *m*; (*for washing*) palangana *f*; (*of pipe*) cazoleta *f*

bowl² /bəʊl/ *n* (*ball*) bola *f*. ● *vt* (*cricket*) arrojar. ● *vi* (*cricket*) arrojar la pelota. ~ **over** derribar

bow-legged /bəʊ'legɪd/ *a* estevado

bowler¹ /'bəʊlə(r)/ *n* (*cricket*) lanzador *m*

bowler² /'bəʊlə(r)/ *n*. ~ (**hat**) hongo *m*, bombín *m*

bowling /'bəʊlɪŋ/ *n* bolos *mpl*

bow-tie /bəʊ'taɪ/ *n* corbata *f* de lazo, pajarita *f*

box¹ /bɒks/ *n* caja *f*; (*for jewels etc*) estuche *m*; (*in theatre*) palco *m*

box² /bɒks/ *vt* boxear contra. ~ **s.o.'s ears** dar una manotada a uno. ● *vi* boxear. ~**er** *n* boxeador *m*. ~**ing** *n* boxeo *m*

box: **B~ing Day** *n* el 26 de diciembre. ~**-office** *n* taquilla *f*. ~**-room** *n* trastero *m*

boy /bɔɪ/ *n* chico *m*, muchacho *m*; (*young*) niño *m*

boycott /'bɔɪkɒt/ *vt* boicotear. ● *n* boicoteo *m*

boy: ~**friend** *n* novio *m*. ~**hood** *n* niñez *f*. ~**ish** *a* de muchacho; (*childish*) infantil

bra /brɑ:/ *n* sostén *m*, sujetador *m*

brace /breɪs/ *n* abrazadera *f*; (*dental*) aparato *m*. ● *vt* asegurar. ~ **o.s.** prepararse. ~**s** *npl* tirantes *mpl*

bracelet /'breɪslɪt/ *n* pulsera *f*

bracing /'breɪsɪŋ/ *a* vigorizante

bracken /'brækən/ *n* helecho *m*

bracket /'brækɪt/ *n* soporte *m*; (*group*) categoría *f*; (*typ*) paréntesis *m invar*. **square** ~**s** corchetes *mpl*.

● *vt* poner entre paréntesis; (*join together*) agrupar

brag /bræg/ *vi* (*pt* **bragged**) jactarse (*about* de)

braid /breɪd/ *n* galón *m*; (*of hair*) trenza *f*

brain /breɪn/ *n* cerebro *m*. ● *vt* romper la cabeza

brain-child /'breɪntʃaɪld/ *n* invento *m*

brain: ~ **drain** (*fam*) fuga *f* de cerebros. ~**less** *a* estúpido. ~**s** *npl* (*fig*) inteligencia *f*

brainstorm /'breɪnstɔ:m/ *n* ataque *m* de locura; (*Amer, brainwave*) idea *f* genial

brainwash /'breɪnwɒʃ/ *vt* lavar el cerebro

brainwave /'breɪnweɪv/ *n* idea *f* genial

brainy /'breɪnɪ/ *a* (**-ier, -iest**) inteligente

braise /breɪz/ *vt* cocer a fuego lento

brake /breɪk/ *n* freno *m*. **disc** ~ freno de disco. **hand** ~ freno de mano. ● *vt*/*i* frenar. ~ **fluid** *n* líquido *m* de freno. ~ **lining** *n* forro *m* del freno. ~ **shoe** *n* zapata *f* del freno

bramble /bræmbl/ *n* zarza *f*

bran /bræn/ *n* salvado *m*

branch /brɑ:ntʃ/ *n* rama *f*; (*of road*) bifurcación *f*; (*com*) sucursal *m*; (*fig*) ramo *m*. ● *vi*. ~ **off** bifurcarse. ~ **out** ramificarse

brand /brænd/ *n* marca *f*; (*iron*) hierro *m*. ● *vt* marcar; (*reputation*) tildar de

brandish /'brændɪʃ/ *vt* blandir

brand-new /brænd'nju:/ *a* flamante

brandy /'brændɪ/ *n* coñac *m*

brash /bræʃ/ *a* descarado

brass /brɑ:s/ *n* latón *m*. **get down to** ~ **tacks** (*fig*) ir al grano. **top** ~ (*sl*) peces *mpl* gordos. ~**y** *a* (**-ier, -iest**) descarado

brassière /'bræsjeə(r)/ *n* sostén *m*, sujetador *m*

brat /bræt/ *n* (*pej*) mocoso *m*

bravado /brə'vɑ:dəʊ/ *n* bravata *f*

brave /breɪv/ *a* (**-er, -est**) valiente. ● *n* (*Red Indian*) guerrero *m* indio. ● *vt* afrontar. ~**ry** /-ərɪ/ *n* valentía *f*, valor *m*

brawl /brɔ:l/ *n* alboroto *m*. ● *vi* pelearse

brawn /brɔ:n/ *n* músculo *m*; (*strength*) fuerza *f* muscular. ~**y** *a* musculoso

bray /breɪ/ *n* rebuzno *m.* ● *vi* rebuznar

brazen /'breɪzn/ *a* descarado

brazier /'breɪzɪə(r)/ *n* brasero *m*

Brazil /brə'zɪl/ *n* el Brasil *m.* ~**ian** *a & n* brasileño (*m*)

breach /bri:tʃ/ *n* violación *f*; (*of contract*) incumplimiento *m*; (*gap*) brecha *f.* ● *vt* abrir una brecha en

bread /bred/ *n* pan *m.* **loaf of** ~ pan. ~**crumbs** /'bredkrʌmz/ *npl* migajas *fpl*; (*culin*) pan rallado. ~**line** *n.* **on the** ~**line** en la miseria

breadth /bredθ/ *n* anchura *f*

bread-winner /'bredwɪnə(r)/ *n* sostén *m* de la familia, cabeza *f* de familia

break /breɪk/ *vt* (*pt* **broke**, *pp* **broken**) romper; quebrantar ⟨*law*⟩; batir ⟨*record*⟩; comunicar ⟨*news*⟩; interrumpir ⟨*journey*⟩. ● *vi* romperse; ⟨*news*⟩ divulgarse. ● *n* ruptura *f*; (*interval*) intervalo *m*; (*chance, fam*) oportunidad *f*; (*in weather*) cambio *m.* ~ **away** escapar. ~ **down** *vt* derribar; analizar ⟨*figures*⟩. ● *vi* estropearse; (*auto*) averiarse; (*med*) sufrir un colapso; (*cry*) deshacerse en lágrimas. ~ **into** forzar ⟨*house etc*⟩; (*start doing*) ponerse a. ~ **off** interrumpirse. ~ **out** ⟨*war, disease*⟩ estallar; (*run away*) escaparse. ~ **up** romperse; ⟨*schools*⟩ terminar. ~**able** *a* frágil. ~**age** *n* rotura *f*

breakdown /'breɪkdaʊn/ *n* (*tec*) falla *f*; (*med*) colapso *m*, crisis *f* nerviosa; (*of figures*) análisis *f*

breaker /'breɪkə(r)/ *n* (*wave*) cachón *m*

breakfast /'brekfəst/ *n* desayuno *m*

breakthrough /'breɪkθru:/ *n* adelanto *m*

breakwater /'breɪkwɔ:tə(r)/ *n* rompeolas *m invar*

breast /brest/ *n* pecho *m*; (*of chicken etc*) pechuga *f.* ~**stroke** *n* braza *f* de pecho

breath /breθ/ *n* aliento *m*, respiración *f.* **out of** ~ sin aliento. **under one's** ~ a media voz. ~**alyser** /'breθəlaɪzə(r)/ *n* alcoholímetro *m*

breathe /bri:ð/ *vt/i* respirar. ~**er** /'bri:ðə(r)/ *n* descanso *m*, pausa *f.* ~**ing** *n* respiración *f*

breathtaking /'breθteɪkɪŋ/ *a* impresionante

bred /bred/ *see* **breed**

breeches /'brɪtʃɪz/ *npl* calzones *mpl*

breed /bri:d/ *vt/i* (*pt* **bred**) reproducirse; (*fig*) engendrar. ● *n* raza *f.* ~**er** *n* criador *m.* ~**ing** *n* cría *f*; (*manners*) educación *f*

breeze /bri:z/ *n* brisa *f.* ~**y** *a* de mucho viento; ⟨*person*⟩ despreocupado. **it is** ~**y** hace viento

Breton /'bretən/ *a & n* bretón (*m*)

brew /bru:/ *vt* hacer. ● *vi* fermentar; ⟨*tea*⟩ reposar; (*fig*) prepararse. ● *n* infusión *f.* ~**er** *n* cervecero *m.* ~**ery** *n* fábrica *f* de cerveza, cervecería *f*

bribe /braɪb/ *n* soborno *m.* ● *vt* sobornar. ~**ry** /-ərɪ/ *n* soborno *m*

brick /brɪk/ *n* ladrillo *m.* ● *vt.* ~ **up** tapar con ladrillos. ~**layer** /'brɪkleɪə(r)/ *n* albañil *m*

bridal /'braɪdl/ *a* nupcial

bride /braɪd/ *n* novia *f.* ~**groom** /'braɪdgrʊm/ *n* novio *m.* ~**smaid** /'braɪdzmeɪd/ *n* dama *f* de honor

bridge[1] /brɪdʒ/ *n* puente *m*; (*of nose*) caballete *m.* ● *vt* tender un puente sobre. ~ **a gap** llenar un vacío

bridge[2] /brɪdʒ/ *n* (*cards*) bridge *m*

bridle /'braɪdl/ *n* brida *f.* ● *vt* embridar. ~**path** *n* camino *m* de herradura

brief /bri:f/ *a* (**-er, -est**) breve. ● *n* (*jurid*) escrito *m.* ● *vt* dar instrucciones a. ~**case** /'bri:fkeɪs/ *n* maletín *m.* ~**ly** *adv* brevemente. ~**s** *npl* (*man's*) calzoncillos *mpl*; (*woman's*) bragas *fpl*

brigade /brɪ'geɪd/ *n* brigada *f.* ~**ier** /-ə'dɪə(r)/ *n* general *m* de brigada

bright /braɪt/ *a* (**-er, -est**) brillante, claro; (*clever*) listo; (*cheerful*) alegre. ~**en** /'braɪtn/ *vt* aclarar; hacer más alegre ⟨*house etc*⟩. ● *vi* ⟨*weather*⟩ aclararse; ⟨*face*⟩ animarse. ~**ly** *adv* brillantemente. ~**ness** *n* claridad *f*

brillian|ce /'brɪljəns/ *n* brillantez *f*, brillo *m.* ~**t** *a* brillante

brim /brɪm/ *n* borde *m*; (*of hat*) ala *f.* ● *vi* (*pt* **brimmed**). ~ **over** desbordarse

brine /braɪn/ *n* salmuera *f*

bring /brɪŋ/ *vt* (*pt* **brought**) traer ⟨*thing*⟩; conducir ⟨*person, vehicle*⟩. ~ **about** causar. ~ **back** devolver. ~ **down** derribar; rebajar ⟨*price*⟩. ~ **off** lograr. ~ **on** causar. ~ **out** sacar; lanzar ⟨*product*⟩; publicar ⟨*book*⟩. ~ **round/to** hacer volver en sí ⟨*unconscious person*⟩. ~ **up** (*med*) vomitar; educar ⟨*children*⟩; plantear ⟨*question*⟩

brink /brɪŋk/ n borde m
brisk /brɪsk/ a (-er, -est) enérgico, vivo. **~ness** n energía f
bristl|e /'brɪsl/ n cerda f. ● vi erizarse. **~ing with** erizado de
Brit|ain /'brɪtən/ n Gran Bretaña f. **~ish** /'brɪtɪʃ/ a británico. **the ~ish** los británicos. **~on** /'brɪtən/ n británico m
Brittany /'brɪtənɪ/ n Bretaña f
brittle /'brɪtl/ a frágil, quebradizo
broach /brəʊtʃ/ vt abordar ⟨subject⟩; espitar ⟨cask⟩
broad /brɔːd/ a (-er, -est) ancho. **in ~ daylight** en pleno día. **~ bean** n haba f
broadcast /'brɔːdkɑːst/ n emisión f. ● vt (pt broadcast) emitir. ● vi hablar por la radio. **~ing** a de radiodifusión. ● n radio-difusión f
broad: ~en /'brɔːdn/ vt ensanchar. ● vi ensancharse. **~ly** adv en general. **~-minded** a de miras amplias, tolerante, liberal
brocade /brə'keɪd/ n brocado m
broccoli /'brɒkəlɪ/ n invar brécol m
brochure /'brəʊʃə(r)/ n folleto m
brogue /brəʊg/ n abarca f, ⟨accent⟩ acento m regional
broke /brəʊk/ see **break**. ● a (sl) sin blanca
broken /'brəʊkən/ see **break**. ● a. **~ English** inglés m chapurreado. **~-hearted** a con el corazón destrozado
broker /'brəʊkə(r)/ n corredor m
brolly /'brɒlɪ/ n (fam) paraguas m invar
bronchitis /brɒŋ'kaɪtɪs/ n bronquitis f
bronze /brɒnz/ n bronce m. ● vt broncear. ● vi broncearse
brooch /brəʊtʃ/ n broche m
brood /bruːd/ n cría f, (joc) prole m. ● vi empollar; (fig) meditar. **~y** a contemplativo
brook[1] /brʊk/ n arroyo m
brook[2] /brʊk/ vt soportar
broom /bruːm/ n hiniesta f; (brush) escoba f. **~stick** /'bruːmstɪk/ n palo m de escoba
broth /brɒθ/ n caldo m
brothel /'brɒθl/ n burdel m
brother /'brʌðə(r)/ n hermano m. **~hood** n fraternidad f, (relig) hermandad f. **~-in-law** n cuñado m. **~ly** a fraternal
brought /brɔːt/ see **bring**

brow /braʊ/ n frente f; (of hill) cima f
browbeat /'braʊbiːt/ vt (pt -beat, pp -beaten) intimidar
brown /braʊn/ a (-er, -est) marrón; ⟨skin⟩ moreno; ⟨hair⟩ castaño. ● n marrón m. ● vt poner moreno; (culin) dorar. ● vi ponerse moreno; (culin) dorarse. **be ~ed off** (sl) estar hasta la coronilla
Brownie /'braʊnɪ/ n niña f exploradora
browse /braʊz/ vi (in a shop) curiosear; ⟨animal⟩ pacer
bruise /bruːz/ n magulladura f. ● vt magullar; machucar ⟨fruit⟩. ● vi magullarse; ⟨fruit⟩ machacarse
brunch /brʌntʃ/ n (fam) desayuno m tardío
brunette /bruː'net/ n morena f
brunt /brʌnt/ n. **the ~ of** lo más fuerte de
brush /brʌʃ/ n cepillo m; (large) escoba; (for decorating) brocha f; (artist's) pincel; (skirmish) escaramuza f. ● vt cepillar. **~ against** rozar. **~ aside** rechazar. **~ off** (rebuff) desairar. **~ up (on)** refrescar
brusque /bruːsk/ a brusco. **~ly** adv bruscamente
Brussels /'brʌslz/ n Bruselas f. **~ sprout** col m de Bruselas
brutal /'bruːtl/ a brutal. **~ity** /-'tælətɪ/ n brutalidad f
brute /bruːt/ n bestia f. **~ force** fuerza f bruta
BSc abbr see **bachelor**
bubble /'bʌbl/ n burbuja f. ● vi burbujear. **~ over** desbordarse
bubbly /'bʌblɪ/ a burbujeante. ● n (fam) champaña m, champán m (fam)
buck[1] /bʌk/ a macho. ● n (deer) ciervo m. ● vi (of horse) corcovear. **~ up** (hurry, sl) darse prisa; (cheer up, sl) animarse
buck[2] /bʌk/ (Amer, sl) dólar m
buck[3] /bʌk/ n. **pass the ~ to s.o.** echarle a uno el muerto
bucket /'bʌkɪt/ n cubo m
buckle /'bʌkl/ n hebilla f. ● vt abrochar. ● vi torcerse. **~ down to** dedicarse con empeño a
bud /bʌd/ n brote m. ● vi (pt budded) brotar.
Buddhis|m /'bʊdɪzəm/ n budismo m. **~t** /'bʊdɪst/ a & n budista (m & f)
budding /'bʌdɪŋ/ a (fig) en ciernes

buddy /'bʌdɪ/ n (fam) compañero m, amigote m (fam)

budge /bʌdʒ/ vt mover. ● vi moverse

budgerigar /'bʌdʒərɪgɑː(r)/ n periquito m

budget /'bʌdʒɪt/ n presupuesto m. ● vi (pt **budgeted**) presupuestar

buff /bʌf/ n (colour) color m de ante; (fam) aficionado m. ● vt pulir

buffalo /'bʌfələʊ/ n (pl **-oes** or **-o**) búfalo m

buffer /'bʌfə(r)/ n parachoques invar. ~ **state** n estado m tapón

buffet /'bʊfeɪ/ n (meal, counter) bufé m. /'bʌfɪt/ n golpe m; (slap) bofetada f. ● vt (pt **buffeted**) golpear

buffoon /bə'fuːn/ n payaso m, bufón m

bug /bʌg/ n bicho m; (germ, sl) microbio m; (device, sl) micrófono m oculto. ● vt (pt **bugged**) ocultar un micrófono en; intervenir ‹telephone›; (Amer, sl) molestar

bugbear /'bʌgbeə(r)/ n pesadilla f

buggy /'bʌgɪ/ n. **baby** ~ (esp Amer) cochecito m de niño

bugle /'bjuːgl/ n corneta f

build /bɪld/ vt/i (pt **built**) construir. ~ **up** vt urbanizar; (increase) aumentar. ● n (of person) figura f, tipo m. ~**er** n constructor m. ~**-up** n aumento m; (of gas etc) acumulación f; (fig) propaganda f

built /bɪlt/ see **build**. ~**-in** a empotrado. ~**-up area** n zona f urbanizada

bulb /bʌlb/ n bulbo m; (elec) bombilla f. ~**ous** a bulboso

Bulgaria /bʌl'geərɪə/ n Bulgaria f. ~**n** a & n búlgaro (m)

bulge /bʌldʒ/ n protuberancia f. ● vi pandearse; (jut out) sobresalir. ~**ing** a abultado; ‹eyes› saltón

bulk /bʌlk/ n bulto m, volumen m. **in** ~ a granel; (loose) suelto. **the** ~ **of** la mayor parte de. ~**y** a voluminoso

bull /bʊl/ n toro m

bulldog /'bʊldɒg/ n buldog m

bulldozer /'bʊldəʊzə(r)/ n oruga f aplanadora, bulldozer m

bullet /'bʊlɪt/ n bala f

bulletin /'bʊlɪtɪn/ n anuncio m; (journal) boletín m

bullet-proof /'bʊlɪtpruːf/ a a prueba de balas

bullfight /'bʊlfaɪt/ n corrida f (de toros). ~**er** n torero m

bullion /'bʊljən/ n (gold) oro m en barras; (silver) plata f en barras

bull: ~**ring** /'bʊlrɪŋ/ n plaza f de toros. ~**'s-eye** n centro m del blanco, diana f

bully /'bʊlɪ/ n matón m. ● vt intimidar. ~**ing** n intimidación f

bum[1] /bʌm/ n (bottom, sl) trasero m

bum[2] /bʌm/ n (Amer, sl) holgazán m

bumble-bee /'bʌmblbiː/ n abejorro m

bump /bʌmp/ vt chocar contra. ● vi dar sacudidas. ● n choque m; (swelling) chichón m. ~ **into** chocar contra; (meet) encontrar

bumper /'bʌmpə(r)/ n parachoques m invar. ● a abundante. ~ **edition** n edición f especial

bumpkin /'bʌmpkɪn/ n patán m, paleto m (fam)

bumptious /'bʌmpʃəs/ a presuntuoso

bun /bʌn/ n bollo m; (hair) moño m

bunch /bʌntʃ/ n manojo m; (of people) grupo m; (of bananas, grapes) racimo m, (of flowers) ramo m

bundle /'bʌndl/ n bulto m; (of papers) legajo m; (of nerves) manojo m. ● vt. ~ **up** atar

bung /bʌŋ/ n tapón m. ● vt tapar; (sl) tirar

bungalow /'bʌŋgələʊ/ n casa f de un solo piso, chalé m, bungalow m

bungle /'bʌŋgl/ vt chapucear

bunion /'bʌnjən/ n juanete m

bunk /bʌŋk/ n litera f

bunker /'bʌŋkə(r)/ n carbonera f; (golf) obstáculo m; (mil) refugio m, búnker m

bunkum /'bʌŋkəm/ n tonterías fpl

bunny /'bʌnɪ/ n conejito m

buoy /bɔɪ/ n boya f. ● vt. ~ **up** hacer flotar; (fig) animar

buoyan|**cy** /'bɔɪənsɪ/ n flotabilidad f; (fig) optimismo m. ~**t** /'bɔɪənt/ a boyante; (fig) alegre

burden /'bɜːdn/ n carga f. ● vt cargar (**with** de). ~**some** a pesado

bureau /'bjʊərəʊ/ n (pl **-eaux** /-əʊz/) escritorio m; (office) oficina f

bureaucra|**cy** /bjʊə'rɒkrəsɪ/ n burocracia f. ~**t** /'bjʊərəkræt/ n burócrata m & f. ~**tic** /-'krætɪk/ a burocrático

burgeon /'bɜːdʒən/ vi brotar; (fig) crecer

burgl|**ar** /'bɜːglə(r)/ n ladrón m. ~**ary** n robo m con allanamiento de morada. **~e** /'bɜːgl/ *vt* robar con allanamiento

Burgundy /'bɜːgəndɪ/ *n* Borgoña *f*; *(wine)* vino *m* de Borgoña

burial /'berɪəl/ *n* entierro *m*

burlesque /bɜː'lesk/ *n* burlesco *m*

burly /'bɜːlɪ/ *a* (**-ier, -iest**) corpulento

Burm|a /'bɜːmə/ Birmania *f*. **~ese** /-'miːz/ *a & n* birmano (*m*)

burn /bɜːn/ *vt* (*pt* **burned** *or* **burnt**) quemar. ● *vi* quemarse. **~ down** *vt* destruir con fuego. ● *n* quemadura *f*. **~er** *n* quemador *m*. **~ing** *a* ardiente; *(food)* que quema; *(question)* candente

burnish /'bɜːnɪʃ/ *vt* lustrar, pulir

burnt /bɜːnt/ *see* **burn**

burp /bɜːp/ *n* (*fam*) eructo *m*. ● *vi* (*fam*) eructar

burr /bɜː(r)/ *n* (*bot*) erizo *m*

burrow /'bʌrəʊ/ *n* madriguera *f*. ● *vt* excavar

bursar /'bɜːsə(r)/ *n* tesorero *m*. **~y** /'bɜːsərɪ/ *n* beca *f*

burst /bɜːst/ *vt* (*pt* **burst**) reventar. ● *vi* reventarse; *(tyre)* pincharse. ● *n* reventón *m*; (*mil*) ráfaga *f*; (*fig*) explosión *f*. **~ of laughter** carcajada *f*

bury /'berɪ/ *vt* enterrar; *(hide)* ocultar

bus /bʌs/ *n* (*pl* **buses**) autobús *m*, camión *m* (*Mex*). ● *vi* (*pt* **bussed**) ir en autobús

bush /bʊʃ/ *n* arbusto *m*; (*land*) monte *m*. **~y** *a* espeso

busily /'bɪzɪlɪ/ *adv* afanosamente

business /'bɪznɪs/ *n* negocio *m*; (*com*) negocios *mpl*; (*profession*) ocupación *f*; (*fig*) asunto *m*. **mind one's own ~** ocuparse de sus propios asuntos. **~-like** *a* práctico, serio. **~man** *n* hombre *m* de negocios

busker /'bʌskə(r)/ *n* músico *m* ambulante

bus-stop /'bʌsstɒp/ *n* parada *f* de autobús

bust[1] /bʌst/ *n* busto *m*; (*chest*) pecho *m*

bust[2] /bʌst/ *vt* (*pt* **busted** *or* **bust**) (*sl*) romper. ● *vi* romperse. ● *a* roto. **go ~** (*sl*) quebrar

bustle /'bʌsl/ *vi* apresurarse. ● *n* bullicio *m*

bust-up /'bʌstʌp/ *n* (*sl*) riña *f*

busy /'bɪzɪ/ *a* (**-ier, -iest**) ocupado; *(street)* concurrido. ● *vt*. **~ o.s. with** ocuparse de

busybody /'bɪzɪbɒdɪ/ *n* entrometido *m*

but /bʌt/ *conj* pero; *(after negative)* sino. ● *prep* menos. **~ for** si no fuera por. **last ~ one** penúltimo. ● *adv* solamente

butane /'bjuːteɪn/ *n* butano *m*

butcher /'bʊtʃə(r)/ *n* carnicero *m*. ● *vt* matar; (*fig*) hacer una carnicería con. **~y** *n* carnicería *f*, matanza *f*

butler /'bʌtlə(r)/ *n* mayordomo *m*

butt /bʌt/ *n* (*of gun*) culata *f*; (*of cigarette*) colilla *f*; (*target*) blanco *m*. ● *vi* topar. **~ in** interrumpir

butter /'bʌtə(r)/ *n* mantequilla *f*. ● *vt* untar con mantequilla. **~ up** *vt* (*fam*) lisonjear, dar jabón a. **~bean** *n* judía *f*

buttercup /'bʌtəkʌp/ *n* ranúnculo *m*

butter-fingers /'bʌtəfɪŋgəz/ *n* manazas *m invar*, torpe *m*

butterfly /'bʌtəflaɪ/ *n* mariposa *f*

buttock /'bʌtək/ *n* nalga *f*

button /'bʌtn/ *n* botón *m*. ● *vt* abotonar. ● *vi* abotonarse. **~hole** /'bʌtnhəʊl/ *n* ojal *m*. ● *vt* (*fig*) detener

buttress /'bʌtrɪs/ *n* contrafuerte *m*. ● *vt* apoyar

buxom /'bʌksəm/ *a* (*woman*) rollizo

buy /baɪ/ *vt* (*pt* **bought**) comprar. ● *n* compra *f*. **~er** *n* comprador *m*

buzz /bʌz/ *n* zumbido *m*; (*phone call*, *fam*) llamada *f*. ● *vi* zumbar. **~ off** (*sl*) largarse. **~er** *n* timbre *m*

by /baɪ/ *prep* por; (*near*) cerca de; (*before*) antes de; (*according to*) según. **~ and large** en conjunto, en general. **~ car** en coche. **~ oneself** por sí solo

bye-bye /'baɪbaɪ/ *int* (*fam*) ¡adiós!

by-election /'baɪɪlekʃn/ *n* elección *f* parcial

bygone /'baɪgɒn/ *a* pasado

by-law /'baɪlɔː/ *n* reglamento *m* (local)

bypass /'baɪpɑːs/ *n* carretera *f* de circunvalación. ● *vt* evitar

by-product /'baɪprɒdʌkt/ *n* subproducto *m*

bystander /'baɪstændə(r)/ *n* espectador *m*

byword /'baɪwɜːd/ *n* sinónimo *m*. **be a ~ for** ser conocido por

C

cab /kæb/ n taxi m; (of lorry, train) cabina f

cabaret /'kæbəreɪ/ n espectáculo m

cabbage /'kæbɪdʒ/ n col m, repollo m

cabin /'kæbɪn/ n cabaña f; (in ship) camarote m; (in plane) cabina f

cabinet /'kæbɪnɪt/ n (cupboard) armario m; (for display) vitrina f. **C~** (pol) gabinete m. **~-maker** n ebanista m & f

cable /'keɪbl/ n cable m. ● vt cablegrafiar. **~ railway** n funicular m

cache /kæʃ/ n (place) escondrijo m; (things) reservas fpl escondidas. ● vt ocultar

cackle /'kækl/ n (of hen) cacareo m; (laugh) risotada f. ● vi cacarear; (laugh) reírse a carcajadas

cacophon|ous /kə'kɒfənəs/ a cacofónico. **~y** n cacofonía f

cactus /'kæktəs/ n (pl -ti /-taɪ/) cacto m

cad /kæd/ n sinvergüenza m. **~dish** a desvergonzado

caddie /'kædɪ/ n (golf) portador m de palos

caddy /'kædɪ/ n cajita f

cadence /'keɪdəns/ n cadencia f

cadet /kə'det/ n cadete m

cadge /kædʒ/ vt/i gorronear. **~r** /-ə(r)/ n gorrón m

Caesarean /sɪ'zeərɪən/ a cesáreo. **~ section** n cesárea f

café /'kæfeɪ/ n cafetería f

cafeteria /kæfɪ'tɪərɪə/ n autoservicio m

caffeine /'kæfiːn/ n cafeína f

cage /keɪdʒ/ n jaula f. ● vt enjaular

cagey /'keɪdʒɪ/ a (fam) evasivo

Cairo /'kaɪərəʊ/ n el Cairo m

cajole /kə'dʒəʊl/ vt engatusar. **~ry** n engatusamiento m

cake /keɪk/ n pastel m, tarta f; (sponge) bizcocho m. **~ of soap** pastilla f de jabón. **~d** a incrustado

calamit|ous /kə'læmɪtəs/ a desastroso. **~y** /kə'læmətɪ/ n calamidad f

calcium /'kælsɪəm/ n calcio m

calculat|e /'kælkjʊleɪt/ vt/i calcular; (Amer) suponer. **~ing** a calculador. **~ion** /-'leɪʃn/ n cálculo m. **~or** n calculadora f

calculus /'kælkjʊləs/ n (pl -li) cálculo m

calendar /'kælɪndə(r)/ n calendario m

calf¹ /kɑːf/ n (pl calves) ternero m

calf² /kɑːf/ n (pl calves) (of leg) pantorrilla f

calibre /'kælɪbə(r)/ n calibre m

calico /'kælɪkəʊ/ n calicó m

call /kɔːl/ vt/i llamar. ● n llamada f; (shout) grito m; (visit) visita f. **be on ~** estar de guardia. **long distance ~** conferencia f. **~ back** vt hacer volver; (on phone) volver a llamar. ● vi volver; (on phone) volver a llamar. **~ for** pedir; (fetch) ir a buscar. **~ off** cancelar. **~ on** visitar. **~ out** dar voces. **~ together** convocar. **~ up** (mil) llamar al servicio militar; (phone) llamar. **~-box** n cabina f telefónica. **~er** n visita f; (phone) el que llama m. **~ing** n vocación f

callous /'kæləs/ a insensible, cruel. **~ness** n crueldad f

callow /'kæləʊ/ a (-er, -est) inexperto

calm /kɑːm/ a (-er, -est) tranquilo; (weather) calmoso. ● n tranquilidad f, calma f. ● vt calmar. ● vi calmarse. **~ness** n tranquilidad f, calma f

calorie /'kælərɪ/ n caloría f

camber /'kæmbə(r)/ n curvatura f

came /keɪm/ see **come**

camel /'kæml/ n camello m

camellia /kə'miːljə/ n camelia f

cameo /'kæmɪəʊ/ n (pl -os) camafeo m

camera /'kæmərə/ n máquina f (fotográfica); (TV) cámara f. **~man** n (pl -men) operador m, cámara m

camouflage /'kæməflɑːʒ/ n camuflaje m. ● vt encubrir; (mil) camuflar

camp¹ /kæmp/ n campamento m. ● vi acamparse

camp² /kæmp/ a (affected) amanerado

campaign /kæm'peɪn/ n campaña f. ● vi hacer campaña

camp: ~bed n catre m de tijera. **~er** n campista m & f; (vehicle) caravana f. **~ing** n camping m. **go ~ing** hacer camping. **~site** /'kæmpsaɪt/ n camping m

campus /'kæmpəs/ n (pl -puses) ciudad f universitaria

can¹ /kæn/ v aux (pt could) (be able to) poder; (know how to) saber. **~not** (neg), **~'t** (neg, fam). **I ~not ~'t go** no puedo ir

can² /kæn/ *n* lata *f*. ● *vt* (*pt* **canned**) enlatar. **∼ned music** música *f* grabada

Canada /'kænədə/ *n* el Canadá *m*. **∼ian** /kə'neɪdɪən/ *a & n* canadiense (*m & f*)

canal /kə'næl/ *n* canal *m*

canary /kə'neərɪ/ *n* canario *m*

cancel /'kænsl/ *vt/i* (*pt* **cancelled**) anular; cancelar ‹*contract etc*›; suspender ‹*appointment etc*›; (*delete*) tachar. **∼lation** /-'leɪʃn/ *n* cancelación *f*

cancer /'kænsə(r)/ *n* cáncer *m*. **C∼** *n* (*Astr*) Cáncer *m*. **∼ous** *a* canceroso

candid /'kændɪd/ *a* franco

candida|cy /'kændɪdəsɪ/ *n* candidatura *f*. **∼te** /'kændɪdeɪt/ *n* candidato *m*

candle /'kændl/ *n* vela *f*. **∼stick** /'kændlstɪk/ *n* candelero *m*

candour /'kændə(r)/ *n* franqueza *f*

candy /'kændɪ/ *n* (*Amer*) caramelo *m*. **∼floss** *n* algodón *m* de azúcar

cane /keɪn/ *n* caña *f*; (*for baskets*) mimbre *m*; (*stick*) bastón *m*. ● *vt* (*strike*) castigar con palmeta

canine /'keɪnaɪn/ *a* canino

canister /'kænɪstə(r)/ *n* bote *m*

cannabis /'kænəbɪs/ *n* cáñamo *m* índico, hachís *m*, mariguana *f*

cannibal /'kænɪbl/ *n* caníbal *m*. **∼ism** *n* canibalismo *m*

cannon /'kænən/ *n invar* cañón *m*. **∼ shot** cañonazo *m*

cannot /'kænət/ *see* **can**¹

canny /'kænɪ/ *a* astuto

canoe /kə'nu:/ *n* canoa *f*, piragua *f*. ● *vi* ir en canoa. **∼ist** *n* piragüista *m & f*

canon /'kænən/ *n* canon *m*; (*person*) canónigo *m*. **∼ize** /'kænənaɪz/ *vt* canonizar

can-opener /'kænəʊpnə(r)/ *n* abrelatas *m invar*

canopy /'kænəpɪ/ *n* dosel *m*; (*of parachute*) casquete *m*

cant /kænt/ *n* jerga *f*

can't /kɑ:nt/ *see* **can**¹

cantankerous /kæn'tæŋkərəs/ *a* malhumorado

canteen /kæn'ti:n/ *n* cantina *f*; (*of cutlery*) juego *m*; (*flask*) cantimplora *f*

canter /'kæntə(r)/ *n* medio galope *m*. ● *vi* ir a medio galope

canvas /'kænvəs/ *n* lona *f*; (*artist's*) lienzo *m*

canvass /'kænvəs/ *vi* hacer campaña, solicitar votos. **∼ing** *n* solicitación *f* (de votos)

canyon /'kænjən/ *n* cañón *m*

cap /kæp/ *n* gorra *f*; (*lid*) tapa *f*; (*of cartridge*) cápsula *f*; (*academic*) birrete *m*; (*of pen*) capuchón *m*; (*mec*) casquete *m*. ● *vt* (*pt* **capped**) tapar, poner cápsula a; (*outdo*) superar

capab|ility /keɪpə'bɪlətɪ/ *n* capacidad *f*. **∼le** /'keɪpəbl/ *a* capaz. **∼ly** *adv* competentemente

capacity /kə'pæsətɪ/ *n* capacidad *f*; (*function*) calidad *f*

cape¹ /keɪp/ *n* (*cloak*) capa *f*

cape² /keɪp/ *n* (*geog*) cabo *m*

caper¹ /'keɪpə(r)/ *vi* brincar. ● *n* salto *m*; (*fig*) travesura *f*

caper² /'keɪpə(r)/ *n* (*culin*) alcaparra *f*

capital /'kæpɪtl/ *a* capital. **∼ letter** *n* mayúscula *f*. ● *n* (*town*) capital *f*; (*money*) capital *m*

capitalis|m /'kæpɪtəlɪzəm/ *n* capitalismo *m*. **∼t** *a & n* capitalista (*m & f*)

capitalize /'kæpɪtəlaɪz/ *vt* capitalizar; (*typ*) escribir con mayúsculas. **∼ on** aprovechar

capitulat|e /kə'pɪtʃʊleɪt/ *vi* capitular. **∼ion** /-'leɪʃn/ *n* capitulación *f*

capon /'keɪpən/ *n* capón *m*

capricious /kə'prɪʃəs/ *a* caprichoso

Capricorn /'kæprɪkɔ:n/ *n* Capricornio *m*

capsicum /'kæpsɪkəm/ *n* pimiento *m*

capsize /kæp'saɪz/ *vt* hacer zozobrar. ● *vi* zozobrar

capsule /'kæpsju:l/ *n* cápsula *f*

captain /'kæptɪn/ *n* capitán *m*. ● *vt* capitanear

caption /'kæpʃn/ *n* (*heading*) título *m*; (*of cartoon etc*) leyenda *f*

captivate /'kæptɪveɪt/ *vt* encantar

captiv|e /'kæptɪv/ *a & n* cautivo (*m*). **∼ity** /-'tɪvətɪ/ *n* cautiverio *m*, cautividad *f*

capture /'kæptʃə(r)/ *vt* prender; llamar ‹*attention*›; (*mil*) tomar. ● *n* apresamiento *m*; (*mil*) toma *f*

car /kɑ:(r)/ *n* coche *m*, carro *m* (*LAm*)

carafe /kə'ræf/ *n* jarro *m*, garrafa *f*

caramel /'kærəmel/ *n* azúcar *m* quemado; (*sweet*) caramelo *m*

carat /'kærət/ *n* quilate *m*

caravan /'kærəvæn/ *n* caravana *f*

carbohydrate /kɑ:bəʊ'haɪdreɪt/ *n* hidrato *m* de carbono

carbon /'kɑːbən/ n carbono m; (paper) carbón m. ~ **copy** copia f al carbón

carburettor /kɑːbjʊ'retə(r)/ n carburador m

carcass /'kɑːkəs/ n cadáver m, esqueleto m

card /kɑːd/ n tarjeta f; (for games) carta f; (membership) carnet m; (records) ficha f

cardboard /'kɑːdbɔːd/ n cartón m

cardiac /'kɑːdɪæk/ a cardíaco

cardigan /'kɑːdɪɡən/ n chaqueta f de punto, rebeca f

cardinal /'kɑːdɪnəl/ a cardinal. ● n cardenal m

card-index /'kɑːdɪndeks/ n fichero m

care /keə(r)/ n cuidado m; (worry) preocupación f; (protection) cargo m. ~ **of** a cuidado de, en casa de. **take** ~ **of** cuidar de ⟨person⟩; ocuparse de ⟨matter⟩. ● vi interesarse. **I don't** ~ me es igual. ~ **about** interesarse por. ~ **for** cuidar de; (like) querer

career /kə'rɪə(r)/ n carrera f. ● vi correr a toda velocidad

carefree /'keəfriː/ a despreocupado

careful /'keəfʊl/ a cuidadoso; (cautious) prudente. ~**ly** adv con cuidado

careless /'keəlɪs/ a negligente; (not worried) indiferente. ~**ly** adv descuidadamente. ~**ness** n descuido m

caress /kə'res/ n caricia f. ● vt acariciar

caretaker /'keəteɪkə(r)/ n vigilante m; (of flats etc) portero m

car-ferry /'kɑːferɪ/ n transbordador m de coches

cargo /'kɑːɡəʊ/ n (pl -oes) carga f

Caribbean /kærɪ'biːən/ a caribe. **Sea** n mar m Caribe

caricature /'kærɪkətʃʊə(r)/ n caricatura f. ● vt caricaturizar

carnage /'kɑːnɪdʒ/ n carnicería f, matanza f

carnal /'kɑːnl/ a carnal

carnation /kɑː'neɪʃn/ n clavel m

carnival /'kɑːnɪvl/ n carnaval m

carol /'kærəl/ n villancico m

carouse /kə'raʊz/ vi correrse una juerga

carousel /kærə'sel/ n tiovivo m

carp[1] /kɑːp/ n invar carpa f

carp[2] /kɑːp/ vi. ~ **at** quejarse de

car park /'kɑːpɑːk/ n aparcamiento m

carpent|er /'kɑːpɪntə(r)/ n carpintero m. ~**ry** n carpintería f

carpet /'kɑːpɪt/ n alfombra f. **be on the** ~ (fam) recibir un rapapolvo; (under consideration) estar sobre el tapete. ● vt alfombrar. ~**sweeper** n escoba f mecánica

carriage /'kærɪdʒ/ n coche m; (mec) carro m; (transport) transporte m; (cost, bearing) porte m

carriageway /'kærɪdʒweɪ/ n calzada f, carretera f

carrier /'kærɪə(r)/ n transportista m & f; (company) empresa f de transportes; (med) portador m. ~**bag** n bolsa f

carrot /'kærət/ n zanahoria f

carry /'kærɪ/ vt llevar; transportar ⟨goods⟩; (involve) llevar consigo, implicar. ● vi ⟨sounds⟩ llegar, oírse. ~ **off** llevarse. ~ **on** continuar; (complain, fam) quejarse. ~ **out** realizar; cumplir ⟨promise, threat⟩. ~**cot** n capazo m

cart /kɑːt/ n carro m. ● vt acarrear; (carry, fam) llevar

cartilage /'kɑːtɪlɪdʒ/ n cartílago m

carton /'kɑːtən/ n caja f (de cartón)

cartoon /kɑː'tuːn/ n caricatura f, chiste m; (strip) historieta f; (film) dibujos mpl animados. ~**ist** n caricaturista m & f

cartridge /'kɑːtrɪdʒ/ n cartucho m

carve /kɑːv/ vt tallar; trinchar ⟨meat⟩

cascade /kæs'keɪd/ n cascada f. ● vi caer en cascadas

case /keɪs/ n caso m; (jurid) proceso m; (crate) cajón m; (box) caja f; (suitcase) maleta f. **in any** ~ en todo caso. **in** ~ **he comes** por si viene. **in** ~ **of** en caso de. **lower** ~ caja f baja, minúscula f. **upper** ~ caja f alta, mayúscula f

cash /kæʃ/ n dinero m efectivo. **pay (in)** ~ pagar al contado. ● vt cobrar. ~ **in (on)** aprovecharse de. ~ **desk** n caja f

cashew /'kæʃuː/ n anacardo m

cashier /kæ'ʃɪə(r)/ n cajero m

cashmere /kæʃ'mɪə(r)/ n casimir m, cachemir m

casino /kə'siːnəʊ/ n (pl -os) casino m

cask /kɑːsk/ n barril m

casket /'kɑːskɪt/ n cajita f

casserole /'kæsərəʊl/ n cacerola f; (stew) cazuela f

cassette /kə'set/ n casete m

cast /kɑːst/ vt (pt cast) arrojar; fundir ⟨metal⟩; dar ⟨vote⟩; (in theatre) repartir. ● *n* lanzamiento *m*; (*in play*) reparto *m*; (*mould*) molde *m*

castanets /ˌkæstəˈnets/ *npl* castañuelas *fpl*

castaway /ˈkɑːstəweɪ/ *n* náufrago *m*

caste /kɑːst/ *n* casta *f*

cast: ~ **iron** *n* hierro *m* fundido. ~**iron** *a* de hierro fundido; (*fig*) sólido

castle /ˈkɑːsl/ *n* castillo *m*; (*chess*) torre *f*

cast-offs /ˈkɑːstɒfs/ *npl* desechos *mpl*

castor /ˈkɑːstə(r)/ *n* ruedecilla *f*

castor oil /ˈkɑːstərˈɔɪl/ *n* aceite *m* de ricino

castor sugar /ˈkɑːstəʃʊgə(r)/ *n* azúcar *m* extrafino

castrat|e /kæˈstreɪt/ *vt* castrar. ~**ion** /-ʃn/ *n* castración *f*

casual /ˈkæʒʊəl/ *a* casual; ⟨*meeting*⟩ fortuito; (*work*) ocasional; (*attitude*) despreocupado; (*clothes*) informal, de sport. ~**ly** *adv* de paso

casualt|y /ˈkæʒʊəltɪ/ *n* accidente *m*; (*injured*) víctima *f*, herido *m*; (*dead*) víctima *f*, muerto *m*. ~**ies** *npl* (*mil*) bajas *fpl*

cat /kæt/ *n* gato *m*

cataclysm /ˈkætəklɪzəm/ *n* cataclismo *m*

catacomb /ˈkætəkuːm/ *n* catacumba *f*

catalogue /ˈkætəlɒg/ *n* catálogo *m*. ● *vt* catalogar

catalyst /ˈkætəlɪst/ *n* catalizador *m*

catamaran /ˈkætəməˈræn/ *n* catamarán *n*

catapult /ˈkætəpʌlt/ *n* catapulta *f*; (*child's*) tirador *m*, tirachinos *m invar*

cataract /ˈkætərækt/ *n* catarata *f*

catarrh /kəˈtɑː(r)/ *n* catarro *m*

catastroph|e /kəˈtæstrəfɪ/ *n* catástrofe *m*. ~**ic** /kætəˈstrɒfɪk/ *a* catastrófico

catch /kætʃ/ *vt* (*pt* caught) coger (*not LAm*), agarrar; (*grab*) asir; tomar ⟨*train, bus*⟩; (*unawares*) sorprender; (*understand*) comprender; contraer ⟨*disease*⟩. ~ **a cold** resfriarse. ~ **sight of** avistar. ● *vi* (*get stuck*) engancharse; ⟨*fire*⟩ prenderse. ● *n* cogida *f*; (*of fish*) pesca *f*; (*on door*) pestillo *m*; (*on window*) cerradura *f*. ~ **on** (*fam*) hacerse popular. ~ **up** poner al día. ~ **up with** alcanzar; ponerse al corriente de ⟨*news etc*⟩

catching /ˈkætʃɪŋ/ *a* contagioso

catchment /ˈkætʃmənt/ *n*. ~ **area** *n* zona *f* de captación

catch-phrase /ˈkætʃfreɪz/ *n* eslogan *m*

catchword /ˈkætʃwɜːd/ *n* eslogan *m*, consigna *f*

catchy /ˈkætʃɪ/ *a* pegadizo

catechism /ˈkætɪkɪzəm/ *n* catecismo *m*

categorical /kætɪˈgɒrɪkl/ *a* categórico

category /ˈkætɪgərɪ/ *n* categoría *f*

cater /ˈkeɪtə(r)/ *vi* proveer comida a. ~ **for** proveer a ⟨*needs*⟩. ~**er** *n* proveedor *m*

caterpillar /ˈkætəpɪlə(r)/ *n* oruga *f*

cathedral /kəˈθiːdrəl/ *n* catedral *f*

catholic /ˈkæθəlɪk/ *a* universal. **C**~ *a* & *n* católico (*m*). **C**~**ism** /kəˈθɒlɪsɪzəm/ *n* catolicismo *m*

catnap /ˈkætnæp/ *n* sueñecito *m*

cat's eyes /ˈkætsaɪz/ *npl* catafotos *mpl*

cattle /ˈkætl/ *npl* ganado *m* (vacuno)

cat|ty /ˈkætɪ/ *a* malicioso. ~**walk** /ˈkætwɔːk/ *n* pasarela *f*

caucus /ˈkɔːkəs/ *n* comité *m* electoral

caught /kɔːt/ *see* catch

cauldron /ˈkɔːldrən/ *n* caldera *f*

cauliflower /ˈkɒlɪflaʊə(r)/ *n* coliflor *f*

cause /kɔːz/ *n* causa *f*, motivo *m*. ● *vt* causar

causeway /ˈkɔːzweɪ/ *n* calzada *f* elevada, carretera *f* elevada

caustic /ˈkɔːstɪk/ *a* & *n* cáustico (*m*)

cauterize /ˈkɔːtəraɪz/ *vt* cauterizar

caution /ˈkɔːʃn/ *n* cautela *f*; (*warning*) advertencia *f*. ● *vt* advertir; (*jurid*) amonestar

cautious /ˈkɔːʃəs/ *a* cauteloso, prudente. ~**ly** *adv* con precaución, cautelosamente

cavalcade /kævəlˈkeɪd/ *n* cabalgata *f*

cavalier /kævəˈlɪə(r)/ *a* arrogante

cavalry /ˈkævəlrɪ/ *n* caballería *f*

cave /keɪv/ *n* cueva *f*. ● *vi*. ~ **in** hundirse. ~**man** *n* (*pl* -men) troglodita *m*

cavern /ˈkævən/ *n* caverna *f*, cueva *f*

caviare /ˈkævɪɑː(r)/ *n* caviar *m*

caving /ˈkeɪvɪŋ/ *n* espeleología *f*

cavity /ˈkævətɪ/ *n* cavidad *f*; (*in tooth*) caries *f*

cavort /kəˈvɔːt/ *vi* brincar

cease /siːs/ *vt/i* cesar. ● *n*. **without** ~ sin cesar. ~**fire** *n* tregua *f*, alto *m* el fuego. ~**less** *a* incesante

cedar /ˈsiːdə(r)/ *n* cedro *m*

cede /si:d/ *vt* ceder

cedilla /sɪ'dɪlə/ *n* cedilla *f*

ceiling /'si:lɪŋ/ *n* techo *m*

celebrat|e /'selɪbreɪt/ *vt* celebrar. ● *vi* divertirse. **~ed** /'selɪbreɪtɪd/ *a* célebre. **~ion** /-'breɪʃn/ *n* celebración *f*; (*party*) fiesta *f*

celebrity /sɪ'lebrətɪ/ *n* celebridad *f*

celery /'selərɪ/ *n* apio *m*

celestial /sɪ'lestjəl/ *a* celestial

celiba|cy /'selɪbəsɪ/ *n* celibato *m*. **~te** /'selɪbət/ *a & n* célibe (*m & f*)

cell /sel/ *n* celda *f*; (*biol*) célula *f*; (*elec*) pila *f*

cellar /'selə(r)/ *n* sótano *m*; (*for wine*) bodega *f*

cell|ist /'tʃelɪst/ *n* violonc(h)elo *m & f*, violonc(h)elista *m & f*. **~o** /'tʃeləʊ/ *n* (*pl* **-os**) violonc(h)elo *m*

Cellophane /'seləfeɪn/ *n* (*P*) celofán *m* (*P*)

cellular /'seljʊlə(r)/ *a* celular

celluloid /'seljʊlɔɪd/ *n* celuloide *m*

cellulose /'seljʊləʊs/ *n* celulosa *f*

Celt /kelt/ *n* celta *m & f*. **~ic** *a* céltico

cement /sɪ'ment/ *n* cemento *m*. ● *vt* cementar; (*fig*) consolidar

cemetery /'semətrɪ/ *n* cementerio *m*

cenotaph /'senəta:f/ *n* cenotafio *m*

censor /'sensə(r)/ *n* censor *m*. ● *vt* censurar. **~ship** *n* censura *f*

censure /'senʃə(r)/ *n* censura *f*. ● *vt* censurar

census /'sensəs/ *n* censo *m*

cent /sent/ *n* centavo *m*

centenary /sen'ti:nərɪ/ *n* centenario *m*

centigrade /'sentɪgreɪd/ *a* centígrado

centilitre /'sentɪli:tə(r)/ *n* centilitro *m*

centimetre /'sentɪmi:tə(r)/ *n* centímetro *m*

centipede /'sentɪpi:d/ *n* ciempiés *m* invar

central /'sentrəl/ *a* central; (*of town*) céntrico. **~ heating** *n* calefacción *f* central. **~ize** *vt* centralizar. **~ly** *adv* (*situated*) en el centro

centre /'sentə(r)/ *n* centro *m*. ● *vt* (*pt* **centred**) *vi* concentrarse

centrifugal /sen'trɪfjʊgəl/ *a* centrífugo

century /'sentʃərɪ/ *n* siglo *m*

ceramic /sɪ'ræmɪk/ *a* cerámico. **~s** *npl* cerámica *f*

cereal /'sɪərɪəl/ *n* cereal *m*

cerebral /'serɪbrəl/ *a* cerebral

ceremon|ial /serɪ'məʊnɪəl/ *a & n* ceremonial (*m*). **~ious** /-'məʊnɪəs/ *a* ceremonioso. **~y** /'serɪmənɪ/ *n* ceremonia *f*

certain /'sɜ:tn/ *a* cierto. **for ~** seguro. **make ~ of** asegurarse de. **~ly** *adv* desde luego. **~ty** *n* certeza *f*

certificate /sə'tɪfɪkət/ *n* certificado *m*; (*of birth, death etc*) partida *f*

certify /'sɜ:tɪfaɪ/ *vt* certificar

cessation /se'seɪʃən/ *n* cesación *f*

cesspit /'sespɪt/ *n*, **cesspool** /'sespu:l/ *n* pozo *m* negro; (*fam*) sentina *f*

chafe /tʃeɪf/ *vt* rozar. ● *vi* rozarse; (*fig*) irritarse

chaff /tʃæf/ *vt* zumbarse de

chaffinch /'tʃæfɪntʃ/ *n* pinzón *m*

chagrin /'ʃægrɪn/ *n* disgusto *m*

chain /tʃeɪn/ *n* cadena *f*. ● *vt* encadenar. **~ reaction** *n* reacción *f* en cadena. **~-smoker** *n* fumador *m* que siempre tiene un cigarrillo encendido. **~ store** *n* sucursal *m*

chair /tʃeə(r)/ *n* silla *f*; (*univ*) cátedra *f*. ● *vt* presidir. **~-lift** *n* telesilla *m*

chairman /'tʃeəmən/ *n* (*pl* **-men**) presidente *m*

chalet /'ʃæleɪ/ *n* chalé *m*

chalice /'tʃælɪs/ *n* cáliz *m*

chalk /tʃɔ:k/ *n* creta *f*; (*stick*) tiza *f*. **~y** *a* cretáceo

challeng|e /'tʃælɪndʒ/ *n* desafío *m*; (*fig*) reto *m*. ● *vt* desafiar; (*question*) poner en duda. **~ing** *a* estimulante

chamber /'tʃeɪmbə(r)/ *n* (*old use*) cámara *f*. **~maid** /'tʃeɪmbəmeɪd/ *n* camarera *f*. **~-pot** *n* orinal *m*. **~s** *npl* despacho *m*, bufete *m*

chameleon /kə'mi:ljən/ *n* camaleón *m*

chamois /'ʃæmɪ/ *n* gamuza *f*

champagne /ʃæm'peɪn/ *n* champaña *m*, champán *m* (*fam*)

champion /'tʃæmpɪən/ *n* campeón *m*. ● *vt* defender. **~ship** *n* campeonato *m*

chance /tʃɑ:ns/ *n* casualidad *f*; (*likelihood*) probabilidad *f*; (*opportunity*) oportunidad *f*; (*risk*) riesgo *m*. **by ~** por casualidad. ● *a* fortuito. ● *vt* arriesgar. ● *vi* suceder. **~ upon** tropezar con

chancellor /'tʃɑ:nsələ(r)/ *n* canciller *m*; (*univ*) rector *m*. **C~ of the Exchequer** Ministro *m* de Hacienda

chancy /'tʃɑ:nsɪ/ *a* arriesgado; (*uncertain*) incierto

chandelier /ʃændə'lɪə(r)/ n araña f (de luces)

change /tʃeɪndʒ/ vt cambiar; (substitute) reemplazar. ~ one's mind cambiar de idea. • vi cambiarse. • n cambio m; (small coins) suelto m. ~ of life menopausia f. ~able a cambiable; ⟨weather⟩ variable. ~over n cambio m

channel /'tʃænl/ n canal m; (fig) medio m. the C~ Islands npl las islas fpl Anglonormandàs. the (English) C~ el canal de la Mancha. • vt (pt channelled) acanalar; (fig) encauzar

chant /tʃɑ:nt/ n canto m. • vt/i cantar; (fig) salmodiar

chao|s /'keɪɒs/ n caos m, desorden m. ~tic /-'ɒtɪk/ a caótico, desordenado

chap¹ /tʃæp/ n (crack) grieta f. • vt (pt chapped) agrietar. • vi agrietarse

chap² /tʃæp/ n (fam) hombre m, tío m (fam)

chapel /'tʃæpl/ n capilla f

chaperon /'ʃæpərəʊn/ n acompañanta f. • vt acompañar

chaplain /'tʃæplɪn/ n capellán m

chapter /'tʃæptə(r)/ n capítulo m

char¹ /tʃɑ:(r)/ vt (pt charred) carbonizar

char² /tʃɑ:(r)/ n asistenta f

character /'kærəktə(r)/ n carácter m; (in play) personaje m. in ~ característico

characteristic /kærəktə'rɪstɪk/ a característico. ~ally adv típicamente

characterize /'kærəktəraɪz/ vt caracterizar

charade /ʃə'rɑ:d/ n charada f, farsa f

charcoal /'tʃɑ:kəʊl/ n carbón m vegetal; (for drawing) carboncillo m

charge /tʃɑ:dʒ/ n precio m; (elec, mil) carga f; (jurid) acusación f; (task, custody) encargo m; (responsibility) responsabilidad f. in ~ of responsable de, encargado de. take ~ of encargarse de. • vt pedir; (elec, mil) cargar; (jurid) acusar; (entrust) encargar. • vi cargar; (money) cobrar. ~able a a cargo (de)

chariot /'tʃærɪət/ n carro m

charisma /kə'rɪzmə/ n carisma m. ~tic /-'mætɪk/ a carismático

charitable /'tʃærɪtəbl/ a caritativo

charity /'tʃærɪtɪ/ n caridad f; (society) institución f benéfica

charlatan /'ʃɑ:lətən/ n charlatán m

charm /tʃɑ:m/ n encanto m; (spell) hechizo m; (on bracelet) dije m, amuleto m. • vt encantar. ~ing a encantador

chart /tʃɑ:t/ n (naut) carta f de marear; (table) tabla f. • vt poner en una carta de marear

charter /'tʃɑ:tə(r)/ n carta f. • vt conceder carta a, estatuir; alquilar ⟨bus, train⟩; fletar ⟨plane, ship⟩. ~ed accountant n contador m titulado. ~ flight n vuelo m charter

charwoman /'tʃɑ:wʊmən/ n (pl -women) asistenta f

chary /'tʃeərɪ/ a cauteloso

chase /tʃeɪs/ vt perseguir. • vi correr. • n persecución f. ~ away, ~ off ahuyentar

chasm /'kæzəm/ n abismo m

chassis /'ʃæsɪ/ n chasis m

chaste /tʃeɪst/ a casto

chastise /tʃæs'taɪz/ vt castigar

chastity /'tʃæstɪtɪ/ n castidad f

chat /tʃæt/ n charla f. have a ~ charlar. • vi (pt chatted) charlar

chattels /'tʃætlz/ n bienes mpl muebles

chatter /'tʃætə(r)/ n charla f. • vi charlar. his teeth are ~ing le castañetean los dientes. ~box /'tʃætəbɒks/ n parlanchín m

chatty a hablador; ⟨style⟩ familiar

chauffeur /'ʃəʊfə(r)/ n chófer m

chauvinis|m /'ʃəʊvɪnɪzəm/ n patriotería f; (male) machismo m. ~t /'ʃəʊvɪnɪst/ n patriotero m; (male) machista m & f

cheap /tʃi:p/ a (-er, -est) barato; (poor quality) de baja calidad; ⟨rate⟩ económico. ~en /'tʃi:pən/ vt abaratar. ~(ly) adv barato, a bajo precio. ~ness n baratura f

cheat /tʃi:t/ vt defraudar; (deceive) engañar. • vi (at cards) hacer trampas. • n trampa f; (person) tramposo m

check¹ /tʃek/ vt comprobar; (examine) inspeccionar; (curb) detener; (chess) dar jaque a. • vi comprobar. • n comprobación f; (of tickets) control m; (curb) freno m; (chess) jaque m; (bill, Amer) cuenta f. ~ in registrarse; (at airport) facturar el equipaje. ~ out pagar la cuenta y marcharse. ~ up comprobar. ~ up on investigar

check² /tʃek/ n (pattern) cuadro m. ~ed a a cuadros

checkmate /'tʃekmeɪt/ n jaque m mate. ● vt dar mate a

check-up /'tʃekʌp/ n examen m

cheek /tʃiːk/ n mejilla f; (fig) descaro m. ~**bone** n pómulo m. ~**y** a descarado

cheep /tʃiːp/ vi piar

cheer /tʃɪə(r)/ n alegría f; (applause) viva m. ● vt alegrar; (applaud) aplaudir. ● vi alegrarse; (applaud) aplaudir. ~ **up!** ¡anímate! ~**ful** a alegre. ~**fulness** n alegría f

cheerio /tʃɪərɪ'əʊ/ int (fam) ¡adiós!, ¡hasta luego!

cheer: ~**less** /'tʃɪəlɪs/ a triste. ~**s!** ¡salud!

cheese /tʃiːz/ n queso m

cheetah /'tʃiːtə/ n guepardo m

chef /ʃef/ n cocinero m

chemical /'kemɪkl/ a químico. ● n producto m químico

chemist /'kemɪst/ n farmacéutico m; (scientist) químico m. ~**ry** n química f. ~**'s (shop)** n farmacia f

cheque /tʃek/ n cheque m, talón m. ~**book** n talonario m

chequered /'tʃekəd/ a a cuadros; (fig) con altibajos

cherish /'tʃerɪʃ/ vt cuidar; (love) querer; abrigar (hope)

cherry /'tʃerɪ/ n cereza f. ~**tree** n cerezo m

cherub /'tʃerəb/ n (pl -im) (angel) querubín m

chess /tʃes/ n ajedrez m. ~**board** n tablero m de ajedrez

chest /tʃest/ n pecho m; (box) cofre m, cajón m. ~ **of drawers** n cómoda f

chestnut /'tʃesnʌt/ n castaña f. ~**tree** n castaño m

chew /tʃuː/ vt masticar; (fig) rumiar. ~**ing-gum** n chicle m

chic /ʃiːk/ a elegante. ● n elegancia f

chick /tʃɪk/ n polluelo m. ~**en** /'tʃɪkɪn/ n pollo m. ● a (sl) cobarde. ● vi. ~**en out** (sl) retirarse. ~**en-pox** n varicela f

chicory /'tʃɪkərɪ/ n (in coffee) achicoria f; (in salad) escarola f

chide /tʃaɪd/ vt (pt chided) reprender

chief /tʃiːf/ n jefe m. ● a principal. ~**ly** adv principalmente

chilblain /'tʃɪlbleɪn/ n sabañón m

child /tʃaɪld/ n (pl children /'tʃɪldrən/) niño m; (offspring) hijo m. ~**birth** /'tʃaɪldbɜːθ/ n parto m. ~**hood** n niñez f. ~**ish** a infantil.

~**less** a sin hijos. ~**like** a inocente, infantil

Chile /'tʃɪlɪ/ n Chile m. ~**an** a & n chileno (m)

chill /tʃɪl/ n frío m; (illness) resfriado m. ● a frío. ● vt enfriar; refrigerar (food)

chilli /'tʃɪlɪ/ n (pl -ies) chile m

chilly /'tʃɪlɪ/ a frío

chime /tʃaɪm/ n carillón m. ● vt tocar (bells); dar (hours). ● vi repicar

chimney /'tʃɪmnɪ/ n (pl -eys) chimenea f. ~**pot** n cañón m de chimenea. ~**sweep** n deshollinador m

chimpanzee /tʃɪmpæn'ziː/ n chimpancé m

chin /tʃɪn/ n barbilla f

china /'tʃaɪnə/ n porcelana f

Chin|a /'tʃaɪnə/ n China f. ~**ese** /-'niːz/ a & n chino (m)

chink[1] /tʃɪŋk/ n (crack) grieta f

chink[2] /tʃɪŋk/ n (sound) tintín m. ● vt hacer tintinear. ● vi tintinear

chip /tʃɪp/ n pedacito m; (splinter) astilla f; (culin) patata f frita; (gambling) ficha f. **have a ~ on one's shoulder** guardar rencor. ● vt (pt chipped) desportillar. ● vi desportillarse. ~ **in** (fam) interrumpir; (with money) contribuir

chiropodist /kɪ'rɒpədɪst/ n callista m & f

chirp /tʃɜːp/ n pío m. ● vi piar

chirpy /'tʃɜːpɪ/ a alegre

chisel /'tʃɪzl/ n formón m. ● vt (pt chiselled) cincelar

chit /tʃɪt/ n vale m, nota f

chit-chat /'tʃɪttʃæt/ n cháchara f

chivalr|ous a /'ʃɪvəlrəs/ a caballeroso. ~**y** /'ʃɪvəlrɪ/ n caballerosidad f

chive /tʃaɪv/ n cebollino m

chlorine /'klɔːriːn/ n cloro m

chock /tʃɒk/ n calzo m. ~**a-block** a, ~**full** a atestado

chocolate /'tʃɒklɪt/ n chocolate m; (individual sweet) bombón m

choice /tʃɔɪs/ n elección f; (preference) preferencia f. ● a escogido

choir /'kwaɪə(r)/ n coro m. ~**boy** /'kwaɪəbɔɪ/ n niño m de coro

choke /tʃəʊk/ vt sofocar. ● vi sofocarse. ● n (auto) estrangulador m, estárter m

cholera /'kɒlərə/ n cólera m

cholesterol /kə'lestərɒl/ n colesterol m

choose /tʃuːz/ vt/i (pt **chose**, pp **chosen**) elegir. ∼**y** /'tʃuːzɪ/ a (fam) exigente

chop /tʃɒp/ vt (pt **chopped**) cortar. ● n (culin) chuleta f. ∼ **down** talar. ∼ **off** cortar. ∼**per** n hacha f; (butcher's) cuchilla f; (sl) helicóptero m

choppy /'tʃɒpɪ/ a picado

chopstick /'tʃɒpstɪk/ n palillo m (chino)

choral /'kɔːrəl/ a coral

chord /kɔːd/ n cuerda f; (mus) acorde m

chore /tʃɔː(r)/ n tarea f, faena f. **household** ∼s npl faenas fpl domésticas

choreographer /kɒrɪ'ɒgrəfə(r)/ n coreógrafo m

chorister /'kɒrɪstə(r)/ n (singer) corista m & f

chortle /'tʃɔːtl/ n risita f alegre. ● vi reírse alegremente

chorus /'kɔːrəs/ n coro m; (of song) estribillo m

chose, chosen /tʃəʊz, 'tʃəʊzn/ see **choose**

Christ /kraɪst/ n Cristo m

christen /'krɪsn/ vt bautizar. ∼**ing** n bautizo m

Christian /'krɪstjən/ a & n cristiano (m). ∼ **name** n nombre m de pila

Christmas /'krɪsməs/ n Navidad f; (period) Navidades fpl. ● a de Navidad, navideño. ∼**box** n aguinaldo m. ∼ **day** n día m de Navidad. ∼ **Eve** n Nochebuena f. **Father** ∼ n Papá m Noel. **Happy** ∼! ¡Felices Pascuas!

chrom|e /krəʊm/ n cromo m. ∼**ium** /'krəʊmɪəm/ n cromo m. ∼**ium plating** n cromado m

chromosome /'krəʊməsəʊm/ n cromosoma m

chronic /'krɒnɪk/ a crónico; (bad, fam) terrible

chronicle /'krɒnɪkl/ n crónica f. ● vt historiar

chronolog|ical /krɒnə'lɒdʒɪkl/ a cronológico. ∼**y** /krə'nɒlədʒɪ/ n cronología f

chrysanthemum /krɪ'sænθəməm/ n crisantemo m

chubby /'tʃʌbɪ/ a (-ier, -iest) regordete; (face) mofletudo

chuck /tʃʌk/ vt (fam) arrojar. ∼ **out** tirar

chuckle /'tʃʌkl/ n risa f ahogada. ● vi reírse entre dientes

chuffed /tʃʌft/ a (sl) contento

chug /tʃʌg/ vi (pt **chugged**) (of motor) traquetear

chum /tʃʌm/ n amigo m, compinche m. ∼**my** a. be ∼**my** (2 people) ser muy amigos. be ∼**my with** ser muy amigo de

chump /tʃʌmp/ n (sl) tonto m. ∼ **chop** n chuleta f

chunk /tʃʌŋk/ n trozo m grueso. ∼**y** /'tʃʌŋkɪ/ a macizo

church /tʃɜːtʃ/ n iglesia f. ∼**yard** /'tʃɜːtʃjɑːd/ n cementerio m

churlish /'tʃɜːlɪʃ/ a grosero

churn /tʃɜːn/ n (for milk) lechera f, cántara f; (for butter) mantequera f. ● vt agitar. ∼ **out** producir en profusión

chute /ʃuːt/ n tobogán m

chutney /'tʃʌtnɪ/ n (pl -eys) condimento m agridulce

cider /'saɪdə(r)/ n sidra f

cigar /sɪ'gɑː(r)/ n puro m

cigarette /sɪgə'ret/ n cigarrillo m. ∼**holder** n boquilla f

cine-camera /'sɪnɪkæmərə/ n cámara f, tomavistas m invar

cinema /'sɪnəmə/ n cine m

cinnamon /'sɪnəmən/ n canela f

cipher /'saɪfə(r)/ n (math, fig) cero m; (secret system) cifra f

circle /'sɜːkl/ n círculo m; (in theatre) anfiteatro m. ● vt girar alrededor de. ● vi dar vueltas

circuit /'sɜːkɪt/ n circuito m; (chain) cadena f

circuitous /sɜː'kjuːɪtəs/ a indirecto

circular /'sɜːkjʊlə(r)/ a & n circular (f)

circularize /'sɜːkjʊləraɪz/ vt enviar circulares a

circulat|e /'sɜːkjʊleɪt/ vt hacer circular. ● vi circular. ∼**ion** /-'leɪʃn/ n circulación f; (of journals) tirada f

circumcis|e /'sɜːkəmsaɪz/ vt circuncidar. ∼**ion** /-'sɪʒn/ n circuncisión f

circumference /sə'kʌmfərəns/ n circunferencia f

circumflex /'sɜːkəmfleks/ a & n circunflejo (m)

circumspect /'sɜːkəmspekt/ a circunspecto

circumstance /'sɜːkəmstəns/ n circunstancia f. ∼**s** (means) npl situación f económica

circus /'sɜːkəs/ n circo m

cistern /'sɪstən/ n depósito m; (of WC) cisterna f

citadel /'sɪtədl/ n ciudadela f

citation /saɪˈteɪʃn/ n citación f
cite /saɪt/ vt citar
citizen /ˈsɪtɪzn/ n ciudadano m; (inhabitant) habitante m & f. **~ship** n ciudadanía f
citrus /ˈsɪtrəs/ n. **~ fruits** cítricos mpl
city /ˈsɪtɪ/ n ciudad f; **the C~** el centro m financiero de Londres
civic /ˈsɪvɪk/ a cívico. **~s** npl cívica f
civil /ˈsɪvl/ a civil, cortés
civilian /sɪˈvɪlɪən/ a & n civil (m & f). **~ clothes** npl traje m de paisano
civility /sɪˈvɪlətɪ/ n cortesía f
civilization /sɪvɪlaɪˈzeɪʃn/ n civilización f. **~e** /ˈsɪvəlaɪz/ vt civilizar
civil: ~ servant n funcionario m. **~ service** n administración f pública
civvies /ˈsɪvɪz/ npl. **in ~** (sl) en traje m de paisano
clad /klæd/ see **clothe**
claim /kleɪm/ vt reclamar; (assert) pretender. ● n reclamación f; (right) derecho m; (jurid) demanda f. **~ant** n demandante m & f; (to throne) pretendiente m
clairvoyant /kleəˈvɔɪənt/ n clarividente m & f
clam /klæm/ n almeja f
clamber /ˈklæmbə(r)/ vi trepar a gatas
clammy /ˈklæmɪ/ a (-ier, -iest) húmedo
clamour /ˈklæmə(r)/ n clamor m. ● vi. **~ for** pedir a voces
clamp /klæmp/ n abrazadera f; (auto) cepo m. ● vt sujetar con abrazadera. **~ down on** reprimir
clan /klæn/ n clan m
clandestine /klænˈdestɪn/ a clandestino
clang /klæŋ/ n sonido m metálico
clanger /ˈklæŋə(r)/ n (sl) metedura f de pata
clap /klæp/ vt (pt clapped) aplaudir; batir ⟨hands⟩. ● vi aplaudir. ● n palmada f; (of thunder) trueno m
claptrap /ˈklæptræp/ n charlatanería f, tonterías fpl
claret /ˈklærət/ n clarete m
clarif|ication /klærɪfɪˈkeɪʃn/ n aclaración f. **~y** /ˈklærɪfaɪ/ vt aclarar. ● vi aclararse
clarinet /klærɪˈnet/ n clarinete m
clarity /ˈklærətɪ/ n claridad f
clash /klæʃ/ n choque m; (noise) estruendo m; (contrast) contraste m; (fig) conflicto m. ● vt golpear. ● vi encontrarse; ⟨dates⟩ coincidir;

⟨opinions⟩ estar en desacuerdo; ⟨colours⟩ desentonar
clasp /klɑːsp/ n cierre m. ● vt agarrar; apretar ⟨hand⟩; (fasten) abrochar
class /klɑːs/ n clase f. **evening ~** n clase nocturna. ● vt clasificar
classic /ˈklæsɪk/ a & n clásico (m). **~al** a clásico. **~s** npl estudios mpl clásicos
classif|ication /klæsɪfɪˈkeɪʃn/ n clasificación f. **~y** /ˈklæsɪfaɪ/ vt clasificar
classroom /ˈklɑːsruːm/ n aula f
classy /ˈklɑːsɪ/ a (sl) elegante
clatter /ˈklætə(r)/ n estrépito m. ● vi hacer ruido
clause /klɔːz/ n cláusula f; (gram) oración f
claustrophobia /klɔːstrəˈfəʊbɪə/ n claustrofobia f
claw /klɔː/ n garra f; (of cat) uña f; (of crab) pinza f; (device) garfio m. ● vt arañar
clay /kleɪ/ n arcilla f
clean /kliːn/ a (-er, -est) limpio; ⟨stroke⟩ neto. ● adv completamente. ● vt limpiar. ● vi hacer la limpieza. **~ up** hacer la limpieza. **~cut** a bien definido. **~er** n mujer f de la limpieza. **~liness** /ˈklenlɪnɪs/ n limpieza f
cleans|e /klenz/ vt limpiar; (fig) purificar. **~ing cream** n crema f desmaquilladora
clear /klɪə(r)/ a (-er, -est) claro; (transparent) transparente; (without obstacles) libre; (profit) neto; ⟨sky⟩ despejado. **keep ~ of** evitar. ● adv claramente. ● vt despejar; liquidar ⟨goods⟩; (jurid) absolver; (jump over) saltar por encima de; quitar ⟨table⟩. ● vi ⟨weather⟩ despejarse; ⟨fog⟩ disolverse. **~ off** vi (sl), **~ out** vi (sl) largarse. **~ up** vt (tidy) poner en orden; aclarar ⟨mystery⟩; ● vi ⟨weather⟩ despejarse
clearance /ˈklɪərəns/ n espacio m libre; (removal of obstructions) despeje m; (authorization) permiso m; (by customs) despacho m; (by security) acreditación f. **~ sale** n liquidación f
clearing /ˈklɪərɪŋ/ n claro m
clearly /ˈklɪəlɪ/ adv evidentemente
clearway /ˈklɪəweɪ/ n carretera f en la que no se permite parar
cleavage /ˈkliːvɪdʒ/ n escote m; (fig) división f
cleave /kliːv/ vt (pt cleaved, clove or cleft; pp cloven or cleft) hender. ● vi henderse

clef /klef/ n (*mus*) clave f

cleft /kleft/ *see* **cleave**

clemen|cy /'klemənsɪ/ n clemencia f. **~t** a clemente

clench /klentʃ/ vt apretar

clergy /'klɜːdʒɪ/ n clero m. **~man** n (*pl* **-men**) clérigo m

cleric /'klerɪk/ n clérigo m. **~al** a clerical; (*of clerks*) de oficina

clerk /klɑːk/ n empleado m; (*jurid*) escribano m

clever /'klevə(r)/ a (**-er, -est**) listo; (*skilful*) hábil. **~ly** adv inteligentemente; (*with skill*) hábilmente. **~ness** n inteligencia f

cliché /'kliːʃeɪ/ n tópico m, frase f hecha

click /klɪk/ n golpecito m. ● vi chascar; (*sl*) llevarse bien

client /'klaɪənt/ n cliente m & f

clientele /kliːən'tel/ n clientela f

cliff /klɪf/ n acantilado m

climat|e /'klaɪmɪt/ n clima m. **~ic** /-'mætɪk/ a climático

climax /'klaɪmæks/ n punto m culminante

climb /klaɪm/ vt subir ⟨stairs⟩; trepar ⟨tree⟩; escalar ⟨mountain⟩. ● vi subir. ● n subida f. **~ down** bajar; (*fig*) volverse atrás, rajarse. **~er** n (*sport*) alpinista m & f; (*plant*) trepadora f

clinch /klɪntʃ/ vt cerrar ⟨deal⟩

cling /klɪŋ/ vi (*pt* **clung**) agarrarse; (*stick*) pegarse

clinic /'klɪnɪk/ n clínica f. **~al** /'klɪnɪkl/ a clínico

clink /klɪŋk/ n sonido m metálico. ● vt hacer tintinear. ● vi tintinear

clinker /'klɪŋkə(r)/ n escoria f

clip[1] /klɪp/ n (*for paper*) sujetapapeles m invar; (*for hair*) horquilla f. ● vt (*pt* **clipped**) (*join*) sujetar

clip[2] /klɪp/ n (*with scissors*) tijeretada f; (*blow, fam*) golpe m. ● vt (*pt* **clipped**) (*cut*) cortar; (*fam*) golpear. **~pers** /'klɪpəz/ npl (*for hair*) maquinilla f para cortar el pelo; (*for nails*) cortauñas m invar. **~ping** n recorte m

clique /kliːk/ n pandilla f

cloak /kləʊk/ n capa f. **~room** /'kləʊkruːm/ n guardarropa m; (*toilet*) servicios mpl

clobber /'klɒbə(r)/ n (*sl*) trastos mpl. ● vt (*sl*) dar una paliza a

clock /klɒk/ n reloj m. **grandfather ~** reloj de caja. ● vi. **~ in** fichar, registrar la llegada. **~wise** /'klɒkwaɪz/ a & adv en el sentido de las agujas del reloj, a la derecha. **~work** /'klɒkwɜːk/ n mecanismo m de relojería. **like ~work** con precisión

clod /klɒd/ n terrón m

clog /klɒg/ n zueco m. ● vt (*pt* **clogged**) atascar. ● vi atascarse

cloister /'klɔɪstə(r)/ n claustro m

close[1] /kləʊs/ a (**-er, -est**) cercano; (*together*) apretado; ⟨friend⟩ íntimo; ⟨weather⟩ bochornoso; ⟨link etc⟩ estrecho; ⟨game, battle⟩ reñido. **have a ~ shave** (*fig*) escaparse de milagro. ● adv cerca. ● n recinto m

close[2] /kləʊz/ vt cerrar. ● vi cerrarse; (*end*) terminar. ● n fin m. **~d shop** n empresa f que emplea solamente a miembros del sindicato

close: **~ly** adv de cerca; (*with attention*) atentamente; (*exactly*) exactamente. **~ness** n proximidad f; (*togetherness*) intimidad f

closet /'klɒzɪt/ n (*Amer*) armario m

close-up /'kləʊsʌp/ n (*cinema etc*) primer plano m

closure /'kləʊʒə(r)/ n cierre m

clot /klɒt/ n (*culin*) grumo m; (*med*) coágulo m; (*sl*) tonto m. ● vi (*pt* **clotted**) cuajarse

cloth /klɒθ/ n tela f; (*duster*) trapo m; (*table-cloth*) mantel m

cloth|e /kləʊð/ vt (*pt* **clothed** *or* **clad**) vestir. **~es** /kləʊðz/ npl, **~ing** n ropa f

cloud /klaʊd/ n nube f. ● vi nublarse. **~burst** /'klaʊdbɜːst/ n chaparrón m. **~y** a (**-ier, -iest**) nublado; ⟨liquid⟩ turbio

clout /klaʊt/ n bofetada f. ● vt abofetear

clove[1] /kləʊv/ n clavo m

clove[2] /kləʊv/ n. **~ of garlic** n diente m de ajo

clove[3] /kləʊv/ *see* **cleave**

clover /'kləʊvə(r)/ n trébol m

clown /klaʊn/ n payaso m. ● vi hacer el payaso

cloy /klɔɪ/ vt empalagar

club /klʌb/ n club m; (*weapon*) porra f; (*at cards*) trébol m. ● vt (*pt* **clubbed**) aporrear. ● vi. **~ together** reunirse, pagar a escote

cluck /klʌk/ vi cloquear

clue /kluː/ n pista f; (*in crosswords*) indicación f. **not to have a ~** no tener la menor idea

clump /klʌmp/ *n* grupo *m*. ● *vt* agrupar. ● *vi* pisar fuertemente

clums|iness /'klʌmzɪnɪs/ *n* torpeza *f*. **~y** /'klʌmzɪ/ *a* (**-ier, -iest**) torpe

clung /klʌŋ/ *see* **cling**

cluster /'klʌstə(r)/ *n* grupo *m*. ● *vi* agruparse

clutch /klʌtʃ/ *vt* agarrar. ● *n* (*auto*) embrague *m*

clutter /'klʌtə(r)/ *n* desorden *m*. ● *vt* llenar desordenadamente

coach /kəʊtʃ/ *n* autocar *m*; (*of train*) vagón *m*; (*horse-drawn*) coche *m*; (*sport*) entrenador *m*. ● *vt* dar clases particulares; (*sport*) entrenar

coagulate /kəʊ'ægjʊleɪt/ *vt* coagular. ● *vi* coagularse

coal /kəʊl/ *n* carbón *m*. **~field** /'kəʊlfi:ld/ *n* yacimiento *m* de carbón

coalition /kəʊə'lɪʃn/ *n* coalición *f*

coarse /kɔːs/ *a* (**-er, -est**) grosero; ⟨*material*⟩ basto. **~ness** *n* grosería *f*; (*texture*) basteza *f*

coast /kəʊst/ *n* costa *f*. ● *vi* (*with cycle*) deslizarse cuesta abajo; (*with car*) ir en punto muerto. **~al** *a* costero. **~er** /'kəʊstə(r)/ *n* (*ship*) barco *m* de cabotaje; (*for glass*) posavasos *m invar*. **~guard** /'kəʊstga:d/ *n* guardacostas *m invar*. **~line** /'kəʊstlaɪn/ *n* litoral *m*

coat /kəʊt/ *n* abrigo *m*; (*jacket*) chaqueta *f*; (*of animal*) pelo *m*; (*of paint*) mano *f*. ● *vt* cubrir, revestir. **~ing** *n* capa *f*. **~ of arms** *n* escudo *m* de armas

coax /kəʊks/ *vt* engatusar

cob /kɒb/ *n* (*of corn*) mazorca *f*

cobble[1] /'kɒbl/ *n* guijarro *m*, adoquín *m*. ● *vt* empedrar con guijarros, adoquinar

cobble[2] /'kɒbl/ *vt* (*mend*) remendar. **~r** /'kɒblə(r)/ *n* (*old use*) remendón *m*

cobweb /'kɒbweb/ *n* telaraña *f*

cocaine /kə'keɪn/ *n* cocaína *f*

cock /kɒk/ *n* gallo *m*; (*mec*) grifo *m*; (*of gun*) martillo *m*. ● *vt* amartillar ⟨*gun*⟩; aguzar ⟨*ears*⟩. **~-and-bull story** *n* patraña *f*. **~erel** /'kɒkərəl/ *n* gallo *m*. **~-eyed** *a* (*sl*) torcido

cockle /'kɒkl/ *n* berberecho *m*

cockney /'kɒknɪ/ *a & n* (*pl* **-eys**) londinense (*m & f*) (del este de Londres)

cockpit /'kɒkpɪt/ *n* (*in aircraft*) cabina *f* del piloto

cockroach /'kɒkrəʊtʃ/ *n* cucaracha *f*

cocksure /kɒk'ʃʊə(r)/ *a* presuntuoso

cocktail /'kɒkteɪl/ *n* cóctel *m*. **fruit ~** macedonia *f* de frutas

cock-up /'kɒkʌp/ *n* (*sl*) lío *m*

cocky /'kɒkɪ/ *a* (**-ier, -iest**) engreído

cocoa /'kəʊkəʊ/ *n* cacao *m*; (*drink*) chocolate *m*

coconut /'kəʊkənʌt/ *n* coco *m*

cocoon /kə'ku:n/ *n* capullo *m*

cod /kɒd/ *n* (*pl* **cod**) bacalao *m*, abadejo *m*

coddle /'kɒdl/ *vt* mimar; (*culin*) cocer a fuego lento

code /kəʊd/ *n* código *m*; (*secret*) cifra *f*

codify /'kəʊdɪfaɪ/ *vt* codificar

cod-liver oil /'kɒdlɪvə(r)ɔɪl/ *n* aceite *m* de hígado de bacalao

coeducational /kəʊedʒʊ'keɪʃənl/ *a* mixto

coerc|e /kəʊ'ɜːs/ *vt* obligar. **~ion** /-ʃn/ *n* coacción *f*

coexist /kəʊɪg'zɪst/ *vi* coexistir. **~ence** *n* coexistencia *f*

coffee /'kɒfɪ/ *n* café *m*. **~-mill** *n* molinillo *m* de café. **~-pot** *n* cafetera *f*

coffer /'kɒfə(r)/ *n* cofre *m*

coffin /'kɒfɪn/ *n* ataúd *m*

cog /kɒg/ *n* diente *m*; (*fig*) pieza *f*

cogent /'kəʊdʒənt/ *a* convincente

cohabit /kəʊ'hæbɪt/ *vi* cohabitar

coherent /kəʊ'hɪərənt/ *a* coherente

coil /kɔɪl/ *vt* enrollar. ● *n* rollo *m*; (*one ring*) vuelta *f*

coin /kɔɪn/ *n* moneda *f*. ● *vt* acuñar. **~age** *n* sistema *m* monetario

coincide /kəʊɪn'saɪd/ *vi* coincidir

coinciden|ce /kəʊ'ɪnsɪdəns/ *n* casualidad *f*. **~tal** /-'dentl/ *a* casual; (*coinciding*) coincidente

coke /kəʊk/ *n* (*coal*) coque *m*

colander /'kʌləndə(r)/ *n* colador *m*

cold /kəʊld/ *a* (**-er, -est**) frío. **be ~** tener frío. **it is ~** hace frío. ● *n* frío *m*; (*med*) resfriado *m*. **have a ~** estar constipado. **~-blooded** *a* insensible. **~ cream** *n* crema *f*. **~ feet** (*fig*) mieditis *f*. **~ness** *n* frialdad *f*. **~-shoulder** *vt* tratar con frialdad. **~ sore** *n* herpes *m* labial. **~ storage** *n* conservación *f* en frigorífico

çoleslaw /'kəʊlslɔː/ *n* ensalada *f* de col

colic /'kɒlɪk/ *n* cólico *m*

collaborat|e /kə'læbəreɪt/ *vi* colaborar. **~ion** /-'reɪʃn/ *n* colaboración *f*. **~or** *n* colaborador *m*

collage /'kɒlɑːʒ/ *n* collage *m*

collaps|e /kə'læps/ *vi* derrumbarse; (*med*) sufrir un colapso. ● *n* derrumbamiento *m*; (*med*) colapso *m*. ~**ible** /kə'læpsəbl/ *a* plegable

collar /'kɒlə(r)/ *n* cuello *m*; (*for animals*) collar *m*. ● *vt* (*fam*) hurtar. ~**bone** *n* clavícula *f*

colleague /'kɒliːg/ *n* colega *m* & *f*

collect /kə'lekt/ *vt* reunir; (*hobby*) coleccionar; (*pick up*) recoger; recaudar ⟨*rent*⟩. ● *vi* ⟨*people*⟩ reunirse; ⟨*things*⟩ acumularse. ~**ed** /kə'lektɪd/ *a* reunido; ⟨*person*⟩ tranquilo. ~**ion** /-ʃn/ *n* colección *f*; (*in church*) colecta *f*; (*of post*) recogida *f*. ~**ive** /kə'lektɪv/ *a* colectivo. ~**or** *n* coleccionista *m* & *f*; (*of taxes*) recaudador *m*

college /'kɒlɪdʒ/ *n* colegio *m*; (*of art, music etc*) escuela *f*; (*univ*) colegio *m* mayor

collide /kə'laɪd/ *vi* chocar

colliery /'kɒlɪərɪ/ *n* mina *f* de carbón

collision /kə'lɪʒn/ *n* choque *m*

colloquial /kə'ləʊkwɪəl/ *a* familiar. ~**ism** *n* expresión *f* familiar

collusion /kə'luːʒn/ *n* connivencia *f*

colon /'kəʊlən/ *n* (*gram*) dos puntos *mpl*; (*med*) colon *m*

colonel /'kɜːnl/ *n* coronel *m*

colon|ial /kə'ləʊnɪəl/ *a* colonial. ~**ize** /'kɒlənaɪz/ *vt* colonizar. ~**y** /'kɒlənɪ/ *n* colonia *f*

colossal /kə'lɒsl/ *a* colosal

colour /'kʌlə(r)/ *n* color *m*. **off** ~ (*fig*) indispuesto. ● *a* de color(es), en color(es). ● *vt* colorar; (*dye*) teñir. ● *vi* (*blush*) sonrojarse. ~ **bar** *n* barrera *f* racial. ~**-blind** *a* daltoniano. ~**ed** /'kʌləd/ *a* de color. ~**ful** *a* lleno de color; (*fig*) pintoresco. ~**less** *a* incoloro. ~**s** *npl* (*flag*) bandera *f*

colt /kəʊlt/ *n* potro *m*

column /'kɒləm/ *n* columna *f*. ~**ist** /'kɒləmnɪst/ *n* columnista *m* & *f*

coma /'kəʊmə/ *n* coma *f*

comb /kəʊm/ *n* peine *m*. ● *vt* peinar; (*search*) registrar

combat /'kɒmbæt/ *n* combate *m*. ● *vt* (*pt* **combated**) combatir. ~**ant** /-ətənt/ *n* combatiente *m* & *f*

combination /kɒmbɪ'neɪʃn/ *n* combinación *f*

combine /kəm'baɪn/ *vt* combinar. ● *vi* combinarse. /'kɒmbaɪn/ *n* asociación *f*. ~**harvester** *n* cosechadora *f*

combustion /kəm'bʌstʃən/ *n* combustión *f*

come /kʌm/ *vi* (*pt* **came**, *pp* **come**) venir; (*occur*) pasar. ~ **about** ocurrir. ~ **across** encontrarse con ⟨*person*⟩; encontrar ⟨*object*⟩. ~ **apart** deshacerse. ~ **away** marcharse. ~ **back** volver. ~ **by** obtener; (*pass*) pasar. ~ **down** bajar. ~ **in** entrar. ~ **in for** recibir. ~ **into** heredar ⟨*money*⟩. ~ **off** desprenderse; (*succeed*) tener éxito. ~ **off it!** (*fam*) ¡no me vengas con eso! ~ **out** salir; (*result*) resultar. ~ **round** (*after fainting*) volver en sí; (*be converted*) cambiar de idea. ~ **to** llegar a ⟨*decision etc*⟩. ~ **up** subir; (*fig*) salir. ~ **up with** proponer ⟨*idea*⟩

comeback /'kʌmbæk/ *n* retorno *m*; (*retort*) réplica *f*

comedian /kə'miːdɪən/ *n* cómico *m*

comedown /'kʌmdaʊn/ *n* revés *m*

comedy /'kɒmədɪ/ *n* comedia *f*

comely /'kʌmlɪ/ *a* (**-ier, -iest**) (*old use*) bonito

comet /'kɒmɪt/ *n* cometa *m*

comeuppance /kʌm'ʌpəns/ *n* (*Amer*) merecido *m*

comf|ort /'kʌmfət/ *n* bienestar *m*; (*consolation*) consuelo *m*. ● *vt* consolar. ~**ortable** *a* cómodo; (*wealthy*) holgado. ~**y** /'kʌmfɪ/ *a* (*fam*) cómodo

comic /'kɒmɪk/ *a* cómico. ● *n* cómico *m*; (*periodical*) tebeo *m*. ~**al** *a* cómico. ~ **strip** *n* historieta *f*

coming /'kʌmɪŋ/ *n* llegada *f*. ● *a* próximo; ⟨*week, month etc*⟩ que viene. ~ **and going** ir y venir

comma /'kɒmə/ *n* coma *f*

command /kə'mɑːnd/ *n* orden *f*; (*mastery*) dominio *m*. ● *vt* mandar; (*deserve*) merecer

commandeer /kɒmən'dɪə(r)/ *vt* requisar

commander /kə'mɑːndə(r)/ *n* comandante *m*

commanding /kə'mɑːndɪŋ/ *a* imponente

commandment /kə'mɑːndmənt/ *n* mandamiento *m*

commando /kə'mɑːndəʊ/ *n* (*pl* **-os**) comando *m*

commemorat|e /kə'meməreɪt/ *vt* conmemorar. ~**ion** /-'reɪʃn/ *n* conmemoración *f*. ~**ive** /-ətɪv/ *a* conmemorativo

commence /kə'mens/ *vt/i* empezar. ~**ment** *n* principio *m*

commend /kə'mend/ *vt* alabar; (*entrust*) encomendar. ∼**able** *a* loable. ∼**ation** /kɒmen'deɪʃn/ *n* elogio *m*

commensurate /kə'menʃərət/ *a* proporcionado

comment /'kɒment/ *n* observación *f*. ● *vi* hacer observaciones

commentary /'kɒməntrɪ/ *n* comentario *m*; (*radio*, *TV*) reportaje *m*

commentat|e /'kɒmənteɪt/ *vi* narrar. ∼**or** *n* (*radio*, *TV*) locutor *m*

commerc|e /'kɒmɜ:s/ *n* comercio *m*. ∼**ial** /kə'mɜ:ʃl/ *a* comercial. ● *n* anuncio *m*. ∼**ialize** *vt* comercializar

commiserat|e /kə'mɪzəreɪt/ *vt* compadecer. ● *vi* compadecerse (**with** de). ∼**ion** /-'reɪʃn/ *n* conmiseración *f*

commission /kə'mɪʃn/ *n* comisión *f*. **out of** ∼ fuera de servicio. ● *vt* encargar; (*mil*) nombrar

commissionaire /kəmɪʃə'neə(r)/ *n* portero *m*

commissioner /kə'mɪʃənə(r)/ *n* comisario *m*; (*of police*) jefe *m*

commit /kə'mɪt/ *vt* (*pt* **committed**) cometer; (*entrust*) confiar. ∼ **o.s.** comprometerse. ∼ **to memory** aprender de memoria. ∼**ment** *n* compromiso *m*

committee /kə'mɪtɪ/ *n* comité *m*

commodity /kə'mɒdətɪ/ *n* producto *m*, artículo *m*

common /'kɒmən/ *a* (**-er**, **-est**) común; (*usual*) corriente; (*vulgar*) ordinario. ● *n* ejido *m*

commoner /'kɒmənə(r)/ *n* plebeyo *m*

common: ∼ **law** *n* derecho *m* consuetudinario. ∼**ly** *adv* comúnmente. **C∼ Market** *n* Mercado *m* Común

commonplace /'kɒmənpleɪs/ *a* banal. ● *n* banalidad *f*

common: ∼**room** *n* sala *f* común, salón *m* común. ∼ **sense** *n* sentido *m* común

Commonwealth /'kɒmənwelθ/ *n*. **the** ∼ la Mancomunidad *f* Británica

commotion /kə'məʊʃn/ *n* confusión *f*

communal /'kɒmjʊnl/ *a* comunal

commune[1] /'kɒmju:n/ *n* comuna *f*

commune[2] /kə'mju:n/ *vi* comunicarse

communicat|e /kə'mju:nɪkeɪt/ *vt* comunicar. ● *vi* comunicarse. ∼**ion** /-'keɪʃn/ *n* comunicación *f*. ∼**ive** /-ətɪv/ *a* comunicativo

communion /kə'mju:nɪən/ *n* comunión *f*

communiqué /kə'mju:nɪkeɪ/ *n* comunicado *m*

communis|m /'kɒmjʊnɪsəm/ *n* comunismo *m*. ∼**t** /'kɒmjʊnɪst/ *n* comunista *m* & *f*

community /kə'mju:nətɪ/ *n* comunidad *f*. ∼ **centre** *n* centro *m* social

commute /kə'mju:t/ *vi* viajar diariamente. ● *vt* (*jurid*) conmutar. ∼**r** /-ə(r)/ *n* viajero *m* diario

compact /kəm'pækt/ *a* compacto. /'kɒmpækt/ *n* (*for powder*) polvera *f*. ∼ **disc** /'kɒm-/ *n* disco *m* compacto

companion /kəm'pænɪən/ *n* compañero *m*. ∼**ship** *n* compañerismo *m*

company /'kʌmpənɪ/ *n* compañía *f*; (*guests*, *fam*) visita *f*; (*com*) sociedad *f*

compar|able /'kɒmpərəbl/ *a* comparable. ∼**ative** /kəm'pærətɪv/ *a* comparativo; (*fig*) relativo. ● *n* (*gram*) comparativo *m*. ∼**e** /kəm'peə(r)/ *vt* comparar. ● *vi* poderse comparar. ∼**ison** /kəm'pærɪsn/ *n* comparación *f*

compartment /kəm'pɑ:tmənt/ *n* compartimiento *m*; (*on train*) departamento *m*

compass /'kʌmpəs/ *n* brújula *f*. ∼**es** *npl* compás *m*

compassion /kəm'pæʃn/ *n* compasión *f*. ∼**ate** *a* compasivo

compatib|ility /kəmpætə'bɪlətɪ/ *n* compatibilidad *f*. ∼**le** /kəm'pætəbl/ *a* compatible

compatriot /kəm'pætrɪət/ *n* compatriota *m* & *f*

compel /kəm'pel/ *vt* (*pt* **compelled**) obligar. ∼**ling** *a* irresistible

compendium /kəm'pendɪəm/ *n* compendio *m*

compensat|e /'kɒmpənseɪt/ *vt* compensar; (*for loss*) indemnizar. ● *vi* compensar. ∼**ion** /-'seɪʃn/ *n* compensación *f*; (*financial*) indemnización *f*

compère /'kɒmpeə(r)/ *n* presentador *m*. ● *vt* presentar

compete /kəm'pi:t/ *vi* competir

competen|ce /'kɒmpətəns/ *n* competencia *f*, aptitud *f*. ∼**t** /'kɒmpɪtənt/ *a* competente, capaz

competit|ion /kɒmpə'tɪʃn/ *n* (*contest*) concurso *m*; (*com*) competencia *f*. ∼**ive** /kəm'petətɪv/ *a*

competidor; ⟨*price*⟩ competitivo.
∼or /kəm'petɪtə(r)/ *n* competidor
m; (*in contest*) concursante *m & f*
compile /kəm'paɪl/ *vt* compilar. **∼r**
/-ə(r)/ *n* recopilador *m*, compilador
m
complacen|cy /kəm'pleɪsənsɪ/ *n*
satisfacción *f* de sí mismo. **∼t**
/kəm'pleɪsnt/ *a* satisfecho de sí
mismo
complain /kəm'pleɪn/ *vi*. **∼** (*about*)
quejarse (de). **∼ of** (*med*) sufrir de.
∼t /kəm'pleɪnt/ *n* queja *f*; (*med*)
enfermedad *f*
complement /'kɒmplɪmənt/ *n* complemento *m*. ● *vt* complementar.
∼ary /-'mentrɪ/ *a* complementario
complet|e /kəm'pli:t/ *a* completo;
(*finished*) acabado; (*downright*)
total. ● *vt* acabar; llenar ⟨*a form*⟩.
∼ely *adv* completamente. **∼ion**
/-ʃn/ *n* conclusión *f*
complex /'kɒmpleks/ *a* complejo.
● *n* complejo *m*
complexion /kəm'plekʃn/ *n* tez *f*;
(*fig*) aspecto *m*
complexity /kəm'pleksətɪ/ *n* com-
plejidad *f*
complian|ce /kəm'plaɪəns/ *n* sumi-
sión *f*. **in ∼ce with** de acuerdo con.
∼t *a* sumiso
complicat|e /'kɒmplɪkeɪt/ *vt* com-
plicar. **∼ed** *a* complicado. **∼ion**
/-'keɪʃn/ *n* complicación *f*
complicity /kəm'plɪsətɪ/ *n* com-
plicidad *f*
compliment /'kɒmplɪmənt/ *n* cumplido *m*; (*amorous*) piropo *m*. ● *vt*
felicitar. **∼ary** /-'mentrɪ/ *a* hal-
agador; (*given free*) de favor. **∼s** *npl*
saludos *mpl*
comply /kəm'plaɪ/ *vi*. **∼ with** conformarse con
component /kəm'pəʊnənt/ *a & n*
componente (*m*)
compose /kəm'pəʊz/ *vt* componer.
∼ o.s. tranquilizarse. **∼d** *a* sereno
compos|er /kəm'pəʊzə(r)/ *n* com-
positor *m*. **∼ition** /kɒmpə'zɪʃn/ *n*
composición *f*
compost /'kɒmpɒst/ *n* abono *m*
composure /kəm'pəʊʒə(r)/ *n* ser-
enidad *f*
compound[1] /'kɒmpaʊnd/ *n* compuesto *m*. ● *a* compuesto; ⟨*fracture*⟩
complicado. /kəm'paʊnd/ *vt* componer; agravar ⟨*problem etc*⟩. ● *vi*
(*settle*) arreglarse

compound[2] /'kɒmpaʊnd/ *n* (*enclosure*) recinto *m*
comprehen|d /kɒmprɪ'hend/ *vt*
comprender. **∼sion** /kɒmprɪ'henʃn/
n comprensión *f*
comprehensive /kɒmprɪ'hensɪv/ *a*
extenso; ⟨*insurance*⟩ a todo riesgo.
∼ school *n* instituto *m*
compress /'kɒmpres/ *n* (*med*) compresa *f*. /kəm'pres/ *vt* comprimir;
(*fig*) condensar. **∼ion** /-ʃn/ *n* com-
presión *f*
comprise /kəm'praɪz/ *vt* comprender
compromise /'kɒmprəmaɪz/ *n*
acuerdo *m*, acomodo *m*, arreglo *m*.
● *vt* comprometer. ● *vi* llegar a un
acuerdo
compuls|ion /kəm'pʌlʃn/ *n* obli-
gación *f*, impulso *m*. **∼ive**
/kəm'pʌlsɪv/ *a* compulsivo. **∼ory**
/kəm'pʌlsərɪ/ *a* obligatorio
compunction /kəm'pʌŋkʃn/ *n*
remordimiento *m*
computer /kəm'pju:tə(r)/ *n* ordenador *m*. **∼ize** *vt* instalar ord-
enadores en. **be ∼ized** tener
ordenador
comrade /'kɒmreɪd/ *n* camarada *m*
& f. **∼ship** *n* camaradería *f*
con[1] /kɒn/ *vt* (*pt* **conned**) (*fam*)
estafar. ● *n* (*fam*) estafa *f*
con[2] /kɒn/ *see* **pro and con**
concave /'kɒŋkeɪv/ *a* cóncavo
conceal /kən'si:l/ *vt* ocultar. **∼ment**
n encubrimiento *m*
concede /kən'si:d/ *vt* conceder
conceit /kən'si:t/ *n* vanidad *f*. **∼ed** *a*
engreído
conceiv|able /kən'si:vəbl/ *a* con-
cebible. **∼ably** *adv*. **may ∼ably** es
concebible que. **∼e** /kən'si:v/ *vt/i*
concebir
concentrat|e /'kɒnsəntreɪt/ *vt* con-
centrar. ● *vi* concentrarse. **∼ion**
/-'treɪʃn/ *n* concentración *f*. **∼ion
camp** *n* campo *m* de concentración
concept /'kɒnsept/ *n* concepto *m*
conception /kən'sepʃn/ *n* con-
cepción *f*
conceptual /kən'septʃʊəl/ *a* conceptual
concern /kən'sɜ:n/ *n* asunto *m*;
(*worry*) preocupación *f*; (*com*)
empresa *f*. ● *vt* tener que ver con;
(*deal with*) tratar de. **as far as I'm
∼ed** en cuanto a mí. **be ∼ed about**
preocuparse por. **∼ing** *prep* acerca
de

concert /'kɒnsət/ n concierto m. in ~ de común acuerdo. ~ed /kən'sɜːtɪd/ a concertado

concertina /kɒnsə'tiːnə/ n concertina f

concerto /kən'tʃɜːtəʊ/ n (pl -os) concierto m

concession /kən'seʃn/ n concesión f

conciliat|e /kən'sɪlɪeɪt/ vt conciliar. ~ion /-'eɪʃn/ n conciliación f

concise /kən'saɪs/ a conciso. ~ly adv concisamente. ~ness n concisión f

conclu|de /kən'kluːd/ vt concluir. ● vi concluirse. ~ding a final. ~sion n conclusión f

conclusive /kən'kluːsɪv/ a decisivo. ~ly adv concluyentemente

concoct /kən'kɒkt/ vt confeccionar; (fig) inventar. ~ion /-ʃn/ n mezcla f; (drink) brebaje m

concourse /'kɒŋkɔːs/ n (rail) vestíbulo m

concrete /'kɒŋkriːt/ n hormigón m. ● a concreto. ● vt cubrir con hormigón

concur /kən'kɜː(r)/ vi (pt concurred) estar de acuerdo

concussion /kən'kʌʃn/ n conmoción f cerebral

condemn /kən'dem/ vt condenar. ~ation /kɒndem'neɪʃn/ n condenación f, condena f; (censure) censura f

condens|ation /kɒnden'seɪʃn/ n condensación f. ~e /kən'dens/ vt condensar. ● vi condensarse

condescend /kɒndɪ'send/ vi dignarse (to a). ~ing a superior

condiment /'kɒndɪmənt/ n condimento m

condition /kən'dɪʃn/ n condición f. on ~ that a condición de que. ● vt condicionar. ~al a condicional. ~er n acondicionador m; (for hair) suavizante m

condolences /kən'dəʊlənsɪz/ npl pésame m

condom /'kɒndɒm/ n condón m

condone /kən'dəʊn/ vt condonar

conducive /kən'djuːsɪv/ a. be ~ to ser favorable a

conduct /kən'dʌkt/ vt conducir; dirigir ⟨orchestra⟩. /'kɒndʌkt/ n conducta f. ~or /kən'dʌktə(r)/ n director m; (of bus) cobrador m. ~ress n cobradora f

cone /kəʊn/ n cono m; (for ice-cream) cucurucho m

confectioner /kən'fekʃənə(r)/ n pastelero m. ~y n dulces mpl, golosinas fpl

confederation /kənfedə'reɪʃn/ n confederación f

confer /kən'fɜː(r)/ vt (pt conferred) conferir. ● vi consultar

conference /'kɒnfərəns/ n congreso m

confess /kən'fes/ vt confesar. ● vi confesarse. ~ion /-ʃn/ n confesión f. ~ional n confes(i)onario m. ~or n confesor m

confetti /kən'fetɪ/ n confeti m, confetis mpl

confide /kən'faɪd/ vt/i confiar

confiden|ce /'kɒnfɪdəns/ n confianza f; (secret) confidencia f. ~ce trick n estafa f, timo m. ~t /'kɒnfɪdənt/ a seguro

confidential /kɒnfɪ'denʃl/ a confidencial

confine /kən'faɪn/ vt confinar; (limit) limitar. ~ment n (imprisonment) prisión f; (med) parto m

confines /'kɒnfaɪnz/ npl confines mpl

confirm /kən'fɜːm/ vt confirmar. ~ation /kɒnfə'meɪʃn/ n confirmación f. ~ed a inveterado

confiscat|e /'kɒnfɪskeɪt/ vt confiscar. ~ion /-'keɪʃn/ n confiscación f

conflagration /kɒnflə'greɪʃn/ n conflagración f

conflict /'kɒnflɪkt/ n conflicto m. /kən'flɪkt/ vi chocar. ~ing /kən-/ a contradictorio

conform /kən'fɔːm/ vt conformar. ● vi conformarse. ~ist n conformista m & f

confound /kən'faʊnd/ vt confundir. ~ed a (fam) maldito

confront /kən'frʌnt/ vt hacer frente a; (face) enfrentarse con. ~ation /kɒnfrʌn'teɪʃn/ n confrontación f

confus|e /kən'fjuːz/ vt confundir. ~ing a desconcertante. ~ion /-ʒn/ n confusión f

congeal /kən'dʒiːl/ vt coagular. ● vi coagularse

congenial /kən'dʒiːnɪəl/ a simpático

congenital /kən'dʒenɪtl/ a congénito

congest|ed /kən'dʒestɪd/ a congestionado. ~ion /-tʃən/ n congestión f

congratulat|e /kən'grætjʊleɪt/ vt felicitar. ~ions /-'leɪʃnz/ npl felicitaciones fpl

congregat|e /'kɒŋgrɪgeɪt/ vi congregarse. **~ion** /-'geɪʃn/ n asamblea f; (relig) fieles mpl, feligreses mpl

congress /'kɒŋgres/ n congreso m. **C~** (Amer) el Congreso

conic(al) /'kɒnɪk(l)/ a cónico

conifer /'kɒnɪfə(r)/ n conífera f

conjecture /kən'dʒektʃə(r)/ n conjetura f. ● vt conjeturar. ● vi hacer conjeturas

conjugal /'kɒndʒʊgl/ a conyugal

conjugat|e /'kɒndʒʊgeɪt/ vt conjugar. **~ion** /-'geɪʃn/ n conjugación f

conjunction /kən'dʒʌŋkʃn/ n conjunción f

conjur|e /'kʌndʒə(r)/ vi hacer juegos de manos. ● vt. **~e up** evocar. **~or** n prestidigitador m

conk /kɒŋk/ vi. **~ out** (sl) fallar; (person) desmayarse

conker /'kɒŋkə(r)/ n (fam) castaña f de Indias

conman /'kɒnmæn/ n (fam) estafador m, timador m

connect /kə'nekt/ vt juntar; (elec) conectar. ● vi unirse; (elec) conectarse. **~ with** (train) enlazar con. **~ed** a unido; (related) relacionado. **be ~ed with** tener que ver con, estar emparentado con

connection /kə'nekʃn/ n unión f; (rail) enlace m; (elec, mec) conexión f; (fig) relación f. **in ~ with** a propósito de, con respecto a. **~s** npl relaciones fpl

conniv|ance /kə'naɪvəns/ n connivencia f. **~e** /kə'naɪv/ vi. **~e at** hacer la vista gorda a

connoisseur /kɒnə'sɜ:(r)/ n experto m

connot|ation /kɒnə'teɪʃn/ n connotación f. **~e** /kə'nəʊt/ vt connotar; (imply) implicar

conquer /'kɒŋkə(r)/ vt conquistar; (fig) vencer. **~or** n conquistador m

conquest /'kɒŋkwest/ n conquista f

conscience /'kɒnʃəns/ n conciencia f

conscientious /kɒnʃɪ'enʃəs/ a concienzudo

conscious /'kɒnʃəs/ a consciente; (deliberate) intencional. **~ly** adv a sabiendas. **~ness** n consciencia f; (med) conocimiento m

conscript /'kɒnskrɪpt/ n recluta m. /kən'skrɪpt/ vt reclutar. **~ion** /kən'skrɪpʃn/ n reclutamiento m

consecrat|e /'kɒnsɪkreɪt/ vt consagrar. **~ion** /-'kreɪʃn/ n consagración f

consecutive /kən'sekjʊtɪv/ a sucesivo

consensus /kən'sensəs/ n consenso m

consent /kən'sent/ vi consentir. ● n consentimiento m

consequen|ce /'kɒnsɪkwəns/ n consecuencia f. **~t** /'kɒnsɪkwənt/ a consiguiente. **~tly** adv por consiguiente

conservation /kɒnsə'veɪʃn/ n conservación f, preservación f. **~ist** /kɒnsə'veɪʃənɪst/ n conservacionista m & f

conservative /kən'sɜ:vətɪv/ a conservador; (modest) prudente, moderado. **C~** a & n conservador (m)

conservatory /kən'sɜ:vətrɪ/ n (greenhouse) invernadero m

conserve /kən'sɜ:v/ vt conservar

consider /kən'sɪdə(r)/ vt considerar; (take into account) tomar en cuenta. **~able** /kən'sɪdərəbl/ a considerable. **~ably** adv considerablemente

considerat|e /kən'sɪdərət/ a considerado. **~ion** /-'reɪʃn/ n consideración f

considering /kən'sɪdərɪŋ/ prep en vista de

consign /kən'saɪn/ vt consignar; (send) enviar. **~ment** n envío m

consist /kən'sɪst/ vi. **~ of** consistir en

consistency /kən'sɪstənsɪ/ n consistencia f; (fig) coherencia f

consistent /kən'sɪstənt/ a coherente; (unchanging) constante. **~ with** compatible con. **~ly** adv constantemente

consolation /kɒnsə'leɪʃn/ n consuelo m

console /kən'səʊl/ vt consolar

consolidat|e /kən'sɒlɪdeɪt/ vt consolidar. ● vi consolidarse. **~ion** /-'deɪʃn/ n consolidación f

consonant /'kɒnsənənt/ n consonante f

consort /'kɒnsɔ:t/ n consorte m & f. /kən'sɔ:t/ vi. **~ with** asociarse con

consortium /kən'sɔ:tɪəm/ n (pl -tia) consorcio m

conspicuous /kən'spɪkjʊəs/ a (easily seen) visible; (showy) llamativo; (noteworthy) notable

conspir|acy /kən'spɪrəsɪ/ n complot m, conspiración f. **~e** /kən'spaɪə(r)/ vi conspirar

constab|le /'kʌnstəbl/ n policía m, guardia m. **~ulary** /kən'stæbjʊlərɪ/ n policía f

constant /'kɒnstənt/ a constante. **~ly** adv constantemente

constellation /kɒnstə'leɪʃn/ n constelación f

consternation /kɒnstə'neɪʃn/ n consternación f

constipat|ed /'kɒnstɪpeɪtɪd/ a estreñido. **~ion** /-'peɪʃn/ n estreñimiento m

constituen|cy /kən'stɪtjʊənsɪ/ n distrito m electoral. **~t** /kən'stɪtjʊənt/ n componente m; (pol) elector m

constitut|e /'kɒnstɪtjuːt/ vt constituir. **~ion** /-'tjuːʃn/ n constitución f. **~ional** /-'tjuːʃənl/ a constitucional. ● n paseo m

constrain /kən'streɪn/ vt forzar, obligar, constreñir. **~t** /kən'streɪnt/ n fuerza f

constrict /kən'strɪkt/ vt apretar. **~ion** /-ʃn/ n constricción f

construct /kən'strʌkt/ vt construir. **~ion** /-ʃn/ n construcción f. **~ive** /kən'strʌktɪv/ a constructivo

construe /kən'struː/ vt interpretar; (gram) construir

consul /'kɒnsl/ n cónsul m. **~ar** /-jʊlə(r)/ a consular. **~ate** /-ət/ n consulado m

consult /kən'sʌlt/ vt/i consultar. **~ant** /kən'sʌltənt/ n asesor m; (med) especialista m & f; (tec) consejero m técnico. **~ation** /kɒnsəl'teɪʃn/ n consulta f

consume /kən'sjuːm/ vt consumir; (eat) comer; (drink) beber. **~r** /-ə(r)/ n consumidor m. ● a de consumo. **~rism** /kən'sjuːmərɪzəm/ n protección f del consumidor, consumismo m

consummat|e /'kɒnsəmeɪt/ vt consumar. **~ion** /-'meɪʃn/ n consumación f

consumption /kən'sʌmpʃn/ n consumo m; (med) tisis f

contact /'kɒntækt/ n contacto m. ● vt ponerse en contacto con

contagious /kən'teɪdʒəs/ a contagioso

contain /kən'teɪn/ vt contener. **~ o.s.** contenerse. **~er** n recipiente m; (com) contenedor m

contaminat|e /kən'tæmɪneɪt/ vt contaminar. **~ion** /-'neɪʃn/ n contaminación f

contemplat|e /'kɒntəmpleɪt/ vt contemplar; (consider) considerar. **~ion** /-'pleɪʃn/ n contemplación f

contemporary /kən'tempərərɪ/ a & n contemporáneo (m)

contempt /kən'tempt/ n desprecio m. **~ible** a despreciable. **~uous** /-tjʊəs/ a desdeñoso

contend /kən'tend/ vt sostener. ● vi contender. **~er** n contendiente m & f

content[1] /kən'tent/ a satisfecho. ● vt contentar

content[2] /'kɒntent/ n contenido m

contented /kən'tentɪd/ a satisfecho

contention /kən'tenʃn/ n contienda f, (opinion) opinión f, argumento m

contentment /kən'tentmənt/ n contento m

contest /'kɒntest/ n (competition) concurso m; (fight) contienda f. /kən'test/ vt disputar. **~ant** n contendiente m & f, concursante m & f

context /'kɒntekst/ n contexto m

continent /'kɒntɪnənt/ n continente m. **the C~** Europa f. **~al** /-'nentl/ a continental

contingency /kən'tɪndʒənsɪ/ n contingencia f

contingent /kən'tɪndʒənt/ a & n contingente m

continu|al /kən'tɪnjʊəl/ a continuo. **~ance** /kən'tɪnjʊəns/ n continuación f. **~ation** /-ʊ'eɪʃn/ n continuación f. **~e** /kən'tɪnjuː/ vt/i continuar; (resume) seguir. **~ed** a continuo. **~ity** /kɒntɪ'njuːətɪ/ n continuidad f. **~ity girl** (cinema, TV) secretaria f de rodaje. **~ous** /kən'tɪnjʊəs/ a continuo. **~ously** adv continuamente

contort /kən'tɔːt/ vt retorcer. **~ion** /-ʃn/ n contorsión f. **~ionist** /-ʃənɪst/ n contorsionista m & f

contour /'kɒntʊə(r)/ n contorno m. **~ line** n curva f de nivel

contraband /'kɒntrəbænd/ n contrabando m

contracepti|on /kɒntrə'sepʃn/ n contracepción f. **~ve** /kɒntrə'septɪv/ a & n anticonceptivo (m)

contract /'kɒntrækt/ n contrato m. /kən'trækt/ vt contraer. ● vi contraerse. **~ion** /kən'trækʃn/ n contracción f. **~or** /kən'træktə(r)/ n contratista m & f

contradict /kɒntrə'dɪkt/ vt contradecir. **~ion** /-ʃn/ n contradicción f. **~ory** a contradictorio

contraption /kən'træpʃn/ n (fam) artilugio m

contrary /'kɒntrərɪ/ a & n contrario (m). **on the ~** al contrario. ● adv. **~ to** contrariamente a. /kən'treərɪ/ a terco

contrast /'kɒntrɑːst/ n contraste m. /kən'trɑːst/ vt poner en contraste. ● vi contrastar. **~ing** a contrastante

contraven|e /kɒntrə'viːn/ vt contravenir. **~tion** /-'venʃn/ n contravención f

contribut|e /kən'trɪbjuːt/ vt/i contribuir. **~e to** escribir para ⟨newspaper⟩. **~ion** /kɒntrɪ'bjuːʃn/ n contribución f; (from salary) cotización f. **~or** n contribuyente m & f; (to newspaper) colaborador m

contrite /'kɒntraɪt/ a arrepentido, pesaroso

contriv|ance /kən'traɪvəns/ n invención f. **~e** /kən'traɪv/ vt idear. **~e to** conseguir

control /kən'trəʊl/ vt (pt controlled) controlar. ● n control m. **~s** npl (mec) mandos mpl

controvers|ial /kɒntrə'vɜːʃl/ a polémico, discutible. **~y** /'kɒntrəvɜːsɪ/ n controversia f

conundrum /kə'nʌndrəm/ n adivinanza f; (problem) enigma m

conurbation /kɒnɜː'beɪʃn/ n conurbación f

convalesce /kɒnvə'les/ vi convalecer. **~nce** n convalecencia f. **~nt** a & n convaleciente (m & f). **~nt home** n casa f de convalecencia

convector /kən'vektə(r)/ n estufa f de convección

convene /kən'viːn/ vt convocar. ● vi reunirse

convenien|ce /kən'viːnɪəns/ n conveniencia f, comodidad f. **all modern ~ces** todas las comodidades. **at your ~ce** según le convenga. **~ces** npl servicios mpl. **~t** /kən'viːnɪənt/ a cómodo; (place) bien situado; (time) oportuno. **be ~t** convenir. **~tly** adv convenientemente

convent /'kɒnvənt/ n convento m

convention /kən'venʃn/ n convención f; (meeting) congreso m. **~al** a convencional

converge /kən'vɜːdʒ/ vi convergir

conversant /kən'vɜːsənt/ a. **~ with** versado en

conversation /kɒnvə'seɪʃn/ n conversación f. **~al** a de la conversación. **~alist** n hábil conversador m

converse[1] /kən'vɜːs/ vi conversar

converse[2] /'kɒnvɜːs/ a inverso. ● n lo contrario. **~ly** adv a la inversa

conver|sion /kən'vɜːʃn/ n conversión f. **~t** /kən'vɜːt/ vt convertir. /'kɒnvɜːt/ n converso m. **~tible** /kən'vɜːtɪbl/ a convertible. ● n (auto) descapotable m

convex /'kɒnveks/ a convexo

convey /kən'veɪ/ vt llevar; transportar ⟨goods⟩; comunicar ⟨idea, feeling⟩. **~ance** n transporte m. **~or belt** n cinta f transportadora

convict /kən'vɪkt/ vt condenar. /'kɒnvɪkt/ n presidiario m. **~ion** /kən'vɪkʃn/ n condena f; (belief) creencia f

convinc|e /kən'vɪns/ vt convencer. **~ing** a convincente

convivial /kən'vɪvɪəl/ a alegre

convoke /kən'vəʊk/ vt convocar

convoluted /'kɒnvəluːtɪd/ a enrollado; (argument) complicado

convoy /'kɒnvɔɪ/ n convoy m

convuls|e /kən'vʌls/ vt convulsionar. **be ~ed with laughter** desternillarse de risa. **~ion** /-ʃn/ n convulsión f

coo /kuː/ vi arrullar

cook /kʊk/ vt cocinar; (alter, fam) falsificar. **~ up** (fam) inventar. ● n cocinero m

cooker /'kʊkə(r)/ n cocina f

cookery /'kʊkərɪ/ n cocina f

cookie /'kʊkɪ/ n (Amer) galleta f

cool /kuːl/ a (-er, -est) fresco; (calm) tranquilo; (unfriendly) frío. ● n fresco m; (sl) calma f. ● vt enfriar. ● vi enfriarse. **~ down** (person) calmarse. **~ly** adv tranquilamente. **~ness** n frescura f

coop /kuːp/ n gallinero m. ● vt. **~ up** encerrar

co-operat|e /kəʊ'ɒpəreɪt/ vi cooperar. **~ion** /-'reɪʃn/ n cooperación f

cooperative /kəʊ'ɒpərətɪv/ a cooperativo. ● n cooperativa f

co-opt /kəʊ'ɒpt/ vt cooptar

co-ordinat|e /kəʊ'ɔːdɪneɪt/ vt coordinar. **~ion** /-'neɪʃn/ n coordinación f

cop /kɒp/ vt (pt copped) (sl) prender. ● n (sl) policía m

cope /kəʊp/ vi (fam) arreglárselas. ∼ **with** enfrentarse con

copious /'kəʊpɪəs/ a abundante

copper[1] /'kɒpə(r)/ n cobre m; (coin) perra f. ● a de cobre

copper[2] /'kɒpə(r)/ n (sl) policía m

coppice /'kɒpɪs/ n, **copse** /kɒps/ n bosquecillo m

Coptic /'kɒptɪk/ a copto

copulat|e /'kɒpjʊleɪt/ vi copular. ∼**ion** /-'leɪʃn/ n cópula f

copy /'kɒpɪ/ n copia f; (typ) material m. ● vt copiar

copyright /'kɒpɪraɪt/ n derechos mpl de autor

copy-writer /'kɒpɪraɪtə(r)/ n redactor m de textos publicitarios

coral /'kɒrəl/ n coral m

cord /kɔːd/ n cuerda f; (fabric) pana f. ∼s npl pantalones mpl de pana

cordial /'kɔːdɪəl/ a & n cordial (m)

cordon /'kɔːdn/ n cordón m. ● vt. ∼ **off** acordonar

corduroy /'kɔːdərɔɪ/ n pana f

core /kɔː(r)/ n (of apple) corazón m; (fig) meollo m

cork /kɔːk/ n corcho m. ● vt taponar. ∼**screw** /'kɔːkskruː/ n sacacorchos m invar

corn[1] /kɔːn/ n (wheat) trigo m; (Amer) maíz m; (seed) grano m

corn[2] /kɔːn/ n (hard skin) callo m

corned /kɔːnd/ a. ∼ **beef** n carne f de vaca en lata

corner /'kɔːnə(r)/ n ángulo m; (inside) rincón m; (outside) esquina f; (football) saque m de esquina. ● vt arrinconar; (com) acaparar. ∼**stone** n piedra f angular

cornet /'kɔːnɪt/ n (mus) corneta f; (for ice-cream) cucurucho m

cornflakes /'kɔːnfleɪks/ npl copos mpl de maíz

cornflour /'kɔːnflaʊə(r)/ n harina f de maíz

cornice /'kɔːnɪs/ n cornisa f

cornucopia /kɔːnjʊ'kəʊpɪə/ n cuerno m de la abundancia

Corn|ish /'kɔːnɪʃ/ a de Cornualles. ∼**wall** /'kɔːnwəl/ n Cornualles m

corny /'kɔːnɪ/ a (trite, fam) gastado; (mawkish) sentimental, sensiblero

corollary /kə'rɒlərɪ/ n corolario m

coronary /'kɒrənərɪ/ n trombosis f coronaria

coronation /kɒrə'neɪʃn/ n coronación f

coroner /'kɒrənə(r)/ n juez m de primera instancia

corporal[1] /'kɔːpərəl/ n cabo m

corporal[2] /'kɔːpərəl/ a corporal

corporate /'kɔːpərət/ a corporativo

corporation /kɔːpə'reɪʃn/ n corporación f; (of town) ayuntamiento m

corps /kɔː(r)/ n (pl corps /kɔːz/) cuerpo m

corpse /kɔːps/ n cadáver m

corpulent /'kɔːpjʊlənt/ a gordo, corpulento

corpuscle /'kɔːpʌsl/ n glóbulo m

corral /kə'rɑːl/ n (Amer) corral m

correct /kə'rekt/ a correcto; ‹time› exacto. ● vt corregir. ∼**ion** /-ʃn/ n corrección f

correlat|e /'kɒrəleɪt/ vt poner en correlación. ∼**ion** /-'leɪʃn/ n correlación f

correspond /kɒrɪ'spɒnd/ vi corresponder; (write) escribirse. ∼**ence** n correspondencia f. ∼**ent** n corresponsal m & f

corridor /'kɒrɪdɔː(r)/ n pasillo m

corroborate /kə'rɒbəreɪt/ vt corroborar

corro|de /kə'rəʊd/ vt corroer. ● vi corroerse. ∼**sion** n corrosión f

corrugated /'kɒrəgeɪtɪd/ a ondulado. ∼ **iron** n hierro m ondulado

corrupt /kə'rʌpt/ a corrompido. ● vt corromper. ∼**ion** /-ʃn/ n corrupción f

corset /'kɔːsɪt/ n corsé m

Corsica /'kɔːsɪkə/ n Córcega f. ∼**n** a & n corso (m)

cortège /'kɔːteɪʒ/ n cortejo m

cos /kɒs/ n lechuga f romana

cosh /kɒʃ/ n cachiporra f. ● vt aporrear

cosiness /'kəʊzɪnɪs/ n comodidad f

cosmetic /kɒz'metɪk/ a & n cosmético (m)

cosmic /'kɒzmɪk/ a cósmico

cosmonaut /'kɒzmənɔːt/ n cosmonauta m & f

cosmopolitan /kɒzmə'pɒlɪtən/ a & n cosmopolita (m & f)

cosmos /'kɒzmɒs/ n cosmos m

Cossack /'kɒsæk/ a & n cosaco (m)

cosset /'kɒsɪt/ vt (pt cosseted) mimar

cost /kɒst/ vi (pt cost) costar, valer. ● vt (pt costed) calcular el coste de. ● n precio m. **at all** ∼**s** cueste lo que cueste. **to one's** ∼ a sus expensas. ∼**s** npl (jurid) costas fpl

Costa Rica /kɒstə'riːkə/ n Costa f Rica. ∼**n** a & n costarricense (m & f), costarriqueño (m)

costly /'kɒstlɪ/ a (-ier, -iest) caro, costoso

costume /'kɒstjuːm/ n traje m

cosy /'kəʊzɪ/ a (-ier, -iest) cómodo; ⟨place⟩ acogedor. ● n cubierta f (de tetera)

cot /kɒt/ n cuna f

cottage /'kɒtɪdʒ/ n casita f de campo. ~ **cheese** n requesón m. ~ **industry** n industria f casera. ~ **pie** n carne f picada con puré de patatas

cotton /'kɒtn/ n algodón m. ● vi. ~ **on** (sl) comprender. ~ **wool** n algodón hidrófilo

couch /kaʊtʃ/ n sofá m. ● vt expresar

couchette /kuː'ʃet/ n litera f

cough /kɒf/ vi toser. ● n tos f. ~ **up** (sl) pagar. ~ **mixture** n jarabe m para la tos

could /kʊd, kəd/ pt of can

couldn't /'kʊdnt/ = could not

council /'kaʊnsl/ n consejo m; (of town) ayuntamiento m. ~ **house** n vivienda f protegida. ~**lor** /'kaʊnsələ(r)/ n concejal m

counsel /'kaʊnsl/ n consejo m; (pl invar) (jurid) abogado m. ~**lor** n consejero m

count[1] /kaʊnt/ n recuento m. ● vt/i contar

count[2] /kaʊnt/ n (nobleman) conde m

countdown /'kaʊntdaʊn/ n cuenta f atrás

countenance /'kaʊntɪnəns/ n semblante m. ● vt aprobar

counter /'kaʊntə(r)/ n (in shop etc) mostrador m; (token) ficha f. ● adv. ~ **to** en contra de. ● a opuesto. ● vt oponerse a; parar ⟨blow⟩. ● vi contraatacar

counter... /'kaʊntə(r)/ pref contra...

counteract /kaʊntər'ækt/ vt contrarrestar

counter-attack /'kaʊntərətæk/ n contraataque m. ● vt/i contraatacar

counterbalance /'kaʊntəbæləns/ n contrapeso m. ● vt/i contrapesar

counterfeit /'kaʊntəfɪt/ a falsificado. ● n falsificación f. ● vt falsificar

counterfoil /'kaʊntəfɔɪl/ n talón m

counterpart /'kaʊntəpɑːt/ n equivalente m; (person) homólogo m

counter-productive /'kaʊntəprə'dʌktɪv/ a contraproducente

countersign /'kaʊntəsaɪn/ vt refrendar

countess /'kaʊntɪs/ n condesa f

countless /'kaʊntlɪs/ a innumerable

countrified /'kʌntrɪfaɪd/ a rústico

country /'kʌntrɪ/ n (native land) país m; (countryside) campo m. ~ **folk** n gente f del campo. **go to the** ~ ir al campo; (pol) convocar elecciones generales

countryman /'kʌntrɪmən/ n (pl -men) campesino m; (of one's own country) compatriota m

countryside /'kʌntrɪsaɪd/ n campo m

county /'kaʊntɪ/ n condado m, provincia f

coup /kuː/ n golpe m

coupé /'kuːpeɪ/ n cupé m

couple /'kʌpl/ n (of things) par m; (of people) pareja f; (married) matrimonio m. **a** ~ **of** un par de. ● vt unir; (tec) acoplar. ● vi copularse

coupon /'kuːpɒn/ n cupón m

courage /'kʌrɪdʒ/ n valor m. ~**ous** /kə'reɪdʒəs/ a valiente. ~**ously** adv valientemente

courgette /kʊə'ʒet/ n calabacín m

courier /'kʊrɪə(r)/ n mensajero m; (for tourists) guía m & f

course /kɔːs/ n curso m; (behaviour) conducta f; (aviat, naut) rumbo m; (culin) plato m; (for golf) campo m. **in due** ~ a su debido tiempo. **in the** ~ **of** en el transcurso de, durante. **of** ~ desde luego, por supuesto

court /kɔːt/ n corte f; (tennis) pista f; (jurid) tribunal m. ● vt cortejar; buscar ⟨danger⟩

courteous /'kɜːtɪəs/ a cortés

courtesan /kɔːtɪ'zæn/ n (old use) cortesana f

courtesy /'kɜːtəsɪ/ n cortesía f

court: ~**ier** /'kɔːtɪə(r)/ n (old use) cortesano m. ~ **martial** n (pl courts martial) consejo m de guerra. ~-**martial** vt (pt ~-**martialled**) juzgar en consejo de guerra. ~**ship** /'kɔːtʃɪp/ n cortejo m

courtyard /'kɔːtjɑːd/ n patio m

cousin /'kʌzn/ n primo m. **first** ~ primo carnal. **second** ~ primo segundo

cove /kəʊv/ n cala f

covenant /'kʌvənənt/ n acuerdo m

Coventry /'kɒvntrɪ/ n. **send to** ~ hacer el vacío

cover /'kʌvə(r)/ vt cubrir; (journalism) hacer un reportaje sobre. ~

up cubrir; (*fig*) ocultar. ● *n* cubierta *f*; (*shelter*) abrigo *m*; (*lid*) tapa *f*; (*for furniture*) funda *f*; (*pretext*) pretexto *m*; (*of magazine*) portada *f*. ~**age** /'kʌvərɪdʒ/ *n* reportaje *m*. ~ **charge** *n* precio *m* del cubierto. ~**ing** *n* cubierta *f*. ~**ing letter** *n* carta *f* explicativa, carta *f* adjunta

covet /'kʌvɪt/ *vt* codiciar

cow /kaʊ/ *n* vaca *f*

coward /'kaʊəd/ *n* cobarde *m*. ~**ly** *a* cobarde. ~**ice** /'kaʊədɪs/ *n* cobardía *f*

cowboy /'kaʊbɔɪ/ *n* vaquero *m*

cower /'kaʊə(r)/ *vi* encogerse, acobardarse

cowl /kaʊl/ *n* capucha *f*; (*of chimney*) sombrerete *m*

cowshed /'kaʊʃed/ *n* establo *m*

coxswain /'koksn/ *n* timonel *m*

coy /kɔɪ/ *a* (**-er, -est**) (falsamente) tímido, remilgado

crab¹ /kræb/ *n* cangrejo *m*

crab² /kræb/ *vi* (*pt* **crabbed**) quejarse

crab-apple /'kræbæpl/ *n* manzana *f* silvestre

crack /kræk/ *n* grieta *f*; (*noise*) crujido *m*; (*of whip*) chasquido *m*; (*joke, sl*) chiste *m*. ● *a* (*fam*) de primera. ● *vt* agrietar; chasquear (*whip, fingers*); cascar (*nut*); gastar (*joke*); resolver (*problem*). ● *vi* agrietarse. **get ~ing** (*fam*) darse prisa. ~ **down on** (*fam*) tomar medidas enérgicas contra. ~ **up** *vi* fallar; (*person*) volverse loco. ~**ed** /krækt/ *a* (*sl*) chiflado

cracker /'krækə(r)/ *n* petardo *m*; (*culin*) galleta *f* (soso); (*culin, Amer*) galleta *f*

crackers /'krækəz/ *a* (*sl*) chiflado

crackl|e /'krækl/ *vi* crepitar. ● *n* crepitación *f*, crujido *m*. ~**ing** /'kræklɪŋ/ *n* crepitación *f*, crujido *m*; (*of pork*) chicharrón *m*

crackpot /'krækpot/ *n* (*sl*) chiflado *m*

cradle /'kreɪdl/ *n* cuna *f*. ● *vt* acunar

craft /krɑːft/ *n* destreza *f*; (*technique*) arte *f*; (*cunning*) astucia *f*. ● *n invar* (*boat*) barco *m*

craftsman /'krɑːftsmən/ *n* (*pl* **-men**) artesano *m*. ~**ship** *n* artesanía *f*

crafty /'krɑːftɪ/ *a* (**-ier, -iest**) astuto

crag /kræg/ *n* despeñadero *m*. ~**gy** *a* peñascoso

cram /kræm/ *vt* (*pt* **crammed**) rellenar. ~ **with** llenar de. ● *vi* (*for exams*) empollar. ~**full** *a* atestado

cramp /kræmp/ *n* calambre *m*

cramped /kræmpt/ *a* apretado

cranberry /'krænbərɪ/ *n* arándano *m*

crane /kreɪn/ *n* grúa *f*; (*bird*) grulla *f*. ● *vt* estirar (*neck*)

crank¹ /kræŋk/ *n* manivela *f*

crank² /kræŋk/ *n* (*person*) excéntrico *m*. ~**y** *a* excéntrico

cranny /'krænɪ/ *n* grieta *f*

crash /kræʃ/ *n* accidente *m*; (*noise*) estruendo *m*; (*collision*) choque *m*; (*com*) quiebra *f*. ● *vt* estrellar. ● *vi* quebrar con estrépito; (*have accident*) tener un accidente; (*car etc*) chocar; (*fail*) fracasar. ~ **course** *n* curso *m* intensivo. ~**helmet** *n* casco *m* protector. ~**land** *vi* hacer un aterrizaje de emergencia, hacer un aterrizaje forzoso

crass /kræs/ *a* craso, burdo

crate /kreɪt/ *n* cajón *m*. ● *vt* embalar

crater /'kreɪtə(r)/ *n* cráter *m*

cravat /krə'væt/ *n* corbata *f*, fular *m*

crav|e /kreɪv/ *vi*. ~**e for** anhelar. ~**ing** *n* ansia *f*

crawl /krɔːl/ *vi* andar a gatas; (*move slowly*) avanzar lentamente; (*drag o.s.*) arrastrarse. ● *n* (*swimming*) crol *m*. **at a** ~ a paso lento. ~ **to** humillarse ante. ~ **with** hervir de

crayon /'kreɪən/ *n* lápiz *m* de color

craze /kreɪz/ *n* manía *f*

craz|iness /'kreɪzɪnɪs/ *n* locura *f*. ~**y** /'kreɪzɪ/ *a* (**-ier, -iest**) loco. **be ~y about** andar loco por. ~**y paving** *n* enlosado *m* irregular

creak /kriːk/ *n* crujido *m*; (*of hinge*) chirrido *m*. ● *vi* crujir; (*hinge*) chirriar

cream /kriːm/ *n* crema *f*; (*fresh*) nata *f*. ● *a* (*colour*) color de crema. ● *vt* (*remove*) desnatar; (*beat*) batir. ~ **cheese** *n* queso *m* de nata. ~**y** *a* cremoso

crease /kriːs/ *n* pliegue *m*; (*crumple*) arruga *f*. ● *vt* plegar; (*wrinkle*) arrugar. ● *vi* arrugarse

creat|e /kriː'eɪt/ *vt* crear. ~**ion** /-ʃn/ *n* creación *f*. ~**ive** *a* creativo. ~**or** *n* creador *m*

creature /'kriːtʃə(r)/ *n* criatura *f*, bicho *m*, animal *m*

crèche /kreʃ/ *n* guardería *f* infantil

credence /'kriːdns/ *n* creencia *f*, fe *f*

credentials /krɪ'denʃlz/ *npl* credenciales *mpl*

credib|ility /kredə'bɪlətɪ/ *n* credibilidad *f*. ~**le** /'kredəbl/ *a* creíble

credit /'kredɪt/ *n* crédito *m*; (*honour*) honor *m*. **take the** ~ **for** atribuirse el mérito de. ● *vt* (*pt* credited) acreditar; (*believe*) creer. ~ with atribuir a uno. ~able *a* loable. ~ card *n* tarjeta *f* de crédito. ~or *n* acreedor *m*

credulous /'krɛdjʊləs/ *a* crédulo

creed /kri:d/ *n* credo *m*

creek /kri:k/ *n* ensenada *f*. up the ~ (*sl*) en apuros

creep /kri:p/ *vi* (*pt* crept) arrastrarse; (*plant*) trepar. ● *n* (*sl*) persona *f* desagradable. ~er *n* enredadera *f*. ~s /kri:ps/ *npl*. give s.o. the ~s dar repugnancia a uno

cremat|e /krɪ'meɪt/ *vt* incinerar. ~ion /-ʃn/ *n* cremación *f*. ~orium /kremə'tɔ:rɪəm/ *n* (*pl* -ia) crematorio *m*

Creole /'kri:əʊl/ *a* & *n* criollo (*m*)

crêpe /kreɪp/ *n* crespón *m*

crept /krept/ *see* creep

crescendo /krɪ'ʃendəʊ/ *n* (*pl* -os) crescendo *m*

crescent /'kresnt/ *n* media luna *f*; (*street*) calle *f* en forma de media luna

cress /kres/ *n* berro *m*

crest /krest/ *n* cresta *f*; (*coat of arms*) blasón *m*

Crete /kri:t/ *n* Creta *f*

cretin /'kretɪn/ *n* cretino *m*

crevasse /krɪ'væs/ *n* grieta *f*

crevice /'krevɪs/ *n* grieta *f*

crew¹ /kru:/ *n* tripulación *f*; (*gang*) pandilla *f*

crew² /kru:/ *see* crow²

crew: ~ cut *n* corte *m* al rape. ~ neck *n* cuello *m* redondo

crib /krɪb/ *n* cuna *f*; (*relig*) belén *m*; (*plagiarism*) plagio *m*. ● *vt/i* (*pt* cribbed) plagiar

crick /krɪk/ *n* calambre *m*; (*in neck*) tortícolis *f*

cricket¹ /'krɪkɪt/ *n* criquet *m*

cricket² /'krɪkɪt/ *n* (*insect*) grillo *m*

cricketer /'krɪkɪtə(r)/ *n* jugador *m* de criquet

crim|e /kraɪm/ *n* crimen *m*; (*acts*) criminalidad *f*. ~inal /'krɪmɪnl/ *a* & *n* criminal *m*

crimp /krɪmp/ *vt* rizar

crimson /'krɪmzn/ *a* & *n* carmesí (*m*)

cringe /krɪndʒ/ *vi* encogerse; (*fig*) humillarse

crinkle /'krɪŋkl/ *vt* arrugar. ● *vi* arrugarse. ● *n* arruga *f*

crinoline /'krɪnəlɪn/ *n* miriñaque *m*

cripple /'krɪpl/ *n* lisiado *m*, mutilado *m*. ● *vt* lisiar; (*fig*) paralizar

crisis /'kraɪsɪs/ *n* (*pl* crises /'kraɪsi:z/) crisis *f*

crisp /krɪsp/ *a* (-er, -est) (*culin*) crujiente; (*air*) vigorizador. ~s *npl* patatas *fpl* fritas a la inglesa

criss-cross /'krɪskrɒs/ *a* entrecruzado. ● *vt* entrecruzar. ● *vi* entrecruzarse

criterion /kraɪ'tɪərɪən/ *n* (*pl* -ia) criterio *m*

critic /'krɪtɪk/ *n* crítico *m*

critical /'krɪtɪkl/ *a* crítico. ~ly *adv* críticamente; (*ill*) gravemente

critici|sm /'krɪtɪsɪzəm/ *n* crítica *f*. ~ze /'krɪtɪsaɪz/ *vt/i* criticar

croak /krəʊk/ *n* (*of person*) gruñido *m*; (*of frog*) canto *m*. ● *vi* gruñir; (*frog*) croar

crochet /'krəʊʃeɪ/ *n* croché *m*, ganchillo *m*. ● *vt* hacer ganchillo

crock¹ /krɒk/ *n* (*person, fam*) vejancón *m*; (*old car*) cacharro *m*

crock² /krɒk/ *n* vasija *f* de loza

crockery /'krɒkərɪ/ *n* loza *f*

crocodile /'krɒkədaɪl/ *n* cocodrilo *m*. ~ tears *npl* lágrimas *fpl* de cocodrilo

crocus /'krəʊkəs/ *n* (*pl* -es) azafrán *m*

crony /'krəʊnɪ/ *n* amigote *m*

crook /krʊk/ *n* (*fam*) maleante *m* & *f*, estafador *m*, criminal *m*; (*stick*) cayado *m*; (*of arm*) pliegue *m*

crooked /'krʊkɪd/ *a* torcido; (*winding*) tortuoso; (*dishonest*) poco honrado

croon /kru:n/ *vt/i* canturrear

crop /krɒp/ *n* cosecha *f*; (*fig*) montón *m*. ● *vt* (*pt* cropped) *vi* cortar. ~ up surgir

cropper /'krɒpər/ *n*. come a ~ (*fall, fam*) caer; (*fail, fam*) fracasar

croquet /'krəʊkeɪ/ *n* croquet *m*

croquette /krə'ket/ *n* croqueta *f*

cross /krɒs/ *n* cruz *f*; (*of animals*) cruce *m*. ● *vt/i* cruzar; (*oppose*) contrariar. ~ off tachar. ~ o.s. santiguarse. ~ out tachar. ~ s.o.'s mind ocurrírsele a uno. ● *a* enfadado. talk at ~ purposes hablar sin entenderse

crossbar /'krɒsbɑ:(r)/ *n* travesaño *m*

cross-examine /krɒsɪg'zæmɪn/ *vt* interrogar

cross-eyed /'krɒsaɪd/ *a* bizco

crossfire /'krɒsfaɪə(r)/ *n* fuego *m* cruzado

crossing /'krɒsɪŋ/ *n* (*by boat*) travesía *f*; (*on road*) paso *m* para peatones

crossly /'krɒslɪ/ adv con enfado

cross-reference /krɒs'refrəns/ n referencia f

crossroads /'krɒsrəʊdz/ n cruce m (de carreteras)

cross-section /krɒs'sekʃn/ n sección f transversal; (fig) muestra f representativa

crosswise /'krɒswaɪz/ adv al través

crossword /'krɒswɜ:d/ n crucigrama m

crotch /krɒtʃ/ n entrepiernas fpl

crotchety /'krɒtʃɪtɪ/ a de mal genio

crouch /kraʊtʃ/ vi agacharse

crow[1] /krəʊ/ n cuervo m. **as the ~ flies** en línea recta

crow[2] /krəʊ/ vi (pt crew) cacarear

crowbar /'krəʊbɑ:(r)/ n palanca f

crowd /kraʊd/ n muchedumbre f. ● vt amontonar; (fill) llenar. ● vi amontonarse; (gather) reunirse. **~ed** a atestado

crown /kraʊn/ n corona f; (of hill) cumbre f; (of head) coronilla f. ● vt coronar; poner una corona a (tooth). **C~ Court** n tribunal m regional. **C~ prince** n príncipe m heredero

crucial /'kru:ʃl/ a crucial

crucifix /'kru:sɪfɪks/ n crucifijo m. **~ion** /-'fɪkʃn/ n crucifixión f

crucify /'kru:sɪfaɪ/ vt crucificar

crude /kru:d/ a (-er, -est) (raw) crudo; (rough) tosco; (vulgar) ordinario

cruel /krʊəl/ a (crueller, cruellest) cruel. **~ty** n crueldad f

cruet /'kru:ɪt/ n vinagreras fpl

cruise /kru:z/ n crucero m. ● vi hacer un crucero; (of car) circular lentamente. **~r** n crucero m

crumb /krʌm/ n migaja f

crumble /'krʌmbl/ vt desmenuzar. ● vi desmenuzarse; (collapse) derrumbarse

crummy /'krʌmɪ/ a (-ier, -iest) (sl) miserable

crumpet /'krʌmpɪt/ n bollo m blando

crumple /'krʌmpl/ vt arrugar; estrujar (paper). ● vi arrugarse

crunch /krʌntʃ/ vt hacer crujir; (bite) ronzar, morder, masticar. ● n crujido m; (fig) momento m decisivo

crusade /kru:'seɪd/ n cruzada f. **~r** /-ə(r)/ n cruzado m

crush /krʌʃ/ vt aplastar; arrugar (clothes); estrujar (paper). ● n (crowd) aglomeración f. **have a ~**

on (sl) estar perdido por. **orange ~** n naranjada f

crust /krʌst/ n corteza f. **~y** a (bread) de corteza dura; (person) malhumorado

crutch /krʌtʃ/ n muleta f; (anat) entrepiernas fpl

crux /krʌks/ n (pl cruxes) punto m más importante, quid m, busilis m

cry /kraɪ/ n grito m. **be a far ~ from** (fig) distar mucho de. ● vi llorar; (call out) gritar. **~ off** rajarse. **~baby** n llorón m

crypt /krɪpt/ n cripta f

cryptic /'krɪptɪk/ a enigmático

crystal /'krɪstl/ n cristal m. **~lize** vt cristalizar. ● vi cristalizarse

cub /kʌb/ n cachorro m. **C~ (Scout)** n niño m explorador

Cuba /'kju:bə/ n Cuba f. **~n** a & n cubano (m)

cubby-hole /'kʌbɪhəʊl/ n casilla f; (room) chiribitil m, cuchitril m

cub|e /kju:b/ n cubo m. **~ic** a cúbico

cubicle /'kju:bɪkl/ n cubículo m; (changing room) caseta f

cubis|m /'kju:bɪzm/ n cubismo m. **~t** a & n cubista (m & f)

cuckold /'kʌkəʊld/ n cornudo m

cuckoo /'kʊku:/ n cuco m, cuclillo m

cucumber /'kju:kʌmbə(r)/ n pepino m

cuddl|e /'kʌdl/ vt abrazar. ● vi abrazarse. ● n abrazo m. **~y** a mimoso

cudgel /'kʌdʒl/ n porra f. ● vt (pt cudgelled) aporrear

cue[1] /kju:/ n indicación f; (in theatre) pie m

cue[2] /kju:/ n (in billiards) taco m

cuff /kʌf/ n puño m; (blow) bofetada f. **speak off the ~** hablar de improviso. ● vt abofetear. **~link** n gemelo m

cul-de-sac /'kʌldəsæk/ n callejón m sin salida

culinary /'kʌlɪnərɪ/ a culinario

cull /kʌl/ vt coger (flowers); entresacar (animals)

culminat|e /'kʌlmɪneɪt/ vi culminar. **~ion** /-'neɪʃn/ n culminación f

culottes /kʊ'lɒts/ npl falda f pantalón

culprit /'kʌlprɪt/ n culpable m

cult /kʌlt/ n culto m

cultivat|e /'kʌltɪveɪt/ vt cultivar. **~ion** /-'veɪʃn/ n cultivo m; (fig) cultura f

cultur|al /ˈkʌltʃərəl/ a cultural. ~**e** /ˈkʌltʃə(r)/ n cultura f; (bot etc) cultivo m. ~**ed** a cultivado; ⟨person⟩ culto

cumbersome /ˈkʌmbəsəm/ a incómodo; (heavy) pesado

cumulative /ˈkjuːmjʊlətɪv/ a cumulativo

cunning /ˈkʌnɪŋ/ a astuto. ● n astucia f

cup /kʌp/ n taza f; (prize) copa f

cupboard /ˈkʌbəd/ n armario m

Cup Final /kʌpˈfaɪnl/ n final f del campeonato

cupful /ˈkʌpfʊl/ n taza f

cupidity /kjuːˈpɪdɪtɪ/ n codicia f

curable /ˈkjʊərəbl/ a curable

curate /ˈkjʊərət/ n coadjutor m

curator /kjʊəˈreɪtə(r)/ n (of museum) conservador m

curb /kɜːb/ n freno m. ● vt refrenar

curdle /ˈkɜːdl/ vt cuajar. ● vi cuajarse; ⟨milk⟩ cortarse

curds /kɜːdz/ npl cuajada f, requesón m

cure /kjʊə(r)/ vt curar. ● n cura f

curfew /ˈkɜːfjuː/ n queda f; (signal) toque m de queda

curio /ˈkjʊərɪəʊ/ n (pl -os) curiosidad f

curio|us /ˈkjʊərɪəs/ a curioso. ~**sity** /-ˈɒsətɪ/ n curiosidad f

curl /kɜːl/ vt rizar ⟨hair⟩. ~ **o.s. up** acurrucarse. ● vi ⟨hair⟩ rizarse; ⟨paper⟩ arrollarse. ● n rizo m. ~**er** /ˈkɜːlə(r)/ n bigudí m, rulo m. ~**y** /ˈkɜːlɪ/ a (-ier, -iest) rizado

currant /ˈkʌrənt/ n pasa f de Corinto

currency /ˈkʌrənsɪ/ n moneda f; (acceptance) uso m (corriente)

current /ˈkʌrənt/ a & n corriente (f). ~ **events** asuntos mpl de actualidad. ~**ly** adv actualmente

curriculum /kəˈrɪkjʊləm/ n (pl -la) programa m de estudios. ~ **vitae** n curriculum m vitae

curry¹ /ˈkʌrɪ/ n curry m

curry² /ˈkʌrɪ/ vt. ~ **favour with** congraciarse con

curse /kɜːs/ n maldición f; (oath) palabrota f. ● vt maldecir. ● vi decir palabrotas

cursory /ˈkɜːsərɪ/ a superficial

curt /kɜːt/ a brusco

curtail /kɜːˈteɪl/ vt abreviar; reducir ⟨expenses⟩

curtain /ˈkɜːtn/ n cortina f; (in theatre) telón m

curtsy /ˈkɜːtsɪ/ n reverencia f. ● vi hacer una reverencia

curve /kɜːv/ n curva f. ● vt encurvar. ● vi encorvarse; ⟨road⟩ torcerse

cushion /ˈkʊʃn/ n cojín m. ● vt amortiguar ⟨a blow⟩; (fig) proteger

cushy /ˈkʊʃɪ/ a (-ier, -iest) (fam) fácil

custard /ˈkʌstəd/ n natillas fpl

custodian /kʌˈstəʊdɪən/ n custodio m

custody /ˈkʌstədɪ/ n custodia f. **be in ~** (jurid) estar detenido

custom /ˈkʌstəm/ n costumbre f; (com) clientela f

customary /ˈkʌstəmərɪ/ a acostumbrado

customer /ˈkʌstəmə(r)/ n cliente m

customs /ˈkʌstəmz/ npl aduana f. ~ **officer** n aduanero m

cut /kʌt/ vt/i (pt cut, pres p cutting) cortar; reducir ⟨prices⟩. ● n corte m; (reduction) reducción f. ~ **across** atravesar. ~ **back**, ~ **down** reducir. ~ **in** interrumpir. ~ **off** cortar; (phone) desconectar; (fig) aislar. ~ **out** recortar; (omit) suprimir. ~ **through** atravesar. ~ **up** cortar en pedazos. **be ~ up about** (fig) afligirse por

cute /kjuːt/ a (-er, -est) (fam) listo; (Amer) mono

cuticle /ˈkjuːtɪkl/ n cutícula f

cutlery /ˈkʌtlərɪ/ n cubiertos mpl

cutlet /ˈkʌtlɪt/ n chuleta f

cut-price /ˈkʌtpraɪs/ a a precio reducido

cut-throat /ˈkʌtθrəʊt/ a despiadado

cutting /ˈkʌtɪŋ/ a cortante; ⟨remark⟩ mordaz. ● n (from newspaper) recorte m; (of plant) esqueje m

cyanide /ˈsaɪənaɪd/ n cianuro m

cybernetics /saɪbəˈnetɪks/ n cibernética f

cyclamen /ˈsɪkləmən/ n ciclamen m

cycle /ˈsaɪkl/ n ciclo m; (bicycle) bicicleta f. ● vi ir en bicicleta

cyclic(al) /ˈsaɪklɪk(l)/ a cíclico

cycli|ng /ˈsaɪklɪŋ/ n ciclismo m. ~**st** n ciclista m & f

cyclone /ˈsaɪkləʊn/ n ciclón m

cylind|er /ˈsɪlɪndə(r)/ n cilindro m. ~**er head** (auto) n culata f. ~**rical** /-ˈlɪndrɪkl/ a cilíndrico

cymbal /ˈsɪmbl/ n címbalo m

cynic /ˈsɪnɪk/ n cínico m. ~**al** a cínico. ~**ism** /-sɪzəm/ n cinismo m

cypress /ˈsaɪprəs/ n ciprés m

Cypr|iot /'sɪprɪət/ a & n chipriota (m & f). **~us** /'saɪprəs/ n Chipre f

cyst /sɪst/ n quiste m

czar /zɑ:(r)/ n zar m

Czech /tʃek/ a & n checo (m). **the ~ Republic** n la república f Checa

Czechoslovak /tʃekəʊ'sləʊvæk/ a & n (history) checoslovaco (m). **~ia** /-ə'vækɪə/ n (history) Checoslovaquia f

D

dab /dæb/ vt (pt dabbed) tocar ligeramente. ● n toque m suave. **a ~ of** un poquito de

dabble /'dæbl/ vi. **~ in** meterse (superficialmente) en. **~r** /-ə(r)/ n aficionado m

dad /dæd/ n (fam) papá m. **~dy** n (children's use) papá m. **~dy-long-legs** n típula f

daffodil /'dæfədɪl/ n narciso m

daft /dɑ:ft/ a (-er, -est) tonto

dagger /'dægə(r)/ n puñal m

dahlia /'deɪlɪə/ n dalia f

daily /'deɪlɪ/ a diario. ● adv diariamente, cada día. ● n diario m; (cleaner, fam) asistenta f

dainty /'deɪntɪ/ a (-ier, -iest) delicado

dairy /'deərɪ/ n vaquería f; (shop) lechería f. ● a lechero

dais /deɪs/ n estrado m

daisy /'deɪzɪ/ n margarita f

dale /deɪl/ n valle m

dally /'dælɪ/ vi tardar; (waste time) perder el tiempo

dam /dæm/ n presa f. ● vt (pt dammed) embalsar

damage /'dæmɪdʒ/ n daño m; (pl, jurid) daños mpl y perjuicios mpl. ● vt (fig) dañar, estropear. **~ing** a perjudicial

damask /'dæməsk/ n damasco m

dame /deɪm/ n (old use) dama f, (Amer, sl) chica f

damn /dæm/ vt condenar; (curse) maldecir. ● int ¡córcholis! ● a maldito. ● n. **I don't care a ~** (no) me importa un comino. **~ation** /-'neɪʃn/ n condenación f, perdición f

damp /dæmp/ n humedad f. ● a (-er, -est) húmedo. ● vt mojar; (fig) ahogar. **~er** /'dæmpə(r)/ n apagador m, sordina f; (fig) aguafiestas m invar. **~ness** n humedad f

damsel /'dæmzl/ n (old use) doncella f

dance /dɑ:ns/ vt/i bailar. ● n baile m. **~-hall** n salón m de baile. **~r** /-ə(r)/ n bailador m; (professional) bailarín m

dandelion /'dændɪlaɪən/ n diente m de león

dandruff /'dændrʌf/ n caspa f

dandy /'dændɪ/ n petimetre m

Dane /deɪn/ n danés m

danger /'deɪndʒə(r)/ n peligro m; (risk) riesgo m. **~ous** a peligroso

dangle /'dæŋgl/ vt balancear. ● vi suspender, colgar

Danish /'deɪnɪʃ/ a danés. ● m (lang) danés m

dank /dæŋk/ a (-er, -est) húmedo, malsano

dare /deə(r)/ vt desafiar. ● vi atreverse a. **I ~ say** probablemente. ● n desafío m

daredevil /'deədevl/ n atrevido m

daring /'deərɪŋ/ a atrevido

dark /dɑ:k/ a (-er, -est) oscuro; (gloomy) sombrío; ⟨skin, hair⟩ moreno. ● n oscuridad f; (nightfall) atardecer. **in the ~** a oscuras. **~en** /'dɑ:kən/ vt oscurecer. ● vi oscurecerse. **~ horse** n persona f de talentos desconocidos. **~ness** n oscuridad f. **~room** n cámara f oscura

darling /'dɑ:lɪŋ/ a querido. ● n querido m

darn /dɑ:n/ vt zurcir

dart /dɑ:t/ n dardo m. ● vi lanzarse; (run) precipitarse. **~board** /'dɑ:tbɔ:d/ n blanco m. **~s** npl los dardos mpl

dash /dæʃ/ vi precipitarse. **~ off** marcharse apresuradamente. **~ out** salir corriendo. ● vt lanzar; (break) romper; defraudar ⟨hopes⟩. ● n carrera f; (small amount) poquito m; (stroke) raya f. **cut a ~** causar sensación

dashboard /'dæʃbɔ:d/ n tablero m de mandos

dashing /'dæʃɪŋ/ a vivo; (showy) vistoso

data /'deɪtə/ npl datos mpl. **~ processing** n proceso m de datos

date[1] /deɪt/ n fecha f; (fam) cita f. **to ~** hasta la fecha. ● vt fechar; (go out with, fam) salir con. ● vi datar; (be old-fashioned) quedar anticuado

date[2] /deɪt/ n (fruit) dátil m

dated /'deɪtɪd/ a pasado de moda

daub /dɔːb/ *vt* embadurnar

daughter /'dɔːtə(r)/ *n* hija *f*. **~-in-law** *n* nuera *f*

daunt /dɔːnt/ *vt* intimidar

dauntless /'dɔːntlɪs/ *a* intrépido

dawdle /'dɔːdl/ *vi* andar despacio; (*waste time*) perder el tiempo. **~r** /-ə(r)/ *n* rezagado *m*

dawn /dɔːn/ *n* amanecer *m*. ● *vi* amanecer; (*fig*) nacer. **it ~ed on me that** caí en la cuenta de que, comprendí que

day /deɪ/ *n* día *m*; (*whole day*) jornada *f*; (*period*) época *f*. **~break** *n* amanecer *m*. **~dream** *n* ensueño *m*. ● *vi* soñar despierto. **~light** /'deɪlaɪt/ *n* luz *f* del día. **~time** /'deɪtaɪm/ *n* día *m*

daze /deɪz/ *vt* aturdir. ● *n* aturdimiento *m*. **in a ~** aturdido

dazzle /'dæzl/ *vt* deslumbrar

deacon /'diːkən/ *n* diácono *m*

dead /ded/ *a* muerto; (*numb*) entumecido. **~ centre** justo en medio. ● *adv* completamente. **~ beat** rendido. **~ on time** justo a tiempo. **~ slow** muy lento. **stop ~** parar en seco. ● *n* muertos *mpl*. **in the ~ of night** en plena noche. **the ~** los muertos *mpl*. **~en** /'dedn/ *vt* amortiguar ⟨*sound, blow*⟩; calmar ⟨*pain*⟩. **~ end** *n* callejón *m* sin salida. **~ heat** *n* empate *m*

deadline /'dedlaɪn/ *n* fecha *f* tope, fin *m* de plazo

deadlock /'dedlɒk/ *n* punto *m* muerto

deadly /'dedlɪ/ *a* (**-ier, -iest**) mortal; (*harmful*) nocivo; (*dreary*) aburrido

deadpan /'dedpæn/ *a* impasible

deaf /def/ *a* (**-er, -est**) sordo. **~-aid** *n* audífono *m*. **~en** /'defn/ *vt* ensordecer. **~ening** *a* ensordecedor. **~mute** *n* sordomudo *m*. **~ness** *n* sordera *f*

deal /diːl/ *n* (*transaction*) negocio *m*; (*agreement*) pacto *m*; (*of cards*) reparto *m*; (*treatment*) trato *m*; (*amount*) cantidad *f*. **a great ~** muchísimo. ● *vt* (*pt* **dealt**) distribuir; dar ⟨*a blow, cards*⟩. ● *vi*. **~ in** comerciar en. **~ with** tratar con ⟨*person*⟩; tratar de ⟨*subject etc*⟩; ocuparse de ⟨*problem etc*⟩. **~er** *n* comerciante *m*. **~ings** /'diːlɪŋz/ *npl* trato *m*

dean /diːn/ *n* deán *m*; (*univ*) decano *m*

dear /dɪə(r)/ *a* (**-er, -est**) querido; (*expensive*) caro. ● *n* querido *m*; (*child*) pequeño *m*. ● *adv* caro. ● *int* ¡Dios mío! **~ me!** ¡Dios mío! **~ly** *adv* tiernamente; (*pay*) caro; (*very much*) muchísimo

dearth /dɜːθ/ *n* escasez *f*

death /deθ/ *n* muerte *f*. **~ duty** *n* derechos *mpl* reales. **~ly** *a* mortal; ⟨*silence*⟩ profundo. ● *adv* como la muerte. **~'s head** *n* calavera *f*. **~trap** *n* lugar *m* peligroso.

débâcle /deɪ'bɑːkl/ *n* fracaso *m*, desastre *m*

debar /dɪ'bɑː(r)/ *vt* (*pt* **debarred**) excluir

debase /dɪ'beɪs/ *vt* degradar

debat|able /dɪ'beɪtəbl/ *a* discutible. **~e** /dɪ'beɪt/ *n* debate *m*. ● *vt* debatir, discutir. ● *vi* discutir; (*consider*) considerar

debauch /dɪ'bɔːtʃ/ *vt* corromper. **~ery** *n* libertinaje *m*

debilit|ate /dɪ'bɪlɪteɪt/ *vt* debilitar. **~y** /dɪ'bɪlətɪ/ *n* debilidad *f*

debit /'debɪt/ *n* debe *m*. ● *vt*. **~ s.o.'s account** cargar en cuenta a uno

debonair /debə'neə(r)/ *a* alegre

debris /'debriː/ *n* escombros *mpl*

debt /det/ *n* deuda *f*. **be in ~** tener deudas. **~or** *n* deudor *m*

debutante /'debjuːtɑːnt/ *n* (*old use*) debutante *f*

decade /'dekeɪd/ *n* década *f*

decaden|ce /'dekədəns/ *n* decadencia *f*. **~t** /'dekədənt/ *a* decadente

decant /dɪ'kænt/ *vt* decantar. **~er** /-ə(r)/ *n* garrafa *f*

decapitate /dɪ'kæpɪteɪt/ *vt* decapitar

decay /dɪ'keɪ/ *vi* decaer; ⟨*tooth*⟩ cariarse. ● *n* decadencia *f*; (*of tooth*) caries *f*

deceased /dɪ'siːst/ *a* difunto

deceit /dɪ'siːt/ *n* engaño *m*. **~ful** *a* falso. **~fully** *adv* falsamente

deceive /dɪ'siːv/ *vt* engañar

December /dɪ'sembə(r)/ *n* diciembre *m*

decen|cy /'diːsənsɪ/ *n* decencia *f*. **~t** /'diːsnt/ *a* decente; (*good, fam*) bueno; (*kind, fam*) amable. **~tly** *adv* decentemente

decentralize /diː'sentrəlaɪz/ *vt* descentralizar

decepti|on /dɪ'sepʃn/ *n* engaño *m*. **~ve** /dɪ'septɪv/ *a* engañoso

decibel /'desɪbel/ *n* decibel(io) *m*

decide /dɪ'saɪd/ vt/i decidir. ~d
/-ɪd/ a resuelto; (unquestionable)
indudable. ~dly /-ɪdlɪ/ adv deci-
didamente; (unquestionably) indudablemente

decimal /'desɪml/ a & n decimal (f).
~ **point** n coma f (decimal)

decimate /'desɪmeɪt/ vt diezmar

decipher /dɪ'saɪfə(r)/ vt descifrar

decision /dɪ'sɪʒn/ n decisión f

decisive /dɪ'saɪsɪv/ a decisivo; (manner) decidido. ~ly adv de manera
decisiva

deck /dek/ n cubierta f; (of cards,
Amer) baraja f. **top** ~ (of bus)
imperial m. ● vt adornar. ~**-chair** n
tumbona f

declaim /dɪ'kleɪm/ vt declamar

declar|ation /deklə'reɪʃn/ n decla-
ración f. ~**e** /dɪ'kleə(r)/ vt declarar

decline /dɪ'klaɪn/ vt rehusar; (gram)
declinar. ● vi disminuir; (deteriorate) deteriorarse; (fall) bajar. ● n
decadencia f; (decrease) disminución f; (fall) baja f

decode /dɪ'kəʊd/ vt descifrar

decompos|e /di:kəm'pəʊz/ vt
descomponer. ● vi descomponerse.
~**ition** /-ɒmpə'zɪʃn/ n descom-
posición f

décor /'deɪkɔ:(r)/ n decoración f

decorat|e /'dekəreɪt/ vt decorar;
empapelar y pintar (room). ~**ion**
/-'reɪʃn/ n (act) decoración f; (ornament) adorno m. ~**ive** /-ətɪv/ a
decorativo. ~**or** /'dekəreɪtə(r)/ n
pintor m decorador. **interior** ~**or**
decorador m de interiores

decorum /dɪ'kɔ:rəm/ n decoro m

decoy /'di:kɔɪ/ n señuelo m. /dɪ'kɔɪ/
vt atraer con señuelo

decrease /dɪ'kri:s/ vt disminuir. ● vi
disminuirse. /'di:kri:s/ n disminución f

decree /dɪ'kri:/ n decreto m; (jurid)
sentencia f. ● vt (pt **decreed**)
decretar

decrepit /dɪ'krepɪt/ a decrépito

decry /dɪ'kraɪ/ vt denigrar

dedicat|e /'dedɪkeɪt/ vt dedicar.
~**ion** /-'keɪʃn/ n dedicación f; (in
book) dedicatoria f

deduce /dɪ'dju:s/ vt deducir

deduct /dɪ'dʌkt/ vt deducir. ~**ion**
/-ʃn/ n deducción f

deed /di:d/ n hecho m; (jurid) escritura f

deem /di:m/ vt juzgar, considerar

deep /di:p/ a (**-er, est**) adv profundo.
get into ~ **waters** meterse en honduras. **go off the** ~ **end** enfadarse.
● adv profundamente. **be** ~ **in
thought** estar absorto en sus pensamientos. ~**en** /'di:pən/ vt pro-
fundizar. ● vi hacerse más
profundo. ~**-freeze** n congelador
m. ~**ly** adv profundamente

deer /dɪə(r)/ n invar ciervo m

deface /dɪ'feɪs/ vt desfigurar

defamation /defə'meɪʃn/ n difa-
mación f

default /dɪ'fɔ:lt/ vi faltar. ● n. **by** ~
en rebeldía. **in** ~ **of** en ausencia de

defeat /dɪ'fi:t/ vt vencer; (frustrate)
frustrar. ● n derrota f; (of plan etc)
fracaso m. ~**ism** /dɪ'fi:tɪzm/ n
derrotismo m. ~**ist** /dɪ'fi:tɪst/ n
derrotista m & f

defect /'di:fekt/ n defecto m.
/dɪ'fekt/ vi desertar. ~ **to** pasar a.
~**ion** /dɪ'fekʃn/ n deserción f. ~**ive**
/dɪ'fektɪv/ a defectuoso

defence /dɪ'fens/ n defensa f. ~**less**
a indefenso

defend /dɪ'fend/ vt defender. ~**ant**
n (jurid) acusado m

defensive /dɪ'fensɪv/ a defensivo.
● n defensiva f

defer /dɪ'fɜ:(r)/ vt (pt **deferred**)
aplazar

deferen|ce /'defərəns/ n deferencia
f. ~**tial** /-'renʃl/ a deferente

defian|ce /dɪ'faɪəns/ n desafío m. **in**
~**ce of** a despecho de. ~**t** a desafi-
ante. ~**tly** adv con tono retador

deficien|cy /dɪ'fɪʃənsɪ/ n falta f. ~**t**
/dɪ'fɪʃnt/ a deficiente. **be** ~**t in** carecer de

deficit /'defɪsɪt/ n déficit m

defile /dɪ'faɪl/ vt ensuciar; (fig)
deshonrar

define /dɪ'faɪn/ vt definir

definite /'defɪnɪt/ a determinado;
(clear) claro; (firm) categórico. ~**ly**
adv claramente; (certainly)
seguramente

definition /defɪ'nɪʃn/ n definición f

definitive /dɪ'fɪnətɪv/ a definitivo

deflat|e /dɪ'fleɪt/ vt desinflar. ● vi
desinflarse. ~**ion** /-ʃn/ n (com)
deflación f

deflect /dɪ'flekt/ vt desviar. ● vi
desviarse

deform /dɪ'fɔ:m/ vt deformar. ~**ed**
a deforme. ~**ity** n deformidad f

defraud /dɪ'frɔ:d/ vt defraudar

defray /dɪ'freɪ/ vt pagar

defrost /diːˈfrɒst/ *vt* descongelar

deft /deft/ *a* (**-er, -est**) hábil. **~ness** *n* destreza *f*

defunct /dɪˈfʌŋkt/ *a* difunto

defuse /diːˈfjuːz/ *vt* desactivar ‹*bomb*›; (*fig*) calmar

defy /dɪˈfaɪ/ *vt* desafiar; (*resist*) resistir

degenerate /dɪˈdʒenəreɪt/ *vi* degenerar. /dɪˈdʒenərət/ *a & n* degenerado (*m*)

degrad|ation /degrəˈdeɪʃn/ *n* degradación *f*. **~e** /dɪˈɡreɪd/ *vt* degradar

degree /dɪˈɡriː/ *n* grado *m*; (*univ*) licenciatura *f*; (*rank*) rango *m*. **to a certain ~** hasta cierto punto. **to a ~** (*fam*) sumamente

dehydrate /diːˈhaɪdreɪt/ *vt* deshidratar

de-ice /diːˈaɪs/ *vt* descongelar

deign /deɪn/ *vi*. **~ to** dignarse

deity /ˈdiːɪtɪ/ *n* deidad *f*

deject|ed /dɪˈdʒektɪd/ *a* desanimado. **~ion** /-ʃn/ *n* abatimiento *m*

delay /dɪˈleɪ/ *vt* retardar; (*postpone*) aplazar. ● *vi* demorarse. ● *n* demora *f*

delectable /dɪˈlektəbl/ *a* deleitable

delegat|e /ˈdelɪɡeɪt/ *vt* delegar. /ˈdelɪɡət/ *n* delegado *m*. **~ion** /-ˈɡeɪʃn/ *n* delegación *f*

delet|e /dɪˈliːt/ *vt* tachar. **~ion** /-ʃn/ *n* tachadura *f*

deliberat|e /dɪˈlɪbəreɪt/ *vt/i* deliberar. /dɪˈlɪbərət/ *a* intencionado; ‹*steps etc*› pausado. **~ely** *adv* a propósito. **~ion** /-ˈreɪʃn/ *n* deliberación *f*

delica|cy /ˈdelɪkəsɪ/ *n* delicadeza *f*; (*food*) manjar *m*; (*sweet food*) golosina *f*. **~te** /ˈdelɪkət/ *a* delicado

delicatessen /delɪkəˈtesn/ *n* charcutería *f* fina

delicious /dɪˈlɪʃəs/ *a* delicioso

delight /dɪˈlaɪt/ *n* placer *m*. ● *vt* encantar. ● *vi* deleitarse. **~ed** *a* encantado. **~ful** *a* delicioso

delineat|e /dɪˈlɪnɪeɪt/ *vt* delinear. **~ion** /-ˈeɪʃn/ *n* delineación *f*

delinquen|cy /dɪˈlɪŋkwənsɪ/ *n* delincuencia *f*. **~t** /dɪˈlɪŋkwənt/ *a & n* delincuente (*m & f*)

deliri|ous /dɪˈlɪrɪəs/ *a* delirante. **~um** *n* delirio *m*

deliver /dɪˈlɪvə(r)/ *vt* entregar; (*utter*) pronunciar; (*aim*) lanzar; (*set free*) librar; (*med*) asistir al parto de. **~ance** *n* liberación *f*. **~y** *n*

entrega *f*; (*of post*) reparto *m*; (*med*) parto *m*

delta /ˈdeltə/ *n* (*geog*) delta *m*

delude /dɪˈluːd/ *vt* engañar. **~ o.s.** engañarse

deluge /ˈdeljuːdʒ/ *n* diluvio *m*

delusion /dɪˈluːʒn/ *n* ilusión *f*

de luxe /dɪˈlʌks/ *a* de lujo

delve /delv/ *vi* cavar. **~ into** (*investigate*) investigar

demagogue /ˈdeməɡɒɡ/ *n* demagogo *m*

demand /dɪˈmɑːnd/ *vt* exigir. ● *n* petición *f*; (*claim*) reclamación *f*; (*com*) demanda *f*. **in ~** muy popular, muy solicitado. **on ~** a solicitud. **~ing** *a* exigente. **~s** *npl* exigencias *fpl*

demarcation /diːmɑːˈkeɪʃn/ *n* demarcación *f*

demean /dɪˈmiːn/ *vt*. **~ o.s.** degradarse. **~our** /dɪˈmiːnə(r)/ *n* conducta *f*

demented /dɪˈmentɪd/ *a* demente

demerara /deməˈreərə/ *n*. **~ (sugar)** *n* azúcar *m* moreno

demise /dɪˈmaɪz/ *n* fallecimiento *m*

demo /ˈdeməʊ/ *n* (*pl* **-os**) (*fam*) manifestación *f*

demobilize /diːˈməʊbəlaɪz/ *vt* desmovilizar

democra|cy /dɪˈmɒkrəsɪ/ *n* democracia *f*. **~t** /ˈdeməkræt/ *n* demócrata *m & f*. **~tic** /-ˈkrætɪk/ *a* democrático

demoli|sh /dɪˈmɒlɪʃ/ *vt* derribar. **~tion** /deməˈlɪʃn/ *n* demolición *f*

demon /ˈdiːmən/ *n* demonio *m*

demonstrat|e /ˈdemənstreɪt/ *vt* demostrar. ● *vi* manifestarse, hacer una manifestación. **~ion** /-ˈstreɪʃn/ *n* demostración *f*; (*pol etc*) manifestación *f*

demonstrative /dɪˈmɒnstrətɪv/ *a* demostrativo

demonstrator /ˈdemənstreɪtə(r)/ *n* demostrador *m*: (*pol etc*) manifestante *m & f*

demoralize /dɪˈmɒrəlaɪz/ *vt* desmoralizar

demote /dɪˈməʊt/ *vt* degradar

demure /dɪˈmjʊə(r)/ *a* recatado

den /den/ *n* (*of animal*) guarida *f*, madriguera *f*

denial /dɪˈnaɪəl/ *n* denegación *f*; (*statement*) desmentimiento *m*

denigrate /ˈdenɪɡreɪt/ *vt* denigrar

denim /ˈdenɪm/ *n* dril *m* (de algodón azul grueso). **~s** *npl* pantalón *m* vaquero

Denmark /'denmɑːk/ *n* Dinamarca *f*

denomination /dɪnɒmɪ'neɪʃn/ *n* denominación *f*; (*relig*) secta *f*

denote /dɪ'nəʊt/ *vt* denotar

denounce /dɪ'naʊns/ *vt* denunciar

dens|e /dens/ *a* (**-er, -est**) espeso; ⟨*person*⟩ torpe. **~ely** *adv* densamente. **~ity** *n* densidad *f*

dent /dent/ *n* abolladura *f*. ● *vt* abollar

dental /'dentl/ *a* dental. **~ surgeon** *n* dentista *m & f*

dentist /'dentɪst/ *n* dentista *m & f*. **~ry** *n* odontología *f*

denture /'dentʃə(r)/ *n* dentadura *f* postiza

denude /dɪ'njuːd/ *vt* desnudar; (*fig*) despojar

denunciation /dɪnʌnsɪ'eɪʃn/ *n* denuncia *f*

deny /dɪ'naɪ/ *vt* negar; desmentir ⟨*rumour*⟩; (*disown*) renegar

deodorant /diː'əʊdərənt/ *a & n* desodorante (*m*)

depart /dɪ'pɑːt/ *vi* marcharse; ⟨*train etc*⟩ salir. **~ from** apartarse de

department /dɪ'pɑːtmənt/ *n* departamento *m*; (*com*) sección *f*. **~ store** *n* grandes almacenes *mpl*

departure /dɪ'pɑːtʃə(r)/ *n* partida *f*; (*of train etc*) salida *f*. **~ from** (*fig*) desviación *f*

depend /dɪ'pend/ *vi* depender. **~ on** depender de; (*rely*) contar con. **~able** *a* seguro. **~ant** /dɪ'pendənt/ *n* familiar *m & f* dependiente. **~ence** *n* dependencia *f*. **~ent** *a* dependiente. **be ~ent on** depender de

depict /dɪ'pɪkt/ *vt* pintar; (*in words*) describir

deplete /dɪ'pliːt/ *vt* agotar

deplor|able /dɪ'plɔːrəbl/ *a* lamentable. **~e** /dɪ'plɔː(r)/ *vt* lamentar

deploy /dɪ'plɔɪ/ *vt* desplegar. ● *vi* desplegarse

depopulate /diː'pɒpjʊleɪt/ *vt* despoblar

deport /dɪ'pɔːt/ *vt* deportar. **~ation** /diːpɔː'teɪʃn/ *n* deportación *f*

depose /dɪ'pəʊz/ *vt* deponer

deposit /dɪ'pɒzɪt/ *vt* (*pt* **deposited**) depositar. ● *n* depósito *m*. **~or** *n* depositante *m & f*

depot /'depəʊ/ *n* depósito *m*; (*Amer*) estación *f*

deprav|e /dɪ'preɪv/ *vt* depravar. **~ity** /-'prævətɪ/ *n* depravación *f*

deprecate /'deprɪkeɪt/ *vt* desaprobar

depreciat|e /dɪ'priːʃɪeɪt/ *vt* depreciar. ● *vi* depreciarse. **~ion** /-'eɪʃn/ *n* depreciación *f*

depress /dɪ'pres/ *vt* deprimir; (*press down*) apretar. **~ion** /-ʃn/ *n* depresión *f*

depriv|ation /deprɪ'veɪʃn/ *n* privación *f*. **~e** /dɪ'praɪv/ *vt*. **~ of** privar de

depth /depθ/ *n* profundidad *f*. **be out of one's ~** perder pie; (*fig*) meterse en honduras. **in the ~s of** en lo más hondo de

deputation /depjʊ'teɪʃn/ *n* diputación *f*

deputize /'depjʊtaɪz/ *vi*. **~ for** sustituir a

deputy /'depjʊtɪ/ *n* sustituto *m*. **~ chairman** *n* vicepresidente *m*

derail /dɪ'reɪl/ *vt* hacer descarrilar. **~ment** *n* descarrilamiento *m*

deranged /dɪ'reɪndʒd/ *a* ⟨*mind*⟩ trastornado

derelict /'derəlɪkt/ *a* abandonado

deri|de /dɪ'raɪd/ *vt* mofarse de. **~sion** /-'rɪʒn/ *n* mofa *f*. **~sive** *a* burlón. **~sory** /dɪ'raɪsərɪ/ *a* mofador; (*offer etc*) irrisorio

deriv|ation /derɪ'veɪʃn/ *n* derivación *f*. **~ative** /dɪ'rɪvətɪv/ *a & n* derivado (*m*). **~e** /dɪ'raɪv/ *vt/i* derivar

derogatory /dɪ'rɒgətrɪ/ *a* despectivo

derv /dɜːv/ *n* gasóleo *m*

descen|d /dɪ'send/ *vt/i* descender, bajar. **~dant** *n* descendiente *m & f*. **~t** /dɪ'sent/ *n* descenso *m*; (*lineage*) descendencia *f*

descri|be /dɪs'kraɪb/ *vt* describir. **~ption** /-'krɪpʃn/ *n* descripción *f*. **~ptive** /-'krɪptɪv/ *a* descriptivo

desecrat|e /'desɪkreɪt/ *vt* profanar. **~ion** /-'kreɪʃn/ *n* profanación *f*

desert[1] /dɪ'zɜːt/ *vt* abandonar. ● *vi* (*mil*) desertar

desert[2] /'dezət/ *a & n* desierto (*m*)

deserter /dɪ'zɜːtə(r)/ *n* desertor *m*

deserts /dɪ'zɜːts/ *npl* lo merecido. **get one's ~** llevarse su merecido

deserv|e /dɪ'zɜːv/ *vt* merecer. **~edly** *adv* merecidamente. **~ing** *a* ⟨*person*⟩ digno de; ⟨*action*⟩ meritorio

design /dɪ'zaɪn/ *n* diseño *m*; (*plan*) proyecto *m*; (*pattern*) modelo *m*; (*aim*) propósito *m*. **have ~s on**

poner la mira en. ● *vt* diseñar; (*plan*) proyectar

designat|e /'dezɪgneɪt/ *vt* designar; (*appoint*) nombrar. **~ion** /-'neɪʃn/ *n* denominación *f*; (*appointment*) nombramiento *m*

designer /dɪ'zaɪnə(r)/ *n* diseñador *m*; (*of clothing*) modisto *m*; (*in theatre*) escenógrafo *m*

desirab|ility /dɪzaɪərə'bɪlətɪ/ *n* conveniencia *f*. **~le** /dɪ'zaɪrəbl/ *a* deseable

desire /dɪ'zaɪə(r)/ *n* deseo *m*. ● *vt* desear

desist /dɪ'zɪst/ *vi* desistir

desk /desk/ *n* escritorio *m*; (*at school*) pupitre *m*; (*in hotel*) recepción *f*; (*com*) caja *f*

desolat|e /'desələt/ *a* desolado; (*uninhabited*) deshabitado. **~ion** /-'leɪʃn/ *n* desolación *f*

despair /dɪ'speə(r)/ *n* desesperación *f*. ● *vi*. **~ of** desesperarse de

desperat|e /'despərət/ *a* desesperado; (*dangerous*) peligroso. **~ely** *adv* desesperadamente. **~ion** /-'reɪʃn/ *n* desesperación *f*

despicable /dɪ'spɪkəbl/ *a* despreciable

despise /dɪ'spaɪz/ *vt* despreciar

despite /dɪ'spaɪt/ *prep* a pesar de

desponden|cy /dɪ'spɒndənsɪ/ *n* abatimiento *m*. **~t** /dɪ'spɒndənt/ *a* desanimado

despot /'despɒt/ *n* déspota *m*

dessert /dɪ'zɜːt/ *n* postre *m*. **~spoon** *n* cuchara *f* de postre

destination /destɪ'neɪʃn/ *n* destino *m*

destine /'destɪn/ *vt* destinar

destiny /'destɪnɪ/ *n* destino *m*

destitute /'destɪtjuːt/ *a* indigente. **~ of** desprovisto de

destroy /dɪ'strɔɪ/ *vt* destruir

destroyer /dɪ'strɔɪə(r)/ *n* (*naut*) destructor *m*

destructi|on /dɪ'strʌkʃn/ *n* destrucción *f*. **~ve** *a* destructivo

desultory /'desəltrɪ/ *a* irregular

detach /dɪ'tætʃ/ *vt* separar. **~able** *a* separable. **~ed** *a* separado. **~ed house** *n* chalet *m*. **~ment** /dɪ'tætʃmənt/ *n* separación *f*; (*mil*) destacamento *m*; (*fig*) indiferencia *f*

detail /'diːteɪl/ *n* detalle *m*. ● *vt* detallar; (*mil*) destacar. **~ed** *a* detallado

detain /dɪ'teɪn/ *vt* detener; (*delay*) retener. **~ee** /diːteɪ'niː/ *n* detenido *m*

detect /dɪ'tekt/ *vt* percibir; (*discover*) descubrir. **~ion** /-ʃn/ *n* descubrimiento *m*, detección *f*. **~or** *n* detector *m*

detective /dɪ'tektɪv/ *n* detective *m*. **~ story** *n* novela *f* policíaca

detention /dɪ'tenʃn/ *n* detención *f*

deter /dɪ'tɜː(r)/ *vt* (*pt* **deterred**) disuadir; (*prevent*) impedir

detergent /dɪ'tɜːdʒənt/ *a & n* detergente (*m*)

deteriorat|e /dɪ'tɪərɪəreɪt/ *vi* deteriorarse. **~ion** /-'reɪʃn/ *n* deterioro *m*

determination /dɪtɜːmɪ'neɪʃn/ *n* determinación *f*

determine /dɪ'tɜːmɪn/ *vt* determinar; (*decide*) decidir. **~d** *a* determinado; (*resolute*) resuelto

deterrent /dɪ'terənt/ *n* fuerza *f* de disuasión

detest /dɪ'test/ *vt* aborrecer. **~able** *a* odioso

detonat|e /'detəneɪt/ *vt* hacer detonar. ● *vi* detonar. **~ion** /-'neɪʃn/ *n* detonación *f*. **~or** *n* detonador *m*

detour /'diːtʊə(r)/ *n* desviación *f*

detract /dɪ'trækt/ *vi*. **~ from** (*lessen*) disminuir

detriment /'detrɪmənt/ *n* perjuicio *m*. **~al** /-'mentl/ *a* perjudicial

devalu|ation /diːvæljuː'eɪʃn/ *n* desvalorización *f*. **~e** /diː'væljuː/ *vt* desvalorizar

devastat|e /'devəsteɪt/ *vt* devastar. **~ing** *a* devastador; (*fig*) arrollador

develop /dɪ'veləp/ *vt* desarrollar; contraer ⟨*illness*⟩; urbanizar ⟨*land*⟩. ● *vi* desarrollarse; (*show*) aparecerse. **~er** *n* (*foto*) revelador *m*. **~ing country** *n* país *m* en vías de desarrollo. **~ment** *n* desarrollo *m*. (**new**) **~ment** novedad *f*

deviant /'diːvɪənt/ *a* desviado

deviat|e /'diːvɪeɪt/ *vi* desviarse. **~ion** /-'eɪʃn/ *n* desviación *f*

device /dɪ'vaɪs/ *n* dispositivo *m*; (*scheme*) estratagema *f*

devil /'devl/ *n* diablo *m*. **~ish** *a* diabólico

devious /'diːvɪəs/ *a* tortuoso

devise /dɪ'vaɪz/ *vt* idear

devoid /dɪ'vɔɪd/ *a*. **~ of** desprovisto de

devolution /diːvə'luːʃn/ *n* descentralización *f*; (*of power*) delegación *f*

devot|e /dɪ'vəʊt/ *vt* dedicar. **~ed** *a* leal. **~edly** *adv* con devoción *f*. **~ee**

/devə'ti:/ *n* partidario *m*. ~**ion** /-ʃn/ *n* dedicación *f*. ~**ions** *npl* (*relig*) oraciones *fpl*

devour /dɪ'vaʊə(r)/ *vt* devorar

devout /dɪ'vaʊt/ *a* devoto

dew /dju:/ *n* rocío *m*

dext|erity /dek'sterətɪ/ *n* destreza *f*. ~**(e)rous** /'dekstrəs/ *a* diestro

diabet|es /daɪə'bi:ti:z/ *n* diabetes *f*. ~**ic** /-'betɪk/ *a* & *n* diabético (*m*)

diabolical /daɪə'bɒlɪkl/ *a* diabólico

diadem /'daɪədem/ *n* diadema *f*

diagnos|e /'daɪəgnəʊz/ *vt* diagnosticar. ~**is** /daɪəg'nəʊsɪs/ *n* (*pl* -**oses** /-si:z/) diagnóstico *m*

diagonal /daɪ'ægənl/ *a* & *n* diagonal (*f*)

diagram /'daɪəgræm/ *n* diagrama *m*

dial /'daɪəl/ *n* cuadrante *m*; (*on phone*) disco *m*. ● *vt* (*pt* **dialled**) marcar

dialect /'daɪəlekt/ *n* dialecto *m*

dial: ~**ling code** *n* prefijo *m*. ~**ling tone** *n* señal *f* para marcar

dialogue /'daɪəlɒg/ *n* diálogo *m*

diameter /daɪ'æmɪtə(r)/ *n* diámetro *m*

diamond /'daɪəmənd/ *n* diamante *m*; (*shape*) rombo *m*. ~**s** *npl* (*cards*) diamantes *mpl*

diaper /'daɪəpə(r)/ *n* (*Amer*) pañal *m*

diaphanous /daɪ'æfənəs/ *a* diáfano

diaphragm /'daɪəfræm/ *n* diafragma *m*

diarrhoea /daɪə'rɪə/ *n* diarrea *f*

diary /'daɪərɪ/ *n* diario *m*; (*book*) agenda *f*

diatribe /'daɪətraɪb/ *n* diatriba *f*

dice /daɪs/ *n invar* dado *m*. ● *vt* (*culin*) cortar en cubitos

dicey /'daɪsɪ/ *a* (*sl*) arriesgado

dictat|e /dɪk'teɪt/ *vt/i* dictar. ~**es** /'dɪkteɪts/ *npl* dictados *mpl*. ~**ion** /dɪk'teɪʃn/ *n* dictado *m*

dictator /dɪk'teɪtə(r)/ *n* dictador *m*. ~**ship** *n* dictadura *f*

diction /'dɪkʃn/ *n* dicción *f*

dictionary /'dɪkʃənərɪ/ *n* diccionario *m*

did /dɪd/ *see* **do**

didactic /daɪ'dæktɪk/ *a* didáctico

diddle /'dɪdl/ *vt* (*sl*) estafar

didn't /'dɪdnt/ = **did not**

die[1] /daɪ/ *vi* (*pres p* **dying**) morir. **be dying to** morirse por. ~ **down** disminuir. ~ **out** extinguirse

die[2] /daɪ/ *n* (*tec*) cuño *m*

die-hard /'daɪhɑːd/ *n* intransigente *m* & *f*

diesel /'di:zl/ *n* (*fuel*) gasóleo *m*. ~ **engine** *n* motor *m* diesel

diet /'daɪət/ *n* alimentación *f*; (*restricted*) régimen *m*. ● *vi* estar a régimen. ~**etic** /daɪə'tetɪk/ *a* dietético. ~**itian** *n* dietético *m*

differ /'dɪfə(r)/ *vi* ser distinto; (*disagree*) no estar de acuerdo. ~**ence** /'dɪfrəns/ *n* diferencia *f*; (*disagreement*) desacuerdo *m*. ~**ent** /'dɪfrənt/ *a* distinto, diferente

differentia|l /dɪfə'renʃl/ *a* & *n* diferencial (*f*). ~**te** /dɪfə'renʃɪeɪt/ *vt* diferenciar. ● *vi* diferenciarse

differently /'dɪfrəntlɪ/ *adv* de otra manera

difficult /'dɪfɪkəlt/ *a* difícil. ~**y** *n* dificultad *f*

diffiden|ce /'dɪfɪdəns/ *n* falta *f* de confianza. ~**t** /'dɪfɪdənt/ *a* que falta confianza

diffus|e /dɪ'fju:s/ *a* difuso. /dɪ'fju:z/ *vt* difundir. ● *vi* difundirse. ~**ion** /-ʒn/ *n* difusión *f*

dig /dɪg/ *n* (*poke*) empujón *m*; (*poke with elbow*) codazo *m*; (*remark*) indirecta *f*; (*archaeol*) excavación *f*. ● *vt* (*pt* **dug**, *pres p* **digging**) cavar; (*thrust*) empujar. ● *vi* cavar. ~ **out** extraer. ~ **up** desenterrar. ~**s** *npl* (*fam*) alojamiento *m*

digest /'daɪdʒest/ *n* resumen *m*. ● *vt* digerir. ~**ible** *a* digerible. ~**ion** /-ʃn/ *n* digestión *f*. ~**ive** *a* digestivo

digger /'dɪgə(r)/ *n* (*mec*) excavadora *f*

digit /'dɪdʒɪt/ *n* cifra *f*; (*finger*) dedo *m*. ~**al** /'dɪdʒɪtl/ *a* digital

dignif|ied /'dɪgnɪfaɪd/ *a* solemne. ~**y** /'dɪgnɪfaɪ/ *vt* dignificar

dignitary /'dɪgnɪtərɪ/ *n* dignatario *m*

dignity /'dɪgnətɪ/ *n* dignidad *f*

digress /daɪ'gres/ *vi* divagar. ~ **from** apartarse de. ~**ion** /-ʃn/ *n* digresión *f*

dike /daɪk/ *n* dique *m*

dilapidated /dɪ'læpɪdeɪtɪd/ *a* ruinoso

dilat|e /daɪ'leɪt/ *vt* dilatar. ● *vi* dilatarse. ~**ion** /-ʃn/ *n* dilatación *f*

dilatory /'dɪlətərɪ/ *a* dilatorio, lento

dilemma /daɪ'lemə/ *n* dilema *m*

diligen|ce /'dɪlɪdʒəns/ *n* diligencia *f*. ~**t** /'dɪlɪdʒənt/ *a* diligente

dilly-dally /'dɪlɪdælɪ/ *vi* (*fam*) perder el tiempo

dilute /daɪ'lju:t/ *vt* diluir

dim /dɪm/ *a* (**dimmer, dimmest**) (*weak*) débil; (*dark*) oscuro; (*stupid*,

fam) torpe. ● *vt* (*pt* **dimmed**) amortiguar. ● *vi* apagarse. ~ **the head-
lights** bajar los faros
dime /daɪm/ *n* (*Amer*) moneda *f* de
diez centavos
dimension /daɪ'menʃn/ *n* dimensión
f
diminish /dɪ'mɪnɪʃ/ *vt/i* disminuir
diminutive   /dɪ'mɪnjʊtɪv/   *a*
diminuto. ● *n* diminutivo *m*
dimness /'dɪmnɪs/ *n* debilidad *f*; (*of
room etc*) oscuridad *f*
dimple /'dɪmpl/ *n* hoyuelo *m*
din /dɪn/ *n* jaleo *m*
dine /daɪn/ *vi* cenar. ~**r** /-ə(r)/ *n*
comensal *m* & *f*; (*rail*) coche *m*
restaurante
dinghy /'dɪŋgɪ/ *n* (*inflatable*) bote *m*
neumático
ding|**iness** /'dɪndʒɪnɪs/ *n* suciedad *f*.
~**y** /'dɪndʒɪ/ *a* (**-ier, -iest**) miserable,
sucio
dining-room /'daɪnɪŋruːm/ *n* comedor *m*
dinner /'dɪnə(r)/ *n* cena *f*. ~**jacket** *n*
esmoquin *m*. ~ **party** *n* cena *f*
dinosaur /'daɪnəsɔː(r)/ *n* dinosaurio
m
dint /dɪnt/ *n*. **by** ~ **of** a fuerza de
diocese /'daɪəsɪs/ *n* diócesis *f*
dip /dɪp/ *vt* (*pt* **dipped**) sumergir.
● *vi* bajar. ~ **into** hojear (*book*). ● *n*
(*slope*) inclinación *f*; (*in sea*) baño *m*
diphtheria /dɪf'θɪərɪə/ *n* difteria *f*
diphthong /'dɪfθɒŋ/ *n* diptongo *m*
diploma /dɪ'pləʊmə/ *n* diploma *m*
diplomacy /dɪ'pləʊməsɪ/ *n* diplomacia *f*
diplomat /'dɪpləmæt/ *n* diplomático
m. ~**ic** /-'mætɪk/ *a* diplomático
dipstick /'dɪpstɪk/ *n* (*auto*) varilla *f*
del nivel de aceite
dire /daɪə(r)/ *a* (**-er, -est**) terrible;
(*need, poverty*) extremo
direct /dɪ'rekt/ *a* directo. ● *adv* directamente. ● *vt* dirigir; (*show the
way*) indicar
direction /dɪ'rekʃn/ *n* dirección *f*.
~**s** *npl* instrucciones *fpl*
directly /dɪ'rektlɪ/ *adv* directamente; (*at once*) en seguida. ● *conj*
(*fam*) en cuanto
director /dɪ'rektə(r)/ *n* director *m*
directory /dɪ'rektərɪ/ *n* guía *f*
dirge /dɜːdʒ/ *n* canto *m* fúnebre
dirt /dɜːt/ *n* suciedad *f*. ~**-track** *n*
(*sport*) pista *f* de ceniza. ~**y** /'dɜːtɪ/
a (**-ier, -iest**) sucio. ~**y trick** *n* mala

jugada *f*. ~**y word** *n* palabrota *f*.
● *vt* ensuciar
disability /dɪsə'bɪlətɪ/ *n* invalidez *f*
disable /dɪs'eɪbl/ *vt* incapacitar. ~**d**
a minusválido
disabuse /dɪsə'bjuːz/ *vt* desengañar
disadvantage   /dɪsəd'vɑːntɪdʒ/   *n*
desventaja *f*. ~**d** *a* desventajado
disagree /dɪsə'griː/ *vi* no estar de
acuerdo; (*food, climate*) sentar mal
a. ~**able** /dɪsə'griːəbl/ *a* desagradable. ~**ment** *n* desacuerdo *m*;
(*quarrel*) riña *f*
disappear /dɪsə'pɪə(r)/ *vi* desaparecer. ~**ance** *n* desaparición *f*
disappoint /dɪsə'pɔɪnt/ *vt* desilusionar, decepcionar. ~**ment** *n*
desilusión *f*, decepción *f*
disapprov|**al** /dɪsə'pruːvl/ *n* desa-
probación *f*. ~**e** /dɪsə'pruːv/ *vi*. ~ **of**
desaprobar
disarm /dɪs'ɑːm/ *vt/i* desarmar.
~**ament** *n* desarme *m*
disarray /dɪsə'reɪ/ *n* desorden *m*
disast|**er** /dɪ'zɑːstə(r)/ *n* desastre *m*.
~**rous** *a* catastrófico
disband /dɪs'bænd/ *vt* disolver. ● *vi*
disolverse
disbelief /dɪsbɪ'liːf/ *n* incredulidad *f*
disc /dɪsk/ *n* disco *m*
discard /dɪs'kɑːd/ *vt* descartar; abandonar (*beliefs etc*)
discern /dɪ'sɜːn/ *vt* percibir. ~**ible** *a*
perceptible. ~**ing** *a* perspicaz
discharge /dɪs'tʃɑːdʒ/ *vt* descargar;
cumplir (*duty*); (*dismiss*) despedir;
poner en libertad (*prisoner*); (*mil*)
licenciar. /'dɪstʃɑːdʒ/ *n* descarga *f*;
(*med*) secreción *f*; (*mil*) licen-
ciamiento *m*; (*dismissal*) despedida
f
disciple /dɪ'saɪpl/ *n* discípulo *m*
disciplin|**arian** /dɪsəplɪ'neərɪən/ *n*
ordenancista *m* & *f*. ~**ary** *a* disciplinario. ~**e** /'dɪsɪplɪn/ *n* disciplina *f*. ● *vt* disciplinar; (*punish*)
castigar
disc jockey /'dɪskdʒɒkɪ/ *n* (*on radio*)
pinchadiscos *m* & *f invar*
disclaim /dɪs'kleɪm/ *vt* desconocer.
~**er** *n* renuncia *f*
disclos|**e** /dɪs'kləʊz/ *vt* revelar.
~**ure** /-ʒə(r)/ *n* revelación *f*
disco /'dɪskəʊ/ *n* (*pl* **-os**) (*fam*) discoteca *f*
discolo|**ur** /dɪs'kʌlə(r)/ *vt* decolorar.
● *vi* decolorarse. ~**ration** /-'reɪʃn/ *n*
decoloración *f*

discomfort /dɪs'kʌmfət/ *n* malestar *m*; (*lack of comfort*) incomodidad *f*
disconcert /dɪskən'sɜːt/ *vt* desconcertar
disconnect /dɪskə'nekt/ *vt* separar; (*elec*) desconectar
disconsolate /dɪs'kɒnsələt/ *a* desconsolado
discontent /dɪskən'tent/ *n* descontento *m*. ~**ed** *a* descontento
discontinue /dɪskən'tɪnjuː/ *vt* interrumpir
discord /'dɪskɔːd/ *n* discordia *f*; (*mus*) disonancia *f*. ~**ant** /-'skɔːdənt/ *a* discorde; (*mus*) disonante
discothèque /'dɪskətek/ *n* discoteca *f*
discount /'dɪskaʊnt/ *n* descuento *m*. /dɪs'kaʊnt/ *vt* hacer caso omiso de; (*com*) descontar
discourage /dɪs'kʌrɪdʒ/ *vt* desanimar; (*dissuade*) disuadir
discourse /'dɪskɔːs/ *n* discurso *m*
discourteous /dɪs'kɜːtɪəs/ *a* descortés
discover /dɪs'kʌvə(r)/ *vt* descubrir. ~**y** *n* descubrimiento *m*
discredit /dɪs'kredɪt/ *vt* (*pt* **discredited**) desacreditar. ● *n* descrédito *m*
discreet /dɪs'kriːt/ *a* discreto. ~**ly** *adv* discretamente
discrepancy /dɪ'skrepənsɪ/ *n* discrepancia *f*
discretion /dɪ'skreʃn/ *n* discreción *f*
discriminat|e /dɪs'krɪmɪneɪt/ *vt/i* discriminar. ~**e between** distinguir entre. ~**ing** *a* perspicaz. ~**ion** /-'neɪʃn/ *n* discernimiento *m*; (*bias*) discriminación *f*
discus /'dɪskəs/ *n* disco *m*
discuss /dɪ'skʌs/ *vt* discutir. ~**ion** /-ʃn/ *n* discusión *f*
disdain /dɪs'deɪn/ *n* desdén *m*. ● *vt* desdeñar. ~**ful** *a* desdeñoso
disease /dɪ'ziːz/ *n* enfermedad *f*. ~**d** *a* enfermo
disembark /dɪsɪm'bɑːk/ *vt/i* desembarcar
disembodied /dɪsɪm'bɒdɪd/ *a* incorpóreo
disenchant /dɪsɪn'tʃɑːnt/ *vt* desencantar. ~**ment** *n* desencanto *m*
disengage /dɪsɪn'geɪdʒ/ *vt* soltar. ~ **the clutch** desembragar. ~**ment** *n* soltura *f*
disentangle /dɪsɪn'tæŋgl/ *vt* desenredar

disfavour /dɪs'feɪvə(r)/ *n* desaprobación *f*. **fall into** ~ (*person*) caer en desgracia; (*custom, word*) caer en desuso
disfigure /dɪs'fɪgə(r)/ *vt* desfigurar
disgorge /dɪs'gɔːdʒ/ *vt* arrojar; (*river*) descargar; (*fig*) restituir
disgrace /dɪs'greɪs/ *n* deshonra *f*; (*disfavour*) desgracia *f*. ● *vt* deshonrar. ~**ful** *a* vergonzoso
disgruntled /dɪs'grʌntld/ *a* descontento
disguise /dɪs'gaɪz/ *vt* disfrazar. ● *n* disfraz *m*. **in** ~ disfrazado
disgust /dɪs'gʌst/ *n* repugnancia *f*, asco *m*. ● *vt* repugnar, dar asco. ~**ing** *a* repugnante, asqueroso
dish /dɪʃ/ *n* plato *m*. ● *vt*. ~ **out** (*fam*) distribuir. ~ **up** servir. ~**cloth** /'dɪʃklɒθ/ *n* bayeta *f*
dishearten /dɪs'hɑːtn/ *vt* desanimar
dishevelled /dɪ'ʃevld/ *a* desaliñado; (*hair*) despeinado
dishonest /dɪs'ɒnɪst/ *a* (*person*) poco honrado; (*means*) fraudulento. ~**y** *n* falta *f* de honradez
dishonour /dɪs'ɒnə(r)/ *n* deshonra *f*. ● *vt* deshonrar. ~**able** *a* deshonroso. ~**ably** *adv* deshonrosamente
dishwasher /'dɪʃwɒʃə(r)/ *n* lavaplatos *m* & *f*
disillusion /dɪsɪ'luːʒn/ *vt* desilusionar. ~**ment** *n* desilusión
disincentive /dɪsɪn'sentɪv/ *n* freno *m*
disinclined /dɪsɪn'klaɪnd/ *a* poco dispuesto
disinfect /dɪsɪn'fekt/ *vt* desinfectar. ~**ant** *n* desinfectante *m*
disinherit /dɪsɪn'herɪt/ *vt* desheredar
disintegrate /dɪs'ɪntɪgreɪt/ *vt* desintegrar. ● *vi* desintegrarse
disinterested /dɪs'ɪntrəstɪd/ *a* desinteresado
disjointed /dɪs'dʒɔɪntɪd/ *a* inconexo
disk /dɪsk/ *n* disco *m*
dislike /dɪs'laɪk/ *n* aversión *f*. ● *vt* tener aversión a
dislocat|e /'dɪsləkeɪt/ *vt* dislocar(se) (*limb*). ~**ion** /-'keɪʃn/ *n* dislocación *f*
dislodge /dɪs'lɒdʒ/ *vt* sacar; (*oust*) desalojar
disloyal /dɪs'lɔɪəl/ *a* desleal. ~**ty** *n* deslealtad *f*
dismal /'dɪzməl/ *a* triste; (*bad*) fatal
dismantle /dɪs'mæntl/ *vt* desarmar

dismay /dɪs'meɪ/ n consternación f.
• vt consternar

dismiss /dɪs'mɪs/ vt despedir; (reject)
rechazar. ~al n despedida f; (of
idea) abandono m

dismount /dɪs'maʊnt/ vi apearse

disobedien|ce /dɪsə'biːdɪəns/ n
desobediencia f. ~t /dɪsə'biːdɪənt/ a
desobediente

disobey /dɪsə'beɪ/ vt/i desobedecer

disorder /dɪs'ɔːdə(r)/ n desorden m;
(ailment) trastorno m. ~ly a
desordenado

disorganize /dɪs'ɔːgənaɪz/ vt desorganizar

disorientate /dɪs'ɔːrɪənteɪt/ vt des-
orientar

disown /dɪs'əʊn/ vt repudiar

disparaging /dɪs'pærɪdʒɪŋ/ a
despreciativo. ~ly adv con
desprecio

disparity /dɪs'pærətɪ/ n disparidad f

dispassionate /dɪs'pæʃənət/ a
desapasionado

dispatch /dɪs'pætʃ/ vt enviar. • n
envío m; (report) despacho m.
~-rider n correo m

dispel /dɪs'pel/ vt (pt dispelled)
disipar

dispensable /dɪs'pensəbl/ a
prescindible

dispensary /dɪs'pensərɪ/ n farmacia
f

dispensation /dɪspen'seɪʃn/ n distribución f; (relig) dispensa f

dispense /dɪs'pens/ vt distribuir;
(med) preparar; (relig) dispensar;
administrar ⟨justice⟩. ~ with prescindir de. ~r /-ə(r)/ n (mec) distribuidor m automático; (med) farmacéutico m

dispers|al /dɪs'pɜːsl/ n dispersión f.
~e /dɪ'spɜːs/ vt dispersar. • vi
dispersarse

dispirited /dɪs'pɪrɪtɪd/ a desani-
mado

displace /dɪs'pleɪs/ vt desplazar

display /dɪs'pleɪ/ vt mostrar; exhibir
⟨goods⟩; manifestar ⟨feelings⟩. • n
exposición f; (of feelings) manifestación f; (pej) ostentación f

displeas|e /dɪs'pliːz/ vt desagradar.
be ~ed with estar disgustado con.
~ure /-'pleʒə(r)/ n desagrado m

dispos|able /dɪs'pəʊzəbl/ a dese-
chable. ~al n (of waste) eliminación
f. at s.o.'s ~al a la disposición de
uno. ~e /dɪs'pəʊz/ vt disponer. be

~ed towards estar bien dispuesto hacia. • vi. ~e of deshacerse de

disposition /dɪspə'zɪʃn/ n disposición f

disproportionate /dɪsprə'pɔːʃənət/
a desproporcionado

disprove /dɪs'pruːv/ vt refutar

dispute /dɪs'pjuːt/ vt disputar. • n
disputa f. in ~ disputado

disqualif|ication /dɪskwɒlɪfɪ'keɪʃn/
n descalificación f. ~y
/dɪs'kwɒlɪfaɪ/ vt incapacitar; (sport)
descalificar

disquiet /dɪs'kwaɪət/ n inquietud f

disregard /dɪsrɪ'gɑːd/ vt no hacer
caso de. • n indiferencia f (for a)

disrepair /dɪsrɪ'peə(r)/ n mal estado
m

disreputable /dɪs'repjʊtəbl/ a de
mala fama

disrepute /dɪsrɪ'pjuːt/ n discrédito
m

disrespect /dɪsrɪs'pekt/ n falta f de
respeto

disrobe /dɪs'rəʊb/ vt desvestir. • vi
desvestirse

disrupt /dɪs'rʌpt/ vt interrumpir;
trastornar ⟨plans⟩. ~ion /-ʃn/ n
interrupción f; (disorder) desor-
ganización f. ~ive a desbaratador

dissatisfaction /dɪsætɪs'fækʃn/ n
descontento m

dissatisfied /dɪ'sætɪsfaɪd/ a
descontento

dissect /dɪ'sekt/ vt disecar. ~ion
/-ʃn/ n disección f

disseminat|e /dɪ'semɪneɪt/ vt dis-
eminar. ~ion /-'neɪʃn/ n di-
seminación f

dissent /dɪ'sent/ vi disentir. • n dis-
entimiento m

dissertation /dɪsə'teɪʃn/ n disertación f; (univ) tesis f

disservice /dɪs'sɜːvɪs/ n mal servicio
m

dissident /'dɪsɪdənt/ a & n disidente
(m & f)

dissimilar /dɪ'sɪmɪlə(r)/ a distinto

dissipate /'dɪsɪpeɪt/ vt disipar; (fig)
desvanecer. ~d a disoluto

dissociate /dɪ'səʊʃɪeɪt/ vt disociar

dissolut|e /'dɪsəluːt/ a disoluto.
~ion /dɪsə'luːʃn/ n disolución f

dissolve /dɪ'zɒlv/ vt disolver. • vi
disolverse

dissuade /dɪ'sweɪd/ vt disuadir

distan|ce /'dɪstəns/ n distancia f.
from a ~ce desde lejos. in the ~ce a

lo lejos. **∼t** /'dɪstənt/ a lejano;
(*aloof*) frío

distaste /dɪs'teɪst/ n aversión f. **∼ful**
a desagradable

distemper[1] /dɪ'stempə(r)/ n (*paint*)
temple m. ● vt pintar al temple

distemper[2] /dɪ'stempə(r)/ n (*of dogs*)
moquillo m

distend /dɪs'tend/ vt dilatar. ● vi
dilatarse

distil /dɪs'tɪl/ vt (*pt* distilled) destilar.
∼lation /-'leɪʃn/ n destilación f.
∼lery /dɪs'tɪlərɪ/ n destilería f

distinct /dɪs'tɪŋkt/ a distinto; (*clear*)
claro; (*marked*) marcado. **∼ion**
/-ʃn/ n distinción f; (*in exam*) sobresaliente m. **∼ive** a distintivo.
∼ly adv claramente

distinguish /dɪs'tɪŋgwɪʃ/ vt/i distinguir. **∼ed** a distinguido

distort /dɪs'tɔːt/ vt torcer. **∼ion** /-ʃn/
n deformación f

distract /dɪs'trækt/ vt distraer. **∼ed**
a aturdido. **∼ing** a molesto. **∼ion**
/-ʃn/ n distracción f; (*confusion*)
aturdimiento m

distraught /dɪs'trɔːt/ a aturdido

distress /dɪs'tres/ n angustia f; (*poverty*) miseria f; (*danger*) peligro m.
● vt afligir. **∼ing** a penoso

distribut|e /dɪs'trɪbjuːt/ vt distri-
buir. **∼ion** /-'bjuːʃn/ n distribución
f. **∼or** n distribuidor m; (*auto*) distribuidor m de encendido

district /'dɪstrɪkt/ n districto m; (*of
town*) barrio m

distrust /dɪs'trʌst/ n desconfianza f.
● vt desconfiar de

disturb /dɪs'tɜːb/ vt molestar; (*perturb*) inquietar; (*move*) desordenar;
(*interrupt*) interrumpir. **∼ance** n
disturbio m; (*tumult*) alboroto m.
∼ed a trastornado. **∼ing** a
inquietante

disused /dɪs'juːzd/ a fuera de uso

ditch /dɪtʃ/ n zanja f; (*for irrigation*)
acequia f. ● vt (*sl*) abandonar

dither /'dɪðə(r)/ vi vacilar

ditto /'dɪtəʊ/ adv ídem

divan /dɪ'væn/ n diván m

dive /daɪv/ vi tirarse de cabeza;
(*rush*) meterse (precipitadamente);
(*underwater*) bucear. ● n salto m;
(*of plane*) picado m; (*place, fam*) taberna f. **∼r** n saltador m; (*underwater*) buzo m

diverge /daɪ'vɜːdʒ/ vi divergir. **∼nt**
/daɪ'vɜːdʒənt/ a divergente

divers|e /daɪ'vɜːs/ a diverso. **∼ify**
/daɪ'vɜːsɪfaɪ/ vt diversificar. **∼ity**
/daɪ'vɜːsətɪ/ n diversidad f

diver|sion /daɪ'vɜːʃn/ n desvío m;
(*distraction*) diversión f. **∼t** /daɪ'vɜː
t/ vt desviar; (*entertain*) divertir

divest /daɪ'vest/ vt. **∼ of** despojar de

divide /dɪ'vaɪd/ vt dividir. ● vi
dividirse

dividend /'dɪvɪdend/ n dividendo m

divine /dɪ'vaɪn/ a divino

diving-board /'daɪvɪŋbɔːd/ n trampolín m

diving-suit /'daɪvɪŋsuːt/ n escafandra f

divinity /dɪ'vɪnɪtɪ/ n divinidad f

division /dɪ'vɪʒn/ n división f

divorce /dɪ'vɔːs/ n divorcio m. ● vt
divorciarse de; (*judge*) divorciar.
● vi divorciarse. **∼e** /dɪvɔː'siː/ n
divorciado m

divulge /daɪ'vʌldʒ/ vt divulgar

DIY abbr see **do-it-yourself**

dizz|iness /'dɪzɪnɪs/ n vértigo m. **∼y**
/'dɪzɪ/ a (*-ier, -iest*) mareado; (*speed*)
vertiginoso. **be** or **feel ∼y** marearse

do /duː/ vt (3 sing pres **does**, pt **did**,
pp **done**) hacer; (*swindle, sl*)
engañar. ● vi hacer; (*fare*) ir; (*be
suitable*) convenir; (*be enough*) bastar. ● n (pl **dos** or **do's**) (*fam*) fiesta f.
● v aux. **∼ you speak Spanish? Yes I
∼** ¿habla Vd español? Sí. **doesn't
he?, don't you?** ¿verdad? ∼ **come
in!** (*emphatic*) ¡pase Vd! ∼ **away
with** abolir. ∼ **in** (*exhaust, fam*) agotar; (*kill, sl*) matar. ∼ **out** (*clean*)
limpiar. ∼ **up** abotonar (*coat etc*);
renovar (*house*). ∼ **with** tener que
ver con; (*need*) necesitar. ∼ **without**
prescindir de. **∼ne for** (*fam*) arruinado. **∼ne in** (*fam*) agotado. **well
∼ne** (*culin*) bien hecho. **well ∼ne!**
¡muy bien!

docile /'dəʊsaɪl/ a dócil

dock[1] /dɒk/ n dique m. ● vt poner en
dique. ● vi atracar al muelle

dock[2] /dɒk/ n (*jurid*) banquillo m de
los acusados

dock: ∼er n estibador m. **∼yard**
/'dɒkjɑːd/ n astillero m

doctor /'dɒktə(r)/ n médico m, doctor m; (*univ*) doctor m. ● vt castrar
(*cat*); (*fig*) adulterar

doctorate /'dɒktərət/ n doctorado m

doctrine /'dɒktrɪn/ n doctrina f

document /'dɒkjʊmənt/ n documento m. **∼ary** /-'mentrɪ/ a & n
documental (*m*)

doddering /'dɒdərɪŋ/ a chocho

dodge /dɒdʒ/ vt esquivar. ● vi esquivarse. ● n regate m; (fam) truco m

dodgems /'dɒdʒəmz/ npl autos mpl de choque

dodgy /'dɒdʒɪ/ a (-ier, -iest) (awkward) difícil

does /dʌz/ see do

doesn't /'dʌznt/ = does not

dog /dɒg/ n perro m. ● vt (pt dogged) perseguir. ~collar n (relig, fam) alzacuello m. ~eared a ⟨book⟩ sobado

dogged /'dɒgɪd/ a obstinado

doghouse /'dɒghaʊs/ n (Amer) perrera f. in the ~ (sl) en desgracia

dogma /'dɒgmə/ n dogma m. ~tic /-'mætɪk/ a dogmático

dogsbody /'dɒgzbɒdɪ/ n (fam) burro m de carga

doh /dəʊ/ n (mus, first note of any musical scale) do m

doily /'dɔɪlɪ/ n tapete m

doings /'duːɪŋz/ npl (fam) actividades fpl

do-it-yourself /duːɪtjɔː'self/ (abbr DIY) n bricolaje m. ~ enthusiast n manitas m

doldrums /'dɒldrəmz/ npl. be in the ~ estar abatido

dole /dəʊl/ vt. ~ out distribuir. ● n (fam) subsidio m de paro. on the ~ (fam) parado

doleful /'dəʊlfl/ a triste

doll /dɒl/ n muñeca f. ● vt. ~ up (fam) emperejilar

dollar /'dɒlə(r)/ n dólar m

dollop /'dɒləp/ n (fam) masa f

dolphin /'dɒlfɪn/ n delfín m

domain /dəʊ'meɪn/ n dominio m; (fig) campo m

dome /dəʊm/ n cúpula f. ~d a abovedado

domestic /də'mestɪk/ a doméstico; ⟨trade, flights, etc⟩ nacional

domesticated a ⟨animal⟩ domesticado

domesticity /dɒme'stɪsətɪ/ n domesticidad f

domestic: ~ science n economía f doméstica. **~ servant** n doméstico m

dominant /'dɒmɪnənt/ a dominante

dominate /'dɒmɪneɪt/ vt/i dominar. **~ion** /-'neɪʃn/ n dominación f

domineer /dɒmɪ'nɪə(r)/ vi tiranizar

Dominican Republic /dəmɪnɪkən rɪ'pʌblɪk/ n República f Dominicana

dominion /də'mɪnjən/ n dominio m

domino /'dɒmɪnəʊ/ n (pl ~es) ficha f de dominó. **~es** npl (game) dominó m

don[1] /dɒn/ n profesor m

don[2] /dɒn/ vt (pt donned) ponerse

donat|e /dəʊ'neɪt/ vt donar. **~ion** /-ʃn/ n donativo m

done /dʌn/ see do

donkey /'dɒŋkɪ/ n burro m. **~work** n trabajo m penoso

donor /'dəʊnə(r)/ n donante m & f

don't /dəʊnt/ = do not

doodle /'duːdl/ vi garrapatear

doom /duːm/ n destino m; (death) muerte f. ● vt. be ~ed to ser condenado a

doomsday /'duːmzdeɪ/ n día m del juicio final

door /dɔː(r)/ n puerta f. **~man** /'dɔːmən/ n (pl -men) portero m. **~mat** /'dɔːmæt/ n felpudo m. **~step** /'dɔːstep/ n peldaño m. **~way** /'dɔːweɪ/ n entrada f

dope /dəʊp/ n (fam) droga f; (idiot, sl) imbécil m. ● vt (fam) drogar. **~y** a (sl) torpe

dormant /'dɔːmənt/ a inactivo

dormer /'dɔːmə(r)/ n. **~ (window)** buhardilla f

dormitory /'dɔːmɪtrɪ/ n dormitorio m

dormouse /'dɔːmaʊs/ n (pl -mice) lirón m

dos|age /'dəʊsɪdʒ/ n dosis f. **~e** /dəʊs/ n dosis f

doss /dɒs/ vi (sl) dormir. **~-house** n refugio m

dot /dɒt/ n punto m. on the ~ en punto. ● vt (pt dotted) salpicar. be ~ted with estar salpicado de

dote /dəʊt/ vi. ~ on adorar

dotted line /dɒtɪd'laɪn/ n línea f de puntos

dotty /'dɒtɪ/ a (-ier, -iest) (fam) chiflado

double /'dʌbl/ a doble. ● adv doble, dos veces. ● n doble m; (person) doble m & f. at the ~ corriendo. ● vt doblar; redoblar ⟨efforts etc⟩. ● vi doblarse. **~-bass** n contrabajo m. **~bed** n cama f de matrimonio. **~breasted** a cruzado. **~ chin** n papada f. **~-cross** vt traicionar. **~-dealing** n doblez m & f. **~-decker** n autobús m de dos pisos. **~ Dutch** n galimatías *m.* **~-jointed** *a* con articulaciones dobles. **~s** *npl* (*tennis*) doble *m*

doubt /daʊt/ *n* duda *f.* • *vt* dudar; (*distrust*) dudar de, desconfiar de. **~ful** *a* dudoso. **~less** *adv* sin duda

doubly /'dʌblɪ/ *adv* doblemente

dough /dəʊ/ *n* masa *f*; (*money, sl*) dinero *m*, pasta *f* (*sl*)

doughnut /'dəʊnʌt/ *n* buñuelo *m*

douse /daʊs/ *vt* mojar; apagar (*fire*)

dove /dʌv/ *n* paloma *f*

dowager /'daʊədʒə(r)/ *n* viuda *f* (con bienes o título del marido)

dowdy /'daʊdɪ/ *a* (**-ier, -iest**) poco atractivo

down[1] /daʊn/ *adv* abajo. **~ with** abajo. **come ~** bajar. **go ~** bajar; (*sun*) ponerse. • *prep* abajo. • *a* (*sad*) triste. • *vt* derribar; (*drink, fam*) beber

down[2] /daʊn/ *n* (*feathers*) plumón *m*

down-and-out /'daʊnənd'aʊt/ *n* vagabundo *m*

downcast /'daʊnkɑːst/ *a* abatido

downfall /'daʊnfɔːl/ *n* caída *f*; (*fig*) perdición *f*

downgrade /daʊn'greɪd/ *vt* degradar

down-hearted /daʊn'hɑːtɪd/ *a* abatido

downhill /daʊn'hɪl/ *adv* cuesta abajo

down payment /'daʊnpeɪmənt/ *n* depósito *m*

downpour /'daʊnpɔː(r)/ *n* aguacero *m*

downright /'daʊnraɪt/ *a* completo; (*honest*) franco. • *adv* completamente

downs /daʊnz/ *npl* colinas *fpl*

downstairs /daʊn'steəz/ *adv* abajo. /'daʊnsteəz/ *a* de abajo

downstream /'daʊnstriːm/ *adv* río abajo

down-to-earth /daʊntʊ'ɜːθ/ *a* práctico

downtrodden /'daʊntrɒdn/ *a* oprimido

down: **~ under** en las antípodas; (*in Australia*) en Australia. **~ward** /'daʊnwəd/ *a & adv*, **~wards** *adv* hacia abajo

dowry /'daʊərɪ/ *n* dote *f*

doze /dəʊz/ *vi* dormitar. **~ off** dormirse, dar una cabezada. • *n* sueño *m* ligero

dozen /'dʌzn/ *n* docena *f.* **~s of** (*fam*) miles de, muchos

Dr *abbr* (*Doctor*) Dr, Doctor *m.* **~ Broadley** (el) Doctor Broadley

drab /dræb/ *a* monótono

draft /drɑːft/ *n* borrador *m*; (*outline*) bosquejo *m*; (*com*) letra *f* de cambio; (*Amer, mil*) reclutamiento *m*; (*Amer, of air*) corriente *f* de aire. • *vt* bosquejar; (*mil*) destacar; (*Amer, conscript*) reclutar

drag /dræg/ *vt* (*pt* **dragged**) arrastrar; rastrear (*river*). • *vi* arrastrarse por el suelo. • *n* (*fam*) lata *f.* **in ~** (*man, sl*) vestido de mujer

dragon /'drægən/ *n* dragón *m*

dragon-fly /'drægənflaɪ/ *n* libélula *f*

drain /dreɪn/ *vt* desaguar; apurar (*tank, glass*); (*fig*) agotar. • *vi* escurrirse. • *n* desaguadero *m.* **be a ~ on** agotar. **~ing-board** *n* escurridero *m*

drama /'drɑːmə/ *n* drama *m*; (*art*) arte *m* teatral. **~tic** /drə'mætɪk/ *a* dramático. **~tist** /'dræmətɪst/ *n* dramaturgo *m.* **~tize** /'dræmətaɪz/ *vt* adaptar al teatro; (*fig*) dramatizar

drank /dræŋk/ *see* **drink**

drape /dreɪp/ *vt* cubrir; (*hang*) colgar. **~s** *npl* (*Amer*) cortinas *fpl*

drastic /'dræstɪk/ *a* drástico

draught /drɑːft/ *n* corriente *f* de aire. **~ beer** *n* cerveza *f* de barril. **~s** *n pl* (*game*) juego *m* de damas

draughtsman /'drɑːftsmən/ *n* (*pl* **-men**) diseñador *m*

draughty /'drɑːftɪ/ *a* lleno de corrientes de aire

draw /drɔː/ *vt* (*pt* **drew**, *pp* **drawn**) tirar; (*attract*) atraer; dibujar (*picture*); trazar (*line*); retirar (*money*). **~ the line at** trazar el límite. • *vi* (*sport*) empatar; dibujar (*pictures*); (*in lottery*) sortear. • *n* (*sport*) empate *m*; (*in lottery*) sorteo *m.* **~ in** (*days*) acortarse. **~ out** sacar (*money*). **~ up** pararse; redactar (*document*); acercar (*chair*)

drawback /'drɔːbæk/ *n* desventaja *f*

drawbridge /'drɔːbrɪdʒ/ *n* puente *m* levadizo

drawer /drɔː(r)/ *n* cajón *m.* **~s** /drɔːz/ *npl* calzoncillos *mpl*; (*women's*) bragas *fpl*

drawing /'drɔːɪŋ/ *n* dibujo *m.* **~-pin** *n* chinche *m*, chincheta *f*

drawing-room /'drɔːɪŋruːm/ *n* salón *m*

drawl /drɔːl/ *n* habla *f* lenta

drawn /drɔːn/ *see* **draw.** • *a* (*face*) ojeroso

dread /dred/ n terror m. ● vt temer. ~**ful** /'dredfl/ a terrible. ~**fully** adv terriblemente

dream /driːm/ n sueño m. ● vt/i (pt **dreamed** or **dreamt**) soñar. ● a ideal. ~ **up** idear. ~**er** n soñador m. ~**y** a soñador

drear|iness /'drɪərɪnɪs/ n tristeza f; (monotony) monotonía f. ~**y** /'drɪərɪ/ a (-ier, -iest) triste; (boring) monótono

dredge[1] /dredʒ/ n draga f. ● vt dragar

dredge[2] /dredʒ/ n (culin) espolvorear

dredger[1] /'dredʒə(r)/ n draga f

dredger[2] /'dredʒə(r)/ n (for sugar) espolvoreador m

dregs /dregz/ npl heces fpl; (fig) hez f

drench /drentʃ/ vt empapar

dress /dres/ n vestido m; (clothing) ropa f. ● vt vestir; (decorate) adornar; (med) vendar; (culin) aderezar, aliñar. ● vi vestirse. ~ **circle** n primer palco m

dresser[1] /'dresə(r)/ n (furniture) aparador m

dresser[2] /'dresə(r)/ n (in theatre) camarero m

dressing /'dresɪŋ/ n (sauce) aliño m; (bandage) vendaje m. ~**case** n neceser m. ~**down** n rapapolvo m, reprensión f. ~**gown** n bata f. ~**room** n tocador m; (in theatre) camarín m. ~**table** n tocador m

dressmak|er /'dresmeɪkə(r)/ n modista m & f. ~**ing** n costura f

dress rehearsal /'dresrɪhɜːsl/ n ensayo m general

dressy /'dresɪ/ a (-ier, -iest) elegante

drew /druː/ see **draw**

dribble /'drɪbl/ vi gotear; (baby) babear; (in football) regatear

dribs and drabs /drɪbzn'dræbz/ npl. **in** ~ poco a poco, en cantidades pequeñas

drie|d /draɪd/ a (food) seco; (fruit) paso. ~**r** /'draɪə(r)/ n secador m

drift /drɪft/ vi ir a la deriva; (snow) amontonarse. ● n (movement) dirección f; (of snow) montón m; (meaning) significado m. ~**er** n persona f sin rumbo. ~**wood** /'drɪftwʊd/ n madera f flotante

drill /drɪl/ n (tool) taladro m; (training) ejercicio m; (fig) lo normal. ● vt taladrar, perforar; (train) entrenar. ● vi entrenarse

drily /'draɪlɪ/ adv secamente

drink /drɪŋk/ vt/i (pt **drank**, pp **drunk**) beber. ● n bebida f. ~**able** a bebible; (water) potable. ~**er** n bebedor m. ~**ing-water** n agua f potable

drip /drɪp/ vi (pt **dripped**) gotear. ● n gota f; (med) goteo m intravenoso; (person, sl) mentecato m. ~**dry** a que no necesita plancharse

dripping /'drɪpɪŋ/ n (culin) pringue m

drive /draɪv/ vt (pt **drove**, pp **driven**) empujar; conducir, manejar (LAm) (car etc). ~ **in** clavar (nail). ~ **s.o. mad** volver loco a uno. ● vi conducir. ~ **in** (in car) entrar en coche. ● n paseo m; (road) calle f; (private road) camino m de entrada; (fig) energía f; (pol) campaña f. ~ **at** querer decir. ~**r** /'draɪvə(r)/ n conductor m, chófer m (LAm)

drivel /'drɪvl/ n tonterías fpl

driving /'draɪvɪŋ/ n conducción f. ~**licence** n carné m de conducir. ~ **school** n autoescuela f

drizzl|e /'drɪzl/ n llovizna f. ● vi lloviznar. ~**y** a lloviznoso

dromedary /'drɒmədərɪ/ n dromedario m

drone /drəʊn/ n (noise) zumbido m; (bee) zángano m. ● vi zumbar; (fig) hablar en voz monótona; (idle, fam) holgazanear

drool /druːl/ vi babear

droop /druːp/ vt inclinar. ● vi inclinarse; (flowers) marchitarse

drop /drɒp/ n gota f; (fall) caída f; (decrease) baja f; (of cliff) precipicio m. ● vt (pt **dropped**) dejar caer; (lower) bajar. ● vi caer. ~ **in on** pasar por casa de. ~ **off** (sleep) dormirse. ~ **out** retirarse; (student) abandonar los estudios. ~**out** n marginado m

droppings /'drɒpɪŋz/ npl excremento m

dross /drɒs/ n escoria f

drought /draʊt/ n sequía f

drove[1] /drəʊv/ see **drive**

drove[2] /drəʊv/ n manada f

drown /draʊn/ vt ahogar. ● vi ahogarse

drowsy /'draʊzɪ/ a soñoliento

drudge /drʌdʒ/ n esclavo m del trabajo. ~**ry** /-ərɪ/ n trabajo m pesado

drug /drʌg/ n droga f; (med) medicamento m. ● vt (pt **drugged**) drogar. ~ **addict** n toxicómano m

drugstore /'drʌgstɔ:(r)/ n (Amer) farmacia f (que vende otros artículos también)

drum /drʌm/ n tambor m; (for oil) bidón m. ● vi (pt **drummed**) tocar el tambor. ● vt. ~ **into s.o.** inculcar en la mente de uno. ~**mer** n tambor m; (in group) batería f. ~**s** npl batería f. ~**stick** /'drʌmstɪk/ n baqueta f; (culin) pierna f (de pollo)

drunk /drʌŋk/ see **drink**. ● a borracho. **get** ~ emborracharse. ~**ard** n borracho m. ~**en** a borracho. ~**enness** n embriaguez f

dry /draɪ/ a (**drier, driest**) seco. ● vt secar. ● vi secarse. ~ **up** (fam) secar los platos. ~**clean** vt limpiar en seco. ~**cleaner** n tintorero m. ~**cleaner's** (shop) tintorería f. ~**ness** n sequedad f

dual /'dju:əl/ a doble. ~ **carriageway** n autovía f, carretera f de doble calzada. ~**purpose** a de doble uso

dub /dʌb/ vt (pt **dubbed**) doblar ⟨film⟩; (nickname) apodar

dubious /'dju:bɪəs/ a dudoso; ⟨person⟩ sospechoso

duchess /'dʌtʃɪs/ n duquesa f

duck[1] /dʌk/ n pato m

duck[2] /dʌk/ vt sumergir; bajar ⟨head etc⟩. ● vi agacharse

duckling /'dʌklɪŋ/ n patito m

duct /dʌkt/ n conducto m

dud /dʌd/ a inútil; ⟨cheque⟩ sin fondos; ⟨coin⟩ falso

due /dju:/ a debido; (expected) esperado. ~ **to** debido a. ● adv. ~ **north** n derecho hacia el norte. ~**s** npl derechos mpl

duel /'dju:əl/ n duelo m

duet /dju:'et/ n dúo m

duffle /'dʌfl/ a. ~ **bag** n bolsa f de lona. ~**coat** n trenca f

dug /dʌg/ see **dig**

duke /dju:k/ n duque m

dull /dʌl/ a (-**er, -est**) ⟨weather⟩ gris; ⟨colour⟩ apagado; ⟨person, play, etc⟩ pesado; ⟨sound⟩ sordo; (stupid) torpe. ● vt aliviar ⟨pain⟩; entorpecer ⟨mind⟩

duly /'dju:lɪ/ adv debidamente

dumb /dʌm/ a (-**er, -est**) mudo; (fam) estúpido

dumbfound /dʌm'faʊnd/ vt pasmar

dummy /'dʌmɪ/ n muñeco m; (of tailor) maniquí m; (of baby) chupete m. ● a falso. ~ **run** n prueba f

dump /dʌmp/ vt descargar; (fam) deshacerse de. ● n vertedero m;

(mil) depósito m; (fam) lugar m desagradable. **be down in the** ~**s** estar deprimido

dumpling /'dʌmplɪŋ/ n bola f de masa hervida

dumpy /'dʌmpɪ/ a (-**ier, -iest**) regordete

dunce /dʌns/ n burro m

dung /dʌŋ/ n excremento m; (manure) estiércol m

dungarees /dʌŋgə'ri:z/ npl mono m, peto m

dungeon /'dʌndʒən/ n calabozo m

dunk /dʌŋk/ vt remojar

duo /'dju:əʊ/ n dúo m

dupe /dju:p/ vt engañar. ● n inocentón m

duplicat|e /'dju:plɪkət/ a & n duplicado (m). /'dju:plɪkeɪt/ vt duplicar; (on machine) reproducir. ~**or** n multicopista f

duplicity /dju:'plɪsətɪ/ n doblez f

durable /'djʊərəbl/ a resistente; (enduring) duradero

duration /djʊ'reɪʃn/ n duración f

duress /djʊ'res/ n coacción f

during /'djʊərɪŋ/ prep durante

dusk /dʌsk/ n crepúsculo m

dusky /'dʌskɪ/ a (-**ier, -iest**) oscuro

dust /dʌst/ n polvo m. ● vt quitar el polvo a; (sprinkle) espolvorear

dustbin /'dʌstbɪn/ n cubo m de la basura

dust-cover /'dʌstkʌvə(r)/ n sobrecubierta f

duster /'dʌstə(r)/ n trapo m

dust-jacket /'dʌstdʒækɪt/ n sobrecubierta f

dustman /'dʌstmən/ n (pl -**men**) basurero m

dustpan /'dʌstpæn/ n recogedor m

dusty /'dʌstɪ/ a (-**ier, -iest**) polvoriento

Dutch /dʌtʃ/ a & n holandés (m). **go** ~ pagar a escote. ~**man** m holandés m. ~**woman** n holandesa f

dutiful /'dju:tɪfl/ a obediente

duty /'dju:tɪ/ n deber m; (tax) derechos mpl de aduana. **on** ~ de servicio. ~**free** a libre de impuestos

duvet /'dju:veɪ/ n edredón m

dwarf /dwɔ:f/ n (pl -**s**) enano m. ● vt empequeñecer

dwell /dwel/ vi (pt **dwelt**) morar. ~ **on** dilatarse. ~**er** n habitante m & f. ~**ing** n morada f

dwindle /'dwɪndl/ vi disminuir

dye /daɪ/ vt (pres p **dyeing**) teñir. ● n tinte m

dying /'daɪɪŋ/ see **die**

dynamic /daɪ'næmɪk/ a dinámico. ~s npl dinámica f

dynamite /'daɪnəmaɪt/ n dinamita f. ● vt dinamitar

dynamo /'daɪnəməʊ/ n dinamo f, dínamo f

dynasty /'dɪnəstɪ/ n dinastía f

dysentery /'dɪsəntrɪ/ n disentería f

dyslexia /dɪs'leksɪə/ n dislexia f

E

each /iːtʃ/ a cada. ● pron cada uno. ~ **one** cada uno. ~ **other** uno a otro, el uno al otro. **they love** ~ **other** se aman

eager /'iːɡə(r)/ a impaciente; (enthusiastic) ávido. ~**ly** adv con impaciencia. ~**ness** n impaciencia f, ansia f

eagle /'iːɡl/ n águila f

ear[1] /ɪə(r)/ n oído m; (outer) oreja f

ear[2] /ɪə(r)/ n (of corn) espiga f

ear: ~**ache** /'ɪəreɪk/ n dolor m de oído. ~**drum** n tímpano m

earl /ɜːl/ n conde m

early /'ɜːlɪ/ a (-ier, -iest) temprano; (before expected time) prematuro. **in the** ~ **spring** a principios de la primavera. ● adv temprano; (ahead of time) con anticipación

earmark /'ɪəmɑːk/ vt. ~ **for** destinar a

earn /ɜːn/ vt ganar; (deserve) merecer

earnest /'ɜːnɪst/ a serio. **in** ~ en serio

earnings /'ɜːnɪŋz/ npl ingresos mpl; (com) ganacias fpl

ear: ~**phones** /'ɪəfəʊnz/ npl auricular m. ~**ring** n pendiente m

earshot /'ɪəʃɒt/ n. **within** ~ al alcance del oído

earth /ɜːθ/ n tierra f. ● vt (elec) conectar a tierra. ~**ly** a terrenal

earthenware /'ɜːθnweə(r)/ n loza f de barro

earthquake /'ɜːθkweɪk/ n terremoto m

earthy /'ɜːθɪ/ a terroso; (coarse) grosero

earwig /'ɪəwɪɡ/ n tijereta f

ease /iːz/ n facilidad f; (comfort) tranquilidad f. **at** ~ a gusto; (mil)

en posición de descanso. **ill at** ~ molesto. **with** ~ fácilmente. ● vt calmar; aliviar ⟨pain⟩; tranquilizar ⟨mind⟩; (loosen) aflojar. ● vi calmarse; (lessen) disminuir

easel /'iːzl/ n caballete m

east /iːst/ n este m, oriente m. ● a del este, oriental. ● adv hacia el este.

Easter /'iːstə(r)/ n Semana f Santa; (relig) Pascua f de Resurrección. ~ **egg** n huevo m de Pascua

east: ~**erly** a este; ⟨wind⟩ del este. ~**ern** a del este, oriental. ~**ward** adv, ~**wards** adv hacia el este

easy /'iːzɪ/ a (-ier, -iest) fácil; (relaxed) tranquilo. **go** ~ **on** (fam) tener cuidado con. **take it** ~ no preocuparse. ● int ¡despacio! ~ **chair** n sillón m. ~**going** a acomodadizo

eat /iːt/ vt/i (pt **ate**, pp **eaten**) comer. ~ **into** corroer. ~**able** a comestible. ~**er** n comedor m

eau-de-Cologne /əʊdəkə'ləʊn/ n agua f de colonia

eaves /iːvz/ npl alero m

eavesdrop /'iːvzdrɒp/ vi (pt -**dropped**) escuchar a escondidas

ebb /eb/ n reflujo m. ● vi bajar; (fig) decaer

ebony /'ebənɪ/ n ébano m

ebullient /ɪ'bʌlɪənt/ a exuberante

EC /iː'siː/ abbr (European Community) CE (Comunidad f Europea)

eccentric /ɪk'sentrɪk/ a & n excéntrico (m). ~**ity** /eksen'trɪsətɪ/ n excentricidad f

ecclesiastical /ɪkliːzɪ'æstɪkl/ a eclesiástico

echelon /'eʃəlɒn/ n escalón m

echo /'ekəʊ/ n (pl -**oes**) eco m. ● vt (pt **echoed**, pres p **echoing**) repetir; (imitate) imitar. ● vi hacer eco

eclectic /ɪk'lektɪk/ a & n ecléctico (m)

eclipse /ɪ'klɪps/ n eclipse m. ● vt eclipsar

ecology /ɪ'kɒlədʒɪ/ n ecología f

econom|ic /iːkə'nɒmɪk/ a económico. ~**ical** a económico. ~**ics** n economía f. ~**ist** /ɪ'kɒnəmɪst/ n economista m & f. ~**ize** /ɪ'kɒnəmaɪz/ vi economizar. ~**y** /ɪ'kɒnəmɪ/ n economía f

ecsta|sy /'ekstəsɪ/ n éxtasis f. ~**tic** /ɪk'stætɪk/ a extático. ~**tically** adv con éxtasis

Ecuador /'ekwədɔː(r)/ n el Ecuador m

ecumenical /iːkjuːˈmenɪkl/ *a* ecuménico

eddy /ˈedɪ/ *n* remolino *m*

edge /edʒ/ *n* borde *m*, margen *m*; (*of knife*) filo *m*; (*of town*) afueras *fpl*. **have the ~ on** (*fam*) llevar la ventaja a. **on ~** nervioso. ● *vt* ribetear; (*move*) mover poco a poco. ● *vi* avanzar cautelosamente. **~ways** *adv* de lado

edging /ˈedʒɪŋ/ *n* borde *m*; (*sewing*) ribete *m*

edgy /ˈedʒɪ/ *a* nervioso

edible /ˈedɪbl/ *a* comestible

edict /ˈiːdɪkt/ *n* edicto *m*

edifice /ˈedɪfɪs/ *n* edificio *m*

edify /ˈedɪfaɪ/ *vt* edificar

edit /ˈedɪt/ *vt* dirigir ⟨*newspaper*⟩; preparar una edición de ⟨*text*⟩; (*write*) redactar; montar ⟨*film*⟩. **~ed by** a cargo de. **~ion** /ɪˈdɪʃn/ *n* edición *f*. **~or** /ˈedɪtə(r)/ *n* (*of newspaper*) director *m*; (*of text*) redactor *m*. **~orial** /edɪˈtɔːrɪəl/ *a* editorial. ● *n* artículo *m* de fondo. **~or in chief** *n* jefe *m* de redacción

educat|e /ˈedʒʊkeɪt/ *vt* instruir, educar. **~ed** *a* culto. **~ion** /-ˈkeɪʃn/ *n* enseñanza *f*; (*culture*) cultura *f*; (*upbringing*) educación *f*. **~ional** /-ˈkeɪʃənl/ *a* instructivo

EEC /iːiːˈsiː/ *abbr* (*European Economic Community*) CEE (Comunidad *f* Económica Europea)

eel /iːl/ *n* anguila *f*

eerie /ˈɪərɪ/ *a* (**-ier, -iest**) misterioso

efface /ɪˈfeɪs/ *vt* borrar

effect /ɪˈfekt/ *n* efecto *m*. **in ~** efectivamente. **take ~** entrar en vigor. ● *vt* efectuar

effective /ɪˈfektɪv/ *a* eficaz; (*striking*) impresionante; (*mil*) efectivo. **~ly** *adv* eficazmente. **~ness** *n* eficacia *f*

effeminate /ɪˈfemɪnət/ *a* afeminado

effervescent /efəˈvesnt/ *a* efervescente

effete /ɪˈfiːt/ *a* agotado

efficien|cy /ɪˈfɪʃənsɪ/ *n* eficiencia *f*; (*mec*) rendimiento *m*. **~t** /ɪˈfɪʃnt/ *a* eficiente. **~tly** *adv* eficientemente

effigy /ˈefɪdʒɪ/ *n* efigie *f*

effort /ˈefət/ *n* esfuerzo *m*. **~less** *a* fácil

effrontery /ɪˈfrʌntərɪ/ *n* descaro *m*

effusive /ɪˈfjuːsɪv/ *a* efusivo

e.g. /iːˈdʒiː/ *abbr* (*exempli gratia*) p.ej., por ejemplo

egalitarian /ɪɡælɪˈteərɪən/ *a* & *n* igualitario (*m*)

egg[1] /eɡ/ *n* huevo *m*

egg[2] /eɡ/ *vt*. **~ on** (*fam*) incitar

egg-cup /ˈeɡkʌp/ *n* huevera *f*

egg-plant /ˈeɡplɑːnt/ *n* berenjena *f*

eggshell /ˈeɡʃel/ *n* cáscara *f* de huevo

ego /ˈiːɡəʊ/ *n* (*pl* **-os**) yo *m*. **~ism** *n* egoísmo *m*. **~ist** *n* egoísta *m* & *f*. **~centric** /iːɡəʊˈsentrɪk/ *a* egocéntrico. **~tism** *n* egotismo *m*. **~tist** *n* egotista *m* & *f*

Egypt /ˈiːdʒɪpt/ *n* Egipto *m*. **~ian** /ɪˈdʒɪpʃn/ *a* & *n* egipcio (*m*)

eh /eɪ/ *int* (*fam*) ¡eh!

eiderdown /ˈaɪdədaʊn/ *n* edredón *m*

eight /eɪt/ *a* & *n* ocho (*m*)

eighteen /eɪˈtiːn/ *a* & *n* dieciocho (*m*). **~th** *a* & *n* decimoctavo (*m*)

eighth /eɪtθ/ *a* & *n* octavo (*m*)

eight|ieth /ˈeɪtɪəθ/ *a* & *n* ochenta (*m*), octogésimo *m*. **~y** /ˈeɪtɪ/ *a* & *n* ochenta (*m*)

either /ˈaɪðə(r)/ *a* cualquiera de los dos; (*negative*) ninguno de los dos; (*each*) cada. ● *pron* uno u otro; (*with negative*) ni uno ni otro. ● *adv* (*negative*) tampoco. ● *conj* o. **~ he or o** él o; (*with negative*) ni él ni

ejaculate /ɪˈdʒækjʊleɪt/ *vt/i* (*exclaim*) exclamar

eject /ɪˈdʒekt/ *vt* expulsar, echar

eke /iːk/ *vt*. **~ out** hacer bastar; (*increase*) complementar

elaborate /ɪˈlæbərət/ *a* complicado. /ɪˈlæbəreɪt/ *vt* elaborar. ● *vi* explicarse

elapse /ɪˈlæps/ *vi* (*of time*) transcurrir

elastic /ɪˈlæstɪk/ *a* & *n* elástico (*m*). **~ band** *n* goma *f* (elástica)

elasticity /ɪlæˈstɪsətɪ/ *n* elasticidad *f*

elat|ed /ɪˈleɪtɪd/ *a* regocijado. **~ion** /-ʃn/ *n* regocijo *m*

elbow /ˈelbəʊ/ *n* codo *m*

elder[1] /ˈeldə(r)/ *a* & *n* mayor (*m*)

elder[2] /ˈeldə(r)/ *n* (*tree*) saúco *m*

elderly /ˈeldəlɪ/ *a* mayor, anciano

eldest /ˈeldɪst/ *a* & *n* el mayor (*m*)

elect /ɪˈlekt/ *vt* elegir. **~ to do** decidir hacer. ● *a* electo. **~ion** /-ʃn/ *n* elección *f*

elector /ɪˈlektə(r)/ *n* elector *m*. **~al** *a* electoral. **~ate** *n* electorado *m*

electric /ɪˈlektrɪk/ *a* eléctrico. **~al** *a* eléctrico. **~ blanket** *n* manta *f* eléctrica. **~ian** /ɪlekˈtrɪʃn/ *n* electricista

m & f. ~ity /ɪlek'trɪsətɪ/ n electricidad f

electrify /ɪ'lektrɪfaɪ/ vt electrificar; *(fig)* electrizar

electrocute /ɪ'lektrəkjuːt/ vt electrocutar

electrolysis /ɪlek'trɒlɪsɪs/ n electrólisis f

electron /ɪ'lektrɒn/ n electrón m

electronic /ɪlek'trɒnɪk/ a electrónico. ~s n electrónica f

elegan|ce /'elɪɡəns/ n elegancia f. ~t /'elɪɡənt/ a elegante. ~tly adv elegantemente

element /'elɪmənt/ n elemento m. ~ary /-'mentrɪ/ a elemental

elephant /'elɪfənt/ n elefante m

elevat|e /'elɪveɪt/ vt elevar. ~ion /-'veɪʃn/ n elevación f. ~or /'elɪveɪtə(r)/ n *(Amer)* ascensor m

eleven /ɪ'levn/ a & n once (m). ~th a & n undécimo (m)

elf /elf/ n *(pl* **elves***)* duende m

elicit /ɪ'lɪsɪt/ vt sacar

eligible /'elɪdʒəbl/ a elegible. **be ~ for** tener derecho a

eliminat|e /ɪ'lɪmɪneɪt/ vt eliminar. ~ion /-'neɪʃn/ n eliminación f

élite /eɪ'liːt/ n elite f, élite m

elixir /ɪ'lɪksɪə(r)/ n elixir m

ellip|se /ɪ'lɪps/ n elipse f. ~tical a elíptico

elm /elm/ n olmo m

elocution /elə'kjuːʃn/ n elocución f

elongate /'iːlɒŋɡeɪt/ vt alargar

elope /ɪ'ləʊp/ vi fugarse con el amante. ~ment n fuga f

eloquen|ce /'eləkwəns/ n elocuencia f. ~t /'eləkwənt/ a elocuente. ~tly adv con elocuencia

El Salvador /el'sælvədɔː(r)/ n El Salvador m

else /els/ adv más. **everybody ~** todos los demás. **nobody ~** ningún otro, nadie más. **nothing ~** nada más. **or ~** o bien. **somewhere ~** en otra parte

elsewhere /els'weə(r)/ adv en otra parte

elucidate /ɪ'luːsɪdeɪt/ vt aclarar

elude /ɪ'luːd/ vt eludir

elusive /ɪ'luːsɪv/ a esquivo

emaciated /ɪ'meɪʃɪeɪtɪd/ a esquelético

emanate /'eməneɪt/ vi emanar

emancipat|e /ɪ'mænsɪpeɪt/ vt emancipar. ~ion /-'peɪʃn/ n emancipación f

embalm /ɪm'bɑːm/ vt embalsamar

embankment /ɪm'bæŋkmənt/ n terraplén m; *(of river)* dique m

embargo /ɪm'bɑːɡəʊ/ n *(pl* **-oes***)* prohibición f

embark /ɪm'bɑːk/ vt embarcar. ● vi embarcarse. **~ on** *(fig)* emprender. **~ation** /emboː'keɪʃn/ n *(of people)* embarco m; *(of goods)* embarque m

embarrass /ɪm'bærəs/ vt desconcertar; *(shame)* dar vergüenza. **~ment** n desconcierto m; *(shame)* vergüenza f

embassy /'embəsɪ/ n embajada f

embed /ɪm'bed/ vt *(pt* **embedded***)* embutir; *(fig)* fijar

embellish /ɪm'belɪʃ/ vt embellecer. **~ment** n embellecimiento m

embers /'embəz/ npl ascua f

embezzle /ɪm'bezl/ vt desfalcar. **~ment** n desfalco m

embitter /ɪm'bɪtə(r)/ vt amargar

emblem /'embləm/ n emblema m

embod|iment /ɪm'bɒdɪmənt/ n encarnación f. **~y** /ɪm'bɒdɪ/ vt encarnar; *(include)* incluir

emboss /ɪm'bɒs/ vt grabar en relieve, repujar. **~ed** a en relieve, repujado

embrace /ɪm'breɪs/ vt abrazar; *(fig)* abarcar. ● vi abrazarse. ● n abrazo m

embroider /ɪm'brɔɪdə(r)/ vt bordar. **~y** n bordado m

embroil /ɪm'brɔɪl/ vt enredar

embryo /'embrɪəʊ/ n *(pl* **-os***)* embrión m. **~nic** /-'ɒnɪk/ a embrionario

emend /ɪ'mend/ vt enmendar

emerald /'emərəld/ n esmeralda f

emerge /ɪ'mɜːdʒ/ vi salir. **~nce** /-əns/ n aparición f

emergency /ɪ'mɜːdʒənsɪ/ n emergencia f. **in an ~** en caso de emergencia. **~ exit** n salida f de emergencia

emery /'eməri/ n esmeril m. **~-board** n lima f de uñas

emigrant /'emɪɡrənt/ n emigrante m & f

emigrat|e /'emɪɡreɪt/ vi emigrar. **~ion** /-'ɡreɪʃn/ n emigración f

eminen|ce /'emɪnəns/ n eminencia f. **~t** /'emɪnənt/ a eminente. **~tly** adv eminentemente

emissary /'emɪsərɪ/ n emisario m

emission /ɪ'mɪʃn/ n emisión f

emit /ɪ'mɪt/ vt *(pt* **emitted***)* emitir

emollient /ɪ'mɒlɪənt/ a & n emoliente (m)

emoti|on /ɪ'məʊʃn/ *n* emoción *f*. **~onal** *a* emocional; ⟨*person*⟩ emotivo; ⟨*moving*⟩ conmovedor. **~ve** /ɪ'məʊtɪv/ *a* emotivo

empathy /'empəθɪ/ *n* empatía *f*

emperor /'empərə(r)/ *n* emperador *m*

emphasi|s /'emfəsɪs/ *n* (*pl* **~ses** /-si:z/) énfasis *m*. **~ze** /'emfəsaɪz/ *vt* subrayar; (*single out*) destacar

emphatic /ɪm'fætɪk/ *a* categórico; (*resolute*) decidido

empire /'empaɪə(r)/ *n* imperio *m*

empirical /ɪm'pɪrɪkl/ *a* empírico

employ /ɪm'plɔɪ/ *vt* emplear. **~ee** /emplɔɪ'i:/ *n* empleado *m*. **~er** *n* patrón *m*. **~ment** *n* empleo *m*. **~ment agency** *n* agencia *f* de colocaciones

empower /ɪm'paʊə(r)/ *vt* autorizar (**to do** a hacer)

empress /'emprɪs/ *n* emperatriz *f*

empt|ies /'emptɪz/ *npl* envases *mpl*. **~iness** *n* vacío *m*. **~y** /'emptɪ/ *a* vacío; ⟨*promise*⟩ vano. **on an ~y stomach** con el estómago vacío. ● *vt* vaciar. ● *vi* vaciarse

emulate /'emjʊleɪt/ *vt* emular

emulsion /ɪ'mʌlʃn/ *n* emulsión *f*

enable /ɪ'neɪbl/ *vt*. **~ s.o. to** permitir a uno

enact /ɪ'nækt/ *vt* (*jurid*) decretar; (*in theatre*) representar

enamel /ɪ'næml/ *n* esmalte *m*. ● *vt* (*pt* **enamelled**) esmaltar

enamoured /ɪ'næməd/ *a*. **be ~ of** estar enamorado de

encampment /ɪn'kæmpmənt/ *n* campamento *m*

encase /ɪn'keɪs/ *vt* encerrar

enchant /ɪn'tʃɑːnt/ *vt* encantar. **~ing** *a* encantador. **~ment** *n* encanto *m*

encircle /ɪn'sɜːkl/ *vt* rodear

enclave /'enkleɪv/ *n* enclave *m*

enclos|e /ɪn'kləʊz/ *vt* cercar ⟨*land*⟩; (*with letter*) adjuntar; (*in receptacle*) encerrar. **~ed** *a* ⟨*space*⟩ encerrado; (*com*) adjunto. **~ure** /ɪn'kləʊʒə(r)/ *n* cercamiento *m*; (*area*) recinto *m*; (*com*) documento *m* adjunto

encompass /ɪn'kʌmpəs/ *vt* cercar; (*include*) incluir, abarcar

encore /'ɒŋkɔː(r)/ *int* ¡bis! ● *n* bis *m*, repetición *f*

encounter /ɪn'kaʊntə(r)/ *vt* encontrar. ● *n* encuentro *m*

encourage /ɪn'kʌrɪdʒ/ *vt* animar; (*stimulate*) estimular. **~ment** *n* estímulo *m*

encroach /ɪn'krəʊtʃ/ *vi*. **~ on** invadir ⟨*land*⟩; quitar ⟨*time*⟩. **~ment** *n* usurpación *f*

encumb|er /ɪn'kʌmbə(r)/ *vt* (*hamper*) estorbar; (*burden*) cargar. **be ~ered with** estar cargado de. **~rance** *n* estorbo *m*; (*burden*) carga *f*

encyclical /ɪn'sɪklɪkl/ *n* encíclica *f*

encyclopaedi|a /ɪnsaɪklə'piːdɪə/ *n* enciclopedia *f*. **~c** *a* enciclopédico

end /end/ *n* fin *m*; (*furthest point*) extremo *m*. **in the ~** por fin. **make ~s meet** poder llegar a fin de mes. **no ~** (*fam*) muy. **no ~ of** muchísimos. **on ~** de pie; (*consecutive*) seguido. ● *vt/i* terminar, acabar

endanger /ɪn'deɪndʒə(r)/ *vt* arriesgar

endear|ing /ɪn'dɪərɪŋ/ *a* simpático. **~ment** *n* palabra *f* cariñosa

endeavour /ɪn'devə(r)/ *n* tentativa *f*. ● *vi*. **~ to** esforzarse por

ending /'endɪŋ/ *n* fin *m*

endive /'endɪv/ *n* escarola *f*, endibia *f*

endless /'endlɪs/ *a* interminable; ⟨*patience*⟩ infinito

endorse /ɪn'dɔːs/ *vt* endosar; (*fig*) aprobar. **~ment** *n* endoso *m*; (*fig*) aprobación *f*; (*auto*) nota *f* de inhabilitación

endow /ɪn'daʊ/ *vt* dotar

endur|able /ɪn'djʊərəbl/ *a* aguantable. **~ance** *n* resistencia *f*. **~e** /ɪn'djʊə(r)/ *vt* aguantar. ● *vi* durar. **~ing** *a* perdurable

enemy /'enəmɪ/ *n & a* enemigo (*m*)

energ|etic /enə'dʒetɪk/ *a* enérgico. **~y** /'enədʒɪ/ *n* energía *f*

enervate /'enɜːveɪt/ *vt* debilitar. **~ing** *a* debilitante

enfold /ɪn'fəʊld/ *vt* envolver; (*in arms*) abrazar

enforce /ɪn'fɔːs/ *vt* aplicar; (*impose*) imponer; hacer cumplir ⟨*law*⟩. **~d** *a* forzado

engage /ɪn'geɪdʒ/ *vt* emplear ⟨*staff*⟩; (*reserve*) reservar; ocupar ⟨*attention*⟩; (*mec*) hacer engranar. ● *vi* (*mec*) engranar. **~d** *a* prometido; (*busy*) ocupado. **get ~d** prometerse. **~ment** *n* compromiso *m*; (*undertaking*) obligación *f*

engaging /ɪn'geɪdʒɪŋ/ *a* atractivo

engender /ɪn'dʒendə(r)/ *vt* engendrar

engine /'endʒɪn/ *n* motor *m*; (*of train*) locomotora *f*. **~-driver** *n* maquinista *m*

engineer /endʒɪ'nɪə(r)/ *n* ingeniero *m*; (*mechanic*) mecánico *m*. ● *vt* (*contrive*, *fam*) lograr. ~**ing** *n* ingeniería *f*

England /'ɪŋglənd/ *n* Inglaterra *f*

English /'ɪŋglɪʃ/ *a* inglés. ● *n* (*lang*) inglés *m*; (*people*) ingleses *mpl*. ~**man** *n* inglés *m*. ~**woman** *n* inglesa *f*. **the ~ Channel** *n* el canal *m* de la Mancha

engrav|e /ɪn'greɪv/ *vt* grabar. ~**ing** *n* grabado *m*

engrossed /ɪn'grəʊst/ *a* absorto

engulf /ɪn'gʌlf/ *vt* tragar(se)

enhance /ɪn'hɑːns/ *vt* aumentar

enigma /ɪ'nɪgmə/ *n* enigma *m*. ~**tic** /enɪg'mætɪk/ *a* enigmático

enjoy /ɪn'dʒɔɪ/ *vt* gozar de. ~ **o.s.** divertirse. **I ~ reading** me gusta la lectura. ~**able** *a* agradable. ~**ment** *n* placer *m*

enlarge /ɪn'lɑːdʒ/ *vt* agrandar; (*foto*) ampliar. ● *vi* agrandarse. ~ **upon** extenderse sobre. ~**ment** *n* (*foto*) ampliación *f*

enlighten /ɪn'laɪtn/ *vt* aclarar; (*inform*) informar. ~**ment** *n* aclaración *f*. **the E~ment** el siglo *m* de la luces

enlist /ɪn'lɪst/ *vt* alistar; (*fig*) conseguir. ● *vi* alistarse

enliven /ɪn'laɪvn/ *vt* animar

enmity /'enmətɪ/ *n* enemistad *f*

ennoble /ɪ'nəʊbl/ *vt* ennoblecer

enorm|ity /ɪ'nɔːmətɪ/ *n* enormidad *f*. ~**ous** /ɪ'nɔːməs/ *a* enorme

enough /ɪ'nʌf/ *a* & *adv* bastante. ● *n* bastante *m*, suficiente *m*. ● *int* ¡basta!

enquir|e /ɪn'kwaɪə(r)/ *vt/i* preguntar. ~**e about** informarse de. ~**y** *n* pregunta *f*; (*investigation*) investigación *f*

enrage /ɪn'reɪdʒ/ *vt* enfurecer

enrapture /ɪn'ræptʃə(r)/ *vt* extasiar

enrich /ɪn'rɪtʃ/ *vt* enriquecer

enrol /ɪn'rəʊl/ *vt* (*pt* **enrolled**) inscribir; matricular (*student*). ● *vi* inscribirse; (*student*) matricularse. ~**ment** *n* inscripción *f*; (*of student*) matrícula *f*

ensconce /ɪn'skɒns/ *vt*. ~ **o.s.** arrellanarse

ensemble /ɒn'sɒmbl/ *n* conjunto *m*

enshrine /ɪn'ʃraɪn/ *vt* encerrar

ensign /'ensaɪn/ *n* enseña *f*

enslave /ɪn'sleɪv/ *vt* esclavizar

ensue /ɪn'sjuː/ *vi* resultar, seguirse

ensure /ɪn'ʃʊə(r)/ *vt* asegurar

entail /ɪn'teɪl/ *vt* suponer; acarrear (*trouble etc*)

entangle /ɪn'tæŋgl/ *vt* enredar. ~**ment** *n* enredo *m*; (*mil*) alambrada *f*

enter /'entə(r)/ *vt* entrar en; (*write*) escribir; matricular (*school etc*); hacerse socio de (*club*). ● *vi* entrar

enterprise /'entəpraɪz/ *n* empresa *f*; (*fig*) iniciativa *f*

enterprising /'entəpraɪzɪŋ/ *a* emprendedor

entertain /entə'teɪn/ *vt* divertir; recibir (*guests*); abrigar (*ideas*, *hopes*); (*consider*) considerar. ~**ment** *n* diversión *f*; (*performance*) espectáculo *m*; (*reception*) recepción *f*

enthral /ɪn'θrɔːl/ *vt* (*pt* **enthralled**) cautivar

enthuse /ɪn'θjuːz/ *vi*. ~ **over** entusiasmarse por

enthusias|m /ɪn'θjuːzɪæzəm/ *n* entusiasmo *m*. ~**tic** /-'æstɪk/ *a* entusiasta; (*thing*) entusiástico. ~**tically** /-'æstɪklɪ/ *adv* con entusiasmo. ~**t** /ɪn'θjuːzɪæst/ *n* entusiasta *m* & *f*

entice /ɪn'taɪs/ *vt* atraer. ~**ment** *n* atracción *f*

entire /ɪn'taɪə(r)/ *a* entero. ~**ly** *adv* completamente. ~**ty** /ɪn'taɪərətɪ/ *n*. **in its ~ty** en su totalidad

entitle /ɪn'taɪtl/ *vt* titular; (*give a right*) dar derecho a. **be ~d to** tener derecho a. ~**ment** *n* derecho *m*

entity /'entətɪ/ *n* entidad *f*

entomb /ɪn'tuːm/ *vt* sepultar

entrails /'entreɪlz/ *npl* entrañas *fpl*

entrance[1] /'entrəns/ *n* entrada *f*; (*right to enter*) admisión *f*

entrance[2] /ɪn'trɑːns/ *vt* encantar

entrant /'entrənt/ *n* participante *m* & *f*; (*in exam*) candidato *m*

entreat /ɪn'triːt/ *vt* suplicar. ~**y** *n* súplica *f*

entrench /ɪn'trentʃ/ *vt* atrincherar

entrust /ɪn'trʌst/ *vt* confiar

entry /'entrɪ/ *n* entrada *f*; (*of street*) bocacalle *f*; (*note*) apunte *m*

entwine /ɪn'twaɪn/ *vt* entrelazar

enumerate /ɪ'njuːməreɪt/ *vt* enumerar

enunciate /ɪ'nʌnsɪeɪt/ *vt* pronunciar; (*state*) enunciar

envelop /ɪn'veləp/ *vt* (*pt* **enveloped**) envolver

envelope /'envələʊp/ *n* sobre *m*

enviable /'envɪəbl/ *a* envidiable

envious /'enviəs/ *a* envidioso. **∼ly** *adv* con envidia

environment /ın'vaıərənmənt/ *n* medio *m* ambiente. **∼al** /-'mentl/ *a* ambiental

envisage /ın'vızıdʒ/ *vt* prever; (*imagine*) imaginar

envoy /'envɔı/ *n* enviado *m*

envy /'envı/ *n* envidia *f*. ● *vt* envidiar

enzyme /'enzaım/ *n* enzima *f*

epaulette /'epəʊlet/ *n* charretera *f*

ephemeral /ı'femərəl/ *a* efímero

epic /'epık/ *n* épica *f*. ● *a* épico

epicentre /'episentə(r)/ *n* epicentro *m*

epicure /'epıkjʊə(r)/ *n* sibarita *m* & *f*; (*gourmet*) gastrónomo *m*

epidemic /epı'demık/ *n* epidemia *f*. ● *a* epidémico

epilep|sy /'epılepsı/ *n* epilepsia *f*. **∼tic** /-'leptık/ *a* & *n* epiléptico (*m*)

epilogue /'epılɒg/ *n* epílogo *m*

episode /'epısəʊd/ *n* episodio *m*

epistle /ı'pısl/ *n* epístola *f*

epitaph /'epıtɑ:f/ *n* epitafio *m*

epithet /'epıθet/ *n* epíteto *m*

epitom|e /ı'pıtəmı/ *n* epítome *m*, personificación *f*. **∼ize** *vt* epitomar, personificar, ser la personificación de

epoch /'i:pɒk/ *n* época *f*. **∼-making** *a* que hace época

equal /'i:kwəl/ *a* & *n* igual (*m* & *f*). **∼ to** (*a task*) a la altura de. ● *vt* (*pt* **equalled**) ser igual a; (*math*) ser. **∼ity** /ı'kwɒlətı/ *n* igualdad *f*. **∼ize** /'i:kwəlaız/ *vt/i* igualar. **∼izer** /-ə(r)/ *n* (*sport*) tanto *m* de empate. **∼ly** *adv* igualmente

equanimity /ekwə'nımətı/ *n* ecuanimidad *f*

equate /ı'kweıt/ *vt* igualar

equation /ı'kweıʒn/ *n* ecuación *f*

equator /ı'kweıtə(r)/ *n* ecuador *m*. **∼ial** /ekwə'tɔ:rıəl/ *a* ecuatorial

equestrian /ı'kwestrıən/ *a* ecuestre

equilateral /i:kwı'lætərl/ *a* equilátero

equilibrium /i:kwı'lıbrıəm/ *n* equilibrio *m*

equinox /'i:kwınɒks/ *n* equinoccio *m*

equip /ı'kwıp/ *vt* (*pt* **equipped**) equipar. **∼ment** *n* equipo *m*

equitable /'ekwıtəbl/ *a* equitativo

equity /'ekwətı/ *n* equidad *f*; (*pl, com*) acciones *fpl* ordinarias

equivalen|ce /ı'kwıvələns/ *n* equivalencia *f*. **∼t** /ı'kwıvələnt/ *a* & *n* equivalente (*m*)

equivocal /ı'kwıvəkl/ *a* equívoco

era /'ıərə/ *n* era *f*

eradicate /ı'rædıkeıt/ *vt* extirpar

erase /ı'reız/ *vt* borrar. **∼r** /-ə(r)/ *n* borrador *m*

erect /ı'rekt/ *a* erguido. ● *vt* levantar. **∼ion** /-ʃn/ *n* erección *f*, montaje *m*

ermine /'ɜ:mın/ *n* armiño *m*

ero|de /ı'rəʊd/ *vt* desgastar. **∼sion** /-ʒn/ *n* desgaste *m*

erotic /ı'rɒtık/ *a* erótico. **∼ism** /-sızəm/ *n* erotismo *m*

err /ɜ:(r)/ *vi* errar; (*sin*) pecar

errand /'erənd/ *n* recado *m*

erratic /ı'rætık/ *a* irregular; ⟨*person*⟩ voluble

erroneous /ı'rəʊnıəs/ *a* erróneo

error /'erə(r)/ *n* error *m*

erudit|e /'eru:daıt/ *a* erudito. **∼ion** /-'dıʃn/ *n* erudición *f*

erupt /ı'rʌpt/ *vi* estar en erupción; (*fig*) estallar. **∼ion** /-ʃn/ *n* erupción *f*

escalat|e /'eskəleıt/ *vt* intensificar. ● *vi* intensificarse. **∼ion** /-'leıʃn/ *n* intensificación *f*

escalator /'eskəleıtə(r)/ *n* escalera *f* mecánica

escapade /eskə'peıd/ *n* aventura *f*

escap|e /ı'skeıp/ *vi* escaparse. ● *vt* evitar. ● *n* fuga *f*; (*avoidance*) evasión *f*. **have a narrow ∼e** escapar por un pelo. **∼ism** /ı'skeıpızəm/ *n* escapismo *m*

escarpment /ıs'kɑ:pmənt/ *n* escarpa *f*

escort /'eskɔ:t/ *n* acompañante *m*; (*mil*) escolta *f*. /ı'skɔ:t/ *vt* acompañar; (*mil*) escoltar

Eskimo /'eskıməʊ/ *n* (*pl* **-os, -o**) esquimal (*m* & *f*)

especial /ı'speʃl/ *a* especial. **∼ly** *adv* especialmente

espionage /'espıənɑ:ʒ/ *n* espionaje *m*

esplanade /esplə'neıd/ *n* paseo *m* marítimo

Esq. /ı'skwaıə(r)/ *abbr* (*Esquire*) (*in address*). **E. Ashton, ∼** Sr. D. E. Ashton

essay /'eseı/ *n* ensayo *m*; (*at school*) composición *f*

essence /'esns/ *n* esencia *f*. **in ∼** esencialmente

essential /ı'senʃl/ *a* esencial. ● *n* lo esencial. **∼ly** *adv* esencialmente

establish /ɪ'stæblɪʃ/ vt establecer; (prove) probar. **~ment** n establecimiento m. **the E~ment** los que mandan, el sistema m

estate /ɪ'steɪt/ n finca f; (possessions) bienes mpl. **~ agent** n agente m inmobiliario. **~ car** n furgoneta f

esteem /ɪ'sti:m/ vt estimar. ● n estimación f, estima f

estimat|e /'estɪmət/ n cálculo m; (com) presupuesto m. /'estɪmeɪt/ vt calcular. **~ion** /-'meɪʃn/ n estima f, estimación f; (opinion) opinión f

estranged /ɪs'treɪndʒd/ a alejado

estuary /'estʃʊərɪ/ n estuario m

etc. /et'setrə/ abbr (et cetera) etc., etcétera

etching /'etʃɪŋ/ n aguafuerte m

eternal /ɪ'tɜ:nl/ a eterno

eternity /ɪ'tɜ:nətɪ/ n eternidad f

ether /'i:θə(r)/ n éter m

ethereal /ɪ'θɪərɪəl/ a etéreo

ethic /'eθɪk/ n ética f. **~s** npl ética f. **~al** a ético

ethnic /'eθnɪk/ a étnico

ethos /'i:θɒs/ n carácter m distintivo

etiquette /'etɪket/ n etiqueta f

etymology /etɪ'mɒlədʒɪ/ n etimología f

eucalyptus /ju:kə'lɪptəs/ n (pl -tuses) eucalipto m

eulogy /'ju:lədʒɪ/ n encomio m

euphemism /'ju:fəmɪzəm/ n eufemismo m

euphoria /ju:'fɔ:rɪə/ n euforia f

Europe /'jʊərəp/ n Europa f. **~an** /-'pɪən/ a & n europeo (m)

euthanasia /ju:θə'neɪzɪə/ n eutanasia f

evacuat|e /ɪ'vækjʊeɪt/ vt evacuar; desocupar ⟨building⟩. **~ion** /-'eɪʃn/ n evacuación f

evade /ɪ'veɪd/ vt evadir

evaluate /ɪ'væljʊeɪt/ vt evaluar

evangeli|cal /i:væn'dʒelɪkl/ a evangélico. **~st** /ɪ'vændʒəlɪst/ n evangelista m & f

evaporat|e /ɪ'væpəreɪt/ vi evaporarse. **~ion** /-'reɪʃn/ n evaporación f

evasion /ɪ'veɪʒn/ n evasión f

evasive /ɪ'veɪsɪv/ a evasivo

eve /i:v/ n víspera f

even /'i:vn/ a regular; (flat) llano; ⟨surface⟩ liso; ⟨amount⟩ igual; ⟨number⟩ par. **get ~ with** desquitarse con. ● vt nivelar. **~ up** igualar. ● adv aun, hasta, incluso. **~ if**

aunque. **~ so** aun así. **not ~** ni siquiera

evening /'i:vnɪŋ/ n tarde f; (after dark) noche f. **~ class** n clase f nocturna. **~ dress** n (man's) traje m de etiqueta; (woman's) traje m de noche

evensong /'i:vənsɒŋ/ n vísperas fpl

event /ɪ'vent/ n acontecimiento m; (sport) prueba f. **in the ~ of** en caso de. **~ful** a lleno de acontecimientos

eventual /ɪ'ventʃʊəl/ a final, definitivo. **~ity** /-'ælətɪ/ n eventualidad f. **~ly** adv finalmente

ever /'evə(r)/ adv jamás, nunca; (at all times) siempre. **~ after** desde entonces. **~ since** desde entonces. ● conj después de que. **~ so** (fam) muy. **for ~** para siempre. **hardly ~** casi nunca

evergreen /'evəgri:n/ a de hoja perenne. ● n árbol m de hoja perenne

everlasting /evə'lɑ:stɪŋ/ a eterno

every /'evrɪ/ a cada, todo. **~ child** todos los niños. **~ one** cada uno. **~ other day** cada dos días

everybody /'evrɪbɒdɪ/ pron todo el mundo

everyday /'evrɪdeɪ/ a todos los días

everyone /'evrɪwʌn/ pron todo el mundo. **~ else** todos los demás

everything /'evrɪθɪŋ/ pron todo

everywhere /'evrɪweə(r)/ adv en todas partes

evict /ɪ'vɪkt/ vt desahuciar. **~ion** /-ʃn/ n desahucio m

eviden|ce /'evɪdəns/ n evidencia f; (proof) pruebas fpl; (jurid) testimonio m. **~ce of** señales de. **in ~ce** visible. **~t** /'evɪdənt/ a evidente. **~tly** adv evidentemente

evil /'i:vl/ a malo. ● n mal m, maldad f

evocative /ɪ'vɒkətɪv/ a evocador

evoke /ɪ'vəʊk/ vt evocar

evolution /i:və'lu:ʃn/ n evolución f

evolve /ɪ'vɒlv/ vt desarrollar. ● vi desarrollarse, evolucionar

ewe /ju:/ n oveja f

ex... /eks/ pref ex...

exacerbate /ɪg'zæsəbeɪt/ vt exacerbar

exact /ɪg'zækt/ a exacto. ● vt exigir (from a). **~ing** a exigente. **~itude** n exactitud f. **~ly** adv exactamente

exaggerat|e /ɪg'zædʒəreɪt/ vt exagerar. **~ion** /-'reɪʃn/ n exageración f

exalt /ɪg'zɔ:lt/ vt exaltar

exam /ɪgˈzæm/ n (fam) examen m.
∼ination /ɪgzæmɪˈneɪʃn/ n examen
m. **∼ine** /ɪgˈzæmɪn/ vt examinar;
interrogar ‹witness›. **∼iner** /-ə(r)/ n
examinador m

example /ɪgˈzɑːmpl/ n ejemplo m.
make an ∼ of infligir castigo ejemplar a

exasperat|e /ɪgˈzæspəreɪt/ vt
exasperar. **∼ion** /-ˈreɪʃn/ n
exasperación f

excavat|e /ˈekskəveɪt/ vt excavar.
∼ion /-ˈveɪʃn/ n excavación f

exceed /ɪkˈsiːd/ vt exceder. **∼ingly**
adv extremadamente

excel /ɪkˈsel/ vi (pt **excelled**) sobresalir. ● vt superar

excellen|ce /ˈeksələns/ n excelencia
f. **∼t** /ˈeksələnt/ a excelente. **∼tly**
adv excelentemente

except /ɪkˈsept/ prep excepto, con
excepción de. **∼ for** con excepción
de. ● vt exceptuar. **∼ing** prep con
excepción de

exception /ɪkˈsepʃən/ n excepción f.
take ∼ to ofenderse por. **∼al**
/ɪkˈsepʃənl/ a excepcional. **∼ally**
adv excepcionalmente

excerpt /ˈeksɜːpt/ n extracto m

excess /ɪkˈses/ n exceso m. /ˈekses/ a
excedente. **∼ fare** n suplemento m.
∼ luggage n exceso m de equipaje

excessive /ɪkˈsesɪv/ a excesivo. **∼ly**
adv excesivamente

exchange /ɪkˈstʃeɪndʒ/ vt cambiar.
● n cambio m. **(telephone) ∼** central f telefónica

exchequer /ɪksˈtʃekə(r)/ n (pol) erario m, hacienda f

excise¹ /ˈeksaɪz/ n impuestos mpl
indirectos

excise² /ekˈsaɪz/ vt quitar

excit|able /ɪkˈsaɪtəbl/ a excitable.
∼e /ɪkˈsaɪt/ vt emocionar; (stimulate) excitar. **∼ed** a entusiasmado. **∼ement** n emoción f;
(enthusiasm) entusiasmo m. **∼ing** a
emocionante

excla|im /ɪkˈskleɪm/ vi exclamar.
∼mation /ekskləˈmeɪʃn/ n exclamación f. **∼mation mark** n signo m
de admiración f, punto m de
exclamación

exclu|de /ɪkˈskluːd/ vt excluir.
∼sion /-ʒn/ n exclusión f

exclusive /ɪkˈskluːsɪv/ a exclusivo;
‹club› selecto. **∼ of** excluyendo.
∼ly adv exclusivamente

excomunicate /ekskəˈmjuːnɪkeɪt/ vt
excomulgar

excrement /ˈekskrɪmənt/ n excremento m

excruciating /ɪkˈskruːʃɪeɪtɪŋ/ a
atroz, insoportable

excursion /ɪkˈskɜːʃn/ n excursión f

excus|able a /ɪkˈskjuːzəbl/ a perdonable. **∼e** /ɪkˈskjuːz/ vt perdonar.
∼e from dispensar de. **∼e me!** ¡perdón! /ɪkˈskjuːs/ n excusa f

ex-directory /eksdɪˈrektərɪ/ a que
no está en la guía telefónica

execrable /ˈeksɪkrəbl/ a execrable

execut|e /ˈeksɪkjuːt/ vt ejecutar.
∼ion /eksɪˈkjuːʃn/ n ejecución f.
∼ioner n verdugo m

executive /ɪgˈzekjʊtɪv/ a & n ejecutivo (m)

executor /ɪgˈzekjʊtə(r)/ n (jurid)
testamentario m

exemplary /ɪgˈzemplərɪ/ a ejemplar

exemplify /ɪgˈzemplɪfaɪ/ vt ilustrar

exempt /ɪgˈzempt/ a exento. ● vt dispensar. **∼ion** /-ʃn/ n exención f

exercise /ˈeksəsaɪz/ n ejercicio m.
● vt ejercer. ● vi hacer ejercicios. **∼
book** n cuaderno m

exert /ɪgˈzɜːt/ vt ejercer. **∼ o.s.** esforzarse. **∼ion** /-ʃn/ n esfuerzo m

exhal|ation /ekshəˈleɪʃn/ n exhalación f. **∼e** /eksˈheɪl/ vt/i exhalar

exhaust /ɪgˈzɔːst/ vt agotar. ● n
(auto) tubo m de escape. **∼ed** a agotado. **∼ion** /-stʃən/ n agotamiento
m. **∼ive** /ɪgˈzɔːstɪv/ a exhaustivo

exhibit /ɪgˈzɪbɪt/ vt exponer; (jurid)
exhibir; (fig) mostrar. ● n objeto m
expuesto; (jurid) documento m

exhibition /eksɪˈbɪʃn/ n exposición
f; (act of showing) demostración f;
(univ) beca f. **∼ist** n exhibicionista
m & f

exhibitor /ɪgˈzɪbɪtə(r)/ n expositor m

exhilarat|e /ɪgˈzɪləreɪt/ vt alegrar.
∼ion /-ˈreɪʃn/ n regocijo m

exhort /ɪgˈzɔːt/ vt exhortar

exile /ˈeksaɪl/ n exilio m; (person)
exiliado m. ● vt desterrar

exist /ɪgˈzɪst/ vi existir. **∼ence** n
existencia f. **in ∼ence** existente

existentialism /egzɪsˈtenʃəlɪzəm/ n
existencialismo m

exit /ˈeksɪt/ n salida f

exodus /ˈeksədəs/ n éxodo m

exonerate /ɪgˈzɒnəreɪt/ vt disculpar

exorbitant /ɪgˈzɔːbɪtənt/ a exorbitante

exorcis|e /'eksɔːsaɪz/ vt exorcizar. **∼m** /-sɪzəm/ n exorcismo m

exotic /ɪg'zɒtɪk/ a exótico

expand /ɪk'spænd/ vt extender; dilatar ‹metal›; (develop) desarrollar. ● vi extenderse; (develop) desarrollarse; ‹metal› dilatarse

expanse /ɪk'spæns/ n extensión f

expansion /ɪk'spænʃn/ n extensión f; (of metal) dilatación f

expansive /ɪk'spænsɪv/ a expansivo

expatriate /eks'pætrɪət/ a & n expatriado (m)

expect /ɪk'spekt/ vt esperar; (suppose) suponer; (demand) contar con. **I ∼ so** supongo que sí

expectan|cy /ɪk'spektənsɪ/ n esperanza f. **life ∼cy** esperanza f de vida. **∼t** /ɪk'spektənt/ a expectante. **∼t mother** n futura madre f

expectation /ekspek'teɪʃn/ n esperanza f

expedien|cy /ɪk'spiːdɪənsɪ/ n conveniencia f. **∼t** /ɪk'spiːdɪənt/ a conveniente

expedite /'ekspɪdaɪt/ vt acelerar

expedition /ekspɪ'dɪʃn/ n expedición f. **∼ary** a expedicionario

expel /ɪk'spel/ vt (pt expelled) expulsar

expend /ɪk'spend/ vt gastar. **∼able** a prescindible

expenditure /ɪk'spendɪtʃə(r)/ n gastos mpl

expens|e /ɪk'spens/ n gasto m; (fig) costa f. **at s.o.'s ∼e** a costa de uno. **∼ive** /ɪk'spensɪv/ a caro. **∼ively** adv costosamente

experience /ɪk'spɪərɪəns/ n experiencia. ● vt experimentar. **∼d** a experto

experiment /ɪk'sperɪmənt/ n experimento m. ● vi experimentar. **∼al** /-'mentl/ a experimental

expert /'ekspɜːt/ a & n experto (m). **∼ise** /ekspɜː'tiːz/ n pericia f. **∼ly** adv hábilmente

expir|e /ɪk'spaɪə(r)/ vi expirar. **∼y** n expiración f

expla|in /ɪk'spleɪn/ vt explicar. **∼nation** /eksplə'neɪʃn/ n explicación f. **∼natory** /ɪks'plænətərɪ/ a explicativo

expletive /ɪk'spliːtɪv/ n palabrota f

explicit /ɪk'splɪsɪt/ a explícito

explode /ɪk'spləʊd/ vt hacer explotar; (tec) explosionar. ● vi estallar

exploit /'eksplɔɪt/ n hazaña f. /ɪk'splɔɪt/ vt explotar. **∼ation** /eksplɔɪ'teɪʃn/ n explotación f

explor|ation /eksplə'reɪʃn/ n exploración f. **∼atory** /ɪk'splɒrətrɪ/ a exploratorio. **∼e** /ɪk'splɔː(r)/ vt explorar. **∼er** n explorador m

explosi|on /ɪk'spləʊʒn/ n explosión f. **∼ve** a & n explosivo (m)

exponent /ɪk'spəʊnənt/ n exponente m

export /ɪk'spɔːt/ vt exportar. /'ekspɔːt/ n exportación f. **∼er** /ɪks'pɔːtə(r)/ exportador m

expos|e /ɪk'spəʊz/ vt exponer; (reveal) descubrir. **∼ure** /-ʒə(r)/ n exposición f. **die of ∼ure** morir de frío

expound /ɪk'spaʊnd/ vt exponer

express[1] /ɪk'spres/ vt expresar

express[2] /ɪk'spres/ a expreso; ‹letter› urgente. ● adv (by express post) por correo urgente. ● n (train) rápido m, expreso m

expression /ɪk'spreʃn/ n expresión f

expressive /ɪk'spresɪv/ a expresivo

expressly /ɪk'spreslɪ/ adv expresamente

expulsion /ɪk'spʌlʃn/ n expulsión f

expurgate /'ekspəgeɪt/ vt expurgar

exquisite /'ekskwɪzɪt/ a exquisito. **∼ly** adv primorosamente

ex-serviceman /eks'sɜːvɪsmən/ n (pl -men) excombatiente m

extant /ek'stænt/ a existente

extempore /ek'stempərɪ/ a improvisado. ● adv de improviso

exten|d /ɪk'stend/ vt extender; (prolong) prolongar; ensanchar ‹house›. ● vi extenderse. **∼sion** n extensión f; (of road, time) prolongación f; (building) anejo m; (com) prórroga f

extensive /ɪk'stensɪv/ a extenso. **∼ly** adv extensamente

extent /ɪk'stent/ n extensión f; (fig) alcance m. **to a certain ∼** hasta cierto punto

extenuate /ɪk'stenjʊeɪt/ vt atenuar

exterior /ɪk'stɪərɪə(r)/ a & n exterior (m)

exterminat|e /ɪk'stɜːmɪneɪt/ vt exterminar. **∼ion** /-'neɪʃn/ n exterminio m

external /ɪk'stɜːnl/ a externo. **∼ly** adv externamente

extinct /ɪk'stɪŋkt/ a extinto. **∼ion** /-ʃn/ n extinción f

extinguish /ɪk'stɪŋgwɪʃ/ vt extinguir. **∼er** n extintor m

extol /ɪk'stəʊl/ vt (pt extolled) alabar

extort /ɪkˈstɔːt/ vt sacar por la fuerza. **~ion** /-ʃn/ n exacción f. **~ionate** /ɪkˈstɔːʃənət/ a exorbitante

extra /ˈekstrə/ a suplementario. ● adv extraordinariamente. ● n suplemento m; (cinema) extra m & f

extract /ˈekstrækt/ n extracto m. /ɪkˈstrækt/ vt extraer; (fig) arrancar. **~ion** /-ʃn/ n extracción f; (lineage) origen m

extradit|e /ˈekstrədaɪt/ vt extraditar. **~ion** /-ˈdɪʃn/ n extradición f

extramarital /ekstrəˈmærɪtl/ a fuera del matrimonio

extramural /ekstrəˈmjʊərəl/ a fuera del recinto universitario; (for external students) para estudiantes externos

extraordinary /ɪkˈstrɔːdnrɪ/ a extraordinario

extra-sensory /ekstrəˈsensərɪ/ a extrasensorial

extravagan|ce /ɪkˈstrævəgəns/ n prodigalidad f, extravagancia f. **~t** /ɪkˈstrævəgənt/ a pródigo, extravagante

extrem|e /ɪkˈstriːm/ a & n extremo (m). **~ely** adv extremadamente. **~ist** n extremista m & f. **~ity** /ɪkˈstremətɪ/ n extremidad f

extricate /ˈekstrɪkeɪt/ vt desenredar, librar

extrovert /ˈekstrəvɜːt/ n extrovertido m

exuberan|ce /ɪgˈzjuːbərəns/ n exuberancia f. **~t** /ɪgˈzjuːbərənt/ a exuberante

exude /ɪgˈzjuːd/ vt rezumar

exult /ɪgˈzʌlt/ vi exultar

eye /aɪ/ n ojo m. **keep an ~ on** no perder de vista. **see ~ to ~** estar de acuerdo con. ● vt (pt **eyed**, pres p **eyeing**) mirar. **~ball** /ˈaɪbɔːl/ n globo m del ojo. **~brow** /ˈaɪbraʊ/ n ceja f. **~ful** /ˈaɪfʊl/ n (fam) espectáculo m sorprendente. **~lash** /ˈaɪlæʃ/ n pestaña f. **~let** /ˈaɪlɪt/ n ojete m. **~lid** /ˈaɪlɪd/ n párpado m. **~opener** n (fam) revelación f. **~shadow** n sombra f de ojos, sombreador m. **~sight** /ˈaɪsaɪt/ n vista f. **~sore** /ˈaɪsɔː(r)/ n (fig, fam) monstruosidad f, horror m. **~witness** /ˈaɪwɪtnɪs/ n testigo m ocular

F

fable /ˈfeɪbl/ n fábula f

fabric /ˈfæbrɪk/ n tejido m, tela f

fabrication /fæbrɪˈkeɪʃn/ n invención f

fabulous /ˈfæbjʊləs/ a fabuloso

façade /fəˈsɑːd/ n fachada f

face /feɪs/ n cara f, rostro m; (of watch) esfera f; (aspect) aspecto m. **~ down(wards)** boca abajo. **~ up(wards)** boca arriba. **in the ~ of** frente a. **lose ~** quedar mal. **pull ~s** hacer muecas. ● vt mirar hacia; ⟨house⟩ dar a; (confront) enfrentarse con. ● vi volverse. **~ up to** enfrentarse con. **~ flannel** n paño m (para lavarse la cara). **~less** a anónimo. **~lift** n cirugía f estética en la cara

facet /ˈfæsɪt/ n faceta f

facetious /fəˈsiːʃəs/ a chistoso, gracioso

facial /ˈfeɪʃl/ a facial. ● n masaje m facial

facile /ˈfæsaɪl/ a fácil

facilitate /fəˈsɪlɪteɪt/ vt facilitar

facility /fəˈsɪlɪtɪ/ n facilidad f

facing /ˈfeɪsɪŋ/ n revestimiento m. **~s** npl (on clothes) vueltas fpl

facsimile /fækˈsɪmɪlɪ/ n facsímile m

fact /fækt/ n hecho m. **as a matter of ~, in ~** en realidad, a decir verdad

faction /ˈfækʃn/ n facción f

factor /ˈfæktə(r)/ n factor m

factory /ˈfæktərɪ/ n fábrica f

factual /ˈfæktʃʊəl/ a basado en hechos, factual

faculty /ˈfækəltɪ/ n facultad f

fad /fæd/ n manía f, capricho m

fade /feɪd/ vi ⟨colour⟩ descolorarse; ⟨flowers⟩ marchitarse; ⟨light⟩ apagarse; ⟨memory, sound⟩ desvanecerse

faeces /ˈfiːsiːz/ npl excrementos mpl

fag¹ /fæg/ n (chore, fam) faena f; (cigarette, sl) cigarillo m, pitillo m

fag² /fæg/ n (homosexual, Amer, sl) marica m

fagged /fægd/ a. **~ (out)** rendido

fah /fɑ/ n (mus, fourth note of any musical scale) fa m

fail /feɪl/ vi fallar; (run short) acabarse. **he ~ed to arrive** no llegó. ● vt no aprobar ⟨exam⟩; suspender ⟨candidate⟩; (disappoint) fallar. **~ s.o.** ⟨words etc⟩ faltarle a uno. ● n. **without ~** sin falta

failing /ˈfeɪlɪŋ/ n defecto m. ● prep a falta de

failure /'feɪljə(r)/ n fracaso m; (*person*) fracasado m; (*med*) ataque m; (*mec*) fallo m. ~ **to do** dejar m de hacer

faint /feɪnt/ a (**-er, -est**) (*weak*) débil; (*indistinct*) indistinto. **feel** ~ estar mareado. **the ~est idea** la más remota idea. ● vi desmayarse. ● n desmayo m. **~hearted** a pusilánime, cobarde. **~ly** adv (*weakly*) débilmente; (*indistinctly*) indistintamente. **~ness** n debilidad f

fair[1] /feə(r)/ a (**-er, -est**) (*just*) justo; ⟨*weather*⟩ bueno; ⟨*amount*⟩ razonable; ⟨*hair*⟩ rubio; ⟨*skin*⟩ blanco. ~ **play** n juego m limpio. ● adv limpio

fair[2] /feə(r)/ n feria f

fair: **~ly** adv (*justly*) justamente; (*rather*) bastante. **~ness** n justicia f

fairy /'feərɪ/ n hada f. **~land** n país m de las hadas. ~ **story**, **~tale** cuento m de hadas

fait accompli /feɪtə'kɒmpli:/ n hecho m consumado

faith /feɪθ/ n (*trust*) confianza f; (*relig*) fe f. **~ful** a fiel. **~fully** adv fielmente. **~fulness** n fidelidad f. **~healing** n curación f por la fe

fake /feɪk/ n falsificación f; (*person*) impostor m. ● a falso. ● vt falsificar; (*pretend*) fingir

fakir /'feɪkɪə(r)/ n faquir m

falcon /'fɔːlkən/ n halcón m

Falkland /'fɔːlklənd/ n. **the ~ Islands** npl las islas fpl Malvinas

fall /fɔːl/ vi (pt **fell**, pp **fallen**) caer. ● n caída f; (*autumn, Amer*) otoño m; (*in price*) baja f. ~ **back on** recurrir a. ~ **down** (*fall*) caer; (*be unsuccessful*) fracasar. ~ **for** (*fam*) enamorarse de ⟨*person*⟩; (*fam*) dejarse engañar por ⟨*trick*⟩. ~ **in** (*mil*) formar filas. ~ **off** (*diminish*) disminuir. ~ **out** (*quarrel*) reñir (*with* con); (*drop out*) caer. ~ **over** caer(se). ~ **over sth** tropezar con algo. ~ **short** ser insuficiente. ~ **through** fracasar

fallacy /'fæləsɪ/ n error m

fallible /'fælɪbl/ a falible

fallout /'fɔːlaʊt/ n lluvia f radiactiva

fallow /'fæləʊ/ a en barbecho

false /fɔːls/ a falso. **~hood** n mentira f. **~ly** adv falsamente. **~ness** n falsedad f

falsetto /fɔːl'setəʊ/ n (pl **-os**) falsete m

falsify /'fɔːlsɪfaɪ/ vt falsificar

falter /'fɔːltə(r)/ vi vacilar

fame /feɪm/ n fama f. **~d** a famoso

familiar /fə'mɪlɪə(r)/ a familiar. **be ~ with** conocer. **~ity** /-'ærətɪ/ n familiaridad f. **~ize** vt familiarizar

family /'fæməlɪ/ n familia f. ● a de (la) familia, familiar

famine /'fæmɪn/ n hambre f, hambruna f (*Amer*)

famished /'fæmɪʃt/ a hambriento

famous /'feɪməs/ a famoso. **~ly** adv (*fam*) a las mil maravillas

fan[1] /fæn/ n abanico m; (*mec*) ventilador m. ● vt (pt **fanned**) abanicar; soplar ⟨*fire*⟩. ● vi. ~ **out** desparramarse en forma de abanico

fan[2] /fæn/ n (*of person*) admirador m; (*enthusiast*) aficionado m, entusiasta m & f

fanatic /fə'nætɪk/ n fanático m. **~al** a fanático. **~ism** /-sɪzəm/ n fanatismo m

fan belt /'fænbelt/ n correa f de ventilador

fancier /'fænsɪə(r)/ n aficionado m

fanciful /'fænsɪfl/ a (*imaginative*) imaginativo; (*unreal*) imaginario

fancy /'fænsɪ/ n fantasía f; (*liking*) gusto m. **take a ~ to** tomar cariño a ⟨*person*⟩; aficionarse a ⟨*thing*⟩. ● a de lujo; (*extravagant*) excesivo. ● vt (*imagine*) imaginar; (*believe*) creer; (*want, fam*) apetecer a. ~ **dress** n disfraz m

fanfare /'fænfeə(r)/ n fanfarria f

fang /fæŋ/ n (*of animal*) colmillo m; (*of snake*) diente m

fanlight /'fænlaɪt/ n montante m

fantasize /'fæntəsaɪz/ vi fantasear

fantastic /fæn'tæstɪk/ a fantástico

fantasy /'fæntəsɪ/ n fantasía f

far /fɑː(r)/ adv lejos; (*much*) mucho. **as ~ as** hasta. **as ~ as I know** que yo sepa. **by ~** con mucho. ● a (*further, furthest* or *farther, farthest*) lejano

far-away /'fɑːrəweɪ/ a lejano

farc|e /fɑːs/ n farsa f. **~ical** a ridículo

fare /feə(r)/ n (*for transport*) tarifa f; (*food*) comida f. ● vi irle. **how did you ~?** ¿qué tal te fue?

Far East /fɑː(r)'iːst/ n Extremo/Lejano Oriente m

farewell /feə'wel/ int & n adiós (m)

far-fetched /fɑː'fetʃt/ a improbable

farm /fɑːm/ n granja f. ● vt cultivar. ~ **out** arrendar. ● vi ser agricultor. **~er** n agricultor m. **~house** n granja f. **~ing** n agricultura f. **~yard** n corral m

far: ∼**off** a lejano. ∼**reaching** a trascendental. ∼**seeing** a clarividente. ∼**sighted** a hipermétrope; (*fig*) clarividente

farther,farthest /'fɑːðə(r), 'fɑːðəst/ *see* **far**

fascinat|e /'fæsɪneɪt/ *vt* fascinar. ∼**ion** /-'neɪʃn/ *n* fascinación *f*

fascis|m /'fæʃɪzəm/ *n* fascismo *m*. ∼**t** /'fæʃɪst/ *a & n* fascista (*m & f*)

fashion /'fæʃn/ *n* (*manner*) manera *f*; (*vogue*) moda *f*. ∼**able** *a* de moda

fast[1] /fɑːst/ *a* (**-er, -est**) rápido; (*clock*) adelantado; (*secure*) fijo; (*colours*) sólido. ● *adv* rápidamente; (*securely*) firmemente. ∼ **asleep** profundamente dormido

fast[2] /fɑːst/ *vi* ayunar. ● *n* ayuno *m*

fasten /'fɑːsn/ *vt/i* sujetar; cerrar (*windows, doors*); abrochar (*belt etc*). ∼**er** *n*, ∼**ing** *n* (*on box, window*) cierre *m*; (*on door*) cerrojo *m*

fastidious /fə'stɪdɪəs/ *a* exigente, minucioso

fat /fæt/ *n* grasa *f*. ● *a* (**fatter, fattest**) gordo; (*meat*) que tiene mucha grasa; (*thick*) grueso. **a** ∼ **lot of** (*sl*) muy poco

fatal /'feɪtl/ *a* mortal; (*fateful*) fatídico

fatalis|m /'feɪtəlɪzəm/ *n* fatalismo *m*. ∼**t** *n* fatalista *m & f*

fatality /fə'tælətɪ/ *n* calamidad *f*; (*death*) muerte *f*

fatally /'feɪtlɪ/ *adv* mortalmente; (*by fate*) fatalmente

fate /feɪt/ *n* destino *m*; (*one's lot*) suerte *f*. ∼**d** *a* predestinado. ∼**ful** *a* fatídico

fat-head /'fæthed/ *n* imbécil *m*

father /'fɑːðə(r)/ *n* padre *m*. ∼**hood** *m* paternidad *f*. ∼**-in-law** *m* (*pl* **fathers-in-law**) *m* suegro *m*. ∼**ly** *a* paternal

fathom /'fæðəm/ *n* braza *f*. ● *vt*. ∼ (**out**) comprender

fatigue /fə'tiːg/ *n* fatiga *f*. ● *vt* fatigar

fat: ∼**ness** *n* gordura *f*. ∼**ten** *vt/i* engordar. ∼**tening** *a* que engorda. ∼**ty** *a* graso. ● *n* (*fam*) gordinflón *m*

fatuous /'fætjʊəs/ *a* fatuo

faucet /'fɔːsɪt/ *n* (*Amer*) grifo *m*

fault /fɔːlt/ *n* defecto *m*; (*blame*) culpa *f*; (*tennis*) falta *f*; (*geol*) falla *f*. **at** ∼ culpable. ● *vt* criticar. ∼**less** *a* impecable. ∼**y** *a* defectuoso

fauna /'fɔːnə/ *n* fauna *f*

faux pas /fəʊ'pɑː/ (*pl* **faux pas** /fəʊ'pɑː /*) *n* metedura *f* de pata, paso *m* en falso

favour /'feɪvə(r)/ *n* favor *m*. ● *vt* favorecer; (*support*) estar a favor de; (*prefer*) preferir. ∼**able** *a* favorable. ∼**ably** *adv* favorablemente

favourit|e /'feɪvərɪt/ *a & n* preferido (*m*). ∼**ism** *n* favoritismo *m*

fawn[1] /fɔːn/ *n* cervato *m*. ● *a* color de cervato, beige, beis

fawn[2] /fɔːn/ *vi*. ∼ **on** adular

fax /fæks/ *n* telefacsímil *m*, fax *m*

fear /fɪə(r)/ *n* miedo *m*. ● *vt* temer. ∼**ful** *a* (*frightening*) espantoso; (*frightened*) temeroso. ∼**less** *a* intrépido. ∼**lessness** *n* intrepidez *f*. ∼**some** *a* espantoso

feasib|ility /fiːzə'bɪlətɪ/ *n* viabilidad *f*. ∼**le** /'fiːzəbl/ *a* factible; (*likely*) posible

feast /fiːst/ *n* (*relig*) fiesta *f*; (*meal*) banquete *m*, comilona *f*. ● *vt* banquetear, festejar. ∼ **on** regalarse con

feat /fiːt/ *n* hazaña *f*

feather /'feðə(r)/ *n* pluma *f*. ● *vt*. ∼ **one's nest** hacer su agosto. ∼**-brained** *a* tonto. ∼**weight** *n* peso *m* pluma

feature /'fiːtʃə(r)/ *n* (*on face*) facción *f*; (*characteristic*) característica *f*; (*in newspaper*) artículo *m*; ∼ (**film**) película *f* principal, largometraje *m*. ● *vt* presentar; (*give prominence to*) destacar. ● *vi* figurar

February /'februərɪ/ *n* febrero *m*

feckless /'feklɪs/ *a* inepto; (*irresponsible*) irreflexivo

fed /fed/ *see* **feed**. ● *a*. ∼ **up** (*sl*) harto (**with** de)

federal /'fedərəl/ *a* federal

federation /fedə'reɪʃn/ *n* federación *f*

fee /fiː/ *n* (*professional*) honorarios *mpl*; (*enrolment*) derechos *mpl*; (*club*) cuota *f*

feeble /'fiːbl/ *a* (**-er, -est**) débil. ∼**-minded** *a* imbécil

feed /fiːd/ *vt* (*pt* **fed**) dar de comer a; (*supply*) alimentar. ● *vi* comer. ● *n* (*for animals*) pienso *m*; (*for babies*) comida *f*. ∼**back** *n* reacciones *fpl*, comentarios *mpl*

feel /fiːl/ *vt* (*pt* **felt**) sentir; (*touch*) tocar; (*think*) parecerle. **do you** ∼ **it's a good idea?** te parece buena idea? **I** ∼ **it is necessary** me parece necesario. ∼ **as if** tener la impresión de que. ∼ **hot/hungry** tener calor/hambre. ∼ **like** (*want, fam*) tener ganas de. **~ up to** sentirse capaz de

feeler /'fiːlə(r)/ *n* (*of insects*) antena *f*. **put out a ~** (*fig*) hacer un sondeo

feeling /'fiːlɪŋ/ *n* sentimiento *m*; (*physical*) sensación *f*

feet /fiːt/ *see* **foot**

feign /feɪn/ *vt* fingir

feint /feɪnt/ *n* finta *f*

felicitous /fə'lɪsɪtəs/ *a* feliz, oportuno

feline /'fiːlaɪn/ *a* felino

fell[1] /fel/ *see* **fall**

fell[2] /fel/ *vt* derribar

fellow /'feləʊ/ *n* (*fam*) tipo *m*; (*comrade*) compañero *m*; (*society*) socio *m*. **~countryman** *n* compatriota *m* & *f*. **~ passenger/traveller** *n* compañero *m* de viaje. **~ship** *n* compañerismo *m*; (*group*) asociación *f*

felony /'felənɪ/ *n* crimen *m*

felt[1] /felt/ *n* fieltro *m*

felt[2] /felt/ *see* **feel**

femal|e /'fiːmeɪl/ *a* hembra; (*voice, sex etc*) femenino. ● *n* mujer *f*; (*animal*) hembra *f*

femini|ne /'femənɪn/ *a* & *n* femenino (*m*). **~nity** /-'nɪnətɪ/ *n* feminidad *f*. **~st** *n* feminista *m* & *f*

fenc|e /fens/ *n* cerca *f*; (*person, sl*) perista *m* & *f*. (*fam*). ● *vt*. **~e (in)** encerrar, cercar. ● *vi* (*sport*) practicar la esgrima. **~er** *n* esgrimidor *m*. **~ing** *n* (*sport*) esgrima *f*

fend /fend/ *vi*. **~ for o.s.** valerse por sí mismo. ● *vt*. **~ off** defenderse de

fender /'fendə(r)/ *n* guardafuego *m*; (*mudguard, Amer*) guardabarros *m invar*; (*naut*) defensa *f*

fennel /'fenl/ *n* hinojo *m*

ferment /'fɜːment/ *n* fermento *m*; (*fig*) agitación *f*. /fə'ment/ *vt/i* fermentar. **~ation** /-'teɪʃn/ *n* fermentación *f*

fern /fɜːn/ *n* helecho *m*

feroci|ous /fə'rəʊʃəs/ *a* feroz. **~ty** /fə'rɒsətɪ/ *n* ferocidad *f*

ferret /'ferɪt/ *n* hurón *m*. ● *vi* (*pt* **ferreted**) huronear. ● *vt*. **~ out** descubrir

ferry /'ferɪ/ *n* ferry *m*. ● *vt* transportar

fertil|e /'fɜːtaɪl/ *a* fértil; (*biol*) fecundo. **~ity** /-'tɪlətɪ/ *n* fertilidad *f*; (*biol*) fecundidad *f*

fertilize /'fɜːtəlaɪz/ *vt* abonar; (*biol*) fecundar. **~r** *n* abono *m*

fervent /'fɜːvənt/ *a* ferviente

fervour /'fɜːvə(r)/ *n* fervor *m*

fester /'festə(r)/ *vi* enconarse

festival /'festəvl/ *n* fiesta *f*; (*of arts*) festival *m*

festive /'festɪv/ *a* festivo. **~ season** *n* temporada *f* de fiestas

festivity /fe'stɪvətɪ/ *n* festividad *f*

festoon /fe'stuːn/ *vi*. **~ with** adornar de

fetch /fetʃ/ *vt* (*go for*) ir a buscar; (*bring*) traer; (*be sold for*) venderse por

fetching /'fetʃɪŋ/ *a* atractivo

fête /feɪt/ *n* fiesta *f*. ● *vt* festejar

fetid /'fetɪd/ *a* fétido

fetish /'fetɪʃ/ *n* fetiche *m*; (*psych*) obsesión *f*

fetter /'fetə(r)/ *vt* encadenar. **~s** *npl* grilletes *mpl*

fettle /'fetl/ *n* condición *f*

feud /fjuːd/ *n* enemistad *f* (inveterada)

feudal /'fjuːdl/ *a* feudal. **~ism** *n* feudalismo *m*

fever /'fiːvə(r)/ *n* fiebre *f*. **~ish** *a* febril

few /fjuː/ *a* pocos. ● *n* pocos *mpl*. **a ~** unos (pocos). **a good ~, quite a ~** (*fam*) muchos. **~er** *a* & *n* menos. **~est** *a* & *n* el menor número de

fiancé /fɪ'ɒnseɪ/ *n* novio *m*. **~e** /fɪ'ɒnseɪ/ *n* novia *f*

fiasco /fɪ'æskəʊ/ *n* (*pl* **-os**) fiasco *m*

fib /fɪb/ *n* mentirijilla *f*. **~ber** *n* mentiroso *m*

fibre /'faɪbə(r)/ *n* fibra *f*. **~glass** *n* fibra *f* de vidrio

fickle /'fɪkl/ *a* inconstante

fiction /'fɪkʃn/ *n* ficción *f*. **(works of) ~** novelas *fpl*. **~al** *a* novelesco

fictitious /fɪk'tɪʃəs/ *a* ficticio

fiddle /'fɪdl/ *n* (*fam*) violín *m*; (*swindle, sl*) trampa *f*. ● *vt* (*sl*) falsificar. **~ with** juguetear con, toquetear, manosear. **~r** *n* (*fam*) violinista *m* & *f*; (*cheat, sl*) tramposo *m*

fidelity /fɪ'delətɪ/ *n* fidelidad *f*

fidget /'fɪdʒɪt/ *vi* (*pt* **fidgeted**) moverse, ponerse nervioso. **~ with** juguetear con. ● *n* azogado *m*. **~y** *a* azogado

field /fiːld/ *n* campo *m*. **~ day** *n* gran ocasión *f*. **~ glasses** *npl* gemelos *mpl*. **F~ Marshal** *n* mariscal *m* de campo, capitán *m* general. **~work** *n* investigaciones *fpl* en el terreno

fiend /fiːnd/ *n* demonio *m*. **~ish** *a* diabólico

fierce /fɪəs/ a (-er, -est) feroz; ‹attack› violento. ~ness n ferocidad f, violencia f

fiery /'faɪərɪ/ a (-ier, -iest) ardiente

fifteen /fɪf'tiːn/ a & n quince (m). ~th a & n quince (m), decimoquinto (m). ● n (fraction) quinzavo m

fifth /fɪfθ/ a & n quinto (m). ~ column n quinta columna f

fift|ieth /'fɪftɪəθ/ a & n cincuenta (m). ~y a & n cincuenta (m). ~y-~y mitad y mitad, a medias. a ~y-~y chance una posibilidad f de cada dos

fig /fɪg/ n higo m

fight /faɪt/ vt/i (pt fought) luchar; (quarrel) disputar. ~ shy of evitar. ● n lucha f; (quarrel) disputa f; (mil) combate m. ~ back defenderse. ~ off rechazar ‹attack›; luchar contra ‹illness›. ~er n luchador m; (mil) combatiente m & f; (aircraft) avión m de caza. ~ing n luchas fpl

figment /'fɪgmənt/ n invención f

figurative /'fɪgjʊrətɪv/ a figurado

figure /'fɪgə(r)/ n (number) cifra f; (diagram) figura f; (shape) forma f; (of woman) tipo m. ● vt imaginar. ● vi figurar. that ~s (Amer, fam) es lógico. ~ out explicarse. ~head n testaferro m, mascarón m de proa. ~ of speech n tropo m, figura f. ~s npl (arithmetic) aritmética f

filament /'fɪləmənt/ n filamento m

filch /fɪltʃ/ vt hurtar

file[1] /faɪl/ n carpeta f; (set of papers) expediente m. ● vt archivar ‹papers›

file[2] /faɪl/ n (row) fila f. ● vi. ~ in entrar en fila. ~ past desfilar ante

file[3] /faɪl/ n (tool) lima f. ● vt limar

filings /'faɪlɪŋz/ npl limaduras fpl

fill /fɪl/ vt llenar. ● vi llenarse. ~ in rellenar ‹form›. ~ out (get fatter) engordar. ~ up (auto) llenar, repostar. ● n. eat one's ~ hartarse de comer. have had one's ~ of estar harto de

fillet /'fɪlɪt/ n filete m. ● vt (pt filleted) cortar en filetes

filling /'fɪlɪŋ/ n (in tooth) empaste m. ~ station n estación f de servicio

film /fɪlm/ n película f. ● vt filmar. ~ star n estrella f de cine. ~-strip n tira f de película

filter /'fɪltə(r)/ n filtro m. ● vt filtrar. ● vi filtrarse. ~-tipped a con filtro

filth /fɪlθ/ n inmundicia f. ~iness n inmundicia f. ~y a inmundo

fin /fɪn/ n aleta f

final /'faɪnl/ a último; (conclusive) decisivo. ● n (sport) final f. ~s npl (schol) exámenes mpl de fin de curso

finale /fɪ'nɑːlɪ/ n final m

final: ~ist n finalista m & f. ~ize vt concluir. ~ly adv (lastly) finalmente, por fin; (once and for all) definitivamente

financ|e /'faɪnæns/ n finanzas fpl. ● vt financiar. ~ial /faɪ'nænʃl/ a financiero. ~ially adv económicamente. ~ier /faɪ'nænsɪə(r)/ n financiero m

finch /fɪntʃ/ n pinzón m

find /faɪnd/ vt (pt found) encontrar. ~ out enterarse de. ~er n el m que encuentra, descubridor m. ~ings npl resultados mpl

fine[1] /faɪn/ a (-er, -est) fino; (excellent) excelente. ● adv muy bien; (small) en trozos pequeños

fine[2] /faɪn/ n multa f. ● vt multar

fine: ~ arts npl bellas artes fpl. ~ly adv (admirably) espléndidamente; (cut) en trozos pequeños. ~ry /'faɪnərɪ/ n galas fpl

finesse /fɪ'nes/ n tino m

finger /'fɪŋgə(r)/ n dedo m. ● vt tocar. ~nail n uña f. ~print n huella f dactilar. ~stall n dedil m. ~tip n punta f del dedo

finicking /'fɪnɪkɪŋ/ a, **finicky** /'fɪnɪkɪ/ a melindroso

finish /'fɪnɪʃ/ vt/i terminar. ~ doing terminar de hacer. ~ up doing terminar por hacer. ● n fin m; (of race) llegada f, meta f; (appearance) acabado m

finite /'faɪnaɪt/ a finito

Fin|land /'fɪnlənd/ n Finlandia f. ~n n finlandés m. ~nish a & n finlandés (m)

fiord /fjɔːd/ n fiordo m

fir /fɜː(r)/ n abeto m

fire /faɪə(r)/ n fuego m; (conflagration) incendio m. ● vt disparar ‹bullet etc›; (dismiss) despedir; (fig) excitar, enardecer, inflamar. ● vi tirar. ~arm n arma f de fuego. ~ brigade n cuerpo m de bomberos. ~cracker n (Amer) petardo m. ~ department n (Amer) cuerpo m de bomberos. ~engine n coche m de bomberos. ~escape n escalera f de incendios. ~light n

lumbre *f*. ~**man** *n* bombero *m*.
~**place** *n* chimenea *f*. ~**side** *n* hogar
m. ~ **station** *n* parque *m* de bomberos. ~**wood** *n* leña *f*. ~**work** *n*
fuego *m* artificial
firing-squad /'faɪərɪŋskwɒd/ *n* pelotón *m* de ejecución
firm¹ /fɜːm/ *n* empresa *f*
firm² /fɜːm/ *a* (**-er, -est**) firme. ~**ly**
adv firmemente. ~**ness** *n* firmeza *f*
first /fɜːst/ *a* primero. at ~ **hand** directamente. **at** ~ **sight** a primera
vista. ● *n* primero *m*. ● *adv* primero; (*first time*) por primera vez.
~ **of all** ante todo. ~ **aid** *n* primeros
auxilios *mpl*. ~**-born** *a* primogénito. ~**class** *a* de primera clase.
~ **floor** *n* primer piso *m*; (*Amer*)
planta *f* baja. **F~ Lady** *n* (*Amer*)
Primera Dama *f*. ~**ly** *adv* en primer
lugar. ~ **name** *n* nombre *m* de pila.
~**rate** *a* excelente
fiscal /'fɪskl/ *a* fiscal
fish /fɪʃ/ *n* (*usually invar*) (*alive in
water*) pez *m*; (*food*) pescado *m*. ● *vi*
pescar. ~ **for** pescar. ~ **out** (*take
out, fam*) sacar. **go** ~**ing** ir de pesca.
~**erman** /'fɪʃəmən/ *n* pescador *m*.
~**ing** *n* pesca *f*. ~**ing-rod** *n* caña *f*
de pesca. ~**monger** *n* pescadero *m*.
~**-shop** *n* pescadería *f*. ~**y** *a* (*smell*)
a pescado; (*questionable, fam*)
sospechoso
fission /'fɪʃn/ *n* fisión *f*
fist /fɪst/ *n* puño *m*
fit¹ /fɪt/ *a* (**fitter, fittest**) con-
veniente; (*healthy*) sano; (*good
enough*) adecuado; (*able*) capaz. ● *n*
(*of clothes*) corte *m*. ● *vt* (*pt* **fitted**)
(*adapt*) adaptar; (*be the right size
for*) sentar bien a; (*install*) colocar.
● *vi* encajar; (*in certain space*)
caber; (*clothes*) sentar. ~ **out**
equipar. ~ **up** equipar
fit² /fɪt/ *n* ataque *m*
fitful /'fɪtfl/ *a* irregular
fitment /'fɪtmənt/ *n* mueble *m*
fitness /'fɪtnɪs/ *n* (*buena*) salud *f*; (*of
remark*) conveniencia *f*
fitting /'fɪtɪŋ/ *a* apropiado. ● *n* (*of
clothes*) prueba *f*. ~**s** /'fɪtɪŋz/ *npl* (*in
house*) accesorios *mpl*
five /faɪv/ *a* & *n* cinco (*m*). ~**r**
/'faɪvə(r)/ *n* (*fam*) billete *m* de cinco
libras
fix /fɪks/ *vt* (*make firm, attach,
decide*) fijar; (*mend, deal with*) arreglar. ● *n*. **in a** ~ en un aprieto.

~**ation** /-eɪʃn/ *n* fijación *f*. ~**ed** *a*
fijo
fixture /'fɪkstʃə(r)/ *n* (*sport*) partido *m*.
~**s** (*in house*) accesorios *mpl*
fizz /fɪz/ *vi* burbujear. ● *n* efer-
vescencia *f*. ~**le** /fɪzl/ *vi* burbujear.
~**le out** fracasar. ~**y** *a* efervescente; (*water*) con gas
flab /flæb/ *n* (*fam*) flaccidez *f*
flabbergast /'flæbəgɑːst/ *vt* pasmar
flabby /'flæbɪ/ *a* flojo
flag /flæg/ *n* bandera *f*. ● *vt* (*pt
flagged*). ~ **down** hacer señales de
parada a. ● *vi* (*pt* **flagged**) (*weaken*)
flaquear; (*interest*) decaer; (*conversation*) languidecer
flagon /'flægən/ *n* botella *f* grande,
jarro *m*
flag-pole /'flægpəʊl/ *n* asta *f* de
bandera
flagrant /'fleɪgrənt/ *a* (*glaring*)
flagrante; (*scandalous*) escandaloso
flagstone /'flægstəʊn/ *n* losa *f*
flair /fleə(r)/ *n* don *m* (**for** de)
flak|e /fleɪk/ *n* copo *m*; (*of paint,
metal*) escama *f*. ● *vi* desconcharse.
~**e out** (*fam*) caer rendido. ~**y** *a*
escamoso
flamboyant /flæm'bɔɪənt/ *a* (*clothes*) vistoso; (*manner*) extravagante
flame /fleɪm/ *n* llama *f*. ● *vi* llamear
flamingo /flə'mɪŋgəʊ/ *n* (*pl* **-o(e)s**)
flamenco *m*
flammable /'flæməbl/ *a* inflamable
flan /flæn/ *n* tartaleta *f*, tarteleta *f*
flank /flæŋk/ *n* (*of animal*) ijada *f*,
flanco *m*; (*of person*) costado *m*; (*of
mountain*) falda *f*; (*mil*) flanco *m*
flannel /'flænl/ *n* franela *f* (de lana);
(*for face*) paño *m* (para lavarse la
cara). ~**ette** *n* franela *f* (de
algodón), muletón *m*
flap /flæp/ *vi* (*pt* **flapped**) ondear;
(*wings*) aletear; (*become agitated,
fam*) ponerse nervioso. ● *vt* sacudir; batir (*wings*). ● *n* (*of pocket*)
cartera *f*; (*of table*) ala *f*. **get into a**
~ ponerse nervioso
flare /fleə(r)/ ● *n* llamarada *f*; (*mil*)
bengala *f*; (*in skirt*) vuelo *m*. ● *vi*. ~
up llamear; (*fighting*) estallar; (*person*) encolerizarse. ~**d** *a* (*skirt*)
acampanado
flash /flæʃ/ ● *vi* brillar; (*on and off*)
destellar. ● *vt* despedir; (*aim torch*)
dirigir; (*flaunt*) hacer ostentación
de. ~ **past** pasar como un rayo. ● *n*
relámpago *m*; (*of news, camera*)

flash *m.* ~**back** *n* escena *f* retrospectiva. ~**light** *n* (*torch*) linterna *f*

flashy /'flæʃı/ *a* ostentoso

flask /flɑːsk/ *n* frasco *m*; (*vacuum flask*) termo *m*

flat¹ /flæt/ *a* (**flatter, flattest**) llano; (*tyre*) desinflado; (*refusal*) categórico; (*fare, rate*) fijo; (*mus*) desafinado. ● *adv.* ~ **out** (*at top speed*) a toda velocidad

flat² /flæt/ *n* (*rooms*) piso *m*, apartamento *m*; (*tyre*) (*fam*) pinchazo *m*; (*mus*) bemol *m*

flat: ~**ly** *adv* categóricamente. ~**ness** *n* llanura *f.* ~**ten** /'flætn/ *vt* allanar, aplanar. ● *vi* allanarse, aplanarse

flatter /flætə(r)/ *vt* adular. ~**er** *n* adulador *m.* ~**ing** *a* (*person*) lisonjero; (*clothes*) favorecedor. ~**y** *n* adulación *f*

flatulence /'flætjʊləns/ *n* flatulencia *f*

flaunt /flɔːnt/ *vt* hacer ostentación de

flautist /'flɔːtɪst/ *n* flautista *m & f*

flavour /'fleıvə(r)/ *n* sabor *m.* ● *vt* condimentar. ~**ing** *n* condimento *m*

flaw /flɔː/ *n* defecto *m.* ~**less** *a* perfecto

flax /flæks/ *n* lino *m.* ~**en** *a* de lino; (*hair*) rubio

flea /fliː/ *n* pulga *f*

fleck /flek/ *n* mancha *f*, pinta *f*

fled /fled/ *see* **flee**

fledged /fledʒd/ *a.* **fully** ~ (*doctor etc*) hecho y derecho; (*member*) de pleno derecho

fledg(e)ling /'fledʒlıŋ/ *n* pájaro *m* volantón

flee /fliː/ *vi* (*pt* **fled**) huir. ● *vt* huir de

fleece /fliːs/ *n* vellón *m.* ● *vt* (*rob*) desplumar

fleet /fliːt/ *n* (*naut, aviat*) flota *f*; (*of cars*) parque *m*

fleeting /'fliːtıŋ/ *a* fugaz

Flemish /'flemıʃ/ *a & n* flamenco (*m*)

flesh /fleʃ/ *n* carne *f.* **in the** ~ en persona. **one's own** ~ **and blood** los de su sangre. ~**y** *a* (*fruit*) carnoso

flew /fluː/ *see* **fly¹**

flex /fleks/ *vt* doblar; flexionar (*muscle*). ● *n* (*elec*) cable *m*, flexible *m*

flexib|ility /fleksə'bılətı/ *n* flexibilidad *f.* ~**le** /'fleksəbl/ *a* flexible

flexitime /fleksı'taım/ *n* horario *m* flexible

flick /flık/ *n* golpecito *m.* ● *vt* dar un golpecito a. ~ **through** hojear

flicker /'flıkə(r)/ *vi* temblar; (*light*) parpadear. ● *n* temblor *m*; (*of hope*) resquicio *m*; (*of light*) parpadeo *m*

flick: ~**knife** *n* navaja *f* de muelle. ~**s** *npl* cine *m*

flier /'flaıə(r)/ *n* aviador *m*; (*circular, Amer*) prospecto *m*, folleto *m*

flies /flaız/ *npl* (*on trousers, fam*) bragueta *f*

flight /flaıt/ *n* vuelo *m*; (*fleeing*) huida *f*, fuga *f.* ~ **of stairs** tramo *m* de escalera *f.* **put to** ~ poner en fuga. **take (to)** ~ darse a la fuga. ~**deck** *n* cubierta *f* de vuelo

flighty /'flaıtı/ *a* (**-ier, -iest**) frívolo

flimsy /'flımzı/ *a* (**-ier, -iest**) flojo, débil, poco substancioso

flinch /flıntʃ/ *vi* (*draw back*) retroceder (**from** ante). **without** ~**ing** (*without wincing*) sin pestañear

fling /flıŋ/ *vt* (*pt* **flung**) arrojar. ● *n.* **have a** ~ echar una cana al aire

flint /flınt/ *n* pedernal *m*; (*for lighter*) piedra *f*

flip /flıp/ *vt* (*pt* **flipped**) dar un golpecito a. ~ **through** hojear. ● *n* golpecito *m.* ~ **side** *n* otra cara *f*

flippant /'flıpənt/ *a* poco serio; (*disrespectful*) irrespetuoso

flipper /'flıpə(r)/ *n* aleta *f*

flirt /flɜːt/ *vi* coquetear. ● *n* (*woman*) coqueta *f*; (*man*) mariposón *m*, coqueto *m.* ~**ation** /-'teıʃn/ *n* coqueteo *m*

flit /flıt/ *vi* (*pt* **flitted**) revolotear

float /fləʊt/ *vi* flotar. ● *vt* hacer flotar. ● *n* flotador *m*; (*on fishing line*) corcho *m*; (*cart*) carroza *f*

flock /flɒk/ *n* (*of birds*) bandada *f*; (*of sheep*) rebaño *m*; (*of people*) muchedumbre *f*, multitud *f.* ● *vi* congregarse

flog /flɒg/ *vt* (*pt* **flogged**) (*beat*) azotar; (*sell, fam*) vender

flood /flʌd/ *n* inundación *f*; (*fig*) torrente *m.* ● *vt* inundar. ● *vi* (*building etc*) inundarse; (*river*) desbordar

floodlight /'flʌdlaıt/ *n* foco *m.* ● *vt* (*pt* **floodlit**) iluminar (con focos)

floor /flɔː(r)/ *n* suelo *m*; (*storey*) piso *m*; (*for dancing*) pista *f.* ● *vt* (*knock down*) derribar; (*baffle*) confundir

flop /flɒp/ *vi* (*pt* **flopped**) dejarse caer pesadamente; (*fail, sl*) fracasar. ● *n* (*sl*) fracaso *m*. ∼**py** *a* flojo

flora /'flɔːrə/ *n* flora *f*

floral /'flɔːrəl/ *a* floral

florid /'flɒrɪd/ *a* florido

florist /'flɒrɪst/ *n* florista *m & f*

flounce /flaʊns/ *n* volante *m*

flounder[1] /'flaʊndə(r)/ *vi* avanzar con dificultad, no saber qué hacer

flounder[2] /'flaʊndə(r)/ *n* (*fish*) platija *f*

flour /flaʊə(r)/ *n* harina *f*

flourish /'flʌrɪʃ/ *vi* prosperar. ● *vt* blandir. ● *n* ademán *m* elegante; (*in handwriting*) rasgo *m*. ∼**ing** *a* próspero

floury /'flaʊərɪ/ *a* harinoso

flout /flaʊt/ *vt* burlarse de

flow /fləʊ/ *vi* correr; (*hang loosely*) caer. ∼ **into** (*river*) desembocar en. ● *n* flujo *m*; (*jet*) chorro *m*; (*stream*) corriente *f*; (*of words, tears*) torrente *m*. ∼ **chart** *n* organigrama *m*

flower /'flaʊə(r)/ *n* flor *f*. ∼**bed** *n* macizo *m* de flores. ∼**ed** *a* floreado, de flores. ∼**y** *a* florido

flown /fləʊn/ *see* **fly**[1]

flu /fluː/ *n* (*fam*) gripe *f*

fluctuat|e /'flʌktjʊeɪt/ *vi* fluctuar. ∼**ion** /-eɪʃn/ *n* fluctuación *f*

flue /fluː/ *n* humero *m*

fluen|cy /'fluːənsɪ/ *n* facilidad *f*. ∼**t** *a* (*style*) fluido; (*speaker*) elocuente. **be** ∼**t** (**in a language**) hablar (un idioma) con soltura. ∼**tly** *adv* con fluidez; (*lang*) con soltura

fluff /flʌf/ *n* pelusa *f*. ∼**y** *a* (**-ier, -iest**) velloso

fluid /'fluːɪd/ *a & n* fluido (*m*)

fluke /fluːk/ *n* (*stroke of luck*) chiripa *f*

flung /flʌŋ/ *see* **fling**

flunk /flʌŋk/ *vt* (*Amer, fam*) ser suspendido en (*exam*); suspender (*person*). ● *vi* (*fam*) ser suspendido

fluorescent /flʊə'resnt/ *a* fluorescente

fluoride /'flʊəraɪd/ *n* fluoruro *m*

flurry /'flʌrɪ/ *n* (*squall*) ráfaga *f*; (*fig*) agitación *f*

flush[1] /flʌʃ/ *vi* ruborizarse. ● *vt* limpiar con agua. ∼ **the toilet** tirar de la cadena. ● *n* (*blush*) rubor *m*; (*fig*) emoción *f*

flush[2] /flʌʃ/ *a*. ∼ (**with**) a nivel (con)

flush[3] /flʌʃ/ *vt/i*. ∼ **out** (*drive out*) echar fuera

fluster /'flʌstə(r)/ *vt* poner nervioso

flute /fluːt/ *n* flauta *f*

flutter /'flʌtə(r)/ *vi* ondear; (*bird*) revolotear. ● *n* (*of wings*) revoloteo *m*; (*fig*) agitación *f*

flux /flʌks/ *n* flujo *m*. **be in a state of** ∼ estar siempre cambiando

fly[1] /flaɪ/ *vi* (*pt* **flew**, *pp* **flown**) volar; (*passenger*) ir en avión; (*flag*) flotar; (*rush*) correr. ● *vt* pilotar (*aircraft*); transportar en avión (*passengers, goods*); izar (*flag*). ● *n* (*of trousers*) bragueta *f*

fly[2] /flaɪ/ *n* mosca *f*

flyer /'flaɪə(r)/ *n* aviador *m*; (*circular, Amer*) prospecto *m*, folleto *m*

flying /'flaɪɪŋ/ *a* volante; (*hasty*) relámpago *invar*. ● *n* (*activity*) aviación *f*. ∼ **visit** *n* visita *f* relámpago

fly: ∼**leaf** *n* guarda *f*. ∼**over** *n* paso *m* elevado. ∼**weight** *n* peso *m* mosca

foal /fəʊl/ *n* potro *m*

foam /fəʊm/ *n* espuma *f*. ∼ (**rubber**) *n* goma *f* espuma. ● *vi* espumar

fob /fɒb/ *vt* (*pt* **fobbed**). ∼ **off on s.o.** (*palm off*) encajar a uno

focal /'fəʊkl/ *a* focal

focus /'fəʊkəs/ *n* (*pl* **-cuses** *or* **-ci** /-saɪ/) foco *m*; (*fig*) centro *m*. **in** ∼ enfocado. **out of** ∼ desenfocado. ● *vt/i* (*pt* **focused**) enfocar(se); (*fig*) concentrar

fodder /'fɒdə(r)/ *n* forraje *m*

foe /fəʊ/ *n* enemigo *m*

foetus /'fiːtəs/ *n* (*pl* **-tuses**) feto *m*

fog /fɒg/ *n* niebla *f*. ● *vt* (*pt* **fogged**) envolver en niebla; (*photo*) velar. ● *vi*. ∼ (**up**) empañarse; (*photo*) velarse

fog(e)y /'fəʊgɪ/ *n*. **be an old** ∼ estar chapado a la antigua

foggy /'fɒgɪ/ *a* (**-ier, -iest**) nebuloso. **it is** ∼ hay niebla

foghorn /'fɒghɔːn/ *n* sirena *f* de niebla

foible /'fɔɪbl/ *n* punto *m* débil

foil[1] /fɔɪl/ *vt* (*thwart*) frustrar

foil[2] /fɔɪl/ *n* papel *m* de plata; (*fig*) contraste *m*

foist /fɔɪst/ *vt* encajar (on a)

fold[1] /fəʊld/ *vt* doblar; cruzar (*arms*). ● *vi* doblarse; (*fail*) fracasar. ● *n* pliegue *m*

fold[2] /fəʊld/ *n* (*for sheep*) redil *m*

folder /'fəʊldə(r)/ *n* (*file*) carpeta *f*; (*leaflet*) folleto *m*

folding /'fəʊldɪŋ/ *a* plegable

foliage /'fəʊlɪɪdʒ/ *n* follaje *m*

folk /fəʊk/ n gente f. ● a popular. ∼**lore** n folklore m. ∼**s** npl (one's relatives) familia f

follow /'fɒləʊ/ vt/i seguir. ∼ **up** seguir; (investigate further) investigar. ∼**er** n seguidor m. ∼**ing** n partidarios mpl. ● a siguiente. ● prep después de

folly /'fɒlɪ/ n locura f

foment /fə'ment/ vt fomentar

fond /fɒnd/ a (-er, -est) (loving) cariñoso; ⟨hope⟩ vivo. **be** ∼ **of s.o.** tener(le) cariño a uno. **be** ∼ **of sth** ser aficionado a algo

fondle /'fɒndl/ vt acariciar

fondness /'fɒndnɪs/ n cariño m; (for things) afición f

font /fɒnt/ n pila f bautismal

food /fu:d/ n alimento m, comida f. ∼ **processor** n robot m de cocina, batidora f

fool /fu:l/ n tonto m. ● vt engañar. ● vi hacer el tonto

foolhardy /'fu:lha:dɪ/ a temerario

foolish /'fu:lɪʃ/ a tonto. ∼**ly** adv tontamente. ∼**ness** n tontería f

foolproof /'fu:lpru:f/ a infalible, a toda prueba, a prueba de tontos

foot /fʊt/ n (pl feet) pie m; (measure) pie m (= 30,48 cm); (of animal, furniture) pata f. **get under s.o.'s feet** estorbar a uno. **on** ∼ a pie. **on/to one's feet** de pie. **put one's** ∼ **in it** meter la pata. ● vt pagar ⟨bill⟩. ∼ **it** ir andando

footage /'fʊtɪdʒ/ n (of film) secuencia f

football /'fʊtbɔ:l/ n (ball) balón m; (game) fútbol m. ∼**er** n futbolista m & f

footbridge /'fʊtbrɪdʒ/ n puente m para peatones

foothills /'fʊthɪlz/ npl estribaciones fpl

foothold /'fʊthəʊld/ n punto m de apoyo m

footing /'fʊtɪŋ/ n pie m

footlights /'fʊtlaɪts/ npl candilejas fpl

footloose /'fʊtlu:s/ a libre

footman /'fʊtmən/ n lacayo m

footnote /'fʊtnəʊt/ n nota f (al pie de la página)

foot: ∼**path** n (in country) senda f; (in town) acera f, vereda f (Arg), banqueta f (Mex). ∼**print** n huella f. ∼**sore** a. **be** ∼**sore** tener los pies doloridos. ∼**step** n paso m. ∼**stool** n escabel m. ∼**wear** n calzado m

for /fɔ:(r)/, unstressed /fə(r)/ prep (expressing purpose) para; (on behalf of) por; (in spite of) a pesar de; (during) durante; (in favour of) a favor de. **he has been in Madrid** ∼ **two months** hace dos meses que está en Madrid. ● conj ya que

forage /'fɒrɪdʒ/ vi forrajear. ● n forraje m

foray /'fɒreɪ/ n incursión f

forbade /fə'bæd/ see **forbid**

forbear /fɔ:'beə(r)/ vt/i (pt **forbore**, pp **forborne**) contenerse. ∼**ance** n paciencia f

forbid /fə'bɪd/ vt (pt **forbade**, pp **bidden**) prohibir (**s.o. to do** a uno hacer). ∼ **s.o. sth** prohibir algo a uno

forbidding /fə'bɪdɪŋ/ a imponente

force /fɔ:s/ n fuerza f. **come into** ∼ entrar en vigor. **the** ∼**s** las fuerzas fpl armadas. ● vt forzar. ∼ **on** imponer a. ∼**d** a forzado. ∼**feed** vt alimentar a la fuerza. ∼**ful** /'fɔ:sfʊl/ a enérgico

forceps /'fɔ:seps/ n invar tenazas fpl; (for obstetric use) fórceps m invar; (for dental use) gatillo m

forcibl|e /'fɔ:səbl/ a a la fuerza. ∼**y** adv a la fuerza

ford /fɔ:d/ n vado m, botadero m (Mex). ● vt vadear

fore /fɔ:(r)/ a anterior. ● n. **come to the** ∼ hacerse evidente

forearm /'fɔ:ra:m/ n antebrazo m

foreboding /fɔ:'bəʊdɪŋ/ n presentimiento m

forecast /'fɔ:ka:st/ vt (pt **forecast**) pronosticar. ● n pronóstico m

forecourt /'fɔ:kɔ:t/ n patio m

forefathers /'fɔ:fa:ðəz/ npl antepasados mpl

forefinger /'fɔ:fɪŋgə(r)/ n (dedo m) índice m

forefront /'fɔ:frʌnt/ n vanguardia f. **in the** ∼ a/en vanguardia, en primer plano

foregone /'fɔ:gɒn/ a. ∼ **conclusion** resultado m previsto

foreground /'fɔ:graʊnd/ n primer plano m

forehead /'fɒrɪd/ n frente f

foreign /'fɒrən/ a extranjero; ⟨trade⟩ exterior; ⟨travel⟩ al extranjero, en el extranjero. ∼**er** n extranjero m. **F**∼ **Secretary** n ministro m de Asuntos Exteriores

foreman /'fɔ:mən/ n capataz m, caporal m

foremost /'fɔːməʊst/ a primero. ● adv. **first and** ~ ante todo

forensic /fə'rensɪk/ a forense

forerunner /'fɔːrʌnə(r)/ n precursor m

foresee /fɔː'siː/ vt (pt **-saw**, pp **-seen**) prever. ~**able** a previsible

foreshadow /fɔː'ʃædəʊ/ vt presagiar

foresight /'fɔːsaɪt/ n previsión f

forest /'fɒrɪst/ n bosque m

forestall /fɔː'stɔːl/ vt anticiparse a

forestry /'fɒrɪstrɪ/ n silvicultura f

foretaste /'fɔːteɪst/ n anticipación f

foretell /fɔː'tel/ vt (pt **foretold**) predecir

forever /fə'revə(r)/ adv para siempre

forewarn /fɔː'wɔːn/ vt prevenir

foreword /'fɔːwɜːd/ n prefacio m

forfeit /'fɔːfɪt/ n (penalty) pena f; (in game) prenda f; (fine) multa f. ● vt perder

forgave /fə'geɪv/ see **forgive**

forge[1] /fɔːdʒ/ n fragua f. ● vt fraguar; (copy) falsificar

forge[2] /fɔːdʒ/ vi avanzar. ~**ahead** adelantarse rápidamente

forge: ~**r** /'fɔːdʒə(r)/ n falsificador m. ~**ry** n falsificación f

forget /fə'get/ vt (pt **forgot**, pp **forgotten**) olvidar. ~ **o.s.** propasarse, extralimitarse. ● vi olvidar(se). **I forgot** se me olvidó. ~**ful** a olvidadizo. ~**ful of** olvidando. ~**me-not** n nomeolvides f invar

forgive /fə'gɪv/ vt (pt **forgave**, pp **forgiven**) perdonar. ~**ness** n perdón m

forgo /fɔː'gəʊ/ vt (pt **forwent**, pp **forgone**) renunciar a

fork /fɔːk/ n tenedor m; (for digging) horca f; (in road) bifurcación f. ● vi ⟨road⟩ bifurcarse. ~ **out** (sl) aflojar la bolsa (fam), pagar. ~**ed** a ahorquillado; ⟨road⟩ bifurcado. ~**lift truck** n carretilla f elevadora

forlorn /fə'lɔːn/ a (hopeless) desesperado; (abandoned) abandonado. ~ **hope** n empresa f desesperada

form /fɔːm/ n forma f; (document) impreso m, formulario m; (schol) clase f. ● vt formar. ● vi formarse

formal /'fɔːml/ a formal; ⟨person⟩ formalista; ⟨dress⟩ de etiqueta. ~**ity** /-'mælətɪ/ n formalidad f. ~**ly** adv oficialmente

format /'fɔːmæt/ n formato m

formation /fɔː'meɪʃn/ n formación f

formative /'fɔːmətɪv/ a formativo

former /'fɔːmə(r)/ a anterior; (first of two) primero. ~**ly** adv antes

formidable /'fɔːmɪdəbl/ a formidable

formless /'fɔːmlɪs/ a informe

formula /'fɔːmjʊlə/ n (pl **-ae** /-iː/ or **-as**) fórmula f

formulate /'fɔːmjʊleɪt/ vt formular

fornicat|e /'fɔːnɪkeɪt/ vi fornicar. ~**ion** /-'keɪʃn/ n fornicación f

forsake /fə'seɪk/ vt (pt **forsook**, pp **forsaken**) abandonar

fort /fɔːt/ n (mil) fuerte m

forte /'fɔːteɪ/ n (talent) fuerte m

forth /fɔːθ/ adv en adelante. **and so** ~ y así sucesivamente. **go back and** ~ ir y venir

forthcoming /fɔːθ'kʌmɪŋ/ a próximo, venidero; (sociable, fam) comunicativo

forthright /'fɔːθraɪt/ a directo

forthwith /fɔːθ'wɪθ/ adv inmediatamente

fortieth /'fɔːtɪɪθ/ a cuarenta, cuadragésimo. ● n cuadragésima parte f

fortif|ication /fɔːtɪfɪ'keɪʃn/ n fortificación f. ~**y** /'fɔːtɪfaɪ/ vt fortificar

fortitude /'fɔːtɪtjuːd/ n valor m

fortnight /'fɔːtnaɪt/ n quince días mpl, quincena f. ~**ly** a bimensual. ● adv cada quince días

fortress /'fɔːtrɪs/ n fortaleza f

fortuitous /fɔː'tjuːɪtəs/ a fortuito

fortunate /'fɔːtʃənət/ a afortunado. **be** ~ tener suerte. ~**ly** adv afortunadamente

fortune /'fɔːtʃuːn/ n fortuna f. **have the good** ~ to tener la suerte de. ~**teller** n adivino m

forty /'fɔːtɪ/ a & n cuarenta (m). ~ **winks** un sueñecito m

forum /'fɔːrəm/ n foro m

forward /'fɔːwəd/ a delantero; (advanced) precoz; (pert) impertinente. ● n (sport) delantero m. ● adv adelante. **come** ~ presentarse. **go** ~ avanzar. ● vt hacer seguir ⟨letter⟩; enviar ⟨goods⟩; (fig) favorecer. ~**ness** n precocidad f

forwards /'fɔːwədz/ adv adelante

fossil /'fɒsl/ a & n fósil (m)

foster /'fɒstə(r)/ vt (promote) fomentar; criar ⟨child⟩. ~**child** n hijo m adoptivo. ~**mother** n madre f adoptiva

fought /fɔːt/ see **fight**

foul /faʊl/ a (-er, -est) ⟨smell, weather⟩ asqueroso; (dirty) sucio; ⟨language⟩ obsceno; ⟨air⟩ viciado. ~ play n jugada f sucia; (crime) delito m. ● n (sport) falta f. ● vt ensuciar; manchar ⟨reputation⟩. ~-mouthed a obsceno

found¹ /faʊnd/ see find

found² /faʊnd/ vt fundar

found³ /faʊnd/ vt (tec) fundir

foundation /faʊnˈdeɪʃn/ n fundación f; (basis) fundamento. ~s npl (archit) cimientos mpl

founder¹ /ˈfaʊndə(r)/ n fundador m

founder² /ˈfaʊndə(r)/ vi ⟨ship⟩ hundirse

foundry /ˈfaʊndrɪ/ n fundición f

fountain /ˈfaʊntɪn/ n fuente f. ~-pen n estilográfica f

four /fɔː(r)/ a & n cuatro (m). ~fold a cuádruple. ● adv cuatro veces. ~-poster n cama f con cuatro columnas

foursome /ˈfɔːsəm/ n grupo m de cuatro personas

fourteen /ˈfɔːtiːn/ a & n catorce (m). ~th a & n catorce (m), decimocuarto (m). ● n (fraction) catorceavo m

fourth /fɔːθ/ a & n cuarto (m)

fowl /faʊl/ n ave f

fox /fɒks/ n zorro m, zorra f. ● vt (baffle) dejar perplejo; (deceive) engañar

foyer /ˈfɔɪeɪ/ n (hall) vestíbulo m

fraction /ˈfrækʃn/ n fracción f

fractious /ˈfrækʃəs/ a díscolo

fracture /ˈfræktʃə(r)/ n fractura f. ● vt fracturar. ● vi fracturarse

fragile /ˈfrædʒaɪl/ a frágil

fragment /ˈfrægmənt/ n fragmento m. ~ary a fragmentario

fragran|ce /ˈfreɪgrəns/ n fragancia f. ~t a fragante

frail /freɪl/ a (-er, -est) frágil

frame /freɪm/ n (of picture, door, window) marco m; (of spectacles) montura f; (fig, structure) estructura f; (temporary state) estado m. ~ of mind estado m de ánimo. ● vt enmarcar; (fig) formular; (jurid, sl) incriminar falsamente. ~-up n (sl) complot m

framework /ˈfreɪmwɜːk/ n estructura f; (context) marco m

France /frɑːns/ n Francia f

franchise /ˈfræntʃaɪz/ n (pol) derecho m a votar; (com) concesión f

Franco... /ˈfræŋkəʊ/ pref franco...

frank /fræŋk/ a sincero. ● vt franquear. ~ly adv sinceramente. ~ness n sinceridad f

frantic /ˈfræntɪk/ a frenético. ~ with loco de

fraternal /frəˈtɜːnl/ a fraternal

fraternity /frəˈtɜːnɪtɪ/ n fraternidad f; (club) asociación f

fraternize /ˈfrætənaɪz/ vi fraternizar

fraud /frɔːd/ n (deception) fraude m; (person) impostor m. ~ulent a fraudulento

fraught /frɔːt/ a (tense) tenso. ~ with cargado de

fray¹ /freɪ/ vt desgastar. ● vi deshilacharse

fray² /freɪ/ n riña f

freak /friːk/ n (caprice) capricho m; (monster) monstruo m; (person) chalado m. ● a anormal. ~ish a anormal

freckle /ˈfrekl/ n peca f. ~d a pecoso

free /friː/ a (freer /ˈfriːə(r)/, freest /ˈfriːɪst/) libre; (gratis) gratis; (lavish) generoso. ~ kick n golpe m franco. ~ of charge gratis. ~ speech n libertad f de expresión. give a ~ hand dar carta blanca. ● vt (pt freed) (set at liberty) poner en libertad; (relieve from) liberar (from/of de); (untangle) desenredar; (loosen) soltar

freedom /ˈfriːdəm/ n libertad f

freehold /ˈfriːhəʊld/ n propiedad f absoluta

freelance /ˈfriːlɑːns/ a independiente

freely /ˈfriːlɪ/ adv libremente

Freemason /ˈfriːmeɪsn/ n masón m. ~ry n masonería f

free-range /ˈfriːreɪndʒ/ a ⟨eggs⟩ de granja

freesia /ˈfriːzjə/ n fresia f

freeway /ˈfriːweɪ/ n (Amer) autopista f

freez|e /friːz/ vt (pt froze, pp frozen) helar; congelar ⟨food, wages⟩. ● vi helarse, congelarse; (become motionless) quedarse inmóvil. ● n helada f; (of wages, prices) congelación f. ~er n congelador m. ~ing a glacial. ● n congelación f. below ~ing bajo cero

freight /freɪt/ n (goods) mercancías fpl; (hire of ship etc) flete m. ~er n (ship) buque m de carga

French /frentʃ/ a francés. ● n (lang) francés m. ~man n francés m. ~-speaking a francófono. ~-window n puertaventana f. ~woman f francesa f

frenz|ied /'frenzɪd/ *a* frenético. **~y** *n* frenesí *m*

frequency /'fri:kwənsɪ/ *n* frecuencia *f*

frequent /frɪ'kwent/ *vt* frecuentar. /'fri:kwənt/ *a* frecuente. **~ly** *adv* frecuentemente

fresco /'freskəʊ/ *n* (*pl* **-o(e)s**) fresco *m*

fresh /freʃ/ *a* (**-er, -est**) fresco; (*different, additional*) nuevo; (*cheeky*) fresco, descarado; ⟨*water*⟩ dulce. **~en** *vi* refrescar. **~en up** ⟨*person*⟩ refrescarse. **~ly** *adv* recientemente. **~man** *n* estudiante *m* de primer año. **~ness** *n* frescura *f*

fret /fret/ *vi* (*pt* **fretted**) inquietarse. **~ful** *a* (*discontented*) quejoso; (*irritable*) irritable

Freudian /'frɔɪdjən/ *a* freudiano

friar /'fraɪə(r)/ *n* fraile *m*

friction /'frɪkʃn/ *n* fricción *f*

Friday /'fraɪdeɪ/ *n* viernes *m*. **Good ~** Viernes Santo

fridge /frɪdʒ/ *n* (*fam*) nevera *f*, refrigerador *m*, refrigeradora *f*

fried /fraɪd/ *see* **fry**. ● *a* frito

friend /frend/ *n* amigo *m*. **~liness** /'frendlɪnɪs/ *n* simpatía *f*. **~ly** *a* (**-ier, -iest**) simpático. **F~ly Society** *n* mutualidad *f*. **~ship** /'frendʃɪp/ *n* amistad *f*

frieze /fri:z/ *n* friso *m*

frigate /'frɪɡət/ *n* fragata *f*

fright /fraɪt/ *n* susto *m*; (*person*) espantajo *m*; (*thing*) horror *m*

frighten /'fraɪtn/ *vt* asustar. **~ off** ahuyentar. **~ed** *a* asustado. **be ~ed** tener miedo (**of** de)

frightful /'fraɪtfl/ *a* espantoso, horrible. **~ly** *adv* terriblemente

frigid /'frɪdʒɪd/ *a* frío; (*psych*) frígido. **~ity** /-'dʒɪdətɪ/ *n* frigidez *f*

frill /frɪl/ *n* volante *m*. **~s** *npl* (*fig*) adornos *mpl*. **with no ~s** sencillo

fringe /frɪndʒ/ *n* (*sewing*) fleco *m*; (*ornamental border*) franja *f*; (*of hair*) flequillo *m*; (*of area*) periferia *f*; (*of society*) margen *m*. **~ benefits** *npl* beneficios *mpl* suplementarios. **~ theatre** *n* teatro *m* de vanguardia

frisk /frɪsk/ *vt* (*search*) cachear

frisky /'frɪskɪ/ *a* (**-ier, -iest**) retozón; ⟨*horse*⟩ fogoso

fritter[1] /'frɪtə(r)/ *vt*. **~ away** desperdiciar

fritter[2] /'frɪtə(r)/ *n* buñuelo *m*

frivol|ity /frɪ'vɒlətɪ/ *n* frivolidad *f*. **~ous** /'frɪvələs/ *a* frívolo

frizzy /'frɪzɪ/ *a* crespo

fro /frəʊ/ *see* **to and fro**

frock /frɒk/ *n* vestido *m*; (*of monk*) hábito *m*

frog /frɒɡ/ *n* rana *f*. **have a ~ in one's throat** tener carraspera

frogman /'frɒɡmən/ *n* hombre *m* rana

frolic /'frɒlɪk/ *vi* (*pt* **frolicked**) retozar. ● *n* broma *f*

from /frɒm/, *unstressed* /frəm/ *prep* de; (*with time, prices, etc*) a partir de; (*habit, conviction*) por; (*according to*) según. **take ~** (*away from*) quitar a

front /frʌnt/ *n* parte *f* delantera; (*of building*) fachada *f*; (*of clothes*) delantera *f*; (*mil, pol*) frente *f*; (*of book*) principio *m*; (*fig, appearance*) apariencia *f*; (*sea front*) paseo *m* marítimo. **in ~ of** delante de. **put a bold ~ on** hacer de tripas corazón, mostrar firmeza. (*first*) primero. **~age** *n* fachada *f*. **~al** *a* frontal; ⟨*attack*⟩ de frente. **~ door** *n* puerta *f* principal. **~ page** *n* (*of newspaper*) primera plana *f*

frontier /'frʌntɪə(r)/ *n* frontera *f*

frost /frɒst/ *n* (*freezing*) helada *f*; (*frozen dew*) escarcha *f*. **~-bite** *n* congelación *f*. **~-bitten** *a* congelado. **~ed** *a* ⟨*glass*⟩ esmerilado

frosting /'frɒstɪŋ/ *n* (*icing, Amer*) azúcar *m* glaseado

frosty *a* ⟨*weather*⟩ de helada; ⟨*window*⟩ escarchado; (*fig*) glacial

froth /frɒθ/ *n* espuma *f*. ● *vi* espumar. **~y** *a* espumoso

frown /fraʊn/ *vi* fruncir el entrecejo. **~ on** desaprobar. ● *n* ceño *m*

froze /frəʊz/, **frozen** /'frəʊzn/ *see* **freeze**

frugal /'fru:ɡl/ *a* frugal. **~ly** *adv* frugalmente

fruit /fru:t/ *n* (*bot, on tree, fig*) fruto *m*; (*as food*) fruta *f*. **~erer** *n* frutero *m*. **~ful** /'fru:tfl/ *a* fértil; (*fig*) fructífero. **~less** *a* infructuoso. **~ machine** *n* (máquina *f*) tragaperras *m*. **~ salad** *n* macedonia *f* de frutas. **~y** /'fru:tɪ/ *a* ⟨*taste*⟩ que sabe a fruta

fruition /fru:'ɪʃn/ *n*. **come to ~** realizarse

frump /frʌmp/ *n* espantajo *m*

frustrat|e /frʌ'streɪt/ *vt* frustrar. **~ion** /-ʃn/ *n* frustración *f*; (*disappointment*) decepción *f*

fry[1] /fraɪ/ *vt* (*pt* **fried**) freír. ● *vi* freírse

fry[2] /fraɪ/ *n* (*pl* **fry**). **small ∼** gente *f* de poca monta

frying-pan /'fraɪɪŋpæn/ *n* sartén *f*

fuchsia /'fjuːʃə/ *n* fucsia *f*

fuddy-duddy /'fʌdɪdʌdɪ/ *n*. **be a ∼** (*sl*) estar chapado a la antigua

fudge /fʌdʒ/ *n* dulce *m* de azúcar

fuel /'fjuːəl/ *n* combustible *m*; (*for car engine*) carburante *m*; (*fig*) pábulo *m*. ● *vt* (*pt* **fuelled**) alimentar de combustible

fugitive /'fjuːdʒɪtɪv/ *a* & *n* fugitivo (*m*)

fugue /fjuːg/ *n* (*mus*) fuga *f*

fulfil /fʊl'fɪl/ *vt* (*pt* **fulfilled**) cumplir (con) ⟨*promise, obligation*⟩; satisfacer ⟨*condition*⟩; realizar ⟨*hopes, plans*⟩; llevar a cabo ⟨*task*⟩. **∼ment** *n* (*of promise, obligation*) cumplimiento *m*; (*of conditions*) satisfacción *f*; (*of hopes, plans*) realización *f*; (*of task*) ejecución *f*

full /fʊl/ *a* (**-er, -est**) lleno; ⟨*bus, hotel*⟩ completo; ⟨*skirt*⟩ amplio; ⟨*account*⟩ detallado. **at ∼ speed** a máxima velocidad. **be ∼ (up)** (*with food*) no poder más. **in ∼ swing** en plena marcha. ● *n*. **in ∼** sin quitar nada. **to the ∼** completamente. **write in ∼** escribir con todas las letras. **∼ back** *n* (*sport*) defensa *m* & *f*. **∼-blooded** *a* vigoroso. **∼ moon** *n* plenilunio *m*. **∼-scale** *a* ⟨*drawing*⟩ de tamaño natural; (*fig*) amplio. **∼ stop** *n* punto *m*; (*at end of paragraph, fig*) punto *m* final. **∼ time** *a* de jornada completa. **∼y** *adv* completamente

fulsome /'fʊlsəm/ *a* excesivo

fumble /'fʌmbl/ *vi* buscar (torpemente)

fume /fjuːm/ *vi* humear; (*fig, be furious*) estar furioso. **∼s** *npl* humo *m*

fumigate /'fjuːmɪgeɪt/ *vt* fumigar

fun /fʌn/ *n* (*amusement*) diversión *f*; (*merriment*) alegría *f*. **for ∼** en broma. **have ∼** divertirse. **make ∼ of** burlarse de

function /'fʌŋkʃn/ *n* (*purpose, duty*) función *f*; (*reception*) recepción *f*. ● *vi* funcionar. **∼al** *a* funcional

fund /fʌnd/ *n* fondo *m*. ● *vt* proveer fondos para

fundamental /fʌndə'mentl/ *a* fundamental

funeral /'fjuːnərəl/ *n* funeral *m*, funerales *mpl*. ● *a* fúnebre

fun-fair /'fʌnfeə(r)/ *n* parque *m* de atracciones

fungus /'fʌŋgəs/ *n* (*pl* **-gi** /-gaɪ/) hongo *m*

funicular /fjuː'nɪkjʊlə(r)/ *n* funicular *m*

funk /fʌŋk/ *m* (*fear, sl*) miedo *m*; (*state of depression, Amer, sl*) depresión *f*. **be in a (blue) ∼** tener (mucho) miedo; (*Amer*) estar (muy) deprimido. ● *vi* rajarse

funnel /'fʌnl/ *n* (*for pouring*) embudo *m*; (*of ship*) chimenea *f*

funn|ily /'fʌnɪlɪ/ *adv* graciosamente; (*oddly*) curiosamente. **∼y** *a* (**-ier, -iest**) divertido, gracioso; (*odd*) curioso, raro. **∼y-bone** *n* cóndilo *m* del húmero. **∼y business** *n* engaño *m*

fur /fɜː(r)/ *n* pelo *m*; (*pelt*) piel *f*; (*in kettle*) sarro *m*

furbish /'fɜːbɪʃ/ *vt* pulir; (*renovate*) renovar

furious /'fjʊərɪəs/ *a* furioso. **∼ly** *adv* furiosamente

furnace /'fɜːnɪs/ *n* horno *m*

furnish /'fɜːnɪʃ/ *vt* (*with furniture*) amueblar; (*supply*) proveer. **∼ings** *npl* muebles *mpl*, mobiliario *m*

furniture /'fɜːnɪtʃə(r)/ *n* muebles *mpl*, mobiliario *m*

furrier /'fʌrɪə(r)/ *n* peletero *m*

furrow /'fʌrəʊ/ *n* surco *m*

furry /'fɜːrɪ/ *a* peludo

furthe|r /'fɜːðə(r)/ *a* más lejano; (*additional*) nuevo. ● *adv* más lejos; (*more*) además. ● *vt* fomentar. **∼rmore** *adv* además. **∼rmost** *a* más lejano. **∼st** *a* más lejano. ● *adv* más lejos

furtive /'fɜːtɪv/ *a* furtivo

fury /'fjʊərɪ/ *n* furia *f*

fuse[1] /fjuːz/ *vt* (*melt*) fundir; (*fig, unite*) fusionar. **∼ the lights** fundir los plomos. ● *vi* fundirse; (*fig*) fusionarse. ● *n* fusible *m*, plomo *m*

fuse[2] /fjuːz/ *n* (*of bomb*) mecha *f*

fuse-box /'fjuːzbɒks/ *n* caja *f* de fusibles

fuselage /'fjuːzəlɑːʒ/ *n* fuselaje *m*

fusion /'fjuːʒn/ *n* fusión *f*

fuss /fʌs/ *n* (*commotion*) jaleo *m*. **kick up a ∼** armar un lío, armar una bronca, protestar. **make a ∼ of** tratar con mucha atención. **∼y** *a* (**-ier, -iest**) (*finicky*) remilgado; (*demanding*) exigente; (*ornate*) recargado

fusty /'fʌstɪ/ *a* (**-ier, -iest**) que huele a cerrado

futile /'fju:taɪl/ a inútil, vano

future /'fju:tʃə(r)/ a futuro. ● n futuro m, porvenir m; (gram) futuro m. **in** ~ en lo sucesivo, de ahora en adelante

futuristic /fju:tʃə'rɪstɪk/ a futurista

fuzz /fʌz/ n (fluff) pelusa f; (police, sl) policía f, poli f (fam)

fuzzy /'fʌzɪ/ a ⟨hair⟩ crespo; ⟨photograph⟩ borroso

G

gab /gæb/ n charla f. **have the gift of the** ~ tener un pico de oro

gabardine /gæbə'di:n/ n gabardina f

gabble /'gæbl/ vt decir atropelladamente. ● vi hablar atropelladamente. ● n torrente m de palabras

gable /'geɪbl/ n aguilón m

gad /gæd/ vi (pt gadded). ~ **about** callejear

gadget /'gædʒɪt/ n chisme m

Gaelic /'geɪlɪk/ a & n gaélico (m)

gaffe /gæf/ n plancha f, metedura f de pata

gag /gæg/ n mordaza f; (joke) chiste m. ● vt (pt gagged) amordazar

gaga /'gɑːgɑː/ a (sl) chocho

gaiety /'geɪətɪ/ n alegría f

gaily /'geɪlɪ/ adv alegremente

gain /geɪn/ vt ganar; (acquire) adquirir; (obtain) conseguir. ● vi ⟨clock⟩ adelantar. ● n ganancia f; (increase) aumento m. ~**ful** a lucrativo

gainsay /geɪn'seɪ/ vt (pt gainsaid) (formal) negar

gait /geɪt/ n modo m de andar

gala /'gɑːlə/ n fiesta f; (sport) competición f

galaxy /'gæləksɪ/ n galaxia f

gale /geɪl/ n vendaval m; (storm) tempestad f

gall /gɔːl/ n bilis f; (fig) hiel f; (impudence) descaro m

gallant /'gælənt/ a (brave) valiente; (chivalrous) galante. ~**ry** n valor m

gall-bladder /'gɔːlblædə(r)/ n vesícula f biliar

galleon /'gælɪən/ n galeón m

gallery /'gælərɪ/ n galería f

galley /'gælɪ/ n (ship) galera f; (ship's kitchen) cocina f. ~ **(proof)** n (typ) galerada f

Gallic /'gælɪk/ a gálico. ~**ism** n galicismo m

gallivant /'gælɪvænt/ vi (fam) callejear

gallon /'gælən/ n galón m (imperial = 4,546l; Amer = 3,785l)

gallop /'gæləp/ n galope m. ● vi (pt galloped) galopar

gallows /'gæləʊz/ n horca f

galore /gə'lɔː(r)/ adv en abundancia

galosh /gə'lɒʃ/ n chanclo m

galvanize /'gælvənaɪz/ vt galvanizar

gambit /'gæmbɪt/ n (in chess) gambito m; (fig) táctica f

gamble /'gæmbl/ vt/i jugar. ~**e on** contar con. ● n (venture) empresa f arriesgada; (bet) jugada f; (risk) riesgo m. ~**er** n jugador m. ~**ing** n juego m

game¹ /geɪm/ n juego m; (match) partido m; (animals, birds) caza f. ● a valiente. ~ **for** listo para

game² /geɪm/ a (lame) cojo

gamekeeper /'geɪmki:pə(r)/ n guardabosque m

gammon /'gæmən/ n jamón m ahumado

gamut /'gæmət/ n gama f

gamy /'geɪmɪ/ a manido

gander /'gændə(r)/ n ganso m

gang /gæŋ/ n pandilla f; (of workmen) equipo m. ● vi. ~ **up** unirse (on contra)

gangling /'gæŋglɪŋ/ a larguirucho

gangrene /'gæŋgri:n/ n gangrena f

gangster /'gæŋstə(r)/ n bandido m, gangster m

gangway /'gæŋweɪ/ n pasillo m; (of ship) pasarela f

gaol /dʒeɪl/ n cárcel f. ~**bird** n criminal m empedernido. ~**er** n carcelero m

gap /gæp/ n vacío m; (breach) brecha f; (in time) intervalo m; (deficiency) laguna f; (difference) diferencia f

gape /geɪp/ vi quedarse boquiabierto; (be wide open) estar muy abierto. ~**ing** a abierto; (person) boquiabierto

garage /'gærɑːʒ/ n garaje m; (petrol station) gasolinera f; (for repairs) taller m. ● vt dejar en (el) garaje

garb /gɑːb/ n vestido m

garbage /'gɑːbɪdʒ/ n basura f

garble /'gɑːbl/ vt mutilar

garden /'gɑːdn/ n (of flowers) jardín m; (of vegetables/fruit) huerto m. ● vi trabajar en el jardín/huerto. ~**er** n jardinero/hortelano m. ~**ing** n jardinería/horticultura f

gargantuan /gɑːˈgæntjʊən/ *a* gigantesco

gargle /ˈgɑːgl/ *vi* hacer gárgaras. *n* gargarismo *m*

gargoyle /ˈgɑːgɔɪl/ *n* gárgola *f*

garish /ˈgeərɪʃ/ *a* chillón

garland /ˈgɑːlənd/ *n* guirnalda *f*

garlic /ˈgɑːlɪk/ *n* ajo *m*

garment /ˈgɑːmənt/ *n* prenda *f* (de vestir)

garnet /ˈgɑːnɪt/ *n* granate *m*

garnish /ˈgɑːnɪʃ/ *vt* aderezar. ● *n* aderezo *m*

garret /ˈgærət/ *n* guardilla *f*, buhardilla *f*

garrison /ˈgærɪsn/ *n* guarnición *f*

garrulous /ˈgærələs/ *a* hablador

garter /ˈgɑːtə(r)/ *n* liga *f*

gas /gæs/ *n* (*pl* **gases**) gas *m*; (*med*) anestésico *m*; (*petrol, Amer, fam*) gasolina *f*. ● *vt* (*pt* **gassed**) asfixiar con gas. ● *vi* (*fam*) charlar. ~ **fire** *n* estufa *f* de gas

gash /gæʃ/ *n* cuchillada *f*. ● *vt* acuchillar

gasket /ˈgæskɪt/ *n* junta *f*

gas: ~ **mask** *n* careta *f* antigás *a invar*. ~ **meter** *n* contador *m* de gas

gasoline /ˈgæsəliːn/ *n* (*petrol, Amer*) gasolina *f*

gasometer /gæˈsɒmɪtə(r)/ *n* gasómetro *m*

gasp /gɑːsp/ *vi* jadear; (*with surprise*) quedarse boquiabierto. ● *n* jadeo *m*

gas: ~ **ring** *n* hornillo *m* de gas. ~ **station** *n* (*Amer*) gasolinera *f*

gastric /ˈgæstrɪk/ *a* gástrico

gastronomy /gæˈstrɒnəmɪ/ *n* gastronomía *f*

gate /geɪt/ *n* puerta *f*; (*of metal*) verja *f*; (*barrier*) barrera *f*

gateau /ˈgætəʊ/ *n* (*pl* **gateaux**) tarta *f*

gate: ~**crasher** *n* intruso *m* (que ha entrado sin ser invitado o sin pagar). ~**way** *n* puerta *f*

gather /ˈgæðə(r)/ *vt* reunir ⟨*people, things*⟩; (*accumulate*) acumular; (*pick up*) recoger; recoger ⟨*flowers*⟩; (*fig, infer*) deducir; (*sewing*) fruncir. ~ **speed** acelerar. ● *vi* ⟨*people*⟩ reunirse; ⟨*things*⟩ acumularse. ~**ing** *n* reunión *f*

gauche /gəʊʃ/ *a* torpe

gaudy /ˈgɔːdɪ/ *a* (**-ier, -iest**) chillón

gauge /geɪdʒ/ *n* (*measurement*) medida *f*; (*rail*) entrevía *f*; (*instrument*) indicador *m*. ● *vt* medir; (*fig*) estimar

gaunt /gɔːnt/ *a* macilento; (*grim*) lúgubre

gauntlet /ˈgɔːntlɪt/ *n*. **run the** ~ **of** estar sometido a

gauze /gɔːz/ *n* gasa *f*

gave /geɪv/ *see* **give**

gawk /gɔːk/ *vi*. ~ **at** mirar como un tonto

gawky /ˈgɔːkɪ/ *a* (**-ier, -iest**) torpe

gawp /gɔːp/ *vi*. ~ **at** mirar como un tonto

gay /geɪ/ *a* (**-er, -est**) (*joyful*) alegre; (*homosexual, fam*) homosexual, gay (*fam*)

gaze /geɪz/ *vi*. ~ **(at)** mirar (fijamente). ● *n* mirada *f* (fija)

gazelle /gəˈzel/ *n* gacela *f*

gazette /gəˈzet/ *n* boletín *m* oficial, gaceta *f*

gazump /gəˈzʌmp/ *vt* aceptar un precio más elevado de otro comprador

GB *abbr see* **Great Britain**

gear /gɪə(r)/ *n* equipo *m*; (*tec*) engranaje *m*; (*auto*) marcha *f*. **in** ~ engranado. **out of** ~ desengranado. ● *vt* adaptar. ~**box** *n* (*auto*) caja *f* de cambios

geese /giːs/ *see* **goose**

geezer /ˈgiːzə(r)/ *n* (*sl*) tipo *m*

gelatine /ˈdʒelətiːn/ *n* gelatina *f*

gelignite /ˈdʒelɪgnaɪt/ *n* gelignita *f*

gem /dʒem/ *n* piedra *f* preciosa

Gemini /ˈdʒemɪnaɪ/ *n* (*astr*) Gemelos *mpl*, Géminis *mpl*

gen /dʒen/ *n* (*sl*) información *f*

gender /ˈdʒendə(r)/ *n* género *m*

gene /dʒiːn/ *n* gene *m*

genealogy /dʒiːnɪˈælədʒɪ/ *n* genealogía *f*

general /ˈdʒenərəl/ *a* general. ● *n* general *m*. **in** ~ generalmente. ~ **election** *n* elecciones *fpl* generales

generaliz|ation /dʒenərəlaɪˈzeɪʃn/ *n* generalización *f*. ~**e** *vt/i* generalizar

generally /ˈdʒenərəlɪ/ *adv* generalmente

general practitioner /ˈdʒenərəl prækˈtɪʃənə(r)/ *n* médico *m* de cabecera

generate /ˈdʒenəreɪt/ *vt* producir; (*elec*) generar

generation /dʒenəˈreɪʃn/ *n* generación *f*

generator /ˈdʒenəreɪtə(r)/ *n* (*elec*) generador *m*

genero|sity /dʒenəˈrɒsətɪ/ *n* generosidad *f*. ~**us** /ˈdʒenərəs/ *a* generoso; (*plentiful*) abundante

genetic /dʒɪ'netɪk/ a genético. **~s** n genética f

Geneva /dʒɪ'niːvə/ n Ginebra f

genial /'dʒiːnɪəl/ a simpático, afable; ⟨climate⟩ suave, templado

genital /'dʒenɪtl/ a genital. **~s** npl genitales mpl

genitive /'dʒenɪtɪv/ a & n genitivo (m)

genius /'dʒiːnɪəs/ n (pl **-uses**) genio m

genocide /'dʒenəsaɪd/ n genocidio m

genre /ʒɑ̃ːr/ n género m

gent /dʒent/ n (sl) señor m. **~s** n aseo m de caballeros

genteel /dʒen'tiːl/ a distinguido; (excessively refined) cursi

gentle /'dʒentl/ a (**-er**, **-est**) (mild, kind) amable, dulce; (slight) ligero; ⟨hint⟩ discreto

gentlefolk /'dʒentlfəʊk/ npl gente f de buena familia

gentleman /'dʒentlmən/ n señor m; (well-bred) caballero m

gentleness /'dʒentlnɪs/ n amabilidad f

gentlewoman /'dʒentlwʊmən/ n señora f (de buena familia)

gently /'dʒentlɪ/ adv amablemente; (slowly) despacio

gentry /'dʒentrɪ/ npl pequeña aristocracia f

genuflect /'dʒenjuːflekt/ vi doblar la rodilla

genuine /'dʒenjʊɪn/ a verdadero; ⟨person⟩ sincero

geograph|er /dʒɪ'ɒɡrəfə(r)/ n geógrafo m. **~ical** /dʒɪə'ɡræfɪkl/ a geográfico. **~y** /dʒɪ'ɒɡrəfɪ/ n geografía f

geolog|ical /dʒɪə'lɒdʒɪkl/ a geológico. **~ist** n geólogo m. **~y** /dʒɪ'ɒlədʒɪ/ n geología f

geometr|ic(al) /dʒɪə'metrɪk(l)/ a geométrico. **~y** /dʒɪ'ɒmətrɪ/ n geometría f

geranium /dʒə'reɪnɪəm/ n geranio m

geriatrics /dʒerɪ'ætrɪks/ n geriatría f

germ /dʒɜːm/ n (rudiment, seed) germen m; (med) microbio m

German /'dʒɜːmən/ a & n alemán (m). **~ic** /dʒə'mænɪk/ a germánico. **~ measles** n rubéola f. **~ shepherd (dog)** n (perro m) pastor m alemán. **~y** n Alemania f

germicide /'dʒɜːmɪsaɪd/ n germicida m

germinate /'dʒɜːmɪneɪt/ vi germinar. ● vt hacer germinar

gerrymander /'dʒerɪmændə(r)/ n falsificación f electoral

gestation /dʒe'steɪʃn/ n gestación f

gesticulate /dʒe'stɪkjʊleɪt/ vi hacer ademanes, gesticular

gesture /'dʒestʃə(r)/ n ademán m; (fig) gesto m

get /ɡet/ vt (pt & pp **got**, pp Amer **gotten**, pres p **getting**) obtener, tener; (catch) coger (not LAm), agarrar (esp LAm); (buy) comprar; (find) encontrar; (fetch) buscar; traer; (understand, sl) comprender, caer (fam). **~ s.o. to do sth** conseguir que uno haga algo. ● vi (go) ir; (become) hacerse; (start to) empezar a; (manage) conseguir. **~ married** casarse. **~ ready** prepararse. **~ about** ⟨person⟩ salir mucho; (after illness) levantarse. **~ along** (manage) ir tirando; (progress) hacer progresos. **~ along with** llevarse bien con. **~ at** (reach) llegar a; (imply) querer decir. **~ away** salir; (escape) escaparse. **~ back** vi volver. ● vt (recover) recobrar. **~ by** (manage) ir tirando; (pass) pasar. **~ down** bajar; (depress) deprimir. **~ in** entrar; subir ⟨vehicle⟩; (arrive) llegar. **~ off** bajar de ⟨train, car etc⟩; (leave) irse; (jurid) salir absuelto. **~ on** (progress) hacer progresos; (succeed) tener éxito. **~ on with** (be on good terms with) llevarse bien con; (continue) seguir. **~ out** ⟨person⟩ salir; (take out) sacar. **~ out of** (fig) librarse de. **~ over** reponerse de ⟨illness⟩. **~ round** soslayar ⟨difficulty etc⟩; engatusar ⟨person⟩. **~ through** (pass) pasar; (finish) terminar; (on phone) comunicar con. **~ up** levantarse; (climb) subir; (organize) preparar. **~away** n huida f. **~up** n traje m

geyser /'ɡiːzə(r)/ n calentador m de agua; (geog) géiser m

Ghana /'ɡɑːnə/ n Ghana f

ghastly /'ɡɑːstlɪ/ a (**-ier**, **-iest**) horrible; (pale) pálido

gherkin /'ɡɜːkɪn/ n pepinillo m

ghetto /'ɡetəʊ/ n (pl **-os**) (Jewish quarter) judería f; (ethnic settlement) barrio m pobre habitado por un grupo étnico

ghost /ɡəʊst/ n fantasma m. **~ly** a espectral

ghoulish /'ɡuːlɪʃ/ a macabro

giant /'dʒaɪənt/ n gigante m. ● a gigantesco

gibberish /'dʒɪbərɪʃ/ n jerigonza f

gibe /dʒaɪb/ n mofa f

giblets /'dʒɪblɪts/ npl menudillos mpl

Gibraltar /dʒɪ'brɔːltə(r)/ n Gibraltar m

gidd|iness /'gɪdɪnɪs/ n vértigo m. ~y a (-ier, -iest) mareado; ⟨speed⟩ vertiginoso. **be/feel ~y** estar/sentirse mareado

gift /gɪft/ n regalo m; (ability) don m. ~ed a dotado de talento. ~-wrap vt envolver para regalo

gig /gɪg/ n (fam) concierto m

gigantic /dʒaɪ'gæntɪk/ a gigantesco

giggle /'gɪgl/ vi reírse tontamente. ● n risita f. **the ~s** la risa f tonta

gild /gɪld/ vt dorar

gills /gɪlz/ npl agallas fpl

gilt /gɪlt/ a dorado. ~-edged a (com) de máxima garantía

gimmick /'gɪmɪk/ n truco m

gin /dʒɪn/ n ginebra f

ginger /'dʒɪndʒə(r)/ n jengibre m. ● a rojizo. ● vt. ~ up animar. ~ ale n, ~ beer n cerveza f de jengibre. ~bread n pan m de jengibre

gingerly /'dʒɪndʒəlɪ/ adv cautelosamente

gingham /'gɪŋəm/ n guinga f

gipsy /'dʒɪpsɪ/ n gitano m

giraffe /dʒɪ'rɑːf/ n jirafa f

girder /'gɜːdə(r)/ n viga f

girdle /'gɜːdl/ n (belt) cinturón m; (corset) corsé m

girl /gɜːl/ n chica f, muchacha f; (child) niña f. ~friend n amiga f; (of boy) novia f. ~hood n (up to adolescence) niñez f; (adolescence) juventud f. ~ish a de niña; ⟨boy⟩ afeminado

giro /'dʒaɪrəʊ/ n (pl -os) giro m (bancario)

girth /gɜːθ/ n circunferencia f

gist /dʒɪst/ n lo esencial invar

give /gɪv/ vt (pt gave, pp given) dar; (deliver) entregar; regalar ⟨present⟩; prestar ⟨aid, attention⟩; (grant) conceder; (yield) ceder; (devote) dedicar. ~ o.s. to darse a. ● vi dar; (yield) ceder; (stretch) estirarse. ● n elasticidad f. ~ away regalar; descubrir ⟨secret⟩. ~ back devolver. ~ in (yield) rendirse. ~ off emitir. ~ o.s. up entregarse (a). ~ out distribuir; (announce) anunciar; (become used up) agotarse. ~ over (devote) dedicar; (stop, fam)

dejar (de). ~ up (renounce) renunciar a; (yield) ceder

given /'gɪvn/ see give. ● a dado. ~ name n nombre m de pila

glacier /'glæsɪə(r)/ n glaciar m

glad /glæd/ a contento. ~den vt alegrar

glade /gleɪd/ n claro m

gladiator /'glædɪeɪtə(r)/ n gladiador m

gladiolus /glædɪ'əʊləs/ n (pl -li /-laɪ/) estoque m, gladiolo m, gladíolo m

gladly /'glædlɪ/ adv alegremente; (willingly) con mucho gusto

glamo|rize /'glæməraɪz/ vt embellecer. ~rous a atractivo. ~ur n encanto m

glance /glɑːns/ n ojeada f. ● vi. ~ at dar un vistazo a

gland /glænd/ n glándula f

glar|e /gleə(r)/ vi deslumbrar; (stare angrily) mirar airadamente. ● n deslumbramiento m; (stare, fig) mirada f airada. ~ing a deslumbrador; (obvious) manifiesto

glass /glɑːs/ n (material) vidrio m; (without stem or for wine) vaso m; (with stem) copa f; (for beer) caña f; (mirror) espejo m. ~es npl (spectacles) gafas fpl, anteojos (LAm) mpl. ~y a vítreo

glaze /gleɪz/ vt poner cristales a ⟨windows, doors⟩; vidriar ⟨pottery⟩. ● n barniz m; (for pottery) esmalte m. ~d a ⟨object⟩ vidriado; ⟨eye⟩ vidrioso

gleam /gliːm/ n destello m. ● vi destellar

glean /gliːn/ vt espigar

glee /gliː/ n regocijo m. ~ club n orfeón m. ~ful a regocijado

glen /glen/ n cañada f

glib /glɪb/ a de mucha labia; ⟨reply⟩ fácil. ~ly adv con poca sinceridad

glid|e /glaɪd/ vi deslizarse; ⟨plane⟩ planear. ~er n planeador m. ~ing n planeo m

glimmer /'glɪmə(r)/ n destello m. ● vi destellar

glimpse /glɪmps/ n vislumbre f. **catch a ~ of** vislumbrar. ● vt vislumbrar

glint /glɪnt/ n destello m. ● vi destellar

glisten /'glɪsn/ vi brillar

glitter /'glɪtə(r)/ vi brillar. ● n brillo m

gloat /gləʊt/ vi. ~ on/over regodearse

global /'gləʊbl/ a (world-wide) mundial; (all-embracing) global

globe /gləʊb/ n globo m

globule /'glɒbjuːl/ n glóbulo m

gloom /gluːm/ n oscuridad f; (sadness, fig) tristeza f. ~y a (-ier, -iest) triste; (pessimistic) pesimista

glorify /'glɔːrɪfaɪ/ vt glorificar

glorious /'glɔːrɪəs/ a espléndido; (deed, hero etc) glorioso

glory /'glɔːrɪ/ n gloria f; (beauty) esplendor m. ● vi. ~ in enorgullecerse de. ~hole n (untidy room) leonera f

gloss /glɒs/ n lustre m. ● a brillante. ● vi. ~ over (make light of) minimizar; (cover up) encubrir

glossary /'glɒsərɪ/ n glosario m

glossy /'glɒsɪ/ a brillante

glove /glʌv/ n guante m. ~ compartment n (auto) guantera f, gaveta f. ~d a enguantado

glow /gləʊ/ vi brillar; (with health) rebosar de; (with passion) enardecerse. ● n incandescencia f; (of cheeks) rubor m

glower /'glaʊə(r)/ vi. ~ (at) mirar airadamente

glowing /'gləʊɪŋ/ a incandescente; (account) entusiasta; (complexion) rojo; (with health) rebosante de

glucose /'gluːkəʊs/ n glucosa f

glue /gluː/ n cola f. ● vt (pres p gluing) pegar

glum /glʌm/ a (glummer, glummest) triste

glut /glʌt/ n superabundancia f

glutton /'glʌtn/ n glotón m. ~ous a glotón. ~y n glotonería f

glycerine /'glɪsəriːn/ n glicerina f

gnarled /nɑːld/ a nudoso

gnash /næʃ/ vt. ~ one's teeth rechinar los dientes

gnat /næt/ n mosquito m

gnaw /nɔː/ vt/i roer

gnome /nəʊm/ n gnomo m

go /gəʊ/ vi (pt went, pp gone) ir; (leave) irse; (work) funcionar; (become) hacerse; (be sold) venderse; (vanish) desaparecer. ~ ahead! ¡adelante! ● bad pasarse. ~ riding montar a caballo. ~ shopping ir de compras. be ~ing to do ir a hacer. ● n (pl goes) (energy) energía f. be on the ~ trabajar sin cesar. have a ~ intentar. it's your ~ te toca a ti. make a ~ of tener éxito en. ~ across cruzar. ~ away irse. ~ back volver. ~ back on faltar a

(promise etc). ~ by pasar. ~ down bajar; (sun) ponerse. ~ for buscar, traer; (like) gustar; (attack, sl) atacar. ~ in entrar. ~ in for presentarse para (exam). ~ off (leave) irse; (go bad) pasarse; (explode) estallar. ~ on seguir; (happen) pasar. ~ out salir; (light, fire) apagarse. ~ over (check) examinar. ~ round (be enough) ser bastante. ~ through (suffer) sufrir; (check) examinar. ~ under hundirse. ~ up subir. ~ without pasarse sin

goad /gəʊd/ vt aguijonear

go-ahead /'gəʊəhed/ n luz f verde. ● a dinámico

goal /gəʊl/ n fin m, objeto m; (sport) gol m. ~ie n (fam) portero m. ~keeper n portero m. ~post n poste m (de la portería)

goat /gəʊt/ n cabra f

goatee /gəʊ'tiː/ n perilla f, barbas fpl de chivo

gobble /'gɒbl/ vt engullir

go-between /'gəʊbɪtwiːn/ n intermediario m

goblet /'gɒblɪt/ n copa f

goblin /'gɒblɪn/ n duende m

God /gɒd/ n Dios m. ~forsaken a olvidado de Dios

god /gɒd/ n dios m. ~child n ahijado m. ~daughter n ahijada f. ~dess /'gɒdɪs/ n diosa f. ~father n padrino m. ~ly a devoto. ~mother n madrina f. ~send n beneficio m inesperado. ~son n ahijado m

go-getter /gəʊ'getə(r)/ n persona f ambiciosa

goggle /'gɒgl/ vi. ~ (at) mirar con los ojos desmesuradamente abiertos

goggles /'gɒglz/ npl gafas fpl protectoras

going /'gəʊɪŋ/ n camino m; (racing) (estado m del) terreno m. it is slow/hard ~ es lento/difícil. ● a (price) actual; (concern) en funcionamiento. ~s-on npl actividades fpl anormales, tejemaneje m

gold /gəʊld/ n oro m. ● a de oro. ~en /'gəʊldən/ a de oro; (in colour) dorado; (opportunity) único. ~en wedding n bodas fpl de oro. ~fish n invar pez m de colores, carpa f dorada. ~mine n mina f de oro; (fig) fuente f de gran riqueza. ~-plated a chapado en oro. ~smith n orfebre m

golf /gɒlf/ *n* golf *m*. **~course** *n* campo *m* de golf. **~er** *n* jugador *m* de golf

golly /'gɒlɪ/ *int* ¡caramba!

golosh /gə'lɒʃ/ *n* chanclo *m*

gondol|a /'gɒndələ/ *n* góndola *f*. **~ier** /gɒndə'lɪə(r)/ *n* gondolero *m*

gone /gɒn/ *see* go. ● *a* pasado. **~ six o'clock** después de las seis

gong /gɒŋ/ *n* gong(o) *m*

good /gʊd/ *a* (**better, best**) bueno, (*before masculine singular noun*) buen. **~ afternoon!** ¡buenas tardes! **~ evening!** (*before dark*) ¡buenas tardes!; (*after dark*) ¡buenas noches! **G~ Friday** *n* Viernes *m* Santo. **~ morning!** ¡buenos días! **~ name** *n* (buena) reputación *f*. **~ night!** ¡buenas noches! **a ~ deal** bastante. **as ~ as** (*almost*) casi. **be ~ with** entender. **do ~** hacer bien. **feel ~** sentirse bien. **have a ~ time** divertirse. **it is ~ for you** le sentará bien. ● *n* bien *m*. **for ~** para siempre. **it is no ~ shouting/etc** es inútil gritar/etc.

goodbye /gʊd'baɪ/ *int* ¡adiós! ● *n* adiós *m*. **say ~ to** despedirse de

good: ~for-nothing *a* & *n* inútil (*m*). **~looking** *a* guapo

goodness /'gʊdnɪs/ *n* bondad *f*. **~!, ~ gracious!, ~ me!, my ~!** ¡Dios mío!

goods /gʊdz/ *npl* (*merchandise*) mercancías *fpl*

goodwill /gʊd'wɪl/ *n* buena voluntad *f*

goody /'gʊdɪ/ *n* (*culin, fam*) golosina *f*; (*in film*) bueno *m*. **~goody** *n* mojigato *m*

gooey /'guːɪ/ *a* (**gooier, gooiest**) (*sl*) pegajoso; (*fig*) sentimental

goof /guːf/ *vi* (*Amer, blunder*) cometer una pifia. **~y** *a* (*sl*) necio

goose /guːs/ *n* (*pl* **geese**) oca *f*

gooseberry /'gʊzbərɪ/ *n* uva *f* espina, grosella *f*

goose-flesh /'guːsfleʃ/ *n*, **goosepimples** /'guːspɪmplz/ *n* carne *f* de gallina

gore /gɔː(r)/ *n* sangre *f*. ● *vt* cornear

gorge /gɔːdʒ/ *n* (*geog*) garganta *f*. ● *vt*. **~ o.s.** hartarse (**on** de)

gorgeous /'gɔːdʒəs/ *a* magnífico

gorilla /gə'rɪlə/ *n* gorila *m*

gormless /'gɔːmlɪs/ *a* (*sl*) idiota

gorse /gɔːs/ *n* aulaga *f*

gory /'gɔːrɪ/ *a* (**-ier, -iest**) (*covered in blood*) ensangrentado; (*horrific, fig*) horrible

gosh /gɒʃ/ *int* ¡caramba!

go-slow /gəʊ'sləʊ/ *n* huelga *f* de celo

gospel /'gɒspl/ *n* evangelio *m*

gossip /'gɒsɪp/ *n* (*idle chatter*) charla *f*; (*tittle-tattle*) comadreo *m*; (*person*) chismoso *m*. ● *vi* (*pt* **gossiped**) (*chatter*) charlar; (*repeat scandal*) comadrear. **~y** *a* chismoso

got /gɒt/ *see* get. **have ~** tener. **have ~ to do** tener que hacer

Gothic /'gɒθɪk/ *a* (*archit*) gótico; (*people*) godo

gouge /gaʊdʒ/ *vt*. **~ out** arrancar

gourmet /'gʊəmeɪ/ *n* gastrónomo *m*

gout /gaʊt/ *n* (*med*) gota *f*

govern /'gʌvn/ *vt/i* gobernar

governess /'gʌvənɪs/ *n* institutriz *f*

government /'gʌvənmənt/ *n* gobierno *m*. **~al** /gʌvən'mentl/ *a* gubernamental

governor /'gʌvənə(r)/ *n* gobernador *m*

gown /gaʊn/ *n* vestido *m*; (*of judge, teacher*) toga *f*

GP *abbr see* **general practitioner**

grab /græb/ *vt* (*pt* **grabbed**) agarrar

grace /greɪs/ *n* gracia *f*. **~ful** *a* elegante

gracious /'greɪʃəs/ *a* (*kind*) amable; (*elegant*) elegante

gradation /grə'deɪʃn/ *n* gradación *f*

grade /greɪd/ *n* clase *f*, categoría *f*; (*of goods*) clase *f*, calidad *f*; (*on scale*) grado *m*; (*school mark*) nota *f*; (*class, Amer*) curso *m*. **~ school** *n* (*Amer*) escuela *f* primaria. ● *vt* clasificar; (*schol*) calificar

gradient /'greɪdɪənt/ *n* (*slope*) pendiente *f*

gradual /'grædʒʊəl/ *a* gradual. **~ly** *adv* gradualmente

graduat|e /'grædjʊət/ *n* (*univ*) licenciado. ● *vi* /'grædjʊeɪt/ licenciarse. ● *vt* graduar. **~ion** /-'eɪʃn/ *n* entrega *f* de títulos

graffiti /grə'fiːtɪ/ *npl* pintada *f*

graft[1] /grɑːft/ *n* (*med, bot*) injerto *m*. ● *vt* injertar

graft[2] /grɑːft/ *n* (*bribery, fam*) corrupción *f*

grain /greɪn/ *n* grano *m*

gram /græm/ *n* gramo *m*

gramma|r /'græmə(r)/ *n* gramática *f*. **~tical** /grə'mætɪkl/ *a* gramatical

gramophone /'græməfəʊn/ *n* tocadiscos *m invar*

grand /grænd/ *a* (**-er, -est**) magnífico; (*excellent, fam*) estupendo. **~child** *n* nieto *m*. **~daughter** *n* nieta *f*

grandeur /'grændʒə(r)/ n grandiosidad f
grandfather /'grændfɑːðə(r)/ n abuelo m
grandiose /'grændɪəʊs/ a grandioso
grand: ~**mother** n abuela f. ~**parents** npl abuelos mpl. ~ **piano** n piano m de cola. ~**son** n nieto m
grandstand /'grænstænd/ n tribuna f
granite /'grænɪt/ n granito m
granny /'grænɪ/ n (fam) abuela f, nana f (fam)
grant /grɑːnt/ vt conceder; (give) donar; (admit) admitir (that que). **take for** ~**ed** dar por sentado. ● n concesión f; (univ) beca f
granulated /'grænjʊleɪtɪd/ a. ~ **sugar** n azúcar m granulado
granule /'grænuːl/ n gránulo m
grape /greɪp/ n uva f
grapefruit /'greɪpfruːt/ n invar toronja f, pomelo m
graph /grɑːf/ n gráfica f
graphic /'græfɪk/ a gráfico
grapple /'græpl/ vi. ~ **with** intentar vencer
grasp /grɑːsp/ vt agarrar. ● n (hold) agarro m; (strength of hand) apretón m; (reach) alcance m; (fig) comprensión f
grasping /'grɑːspɪŋ/ a avaro
grass /grɑːs/ n hierba f. ~**hopper** n saltamontes m invar. ~**land** n pradera f. ~ **roots** npl base f popular. ● a popular. ~**y** a cubierto de hierba
grate /greɪt/ n (fireplace) párrilla f. ● vt rallar. ~ **one's teeth** hacer rechinar los dientes. ● vi rechinar
grateful /'greɪtfl/ a agradecido. ~**ly** adv con gratitud
grater /'greɪtə(r)/ n rallador m
gratif|ied /'grætɪfaɪd/ a contento. ~**y** vt satisfacer; (please) agradar a. ~**ying** a agradable
grating /'greɪtɪŋ/ n reja f
gratis /'grɑːtɪs/ a & adv gratis (a invar)
gratitude /'grætɪtjuːd/ n gratitud f
gratuitous /grə'tjuːɪtəs/ a gratuito
gratuity /grə'tjuːətɪ/ n (tip) propina f; (gift of money) gratificación f
grave¹ /greɪv/ n sepultura f
grave² /greɪv/ a (-er, -est) (serious) serio. /grɑːv/ a. ~ **accent** n acento m grave
grave-digger /'greɪvdɪɡə(r)/ n sepulturero m

gravel /'grævl/ n grava f
gravely /'greɪvlɪ/ a (seriously) seriamente
grave: ~**stone** n lápida f. ~**yard** n cementerio m
gravitat|e /'grævɪteɪt/ vi gravitar. ~**ion** /-'teɪʃn/ n gravitación f
gravity /'grævətɪ/ n gravedad f
gravy /'greɪvɪ/ n salsa f
graze¹ /greɪz/ vt/i (eat) pacer
graze² /greɪz/ vt (touch) rozar; (scrape) raspar. ● n rozadura f
greas|e /griːs/ n grasa f. ● vt engrasar. ~**e-paint** n maquillaje m. ~**e-proof paper** n papel m a prueba de grasa, apergaminado m. ~**y** a grasiento
great /greɪt/ a (-er, -est) grande, (before singular noun) gran; (very good, fam) estupendo. **G~ Britain** n Gran Bretaña f. ~**grandfather** n bisabuelo m. ~**grandmother** n bisabuela f. ~**ly** /'greɪtlɪ/ adv (very) muy; (much) mucho. ~**ness** n grandeza f
Greece /griːs/ n Grecia f
greed /griːd/ n avaricia f; (for food) glotonería f. ~**y** a avaro; (for food) glotón
Greek /griːk/ a & n griego (m)
green /griːn/ a (-er, -est) verde; (fig) crédulo. ● n verde m; (grass) césped m. ~ **belt** n zona f verde. ~**ery** n verdor m. ~ **fingers** npl habilidad f con las plantas
greengage /'griːnɡeɪdʒ/ n (plum) claudia f
greengrocer /'griːnɡrəʊsə(r)/ n verdulero m
greenhouse /'griːnhaʊs/ n invernadero m
green: ~ **light** n luz f verde. ~**s** npl verduras fpl
Greenwich Mean Time /grenɪtʃ'miːntaɪm/ n hora f media de Greenwich
greet /griːt/ vt saludar; (receive) recibir. ~**ing** n saludo m. ~**ings** npl (in letter) recuerdos mpl
gregarious /ɡrɪ'ɡeərɪəs/ a gregario
grenade /ɡrɪ'neɪd/ n granada f
grew /ɡruː/ see grow
grey /ɡreɪ/ a & n (-er, -est) gris (m). ● vi (hair) encanecer
greyhound /'ɡreɪhaʊnd/ n galgo m
grid /ɡrɪd/ n reja f; (network, elec) red f; (culin) parrilla f; (on map) cuadrícula f

grief /griːf/ *n* dolor *m*. **come to ~** ⟨*person*⟩ sufrir un accidente; (*fail*) fracasar

grievance /ˈgriːvns/ *n* queja *f*

grieve /griːv/ *vt* afligir. ● *vi* afligirse. **~ for** llorar

grievous /ˈgriːvəs/ *a* doloroso; (*serious*) grave

grill /gril/ *n* (*cooking device*) parrilla *f*; (*food*) parrillada *f*, asado *m*, asada *f*. ● *vt* asar a la parrilla; (*interrogate*) interrogar

grille /gril/ *n* rejilla *f*

grim /grim/ *a* (**grimmer, grimmest**) severo

grimace /ˈgriməs/ *n* mueca *f*. ● *vi* hacer muecas

grim|e /graim/ *n* mugre *f*. **~y** *a* mugriento

grin /grin/ *vt* (*pt* **grinned**) sonreír. ● *n* sonrisa *f* (abierta)

grind /graind/ *vt* (*pt* **ground**) moler ⟨*coffee, corn etc*⟩; (*pulverize*) pulverizar; (*sharpen*) afilar. **~ one's teeth** hacer rechinar los dientes. ● *n* faena *f*

grip /grip/ *vt* (*pt* **gripped**) agarrar; (*interest*) captar la atención de. ● *n* (*hold*) agarro *m*; (*strength of hand*) apretón *m*. **come to ~s** encararse (**with** a/con)

gripe /graip/ *n*. **~s** *npl* (*med*) cólico *m*

grisly /ˈgrizli/ *a* (**-ier, -iest**) horrible

gristle /ˈgrisl/ *n* cartílago *m*

grit /grit/ *n* arena *f*, (*fig*) valor *m*, aguante *m*. ● *vt* (*pt* **gritted**) echar arena en ⟨*road*⟩. **~ one's teeth** (*fig*) acorazarse

grizzle /ˈgrizl/ *vi* lloriquear

groan /grəʊn/ *vi* gemir. ● *n* gemido *m*

grocer /ˈgrəʊsə(r)/ *n* tendero *m*. **~ies** *npl* comestibles *mpl*. **~y** *n* tienda *f* de comestibles

grog /grɒg/ *n* grog *m*

groggy /ˈgrɒgi/ *a* (*weak*) débil; (*unsteady*) inseguro; (*ill*) malucho

groin /grɔin/ *n* ingle *f*

groom /gruːm/ *n* mozo *m* de caballos; (*bridegroom*) novio *m*. ● *vt* almohazar ⟨*horses*⟩; (*fig*) preparar. **well-~ed** *a* bien arreglado

groove /gruːv/ *n* ranura *f*; (*in record*) surco *m*

grope /grəʊp/ *vi* (*find one's way*) moverse a tientas. **~ for** buscar a tientas

gross /grəʊs/ *a* (**-er, -est**) (*coarse*) grosero; (*com*) bruto; (*fat*) grueso; (*flagrant*) grave. ● *n invar* gruesa *f*. **~ly** *adv* groseramente; (*very*) enormemente

grotesque /grəʊˈtesk/ *a* grotesco

grotto /ˈgrɒtəʊ/ *n* (*pl* **-oes**) gruta *f*

grotty /ˈgrɒti/ *a* (*sl*) desagradable; (*dirty*) sucio

grouch /graʊtʃ/ *vi* (*grumble, fam*) rezongar

ground[1] /graʊnd/ *n* suelo *m*; (*area*) terreno *m*; (*reason*) razón *f*; (*elec, Amer*) toma *f* de tierra. ● *vt* varar ⟨*ship*⟩; prohibir despegar ⟨*aircraft*⟩. **~s** *npl* jardines *mpl*; (*sediment*) poso *m*

ground[2] /graʊnd/ *see* **grind**

ground: ~ floor *n* planta *f* baja. **~ rent** *n* alquiler *m* del terreno

grounding /ˈgraʊndiŋ/ *n* base *f*, conocimientos *mpl* (**in** de)

groundless /ˈgraʊndlis/ *a* infundado

ground: ~sheet *n* tela *f* impermeable. **~swell** *n* mar *m* de fondo. **~work** *n* trabajo *m* preparatorio

group /gruːp/ *n* grupo *m*. ● *vt* agrupar. ● *vi* agruparse

grouse[1] /graʊs/ *n invar* (*bird*) urogallo *m*. **red ~** lagópodo *m* escocés

grouse[2] /graʊs/ *vi* (*grumble, fam*) rezongar

grove /grəʊv/ *n* arboleda *f*. **lemon ~** *n* limonar *m*. **olive ~** *n* olivar *m*. **orange ~** *n* naranjal *m*. **pine ~** *n* pinar *m*

grovel /ˈgrɒvl/ *vi* (*pt* **grovelled**) arrastrarse, humillarse. **~ling** *a* servil

grow /grəʊ/ *vi* (*pt* **grew**, *pp* **grown**) crecer; ⟨*cultivated plant*⟩ cultivarse; (*become*) volverse, ponerse. ● *vt* cultivar. **~ up** hacerse mayor. **~er** *n* cultivador *m*

growl /graʊl/ *vi* gruñir. ● *n* gruñido *m*

grown /grəʊn/ *see* **grow**. ● *a* adulto. **~-up** *a* & *n* adulto (*m*)

growth /grəʊθ/ *n* crecimiento *m*; (*increase*) aumento *m*; (*development*) desarrollo *m*; (*med*) tumor *m*

grub /grʌb/ *n* (*larva*) larva *f*; (*food, sl*) comida *f*

grubby /ˈgrʌbi/ *a* (**-ier, -iest**) mugriento

grudg|e /grʌdʒ/ *vt* dar de mala gana; (*envy*) envidiar. **~e doing** molestarle hacer. **he ~ed paying** le molestó pagar. ● *n* rencor *m*. **bear/ have a ~e against s.o.** guardar rencor a alguien. **~ingly** *adv* de mala gana

gruelling /ˈgruːəlɪŋ/ *a* agotador

gruesome /ˈgruːsəm/ *a* horrible

gruff /grʌf/ *a* (**-er, -est**) ⟨*manners*⟩ brusco; ⟨*voice*⟩ ronco

grumble /ˈgrʌmbl/ *vi* rezongar

grumpy /ˈgrʌmpɪ/ *a* (**-ier, -iest**) malhumorado

grunt /grʌnt/ *vi* gruñir. ● *n* gruñido *m*

guarant|ee /gærənˈtiː/ *n* garantía *f*. ● *vt* garantizar. **~or** *n* garante *m* & *f*

guard /gɑːd/ *vt* proteger; ⟨*watch*⟩ vigilar. ● *vi*. **~ against** guardar de. ● *n* (*vigilance, mil group*) guardia *f*; (*person*) guardia *m*; (*on train*) jefe *m* de tren

guarded /ˈgɑːdɪd/ *a* cauteloso

guardian /ˈgɑːdɪən/ *n* guardián *m*; (*of orphan*) tutor *m*

guer(r)illa /gəˈrɪlə/ *n* guerrillero *m*. **~ warfare** *n* guerra *f* de guerrillas

guess /ges/ *vt/i* adivinar; (*suppose, Amer*) creer. ● *n* conjetura *f*. **~work** *n* conjetura(s) *f(pl)*

guest /gest/ *n* invitado *m*; (*in hotel*) huésped *m*. **~house** *n* casa *f* de huéspedes

guffaw /gʌˈfɔː/ *n* carcajada *f*. ● *vi* reírse a carcajadas

guidance /ˈgaɪdəns/ *n* (*advice*) consejos *mpl*; (*information*) información *f*

guide /gaɪd/ *n* (*person*) guía *m* & *f*; (*book*) guía *f*. **Girl G~** exploradora *f*, guía *f* (*fam*). ● *vt* guiar. **~book** *n* guía *f*. **~d missile** *n* proyectil *m* teledirigido. **~lines** *npl* pauta *f*

guild /gɪld/ *n* gremio *m*

guile /gaɪl/ *n* astucia *f*

guillotine /ˈgɪlətiːn/ *n* guillotina *f*

guilt /gɪlt/ *n* culpabilidad *f*. **~y** *a* culpable

guinea-pig /ˈgɪnɪpɪg/ *n* (*including fig*) cobaya *f*

guise /gaɪz/ *n* (*external appearance*) apariencia *f*; (*style*) manera *f*

guitar /gɪˈtɑː(r)/ *n* guitarra *f*. **~ist** *n* guitarrista *m* & *f*

gulf /gʌlf/ *n* (*part of sea*) golfo *m*; (*hollow*) abismo *m*

gull /gʌl/ *n* gaviota *f*

gullet /ˈgʌlɪt/ *n* esófago *m*

gullible /ˈgʌləbl/ *a* crédulo

gully /ˈgʌlɪ/ *n* (*ravine*) barranco *m*

gulp /gʌlp/ *vt*. **~ down** tragarse de prisa. ● *vi* tragar; (*from fear etc*) sentir dificultad para tragar. ● *n* trago *m*

gum[1] /gʌm/ *n* goma *f*; (*for chewing*) chicle *m*. ● *vt* (*pt* **gummed**) engomar

gum[2] /gʌm/ *n* (*anat*) encía *f*. **~boil** /ˈgʌmbɔɪl/ *n* flemón *m*

gumboot /ˈgʌmbuːt/ *n* bota *f* de agua

gumption /ˈgʌmpʃn/ *n* (*fam*) iniciativa *f*; (*common sense*) sentido *m* común

gun /gʌn/ *n* (*pistol*) pistola *f*; (*rifle*) fusil *m*; (*large*) cañón *m*. ● *vt* (*pt* **gunned**). **~ down** abatir a tiros. **~fire** *n* tiros *mpl*

gunge /gʌndʒ/ *n* (*sl*) materia *f* sucia (y pegajosa)

gun: **~man** /ˈgʌnmən/ *n* pistolero *m*. **~ner** /ˈgʌnə(r)/ *n* artillero *m*. **~powder** *n* pólvora *f*. **~shot** *n* disparo *m*

gurgle /ˈgɜːgl/ *n* (*of liquid*) gorgoteo *m*; (*of baby*) gorjeo *m*. ● *vi* ⟨*liquid*⟩ gorgotear; ⟨*baby*⟩ gorjear

guru /ˈgʊruː/ *n* (*pl* **-us**) mentor *m*

gush /gʌʃ/ *vi*. **~ (out)** salir a borbotones. ● *n* (*of liquid*) chorro *m*; (*fig*) torrente *m*. **~ing** *a* efusivo

gusset /ˈgʌsɪt/ *n* escudete *m*

gust /gʌst/ *n* ráfaga *f*; (*of smoke*) bocanada *f*

gusto /ˈgʌstəʊ/ *n* entusiasmo *m*

gusty /ˈgʌstɪ/ *a* borrascoso

gut /gʌt/ *n* tripa *f*, intestino *m*. ● *vt* (*pt* **gutted**) destripar; ⟨*fire*⟩ destruir. **~s** *npl* tripas *fpl*; (*courage, fam*) valor *m*

gutter /ˈgʌtə(r)/ *n* (*on roof*) canalón *m*; (*in street*) cuneta *f*; (*slum, fig*) arroyo *m*. **~snipe** *n* golfillo *m*

guttural /ˈgʌtərəl/ *a* gutural

guy /gaɪ/ *n* (*man, fam*) hombre *m*, tío *m* (*fam*)

guzzle /ˈgʌzl/ *vt/i* soplarse, tragarse

gym /dʒɪm/ *n* (*gymnasium, fam*) gimnasio *m*; (*gymnastics, fam*) gimnasia *f*

gymkhana /dʒɪmˈkɑːnə/ *n* gincana *f*, gymkhana *f*

gymnasium /dʒɪmˈneɪzɪəm/ *n* gimnasio *m*

gymnast /ˈdʒɪmnæst/ *n* gimnasta *m* & *f*. **~ics** *npl* gimnasia *f*

gym-slip /ˈdʒɪmslɪp/ *n* túnica *f* (de gimnasia)

gynaecolog|ist /gaɪnɪˈkɒlədʒɪst/ *n* ginecólogo *m*. **~y** *n* ginecología *f*

gypsy /ˈdʒɪpsɪ/ *n* gitano *m*

gyrate /dʒaɪə'reɪt/ *vi* girar

gyroscope /'dʒaɪərəskəʊp/ *n* giroscopio *m*

H

haberdashery /hæbə'dæʃərɪ/ *n* mercería *f*

habit /'hæbɪt/ *n* costumbre *f*; (*costume, relig*) hábito *m*. **be in the ~ of** (+ *gerund*) tener la costumbre de (+ *infinitive*), soler (+ *infinitive*). **get into the ~ of** (+ *gerund*) acostumbrarse a (+ *infinitive*)

habitable /'hæbɪtəbl/ *a* habitable

habitat /'hæbɪtæt/ *n* hábitat *m*

habitation /hæbɪ'teɪʃn/ *n* habitación *f*

habitual /hə'bɪtjʊəl/ *a* habitual; ⟨*smoker, liar*⟩ inveterado. **~ly** *adv* de costumbre

hack /hæk/ *n* (*old horse*) jamelgo *m*; (*writer*) escritorzuelo *m*. ● *vt* cortar. **~ to pieces** cortar en pedazos

hackney /'hæknɪ/ *a*. **~ carriage** *n* coche *m* de alquiler, taxi *m*

hackneyed /'hæknɪd/ *a* manido

had /hæd/ *see* **have**

haddock /'hædək/ *n invar* eglefino *m*. **smoked ~** *n* eglefino *m* ahumado

haemorrhage /'hemərɪdʒ/ *n* hemorragia *f*

haemorrhoids /'hemərɔɪdz/ *npl* hemorroides *fpl*, almorranas *fpl*

hag /hæg/ *n* bruja *f*

haggard /'hægəd/ *a* ojeroso

haggle /'hægl/ *vi* regatear

Hague /heɪg/ *n*. **The ~** La Haya *f*

hail[1] /heɪl/ *n* granizo *m*. ● *vi* granizar

hail[2] /heɪl/ *vt* (*greet*) saludar; llamar ⟨*taxi*⟩. ● *vi*. **~ from** venir de

hailstone /'heɪlstəʊn/ *n* grano *m* de granizo

hair /heə(r)/ *n* pelo *m*. **~brush** *n* cepillo *m* para el pelo. **~cut** *n* corte *m* de pelo. **have a ~cut** cortarse el pelo. **~do** *n* (*fam*) peinado *m*. **~dresser** *n* peluquero *m*. **~dresser's (shop)** *n* peluquería *f*. **~dryer** *n* secador *m*. **~pin** *n* horquilla *f*. **~pin bend** *n* curva *f* cerrada. **~-raising** *a* espeluznante. **~style** *n* peinado *m*

hairy /'heərɪ/ *a* (**-ier, -iest**) peludo; (*terrifying, sl*) espeluznante

hake /heɪk/ *n invar* merluza *f*

halcyon /'hælsɪən/ *a* sereno. **~ days** *npl* época *f* feliz

hale /heɪl/ *a* robusto

half /hɑːf/ *n* (*pl* **halves**) mitad *f*. ● *a* medio. **~ a dozen** media docena *f*. **~ an hour** media hora *f*. ● *adv* medio, a medias. **~-back** *n* (*sport*) medio *m*. **~-caste** *a & n* mestizo (*m*). **~-hearted** *a* poco entusiasta. **~-term** *n* vacaciones *fpl* de medio trimestre. **~-time** *n* (*sport*) descanso *m*. **~-way** *a* medio. ● *adv* a medio camino. **~-wit** *n* imbécil *m & f*. **at ~-mast** a media asta

halibut /'hælɪbət/ *n invar* hipogloso *m*, halibut *m*

hall /hɔːl/ *n* (*room*) sala *f*; (*mansion*) casa *f* solariega; (*entrance*) vestíbulo *m*. **~ of residence** *n* colegio *m* mayor

hallelujah /hælɪ'luːjə/ *int & n* aleluya (*f*)

hallmark /'hɔːlmɑːk/ *n* (*on gold etc*) contraste *m*; (*fig*) sello *m* (distintivo)

hallo /hə'ləʊ/ *int* = **hello**

hallow /'hæləʊ/ *vt* santificar. **H~e'en** *n* víspera *f* de Todos los Santos

hallucination /həluːsɪ'neɪʃn/ *n* alucinación *f*

halo /'heɪləʊ/ *n* (*pl* **-oes**) aureola *f*

halt /hɔːlt/ *n* alto *m*. ● *vt* parar. ● *vi* pararse

halve /hɑːv/ *vt* dividir por mitad

ham /hæm/ *n* jamón *m*; (*theatre, sl*) racionista *m & f*

hamburger /'hæmbɜːgə(r)/ *n* hamburguesa *f*

hamlet /'hæmlɪt/ *n* aldea *f*, caserío *m*

hammer /'hæmə(r)/ *n* martillo *m*. ● *vt* martill(e)ar; (*defeat, fam*) machacar

hammock /'hæmək/ *n* hamaca *f*

hamper[1] /'hæmpə(r)/ *n* cesta *f*

hamper[2] /'hæmpə(r)/ *vt* estorbar, poner trabas

hamster /'hæmstə(r)/ *n* hámster *m*

hand /'hænd/ *n* (*including cards*) mano *f*; (*of clock*) manecilla *f*; (*writing*) escritura *f*, letra *f*; (*worker*) obrero *m*. **at ~** a mano. **by ~** a mano. **lend a ~** echar una mano. **on ~** a mano. **on one's ~s** (*fig*) en (las) manos de uno. **on the one ~... on the other ~** por un lado... por otro.

out of ~ fuera de control. **to** ~ a mano. • *vt* dar. ~ **down** pasar. ~ **in** entregar. ~ **over** entregar. ~ **out** distribuir. ~**bag** *n* bolso *m*, cartera *f* (*LAm*). ~**book** *n* (*manual*) manual *m*; (*guidebook*) guía *f*. ~**cuffs** *npl* esposas *fpl*. ~**ful** /'hændfʊl/ *n* puñado *m*; (*person, fam*) persona *f* difícil. ~**luggage** *n* equipaje *m* de mano. ~**out** *n* folleto *m*; (*money*) limosna *f*

handicap /'hændɪkæp/ *n* desventaja *f*; (*sport*) handicap *m*. • *vt* (*pt* **han-dicapped**) imponer impedimentos a

handicraft /'hændɪkrɑːft/ *n* artesanía *f*

handiwork /'hændɪwɜːk/ *n* obra *f*, trabajo *m* manual

handkerchief /'hæŋkətʃɪf/ *n* (*pl* **-fs**) pañuelo *m*

handle /'hændl/ *n* (*of door etc*) tirador *m*; (*of implement*) mango *m*; (*of cup, bag, basket etc*) asa *f*. • *vt* manejar; (*touch*) tocar; (*control*) controlar

handlebar /'hændlbɑː(r)/ *n* (*on bicycle*) manillar *m*

handshake /'hændʃeɪk/ *n* apretón *m* de manos

handsome /'hænsəm/ *a* (*good-looking*) guapo; (*generous*) generoso; (*large*) considerable

handwriting /'hændraɪtɪŋ/ *n* escritura *f*, letra *f*

handy /'hændɪ/ *a* (**-ier, -iest**) (*useful*) cómodo; (*person*) diestro; (*near*) a mano. ~**man** *n* hombre *m* habilidoso

hang /hæŋ/ *vt* (*pt* **hung**) colgar; (*pt* **hanged**) (*capital punishment*) ahorcar. • *vi* colgar; (*hair*) caer. • *n*. **get the** ~ **of sth** coger el truco de algo. ~ **about** holgazanear. ~ **on** (*hold out*) resistir; (*wait, sl*) esperar. ~ **out** *vi* tender; (*live, sl*) vivir. ~ **up** (*telephone*) colgar

hangar /'hæŋə(r)/ *n* hangar *m*

hanger /'hæŋə(r)/ *n* (*for clothes*) percha *f*. ~**on** *n* parásito *m*, pegote *m*

hang-gliding /'hæŋglaɪdɪŋ/ *n* vuelo *m* libre

hangman /'hæŋmən/ *n* verdugo *m*

hangover /'hæŋəʊvə(r)/ *n* (*after drinking*) resaca *f*

hang-up /'hæŋʌp/ *n* (*sl*) complejo *m*

hanker /'hæŋkə(r)/ *vi*. ~ **after** anhelar. ~**ing** *n* anhelo *m*

hanky-panky /'hæŋkɪpæŋkɪ/ *n* (*trickery, sl*) trucos *mpl*

haphazard /hæp'hæzəd/ *a* fortuito. ~**ly** *adv* al azar

hapless /'hæplɪs/ *a* desafortunado

happen /'hæpən/ *vi* pasar, suceder, ocurrir. **if he** ~**s to come** si acaso viene. ~**ing** *n* acontecimiento *m*

happ|ily /'hæpɪlɪ/ *adv* felizmente; (*fortunately*) afortunadamente. ~**iness** *n* felicidad *f*. ~**y** *a* (**-ier, -iest**) feliz. ~**y-go-lucky** *a* despreocupado. ~**y medium** *n* término *m* medio

harangue /hə'ræŋ/ *n* arenga *f*. • *vt* arengar

harass /'hærəs/ *vt* acosar. ~**ment** *n* tormento *m*

harbour /'hɑːbə(r)/ *n* puerto *m*. • *vt* encubrir (*criminal*); abrigar (*feelings*)

hard /hɑːd/ *a* (**-er, -est**) duro; (*difficult*) difícil. ~ **of hearing** duro de oído. • *adv* mucho; (*pull*) fuerte. ~ **by** (*muy*) cerca. ~ **done by** tratado injustamente. ~ **up** (*fam*) sin un cuarto. ~**board** *n* chapa *f* de madera, tabla *f*. ~**boiled egg** *n* huevo *m* duro. ~**en** /'hɑːdn/ *vt* endurecer. • *vi* endurecerse. ~**headed** *a* realista

hardly /'hɑːdlɪ/ *adv* apenas. ~ **ever** casi nunca

hardness /'hɑːdnɪs/ *n* dureza *f*

hardship /'hɑːdʃɪp/ *n* apuro *m*

hard: ~ **shoulder** *n* arcén *m*. ~**ware** *n* ferretería *f*; (*computer*) hardware *m*. ~**working** *a* trabajador

hardy /'hɑːdɪ/ *a* (**-ier, -iest**) (*bold*) audaz; (*robust*) robusto; (*bot*) resistente

hare /heə(r)/ *n* liebre *f*. ~**brained** *a* aturdido

harem /'hɑːriːm/ *n* harén *m*

haricot /'hærɪkəʊ/ *n*. ~ **bean** alubia *f*, judía *f*

hark /hɑːk/ *vi* escuchar. ~ **back to** volver a

harlot /'hɑːlət/ *n* prostituta *f*

harm /hɑːm/ *n* daño *m*. **there is no** ~ **in** (+ *gerund*) no hay ningún mal en (+ *infinitive*). • *vt* hacer daño a (*person*); dañar (*thing*); perjudicar (*interests*). ~**ful** *a* perjudical. ~**less** *a* inofensivo

harmonica /hɑːˈmɒnɪkə/ *n* armónica *f*

harmon|ious /hɑːˈməʊnɪəs/ *a* armonioso. ~**ize** *vt/i* armonizar. ~**y** *n* armonía *f*

harness /'hɑːnɪs/ n (for horses) guarniciones fpl; (for children) andadores mpl. ● vt poner guarniciones a ‹horse›; (fig) aprovechar

harp /hɑːp/ n arpa f. ● vi. ~ on (about) machacar. ~ist /'hɑːpɪst/ n arpista m & f

harpoon /hɑːˈpuːn/ n arpón m

harpsichord /'hɑːpsɪkɔːd/ n clavicémbalo m, clave m

harrowing / 'hærəʊɪŋ/ a desgarrador

harsh /hɑːʃ/ a (-er, -est) duro, severo; ‹taste, sound› áspero. ~ly adv severamente. ~ness n severidad f

harvest /'hɑːvɪst/ n cosecha f. ● vt cosechar. ~er n (person) segador; (machine) cosechadora f

has /hæz/ see have

hash /hæʃ/ n picadillo m. make a ~ of sth hacer algo con los pies, estropear algo

hashish /'hæʃiːʃ/ n hachís m

hassle /'hæsl/ n (quarrel) pelea f; (difficulty) problema m, dificultad f; (bother, fam) pena f, follón m, lío m. ● vt (harass) acosar, dar la lata

haste /heɪst/ n prisa f. in ~ de prisa. make ~ darse prisa

hasten /'heɪsn/ vt apresurar. ● vi apresurarse, darse prisa

hast|ily /'heɪstɪlɪ/ adv de prisa. ~y (-ier, -iest) precipitado; (rash) irreflexivo

hat /hæt/ n sombrero m. a ~ trick n tres victorias fpl consecutivas

hatch¹ /hætʃ/ n (for food) ventanilla f; (naut) escotilla f

hatch² /hætʃ/ vt empollar ‹eggs›; tramar ‹plot›. ● vi salir del cascarón

hatchback /'hætʃbæk/ n (coche m) cincopuertas m invar, coche m con puerta trasera

hatchet /'hætʃɪt/ n hacha f

hate /heɪt/ n odio m. ● vt odiar. ~ful a odioso

hatred /'heɪtrɪd/ n odio m

haughty /'hɔːtɪ/ a (-ier, -iest) altivo

haul /hɔːl/ vt arrastrar; transportar ‹goods›. ● n (catch) redada f; (stolen goods) botín m; (journey) recorrido m. ~age n transporte m. ~ier n transportista m & f

haunch /hɔːntʃ/ n anca f

haunt /hɔːnt/ vt frecuentar. ● n sitio m preferido. ~ed house n casa f frecuentada por fantasmas

Havana /həˈvænə/ n La Habana f

have /hæv/ vt (3 sing pres tense has, pt had) tener; (eat, drink) tomar. ~ it out with resolver el asunto. ~ sth done hacer hacer algo. ~ to do tener que hacer. ● v aux haber. ~ just done acabar de hacer. ● n. the ~s and ~nots los ricos mpl y los pobres mpl

haven /'heɪvn/ n puerto m; (refuge) refugio m

haversack /'hævəsæk/ n mochila f

havoc /'hævək/ n estragos mpl

haw /hɔː/ see hum

hawk¹ /hɔːk/ n halcón m

hawk² /hɔːk/ vt vender por las calles. ~er n vendedor m ambulante

hawthorn /'hɔːθɔːn/ n espino m (blanco)

hay /heɪ/ n heno m. ~ fever n fiebre f del heno. ~stack n almiar m

haywire /'heɪwaɪə(r)/ a. go ~ ‹plans› desorganizarse; ‹machine› estropearse

hazard /'hæzəd/ n riesgo m. ● vt arriesgar; aventurar ‹guess›. ~ous a arriesgado

haze /heɪz/ n neblina f

hazel /'heɪzl/ n avellano m. ~nut n avellana f

hazy /'heɪzɪ/ a (-ier, -iest) nebuloso

he /hiː/ pron él. ● n (animal) macho m; (man) varón m

head /hed/ n cabeza f; (leader) jefe m; (of beer) espuma f. ~s or tails cara o cruz. ● a principal. ~ waiter n jefe m de comedor. ● vt encabezar. ~ the ball dar un cabezazo. ~ for dirigirse a. ~ache n dolor m de cabeza. ~dress n tocado m. ~er n (football) cabezazo m. ~ first adv de cabeza. ~gear n tocado m

heading /'hedɪŋ/ n título m, encabezamiento m

headlamp /'hedlæmp/ n faro m

headland /'hedlənd/ n promontorio m

headlight /'hedlaɪt/ n faro m

headline /'hedlaɪn/ n titular m

headlong /'hedlɒŋ/ adv de cabeza; (precipitately) precipitadamente

head: ~master n director m. ~mistress n directora f. ~on a & adv de frente. ~phone n auricular m, audífono m (LAm)

headquarters /hedˈkwɔːtəz/ n (of organization) sede f; (of business) oficina f central; (mil) cuartel m general

headstrong /'hedstrɒŋ/ a testarudo

headway /'hedweɪ/ n progreso m. **make ~** hacer progresos

heady /'hedɪ/ a (**-ier, -iest**) (*impetuous*) impetuoso; (*intoxicating*) embriagador

heal /hiːl/ vt curar. ● vi ‹wound› cicatrizarse; (*fig*) curarse

health /helθ/ n salud f. **~y** a sano

heap /hiːp/ n montón m. ● vt amontonar. **~s of** (*fam*) montones de, muchísimos

hear /hɪə(r)/ vt/i (*pt* **heard** /hɜːd/) oír. **~, ~!** ¡bravo! **not ~ of** (*refuse to allow*) no querer oír. **~ about** oir hablar de. **~ from** recibir noticias de. **~ of** oir hablar de

hearing /'hɪərɪŋ/ n oído m; (*of witness*) audición f. **~-aid** n audífono m

hearsay /'hɪəseɪ/ n rumores mpl. **from ~** según los rumores

hearse /hɜːs/ n coche m fúnebre

heart /hɑːt/ n corazón m. **at ~** en el fondo. **by ~** de memoria. **lose ~** descorozonarse. **~ache** n pena f. **~ attack** n ataque m al corazón. **~break** n pena f. **~breaking** a desgarrador. **~broken** a. **be ~broken** partírsele el corazón

heartburn /'hɑːtbɜːn/ n acedia f

hearten /'hɑːtn/ vt animar

heartfelt /'hɑːtfelt/ a sincero

hearth /hɑːθ/ n hogar m

heartily /'hɑːtɪlɪ/ adv de buena gana; (*sincerely*) sinceramente

heart: ~less a cruel. **~searching** n examen m de conciencia. **~to-~** a abierto

hearty /'hɑːtɪ/ a (*sincere*) sincero; ‹meal› abundante

heat /hiːt/ n calor m; (*contest*) eliminatoria f. ● vt calentar. ● vi calentarse. **~ed** a (*fig*) acalorado. **~er** /'hiːtə(r)/ n calentador m

heath /hiːθ/ n brezal m, descampado m, terreno m baldío

heathen /'hiːðn/ n & a pagano (m)

heather /'heðə(r)/ n brezo m

heat: ~ing n calefacción f. **~stroke** n insolación f. **~wave** n ola f de calor

heave /hiːv/ vt (*lift*) levantar; exhalar ‹sigh›; (*throw, fam*) lanzar. ● vi (*retch*) sentir náuseas

heaven /'hevn/ n cielo m. **~ly** a celestial; (*astronomy*) celeste; (*excellent, fam*) divino

heavily /'hevɪlɪ/ adv pesadamente; (*smoke, drink*) mucho. **~y** a (**-ier,**

-iest) pesado; ‹sea› grueso; ‹traffic› denso; ‹work› duro. **~yweight** n peso m pesado

Hebrew /'hiːbruː/ a & n hebreo (m)

heckle /'hekl/ vt interrumpir ‹speaker›

hectic /'hektɪk/ a febril

hedge /hedʒ/ n seto m vivo. ● vt rodear con seto vivo. ● vi escaparse por la tangente

hedgehog /'hedʒhɒg/ n erizo m

heed /hiːd/ vt hacer caso de. ● n atención f. **pay ~ to** hacer caso de. **~less** a desatento

heel /hiːl/ n talón m; (*of shoe*) tacón m. **down at ~, down at the ~s** (*Amer*) desharrapado

hefty /'heftɪ/ a (**-ier, -iest**) (*sturdy*) fuerte; (*heavy*) pesado

heifer /'hefə(r)/ n novilla f

height /haɪt/ n altura f; (*of person*) estatura f; (*of fame, glory*) cumbre f; (*of joy, folly, days*) colmo m

heighten /'haɪtn/ vt (*raise*) elevar; (*fig*) aumentar

heinous /'heɪnəs/ a atroz

heir /eə(r)/ n heredero m. **~ess** n heredera f. **~loom** /'eəluːm/ n reliquia f heredada

held /held/ *see* **hold**[1]

helicopter /'helɪkɒptə(r)/ n helicóptero m

heliport /'helɪpɔːt/ n helipuerto m

hell /hel/ n infierno m. **~bent** a resuelto. **~ish** a infernal

hello /hə'ləʊ/ int ¡hola!; (*telephone, caller*) ¡oiga!, ¡bueno! (*Mex*), ¡hola! (*Arg*); (*telephone, person answering*) ¡diga!, ¡bueno! (*Mex*), ¡hola! (*Arg*); (*surprise*) ¡vaya! **say ~ to** saludar

helm /helm/ n (*of ship*) timón m

helmet /'helmɪt/ n casco m

help /help/ vt/i ayudar. **he cannot ~ laughing** no puede menos de reír. **~ o.s. to** servirse. **it cannot be ~ed** no hay más remedio. ● n ayuda f; (*charwoman*) asistenta f. **~er** n ayudante m. **~ful** a útil; ‹person› amable

helping /'helpɪŋ/ n porción f

helpless /'helplɪs/ a (*unable to manage*) incapaz; (*powerless*) impotente

helter-skelter /heltə'skeltə(r)/ n tobogán m. ● adv atropelladamente

hem /hem/ n dobladillo m. ● vt (*pt* **hemmed**) hacer un dobladillo. **~ in** encerrar

hemisphere /'hemɪsfɪə(r)/ *n* hemisferio *m*

hemp /hemp/ *n* (*plant*) cáñamo *m*; (*hashish*) hachís *m*

hen /hen/ *n* gallina *f*

hence /hens/ *adv* de aquí. **~forth** *adv* de ahora en adelante

henchman /'hentʃmən/ *n* secuaz *m*

henna /'henə/ *n* alheña *f*

hen-party /'henpɑːtɪ/ *n* (*fam*) reunión *f* de mujeres

henpecked /'henpekt/ *a* dominado por su mujer

her /hɜː(r)/ *pron* (*accusative*) la; (*dative*) le; (*after prep*) ella. **I know ~** la conozco. ● *a* su, sus *pl*

herald /'herəld/ *vt* anunciar

heraldry /'herəldrɪ/ *n* heráldica *f*

herb /hɜːb/ *n* hierba *f*. **~s** *npl* hierbas *fpl* finas

herbaceous /hɜː'beɪʃəs/ *a* herbáceo

herbalist /'hɜːbəlɪst/ *n* herbolario *m*

herculean /hɜːkjʊ'liːən/ *a* hercúleo

herd /hɜːd/ *n* rebaño *m*. ● *vt*. **~ together** reunir

here /hɪə(r)/ *adv* aquí. **~!** (*take this*) ¡tenga! **~abouts** *adv* por aquí. **~after** *adv* en el futuro. **~by** *adv* por este medio; (*in letter*) por la presente

heredit|ary /hɪ'redɪtərɪ/ *a* hereditario. **~y** /hɪ'redətɪ/ *n* herencia *f*

here|sy /'herəsɪ/ *n* herejía *f*. **~tic** *n* hereje *m* & *f*

herewith /hɪə'wɪð/ *adv* adjunto

heritage /'herɪtɪdʒ/ *n* herencia *f*; (*fig*) patrimonio *m*

hermetic /hɜː'metɪk/ *a* hermético

hermit /'hɜːmɪt/ *n* ermitaño *m*

hernia /'hɜːnɪə/ *n* hernia *f*

hero /'hɪərəʊ/ *n* (*pl* -oes) héroe *m*. **~ic** *a* heroico

heroin /'herəʊɪn/ *n* heroína *f*

hero: ~ine /'herəʊɪn/ *n* heroína *f*. **~ism** /'herəʊɪzm/ *n* heroismo *m*

heron /'herən/ *n* garza *f* real

herring /'herɪŋ/ *n* arenque *m*

hers /hɜːz/ *poss pron* suyo *m*, suya *f*, suyos *mpl*, suyas *fpl*, de ella

herself /hɜː'self/ *pron* ella misma; (*reflexive*) se; (*after prep*) sí

hesitant /'hezɪtənt/ *a* vacilante

hesitat|e /'hezɪteɪt/ *vi* vacilar. **~ion** /-'teɪʃn/ *n* vacilación *f*

hessian /'hesɪən/ *n* arpillera *f*

het /het/ *a*. **~ up** (*sl*) nervioso

heterogeneous /hetərəʊ'dʒiːnɪəs/ *a* heterogéneo

heterosexual /hetərəʊ'seksjʊəl/ *a* heterosexual

hew /hjuː/ *vt* (*pp* hewn) cortar; (*cut into shape*) tallar

hexagon /'heksəgən/ *n* hexágono *m*. **~al** /-'æɡənl/ *a* hexagonal

hey /heɪ/ *int* ¡eh!

heyday /'heɪdeɪ/ *n* apogeo *m*

hi /haɪ/ *int* (*fam*) ¡hola!

hiatus /haɪ'eɪtəs/ *n* (*pl* -tuses) hiato *m*

hibernat|e /'haɪbəneɪt/ *vi* hibernar. **~ion** *n* hibernación *f*

hibiscus /hɪ'bɪskəs/ *n* hibisco *m*

hiccup /'hɪkʌp/ *n* hipo *m*. **have (the) ~s** tener hipo. ● *vi* tener hipo

hide[1] /haɪd/ *vt* (*pt* hid, *pp* hidden) esconder. ● *vi* esconderse

hide[2] /haɪd/ *n* piel *f*, cuero *m*

hideous /'hɪdɪəs/ *a* (*dreadful*) horrible; (*ugly*) feo

hide-out /'haɪdaʊt/ *n* escondrijo *m*

hiding[1] /'haɪdɪŋ/ *n* (*thrashing*) paliza *f*

hiding[2] /'haɪdɪŋ/ *n*. **go into ~** esconderse

hierarchy /'haɪərɑːkɪ/ *n* jerarquía *f*

hieroglyph /'haɪərəglɪf/ *n* jeroglífico *m*

hi-fi /'haɪfaɪ/ *a* de alta fidelidad. ● *n* (equipo *m* de) alta fidelidad (*f*)

higgledy-piggledy /hɪgldɪ'pɪgldɪ/ *adv* en desorden

high /haɪ/ *a* (-er, -est) alto; (*price*) elevado; (*number, speed*) grande; (*wind*) fuerte; (*intoxicated, fam*) ebrio; (*voice*) agudo; (*meat*) manido. **in the ~ season** en plena temporada. ● *n* alto nivel *m*. **a (new) ~** un récord *m*. ● *adv* alto

highbrow /'haɪbrəʊ/ *a* & *n* intelectual (*m* & *f*)

higher education /haɪər edʒʊ'keɪʃn/ *n* enseñanza *f* superior

high-falutin /haɪfə'luːtɪn/ *a* pomposo

high-handed /haɪ'hændɪd/ *a* despótico

high jump /haɪdʒʌmp/ *n* salto *m* de altura

highlight /'haɪlaɪt/ *n* punto *m* culminante. ● *vt* destacar

highly /'haɪlɪ/ *adv* muy; (*paid*) muy bien. **~ strung** *a* nervioso

highness /'haɪnɪs/ *n* (*title*) alteza *f*

high: ~-rise building *n* rascacielos *m*. **~ school** *n* instituto *m*. **~-speed** *a* de gran velocidad. **~ spot** *n* (*fam*) punto *m* culminante. **~ street** *n* calle f mayor. **~-strung** a (Amer) nervioso. **~ tea** n merienda f substanciosa

highway /'haɪweɪ/ n carretera f. **~man** n salteador m de caminos

hijack /'haɪdʒæk/ vt secuestrar. ● n secuestro m. **~er** n secuestrador

hike /haɪk/ n caminata f. ● vi darse la caminata. **~r** n excursionista m & f

hilarious /hɪ'leərɪəs/ a (funny) muy divertido

hill /hɪl/ n colina f; (slope) cuesta f. **~billy** n rústico m. **~side** n ladera f. **~y** a montuoso

hilt /hɪlt/ n (of sword) puño m. **to the ~** totalmente

him /hɪm/ pron le, lo; (after prep) él. **I know ~** le/lo conozco

himself /hɪm'self/ pron él mismo; (reflexive) se

hind /haɪnd/ a trasero

hinder /'hɪndə(r)/ vt estorbar; (prevent) impedir

hindrance /'hɪndrəns/ n obstáculo m

hindsight /'haɪnsaɪt/ n. **with ~** retrospectivamente

Hindu /hɪn'duː/ n & a hindú (m & f). **~ism** n hinduismo m

hinge /hɪndʒ/ n bisagra f. ● vi. **~ on** (depend on) depender de

hint /hɪnt/ n indirecta f; (advice) consejo m. ● vt dar a entender. ● vi soltar una indirecta. **~ at** hacer alusión a

hinterland /'hɪntəlænd/ n interior m

hip /hɪp/ n cadera f

hippie /'hɪpɪ/ n hippie m & f

hippopotamus /hɪpə'pɒtəməs/ n (pl -muses or -mi) hipopótamo m

hire /haɪə(r)/ vt alquilar ‹thing›; contratar ‹person›. ● n alquiler m. **~-purchase** n compra f a plazos

hirsute /'hɜːsjuːt/ a hirsuto

his /hɪz/ a su, sus pl. ● poss pron el suyo m, la suya f, los suyos mpl, las suyas fpl

Hispan|ic /hɪ'spænɪk/ a hispánico. **~ist** /'hɪspənɪst/ n hispanista m & f. **~o...** pref hispano...

hiss /hɪs/ n silbido. ● vt/i silbar

histor|ian /hɪ'stɔːrɪən/ n historiador m. **~ic(al)** /hɪ'stɒrɪkl/ a histórico. **~y** /'hɪstrɪ/ n historia f. **make ~y** pasar a la historia

histrionic /hɪstrɪ'ɒnɪk/ a histriónico

hit /hɪt/ vt (pt hit, pres p hitting) golpear; (collide with) chocar con;

(find) dar con; (affect) afectar. **~ it off with** hacer buenas migas con. ● n (blow) golpe m; (fig) éxito m. **~ on** vi encontrar, dar con

hitch /hɪtʃ/ vt (fasten) atar. ● n (snag) problema m. **~ a lift, ~-hike** vi hacer autostop, hacer dedo (Arg), pedir aventón (Mex). **~-hiker** n autostopista m & f

hither /'hɪðə(r)/ adv acá. **~ and thither** acá y allá

hitherto /'hɪðətuː/ adv hasta ahora

hit-or-miss /'hɪtɔː'mɪs/ a (fam) a la buena de Dios, a ojo

hive /haɪv/ n colmena f. ● vt. **~off** separar; (industry) desnacionalizar

hoard /hɔːd/ vt acumular. ● n provisión f; (of money) tesoro m

hoarding /'hɔːdɪŋ/ n cartelera f, valla f publicitaria

hoar-frost /'hɔːfrɒst/ n escarcha f

hoarse /hɔːs/ a (-er, -est) ronco. **~ness** n (of voice) ronquera f; (of sound) ronquedad f

hoax /həʊks/ n engaño m. ● vt engañar

hob /hɒb/ n repisa f; (of cooker) fogón m

hobble /'hɒbl/ vi cojear

hobby /'hɒbɪ/ n pasatiempo m

hobby-horse /'hɒbɪhɔːs/ n (toy) caballito m (de niño); (fixation) caballo m de batalla

hobnail /'hɒbneɪl/ n clavo m

hob-nob /'hɒbnɒb/ vi (pt hob-nobbed). **~ with** codearse con

hock[1] /hɒk/ n vino m del Rin

hock[2] /hɒk/ vt (pawn, sl) empeñar

hockey /'hɒkɪ/ n hockey m

hodgepodge /'hɒdʒpɒdʒ/ n mezcolanza f

hoe /həʊ/ n azada f. ● vt (pres p hoeing) azadonar

hog / hɒg/ n cerdo m. ● vt (pt hogged) (fam) acaparar

hoist /hɔɪst/ vt levantar; izar ‹flag›. ● n montacargas m invar

hold[1] /həʊld/ vt (pt held) tener; (grasp) coger (not LAm), agarrar; (contain) contener; mantener ‹interest›; (believe) creer; contener ‹breath›. **~ one's tongue** callarse. ● vi mantenerse. ● n asidero m; (influence) influencia f. **get ~ of** agarrar; (fig, acquire) adquirir. **~ back** (contain) contener; (conceal) ocultar. **~ on** (stand firm) resistir; (wait) esperar. **~ on to** (keep) guardar; (cling to) agarrarse a. **~**

out *vt* (*offer*) ofrecer. ● *vi* (*resist*) resistir. ~ **over** aplazar. ~ **up** (*support*) sostener; (*delay*) retrasar; (*rob*) atracar. ~ **with** aprobar

hold² /həʊld/ *n* (*of ship*) bodega *f*

holdall /ˈhəʊldɔːl/ *n* bolsa *f* (de viaje)

holder /ˈhəʊldə(r)/ *n* tenedor *m*; (*of post*) titular *m*; (*for object*) soporte *m*

holding /ˈhəʊldɪŋ/ *n* (*land*) propiedad *f*

hold-up /ˈhəʊldʌp/ *n* atraco *m*

hole /həʊl/ *n* agujero *m*; (*in ground*) hoyo *m*; (*in road*) bache *m*. ● *vt* agujerear

holiday /ˈhɒlɪdeɪ/ *n* vacaciones *fpl*; (*public*) fiesta *f*. ● *vi* pasar las vacaciones. ~**maker** *n* veraneante *m*

holiness /ˈhəʊlɪnɪs/ *n* santidad *f*

Holland /ˈhɒlənd/ *n* Holanda *f*

hollow /ˈhɒləʊ/ *a* & *n* hueco (*m*). ● *vt* ahuecar

holly /ˈhɒlɪ/ *n* acebo *m*. ~**hock** *n* malva *f* real

holocaust /ˈhɒləkɔːst/ *n* holocausto *m*

holster /ˈhəʊlstə(r)/ *n* pistolera *f*

holy /ˈhəʊlɪ/ *a* (**-ier, -iest**) santo, sagrado. **H~ Ghost, H~ Spirit** *n* Espíritu *m* Santo. ~ **water** *n* agua *f* bendita

homage /ˈhɒmɪdʒ/ *n* homenaje *m*

home /həʊm/ *n* casa *f*; (*institution*) asilo *m*; (*for soldiers*) hogar *m*; (*native land*) patria *f*. **feel at ~ with** sentirse como en su casa. ● *a* casera, de casa; (*of family*) de familia; (*pol*) interior; (*match*) de casa. ● *adv*. (**at**) ~ **en casa. H~ Counties** *npl* región *f* alrededor de Londres. ~**land** *n* patria *f*. ~**less** *a* sin hogar. ~**ly** /ˈhəʊmlɪ/ *a* (**-ier, -iest**) casero; (*ugly*) feo. **H~ Office** *n* Ministerio *m* del Interior. **H~ Secretary** *n* Ministro *m* del Interior. ~**sick** *a*. **be** ~**sick** tener morriña. ~ **town** *n* ciudad *f* natal. ~ **truths** *npl* las verdades *fpl* del barquero, las cuatro verdades *fpl*. ~**ward** /ˈhəʊmwəd/ *a* (*journey*) de vuelta. ● *adv* hacia casa. ~**work** *n* deberes *mpl*

homicide /ˈhɒmɪsaɪd/ *n* homicidio *m*

homoeopath|ic /həʊmɪəʊˈpæθɪk/ *a* homeopático. ~**y** /-ˈɒpəθɪ/ *n* homeopatía *f*

homogeneous /həʊməʊˈdʒiːnɪəs/ *a* homogéneo

homosexual /həʊməʊˈseksjʊəl/ *a* & *n* homosexual (*m*)

hone /həʊn/ *vt* afilar

honest /ˈɒnɪst/ *a* honrado; (*frank*) sincero. ~**ly** *adv* honradamente. ~**y** *n* honradez *f*

honey /ˈhʌnɪ/ *n* miel *f*; (*person, fam*) cielo *m*, cariño *m*. ~**comb** /ˈhʌnɪkəʊm/ *n* panal *m*

honeymoon /ˈhʌnɪmuːn/ *n* luna *f* de miel

honeysuckle /ˈhʌnɪsʌkl/ *n* madreselva *f*

honk /hɒŋk/ *vi* tocar la bocina

honorary /ˈɒnərərɪ/ *a* honorario

honour /ˈɒnə(r)/ *n* honor *m*. ● *vt* honrar. ~**able** *a* honorable

hood /hʊd/ *n* capucha *f*; (*car roof*) capota *f*; (*car bonnet*) capó *m*

hoodlum /ˈhuːdləm/ *n* gamberro *m*, matón *m*

hoodwink /ˈhʊdwɪŋk/ *vt* engañar

hoof /huːf/ *n* (*pl* **hoofs** or **hooves**) casco *m*

hook /hʊk/ *n* gancho *m*; (*on garment*) corchete *m*; (*for fishing*) anzuelo *m*. **by ~ or by crook** por fas o por nefas, por las buenas o por las malas. **get s.o. off the ~** sacar a uno de un apuro. **off the ~** (*telephone*) descolgado. ● *vt* enganchar. ● *vi* engancharse

hooked /hʊkt/ *a* ganchudo. ~ **on** (*sl*) adicto a

hooker /ˈhʊkə(r)/ *n* (*rugby*) talonador *m*; (*Amer, sl*) prostituta *f*

hookey /ˈhʊkɪ/ *n*. **play** ~ (*Amer, sl*) hacer novillos

hooligan /ˈhuːlɪgən/ *n* gamberro *m*

hoop /huːp/ *n* aro *m*

hooray /hʊˈreɪ/ *int* & *n* ¡viva! (*m*)

hoot /huːt/ *n* (*of horn*) bocinazo *m*; (*of owl*) ululato *m*. ● *vi* tocar la bocina; (*owl*) ulular

hooter /ˈhuːtə(r)/ *n* (*of car*) bocina *f*; (*of factory*) sirena *f*

Hoover /ˈhuːvə(r)/ *n* (*P*) aspiradora *f*. ● *vt* pasar la aspiradora

hop¹ /hɒp/ *vi* (*pt* **hopped**) saltar a la pata coja. ~ **in** (*fam*) subir. ~ **it** (*sl*) largarse. ~ **out** (*fam*) bajar. ● *n* salto *m*; (*flight*) etapa *f*

hop² /hɒp/ *n*. ~**(s)** lúpulo *m*

hope /həʊp/ *n* esperanza *f*. ● *vt/i* esperar. ~ **for** esperar. ~**ful** *a* esperanzador. ~**fully** *adv* con optimismo; (*it is hoped*) se espera. ~**less** *a* desesperado. ~**lessly** *adv* sin esperanza

hopscotch /ˈhɒpskɒtʃ/ *n* tejo *m*

horde /hɔːd/ *n* horda *f*

horizon /hə'raɪzn/ n horizonte m
horizontal /hɒrɪ'zɒntl/ a horizontal.
  ~ly adv horizontalmente
hormone /'hɔːməʊn/ n hormona f
horn /hɔːn/ n cuerno m; (of car) bocina f; (mus) trompa f. ● vt. **~ in** (sl)
  entrometerse. **~ed** a con cuernos
hornet /'hɔːnɪt/ n avispón m
horny /'hɔːnɪ/ a ⟨hands⟩ calloso
horoscope /'hɒrəskəʊp/ n horóscopo m
horri|ble /'hɒrəbl/ a horrible. **~d**
  /'hɒrɪd/ a horrible
horrif|ic /hə'rɪfɪk/ a horroroso. **~y**
  /'hɒrɪfaɪ/ vt horrorizar
horror /'hɒrə(r)/ n horror m. **~ film**
  n película f de miedo
hors-d'oevre /ɔː'dɜːvr/ n entremés
  m
horse /hɔːs/ n caballo m. **~back** n.
  on ~back a caballo
horse chestnut /hɔːs'tʃesnʌt/ n castaña f de Indias
horse: **~man** n jinete m. **~play** n
  payasadas fpl. **~power** n (unit)
  caballo m (de fuerza). **~racing** n
  carreras fpl de caballos
horseradish /'hɔːsrædɪʃ/ n rábano m
  picante
horse: **~ sense** n (fam) sentido m
  común. **~shoe** /'hɔːsʃuː/ n herradura f
horsy /'hɔːsɪ/ a ⟨face etc⟩ caballuno
horticultur|al /hɔːtɪ'kʌltʃərəl/ a hor-
  tícola. **~e** /'hɔːtɪkʌltʃə(r)/ n hor-
  ticultura f
hose /həʊz/ n (tube) manga f. ● vt
  (water) regar con una manga;
  (clean) limpiar con una manga.
  ~pipe n manga f
hosiery /'həʊzɪərɪ/ n calcetería f
hospice /'hɒspɪs/ n hospicio m
hospitabl|e /hɒ'spɪtəbl/ a hos-
  pitalario. **~y** adv con hospitalidad
hospital /'hɒspɪtl/ n hospital m
hospitality /hɒspɪ'tælətɪ/ n hospitalidad f
host[1] /həʊst/ n. **a ~ of** un montón de
host[2] /həʊst/ n (master of house)
  huésped m, anfitrión m
host[3] /həʊst/ n ⟨relig⟩ hostia f
hostage /'hɒstɪdʒ/ n rehén m
hostel /'hɒstl/ n (for students) residencia f. **youth ~** albergue m
  juvenil
hostess /'həʊstɪs/ n huéspeda f,
  anfitriona f
hostil|e /'hɒstaɪl/ a hostil. **~ity** n
  hostilidad f

hot /hɒt/ a (**hotter, hottest**) caliente; (culin) picante; ⟨news⟩ de
  última hora. **be/feel ~** tener calor.
  in ~ water (fam) en un apuro. **it is
  ~** hace calor. ● vt/i. **~ up** (fam)
  calentarse
hotbed /'hɒtbed/ n (fig) semillero m
hotchpotch /'hɒtʃpɒtʃ/ n mezcolanza f
hot dog /hɒt'dɒg/ n perrito m
  caliente
hotel /həʊ'tel/ n hotel m. **~ier** n hot-
  elero m
hot: **~head** n impetuoso m.
  ~headed a impetuoso. **~house** n invernadero m. **~line** n teléfono m rojo.
  ~plate n calentador m. **~water
  bottle** n bolsa f de agua caliente
hound /haʊnd/ n perro m de caza.
  ● vt perseguir
hour /aʊə(r)/ n hora f. **~ly** a & adv
  cada hora. **~ly pay** n sueldo m por
  hora. **paid ~ly** pagado por hora
house /haʊs/ n (pl **-s** /'haʊzɪz/) casa
  f; (theatre building) sala f; (theatre
  audience) público m; (pol) cámara f.
  /haʊz/ vt alojar; (keep) guardar.
  ~boat n casa f flotante. **~breaking**
  n robo m de casa. **~hold**
  /'haʊshəʊld/ n casa f, familia f.
  ~holder n dueño m de una casa;
  (head of household) cabeza f de familia. **~keeper** n ama f de llaves.
  ~keeping n gobierno m de la casa.
  ~maid n criada f, mucama f (LAm).
  H~ of Commons n Cámara f de los
  Comunes. **~proud** a meticuloso.
  ~warming n inauguración f de
  una casa. **~wife** /'haʊswaɪf/ n ama
  f de casa. **~work** n quehaceres mpl
  domésticos
housing /'haʊzɪŋ/ n alojamiento m.
  ~ estate n urbanización f
hovel /'hɒvl/ n casucha f
hover /'hɒvə(r)/ vi ⟨bird, threat etc⟩
  cernerse; (loiter) rondar. **~craft** n
  aerodeslizador m
how /haʊ/ adv cómo. **~ about a
  walk?** ¿qué le parece si damos un
  paseo? **~ are you?** ¿cómo está Vd?
  ~ do you do? (in introduction)
  mucho gusto. **~ long?** ¿cuánto
  tiempo? **~ many?** ¿cuántos? **~
  much?** ¿cuánto? **~ often?** ¿cuántas
  veces? **and ~!** ¡y cómo!
however /haʊ'evə(r)/ adv (with
  verb) de cualquier manera que (+
  subjunctive); (with adjective or
  adverb) por... que (+ subjunctive);

(*nevertheless*) no obstante, sin
embargo. **~ much it rains** por
mucho que llueva
howl /haʊl/ n aullido. ● vi aullar
howler /ˈhaʊlə(r)/ n (*fam*) plancha f
HP *abbr see* **hire-purchase**
hp *abbr see* **horsepower**
hub /hʌb/ n (*of wheel*) cubo m; (*fig*)
centro m
hubbub /ˈhʌbʌb/ n barahúnda f
hub-cap /ˈhʌbkæp/ n tapacubos m
invar
huddle /ˈhʌdl/ vi apiñarse
hue¹ /hjuː/ n (*colour*) color m
hue² /hjuː/ n. ~ **and cry** clamor m
huff /hʌf/ n. **in a ~** enojado
hug /hʌɡ/ vt (*pt* hugged) abrazar;
(*keep close to*) no apartarse de. ● n
abrazo m
huge /hjuːdʒ/ a enorme. **~ly** adv
enormemente
hulk /hʌlk/ n (*of ship*) barco m viejo;
(*person*) armatoste m
hull /hʌl/ n (*of ship*) casco m
hullabaloo /hʌləbəˈluː/ n tumulto m
hullo /həˈləʊ/ int = **hello**
hum /hʌm/ vt/i (*pt* hummed) ⟨person⟩ canturrear; ⟨insect, engine⟩
zumbar. ● n zumbido m. ~ **(or hem)
and haw (or ha)** vacilar
human /ˈhjuːmən/ a & n humano
(m). ~ **being** n ser m humano
humane /hjuːˈmeɪn/ a humano
humanism /ˈhjuːmənɪzəm/ n humanismo m
humanitarian /hjuːmænɪˈteərɪən/ a
humanitario
humanity /hjuːˈmænətɪ/ n humanidad f
humbl|e /ˈhʌmbl/ a (-er, -est)
humilde. ● vt humillar. ~**y** adv
humildemente
humbug /ˈhʌmbʌɡ/ n (*false talk*)
charlatanería f; (*person*) charlatán
m; (*sweet*) caramelo m de menta
humdrum /ˈhʌmdrʌm/ a monótono
humid /ˈhjuːmɪd/ a húmedo. ~**ifier**
n humedecedor m. ~**ity** /hjuː-
ˈmɪdətɪ/ n humedad f
humiliat|e /hjuːˈmɪlieɪt/ vt humillar.
~**ion** /-ˈeɪʃn/ n humillación f
humility /hjuːˈmɪlətɪ/ n humildad f
humorist /ˈhjuːmərɪst/ n humorista
m & f
humo|rous /ˈhjuːmərəs/ a divertido.
~**rously** adv con gracia. ~**ur** n
humorismo m; (*mood*) humor m.
sense of ~ur n sentido m del humor

hump /hʌmp/ n montecillo m; (*of the
spine*) joroba f. **the ~** (*sl*) malhumor
m. ● vt encorvarse; (*hoist up*) llevar
al hombro
hunch /hʌntʃ/ vt encorvar. ~**ed up**
encorvado. ● n presentimiento m;
(*lump*) joroba f. ~**back** /ˈhʌntʃbæk/
n jorobado m
hundred /ˈhʌndrəd/ a ciento, (*before
noun*) cien. ● n ciento m. ~**fold** a
céntuplo. ● adv cien veces. ~**s of**
centenares de. ~**th** a centésimo.
● n centésimo m, centésima parte f
hundredweight /ˈhʌndrədweɪt/ n
50,8kg; (*Amer*) 45,36kg
hung /hʌŋ/ *see* **hang**
Hungar|ian /hʌŋˈɡeərɪən/ a & n húngaro (m). ~**y** /ˈhʌŋɡərɪ/ n Hungría f
hunger /ˈhʌŋɡə(r)/ n hambre f. ● vi.
~ **for** tener hambre de. ~**-strike** n
huelga f de hambre
hungr|ily /ˈhʌŋɡrəlɪ/ adv ávidamente. ~**y** a (-ier, -iest) hambriento. **be ~y** tener hambre
hunk /hʌŋk/ n (*buen*) pedazo m
hunt /hʌnt/ vt/i cazar. ~ **for** buscar.
● n caza f. ~**er** n cazador m. ~**ing** n
caza f
hurdle /ˈhɜːdl/ n (*sport*) valla f; (*fig*)
obstáculo m
hurdy-gurdy /ˈhɜːdɪɡɜːdɪ/ n organillo m
hurl /hɜːl/ vt lanzar
hurly-burly /ˈhɜːlɪbɜːlɪ/ n tumulto m
hurrah /hʊˈrɑː/, **hurray** /hʊˈreɪ/ int &
n ¡viva! (m)
hurricane /ˈhʌrɪkən/ n huracán m
hurried /ˈhʌrɪd/ a apresurado. ~**ly**
adv apresuradamente
hurry /ˈhʌrɪ/ vi apresurarse, darse
prisa. ● vt apresurar, dar prisa a.
● n prisa f. **be in a ~** tener prisa
hurt /hɜːt/ vt/i (*pt* hurt) herir. ● n
(*injury*) herida f; (*harm*) daño m.
~**ful** a hiriente; (*harmful*) dañoso
hurtle /ˈhɜːtl/ vt lanzar. ● vi. ~
along mover rápidamente
husband /ˈhʌzbənd/ n marido m
hush /hʌʃ/ vt acallar. ● n silencio m.
~ **up** ocultar ⟨affair⟩. ~~ a (*fam*)
muy secreto
husk /hʌsk/ n cáscara f
husky /ˈhʌskɪ/ a (-ier, -iest) (*hoarse*)
ronco; (*burly*) fornido
hussy /ˈhʌsɪ/ n desvergonzada f
hustle /ˈhʌsl/ vt (*jostle*) empujar.
● vi (*hurry*) darse prisa. ● n empuje
m. ~ **and bustle** n bullicio m
hut /hʌt/ n cabaña f

hutch /hʌtʃ/ n conejera f
hyacinth /'haɪəsɪnθ/ n jacinto m
hybrid /'haɪbrɪd/ a & n híbrido (m)
hydrangea /haɪ'dreɪndʒə/ n hortensia f
hydrant /'haɪdrənt/ n. (fire) ~ n boca f de riego
hydraulic /haɪ'drɔ:lɪk/ a hidráulico
hydroelectric /haɪdrəʊɪ'lektrɪk/ a hidroeléctrico
hydrofoil /'haɪdrəfɔɪl/ n aerodeslizador m
hydrogen /'haɪdrədʒən/ n hidrógeno m. ~ **bomb** n bomba f de hidrógeno. ~ **peroxide** n peróxido m de hidrógeno
hyena /haɪ'i:nə/ n hiena f
hygien|e /'haɪdʒi:n/ n higiene f. ~**ic** a higiénico
hymn /hɪm/ n himno m
hyper... /'haɪpə(r)/ pref hiper...
hypermarket /'haɪpəma:kɪt/ n hipermercado m
hyphen /'haɪfn/ n guión m. ~**ate** vt escribir con guión
hypno|sis /hɪp'nəʊsɪs/ n hipnosis f. ~**tic** /-'nɒtɪk/ a hipnótico. ~**tism** /hɪpnə'tɪzəm/ n hipnotismo m. ~**tist** n hipnotista m & f. ~**tize** vt hipnotizar
hypochondriac /haɪpə'kɒndrɪæk/ n hipocondríaco m
hypocrisy /hɪ'pɒkrəsɪ/ n hipocresía f
hypocrit|e /'hɪpəkrɪt/ n hipócrita m & f. ~**ical** a hipócrita
hypodermic /haɪpə'dɜ:mɪk/ a hipodérmico. ● n jeringa f hipodérmica
hypothe|sis /haɪ'pɒθəsɪs/ n (pl -theses /-si:z/) hipótesis f. ~**tical** /-ə'θetɪkl/ a hipotético
hysteri|a /hɪ'stɪərɪə/ n histerismo m. ~**cal** /-'terɪkl/ a histérico. ~**cs** /hɪ'sterɪks/ npl histerismo m. have ~**cs** ponerse histérico; (laugh) morir de risa

I

I /aɪ/ pron yo
ice /aɪs/ n hielo m. ● vt helar; glasear ⟨cake⟩. ● vi. ~ (**up**) helarse. ~**berg** n iceberg m, témpano m. ~**cream** n helado m. ~**cube** n cubito m de hielo. ~ **hockey** n hockey m sobre hielo

Iceland /'aɪslənd/ n Islandia f. ~**er** n islandés m. ~**ic** /-'lændɪk/ a islandés
ice lolly /aɪs'lɒlɪ/ polo m, paleta f (LAm)
icicle /'aɪsɪkl/ n carámbano m
icing /'aɪsɪŋ/ n (sugar) azúcar m glaseado
icon /'aɪkɒn/ n icono m
icy /'aɪsɪ/ a (-ier, -iest) glacial
idea /aɪ'dɪə/ n idea f
ideal /aɪ'dɪəl/ a ideal. ● n ideal m. ~**ism** n idealismo m. ~**ist** n idealista m & f. ~**istic** /-'lɪstɪk/ a idealista. ~**ize** vt idealizar. ~**ly** adv idealmente
identical /aɪ'dentɪkl/ a idéntico
identif|ication /aɪdentɪfɪ'keɪʃn/ n identificación f. ~**y** /aɪ'dentɪfaɪ/ vt identificar. ● vi. ~**y with** identificarse con
identikit /aɪ'dentɪkɪt/ n retrato-robot m
identity /aɪ'dentɪtɪ/ n identidad f
ideolog|ical /aɪdɪə'lɒdʒɪkl/ a ideológico. ~**y** /aɪdɪ'ɒlədʒɪ/ n ideología f
idiocy /'ɪdɪəsɪ/ n idiotez f
idiom /'ɪdɪəm/ n locución f. ~**atic** /-'mætɪk/ a idiomático
idiosyncrasy /ɪdɪəʊ'sɪnkrəsɪ/ n idiosincrasia f
idiot /'ɪdɪət/ n idiota m & f. ~**ic** /-'ɒtɪk/ a idiota
idle /'aɪdl/ a (-er, -est) ocioso; (lazy) holgazán; (out of work) desocupado; ⟨machine⟩ parado. ● vi ⟨engine⟩ marchar en vacío. ● vt. ~ **away** perder. ~**ness** n ociosidad f. ~**r** /-ə(r)/ n ocioso m
idol /'aɪdl/ n ídolo m. ~**ize** vt idolatrar
idyllic /ɪ'dɪlɪk/ a idílico
i.e. /aɪ'i:/ abbr (id est) es decir
if /ɪf/ conj si
igloo /'ɪglu:/ n iglú m
ignite /ɪg'naɪt/ vt encender. ● vi encenderse
ignition /ɪg'nɪʃn/ n ignición f; (auto) encendido m. ~ (**switch**) n contacto m
ignoramus /ɪgnə'reɪməs/ n (pl -muses) ignorante
ignoran|ce /'ɪgnərəns/ n ignorancia f. ~**t** a ignorante. ~**tly** adv por ignorancia
ignore /ɪg'nɔ:(r)/ vt no hacer caso de
ilk /ɪlk/ n ralea f
ill /ɪl/ a enfermo; (bad) malo. ~ **will** n mala voluntad f. ● adv mal. ~ **at**

ease inquieto. ● *n* mal *m.* **~ad-vised** *a* imprudente. **~bred** *a* mal educado

illegal /ɪˈliːgl/ *a* ilegal

illegible /ɪˈledʒəbl/ *a* ilegible

illegitima|cy /ɪlɪˈdʒɪtɪməsɪ/ *n* ilegitimidad *f.* **~te** *a* ilegítimo

ill: **~fated** *a* malogrado. **~gotten** *a* mal adquirido

illitera|cy /ɪˈlɪtərəsɪ/ *n* analfabetismo *m.* **~te** *a & n* analfabeto (*m*)

ill: **~natured** *a* poco afable. **~ness** *n* enfermedad *f*

illogical /ɪˈlɒdʒɪkl/ *a* ilógico

ill: **~starred** *a* malogrado. **~treat** *vt* maltratar

illuminat|e /ɪˈluːmɪneɪt/ *vt* iluminar. **~ion** /-ˈneɪʃn/ *n* iluminación *f*

illus|ion /ɪˈluːʒn/ *n* ilusión *f.* **~sory** *a* ilusorio

illustrat|e /ˈɪləstreɪt/ *vt* ilustrar. **~ion** *n* (*example*) ejemplo *m*; (*picture in book*) grabado *m*, lámina *f.* **~ive** *a* ilustrativo

illustrious /ɪˈlʌstrɪəs/ *a* ilustre

image /ˈɪmɪdʒ/ *n* imagen *f.* **~ry** *n* imágenes *fpl*

imagin|able /ɪˈmædʒɪnəbl/ *a* imaginable. **~ary** *a* imaginario. **~ation** /-ˈneɪʃn/ *n* imaginación *f.* **~ative** *a* imaginativo. **~e** *vt* imaginar(se)

imbalance /ɪmˈbæləns/ *n* desequilibrio *m*

imbecil|e /ˈɪmbəsiːl/ *a & n* imbécil (*m & f*). **~ity** /-ˈsɪlətɪ/ *n* imbecilidad *f*

imbibe /ɪmˈbaɪb/ *vt* embeber; (*drink*) beber

imbue /ɪmˈbjuː/ *vt* empapar (**with** de)

imitat|e /ˈɪmɪteɪt/ *vt* imitar. **~ion** /-ˈteɪʃn/ *n* imitación *f.* **~or** *n* imitador *m*

immaculate /ɪˈmækjʊlət/ *a* inmaculado

immaterial /ɪməˈtɪərɪəl/ *a* inmaterial; (*unimportant*) insignificante

immature /ɪməˈtjʊə(r)/ *a* inmaduro

immediate /ɪˈmiːdɪət/ *a* inmediato. **~ly** *adv* inmediatamente. **~ly you hear me** en cuanto me oigas. ● *conj* en cuanto (+ *subj*)

immens|e /ɪˈmens/ *a* inmenso. **~ely** *adv* inmensamente; (*very much*, *fam*) muchísimo. **~ity** *n* inmensidad *f*

immers|e /ɪˈmɜːs/ *vt* sumergir. **~ion** /ɪˈmɜːʃn/ *n* inmersión *f.* **~ion heater** *n* calentador *m* de inmersión

immigra|nt /ˈɪmɪgrənt/ *a & n* inmigrante (*m & f*). **~te** *vi* inmigrar. **~tion** /-ˈɡreɪʃn/ *n* inmigración *f*

imminen|ce /ˈɪmɪnəns/ *n* inminencia *f.* **~t** *a* inminente

immobil|e /ɪˈməʊbaɪl/ *a* inmóvil. **~ize** /-bɪlaɪz/ *vt* inmovilizar

immoderate /ɪˈmɒdərət/ *a* inmoderado

immodest /ɪˈmɒdɪst/ *a* inmodesto

immoral /ɪˈmɒrəl/ *a* inmoral. **~ity** /ɪməˈrælətɪ/ *n* inmoralidad *f*

immortal /ɪˈmɔːtl/ *a* inmortal. **~ity** /-ˈtælətɪ/ *n* inmortalidad *f.* **~ize** *vt* inmortalizar

immun|e /ɪˈmjuːn/ *a* inmune (**from**, **to** a, contra). **~ity** *n* inmunidad *f.* **~ization** /ɪmjʊnaɪˈzeɪʃn/ *n* inmunización *f.* **~ize** *vt* inmunizar

imp /ɪmp/ *n* diablillo *m*

impact /ˈɪmpækt/ *n* impacto *m*

impair /ɪmˈpeə(r)/ *vt* perjudicar

impale /ɪmˈpeɪl/ *vt* empalar

impart /ɪmˈpɑːt/ *vt* comunicar

impartial /ɪmˈpɑːʃl/ *a* imparcial. **~ity** /-ɪˈælətɪ/ *n* imparcialidad *f*

impassable /ɪmˈpɑːsəbl/ *a* ⟨*barrier etc*⟩ infranqueable; ⟨*road*⟩ impracticable

impasse /æmˈpɑːs/ *n* callejón *m* sin salida

impassioned /ɪmˈpæʃnd/ *a* apasionado

impassive /ɪmˈpæsɪv/ *a* impasible

impatien|ce /ɪmˈpeɪʃəns/ *n* impaciencia *f.* **~t** *a* impaciente. **~tly** *adv* con impaciencia

impeach /ɪmˈpiːtʃ/ *vt* acusar

impeccable /ɪmˈpekəbl/ *a* impecable

impede /ɪmˈpiːd/ *vt* estorbar

impediment /ɪmˈpedɪmənt/ *n* obstáculo *m.* (**speech**) **~** *n* defecto *m* del habla

impel /ɪmˈpel/ *vt* (*pt* **impelled**) impeler

impending /ɪmˈpendɪŋ/ *a* inminente

impenetrable /ɪmˈpenɪtrəbl/ *a* impenetrable

imperative /ɪmˈperətɪv/ *a* imprescindible. ● *n* (*gram*) imperativo *m*

imperceptible /ɪmpəˈseptəbl/ *a* imperceptible

imperfect /ɪmˈpɜːfɪkt/ *a* imperfecto. **~ion** /-ˈfekʃn/ *n* imperfección *f*

imperial /ɪmˈpɪərɪəl/ *a* imperial. **~ism** *n* imperialismo *m*

imperil /ɪm'perəl/ vt (pt **imperilled**) poner en peligro

imperious /ɪm'pɪərɪəs/ a imperioso

impersonal /ɪm'pɜːsənl/ a impersonal

impersonat|e /ɪm'pɜːsəneɪt/ vt hacerse pasar por; (mimic) imitar. **~ion** /-'neɪʃn/ n imitación f. **~or** n imitador m

impertinen|ce /ɪm'pɜːtɪnəns/ n impertinencia f. **~t** a impertinente. **~tly** adv impertinentemente

impervious /ɪm'pɜːvɪəs/ a. **~ to** impermeable a; (fig) insensible a

impetuous /ɪm'petjʊəs/ a impetuoso

impetus /'ɪmpɪtəs/ n ímpetu m

impinge /ɪm'pɪndʒ/ vi. **~ on** afectar a

impish /'ɪmpɪʃ/ a travieso

implacable /ɪm'plækəbl/ a implacable

implant /ɪm'plɑːnt/ vt implantar

implement /'ɪmplɪmənt/ n herramienta f. /'ɪmplɪment/ vt realizar

implicat|e /'ɪmplɪkeɪt/ vt implicar. **~ion** /-'keɪʃn/ n implicación f

implicit /ɪm'plɪsɪt/ a (implied) implícito; (unquestioning) absoluto

implied /ɪm'plaɪd/ a implícito

implore /ɪm'plɔː(r)/ vt implorar

imply /ɪm'plaɪ/ vt implicar; (mean) querer decir; (insinuate) dar a entender

impolite /ɪmpə'laɪt/ a mal educado

imponderable /ɪm'pɒndərəbl/ a & n imponderable (m)

import /ɪm'pɔːt/ vt importar. /'ɪmpɔːt/ n (article) importación f; (meaning) significación f

importan|ce /ɪm'pɔːtəns/ n importancia f. **~t** a importante

importation /ɪmpɔː'teɪʃn/ n importación f

importer /ɪm'pɔːtə(r)/ n importador m

impose /ɪm'pəʊz/ vt imponer. ● vi. **~ on** abusar de la amabilidad de

imposing /ɪm'pəʊzɪŋ/ a imponente

imposition /ɪmpə'zɪʃn/ n imposición f; (fig) molestia f

impossib|ility /ɪmpɒsə'bɪlətɪ/ n imposibilidad f. **~le** a imposible

impostor /ɪm'pɒstə(r)/ n impostor m

impoten|ce /'ɪmpətəns/ n impotencia f. **~t** a impotente

impound /ɪm'paʊnd/ vt confiscar

impoverish /ɪm'pɒvərɪʃ/ vt empobrecer

impracticable /ɪm'præktɪkəbl/ a impracticable

impractical /ɪm'præktɪkl/ a poco práctico

imprecise /ɪmprɪ'saɪs/ a impreciso

impregnable /ɪm'pregnəbl/ a inexpugnable

impregnate /'ɪmpregneɪt/ vt impregnar (with de)

impresario /ɪmprɪ'sɑːrɪəʊ/ n (pl **-os**) empresario m

impress /ɪm'pres/ vt impresionar; (imprint) imprimir. **~ on s.o.** hacer entender a uno

impression /ɪm'preʃn/ n impresión f. **~able** a impresionable

impressive /ɪm'presɪv/ a impresionante

imprint /'ɪmprɪnt/ n impresión f. /ɪm'prɪnt/ vt imprimir

imprison /ɪm'prɪzn/ vt encarcelar. **~ment** n encarcelamiento m

improbab|ility /ɪmprɒbə'bɪlətɪ/ n improbabilidad f. **~le** a improbable

impromptu /ɪm'prɒmptjuː/ a improvisado. ● adv de improviso

improper /ɪm'prɒpə(r)/ a impropio; (incorrect) incorrecto

impropriety /ɪmprə'praɪətɪ/ n inconveniencia f

improve /ɪm'pruːv/ vt mejorar. ● vi mejorar(se). **~ment** n mejora f

improvis|ation /ɪmprəvaɪ'zeɪʃn/ n improvisación f. **~e** vt/i improvisar

imprudent /ɪm'pruːdənt/ a imprudente

impuden|ce /'ɪmpjʊdəns/ n insolencia f. **~t** a insolente

impulse /'ɪmpʌls/ n impulso m. **on ~** sin reflexionar

impulsive /ɪm'pʌlsɪv/ a irreflexivo. **~ly** adv sin reflexionar

impunity /ɪm'pjuːnətɪ/ n impunidad f. **with ~** impunemente

impur|e /ɪm'pjʊə(r)/ a impuro. **~ity** n impureza f

impute /ɪm'pjuːt/ vt imputar

in /ɪn/ prep en, dentro de. **~ a firm manner** de una manera terminante. **~ an hour('s time)** dentro de una hora. **~ doing** al hacer. **~ so far as** en cuanto que. **~ the evening** por la tarde. **~ the main** por la mayor parte. **~ the rain** bajo la lluvia. **~ the sun** al sol. **one ~ ten** uno de cada diez. **the best ~** el mejor de. ● adv (inside) dentro; (at home) en

casa; (*in fashion*) de moda. ● *n.* the
~s and outs of los detalles *mpl* de

inability /ɪnəˈbɪlətɪ/ *n* incapacidad *f*

inaccessible /ɪnækˈsesəbl/ *a*
inaccesible

inaccura|cy /ɪnˈækjʊrəsɪ/ *n* inex-
actitud *f.* ~te *a* inexacto

inaction /ɪnˈækʃn/ *n* inacción *f*

inactiv|e /ɪnˈæktɪv/ *a* inactivo. ~ity
/-ˈtɪvətɪ/ *n* inactividad *f*

inadequa|cy /ɪnˈædɪkwəsɪ/ *a*
insuficiencia *f.* ~te *a* insuficiente

inadmissible /ɪnədˈmɪsəbl/ *a*
inadmisible

inadvertently /ɪnədˈvɜːtntlɪ/ *adv*
por descuido

inadvisable /ɪnədˈvaɪzəbl/ *a* no
aconsejable

inane /ɪˈneɪn/ *a* estúpido

inanimate /ɪnˈænɪmət/ *a* inanimado

inappropriate /ɪnəˈprəʊprɪət/ *a*
inoportuno

inarticulate /ɪnɑːˈtɪkjʊlət/ *a* incapaz
de expresarse claramente

inasmuch as /ɪnəzˈmʌtʃəz/ *adv* ya
que

inattentive /ɪnəˈtentɪv/ *a* desatento

inaudible /ɪnˈɔːdəbl/ *a* inaudible

inaugural /ɪˈnɔːgjʊrəl/ *a* inaugural

inaugurat|e /ɪˈnɔːgjʊreɪt/ *vt* in-
augurar. ~ion /-ˈreɪʃn/ *n* inauguración *f*

inauspicious /ɪnɔːˈspɪʃəs/ *a* poco
propicio

inborn /ˈɪnbɔːn/ *a* innato

inbred /ɪnˈbred/ *a* (*inborn*) innato

incalculable /ɪnˈkælkjʊləbl/ *a*
incalculable

incapab|ility /ɪnkeɪpəˈbɪlətɪ/ *n* inca-
pacidad *f.* ~le *a* incapaz

incapacit|ate /ɪnkəˈpæsɪteɪt/ *vt* inca-
pacitar. ~y *n* incapacidad *f*

incarcerat|e /ɪnˈkɑːsəreɪt/ *vt* encar-
celar. ~ion /-ˈreɪʃn/ *n* encarcelamiento *m*

incarnat|e /ɪnˈkɑːnət/ *a* encarnado.
~ion /-ˈneɪʃn/ *n* encarnación *f*

incautious /ɪnˈkɔːʃəs/ *a* incauto. ~ly
adv incautamente

incendiary /ɪnˈsendɪərɪ/ *a* incendiario. ● *n* (*person*) incendiario *m*;
(*bomb*) bomba *f* incendiaria

incense[1] /ˈɪnsens/ *n* incienso *m*

incense[2] /ɪnˈsens/ *vt* enfurecer

incentive /ɪnˈsentɪv/ *n* incentivo *m*;
(*payment*) prima *f* de incentivo

inception /ɪnˈsepʃn/ *n* principio *m*

incertitude /ɪnˈsɜːtɪtjuːd/ *n* incertidumbre *f*

incessant /ɪnˈsesnt/ *a* incesante.
~ly *adv* sin cesar

incest /ˈɪnsest/ *n* incesto *m.* ~uous
/-ˈsestjʊəs/ *a* incestuoso

inch /ɪntʃ/ *n* pulgada *f* (= 2,54cm).
● *vi* avanzar palmo a palmo

incidence /ˈɪnsɪdəns/ *n* frecuencia *f*

incident /ˈɪnsɪdənt/ *n* incidente *m*

incidental /ɪnsɪˈdentl/ *a* fortuito.
~ly *adv* incidentemente; (*by the
way*) a propósito

incinerat|e /ɪnˈsɪnəreɪt/ *vt*
incinerar. ~or *n* incinerador *m*

incipient /ɪnˈsɪpɪənt/ *a* incipiente

incision /ɪnˈsɪʒn/ *n* incisión *f*

incisive /ɪnˈsaɪsɪv/ *a* incisivo

incite /ɪnˈsaɪt/ *vt* incitar. ~ment *n*
incitación *f*

inclement /ɪnˈklemənt/ *a* incle-
mente

inclination /ɪnklɪˈneɪʃn/ *n* inclinación *f*

incline[1] /ɪnˈklaɪn/ *vt* inclinar. ● *vi*
inclinarse. be ~d to tener ten-
dencia a

incline[2] /ˈɪnklaɪn/ *n* cuesta *f*

inclu|de /ɪnˈkluːd/ *vt* incluir. ~ding
prep incluso. ~sion /-ʒn/ *n* inclu-
sión *f*

inclusive /ɪnˈkluːsɪv/ *a* inclusivo. be
~ of incluir. ● *adv* inclusive

incognito /ɪnkɒgˈniːtəʊ/ *adv* de
incógnito

incoherent /ɪnkəʊˈhɪərənt/ *a* in-
coherente

income /ˈɪnkʌm/ *n* ingresos *mpl.* ~
tax *n* impuesto *m* sobre la renta

incoming /ˈɪnkʌmɪŋ/ *a* ⟨tide⟩ ascendente; ⟨tenant etc⟩ nuevo

incomparable /ɪnˈkɒmpərəbl/ *a* incomparable

incompatible /ɪnkəmˈpætəbl/ *a* incompatible

incompeten|ce /ɪnˈkɒmpɪtəns/ *n*
incompetencia *f.* ~t *a* incompetente

incomplete /ɪnkəmˈpliːt/ *a* incompleto

incomprehensible /ɪnkɒmprɪ-
ˈhensəbl/ *a* incomprensible

inconceivable /ɪnkənˈsiːvəbl/ *a* inconcebible

inconclusive /ɪnkənˈkluːsɪv/ *a* poco
concluyente

incongruous /ɪnˈkɒŋgrʊəs/ *a* incongruente

inconsequential /ɪnkɒnsɪˈkwenʃl/ *a*
sin importancia

inconsiderate /ɪnkən'sɪdərət/ a desconsiderado

inconsisten|cy /ɪnkən'sɪstənsɪ/ n inconsecuencia f. ~t a inconsecuente. be ~t with no concordar con

inconspicuous /ɪnkən'spɪkjʊəs/ a que no llama la atención. ~ly adv sin llamar la atención

incontinen|ce /ɪn'kɒntɪnəns/ a incontinencia f. ~t a incontinente

inconvenien|ce /ɪnkən'vi:nɪəns/ a incomodidad f; (drawback) inconveniente m. ~t a incómodo; ⟨time⟩ inoportuno

incorporat|e /ɪn'kɔ:pəreɪt/ vt incorporar; (include) incluir. ~ion /-'reɪʃn/ n incorporación f

incorrect /ɪnkə'rekt/ a incorrecto

incorrigible /ɪn'kɒrɪdʒəbl/ a incorregible

incorruptible /ɪnkə'rʌptəbl/ a incorruptible

increase /'ɪnkri:s/ n aumento m (in, of de). /ɪn'kri:s/ vt/i aumentar

increasing /ɪn'kri:sɪŋ/ a creciente. ~ly adv cada vez más

incredible /ɪn'kredəbl/ a increíble

incredulous /ɪn'kredjʊləs/ a incrédulo

increment /'ɪnkrɪmənt/ n aumento m

incriminat|e /ɪn'krɪmɪneɪt/ vt acriminar. ~ing a acriminador

incubat|e /'ɪŋkjʊbeɪt/ vt incubar. ~ion /-'beɪʃn/ n incubación f. ~or n incubadora f

inculcate /'ɪnkʌlkeɪt/ vt inculcar

incumbent /ɪn'kʌmbənt/ n titular. ● a. be ~ on incumbir a

incur /ɪn'kɜ:(r)/ vt (pt incurred) incurrir en; contraer ⟨debts⟩

incurable /ɪn'kjʊərəbl/ a incurable

incursion /ɪn'kɜ:ʃn/ n incursión f

indebted /ɪn'detɪd/ a. ~ to s.o. estar en deuda con uno

indecen|cy /ɪn'di:snsɪ/ n indecencia f. ~t a indecente

indecisi|on /ɪndɪ'sɪʒn/ n indecisión f. ~ve /ɪndɪ'saɪsɪv/ a indeciso

indeed /ɪn'di:d/ adv en efecto; (really?) ¿de veras?

indefatigable /ɪndɪ'fætɪgəbl/ a incansable

indefinable /ɪndɪ'faɪnəbl/ a indefinible

indefinite /ɪn'defɪnət/ a indefinido. ~ly adv indefinidamente

indelible /ɪn'delɪbl/ a indeleble

indemni|fy /ɪn'demnɪfaɪ/ vt indemnizar. ~ty /-ətɪ/ n indemnización f

indent /ɪn'dent/ vt endentar ⟨text⟩. ~ation /-'teɪʃn/ n mella f

independen|ce /ɪndɪ'pendəns/ n independencia f. ~t a independiente. ~tly adv independientemente. ~tly of independientemente de

indescribable /ɪndɪ'skraɪbəbl/ a indescriptible

indestructible /ɪndɪ'strʌktəbl/ a indestructible

indeterminate /ɪndɪ'tɜ:mɪnət/ a indeterminado

index /'ɪndeks/ n (pl indexes) índice m. ● vt poner índice a; (enter in the/ an index) poner en el/un índice. ~ finger n (dedo m) índice m. ~-linked a indexado

India /'ɪndɪə/ n la India f. ~n a & n indio (m). ~n summer n veranillo m de San Martín

indicat|e /'ɪndɪkeɪt/ vt indicar. ~ion /-'keɪʃn/ n indicación f. ~ive /ɪn'dɪkətɪv/ a &~n indicativo (m). ~or /'ɪndɪkeɪtə(r)/ n indicador m

indict /ɪn'daɪt/ vt acusar. ~ment n acusación f

indifferen|ce /ɪn'dɪfrəns/ n indiferencia f. ~t a indiferente; (not good) mediocre

indigenous /ɪn'dɪdʒɪnəs/ a indígena

indigesti|ble /ɪndɪ'dʒestəbl/ a indigesto. ~on /-tʃən/ n indigestión f

indigna|nt /ɪn'dɪgnənt/ a indignado. ~tion /-'neɪʃn/ n indignación f

indignity /ɪn'dɪgnətɪ/ n indignidad f

indigo /'ɪndɪgəʊ/ n añil (m)

indirect /ɪndɪ'rekt/ a indirecto. ~ly adv indirectamente

indiscre|et /ɪndɪ'skri:t/ a indiscreto. ~tion /-'kreʃn/ n indiscreción f

indiscriminate /ɪndɪ'skrɪmɪnət/ a indistinto. ~ly adv indistintamente

indispensable /ɪndɪ'spensəbl/ a imprescindible

indispos|ed /ɪndɪ'spəʊzd/ a indispuesto. ~ition /-ə'zɪʃn/ n indisposición f

indisputable /ɪndɪ'spju:təbl/ a indiscutible

indissoluble /ɪndɪ'sɒljʊbl/ a indisoluble

indistinct /ɪndɪ'stɪŋkt/ a indistinto

indistinguishable /ɪndɪ'stɪŋgwɪʃəbl/ a indistinguible

individual /ɪndɪ'vɪdjʊəl/ a individual. ● n individuo m. ~ist n individualista m & · f. ~ity n individualidad *f*. ~ly *adv* individualmente

indivisible /ɪndɪˈvɪzəbl/ *a* indivisible

Indo-China /ˌɪndəʊˈtʃaɪnə/ *n* Indochina *f*

indoctrinat|e /ɪnˈdɒktrɪneɪt/ *vt* adoctrinar. ~ion /-ˈneɪʃn/ *n* adoctrinamiento *m*

indolen|ce /ˈɪndələns/ *n* indolencia *f*. ~t *a* indolente

indomitable /ɪnˈdɒmɪtəbl/ *a* indomable

Indonesia /ˌɪndəʊˈniːzɪə/ *n* Indonesia *f*. ~n *a* & *n* indonesio (*m*)

indoor /ˈɪndɔː(r)/ *a* interior; ‹*clothes etc*› de casa; (*covered*) cubierto. ~s *adv* dentro; (*at home*) en casa

induce /ɪnˈdjuːs/ *vt* inducir; (*cause*) provocar. ~ment *n* incentivo *m*

induct /ɪnˈdʌkt/ *vt* instalar; (*mil*, *Amer*) incorporar

indulge /ɪnˈdʌldʒ/ *vt* satisfacer ‹*desires*›; complacer ‹*person*›. ● *vi*. ~ **in** entregarse a. ~nce /ɪnˈdʌldʒəns/ *n* (*of desires*) satisfacción *f*; (*relig*) indulgencia *f*. ~nt *a* indulgente

industrial /ɪnˈdʌstrɪəl/ *a* industrial; ‹*unrest*› laboral. ~ist *n* industrial *m* & *f*. ~ized *a* industrializado

industrious /ɪnˈdʌstrɪəs/ *a* trabajador

industry /ˈɪndəstrɪ/ *n* industria *f*; (*zeal*) aplicación *f*

inebriated /ɪˈniːbrɪeɪtɪd/ *a* borracho

inedible /ɪnˈedɪbl/ *a* incomible

ineffable /ɪnˈefəbl/ *a* inefable

ineffective /ɪnɪˈfektɪv/ *a* ineficaz; ‹*person*› incapaz

ineffectual /ɪnɪˈfektjʊəl/ *a* ineficaz

inefficien|cy /ɪnɪˈfɪʃnsɪ/ *n* ineficacia *f*; (*of person*) incompetencia *f*. ~t *a* ineficaz; ‹*person*› incompetente

ineligible /ɪnˈelɪdʒəbl/ *a* inelegible. **be ~ for** no tener derecho a

inept /ɪˈnept/ *a* inepto

inequality /ɪnɪˈkwɒlətɪ/ *n* desigualdad *f*

inert /ɪˈnɜːt/ *a* inerte

inertia /ɪˈnɜːʃə/ *n* inercia *f*

inescapable /ɪnɪˈskeɪpəbl/ *a* ineludible

inestimable /ɪnˈestɪməbl/ *a* inestimable

inevitabl|e /ɪnˈevɪtəbl/ *a* inevitable. ~ly *adv* inevitablemente

inexact /ɪnɪgˈzækt/ *a* inexacto

inexcusable /ɪnɪkˈskjuːsəbl/ *a* imperdonable

inexhaustible /ɪnɪgˈzɔːstəbl/ *a* inagotable

inexorable /ɪnˈeksərəbl/ *a* inexorable

inexpensive /ɪnɪkˈspensɪv/ *a* económico, barato

inexperience /ɪnɪkˈspɪərɪəns/ *n* falta *f* de experiencia. ~d *a* inexperto

inexplicable /ɪnɪkˈsplɪkəbl/ *a* inexplicable

inextricable /ɪnɪkˈstrɪkəbl/ *a* inextricable

infallib|ility /ɪnˈfæləbɪlətɪ/ *n* infalibilidad *f*. ~le *a* infalible

infam|ous /ˈɪnfəməs/ *a* infame. ~y *n* infamia *f*

infan|cy /ˈɪnfənsɪ/ *n* infancia *f*. ~t *n* niño *m*. ~tile /ˈɪnfəntaɪl/ *a* infantil

infantry /ˈɪnfəntrɪ/ *n* infantería *f*

infatuat|ed /ɪnˈfætjʊeɪtɪd/ *a*. **be ~ed with** encapricharse por. ~ion /-ˈeɪʃn/ *n* encaprichamiento *m*

infect /ɪnˈfekt/ *vt* infectar; (*fig*) contagiar. ~ **s.o. with** contagiar a uno. ~ion /-ˈfekʃn/ *n* infección *f*; (*fig*) contagio *m*. ~ious /ɪnˈfekʃəs/ *a* contagioso

infer /ɪnˈfɜː(r)/ *vt* (*pt* **inferred**) deducir. ~ence /ˈɪnfərəns/ *n* deducción *f*

inferior /ɪnˈfɪərɪə(r)/ *a* inferior. ● *n* inferior *m* & *f*. ~ity /-ˈɒrətɪ/ *n* inferioridad *f*

infernal /ɪnˈfɜːnl/ *a* infernal. ~ly *adv* (*fam*) atrozmente

inferno /ɪnˈfɜːnəʊ/ *n* (*pl* **-os**) infierno *m*

infertil|e /ɪnˈfɜːtaɪl/ *a* estéril. ~ity /-ˈtɪlətɪ/ *n* esterilidad *f*

infest /ɪnˈfest/ *vt* infestar. ~ation /-ˈsteɪʃn/ *n* infestación *f*

infidelity /ɪnfɪˈdelətɪ/ *n* infidelidad *f*

infighting /ˈɪnfaɪtɪŋ/ *n* lucha *f* cuerpo a cuerpo; (*fig*) riñas *fpl* (internas)

infiltrat|e /ˈɪnfɪlˈtreɪt/ *vt* infiltrar. ● *vi* infiltrarse. ~ion /-ˈtreɪʃn/ *n* infiltración *f*

infinite /ˈɪnfɪnət/ *a* infinito. ~ly *adv* infinitamente

infinitesimal /ɪnfɪnɪˈtesɪml/ *a* infinitesimal

infinitive /ɪnˈfɪnɪtɪv/ *n* infinitivo *m*

infinity /ɪnˈfɪnətɪ/ *n* (*infinite distance*) infinito *m*; (*infinite quantity*) infinidad *f*

infirm /ɪnˈfɜːm/ *a* enfermizo

infirmary /ɪnˈfɜːmərɪ/ *n* hospital *m*; (*sick bay*) enfermería *f*

infirmity /ɪnˈfɜːmətɪ/ n enfermedad f; (weakness) debilidad f

inflam|e /ɪnˈfleɪm/ vt inflamar. ~**mable** /ɪnˈflæməbl/ a inflamable. ~**mation** /-əˈmeɪʃn/ n inflamación f. ~**matory** /ɪnˈflæmətərɪ/ a inflamatorio

inflate /ɪnˈfleɪt/ vt inflar

inflation /ɪnˈfleɪʃn/ n inflación f. ~**ary** a inflacionario

inflection /ɪnˈflekʃn/ n inflexión f

inflexible /ɪnˈfleksəbl/ a inflexible

inflict /ɪnˈflɪkt/ vt infligir (on a)

inflow /ˈɪnfləʊ/ n afluencia f

influence /ˈɪnflʊəns/ n influencia f. **under the** ~ (drunk, fam) borracho. ● vt influir, influenciar (esp LAm)

influential /ɪnflʊˈenʃl/ a influyente

influenza /ɪnflʊˈenzə/ n gripe f

influx /ˈɪnflʌks/ n afluencia f

inform /ɪnˈfɔːm/ vt informar. **keep** ~**ed** tener al corriente

informal /ɪnˈfɔːml/ a (simple) sencillo, sin ceremonia; (unofficial) oficioso. ~**ity** /ˈmælətɪ/ n falta f de ceremonia. ~**ly** adv sin ceremonia

inform|ant /ɪnˈfɔːmənt/ n informador m. ~**ation** /ɪnfəˈmeɪʃn/ n información f. ~**ative** /ɪnˈfɔːmətɪv/ a informativo. ~**er** /ɪnˈfɔːmə(r)/ n denunciante m

infra-red /ɪnfrəˈred/ a infrarrojo

infrequent /ɪnˈfriːkwənt/ a poco frecuente. ~**ly** adv raramente

infringe /ɪnˈfrɪndʒ/ vt infringir. ~ **on** usurpar. ~**ment** n infracción f

infuriate /ɪnˈfjʊərɪeɪt/ vt enfurecer

infus|e /ɪnˈfjuːz/ vt infundir. ~**ion** /-ʒn/ n infusión f

ingen|ious /ɪnˈdʒiːnɪəs/ a ingenioso. ~**uity** /ɪndʒɪˈnjuːətɪ/ n ingeniosidad f

ingenuous /ɪnˈdʒenjʊəs/ a ingenuo

ingest /ɪnˈdʒest/ vt ingerir

ingot /ˈɪŋgət/ n lingote m

ingrained /ɪnˈgreɪnd/ a arraigado

ingratiate /ɪnˈgreɪʃɪeɪt/ vt. ~ **o.s. with** congraciarse con

ingratitude /ɪnˈgrætɪtjuːd/ n ingratitud f

ingredient /ɪnˈgriːdɪənt/ n ingrediente m

ingrowing /ˈɪngrəʊɪŋ/ a. ~ **nail** uñero m, uña f encarnada

inhabit /ɪnˈhæbɪt/ vt habitar. ~**able** a habitable. ~**ant** n habitante m

inhale /ɪnˈheɪl/ vt aspirar. ● vi (tobacco) aspirar el humo

inherent /ɪnˈhɪərənt/ a inherente. ~**ly** adv intrínsecamente

inherit /ɪnˈherɪt/ vt heredar. ~**ance** n herencia f

inhibit /ɪnˈhɪbɪt/ vt inhibir. **be** ~**ed** tener inhibiciones. ~**ion** /-ˈbɪʃn/ n inhibición f

inhospitable /ɪnhəˈspɪtəbl/ a (place) inhóspito; (person) inhospitalario

inhuman /ɪnˈhjuːmən/ a inhumano. ~**e** /ɪnhjuːˈmeɪn/ a inhumano. ~**ity** /ɪnhjuːˈmænətɪ/ n inhumanidad f

inimical /ɪˈnɪmɪkl/ a hostil

inimitable /ɪˈnɪmɪtəbl/ a inimitable

iniquit|ous /ɪˈnɪkwɪtəs/ a inicuo. ~**y** /-ətɪ/ n iniquidad f

initial /ɪˈnɪʃl/ n inicial f. ● vt (pt **initialled**) firmar con iniciales. **he** ~**led the document** firmó el documento con sus iniciales. ● a inicial. ~**ly** adv al principio

initiat|e /ɪˈnɪʃɪeɪt/ vt iniciar; promover (scheme etc). ~**ion** /-ˈeɪʃn/ n iniciación f

initiative /ɪˈnɪʃətɪv/ n iniciativa f

inject /ɪnˈdʒekt/ vt inyectar; (fig) injertar (new element). ~**ion** /-ʃn/ n inyección f

injunction /ɪnˈdʒʌŋkʃn/ n (court order) entredicho m

injur|e /ˈɪndʒə(r)/ vt (wound) herir; (fig, damage) perjudicar. ~**y** /ˈɪndʒərɪ/ n herida f; (damage) perjuicio m

injustice /ɪnˈdʒʌstɪs/ n injusticia f

ink /ɪŋk/ n tinta f

inkling /ˈɪŋklɪŋ/ n atisbo m

ink: ~**well** n tintero m. ~**y** a manchado de tinta

inland /ˈɪnlənd/ a interior. ● adv tierra adentro. **I**~ **Revenue** n Hacienda f

in-laws /ˈɪnlɔːz/ npl parientes mpl políticos

inlay /ɪnˈleɪ/ vt (pt **inlaid**) taracear, incrustar. /ˈɪnleɪ/ n taracea f, incrustación f

inlet /ˈɪnlet/ n ensenada f; (tec) entrada f

inmate /ˈɪnmeɪt/ n (of asylum) internado m; (of prison) preso m

inn /ɪn/ n posada f

innards /ˈɪnədz/ npl tripas fpl

innate /ɪˈneɪt/ a innato

inner /ˈɪnə(r)/ a interior; (fig) íntimo. ~**most** a más íntimo. ~**tube** n cámara f de aire, llanta f (LAm)

innings /ˈɪnɪŋz/ n invar turno m

innkeeper /ˈɪnkiːpə(r)/ n posadero m

innocen|ce /ˈɪnəsns/ n inocencia f. **~t** a & n inocente (m & f)

innocuous /ɪˈnɒkjʊəs/ a inocuo

innovat|e /ˈɪnəveɪt/ vi innovar. **~ion** /-ˈveɪʃn/ n innovación f. **~or** n innovador m

innuendo /ɪnjuˈendəʊ/ n (pl -oes) insinuación f

innumerable /ɪˈnjuːmərəbl/ a innumerable

inoculat|e /ɪˈnɒkjʊleɪt/ vt inocular. **~ion** /-ˈleɪʃn/ n inoculación f

inoffensive /ɪnəˈfensɪv/ a inofensivo

inoperative /ɪnˈɒpərətɪv/ a inoperante

inopportune /ɪnˈɒpətjuːn/ a inoportuno

inordinate /ɪˈnɔːdɪnət/ a excesivo. **~ly** adv excesivamente

in-patient /ˈɪnpeɪʃnt/ n paciente m interno

input /ˈɪnpʊt/ n (data) datos mpl; (comput process) entrada f, input m; (elec) energía f

inquest /ˈɪnkwest/ n investigación f judicial

inquir|e /ɪnˈkwaɪə(r)/ vi preguntar. **~y** n (question) pregunta f; (investigation) investigación f

inquisition /ɪnkwɪˈzɪʃn/ n inquisición f

inquisitive /ɪnˈkwɪzətɪv/ a inquisitivo

inroad /ˈɪnrəʊd/ n incursión f

inrush /ˈɪnrʌʃ/ n irrupción f

insan|e /ɪnˈseɪn/ a loco. **~ity** /-ˈsænətɪ/ n locura f

insanitary /ɪnˈsænɪtərɪ/ a insalubre

insatiable /ɪnˈseɪʃəbl/ a insaciable

inscri|be /ɪnˈskraɪb/ vt inscribir; dedicar ⟨book⟩. **~ption** /-ɪpʃn/ n inscripción f; (in book) dedicatoria f

inscrutable /ɪnˈskruːtəbl/ a inescrutable

insect /ˈɪnsekt/ n insecto m. **~icide** /ɪnˈsektɪsaɪd/ n insecticida f

insecur|e /ɪnsɪˈkjʊə(r)/ a inseguro. **~ity** n inseguridad f

insemination /ɪnsemɪˈneɪʃn/ n inseminación f

insensible /ɪnˈsensəbl/ a insensible; (unconscious) sin conocimiento

insensitive /ɪnˈsensətɪv/ a insensible

inseparable /ɪnˈsepərəbl/ a inseparable

insert /ˈɪnsɜːt/ n materia f insertada. /ɪnˈsɜːt/ vt insertar. **~ion** /-ʃn/ n inserción f

inshore /ɪnˈʃɔː(r)/ a costero

inside /ɪnˈsaɪd/ n interior m. **~ out** al revés; (thoroughly) a fondo. ● a interior. ● adv dentro. ● prep dentro de. **~s** npl tripas fpl

insidious /ɪnˈsɪdɪəs/ a insidioso

insight /ˈɪnsaɪt/ n (perception) penetración f, revelación f

insignia /ɪnˈsɪgnɪə/ npl insignias fpl

insignificant /ɪnsɪgˈnɪfɪkənt/ a insignificante

insincer|e /ɪnsɪnˈsɪə(r)/ a poco sincero. **~ity** /-ˈserətɪ/ n falta f de sinceridad f

insinuat|e /ɪnˈsɪnjʊeɪt/ vt insinuar. **~ion** /-ˈeɪʃn/ n insinuación f

insipid /ɪnˈsɪpɪd/ a insípido

insist /ɪnˈsɪst/ vt/i insistir. **~ on** insistir en; (demand) exigir

insisten|ce /ɪnˈsɪstəns/ n insistencia f. **~t** a insistente. **~tly** adv con insistencia

insolen|ce /ˈɪnsələns/ n insolencia f. **~t** a insolente

insoluble /ɪnˈsɒljʊbl/ a insoluble

insolvent /ɪnˈsɒlvənt/ a insolvente

insomnia /ɪnˈsɒmnɪə/ n insomnio m. **~c** /-ræk/ n insomne m & f

inspect /ɪnˈspekt/ vt inspeccionar; revisar ⟨ticket⟩. **~ion** /-ʃn/ n inspección f. **~or** n inspector m; (on train, bus) revisor m

inspir|ation /ɪnspəˈreɪʃn/ n inspiración f. **~e** /ɪnˈspaɪə(r)/ vt inspirar

instability /ɪnstəˈbɪlətɪ/ n inestabilidad f

install /ɪnˈstɔːl/ vt instalar. **~ation** /-əˈleɪʃn/ n instalación f

instalment /ɪnˈstɔːlmənt/ n (payment) plazo m; (of serial) entrega f

instance /ˈɪnstəns/ n ejemplo m; (case) caso m. **for ~** por ejemplo. **in the first ~** en primer lugar

instant /ˈɪnstənt/ a inmediato; ⟨food⟩ instantáneo. ● n instante m. **~aneous** /ɪnstənˈteɪnɪəs/ a instantáneo. **~ly** /ˈɪnstəntlɪ/ adv inmediatamente

instead /ɪnˈsted/ adv en cambio. **~ of doing** en vez de hacer. **~ of s.o.** en lugar de uno

instep /ˈɪnstep/ n empeine m

instigat|e /ˈɪnstɪgeɪt/ vt instigar. **~ion** /-ˈgeɪʃn/ n instigación f. **~or** n instigador m

instil /ɪnˈstɪl/ vt (pt instilled) infundir

instinct /ˈɪnstɪŋkt/ n instinto m. **~ive** /ɪnˈstɪŋktɪv/ a instintivo

institut|e /'ɪnstɪtjuːt/ n instituto m.
● vt instituir; iniciar ⟨enquiry etc⟩.
∼ion /-'tjuːʃn/ n institución f
instruct /ɪn'strʌkt/ vt instruir;
(order) mandar. ∼ s.o. in sth
enseñar algo a uno. ∼ion /-ʃn/ n
instrucción f. ∼ions /-ʃnz/ npl (for
use) modo m de empleo. ∼ive a
instructivo
instrument /'ɪnstrəmənt/ n instrumento m. ∼al /ɪnstrə'mentl/ a
instrumental. **be** ∼al in contribuir
a. ∼alist n instrumentalista m & f
insubordinat|e /ɪnsə'bɔːdɪnət/ a
insubordinado. ∼ion /-'neɪʃn/ n
insubordinación f
insufferable /ɪn'sʌfərəbl/ a insufrible, insoportable
insufficient /ɪnsə'fɪʃnt/ a insuficiente. ∼ly adv insuficientemente
insular /'ɪnsjʊlə(r)/ a insular;
(narrow-minded) de miras
estrechas
insulat|e /'ɪnsjʊleɪt/ vt aislar. ∼ing
tape n cinta f aisladora/aislante.
∼ion /-'leɪʃn/ n aislamiento m
insulin /'ɪnsjʊlɪn/ n insulina f
insult /ɪn'sʌlt/ vt insultar. /'ɪnsʌlt/ n
insulto m
insuperable /ɪn'sjuːpərəbl/ a
insuperable
insur|ance /ɪn'ʃʊərəns/ n seguro m.
∼e vt asegurar. ∼e that asegurarse
de que
insurgent /ɪn'sɜːdʒənt/ a & n insur-
recto (m)
insurmountable /ɪnsə'maʊntəbl/ a
insuperable
insurrection /ɪnsə'rekʃn/ n in-
surrección f
intact /ɪn'tækt/ a intacto
intake /'ɪnteɪk/ n (quantity) número
m; (mec) admisión f; (of food) consumo m
intangible /ɪn'tændʒəbl/ a
intangible
integral /'ɪntɪɡrəl/ a íntegro. **be an**
∼ **part of** ser parte integrante de
integrat|e /'ɪntɪɡreɪt/ vt integrar.
● vi integrarse. ∼ion /-'ɡreɪʃn/ n
integración f
integrity /ɪn'teɡrəti/ n integridad f
intellect /'ɪntəlekt/ n intelecto m.
∼ual a & n intelectual (m)
intelligen|ce /ɪn'telɪdʒəns/ n inte-
ligencia f; (information) información f. ∼t a inteligente. ∼tly

adv inteligentemente. ∼tsia
/ɪntelɪ'dʒentsɪə/ n intelectualidad f
intelligible /ɪn'telɪdʒəbl/ a inteligible
intemperance /ɪn'tempərəns/ n in-
moderación f
intend /ɪn'tend/ vt destinar. ∼ **to do**
tener la intención de hacer. ∼ed a
intencionado. ● n (future spouse)
novio m
intense /ɪn'tens/ a intenso; ⟨person⟩
apasionado. ∼ly adv intensamente;
(very) sumamente
intensif|ication /ɪntensɪfɪ'keɪʃn/ n
intensificación f. ∼y /-faɪ/ vt
intensificar
intensity /ɪn'tensəti/ n intensidad f
intensive /ɪn'tensɪv/ a intensivo. ∼
care n asistencia f intensiva, cui-
dados mpl intensivos
intent /ɪn'tent/ n propósito m. ● a
atento. ∼ **on** absorto en. ∼ **on**
doing resuelto a hacer
intention /ɪn'tenʃn/ n intención f.
∼al a intencional
intently /ɪn'tentlɪ/ adv atentamente
inter /ɪn'tɜː(r)/ vt (pt **interred**)
enterrar
inter... /'ɪntə(r)/ pref inter..., entre...
interact /ɪntər'ækt/ vi obrar recí-
procamente. ∼ion /-ʃn/ n interacción f
intercede /ɪntə'siːd/ vi interceder
intercept /ɪntə'sept/ vt interceptar.
∼ion /-ʃn/ n interceptación f; (in
geometry) intersección f
interchange /'ɪntətʃeɪndʒ/ n (road
junction) cruce m. ∼**able**
/-'tʃeɪndʒəbl/ a intercambiable
intercom /'ɪntəkɒm/ n inter-
comunicador m
interconnected /ɪntəkə'nektɪd/ a
relacionado
intercourse /'ɪntəkɔːs/ n trato m;
(sexual) trato m sexual
interest /'ɪntrest/ n interés m;
(advantage) ventaja f. ● vt inter-
esar. ∼ed a interesado. **be** ∼**ed in**
interesarse por. ∼**ing** a interesante
interfere /ɪntə'fɪə(r)/ vi entrometerse. ∼ **in** entrometerse en. ∼
with entrometerse en, interferir en;
interferir ⟨radio⟩. ∼**nce** n inter-
ferencia f
interim /'ɪntərɪm/ a provisional. ● n. **in the** ∼
entre tanto
interior /ɪn'tɪərɪə(r)/ a & n interior
(m)

interjection /ɪntə'dʒekʃn/ n interjección f

interlock /ɪntə'lɒk/ vt/i (tec) engranar

interloper /'ɪntələʊpə(r)/ n intruso m

interlude /'ɪntəluːd/ n intervalo m; (theatre, music) interludio m

intermarr|iage /ɪntə'mærɪdʒ/ n matrimonio m entre personas de distintas razas. ∼y vi casarse (con personas de distintas razas)

intermediary /ɪntə'miːdɪərɪ/ a & n intermediario (m)

intermediate /ɪntə'miːdɪət/ a intermedio

interminable /ɪn'tɜːmɪnəbl/ a interminable

intermission /ɪntə'mɪʃn/ n pausa f; (theatre) descanso m

intermittent /ɪntə'mɪtnt/ a intermitente. ∼ly adv con discontinuidad

intern /ɪn'tɜːn/ vt internar. /'ɪntɜːn/ n (doctor, Amer) interno m

internal /ɪn'tɜːnl/ a interior. ∼ly adv interiormente

international /ɪntə'næʃənl/ a & n internacional (m)

internee /ɪntɜː'niː/ n internado m

internment /ɪn'tɜːnmənt/ n internamiento m

interplay /'ɪntəpleɪ/ n interacción f

interpolate /ɪn'tɜːpəleɪt/ vt interpolar

interpret /ɪn'tɜːprɪt/ vt/i interpretar. ∼ation /-'teɪʃn/ n interpretación f. ∼er n intérprete m & f

interrelated /ɪntərɪ'leɪtɪd/ a interrelacionado

interrogat|e /ɪn'terəgeɪt/ vt interrogar. ∼ion /-'geɪʃn/ n interrogación f; (session of questions) interrogatorio m

interrogative /ɪntə'rɒgətɪv/ a & n interrogativo (m)

interrupt /ɪntə'rʌpt/ vt interrumpir. ∼ion /-ʃn/ n interrupción f

intersect /ɪntə'sekt/ vt cruzar. ● vi (roads) cruzarse; (geometry) intersecarse. ∼ion /-ʃn/ n (roads) cruce m; (geometry) intersección f

interspersed /ɪntə'spɜːst/ a disperso. ∼ with salpicado de

intertwine /ɪntə'twaɪn/ vt entrelazar. ● vi entrelazarse

interval /'ɪntəvl/ n intervalo m; (theatre) descanso m. at ∼s a intervalos

interven|e /ɪntə'viːn/ vi intervenir. ∼tion /-'venʃn/ n intervención f

interview /'ɪntəvjuː/ n entrevista f. ● vt entrevistarse con. ∼er n entrevistador m

intestin|al /ɪnte'staɪnl/ a intestinal. ∼e /ɪn'testɪn/ n intestino m

intimacy /'ɪntɪməsɪ/ n intimidad f

intimate[1] /'ɪntɪmət/ a íntimo

intimate[2] /'ɪntɪmeɪt/ vt (state) anunciar; (imply) dar a entender

intimately /'ɪntɪmətlɪ/ adv íntimamente

intimidat|e /ɪn'tɪmɪdeɪt/ vt intimidar. ∼ion /-'deɪʃn/ n intimidación f

into /'ɪntuː/, unstressed /'ɪntə/ prep en; (translate) a

intolerable /ɪn'tɒlərəbl/ a intolerable

intoleran|ce /ɪn'tɒlərəns/ n intolerancia f. ∼t a intolerante

intonation /ɪntə'neɪʃn/ n entonación f

intoxicat|e /ɪn'tɒksɪkeɪt/ vt embriagar; (med) intoxicar. ∼ed a ebrio. ∼ion /-'keɪʃn/ n embriaguez f; (med) intoxicación f

intra... /'ɪntrə/ pref intra...

intractable /ɪn'træktəbl/ a (person) intratable; (thing) muy difícil

intransigent /ɪn'trænsɪdʒənt/ a intransigente

intransitive /ɪn'trænsɪtɪv/ a intransitivo

intravenous /ɪntrə'viːnəs/ a intravenoso

intrepid /ɪn'trepɪd/ a intrépido

intrica|cy /'ɪntrɪkəsɪ/ n complejidad f. ∼te a complejo

intrigu|e /ɪn'triːg/ vt/i intrigar. ● n intriga f. ∼ing a intrigante

intrinsic /ɪn'trɪnsɪk/ a intrínseco. ∼ally adv intrínsecamente

introduc|e /ɪntrə'djuːs/ vt introducir; presentar (person). ∼tion /ɪntrə'dʌkʃn/ n introducción f; (to person) presentación f. ∼tory /-tərɪ/ a preliminar

introspective /ɪntrə'spektɪv/ a introspectivo

introvert /'ɪntrəvɜːt/ n introvertido m

intru|de /ɪn'truːd/ vi entrometerse; (disturb) molestar. ∼der n intruso m. ∼sion n intrusión f

intuiti|on /ɪntjuː'ɪʃn/ n intuición f. ∼ve /ɪn'tjuːɪtɪv/ a intuitivo

inundat|e /'ɪnʌndeɪt/ *vt* inundar.
~ion /-'deɪʃn/ *n* inundación *f*

invade /ɪn'veɪd/ *vt* invadir. **~r**
/-ə(r)/ *n* invasor *m*

invalid[1] /'ɪnvəlɪd/ *n* enfermo *m*,
inválido *m*

invalid[2] /ɪn'vælɪd/ *a* nulo. **~ate** *vt*
invalidar

invaluable /ɪn'væljʊəbl/ *a* inestimable

invariabl|e /ɪn'veərɪəbl/ *a* invari-
able. **~y** *adv* invariablemente

invasion /ɪn'veɪʒn/ *n* invasión *f*

invective /ɪn'vektɪv/ *n* invectiva *f*

inveigh /ɪn'veɪ/ *vi* dirigir invectivas
(**against** contra)

inveigle /ɪn'veɪgl/ *vt* engatusar,
persuadir

invent /ɪn'vent/ *vt* inventar. **~ion**
/-'venʃn/ *n* invención *f*. **~ive** *a*
inventivo. **~or** *n* inventor *m*

inventory /'ɪnvəntərɪ/ *n* inventario
m

invers|e /ɪn'vɜːs/ *a & n* inverso (*m*).
~ely *adv* inversamente. **~ion**
/ɪn'vɜːʃn/ *n* inversión *f*

invert /ɪn'vɜːt/ *vt* invertir. **~ed commas** *npl* comillas *fpl*

invest /ɪn'vest/ *vt* invertir. ● *vi*. **~ in**
hacer una inversión *f*

investigat|e /ɪn'vestɪgeɪt/ *vt* invest-
igar. **~ion** /-'geɪʃn/ *n* investigación
f. **under ~ion** sometido a examen.
~or *n* investigador *m*

inveterate /ɪn'vetərət/ *a* inveterado

invidious /ɪn'vɪdɪəs/ *a* (*hateful*)
odioso; (*unfair*) injusto

invigilat|e /ɪn'vɪdʒɪleɪt/ *vi* vigilar.
~or *n* celador *m*

invigorate /ɪn'vɪgəreɪt/ *vt* vigorizar;
(*stimulate*) estimular

invincible /ɪn'vɪnsɪbl/ *a* invencible

invisible /ɪn'vɪzəbl/ *a* invisible

invit|ation /ɪnvɪ'teɪʃn/ *n* invitación
f. **~e** /ɪn'vaɪt/ *vt* invitar; (*ask for*)
pedir. **~ing** *a* atrayente

invoice /'ɪnvɔɪs/ *n* factura *f*. ● *vt*
facturar

invoke /ɪn'vəʊk/ *vt* invocar

involuntary /ɪn'vɒləntərɪ/ *a*
involuntario

involve /ɪn'vɒlv/ *vt* enredar. **~d** *a*
(*complex*) complicado. **~d in**
embrollado en. **~ment** *n* enredo *m*

invulnerable /ɪn'vʌlnərəbl/ *a*
invulnerable

inward /'ɪnwəd/ *a* interior. ● *adv*
interiormente. **~s** *adv* hacia/para
dentro

iodine /'aɪədiːn/ *n* yodo *m*

iota /aɪ'əʊtə/ *n* (*amount*) pizca *f*

IOU /aɪəʊ'juː/ *abbr* (*I owe you*)
pagaré *m*

IQ /aɪ'kjuː/ *abbr* (*intelligence quotient*) cociente *m* intelectual

Iran /ɪ'rɑːn/ *n* Irán *m*. **~ian** /ɪ'reɪnɪən/
a & n iraní (*m*)

Iraq /ɪ'rɑːk/ *n* Irak *m*. **~i** *a & n* iraquí
(*m*)

irascible /ɪ'ræsəbl/ *a* irascible

irate /aɪ'reɪt/ *a* colérico

ire /aɪə(r)/ *n* ira *f*

Ireland /'aɪələnd/ *n* Irlanda *f*

iris /'aɪərɪs/ *n* (*anat*) iris *m*; (*bot*) lirio
m

Irish /'aɪərɪʃ/ *a* irlandés. ● *n* (*lang*)
irlandés *m*. **~man** *n* irlandés *m*.
~woman *n* irlandesa *f*

irk /ɜːk/ *vt* fastidiar. **~some** *a*
fastidioso

iron /'aɪən/ *n* hierro *m*; (*appliance*)
plancha *f*. ● *a* de hierro. ● *vt* planchar. **~ out** allanar. **I~ Curtain** *n*
telón *m* de acero

ironic(al) /aɪ'rɒnɪk(l)/ *a* irónico

ironing-board /'aɪənɪŋbɔːd/ *n* tabla
f de planchar

ironmonger /'aɪənmʌŋgə(r)/ *n* fer-
retero *m*. **~y** *n* ferretería *f*

ironwork /'aɪənwɜːk/ *n* herraje *m*

irony /'aɪərənɪ/ *n* ironía *f*

irrational /ɪ'ræʃənl/ *a* irracional

irreconcilable /ɪrekən'saɪləbl/ *a*
irreconciliable

irrefutable /ɪrɪ'fjuːtəbl/ *a*
irrefutable

irregular /ɪ'regjʊlə(r)/ *a* irregular.
~ity /-'lærətɪ/ *n* irregularidad *f*

irrelevan|ce /ɪ'reləvəns/ *n* in-
oportunidad *f*, impertinencia *f*. **~t**
a no pertinente

irreparable /ɪ'repərəbl/ *a*
irreparable

irreplaceable /ɪrɪ'pleɪsəbl/ *a*
irreemplazable

irrepressible /ɪrɪ'presəbl/ *a*
irreprimible

irresistible /ɪrɪ'zɪstəbl/ *a* irresistible

irresolute /ɪ'rezəluːt/ *a* irresoluto,
indeciso

irrespective /ɪrɪ'spektɪv/ *a*. **~ of** sin
tomar en cuenta

irresponsible /ɪrɪ'spɒnsəbl/ *a*
irresponsable

irretrievable /ɪrɪ'triːvəbl/ *a*
irrecuperable

irreverent /ɪ'revərənt/ *a* irreverente

irreversible /ɪrɪ'vɜːsəbl/ a irreversible; ⟨*decision*⟩ irrevocable

irrevocable /ɪ'revəkəbl/ a irrevocable

irrigat|e /'ɪrɪgeɪt/ vt regar; (*med*) irrigar. ∼**ion** /-'geɪʃn/ n riego m; (*med*) irrigación f

irritable /'ɪrɪtəbl/ a irritable

irritat|e /'ɪrɪteɪt/ vt irritar. ∼**ion** /-'teɪʃn/ n irritación f

is /ɪz/ *see* be

Islam /'ɪzlɑːm/ n Islam m. ∼**ic** /ɪz'læmɪk/ a islámico

island /'aɪlənd/ n isla f. **traffic** ∼ n refugio m (en la calle). ∼**er** n isleño m

isle /aɪl/ n isla f

isolat|e /'aɪsəleɪt/ vt aislar. ∼**ion** /-'leɪʃn/ n aislamiento m

isotope /'aɪsətəʊp/ n isotopo m

Israel /'ɪzreɪl/ n Israel m. ∼**i** /ɪz'reɪlɪ/ a & n israelí (m)

issue /'ɪʃuː/ n asunto m; (*outcome*) resultado m; (*of magazine etc*) número m; (*of stamps*) emisión f; (*offspring*) descendencia f. **at** ∼ en cuestión. **take** ∼ **with** oponerse a. ● vt distribuir; emitir ⟨*stamps etc*⟩; publicar ⟨*book*⟩. ● vi. ∼ **from** salir de

isthmus /'ɪsməs/ n istmo m

it /ɪt/ pron (*subject*) el, ella, ello; (*direct object*) lo, la; (*indirect object*) le; (*after preposition*) él, ella, ello. ∼ **is hot** hace calor. ∼ **is me** soy yo. **far from** ∼ ni mucho menos. **that's** ∼ eso es. **who is** ∼? ¿quién es?

italic /ɪ'tælɪk/ a bastardillo m. ∼**s** npl (letra f) bastardilla f

ital|ian /ɪ'tæljən/ a & n italiano (m). **I∼y** /'ɪtəlɪ/ n Italia f

itch /ɪtʃ/ n picazón f. ● vi picar. **I'm ∼ing to** rabio por. **my arm ∼es** me pica el brazo. ∼**y** a que pica

item /'aɪtəm/ n artículo m; (*on agenda*) asunto m. **news** ∼ n noticia f. ∼**ize** vt detallar

itinerant /aɪ'tɪnərənt/ a ambulante

itinerary /aɪ'tɪnərərɪ/ n itinerario m

its /ɪts/ a su, sus (*pl*). ● pron (el) suyo m, (la) suya f, (los) suyos mpl, (las) suyas fpl

it's /ɪts/ = **it is, it has**

itself /ɪt'self/ pron él mismo, ella misma, ello mismo; (*reflexive*) se; (*after prep*) sí mismo, sí misma

ivory /'aɪvərɪ/ n marfil m. ∼ **tower** n torre f de marfil

ivy /'aɪvɪ/ n hiedra f

J

jab /dʒæb/ vt (*pt* **jabbed**) pinchar; (*thrust*) hurgonear. ● n pinchazo m

jabber /'dʒæbə(r)/ vi barbullar. ● n farfulla f

jack /dʒæk/ n (*mec*) gato m; (*cards*) sota f. ● vt. ∼ **up** alzar con gato

jackal /'dʒækl/ n chacal m

jackass /'dʒækæs/ n burro m

jackdaw /'dʒækdɔː/ n grajilla f

jacket /'dʒækɪt/ n chaqueta f, saco m (*LAm*); (*of book*) sobrecubierta f, camisa f

jack-knife /'dʒæknaɪf/ n navaja f

jackpot /'dʒækpɒt/ n premio m gordo. **hit the** ∼ sacar el premio gordo

jade /dʒeɪd/ n (*stone*) jade m

jaded /'dʒeɪdɪd/ a cansado

jagged /'dʒægɪd/ a dentado

jaguar /'dʒægjʊə(r)/ n jaguar m

jail /dʒeɪl/ n cárcel m. ∼**bird** n criminal m emperdernido. ∼**er** n carcelero m

jalopy /dʒə'lɒpɪ/ n cacharro m

jam¹ /dʒæm/ vt (*pt* **jammed**) interferir con ⟨*radio*⟩; ⟨*traffic*⟩ embotellar; ⟨*people*⟩ agolparse en. ● vi obstruirse; ⟨*mechanism etc*⟩ atascarse. ● n (*of people*) agolpamiento m; (*of traffic*) embotellamiento m; (*situation, fam*) apuro m

jam² /dʒæm/ n mermelada f

Jamaica /dʒə'meɪkə/ n Jamaica f

jamboree /dʒæmbə'riː/ n reunión f

jam-packed /'dʒæm'pækt/ a atestado

jangle /'dʒæŋgl/ n sonido m metálico (y áspero). ● vt/i sonar discordemente

janitor /'dʒænɪtə(r)/ n portero m

January /'dʒænjʊərɪ/ n enero m

Japan /dʒə'pæn/ n el Japón m. ∼**ese** /dʒæpə'niːz/ a & n japonés (m)

jar¹ /dʒɑː(r)/ n tarro m, frasco m

jar² /dʒɑː(r)/ vi (*pt* **jarred**) ⟨*sound*⟩ sonar mal; ⟨*colours*⟩ chillar. ● vt sacudir

jar³ /dʒɑː(r)/ n. **on the** ∼ (*ajar*) entreabierto

jargon /'dʒɑːgən/ n jerga f

jarring /'dʒɑːrɪŋ/ a discorde

jasmine /'dʒæsmɪn/ n jazmín m

jaundice /'dʒɔːndɪs/ n ictericia f. ∼**d** a (*envious*) envidioso; (*bitter*) amargado

jaunt /dʒɔːnt/ n excursión f

jaunty /'dʒɔːntɪ/ *a* (**-ier, -iest**) garboso

javelin /'dʒævəlɪn/ *n* jabalina *f*

jaw /dʒɔː/ *n* mandíbula *f*. ● *vi* (*talk lengthily, sl*) hablar por los codos

jay /dʒeɪ/ *n* arrendajo *m*. ∼**walk** *vi* cruzar la calle descuidadamente

jazz /dʒæz/ *n* jazz *m*. ● *vt.* ∼ **up** animar. ∼**y** *a* chillón

jealous /'dʒeləs/ *a* celoso. ∼**y** *n* celos *mpl*

jeans /dʒiːnz/ *npl* (pantalones *mpl*) vaqueros *mpl*

jeep /dʒiːp/ *n* jeep *m*

jeer /dʒɪə(r)/ *vt/i.* ∼ **at** mofarse de, befar; (*boo*) abuchear. ● *n* mofa *f*; (*boo*) abucheo *m*

jell /dʒel/ *vi* cuajar. ∼**ied** *a* en gelatina

jelly /'dʒelɪ/ *n* jalea *f*. ∼**fish** *n* medusa *f*

jeopard|ize /'dʒepədaɪz/ *vt* arriesgar. ∼**y** *n* peligro *m*

jerk /dʒɜːk/ *n* sacudida *f*; (*fool, sl*) idiota *m* & *f*. ● *vt* sacudir. ∼**ily** *adv* a sacudidas. ∼**y** *a* espasmódico

jersey /'dʒɜːzɪ/ *n* (*pl* **-eys**) jersey *m*

jest /dʒest/ *n* broma *f*. ● *vi* bromear. ∼**er** *n* bufón *m*

Jesus /'dʒiːzəs/ *n* Jesús *m*

jet[1] /dʒet/ *n* (*stream*) chorro *m*; (*plane*) yet *m*, avión *m* de propulsión por reacción

jet[2] /dʒet/ *n* (*mineral*) azabache *m*. ∼**-black** *a* de azabache, como el azabache

jet: ∼ **lag** *n* cansancio *m* retardado después de un vuelo largo. **have** ∼ **lag** estar desfasado. ∼**-propelled** *a* (de propulsión) a reacción

jettison /'dʒetɪsn/ *vt* echar al mar; (*fig, discard*) deshacerse de

jetty /'dʒetɪ/ *n* muelle *m*

Jew /dʒuː/ *n* judío *m*

jewel /'dʒuːəl/ *n* joya *f*. ∼**led** *a* enjoyado. ∼**ler** *n* joyero *m*. ∼**lery** *n* joyas *fpl*

Jew: ∼**ess** *n* judía *f*. ∼**ish** *a* judío. ∼**ry** /'dʒuərɪ/ *n* los judíos *mpl*

jib[1] /dʒɪb/ *n* (*sail*) foque *m*

jib[2] /dʒɪb/ *vi* (*pt* **jibbed**) rehusar. ∼ **at** oponerse a.

jiffy /'dʒɪfɪ/ *n* momentito *m*. **do sth in a** ∼ hacer algo en un santiamén

jig /dʒɪg/ *n* (*dance*) giga *f*

jiggle /'dʒɪgl/ *vt* zangolotear

jigsaw /'dʒɪgsɔː/ *n* rompecabezas *m invar*

jilt /dʒɪlt/ *vt* plantar, dejar plantado

jingle /'dʒɪŋgl/ *vt* hacer sonar. ● *vi* tintinear. ● *n* tintineo *m*; (*advert*) anuncio *m* cantado

jinx /dʒɪŋks/ *n* (*person*) gafe *m*; (*spell*) maleficio *m*

jitter|s /'dʒɪtəz/ *npl.* **have the** ∼**s** estar nervioso. ∼**y** /-ərɪ/ *a* nervioso. **be** ∼**y** estar nervioso

job /dʒɒb/ *n* trabajo *m*; (*post*) empleo *m*, puesto *m*. **have a** ∼ **doing** costar trabajo hacer. **it is a good** ∼ **that** menos mal que. ∼**centre** *n* bolsa *f* de trabajo. ∼**less** *a* sin trabajo.

jockey /'dʒɒkɪ/ *n* jockey *m*. ● *vi* (*manoeuvre*) maniobrar (**for** para)

jocular /'dʒɒkjʊlə(r)/ *a* jocoso

jog /dʒɒg/ *vt* (*pt* **jogged**) empujar; refrescar (*memory*). ● *vi* hacer footing. ∼**ging** *n* jogging *m*

join /dʒɔɪn/ *vt* unir, juntar; hacerse socio de (*club*); hacerse miembro de (*political group*); alistarse en (*army*); reunirse con (*another person*). ● *vi* (*roads etc*) empalmar; (*rivers*) confluir. ∼ **in** participar (en). ∼ **up** (*mil*) alistarse. ● *n* juntura *f*

joiner /'dʒɔɪnə(r)/ *n* carpintero *m*

joint /dʒɔɪnt/ *a* común. ∼ **author** *n* coautor *m*. ● *n* (*join*) juntura *f*; (*anat*) articulación *f*; (*culin*) asado *m*; (*place, sl*) garito *m*; (*marijuana, sl*) cigarillo *m* de marijuana. **out of** ∼ descoyuntado. ∼**ly** *adv* conjuntamente

joist /dʒɔɪst/ *n* viga *f*

jok|e /dʒəʊk/ *n* broma *f*; (*funny story*) chiste *m*. ● *vi* bromear. ∼**er** *n* bromista *m* & *f*; (*cards*) comodín *m*. ∼**ingly** *adv* en broma

joll|ification /dʒɒlɪfɪ'keɪʃn/ *n* jolgorio *m*. ∼**ity** *n* jolgorio *m*. ∼**y** *a* (**-ier, -iest**) alegre. ● *adv* (*fam*) muy

jolt /dʒɒlt/ *vt* sacudir. ● *vt* (*vehicle*) traquetear. ● *n* sacudida *f*

Jordan /'dʒɔːdən/ *n* Jordania *f*. ∼**ian** *a* & *n* /-'deɪnɪən/ jordano (*m*)

jostle /'dʒɒsl/ *vt/i* empujar(se)

jot /dʒɒt/ *n* pizca *f*. ● *vt* (*pt* **jotted**) apuntar. ∼**ter** *n* bloc *m*

journal /'dʒɜːnl/ *n* (*diary*) diario *m*; (*newspaper*) periódico *m*; (*magazine*) revista *f*. ∼**ese** /dʒɜːnə'liːz/ *n* jerga *f* periodística. ∼**ism** *n* periodismo *m*. ∼**ist** *n* periodista *m* & *f*

journey /'dʒɜːnɪ/ *n* viaje *m*. ● *vi* viajar

jovial /'dʒəʊvɪəl/ *a* jovial

jowl /dʒaʊl/ *n* (*jaw*) quijada *f*; (*cheek*) mejilla *f*. **cheek by** ∼ muy cerca

joy /dʒɔɪ/ n alegría f. **~ful** a alegre. **~ride** n paseo m en coche sin permiso del dueño. **~ous** a alegre

jubila|nt /'dʒuːbɪlənt/ a jubiloso. **~tion** /-'leɪʃn/ n júbilo m

jubilee /'dʒuːbɪliː/ n aniversario m especial

Judaism /'dʒuːdeɪɪzəm/ n judaísmo m

judder /'dʒʌdə(r)/ vi vibrar. ● n vibración f

judge /dʒʌdʒ/ n juez m. ● vt juzgar. **~ment** n juicio m

judicia|l /dʒuː'dɪʃl/ a judicial. **~ry** n magistratura f

judicious /dʒuː'dɪʃəs/ a juicioso

judo /'dʒuːdəʊ/ n judo m

jug /dʒʌg/ n jarra f

juggernaut /'dʒʌgənɔːt/ n (lorry) camión m grande

juggle /'dʒʌgl/ vt/i hacer juegos malabares (con). **~r** n malabarista m & f

juic|e /dʒuːs/ n jugo m, zumo m. **~y** a jugoso, zumoso; ⟨story etc⟩ (fam) picante

juke-box /'dʒuːkbɒks/ n tocadiscos m invar tragaperras

July /dʒuː'laɪ/ n julio m

jumble /'dʒʌmbl/ vt mezclar. ● n (muddle) revoltijo m. **~ sale** n venta f de objetos usados, mercadillo m

jumbo /'dʒʌmbəʊ/ a. **~ jet** n jumbo m

jump /dʒʌmp/ vt/i saltar. **~ the gun** obrar prematuramente. **~ the queue** colarse. ● vi saltar; (start) asustarse; ⟨prices⟩ alzarse. **~ at** apresurarse a aprovechar. ● n salto m; (start) susto m; (increase) aumento m

jumper /'dʒʌmpə(r)/ n jersey m; (dress, Amer) mandil m, falda f con peto

jumpy /'dʒʌmpɪ/ a nervioso

junction /'dʒʌŋkʃn/ n juntura f; (of roads) cruce m, entronque m (LAm); (rail) empalme m, entronque m (LAm)

juncture /'dʒʌŋktʃə(r)/ n momento m; (state of affairs) coyuntura f

June /dʒuːn/ n junio m

jungle /'dʒʌŋgl/ n selva f

junior /'dʒuːnɪə(r)/ a (in age) más joven (**to** que); (in rank) subalterno. ● n menor m. **~ school** n escuela f

junk /dʒʌŋk/ n trastos mpl viejos. ● vt (fam) tirar

junkie /'dʒʌŋkɪ/ n (sl) drogadicto m

junk shop /'dʒʌŋkʃɒp/ n tienda f de trastos viejos

junta /'dʒʌntə/ n junta f

jurisdiction /dʒʊərɪs'dɪkʃn/ n jurisdicción f

jurisprudence /dʒʊərɪs'pruːdəns/ n jurisprudencia f

juror /'dʒʊərə(r)/ n jurado m

jury /'dʒʊərɪ/ n jurado m

just /dʒʌst/ a (fair) justo. ● adv exactamente; (slightly) apenas; (only) sólo, solamente. **~ as tall** tan alto (as como). **~ listen!** ¡escucha! **he has ~ left** acaba de marcharse

justice /'dʒʌstɪs/ n justicia f. **J~ of the Peace** juez m de paz

justif|iable /dʒʌstɪ'faɪəbl/ a justificable. **~iably** adv con razón. **~ication** /dʒʌstɪfɪ'keɪʃn/ n justificación f. **~y** /'dʒʌstɪfaɪ/ vt justificar

justly /'dʒʌstlɪ/ adv con justicia

jut /dʒʌt/ vi (pt jutted). **~ out** sobresalir

juvenile /'dʒuːvənaɪl/ a juvenil; (childish) infantil. ● n joven m & f. **~ court** n tribunal m de menores

juxtapose /dʒʌkstə'pəʊz/ vt yuxtaponer

K

kaleidoscope /kə'laɪdəskəʊp/ n caleidoscopio m

kangaroo /kæŋgə'ruː/ n canguro m

kapok /'keɪpɒk/ n miraguano m

karate /kə'rɑːtɪ/ n karate m

kebab /kɪ'bæb/ n broqueta f

keel /kiːl/ n (of ship) quilla f. ● vi. **~ over** volcarse

keen /kiːn/ a (-er, -est) ⟨interest, feeling⟩ vivo; ⟨wind, mind, analysis⟩ penetrante; ⟨edge⟩ afilado; ⟨appetite⟩ bueno; ⟨eyesight⟩ agudo; (eager) entusiasta. **be ~ on** gustarle a uno. **he's ~ on Shostakovich** le gusta Shostakovich. **~ly** adv vivamente; (enthusiastically) con entusiasmo. **~ness** n intensidad f; (enthusiasm) entusiasmo m.

keep /kiːp/ vt (pt kept) guardar; cumplir ⟨promise⟩; tener ⟨shop, animals⟩; mantener ⟨family⟩; observar ⟨rule⟩; (celebrate) celebrar; (delay) detener; (prevent) impedir. ● vi ⟨food⟩ conservarse; (remain) quedarse. ● n subsistencia f; (of castle) torreón *m*. **for** ~**s** (*fam*) para siempre. ~ **back** *vt* retener. ● *vi* no acercarse. ~ **in** no dejar salir. ~ **in with** mantenerse en buenas relaciones con. ~ **out** no dejar entrar. ~ **up** mantener. ~ **up (with)** estar al día (en). ~**er** *n* guarda *m*

keeping /'ki:pɪŋ/ *n* cuidado *m*. **in** ~ **with** de acuerdo con

keepsake /'ki:pseɪk/ *n* recuerdo *m*

keg /keg/ *n* barrilete *m*

kennel /'kenl/ *n* perrera *f*

Kenya /'kenjə/ *n* Kenia *f*

kept /kept/ *see* **keep**

kerb /kɜːb/ *n* bordillo *m*

kerfuffle /kə'fʌfl/ *n* (*fuss, fam*) lío *m*

kernel /'kɜːnl/ *n* almendra *f*; (*fig*) meollo *m*

kerosene /'kerəsiːn/ *n* queroseno *m*

ketchup /'ketʃʌp/ *n* salsa *f* de tomate

kettle /'ketl/ *n* hervidor *m*

key /kiː/ *n* llave *f*; (*of typewriter, piano etc*) tecla *f*. ● *vt*. ~ **up** excitar. ~**board** *n* teclado *m*. ~**hole** *n* ojo *m* de la cerradura. ~**note** *n* (*mus*) tónica *f*; (*speech*) idea *f* fundamental. ~**ring** *n* llavero *m*. ~**stone** *n* piedra *f* clave

khaki /'kɑːkɪ/ *a* caqui

kibbutz /kɪ'bʊts/ *n* (*pl* -**im** /-iːm/ *or* -**es**) kibbutz *m*

kick /kɪk/ *vt* dar una patada a; ⟨*animals*⟩ tirar una coz a. ● *vi* dar patadas; ⟨*firearm*⟩ dar culatazo. ● *n* patada *f*; (*of animal*) coz *f*; (*of firearm*) culatazo *m*; (*thrill, fam*) placer *m*. ~ **out** (*fam*) echar a patadas. ~ **up** armar ⟨*fuss etc*⟩. ~**back** *n* culatazo *m*; (*payment*) soborno *m*. ~**off** *n* (*sport*) saque *m* inicial

kid /kɪd/ *n* (*young goat*) cabrito *m*; (*leather*) cabritilla *f*; (*child, sl*) chaval *m*. ● *vt* (*pt* **kidded**) tomar el pelo a. ● *vi* bromear

kidnap /'kɪdnæp/ *vt* (*pt* **kidnapped**) secuestrar. ~**ping** *n* secuestro *m*

kidney /'kɪdnɪ/ *n* riñón *m*. ● *a* renal

kill /kɪl/ *vt* matar; (*fig*) acabar con. ● *n* matanza *f*; (*in hunt*) pieza(s) *f*(*pl*). ~**er** *n* matador *m*; (*murderer*) asesino *m*. ~**ing** *n* matanza *f*; (*murder*) asesinato *m*. ● *a* (*funny, fam*) para morirse de risa; (*tiring, fam*) agotador. ~**joy** *n* aguafiestas *m & f* invar

kiln /kɪln/ *n* horno *m*

kilo /'kiːləʊ/ *n* (*pl* -**os**) kilo *m*

kilogram(me) /'kɪləgræm/ *n* kilogramo *m*

kilohertz /'kɪləhɜːts/ *n* kilohercio *m*

kilometre /'kɪləmiːtə(r)/ *n* kilómetro *m*

kilowatt /'kɪləwɒt/ *n* kilovatio *m*

kilt /kɪlt/ *n* falda *f* escocesa

kin /kɪn/ *n* parientes *mpl*. **next of** ~ pariente *m* más próximo, parientes *mpl* más próximos

kind[1] /kaɪnd/ *n* clase *f*. ~ **of** (*somewhat, fam*) un poco. **in** ~ en especie. **be two of a** ~ ser tal para cual

kind[2] /kaɪnd/ *a* amable

kindergarten /'kɪndəgaːtn/ *n* escuela *f* de párvulos

kind-hearted /kaɪnd'haːtɪd/ *a* bondadoso

kindle /'kɪndl/ *vt/i* encender(se)

kind: ~**liness** *n* bondad *f*. ~**ly** *a* (-**ier**, -**iest**) bondadoso. ● *adv* bondadosamente; (*please*) haga el favor de. ~**ness** *n* bondad *f*

kindred /'kɪndrɪd/ *a* emparentado. ~ **spirits** *npl* almas *fpl* afines

kinetic /kɪ'netɪk/ *a* cinético

king /kɪŋ/ *n* rey *m*

kingdom /'kɪŋdəm/ *n* reino *m*

kingpin /'kɪŋpɪn/ *n* (*person*) persona *f* clave; (*thing*) piedra *f* angular

king-size(d) /'kɪŋsaɪz(d)/ *a* extraordinariamente grande

kink /kɪŋk/ *n* (*in rope*) retorcimiento *m*; (*fig*) manía *f*. ~**y** *a* (*fam*) pervertido

kiosk /'kiːɒsk/ *n* quiosco *m*. **telephone** ~ cabina *f* telefónica

kip /kɪp/ *n* (*sl*) sueño *m*. ● *vi* (*pt* **kipped**) dormir

kipper /'kɪpə(r)/ *n* arenque *m* ahumado

kiss /kɪs/ *n* beso *m*. ● *vt/i* besar(se)

kit /kɪt/ *n* avíos *mpl*; (*tools*) herramientos *mpl*. ● *vt* (*pt* **kitted**). ~ **out** equipar de. ~**bag** *n* mochila *f*

kitchen /'kɪtʃɪn/ *n* cocina *f*. ~**ette** /kɪtʃɪ'net/ *n* cocina *f* pequeña. ~ **garden** *n* huerto *m*

kite /kaɪt/ *n* (*toy*) cometa *f*

kith /kɪθ/ *n*. ~ **and kin** amigos *mpl* y parientes *mpl*

kitten /'kɪtn/ *n* gatito *m*

kitty /'kɪtɪ/ *n* (*fund*) fondo *m* común

kleptomaniac /kleptəʊ'meɪnɪæk/ *n* cleptómano *m*

knack /næk/ *n* truco *m*

knapsack /'næpsæk/ *n* mochila *f*

knave /neɪv/ *n* (*cards*) sota *f*

knead /niːd/ *vt* amasar

knee /niː/ *n* rodilla *f*. ~**cap** *n* rótula *f*

kneel /niːl/ *vi* (*pt* **knelt**). **~ (down)** arrodillarse

knees-up /'niːzʌp/ *n* (*fam*) baile *m*

knell /nel/ *n* toque *m* de difuntos

knelt /nelt/ *see* **kneel**

knew /njuː/ *see* **know**

knickerbockers /'nɪkəbɒkəz/ *npl* pantalón *m* bombacho

knickers /'nɪkəz/ *npl* bragas *fpl*

knick-knack /'nɪknæk/ *n* chuchería *f*

knife /naɪf/ *n* (*pl* **knives**) cuchillo *m*. ● *vt* acuchillar

knight /naɪt/ *n* caballero *m*; (*chess*) caballo *m*. ● *vt* conceder el título de Sir a. **~hood** *n* título *m* de Sir

knit /nɪt/ *vt* (*pt* **knitted** *or* **knit**) tejer. ● *vi* hacer punto. **~ one's brow** fruncir el ceño. **~ting** *n* labor *f* de punto. **~wear** *n* artículos *mpl* de punto

knob /nɒb/ *n* botón *m*; (*of door, drawer etc*) tirador *m*. **~bly** *a* nudoso

knock /nɒk/ *vt* golpear; (*criticize*) criticar. ● *vi* golpear; (*at door*) llamar. ● *n* golpe *m*. **~ about** *vt* maltratar. ● *vi* rodar. **~ down** derribar; atropellar ⟨*person*⟩; rebajar ⟨*prices*⟩. **~ off** *vt* hacer caer; (*complete quickly, fam*) despachar; (*steal, sl*) birlar. ● *vi* (*finish work, fam*) terminar, salir del trabajo. **~ out** (*by blow*) dejar sin conocimiento; (*eliminate*) eliminar; (*tire*) agotar. **~ over** tirar; atropellar ⟨*person*⟩. **~ up** preparar de prisa ⟨*meal etc*⟩. **~down** *a* ⟨*price*⟩ de saldo. **~er** *n* aldaba *f*. **~-kneed** *a* patizambo. **~out** *n* (*boxing*) knock-out *m*

knot /nɒt/ *n* nudo *m*. ● *vt* (*pt* **knotted**) anudar. **~ty** /'nɒtɪ/ *a* nudoso

know /nəʊ/ *vt* (*pt* **knew**) saber; (*be acquainted with*) conocer. ● *vi* saber. ● *n*. **be in the ~** estar al tanto. **~ about** entender de ⟨*cars etc*⟩. **~ of** saber de. **~-all** *n*, **~-it-all** (*Amer*) *n* sabelotodo *m* & *f*. **~-how** *n* habilidad *f*. **~ingly** *adv* deliberadamente

knowledge /'nɒlɪdʒ/ *n* conocimiento *m*; (*learning*) conocimientos *mpl*. **~able** *a* informado

known /nəʊn/ *see* **know**. ● *a* conocido

knuckle /'nʌkl/ *n* nudillo *m*. ● *vi*. **~ under** someterse

Koran /kəˈrɑːn/ *n* Corán *m*, Alcorán *m*

Korea /kəˈrɪə/ *n* Corea *f*

kosher /'kəʊʃə(r)/ *a* preparado según la ley judía

kowtow /kaʊˈtaʊ/ *vi* humillarse (**to** ante)

kudos /'kjuːdɒs/ *n* prestigio *m*

L

lab /læb/ *n* (*fam*) laboratorio *m*

label /'leɪbl/ *n* etiqueta *f*. ● *vt* (*pt* **labelled**) poner etiqueta a; (*fig, describe as*) describir como

laboratory /ləˈbɒrətərɪ/ *n* laboratorio *m*

laborious /ləˈbɔːrɪəs/ *a* penoso

labour /'leɪbə(r)/ *n* trabajo *m*; (*workers*) mano *f* de obra. **in ~** de parto. ● *vi* trabajar. ● *vt* insistir en

Labour /'leɪbə(r)/ *n* el partido *m* laborista. ● *a* laborista

laboured /'leɪbəd/ *a* penoso

labourer /'leɪbərə(r)/ *n* obrero *m*; (*on farm*) labriego *m*

labyrinth /'læbərɪnθ/ *n* laberinto *m*

lace /leɪs/ *n* encaje *m*; (*of shoe*) cordón *m*, agujeta *f* (*Mex*). ● *vt* (*fasten*) atar. **~ with** echar a ⟨*a drink*⟩

lacerate /'læsəreɪt/ *vt* lacerar

lack /læk/ *n* falta *f*. **for ~ of** por falta de. ● *vt* faltarle a uno. **he ~s money** carece de dinero. **be ~ing** faltar

lackadaisical /lækəˈdeɪzɪkl/ *a* indolente, apático

lackey /'lækɪ/ *n* lacayo *m*

laconic /ləˈkɒnɪk/ *a* lacónico

lacquer /'lækə(r)/ *n* laca *f*

lad /læd/ *n* muchacho *m*

ladder /'lædə(r)/ *n* escalera *f* (de mano); (*in stocking*) carrera *f*. ● *vt* hacer una carrera en. ● *vi* hacerse una carrera

laden /'leɪdn/ *a* cargado (**with** de)

ladle /'leɪdl/ *n* cucharón *m*

lady /'leɪdɪ/ *n* señora *f*, señorita *f*. **~bird** *n*, **~bug** *n* (*Amer*) mariquita *f*. **~ friend** *n* amiga *f*. **~-in-waiting** *n* dama *f* de honor. **~like** *a* distinguido. **~ship** *n* Señora *f*

lag¹ /læg/ *vi* (*pt* **lagged**). **~ (behind)** retrasarse. ● *n* (*interval*) intervalo *m*

lag² /læg/ *vt* (*pt* **lagged**) revestir ⟨*pipes*⟩

lager /'lɑːgə(r)/ *n* cerveza *f* dorada

laggard /'lægəd/ *n* holgazán *m*

lagging /'lægɪŋ/ n revestimiento m calorífugo

lagoon /lə'guːn/ n laguna f

lah /lɑː/ n (mus, sixth note of any musical scale) la m

laid /leɪd/ see **lay**¹

lain /leɪn/ see **lie**¹

lair /leə(r)/ n guarida f

laity /'leɪɪtɪ/ n laicado m

lake /leɪk/ n lago m

lamb /læm/ n cordero m. ~swool n lana f de cordero

lame /leɪm/ a (-er, -est) cojo; ⟨excuse⟩ poco convincente. ~ly adv ⟨argue⟩ con poca convicción f

lament /lə'ment/ n lamento m. • vt/i lamentarse (de). ~able /'læməntəbl/ a lamentable

laminated /'læmɪneɪtɪd/ a laminado

lamp /læmp/ n lámpara f. ~post n farol m. ~shade n pantalla f

lance /lɑːns/ n lanza f. • vt (med) abrir con lanceta. ~corporal n cabo m interino

lancet /'lɑːnsɪt/ n lanceta f

land /lænd/ n tierra f; ⟨country⟩ país m; ⟨plot⟩ terreno m. • a terrestre; ⟨breeze⟩ de tierra; ⟨policy, reform⟩ agrario. • vt desembarcar; ⟨obtain⟩ conseguir; dar ⟨blow⟩; ⟨put⟩ meter. • vi ⟨from ship⟩ desembarcar; ⟨aircraft⟩ aterrizar; ⟨fall⟩ caer. ~ up ir a parar

landed /'lændɪd/ a hacendado

landing /'lændɪŋ/ n desembarque m; ⟨aviat⟩ aterrizaje m; ⟨top of stairs⟩ descanso m. ~stage n desembarcadero m

landlady /'lændleɪdɪ/ n propietaria f; ⟨of inn⟩ patrona f

land-locked /'lændlɒkt/ a rodeado de tierra

landlord /'lændlɔːd/ n propietario m; ⟨of inn⟩ patrón m

land: ~mark n punto m destacado. ~scape /'lændskeɪp/ n paisaje m. • vt ajardinar. ~slide n desprendimiento m de tierras; ⟨pol⟩ victoria f arrolladora

lane /leɪn/ n ⟨path, road⟩ camino m; ⟨strip of road⟩ carril m; ⟨aviat⟩ ruta f

language /'læŋgwɪdʒ/ n idioma m; ⟨speech, style⟩ lenguaje m

langu|**id** /'læŋgwɪd/ a lánguido. ~ish /'læŋgwɪʃ/ vi languidecer. ~or /'læŋgə(r)/ n languidez f

lank /læŋk/ a larguirucho; ⟨hair⟩ lacio. ~y /'læŋkɪ/ a (-ier, -iest) larguirucho

lantern /'læntən/ n linterna f

lap¹ /læp/ n regazo m

lap² /læp/ n ⟨sport⟩ vuelta f. • vt/i (pt **lapped**). ~ **over** traslapar(se)

lap³ /læp/ vt (pt **lapped**). ~ **up** beber a lengüetazos; ⟨fig⟩ aceptar con entusiasmo. • vi ⟨waves⟩ chapotear

lapel /lə'pel/ n solapa f

lapse /læps/ vi ⟨decline⟩ degradarse; ⟨expire⟩ caducar; ⟨time⟩ transcurrir. ~ **into** recaer en. • n error m; ⟨of time⟩ intervalo m

larceny /'lɑːsənɪ/ n robo m

lard /lɑːd/ n manteca f de cerdo

larder /'lɑːdə(r)/ n despensa f

large /lɑːdʒ/ a (-er, -est) grande, ⟨before singular noun⟩ gran. • n. at ~ en libertad. ~ly adv en gran parte. ~ness n ⟨gran⟩ tamaño m

largesse /lɑː'ʒes/ n generosidad f

lark¹ /lɑːk/ n alondra f

lark² /lɑːk/ n broma f; ⟨bit of fun⟩ travesura f. • vi andar de juerga

larva /'lɑːvə/ n (pl **-vae** /-viː/) larva f

laryn|**gitis** /lærɪn'dʒaɪtɪs/ n laringitis f. ~x /'lærɪŋks/ n laringe f

lascivious /lə'sɪvɪəs/ a lascivo

laser /'leɪzə(r)/ n láser m

lash /læʃ/ vt azotar. ~ **out** ⟨spend⟩ gastar. ~ **out against** atacar. • n latigazo m; ⟨eyelash⟩ pestaña f

lashings /'læʃɪŋz/ npl. ~ **of** ⟨cream etc, sl⟩ montones de

lass /læs/ n muchacha f

lassitude /'læsɪtjuːd/ n lasitud f

lasso /læ'suː/ n (pl **-os**) lazo m

last¹ /lɑːst/ a último; ⟨week etc⟩ pasado. ~ **Monday** n el lunes pasado. **have the** ~ **word** decir la última palabra. **the** ~ **straw** n el colmo m. • adv por último; ⟨most recently⟩ la última vez. **he came** ~ llegó el último. • n último m; ⟨remainder⟩ lo que queda. ~ **but one** penúltimo. **at (long)** ~ en fin.

last² /lɑːst/ vi durar. ~ **out** sobrevivir

last³ /lɑːst/ n horma f

lasting /'lɑːstɪŋ/ a duradero

last: ~ly adv por último. ~ **night** n anoche m

latch /lætʃ/ n picaporte m

late /leɪt/ a (-er, -est) ⟨not on time⟩ tarde; ⟨recent⟩ reciente; ⟨former⟩ antiguo, ex; ⟨fruit⟩ tardío; ⟨hour⟩ avanzado; ⟨deceased⟩ difunto. **in** ~ **July** a fines de julio. **the** ~ **Dr Phillips** el difunto Dr. Phillips. • adv tarde. **of** ~ últimamente. ~ly adv últimamente. ~ness n ⟨delay⟩ retraso m; ⟨of hour⟩ lo avanzado

latent /'leɪtnt/ a latente

lateral /'lætərəl/ a lateral

latest /'leɪtɪst/ a último. **at the ~** a más tardar

lathe /leɪð/ n torno m

lather /'lɑːðə(r)/ n espuma f. ● vt enjabonar. ● vi hacer espuma

Latin /'lætɪn/ n (lang) latín m. ● a latino

latitude /'lætɪtjuːd/ n latitud m

latrine /lə'triːn/ n letrina f

latter /'lætə(r)/ a último; (of two) segundo. ● n. **the ~** éste m, ésta f, éstos mpl, éstas fpl. **~day** a moderno. **~ly** adv últimamente

lattice /'lætɪs/ n enrejado m

laudable /'lɔːdəbl/ a laudable

laugh /lɑːf/ vi reír(se) (**at** de). ● n risa f. **~able** a ridículo. **~ing-stock** n hazmerreír m invar. **~ter** /'lɑːftə(r)/ n (act) risa f; (sound of laughs) risas fpl

launch[1] /lɔːntʃ/ vt lanzar. ● n lanzamiento m. **~ (out) into** lanzarse a

launch[2] /lɔːntʃ/ n (boat) lancha f

launching pad /'lɔːntʃɪŋpæd/ n plataforma f de lanzamiento

laund|er /'lɔːndə(r)/ vt lavar (y planchar). **~erette** n lavandería f automática. **~ress** n lavandera f. **~ry** /'lɔːndrɪ/ n (place) lavandería f; (dirty clothes) ropa f sucia; (clean clothes) colada f

laurel /'lɒrəl/ n laurel m

lava /'lɑːvə/ n lava f

lavatory /'lævətərɪ/ n retrete m. **public ~** servicios mpl

lavender /'lævəndə(r)/ n lavanda f

lavish /'lævɪʃ/ a (person) pródigo; (plentiful) abundante; (lush) suntuoso. ● vt prodigar. **~ly** adv profusamente

law /lɔː/ n ley f; (profession, subject of study) derecho m. **~abiding** a observante de la ley. **~ and order** n orden m público. **~ court** n tribunal m. **~ful** a (permitted by law) lícito; (recognized by law) legítimo. **~fully** adv legalmente. **~less** a sin leyes

lawn /lɔːn/ n césped m. **~mower** n cortacésped f. **~ tennis** n tenis m (sobre hierba)

lawsuit /'lɔːsuːt/ n pleito m

lawyer /'lɔɪə(r)/ n abogado m

lax /læks/ a descuidado; (morals etc) laxo

laxative /'læksətɪv/ n laxante m

laxity /'læksətɪ/ n descuido m

lay[1] /leɪ/ vt (pt laid) poner (incl table, eggs); tender (trap); formar (plan). **~ hands on** echar mano a. **~ hold of** agarrar. **~ waste** asolar. **~ aside** dejar a un lado. **~ down** dejar a un lado; imponer (condition). **~ into** (sl) dar una paliza a. **~ off** vt despedir (worker); ● vi (fam) terminar. **~ on** (provide) proveer. **~ out** (design) disponer; (display) exponer; desembolsar (money). **~ up** (store) guardar; obligar a guardar cama (person)

lay[2] /leɪ/ a (non-clerical) laico; (opinion etc) profano

lay[3] /leɪ/ see **lie**

layabout /'leɪəbaʊt/ n holgazán m

lay-by /'leɪbaɪ/ n apartadero m

layer /'leɪə(r)/ n capa f

layette /leɪ'et/ n canastilla f

layman /'leɪmən/ n lego m

lay-off /'leɪɒf/ n paro m forzoso

layout /'leɪaʊt/ n disposición f

laze /leɪz/ vi holgazanear; (relax) descansar

laz|iness /'leɪzɪnɪs/ n pereza f. **~y** a perezoso. **~y-bones** n holgazán m

lb. abbr (pound) libra f

lead[1] /liːd/ vt (pt led) conducir; dirigir (team); llevar (life); (induce) inducir a. ● vi (go first) ir delante; (road) ir, conducir; (in cards) salir. ● n mando m; (clue) pista f; (leash) correa f; (in theatre) primer papel m; (wire) cable m; (example) ejemplo m. **in the ~** en cabeza. **~ away** llevar. **~ up to** preparar el terreno para

lead[2] /led/ n plomo m; (of pencil) mina f. **~en** /'ledn/ a de plomo

leader /'liːdə(r)/ n jefe m; (leading article) editorial m. **~ship** n dirección f

leading /'liːdɪŋ/ a principal; (in front) delantero. **~ article** n editorial m

leaf /liːf/ n (pl leaves) hoja f. ● vi. **~ through** hojear

leaflet /'liːflɪt/ n folleto m

leafy /'liːfɪ/ a frondoso

league /liːg/ n liga f. **be in ~ with** conchabarse con

leak /liːk/ n (hole) agujero m; (of gas, liquid) escape m; (of information) filtración f; (in roof) gotera f; (in boat) vía f de agua. ● vi (receptacle, gas, liquid) salirse; (information) filtrarse; (drip) gotear; (boat) hacer agua. ● vt dejar escapar; filtrar (in-

formation⟩. **~age** n = **leak**. **~y** a ⟨*re-ceptacle*⟩ agujereado; ⟨*roof*⟩ que tiene goteras; ⟨*boat*⟩ que hace agua

lean¹ /liːn/ vt (pt **leaned** or **leant** /lent/) apoyar. ● vi inclinarse. **~ against** apoyarse en. **~ on** apoyarse en. **~out** asomarse (**of** a). **~ over** inclinarse

lean² /liːn/ a (**-er, -est**) magro. ● n carne f magra

leaning /'liːnɪŋ/ a inclinado. ● n inclinación f

leanness /'liːnnɪs/ n (*of meat*) magrez f; (*of person*) flaqueza f

lean-to /'liːntuː/ n colgadizo m

leap /liːp/ vi (pt **leaped** or **leapt** /lept/) saltar. ● n salto m. **~frog** n salto m, saltacabrilla f. ● vi (pt **-frogged**) jugar a saltacabrilla. **~ year** n año m bisiesto

learn /lɜːn/ vt/i (pt **learned** or **learnt**) aprender (**to do** a hacer). **~ed** /'lɜː nɪd/ a culto. **~er** /'lɜːnə(r)/ n principiante m; (*apprentice*) aprendiz m; (*student*) estudiante m & f. **~ing** n saber m

lease /liːs/ n arriendo m. ● vt arrendar

leash /liːʃ/ n correa f

least /liːst/ a. **the ~** (*smallest amount of*) mínimo; (*slightest*) menor; (*smallest*) más pequeño. ● n lo menos. **at ~** por lo menos. **not in the ~** en absoluto. ● adv menos

leather /'leðə(r)/ n piel f, cuero m

leave /liːv/ vt (pt **left**) dejar; (*depart from*) marcharse de. **~ alone** dejar de tocar ⟨*thing*⟩; dejar en paz ⟨*person*⟩. **be left (over)** quedar. ● vi marcharse; ⟨*train*⟩ salir. ● n permiso m. **on ~** (*mil*) de permiso. **take one's ~ of** despedirse de. **~ out** omitir

leavings /'liːvɪŋz/ npl restos mpl

Leban|on /'lebənən/ n el Líbano m. **~ese** /-'niːz/ a & n libanés (m)

lecher /'letʃə(r)/ n libertino m. **~ous** a lascivo. **~y** n lascivia f

lectern /'lektɜːn/ n atril m; (*in church*) facistol m

lecture /'lektʃə(r)/ n conferencia f; (*univ*) clase f; (*rebuke*) sermón m. ● vt/i dar una conferencia (a); (*univ*) dar clases (a); (*rebuke*) sermonear. **~r** n conferenciante m; (*univ*) profesor m

led /led/ see **lead**¹

ledge /ledʒ/ n repisa f; (*of window*) antepecho m

ledger /'ledʒə(r)/ n libro m mayor

lee /liː/ n sotavento m; (*fig*) abrigo m

leech /liːtʃ/ n sanguijuela f

leek /liːk/ n puerro m

leer /'lɪə(r)/ vi. **~ (at)** mirar impúdicamente. ● n mirada f impúdica

leeway /'liːweɪ/ n deriva f; (*fig, freedom of action*) libertad f de acción. **make up ~** recuperar los atrasos

left¹ /left/ a izquierdo. ● adv a la izquierda. ● n izquierda f

left² /left/ see **leave**

left: ~-hand a izquierdo. **~-handed** a zurdo. **~ist** n izquierdista m & f. **~ luggage** n consigna f. **~overs** npl restos mpl

left-wing /left'wɪŋ/ a izquierdista

leg /leg/ n pierna f; (*of animal, furniture*) pata f; (*of pork*) pernil m; (*of lamb*) pierna f; (*of journey*) etapa f. **on its last ~s** en las últimas

legacy /'legəsɪ/ n herencia f

legal /'liːgl/ a (*permitted by law*) lícito; (*recognized by law*) legítimo; (*affairs etc*) jurídico. **~ aid** n abogacía f de pobres. **~ity** /-'gælətɪ/ n legalidad f. **~ize** vt legalizar. **~ly** adv legalmente

legation /lɪ'geɪʃn/ n legación f

legend /'ledʒənd/ n leyenda f. **~ary** a legendario

leggings /'legɪnz/ npl polainas fpl

legib|ility /ledʒəbɪlətɪ/ n legibilidad f. **~le** a legible. **~ly** a legiblemente

legion /'liːdʒən/ n legión f

legislat|e /'ledʒɪsleɪt/ vi legislar. **~ion** /-'leɪʃn/ n legislación f. **~ive** a legislativo. **~ure** /-eɪtʃə(r)/ n cuerpo m legislativo

legitima|cy /lɪ'dʒɪtɪməsɪ/ f legitimidad f. **~te** a legítimo

leisure /'leʒə(r)/ n ocio m. **at one's ~** cuando tenga tiempo. **~ly** adv sin prisa

lemon /'lemən/ n limón m. **~ade** /lemə'neɪd/ n (*fizzy*) gaseosa f (de limón); (*still*) limonada f

lend /lend/ vt (pt **lent**) prestar. **~ itself to** prestarse a. **~er** n prestador m; (*moneylender*) prestamista m & f. **~ing** n préstamo m. **~ing library** n biblioteca f de préstamo

length /leŋθ/ n largo m; (*in time*) duración f; (*of cloth*) largo m; (*of road*) tramo m. **at ~** (*at last*) por fin. **at (great) ~** detalladamente. **~en**

/'leŋθən/ vt alargar. ● vi alargarse.
~**ways** adv a lo largo. ~**y** a largo
lenien|cy /'li:nɪənsɪ/ n indulgencia f.
~**t** a indulgente. ~**tly** adv con
indulgencia
lens /lenz/ n lente f. **contact** ~**es** npl
lentillas fpl
lent /lent/ see **lend**
Lent /lent/ n cuaresma f
lentil /'lentl/ n (bean) lenteja f
Leo /'li:əʊ/ n (astr) Leo m
leopard /'lepəd/ n leopardo m
leotard /'li:əta:d/ n leotardo m
lep|er /'lepə(r)/ n leproso m. ~**rosy**
/'leprəsɪ/ n lepra f
lesbian /'lezbɪən/ n lesbiana f. ● a
lesbiano
lesion /'li:ʒn/ n lesión f
less /les/ a (in quantity) menos; (in
size) menor. ● adv & prep menos. ~
than menos que; (with numbers)
menos de. ● n menor m. ~ **and** ~
cada vez menos. **none the** ~ sin
embargo. ~**en** /'lesn/ vt/i disminuir. ~**er** /'lesə(r)/ a menor
lesson /'lesn/ n clase f
lest /lest/ conj por miedo de que
let /let/ vt (pt **let**, pres p **letting**)
dejar; (lease) alquilar. ~ **me do it**
déjame hacerlo. ● v aux. ~**'s go!**
¡vamos!, ¡vámonos! ~**'s see** (vamos)
a ver. ~**'s talk/drink** hablemos/
bebamos. ● n alquiler m. ~ **down**
bajar; (deflate) desinflar; (fig)
defraudar. ~ **go** soltar. ~ **in** dejar
entrar. ~ **off** disparar ⟨gun⟩; (cause
to explode) hacer explotar; hacer
estallar ⟨firework⟩; (excuse)
perdonar. ~ **off steam** (fig)
desfogarse. ~ **on** (sl) revelar. ~ **o.s.
in for** meterse en. ~ **out** dejar salir.
~ **through** dejar pasar. ~ **up** disminuir. ~**down** n desilusión f
lethal /'li:θl/ a ⟨dose, wound⟩ mortal;
⟨weapon⟩ mortífero
letharg|ic /lɪ'tɑ:dʒɪk/ a letárgico. ~**y**
/'leθədʒɪ/ n letargo m
letter /'letə(r)/ n (of alphabet) letra f;
(written message) carta f. ~**bomb** n
carta f explosiva. ~**box** n buzón m.
~**head** n membrete m. ~**ing** n
letras fpl
lettuce /'letɪs/ n lechuga f
let-up /'letʌp/ n (fam) descanso m
leukaemia /lu:'ki:mɪə/ n leucemia f
level /'levl/ a (flat) llano; (on surface)
horizontal; (in height) a nivel; (in
score) igual; ⟨spoonful⟩ raso. ● n

nivel m. **be on the** ~ (fam) ser honrado. ● vt (pt **levelled**) nivelar;
(aim) apuntar. ~ **crossing** n paso m
a nivel. ~**headed** a juicioso
lever /'li:və(r)/ n palanca f. ● vt apalancar. ~**age** /'li:vərɪdʒ/ n apa-
lancamiento m
levity /'levɪtɪ/ n ligereza f
levy /'levɪ/ vt exigir ⟨tax⟩. ● n
impuesto m
lewd /lu:d/ a (**-er, -est**) lascivo
lexicography /leksɪ'kɒgrəfɪ/ n lexicografía f
lexicon /'leksɪkən/ n léxico m
liable /'laɪəbl/ a. **be** ~ **to do** tener
tendencia a hacer. ~ **for** responsable de. ~ **to** susceptible de;
expuesto a ⟨fine⟩
liability /laɪə'bɪlətɪ/ n responsabilidad f; (disadvantage, fam)
inconveniente m. **liabilities** npl
(debts) deudas fpl
liais|e /lɪ'eɪz/ vi hacer un enlace,
enlazar. ~**on** /lɪ'eɪzɒn/ n enlace m;
(love affair) lío m
liar /'laɪə(r)/ n mentiroso m
libel /'laɪbl/ n libelo m. ● vt (pt
libelled) difamar (por escrito)
Liberal /'lɪbərəl/ a & n liberal (m & f)
liberal /'lɪbərəl/ a liberal; (generous)
generoso; (tolerant) tolerante. ~**ly**
adv liberalmente; (generously) gen-
erosamente; (tolerantly) tolerant-
emente
liberat|e /'lɪbəreɪt/ vt liberar. ~**ion**
/-'reɪʃn/ n liberación f
libertine /'lɪbəti:n/ n libertino m
liberty /'lɪbətɪ/ n libertad f. **be at** ~
to estar autorizado para. **take lib-
erties** tomarse libertades. **take the**
~ **of** tomarse la libertad de
libido /lɪ'bi:dəʊ/ n (pl **-os**) libido m
Libra /'li:brə/ n (astr) Libra f
librar|ian /laɪ'breərɪən/ n biblio-
tecario m. ~**y** /'laɪbrərɪ/ n biblioteca f
libretto /lɪ'bretəʊ/ n (pl **-os**) libreto
m
Libya /'lɪbɪə/ n Libia f. ~**n** a & n libio
(m)
lice /laɪs/ see **louse**
licence /'laɪsns/ n licencia f, permiso
m; (fig, liberty) libertad f. ~ **plate** n
(placa f de) matrícula f. **driving** ~
carné m de conducir
license /'laɪsns/ vt autorizar
licentious /laɪ'senʃəs/ a licencioso
lichen /'laɪkən/ n liquen m

lick /lɪk/ vt lamer; (*defeat, sl*) dar una paliza a. ~ **one's chops** relamerse. ● *n* lametón *m*

licorice /'lɪkərɪs/ *n* (*Amer*) regaliz *m*

lid /lɪd/ *n* tapa *f*; (*of pan*) cobertera *f*

lido /'liːdəʊ/ *n* (*pl* -os) piscina *f*

lie¹ /laɪ/ *vi* (*pt* lay, *pp* lain, *pres p* lying) echarse; (*state*) estar echado; (*remain*) quedarse; (*be*) estar, encontrarse; (*in grave*) yacer. **be lying** estar echado. ~ **down** acostarse. ~ **low** quedarse escondido

lie² /laɪ/ *n* mentira *f*. ● *vi* (*pt* lied, *pres p* lying) mentir. **give the ~ to** desmentir

lie-in /laɪ'ɪn/ *n*. **have a ~-in** quedarse en la cama

lieu /ljuː/ *n*. **in ~ of** en lugar de

lieutenant /lef'tenənt/ *n* (*mil*) teniente *m*

life /laɪf/ *n* (*pl* lives) vida *f*. ~**belt** *n* cinturón *m* salvavidas. ~**boat** *n* lancha *f* de salvamento; (*on ship*) bote *m* salvavidas. ~**buoy** *n* boya *f* salvavidas. ~ **cycle** *n* ciclo *m* vital. ~**guard** *n* bañero *m*. ~**jacket** *n* chaleco *m* salvavidas. ~**less** *a* sin vida. ~**like** *a* natural. ~**line** *n* cuerda *f* salvavidas; (*fig*) cordón *m* umbilical. ~**long** *a* de toda la vida. ~**size(d)** *a* de tamaño natural. ~**time** *n* vida *f*

lift /lɪft/ *vt* levantar; (*steal, fam*) robar. ● *vi* (*fog*) disiparse. ● *n* ascensor *m*, elevador *m* (*LAm*). **give a ~ to s.o.** llevar a uno en su coche, dar aventón a uno (*LAm*). ~**-off** *n* (*aviat*) despegue *m*

ligament /'lɪgəmənt/ *n* ligamento *m*

light¹ /laɪt/ *n* luz *f*; (*lamp*) lámpara *f*, luz *f*; (*flame*) fuego *m*; (*headlight*) faro *m*. **bring to ~** sacar a luz. **come to ~** salir a luz. **have you got a ~?** ¿tienes fuego? **the ~s** *npl* (*auto, traffic signals*) el semáforo *m*. ● *a* claro. ● *vt* (*pt* lit *or* lighted) encender; (*illuminate*) alumbrar. ~ **up** *vt/i* iluminar(se)

light² /laɪt/ *a* (-er, -est) (*not heavy*) ligero

lighten¹ /'laɪtn/ *vt* (*make less heavy*) aligerar

lighten² /'laɪtn/ *vt* (*give light to*) iluminar; (*make brighter*) aclarar

lighter /'laɪtə(r)/ *n* (*for cigarettes*) mechero *m*

light-fingered /laɪt'fɪŋgəd/ *a* largo de uñas

light-headed /laɪt'hedɪd/ *a* (*dizzy*) mareado; (*frivolous*) casquivano

light-hearted /laɪt'hɑːtɪd/ *a* alegre

lighthouse /'laɪthaʊs/ *n* faro *m*

lighting /'laɪtɪŋ/ *n* (*system*) alumbrado *m*; (*act*) iluminación *f*

light: ~**ly** *adv* ligeramente. ~**ness** *n* ligereza *f*

lightning /'laɪtnɪŋ/ *n* relámpago *m*. ● *a* relámpago

lightweight /'laɪtweɪt/ *a* ligero. ● *n* (*boxing*) peso *m* ligero

light-year /'laɪtjɪə(r)/ *n* año *m* luz

like¹ /laɪk/ *a* parecido. ● *prep* como. ● *conj* (*fam*) como. ● *n* igual *m*. **the ~s of you** la gente como tú

like² /laɪk/ *vt* gustarle (a uno). **I ~ chocolate** me gusta el chocolate. **I should ~** quisiera. **they ~ swimming** (a ellos) les gusta nadar. **would you ~?** ¿quieres? ~**able** *a* simpático. ~**s** *npl* gustos *mpl*

likelihood /'laɪklɪhʊd/ *n* probabilidad *f*

likely *a* (-ier, -iest) probable. **he is ~ to come** es probable que venga. ● *adv* probablemente. **not ~!** ¡ni hablar!

like-minded /laɪk'maɪndɪd/ *a*. **be ~** tener las mismas opiniones

liken /'laɪkən/ *vt* comparar

likeness /'laɪknɪs/ *n* parecido *m*. **be a good ~** parecerse mucho

likewise /'laɪkwaɪz/ *adv* (*also*) también; (*the same way*) lo mismo

liking /'laɪkɪŋ/ *n* (*for thing*) afición *f*; (*for person*) simpatía *f*

lilac /'laɪlək/ *n* lila *f*. ● *a* color de lila

lilt /lɪlt/ *n* ritmo *m*

lily /'lɪlɪ/ *n* lirio *m*. ~ **of the valley** lirio *m* de los valles

limb /lɪm/ *n* miembro *m*. **out on a ~** aislado

limber /'lɪmbə(r)/ *vi*. ~ **up** hacer ejercicios preliminares

limbo /'lɪmbəʊ/ *n* limbo *m*. **be in ~** (*forgotten*) estar olvidado

lime¹ /laɪm/ *n* (*white substance*) cal *f*

lime² /laɪm/ *n* (*fruit*) lima *f*

lime³ /laɪm/ *n*. ~**(-tree)** (*linden tree*) tilo *m*

limelight /'laɪmlaɪt/ *n*. **be in the ~** estar muy a la vista

limerick /'lɪmərɪk/ *n* quintilla *f* humorística

limestone /'laɪmstəʊn/ *n* caliza *f*

limit /'lɪmɪt/ *n* límite *m*. ● *vt* limitar. ~**ation** /-'teɪʃn/ *n* limitación *f*. ~**ed**

a limitado. **~ed company** *n* sociedad *f* anónima

limousine /'lɪməziːn/ *n* limusina *f*

limp¹ /lɪmp/ *vi* cojear. ● *n* cojera *f*. **have a ~** cojear

limp² /lɪmp/ *a* (**-er, -est**) flojo

limpid /'lɪmpɪd/ *a* límpido

linctus /'lɪŋktəs/ *n* jarabe *m* (para la tos)

line¹ /laɪn/ *n* línea *f*; (*track*) vía *f*; (*wrinkle*) arruga *f*; (*row*) fila *f*; (*of poem*) verso *m*; (*rope*) cuerda *f*; (*of goods*) surtido *m*; (*queue, Amer*) cola *f*. **in ~ with** de acuerdo con. ● *vt* (*on paper etc*) rayar; bordear ⟨*streets etc*⟩. **~ up** alinearse; (*in queue*) hacer cola

line² /laɪn/ *vt* forrar; (*fill*) llenar

lineage /'lɪnɪɪdʒ/ *n* linaje *m*

linear /'lɪnɪə(r)/ *a* lineal

linen /'lɪnɪn/ *n* (*sheets etc*) ropa *f* blanca; (*material*) lino *m*

liner /'laɪnə(r)/ *n* transatlántico *m*

linesman /'laɪnzmən/ *n* (*football*) juez *m* de línea

linger /'lɪŋɡə(r)/ *vi* tardar en marcharse; ⟨*smells etc*⟩ persistir. **~ over** dilatarse en

lingerie /'lænʒərɪ/ *n* ropa *f* interior, lencería *f*

lingo /'lɪŋɡəʊ/ *n* (*pl* **-os**) idioma *m*; (*specialized vocabulary*) jerga *f*

linguist /'lɪŋgwɪst/ *n* (*specialist in languages*) políglota *m & f*; (*specialist in linguistics*) lingüista *m & f*. **~ic** /lɪŋ'gwɪstɪk/ *a* lingüístico. **~ics** *n* lingüística *f*

lining /'laɪnɪŋ/ *n* forro *m*; (*auto, of brakes*) guarnición *f*

link /lɪŋk/ *n* (*of chain*) eslabón *m*; (*fig*) lazo *m*. ● *vt* eslabonar; (*fig*) enlazar. **~ up with** reunirse con. **~age** *n* enlace *m*

links /lɪŋks/ *n invar* campo *m* de golf

lino /'laɪnəʊ/ *n* (*pl* **-os**) linóleo *m*. **~leum** /lɪ'nəʊlɪəm/ *n* linóleo *m*

lint /lɪnt/ *n* (*med*) hilas *fpl*; (*fluff*) pelusa *f*

lion /'laɪən/ *n* león *m*. **the ~'s share** la parte *f* del león. **~ess** *n* leona *f*

lionize /'laɪənaɪz/ *vt* tratar como una celebridad

lip /lɪp/ *n* labio *m*; (*edge*) borde *m*. **pay ~ service to** aprobar de boquilla. **stiff upper ~** *n* imperturbabilidad *f*. **~-read** *vt/i* leer en los labios. **~salve** *n* crema *f* para los labios. **~stick** *n* lápiz *m* de labios.

liquefy /'lɪkwɪfaɪ/ *vt/i* licuar(se)

liqueur /lɪ'kjʊə(r)/ *n* licor *m*

liquid /'lɪkwɪd/ *a & n* líquido (*m*)

liquidat|e /'lɪkwɪdeɪt/ *vt* liquidar. **~ion** /-'deɪʃn/ *n* liquidación *f*

liquidize /'lɪkwɪdaɪz/ *vt* licuar. **~r** *n* licuadora *f*

liquor /'lɪkə(r)/ *n* bebida *f* alcohólica

liquorice /'lɪkərɪs/ *n* regaliz *m*

lira /'lɪərə/ *n* (*pl* **lire** /'lɪəreɪ/ *or* **liras**) lira *f*

lisle /laɪl/ *n* hilo *m* de Escocia

lisp /lɪsp/ *n* ceceo *m*. **speak with a ~** cecear. ● *vi* cecear

lissom /'lɪsəm/ *a* flexible, ágil

list¹ /lɪst/ *n* lista *f*. ● *vt* hacer una lista de; (*enter in a list*) inscribir

list² /lɪst/ *vi* ⟨*ship*⟩ escorar

listen /'lɪsn/ *vi* escuchar. **~ in (to)** escuchar. **~ to** escuchar. **~er** *n* oyente *m & f*

listless /'lɪstlɪs/ *a* apático

lit /lɪt/ *see* **light¹**

litany /'lɪtənɪ/ *n* letanía *f*

literacy /'lɪtərəsɪ/ *n* capacidad *f* de leer y escribir

literal /'lɪtərəl/ *a* literal; (*fig*) prosaico. **~ly** *adv* al pie de la letra, literalmente

literary /'lɪtərərɪ/ *a* literario

literate /'lɪtərət/ *a* que sabe leer y escribir

literature /'lɪtərətʃə(r)/ *n* literatura *f*; (*fig*) impresos *mpl*

lithe /laɪð/ *a* ágil

lithograph /'lɪθəgrɑːf/ *n* litografía *f*

litigation /lɪtɪ'geɪʃn/ *n* litigio *m*

litre /'liːtə(r)/ *n* litro *m*

litter /'lɪtə(r)/ *n* basura *f*; (*of animals*) camada *f*. ● *vt* ensuciar; (*scatter*) esparcir. **~ed with** lleno de. **~bin** *n* papelera *f*

little /'lɪtl/ *a* pequeño; (*not much*) poco de. ● *n* poco *m*. **a ~** un poco. **a ~ water** un poco de agua. ● *adv* poco. **~ by ~** poco a poco. **~ finger** *n* meñique *m*

liturgy /'lɪtədʒɪ/ *n* liturgia *f*

live¹ /lɪv/ *vt/i* vivir. **~ down** lograr borrar. **~ it up** echar una cana al aire. **~ on** ⟨*feed o.s. on*⟩ vivir de; (*continue*) perdurar. **~ up to** vivir de acuerdo con; cumplir ⟨*a promise*⟩

live² /laɪv/ *a* vivo; ⟨*wire*⟩ con corriente; ⟨*broadcast*⟩ en directo. **be a ~ wire** ser una persona enérgica

livelihood /'laɪvlɪhʊd/ *n* sustento *m*

livel|iness /'laɪvlɪnɪs/ *n* vivacidad *f*. **~y** *a* (**-ier, -iest**) vivo

liven /ˈlaɪvn/ vt/i. ~ **up** animar(se); (*cheer up*) alegrar(se)

liver /ˈlɪvə(r)/ n hígado m

livery /ˈlɪvərɪ/ n librea f

livestock /ˈlaɪvstɒk/ n ganado m

livid /ˈlɪvɪd/ a lívido; (*angry, fam*) furioso

living /ˈlɪvɪŋ/ a vivo. ● n vida f. ~**room** cuarto m de estar, cuarto m de estancia (*LAm*)

lizard /ˈlɪzəd/ n lagartija f; (*big*) lagarto m

llama /ˈlɑːmə/ n llama f

load /ləʊd/ n (*incl elec*) carga f; (*quantity*) cantidad f; (*weight, strain*) peso m. ● vt cargar. ~**ed** a *incl dice*) cargado; (*wealthy, sl*) muy rico. ~**s of** (*fam*) montones de

loaf[1] /ləʊf/ n (*pl loaves*) pan m; (*stick of bread*) barra f

loaf[2] /ləʊf/ vi. ~ (**about**) holgazanear. ~**er** n holgazán m

loam /ləʊm/ n marga f

loan /ləʊn/ n préstamo m. on ~ prestado. ● vt prestar

loath /ləʊθ/ a poco dispuesto (**to** a)

loath|**e** /ləʊð/ vt odiar. ~**ing** n odio m (**of** a). ~**some** a odioso

lobby /ˈlɒbɪ/ n vestíbulo m; (*pol*) grupo m de presión. ● vt hacer presión sobre

lobe /ləʊb/ n lóbulo m

lobster /ˈlɒbstə(r)/ n langosta f

local /ˈləʊkl/ a local. ● n (*pub, fam*) bar m. **the** ~**s** los vecinos mpl

locale /ləʊˈkɑːl/ n escenario m

local government /ləʊkl-ˈɡʌvənmənt/ n gobierno m municipal

locality /ləʊˈkælətɪ/ n localidad f

localized /ˈləʊkəlaɪzd/ a localizado

locally /ˈləʊkəlɪ/ adv localmente; (*nearby*) en la localidad

locate /ləʊˈkeɪt/ vt (*situate*) situar; (*find*) encontrar

location /ləʊˈkeɪʃn/ n colocación f; (*place*) situación f. **to film on** ~ **in Andalusia** rodar en Andalucía

lock[1] /lɒk/ n (*of door etc*) cerradura f; (*on canal*) esclusa f. ● vt/i cerrar(se) con llave. ~ **in** encerrar. ~ **out** cerrar la puerta a. ~ **up** encerrar

lock[2] /lɒk/ n (*of hair*) mechón m. ~**s** npl pelo m

locker /ˈlɒkə(r)/ n armario m

locket /ˈlɒkɪt/ n medallón m

lock-out /ˈlɒkaʊt/ n lock-out m

locksmith /ˈlɒksmɪθ/ n cerrajero m

locomotion /ləʊkəˈməʊʃn/ n locomoción f

locomotive /ləʊkəˈməʊtɪv/ n locomotora f

locum /ˈləʊkəm/ n interino m

locust /ˈləʊkəst/ n langosta f

lodge /lɒdʒ/ n (*in park*) casa f del guarda; (*of porter*) portería f. ● vt alojar; presentar ‹*complaint*›; depositar ‹*money*›. ● vi alojarse. ~**r** /-ə(r)/ n huésped m

lodgings /ˈlɒdʒɪŋz/ n alojamiento m; (*room*) habitación f

loft /lɒft/ n desván m

lofty /ˈlɒftɪ/ a (**-ier, -iest**) elevado; (*haughty*) altanero

log /lɒɡ/ n (*of wood*) leño m; (*naut*) cuaderno m de bitácora. **sleep like a** ~ dormir como un lirón. ● vt (*pt* **logged**) apuntar; (*travel*) recorrer

logarithm /ˈlɒɡərɪðəm/ n logaritmo m

log-book /ˈlɒɡbʊk/ n cuaderno m de bitácora; (*aviat*) diario m de vuelo

loggerheads /ˈlɒɡəhedz/ npl. **be at** ~ **with** estar a matar con

logic /ˈlɒdʒɪk/ a lógica f. ~**al** a lógico. ~**ally** adv lógicamente

logistics /ləˈdʒɪstɪks/ n logística f

logo /ˈləʊɡəʊ/ n (*pl* **-os**) logotipo m

loin /lɔɪn/ n (*culin*) solomillo m. ~**s** npl ijadas fpl

loiter /ˈlɔɪtə(r)/ vi holgazanear

loll /lɒl/ vi repantigarse

loll|**ipop** /ˈlɒlɪpɒp/ n (*boiled sweet*) piruli m. ~**y** n (*iced*) polo m; (*money, sl*) dinero m

London /ˈlʌndən/ n Londres m. ● a londinense. ~**er** n londinense m & f

lone /ləʊn/ a solitario. ~**ly** /ˈləʊnlɪ/ a (**-ier, -iest**) solitario. **feel** ~**ly** sentirse muy solo. ~**r** /ˈləʊnə(r)/ n solitario m. ~**some** a solitario

long[1] /lɒŋ/ a (**-er, -est**) largo. **a** ~ **time** mucho tiempo. **how** ~ **is it?** ¿cuánto tiene de largo? **in the** ~ **run** a la larga. ● adv largo/mucho tiempo. **as** ~ **as** (*while*) mientras; (*provided that*) con tal que (+ *subjunctive*). **before** ~ dentro de poco. **so** ~**!** ¡hasta luego! **so** ~ **as** (*provided that*) con tal que (+ *subjunctive*)

long[2] /lɒŋ/ vi. ~ **for** anhelar

long-distance /lɒŋˈdɪstəns/ a de larga distancia. ~ **(tele)phone call** n conferencia f

longer /ˈlɒŋɡə(r)/ adv. **no** ~**er** ya no

longevity /lɒnˈdʒevətɪ/ n longevidad f

long: ~ **face** n cara f triste. ~**hand** n escritura f a mano. ~ **johns** npl (fam) calzoncillos mpl largos. ~ **jump** n salto m de longitud

longing /ˈlɒŋɪŋ/ n anhelo m, ansia f

longitude /ˈlɒŋɡɪtjuːd/ n longitud f

long: ~**playing record** n elepé m. ~**range** a de gran alcance. ~**sighted** a présbita. ~**standing** a de mucho tiempo. ~**suffering** a sufrido. ~**term** a a largo plazo. ~ **wave** n onda f larga. ~**winded** a ⟨speaker etc⟩ prolijo

loo /luː/ n (fam) servicios mpl

look /lʊk/ vt mirar; (seem) parecer; representar ⟨age⟩. ● vi mirar; (seem) parecer; (search) buscar. ● n mirada f; (appearance) aspecto m. ~ **after** ocuparse de; cuidar ⟨person⟩. ~ **at** mirar. ~ **down on** despreciar. ~ **for** buscar. ~ **forward to** esperar con ansia. ~ **in on** pasar por casa de. ~ **into** investigar. ~ **like** (resemble) parecerse a. ~ **on to** ⟨room, window⟩ dar a. ~ **out** tener cuidado. ~ **out for** buscar; (watch) tener cuidado con. ~ **round** volver la cabeza. ~ **through** hojear. ~ **up** buscar ⟨word⟩; (visit) ir a ver. ~ **up to** respetar. ~**er-on** n espectador m. ~**ing-glass** n espejo m. ~**out** n (mil) atalaya f; (person) vigía m. ~**s** npl belleza f. **good** ~**s** mpl belleza f

loom¹ /luːm/ n telar m

loom² /luːm/ vi aparecerse

loony /ˈluːnɪ/ a & n (sl) chiflado (m) (fam), loco (m). ~ **bin** n (sl) manicomio m

loop /luːp/ n lazo m. ● vt hacer presilla con

loophole /ˈluːphəʊl/ n (in rule) escapatoria f

loose /luːs/ a (-er, -est) (untied) suelto; (not tight) flojo; (inexact) vago; (immoral) inmoral; (not packed) suelto. **be at a** ~ **end, be at** ~ **ends** (Amer) no tener nada que hacer. ~**ly** adv sueltamente; (roughly) aproximadamente. ~**n** /ˈluːsn/ vt (slacken) aflojar; (untie) desatar

loot /luːt/ n botín m. ● vt saquear. ~**er** n saqueador m. ~**ing** n saqueo m

lop /lɒp/ vt (pt lopped). ~ **off** cortar

lop-sided /lɒpˈsaɪdɪd/ a ladeado

loquacious /ləˈkweɪʃəs/ a locuaz

lord /lɔːd/ n señor m; (British title) lord m. **(good) L~!** ¡Dios mío! **the L~** el Señor m. **the (House of) L~s** la Cámara f de los Lores. ~**ly** señorial; (haughty) altivo. ~**ship** n señoría f

lore /lɔː(r)/ n tradiciones fpl

lorgnette /lɔːˈnjet/ n impertinentes mpl

lorry /ˈlɒrɪ/ n camión m

lose /luːz/ vt/i (pt lost) perder. ~**r** n perdedor m

loss /lɒs/ n pérdida f. **be at a** ~ estar perplejo. **be at a** ~ **for words** no encontrar palabras. **be at a** ~ **to** no saber cómo

lost /lɒst/ see **lose**. ● a perdido. ~ **property** n, ~ **and found** (Amer) n oficina f de objetos perdidos. **get** ~ perderse

lot /lɒt/ n (fate) suerte f; (at auction) lote m; (land) solar m. **a** ~ **(of)** muchos. **quite a** ~ **of** (fam) bastante. ~**s (of)** (fam) muchos. **the** ~ todos mpl

lotion /ˈləʊʃn/ n loción f

lottery /ˈlɒtərɪ/ n lotería f

lotto /ˈlɒtəʊ/ n lotería f

lotus /ˈləʊtəs/ n (pl -uses) loto m

loud /laʊd/ a (-er, -est) fuerte; (noisy) ruidoso; (gaudy) chillón. **out** ~ en voz alta. ~ **hailer** n megáfono m. ~**ly** adv (speak etc) en voz alta; (noisily) ruidosamente. ~**speaker** n altavoz m

lounge /laʊndʒ/ vi repantigarse. ● n salón m. ~ **suit** n traje m de calle

louse /laʊs/ n (pl lice) piojo m

lousy /ˈlaʊzɪ/ a (-ier, -iest) piojoso; (bad, sl) malísimo

lout /laʊt/ n patán m

lovable /ˈlʌvəbl/ a adorable

love /lʌv/ n amor m; (tennis) cero m. **be in** ~ **with** estar enamorado de. **fall in** ~ **with** enamorarse de. ● vt querer ⟨person⟩; gustarle mucho a uno, encantarle a uno ⟨things⟩. **I** ~ **milk** me encanta la leche. ~ **affair** n amores mpl

lovely /ˈlʌvlɪ/ a (-ier, -iest) hermoso; (delightful, fam) precioso. **have a** ~ **time** divertirse

lover /ˈlʌvə(r)/ n amante m & f

lovesick /ˈlʌvsɪk/ a atortolado

loving /ˈlʌvɪŋ/ a cariñoso

low¹ /ləʊ/ a & adv (-er, -est) bajo. ● n (low pressure) área f de baja presión

low² /ləʊ/ vi mugir

lowbrow /'ləʊbraʊ/ a poco culto
low-cut /'ləʊkʌt/ a escotado
low-down /'ləʊdaʊn/ a bajo. ● n (sl) informes mpl
lower /'ləʊə(r)/ a & adv see **low²**. ● vt bajar. ~ **o.s.** envilecerse
low-key /'ləʊ'kiː/ a moderado
lowlands /'ləʊləndz/ npl tierra f baja
lowly /'ləʊlɪ/ a (-ier, -iest) humilde
loyal /'lɔɪəl/ a leal. ~ly adv lealmente. ~ty n lealtad f
lozenge /'lɒzɪndʒ/ n (shape) rombo m; (tablet) pastilla f
LP /el'piː/ abbr (long-playing record) elepé m
Ltd /'lɪmɪtɪd/ abbr (Limited) S.A., Sociedad Anónima
lubrica|nt /'luːbrɪkənt/ n lubricante m. ~te /-'keɪt/ vt lubricar. ~tion /-'keɪʃn/ n lubricación f
lucid /'luːsɪd/ a lúcido. ~ity /-'sɪdətɪ/ n lucidez f
luck /lʌk/ n suerte f. **bad** ~ n mala suerte f. ~ily /'lʌkɪlɪ/ adv afortunadamente. ~y a (-ier, -iest) afortunado
lucrative /'luːkrətɪv/ a lucrativo
lucre /'luːkə(r)/ n (pej) dinero m. **filthy** ~ vil metal m
ludicrous /'luːdɪkrəs/ a ridículo
lug /lʌg/ vt (pt lugged) arrastrar
luggage /'lʌgɪdʒ/ n equipaje m. ~-rack n rejilla f. ~-van n furgón m
lugubrious /luː'guːbrɪəs/ a lúgubre
lukewarm /'luːkwɔːm/ a tibio
lull /lʌl/ vt (soothe, send to sleep) adormecer; (calm) calmar. ● n periodo m de calma
lullaby /'lʌləbaɪ/ n canción f de cuna
lumbago /lʌm'beɪgəʊ/ n lumbago m
lumber /'lʌmbə(r)/ n trastos mpl viejos; (wood) maderas mpl. ● vt. ~ **s.o. with** hacer que uno cargue con. ~jack n leñador m
luminous /'luːmɪnəs/ a luminoso
lump¹ /lʌmp/ n protuberancia f; (in liquid) grumo m; (of sugar) terrón m; (in throat) nudo m. ● vt. ~ **together** agrupar
lump² /lʌmp/ vt. ~ **it** (fam) aguantarlo
lump: ~ **sum** n suma f global. ~y a ⟨sauce⟩ grumoso; (bumpy) cubierto de protuberancias
lunacy /'luːnəsɪ/ n locura f
lunar /'luːnə(r)/ a lunar
lunatic /'luːnətɪk/ n loco m
lunch /lʌntʃ/ n comida f, almuerzo m. ● vi comer

luncheon /'lʌntʃən/ n comida f, almuerzo m. ~ **meat** n carne f en lata. ~ **voucher** n vale m de comida
lung /lʌŋ/ n pulmón m
lunge /lʌndʒ/ n arremetida f
lurch¹ /lɜːtʃ/ vi tambalearse
lurch² /lɜːtʃ/ n. **leave in the** ~ dejar en la estacada
lure /ljʊə(r)/ vt atraer. ● n (attraction) atractivo m
lurid /'ljʊərɪd/ a chillón; (shocking) espeluznante
lurk /lɜːk/ vi esconderse; (in ambush) estar al acecho; (prowl) rondar
luscious /'lʌʃəs/ a delicioso
lush /lʌʃ/ a exuberante. ● n (Amer, sl) borracho m
lust /lʌst/ n lujuria f; (fig) ansia f. ● vi. ~ **after** codiciar. ~ful a lujurioso
lustre /'lʌstə(r)/ n lustre m
lusty /'lʌstɪ/ a (-ier, -iest) fuerte
lute /luːt/ n laúd m
Luxemburg /'lʌksəmbɜːg/ n Luxemburgo m
luxuriant /lʌg'zjʊərɪənt/ a exuberante
luxur|ious /lʌg'zjʊərɪəs/ a lujoso. ~y /'lʌkʃərɪ/ n lujo m. ● a de lujo
lye /laɪ/ n lejía f
lying /'laɪɪŋ/ see **lie¹**, **lie²**. ● n mentiras fpl
lynch /lɪntʃ/ vt linchar
lynx /lɪŋks/ n lince m
lyre /'laɪə(r)/ n lira f
lyric /'lɪrɪk/ a lírico. ~al a lírico. ~ism /-sɪzəm/ n lirismo m. ~s npl letra f

M

MA abbr (Master of Arts) Master m, grado m universitario entre el de licenciado y doctor
mac /mæk/ n (fam) impermeable m
macabre /mə'kɑːbrə/ a macabro
macaroni /mækə'rəʊnɪ/ n macarrones mpl
macaroon /mækə'ruːn/ n mostachón m
mace¹ /meɪs/ n (staff) maza f
mace² /meɪs/ n (spice) macis f
Mach /mɑːk/ n. ~ **(number)** n (número m de) Mach (m)
machiavellian /mækɪə'velɪən/ a maquiavélico

machinations /ˌmækɪ'neɪʃnz/ *npl* maquinaciones *fpl*

machine /mə'ʃi:n/ *n* máquina *f*. ● *vt* (*sew*) coser a máquina; (*tec*) trabajar a máquina. ~**gun** *n* ametralladora *f*. ~**ry** /mə'ʃi:nərɪ/ *n* maquinaria *f*; (*working parts, fig*) mecanismo *m*. ~ **tool** *n* máquina *f* herramienta

machinist /mə'ʃi:nɪst/ *n* maquinista *m & f*

mach|ismo /mæ'tʃɪzməʊ/ *n* machismo *m*. ~**o** *a* macho

mackerel /'mækrəl/ *n invar* (*fish*) caballa *f*

mackintosh /'mækɪntɒʃ/ *n* impermeable *m*

macrobiotic /ˌmækrəʊbaɪ'ɒtɪk/ *a* macrobiótico

mad /mæd/ *a* (**madder, maddest**) loco; (*foolish*) insensato; (*dog*) rabioso; (*angry, fam*) furioso. **be ~ about** estar loco por. **like ~** como un loco; (*a lot*) muchísimo

Madagascar /ˌmædə'gæskə(r)/ *n* Madagascar *m*

madam /'mædəm/ *n* señora *f*; (*unmarried*) señorita *f*

madcap /'mædkæp/ *a* atolondrado. ● *n* locuelo *m*

madden /'mædn/ *vt* (*make mad*) enloquecer; (*make angry*) enfurecer

made /meɪd/ *see* **make**. ~ **to measure** hecho a la medida

Madeira /mə'dɪərə/ *n* (*wine*) vino *m* de Madera

mad: ~**house** *n* manicomio *m*. ~**ly** *adv* (*interested, in love etc*) locamente; (*frantically*) como un loco. ~**man** *n* loco *m*. ~**ness** *n* locura *f*

madonna /mə'dɒnə/ *n* Virgen *f* María

madrigal /'mædrɪgl/ *n* madrigal *m*

maelstrom /'meɪlstrəm/ *n* remolino *m*

maestro /'maɪstrəʊ/ *n* (*pl* **maestri** /-stri:/ *or* **os**) maestro *m*

Mafia /'mæfɪə/ *n* mafia *f*

magazine /ˌmægə'zi:n/ *n* revista *f*; (*of gun*) recámara *f*

magenta /mə'dʒentə/ *a* rojo purpúreo

maggot /'mægət/ *n* gusano *m*. ~**y** *a* agusanado

Magi /'meɪdʒaɪ/ *npl*. **the ~** los Reyes *mpl* Magos

magic /'mædʒɪk/ *n* magia *f*. ● *a* mágico. ~**al** *a* mágico. ~**ian** /mə'dʒɪʃn/ *n* mago *m*

magisterial /ˌmædʒɪ'stɪərɪəl/ *a* magistral; (*imperious*) autoritario

magistrate /'mædʒɪstreɪt/ *n* magistrado *m*, juez *m*

magnanim|ity /ˌmægnə'nɪmətɪ/ *n* magnanimidad *f*. ~**ous** /-'nænɪməs/ *a* magnánimo

magnate /'mægneɪt/ *n* magnate *m*

magnesia /mæg'ni:ʒə/ *n* magnesia *f*

magnet /'mægnɪt/ *n* imán *m*. ~**ic** /-'netɪk/ *a* magnético. ~**ism** *n* magnetismo *m*. ~**ize** *vt* magnetizar

magnificen|ce /mæg'nɪfɪsns/ *a* magnificencia *f*. ~**t** *a* magnífico

magnif|ication /ˌmægnɪfɪ'keɪʃn/ *n* aumento *m*. ~**ier** /-'faɪə(r)/ *n* lupa *f*, lente *f* de aumento. ~**y** /-'faɪ/ *vt* aumentar. ~**ying-glass** *n* lupa *f*, lente *f* de aumento

magnitude /'mægnɪtjuːd/ *n* magnitud *f*

magnolia /mæg'nəʊlɪə/ *n* magnolia *f*

magnum /'mægnəm/ *n* botella *f* de litro y medio

magpie /'mægpaɪ/ *n* urraca *f*

mahogany /mə'hɒgənɪ/ *n* caoba *f*

maid /meɪd/ *n* (*servant*) criada *f*; (*girl, old use*) doncella *f*. **old ~** solterona *f*

maiden /'meɪdn/ *n* doncella *f*. ● *a* (*aunt*) soltera; (*voyage*) inaugural. ~**hood** *n* doncellez *f*, virginidad *f*, soltería *f*. ~**ly** *adv* virginal. ~ **name** *n* apellido *m* de soltera

mail[1] /meɪl/ *n* correo *m*; (*letters*) cartas *fpl*. ● *a* postal, de correos. ● *vt* (*post*) echar al correo; (*send*) enviar por correo

mail[2] /meɪl/ *n* (*armour*) (cota *f* de) malla *f*

mail: ~**ing list** *n* lista *f* de direcciones. ~**man** *n* (*Amer*) cartero *m*. ~ **order** *n* venta *f* por correo

maim /meɪm/ *vt* mutilar

main /meɪn/ *n*. (**water**)**gas** ~ cañería *f* principal. **in the ~** en su mayor parte. **the ~s** *npl* (*elec*) la red *f* eléctrica. ● *a* principal. **a ~ road** *n* una carretera *f*. ~**land** *n* continente *m*. ~**ly** *adv* principalmente. ~**spring** *n* muelle *m* real; (*fig, motive*) móvil *m* principal. ~**stay** *n* sostén *m*. ~**stream** *n* corriente *f* principal. ~ **street** *n* calle *f* principal

maintain /meɪn'teɪn/ *vt* mantener

maintenance /'meɪntənəns/ *n* mantenimiento *m*; (*allowance*) pensión *f* alimenticia

maisonette 349 **manage**

maisonette /meɪzə'net/ n (small house) casita f; (part of house) dúplex m

maize /meɪz/ n maíz m

majestic /mə'dʒestɪk/ a majestuoso

majesty /'mædʒəstɪ/ n majestad f

major /'meɪdʒə(r)/ a mayor. **a ~ road** una calle f prioritaria. • n comandante m. • vi. **~ in** (univ, Amer) especializarse en

Majorca /mə'jɔːkə/ n Mallorca f

majority /mə'dʒɒrətɪ/ n mayoría f. **the ~ of people** la mayoría f de la gente. • a mayoritario

make /meɪk/ vt/i (pt **made**) hacer; (manufacture) fabricar; ganar ‹money›; tomar ‹decision›; llegar a ‹destination›. **~ s.o. do sth** obligar a uno a hacer algo. **be made of** estar hecho de. **I cannot ~ anything of it** no me lo explico. **I ~ it two o'clock** yo tengo las dos. • n fabricación f; (brand) marca f. **~ as if to** estar a punto de. **~ believe** fingir. **~ do** (manage) arreglarse. **~ do with** (content o.s.) contentarse con. **~ for** dirigirse a. **~ good** vi tener éxito. • vt compensar; (repair) reparar. **~ it** llegar; (succeed) tener éxito. **~ it up** (become reconciled) hacer las paces. **~ much of** dar mucha importancia a. **~ off** escaparse (with con). **~ out** vt distinguir; (understand) entender; (draw up) extender; (assert) dar a entender. • vi arreglárselas. **~ over** ceder (to a). **~ up** formar; (prepare) preparar; inventar ‹story›; (compensate) compensar. • vi hacer las paces. **~ up** (one's face) maquillarse. **~ up for** compensar; recuperar ‹time›. **~ up to** congraciarse con. **~believe** a fingido, simulado. **~** n ficción f

maker /'meɪkə(r)/ n fabricante m & f. **the M~** el Hacedor m, el Creador m

makeshift /'meɪkʃɪft/ n expediente m. • a (temporary) provisional; (improvised) improvisado

make-up /'meɪkʌp/ n maquillaje m

makeweight /'meɪkweɪt/ n complemento m

making /'meɪkɪŋ/ n. **be the ~ of** ser la causa del éxito de. **he has the ~s of** tiene madera de. **in the ~** en vías de formación

maladjust|ed /mælə'dʒʌstɪd/ a inadaptado. **~ment** n inadaptación f

maladministration /mæləd mɪnɪ'streɪʃn/ n mala administración f

malady /'mælədɪ/ n enfermedad f

malaise /mæ'leɪz/ n malestar m

malaria /mə'leərɪə/ n paludismo m

Malay /mə'leɪ/ a & n malayo (m). **~sia** n Malasia f

male /meɪl/ a masculino; (bot, tec) macho. • n macho m; (man) varón m

malefactor /'mælɪfæktə(r)/ n malhechor m

malevolen|ce /mə'levəlns/ n malevolencia f. **~t** a malévolo

malform|ation /mælfɔː'meɪʃn/ n malformación f. **~ed** a deforme

malfunction /mæl'fʌŋkʃn/ n funcionamiento m defectuoso. • vi funcionar mal

malic|e /'mælɪs/ n rencor m. **bear s.o. ~e** guardar rencor a uno. **~ious** /mə'lɪʃəs/ a malévolo. **~iously** adv con malevolencia

malign /mə'laɪn/ a maligno. • vt calumniar

malignan|cy /mə'lɪɡnənsɪ/ n malignidad f. **~t** a maligno

malinger /mə'lɪŋɡə(r)/ vi fingirse enfermo. **~er** n enfermo m fingido

malleable /'mælɪəbl/ a maleable

mallet /'mælɪt/ n mazo m

malnutrition /mælnjuː'trɪʃn/ n desnutrición f

malpractice /mæl'præktɪs/ n falta f profesional

malt /mɔːlt/ n malta f

Malt|a /'mɔːltə/ n Malta f. **~ese** /-'tiːz/ a & n maltés (m)

maltreat /mæl'triːt/ vt maltratar. **~ment** n maltrato m

malt whisky /mɔːlt'wɪskɪ/ n güisqui m de malta

mammal /'mæml/ n mamífero m

mammoth /'mæməθ/ n mamut m. • a gigantesco

man /mæn/ n (pl men) hombre m; (in sports team) jugador m; (chess) pieza f. **~ in the street** hombre m de la calle. **to ~ to ~** de hombre a hombre. • vt (pt **manned**) guarnecer (de hombres); tripular ‹ship›; servir ‹guns›

manacle /'mænəkl/ n manilla f. • vt poner esposas a

manage /'mænɪdʒ/ vt dirigir; llevar ‹shop, affairs›; (handle) manejar. • vi arreglárselas. **~ to do** lograr

hacer. ~able *a* manejable. ~ment
n dirección *f*

manager /'mænɪdʒə(r)/ *n* director *m*;
(*of actor*) empresario *m*. ~ess
/-'res/ *n* directora *f*. ~ial /-'dʒɪərɪəl/
a directivo. ~ial staff *n* personal *m*
dirigente

managing director /mænɪdʒɪŋ
daɪ'rektə(r)/ *n* director *m* gerente

mandarin /'mændərɪn/ *n* mandarín
m; (*orange*) mandarina *f*

mandate /'mændeɪt/ *n* mandato *m*

mandatory /'mændətərɪ/ *a* obligatorio

mane /meɪn/ *n* (*of horse*) crin *f*; (*of lion*) melena *f*

manful /'mænfl/ *a* valiente

manganese /'mæŋgəniːz/ *n* manganeso *m*

manger /'meɪndʒə(r)/ *n* pesebre *m*

mangle[1] /'mæŋgl/ *n* (*for wringing*)
exprimidor *m*; (*for smoothing*)
máquina *f* de planchar

mangle[2] /'mæŋgl/ *vt* destrozar

mango /'mæŋgəʊ/ *n* (*pl* **-oes**) mango *m*

mangy /'meɪndʒɪ/ *a* sarnoso

man: ~handle *vt* maltratar. ~hole
n registro *m*. ~hole cover *n* tapa *f*
de registro. ~hood *n* edad *f* viril;
(*quality*) virilidad *f*. ~hour *n* hora-hombre *f*. ~hunt *n* persecución
f

mania /'meɪnɪə/ *n* manía *f*. ~c /-ɪæk/
n maníaco *m*

manicur|e /'mænɪkjʊə(r)/ *n* manicura *f*. ● *vt* hacer la manicura a (*person*). ~ist *n* manicuro *m*

manifest /'mænɪfest/ *a* manifiesto.
● *vt* mostrar. ~ation /-'steɪʃn/ *n*
manifestación *f*

manifesto /mænɪ'festəʊ/ *n* (*pl* **-os**)
manifiesto *m*

manifold /'mænɪfəʊld/ *a* múltiple

manipulat|e /mə'nɪpjʊleɪt/ *vt* manipular. ~ion /-'leɪʃn/ *n* manipulación *f*

mankind /mæn'kaɪnd/ *n* la humanidad *f*

man: ~ly *adv* viril. ~made *a*
artificial

mannequin /'mænɪkɪn/ *n* maniquí
m

manner /'mænə(r)/ *n* manera *f*;
(*behaviour*) comportamiento *m*;
(*kind*) clase *f*. ~ed *a* amanerado.
bad-~ed *a* mal educado. ~s *npl*
(*social behaviour*) educación *f*. have
no ~s no tener educación

mannerism /'mænərɪzəm/ *n* peculiaridad *f*

mannish /'mænɪʃ/ *a* (*woman*)
hombruna

manoeuvre /mə'nuːvə(r)/ *n* maniobra
f. ● *vt/i* maniobrar

man-of-war /mænəv'wɔː(r)/ *n* buque
m de guerra

manor /'mænə(r)/ *n* casa *f* solariega

manpower /'mænpaʊə(r)/ *n* mano *f*
de obra

manservant /'mænsɜːvənt/ *n* criado
m

mansion /'mænʃn/ *n* mansión *f*

man: ~size(d) *a* grande. ~slaughter *n* homicidio *m* impremeditado

mantelpiece /'mæntlpiːs/ *n* repisa *f*
de chimenea

mantilla /mæn'tɪlə/ *n* mantilla *f*

mantle /'mæntl/ *n* manto *m*

manual /'mænjʊəl/ *a* manual. ● *n*
(*handbook*) manual *m*

manufacture /mænjʊ'fæktʃə(r)/ *vt*
fabricar. ● *n* fabricación *f*. ~r /-ə(r)/
n fabricante *m*

manure /mə'njʊə(r)/ *n* estiércol *m*

manuscript /'mænjʊskrɪpt/ *n* manuscrito *m*

many /'menɪ/ *a & n* muchos (*mpl*).
~ people mucha gente *f*. ~ a time
muchas veces. a great/good ~
muchísimos

map /mæp/ *n* mapa *m*; (*of streets etc*)
plano *m*. ● *vt* (*pt* **mapped**) levantar
un mapa de. ~ out organizar

maple /'meɪpl/ *n* arce *m*

mar /mɑː/ *vt* (*pt* **marred**) estropear;
aguar (*enjoyment*)

marathon /'mærəθən/ *n* maratón *m*

maraud|er /mə'rɔːdə(r)/ *n* merodeador *m*. ~ing *a* merodeador

marble /'mɑːbl/ *n* mármol *m*; (*for game*) canica *f*

March /mɑːtʃ/ *n* marzo *m*

march /mɑːtʃ/ *vi* (*mil*) marchar. ~ off
irse. ● *vt*. ~ off (*lead away*)
llevarse. ● *n* marcha *f*

marchioness /mɑːʃə'nes/ *n* marquesa
f

march-past /'mɑːtʃpɑːst/ *n* desfile *m*

mare /meə(r)/ *n* yegua *f*

margarine /mɑːdʒə'riːn/ *n* margarina
f

margin /'mɑːdʒɪn/ *n* margen *f*. ~al *a*
marginal. ~al seat *n* (*pol*) escaño *m*
inseguro. ~ally *adv* muy poco

marguerite /mɑːgə'riːt/ *n* margarita *f*

marigold /'mærɪgəʊld/ *n* caléndula *f*

marijuana /ˌmærɪˈhwɑːnə/ n marihuana f

marina /məˈriːnə/ n puerto m deportivo

marina|de /ˌmærɪˈneɪd/ n escabeche m. ~te /ˈmærɪneɪt/ vt escabechar

marine /məˈriːn/ a marino. ● n (sailor) soldado m de infantería de marina; (shipping) marina f

marionette /ˌmærɪəˈnet/ n marioneta f

marital /ˈmærɪtl/ a marital, matrimonial. ~ status n estado m civil

maritime /ˈmærɪtaɪm/ a marítimo

marjoram /ˈmɑːdʒərəm/ n mejorana f

mark[1] /mɑːk/ n marca f; (trace) huella f; (schol) nota f; (target) blanco m. ● vt marcar; poner nota a ⟨exam⟩. ~ time marcar el paso. ~ out trazar; escoger ⟨person⟩

mark[2] /mɑːk/ n (currency) marco m

marked /mɑːkt/ a marcado. ~ly /-kɪdlɪ/ adv marcadamente

marker /ˈmɑːkə(r)/ n marcador m; (for book) registro m

market /ˈmɑːkɪt/ n mercado m. on the ~ en venta. ● vt (sell) vender; (launch) comercializar. ~ garden n huerto m. ~ing n marketing m

marking /ˈmɑːkɪŋ/ n (marks) marcas fpl

marksman /ˈmɑːksmən/ n tirador m. ~ship n puntería f

marmalade /ˈmɑːməleɪd/ n mermelada f de naranja

marmot /ˈmɑːmət/ n marmota f

maroon /məˈruːn/ n granate m. ● a de color granate

marooned /məˈruːnd/ a abandonado; (snow-bound etc) aislado

marquee /mɑːˈkiː/ n tienda f de campaña f grande; (awning, Amer) marquesina f

marquetry /ˈmɑːkɪtrɪ/ n marquetería f

marquis /ˈmɑːkwɪs/ n marqués m

marriage /ˈmærɪdʒ/ n matrimonio m; (wedding) boda f. ~able a casadero

married /ˈmærɪd/ a casado; ⟨life⟩ conjugal

marrow /ˈmærəʊ/ n (of bone) tuétano m; (vegetable) calabacín m

marry /ˈmærɪ/ vt casarse con; (give or unite in marriage) casar. ● vi casarse. get married casarse

marsh /mɑːʃ/ n pantano m

marshal /ˈmɑːʃl/ n (mil) mariscal m; (master of ceremonies) maestro m de ceremonias; (at sports events) oficial m. ● vt (pt marshalled) ordenar; formar ⟨troops⟩

marsh mallow /mɑːʃˈmæləʊ/ n (plant) malvavisco m

marshmallow /mɑːʃˈmæləʊ/ n (sweet) caramelo m blando

marshy /ˈmɑːʃɪ/ a pantanoso

martial /ˈmɑːʃl/ a marcial. ~ law n ley f marcial

Martian /ˈmɑːʃn/ a & n marciano (m)

martinet /ˌmɑːtɪˈnet/ n ordenancista m & f

martyr /ˈmɑːtə(r)/ n mártir m & f. ● vt martirizar. ~dom n martirio m

marvel /ˈmɑːvl/ n maravilla f. ● vi (pt marvelled) maravillarse (at con, de). ~lous /ˈmɑːvələs/ a maravilloso

Marxis|m /ˈmɑːksɪzəm/ n marxismo m. ~t a & n marxista (m & f)

marzipan /ˈmɑːzɪpæn/ n mazapán m

mascara /mæˈskɑːrə/ n rimel m

mascot /ˈmæskɒt/ n mascota f

masculin|e /ˈmæskjʊlɪn/ a & n masculino (m). ~ity /-ˈlɪnətɪ/ n masculinidad f

mash /mæʃ/ n mezcla f; (potatoes, fam) puré m de patatas. ● vt (crush) machacar; (mix) mezclar. ~ed potatoes n puré m de patatas

mask /mɑːsk/ n máscara f. ● vt enmascarar

masochis|m /ˈmæsəkɪzəm/ n masoquismo m. ~t n masoquista m & f

mason /ˈmeɪsn/ n (builder) albañil m

Mason /ˈmeɪsn/ n. ~ masón m. ~ic /məˈsɒnɪk/ a masónico

masonry /ˈmeɪsnrɪ/ n albañilería f

masquerade /ˌmɑːskəˈreɪd/ n mascarada f. ● vi. ~ as hacerse pasar por

mass[1] /mæs/ n masa f; (large quantity) montón m. the ~es npl las masas fpl. ● vt/i agrupar(se)

mass[2] /mæs/ n (relig) misa f. high ~ misa f mayor

massacre /ˈmæsəkə(r)/ n masacre f, matanza f. ● vt masacrar

massage /ˈmæsɑːʒ/ n masaje m. ● vt dar masaje a

masseu|r /mæˈsɜː(r)/ n masajista m. ~se /mæˈsɜːz/ n masajista f

massive /ˈmæsɪv/ a masivo; (heavy) macizo; (huge) enorme

mass: ~ media n medios mpl de comunicación. ~-produce vt fabricar en serie

mast /mɑ:st/ n mástil m; (*for radio, TV*) torre f

master /'mɑ:stə(r)/ n maestro m; (*in secondary school*) profesor m; (*of ship*) capitán m. ● vt dominar. **~key** n llave f maestra. **~ly** a magistral. **~mind** n cerebro m. ● vt dirigir. **M~ of Arts** master m, grado m universitario entre el de licenciado y el de doctor

masterpiece /'mɑ:stəpi:s/ n obra f maestra

master-stroke /'mɑ:stəstrəuk/ n golpe m maestro

mastery /'mɑ:stərɪ/ n dominio m; (*skill*) maestría f

masturbat|e /'mæstəbeɪt/ vi masturbarse. **~ion** /-'beɪʃn/ n masturbación f

mat /mæt/ n estera f; (*at door*) felpudo m

match[1] /mætʃ/ n (*sport*) partido m; (*equal*) igual m; (*marriage*) matrimonio m; (*s.o. to marry*) partido m. ● vt emparejar; (*equal*) igualar; (*clothes, colours*) hacer juego con. ● vi hacer juego

match[2] /mætʃ/ n (*of wood*) fósforo m; (*of wax*) cerilla f. **~box** /'mætʃbɒks/ n (*for wooden matches*) caja f de fósforos; (*for wax matches*) caja f de cerillas

matching /'mætʃɪŋ/ a que hace juego

mate[1] /meɪt/ n compañero m; (*of animals*) macho m, hembra f; (*assistant*) ayudante m. ● vt/i acoplar(se)

mate[2] /meɪt/ n (*chess*) mate m

material /mə'tɪərɪəl/ n material m; (*cloth*) tela f. ● a material; (*fig*) importante. **~istic** /-'lɪstɪk/ a materialista. **~s** npl materiales mpl. **raw ~s** npl materias fpl primas

materialize /mə'tɪərɪəlaɪz/ vi materializarse

maternal /mə'tɜ:nl/ a maternal; (*relation*) materno

maternity /mə'tɜ:nɪtɪ/ n maternidad f. ● a de maternidad. **~ clothes** npl vestido m pre-mamá. **~ hospital** n maternidad f

matey /'meɪtɪ/ a (*fam*) simpático

mathematic|ian /mæθəmə'tɪʃn/ n matemático m. **~al** /-'mætɪkl/ a matemático. **~s** /-'mætɪks/ n & npl matemáticas fpl

maths /mæθs/, **math** (*Amer*) n & npl matemáticas fpl

matinée /'mætɪneɪ/ n función f de tarde

matriculat|e /mə'trɪkjʊleɪt/ vt/i matricular(se). **~ion** /-'leɪʃn/ n matriculación f

matrimon|ial /mætrɪ'məʊnɪəl/ a matrimonial. **~y** /'mætrɪmənɪ/ n matrimonio m

matrix /'meɪtrɪks/ n (*pl* **matrices** /-sɪ:z/) matriz f

matron /'meɪtrən/ n (*married, elderly*) matrona f; (*in school*) ama f de llaves; (*former use, in hospital*) enfermera f jefe. **~ly** a matronil

matt /mæt/ a mate

matted /'mætɪd/ a enmarañado

matter /'mætə(r)/ n (*substance*) materia f; (*affair*) asunto m; (*pus*) pus m. **as a ~ of fact** en realidad. **no ~** no importa. **what is the ~?** ¿qué pasa? ● vi importar. **it does not ~** no importa. **~-of-fact** a realista

matting /'mætɪŋ/ n estera f

mattress /'mætrɪs/ n colchón m

matur|e /mə'tjʊə(r)/ a maduro. ● vt/i madurar. **~ity** n madurez f

maul /mɔ:l/ vt maltratar

Mauritius /mə'rɪʃəs/ n Mauricio m

mausoleum /mɔ:sə'lɪəm/ n mausoleo m

mauve /məʊv/ a & n color (m) de malva

mawkish /'mɔ:kɪʃ/ a empalagoso

maxim /'mæksɪm/ n máxima f

maxim|ize /'mæksɪmaɪz/ vt llevar al máximo. **~um** a & n (*pl* **-ima**) máximo (m)

may /meɪ/ v aux (*pt* **might**) poder. **~ I smoke?** ¿se permite fumar? **~ he be happy** ¡que sea feliz! **he ~/might come** puede que venga. **I ~/might as well stay** más vale quedarme. **it ~/might be true** puede ser verdad

May /meɪ/ n mayo m. **~ Day** n el primero m de mayo

maybe /'meɪbɪ/ adv quizá(s)

mayhem /'meɪhem/ n (*havoc*) alboroto m

mayonnaise /meɪə'neɪz/ n mayonesa f

mayor /meə(r)/ n alcalde m, alcaldesa f. **~ess** n alcaldesa f

maze /meɪz/ n laberinto m

me[1] /mi:/ pron me; (*after prep*) mí. **he knows ~** me conoce. **it's ~** soy yo

me[2] /mi:/ n (*mus, third note of any musical scale*) mi m

meadow /'medəʊ/ n prado m

meagre /'mi:gə(r)/ a escaso

meal[1] /mi:l/ n comida f

meal[2] /mi:l/ n (grain) harina f

mealy-mouthed /mi:lɪ'maʊðd/ a hipócrita

mean[1] /mi:n/ vt (pt meant) (intend) tener la intención de, querer; (signify) querer decir, significar. ~ **to do** tener la intención de hacer. ~ **well** tener buenas intenciones. **be meant for** estar destinado a

mean[2] /mi:n/ a (-er, -est) (miserly) tacaño; (unkind) malo; (poor) pobre

mean[3] /mi:n/ a medio. ● n medio m; (average) promedio m

meander /mɪ'ændə(r)/ vi (river) serpentear; (person) vagar

meaning /'mi:nɪŋ/ n sentido m. ~**ful** a significativo. ~**less** a sin sentido

meanness /'mi:nnɪs/ n (miserliness) tacañería f; (unkindness) maldad f

means /mi:nz/ n medio m. **by all** ~ por supuesto. **by no** ~ de ninguna manera. ● npl (wealth) recursos mpl. ~ **test** n investigación f financial

meant /ment/ see **mean**[1]

meantime /'mi:nataɪm/ adv entretanto. **in the** ~ entretanto

meanwhile /'mi:nwaɪl/ adv entretanto

measles /'mi:zlz/ n sarampión m

measly /'mi:zlɪ/ a (sl) miserable

measurable /'meʒərəbl/ a mensurable

measure /'meʒə(r)/ n medida f; (ruler) regla f. ● vt/i medir. ~ **up to** estar a la altura de. ~**d** a (rhythmical) acompasado; (carefully considered) prudente. ~**ment** n medida f

meat /mi:t/ n carne f. ~**y** a carnoso; (fig) sustancioso

mechanic /mɪ'kænɪk/ n mecánico m. ~**al** /mɪ'kænɪkl/ a mecánico. ~**s** n mecánica f

mechani|sm /'mekənɪzəm/ n mecanismo m. ~**ze** vt mecanizar

medal /medl/ n medalla f

medallion /mɪ'dælɪən/ n medallón m

medallist /'medəlɪst/ n ganador m de una medalla. **be a gold** ~ ganar una medalla de oro

meddle /'medl/ vi entrometerse (**in** en); (tinker) tocar. ~ **with** (tinker) tocar. ~**some** a entrometido

media /'mi:dɪə/ see **medium**. ● npl. **the** ~ npl los medios mpl de comunicación

mediat|e /'mi:dɪeɪt/ vi mediar. ~**ion** /-eɪʃn/ n mediación f. ~**or** n mediador m

medical /'medɪkl/ a médico; (student) de medicina. ● n (fam) reconocimiento m médico

medicat|ed /'medɪkeɪtɪd/ a medicinal. ~**ion** /-'keɪʃn/ n medicación f

medicin|e /'medsɪn/ n medicina f. ~**al** /mɪ'dɪsɪnl/ a medicinal

medieval /medɪ'i:vl/ a medieval

mediocr|e /mi:dɪ'əʊkə(r)/ a mediocre. ~**ity** /-'ɒkrətɪ/ n mediocridad f

meditat|e /'medɪteɪt/ vt/i meditar. ~**ion** /-'teɪʃn/ n meditación f

Mediterranean /medɪtə'reɪnɪən/ a mediterráneo. ● n. **the** ~ el Mediterráneo m

medium /'mi:dɪəm/ n (pl media) medio m; (pl mediums) (person) médium m. ● a mediano

medley /'medlɪ/ n popurrí m

meek /mi:k/ a (-er, -est) manso

meet /mi:t/ vt (pt met) encontrar; (bump into s.o.) encontrarse con; (see again) ver; (fetch) ir a buscar; (get to know, be introduced to) conocer. ~ **the bill** pagar la cuenta. ● vi encontrarse; (get to know) conocerse; (in session) reunirse. ~ **with** tropezar con (obstacles)

meeting /'mi:tɪŋ/ n reunión f; (accidental between two people) encuentro m; (arranged between two people) cita f

megalomania /megələʊ'meɪnɪə/ n megalomanía f

megaphone /'megəfəʊn/ n megáfono m

melanchol|ic /melən'kɒlɪk/ a melancólico. ~**y** /'melənkɒlɪ/ n melancolía f. ● a melancólico

mêlée /'meleɪ/ n pelea f confusa

mellow /'meləʊ/ a (-er, -est) (fruit, person) maduro; (sound, colour) dulce. ● vt/i madurar(se)

melodi|c /mɪ'lɒdɪk/ a melódico. ~**ous** /mɪ'ləʊdɪəs/ a melodioso

melodrama /'melədrɑːmə/ n melodrama m. ~**tic** /-ə'mætɪk/ a melodramático

melody /'melədɪ/ n melodía f

melon /'melən/ n melón m

melt /melt/ vt (make liquid) derretir; fundir (metals). ● vi (become liquid) derretirse; (metals) fundirse. ~**ing-pot** n crisol m

member /'membə(r)/ n miembro m. **M~ of Parliament** n diputado m.

~**ship** n calidad f. de miembro; (*members*) miembros *mpl*

membrane /'membreɪn/ n membrana f

memento /mɪ'mentəʊ/ n (pl **-oes**) recuerdo m

memo /'meməʊ/ n (pl **-os**) (*fam*) nota f

memoir /'memwɑ:(r)/ n memoria f

memorable /'memərəbl/ a memorable

memorandum /memə'rændəm/ n (pl **-ums**) nota f

memorial /mɪ'mɔ:rɪəl/ n monumento m. ● a conmemorativo

memorize /'meməraɪz/ vt aprender de memoria

memory /'memərɪ/ n (*faculty*) memoria f; (*thing remembered*) recuerdo m. **from** ~ de memoria. **in** ~ **of** en memoria de

men /men/ *see* **man**

menac|e /'menəs/ n amenaza f; (*nuisance*) pesado m. ● vt amenazar. ~**ingly** adv de manera amenazadora

menagerie /mɪ'nædʒərɪ/ n casa f de fieras

mend /mend/ vt reparar; (*darn*) zurcir. ~ **one's ways** enmendarse. ● n remiendo m. **be on the** ~ ir mejorando

menfolk /'menfəʊk/ n hombres *mpl*

menial /'mi:nɪəl/ a servil

meningitis /menɪn'dʒaɪtɪs/ n meningitis f

menopause /'menəpɔ:z/ n menopausia f

menstruat|e /'menstrʊeɪt/ vi menstruar. ~**ion** /-eɪʃn/ n menstruación f

mental /'mentl/ a mental; ⟨*hospital*⟩ psiquiátrico

mentality /men'tælətɪ/ n mentalidad f

menthol /'menθɒl/ n mentol m. ~**ated** a mentolado

mention /'menʃn/ vt mencionar. **don't** ~ **it!** ¡no hay de qué! ● n mención f

mentor /'mentɔ:(r)/ n mentor m

menu /'menju:/ n (*set meal*) menú m; (*a la carte*) lista f (de platos)

mercantile /'mɜ:kəntaɪl/ a mercantil

mercenary /'mɜ:sɪnərɪ/ a & n mercenario (m)

merchandise /'mɜ:tʃəndaɪz/ n mercancias *fpl*

merchant /'mɜ:tʃənt/ n comerciante m. ● a ⟨*ship, navy*⟩ mercante. ~ **bank** n banco m mercantil

merci|ful /'mɜ:sɪfl/ a misericordioso. ~**fully** adv (*fortunately, fam*) gracias a Dios. ~**less** /'mɜ:sɪlɪs/ a despiadado

mercur|ial /mɜ:'kjʊərɪəl/ a mercurial; (*fig, active*) vivo. ~**y** /'mɜ:kjʊrɪ/ n mercurio m

mercy /'mɜ:sɪ/ n compasión f. **at the** ~ **of** a merced de

mere /mɪə(r)/ a simple. ~**ly** adv simplemente

merest /'mɪərɪst/ a mínimo

merge /mɜ:dʒ/ vt unir; fusionar ⟨*companies*⟩. ● vi unirse; ⟨*companies*⟩ fusionarse. ~**r** /-ə(r)/ n fusión f

meridian /mə'rɪdɪən/ n meridiano m

meringue /mə'ræŋ/ n merengue m

merit /'merɪt/ n mérito m. ● vt (pt **merited**) merecer. ~**orious** /-'tɔ:rɪəs/ a meritorio

mermaid /'mɜ:meɪd/ n sirena f

merr|ily /'merəlɪ/ adv alegremente. ~**iment** /'merɪmənt/ n alegría f. ~**y** /'merɪ/ a (**-ier, -iest**) alegre. **make** ~ divertirse. ~**y-go-round** n tiovivo m. ~**y-making** n holgorio m

mesh /meʃ/ n malla f; (*network*) red f

mesmerize /'mezməraɪz/ vt hipnotizar

mess /mes/ n desorden m; (*dirt*) suciedad f; (*mil*) rancho m. **make a** ~ **of** chapucear, estropear. ● vt. ~ **up** desordenar; (*dirty*) ensuciar. ● vi. ~ **about** entretenerse. ~ **with** (*tinker with*) manosear

message /'mesɪdʒ/ n recado m

messenger /'mesɪndʒə(r)/ n mensajero m

Messiah /mɪ'saɪə/ n Mesías m

Messrs /'mesəz/ *npl*. ~ **Smith** los señores *mpl or* Sres. Smith

messy /'mesɪ/ a (**-ier, -iest**) en desorden; (*dirty*) sucio

met /met/ *see* **meet**

metabolism /mɪ'tæbəlɪzəm/ n metabolismo m

metal /'metl/ n metal. ● a de metal. ~**lic** /mɪ'tælɪk/ a metálico

metallurgy /mɪ'tælədʒɪ/ n metalurgia f

metamorphosis /metə'mɔ:fəsɪs/ n (pl **-phoses** /-sɪ:z/) metamorfosis f

metaphor /'metəfə(r)/ n metáfora f. ~**ical** /-'fɒrɪkl/ a metafórico

mete /mi:t/ vt. ~ **out** repartir; dar ⟨punishment⟩

meteor /'mi:tɪə(r)/ n meteoro m

meteorite /'mi:tɪərait/ n meteorito m

meteorolog|ical /mi:tɪərə'lɒdʒɪkl/ a meteorológico. ~**y** /-'rɒlədʒɪ/ n meteorología f

meter[1] /'mi:tə(r)/ n contador m

meter[2] /'mi:tə(r)/ n (Amer) = **metre**

method /'meθəd/ n método m

methodical /mɪ'θɒdɪkl/ a metódico

Methodist /'meθədɪst/ a & n metodista (m & f)

methylated /'meθɪleɪtɪd/ a. ~ **spirit** n alcohol m desnaturalizado

meticulous /mɪ'tɪkjʊləs/ a meticuloso

metre /'mi:tə(r)/ n metro m

metric /'metrɪk/ a métrico. ~**ation** /-'keɪʃn/ n cambio m al sistema métrico

metropolis /mɪ'trɒpəlɪs/ n metrópoli f

metropolitan /metrə'pɒlɪtən/ a metropolitano

mettle /'metl/ n valor m

mew /mju:/ n maullido m. ● vi maullar

mews /mju:z/ npl casas fpl pequeñas (que antes eran caballerizas)

Mexic|an /'meksɪkən/ a & n mejicano (m); (in Mexico) mexicano (m). ~**o** /-kəʊ/ n Méjico m; (in Mexico) México m

mezzanine /'metsəni:n/ n entresuelo m

mi /mi:/ n (mus, third note of any musical scale) mi m

miaow /mi:'aʊ/ n & vi = **mew**

mice /maɪs/ see **mouse**

mickey /'mɪkɪ/ n. **take the** ~ **out of** (sl) tomar el pelo a

micro... /'maɪkrəʊ/ pref micro...

microbe /'maɪkrəʊb/ n microbio m

microchip /'maɪkrəʊtʃɪp/ n pastilla f

microfilm /'maɪkrəʊfɪlm/ n microfilme m

microphone /'maɪkrəfəʊn/ n micrófono m

microprocessor /maɪkrəʊ'prəʊsesə(r)/ n microprocesador m

microscop|e /'maɪkrəskəʊp/ n microscopio m. ~**ic** /-'skɒpɪk/ a microscópico

microwave /'maɪkrəʊweɪv/ n microonda f. ~ **oven** n horno m de microondas

mid /mɪd/ a. **in** ~ **air** en pleno aire. **in** ~ **March** a mediados de marzo. **in** ~ **ocean** en medio del océano

midday /mɪd'deɪ/ n mediodía m

middle /'mɪdl/ a de en medio; ⟨quality⟩ mediano. ● n medio m. **in the** ~ **of** en medio de. ~**aged** a de mediana edad. **M**~ **Ages** npl Edad f Media. ~ **class** n clase f media. ~**class** a de la clase media. **M**~ **East** n Oriente m Medio. ~**man** n intermediario m

middling /'mɪdlɪŋ/ a regular

midge /mɪdʒ/ n mosquito m

midget /'mɪdʒɪt/ n enano m. ● a minúsculo

Midlands /'mɪdləndz/ npl región f central de Inglaterra

midnight /'mɪdnaɪt/ n medianoche f

midriff /'mɪdrɪf/ n diafragma m; (fam) vientre m

midst /mɪdst/ n. **in our** ~ entre nosotros. **in the** ~ **of** en medio de

midsummer /mɪd'sʌmə(r)/ n pleno verano m; (solstice) solsticio m de verano

midway /mɪd'weɪ/ adv a medio camino

midwife /'mɪdwaɪf/ n comadrona f

midwinter /mɪd'wɪntə(r)/ n pleno invierno m

might[1] /maɪt/ see **may**

might[2] /maɪt/ n (strength) fuerza f; (power) poder m. ~**y** a (strong) fuerte; (powerful) poderoso; (very great, fam) enorme. ● adv (fam) muy

migraine /'mi:greɪn/ n jaqueca f

migrant /'maɪgrənt/ a migratorio. ● n (person) emigrante m & f

migrat|e /maɪ'greɪt/ vi emigrar. ~**ion** /-ʃn/ n migración f

mike /maɪk/ n (fam) micrófono m

mild /maɪld/ a (-er, -est) ⟨person⟩ apacible; ⟨climate⟩ templado; ⟨slight⟩ ligero; ⟨taste⟩ suave; ⟨illness⟩ benigno

mildew /'mɪldju:/ n moho m

mild: ~ly adv (slightly) ligeramente. ~**ness** n (of person) apacibilidad f; (of climate, illness) benignidad f; (of taste) suavidad f

mile /maɪl/ n milla f. ~**s better** (fam) mucho mejor. ~**s too big** (fam) demasiado grande. ~**age** n (loosely) kilometraje m. ~**stone** n mojón m; (event, stage, fig) hito m

milieu /mɪ'ljɜ:/ n ambiente m

militant /'mɪlɪtənt/ a & n militante
(m & f)

military /'mɪlɪtərɪ/ a militar

militate /'mɪlɪteɪt/ vi militar
(**against** contra)

militia /mɪ'lɪʃə/ n milicia f

milk /mɪlk/ n leche f. ● a ⟨product⟩
lácteo; ⟨chocolate⟩ con leche. ● vt
ordeñar ⟨cow⟩; (exploit) chupar.
~man n repartidor m de leche. **~
shake** n batido m de leche. **~y** a
lechoso. **M~y Way** n Vía f Láctea

mill /mɪl/ n molino m; (for coffee, pepper) molinillo m; (factory) fábrica f.
● vt moler. ● vi. **~ about/around**
apiñarse, circular

millennium /mɪ'lenɪəm/ n (pl -ia or
-iums) milenio m

miller /'mɪlə(r)/ n molinero m

millet /'mɪlɪt/ n mijo m

milli... /'mɪlɪ/ pref mili...

milligram(me) /'mɪlɪgræm/ n mili-
gramo m

millimetre /'mɪlɪmiːtə(r)/ n milímetro m

milliner /'mɪlɪnə(r)/ n sombrerero m

million /'mɪlɪən/ n millón m. **a ~
pounds** un millón m de libras.
~aire n millonario m

millstone /'mɪlstəʊn/ n muela f (de
molino); (fig, burden) losa f

mime /maɪm/ n pantomima f. ● vt
hacer en pantomima. ● vi actuar de
mimo

mimic /'mɪmɪk/ vt (pt **mimicked**)
imitar. ● n imitador m. **~ry** n imitación f

mimosa /mɪ'məʊzə/ n mimosa f

minaret /mɪnə'ret/ n alminar m

mince /mɪns/ vt desmenuzar; picar
⟨meat⟩. **not to ~ matters/words** no
tener pelos en la lengua. ● n carne f
picada. **~meat** n conserva f de fruta
picada. **make ~meat of s.o.** hacer
trizas a uno. **~ pie** n pastel m con
frutas picadas. **~r** n máquina f de
picar carne

mind /maɪnd/ n mente f; (sanity) juicio m; (opinion) parecer m; (intention) intención f. **be on one's ~**
preocuparle a uno. ● vt (look after)
cuidar; (heed) hacer caso de. **I don't
~ me da igual. I don't ~ the noise**
no me molesta el ruido. **never ~** no
te preocupes, no se preocupe. **~er**
n cuidador m. **~ful** a atento (**of** a).
~less a estúpido

mine¹ /maɪn/ poss pron (el) mío m,
(la) mía f, (los) míos mpl, (las) mías
fpl. **it is ~** es mío

mine² /maɪn/ n mina f. ● vt extraer.
~field n campo m de minas. **~r** n
minero m

mineral /'mɪnərəl/ a & n mineral
(m). **~ (water)** n (fizzy soft drink)
gaseosa f. **~ water** n (natural) agua
f mineral

minesweeper /'maɪnswiːpə(r)/ n
(ship) dragaminas m invar

mingle /'mɪŋgl/ vt/i mezclar(se)

mingy /'mɪndʒɪ/ a tacaño

mini... /'mɪnɪ/ pref mini...

miniature /'mɪnɪtʃə(r)/ a & n miniatura (f)

mini: **~bus** n microbús m. **~cab** n
taxi m

minim /'mɪnɪm/ n (mus) blanca f

minim|al /'mɪnɪml/ a mínimo. **~ize**
vt minimizar. **~um** a & n (pl -ima)
mínimo (m)

mining /'maɪnɪŋ/ n explotación f.
● a minero

miniskirt /'mɪnɪskɜːt/ n minifalda f

minist|er /'mɪnɪstə(r)/ n ministro m;
(relig) pastor m. **~erial** /-'stɪərɪəl/ a
ministerial. **~ry** n ministerio m

mink /mɪŋk/ n visón m

minor /'maɪnə(r)/ a (incl mus)
menor; (of little importance) sin
importancia. ● n menor m & f de
edad

minority /maɪ'nɒrətɪ/ n minoría f.
● a minoritario

minster /'mɪnstə(r)/ n catedral f

minstrel /'mɪnstrəl/ n juglar m

mint¹ /mɪnt/ n (plant) menta f;
(sweet) caramelo m de menta

mint² /mɪnt/ n. **the M~** n casa f de
la moneda. **a ~** un dineral m. ● vt
acuñar. **in ~ condition** como nuevo

minuet /mɪnjʊ'et/ n minué m

minus /'maɪnəs/ prep menos; (without, fam) sin. ● n (sign) menos m. **~
sign** n menos m

minuscule /'mɪnəskjuːl/ a minúsculo

minute¹ /'mɪnɪt/ n minuto m. **~s** npl
(of meeting) actas fpl

minute² /maɪ'njuːt/ a minúsculo;
(detailed) minucioso

minx /mɪŋks/ n chica f descarada

mirac|le /'mɪrəkl/ n milagro m. **~u-
lous** /mɪ'rækjʊləs/ a milagroso

mirage /'mɪrɑːʒ/ n espejismo m

mire /maɪə(r)/ n fango m

mirror /'mɪrə(r)/ n espejo m. ● vt
reflejar

mirth /mɜːθ/ n (merriment) alegría f;
(laughter) risas fpl

misadventure /mɪsəd'ventʃə(r)/ *n* desgracia *f*

misanthropist /mɪ'zænθrəpɪst/ *n* misántropo *m*

misapprehension /mɪsæpri'henʃŋ/ *n* malentendido *m*

misbehav|e /mɪsbɪ'heɪv/ *vi* portarse mal. ∼**iour** *n* mala conducta *f*

miscalculat|e /mɪs'kælkjʊleɪt/ *vt/i* calcular mal. ∼**ion** /-'leɪʃn/ *n* desacierto *m*

miscarr|iage /'mɪskærɪdʒ/ *n* aborto *m*. ∼**iage of justice** *n* error *m* judicial. ∼**y** *vi* abortar

miscellaneous /mɪsə'leɪnɪəs/ *a* vario

mischief /'mɪstʃɪf/ *n* (*foolish conduct*) travesura *f*; (*harm*) daño *m*. **get into** ∼ cometer travesuras. **make** ∼ armar un lío

mischievous /'mɪstʃɪvəs/ *a* travieso; (*malicious*) perjudicial

misconception /mɪskən'sepʃn/ *n* equivocación *f*

misconduct /mɪs'kɒndʌkt/ *n* mala conducta *f*

misconstrue /mɪskən'stru:/ *vt* interpretar mal

misdeed /mɪs'di:d/ *n* fechoría *f*

misdemeanour /mɪsdɪ'mi:nə(r)/ *n* fechoría *f*

misdirect /mɪsdɪ'rekt/ *vt* dirigir mal ⟨*person*⟩

miser /'maɪzə(r)/ *n* avaro *m*

miserable /'mɪzərəbl/ *a* (*sad*) triste; (*wretched*) miserable; ⟨*weather*⟩ malo

miserly /'maɪzəlɪ/ *a* avariento

misery /'mɪzərɪ/ *n* (*unhappiness*) tristeza *f*; (*pain*) sufrimiento *m*; (*poverty*) pobreza *f*; (*person, fam*) aguafiestas *m & f*

misfire /mɪs'faɪə(r)/ *vi* fallar

misfit /'mɪsfɪt/ *n* (*person*) inadaptado *m*; (*thing*) cosa *f* mal ajustada

misfortune /mɪs'fɔ:tʃu:n/ *n* desgracia *f*

misgiving /mɪs'gɪvɪŋ/ *n* (*doubt*) duda *f*; (*apprehension*) presentimiento *m*

misguided /mɪs'gaɪdɪd/ *a* equivocado. **be** ∼ equivocarse

mishap /'mɪshæp/ *n* desgracia *f*

misinform /mɪsɪn'fɔ:m/ *vt* informar mal

misinterpret /mɪsɪn'tɜ:prɪt/ *vt* interpretar mal

misjudge /mɪs'dʒʌdʒ/ *vt* juzgar mal

mislay /mɪs'leɪ/ *vt* (*pt* **mislaid**) extraviar

mislead /mɪs'li:d/ *vt* (*pt* **misled**) engañar. ∼**ing** *a* engañoso

mismanage /mɪs'mænɪdʒ/ *vt* administrar mal. ∼**ment** *n* mala administración *f*

misnomer /mɪs'nəʊmə(r)/ *n* nombre *m* equivocado

misplace /mɪs'pleɪs/ *vt* colocar mal; (*lose*) extraviar

misprint /'mɪsprɪnt/ *n* errata *f*

misquote /mɪs'kwəʊt/ *vt* citar mal

misrepresent /mɪsreprɪ'zent/ *vt* describir engañosamente

miss[1] /mɪs/ *vt* (*fail to hit*) errar; (*notice absence of*) echar de menos; perder ⟨*train*⟩. ∼ **the point** no comprender. ● *n* fallo *m*. ∼ **out** omitir

miss[2] /mɪs/ *n* (*pl* **misses**) señorita *f*

misshapen /mɪs'ʃeɪpən/ *a* deforme

missile /'mɪsaɪl/ *n* proyectil *m*

missing /'mɪsɪŋ/ *a* ⟨*person*⟩ (*absent*) ausente; ⟨*person*⟩ (*after disaster*) desaparecido; (*lost*) perdido. **be** ∼ faltar

mission /'mɪʃn/ *n* misión *f*. ∼**ary** /'mɪʃənərɪ/ *n* misionero *m*

missive /'mɪsɪv/ *n* misiva *f*

misspell /mɪs'spel/ *vt* (*pt* **misspelt** *or* **misspelled**) escribir mal

mist /mɪst/ *n* neblina *f*; (*at sea*) bruma *f*. ● *vt/i* empañar(se)

mistake /mɪ'steɪk/ *n* error *m*. ● *vt* (*pt* **mistook**, *pp* **mistaken**) equivocarse de; (*misunderstand*) entender mal. ∼ **for** tomar por. ∼**n** /-ən/ *a* equivocado. **be** ∼**n** equivocarse. ∼**nly** *adv* equivocadamente

mistletoe /'mɪsltəʊ/ *n* muérdago *m*

mistreat /mɪs'tri:t/ *vt* maltratar

mistress /'mɪstrɪs/ *n* (*of house*) señora *f*; (*primary school teacher*) maestra *f*; (*secondary school teacher*) profesora *f*; (*lover*) amante *f*

mistrust /mɪs'trʌst/ *vt* desconfiar de. ● *n* desconfianza *f*

misty /'mɪstɪ/ *a* (**-ier**, **-iest**) nebuloso; ⟨*day*⟩ de niebla; ⟨*glass*⟩ empañado. **it is** ∼ hay neblina

misunderstand /mɪsʌndə'stænd/ *vt* (*pt* **-stood**) entender mal. ∼**ing** *n* malentendido *m*

misuse /mɪs'ju:z/ *vt* emplear mal; abusar de ⟨*power etc*⟩. /mɪs'ju:s/ *n* mal uso *m*; (*unfair use*) abuso *m*

mite /maɪt/ *n* (*insect*) ácaro *m*, garrapata *f*; (*child*) niño *m* pequeño

mitigate /'mɪtɪgeɪt/ *vt* mitigar

mitre /'maɪtə(r)/ n (head-dress) mitra f

mitten /'mɪtn/ n manopla f; (leaving fingers exposed) mitón m

mix /mɪks/ vt/i mezclar(se). ~ up mezclar; (confuse) confundir. ~ with frecuentar ⟨people⟩. ● n mezcla f

mixed /mɪkst/ a ⟨school etc⟩ mixto; (assorted) variado. be ~ up estar confuso

mixer /'mɪksə(r)/ n (culin) batidora f. be a good ~ tener don de gentes

mixture /'mɪkstʃə(r)/ n mezcla f

mix-up /'mɪksʌp/ n lío m

moan /məʊn/ n gemido m. ● vi gemir; (complain) quejarse (about de). ~er n refunfuñador m

moat /məʊt/ n foso m

mob /mɒb/ n (crowd) muchedumbre f; (gang) pandilla f; (masses) populacho m. ● vt (pt mobbed) acosar

mobil|e /'məʊbaɪl/ a móvil. ~e home n caravana f. ● n móvil m. ~ity /mə'bɪlətɪ/ n movilidad f

mobiliz|ation /məʊbɪlaɪ'zeɪʃn/ n movilización f. ~e /'məʊbɪlaɪz/ vt/i movilizar

moccasin /'mɒkəsɪn/ n mocasín m

mocha /'mɒkə/ n moca m

mock /mɒk/ vt burlarse de. ● vi burlarse. ● a fingido

mockery /'mɒkərɪ/ n burla f. a ~ of una parodia f de

mock-up /'mɒkʌp/ n maqueta f

mode /məʊd/ n (way, method) modo m; (fashion) moda f

model /'mɒdl/ n modelo m; (mock-up) maqueta f; (for fashion) maniquí m. ● a (exemplary) ejemplar; ⟨car etc⟩ en miniatura. ● vt (pt modelled) modelar; presentar ⟨clothes⟩. ● vi ser maniquí; (pose) posar. ~ling n profesión f de maniquí

moderate /'mɒdərət/ a & n moderado (m). /'mɒdəreɪt/ vt/i moderar(se). ~ly /'mɒdərətlɪ/ adv (in moderation) moderadamente; (fairly) medianamente

moderation /mɒdə'reɪʃn/ n moderación f. in ~ con moderación

modern /'mɒdn/ a moderno. ~ize vt modernizar

modest /'mɒdɪst/ a modesto. ~y n modestia f

modicum /'mɒdɪkəm/ n. a ~ of un poquito m de

modif|ication /mɒdɪfɪ'keɪʃn/ n modificación f. ~y /-faɪ/ vt/i modificar(se)

modulat|e /'mɒdjʊleɪt/ vt/i modular. ~ion /-'leɪʃn/ n modulación f

module /'mɒdjuːl/ n módulo m

mogul /'məʊgəl/ n (fam) magnate m

mohair /'məʊheə(r)/ n mohair m

moist /mɔɪst/ a (-er, -est) húmedo. ~en /'mɔɪsn/ vt humedecer

moistur|e /'mɔɪstʃə(r)/ n humedad f. ~ize /'mɔɪstʃəraɪz/ vt humedecer. ~izer n crema f hidratante

molar /'məʊlə(r)/ n muela f

molasses /mə'læsɪz/ n melaza f

mold /məʊld/ (Amer) = **mould**

mole¹ /məʊl/ n (animal) topo m

mole² /məʊl/ n (on skin) lunar m

mole³ /məʊl/ n (breakwater) malecón m

molecule /'mɒlɪkjuːl/ n molécula f

molehill /'məʊlhɪl/ n topera f

molest /mə'lest/ vt importunar

mollify /'mɒlɪfaɪ/ vt apaciguar

mollusc /'mɒləsk/ n molusco m

mollycoddle /'mɒlɪkɒdl/ vt mimar

molten /'məʊltən/ a fundido

mom /mɒm/ n (Amer) mamá f

moment /'məʊmənt/ n momento m. ~arily /'məʊməntərɪlɪ/ adv momentáneamente. ~ary a momentáneo

momentous /mə'mentəs/ a importante

momentum /mə'mentəm/ n momento m; (speed) velocidad f; (fig) ímpetu m

Monaco /'mɒnəkəʊ/ n Mónaco m

monarch /'mɒnək/ n monarca m. ~ist n monárquico m. ~y n monarquía f

monast|ery /'mɒnəstərɪ/ n monasterio m. ~ic /mə'næstɪk/ a monástico

Monday /'mʌndeɪ/ n lunes m

monetar|ist /'mʌnɪtərɪst/ n monetarista m & f. ~y a monetario

money /'mʌnɪ/ n dinero m. ~-box n hucha f. ~ed a adinerado. ~lender n prestamista m & f. ~ order n giro m postal. ~s npl cantidades fpl de dinero. ~spinner n mina f de dinero

mongol /'mɒŋgl/ n & a (med) mongólico (m)

mongrel /'mʌŋgrəl/ n perro m mestizo

monitor /'mɒnɪtə(r)/ n (pupil) monitor m & f; (tec) monitor m. ● vt controlar; escuchar ⟨a broadcast⟩

monk /mʌŋk/ n monje m

monkey /'mʌŋkɪ/ n mono m. ∼-nut n cacahuete m, maní m (LAm). ∼-wrench n llave f inglesa

mono /'mɒnəʊ/ a monofónico

monocle /'mɒnəkl/ n monóculo m

monogram /'mɒnəgræm/ n monograma m

monologue /'mɒnəlɒg/ n monólogo m

monopol|ize /mə'nɒpəlaɪz/ vt monopolizar. ∼y n monopolio m

monosyllab|ic /mɒnəsɪ'læbɪk/ a monosilábico. ∼le /-'sɪləbl/ n monosílabo m

monotone /'mɒnətəʊn/ n monotonía f. speak in a ∼ hablar con una voz monótona

monoton|ous /mə'nɒtənəs/ a monótono. ∼y n monotonía f

monsoon /mɒn'suːn/ n monzón m

monster /'mɒnstə(r)/ n monstruo m

monstrosity /mɒn'strɒsətɪ/ n monstruosidad f

monstrous /'mɒnstrəs/ a monstruoso

montage /mɒn'tɑːʒ/ n montaje m

month /mʌnθ/ n mes m. ∼ly /'mʌnθlɪ/ a mensual. ● adv mensualmente. ● n (periodical) revista f mensual

monument /'mɒnjʊmənt/ n monumento m. ∼al /-'mentl/ a monumental

moo /muː/ n mugido m. ● vi mugir

mooch /muːtʃ/ vi (sl) haraganear. ● vt (Amer, sl) birlar

mood /muːd/ n humor m. be in the ∼ for tener ganas de. in a good/bad ∼ de buen/mal humor. ∼y a (-ier, -iest) de humor cambiadizo; (bad-tempered) malhumorado

moon /muːn/ n luna f. ∼light n luz f de la luna. ∼lighting n (fam) pluriempleo m. ∼lit a iluminado por la luna; ⟨night⟩ de luna

moor¹ /mʊə(r)/ n (open land) páramo m

moor² /mʊə(r)/ vt amarrar. ∼ings npl (ropes) amarras fpl; (place) amarradero m

Moor /mʊə(r)/ n moro m

moose /muːs/ n invar alce m

moot /muːt/ a discutible. ● vt proponer ⟨question⟩

mop /mɒp/ n fregona f. ∼ of hair pelambrera f. ● vt (pt mopped) fregar. ∼ (up) limpiar

mope /məʊp/ vi estar abatido

moped /'məʊped/ n ciclomotor m

moral /'mɒrəl/ a moral. ● n moraleja f. ∼s npl moralidad f

morale /mə'rɑːl/ n moral f

moral|ist /'mɒrəlɪst/ n moralista m & f. ∼ity /mə'rælətɪ/ n moralidad f. ∼ize vi moralizar. ∼ly adv moralmente

morass /mə'ræs/ n (marsh) pantano m; (fig, entanglement) embrollo m

morbid /'mɔːbɪd/ a morboso

more /mɔː(r)/ a & n & adv más. ∼ and ∼ cada vez más. ∼ or less más o menos. once ∼ una vez más. some ∼ más

moreover /mɔː'rəʊvə(r)/ adv además

morgue /mɔːg/ n depósito m de cadáveres

moribund /'mɒrɪbʌnd/ a moribundo

morning /'mɔːnɪŋ/ n mañana f; (early hours) madrugada f. at 11 o'clock in the ∼ a las once de la mañana. in the ∼ por la mañana

Morocc|an /mə'rɒkən/ a & n marroquí (m & f). ∼o /-kəʊ/ n Marruecos mpl

moron /'mɔːrɒn/ n imbécil m & f

morose /mə'rəʊs/ a malhumorado

morphine /'mɔːfiːn/ n morfina f

Morse /mɔːs/ n Morse m. ∼ (code) n alfabeto m Morse

morsel /'mɔːsl/ n pedazo m; (mouthful) bocado m

mortal /'mɔːtl/ a & n mortal (m). ∼ity /-'tælətɪ/ n mortalidad f

mortar /'mɔːtə(r)/ n (all senses) mortero m

mortgage /'mɔːgɪdʒ/ n hipoteca f. ● vt hipotecar

mortify /'mɔːtɪfaɪ/ vt mortificar

mortuary /'mɔːtjʊərɪ/ n depósito m de cadáveres

mosaic /məʊ'zeɪk/ n mosaico m

Moscow /'mɒskəʊ/ n Moscú m

Moses /'məʊzɪz/ a. ∼ basket n moisés m

mosque /mɒsk/ n mezquita f

mosquito /mɒs'kiːtəʊ/ n (pl -oes) mosquito m

moss /mɒs/ n musgo m. ∼y a musgoso

most /məʊst/ a más. for the ∼ part en su mayor parte. ● n la mayoría f. ∼ of la mayor parte de. at ∼ a lo más. make the ∼ of aprovechar al máximo. ● adv más; (very) muy. ∼ly adv principalmente

MOT *abbr* (*Ministry of Transport*). **~ (test)** ITV, inspección *f* técnica de vehículos

motel /məʊˈtel/ *n* motel *m*

moth /mɒθ/ *n* mariposa *f* (nocturna); (*in clothes*) polilla *f*. **~ball** *n* bola *f* de naftalina. **~eaten** *a* apolillado

mother /ˈmʌðə(r)/ *n* madre *f*. ● *vt* cuidar como a un hijo. **~hood** *n* maternidad *f*. **~in-law** *n* (*pl* **~s-in-law**) suegra *f*. **~land** *n* patria *f*. **~ly** *adv* maternalmente. **~of-pearl** *n* nácar *m*. **M~'s Day** *n* el día *m* de la Madre. **~to-be** *n* futura madre *f*. **~ tongue** *n* lengua *f* materna

motif /məʊˈtiːf/ *n* motivo *m*

motion /ˈməʊʃn/ *n* movimiento *m*; (*proposal*) moción *f*. ● *vt/i*. **~ (to) s.o. to** hacer señas a uno para que. **~less** *a* inmóvil

motivat|e /ˈməʊtɪveɪt/ *vt* motivar. **~ion** /-ˈveɪʃn/ *n* motivación *f*

motive /ˈməʊtɪv/ *n* motivo *m*

motley /ˈmɒtlɪ/ *a* abigarrado

motor /ˈməʊtə(r)/ *n* motor *m*; (*car*) coche *m*. ● *a* motor; (*fem*) motora, motriz. ● *vi* ir en coche. **~ bike** *n* (*fam*) motocicleta, moto *f* (*fam*). **~ boat** *n* lancha *f* motora. **~cade** /ˈməʊtəkeɪd/ *n* (*Amer*) desfile *m* de automóviles. **~ car** *n* coche *m*, automóvil *m*. **~ cycle** *n* motocicleta *f*. **~cyclist** *n* motociclista *m* & *f*. **~ing** *n* automovilismo *m*. **~ist** *n* automovilista *m* & *f*. **~ize** *vt* motorizar. **~way** *n* autopista *f*

mottled /ˈmɒtld/ *a* abigarrado

motto /ˈmɒtəʊ/ *n* (*pl* **-oes**) lema *m*

mould[1] /məʊld/ *n* molde *m*. ● *vt* moldear

mould[2] /məʊld/ *n* (*fungus, rot*) moho *m*

moulding /ˈməʊldɪŋ/ *n* (*on wall etc*) moldura *f*

mouldy /ˈməʊldɪ/ *a* mohoso

moult /məʊlt/ *vi* mudar

mound /maʊnd/ *n* montículo *m*; (*pile, fig*) montón *m*

mount[1] /maʊnt/ *vt/i* subir. ● *n* montura *f*. **~ up** aumentar

mount[2] /maʊnt/ *n* (*hill*) monte *m*

mountain /ˈmaʊntɪn/ *n* montaña *f*. **~eer** /maʊntɪˈnɪə(r)/ *n* alpinista *m* & *f*. **~eering** *n* alpinismo *m*. **~ous** /ˈmaʊntɪnəs/ *a* montañoso

mourn /mɔːn/ *vt* llorar. ● *vi* lamentarse. **~ for** llorar la muerte de. **~er** *n* persona *f* que acompaña el cortejo fúnebre. **~ful** *a* triste. **~ing** *n* luto *m*

mouse /maʊs/ *n* (*pl* **mice**) ratón *m*. **~trap** *n* ratonera *f*

mousse /muːs/ *n* (*dish*) crema *f* batida

moustache /məˈstɑːʃ/ *n* bigote *m*

mousy /ˈmaʊsɪ/ *a* (*hair*) pardusco; (*fig*) tímido

mouth /maʊð/ *vt* formar con los labios. /maʊθ/ *n* boca *f*. **~ful** *n* bocado *m*. **~organ** *n* armónica *f*. **~piece** *n* (*mus*) boquilla *f*; (*fig, person*) portavoz *f*, vocero *m* (*LAm*). **~wash** *n* enjuague *m*

movable /ˈmuːvəbl/ *a* móvil, movible

move /muːv/ *vt* mover; mudarse de (*house*); (*with emotion*) conmover; (*propose*) proponer. ● *vi* moverse; (*be in motion*) estar en movimiento; (*progress*) hacer progresos; (*take action*) tomar medidas; (*depart*) irse. **~ (out)** irse. ● *n* movimiento *m*; (*in game*) jugada *f*; (*player's turn*) turno *m*; (*removal*) mudanza *f*. **on the ~** en movimiento. **~ along** (hacer) circular. **~ away** alejarse. **~ back** (hacer) retroceder. **~ forward** (hacer) avanzar. **~ in** instalarse. **~ on** (hacer) circular. **~ over** apartarse. **~ment** /ˈmuːvmənt/ *n* movimiento *m*

movie /ˈmuːvɪ/ *n* (*Amer*) película *f*. **the ~s** *npl* el cine *m*

moving /ˈmuːvɪŋ/ *a* en movimiento; (*touching*) conmovedor

mow /məʊ/ *vt* (*pt* **mowed** *or* **mown**) segar. **~ down** derribar. **~er** *n* (*for lawn*) cortacésped *m* *inv*

MP *abbr see* **Member of Parliament**

Mr /ˈmɪstə(r)/ *abbr* (*pl* **Messrs**) (*Mister*) señor *m*. **~ Coldbeck** (el) Sr. Coldbeck

Mrs /ˈmɪsɪz/ *abbr* (*pl* **Mrs**) (*Missis*) señora *f*. **~ Andrews** (la) Sra. Andrews. **the ~ Andrews** (las) Sras. Andrews

Ms /mɪz/ *abbr* (*title of married or unmarried woman*) señora *f*, señorita *f*. **Ms Lawton** (la) Sra. Lawton

much /mʌtʃ/ *a* & *n* mucho (*m*). ● *adv* mucho; (*before pp*) muy. **~ as** por mucho que. **~ the same** más o menos lo mismo. **so ~** tanto. **too ~** demasiado

muck /mʌk/ *n* estiércol *m*; (*dirt, fam*) suciedad *f*. ● *vi*. **~ about** (*sl*) perder el tiempo. **~ about with** (*sl*) juguetear con. ● vt. ~ up (sl) echar a perder. ~ in (sl) participar. ~y a sucio

mucus /'mjuːkəs/ n moco m

mud /mʌd/ n lodo m, barro m

muddle /'mʌdl/ vt embrollar. ● vi. ~ **through** salir del paso. ● n desorden m; (mix-up) lío m

muddy /'mʌdɪ/ a lodoso; ⟨hands etc⟩ cubierto de lodo

mudguard /'mʌdgɑːd/ n guardabarros m invar

muff /mʌf/ n manguito m

muffin /'mʌfɪn/ n mollete m

muffle /'mʌfl/ vt tapar; amortiguar ⟨a sound⟩. ~r n (scarf) bufanda f

mug /mʌg/ n tazón m; (for beer) jarra f; (face, sl) cara f, jeta f (sl); (fool, sl) primo m. ● vt (pt mugged) asaltar. ~ger n asaltador m. ~ging n asalto m

muggy /'mʌgɪ/ a bochornoso

Muhammadan /mə'hæmɪdən/ a & n mahometano (m)

mule[1] /mjuːl/ n mula f, mulo m

mule[2] /mjuːl/ n (slipper) babucha f

mull[1] /mʌl/ vt. ~ over reflexionar sobre

mull[2] /mʌl/ vt calentar con especias ⟨wine⟩

multi... /'mʌltɪ/ pref multi...

multicoloured /mʌltɪ'kʌləd/ a multicolor

multifarious /mʌltɪ'feərɪəs/ a múltiple

multinational /mʌltɪ'næʃənl/ a & n multinacional (f)

multipl|e /'mʌltɪpl/ a & n múltiplo (m). ~ication /mʌltɪplɪ'keɪʃn/ n multiplicación f. ~y /'mʌltɪplaɪ/ vt/i multiplicar(se)

multitude /'mʌltɪtjuːd/ n multitud f

mum[1] /mʌm/ n (fam) mamá f (fam)

mum[2] /mʌm/ a. keep ~ (fam) guardar silencio

mumble /'mʌmbl/ vt decir entre dientes. ● vi hablar entre dientes

mummify /'mʌmɪfaɪ/ vt/i momificar(se)

mummy[1] /'mʌmɪ/ n (mother, fam) mamá f (fam)

mummy[2] /'mʌmɪ/ n momia f

mumps /mʌmps/ n paperas fpl

munch /mʌntʃ/ vt/i mascar

mundane /mʌn'deɪn/ a mundano

municipal /mjuː'nɪsɪpl/ a municipal. ~ity /-'pælətɪ/ n municipio m

munificent /mjuː'nɪfɪsənt/ a munífico

munitions /mjuː'nɪʃnz/ npl municiones fpl

mural /'mjʊərəl/ a & n mural (f)

murder /'mɜːdə(r)/ n asesinato m. ● vt asesinar. ~er n asesino m. ~ess n asesina f. ~ous a homicida

murky /'mɜːkɪ/ a (-ier, -iest) oscuro

murmur /'mɜːmə(r)/ n murmullo m. ● vt/i murmurar

muscle /'mʌsl/ n músculo m. ● vi. ~ in (Amer, sl) meterse por fuerza en

muscular /'mʌskjʊlə(r)/ a muscular; (having well-developed muscles) musculoso

muse /mjuːz/ vi meditar

museum /mjuː'zɪəm/ n museo m

mush /mʌʃ/ n pulpa f

mushroom /'mʌʃrʊm/ n champiñón m; (bot) seta f. ● vi (appear in large numbers) crecer como hongos

mushy /'mʌʃɪ/ a pulposo

music /'mjuːzɪk/ n música f. ~al a musical; ⟨instrument⟩ de música; (talented) que tiene don de música. ● n comedia f musical. ~ hall n teatro m de variedades. ~ian /mjuː'zɪʃn/ n músico m

musk /mʌsk/ n almizcle m

Muslim /'mʊzlɪm/ a & n musulmán (m)

muslin /'mʌzlɪn/ n muselina f

musquash /'mʌskwɒʃ/ n ratón m almizclero

mussel /'mʌsl/ n mejillón m

must /mʌst/ v aux deber, tener que. he ~ be old debe ser viejo. I ~ have done it debo haberlo hecho. you ~ go debes marcharte. ● n. be a ~ ser imprescindible

mustard /'mʌstəd/ n mostaza f

muster /'mʌstə(r)/ vt/i reunir(se)

musty /'mʌstɪ/ a (-ier, -iest) que huele a cerrado

mutation /mjuː'teɪʃn/ n mutación f

mute /mjuːt/ a & n mudo (m). ~d a ⟨sound⟩ sordo; ⟨criticism⟩ callado

mutilat|e /'mjuːtɪleɪt/ vt mutilar. ~ion /-'leɪʃn/ n mutilación f

mutin|ous /'mjuːtɪnəs/ a ⟨sailor etc⟩ amotinado; (fig) rebelde. ~y n motín m. ● vi amotinarse

mutter /'mʌtə(r)/ vt/i murmurar

mutton /'mʌtn/ n cordero m

mutual /'mjuːtʃʊəl/ a mutuo; (common, fam) común. ~ly adv mutuamente

muzzle /mʌzl/ n (snout) hocico m; (device) bozal m; (of gun) boca f. ● vt poner el bozal a

my /maɪ/ a mi, mis pl

myopic /maɪˈɒpɪk/ a miope

myriad /ˈmɪrɪəd/ n miríada f

myself /maɪˈself/ pron yo mismo m, yo misma f; (reflexive) me; (after prep) mí (mismo) m, mí (misma) f

myster|ious /mɪˈstɪərɪəs/ a misterioso. ~**y** /ˈmɪstərɪ/ n misterio m

mystic /ˈmɪstɪk/ a & n místico (m). ~**al** a místico. ~**ism** /-sɪzəm/ n misticismo m

mystif|ication /mɪstɪfɪˈkeɪʃn/ n confusión f. ~**y** /-faɪ/ vt dejar perplejo

mystique /mɪˈstiːk/ n mística f

myth /mɪθ/ n mito m. ~**ical** a mítico. ~**ology** /mɪˈθɒlədʒɪ/ n mitología f

N

N abbr (north) norte m

nab /næb/ vt (pt nabbed) (arrest, sl) coger (not LAm), agarrar (esp LAm)

nag /næg/ vt (pt nagged) fastidiar; (scold) regañar. ● vi criticar

nagging /ˈnægɪŋ/ a persistente, regañón

nail /neɪl/ n clavo m; (of finger, toe) uña f. **pay on the** ~ pagar a tocateja. ● vt clavar. ~ **polish** n esmalte m para las uñas

naïve /naɪˈiːv/ a ingenuo

naked /ˈneɪkɪd/ a desnudo. **to the** ~ **eye** a simple vista. ~**ly** adv desnudamente. ~**ness** n desnudez f

namby-pamby /næmbɪˈpæmbɪ/ a & n ñoño (m)

name /neɪm/ n nombre m; (fig) fama f. ● vt nombrar; (fix) fijar. **be** ~**d after** llevar el nombre de. ~**less** a anónimo. ~**ly** /ˈneɪmlɪ/ adv a saber. ~**sake** /ˈneɪmseɪk/ n (person) tocayo m

nanny /ˈnænɪ/ n niñera f. ~**goat** n cabra f

nap[1] /næp/ n (sleep) sueñecito m; (after lunch) siesta f. ● vi (pt napped) echarse un sueño. **catch s.o.** ~**ping** coger a uno desprevenido

nap[2] /næp/ n (fibres) lanilla f

nape /neɪp/ n nuca f

napkin /ˈnæpkɪn/ n (at meals) servilleta f; (for baby) pañal m

nappy /ˈnæpɪ/ n pañal m

narcotic /naːˈkɒtɪk/ a & n narcótico (m)

narrat|e /nəˈreɪt/ vt contar. ~**ion** /-ʃn/ n narración f. ~**ive** /ˈnærətɪv/ n relato m. ~**or** /nəˈreɪtə(r)/ n narrador m

narrow /ˈnærəʊ/ a (-er, -est) estrecho. **have a** ~ **escape** escaparse por los pelos. ● vt estrechar; (limit) limitar. ● vi estrecharse. ~**ly** adv estrechamente; (just) por poco. ~**-minded** a de miras estrechas. ~**ness** n estrechez f

nasal /ˈneɪzl/ a nasal

nast|ily /ˈnaːstɪlɪ/ adv desagradablemente; (maliciously) con malevolencia. ~**iness** n (malice) malevolencia f. ~**y** a /ˈnaːstɪ/ (-ier, -iest) desagradable; (malicious) malévolo; ⟨weather⟩ malo; ⟨taste, smell⟩ asqueroso; ⟨wound⟩ grave; ⟨person⟩ antipático

natal /ˈneɪtl/ a natal

nation /ˈneɪʃn/ n nación f

national /ˈnæʃənl/ a nacional. ● n súbdito m. ~ **anthem** n himno m nacional. ~**ism** n nacionalismo m. ~**ity** /næʃəˈnælətɪ/ n nacionalidad f. ~**ize** vt nacionalizar. ~**ly** adv a nivel nacional

nationwide /ˈneɪʃnwaɪd/ a nacional

native /ˈneɪtɪv/ n natural m & f. **be a** ~ **of** ser natural de. ● a nativo; ⟨country, town⟩ natal; (inborn) innato. ~ **speaker of Spanish** hispanohablante m & f. ~ **language** n lengua f materna

Nativity /nəˈtɪvətɪ/ n. **the** ~ la Natividad f

NATO /ˈneɪtəʊ/ abbr (North Atlantic Treaty Organization) OTAN f, Organización f del Tratado del Atlántico Norte

natter /ˈnætə(r)/ vi (fam) charlar. ● n (fam) charla f

natural /ˈnætʃərəl/ a natural. ~ **history** n historia f natural. ~**ist** n naturalista m & f

naturaliz|ation /nætʃərəlaɪˈzeɪʃn/ n naturalización f. ~**e** vt naturalizar

naturally /ˈnætʃərəlɪ/ adv (of course) naturalmente; (by nature) por naturaleza

nature /ˈneɪtʃə(r)/ n naturaleza f; (kind) género m; (of person) carácter m

naught /nɔːt/ n (old use) nada f; (maths) cero m

naught|ily /ˈnɔːtɪlɪ/ adv mal. ~**y** a (-ier, -iest) malo; ⟨child⟩ travieso; ⟨joke⟩ verde

nause|a /'nɔ:zɪə/ n náusea f. ~**ate** vt dar náuseas a. ~**ous** a nauseabundo

nautical /'nɔ:tɪkl/ a náutico. ~ **mile** n milla f marina

naval /'neɪvl/ a naval; ‹officer› de marina

Navarre /nə'vɑː(r)/ n Navarra f. ~**se** a navarro

nave /neɪv/ n (of church) nave f

navel /'neɪvl/ n ombligo m

navigable /'nævɪgəbl/ a navegable

navigat|e /'nævɪgeɪt/ vt navegar por ‹sea etc›; gobernar ‹ship›. ● vi navegar. ~**ion** n navegación f. ~**or** n navegante m

navvy /'nævɪ/ n peón m caminero

navy /'neɪvɪ/ n marina f. ~ **(blue)** azul m marino

NE abbr (north-east) noreste m

near /'nɪə(r)/ adv cerca. ~ **at hand** muy cerca. ~ **by** adv cerca. **draw** ~ acercarse. ● prep. ~ **(to)** cerca de. ● a cercano. ● vt acercarse a. ~**by** a cercano. **N**~ **East** n Oriente m Próximo. ~**ly** /'nɪəlɪ/ adv casi. **not** ~**ly as pretty as** no es ni con mucho tan guapa como. ~**ness** /'nɪənɪs/ n proximidad f

neat /ni:t/ a (-er, -est) pulcro; ‹room etc› bien arreglado; ‹clever› diestro; ‹ingenious› hábil; ‹whisky, brandy etc› solo. ~**ly** adv pulcramente. ~**ness** n pulcritud f

nebulous /'nebjʊləs/ a nebuloso

necessar|ies /'nesəsərɪz/ npl lo indispensable. ~**ily** /nesə'serɪlɪ/ adv necesariamente. ~**y** a necesario, imprescindible

necessit|ate /nə'sesɪteɪt/ vt necesitar. ~**y** /nɪ'sesətɪ/ n necesidad f; ‹thing› cosa f indispensable

neck /nek/ n (of person, bottle, dress) cuello m; (of animal) pescuezo m. ~ **and** ~ parejas. ~**lace** /'nekləs/ n collar m. ~**line** n escote m. ~**tie** n corbata f

nectar /'nektə(r)/ n néctar m

nectarine /'nektə'ri:n/ n nectarina f

née /neɪ/ a de soltera

need /ni:d/ n necesidad f. ● vt necesitar; ‹demand› exigir. **you** ~ **not speak** no tienes que hablar

needle /'ni:dl/ n aguja f. ● vt (annoy, fam) pinchar

needless /'ni:dlɪs/ a innecesario. ~**ly** adv innecesariamente

needlework /'ni:dlwɜːk/ n costura f; (embroidery) bordado m

needy /'ni:dɪ/ a (-ier, -iest) necesitado

negation /nɪ'geɪʃn/ n negación f

negative /'negətɪv/ a negativo. ● n (of photograph) negativo m; (word, gram) negativa f. ~**ly** adv negativamente

neglect /nɪ'glekt/ vt descuidar; no cumplir con ‹duty›. ~ **to do** dejar de hacer. ● n descuido m, negligencia f. **(state of)** ~ abandono m. ~**ful** a descuidado

négligé /'neglɪʒeɪ/ n bata f, salto m de cama

negligen|ce /'neglɪdʒəns/ n negligencia f, descuido m. ~**t** a descuidado

negligible /'neglɪdʒəbl/ a insignificante

negotiable /nɪ'gəʊʃəbl/ a negociable

negotiat|e /nɪ'gəʊʃɪeɪt/ vt/i negociar. ~**ion** /-'eɪʃn/ n negociación f. ~**or** n negociador m

Negr|ess /'ni:grɪs/ n negra f. ~**o** n (pl -oes) negro m. ● a negro

neigh /neɪ/ n relincho m. ● vi relinchar

neighbour /'neɪbə(r)/ n vecino m. ~**hood** n vecindad f, barrio m. **in the** ~**hood of** alrededor de. ~**ing** a vecino. ~**ly** /'neɪbəlɪ/ a amable

neither /'naɪðə(r)/ a & pron ninguno m de los dos, ni el uno m ni el otro m. ● adv ni. ~ **big nor small** ni grande ni pequeño. ~ **shall I come** no voy yo tampoco. ● conj tampoco

neon /'ni:ɒn/ n neón m. ● a ‹lamp etc› de neón

nephew /'nevju:/ n sobrino m

nepotism /'nepətɪzəm/ m nepotismo m

nerve /nɜːv/ n nervio m; (courage) valor m; (calm) sangre f fría; (impudence, fam) descaro m. ~**racking** a exasperante. ~**s** npl (before exams etc) nervios mpl

nervous /'nɜːvəs/ a nervioso. **be/feel** ~ (afraid) tener miedo (**of** a). ~**ly** adv (tensely) nerviosamente; (timidly) tímidamente. ~**ness** n nerviosidad f; (fear) miedo m

nervy /'nɜːvɪ/ a see **nervous**; (Amer, fam) descarado

nest /nest/ n nido m. ● vi anidar. ~**egg** n (money) ahorros mpl

nestle /'nesl/ vi acomodarse. ~ **up to** arrimarse a

net /net/ *n* red *f*. ● *vt* (*pt* **netted**) coger (*not LAm*), agarrar (*esp LAm*). ● *a* (*weight etc*) neto

netball /'netbɔːl/ *n* baloncesto *m*

Netherlands /'neðələndz/ *npl*. **the ∼** los Países *mpl* Bajos

netting /'netɪŋ/ *n* (*nets*) redes *fpl*; (*wire*) malla *f*; (*fabric*) tul *m*

nettle /'netl/ *n* ortiga *f*

network /'netwɜːk/ *n* red *f*

neuralgia /njʊə'rældʒɪə/ *n* neuralgia *f*

neuro|sis /njʊə'rəʊsɪs/ *n* (*pl* **-oses** /-siːz/) neurosis *f*. **∼tic** *a* & *n* neurótico (*m*)

neuter /'njuːtə(r)/ *a* & *n* neutro (*m*). ● *vt* castrar ⟨*animals*⟩

neutral /'njuːtrəl/ *a* neutral; ⟨*colour*⟩ neutro; (*elec*) neutro. **∼ (gear)** (*auto*) punto *m* muerto. **∼ity** /-'trælətɪ/ *n* neutralidad *f*

neutron /'njuːtrɒn/ *n* neutrón *m*. **∼ bomb** *n* bomba *f* de neutrones

never /'nevə(r)/ *adv* nunca, jamás; (*not, fam*) no. **∼ again** nunca más. **∼ mind** (*don't worry*) no te preocupes, no se preocupe; (*it doesn't matter*) no importa. **he ∼ smiles** no sonríe nunca. **I ∼ saw him** (*fam*) no le vi. **∼-ending** *a* interminable

nevertheless /nevəðə'les/ *adv* sin embargo, no obstante

new /njuː/ *a* (**-er, -est**) (*new to owner*) nuevo (*placed before noun*); (*brand new*) nuevo (*placed after noun*). **∼-born** *a* recién nacido. **∼comer** *n* recién llegado *m*. **∼fangled** *a* (*pej*) moderno. **∼-laid egg** *n* huevo *m* fresco. **∼ly** *adv* nuevamente; (*recently*) recién. **∼ly-weds** *npl* recién casados *mpl*. **∼ moon** *n* luna *f* nueva. **∼ness** *n* novedad *f*

news /njuːz/ *n* noticias *fpl*; (*broadcasting, press*) informaciones *fpl*; (*on TV*) telediario *m*; (*on radio*) diario *m* hablado. **∼agent** *n* vendedor *m* de periódicos. **∼caster** *n* locutor *m*. **∼letter** *n* boletín *m*. **∼paper** *n* periódico *m*. **∼reader** *n* locutor *m*. **∼reel** *n* noticiario *m*, nodo *m* (*in Spain*)

newt /njuːt/ *n* tritón *m*

new year /njuː'jɪə(r)/ *n* año *m* nuevo. **N∼'s Day** *n* día *m* de Año Nuevo. **N∼'s Eve** *n* noche *f* vieja

New Zealand /njuː'ziːlənd/ *n* Nueva Zelanda *f*. **∼er** *n* neozelandés *m*

next /nekst/ *a* próximo; ⟨*week, month etc*⟩ que viene, próximo;

⟨*adjoining*⟩ vecino; ⟨*following*⟩ siguiente. ● *adv* la próxima vez; (*afterwards*) después. ● *n* siguiente *m*. **∼ to** junto a. **∼ to nothing** casi nada. **∼ door** al lado (**to** de). **∼-door** de al lado. **∼-best** mejor alternativa *f*. **∼ of kin** *n* pariente *m* más próximo, parientes *mpl* más próximos

nib /nɪb/ *n* (*of pen*) plumilla *f*

nibble /'nɪbl/ *vt/i* mordisquear. ● *n* mordisco *m*

nice /naɪs/ *a* (**-er, -est**) agradable; (*likeable*) simpático; (*kind*) amable; (*pretty*) bonito; ⟨*weather*⟩ bueno; (*subtle*) sutil. **∼ly** *adv* agradablemente; (*kindly*) amablemente; (*well*) bien

nicety /'naɪsətɪ/ *n* (*precision*) precisión *f*; (*detail*) detalle. **to a ∼** exactamente

niche /nɪtʃ, niːʃ/ *n* (*recess*) nicho *m*; (*fig*) buena posición *f*

nick /nɪk/ *n* corte *m* pequeño; (*prison, sl*) cárcel *f*. **in the ∼ of time** justo a tiempo. ● *vt* (*steal, arrest, sl*) birlar

nickel /'nɪkl/ *n* níquel *m*; (*Amer*) moneda *f* de cinco centavos

nickname /'nɪkneɪm/ *n* apodo *m*; (*short form*) diminutivo *m*. ● *vt* apodar

nicotine /'nɪkətiːn/ *n* nicotina *f*

niece /niːs/ *n* sobrina *f*

nifty /'nɪftɪ/ *a* (*sl*) (*smart*) elegante

Nigeria /naɪ'dʒɪərɪə/ *n* Nigeria *f*. **∼n** *a* & *n* nigeriano (*m*)

niggardly /'nɪgədlɪ/ *a* ⟨*person*⟩ tacaño; ⟨*thing*⟩ miserable

niggling /'nɪglɪŋ/ *a* molesto

night /naɪt/ *n* noche *f*; (*evening*) tarde *f*. ● *a* nocturno, de noche. **∼cap** *n* (*hat*) gorro *m* de dormir; (*drink*) bebida *f* (*tomada antes de acostarse*). **∼club** *n* sala *f* de fiestas, boîte *f*. **∼dress** *n* camisón *m*. **∼fall** *n* anochecer *m*. **∼gown** *n* camisón *m*

nightingale /'naɪtɪŋgeɪl/ *n* ruiseñor *m*

night: ∼life *n* vida *f* nocturna. **∼ly** *adv* todas las noches. **∼mare** *n* pesadilla *f*. **∼school** *n* escuela *f* nocturna. **∼-time** *n* noche *f*. **∼watchman** *n* sereno *m*

nil /nɪl/ *n* nada *f*; (*sport*) cero *m*

nimble /'nɪmbl/ *a* (**-er, -est**) ágil

nine /naɪn/ *a* & *n* nueve (*m*)

nineteen /naɪn'tiːn/ *a* & *n* diecinueve (*m*). **∼th** *a* & *n* diecinueve (*m*), decimonoveno (*m*)

ninet|ieth /'naɪntɪəθ/ a noventa, nonagésimo. **~y** a & n noventa (m)

ninth /'naɪnθ/ a & n noveno (m)

nip¹ /nɪp/ vt (pt **nipped**) (pinch) pellizcar; (bite) mordisquear. • vi (rush, sl) correr. • n (pinch) pellizco m; (cold) frío m

nip² /nɪp/ n (of drink) trago m

nipper /'nɪpə(r)/ n (sl) chaval m

nipple /'nɪpl/ n pezón m; (of baby's bottle) tetilla f

nippy /'nɪpɪ/ a (-ier, -iest) (nimble, fam) ágil; (quick, fam) rápido; (chilly, fam) fresquito

nitrogen /'naɪtrədʒən/ n nitrógeno m

nitwit /'nɪtwɪt/ n (fam) imbécil m & f

no /nəʊ/ a ninguno. **~ entry** prohibido el paso. **~ man's land** n tierra f de nadie. **~ smoking** se prohibe fumar. **~ way!** (Amer, fam) ¡ni hablar! • adv no. • n (pl **noes**) no m

nobility /nəʊ'bɪlətɪ/ n nobleza f

noble /'nəʊbl/ a (-er, -est) noble. **~man** n noble m

nobody /'nəʊbədɪ/ pron nadie m. • n nadie m. **~ is there** no hay nadie. **he knows ~** no conoce a nadie

nocturnal /nɒk'tɜ:nl/ a nocturno

nod /nɒd/ vt (pt **nodded**). **~ one's head** asentir con la cabeza. • vi (in agreement) asentir con la cabeza; (in greeting) saludar; (be drowsy) dar cabezadas. • n inclinación f de cabeza

nodule /'nɒdju:l/ n nódulo m

nois|e /nɔɪz/ n ruido m. **~eless** a silencioso. **~ily** /'nɔɪzɪlɪ/ adv ruidosamente. **~y** a (-ier, -iest) ruidoso

nomad /'nəʊmæd/ n nómada m & f. **~ic** /-'mædɪk/ a nómada

nominal /'nɒmɪnl/ a nominal

nominat|e /'nɒmɪneɪt/ vt nombrar; (put forward) proponer. **~ion** /-'neɪʃn/ n nombramiento m

non-... /nɒn/ pref no ...

nonagenarian /nəʊnədʒɪ'neərɪən/ a & n nonagenario (m), noventón (m)

nonchalant /'nɒnʃələnt/ a imperturbable

non-commissioned /nɒnkə'mɪʃnd/ a. **~ officer** n suboficial m

non-committal /nɒnkə'mɪtl/ a evasivo

nondescript /'nɒndɪskrɪpt/ a inclasificable, anodino

none /nʌn/ pron (person) nadie, ninguno; (thing) ninguno, nada. **~ of** nada de. **~ of us** ninguno de nosotros. **I have ~** no tengo nada. • adv no, de ninguna manera. **he is ~ the happier** no está más contento

nonentity /nɒ'nentətɪ/ n nulidad f

non-existent /nɒnɪg'zɪstənt/ a inexistente

nonplussed /nɒn'plʌst/ a perplejo

nonsens|e /'nɒnsns/ n tonterías fpl, disparates mpl. **~ical** /-'sensɪkl/ a absurdo

non-smoker /nɒn'sməʊkə(r)/ n persona f que no fuma; (rail) departamento m de no fumadores

non-starter /nɒn'stɑ:tə(r)/ n (fam) proyecto m imposible

non-stop /nɒn'stɒp/ a ⟨train⟩ directo; ⟨flight⟩ sin escalas. • adv sin parar; (by train) directamente; (by air) sin escalas

noodles /'nu:dlz/ npl fideos mpl

nook /nʊk/ n rincón m

noon /nu:n/ n mediodía m

no-one /'nəʊwʌn/ pron nadie. see **nobody**

noose /nu:s/ n nudo m corredizo

nor /nɔ:(r)/ conj ni, tampoco. **neither blue ~ red** ni azul ni rojo. **he doesn't play the piano, ~ do I** no sabe tocar el piano, ni yo tampoco

Nordic /'nɔ:dɪk/ a nórdico

norm /nɔ:m/ n norma f; (normal) lo normal

normal /'nɔ:ml/ a normal. **~cy** n (Amer) normalidad f. **~ity** /-'mælətɪ/ n normalidad f. **~ly** adv normalmente

Norman /'nɔ:mən/ a & n normando (m)

Normandy /'nɔ:məndɪ/ n Normandia f

north /nɔ:θ/ n norte m. • a del norte, norteño. • adv hacia el norte. **N~ America** n América f del Norte, Norteamérica f. **N~ American** a & n norteamericano (m). **~east** n nordeste m. **~erly** /'nɔ:ðəlɪ/ a del norte. **~ern** /'nɔ:ðən/ a del norte. **~erner** n norteño m. **N~ Sea** n mar m del Norte. **~ward** a hacia el norte. **~wards** adv hacia el norte. **~west** n noroeste m

Norw|ay /'nɔ:weɪ/ n Noruega f. **~egian** a & n noruego (m)

nose /nəʊz/ n nariz f. • vi. **~ about** curiosear. **~bleed** n hemorragia f nasal. **~dive** n picado m

nostalgi|a /nɒ'stældʒə/ n nostalgia f. **~c** a nostálgico

nostril /'nɒstrɪl/ n nariz f; (of horse) ollar m

nosy /'nəʊzɪ/ a (-ier, -iest) (fam) entrometido

not /nɒt/ adv no. ~ **at all** no... nada; (after thank you) de nada. ~ **yet** aún no. **I do ~ know** no sé. **I suppose ~** supongo que no

notabl|e /'nəʊtəbl/ a notable. ● n (person) notabilidad f. ~**y** /'nəʊtəblɪ/ adv notablemente

notary /'nəʊtərɪ/ n notario m

notation /nəʊ'teɪʃn/ n notación f

notch /nɒtʃ/ n muesca f. ● vt. ~ **up** apuntar ⟨score etc⟩

note /nəʊt/ n nota f; (banknote) billete m. **take ~s** tomar apuntes. ● vt notar. ~**book** n libreta f. ~**d** a célebre. ~**paper** n papel m de escribir. ~**worthy** a notable

nothing /'nʌθɪŋ/ pron nada. **he eats ~** no come nada. **for ~** (free) gratis; (in vain) inútilmente. ● n nada f; (person) nulidad f; (thing of no importance) frusleria f; (zero) cero m. ● adv de ninguna manera. ~ **big** nada grande. ~ **else** nada más. ~ **much** poca cosa

notice /'nəʊtɪs/ n (attention) atención f; (advert) anuncio m; (sign) letrero m; (poster) cartel m; (termination of employment) despido m; (warning) aviso m. **(advance)** ~ previo aviso m. ~ **(of dismissal)** despido m. **take ~ of** prestar atención a, hacer caso a ⟨person⟩; hacer caso de ⟨thing⟩. ● vt notar. ~**able** a evidente. ~**ably** adv visiblemente. ~**board** n tablón m de anuncios

notif|ication /nəʊtɪfɪ'keɪʃn/ n aviso m, notificación f. ~**y** vt avisar

notion /'nəʊʃn/ n (concept) concepto m; (idea) idea f. ~**s** npl (sewing goods etc, Amer) artículos mpl de mercería

notori|ety /nəʊtə'raɪətɪ/ n notoriedad f; (pej) mala fama f. ~**ous** /nəʊ'tɔːrɪəs/ a notorio. ~**ously** adv notoriamente

notwithstanding /nɒtwɪθ'stændɪŋ/ prep a pesar de. ● adv sin embargo

nougat /'nuːgɑː/ n turrón m

nought /nɔːt/ n cero m

noun /naʊn/ n sustantivo m, nombre m

nourish /'nʌrɪʃ/ vt alimentar; (incl fig) nutrir. ~**ment** n alimento m

novel /'nɒvl/ n novela f. ● a nuevo. ~**ist** n novelista m & f. ~**ty** n novedad f

November /nəʊ'vembə(r)/ n noviembre m

novice /'nɒvɪs/ n principiante m & f

now /naʊ/ adv ahora. ~ **and again**, ~ **and then** de vez en cuando. **just ~** ahora mismo; (a moment ago) hace poco. ● conj ahora que

nowadays /'naʊədeɪz/ adv hoy (en) día

nowhere /'nəʊweə(r)/ adv en/por ninguna parte; (after motion towards) a ninguna parte

noxious /'nɒkʃəs/ a nocivo

nozzle /'nɒzl/ n boquilla f; (tec) tobera f

nuance /'njuːɑːns/ n matiz m

nuclear /'njuːklɪə(r)/ a nuclear

nucleus /'njuːklɪəs/ n (pl -**lei** /-lɪaɪ/) núcleo m

nude /njuːd/ a & n desnudo (m). **in the ~** desnudo

nudge /nʌdʒ/ vt dar un codazo a. ● n codazo m

nudi|sm /'njuːdɪzəm/ n desnudismo m. ~**st** n nudista m & f. ~**ty** /'njuːdətɪ/ n desnudez f

nuisance /'njuːsns/ n (thing, event) fastidio m; (person) pesado m. **be a ~** dar la lata

null /nʌl/ a nulo. ~**ify** vt anular

numb /nʌm/ a entumecido. ● vt entumecer

number /'nʌmbə(r)/ n número m. ● vt numerar; (count, include) contar. ~**plate** n matrícula f

numeracy /'njuːmərəsɪ/ n conocimientos mpl de matemáticas

numeral /'njuːmərəl/ n número m

numerate /'njuːmərət/ a que tiene buenos conocimientos de matemáticas

numerical /njuː'merɪkl/ a numérico

numerous /'njuːmərəs/ a numeroso

nun /nʌn/ n monja f

nurse /nɜːs/ n enfermera f, enfermero m; (nanny) niñera f. **wet ~** n nodriza f. ● vt cuidar; abrigar ⟨hope etc⟩. ~**maid** n niñera f

nursery /'nɜːsərɪ/ n cuarto m de los niños; (for plants) vivero m. **(day) ~** n guardería f infantil. ~ **rhyme** n canción f infantil. ~ **school** n escuela f de párvulos

nursing home /'nɜːsɪŋhəʊm/ n (for old people) asilo m de ancianos

nurture /'nɜːtʃə(r)/ vt alimentar

nut /nʌt/ n (walnut, Brazil nut etc) nuez f; (hazelnut) avellana f; (peanut) cacahuete m; (tec) tuerca f;

(*crazy person, sl*) chiflado *m*.
~**crackers** *npl* cascanueces *m invar*
nutmeg /ˈnʌtmeg/ *n* nuez *f* moscada
nutrient /ˈnjuːtrɪənt/ *n* alimento *m*
nutrit|ion /njuːˈtrɪʃn/ *n* nutrición *f*.
~**ious** *a* nutritivo
nuts /nʌtz/ *a* (*crazy, sl*) chiflado
nutshell /ˈnʌtʃel/ *n* cáscara *f* de
nuez. **in a** ~ en pocas palabras
nuzzle /ˈnʌzl/ *vt* acariciar con el
hocico
NW *abbr* (*north-west*) noroeste *m*
nylon /ˈnaɪlɒn/ *n* nailon *m*. ~**s** *npl*
medias *fpl* de nailon
nymph /nɪmf/ *n* ninfa *f*

O

oaf /əʊf/ *n* (*pl* **oafs**) zoquete *m*
oak /əʊk/ *n* roble *m*
OAP /əʊeɪˈpiː/ *abbr* (*old-age pensioner*) *n* pensionista *m & f*
oar /ɔː(r)/ *n* remo *m*. ~**sman** /ˈɔːzmən/ *n* (*pl* **-men**) remero *m*
oasis /əʊˈeɪsɪs/ *n* (*pl* **oases** /-siːz/) oasis *m invar*
oath /əʊθ/ *n* juramento *m*; (*swearword*) palabrota *f*
oat|meal /ˈəʊtmiːl/ *n* harina *f* de avena. ~**s** /əʊts/ *npl* avena *f*
obedien|ce /əʊˈbiːdɪəns/ *n* obediencia *f*. ~**t** /əʊˈbiːdɪənt/ *a* obediente. ~**tly** *adv* obedientemente
obelisk /ˈɒbəlɪsk/ *n* obelisco *m*
obes|e /əʊˈbiːs/ *a* obeso. ~**ity** *n* obesidad *f*
obey /əʊˈbeɪ/ *vt* obedecer; cumplir ⟨*instructions etc*⟩
obituary /əˈbɪtʃʊərɪ/ *n* necrología *f*
object /ˈɒbdʒɪkt/ *n* objeto *m*. /əbˈdʒekt/ *vi* oponerse
objection /əbˈdʒekʃn/ *n* objeción *f*. ~**able** /əbˈdʒekʃnəbl/ *a* censurable; (*unpleasant*) desagradable
objective /əbˈdʒektɪv/ *a & n* objetivo (*m*). ~**ively** *adv* objetivamente
objector /əbˈdʒektə(r)/ *n* objetante *m & f*
oblig|ation /ɒblɪˈgeɪʃn/ *n* obligación *f*. **be under an** ~**ation to** tener obligación de. ~**atory** /əˈblɪgətrɪ/ *a* obligatorio. ~**e** /əˈblaɪdʒ/ *vt* obligar; (*do a small service*) hacer un favor a. ~**ed** *a* agradecido. **much** ~**ed!** ¡muchas gracias! ~**ing** *a* atento
oblique /əˈbliːk/ *a* oblicuo

obliterat|e /əˈblɪtəreɪt/ *vt* borrar. ~**ion** /-ˈreɪʃn/ *n* borradura *f*
oblivio|n /əˈblɪvɪən/ *n* olvido *m*. ~**us** /əˈblɪvɪəs/ *a* (*unaware*) inconsciente (**to, of** de)
oblong /ˈɒblɒŋ/ *a & n* oblongo (*m*)
obnoxious /əbˈnɒkʃəs/ *a* odioso
oboe /ˈəʊbəʊ/ *n* oboe *m*
obscen|e /əbˈsiːn/ *a* obsceno. ~**ity** /-enətɪ/ *n* obscenidad *f*
obscur|e /əbˈskjʊə(r)/ *a* oscuro. ● *vt* oscurecer; (*conceal*) esconder; (*confuse*) confundir. ~**ity** *n* oscuridad *f*
obsequious /əbˈsiːkwɪəs/ *a* obsequioso
observan|ce /əbˈzɜːvəns/ *n* observancia *f*. ~**t** /əbˈzɜːvənt/ *a* observador
observation /ɒbzəˈveɪʃn/ *n* observación *f*
observatory /əbˈzɜːvətrɪ/ *n* observatorio *m*
observe /əbˈzɜːv/ *vt* observar. ~**r** *n* observador *m*
obsess /əbˈses/ *vt* obsesionar. ~**ion** /-ʃn/ *n* obsesión *f*. ~**ive** *a* obsesivo
obsolete /ˈɒbsəliːt/ *a* desusado
obstacle /ˈɒbstəkl/ *n* obstáculo *m*
obstetrics /əbˈstetrɪks/ *n* obstetricia *f*
obstina|cy /ˈɒbstɪnəsɪ/ *n* obstinación *f*. ~**te** /ˈɒbstɪnət/ *a* obstinado. ~**tely** *adv* obstinadamente
obstreperous /ɒbˈstrepərəs/ *a* turbulento, ruidoso, protestón
obstruct /əbˈstrʌkt/ *vt* obstruir. ~**ion** /-ʃn/ *n* obstrucción *f*
obtain /əbˈteɪn/ *vt* obtener. ● *vi* prevalecer. ~**able** *a* asequible
obtrusive /əbˈtruːsɪv/ *a* importuno
obtuse /əbˈtjuːs/ *a* obtuso
obviate /ˈɒbvɪeɪt/ *vt* evitar
obvious /ˈɒbvɪəs/ *a* obvio. ~**ly** obviamente
occasion /əˈkeɪʒn/ *n* ocasión *f*, oportunidad *f*. **on** ~ de vez en cuando. ● *vt* ocasionar. ~**al** /əˈkeɪʒnl/ *a* poco frecuente. ~**ally** *adv* de vez en cuando
occult /ɒˈkʌlt/ *a* oculto
occup|ant /ˈɒkjʊpənt/ *n* ocupante *m & f*. ~**ation** /ɒkjʊˈpeɪʃn/ *n* ocupación *f*; (*job*) trabajo *m*, profesión *f*. ~**ational** *a* profesional. ~**ier** *n* ocupante *m & f*. ~**y** /ˈɒkjʊpaɪ/ *vt* ocupar
occur /əˈkɜː(r)/ *vi* (*pt* **occurred**) ocurrir, suceder; (*exist*) encontrarse. **it** ~**red to me that** se me ocurrió que.

~rence /ə'kʌrəns/ n suceso m, acontecimiento m

ocean /'əʊʃn/ n océano m

o'clock /ə'klɒk/ adv. it is 7 ~ son las siete

octagon /'ɒktəgən/ n octágono m

octane /'ɒkteɪn/ n octano m

octave /'ɒktɪv/ n octava f

October /ɒk'təʊbə(r)/ n octubre m

octopus /'ɒktəpəs/ n (pl -puses) pulpo m

oculist /'ɒkjʊlɪst/ n oculista m & f

odd /ɒd/ a (-er, -est) extraño, raro; ⟨number⟩ impar; (one of pair) sin pareja; (occasional) poco frecuente; (left over) sobrante. fifty-~ unos cincuenta, cincuenta y pico. the ~ one out la excepción f. ~ity n (thing) curiosidad f; (person) excéntrico m. ~ly adv extrañamente. ~ly enough por extraño que parezca. ~ment /'ɒdmənt/ n retazo m. ~s /ɒdz/ npl probabilidades fpl; (in betting) apuesta f. ~s and ends retazos mpl. at ~s de punta, de malas

ode /əʊd/ n oda f

odious /'əʊdɪəs/ a odioso

odour /'əʊdə(r)/ n olor m. ~less a inodoro

of /əv, ɒv/ prep de. a friend ~ mine un amigo mío. how kind ~ you es Vd muy amable

off /ɒf/ adv lejos; ⟨light etc⟩ apagado; ⟨tap⟩ cerrado; ⟨food⟩ pasado. ● prep de, desde; (away from) fuera de; (distant from) lejos de. be better ~ estar mejor. be ~ marcharse. day ~ n día m de asueto, día m libre

offal /'ɒfl/ n menudos mpl, asaduras fpl

off: ~beat a insólito. ~ chance n posibilidad f remota. ~ colour a indispuesto

offen|ce /ə'fens/ n ofensa f; (illegal act) delito m. take ~ce ofenderse. ~d /ə'fend/ vt ofender. ~der n delincuente m & f. ~sive /ə'fensɪv/ a ofensivo; (disgusting) repugnante. ● n ofensiva f

offer /'ɒfə(r)/ vt ofrecer. ● n oferta f. on ~ en oferta

offhand /ɒf'hænd/ a (casual) desenvuelto; (brusque) descortés. ● adv de improviso

office /'ɒfɪs/ n oficina f; (post) cargo m

officer /'ɒfɪsə(r)/ n oficial m; (policeman) policía f, guardia m; (of organization) director m

official /ə'fɪʃl/ a & n oficial (m). ~ly adv oficialmente

officiate /ə'fɪʃɪeɪt/ vi oficiar. ~ as desempeñar las funciones de

officious /ə'fɪʃəs/ a oficioso

offing /'ɒfɪŋ/ n. in the ~ en perspectiva

off: ~licence n tienda f de bebidas alcohólicas. ~load vt descargar. ~putting a (disconcerting, fam) desconcertante; (repellent) repugnante. ~set /'ɒfset/ vt (pt -set, pres p -setting) contrapesar. ~shoot /'ɒfʃuːt/ n retoño m; (fig) ramificación f. ~side /ɒf'saɪd/ a (sport) fuera de juego. ~spring /'ɒfsprɪŋ/ n invar progenie f. ~stage a entre bastidores. ~white a blancuzco, color hueso

often /'ɒfn/ adv muchas veces, con frecuencia, a menudo. how ~? ¿cuántas veces?

ogle /'əʊgl/ vt comerse con los ojos

ogre /'əʊgə(r)/ n ogro m

oh /əʊ/ int ¡oh!, ¡ay!

oil /ɔɪl/ n aceite m; (petroleum) petróleo m. ● vt lubricar. ~field /'ɔɪlfiːld/ n yacimiento m petrolífero. ~painting n pintura f al óleo. ~rig /'ɔɪlrɪg/ n plataforma f de perforación. ~skins /'ɔɪlskɪnz/ npl chubasquero m. ~y a aceitoso; ⟨food⟩ grasiento

ointment /'ɔɪntmənt/ n ungüento m

OK /əʊ'keɪ/ int ¡vale!, ¡de acuerdo! ● a bien; (satisfactory) satisfactorio. ● adv muy bien

old /əʊld/ a (-er, -est) viejo; (not modern) anticuado; (former) antiguo. how ~ is she? ¿cuántos años tiene? she is ten years ~ tiene diez años. of ~ de antaño. ~ age n vejez f. ~fashioned a anticuado. ~ maid n soltera f. ~world a antiguo

oleander /əʊlɪ'ændə(r)/ n adelfa f

olive /'ɒlɪv/ n (fruit) aceituna f; (tree) olivo m. ● a de oliva; (colour) aceitunado

Olympic /ə'lɪmpɪk/ a olímpico. ~s npl, ~ Games npl Juegos mpl Olímpicos

omelette /'ɒmlɪt/ n tortilla f, tortilla f de huevos (Mex)

om|en /'əʊmen/ n agüero m. ~inous /'ɒmɪnəs/ a siniestro

omi|ssion /ə'mɪʃn/ n omisión f. ~t /ə'mɪt/ vt (pt omitted) omitir

omnipotent /ɒm'nɪpətənt/ a omnipotente

on /ɒn/ *prep* en, sobre. ~ **foot** a pie. ~ **Monday** el lunes. ~ **Mondays** los lunes. ~ **seeing** al ver. ~ **the way** de camino. ● *adv* (*light etc*) encendido; (*put on*) puesto, poco natural; (*machine*) en marcha; (*tap*) abierto. ~ **and off** de vez en cuando. ~ **and** ~ sin cesar. **and so** ~ y así sucesivamente. **be** ~ **at** (*fam*) criticar. **go** ~ continuar. **later** ~ más tarde

once /wʌns/ *adv* una vez; (*formerly*) antes. ● *conj* una vez que. **at** ~ en seguida. ~-**over** *n* (*fam*) ojeada *f*

oncoming /ˈɒnkʌmɪŋ/ *a* que se acerca; (*traffic*) que viene en sentido contrario, de frente

one /wʌn/ *a* & *n* uno (*m*). ● *pron* uno. ~ **another** el uno al otro. ~ **by** ~ uno a uno. ~ **never knows** nunca se sabe. **the blue** ~ el azul. **this** ~ éste. ~-**off** *a* (*fam*) único

onerous /ˈɒnərəs/ *a* oneroso

one: ~**self** /wʌnˈself/ *pron* (*subject*) uno mismo; (*object*) se; (*after prep*) sí (mismo). **by** ~**self** solo. ~-**sided** *a* unilateral. ~-**way** (*street*) de dirección única; (*ticket*) de ida

onion /ˈʌnɪən/ *n* cebolla *f*

onlooker /ˈɒnlʊkə(r)/ *n* espectador *m*

only /ˈəʊnlɪ/ *a* único. ~ **son** *n* hijo *m* único. ● *adv* sólo, solamente. ~ **just** apenas. ~ **too** de veras. ● *conj* pero, sólo que

onset /ˈɒnset/ *n* principio *m*; (*attack*) ataque *m*

onslaught /ˈɒnslɔːt/ *n* ataque *m* violento

onus /ˈəʊnəs/ *n* responsabilidad *f*

onward(s) /ˈɒnwəd(z)/ *a* & *adv* hacia adelante

onyx /ˈɒnɪks/ *n* ónice *f*

ooze /uːz/ *vt/i* rezumar

opal /ˈəʊpl/ *n* ópalo *m*

opaque /əʊˈpeɪk/ *a* opaco

open /ˈəʊpən/ *a* abierto; (*free to all*) público; (*undisguised*) manifiesto; (*question*) discutible; (*view*) despejado. ~ **sea** *n* alta mar *f*. ~ **secret** *n* secreto *m* a voces. **O**~ **University** *n* Universidad *f* a Distancia. **half**-~ *a* medio abierto. **in the** ~ *n* al aire libre. ● *vt/i* abrir. ~-**ended** *a* abierto. ~**er** /ˈəʊpənə(r)/ *n* (*for tins*) abrelatas *m invar*; (*for bottles with caps*) abrebotellas *m invar*; (*corkscrew*) sacacorchos *m invar*. **eye**-~**er** *n* (*fam*) revelación *f*. ~**ing** /ˈəʊpənɪŋ/ *n* abertura *f*; (*beginning*)

principio *m*; (*job*) vacante *m*. ~**ly** /ˈəʊpənlɪ/ *adv* abiertamente. ~-**minded** *a* imparcial

opera /ˈɒprə/ *n* ópera *f*. ~-**glasses** *npl* gemelos *mpl* de teatro

operate /ˈɒpəreɪt/ *vt* hacer funcionar. ● *vi* funcionar; (*medicine etc*) operar. ~ **on** (*med*) operar a

operatic /ɒpəˈrætɪk/ *a* operístico

operation /ɒpəˈreɪʃn/ *n* operación *f*; (*mec*) funcionamiento *m*. **in** ~ en vigor. ~**al** /ɒpəˈreɪʃnl/ *a* operacional

operative /ˈɒpərətɪv/ *a* operativo; (*law etc*) en vigor

operator *n* operario *m*; (*telephonist*) telefonista *m* & *f*

operetta /ɒpəˈretə/ *n* opereta *f*

opinion /əˈpɪnɪən/ *n* opinión *f*. **in my** ~ a mi parecer. ~**ated** *a* dogmático

opium /ˈəʊpɪəm/ *n* opio *m*

opponent /əˈpəʊnənt/ *n* adversario *m*

opportun|**e** /ˈɒpətjuːn/ *a* oportuno. ~**ist** /ɒpəˈtjuːnɪst/ *n* oportunista *m* & *f*. ~**ity** /ɒpəˈtjuːnətɪ/ *n* oportunidad *f*

oppos|**e** /əˈpəʊz/ *vt* oponerse a. ~**ed to** en contra de. **be** ~**ed to** oponerse a. ~**ing** *a* opuesto

opposite /ˈɒpəzɪt/ *a* opuesto; (*facing*) de enfrente. ● *n* contrario *m*. ● *adv* enfrente. ● *prep* enfrente de. ~ **number** *n* homólogo *m*

opposition /ɒpəˈzɪʃn/ *n* oposición *f*; (*resistence*) resistencia *f*

oppress /əˈpres/ *vt* oprimir. ~**ion** /-ʃn/ *n* opresión *f*. ~**ive** *a* (*cruel*) opresivo; (*heat*) sofocante. ~**or** *n* opresor *m*

opt /ɒpt/ *vi.* ~ **for** elegir. ~ **out** negarse a participar

optic|**al** /ˈɒptɪkl/ *a* óptico. ~**ian** /ɒpˈtɪʃn/ *n* óptico *m*

optimis|**m** /ˈɒptɪmɪzəm/ *n* optimismo *m*. ~**t** /ˈɒptɪmɪst/ *n* optimista *m* & *f*. ~**tic** /-ˈmɪstɪk/ *a* optimista

optimum /ˈɒptɪməm/ *n* lo óptimo, lo mejor

option /ˈɒpʃn/ *n* opción *f*. ~**al** /ˈɒpʃənl/ *a* facultativo

opulen|**ce** /ˈɒpjʊləns/ *n* opulencia *f*. ~**t** /ˈɒpjʊlənt/ *a* opulento

or /ɔː(r)/ *conj* o; (*before Spanish o- and* ho-) u; (*after negative*) ni. ~ **else** si no, o bien

oracle /ˈɒrəkl/ *n* oráculo *m*

oral /'ɔːrəl/ *a* oral. ● *n* (*fam*) examen *m* oral

orange /'ɒrɪndʒ/ *n* naranja *f*; (*tree*) naranjo *m*; (*colour*) color *m* naranja. ● *a* de color naranja. **~ade** *n* naranjada *f*

orator /'ɒrətə(r)/ *n* orador *m*

oratorio /ɒrə'tɔːrɪəʊ/ *n* (*pl* -**os**) oratorio *m*

oratory /'ɒrətrɪ/ *n* oratoria *f*

orb /ɔːb/ *n* orbe *m*

orbit /'ɔːbɪt/ *n* órbita *f*. ● *vt* orbitar

orchard /'ɔːtʃəd/ *n* huerto *m*

orchestra /'ɔːkɪstrə/ *n* orquesta *f*. **~l** /-'kestrəl/ *a* orquestal. **~te** /'ɔːkɪstreɪt/ *vt* orquestar

orchid /'ɔːkɪd/ *n* orquídea *f*

ordain /ɔː'deɪn/ *vt* ordenar

ordeal /ɔː'diːl/ *n* prueba *f* dura

order /'ɔːdə(r)/ *n* orden *m*; (*com*) pedido *m*. **in ~ that** para que. **in ~ to** para. ● *vt* (*command*) mandar; (*com*) pedir

orderly /'ɔːdəlɪ/ *a* ordenado. ● *n* asistente *m & f*

ordinary /'ɔːdɪnrɪ/ *a* corriente; (*average*) medio; (*mediocre*) ordinario

ordination /ɔːdɪ'neɪʃn/ *n* ordenación *f*

ore /ɔː(r)/ *n* mineral *m*

organ /'ɔːgən/ *n* órgano *m*

organic /ɔː'gænɪk/ *a* orgánico

organism /'ɔːgənɪzəm/ *n* organismo *m*

organist /'ɔːgənɪst/ *n* organista *m & f*

organiz|ation /ɔːgənaɪ'zeɪʃn/ *n* organización *f*. **~e** /'ɔːgənaɪz/ *vt* organizar. **~er** *n* organizador *m*

orgasm /'ɔːgæzəm/ *n* orgasmo *m*

orgy /'ɔːdʒɪ/ *n* orgía *f*

Orient /'ɔːrɪənt/ *n* Oriente *m*. **~al** /-'entl/ *a & n* oriental (*m & f*)

orientat|e /'ɔːrɪənteɪt/ *vt* orientar. **~ion** /-'teɪʃn/ *n* orientación *f*

orifice /'ɒrɪfɪs/ *n* orificio *m*

origin /'ɒrɪdʒɪn/ *n* origen *m*. **~al** /ə'rɪdʒənl/ *a* original. **~ality** /-'nælətɪ/ *n* originalidad *f*. **~ally** *adv* originalmente. **~ate** /ə'rɪdʒɪneɪt/ *vi*. **~ate from** provenir de. **~ator** *n* autor *m*

ormolu /'ɔːməluː/ *n* similor *m*

ornament /'ɔːnəmənt/ *n* adorno *m*. **~al** /-'mentl/ *a* de adorno. **~ation** /-en'teɪʃn/ *n* ornamentación *f*

ornate /ɔː'neɪt/ *a* adornado; ⟨*style*⟩ florido

ornithology /ɔːnɪ'θɒlədʒɪ/ *n* ornitología *f*

orphan /'ɔːfn/ *n* huérfano *m*. ● *vt* dejar huérfano. **~age** *n* orfanato *m*

orthodox /'ɔːθədɒks/ *a* ortodoxo. **~y** *n* ortodoxia *f*

orthopaedic /ɔːθə'piːdɪk/ *a* ortopédico. **~s** *n* ortopedia *f*

oscillate /'ɒsɪleɪt/ *vi* oscilar

ossify /'ɒsɪfaɪ/ *vt* osificar. ● *vi* osificarse

ostensibl|e /ɒs'tensɪbl/ *a* aparente. **~y** *adv* aparentemente

ostentat|ion /ɒsten'teɪʃn/ *n* ostentación *f*. **~ious** *a* ostentoso

osteopath /'ɒstɪəpæθ/ *n* osteópata *m & f*. **~y** /-'ɒpəθɪ/ *n* osteopatía *f*

ostracize /'ɒstrəsaɪz/ *vt* excluir

ostrich /'ɒstrɪtʃ/ *n* avestruz *m*

other /'ʌðə(r)/ *a & n & pron* otro (*m*). **~ than** de otra manera que. **the ~ one** el otro. **~wise** /'ʌðəwaɪz/ *adv* de otra manera; (*or*) si no

otter /'ɒtə(r)/ *n* nutria *f*

ouch /aʊtʃ/ *int* ¡ay!

ought /ɔːt/ *v aux* deber. **I ~ to see it** debería verlo. **he ~ to have done it** debería haberlo hecho

ounce /aʊns/ *n* onza *f* (= 28.35 *gr*.)

our /'aʊə(r)/ *a* nuestro. **~s** /'aʊəz/ *poss pron* el nuestro, la nuestra, los nuestros, las nuestras. **~selves** /aʊə'selvz/ *pron* (*subject*) nosotros mismos, nosotras mismas; (*reflexive*) nos; (*after prep*) nosotros (mismos), nosotras (mismas)

oust /aʊst/ *vt* expulsar, desalojar

out /aʊt/ *adv* fuera; ⟨*light*⟩ apagado; (*in blossom*) en flor; (*in error*) equivocado. **~-and-~** *a* cien por cien. **~ of date** anticuado; (*not valid*) caducado. **~ of doors** fuera. **~ of order** estropeado; (*sign*) no funciona. **~ of pity** por compasión. **~ of place** fuera de lugar; (*fig*) inoportuno. **~ of print** agotado. **~ of sorts** indispuesto. **~ of stock** agotado. **~ of tune** desafinado. **~ of work** parado, desempleado. **be ~** equivocarse. **be ~ of** quedarse sin. **be ~ to** estar resuelto a. **five ~ of six** cinco de cada seis. **made ~ of** hecho de

outbid /aʊt'bɪd/ *vt* (*pt* -**bid**, *pres p* -**bidding**) ofrecer más que

outboard /'aʊtbɔːd/ *a* fuera borda

outbreak /'aʊtbreɪk/ *n* (*of anger*) arranque *m*; (*of war*) comienzo *m*; (*of disease*) epidemia *f*

outbuilding /'aʊtbɪldɪŋ/ *n* dependencia *f*

outburst /'aʊtbɜːst/ *n* explosión *f*

outcast /'aʊtkɑːst/ *n* paria *m* & *f*

outcome /'aʊtkʌm/ *n* resultado *m*

outcry /'aʊtkraɪ/ *n* protesta *f*

outdated /aʊt'deɪtɪd/ *a* anticuado

outdo /aʊt'duː/ *vt* (*pt* -**did**, *pp* -**done**) superar

outdoor /'aʊtdɔː(r)/ *a* al aire libre. ~**s** /-'dɔːz/ *adv* al aire libre

outer /'aʊtə(r)/ *a* exterior

outfit /'aʊtfɪt/ *n* equipo *m*; (*clothes*) traje *m*. ~**ter** *n* camisero *m*

outgoing /'aʊtgəʊɪŋ/ *a* ‹*minister etc*› saliente; (*sociable*) abierto. ~**s** *npl* gastos *mpl*

outgrow /æʊt'grəʊ/ *vt* (*pt* -**grew**, *pp* -**grown**) crecer más que ‹*person*›; hacerse demasiado grande para ‹*clothes*›. **he's** ~**n his trousers** le quedan pequeños los pantalones

outhouse /'aʊthaʊs/ *n* dependencia *f*

outing /'aʊtɪŋ/ *n* excursión *f*

outlandish /aʊt'lændɪʃ/ *a* extravagante

outlaw /'aʊtlɔː/ *n* proscrito *m*. ● *vt* proscribir

outlay /'aʊtleɪ/ *n* gastos *mpl*

outlet /'aʊtlet/ *n* salida *f*

outline /'aʊtlaɪn/ *n* contorno *m*; (*summary*) resumen *m*. ● *vt* trazar; (*describe*) dar un resumen de

outlive /aʊt'lɪv/ *vt* sobrevivir a

outlook /'aʊtlʊk/ *n* perspectiva *f*

outlying /'aʊtlaɪɪŋ/ *a* remoto

outmoded /aʊt'məʊdɪd/ *a* anticuado

outnumber /aʊt'nʌmbə(r)/ *vt* sobrepasar en número

outpatient /aʊt'peɪʃnt/ *n* paciente *m* externo

outpost /'aʊtpəʊst/ *n* avanzada *f*

output /'aʊtpʊt/ *n* producción *f*

outrage /'aʊtreɪdʒ/ *n* ultraje *m*. ● *vt* ultrajar. ~**ous** /aʊt'reɪdʒəs/ *a* escandaloso, atroz

outright /'aʊtraɪt/ *adv* completamente; (*at once*) inmediatamente; (*frankly*) francamente. ● *a* completo; ‹*refusal*› rotundo

outset /'aʊtset/ *n* principio *m*

outside /'aʊtsaɪd/ *a* & *n* exterior (*m*). /aʊt'saɪd/ *adv* fuera. ● *prep* fuera de. ~**r** /aʊt'saɪdə(r)/ *n* forastero *m*; (*in race*) caballo *m* no favorito

outsize /'aʊtsaɪz/ *a* de tamaño extraordinario

outskirts /'aʊtskɜːts/ *npl* afueras *fpl*

outspoken /aʊt'spəʊkn/ *a* franco. **be** ~ no tener pelos en la lengua

outstanding /aʊt'stændɪŋ/ *a* excepcional; (*not settled*) pendiente; (*conspicuous*) sobresaliente

outstretched /aʊt'stretʃt/ *a* extendido

outstrip /aʊt'strɪp/ *vt* (*pt* -**stripped**) superar

outward /'aʊtwəd/ *a* externo; ‹*journey*› de ida. ~**ly** *adv* por fuera, exteriormente. ~**(s)** *adv* hacia fuera

outweigh /aʊt'weɪ/ *vt* pesar más que; (*fig*) valer más que

outwit /aʊt'wɪt/ *vt* (*pt* -**witted**) ser más listo que

oval /'əʊvl/ *a* oval(ado). ● *n* óvalo *m*

ovary /'əʊvərɪ/ *n* ovario *m*

ovation /əʊ'veɪʃn/ *n* ovación *f*

oven /'ʌvn/ *n* horno *m*

over /'əʊvə(r)/ *prep* por encima de; (*across*) al otro lado de; (*during*) durante; (*more than*) más de. ~ **and above** por encima de. ● *adv* por encima; (*ended*) terminado; (*more*) más; (*in excess*) de sobra. ~ **again** otra vez. ~ **and** ~ una y otra vez. ~ **here** por aquí. ~ **there** por allí. **all** ~ por todas partes

over... /'əʊvə(r)/ *pref* sobre..., super...

overall /əʊvər'ɔːl/ *a* global; ‹*length, cost*› total. ● *adv* en conjunto. /'əʊvərɔːl/ *n*, ~**s** *npl* mono *m*

overawe /əʊvər'ɔː/ *vt* intimidar

overbalance /əʊvə'bæləns/ *vt* hacer perder el equilibrio. ● *vi* perder el equilibrio

overbearing /əʊvə'beərɪŋ/ *a* dominante

overboard /'əʊvəbɔːd/ *adv* al agua

overbook /əʊvə'bʊk/ *vt* aceptar demasiadas reservaciones para

overcast /əʊvə'kɑːst/ *a* nublado

overcharge /əʊvə'tʃɑːdʒ/ *vt* (*fill too much*) sobrecargar; (*charge too much*) cobrar demasiado

overcoat /'əʊvəkəʊt/ *n* abrigo *m*

overcome /əʊvə'kʌm/ *vt* (*pt* -**came**, *pp* -**come**) superar, vencer. **be** ~ **by** estar abrumado de

overcrowded /əʊvə'kraʊdɪd/ *a* atestado (de gente)

overdo /əʊvə'duː/ *vt* (*pt* -**did**, *pp* -**done**) exagerar; (*culin*) cocer demasiado

overdose /ˈəʊvədəʊs/ n sobredosis f

overdraft /ˈəʊvədrɑːft/ n giro m en descubierto

overdraw /əʊvəˈdrɔː/ vt (pt **-drew**, pp **-drawn**) girar en descubierto. **be ~n** tener un saldo deudor

overdue /əʊvəˈdjuː/ a retrasado; (belated) tardío; (bill) vencido y no pagado

overestimate /əʊvərˈestɪmeɪt/ vt sobrestimar

overflow /əʊvəˈfləʊ/ vi desbordarse. /ˈəʊvəfləʊ/ n (excess) exceso m; (outlet) rebosadero m

overgrown /əʊvəˈɡrəʊn/ a demasiado grande; (garden) cubierto de hierbas

overhang /əʊvəˈhæŋ/ vt (pt **-hung**) sobresalir por encima de; (fig) amenazar. ● vi sobresalir. /ˈəʊvəhæŋ/ n saliente f

overhaul /əʊvəˈhɔːl/ vt revisar. /ˈəʊvəhɔːl/ n revisión f

overhead /əʊvəˈhed/ adv por encima. /ˈəʊvəhed/ a de arriba. **~s** npl gastos mpl generales

overhear /əʊvəˈhɪə(r)/ vt (pt **-heard**) oír por casualidad

overjoyed /əʊvəˈdʒɔɪd/ a muy contento. **he was ~** rebosaba de alegría

overland /ˈəʊvəlænd/ a terrestre. ● adv por tierra

overlap /əʊvəˈlæp/ vt (pt **-lapped**) traslapar. ● vi traslaparse

overleaf /əʊvəˈliːf/ adv a la vuelta. **see ~** véase al dorso

overload /əʊvəˈləʊd/ vt sobrecargar

overlook /əʊvəˈlʊk/ vt dominar; (building) dar a; (forget) olvidar; (oversee) inspeccionar; (forgive) perdonar

overnight /əʊvəˈnaɪt/ adv por la noche, durante la noche; (fig, instantly) de la noche a la mañana. **stay ~** pasar la noche. ● a de noche

overpass /ˈəʊvəpɑːs/ n paso m a desnivel, paso m elevado

overpay /əʊvəˈpeɪ/ vt (pt **-paid**) pagar demasiado

overpower /əʊvəˈpaʊə(r)/ vt subyugar; dominar (opponent); (fig) abrumar. **~ing** a abrumador

overpriced /əʊvəˈpraɪst/ a demasiado caro

overrate /əʊvəˈreɪt/ vt supervalorar

overreach /əʊvəˈriːtʃ/ vr. **~ o.s.** extralimitarse

overreact /əʊvərɪˈækt/ vi reaccionar excesivamente

overrid|e /əʊvəˈraɪd/ vt (pt **-rode**, pp **-ridden**) pasar por encima de. **~ing** a dominante

overripe /ˈəʊvəraɪp/ a pasado, demasiado maduro

overrule /əʊvəˈruːl/ vt anular; denegar (claim)

overrun /əʊvəˈrʌn/ vt (pt **-ran**, **-run**, pres p **-running**) invadir; exceder (limit)

overseas /əʊvəˈsiːz/ a de ultramar. ● adv al extranjero, en ultramar

oversee /əʊvəˈsiː/ vt (pt **-saw**, pp **-seen**) vigilar. **~r** /ˈəʊvəsɪə(r)/ n supervisor m

overshadow /əʊvəˈʃædəʊ/ vt (darken) sombrear; (fig) eclipsar

overshoot /əʊvəˈʃuːt/ vt (pt **-shot**) excederse. **~ the mark** pasarse de la raya

oversight /ˈəʊvəsaɪt/ n descuido m

oversleep /əʊvəˈsliːp/ vi (pt **-slept**) despertarse tarde. **I overslept** se me pegaron las sábanas

overstep /əʊvəˈstep/ vt (pt **-stepped**) pasar de. **~ the mark** pasarse de la raya

overt /ˈəʊvɜːt/ a manifiesto

overtak|e /əʊvəˈteɪk/ vt/i (pt **-took**, pp **-taken**) sobrepasar; (auto) adelantar. **~ing** n adelantamiento m

overtax /əʊvəˈtæks/ vt exigir demasiado

overthrow /əʊvəˈθrəʊ/ vt (pt **-threw**, pp **-thrown**) derrocar. /ˈəʊvəθrəʊ/ n derrocamiento m

overtime /ˈəʊvətaɪm/ n horas fpl extra

overtone /ˈəʊvətəʊn/ n (fig) matiz m

overture /ˈəʊvətjʊə(r)/ n obertura f. **~s** npl (fig) propuestas fpl

overturn /əʊvəˈtɜːn/ vt/i volcar

overweight /əʊvəˈweɪt/ a demasiado pesado. **be ~** pesar demasiado, ser gordo

overwhelm /əʊvəˈwelm/ vt aplastar; (with emotion) abrumar. **~ing** a aplastante; (fig) abrumador

overwork /əʊvəˈwɜːk/ vt hacer trabajar demasiado. ● vi trabajar demasiado. ● n trabajo m excesivo

overwrought /əʊvəˈrɔːt/ a agotado, muy nervioso

ovulation /ɒvjʊˈleɪʃn/ n ovulación f

ow|e /əʊ/ vt deber. **~ing** a debido. **~ing to** a causa de

owl /aʊl/ n lechuza f, búho m

own /əʊn/ a propio. **get one's ~ back** (fam) vengarse. **hold one's ~**

mantenerse firme, saber defenderse. **on one's ~** por su cuenta. ● *vt* poseer, tener. ● *vi.* **~ up (to)** (*fam*) confesar. **~er** *n* propietario *m*, dueño *m*. **~ership** *n* posesión *f*; (*right*) propiedad *f*

ox /ɒks/ *n* (*pl* **oxen**) buey *m*

oxide /'ɒksaɪd/ *n* óxido *m*

oxygen /'ɒksɪdʒən/ *n* oxígeno *m*

oyster /'ɔɪstə(r)/ *n* ostra *f*

P

p /piː/ *abbr* (*pence, penny*) penique(s) (*m(pl)*)

pace /peɪs/ *n* paso *m*. ● *vi.* **~ up and down** pasearse de aquí para allá. **~maker** *n* (*runner*) el que marca el paso; (*med*) marcapasos *m invar*. **keep ~ with** andar al mismo paso que

Pacific /pə'sɪfɪk/ *a* pacífico. ● *n.* **~ (Ocean)** (Océano *m*) Pacífico *m*

pacif|ist /'pæsɪfɪst/ *n* pacifista *m & f*. **~y** /'pæsɪfaɪ/ *vt* apaciguar

pack /pæk/ *n* fardo *m*; (*of cards*) baraja *f*; (*of hounds*) jauría *f*; (*of wolves*) manada *f*; (*large amount*) montón *m*. ● *vt* empaquetar; hacer ‹*suitcase*›; (*press down*) apretar. ● *vi* hacer la maleta. **~age** /'pækɪdʒ/ *n* paquete *m*. ● *vt* empaquetar. **~age deal** *n* acuerdo *m* global. **~age tour** *n* viaje *m* organizado. **~ed lunch** *n* almuerzo *m* frío. **~ed out** (*fam*) de bote en bote. **~et** /'pækɪt/ *n* paquete *m*. **send ~ing** echar a paseo

pact /pækt/ *n* pacto *m*, acuerdo *m*

pad /pæd/ *n* almohadilla *f*; (*for writing*) bloc *m*; (*for ink*) tampón *m*; (*flat, fam*) piso *m*. ● *vt* (*pt* **padded**) rellenar. **~ding** *n* relleno *m*. ● *vi* andar a pasos quedos. **launching ~** plataforma *f* de lanzamiento

paddle[1] /'pædl/ *n* canalete *m*

paddle[2] /'pædl/ *vi* mojarse los pies

paddle-steamer /'pædlstiːmə(r)/ *n* vapor *m* de ruedas

paddock /'pædək/ *n* recinto *m*; (*field*) prado *m*

paddy /'pædɪ/ *n* arroz *m* con cáscara. **~-field** *n* arrozal *m*

padlock /'pædlɒk/ *n* candado *m*. ● *vt* cerrar con candado

paediatrician /piːdɪə'trɪʃn/ *n* pediatra *m & f*

pagan /'peɪɡən/ *a & n* pagano (*m*)

page[1] /peɪdʒ/ *n* página *f*. ● *vt* paginar

page[2] /peɪdʒ/ (*in hotel*) botones *m invar*. ● *vt* llamar

pageant /'pædʒənt/ *n* espectáculo *m* (histórico). **~ry** *n* boato *m*

pagoda /pə'ɡəʊdə/ *n* pagoda *f*

paid /peɪd/ *see* **pay**. ● *a.* **put ~ to** (*fam*) acabar con

pail /peɪl/ *n* cubo *m*

pain /peɪn/ *n* dolor *m.* **~ in the neck** (*fam*) ‹*persona*› pesado *m*; ‹*thing*› lata *f*. **be in ~** tener dolores. **~s** *npl* (*effort*) esfuerzos *mpl*. **be at ~s** esmerarse. ● *vt* doler. **~ful** /'peɪnfl/ *a* doloroso; (*laborious*) penoso. **~killer** *n* calmante *m*. **~less** *a* indoloro. **~staking** /'peɪnzteɪkɪŋ/ *a* esmerado

paint /peɪnt/ *n* pintura *f*. ● *vt/i* pintar. **~er** *n* pintor *m*. **~ing** *n* pintura *f*

pair /peə(r)/ *n* par *m*; (*of people*) pareja *f*. **~ of trousers** pantalón *m*, pantalones *mpl*. ● *vi* emparejarse. **~ off** emparejarse

pajamas /pə'dʒɑːməz/ *npl* pijama *m*

Pakistan /pɑːkɪ'stɑːn/ *n* el Pakistán *m*. **~i** *a & n* paquistaní (*m & f*)

pal /pæl/ *n* (*fam*) amigo *m*

palace /'pælɪs/ *n* palacio *m*

palat|able /'pælətəbl/ *a* sabroso; (*fig*) aceptable. **~e** /'pælət/ *n* paladar *m*

palatial /pə'leɪʃl/ *a* suntuoso

palaver /pə'lɑːvə(r)/ *n* (*fam*) lío *m*

pale[1] /peɪl/ *a* (**-er, -est**) pálido; ‹*colour*› claro. ● *vi* palidecer

pale[2] /peɪl/ *n* estaca *n*

paleness /'peɪlnɪs/ *n* palidez *f*

Palestin|e /'pælɪstaɪn/ *n* Palestina *f*. **~ian** /-'stɪnɪən/ *a & n* palestino (*m*)

palette /'pælɪt/ *n* paleta *f*. **~-knife** *n* espátula *f*

pall[1] /pɔːl/ *n* paño *m* mortuorio; (*fig*) capa *f*

pall[2] /pɔːl/ *vi.* **~ (on)** perder su sabor (para)

pallid /'pælɪd/ *a* pálido

palm /pɑːm/ *n* palma *f*. ● *vt.* **~ off** encajar (**on** a). **~ist** /'pɑːmɪst/ *n* quiromántico *m*. **P~ Sunday** *n* Domingo *m* de Ramos

palpable /'pælpəbl/ *a* palpable

palpitat|e /'pælpɪteɪt/ *vi* palpitar. **~ion** /-'teɪʃn/ *n* palpitación *f*

paltry /'pɔːltrɪ/ *a* (**-ier, -iest**) insignificante

pamper /'pæmpə(r)/ *vt* mimar

pamphlet /'pæmflɪt/ n folleto m
pan /pæn/ n cacerola f; (for frying) sartén f; (of scales) platillo m; (of lavatory) taza f
panacea /pænə'sɪə/ n panacea f
panache /pæ'næʃ/ n brío m
pancake /'pænkeɪk/ n hojuela f, crêpe f
panda /'pændə/ n panda m. ~ **car** n coche m de la policía
pandemonium /pændɪ'məʊnɪəm/ n pandemonio m
pander /'pændə(r)/ vi. ~ **to** complacer
pane /peɪn/ n (of glass) vidrio m
panel /'pænl/ n panel m; (group of people) jurado m. ~**ling** n paneles mpl
pang /pæŋ/ n punzada f
panic /'pænɪk/ n pánico m. ● vi (pt panicked) ser preso de pánico. ~**-stricken** a preso de pánico
panoram|a /pænə'rɑːmə/ n panorama m. ~**ic** /-'ræmɪk/ a panorámico
pansy /'pænzɪ/ n pensamiento m; (effeminate man, fam) maricón m
pant /pænt/ vi jadear
pantechnicon /pæn'teknɪkən/ n camión m de mudanzas
panther /'pænθə(r)/ n pantera f
panties /'pæntɪz/ npl bragas fpl
pantomime /'pæntəmaɪm/ n pantomima f
pantry /'pæntrɪ/ n despensa f
pants /pænts/ npl (man's underwear, fam) calzoncillos mpl; (woman's underwear, fam) bragas fpl; (trousers, fam) pantalones mpl
papa|cy /'peɪpəsɪ/ n papado m. ~**l** a papal
paper /'peɪpə(r)/ n papel m; (newspaper) periódico m; (exam) examen m; (document) documento m. **on** ~ en teoría. ● vt empapelar, tapizar (LAm). ~**back** /'peɪpəbæk/ a en rústica. ● n libro m en rústica. ~**clip** n sujetapapeles m invar, clip m. ~**weight** /'peɪpəweɪt/ n pisapapeles m invar. ~**work** n papeleo m, trabajo m de oficina
papier mâché /pæpɪeɪ'mæʃeɪ/ n cartón m piedra
par /pɑː(r)/ n par f; (golf) par m. **feel below** ~ no estar en forma. **on a** ~ **with** a la par con
parable /'pærəbl/ n parábola f
parachut|e /'pærəʃuːt/ n paracaídas m invar. ● vi lanzarse en paracaídas. ~**ist** n paracaidista m & f

parade /pə'reɪd/ n desfile m; (street) paseo m; (display) alarde m. ● vi desfilar. ● vt hacer alarde de
paradise /'pærədaɪs/ n paraíso m
paradox /'pærədɒks/ n paradoja f. ~**ical** /-'dɒksɪkl/ a paradójico
paraffin /'pærəfɪn/ n queroseno m
paragon /'pærəgən/ n dechado m
paragraph /'pærəgrɑːf/ n párrafo m
parallel /'pærəlel/ a paralelo. ● n paralelo m; (line) paralela f. ● vt ser paralelo a
paraly|se /'pærəlaɪz/ vt paralizar. ~**sis** /pə'ræləsɪs/ n (pl -ses /-siːz/) parálisis f. ~**tic** /pærə'lɪtɪk/ a & n paralítico (m)
parameter /pə'ræmɪtə(r)/ n parámetro m
paramount /'pærəmaʊnt/ a supremo
paranoia /pærə'nɔɪə/ n paranoia f
parapet /'pærəpɪt/ n parapeto m
paraphernalia /pærəfə'neɪlɪə/ n trastos mpl
paraphrase /'pærəfreɪz/ n paráfrasis f. ● vt parafrasear
paraplegic /pærə'pliːdʒɪk/ n parapléjico m
parasite /'pærəsaɪt/ n parásito m
parasol /'pærəsɒl/ n sombrilla f
paratrooper /'pærətruːpə(r)/ n paracaidista m
parcel /'pɑːsl/ n paquete m
parch /pɑːtʃ/ vt resecar. **be** ~**ed** tener mucha sed
parchment /'pɑːtʃmənt/ n pergamino m
pardon /'pɑːdn/ n perdón m; (jurid) indulto m. **I beg your** ~! ¡perdone Vd! **I beg your** ~? ¿cómo?, ¿mande? (Mex). ● vt perdonar
pare /peə(r)/ vt cortar ‹nails›; (peel) pelar, mondar
parent /'peərənt/ n (father) padre m; (mother) madre f; (source) origen m. ~**s** npl padres mpl. ~**al** /pə'rentl/ a de los padres
parenthesis /pə'renθəsɪs/ n (pl -theses /-siːz/) paréntesis m invar
parenthood /'peərənthʊd/ n paternidad f, maternidad f
Paris /'pærɪs/ n París m
parish /'pærɪʃ/ n parroquia f; (municipal) municipio m. ~**ioner** /pə'rɪʃənə(r)/ n feligrés m
Parisian /pə'rɪzɪən/ a & n parisino (m)
parity /'pærətɪ/ n igualdad f

park /pɑːk/ *n* parque *m.* ● *vt/i* aparcar. ~ **oneself** *vr* (*fam*) instalarse

parka /'pɑːkə/ *n* anorak *m*

parking-meter /'pɑːkɪŋmiːtə(r)/ *n* parquímetro *m*

parliament /'pɑːləmənt/ *n* parlamento *m.* ~**ary** /-'mentrɪ/ *a* parlamentario

parlour /'pɑːlə(r)/ *n* salón *m*

parochial /pə'rəʊkɪəl/ *a* parroquial; (*fig*) pueblerino

parody /'pærədɪ/ *n* parodia *f.* ● *vt* parodiar

parole /pə'rəʊl/ *n* libertad *f* bajo palabra, libertad *f* provisional. **on** ~ libre bajo palabra. ● *vt* liberar bajo palabra

paroxysm /'pærəksɪzəm/ *n* paroxismo *m*

parquet /'pɑːkeɪ/ *n.* ~ **floor** *n* parqué *m*

parrot /'pærət/ *n* papagayo *m*

parry /'pærɪ/ *vt* parar; (*avoid*) esquivar. ● *n* parada *f*

parsimonious /pɑːsɪ'məʊnɪəs/ *a* parsimonioso

parsley /'pɑːslɪ/ *n* perejil *m*

parsnip /'pɑːsnɪp/ *n* pastinaca *f*

parson /'pɑːsn/ *n* cura *m*, párroco *m*

part /pɑːt/ *n* parte *f*; (*of machine*) pieza *f*; (*of serial*) entrega *f*; (*in play*) papel *m*; (*side in dispute*) partido *m*. **on the** ~ **of** por parte de. ● *adv* en parte. ● *vt* separar. ~ **with** *vt* separarse de. ● *vi* separarse

partake /pɑː'teɪk/ *vt* (*pt* -**took**, *pp* -**taken**) participar. ~ **of** compartir

partial /'pɑːʃl/ *a* parcial. **be** ~ **to** ser aficionado a. ~**ity** /-ɪ'ælətɪ/ *n* parcialidad *f.* ~**ly** *adv* parcialmente

participa|nt /pɑː'tɪsɪpənt/ *n* participante *m & f.* ~**te** /pɑː'tɪsɪpeɪt/ *vi* participar. ~**tion** /-'peɪʃn/ *n* participación *f*

participle /'pɑːtɪsɪpl/ *n* participio *m*

particle /'pɑːtɪkl/ *n* partícula *f*

particular /pə'tɪkjʊlə(r)/ *a* particular; (*precise*) meticuloso; (*fastidious*) quisquilloso. ● *n.* **in** ~ especialmente. ~**ly** *adv* especialmente. ~**s** *npl* detalles *mpl*

parting /'pɑːtɪŋ/ *n* separación *f*; (*in hair*) raya *f.* ● *a* de despedida

partisan /pɑːtɪ'zæn/ *n* partidario *m*

partition /pɑː'tɪʃn/ *n* partición *f*; (*wall*) tabique *m.* ● *vt* dividir

partly /'pɑːtlɪ/ *adv* en parte

partner /'pɑːtnə(r)/ *n* socio *m*; (*sport*) pareja *f.* ~**ship** *n* asociación *f*; (*com*) sociedad *f*

partridge /'pɑːtrɪdʒ/ *n* perdiz *f*

part-time /pɑːt'taɪm/ *a & adv* a tiempo parcial

party /'pɑːtɪ/ *n* reunión *f*, fiesta *f*; (*group*) grupo *m*; (*pol*) partido *m*; (*jurid*) parte *f.* ~ **line** *n* (*telephone*) línea *f* colectiva

pass /pɑːs/ *vt* pasar; (*in front of*) pasar por delante de; (*overtake*) adelantar; (*approve*) aprobar ⟨*exam*, *bill*, *law*⟩; hacer ⟨*remark*⟩; pronunciar ⟨*judgement*⟩. ~ **down** transmitir. ~ **over** pasar por alto de. ~ **round** distribuir. ~ **through** pasar por; (*cross*) atravesar. ~ **up** (*fam*) dejar pasar. ● *vi* pasar; (*in exam*) aprobar. ~ **away** morir. ~ **out** (*fam*) desmayarse. ● *n* (*permit*) permiso *m*; (*in mountains*) puerto *m*, desfiladero *m*; (*sport*) pase *m*; (*in exam*) aprobado *m.* **make a** ~ **at** (*fam*) hacer proposiciones amorosas a. ~**able** /'pɑːsəbl/ *a* pasable; ⟨*road*⟩ transitable

passage /'pæsɪdʒ/ *n* paso *m*; (*voyage*) travesía *f*; (*corridor*) pasillo *m*; (*in book*) pasaje *m*

passenger /'pæsɪndʒə(r)/ *n* pasajero *m*

passer-by /pɑːsə'baɪ/ *n* (*pl* **passers-by**) transeúnte *m & f*

passion /'pæʃn/ *n* pasión *f.* ~**ate** *a* apasionado. ~**ately** *adv* apasionadamente

passive /'pæsɪv/ *a* pasivo. ~**ness** *n* pasividad *f*

passmark /'pɑːsmɑːk/ *n* aprobado *m*

Passover /'pɑːsəʊvə(r)/ *n* Pascua *f* de los hebreos

passport /'pɑːspɔːt/ *n* pasaporte *m*

password /'pɑːswɜːd/ *n* contraseña *f*

past /pɑːst/ *a & n* pasado (*m*). **in times** ~ en tiempos pasados. **the** ~ **week** *n* la semana *f* pasada. ● *prep* por delante de; (*beyond*) más allá de. ● *adv* por delante. **drive** ~ pasar en coche. **go** ~ pasar

paste /peɪst/ *n* pasta *f*; (*adhesive*) engrudo *m.* ● *vt* (*fasten*) pegar; (*cover*) engrudar. ~**board** /'peɪstbɔːd/ *n* cartón *m.* ~ **jewellery** *n* joyas *fpl* de imitación

pastel /'pæstl/ *a & n* pastel (*m*)

pasteurize /'pæstʃəraɪz/ *vt* pasteurizar

pastiche /pæ'stiːʃ/ *n* pastiche *m*

pastille /'pæstɪl/ n pastilla f

pastime /'pɑːstaɪm/ n pasatiempo m

pastoral /'pɑːstərəl/ a pastoral

pastr|ies npl pasteles mpl, pastas fpl. **~y** /'peɪstrɪ/ n pasta f

pasture /'pɑːstʃə(r)/ n pasto m

pasty[1] /'pæstɪ/ n empanada f

pasty[2] /'peɪstɪ/ a pastoso; (pale) pálido

pat[1] /pæt/ vt (pt **patted**) dar palmaditas en; acariciar ⟨dog etc⟩. ● n palmadita f; (of butter) porción f

pat[2] /pæt/ adv en el momento oportuno

patch /pætʃ/ n pedazo m; (period) período m; (repair) remiendo m; (piece of ground) terreno m. **not a ~ on** (fam) muy inferior a. ● vt remendar. **~ up** arreglar. **~work** n labor m de retazos; (fig) mosaico m. **~y** a desigual

pâté /'pæteɪ/ n pasta f, paté m

patent /'peɪtnt/ a patente. ● n patente f. ● vt patentar. **~ leather** n charol m. **~ly** adv evidentemente

patern|al /pə'tɜːnl/ a paterno. **~ity** /pə'tɜːnətɪ/ n paternidad f

path /pɑːθ/ n (pl -s /pɑːðz/) sendero m; (sport) pista f; (of rocket) trayectoria f; (fig) camino m

pathetic /pə'θetɪk/ a patético, lastimoso

pathology /pə'θɒlədʒɪ/ n patología f

pathos /'peɪθɒs/ n patetismo m

patien|ce /'peɪʃns/ n paciencia f. **~t** /'peɪʃnt/ a & n paciente (m & f). **~tly** adv con paciencia

patio /'pætɪəʊ/ n (pl -os) patio m

patriarch /'peɪtrɪɑːk/ n patriarca m

patrician /pə'trɪʃn/ a & n patricio (m)

patriot /'pætrɪət/ n patriota m & f. **~ic** /-'ɒtɪk/ a patriótico. **~ism** n patriotismo m

patrol /pə'trəʊl/ n patrulla f. ● vt/i patrullar

patron /'peɪtrən/ n (of the arts etc) mecenas m & f; (customer) cliente m & f; (of charity) patrocinador m. **~age** /'pætrənɪdʒ/ n patrocinio m; (of shop etc) clientela f. **~ize** vt ser cliente de; (fig) tratar con condescendencia

patter[1] /'pætə(r)/ n (of steps) golpeteo m; (of rain) tamborileo m. ● vi correr con pasos ligeros; ⟨rain⟩ tamborilear

patter[2] /'pætə(r)/ (speech) jerga f; (chatter) parloteo m

pattern /'pætn/ n diseño m; (model) modelo m; (sample) muestra f; (manner) modo m; (in dressmaking) patrón m

paunch /pɔːntʃ/ n panza f

pauper /'pɔːpə(r)/ n indigente m & f, pobre m & f

pause /pɔːz/ n pausa f. ● vi hacer una pausa

pave /peɪv/ vt pavimentar. **~ the way for** preparar el terreno para

pavement /'peɪvmənt/ n pavimento m; (at side of road) acera f

pavilion /pə'vɪlɪən/ n pabellón m

paving-stone /'peɪvɪŋstəʊn/ n losa f

paw /pɔː/ n pata f; (of cat) garra f. ● vi tocar con la pata; ⟨person⟩ manosear

pawn[1] /pɔːn/ n (chess) peón m; (fig) instrumento m

pawn[2] /pɔːn/ vt empeñar. ● n. **in ~** en prenda. **~broker** /'pɔːnbrəʊkə(r)/ n prestamista m & f. **~shop** n monte m de piedad

pawpaw /'pɔːpɔː/ n papaya f

pay /peɪ/ vt (pt **paid**) pagar; prestar ⟨attention⟩; hacer ⟨compliment, visit⟩. **~ back** devolver. **~ cash** pagar al contado. **~ in** ingresar. **~ off** pagar. **~ out** pagar. ● vi pagar; (be profitable) rendir. ● n paga f. **in the ~ of** al servicio de. **~able** /'peɪəbl/ a pagadero. **~ment** /'peɪmənt/ n pago m. **~off** n (sl) liquidación f; (fig) ajuste m de cuentas. **~roll** /'peɪrəʊl/ n nómina f. **~ up** pagar

pea /piː/ n guisante m

peace /piːs/ n paz f. **~ of mind** tranquilidad f. **~able** a pacífico. **~ful** /'piːsfl/ a tranquilo. **~maker** /'piːsmeɪkə(r)/ n pacificador m

peach /piːtʃ/ n melocotón m, durazno m (LAm); (tree) melocotonero m, duraznero m (LAm)

peacock /'piːkɒk/ n pavo m real

peak /piːk/ n cumbre f; (maximum) máximo m. **~ hours** npl horas fpl punta. **~ed cap** n gorra f de visera

peaky /'piːkɪ/ a pálido

peal /piːl/ n repique m. **~s of laughter** risotadas fpl

peanut /'piːnʌt/ n cacahuete m, maní m (Mex). **~s** (sl) una bagatela f

pear /peə(r)/ n pera f; (tree) peral m

pearl /pɜːl/ n perla f. **~y** a nacarado

peasant /'peznt/ n campesino m

peat /piːt/ n turba f

pebble /'pebl/ n guijarro m

peck /pek/ vt picotear; (kiss, fam) dar un besito a. ● n picotazo m; (kiss) besito m. ~ish /'pekɪʃ/ a. be ~ish (fam) tener hambre, tener gazuza (fam)

peculiar /pɪ'kjuːlɪə(r)/ a raro; (special) especial. ~ity /-'ærətɪ/ n rareza f; (feature) particularidad f

pedal /'pedl/ n pedal m. ● vi pedalear

pedantic /pɪ'dæntɪk/ a pedante

peddle /'pedl/ vt vender por las calles

pedestal /'pedɪstl/ n pedestal m

pedestrian /pɪ'destrɪən/ n peatón m. ● a de peatones; (dull) prosaico. ~ crossing n paso m de peatones

pedigree /'pedɪgriː/ n linaje m; (of animal) pedigrí m. ● a ⟨animal⟩ de raza

pedlar /'pedlə(r)/ n buhonero m, vendedor m ambulante

peek /piːk/ vi mirar a hurtadillas

peel /piːl/ n cáscara f; (for washing) ⟨fruit, vegetables⟩. ● vi pelarse. ~ings npl peladuras fpl, monda f

peep[1] /piːp/ vi mirar a hurtadillas. ● n mirada f furtiva

peep[2] /piːp/ ⟨bird⟩ piar. ● n pío m

peep-hole /'piːphəʊl/ n mirilla f

peer[1] /pɪə(r)/ vi mirar. ~ at escudriñar

peer[2] /pɪə(r)/ n par m, compañero m. ~age n pares mpl

peev|ed /piːvd/ a (sl) irritado. ~ish /'piːvɪʃ/ a picajoso

peg /peg/ n clavija f; (for washing) pinza f; (hook) gancho m; (for tent) estaca f. **off the** ~ de percha. ● vt (pt pegged) fijar ⟨precios⟩. ~ away at afanarse por

pejorative /pɪ'dʒɒrətɪv/ a peyorativo, despectivo

pelican /'pelɪkən/ n pelícano m. ~ crossing n paso m de peatones (con semáforo)

pellet /'pelɪt/ n pelotilla f; (for gun) perdigón m

pelt[1] /pelt/ n pellejo m

pelt[2] /pelt/ vt tirar. ● vi llover a cántaros

pelvis /'pelvɪs/ n pelvis f

pen[1] /pen/ n (enclosure) recinto m

pen[2] /pen/ (for writing) pluma f, estilográfica f; (ball-point) bolígrafo m

penal /'piːnl/ a penal. ~ize vt castigar. ~ty /'penltɪ/ n castigo m; (fine)

multa f. ~ty kick n (football) penalty m

penance /'penəns/ n penitencia f

pence /pens/ see **penny**

pencil /'pensl/ n lápiz m. ● vt (pt pencilled) escribir con lápiz. ~sharpener n sacapuntas m invar

pendant /'pendənt/ n dije m, medallón m

pending /'pendɪŋ/ a pendiente. ● prep hasta

pendulum /'pendjʊləm/ n péndulo m

penetrat|e /'penɪtreɪt/ vt/i penetrar. ~ing a penetrante. ~ion /-'treɪʃn/ n penetración f

penguin /'peŋgwɪn/ n pingüino m

penicillin /penɪ'sɪlɪn/ n penicilina f

peninsula /pə'nɪnsjʊlə/ n península f

penis /'piːnɪs/ n pene m

peniten|ce /'penɪtəns/ n penitencia f. ~t /'penɪtənt/ a & n penitente (m & f). ~tiary /penɪ'tenʃərɪ/ n (Amer) cárcel m

pen: ~**knife** /'pennaɪf/ n (pl penknives) navaja f; (small) cortaplumas m invar. ~**name** n seudónimo m

pennant /'penənt/ n banderín m

penn|iless /'penɪlɪs/ a sin un céntimo. ~**y** /'penɪ/ n (pl pennies or pence) penique m

pension /'penʃn/ n pensión f; (for retirement) jubilación f. ● vt pensionar. ~**able** a con derecho a pensión; ⟨age⟩ de la jubilación. ~**er** n jubilado m. ~ **off** jubilar

pensive /'pensɪv/ a pensativo

pent-up /'pentʌp/ a reprimido; (confined) encerrado

pentagon /'pentəgən/ n pentágono m

Pentecost /'pentɪkɒst/ n Pentecostés m

penthouse /'penthaʊs/ n ático m

penultimate /pen'ʌltɪmət/ a penúltimo

penury /'penjʊərɪ/ n penuria f

peony /'piːənɪ/ n peonía f

people /'piːpl/ npl gente f; (citizens) pueblo m. ~ **say** se dice. **English** ~ los ingleses mpl. **my** ~ (fam) mi familia f. ● vt poblar

pep /pep/ n vigor m. ● vt. ~ **up** animar

pepper /'pepə(r)/ n pimienta f; (vegetable) pimiento m. ● vt sazonar con pimienta. ~**y** a picante. ~**corn**

/'pepǝkɔ:n/ n grano m de pimienta. ~corn rent n alquiler m nominal

peppermint /'pepǝmɪnt/ n menta f; (sweet) pastilla f de menta

pep talk /'peptɔ:k/ n palabras fpl animadoras

per /pɜ:(r)/ prep por. ~ **annum** al año. ~ **cent** por ciento. ~ **head** por cabeza, por persona. **ten miles** ~ **hour** diez millas por hora

perceive /pǝ'si:v/ vt percibir; (notice) darse cuenta de

percentage /pǝ'sentɪdʒ/ n porcentaje m

percepti|ble /pǝ'septǝbl/ a perceptible. ~**on** /pǝ'sepʃn/ n percepción f. ~**ve** a perspicaz

perch[1] /pɜ:tʃ/ n (of bird) percha f. ● vi posarse

perch[2] /pɜ:tʃ/ (fish) perca f

percolat|e /'pɜ:kǝleɪt/ vt filtrar. ● vi filtrarse. ~**or** n cafetera f

percussion /pǝ'kʌʃn/ n percusión f

peremptory /pǝ'remptǝrɪ/ a perentorio

perennial /pǝ'renɪǝl/ a & n perenne (m)

perfect /'pɜ:fɪkt/ a perfecto. /pǝ'fekt/ vt perfeccionar. ~**ion** /pǝ'fekʃn/ n perfección f. **to** ~**ion** a la perfección. ~**ionist** n perfeccionista m & f. ~**ly** /'pɜ:fɪktlɪ/ adv perfectamente

perforat|e /'pɜ:fǝreɪt/ vt perforar. ~**ion** /-'reɪʃn/ n perforación f

perform /pǝ'fɔ:m/ vt hacer, realizar; representar (play); desempeñar (role); (mus) interpretar. ~ **an operation** (med) operar. ~**ance** n ejecución f; (of play) representación f; (of car) rendimiento m; (fuss, fam) jaleo m. ~**er** n artista m & f

perfume /'pɜ:fju:m/ n perfume m

perfunctory /pǝ'fʌŋktǝrɪ/ a superficial

perhaps /pǝ'hæps/ adv quizá(s), tal vez

peril /'perǝl/ n peligro m. ~**ous** a arriesgado, peligroso

perimeter /pǝ'rɪmɪtǝ(r)/ n perímetro m

period /'pɪǝrɪǝd/ n período m; (lesson) clase f; (gram) punto m. ● a de (la) época. ~**ic** /-'ɒdɪk/ a periódico. ~**ical** /pɪǝrɪ'ɒdɪkl/ n revista f. ~**ically** /-'ɒdɪklɪ/ adv periódico

peripher|al /pǝ'rɪfǝrǝl/ a periférico. ~**y** /pǝ'rɪfǝrɪ/ n periferia f

periscope /'perɪskǝʊp/ n periscopio m

perish /'perɪʃ/ vi perecer; (rot) estropearse. ~**able** a perecedero. ~**ing** a (fam) glacial

perjur|e /'pɜ:dʒǝ(r)/ vr. ~**e o.s.** perjurarse. ~**y** n perjurio m

perk[1] /pɜ:k/ n gaje m

perk[2] /pɜ:k/ vt/i. ~ **up** vt reanimar. ● vi reanimarse. ~**y** a alegre

perm /pɜ:m/ n permanente f. ● vt hacer una permanente a

permanen|ce /'pɜ:mǝnǝns/ n permanencia f. ~**t** /'pɜ:mǝnǝnt/ a permanente. ~**tly** adv permanentemente

permea|ble /'pɜ:mɪǝbl/ a permeable. ~**te** /'pɜ:mɪeɪt/ vt penetrar; (soak) empapar

permissible /pǝ'mɪsǝbl/ a permisible

permission /pǝ'mɪʃn/ n permiso m

permissive /pǝ'mɪsɪv/ a indulgente. ~**ness** n tolerancia f. ~ **society** n sociedad f permisiva

permit /pǝ'mɪt/ vt (pt permitted) permitir. /'pɜ:mɪt/ n permiso m

permutation /pɜ:mju:'teɪʃn/ n permutación f

pernicious /pǝ'nɪʃǝs/ a pernicioso

peroxide /pǝ'rɒksaɪd/ n peróxido m

perpendicular /pɜ:pǝn'dɪkjʊlǝ(r)/ a & n perpendicular (f)

perpetrat|e /'pɜ:pɪtreɪt/ vt cometer. ~**or** n autor m

perpetua|l /pǝ'petʃʊǝl/ a perpetuo. ~**te** /pǝ'petʃʊeɪt/ vt perpetuar. ~**tion** /-'eɪʃn/ n perpetuación f

perplex /pǝ'pleks/ vt dejar perplejo. ~**ed** a perplejo. ~**ing** a desconcertante. ~**ity** n perplejidad f

persecut|e /'pɜ:sɪkju:t/ vt perseguir. ~**ion** /-'kju:ʃn/ n persecución f

persever|ance /pɜ:sɪ'vɪǝrǝns/ n perseverancia f. ~**e** /pɜ:sɪ'vɪǝ(r)/ vi perseverar, persistir

Persian /'pɜ:ʃn/ a persa. **the** ~ **Gulf** n el golfo m Pérsico. ● n persa (m & f); (lang) persa m

persist /pǝ'sɪst/ vi persistir. ~**ence** n persistencia f. ~**ent** a persistente; (continual) continuo. ~**ently** adv persistentemente

person /'pɜ:sn/ n persona f

personal /'pɜ:sǝnl/ a personal

personality /pɜ:sǝ'nælǝtɪ/ n personalidad f; (on T'V) personaje m

personally /'pɜ:sǝnǝlɪ/ adv personalmente; (in person) en persona

personify /pə'sɒnɪfaɪ/ vt personificar

personnel /pɜːsə'nel/ n personal m

perspective /pə'spektɪv/ n perspectiva f

perspicacious /pɜːspɪ'keɪʃəs/ a perspicaz

perspir|ation /pɜːspə'reɪʃn/ n sudor m. ~e /pəs'paɪə(r)/ vi sudar

persua|de /pə'sweɪd/ vt persuadir. ~sion n persuasión f. ~sive /pə'sweɪsɪv/ a persuasivo. ~sively adv de manera persuasiva

pert /pɜːt/ a (saucy) impertinente; (lively) animado

pertain /pə'teɪn/ vi. ~ to relacionarse con

pertinent /'pɜːtɪnənt/ a pertinente. ~ly adv pertinentemente

pertly /'pɜːtlɪ/ adv impertinentemente

perturb /pə'tɜːb/ vt perturbar

Peru /pə'ruː/ n el Perú m

perus|al /pə'ruːzl/ n lectura f cuidadosa. ~e /pə'ruːz/ vt leer cuidadosamente

Peruvian /pə'ruːvɪan/ a & n peruano (m)

perva|de /pə'veɪd/ vt difundirse por. ~sive a penetrante

perver|se /pə'vɜːs/ a (stubborn) terco; (wicked) perverso. ~sity n terquedad f; (wickedness) perversidad f. ~sion n perversión f. ~t /pə'vɜːt/ vt pervertir. /'pɜːvɜːt/ n pervertido m

pessimis|m /'pesɪmɪzəm/ n pesimismo m. ~t /'pesɪmɪst/ n pesimista m & f. ~tic /-'mɪstɪk/ a pesimista

pest /pest/ n insecto m nocivo, plaga f; (person) pelma m; (thing) lata f

pester /'pestə(r)/ vt importunar

pesticide /'pestɪsaɪd/ n pesticida f

pet /pet/ n animal m doméstico; (favourite) favorito m. ● a preferido. ● vt (pt petted) acariciar

petal /'petl/ n pétalo m

peter /'piːtə(r)/ vi. ~ out ⟨supplies⟩ agotarse; (disappear) desaparecer

petite /pə'tiːt/ a (of woman) chiquita

petition /pɪ'tɪʃn/ n petición f. ● vt dirigir una petición a

pet name /'petneɪm/ n apodo m cariñoso

petrify /'petrɪfaɪ/ vt petrificar. ● vi petrificarse

petrol /'petrəl/ n gasolina f. ~eum /pɪ'trəʊlɪəm/ n petróleo m. ~ gauge

n indicador m de nivel de gasolina. ~ pump n (in car) bomba f de gasolina; (at garage) surtidor m de gasolina. ~ station n gasolinera f. ~ tank n depósito m de gasolina

petticoat /'petɪkəʊt/ n enaguas fpl

pett|iness /'petɪnɪs/ n mezquindad f. ~y /'petɪ/ a (-ier, -iest) insignificante; (mean) mezquino. ~y cash n dinero m para gastos menores. ~y officer n suboficial m de marina

petulan|ce /'petjʊləns/ n irritabilidad f. ~t /'petjʊlənt/ a irritable

pew /pjuː/ n banco m (de iglesia)

pewter /'pjuːtə(r)/ n peltre m

phallic /'fælɪk/ a fálico

phantom /'fæntəm/ n fantasma m

pharmaceutical /faːmə'sjuːtɪkl/ a farmacéutico

pharmac|ist /'faːməsɪst/ n farmacéutico m. ~y /'faːməsɪ/ n farmacia f

pharyngitis /færɪn'dʒaɪtɪs/ n faringitis f

phase /feɪz/ n etapa f. ● vt. ~ in introducir progresivamente. ~ out retirar progresivamente

PhD abbr (Doctor of Philosophy) n Doctor m en Filosofía

pheasant /'feznt/ n faisán m

phenomenal /fɪ'nɒmɪnl/ a fenomenal

phenomenon /fɪ'nɒmɪnən/ n (pl -ena) fenómeno m

phew /fjuː/ int ¡uy!

phial /'faɪəl/ n frasco m

philanderer /fɪ'lændərə(r)/ n mariposón m

philanthrop|ic /fɪlən'θrɒpɪk/ a filantrópico. ~ist /fɪ'lænθrəpɪst/ n filántropo m

philatel|ist /fɪ'lætəlɪst/ n filatelista m & f. ~y /fɪ'lætəlɪ/ n filatelia f

philharmonic /fɪlhɑː'mɒnɪk/ a filarmónico

Philippines /'fɪlɪpiːnz/ npl Filipinas fpl

philistine /'fɪlɪstaɪn/ a & n filisteo (m)

philosoph|er /fɪ'lɒsəfə(r)/ n filósofo m. ~ical /-ə'sɒfɪkl/ a filosófico. ~y /fɪ'lɒsəfɪ/ n filosofía f

phlegm /flem/ n flema f. ~atic /fleg'mætɪk/ a flemático

phobia /'fəʊbɪə/ n fobia f

phone /fəʊn/ n (fam) teléfono m. ● vt/i llamar por teléfono. ~ back

⟨caller⟩ volver a llamar; ⟨person called⟩ llamar. ~ box n cabina f telefónica

phonetic /fə'netɪk/ a fonético. ~s n fonética f

phoney /'fəʊnɪ/ a (-ier, -iest) (sl) falso. ● n (sl) farsante m & f

phosphate /'fɒsfeɪt/ n fosfato m

phosphorus /'fɒsfərəs/ n fósforo m

photo /'fəʊtəʊ/ n (pl -os) (fam) fotografía f, foto f (fam)

photocopy /'fəʊtəʊkɒpɪ/ n fotocopia f. ● vt fotocopiar

photogenic /fəʊtəʊ'dʒenɪk/ a fotogénico

photograph /'fəʊtəgrɑːf/ n fotografía f. ● vt hacer una fotografía de, sacar fotos de. ~er /fə'tɒgrəfə(r)/ n fotógrafo m. ~ic /-'græfɪk/ a fotográfico ~y /fə'tɒgrəfɪ/ n fotografía f

phrase /freɪz/ n frase f, locución f, expresión f. ● vt expresar. ~-book n libro m de frases

physical /'fɪzɪkl/ a físico

physician /fɪ'zɪʃn/ n médico m

physic|ist /'fɪzɪsɪst/ n físico m. ~s /'fɪzɪks/ n física f

physiology /fɪzɪ'ɒlədʒɪ/ n fisiología f

physiotherap|ist /fɪzɪəʊ'θerəpɪst/ n fisioterapeuta m & f. ~y /fɪzɪəʊ'θerəpɪ/ n fisioterapia f

physique /fɪ'ziːk/ n constitución f; (appearance) físico m

pian|ist /'pɪənɪst/ n pianista m & f. ~o /pɪ'ænəʊ/ n (pl -os) piano m

piccolo /'pɪkələʊ/ n flautín m, piccolo m

pick¹ /pɪk/ (tool) pico m

pick² /pɪk/ vt escoger; recoger ⟨flowers etc⟩; forzar ⟨a lock⟩; (dig) picar. ~ a quarrel buscar camorra. ~ holes in criticar. ● n (choice) selección f; (the best) lo mejor. ~ on vt (nag) meterse con. ~ out vt escoger; (identify) identificar; destacar ⟨colour⟩. ~ up vt recoger; (lift) levantar; (learn) aprender; adquirir ⟨habit, etc⟩; obtener ⟨information⟩; contagiarse de ⟨illness⟩. ● vi mejorar; (med) reponerse

pickaxe /'pɪkæks/ n pico m

picket /'pɪkɪt/ n (striker) huelguista m & f; (group of strikers) piquete m; (stake) estaca f. ~ line n piquete m. ● vt vigilar por piquetes. ● vi estar de guardia

pickle /'pɪkl/ n (in vinegar) encurtido m; (in brine) salmuera f. in a ~

(fam) en un apuro. ● vt encurtir. ~s npl encurtido m

pick: ~pocket /'pɪkpɒkɪt/ n ratero m. ~-up n (sl) ligue m; (truck) camioneta f; (stylus-holder) fonocaptor m, brazo m

picnic /'pɪknɪk/ n comida f campestre. ● vi (pt picnicked) merendar en el campo

pictorial /pɪk'tɔːrɪəl/ a ilustrado

picture /'pɪktʃə(r)/ n (painting) cuadro m; (photo) fotografía f; (drawing) dibujo m; (beautiful thing) preciosidad f; (film) película f; (fig) descripción f. the ~s npl el cine m. ● vt imaginarse; (describe) describir

picturesque /pɪktʃə'resk/ a pintoresco

piddling /'pɪdlɪŋ/ a (fam) insignificante

pidgin /'pɪdʒɪn/ a. ~ English n inglés m corrompido

pie /paɪ/ n empanada f; (sweet) pastel m, tarta f

piebald /'paɪbɔːld/ a pío

piece /piːs/ n pedazo m; (coin) moneda f; (in game) pieza f. a ~ of advice un consejo m. a ~ of news una noticia f. take to ~s desmontar. ● vt. ~ together juntar. ~meal /'piːsmiːl/ a gradual; (unsystematic) poco sistemático. —adv poco a poco. ~-work n trabajo m a destajo

pier /pɪə(r)/ n muelle m

pierc|e /pɪəs/ vt perforar. ~ing a penetrante

piety /'paɪətɪ/ n piedad f

piffl|e /'pɪfl/ n (sl) tonterías fpl. ~ing a (sl) insignificante

pig /pɪg/ n cerdo m

pigeon /'pɪdʒɪn/ n paloma f; (culin) pichón m. ~-hole n casilla f

pig: ~gy /'pɪgɪ/ a (greedy, fam) glotón. ~gy-back adv a cuestas. ~gy bank n hucha f. ~-headed a terco

pigment /'pɪgmənt/ n pigmento m. ~ation /-'teɪʃn/ n pigmentación f

pig: ~skin /'pɪgskɪn/ n piel m de cerdo. ~sty /'pɪgstaɪ/ n pocilga f

pigtail /'pɪgteɪl/ n (plait) trenza f

pike /paɪk/ n invar (fish) lucio m

pilchard /'pɪltʃəd/ n sardina f

pile¹ /paɪl/ n (heap) montón m. ● vt amontonar. ~ it on exagerar. ● vi amontonar. ~ up vt amontonar. ● vi amontonarse. ~s /paɪlz/ npl (med) almorranas fpl

pile² /paɪl/ n (of fabric) pelo m

pile-up /'paɪlʌp/ n accidente m múltiple

pilfer /'pɪlfə(r)/ vt/i hurtar. ~**age** n, ~**ing** n hurto m

pilgrim /'pɪlgrɪm/ n peregrino. ~**age** n peregrinación f

pill /pɪl/ n píldora f

pillage /'pɪlɪdʒ/ n saqueo m. ● vt saquear

pillar /'pɪlə(r)/ n columna f. ~**box** n buzón m

pillion /'pɪlɪən/ n asiento m trasero. **ride** ~ ir en el asiento trasero

pillory /'pɪlərɪ/ n picota f

pillow /'pɪləʊ/ n almohada f. ~**case** /'pɪləʊkeɪs/ n funda f de almohada

pilot /'paɪlət/ n piloto m. ● vt pilotar. ~**light** n fuego m piloto

pimp /pɪmp/ n alcahuete m

pimple /'pɪmpl/ n grano m

pin /pɪn/ n alfiler m; (mec) perno m. ~**s and needles** hormigueo m. ● vt (pt **pinned**) prender con alfileres; (hold down) enclavijar; (fix) sujetar. ~ **s.o. down** obligar a uno a que se decida. ~ **up** fijar

pinafore /'pɪnəfɔ:(r)/ n delantal m. ~ **dress** n mandil m

pincers /'pɪnsəz/ npl tenazas fpl

pinch /pɪntʃ/ vt pellizcar; (steal, sl) hurtar. ● vi ⟨shoe⟩ apretar. ● n pellizco m; (small amount) pizca f. **at a** ~ en caso de necesidad

pincushion /'pɪnkʊʃn/ n acerico m

pine[1] /paɪn/ n pino m

pine[2] /paɪn/ vi. ~ **away** consumirse. ~ **for** suspirar por

pineapple /'paɪnæpl/ n piña f, ananás m

ping /pɪŋ/ n sonido m agudo. ~**pong** /'pɪŋpɒŋ/ n pimpón m, ping-pong m

pinion /'pɪnjən/ vt maniatar

pink /pɪŋk/ a & n color (m) de rosa

pinnacle /'pɪnəkl/ n pináculo m

pin: ~**point** vt determinar con precisión f. ~**stripe** /'pɪnstraɪp/ n raya f fina

pint /paɪnt/ n pinta f (= 0.57 litre)

pin-up /'pɪnʌp/ n (fam) fotografía f de mujer

pioneer /paɪə'nɪə(r)/ n pionero m. ● vt ser el primero, promotor de, promover

pious /'paɪəs/ a piadoso

pip[1] /pɪp/ n (seed) pepita f

pip[2] /pɪp/ (time signal) señal f

pip[3] /pɪp/ (on uniform) estrella f

pipe /paɪp/ n tubo m; (mus) caramillo m; (for smoking) pipa f. ● vt conducir por tuberías. ~**down** (fam) bajar la voz, callarse. ~**cleaner** n limpiapipas m invar. ~**dream** n ilusión f. ~**line** /'paɪplaɪn/ n tubería f; (for oil) oleoducto m. **in the** ~**line** en preparación f. ~**r** n flautista m & f

piping /'paɪpɪŋ/ n tubería f. ~ **hot** muy caliente, hirviendo

piquant /'pi:kənt/ a picante

pique /pi:k/ n resentimiento m

pira|cy /'paɪərəsɪ/ n piratería f. ~**te** /'paɪərət/ n pirata m

pirouette /pɪru'et/ n pirueta f. ● vi piruetear

Pisces /'paɪsi:z/ n (astr) Piscis m

pistol /'pɪstl/ n pistola f

piston /'pɪstən/ n pistón m

pit /pɪt/ n foso m; (mine) mina f; (of stomach) boca f. ● vt (pt **pitted**) marcar con hoyos; (fig) oponer. ~ **o.s. against** medirse con

pitch[1] /pɪtʃ/ n brea f

pitch[2] /pɪtʃ/ (degree) grado m; (mus) tono m; (sport) campo m. ● vt lanzar; armar ⟨tent⟩. ~ **into** (fam) atacar. ● vi caerse; ⟨ship⟩ cabecear. ~ **in** (fam) contribuir. ~**ed battle** n batalla f campal

pitch-black /pɪtʃ'blæk/ a oscuro como boca de lobo

pitcher /'pɪtʃə(r)/ n jarro m

pitchfork /'pɪtʃfɔ:k/ n horca f

piteous /'pɪtɪəs/ a lastimoso

pitfall /'pɪtfɔ:l/ n trampa f

pith /pɪθ/ n (of orange, lemon) médula f; (fig) meollo m

pithy /'pɪθɪ/ a (-ier, -iest) conciso

piti|ful /'pɪtɪfl/ a lastimoso. ~**less** a despiadado

pittance /'pɪtns/ n sueldo m irrisorio

pity /'pɪtɪ/ n piedad f; (regret) lástima f. ● vt compadecerse de

pivot /'pɪvət/ n pivote m. ● vt montonar sobre un pivote. ● vi girar sobre un pivote; (fig) depender (**on** de)

pixie /'pɪksɪ/ n duende m

placard /'plækɑ:d/ n pancarta f; (poster) cartel m

placate /plə'keɪt/ vt apaciguar

place /pleɪs/ n lugar m; (seat) asiento m; (post) puesto m; (house, fam) casa f. **take** ~ tener lugar. ● vt poner, colocar; (remember) recordar; (identify) identificar. **be**

~d (*in race*) colocarse. ~mat *n* salvamanteles *m invar.* ~ment /'pleɪsmənt/ *n* colocación *f*

placid /'plæsɪd/ *a* plácido

plagiari|sm /'pleɪdʒərɪzm/ *n* plagio *m.* ~ze /'pleɪdʒəraɪz/ *vt* plagiar

plague /pleɪg/ *n* peste *f*; (*fig*) plaga *f.*
● *vt* atormentar

plaice /pleɪs/ *n invar* platija *f*

plaid /plæd/ *n* tartán *m*

plain /pleɪn/ *a* (-er, -est) claro; (*simple*) sencillo; (*candid*) franco; (*ugly*) feo. in ~ clothes en traje de paisano. ● *adv* claramente. ● *n* llanura *f.* ~ly *adv* claramente; (*frankly*) francamente; (*simply*) sencillamente. ~ness *n* claridad *f*; (*simplicity*) sencillez *f*

plaintiff /'pleɪntɪf/ *n* demandante *m & f*

plait /plæt/ *vt* trenzar. ● *n* trenza *f*

plan /plæn/ *n* proyecto *m*; (*map*) plano *m.* ● *vt* (*pt* planned) planear, proyectar; (*intend*) proponerse

plane[1] /pleɪn/ *n* (*tree*) plátano *m*

plane[2] /pleɪn/ (*level*) nivel *m*; (*aviat*) avión *m.* ● *a* plano

plane[3] /pleɪn/ (*tool*) cepillo *m.* ● *vt* cepillar

planet /'plænɪt/ *n* planeta *m.* ~ary *a* planetario

plank /plæŋk/ *n* tabla *f*

planning ~ /'plænɪŋ/ *n* planificación *f.* family ~ *n* planificación familiar. town ~ *n* urbanismo *m*

plant /plɑːnt/ *n* planta *f*; (*mec*) maquinaria *f*; (*factory*) fábrica *f.* ● *vt* plantar; (*place in position*) colocar. ~ation /plæn'teɪʃn/ *n* plantación *f*

plaque /plæk/ *n* placa *f*

plasma /'plæzmə/ *n* plasma *m*

plaster /'plɑːstə(r)/ *n* yeso *m*; (*adhesive*) esparadrapo *m*; (*for setting bones*) escayola *f.* ~ of Paris *n* yeso *m* mate. ● *vt* enyesar; (*med*) escayolar ⟨broken bone⟩; (*cover*) cubrir (with de). ~ed *a* (*fam*) borracho

plastic /'plæstɪk/ *a & n* plástico (*m*)

Plasticine /'plæstɪsiːn/ *n* (*P*) pasta *f* de modelar, plastilina *f* (*P*)

plastic surgery /plæstɪk'sɜːdʒərɪ/ *n* cirugía *f* estética

plate /pleɪt/ *n* plato *m*; (*of metal*) chapa *f*; (*silverware*) vajilla *f* de plata; (*in book*) lámina *f.* ● *vt* (*cover with metal*) chapear

plateau /'plætəʊ/ *n* (*pl* plateaux) *n* meseta *f*

plateful /'pleɪtfl/ *n* (*pl* -fuls) plato *m*

platform /'plætfɔːm/ *n* plataforma *f*; (*rail*) andén *m*

platinum /'plætɪnəm/ *n* platino *m*

platitude /'plætɪtjuːd/ *n* tópico *m*, perogrullada *f*, lugar *m* común

platonic /plə'tɒnɪk/ *a* platónico

platoon /plə'tuːn/ *n* pelotón *m*

platter /'plætə(r)/ *n* fuente *f*, plato *m* grande

plausible /'plɔːzəbl/ *a* plausible; ⟨person⟩ convincente

play /pleɪ/ *vt* jugar; (*act role*) desempeñar el papel de; tocar ⟨instrument⟩. ~ safe no arriesgarse. ~ up to halagar. ● *vi* jugar. ~ed out agotado. ● *n* juego *m*; (*drama*) obra *f* de teatro. ~ on words *n* juego *m* de palabras. ~ down *vt* minimizar. ~ on *vt* aprovecharse de. ~ up *vi* (*fam*) causar problemas. ~act *vi* hacer la comedia. ~boy /'pleɪbɔɪ/ *n* calavera *m.* ~er *n* jugador *m*; (*mus*) músico *m.* ~ful /'pleɪfl/ *a* juguetón. ~fully *adv* jugando; (*jokingly*) en broma. ~ground /'pleɪgraʊnd/ *n* parque *m* de juegos infantiles; (*in school*) campo *m* de recreo. ~group *n* jardín *m* de la infancia. ~ing /'pleɪɪŋ/ *n* juego *m.* ~ing-card *n* naipe *m.* ~ing-field *n* campo *m* de deportes. ~mate /'pleɪmeɪt/ *n* compañero *m* (de juego). ~pen *n* corralito *m.* ~thing *n* juguete *m.* ~wright /'pleɪraɪt/ *n* dramaturgo *m*

plc /piːel'siː/ *abbr* (*public limited company*) S.A., sociedad *f* anónima

plea /pliː/ *n* súplica *f*; (*excuse*) excusa *f*; (*jurid*) defensa *f*

plead /pliːd/ *vt* (*jurid*) alegar; (*as excuse*) pretextar. ● *vi* suplicar; (*jurid*) abogar. ~ with suplicar

pleasant /'pleznt/ *a* agradable

pleas|e /pliːz/ *int* por favor. ● *vt* agradar, dar gusto a. ● *vi* agradar; (*wish*) querer. ~ o.s. hacer lo que quiera. do as you ~e haz lo que quieras. ~ed *a* contento. ~ed with satisfecho de. ~ing *a* agradable

pleasur|e /'pleʒə(r)/ *n* placer *m.* ~able *a* agradable

pleat /pliːt/ *n* pliegue *m.* ● *vt* hacer pliegues en

plebiscite /'plebɪsɪt/ *n* plebiscito *m*

plectrum /'plektrəm/ *n* plectro *m*

pledge /pledʒ/ *n* prenda *f*; (*promise*) promesa *f.* ● *vt* empeñar; (*promise*) prometer

plent|iful /'plentɪfl/ *a* abundante. ~y /'plentɪ/ *n* abundancia *f.* ~y (of) muchos (de)

pleurisy /'plʊərəsɪ/ n pleuresía f

pliable /'plaɪəbl/ a flexible

pliers /'plaɪəz/ npl alicates mpl

plight /plaɪt/ n situación f (difícil)

plimsolls /'plɪmsəlz/ npl zapatillas fpl de lona

plinth /plɪnθ/ n plinto m

plod /plɒd/ vi (pt **plodded**) caminar con paso pesado; (work hard) trabajar laboriosamente. **~der** n empollón m

plonk /plɒŋk/ n (sl) vino m peleón

plop /plɒp/ n paf m. ● vi (pt **plopped**) caerse con un paf

plot /plɒt/ n complot m; (of novel etc) argumento m; (piece of land) parcela f. ● vt (pt **plotted**) tramar; (mark out) trazar. ● vi conspirar

plough /plaʊ/ n arado m. ● vt/i arar. **~ through** avanzar laboriosamente por

ploy /plɔɪ/ n (fam) estratagema f, truco m

pluck /plʌk/ vt arrancar; depilarse (eyebrows); desplumar (bird); recoger (flowers). **~ up courage** hacer de tripas corazón. ● n valor m. **~y** a (-ier, -iest) valiente

plug /plʌg/ n tapón m; (elec) enchufe m; (auto) bujía f. ● vt (pt **plugged**) tapar; (advertise, fam) dar publicidad a. **~ in** (elec) enchufar

plum /plʌm/ n ciruela f; (tree) ciruelo m

plumage /'pluːmɪdʒ/ n plumaje m

plumb /plʌm/ a vertical. ● n plomada f. ● adv verticalmente; (exactly) exactamente. ● vt sondar

plumb|er /'plʌmə(r)/ n fontanero m. **~ing** n instalación f sanitaria, instalación f de cañerías

plume /pluːm/ n pluma f

plum job /plʌm'dʒɒb/ n (fam) puesto m estupendo

plummet /'plʌmɪt/ n plomada f. ● vi caer a plomo, caer en picado

plump /plʌmp/ a (-er, -est) rechoncho. ● vt. **~ for** elegir. **~ness** n gordura f

plum pudding /plʌm'pʊdɪŋ/ n budín m de pasas

plunder /'plʌndə(r)/ n (act) saqueo m; (goods) botín m. ● vt saquear

plung|e /plʌndʒ/ vt hundir; (in water) sumergir. ● vi zambullirse; (fall) caer. ● n salto m. **~er** n (for sink) desatascador m; (mec) émbolo m. **~ing** a (neckline) bajo, escotado

plural /'plʊərəl/ a & n plural (m)

plus /plʌs/ prep más. ● a positivo. ● n signo m más; (fig) ventaja f. **five ~** más de cinco

plush /plʌʃ/ n felpa f. ● a de felpa, afelpado; (fig) lujoso. **~y** a lujoso

plutocrat /'pluːtəkræt/ n plutócrata m & f

plutonium /pluːˈtəʊnjəm/ n plutonio m

ply /plaɪ/ vt manejar (tool); ejercer (trade). **~ s.o. with drink** dar continuamente de beber a uno. **~wood** n contrachapado m

p.m. /piːˈem/ abbr (post meridiem) de la tarde

pneumatic /njuːˈmætɪk/ a neumático

pneumonia /njuːˈməʊnjə/ n. pulmonía f

PO /piːˈəʊ/ abbr (Post Office) oficina f de correos

poach /pəʊtʃ/ vt escalfar (egg); cocer (fish etc); (steal) cazar en vedado. **~er** n cazador m furtivo

pocket /'pɒkɪt/ n bolsillo m; (of air, resistance) bolsa f. **be in ~** salir ganado. **be out of ~** salir perdiendo. ● vt poner en el bolsillo. **~book** n (notebook) libro m de bolsillo; (purse, Amer) cartera f; (handbag, Amer) bolso m. **~money** n dinero m para los gastos personales

pock-marked /'pɒkmɑːkt/ a (face) picado de viruelas

pod /pɒd/ n vaina f

podgy /'pɒdʒɪ/ a (-ier, -iest) rechoncho

poem /'pəʊɪm/ n poesía f

poet /'pəʊɪt/ n poeta m. **~ess** n poetisa f. **~ic** /-'etɪk/ a, **~ical** /-'etɪkl/ a poético. **P~ Laureate** n poeta laureado. **~ry** /'pəʊɪtrɪ/ n poesía f

poignant /'pɔɪnjənt/ a conmovedor

point /pɔɪnt/ n punto m; (sharp end) punta f; (significance) lo importante; (elec) toma f de corriente. **good ~s** cualidades fpl. **to the ~** pertinente. **up to a ~** hasta cierto punto. **what is the ~?** ¿para qué?, ¿a qué fin? ● vt (aim) apuntar; (show) indicar. **~ out** señalar. ● vi señalar. **~-blank** a & adv a boca de jarro, a quemarropa. **~ed** /'pɔɪntɪd/ a puntiagudo; (fig) mordaz. **~er** /'pɔɪntə(r)/ n indicador m; (dog) perro m de muestra; (clue, fam) indicación f. **~less** /'pɔɪntlɪs/ a inútil

poise /pɔɪz/ n equilibrio m; (elegance) elegancia f; (fig) aplomo m. ~d a en equilibrio. ~d for listo para

poison /'pɔɪzn/ n veneno m. ● vt envenenar. ~ous a venenoso; (chemical etc) tóxico

poke /pəʊk/ vt empujar; atizar (fire). ~ fun at burlarse de. ~ out asomar (head). ● vi hurgar; (pry) meterse. ~ about fisgonear. ● n empuje m

poker[1] /'pəʊkə(r)/ n atizador m

poker[2] /'pəʊkə(r)/ (cards) póquer m. ~-face cara f inmutable

poky /'pəʊkɪ/ a (-ier, -iest) estrecho

Poland /'pəʊlənd/ n Polonia f

polar /'pəʊlə(r)/ a polar. ~ bear n oso m blanco

polarize /'pəʊləraɪz/ vt polarizar

Pole /pəʊl/ polaco n

pole[1] /pəʊl/ n palo m; (for flag) asta f

pole[2] /pəʊl/ (geog) polo m. ~-star n estrella f polar

polemic /pə'lemɪk/ a polémico. ● n polémica f

police /pə'liːs/ n policía f. ● vt vigilar. ~man /pə'liːsmən/ n (pl -men) policía m, guardia m. ~ record n antecedentes mpl penales. ~ state n estado m policíaco. ~ station n comisaría f. ~woman /-wʊmən/ n (pl -women) mujer m policía

policy[1] /'pɒlɪsɪ/ n política f

policy[2] /'pɒlɪsɪ/ (insurance) póliza f (de seguros)

polio(myelitis) /'pəʊlɪəʊ(maɪə'laɪtɪs)/ n polio(mielitis) f

polish /'pɒlɪʃ/ n (for shoes) betún m; (for floor) cera f; (for nails) esmalte m de uñas; (shine) brillo m; (fig) finura f. nail ~ esmalte m de uñas. ● vt pulir; limpiar (shoes); encerar (floor). ~ off despachar. ~ed a pulido; (manner) refinado. ~er n pulidor m; (machine) pulidora f

Polish /'pəʊlɪʃ/ a & n polaco (m)

polite /pə'laɪt/ a cortés. ~ly adv cortésmente. ~ness n cortesía f

politic|al /pə'lɪtɪkl/ a político. ~ian /pɒlɪ'tɪʃn/ n político m. ~s /'pɒlətɪks/ n política f

polka /'pɒlkə/ n polca f. ~ dots npl diseño m de puntos

poll /pəʊl/ n elección f; (survey) encuesta f. ● vt obtener (votes)

pollen /'pɒlən/ n polen m

polling-booth /'pəʊlɪŋbuːð/ n cabina f de votar

pollut|e /pə'luːt/ vt contaminar. ~ion /-ʃn/ n contaminación f

polo /'pəʊləʊ/ n polo m. ~-neck n cuello m vuelto

poltergeist /'pɒltəgaɪst/ n duende m

polyester /pɒlɪ'estə(r)/ n poliéster m

polygam|ist /pə'lɪgəmɪst/ n polígamo m. ~ous a polígamo. ~y /pə'lɪgəmɪ/ n poligamia f

polyglot /'pɒlɪglɒt/ a & n políglota (m & f)

polygon /'pɒlɪgən/ n polígono m

polyp /'pɒlɪp/ n pólipo m

polystyrene /pɒlɪ'staɪriːn/ n poliestireno m

polytechnic /pɒlɪ'teknɪk/ n escuela f politécnica

polythene /'pɒlɪθiːn/ n polietileno m. ~ bag n bolsa f de plástico

pomegranate /'pɒmɪgrænɪt/ n (fruit) granada f

pommel /'pʌml/ n pomo m

pomp /pɒmp/ n pompa f

pompon /'pɒmpɒn/ n pompón m

pompo|sity /pɒm'pɒsətɪ/ n pomposidad f. ~us /'pɒmpəs/ a pomposo

poncho /'pɒntʃəʊ/ n (pl -os) poncho m

pond /pɒnd/ n charca f; (artificial) estanque m

ponder /'pɒndə(r)/ vt considerar. ● vi reflexionar. ~ous /'pɒndərəs/ a pesado

pong /pɒŋ/ n (sl) hedor m. ● vi (sl) apestar

pontif|f /'pɒntɪf/ n pontífice m. ~ical /-'tɪfɪkl/ a pontifical; (fig) dogmático. ~icate /pɒn'tɪfɪkeɪt/ vi pontificar

pontoon /pɒn'tuːn/ n pontón m. ~ bridge n puente m de pontones

pony /'pəʊnɪ/ n poni m. ~-tail n cola f de caballo. ~-trekking n excursionismo m en poni

poodle /'puːdl/ n perro m de lanas, caniche m

pool[1] /puːl/ n charca f; (artificial) estanque m. (swimming-)~ n piscina f

pool[2] /puːl/ (common fund) fondos mpl comunes; (snooker) billar m americano. ● vt aunar. ~s npl quinielas fpl

poor /pʊə(r)/ a (-er, -est) pobre; (not good) malo. be in ~ health estar mal de salud. ~ly a (fam) indispuesto. ● adv pobremente; (badly) mal

pop[1] /pɒp/ n ruido m seco; (of bottle) taponazo m. ● vt (pt **popped**) hacer reventar; (put) poner. ~ **in** vi entrar; (visit) pasar por. ~ **out** vi saltar; ⟨person⟩ salir un rato. ~ **up** vi surgir, aparecer

pop[2] /pɒp/ a (popular) pop invar. ● n (fam) música f pop. ~ **art** n arte m pop

popcorn /'pɒpkɔːn/ n palomitas fpl

pope /pəʊp/ n papa m

popgun /'pɒpgʌn/ n pistola f de aire comprimido

poplar /'pɒplə(r)/ n chopo m

poplin /'pɒplɪn/ n popelina f

poppy /'pɒpɪ/ n amapola f

popular /'pɒpjʊlə(r)/ a popular. ~**ity** /-'lærətɪ/ n popularidad f. ~**ize** vt popularizar

populat|e /'pɒpjʊleɪt/ vt poblar. ~**ion** /-'leɪʃn/ n población f; (number of inhabitants) habitantes mpl

porcelain /'pɔːsəlɪn/ n porcelana f

porch /pɔːtʃ/ n porche m

porcupine /'pɔːkjʊpaɪn/ n puerco m espín

pore[1] /pɔː(r)/ n poro m

pore[2] /pɔː(r)/ vi. ~ **over** estudiar detenidamente

pork /pɔːk/ n cerdo m

porn /pɔːn/ n (fam) pornografía f. ~**ographic** /-ə'græfɪk/ a pornográfico. ~**ography** /pɔː'nɒgrəfɪ/ n pornografía f

porous /'pɔːrəs/ a poroso

porpoise /'pɔːpəs/ n marsopa f

porridge /'pɒrɪdʒ/ n gachas fpl de avena

port[1] /pɔːt/ n puerto m; (porthole) portilla f. ~ **of call** puerto de escala

port[2] /pɔːt/ (naut, left) babor m. ● a de babor

port[3] /pɔːt/ (wine) oporto m

portable /'pɔːtəbl/ a portátil

portal /'pɔːtl/ n portal m

portent /'pɔːtent/ n presagio m

porter /'pɔːtə(r)/ n portero m; (for luggage) mozo m. ~**age** n porte m

portfolio /pɔːt'fəʊljəʊ/ n (pl -os) cartera f

porthole /'pɔːthəʊl/ n portilla f

portico /'pɔːtɪkəʊ/ n (pl -oes) pórtico m

portion /'pɔːʃn/ n porción f. ● vt repartir

portly /'pɔːtlɪ/ a (-ier, -iest) corpulento

portrait /'pɔːtrɪt/ n retrato m

portray /pɔː'treɪ/ vt retratar; (represent) representar. ~**al** n retrato m

Portug|al /'pɔːtjʊgl/ n Portugal m. ~**uese** /-'giːz/ a & n portugués (m)

pose /pəʊz/ n postura f. ● vt colocar; hacer ⟨question⟩; plantear ⟨problem⟩. ● vi posar. ~ **as** hacerse pasar por. ~**r** /'pəʊzə(r)/ n pregunta f difícil

posh /pɒʃ/ a (sl) elegante

position /pə'zɪʃn/ n posición f; (job) puesto m; (status) rango m. ● vt colocar

positive /'pɒzətɪv/ a positivo; (real) verdadero; (certain) seguro. ● n (foto) positiva f. ~**ly** adv positivamente

possess /pə'zes/ vt poseer. ~**ion** /pə'zeʃn/ n posesión f. **take** ~**ion of** tomar posesión de. ~**ions** npl posesiones fpl; (jurid) bienes mpl. ~**ive** /pə'zesɪv/ a posesivo. ~**or** n poseedor m

possib|ility /pɒsə'bɪlətɪ/ n posibilidad f. ~**le** /'pɒsəbl/ a posible. ~**ly** adv posiblemente

post[1] /pəʊst/ n (pole) poste m. ● vt fijar ⟨notice⟩

post[2] /pəʊst/ (place) puesto m

post[3] /pəʊst/ (mail) correo m. ● vt echar ⟨letter⟩. **keep s.o.** ~**ed** tener a uno al corriente

post... /pəʊst/ pref post

post: ~age /'pəʊstɪdʒ/ n franqueo m. ~**al** /'pəʊstl/ a postal. ~**al order** n giro m postal. ~**box** n buzón m. ~**card** /'pəʊstkɑːd/ n (tarjeta f) postal f. ~**code** n código m postal

post-date /pəʊst'deɪt/ vt poner fecha posterior a

poster /'pəʊstə(r)/ n cartel m

poste restante /pəʊst'restɑːnt/ n lista f de correos

posteri|or /pɒ'stɪərɪə(r)/ a posterior. ● n trasero m. ~**ty** /pɒs'terətɪ/ n posteridad f

posthumous /'pɒstjʊməs/ a póstumo. ~**ly** adv después de la muerte

post: ~man /'pəʊstmən/ n (pl -men) cartero m. ~**mark** /'pəʊstmɑːk/ n matasellos m invar. ~**master** /'pəʊstmɑːstə(r)/ n administrador m de correos. ~**mistress** /'pəʊstmɪstrɪs/ n administradora f de correos

post-mortem /'pəʊstmɔːtəm/ n autopsia f

Post Office /'pəʊstɒfɪs/ n oficina f de correos, correos mpl

postpone /pəʊst'pəʊn/ *vt* aplazar. **~ment** *n* aplazamiento *m*

postscript /'pəʊstskrɪpt/ *n* posdata *f*

postulant /'pɒstjʊlənt/ *n* postulante *m & f*

postulate /'pɒstjʊleɪt/ *vt* postular

posture /'pɒstʃə(r)/ *n* postura *f*. ● *vi* adoptar una postura

posy /'pəʊzi/ *n* ramillete *m*

pot /pɒt/ *n* (*for cooking*) olla *f*; (*for flowers*) tiesto *m*; (*marijuana, sl*) mariguana *f*. **go to ~** (*sl*) echarse a perder. ● *vt* (*pt* **potted**) poner en tiesto

potassium /pə'tæsjəm/ *n* potasio *m*

potato /pə'teɪtəʊ/ *n* (*pl* **-oes**) patata *f*, papa *f* (*LAm*)

pot: **~-belly** *n* barriga *f*. **~-boiler** *n* obra *f* literaria escrita sólo para ganar dinero

poten|cy /'pəʊtənsɪ/ *n* potencia *f*. **~t** /'pəʊtnt/ *a* potente; (*drink*) fuerte

potentate /'pəʊtənteɪt/ *n* potentado *m*

potential /pəʊ'tenʃl/ *a & n* potencial (*m*). **~ity** /-ʃɪ'ælətɪ/ *n* potencialidad *f*. **~ly** *adv* potencialmente

pot-hole /'pɒthəʊl/ *n* caverna *f*; (*in road*) bache *m*. **~r** *n* espeleólogo *m*

potion /'pəʊʃn/ *n* poción *f*

pot: **~ luck** *n* lo que haya. **~-shot** *n* tiro *m* al azar. **~ted** /'pɒtɪd/ *see* **pot**. ● *a* (*food*) en conserva

potter[1] /'pɒtə(r)/ *n* alfarero *m*

potter[2] /'pɒtə(r)/ *vi* hacer pequeños trabajos agradables, no hacer nada de particular

pottery /'pɒtərɪ/ *n* cerámica *f*

potty /'pɒtɪ/ *a* (**-ier**, **-iest**) (*sl*) chiflado. ● *n* orinal *m*

pouch /paʊtʃ/ *n* bolsa *f* pequeña

pouffe /pu:f/ *n* (*stool*) taburete *m*

poulterer /'pəʊltərə(r)/ *n* pollero *m*

poultice /'pəʊltɪs/ *n* cataplasma *f*

poultry /'pəʊltrɪ/ *n* aves *fpl* de corral

pounce /paʊns/ *vi* saltar, atacar de repente. ● *n* salto *m*, ataque *m* repentino

pound[1] /paʊnd/ *n* (*weight*) libra *f* (= 454g); (*money*) libra *f* (esterlina)

pound[2] /paʊnd/ *n* (*for cars*) depósito *m*

pound[3] /paʊnd/ *vt* (*crush*) machacar; (*bombard*) bombardear. ● *vi* golpear; (*heart*) palpitar; (*walk*) ir con pasos pesados

pour /pɔ:(r)/ *vt* verter. **~ out** servir (*drink*). ● *vi* fluir; (*rain*) llover a cántaros. **~ in** (*people*) entrar en tropel. **~ing rain** *n* lluvia *f* torrencial. **~ out** (*people*) salir en tropel

pout /paʊt/ *vi* hacer pucheros. ● *n* puchero *m*, mala cara *f*

poverty /'pɒvətɪ/ *n* pobreza *f*

powder /'paʊdə(r)/ *n* polvo *m*; (*cosmetic*) polvos *mpl*. ● *vt* polvorear; (*pulverize*) pulverizar. **~ one's face** ponerse polvos en la cara. **~ed** *a* en polvo. **~y** *a* polvoriento

power /'paʊə(r)/ *n* poder *m*; (*elec*) corriente *f*; (*energy*) energía *f*; (*nation*) potencia *f*. **~ cut** *n* apagón *m*. **~ed** *a* con motor. **~ed by** impulsado por. **~ful** *a* poderoso. **~less** *a* impotente. **~-station** *n* central *f* eléctrica

practicable /'præktɪkəbl/ *a* practicable

practical /'præktɪkl/ *a* práctico. **~ joke** *n* broma *f* pesada. **~ly** *adv* prácticamente

practi|ce /'præktɪs/ *n* práctica *f*; (*custom*) costumbre *f*; (*exercise*) ejercicio *m*; (*sport*) entrenamiento *m*; (*clients*) clientela *f*. **be in ~ce** (*doctor, lawyer*) ejercer. **be out of ~ce** no estar en forma. **in ~ce** (*in fact*) en la práctica; (*on form*) en forma. **~se** /'præktɪs/ *vt* hacer ejercicios en; (*put into practice*) poner en práctica; (*sport*) entrenarse en; ejercer (*profession*). ● *vi* ejercitarse; (*professional*) ejercer. — **~sed** *a* experto

practitioner /præk'tɪʃənə(r)/ *n* profesional *m & f*. **general ~** médico *m* de cabecera. **medical ~** médico *m*

pragmatic /præg'mætɪk/ *a* pragmático

prairie /'preərɪ/ *n* pradera *f*

praise /preɪz/ *vt* alabar. ● *n* alabanza *f*. **~worthy** *a* loable

pram /præm/ *n* cochecito *m* de niño

prance /prɑːns/ *vi* (*horse*) hacer cabriolas; (*person*) pavonearse

prank /præŋk/ *n* travesura *f*

prattle /'prætl/ *vi* parlotear. ● *n* parloteo *m*

prawn /prɔːn/ *n* gamba *f*

pray /preɪ/ *vi* rezar. **~er** /preə(r)/ *n* oración *f*. **~ for** rogar

pre.. /pri:/ *pref* pre...

preach /priːtʃ/ *vt/i* predicar. **~er** *n* predicador *m*

preamble /priː'æmbl/ *n* preámbulo *m*

pre-arrange /priːəˈreɪndʒ/ vt arreglar de antemano. ∼**ment** n arreglo m previo

precarious /prɪˈkeərɪəs/ a precario. ∼**ly** adv precariamente

precaution /prɪˈkɔːʃn/ n precaución f. ∼**ary** a de precaución; (preventive) preventivo

precede /prɪˈsiːd/ vt preceder

preceden|ce /ˈpresɪdəns/ n precedencia f. ∼**t** /ˈpresɪdənt/ n precedente m

preceding /prɪˈsiːdɪŋ/ a precedente

precept /ˈpriːsept/ n precepto m

precinct /ˈpriːsɪŋkt/ n recinto m. **pedestrian** ∼ zona f peatonal. ∼**s** npl contornos mpl

precious /ˈpreʃəs/ a precioso. ● adv (fam) muy

precipice /ˈpresɪpɪs/ n precipicio m

precipitat|e /prɪˈsɪpɪteɪt/ vt precipitar. /prɪˈsɪpɪtət/ n precipitado m. ● a precipitado. ∼**ion** /-ˈteɪʃn/ n precipitación f

precipitous /prɪˈsɪpɪtəs/ a escarpado

précis /ˈpreɪsiː/ n (pl précis /-siːz/) resumen m

precis|e /prɪˈsaɪs/ a preciso; (careful) meticuloso. ∼**ely** adv precisamente. ∼**ion** /-ˈsɪʒn/ n precisión f

preclude /prɪˈkluːd/ vt (prevent) impedir; (exclude) excluir

precocious /prɪˈkəʊʃəs/ a precoz. ∼**ly** adv precozmente

preconce|ived /priːkənˈsiːvd/ a preconcebido. ∼**ption** /-ˈsepʃn/ n preconcepción f

precursor /priːˈkɜːsə(r)/ n precursor m

predator /ˈpredətə(r)/ n animal m de rapiña. ∼**y** a de rapiña

predecessor /ˈpriːdɪsesə(r)/ n predecesor m, antecesor m

predestin|ation /prɪdestɪˈneɪʃn/ n predestinación f. ∼**e** /priːˈdestɪn/ vt predestinar

predicament /prɪˈdɪkəmənt/ n apuro m

predicat|e /ˈpredɪkət/ n predicado m. ∼**ive** /prɪˈdɪkətɪv/ a predicativo

predict /prɪˈdɪkt/ vt predecir. ∼**ion** /-ʃn/ n predicción f

predilection /priːdɪˈlekʃn/ n predilección f

predispose /priːdɪˈspəʊz/ vt predisponer

predomina|nt /prɪˈdɒmɪnənt/ a predominante. ∼**te** /prɪˈdɒmɪneɪt/ vi predominar

pre-eminent /priːˈemɪnənt/ a preeminente

pre-empt /priːˈempt/ vt adquirir por adelantado, adelantarse a

preen /priːn/ vt limpiar, arreglar. ∼ **o.s.** atildarse

prefab /ˈpriːfæb/ n (fam) casa f prefabricada. ∼**ricated** /-ˈfæbrɪkeɪtɪd/ a prefabricado

preface /ˈprefəs/ n prólogo m

prefect /ˈpriːfekt/ n monitor m; (official) prefecto m

prefer /prɪˈfɜː(r)/ vt (pt **preferred**) preferir. ∼**able** /ˈprefrəbl/ a preferible. ∼**ence** /ˈprefrəns/ n preferencia f. ∼**ential** /-əˈrenʃl/ a preferente

prefix /ˈpriːfɪks/ n (pl **-ixes**) prefijo m

pregnan|cy /ˈpregnənsi/ n embarazo m. ∼**t** /ˈpregnənt/ a embarazada

prehistoric /priːhɪˈstɒrɪk/ a prehistórico

prejudge /priːˈdʒʌdʒ/ vt prejuzgar

prejudice /ˈpredʒʊdɪs/ n prejuicio m; (harm) perjuicio m. ● vt predisponer; (harm) perjudicar. ∼**d** a parcial

prelate /ˈprelət/ n prelado m

preliminar|ies /prɪˈlɪmɪnərɪz/ npl preliminares mpl. ∼**y** /prɪˈlɪmɪnəri/ a preliminar

prelude /ˈpreljuːd/ n preludio m

pre-marital /priːˈmærɪtl/ a prematrimonial

premature /ˈpremətjʊə(r)/ a prematuro

premeditated /priːˈmedɪteɪtɪd/ a premeditado

premier /ˈpremɪə(r)/ a primero. ● n (pol) primer ministro

première /ˈpremɪə(r)/ n estreno m

premises /ˈpremɪsɪz/ npl local m. **on the** ∼ en el local

premiss /ˈpremɪs/ n premisa f

premium /ˈpriːmɪəm/ n premio m. **at a** ∼ muy solicitado

premonition /priːməˈnɪʃn/ n presentimiento m

preoccup|ation /priːɒkjʊˈpeɪʃn/ n preocupación f. ∼**ied** /-ˈɒkjʊpaɪd/ a preocupado

prep /prep/ n deberes mpl

preparation /prepəˈreɪʃn/ n preparación f. ∼**s** npl preparativos mpl

preparatory /prɪˈpærətrɪ/ a preparatorio. ~ **school** n escuela f primaria privada

prepare /prɪˈpeə(r)/ vt preparar. • vi prepararse. ~**d to** dispuesto a

prepay /priːˈpeɪ/ vt (pt **-paid**) pagar por adelantado

preponderance /prɪˈpɒndərəns/ n preponderancia f

preposition /prepəˈzɪʃn/ n preposición f

prepossessing /priːpəˈzesɪŋ/ a atractivo

preposterous /prɪˈpɒstərəs/ a absurdo

prep school /ˈprepskuːl/ n escuela f primaria privada

prerequisite /priːˈrekwɪzɪt/ n requisito m previo

prerogative /prɪˈrɒgətɪv/ n prerrogativa f

Presbyterian /prezbɪˈtɪərɪən/ a & n presbiteriano (m)

prescri|be /prɪˈskraɪb/ vt prescribir; (med) recetar. ~**ption** /-ˈɪpʃn/ n prescripción f; (med) receta f

presence /ˈprezns/ n presencia f; (attendance) asistencia f. ~ **of mind** presencia f de ánimo

present[1] /ˈpreznt/ a & n presente (m & f). **at** ~ actualmente. **for the** ~ por ahora

present[2] /ˈpreznt/ n (gift) regalo m

present[3] /prɪˈzent/ vt presentar; (give) obsequiar. ~ **s.o. with** obsequiar a uno con. ~**able** a presentable. ~**ation** /prezn'teɪʃn/ n presentación f; (ceremony) ceremonia f de entrega

presently /ˈprezntlɪ/ adv dentro de poco

preserv|ation /prezəˈveɪʃn/ n conservación f. ~**ative** /prɪˈzɜːvətɪv/ n preservativo m. ~**e** /prɪˈzɜːv/ vt conservar; (maintain) mantener; (culin) poner en conserva. • n coto m; (jam) confitura f

preside /prɪˈzaɪd/ vi presidir. ~ **over** presidir

presiden|cy /ˈprezɪdənsɪ/ n presidencia f. ~**t** /ˈprezɪdənt/ n presidente m. ~**tial** /-ˈdenʃl/ a presidencial

press /pres/ vt apretar; exprimir (fruit etc); (insist on) insistir en; (iron) planchar. **be** ~**ed for** tener poco. • vi apretar; (time) apremiar; (fig) urgir. ~ **on** seguir adelante. • n presión f; (mec, newspapers)

prensa f; (printing) imprenta f. ~ **conference** n rueda f de prensa. ~ **cutting** n recorte m de periódico. ~**ing** /ˈpresɪŋ/ a urgente. ~**stud** n automático m. ~**up** n plancha f

pressure /ˈpreʃə(r)/ n presión f. • vt hacer presión sobre. ~**cooker** n olla f a presión. ~ **group** n grupo m de presión

pressurize /ˈpreʃəraɪz/ vt hacer presión sobre

prestig|e /preˈstiːʒ/ n prestigio m. ~**ious** /preˈstɪdʒəs/ a prestigioso

presum|ably /prɪˈzjuːməblɪ/ adv presumiblemente, probablemente. ~**e** /prɪˈzjuːm/ vt presumir. ~**e (up)on** vi abusar de. ~**ption** /-ˈzʌmpʃn/ n presunción f. ~**ptuous** /prɪˈzʌmptʃʊəs/ a presuntuoso

presuppose /priːsəˈpəʊz/ vt presuponer

preten|ce /prɪˈtens/ n fingimiento m; (claim) pretensión f; (pretext) pretexto m. ~**d** /prɪˈtend/ vt/i fingir. ~**d to** (lay claim) pretender

pretentious /prɪˈtenʃəs/ a pretencioso

pretext /ˈpriːtekst/ n pretexto m

pretty /ˈprɪtɪ/ a (**-ier, -iest**) adv bonito, lindo (esp LAm); (person) guapo

prevail /prɪˈveɪl/ vi predominar; (win) prevalecer. ~ **on** persuadir

prevalen|ce /ˈprevələns/ n costumbre f. ~**t** /ˈprevələnt/ a extendido

prevaricate /prɪˈværɪkeɪt/ vi despistar

prevent /prɪˈvent/ vt impedir. ~**able** a evitable. ~**ion** /-ʃn/ n prevención f. ~**ive** a preventivo

preview /ˈpriːvjuː/ n preestreno m, avance m

previous /ˈpriːvɪəs/ a anterior. ~ **to** antes de. ~**ly** adv anteriormente, antes

pre-war /priːˈwɔː(r)/ a de antes de la guerra

prey /preɪ/ n presa f; (fig) víctima f. **bird of** ~ n ave f de rapiña. • vi. ~ **on** alimentarse de; (worry) atormentar

price /praɪs/ n precio m. • vt fijar el precio de. ~**less** a inapreciable; (amusing, fam) muy divertido. ~**y** a (fam) caro

prick /prɪk/ vt/i pinchar. ~ **up one's ears** aguzar las orejas. • n pinchazo m

prickl|e /'prɪkl/ n (bot) espina f; (of animal) púa f; (sensation) picor m. **~y** a espinoso; ⟨animal⟩ lleno de púas; ⟨person⟩ quisquilloso

pride /praɪd/ n orgullo m. ~ **of place** n puesto de honor. ● vr. ~ **o.s. on** enorgullecerse de

priest /priːst/ n sacerdote m. **~hood** n sacerdocio m. **~ly** a sacerdotal

prig /prɪg/ n mojigato m. **~gish** a mojigato

prim /prɪm/ a (primmer, primmest) estirado; (prudish) gazmoño

primarily /'praɪmərɪlɪ/ adv en primer lugar

primary /'praɪmərɪ/ a primario; (chief) principal. ~ **school** n escuela f primaria

prime[1] /praɪm/ vt cebar ⟨gun⟩; (prepare) preparar; aprestar ⟨surface⟩

prime[2] /praɪm/ a principal; (first rate) excelente. ~ **minister** n primer ministro m. ● n. **be in one's** ~ estar en la flor de la vida

primer[1] /'praɪmə(r)/ n (of paint) primera mano f

primer[2] /'praɪmə(r)/ (book) silabario m

primeval /praɪ'miːvl/ a primitivo

primitive /'prɪmɪtɪv/ a primitivo

primrose /'prɪmrəʊz/ n primavera f

prince /prɪns/ n príncipe m. **~ly** a principesco. **~ss** /prɪn'ses/ n princesa f

principal /'prɪnsəpl/ a principal. ● n (of school etc) director m

principality /prɪnsɪ'pælətɪ/ n principado m

principally /'prɪnsɪpəlɪ/ adv principalmente

principle /'prɪnsəpl/ n principio m. **in** ~ en principio. **on** ~ por principio

print /prɪnt/ vt imprimir; (write in capitals) escribir con letras de molde. ● n (of finger, foot) huella f; (letters) caracteres mpl; (of design) estampado m; (picture) grabado m; (photo) copia f. **in** ~ ⟨book⟩ disponible. **out of** ~ agotado. **~ed matter** n impresos mpl. **~er** /'prɪntə(r)/ n impresor m; (machine) impresora f. **~ing** n tipografía f. **~out** n listado m

prior /'praɪə(r)/ n prior m. ● a anterior. ~ **to** antes de

priority /praɪ'ɒrətɪ/ n prioridad f

priory /'praɪərɪ/ n priorato m

prise /praɪz/ vt apalancar. ~ **open** abrir por fuerza

prism /'prɪzəm/ n prisma m

prison /'prɪzn/ n cárcel m. **~er** n prisionero m; (in prison) preso m; (under arrest) detenido m. ~ **officer** n carcelero m

pristine /'prɪstiːn/ a prístino

privacy /'prɪvəsɪ/ n intimidad f; (private life) vida f privada. **in** ~ en la intimidad

private /'praɪvət/ a privado; (confidential) personal; ⟨lessons, house⟩ particular; ⟨ceremony⟩ en la intimidad. ● n soldado m raso. **in** ~ en privado; (secretly) en secreto. ~ **eye** n (fam) detective m privado. **~ly** adv en privado; (inwardly) interiormente

privation /praɪ'veɪʃn/ n privación f

privet /'prɪvɪt/ n alheña f

privilege /'prɪvəlɪdʒ/ n privilegio m. **~d** a privilegiado

privy /'prɪvɪ/ a. ~ **to** al corriente de

prize /praɪz/ n premio m. ● a ⟨idiot etc⟩ de remate. ● vt estimar. **~fighter** n boxeador m profesional. **~giving** n reparto m de premios. **~winner** n premiado m

pro /prəʊ/ n. **~s and cons** el pro m y el contra m

probab|ility /prɒbə'bɪlətɪ/ n probabilidad f. **~le** /'prɒbəbl/ a probable. **~ly** adv probablemente

probation /prə'beɪʃn/ n prueba f; (jurid) libertad f condicional. **~ary** a de prueba

probe /prəʊb/ n sonda f; (fig) encuesta f. ● vt sondar. ● vi. ~ **into** investigar

problem /'prɒbləm/ n problema m. ● a difícil. **~atic** /-'mætɪk/ a problemático

procedure /prə'siːdʒə(r)/ n procedimiento m

proceed /prə'siːd/ vi proceder. **~ing** n procedimiento m. **~ings** /prə'siːdɪŋz/ npl (report) actas fpl; (jurid) proceso m

proceeds /'prəʊsiːdz/ npl ganancias fpl

process /'prəʊses/ n proceso m. **in** ~ **of** en vías de. **in the** ~ **of time** con el tiempo. ● vt tratar; revelar ⟨photo⟩. **~ion** /prə'seʃn/ n desfile m

procla|im /prə'kleɪm/ vt proclamar. **~mation** /prɒklə'meɪʃn/ n proclamación f

procrastinate /prəʊˈkræstɪneɪt/ *vi* aplazar, demorar, diferir

procreation /prəʊkrɪˈeɪʃn/ *n* procreación *f*

procure /prəˈkjʊə(r)/ *vt* obtener

prod /prɒd/ *vt* (*pt* **prodded**) empujar; (*with elbow*) dar un codazo a. ● *vi* dar con el dedo. ● *n* empuje *m*; (*with elbow*) codazo *m*

prodigal /ˈprɒdɪgl/ *a* pródigo

prodigious /prəˈdɪdʒəs/ *a* prodigioso

prodigy /ˈprɒdɪdʒɪ/ *n* prodigio *m*

produce /prəˈdjuːs/ *vt* (*show*) presentar; (*bring out*) sacar; poner en escena ⟨*play*⟩; (*cause*) causar; (*manufacture*) producir. /ˈprɒdjuːs/ *n* productos *mpl*. **~er** /prəˈdjuːsə(r)/ *n* productor *m*; (*in theatre*) director *m*

product /ˈprɒdʌkt/ *n* producto *m*. **~ion** /prəˈdʌkʃn/ *n* producción *f*; (*of play*) representación *f*

productiv|e /prəˈdʌktɪv/ *a* productivo. **~ity** /prɒdʌkˈtɪvətɪ/ *n* productividad *f*

profan|e /prəˈfeɪn/ *a* profano; (*blasphemous*) blasfemo. **~ity** /-ˈfænətɪ/ *n* profanidad *f*

profess /prəˈfes/ *vt* profesar; (*pretend*) pretender

profession /prəˈfeʃn/ *n* profesión *f*. **~al** *a & n* profesional (*m & f*)

professor /prəˈfesə(r)/ *n* catedrático *m*; (*Amer*) profesor *m*

proffer /ˈprɒfə(r)/ *vt* ofrecer

proficien|cy /prəˈfɪʃənsɪ/ *n* competencia *f*. **~t** /prəˈfɪʃnt/ *a* competente

profile /ˈprəʊfaɪl/ *n* perfil *m*

profit /ˈprɒfɪt/ *n* (*com*) ganancia *f*; (*fig*) provecho *m*. ● *vi*. **~ from** sacar provecho de. **~able** *a* provechoso

profound /prəˈfaʊnd/ *a* profundo. **~ly** *adv* profundamente

profus|e /prəˈfjuːs/ *a* profuso. **~ely** *adv* profusamente. **~ion** /-ʒn/ *n* profusión *f*

progeny /ˈprɒdʒənɪ/ *n* progenie *f*

prognosis /prɒgˈnəʊsɪs/ *n* (*pl* -**oses**) pronóstico *m*

program(|me) /ˈprəʊɡræm/ *n* programa *m*. ● *vt* (*pt* **programmed**) programar. **~mer** *n* programador *m*

progress /ˈprəʊgres/ *n* progreso *m*, progresos *mpl*; (*development*) desarrollo *m*. **in ~** en curso. /prəˈgres/ *vi* hacer progresos; (*develop*) desarrollarse. **~ion** /prəˈgreʃn/ *n* progresión *f*

progressive /prəˈgresɪv/ *a* progresivo; (*reforming*) progresista. **~ly** *adv* progresivamente

prohibit /prəˈhɪbɪt/ *vt* prohibir. **~ive** /-bətɪv/ *a* prohibitivo

project /prəˈdʒekt/ *vt* proyectar. ● *vi* (*stick out*) sobresalir. /ˈprɒdʒekt/ *n* próyecto *m*

projectile /prəˈdʒektaɪl/ *n* proyectil *m*

projector /prəˈdʒektə(r)/ *n* proyector *m*

proletari|an /prəʊlɪˈteərɪən/ *a & n* proletario (*m*). **~at** /prəʊlɪˈteərɪət/ *n* proletariado *m*

prolif|erate /prəˈlɪfəreɪt/ *vi* proliferar. **~eration** /-ˈreɪʃn/ *n* proliferación *f*. **~ic** /prəˈlɪfɪk/ *a* prolífico

prologue /ˈprəʊlɒg/ *n* prólogo *m*

prolong /prəˈlɒŋ/ *vt* prolongar

promenade /prɒməˈnɑːd/ *n* paseo *m*; (*along beach*) paseo *m* marítimo. ● *vt* pasear. ● *vi* pasearse. **~ concert** *n* concierto *m* (que forma parte de un festival de música clásica en Londres, en que no todo el público tiene asientos)

prominen|ce /ˈprɒmɪnəns/ *n* prominencia *f*; (*fig*) importancia *f*. **~t** /ˈprɒmɪnənt/ *a* prominente; (*important*) importante; (*conspicuous*) conspicuo

promiscu|ity /prɒmɪˈskjuːətɪ/ *n* libertinaje *m*. **~ous** /prəˈmɪskjʊəs/ *a* libertino

promis|e /ˈprɒmɪs/ *n* promesa *f*. ● *vt/i* prometer. **~ing** *a* prometedor; ⟨*person*⟩ que promete

promontory /ˈprɒməntrɪ/ *n* promontorio *m*

promot|e /prəˈməʊt/ *vt* promover. **~ion** /-ˈməʊʃn/ *n* promoción *f*

prompt /prɒmpt/ *a* pronto; (*punctual*) puntual. ● *adv* en punto. ● *vt* incitar; apuntar ⟨*actor*⟩. **~er** *n* apuntador *m*. **~ly** *adv* puntualmente. **~ness** *n* prontitud *f*

promulgate /ˈprɒməlgeɪt/ *vt* promulgar

prone /prəʊn/ *a* echado boca abajo. **~ to** propenso a

prong /prɒŋ/ *n* (*of fork*) diente *m*

pronoun /ˈprəʊnaʊn/ *n* pronombre *m*

pronounc|e /prəˈnaʊns/ *vt* pronunciar; (*declare*) declarar. **~ement** *n* declaración *f*. **~ed**

/prə'naʊnst/ *a* pronunciado;
(*noticeable*) marcado

pronunciation /prənʌnsɪ'eɪʃn/ *n*
pronunciación *f*

proof /pru:f/ *n* prueba *f*; (*of alcohol*)
graduación *f* normal. ● *a*. ~ **against**
a prueba de. ~**reading** *n* corrección *f* de pruebas

prop[1] /prɒp/ *n* puntal *m*; (*fig*) apoyo
m. ● *vt* (*pt* **propped**) apoyar. ~
against (*lean*) apoyar en

prop[2] /prɒp/ (*in theatre, fam*) accesorio *m*

propaganda /prɒpə'gændə/ *n* propaganda *f*

propagat|e /'prɒpəgeɪt/ *vt* propa-
gar. ● *vi* propagarse. ~**ion** /-'geɪʃn/
n propagación *f*

propel /prə'pel/ *vt* (*pt* **propelled**)
propulsar. ~**ler** /prə'pelə(r)/ *n* hélice *f*

propensity /prə'pensətɪ/ *n* pro-
pensión *f*

proper /'prɒpə(r)/ *a* correcto; (*suitable*) apropiado; (*gram*) propio;
(*real, fam*) verdadero. ~**ly** *adv*
correctamente

property /'prɒpətɪ/ *n* propiedad *f*;
(*things owned*) bienes *mpl*. ● *a*
inmobiliario

prophe|cy /'prɒfəsɪ/ *n* profecía *f*.
~**sy** /'prɒfɪsaɪ/ *vt/i* profetizar. ~**t**
/'prɒfɪt/ *n* profeta *m*. ~**tic**
/prə'fetɪk/ *a* profético

propitious /prə'pɪʃəs/ *a* propicio

proportion /prə'pɔ:ʃn/ *n* proporción
f. ~**al a, ~ate** *a* proporcional

propos|al /prə'pəʊzl/ *n* propuesta *f*.
~**al of marriage** oferta *f* de matrimonio. ~**e** /prə'pəʊz/ *vt* proponer.
● *vi* hacer una oferta de
matrimonio

proposition /prɒpə'zɪʃn/ *n* proposición *f*; (*project, fam*) asunto *m*

propound /prə'paʊnd/ *vt* proponer

proprietor /prə'praɪətə(r)/ *n* propietario *m*

propriety /prə'praɪətɪ/ *n* decoro *m*

propulsion /prə'pʌlʃn/ *n* propulsión
f

prosaic /prə'zeɪk/ *a* prosaico

proscribe /prə'skraɪb/ *vt* proscribir

prose /prəʊz/ *n* prosa *f*

prosecut|e /'prɒsɪkju:t/ *vt* procesar;
(*carry on*) proseguir. ~**ion** /-'kju:ʃn/
n proceso *m*. ~**or** *n* acusador *m*.
Public P~or fiscal *m*

prospect /'prɒspekt/ *n* vista *f*;
(*expectation*) perspectiva *f*.
/prə'spekt/ *vi* prospectar

prospective /prə'spektɪv/ *a* probable; (*future*) futuro

prospector /prə'spektə(r)/ *n* prospector *m*, explorador *m*

prospectus /prə'spektəs/ *n* prospecto *m*

prosper /'prɒspə(r)/ *vi* prosperar.
~**ity** /-'sperətɪ/ *n* prosperidad *f*.
~**ous** /'prɒspərəs/ *a* próspero

prostitut|e /'prɒstɪtju:t/ *n* prostituta
f. ~**ion** /-'tju:ʃn/ *n* prostitución *f*

prostrate /'prɒstreɪt/ *a* echado boca
abajo; (*fig*) postrado

protagonist /prə'tægənɪst/ *n* protagonista *m* & *f*

protect /prə'tekt/ *vt* proteger. ~**ion**
/-ʃn/ *n* protección *f*. ~**ive**
/prə'tektɪv/ *a* protector. ~**or** *n* protector *m*

protégé /'prɒtɪʒeɪ/ *n* protegido *m*.
~**e** *n* protegida *f*

protein /'prəʊti:n/ *n* proteína *f*

protest /'prəʊtest/ *n* protesta *f*.
under ~ bajo protesta. /prə'test/
vt/i protestar. ~**er** *n* (*demonstrator*)
manifestante *m* & *f*

Protestant /'prɒtɪstənt/ *a* & *n* protestante (*m* & *f*)

protocol /'prəʊtəkɒl/ *n* protocolo *m*

prototype /'prəʊtətaɪp/ *n* prototipo
m

protract /prə'trækt/ *vt* prolongar

protractor /prə'træktə(r)/ *n* trans-
portador *m*

protrude /prə'tru:d/ *vi* sobresalir

protuberance /prə'tju:bərəns/ *n*
protuberancia *f*

proud /praʊd/ *a* orgulloso. ~**ly** *adv*
orgullosamente

prove /pru:v/ *vt* probar. ● *vi*
resultar. ~**n** *a* probado

provenance /'prɒvənəns/ *n* procedencia *f*

proverb /'prɒvɜ:b/ *n* proverbio *m*.
~**ial** /prə'vɜ:bɪəl/ *a* proverbial

provide /prə'vaɪd/ *vt* proveer. ● *vi*.
~ **against** precaverse de. ~ **for**
(*allow for*) prever; mantener (*person*). ~**d** /prə'vaɪdɪd/ *conj*. ~ (**that**)
con tal que

providen|ce /'prɒvɪdəns/ *n* pro-
videncia *f*. ~**t** *a* providente. ~**tial**
/prɒvɪ'denʃl/ *a* providencial

providing /prə'vaɪdɪŋ/ *conj*. ~ **that**
con tal que

provinc|e /'prɒvɪns/ *n* provincia *f*;
(*fig*) competencia *f*. ~**ial** /prə'vɪnʃl/
a provincial

provision /prə'vɪʒn/ *n* provisión *f*; (*supply*) suministro *m*; (*stipulation*) condición *f*. **~s** *npl* comestibles *mpl*

provisional /prə'vɪʒənl/ *a* provisional. **~ly** *adv* provisionalmente

proviso /prə'vaɪzəʊ/ *n* (*pl* **-os**) condición *f*

provo|cation /prɒvə'keɪʃn/ *n* provocación *f*. **~cative** /-'vɒkətɪv/ *a* provocador. **~ke** /prə'vəʊk/ *vt* provocar

prow /praʊ/ *n* proa *f*

prowess /'praʊɪs/ *n* habilidad *f*; (*valour*) valor *m*

prowl /praʊl/ *vi* merodear. ● *n* ronda *f*. **be on the ~** merodear. **~er** *n* merodeador *m*

proximity /prɒk'sɪmətɪ/ *n* proximidad *f*

proxy /'prɒksɪ/ *n* poder *m*. **by ~** por poder

prude /pruːd/ *n* mojigato *m*

pruden|ce /'pruːdəns/ *n* prudencia *f*. **~t** /'pruːdənt/ *a* prudente. **~tly** *adv* prudentemente

prudish /'pruːdɪʃ/ *a* mojigato

prune[1] /pruːn/ *n* ciruela *f* pasa

prune[2] /pruːn/ *vt* podar

pry /praɪ/ *vi* entrometerse

psalm /sɑːm/ *n* salmo *m*

pseudo... /'sjuːdəʊ/ *pref* seudo...

pseudonym /'sjuːdənɪm/ *n* seudónimo *m*

psychiatr|ic /saɪkɪ'ætrɪk/ *a* psiquiátrico. **~ist** /saɪ'kaɪətrɪst/ *n* psiquiatra *m* & *f*. **~y** /saɪ'kaɪətrɪ/ *n* psiquiatría *f*

physic /'saɪkɪk/ *a* psíquico

psycho-analys|e /saɪkəʊ'ænəlaɪz/ *vt* psicoanalizar. **~is** /saɪkəʊ'næləsɪs/ *n* psicoanálisis *m*. **~t** /-ɪst/ *n* psicoanalista *m* & *f*

psycholog|ical /saɪkə'lɒdʒɪkl/ *a* psicológico. **~ist** /saɪ'kɒlədʒɪst/ *n* psicólogo *m*. **~y** /saɪ'kɒlədʒɪ/ *n* psicología *f*

psychopath /'saɪkəpæθ/ *n* psicópata *m* & *f*

pub /pʌb/ *n* bar *m*

puberty /'pjuːbətɪ/ *n* pubertad *f*

pubic /'pjuːbɪk/ *a* pubiano, púbico

public /'pʌblɪk/ *a* público

publican /'pʌblɪkən/ *n* tabernero *m*

publication /pʌblɪ'keɪʃn/ *n* publicación *f*

public house /pʌblɪk'haʊs/ *n* bar *m*

publicity /pʌb'lɪsətɪ/ *n* publicidad *f*

publicize /'pʌblɪsaɪz/ *vt* publicar, anunciar

publicly /'pʌblɪklɪ/ *adv* públicamente

public school /pʌblɪk'skuːl/ *n* colegio *m* privado; (*Amer*) instituto *m*

public-spirited /pʌblɪk'spɪrɪtɪd/ *a* cívico

publish /'pʌblɪʃ/ *vt* publicar. **~er** *n* editor *m*. **~ing** *n* publicación *f*

puck /pʌk/ *n* (*ice hockey*) disco *m*

pucker /'pʌkə(r)/ *vt* arrugar. ● *vi* arrugarse

pudding /'pʊdɪŋ/ *n* postre *m*; (*steamed*) budín *m*

puddle /'pʌdl/ *n* charco *m*

pudgy /'pʌdʒɪ/ *a* (**-ier, -iest**) rechoncho

puerile /'pjʊəraɪl/ *a* pueril

puff /pʌf/ *n* soplo *m*; (*for powder*) borla *f*. ● *vt/i* soplar. **~ at** chupar ⟨*pipe*⟩. **~ out** apagar ⟨*candle*⟩; (*swell up*) hinchar. **~ed** *a* (*out of breath*) sin aliento. **~ pastry** *n* hojaldre *m*. **~y** /'pʌfɪ/ *a* hinchado

pugnacious /pʌg'neɪʃəs/ *a* belicoso

pug-nosed /'pʌgnəʊzd/ *a* chato

pull /pʊl/ *vt* tirar de; sacar ⟨*tooth*⟩; torcer ⟨*muscle*⟩. **~ a face** hacer una mueca. **~ a fast one** hacer una mala jugada. **~ down** derribar ⟨*building*⟩. **~ off** quitarse; (*fig*) lograr. **~ one's weight** poner de su parte. **~ out** sacar. **~ s.o.'s leg** tomarle el pelo a uno. **~ up** (*uproot*) desarraigar; (*reprimand*) reprender. ● *vi* tirar (**at** de). **~ away** (*auto*) alejarse. **~ back** retirarse. **~ in** (*enter*) entrar; (*auto*) parar. **~ o.s. together** tranquilizarse. **~ out** (*auto*) salirse. **~ through** recobrar la salud. **~ up** (*auto*) parar. ● *n* tirón *m*; (*fig*) atracción *f*; (*influence*) influencia *f*. **give a ~** tirar

pulley /'pʊlɪ/ *n* polea *f*

pullover /'pʊləʊvə(r)/ *n* jersey *m*

pulp /pʌlp/ *n* pulpa *f*; (*for paper*) pasta *f*

pulpit /'pʊlpɪt/ *n* púlpito *m*

pulsate /'pʌlseɪt/ *vi* pulsar

pulse /pʌls/ *n* (*med*) pulso *m*

pulverize /'pʌlvəraɪz/ *vt* pulverizar

pumice /'pʌmɪs/ *n* piedra *f* pómez

pummel /'pʌml/ *vt* (*pt* **pummelled**) aporrear

pump[1] /pʌmp/ *n* bomba *f*; ● *vt* sacar con una bomba; (*fig*) sonsacar. **~ up** inflar

pump[2] /pʌmp/ (*plimsoll*) zapatilla *f* de lona; (*dancing shoe*) escarpín *m*

pumpkin /'pʌmpkɪn/ *n* calabaza *f*

pun /pʌn/ *n* juego *m* de palabras

punch[1] /pʌntʃ/ *vt* dar un puñetazo a; (*perforate*) perforar; hacer ⟨hole⟩. ● *n* puñetazo *m*; (*vigour*, *sl*) empuje *m*; (*device*) punzón *m*

punch[2] /pʌntʃ/ (*drink*) ponche *m*

punch: **~drunk** *a* aturdido a golpes. **~ line** *n* gracia *f*. **~-up** *n* riña *f*

punctilious /pʌŋk'tɪlɪəs/ *a* meticuloso

punctual /'pʌŋktʃʊəl/ *a* puntual. **~ity** /-'æləti/ *n* puntualidad *f*. **~ly** *adv* puntualmente

punctuat|e /'pʌŋktʃʊeɪt/ *vt* puntuar. **~ion** /-'eɪʃn/ *n* puntuación *f*

puncture /'pʌŋktʃə(r)/ *n* (*in tyre*) pinchazo *m*. ● *vt* pinchar. ● *vi* pincharse

pundit /'pʌndɪt/ *n* experto *m*

pungen|cy /'pʌndʒənsɪ/ *n* acritud *f*; (*fig*) mordacidad *f*. **~t** /'pʌndʒənt/ *a* acre; ⟨remark⟩ mordaz

punish /'pʌnɪʃ/ *vt* castigar. **~able** *a* castigable. **~ment** *n* castigo *m*

punitive /'pju:nɪtɪv/ *a* punitivo

punk /pʌŋk/ *a* ⟨music, person⟩ punk

punnet /'pʌnɪt/ *n* canastilla *f*

punt[1] /pʌnt/ *n* (*boat*) batea *f*

punt[2] /pʌnt/ *vi* apostar. **~er** *n* apostante *m & f*

puny /'pju:nɪ/ *a* (**-ier**, **-iest**) diminuto; (*weak*) débil; (*petty*) insignificante

pup /pʌp/ *n* cachorro *m*

pupil[1] /'pju:pl/ *n* alumno *m*

pupil[2] /'pju:pl/ (*of eye*) pupila *f*

puppet /'pʌpɪt/ *n* títere *m*

puppy /'pʌpɪ/ *n* cachorro *m*

purchase /'pɜ:tʃəs/ *vt* comprar. ● *n* compra *f*. **~r** *n* comprador *m*

pur|e /'pjʊə(r)/ *a* (**-er**, **-est**) puro. **~ely** *adv* puramente. **~ity** *n* pureza *f*

purée /'pjʊəreɪ/ *n* puré *m*

purgatory /'pɜ:gətrɪ/ *n* purgatorio *m*

purge /pɜ:dʒ/ *vt* purgar. ● *n* purga *f*

purif|ication /pjʊərɪfɪ'keɪʃn/ *n* purificación *f*. **~y** /'pjʊərɪfaɪ/ *vt* purificar

purist /'pjʊərɪst/ *n* purista *m & f*

puritan /'pjʊərɪtən/ *n* puritano *m*. **~ical** /-'tænɪkl/ *a* puritano

purl /pɜ:l/ *n* (*knitting*) punto *m* del revés

purple /'pɜ:pl/ *a* purpúreo, morado. ● *n* púrpura *f*

purport /pə'pɔ:t/ *vt*. **~ to be** pretender ser

purpose /'pɜ:pəs/ *n* propósito *m*; (*determination*) resolución *f*. **on ~** a propósito. **to no ~** en vano. **~-built** *a* construido especialmente. **~ful** *a* (*resolute*) resuelto. **~ly** *adv* a propósito

purr /pɜ:(r)/ *vi* ronronear

purse /pɜ:s/ *n* monedero *m*; (*Amer*) bolso *m*, cartera *f* (*LAm*). ● *vt* fruncir

pursu|e /pə'sju:/ *vt* perseguir, seguir. **~er** *n* perseguidor *m*. **~it** /pə'sju:t/ *n* persecución *f*; (*fig*) ocupación *f*

purveyor /pə'veɪə(r)/ *n* proveedor *m*

pus /pʌs/ *n* pus *m*

push /pʊʃ/ *vt* empujar; apretar ⟨button⟩. ● *vi* empujar. ● *n* empuje *m*; (*effort*) esfuerzo *m*; (*drive*) dinamismo *m*. **at a ~** en caso de necesidad. **get the ~** (*sl*) ser despedido. **~ aside** *vt* apartar. **~ back** *vt* hacer retroceder. **~ off** *vi* (*sl*) marcharse. **~ on** *vi* seguir adelante. **~ up** *vt* levantar. **~-button telephone** *n* teléfono *m* de teclas. **~-chair** *n* sillita *f* con ruedas. **~ing** /'pʊʃɪŋ/ *a* ambicioso. **~-over** *n* (*fam*) cosa *f* muy fácil, pan comido. **~y** *a* (*pej*) ambicioso

puss /pʊs/ *n* minino *m*

put /pʊt/ *vt* (*pt* put, *pres p* putting) poner; (*express*) expresar; (*say*) decir; (*estimate*) estimar; hacer ⟨question⟩. **~ across** comunicar; (*deceive*) engañar. **~ aside** poner aparte. **~ away** guardar. **~ back** devolver; retrasar ⟨clock⟩. **~ by** guardar; ahorrar ⟨money⟩. **~ down** depositar; (*suppress*) suprimir; (*write*) apuntar; (*kill*) sacrificar. **~ forward** avanzar. **~ in** introducir; (*submit*) presentar. **~ in for** pedir. **~ off** aplazar; (*disconcert*) desconcertar. **~ on** (*wear*) ponerse; cobrar ⟨speed⟩; encender ⟨light⟩. **~ one's foot down** mantenerse firme. **~ out** (*extinguish*) apagar; (*inconvenience*) incomodar; extender ⟨hand⟩; (*disconcert*) desconcertar. **~ to sea** hacerse a la mar. **~ through** (*phone*) poner. **~ up** levantar; subir ⟨price⟩; alojar ⟨guest⟩. **~ up with** soportar. **stay ~** (*fam*) no moverse

putrefy /'pju:trɪfaɪ/ *vi* pudrirse

putt /pʌt/ *n* (*golf*) golpe *m* suave

putty /'pʌtɪ/ *n* masilla *f*

put-up /'pʊtʌp/ *a*. **~ job** *n* confabulación *f*

puzzl|e /'pʌzl/ *n* enigma *m*; (*game*) rompecabezas *m invar*. ● *vt* dejar perplejo. ● *vi* calentarse los sesos. ~**ing** *a* incomprensible; (*odd*) curioso

pygmy /'pɪgmɪ/ *n* pigmeo *m*

pyjamas /pə'dʒɑːməz/ *npl* pijama *m*

pylon /'paɪlən/ *n* pilón *m*

pyramid /'pɪrəmɪd/ *n* pirámide *f*

python /'paɪθn/ *n* pitón *m*

Q

quack[1] /kwæk/ *n* (*of duck*) graznido *m*

quack[2] /kwæk/ (*person*) charlatán *m*. ~ **doctor** *n* curandero *m*

quadrangle /'kwɒdræŋgl/ *n* cuadrilátero *m*; (*court*) patio *m*

quadruped /'kwɒdruped/ *n* cuadrúpedo *m*

quadruple /'kwɒdrupl/ *a & n* cuádruplo (*m*). ● *vt* cuadruplicar. ~**t** /-plət/ *n* cuatrillizo *m*

quagmire /'kwægmaɪə(r)/ *n* ciénaga *f*; (*fig*) atolladero *m*

quail /kweɪl/ *n* codorniz *f*

quaint /kweɪnt/ *a* (**-er, -est**) pintoresco; (*odd*) curioso

quake /kweɪk/ *vi* temblar. ● *n* (*fam*) terremoto *m*

Quaker /'kweɪkə(r)/ *n* cuáquero (*m*)

qualification /kwɒlɪfɪ'keɪʃn/ *n* título *m*; (*requirement*) requisito *m*; (*ability*) capacidad *f*; (*fig*) reserva *f*

qualif|ied /'kwɒlɪfaɪd/ *a* cualificado; (*limited*) limitado; (*with degree, diploma*) titulado. ~**y** /'kwɒlɪfaɪ/ *vt* calificar; (*limit*) limitar. ● *vi* sacar el título; (*sport*) clasificarse; (*fig*) llenar los requisitos

qualitative /'kwɒlɪtətɪv/ *a* cualitativo

quality /'kwɒlɪtɪ/ *n* calidad *f*; (*attribute*) cualidad *f*

qualm /kwɑːm/ *n* escrúpulo *m*

quandary /'kwɒndrɪ/ *n*. **in a** ~ en un dilema

quantitative /'kwɒntɪtətɪv/ *a* cuantitativo

quantity /'kwɒntɪtɪ/ *n* cantidad *f*

quarantine /'kwɒrəntiːn/ *n* cuarentena *f*

quarrel /'kwɒrəl/ *n* riña *f*. ● *vi* (*pt* **quarrelled**) reñir. ~**some** *a* pendenciero

quarry[1] /'kwɒrɪ/ *n* (*excavation*) cantera *f*

quarry[2] /'kwɒrɪ/ *n* (*animal*) presa *f*

quart /kwɔːt/ *n* (poco más de un) litro *m*

quarter /'kwɔːtə(r)/ *n* cuarto *m*; (*of year*) trimestre *m*; (*district*) barrio *m*. **from all** ~**s** de todas partes. ● *vt* dividir en cuartos; (*mil*) acuartelar. ~**s** *npl* alojamiento *m*

quartermaster /'kwɔːtəmɑːstə(r)/ *n* intendente *m*

quarter: ** ~-final** *n* cuarto *m* de final. ~**ly** *a* trimestral. ● *adv* cada tres meses

quartet /kwɔː'tet/ *n* cuarteto *m*

quartz /kwɔːts/ *n* cuarzo *m*. ● *a* ⟨*watch etc*⟩ de cuarzo

quash /kwɒʃ/ *vt* anular

quasi.. /'kweɪsaɪ/ *pref* cuasi...

quaver /'kweɪvə(r)/ *vi* temblar. ● *n* (*mus*) corchea *f*

quay /kiː/ *n* muelle *m*

queasy /'kwiːzɪ/ *a* ⟨*stomach*⟩ delicado

queen /kwiːn/ *n* reina *f*. ~ **mother** *n* reina *f* madre

queer /kwɪə(r)/ *a* (**-er, -est**) extraño; (*dubious*) sospechoso; (*ill*) indispuesto. ● *n* (*sl*) homosexual *m*

quell /kwel/ *vt* reprimir

quench /kwentʃ/ *vt* apagar; sofocar ⟨*desire*⟩

querulous /'kwerʊləs/ *a* quejumbroso

query /'kwɪərɪ/ *n* pregunta *f*. ● *vt* preguntar; (*doubt*) poner en duda

quest /kwest/ *n* busca *f*

question /'kwestʃən/ *n* pregunta *f*; (*for discussion*) cuestión *f*. **in** ~ en cuestión. **out of the** ~ imposible. **without** ~ sin duda. ● *vt* preguntar; ⟨*police etc*⟩ interrogar; (*doubt*) poner en duda. ~**able** /'kwestʃənəbl/ *a* discutible. ~ **mark** *n* signo *m* de interrogación. ~**naire** /kwestʃə'neə(r)/ *n* cuestionario *m*

queue /kjuː/ *n* cola *f*. ● *vi* (*pres p* **queuing**) hacer cola

quibble /'kwɪbl/ *vi* discutir; (*split hairs*) sutilizar

quick /kwɪk/ *a* (**-er, -est**) rápido. **be** ~! ¡date prisa! ● *adv* rápidamente. ● *n*. **to the** ~ en lo vivo. ~**en** /'kwɪkən/ *vt* acelerar. ● *vi* acelerarse. ~**ly** *adv* rápidamente. ~**sand** /'kwɪksænd/ *n* arena *f* movediza. ~**-tempered** *a* irascible

quid /kwɪd/ *n invar* (*sl*) libra *f* (esterlina)

quiet /'kwaɪət/ *a* (**-er, -est**) tranquilo; (*silent*) callado; (*discreet*) discreto. ● *n* tranquilidad *f*. **on the ~** a escondidas. **~en** /'kwaɪətn/ *vt* calmar. ● *vi* calmarse. **~ly** *adv* tranquilamente; (*silently*) silenciosamente; (*discreetly*) discretamente. **~ness** *n* tranquilidad *f*

quill /kwɪl/ *n* pluma *f*

quilt /kwɪlt/ *n* edredón *m*. ● *vt* acolchar

quince /kwɪns/ *n* membrillo *m*

quinine /kwɪ'niːn/ *n* quinina *f*

quintessence /kwɪn'tesns/ *n* quintaesencia *f*

quintet /kwɪn'tet/ *n* quinteto *m*

quintuplet /'kwɪntjuːplət/ *n* quintillizo *m*

quip /kwɪp/ *n* ocurrencia *f*

quirk /kwɜːk/ *n* peculiaridad *f*

quit /kwɪt/ *vt* (*pt* **quitted**) dejar. ● *vi* abandonar; (*leave*) marcharse; (*resign*) dimitir. **~ doing** (*cease, Amer*) dejar de hacer

quite /kwaɪt/ *adv* bastante; (*completely*) totalmente; (*really*) verdaderamente. **~ (so)!** ¡claro! **~ a few** bastante

quits /kwɪts/ *a* a la par. **call it ~** darlo por terminado

quiver /'kwɪvə(r)/ *vi* temblar

quixotic /kwɪk'sɒtɪk/ *a* quijotesco

quiz /kwɪz/ *n* (*pl* **quizzes**) serie *f* de preguntas; (*game*) concurso *m*. ● *vt* (*pt* **quizzed**) interrogar. **~zical** /'kwɪzɪkl/ *a* burlón

quorum /'kwɔːrəm/ *n* quórum *m*

quota /'kwəʊtə/ *n* cuota *f*

quot|ation /kwəʊ'teɪʃn/ *n* cita *f*; (*price*) presupuesto *m*. **~ation marks** *npl* comillas *fpl*. **~e** /kwəʊt/ *vt* citar; (*com*) cotizar. ● *n* (*fam*) cita *f*; (*price*) presupuesto *m*. **in ~es** *npl* entre comillas

quotient /'kwəʊʃnt/ *n* cociente *m*

R

rabbi /'ræbaɪ/ *n* rabino *m*

rabbit /'ræbɪt/ *n* conejo *m*

rabble /'ræbl/ *n* gentío *m*. **the ~** (*pej*) el populacho *m*

rabi|d /'ræbɪd/ *a* feroz; (*dog*) rabioso. **~es** /'reɪbiːz/ *n* rabia *f*

race¹ /reɪs/ *n* carrera *f*. ● *vt* hacer correr (*horse*); acelerar (*engine*). ● *vi* (*run*) correr, ir corriendo; (*rush*) ir de prisa

race² /reɪs/ (*group*) raza *f*

race: ~course /'reɪskɔːs/ *n* hipódromo *m*. **~horse** /'reɪshɔːs/ *n* caballo *m* de carreras. **~riots** /'reɪsraɪəts/ *npl* disturbios *mpl* raciales. **~track** /'reɪstræk/ *n* hipódromo *m*

racial /'reɪʃl/ *a* racial. **~ism** /-ɪzəm/ *n* racismo *m*

racing /'reɪsɪŋ/ *n* carreras *fpl*. **~ car** *n* coche *m* de carreras

racis|m /'reɪsɪzəm/ *n* racismo *m*. **~t** /'reɪsɪst/ *a & n* racista (*m & f*)

rack¹ /ræk/ *n* (*shelf*) estante *m*; (*for luggage*) rejilla *f*; (*for plates*) escurreplatos *m invar*. ● *vt*. **~ one's brains** devanarse los sesos

rack² /ræk/ *n*. **go to ~ and ruin** quedarse en la ruina

racket¹ /'rækɪt/ *n* (*for sports*) raqueta *f*

racket² /'rækɪt/ *n* (*din*) alboroto *m*; (*swindle*) estafa *f*. **~eer** /-ə'tɪə(r)/ *n* estafador *m*

raconteur /rækɒn'tɜː/ *n* anecdotista *m & f*

racy /'reɪsɪ/ *a* (**-ier, -iest**) vivo

radar /'reɪdɑː(r)/ *n* radar *m*

radian|ce /'reɪdɪəns/ *n* resplandor *m*. **~t** /'reɪdɪənt/ *a* radiante. **~tly** *adv* con resplandor

radiat|e /'reɪdɪeɪt/ *vt* irradiar. ● *vi* divergir. **~ion** /-'eɪʃn/ *n* radiación *f*. **~or** /'reɪdɪeɪtə(r)/ *n* radiador *m*

radical /'rædɪkl/ *a & n* radical (*m*)

radio /'reɪdɪəʊ/ *n* (*pl* **-os**) radio *f*. ● *vt* transmitir por radio

radioactiv|e /reɪdɪəʊ'æktɪv/ *a* radiactivo. **~ity** /-'tɪvətɪ/ *n* radiactividad *f*

radiograph|er /reɪdɪ'ɒɡrəfə(r)/ *n* radiógrafo *m*. **~y** *n* radiografía *f*

radish /'rædɪʃ/ *n* rábano *m*

radius /'reɪdɪəs/ *n* (*pl* **-dii** /-dɪaɪ/) radio *m*

raffish /'ræfɪʃ/ *a* disoluto

raffle /'ræfl/ *n* rifa *f*

raft /rɑːft/ *n* balsa *f*

rafter /'rɑːftə(r)/ *n* cabrio *m*

rag¹ /ræɡ/ *n* andrajo *m*; (*for wiping*) trapo *m*; (*newspaper*) periodicucho *m*. **in ~s** (*person*) andrajoso; (*clothes*) hecho jirones

rag² /ræɡ/ *n* (*univ*) festival *m* estudiantil; (*prank, fam*) broma *f* pesada. ● *vt* (*pt* **ragged**) (*sl*) tomar el pelo a

ragamuffin /'rægəmʌfɪn/ *n* granuja *m*, golfo *m*

rage /reɪdʒ/ *n* rabia *f*; (*fashion*) moda *f*. ● *vi* estar furioso; ‹*storm*› bramar

ragged /'rægɪd/ *a* ‹person› andrajoso; ‹*clothes*› hecho jirones; ‹*edge*› mellado

raid /reɪd/ *n* (*mil*) incursión *f*; (*by police, etc*) redada *f*; (*by thieves*) asalto *m*. ● *vt* (*mil*) atacar; ‹*police*› hacer una redada en; ‹*thieves*› asaltar. **~er** *n* invasor *m*; (*thief*) ladrón *m*

rail[1] /reɪl/ *n* barandilla *f*; (*for train*) riel *m*; (*rod*) barra *f*. **by ~** por ferrocarril

rail[2] /reɪl/ *vi*. **~ against, ~ at** insultar

railing /'reɪlɪŋ/ *n* barandilla *f*; (*fence*) verja *f*

rail|road /'reɪlrəʊd/ *n* (*Amer*), **~way** /'reɪlweɪ/ *n* ferrocarril *m*. **~way-man** (*pl* **-men**) ferroviario *m*. **~way station** *n* estación *f* de ferrocarril

rain /reɪn/ *n* lluvia *f*. ● *vi* llover. **~bow** /'reɪnbəʊ/ *n* arco *m* iris. **~coat** /'reɪnkəʊt/ *n* impermeable *m*. **~fall** /'reɪnfɔːl/ *n* precipitación *f*. **~water** *n* agua *f* de lluvia. **~y** /'reɪnɪ/ *a* (**-ier, -iest**) lluvioso

raise /reɪz/ *vt* levantar; (*breed*) criar; obtener ‹*money etc*›; hacer ‹*question*›; plantear ‹*problem*›; subir ‹*price*›. **~ one's glass** to brindar por. **~ one's hat** descubrirse. ● *n* (*Amer*) aumento *m*

raisin /'reɪzn/ *n* (uva *f*) pasa *f*

rake[1] /reɪk/ *n* rastrillo *m*. ● *vt* rastrillar; (*search*) buscar en. **~ up** remover

rake[2] /reɪk/ *n* (*man*) calavera *m*

rake-off /'reɪkɒf/ *n* (*fam*) comisión *f*

rally /'rælɪ/ *vt* reunir; (*revive*) reanimar. ● *vi* reunirse; (*in sickness*) recuperarse. ● *n* reunión *f*; (*recovery*) recuperación *f*; (*auto*) rallye *m*

ram /ræm/ *n* carnero *m*. ● *vt* (*pt* **rammed**) (*thrust*) meter por la fuerza; (*crash into*) chocar con

rambl|e /'ræmbl/ *n* excursión *f* a pie. ● *vi* ir de paseo; (*in speech*) divagar. **~e on** divagar. **~er** *n* excursionista *m* & *f*. **~ing** *a* ‹speech› divagador

ramification /ræmɪfɪ'keɪʃn/ *n* ramificación *f*

ramp /ræmp/ *n* rampa *f*

rampage /ræm'peɪdʒ/ *vi* alborotarse. /'ræmpeɪdʒ/ *n*. **go on the ~** alborotarse

rampant /'ræmpənt/ *a*. **be ~** ‹disease etc› estar extendido

rampart /'ræmpɑːt/ *n* muralla *f*

ramshackle /'ræmʃækl/ *a* desvencijado

ran /ræn/ *see* **run**

ranch /rɑːntʃ/ *n* hacienda *f*

rancid /'rænsɪd/ *a* rancio

rancour /'ræŋkə(r)/ *n* rencor *m*

random /'rændəm/ *a* hecho al azar; (*chance*) fortuito. ● *n*. **at ~** al azar

randy /'rændɪ/ *a* (**-ier, -iest**) lujurioso, cachondo (*fam*)

rang /ræŋ/ *see* **ring**[2]

range /reɪndʒ/ *n* alcance *m*; (*distance*) distancia *f*; (*series*) serie *f*; (*of mountains*) cordillera *f*; (*extent*) extensión *f*; (*com*) surtido *m*; (*open area*) dehesa *f*; (*stove*) cocina *f* económica. ● *vi* extenderse; (*vary*) variar

ranger /'reɪndʒə(r)/ *n* guardabosque *m*

rank[1] /ræŋk/ *n* posición *f*, categoría *f*; (*row*) fila *f*; (*for taxis*) parada *f*. **the ~ and file** la masa *f*. ● *vt* clasificar. ● *vi* clasificarse. **~s** *npl* soldados *mpl* rasos

rank[2] /ræŋk/ *a* (**-er, -est**) exuberante; (*smell*) fétido; (*fig*) completo

rankle /'ræŋkl/ *vi* (*fig*) causar rencor

ransack /'rænsæk/ *vt* registrar; (*pillage*) saquear

ransom /'rænsəm/ *n* rescate *m*. **hold s.o. to ~** exigir rescate por uno; (*fig*) hacer chantaje a uno. ● *vt* rescatar; (*redeem*) redimir

rant /rænt/ *vi* vociferar

rap /ræp/ *n* golpe *m* seco. ● *vt/i* (*pt* **rapped**) golpear

rapacious /rə'peɪʃs/ *a* rapaz

rape /reɪp/ *vt* violar. ● *n* violación *f*

rapid /'ræpɪd/ *a* rápido. **~ity** /rə'pɪdətɪ/ *n* rapidez *f*. **~s** /'ræpɪdz/ *npl* rápido *m*

rapist /'reɪpɪst/ *n* violador *m*

rapport /ræ'pɔː(r)/ *n* armonía *f*, relación *f*

rapt /ræpt/ *a* ‹attention› profundo. **~ in** absorto en

raptur|e /'ræptʃə(r)/ *n* éxtasis *m*. **~ous** *a* extático

rare[1] /reə(r)/ *a* (**-er, -est**) raro

rare[2] /reə(r)/ *a* (*culin*) poco hecho

rarefied /'reərɪfaɪd/ *a* enrarecido

rarely /'reəlɪ/ adv raramente

rarity /'reərətɪ/ n rareza f

raring /'reərɪŋ/ a (fam). ~ **to** impaciente por

rascal /'rɑːskl/ n tunante m & f

rash[1] /ræʃ/ a (-er, -est) imprudente, precipitado

rash[2] /ræʃ/ n erupción f

rasher /'ræʃə(r)/ n loncha f

rash|ly /'ræʃlɪ/ adv imprudentemente, a la ligera. ~**ness** n imprudencia f

rasp /rɑːsp/ n (file) escofina f

raspberry /'rɑːzbrɪ/ n frambuesa f

rasping /'rɑːspɪŋ/ a áspero

rat /ræt/ n rata f. ● vi (pt ratted). ~ **on** (desert) desertar; (inform on) denunciar, chivarse

rate /reɪt/ n (ratio) proporción f; (speed) velocidad f; (price) precio m; (of interest) tipo m. **at any** ~ de todas formas. **at the** ~ **of** (on the basis of) a razón de. **at this** ~ así. ● vt valorar; (consider) considerar; (deserve, Amer) merecer. ● vi ser considerado. ~**able value** n valor m imponible. ~**payer** /'reɪtpeɪə(r)/ n contribuyente m & f. ~**s** npl (taxes) impuestos mpl municipales

rather /'rɑːðə(r)/ adv mejor dicho; (fairly) bastante; (a little) un poco. ● int claro. **I would** ~ **not** prefiero no

ratif|ication /rætɪfɪ'keɪʃn/ n ratificación f. ~**y** /'rætɪfaɪ/ vt ratificar

rating /'reɪtɪŋ/ n clasificación f; (sailor) marinero m; (number, TV) índice m

ratio /'reɪʃɪəʊ/ n (pl -os) proporción f

ration /'ræʃn/ n ración f. ● vt racionar

rational /'ræʃənəl/ a racional. ~**ize** /'ræʃənəlaɪz/ vt racionalizar

rat race /'rætreɪs/ n lucha f incesante para triunfar

rattle /'rætl/ vi traquetear. ● vt (shake) agitar; (sl) desconcertar. ● n traqueteo m; (toy) sonajero m. ~ **off** (fig) decir de corrida

rattlesnake /'rætlsneɪk/ n serpiente f de cascabel

ratty /'rætɪ/ a (-ier, -iest) (sl) irritable

raucous /'rɔːkəs/ a estridente

ravage /'rævɪdʒ/ vt estragar. ~**s** /'rævɪdʒɪz/ npl estragos mpl

rave /reɪv/ vi delirar; (in anger) enfurecerse. ~ **about** entusiasmarse por

raven /'reɪvn/ n cuervo m. ● a ⟨hair⟩ negro

ravenous /'rævənəs/ a voraz; ⟨person⟩ hambriento. **be** ~ morirse de hambre

ravine /rə'viːn/ n barranco m

raving /'reɪvɪŋ/ a. ~ **mad** loco de atar. ~**s** npl divagaciones fpl

ravish /'rævɪʃ/ vt (rape) violar. ~**ing** a (enchanting) encantador

raw /rɔː/ a (-er, -est) crudo; (not processed) bruto; ⟨wound⟩ en carne viva; (inexperienced) inexperto; ⟨weather⟩ crudo. ~ **deal** n tratamiento m injusto, injusticia f. ~ **materials** npl materias fpl primas

ray /reɪ/ n rayo m

raze /reɪz/ vt arrasar

razor /'reɪzə(r)/ n navaja f de afeitar; (electric) maquinilla f de afeitar

Rd abbr (Road) C/, Calle f

re[1] /riː/ prep con referencia a. ● pref re...

re[2] /reɪ/ n (mus, second note of any musical scale) re m

reach /riːtʃ/ vt alcanzar; (extend) extender; (arrive at) llegar a; (achieve) lograr; (hand over) pasar, dar. ● vi extenderse. ● n alcance m; (of river) tramo m recto. **within** ~ **of** al alcance de; (close to) a corta distancia de

react /rɪ'ækt/ vi reaccionar. ~**ion** /rɪ'ækʃn/ n reacción f. ~**ionary** a & n reaccionario (m)

reactor /rɪ'æktə(r)/ n reactor m

read /riːd/ vt (pt read /red/) leer; (study) estudiar; (interpret) interpretar. ● vi leer; ⟨instrument⟩ indicar. ● n (fam) lectura f. ~ **out** vt leer en voz alta. ~**able** a interesante, agradable; (clear) legible. ~**er** /'riːdə(r)/ n lector m. ~**ership** n lectores m

readi|ly /'redɪlɪ/ adv (willingly) de buena gana; (easily) fácilmente. ~**ness** /'redɪnɪs/ n prontitud f. **in** ~**ness** preparado, listo

reading /'riːdɪŋ/ n lectura f

readjust /riːə'dʒʌst/ vt reajustar. ● vi readaptarse (**to** a)

ready /'redɪ/ a (-ier, -iest) listo, preparado; (quick) pronto. ~**-made** a confeccionado. ~ **money** n dinero m contante. ~ **reckoner** n baremo m. **get** ~ preparase

real /rɪəl/ a verdadero. ● adv (Amer, fam) verdaderamente. ~ **estate** n bienes mpl raíces

realis|m /'rɪəlɪzəm/ n realismo m. **~t** /'rɪəlɪst/ n realista m & f. **~tic** /-'lɪstɪk/ a realista. **~tically** /-'lɪstɪklɪ/ adv de manera realista

reality /rɪ'ælətɪ/ n realidad f

realiz|ation /rɪəlaɪ'zeɪʃn/ n comprensión f; (com) realización f. **~e** /'rɪəlaɪz/ vt darse cuenta de; (fulfil, com) realizar

really /'rɪəlɪ/ adv verdaderamente

realm /relm/ n reino m

ream /riːm/ n resma f

reap /riːp/ vt segar; (fig) cosechar

re: ~appear /riːə'pɪə(r)/ vi reaparecer. **~appraisal** /riːə'preɪzl/ n revaluación f

rear[1] /rɪə(r)/ n parte f de atrás. ● a posterior, trasero

rear[2] /rɪə(r)/ vt (bring up, breed) criar. **~ one's head** levantar la cabeza. ● vi ⟨horse⟩ encabritarse. **~ up** ⟨horse⟩ encabritarse

rear: ~admiral n contraalmirante m. **~guard** /'rɪəgɑːd/ n retaguardia f

re: ~arm /riː'ɑːm/ vt rearmar. ● vi rearmarse. **~arrange** /riːə'reɪndʒ/ vt arreglar de otra manera

reason /'riːzn/ n razón f, motivo m. **within ~** dentro de lo razonable. ● vi razonar

reasonable /'riːzənəbl/ a razonable

reasoning /'riːznɪŋ/ n razonamiento m

reassur|ance /riːə'ʃʊərəns/ n promesa f tranquilizadora; (guarantee) garantía f. **~e** /riːə'ʃʊə(r)/ vt tranquilizar

rebate /'riːbeɪt/ n reembolso m; (discount) rebaja f

rebel /'rebl/ n rebelde m & f. /rɪ'bel/ vi (pt rebelled) rebelarse. **~lion** n rebelión f. **~lious** a rebelde

rebound /rɪ'baʊnd/ vi rebotar; (fig) recaer. /'riːbaʊnd/ n rebote m. **on the ~** (fig) por reacción

rebuff /rɪ'bʌf/ vt rechazar. ● n desaire m

rebuild /riː'bɪld/ vt (pt rebuilt) reconstruir

rebuke /rɪ'bjuːk/ vt reprender. ● n reprensión f

rebuttal /rɪ'bʌtl/ n refutación f

recall /rɪ'kɔːl/ vt (call s.o. back) llamar; (remember) recordar. ● n llamada f

recant /rɪ'kænt/ vi retractarse

recap /'riːkæp/ vt/i (pt recapped) (fam) resumir. ● n (fam) resumen m

recapitulat|e /riːkə'pɪtʃʊleɪt/ vt/i resumir. **~ion** /-'leɪʃn/ n resumen m

recapture /riː'kæptʃə(r)/ vt recobrar; (recall) hacer revivir

reced|e /rɪ'siːd/ vi retroceder. **~ing** a ⟨forehead⟩ huidizo

receipt /rɪ'siːt/ n recibo m. **~s** npl (com) ingresos mpl

receive /rɪ'siːv/ vt recibir. **~r** /-ə(r)/ n (of stolen goods) perista m & f; (of phone) auricular m

recent /'riːsnt/ a reciente. **~ly** adv recientemente

receptacle /rɪ'septəkl/ n recipiente m

reception /rɪ'sepʃn/ n recepción f; (welcome) acogida f. **~ist** n recepcionista m & f

receptive /rɪ'septɪv/ a receptivo

recess /rɪ'ses/ n hueco m; (holiday) vacaciones fpl; (fig) parte f recóndita

recession /rɪ'seʃn/ n recesión f

recharge /riː'tʃɑːdʒ/ vt cargar de nuevo, recargar

recipe /'resəpɪ/ n receta f

recipient /rɪ'sɪpɪənt/ n recipiente m & f; (of letter) destinatario m

reciprocal /rɪ'sɪprəkl/ a recíproco

reciprocate /rɪ'sɪprəkeɪt/ vt corresponder a

recital /rɪ'saɪtl/ n (mus) recital m

recite /rɪ'saɪt/ vt recitar; (list) enumerar

reckless /'reklɪs/ a imprudente. **~ly** adv imprudentemente. **~ness** n imprudencia f

reckon /'rekən/ vt/i calcular; (consider) considerar; (think) pensar. **~ on** (rely) contar con. **~ing** n cálculo m

reclaim /rɪ'kleɪm/ vt reclamar; recuperar ⟨land⟩

reclin|e /rɪ'klaɪn/ vi recostarse. **~ing** a acostado; ⟨seat⟩ reclinable

recluse /rɪ'kluːs/ n solitario m

recogni|tion /rekəg'nɪʃn/ n reconocimiento m. **beyond ~tion** irreconocible. **~ze** /'rekəgnaɪz/ vt reconocer

recoil /rɪ'kɔɪl/ vi retroceder. ● n (of gun) culatazo m

recollect /rekə'lekt/ vt recordar. **~ion** /-ʃn/ n recuerdo m

recommend /rekə'mend/ vt recomendar. **~ation** /-'deɪʃn/ n recomendación f

recompense /'rekəmpens/ *vt* recompensar. ● *n* recompensa *f*

reconcil|e /'rekənsaɪl/ *vt* reconciliar ⟨*people*⟩; conciliar ⟨*facts*⟩. **~e o.s.** resignarse (**to** a). **~iation** /-sɪlɪ'eɪʃn/ *n* reconciliación *f*

recondition /ri:kən'dɪʃn/ *vt* reacondicionar, arreglar

reconnaissance /rɪ'kɒnɪsns/ *n* reconocimiento *m*

reconnoitre /rekə'nɔɪtə(r)/ *vt* (*pres p* -**tring**) (*mil*) reconocer. ● *vi* hacer un reconocimiento

re: **~consider** /ri:kən'sɪdə(r)/ *vt* volver a considerar. **~construct** /ri:kən'strʌkt/ *vt* reconstruir. **~construction** /-ʃn/ *n* reconstrucción *f*

record /rɪ'kɔ:d/ *vt* (*in register*) registrar; (*in diary*) apuntar; (*mus*) grabar. /'rekɔ:d/ *n* (*file*) documentación *f*, expediente *m*; (*mus*) disco *m*; (*sport*) récord *m*. **off the ~** en confianza. **~er** /rɪ'kɔ:də(r)/ *n* registrador *m*; (*mus*) flauta *f* dulce. **~ing** *n* grabación *f*. **~player** *n* tocadiscos *m invar*

recount /rɪ'kaʊnt/ *vt* contar, relatar, referir

re-count /ri:'kaʊnt/ *vt* recontar. /'ri:kaʊnt/ *n* (*pol*) recuento *m*

recoup /rɪ'ku:p/ *vt* recuperar

recourse /rɪ'kɔ:s/ *n* recurso *m*. **have ~ to** recurrir a

recover /rɪ'kʌvə(r)/ *vt* recuperar. ● *vi* reponerse. **~y** *n* recuperación *f*

recreation /rekrɪ'eɪʃn/ *n* recreo *m*. **~al** *a* de recreo

recrimination /rɪkrɪmɪ'neɪʃn/ *n* recriminación *f*

recruit /rɪ'kru:t/ *n* recluta *m*. ● *vt* reclutar. **~ment** *n* reclutamiento *m*

rectang|le /'rektæŋgl/ *n* rectángulo *m*. **~ular** /-'tæŋgjʊlə(r)/ *a* rectangular

rectif|ication /rektɪfɪ'keɪʃn/ *n* rectificación *f*. **~y** /'rektɪfaɪ/ *vt* rectificar

rector /'rektə(r)/ *n* párroco *m*; (*of college*) rector *m*. **~y** *n* rectoría *f*

recumbent /rɪ'kʌmbənt/ *a* recostado

recuperat|e /rɪ'ku:pəreɪt/ *vt* recuperar. ● *vi* reponerse. **~ion** /-'reɪʃn/ *n* recuperación *f*

recur /rɪ'kɜ:(r)/ *vi* (*pt* **recurred**) repetirse. **~rence** /rɪ'kʌrns/ *n* repetición *f*. **~rent** /rɪ'kʌrənt/ *a* repetido

recycle /ri:'saɪkl/ *vt* reciclar

red /red/ *a* (**redder**, **reddest**) rojo. ● *n* rojo. **in the ~** ⟨*account*⟩ en descubierto. **~breast** /'redbrest/ *n* petirrojo *m*. **~brick** /'redbrɪk/ *a* ⟨*univ*⟩ de reciente fundación. **~den** /'redn/ *vt* enrojecer. ● *vi* enrojecerse. **~dish** *a* rojizo

redecorate /ri:'dekəreɪt/ *vt* pintar de nuevo

rede|em /rɪ'di:m/ *vt* redimir. **~eming quality** *n* cualidad *f* compensadora. **~mption** /-'dempʃn/ *n* redención *f*

redeploy /ri:dɪ'plɔɪ/ *vt* disponer de otra manera; (*mil*) cambiar de frente

red: **~handed** *a* en flagrante. **~ herring** *n* (*fig*) pista *f* falsa. **~hot** *a* al rojo; ⟨*news*⟩ de última hora

Red Indian /red'ɪndjən/ *n* piel *m* & *f* roja

redirect /ri:daɪ'rekt/ *vt* reexpedir

red: **~letter day** *n* día *m* señalado, día *m* memorable. **~ light** *n* luz *f* roja. **~ness** *n* rojez *f*

redo /ri:'du:/ *vt* (*pt* **redid**, *pp* **redone**) rehacer

redouble /rɪ'dʌbl/ *vt* redoblar

redress /rɪ'dres/ *vt* reparar. ● *n* reparación *f*

red tape /red'teɪp/ *n* (*fig*) papeleo *m*

reduc|e /rɪ'dju:s/ *vt* reducir. ● *vi* reducirse; (*slim*) adelgazar. **~tion** /'dʌkʃn/ *n* reducción *f*

redundan|cy /rɪ'dʌndənsɪ/ *n* superfluidad *f*; (*unemployment*) desempleo *m*. **~t** /rɪ'dʌndənt/ *a* superfluo. **be made ~t** perder su empleo

reed /ri:d/ *n* caña *f*; (*mus*) lengüeta *f*

reef /ri:f/ *n* arrecife *m*

reek /ri:k/ *n* mal olor *m*. ● *vi*. **~ (of)** apestar a

reel /ri:l/ *n* carrete *m*. ● *vi* dar vueltas; (*stagger*) tambalearse. ● *vt*. **~ off** (*fig*) enumerar

refectory /rɪ'fektərɪ/ *n* refectorio *m*

refer /rɪ'fɜ:(r)/ *vt* (*pt* **referred**) remitir. ● *vi* referirse. **~ to** referirse a; (*consult*) consultar

referee /refə'ri:/ *n* árbitro *m*; (*for job*) referencia *f*. ● *vi* (*pt* **refereed**) arbitrar

reference /'refrəns/ *n* referencia *f*. **~ book** *n* libro *m* de consulta. **in ~ to, with ~ to** en cuanto a; (*com*) respecto a

referendum /refə'rendəm/ *n* (*pl* -**ums**) referéndum *m*

refill /ri:'fɪl/ *vt* rellenar. /'ri:fɪl/ *n* recambio *m*

refine /rɪ'faɪn/ vt refinar. **~d** a refinado. **~ment** n refinamiento m; (tec) refinación f. **~ry** /-ərɪ/ n refinería f

reflect /rɪ'flekt/ vt reflejar. ● vi reflejar; (think) reflexionar. **~ upon** perjudicar. **~ion** /-ʃn/ n reflexión f; (image) reflejo m. **~ive** /rɪ'flektɪv/ a reflector; (thoughtful) pensativo. **~or** n reflector m

reflex /'ri:fleks/ a & n reflejo (m)

reflexive /rɪ'fleksɪv/ a (gram) reflexivo

reform /rɪ'fɔ:m/ vt reformar. ● vi reformarse. ● n reforma f. **~er** n reformador m

refract /rɪ'frækt/ vt refractar

refrain[1] /rɪ'freɪn/ n estribillo m

refrain[2] /rɪ'freɪn/ vi abstenerse (from de)

refresh /rɪ'freʃ/ vt refrescar. **~er** /rɪ'freʃə(r)/ a ⟨course⟩ de repaso. **~ing** a refrescante. **~ments** npl (food and drink) refrigerio m

refrigerat|e /rɪ'frɪdʒəreɪt/ vt refrigerar. **~or** n nevera f, refrigeradora f (LAm)

refuel /ri:'fju:əl/ vt/i (pt refuelled) repostar

refuge /'refju:dʒ/ n refugio m. **take ~** refugiarse. **~e** /refju'dʒi:/ n refugiado m

refund /rɪ'fʌnd/ vt reembolsar. /'ri:fʌnd/ n reembolso m

refurbish /ri:'fɜ:bɪʃ/ vt renovar

refusal /rɪ'fju:zl/ n negativa f

refuse[1] /rɪ'fju:z/ vt rehusar. ● vi negarse

refuse[2] /'refju:s/ n basura f

refute /rɪ'fju:t/ vt refutar

regain /rɪ'geɪn/ vt recobrar

regal /'ri:gl/ a real

regale /rɪ'geɪl/ vt festejar

regalia /rɪ'geɪlɪə/ npl insignias fpl

regard /rɪ'gɑ:d/ vt mirar; (consider) considerar. **as ~s** en cuanto a. ● n mirada f; (care) atención f; (esteem) respeto m. **~ing** prep en cuanto a. **~less** /rɪ'gɑ:dlɪs/ adv a pesar de todo. **~less of** sin tener en cuenta. **~s** npl saludos mpl. **kind ~s** npl recuerdos mpl

regatta /rɪ'gætə/ n regata f

regency /'ri:dʒənsɪ/ n regencia f

regenerate /rɪ'dʒenəreɪt/ vt regenerar

regent /'ri:dʒənt/ n regente m & f

regime /reɪ'ʒi:m/ n régimen m

regiment /'redʒɪmənt/ n regimiento m. **~al** /-'mentl/ a del regimiento. **~ation** /-en'teɪʃn/ n reglamentación f rígida

region /'ri:dʒən/ n región f. **in the ~ of** alrededor de. **~al** a regional

register /'redʒɪstə(r)/ n registro m. ● vt registrar; matricular ⟨vehicle⟩; declarar ⟨birth⟩; certificar ⟨letter⟩; facturar ⟨luggage⟩; (indicate) indicar; (express) expresar. ● vi (enrol) inscribirse; (fig) producir impresión. **~ office** n registro m civil

registrar /redʒɪ'strɑ:(r)/ n secretario m del registro civil; (univ) secretario m general

registration /redʒɪ'streɪʃn/ n registración f; (in register) inscripción f; (of vehicle) matrícula f

registry /'redʒɪstrɪ/ n. **~ office** n registro m civil

regression /rɪ'greʃn/ n regresión f

regret /rɪ'gret/ n pesar m. ● vt (pt regretted) lamentar. **I ~ that** siento (que). **~fully** adv con pesar. **~table** a lamentable. **~tably** adv lamentablemente

regular /'regjʊlə(r)/ a regular; (usual) habitual. ● n (fam) cliente m habitual. **~ity** /-'lærətɪ/ n regularidad f. **~ly** adv regularmente

regulat|e /'regjʊleɪt/ vt regular. **~ion** /-'leɪʃn/ n arreglo m; (rule) regla f

rehabilitat|e /ri:hə'bɪlɪteɪt/ vt rehabilitar. **~ion** /-'teɪʃn/ n rehabilitación f

rehash /ri:'hæʃ/ vt volver a presentar. /'ri:hæʃ/ n refrito m

rehears|al /rɪ'hɜ:sl/ n ensayo m. **~e** /rɪ'hɜ:s/ vt ensayar

reign /reɪn/ n reinado m. ● vi reinar

reimburse /ri:ɪm'bɜ:s/ vt reembolsar

reins /reɪnz/ npl riendas fpl

reindeer /'reɪndɪə(r)/ n invar reno m

reinforce /ri:ɪn'fɔ:s/ vt reforzar. **~ment** n refuerzo m

reinstate /ri:ɪn'steɪt/ vt reintegrar

reiterate /ri:'ɪtəreɪt/ vt reiterar

reject /rɪ'dʒekt/ vt rechazar. /'ri:dʒekt/ n producto m defectuoso. **~ion** /'dʒekʃn/ n rechazamiento m, rechazo m

rejoic|e /rɪ'dʒɔɪs/ vi regocijarse. **~ing** n regocijo m

rejoin /rɪ'dʒɔɪn/ vt reunirse con; (answer) replicar. **~der** /rɪ'dʒɔɪndə(r)/ n réplica f

rejuvenate /rɪ'dʒuːvəneɪt/ vt rejuvenecer

rekindle /riː'kɪndl/ vt reavivar

relapse /rɪ'læps/ n recaída f. ● vi recaer; (into crime) reincidir

relate /rɪ'leɪt/ vt contar; (connect) relacionar. ● vi relacionarse (to con). ~d a emparentado; ⟨ideas etc⟩ relacionado

relation /rɪ'leɪʃn/ n relación f; (person) pariente m & f. ~ship n relación f; (blood tie) parentesco m; (affair) relaciones fpl

relative /'relətɪv/ n pariente m & f. ● a relativo. ~ly adv relativamente

relax /rɪ'læks/ vt relajar. ● vi relajarse. ~ation /riːlæk'seɪʃn/ n relajación f; (rest) descanso m; (recreation) recreo m. ~ing a relajante

relay /'riːleɪ/ n relevo m. ~ (race) n carrera f de relevos. /rɪ'leɪ/ vt retransmitir

release /rɪ'liːs/ vt soltar; poner en libertad ⟨prisoner⟩; lanzar ⟨bomb⟩; estrenar ⟨film⟩; (mec) desenganchar; publicar ⟨news⟩; emitir ⟨smoke⟩. ● n liberación f; (of film) estreno m; (record) disco m nuevo

relegate /'relɪgeɪt/ vt relegar

relent /rɪ'lent/ vi ceder. ~less a implacable; (continuous) incesante

relevan|ce /'reləvəns/ n pertinencia f. ~t /'reləvənt/ a pertinente

reliab|ility /rɪlaɪə'bɪlətɪ/ n fiabilidad f. ~le /rɪ'laɪəbl/ a seguro; ⟨person⟩ de fiar; (com) serio

relian|ce /rɪ'laɪəns/ n dependencia f; (trust) confianza f. ~t a confiado

relic /'relɪk/ n reliquia f. ~s npl restos mpl

relie|f /rɪ'liːf/ n alivio m; (assistance) socorro m; (outline) relieve m. ~ve /rɪ'liːv/ vt aliviar; (take over from) relevar

religio|n /rɪ'lɪdʒən/ n religión f. ~us /rɪ'lɪdʒəs/ a religioso

relinquish /rɪ'lɪnkwɪʃ/ vt abandonar, renunciar

relish /'relɪʃ/ n gusto m; (culin) salsa f. ● vt saborear. **I don't ~ the idea** no me gusta la idea

relocate /riːləʊ'keɪt/ vt colocar de nuevo

reluctan|ce /rɪ'lʌktəns/ n desgana f. ~t /rɪ'lʌktənt/ a mal dispuesto. **be ~t to** no tener ganas de. ~tly adv de mala gana

rely /rɪ'laɪ/ vi. ~ **on** contar con; (trust) fiarse de; (depend) depender

remain /rɪ'meɪn/ vi quedar. ~der /rɪ'meɪndə(r)/ n resto m. ~s npl restos mpl; (left-overs) sobras fpl

remand /rɪ'mɑːnd/ vt. ~ **in custody** mantener bajo custodia. ● n. **on ~** bajo custodia

remark /rɪ'mɑːk/ n observación f. ● vt observar. ~able a notable

remarry /riː'mærɪ/ vi volver a casarse

remedial /rɪ'miːdɪəl/ a remediador

remedy /'remədɪ/ n remedio m. ● vt remediar

rememb|er /rɪ'membə(r)/ vt acordarse de. ● vi acordarse. ~rance n recuerdo m

remind /rɪ'maɪnd/ vt recordar. ~er n recordatorio m; (letter) notificación f

reminisce /remɪ'nɪs/ vi recordar el pasado. ~nces npl recuerdos mpl. ~nt /remɪ'nɪsnt/ a. **be ~nt of** recordar

remiss /rɪ'mɪs/ a negligente

remission /rɪ'mɪʃn/ n remisión f; (of sentence) reducción f de condena

remit /rɪ'mɪt/ vt (pt remitted) perdonar; enviar ⟨money⟩. ● vi moderarse. ~tance n remesa f

remnant /'remnənt/ n resto m; (of cloth) retazo m; (trace) vestigio m

remonstrate /'remənstreɪt/ vi protestar

remorse /rɪ'mɔːs/ n remordimiento m. ~ful a lleno de remordimiento. ~less a implacable

remote /rɪ'məʊt/ a remoto; (slight) leve; ⟨person⟩ distante. ~ **control** n mando m a distancia. ~ly adv remotamente. ~ness n lejanía f; (isolation) aislamiento m, alejamiento m; (fig) improbabilidad f

remov|able /rɪ'muːvəbl/ a movible; (detachable) de quita y pon, separable. ~al n eliminación f; (from house) mudanza f. ~e /rɪ'muːv/ vt quitar; (dismiss) despedir; (get rid of) eliminar; (do away with) suprimir

remunerat|e /rɪ'mjuːnəreɪt/ vt remunerar. ~ion /-'reɪʃn/ n remuneración f. ~ive a remunerador

Renaissance /rə'neɪsəns/ n Renacimiento m

rend /rend/ vt (pt rent) rasgar

render /'rendə(r)/ *vt* rendir; (*com*) presentar; (*mus*) interpretar; prestar ‹*help etc*›. **~ing** *n* (*mus*) interpretación *f*

rendezvous /'rɒndɪvu:/ *n* (*pl* **-vous** /-vu:z/) cita *f*

renegade /'renɪgeɪd/ *n* renegado

renew /rɪ'nju:/ *vt* renovar; (*resume*) reanudar. **~able** *a* renovable. **~al** *n* renovación *f*

renounce /rɪ'naʊns/ *vt* renunciar a; (*disown*) repudiar

renovat|e /'renəveɪt/ *vt* renovar. **~ion** /-'veɪʃn/ *n* renovación *f*

renown /rɪ'naʊn/ *n* fama *f*. **~ed** *a* célebre

rent[1] /rent/ *n* alquiler *m*. ● *vt* alquilar

rent[2] /rent/ *see* **rend**

rental /rentl/ *n* alquiler *m*

renunciation /rɪnʌnsɪ'eɪʃn/ *n* renuncia *f*

reopen /ri:'əʊpən/ *vt* reabrir. ● *vi* reabrirse. **~ing** *n* reapertura *f*

reorganize /ri:'ɔ:gənaɪz/ *vt* reorganizar

rep[1] /rep/ *n* (*com*, *fam*) representante *m* & *f*

rep[2] /rep/ (*theatre*, *fam*) teatro *m* de repertorio

repair /rɪ'peə(r)/ *vt* reparar; remendar ‹*clothes*, *shoes*›. ● *n* reparación *f*; (*patch*) remiendo *m*. **in good ~** en buen estado

repartee /repɑ:'ti:/ *n* ocurrencias *fpl*

repatriat|e /ri:'pætrɪeɪt/ *vt* repatriar. **~ion** /-'eɪʃn/ *n* repatriación *f*

repay /ri:'peɪ/ *vt* (*pt* **repaid**) reembolsar; pagar ‹*debt*›; (*reward*) recompensar. **~ment** *n* reembolso *m*, pago *m*

repeal /rɪ'pi:l/ *vt* abrogar. ● *n* abrogación *f*

repeat /rɪ'pi:t/ *vt* repetir. ● *vi* repetir(se). ● *n* repetición *f*. **~edly** /rɪ'pi:tɪdlɪ/ *adv* repetidas veces

repel /rɪ'pel/ *vt* (*pt* **repelled**) repeler. **~lent** *a* repelente

repent /rɪ'pent/ *vi* arrepentirse. **~ance** *n* arrepentimiento *m*. **~ant** *a* arrepentido

repercussion /ri:pə'kʌʃn/ *n* repercusión *f*

reperto|ire /'repətwɑ:(r)/ *n* repertorio *m*. **~ry** /'repətrɪ/ *n* repertorio *m*. **~ry** (**theatre**) *n* teatro *m* de repertorio

repetit|ion /repɪ'tɪʃn/ *n* repetición *f*. **~ious** /-'tɪʃəs/ *a*, **~ive** /rɪ'petətɪv/ *a* que se repite; (*dull*) monótono

replace /rɪ'pleɪs/ *vt* reponer; (*take the place of*) sustituir. **~ment** *n* sustitución *f*; (*person*) sustituto *m*. **~ment part** *n* recambio *m*

replay /'ri:pleɪ/ *n* (*sport*) repetición *f* del partido; (*recording*) repetición *f* inmediata

replenish /rɪ'plenɪʃ/ *vt* reponer; (*refill*) rellenar

replete /rɪ'pli:t/ *a* repleto

replica /'replɪkə/ *n* copia *f*

reply /rɪ'plaɪ/ *vt/i* contestar. ● *n* respuesta *f*

report /rɪ'pɔ:t/ *vt* anunciar; (*denounce*) denunciar. ● *vi* presentar un informe; (*present o.s.*) presentarse. ● *n* informe *m*; (*schol*) boletín *m*; (*rumour*) rumor *m*; (*newspaper*) reportaje *m*; (*sound*) estallido *m*. **~age** /repɔ:'tɑ:ʒ/ *n* reportaje *m*. **~edly** *adv* según se dice. **~er** /rɪ'pɔ:tə(r)/ *n* reportero *m*, informador *m*

repose /rɪ'pəʊz/ *n* reposo *m*

repository /rɪ'pɒzɪtrɪ/ *n* depósito *m*

repossess /ri:pə'zes/ *vt* recuperar

reprehen|d /reprɪ'hend/ *vt* reprender. **~sible** /-səbl/ *a* reprensible

represent /reprɪ'zent/ *vt* representar. **~ation** /-'teɪʃn/ *n* representación *f*. **~ative** /reprɪ'zentətɪv/ *a* representativo. ● *n* representante *m* & *f*

repress /rɪ'pres/ *vt* reprimir. **~ion** /-ʃn/ *n* represión *f*. **~ive** *a* represivo

reprieve /rɪ'pri:v/ *n* indulto *m*; (*fig*) respiro *m*. ● *vt* indultar; (*fig*) aliviar

reprimand /'reprɪmɑ:nd/ *vt* reprender. ● *n* reprensión *f*

reprint /'ri:prɪnt/ *n* reimpresión *f*; (*offprint*) tirada *f* aparte. /ri:'prɪnt/ *vt* reimprimir

reprisal /rɪ'praɪzl/ *n* represalia *f*

reproach /rɪ'prəʊtʃ/ *vt* reprochar. ● *n* reproche *m*. **~ful** *a* de reproche, reprobador. **~fully** *adv* con reproche

reprobate /'reprəbeɪt/ *n* malvado *m*; (*relig*) réprobo *m*

reproduc|e /ri:prə'dju:s/ *vt* reproducir. ● *vi* reproducirse. **~tion** /-'dʌkʃn/ *n* reproducción *f*. **~tive** /-'dʌktɪv/ *a* reproductor

reprove /rɪ'pru:v/ *vt* reprender

reptile /'reptaɪl/ *n* reptil *m*

republic /rɪ'pʌblɪk/ n república f.
~**an** a & n republicano (m)
repudiate /rɪ'pju:dɪeɪt/ vt repudiar;
(refuse to recognize) negarse a
reconocer
repugnan|ce /rɪ'pʌgnəns/ n repugnancia f. ~**t** /rɪ'pʌgnənt/ a
repugnante
repuls|e /rɪ'pʌls/ vt rechazar,
repulsar. ~**ion** /-ʃn/ n repulsión f.
~**ive** a repulsivo
reputable /'repjʊtəbl/ a acreditado,
de confianza, honroso
reputation /repjʊ'teɪʃn/ n reputación f
repute /rɪ'pju:t/ n reputación f. ~**d**
/-ɪd/ a supuesto. ~**dly** adv según se
dice
request /rɪ'kwest/ n petición f. ● vt
pedir. ~ **stop** n parada f
discrecional
require /rɪ'kwaɪə(r)/ vt requerir;
(need) necesitar; (demand) exigir.
~**d** a necesario. ~**ment** n requisito
m
requisite /'rekwɪzɪt/ a necesario.
● n requisito m
requisition /rekwɪ'zɪʃn/ n requisición f. ● vt requisar
resale /'ri:seɪl/ n reventa f
rescind /rɪ'sɪnd/ vt rescindir
rescue /'reskju:/ vt salvar. ● n salvamento m. ~**r** /-ə(r)/ n salvador m
research /rɪ'sɜ:tʃ/ n investigación f.
● vt investigar. ~**er** n investigador
m
resembl|ance /rɪ'zembləns/ n parecido m. ~**e** /rɪ'zembl/ vt parecerse a
resent /rɪ'zent/ vt resentirse por.
~**ful** a resentido. ~**ment** n resentimiento m
reservation /rezə'veɪʃn/ n reserva f;
(booking) reservación f
reserve /rɪ'zɜ:v/ vt reservar. ● n
reserva f; (in sports) suplente m & f.
~**d** a reservado
reservist /rɪ'zɜ:vɪst/ n reservista m
& f
reservoir /'rezəvwɑ:(r)/ n embalse m;
(tank) depósito m
reshape /ri:'ʃeɪp/ vt formar de
nuevo, reorganizar
reshuffle /ri:'ʃʌfl/ vt (pol)
reorganizar. ● n (pol) reorganización f
reside /rɪ'zaɪd/ vi residir
residen|ce /'rezɪdəns/ n residencia f.
~**ce permit** n permiso m de residencia. **be in** ~**ce** ⟨doctor etc⟩

interno. ~**t** /'rezɪdənt/ a & n residente (m & f). ~**tial** /rezɪ'denʃl/ a
residencial
residue /'rezɪdju:/ n residuo m
resign /rɪ'zaɪn/ vt/i dimitir. ~ **o.s. to**
resignarse a. ~**ation** /rezɪg'neɪʃn/ n
resignación f; (from job) dimisión f.
~**ed** a resignado
resilien|ce /rɪ'zɪlɪəns/ n elasticidad f;
(of person) resistencia f. ~**t**
/rɪ'zɪlɪənt/ a elástico; ⟨person⟩
resistente
resin /'rezɪn/ n resina f
resist /rɪ'zɪst/ vt resistir. ● vi resistirse. ~**ance** n resistencia f.
~**ant** a resistente
resolut|e /'rezəlu:t/ a resuelto. ~**ion**
/-'lu:ʃn/ n resolución f
resolve /rɪ'zɒlv/ vt resolver. ~ **to do**
resolverse a hacer. ● n resolución f.
~**d** a resuelto
resonan|ce /'rezənəns/ n resonancia
f. ~**t** /'rezənənt/ a resonante
resort /rɪ'zɔ:t/ vi. ~ **to** recurrir a.
● n recurso m; (place) lugar m turístico. **in the last** ~ como último
recurso
resound /rɪ'zaʊnd/ vi resonar. ~**ing**
a resonante
resource /rɪ'sɔ:s/ n recurso m. ~**ful**
a ingenioso. ~**fulness** n ingeniosidad f
respect /rɪ'spekt/ n (esteem) respeto
m; (aspect) respecto m. **with** ~ **to**
con respecto a. ● vt respetar
respectab|ility /rɪspektə'bɪlətɪ/ n
respetabilidad f. ~**le** /rɪ'spektəbl/ a
respetable. ~**ly** adv respetablemente
respectful /rɪ'spektfl/ a respetuoso
respective /rɪ'spektɪv/ a respectivo.
~**ly** adv respectivamente
respiration /respə'reɪʃn/ n respiración f
respite /'respaɪt/ n respiro m, tregua
f
resplendent /rɪ'splendənt/ a
resplandeciente
respon|d /rɪ'spɒnd/ vi responder.
~**se** /rɪ'spɒns/ n respuesta f; (reaction) reacción f
responsib|ility /rɪspɒnsə'bɪlətɪ/ n
responsabilidad f. ~**le** /rɪ'spɒnsəbl/
a responsable; ⟨job⟩ de responsabilidad. ~**ly** adv con formalidad
responsive /rɪ'spɒnsɪv/ a que reacciona bien. ~ **to** sensible a
rest¹ /rest/ vt descansar; (lean)
apoyar; (place) poner, colocar. ● vi

descansar; (*lean*) apoyarse. ● *n*
descanso *m*; (*mus*) pausa *f*

rest[2] /rest/ *n* (*remainder*) resto *m*, lo
demás; (*people*) los demás, los otros
mpl. ● *vi* (*remain*) quedar

restaurant /'restərɒnt/ *n* restaurante *m*

restful /'restfl/ *a* sosegado

restitution /restɪ'tjuːʃn/ *n* resti-
tución *f*

restive /'restɪv/ *a* inquieto

restless /'restlɪs/ *a* inquieto. ~ly
adv inquietamente. ~ness *n*
inquietud *f*

restor|ation /restə'reɪʃn/ *n* restau-
ración *f*. ~e /rɪ'stɔː(r)/ *vt*
restablecer; restaurar ⟨*building*⟩;
(*put back in position*) reponer;
(*return*) devolver

restrain /rɪ'streɪn/ *vt* contener. ~
o.s. contenerse. ~ed *a* (*moderate*)
moderado; (*in control of self*) comedido. ~t *n* restricción *f*; (*moderation*) moderación *f*

restrict /rɪ'strɪkt/ *vt* restringir.
~ion /-ʃn/ *n* restricción *f*. ~ive
/rɪ'strɪktɪv/ *a* restrictivo

result /rɪ'zʌlt/ *n* resultado *m*. ● *vi*. ~
from resultar de. ~ **in** dar como
resultado

resume /rɪ'zjuːm/ *vt* reanudar. ● *vi*
continuar

résumé /'rezjʊmeɪ/ *n* resumen *m*

resumption /rɪ'zʌmpʃn/ *n* continuación *f*

resurgence /rɪ'sɜːdʒəns/ *n* resur-
gimiento *m*

resurrect /rezə'rekt/ *vt* resucitar.
~ion /-ʃn/ *n* resurrección *f*

resuscitat|e /rɪ'sʌsɪteɪt/ *vt* resu-
citar. ~ion /-'teɪʃn/ *n* resucitación *f*

retail /'riːteɪl/ *n* venta *f* al por menor.
● *a & adv* al por menor. ● *vt* vender
al por menor. ● *vi* venderse al por
menor. ~er *n* minorista *m & f*

retain /rɪ'teɪn/ *vt* retener; (*keep*)
conservar

retainer /rɪ'teɪnə(r)/ *n* (*fee*) anticipo
m

retaliat|e /rɪ'tælɪeɪt/ *vi* desquitarse.
~ion /-'eɪʃn/ *n* represalias *fpl*

retarded /rɪ'tɑːdɪd/ *a* retrasado

retentive /rɪ'tentɪv/ *a* ⟨*memory*⟩
bueno

rethink /riː'θɪŋk/ *vt* (*pt* **rethought**)
considerar de nuevo

reticen|ce /'retɪsns/ *n* reserva *f*. ~t
/'retɪsnt/ *a* reservado, callado

retina /'retɪnə/ *n* retina *f*

retinue /'retɪnjuː/ *n* séquito *m*

retir|e /rɪ'taɪə(r)/ *vi* (*from work*) ju-
bilarse; (*withdraw*) retirarse; (*go to
bed*) acostarse. ● *vt* jubilar. ~ed *a*
jubilado. ~ement *n* jubilación *f*.
~ing /rɪ'taɪərɪŋ/ *a* reservado

retort /rɪ'tɔːt/ *vt/i* replicar. ● *n* réplica *f*

retrace /riː'treɪs/ *vt* repasar. ~
one's steps volver sobre sus pasos

retract /rɪ'trækt/ *vt* retirar. ● *vi*
retractarse

retrain /riː'treɪn/ *vt* reciclar,
reeducar

retreat /rɪ'triːt/ *vi* retirarse. ● *n* retirada *f*; (*place*) refugio *m*

retrial /riː'traɪəl/ *n* nuevo proceso *m*

retribution /retrɪ'bjuːʃn/ *n* justo *m*
castigo

retriev|al /rɪ'triːvl/ *n* recuperación *f*.
~e /rɪ'triːv/ *vt* (*recover*) recuperar;
(*save*) salvar; (*put right*) reparar.
~er *n* (*dog*) perro *m* cobrador

retrograde /'retrəgreɪd/ *a* retrógrado

retrospect /'retrəspekt/ *n* retros-
pección *f*. **in** ~ retrospectivamente. ~ive /-'spektɪv/ *a* retrospectivo

return /rɪ'tɜːn/ *vi* volver; (*reappear*)
reaparecer. ● *vt* devolver; (*com*)
declarar; (*pol*) elegir. ● *n* vuelta *f*;
(*com*) ganancia *f*; (*restitution*) devo-
lución *f*. ~ **of income** *n* declaración
f de ingresos. **in** ~ **for** a cambio de.
many happy ~s! ¡feliz cumpleaños!
~ing /rɪ'tɜːnɪŋ/ *a*. ~ing officer *n*
escrutador *m*. ~ match *n* partido *m*
de desquite. ~ ticket *n* billete *m* de
ida y vuelta. ~s *npl* (*com*) ingresos
mpl

reunion /riː'juːnɪən/ *n* reunión *f*

reunite /riːjuː'naɪt/ *vt* reunir

rev /rev/ *n* (*auto, fam*) revolución *f*.
● *vt/i*. ~ (**up**) (*pt* **revved**) (*auto,
fam*) acelerar(se)

revamp /riː'væmp/ *vt* renovar

reveal /rɪ'viːl/ *vt* revelar. ~ing *a*
revelador

revel /'revl/ *vi* (*pt* **revelled**) jaranear.
~ **in** deleitarse en. ~ry *n* juerga *f*

revelation /revə'leɪʃn/ *n* revelación
f

revenge /rɪ'vendʒ/ *n* venganza *f*;
(*sport*) desquite *m*. **take** ~
vengarse. ● *vt* vengar. ~ful *a* vin-
dicativo, vengativo

revenue /'revənjuː/ *n* ingresos *mpl*

reverberate /rɪ'vɜːbəreɪt/ vi ⟨light⟩ reverberar; ⟨sound⟩ resonar

revere /rɪ'vɪə(r)/ vt venerar

reverence /'revərəns/ n reverencia f

reverend /'revərənd/ a reverendo

reverent /'revərənt/ a reverente

reverie /'revərɪ/ n ensueño m

revers /rɪ'vɪə/ n (pl **revers** /rɪ'vɪəz/) n solapa f

revers|al /rɪ'vɜːsl/ n inversión f. **~e** /rɪ'vɜːs/ a inverso. ● n contrario m; (back) revés m; (auto) marcha f atrás. ● vt invertir; anular ⟨decision⟩; (auto) dar marcha atrás a. ● vi (auto) dar marcha atrás

revert /rɪ'vɜːt/ vi. **~ to** volver a

review /rɪ'vjuː/ n repaso m; (mil) revista f; (of book, play, etc) crítica f. ● vt analizar ⟨situation⟩; reseñar ⟨book, play, etc⟩. **~er** n crítico m

revile /rɪ'vaɪl/ vt injuriar

revis|e /rɪ'vaɪz/ vt revisar; ⟨schol⟩ repasar. **~ion** /-ɪʒn/ n revisión f; (schol) repaso m

reviv|al /rɪ'vaɪvl/ n restablecimiento m; (of faith) despertar m; (of play) reestreno m. **~e** /rɪ'vaɪv/ vt restablecer; resucitar ⟨person⟩. ● vi restablecerse; ⟨person⟩ volver en sí

revoke /rɪ'vəʊk/ vt revocar

revolt /rɪ'vəʊlt/ vi sublevarse. ● vt dar asco a. ● n sublevación f

revolting /rɪ'vəʊltɪŋ/ a asqueroso

revolution /revə'luːʃn/ n revolución f. **~ary** a & n revolucionario (m). **~ize** vt revolucionar

revolve /rɪ'vɒlv/ vi girar

revolver /rɪ'vɒlvə(r)/ n revólver m

revolving /rɪ'vɒlvɪŋ/ a giratorio

revue /rɪ'vjuː/ n revista f

revulsion /rɪ'vʌlʃn/ n asco m

reward /rɪ'wɔːd/ n recompensa f. ● vt recompensar. **~ing** a remunerador; (worthwhile) que vale la pena

rewrite /riː'raɪt/ vt (pt **rewrote**, pp **rewritten**) escribir de nuevo; (change) redactar de nuevo

rhapsody /'ræpsədɪ/ n rapsodia f

rhetoric /'retərɪk/ n retórica f. **~al** /rɪ'tɒrɪkl/ a retórico

rheumati|c /ruː'mætɪk/ a reumático. **~sm** /'ruːmətɪzəm/ n reumatismo m

rhinoceros /raɪ'nɒsərəs/ n (pl **-oses**) rinoceronte m

rhubarb /'ruːbɑːb/ n ruibarbo m

rhyme /raɪm/ n rima f; (poem) poesía f. ● vt/i rimar

rhythm /'rɪðəm/ n ritmo m. **~ic(al)** /'rɪðmɪk(l)/ a rítmico

rib /rɪb/ n costilla f. **—vt** (pt **ribbed**) (fam) tomar el pelo a

ribald /'rɪbld/ a obsceno, verde

ribbon /'rɪbən/ n cinta f

rice /raɪs/ n arroz m. **~ pudding** n arroz con leche

rich /rɪtʃ/ a (**-er, -est**) rico. ● n ricos mpl. **~es** npl riquezas fpl. **~ly** adv ricamente. **~ness** n riqueza f

rickety /'rɪkətɪ/ a (shaky) cojo, desvencijado

ricochet /'rɪkəʃeɪ/ n rebote m. ● vi rebotar

rid /rɪd/ vt (pt **rid**, pres p **ridding**) librar (of de). **get ~ of** deshacerse de. **~dance** /'rɪdns/ n. **good ~dance!** ¡qué alivio!

ridden /'rɪdn/ see **ride**. ● a (infested) infestado. **~ by** (oppressed) agobiado de

riddle[1] /'rɪdl/ n acertijo m

riddle[2] /'rɪdl/ vt acribillar. **be ~d with** estar lleno de

ride /raɪd/ vi (pt **rode**, pp **ridden**) (on horseback) montar; (go) ir (en bicicleta, a caballo etc). **take s.o. for a ~** (fam) engañarle a uno. ● vt montar a ⟨horse⟩; ir en ⟨bicycle⟩; recorrer ⟨distance⟩. ● n (on horse) cabalgata f; (in car) paseo m en coche. **~r** /-ə(r)/ n (on horse) jinete m; (cyclist) ciclista m & f; (in document) cláusula f adicional

ridge /rɪdʒ/ n línea f, arruga f; (of mountain) cresta f; (of roof) caballete m

ridicul|e /'rɪdɪkjuːl/ n irrisión f. ● vt ridiculizar. **~ous** /rɪ'dɪkjʊləs/ a ridículo

riding /'raɪdɪŋ/ n equitación f

rife /raɪf/ a difundido. **~ with** lleno de

riff-raff /'rɪfræf/ n gentuza f

rifle[1] /'raɪfl/ n fusil m

rifle[2] /'raɪfl/ vt saquear

rifle-range /'raɪflreɪndʒ/ n campo m de tiro

rift /rɪft/ n grieta f; (fig) ruptura f

rig[1] /rɪg/ vt (pt **rigged**) aparejar. ● n (at sea) plataforma f de perforación. **~ up** vt improvisar

rig[2] /rɪg/ vt (pej) amañar

right /raɪt/ a (correct, fair) exacto, justo; (morally) bueno; (not left) derecho; (suitable) adecuado. ● n (entitlement) derecho m; (not left) derecha f; (not evil) bien m. **~ of**

way n (auto) prioridad f. **be in the ~** tener razón. **on the ~** a la derecha. **put ~** rectificar. ● vt enderezar; (fig) corregir. ● adv a la derecha; (directly) derecho; (completely) completamente; (well) bien. **~ away** adv inmediatamente. **~ angle** n ángulo m recto

righteous /'raɪtʃəs/ a recto; (cause) justo

right: **~ful** /'raɪtfl/ a legítimo. **~fully** adv legítimamente. **~hand man** n brazo m derecho. **~ly** adv justamente. **~ wing** a (pol) n derechista

rigid /'rɪdʒɪd/ a rígido. **~ity** /-'dʒɪdətɪ/ n rigidez f

rigmarole /'rɪgmərəʊl/ n galimatías m invar

rig|orous /'rɪgərəs/ a riguroso. **~our** /'rɪgə(r)/ n rigor m

rig-out /'rɪgaʊt/ n (fam) atavío m

rile /raɪl/ vt (fam) irritar

rim /rɪm/ n borde m; (of wheel) llanta f; (of glasses) montura f. **~med** a bordeado

rind /raɪnd/ n corteza f; (of fruit) cáscara f

ring[1] /rɪŋ/ n (circle) círculo m; (circle of metal etc) aro m; (on finger) anillo m; (on finger with stone) sortija f; (boxing) cuadrilátero m; (bullring) ruedo m, redondel m, plaza f; (for circus) pista f. ● vt rodear

ring[2] /rɪŋ/ n (of bell) toque m; (tinkle) tintineo m; (telephone call) llamada f. ● vt (pt rang, pp rung) hacer sonar; (telephone) llamar por teléfono. **~ the bell** tocar el timbre. ● v sonar. **~ back** vt/i volver a llamar. **~ off** vi colgar. **~ up** vt llamar por teléfono

ring: **~leader** /'rɪŋliːdə(r)/ n cabecilla f. **~ road** n carretera f de circunvalación

rink /rɪŋk/ n pista f

rinse /rɪns/ vt enjuagar. ● n aclarado m; (of dishes) enjuague m; (for hair) reflejo m

riot /'raɪət/ n disturbio m; (of colours) profusión f. **run ~** desenfrenarse. ● vi amotinarse. **~er** n amotinador m. **~ous** a tumultuoso

rip /rɪp/ vt (pt ripped) rasgar. ● vi rasgarse. **let ~** (fig) soltar. ● n rasgadura f. **~ off** vt (sl) timar. **~cord** n (of parachute) cuerda f de abertura

ripe /raɪp/ a (-er, -est) maduro. **~n** /'raɪpən/ vt/i madurar. **~ness** n madurez f

rip-off /'rɪpɒf/ n (sl) timo m

ripple /'rɪpl/ n rizo m; (sound) murmullo m. ● vt rizar. ● vi rizarse

rise /raɪz/ vi (pt rose, pp risen) levantarse; (rebel) sublevarse; (river) crecer; (prices) subir. ● n subida f; (land) altura f; (increase) aumento m; (to power) ascenso m. **give ~ to** ocasionar. **~r** /-ə(r)/ n. **early ~r** n madrugador m

rising /'raɪzɪŋ/ n (revolt) sublevación f. ● a (sun) naciente. **~ generation** n nueva generación f

risk /rɪsk/ n riesgo m. ● vt arriesgar. **~y** a (-ier, -iest) arriesgado

risqué /'riːskeɪ/ a subido de color

rissole /'rɪsəʊl/ n croqueta f

rite /raɪt/ n rito m

ritual /'rɪtʃʊəl/ a & n ritual (m)

rival /'raɪvl/ a & n rival (m). ● vt (pt rivalled) rivalizar con. **~ry** n rivalidad f

river /'rɪvə(r)/ n río m

rivet /'rɪvɪt/ n remache m. ● vt remachar. **~ing** a fascinante

Riviera /rɪvɪ'eərə/ n. **the (French) ~** la Costa f Azul. **the (Italian) ~** la Riviera f (Italiana)

rivulet /'rɪvjʊlɪt/ n riachuelo m

road /rəʊd/ n (in town) calle f; (between towns) carretera f; (way) camino m. **on the ~** en camino. **~hog** n conductor m descortés. **~house** n albergue m. **~map** n mapa m de carreteras. **~side** /'rəʊdsaɪd/ n borde m de la carretera. **~ sign** n señal f de tráfico. **~way** /'rəʊdweɪ/ n calzada f. **~works** npl obras fpl. **~worthy** /'rəʊdwɜːðɪ/ a (vehicle) seguro

roam /rəʊm/ vi vagar

roar /rɔː(r)/ n rugido m; (laughter) carcajada f. ● vt/i rugir. **~ past** (vehicles) pasar con estruendo. **~ with laughter** reírse a carcajadas. **~ing** /'rɔːrɪŋ/ a (trade etc) activo

roast /rəʊst/ vt asar; tostar (coffee). ● vi asarse; (person, coffee) tostarse. ● a & n asado (m). **~ beef** n rosbif m

rob /rɒb/ vt (pt robbed) robar; asaltar (bank). **~ of** privar de. **~ber** n ladrón m; (of bank) atracador m. **~bery** n robo m

robe /rəʊb/ n manto m; (univ etc) toga f. **bath-~** n albornoz m

robin /'rɒbɪn/ n petirrojo m

robot /ˈrəʊbɒt/ n robot m, autómata m

robust /rəʊˈbʌst/ a robusto

rock[1] /rɒk/ n roca f; (*boulder*) peñasco m; (*sweet*) caramelo m en forma de barra; (*of Gibraltar*) peñón m. **on the ~s** ⟨drink⟩ con hielo; (*fig*) arruinado. **be on the ~s** ⟨marriage etc⟩ andar mal

rock[2] /rɒk/ vt mecer; (*shake*) sacudir. ● vi mecerse; (*shake*) sacudirse. ● n (*mus*) música f rock

rock: ~bottom a (*fam*) bajísimo. **~ery** /ˈrɒkərɪ/ n cuadro m alpino, rocalla f

rocket /ˈrɒkɪt/ n cohete m

rock: ~ing-chair n mecedora f. **~ing-horse** n caballo m de balancín. **~y** /ˈrɒkɪ/ a (**-ier, -iest**) rocoso; (*fig, shaky*) bamboleante

rod /rɒd/ n vara f; (*for fishing*) caña f; (*metal*) barra f

rode /rəʊd/ see **ride**

rodent /ˈrəʊdnt/ n roedor m

rodeo /rəˈdeɪəʊ/ n (*pl* **-os**) rodeo m

roe[1] /rəʊ/ n (*fish eggs*) hueva f

roe[2] /rəʊ/ (*pl* **roe**, *or* **roes**) (*deer*) corzo m

rogu|e /rəʊg/ n pícaro m. **~ish** a picaresco

role /rəʊl/ n papel m

roll /rəʊl/ vt hacer rodar; (*roll up*) enrollar; (*flatten lawn*) allanar; aplanar ⟨pastry⟩. ● vi rodar; ⟨ship⟩ balancearse; (*on floor*) revolcarse. **be ~ing (in money)** (*fam*) nadar (en dinero). ● n rollo m; (*of ship*) balanceo m; (*of drum*) redoble m; (*of thunder*) ruido m; (*bread*) panecillo m; (*list*) lista f. **~ over** vi (*turn over*) dar una vuelta. **~ up** vt enrollar; arremangar ⟨sleeve⟩. ● vi (*fam*) llegar. **~call** n lista f

roller /ˈrəʊlə(r)/ n rodillo m; (*wheel*) rueda f; (*for hair*) rulo m, bigudí m. **~coaster** n montaña f rusa. **~skate** n patín m de ruedas

rollicking /ˈrɒlɪkɪŋ/ a alegre

rolling /ˈrəʊlɪŋ/ a ondulado. **~pin** n rodillo m

Roman /ˈrəʊmən/ a & n romano (m). **~ Catholic** a & n católico (m) (romano)

romance /rəʊˈmæns/ n novela f romántica; (*love*) amor m; (*affair*) aventura f

Romania /rəʊˈmeɪnɪə/ n Rumania f. **~n** a & n rumano (m)

romantic /rəʊˈmæntɪk/ a romántico. **~ism** n romanticismo m

Rome /rəʊm/ n Roma f

romp /rɒmp/ vi retozar. ● n retozo m

rompers /ˈrɒmpəz/ npl pelele m

roof /ruːf/ n techo m, tejado m; (*of mouth*) paladar m. ● vt techar. **~garden** n jardín m en la azotea. **~rack** n baca f. **~top** n tejado m

rook[1] /rʊk/ n grajo m

rook[2] /rʊk/ (*in chess*) torre f

room /ruːm/ n cuarto m, habitación f; (*bedroom*) dormitorio m; (*space*) sitio m; (*large hall*) sala f. **~y** a espacioso; ⟨clothes⟩ holgado

roost /ruːst/ n percha f. ● vi descansar. **~er** n gallo m

root[1] /ruːt/ n raíz f. **take ~** echar raíces. ● vt hacer arraigar. ● vi echar raíces, arraigarse

root[2] /ruːt/ vt/i. **~ about** vi hurgar. **~ for** vi (*Amer, sl*) alentar. **~ out** vt extirpar

rootless /ˈruːtlɪs/ a desarraigado

rope /rəʊp/ n cuerda f. **know the ~s** estar al corriente. ● vt atar. **~ in** vt agarrar

rosary /ˈrəʊzərɪ/ n (*relig*) rosario m

rose[1] /rəʊz/ n rosa f; (*nozzle*) roseta f

rose[2] /rəʊz/ see **rise**

rosé /ˈrəʊzeɪ/ n (vino m) rosado m

rosette /rəʊˈzet/ n escarapela f

roster /ˈrɒstə(r)/ n lista f

rostrum /ˈrɒstrəm/ n tribuna f

rosy /ˈrəʊzɪ/ a (**-ier, -iest**) rosado; ⟨skin⟩ sonrosado

rot /rɒt/ vt (*pt* **rotted**) pudrir. ● vi pudrirse. ● n putrefacción f; (*sl*) tonterías fpl

rota /ˈrəʊtə/ n lista f

rotary /ˈrəʊtərɪ/ a giratorio, rotativo

rotat|e /rəʊˈteɪt/ vt girar; (*change round*) alternar. ● vi girar; (*change round*) alternarse. **~ion** /-ʃn/ n rotación f

rote /rəʊt/ n. **by ~** maquinalmente, de memoria

rotten /ˈrɒtn/ a podrido; (*fam*) desagradable

rotund /rəʊˈtʌnd/ a redondo; ⟨person⟩ regordete

rouge /ruːʒ/ n colorete m

rough /rʌf/ a (**-er, -est**) áspero; ⟨person⟩ tosco; (*bad*) malo; ⟨ground⟩ accidentado; (*violent*) brutal; (*approximate*) aproximado; ⟨diamond⟩ bruto. ● adv duro. **~ copy** n, **~ draft** n borrador m. ● n (*ruffian*) matón *m*. ● *vt*. ~ **it** vivir sin comodidades. ~ **out** *vt* esbozar

roughage /'rʌfɪdʒ/ *n* alimento *m* indigesto, afrecho *m*; (*for animals*) forraje *m*

rough: ~**and-ready** *a* improvisado. ~**and-tumble** *n* riña *f*. ~**ly** *adv* toscamente; (*more or less*) más o menos. ~**ness** *n* aspereza *f*; (*lack of manners*) incultura *f*; (*crudeness*) tosquedad *f*

roulette /ru:'let/ *n* ruleta *f*

round /raʊnd/ *a* (-er, -est) redondo. ● *n* círculo *m*; (*slice*) tajada *f*; (*of visits, drinks*) ronda *f*; (*of competition*) vuelta *f*; (*boxing*) asalto *m*. ● *prep* alrededor de. ● *adv* alrededor. ~ **about** (*approximately*) aproximadamente. **come** ~ **to, go** ~ **to** (*a friend etc*) pasar por casa de. ● *vt* redondear; doblar ⟨*corner*⟩. ~ **off** *vt* terminar. ~ **up** *vt* reunir; redondear ⟨*price*⟩

roundabout /'raʊndəbaʊt/ *n* tiovivo *m*; (*for traffic*) glorieta *f*. ● *a* indirecto

rounders /'raʊndəz/ *n* juego *m* parecido al béisbol

round: ~**ly** *adv* (*bluntly*) francamente. ~ **trip** *n* viaje *m* de ida y vuelta. ~-**up** *n* reunión *f*; (*of suspects*) redada *f*

rous|**e** /raʊz/ *vt* despertar. ~**ing** *a* excitante

rout /raʊt/ *n* derrota *f*. ● *vt* derrotar

route /ru:t/ *n* ruta *f*; (*naut, aviat*) rumbo *m*; (*of bus*) línea *f*

routine /ru:'ti:n/ *n* rutina *f*. ● *a* rutinario

rov|**e** /rəʊv/ *vt/i* vagar (por). ~**ing** *a* errante

row[1] /rəʊ/ *n* fila *f*

row[2] /rəʊ/ *n* (*in boat*) paseo *m* en bote (de remos). ● *vi* remar

row[3] /raʊ/ *n* (*noise, fam*) ruido *m*; (*quarrel*) pelea *f*. ● *vi* (*fam*) pelearse

rowdy /'raʊdɪ/ *a* (-ier, -iest) *n* ruidoso

rowing /'rəʊɪŋ/ *n* remo *m*. ~**boat** *n* bote *m* de remos

royal /'rɔɪəl/ *a* real. ~**ist** *a* & *n* monárquico (*m*). ~**ly** *adv* magníficamente. ~**ty** /'rɔɪəltɪ/ *n* familia *f* real; (*payment*) derechos *mpl* de autor

rub /rʌb/ *vt* (*pt* **rubbed**) frotar. ~ **it in** insistir en algo. ● *n* frotamiento *m*. ~ **off on s.o.** *vi* pegársele a uno. ~ **out** *vt* borrar

rubber /'rʌbə(r)/ *n* goma *f*. ~ **band** *n* goma *f* (elástica). ~ **stamp** *n* sello *m* de goma. ~-**stamp** *vt* (*fig*) aprobar maquinalmente. ~**y** *a* parecido al caucho

rubbish /'rʌbɪʃ/ *n* basura *f*; (*junk*) trastos *mpl*; (*fig*) tonterías *fpl*. ~**y** *a* sin valor

rubble /'rʌbl/ *n* escombros; (*small*) cascajo *m*

ruby /'ru:bɪ/ *n* rubí *m*

rucksack /'rʌksæk/ *n* mochila *f*

rudder /'rʌdə(r)/ *n* timón *m*

ruddy /'rʌdɪ/ *a* (-ier, -iest) rubicundo; (*sl*) maldito

rude /ru:d/ *a* (-er, -est) descortés, mal educado; (*improper*) indecente; (*brusque*) brusco. ~**ly** *adv* con descortesía. ~**ness** *n* descortesía *f*

rudiment /'ru:dɪmənt/ *n* rudimento *m*. ~**ary** /-'mentrɪ/ *a* rudimentario

rueful /'ru:fl/ *a* triste

ruffian /'rʌfɪən/ *n* rufián *m*

ruffle /'rʌfl/ *vt* despeinar ⟨*hair*⟩; arrugar ⟨*clothes*⟩. ● *n* (*frill*) volante *m*, fruncido *m*

rug /rʌg/ *n* tapete *m*; (*blanket*) manta *f*

Rugby /'rʌgbɪ/ *n*. ~ (**football**) *n* rugby *m*

rugged /'rʌgɪd/ *a* desigual; (*landscape*) accidentado; (*fig*) duro

ruin /'ru:ɪn/ *n* ruina *f*. ● *vt* arruinar. ~**ous** *a* ruinoso

rule /ru:l/ *n* regla *f*; (*custom*) costumbre *f*; (*pol*) dominio *m*. **as a** ~ por regla general. ● *vt* gobernar; (*master*) dominar; (*jurid*) decretar; (*decide*) decidir. ~ **out** *vt* descartar. ~**d paper** *n* papel *m* rayado

ruler /'ru:lə(r)/ *n* (*sovereign*) soberano *m*; (*leader*) gobernante *m* & *f*; (*measure*) regla *f*

ruling /'ru:lɪŋ/ *a* ⟨*class*⟩ dirigente. ● *n* decisión *f*

rum /rʌm/ *n* ron *m*

rumble /rʌmbl/ *vi* retumbar; ⟨*stomach*⟩ hacer ruidos. ● *n* retumbo *m*; (*of stomach*) ruido *m*

ruminant /'ru:mɪnənt/ *a* & *n* rumiante (*m*)

rummage /'rʌmɪdʒ/ *vi* hurgar

rumour /'ru:mə(r)/ *n* rumor *m*. ● *vt*. **it is** ~**ed that** se dice que

rump /rʌmp/ *n* (*of horse*) grupa *f*; (*of fowl*) rabadilla *f*. ~ **steak** *n* filete *m*

rumpus /'rʌmpəs/ *n* (*fam*) jaleo *m*

run /rʌn/ *vi* (*pt* **ran**, *pp* **run**, *pres p* **running**) correr; (*flow*) fluir; (*pass*) pasar; (*function*) funcionar; (*melt*) derretirse; ⟨*bus etc*⟩ circular; ⟨*play*⟩ representarse (continuamente); ⟨*colours*⟩ correrse; (*in election*) presentarse. ● *vt* tener ⟨*house*⟩; (*control*) dirigir; correr ⟨*risk*⟩; (*drive*) conducir; (*pass*) pasar; (*present*) presentar; forzar ⟨*blockade*⟩. **~ a temperature** tener fiebre. ● *n* corrida *f*, carrera *f*; (*journey*) viaje *m*; (*outing*) paseo *m*, excursión *f*; (*distance travelled*) recorrido *m*; (*ladder*) carrera *f*; (*ski*) pista *f*; (*series*) serie *f*. **at a ~** corriendo. **have the ~** of tener a su disposición. **in the long ~** a la larga. **on the ~** de fuga. **~ across** *vt* toparse con ⟨*friend*⟩. **~ away** *vi* escaparse. **~ down** *vi* bajar corriendo; ⟨*clock*⟩ quedarse sin cuerda. ● *vt* (*auto*) atropellar; (*belittle*) denigrar. **~ in** *vt* rodar ⟨*vehicle*⟩. ● *vi* entrar corriendo. **~ into** *vt* toparse con ⟨*friend*⟩; (*hit*) chocar con. **~ off** *vt* tirar ⟨*copies etc*⟩. **~ out** *vi* salir corriendo; ⟨*liquid*⟩ salirse; (*fig*) agotarse. **~ out of** quedar sin. **~ over** *vt* (*auto*) atropellar. **~ through** *vt* traspasar; (*revise*) repasar. **~ up** *vt* hacerse ⟨*bill*⟩. ● *vi* subir corriendo. **~ up against** tropezar con ⟨*difficulties*⟩. **~away** /'rʌnəweɪ/ *a* fugitivo; ⟨*success*⟩ decisivo; ⟨*inflation*⟩ galopante. ● *n* fugitivo *m*. **~ down** *a* ⟨*person*⟩ agotado. **~down** *n* informe *m* detallado

rung[1] /rʌŋ/ *n* (*of ladder*) peldaño *m*

rung[2] /rʌŋ/ *see* **ring**

run: **~ner** /'rʌnə(r)/ *n* corredor *m*; (*on sledge*) patín *m*. **~ner bean** *n* judía *f* escarlata. **~ner-up** *n* subcampeón *m*, segundo *m*. **~ning** /'rʌnɪŋ/ *n* (*race*) carrera *f*. **be in the ~ning** tener posibilidades de ganar. ● *a* en marcha; ⟨*water*⟩ corriente; ⟨*commentary*⟩ en directo. **four times ~ning** cuatro veces seguidas. **~ny** /'rʌnɪ/ *a* líquido; ⟨*nose*⟩ que moquea. **~-of-the-mill** *a* ordinario. **~-up** *n* período *m* que precede. **~way** /'rʌnweɪ/ *n* pista *f*

rupture /'rʌptʃə(r)/ *n* ruptura *f*; (*med*) hernia *f*. ● *vt/i* quebrarse

rural /'rʊərəl/ *a* rural

ruse /ru:z/ *n* ardid *m*

rush[1] /rʌʃ/ *n* (*haste*) prisa *f*; (*crush*) bullicio *m*. ● *vi* precipitarse. ● *vt* apresurar; (*mil*) asaltar

rush[2] /rʌʃ/ *n* (*plant*) junco *m*

rush-hour /'rʌʃaʊə(r)/ *n* hora *f* punta

rusk /rʌsk/ *n* galleta *f*, tostada *f*

russet /'rʌsɪt/ *a* rojizo. ● *n* (*apple*) manzana *f* rojiza

Russia /'rʌʃə/ *n* Rusia *f*. **~n** *a* & *n* ruso (*m*)

rust /rʌst/ *n* orín *m*. ● *vt* oxidar. ● *vi* oxidarse

rustic /'rʌstɪk/ *a* rústico

rustle /'rʌsl/ *vt* hacer susurrar; (*Amer*) robar. **~ up** (*fam*) preparar. ● *vi* susurrar

rust: **~proof** *a* inoxidable. **~y** *a* (**-ier, -iest**) oxidado

rut /rʌt/ *n* surco *m*. **in a ~** en la rutina de siempre

ruthless /'ru:θlɪs/ *a* despiadado. **~ness** *n* crueldad *f*

rye /raɪ/ *n* centeno *m*

S

S *abbr* (*south*) sur *m*

sabbath /'sæbəθ/ *n* día *m* de descanso; (*Christian*) domingo *m*; (*Jewish*) sábado *m*

sabbatical /sə'bætɪkl/ *a* sabático

sabot|age /'sæbətɑːʒ/ *n* sabotaje *m*. ● *vt* sabotear. **~eur** /-'tɜː(r)/ *n* saboteador *m*

saccharin /'sækərɪn/ *n* sacarina *f*

sachet /'sæʃeɪ/ *n* bolsita *f*

sack[1] /sæk/ *n* saco *m*. **get the ~** (*fam*) ser despedido. ● *vt* (*fam*) despedir. **~ing** *n* arpillera *f*; (*fam*) despido *m*

sack[2] /sæk/ *vt* (*plunder*) saquear

sacrament /'sækrəmənt/ *n* sacramento *m*

sacred /'seɪkrɪd/ *a* sagrado

sacrifice /'sækrɪfaɪs/ *n* sacrificio *m*. ● *vt* sacrificar

sacrileg|e /'sækrɪlɪdʒ/ *n* sacrilegio *m*. **~ious** /-'lɪdʒəs/ *a* sacrílego

sacrosanct /'sækrəʊsæŋkt/ *a* sacrosanto

sad /sæd/ *a* (**sadder, saddest**) triste. **~den** /'sædn/ *vt* entristecer

saddle /'sædl/ *n* silla *f*. **be in the ~** (*fig*) tener las riendas. ● *vt* ensillar ⟨*horse*⟩. **~ s.o. with** (*fig*) cargar a uno con. **~bag** *n* alforja *f*

sad: **~ly** *adv* tristemente; (*fig*) desgraciadamente. **~ness** *n* tristeza *f*

sadis|m /'seɪdɪzəm/ *n* sadismo *m*. **~t** /'seɪdɪst/ *n* sádico *m*. **~tic** /sə'dɪstɪk/ *a* sádico

safari /səˈfɑːrɪ/ n safari m

safe /seɪf/ a (-er, -est) seguro; (out of danger) salvo; (cautious) prudente. ~ **and sound** sano y salvo. ● n caja f fuerte. ~ **deposit** n caja f de seguridad. ~**guard** /ˈseɪfgɑːd/ n salvaguardia f. ● vt salvaguardar. ~**ly** adv sin peligro; (in safe place) en lugar seguro. ~**ty** /ˈseɪftɪ/ n seguridad f. ~**ty belt** n cinturón m de seguridad. ~**ty-pin** n imperdible m. ~**ty-valve** n válvula f de seguridad

saffron /ˈsæfrən/ n azafrán m

sag /sæg/ vi (pt sagged) hundirse; (give) aflojarse

saga /ˈsɑːgə/ n saga f

sage[1] /seɪdʒ/ n (wise person) sabio m. ● a sabio

sage[2] /seɪdʒ/ n (herb) salvia f

sagging /ˈsægɪŋ/ a hundido; (fig) decaído

Sagittarius /sædʒɪˈteərɪəs/ n (astr) Sagitario m

sago /ˈseɪgəʊ/ n sagú m

said /sed/ see **say**

sail /seɪl/ n vela f; (trip) paseo m (en barco). ● vi navegar; (leave) partir; (sport) practicar la vela; (fig) deslizarse. ● vt manejar ⟨boat⟩. ~**ing** n (sport) vela f. ~**ing-boat** n, ~**ing-ship** n barco m de vela. ~**or** /ˈseɪlə(r)/ n marinero m

saint /seɪnt, before name sənt/ n santo m. ~**ly** a santo

sake /seɪk/ n. **for the ~ of** por, por el amor de

salacious /səˈleɪʃəs/ a salaz

salad /ˈsæləd/ n ensalada f. ~ **bowl** n ensaladera f. ~ **cream** n mayonesa f. ~**dressing** n aliño m

salar|ied /ˈsælərɪd/ a asalariado. ~**y** /ˈsælərɪ/ n sueldo m

sale /seɪl/ n venta f; (at reduced prices) liquidación f. **for ~** (sign) se vende. **on ~** en venta. ~**able** /ˈseɪləbl/ a vendible. ~**sman** /ˈseɪlzmən/ n (pl -men) vendedor m; (in shop) dependiente m; (traveller) viajante m. ~**swoman** n (pl -women) vendedora f; (in shop) dependienta f

salient /ˈseɪlɪənt/ a saliente, destacado

saliva /səˈlaɪvə/ n saliva f

sallow /ˈsæləʊ/ a (-er, -est) amarillento

salmon /ˈsæmən/ n invar salmón m. ~ **trout** n trucha f salmonada

salon /ˈsælɒn/ n salón m

saloon /səˈluːn/ n (on ship) salón m; (Amer, bar) bar m; (auto) turismo m

salt /sɔːlt/ n sal f. ● a salado. ● vt salar. ~**cellar** n salero m. ~**y** a salado

salutary /ˈsæljʊtrɪ/ a saludable

salute /səˈluːt/ n saludo m. ● vt saludar. ● vi hacer un saludo

salvage /ˈsælvɪdʒ/ n salvamento m; (goods) objetos mpl salvados. ● vt salvar

salvation /sælˈveɪʃn/ n salvación f

salve /sælv/ n ungüento m

salver /ˈsælvə(r)/ n bandeja f

salvo /ˈsælvəʊ/ n (pl -os) salva f

same /seɪm/ a igual (as que); (before noun) mismo (as que). **at the ~ time** al mismo tiempo. ● pron. **the ~** el mismo, la misma, los mismos, las mismas. **do the ~ as** hacer como. ● adv. **the ~** de la misma manera. **all the ~** de todas formas

sample /ˈsɑːmpl/ n muestra f. ● vt probar ⟨food⟩

sanatorium /sænəˈtɔːrɪəm/ n (pl -ums) sanatorio m

sanctify /ˈsæŋktɪfaɪ/ vt santificar

sanctimonious /sæŋktɪˈməʊnɪəs/ a beato

sanction /ˈsæŋkʃn/ n sanción f. ● vt sancionar

sanctity /ˈsæŋktətɪ/ n santidad f

sanctuary /ˈsæŋktʃʊərɪ/ n (relig) santuario m; (for wildlife) reserva f; (refuge) asilo m

sand /sænd/ n arena f. ● vt enarenar. ~**s** npl (beach) playa f

sandal /ˈsændl/ n sandalia f

sand: ~**castle** n castillo m de arena. ~**paper** /ˈsændpeɪpə(r)/ n papel m de lija. ● vt lijar. ~**storm** /ˈsændstɔːm/ n tempestad f de arena

sandwich /ˈsænwɪdʒ/ n bocadillo m, sandwich m. ● vt. ~**ed between** intercalado

sandy /ˈsændɪ/ a arenoso

sane /seɪn/ a (-er, -est) ⟨person⟩ cuerdo; ⟨judgement, policy⟩ razonable. ~**ly** adv sensatamente

sang /sæŋ/ see **sing**

sanitary /ˈsænɪtrɪ/ a higiénico; ⟨system etc⟩ sanitario. ~ **towel** n, ~ **napkin** n (Amer) compresa f (higiénica)

sanitation /sænɪˈteɪʃn/ n higiene f; (drainage) sistema m sanitario

sanity /ˈsænɪtɪ/ n cordura f; (fig) sensatez f

sank /sæŋk/ see **sink**

Santa Claus /'sæntəklɔːz/ n Papá m Noel

sap /sæp/ n (in plants) savia f. ● vt (pt **sapped**) agotar

sapling /'sæplɪŋ/ n árbol m joven

sapphire /'sæfaɪə(r)/ n zafiro m

sarcas|m /'sɑːkæzəm/ n sarcasmo m. **~tic** /-'kæstɪk/ a sarcástico

sardine /sɑː'diːn/ n sardina f

Sardinia /sɑː'dɪnɪə/ n Cerdeña f. **~n** a & n sardo (m)

sardonic /sɑː'dɒnɪk/ a sardónico

sash /sæʃ/ n (over shoulder) banda f; (round waist) fajín m. **~window** n ventana f de guillotina

sat /sæt/ see **sit**

satanic /sə'tænɪk/ a satánico

satchel /'sætʃl/ n cartera f

satellite /'sætəlaɪt/ n & a satélite (m)

satiate /'seɪʃɪeɪt/ vt saciar

satin /'sætɪn/ n raso m. ● a de raso; (like satin) satinado

satir|e /'sætaɪə(r)/ n sátira f. **~ical** /sə'tɪrɪkl/ a satírico. **~ist** /'sætərɪst/ n satírico m. **~ize** /'sætəraɪz/ vt satirizar

satisfaction /sætɪs'fækʃn/ n satisfacción f

satisfactor|ily /sætɪs'fæktərɪlɪ/ adv satisfactoriamente. **~y** /sætɪs 'fæktərɪ/ a satisfactorio

satisfy /'sætɪsfaɪ/ vt satisfacer; (convince) convencer. **~ing** a satisfactorio

satsuma /sæt'suːmə/ n mandarina f

saturat|e /'sætʃəreɪt/ vt saturar, empapar. **~ed** a saturado, empapado. **~ion** /-'reɪʃn/ n saturación f

Saturday /'sætədeɪ/ n sábado m

sauce /sɔːs/ n salsa f; (cheek) descaro m. **~pan** /'sɔːspən/ n cazo m

saucer /'sɔːsə(r)/ n platillo m

saucy /'sɔːsɪ/ a (-ier, -iest) descarado

Saudi Arabia /saʊdɪə'reɪbɪə/ n Arabia f Saudí

sauna /'sɔːnə/ n sauna f

saunter /'sɔːntə(r)/ vi deambular, pasearse

sausage /'sɒsɪdʒ/ n salchicha f

savage /'sævɪdʒ/ a salvaje; (fierce) feroz; (furious, fam) rabioso. ● n salvaje m & f. ● vt atacar. **~ry** n ferocidad f

sav|e /seɪv/ vt salvar; ahorrar (money, time); (prevent) evitar. ● n (football) parada f. ● prep salvo, con excepción de. **~er** n ahorrador m. **~ing** n ahorro m. **~ings** npl ahorros mpl

saviour /'seɪvɪə(r)/ n salvador m

savour /'seɪvə(r)/ n sabor m. ● vt saborear. **~y** a (appetizing) sabroso; (not sweet) no dulce. ● n aperitivo m (no dulce)

saw[1] /sɔː/ see **see**[1]

saw[2] /sɔː/ n sierra f. ● vt (pt **sawed**, pp **sawn**) serrar. **~dust** /'sɔːdʌst/ n serrín m. **~n** /sɔːn/ see **saw**

saxophone /'sæksəfəʊn/ n saxófono m

say /seɪ/ vt/i (pt **said** /sed/) decir; rezar (prayer). **I ~!** ¡no me digas! ● n. **have a ~** expresar una opinión; (in decision) tener voz en capítulo. **have no ~** no tener ni voz ni voto. **~ing** /'seɪɪŋ/ n refrán m

scab /skæb/ n costra f; (blackleg, fam) esquirol m

scaffold /'skæfəʊld/ n (gallows) cadalso m, patíbulo m. **~ing** /'skæfəldɪŋ/ n (for workmen) andamio m

scald /skɔːld/ vt escaldar; calentar (milk etc). ● n escaldadura f

scale[1] /skeɪl/ n escala f

scale[2] /skeɪl/ n (of fish) escama f

scale[3] /skeɪl/ vt (climb) escalar. **~ down** vt reducir (proporcionalmente)

scales /skeɪlz/ npl (for weighing) balanza f, peso m

scallop /'skɒləp/ n venera f; (on dress) festón m

scalp /skælp/ n cuero m cabelludo. ● vt quitar el cuero cabelludo a

scalpel /'skælpəl/ n escalpelo m

scamp /skæmp/ n bribón m

scamper /'skæmpə(r)/ vi. **~ away** marcharse corriendo

scampi /'skæmpɪ/ npl gambas fpl grandes

scan /skæn/ vt (pt **scanned**) escudriñar; (quickly) echar un vistazo a; (radar) explorar. ● vi (poetry) estar bien medido

scandal /'skændl/ n escándalo m; (gossip) chismorreo m. **~ize** /'skændəlaɪz/ vt escandalizar. **~ous** a escandaloso

Scandinavia /skændɪ'neɪvɪə/ n Escandinavia f. **~n** a & n escandinavo (m)

scant /skænt/ a escaso. **~ily** adv insuficientemente. **~y** /'skæntɪ/ a (-ier, -iest) escaso

scapegoat /'skeɪpgəʊt/ n cabeza f de turco

scar /skɑ:(r)/ n cicatriz f. ● vt (pt **scarred**) dejar una cicatriz en. ● vi cicatrizarse

scarc|e /skeəs/ a (**-er**, **-est**) escaso. **make o.s. ~e** (fam) mantenerse lejos. **~ely** /ˈskeəslɪ/ adv apenas. **~ity** n escasez f

scare /ˈskeə(r)/ vt asustar. **be ~d** tener miedo. ● n susto m. **~crow** /ˈskeəkrəʊ/ n espantapájaros m invar. **~monger** /ˈskeəmʌŋɡə(r)/ n alarmista m & f

scarf /skɑ:f/ n (pl **scarves**) bufanda f; (over head) pañuelo m

scarlet /ˈskɑ:lət/ a escarlata f. **~ fever** n escarlatina f

scary /ˈskeərɪ/ a (**-ier**, **-iest**) que da miedo

scathing /ˈskeɪðɪŋ/ a mordaz

scatter /ˈskætə(r)/ vt (throw) esparcir; (disperse) dispersar. ● vi dispersarse. **~-brained** a atolondrado. **~ed** a disperso; (occasional) esporádico

scatty /ˈskætɪ/ a (**-ier**, **-iest**) (sl) atolondrado

scavenge /ˈskævɪndʒ/ vi buscar (en la basura). **~r** /-ə(r)/ n (vagrant) persona f que busca objetos en la basura

scenario /sɪˈnɑ:rɪəʊ/ n (pl **-os**) argumento; (of film) guión m

scen|e /si:n/ n escena f; (sight) vista f; (fuss) lío m. **behind the ~es** entre bastidores. **~ery** /ˈsi:nərɪ/ n paisaje m; (in theatre) decorado m. **~ic** /ˈsi:nɪk/ a pintoresco

scent /sent/ n olor m; (perfume) perfume m; (trail) pista f. ● vt presentir; (make fragrant) perfumar

sceptic /ˈskeptɪk/ n escéptico m. **~al** a escéptico. **~ism** /-sɪzəm/ n escepticismo m

sceptre /ˈseptə(r)/ n cetro m

schedule /ˈʃedju:l, ˈskedju:l/ n programa f; (timetable) horario m. **behind ~** con retraso. **on ~** sin retraso. ● vt proyectar. **~d flight** n vuelo m regular

scheme /ski:m/ n proyecto m; (plot) intriga f. ● vi hacer proyectos; (pej) intrigar. **~r** n intrigante m & f

schism /ˈsɪzəm/ n cisma m

schizophrenic /skɪtsəˈfrenɪk/ a & n esquizofrénico (m)

scholar /ˈskɒlə(r)/ n erudito m. **~ly** a erudito. **~ship** n erudición f; (grant) beca f

scholastic /skəˈlæstɪk/ a escolar

school /sku:l/ n escuela f; (of univ) facultad f. ● a ⟨age, holidays, year⟩ escolar. ● vt enseñar; (discipline) disciplinar. **~boy** /ˈsku:lbɔɪ/ n colegial m. **~girl** /-ɡɜ:l/ n colegiala f. **~ing** n instrucción f. **~master** /ˈsku:lmɑ:stə(r)/ n (primary) maestro m; (secondary) profesor m. **~mistress** n (primary) maestra f; (secondary) profesora f. **~teacher** n (primary) maestro m; (secondary) profesor m

schooner /ˈsku:nə(r)/ n goleta f; (glass) vaso m grande

sciatica /saɪˈætɪkə/ n ciática f

scien|ce /ˈsaɪəns/ n ciencia f. **~ce fiction** n ciencia f ficción. **~tific** /-ˈtɪfɪk/ a científico. **~tist** /ˈsaɪəntɪst/ n científico m

scintillate /ˈsɪntɪleɪt/ vi centellear

scissors /ˈsɪsəz/ npl tijeras fpl

sclerosis /skləˈrəʊsɪs/ n esclerosis f

scoff /skɒf/ vt (sl) zamparse. ● vi. **~ at** mofarse de

scold /skəʊld/ vt regañar. **~ing** n regaño m

scone /skɒn/ n (tipo m de) bollo m

scoop /sku:p/ n paleta f; (news) noticia f exclusiva. ● vt. **~ out** excavar. **~ up** recoger

scoot /sku:t/ vi (fam) largarse corriendo. **~er** /ˈsku:tə(r)/ n escúter m; (for child) patinete m

scope /skəʊp/ n alcance m; (opportunity) oportunidad f

scorch /skɔ:tʃ/ vt chamuscar. **~er** n (fam) día m de mucho calor. **~ing** a (fam) de mucho calor

score /skɔ:(r)/ n tanteo m; (mus) partitura f; (twenty) veintena f; (reason) motivo m. **on that ~** en cuanto a eso. ● vt marcar; (slash) rayar; (mus) instrumentar; conseguir ⟨success⟩. ● vi marcar un tanto; (keep score) tantear. **~ over** s.o. aventajar a. **~r** /-ə(r)/ n tanteador m

scorn /skɔ:n/ n desdén m. ● vt desdeñar. **~ful** a desdeñoso. **~fully** adv desdeñosamente

Scorpio /ˈskɔ:pɪəʊ/ n (astr) Escorpión m

scorpion /ˈskɔ:pɪən/ n escorpión m

Scot /skɒt/ n escocés m. **~ch** /skɒtʃ/ a escocés. ● n güisqui m

scotch /skɒtʃ/ vt frustrar; (suppress) suprimir

scot-free /skɒtˈfri:/ a impune; (gratis) sin pagar

Scot: ~**land** /'skɒtlənd/ n Escocia f. ~**s** a escocés. ~**sman** n escocés m. ~**swoman** n escocesa f. ~**tish** a escocés

scoundrel /'skaʊndrəl/ n canalla f

scour /'skaʊə(r)/ vt estregar; (search) registrar. ~**er** n estropajo m

scourge /skɜːdʒ/ n azote m

scout /skaʊt/ n explorador m. **Boy S**~ explorador m. ● vi. ~ **(for)** buscar

scowl /skaʊl/ n ceño m. ● vi fruncir el entrecejo

scraggy /'skrægɪ/ a (-ier, -iest) descarnado

scram /skræm/ vi (sl) largarse

scramble /'skræmbl/ vi (clamber) gatear. ~ **for** pelearse para obtener. ● vt revolver ⟨eggs⟩. ● n (difficult climb) subida f difícil; (struggle) lucha f

scrap /skræp/ n pedacito m; (fight, fam) pelea f. ● vt (pt scrapped) desechar. ~**book** n álbum m de recortes. ~**s** npl sobras fpl

scrape /skreɪp/ n raspadura f; (fig) apuro m. ● vt raspar; (graze) arañar; (rub) frotar. ● vi. ~ **through** lograr pasar; aprobar por los pelos ⟨exam⟩. ~ **together** reunir. ~**r** /-ə(r)/ n raspador m

scrap: ~ **heap** n montón m de deshechos. ~**iron** n chatarra f

scrappy /'skræpɪ/ a fragmentario, pobre, de mala calidad

scratch /skrætʃ/ vt rayar; (with nail etc) arañar; rascar ⟨itch⟩. ● vi arañar. ● n raya f; (from nail etc) arañazo m. **start from** ~ empezar sin nada, empezar desde el principio. **up to** ~ al nivel requerido

scrawl /skrɔːl/ n garrapato m. ● vt/i garrapatear

scrawny /'skrɔːnɪ/ a (-ier, -iest) descarnado

scream /skriːm/ vt/i gritar. ● n grito m

screech /skriːtʃ/ vi gritar; ⟨brakes etc⟩ chirriar. ● n grito m; (of brakes etc) chirrido m

screen /skriːn/ n pantalla f; (folding) biombo m. ● vt (hide) ocultar; (protect) proteger; proyectar ⟨film⟩; seleccionar ⟨candidates⟩

screw /skruː/ n tornillo m. ● vt atornillar. ~**driver** /'skruːdraɪvə(r)/ n destornillador m. ~ **up** atornillar; entornar ⟨eyes⟩; torcer ⟨face⟩; (ruin,

sl) arruinar. ~**y** /'skruːɪ/ a (-ier, -iest) (sl) chiflado

scribble /'skrɪbl/ vt/i garrapatear. ● n garrapato m

scribe /skraɪb/ n copista m & f

script /skrɪpt/ n escritura f; (of film etc) guión m

Scriptures /'skrɪptʃəz/ npl Sagradas Escrituras fpl

script-writer /'skrɪptraɪtə(r)/ n guionista m & f

scroll /skrəʊl/ n rollo m (de pergamino)

scrounge /skraʊndʒ/ vt/i obtener de gorra; (steal) birlar. ~**r** /-ə(r)/ n gorrón m

scrub /skrʌb/ n (land) maleza f; (clean) fregado m. ● vt/i (pt scrubbed) fregar

scruff /skrʌf/ n. **the** ~ **of the neck** el cogote m

scruffy /'skrʌfɪ/ a (-ier, -iest) desaliñado

scrum /skrʌm/ n, **scrummage** /'skrʌmɪdʒ/ n (Rugby) melée f

scrup|le /'skruːpl/ n escrúpulo m. ~**ulous** /'skruːpjʊləs/ a escrupuloso. ~**ulously** adv escrupulosamente

scrutin|ize /'skruːtɪnaɪz/ vt escudriñar. ~**y** /'skruːtɪnɪ/ n examen m minucioso

scuff /skʌf/ vt arañar ⟨shoes⟩

scuffle /'skʌfl/ n pelea f

scullery /'skʌlərɪ/ n trascocina f

sculpt /skʌlpt/ vt/i esculpir. ~**or** n escultor m. ~**ure** /-tʃə(r)/ n escultura f. ● vt/i esculpir

scum /skʌm/ n espuma f; (people, pej) escoria f

scurf /skɜːf/ n caspa f

scurrilous /'skʌrɪləs/ a grosero

scurry /'skʌrɪ/ vi correr

scurvy /'skɜːvɪ/ n escorbuto m

scuttle[1] /'skʌtl/ n cubo m del carbón

scuttle[2] /'skʌtl/ vt barrenar ⟨ship⟩

scuttle[3] /'skʌtl/ vi. ~ **away** correr, irse de prisa

scythe /saɪð/ n guadaña f

SE abbr (south-east) sudeste m

sea /siː/ n mar m. **at** ~ en el mar; (fig) confuso. **by** ~ por mar. ~**board** /'siːbɔːd/ n litoral m. ~**farer** /'siːfeərə(r)/ n marinero m. ~**food** /'siːfuːd/ n mariscos mpl. ~**gull** /'siːgʌl/ n gaviota f. ~**horse** n caballito m de mar, hipocampo m

seal[1] /siːl/ n sello m. ● vt sellar. ~ **off** acordonar ⟨area⟩

seal² /si:l/ (*animal*) foca *f*

sea level /'si:levl/ *n* nivel *m* del mar

sealing-wax /'si:lɪŋwæks/ *n* lacre *m*

sea lion /'si:laɪən/ *n* león *m* marino

seam /si:m/ *n* costura *f*; (*of coal*) veta *f*

seaman /'si:mən/ *n* (*pl* -men) marinero *m*

seamy /'si:mɪ/ *a*. the ~ side *n* el lado *m* sórdido, el revés *m*

seance /'seɪɑ:ns/ *n* sesión *f* de espiritismo

sea: ~plane /'si:pleɪn/ *n* hidroavión *f*. ~port /'si:pɔ:t/ *n* puerto *m* de mar

search /sɜ:tʃ/ *vt* registrar; (*examine*) examinar. ● *vi* buscar. ● *n* (*for sth*) búsqueda *f*; (*of sth*) registro *m*. in ~ of en busca de. ~ for buscar. ~ing *a* penetrante. ~party *n* equipo *m* de salvamento. ~light /'sɜ:tʃlaɪt/ *n* reflector *m*

sea: ~scape /'si:skeɪp/ *n* marina *f*. ~shore *n* orilla *f* del mar. ~sick /'si:sɪk/ *a* mareado. be ~sick marearse. ~side /'si:saɪd/ *n* playa *f*

season /'si:zn/ *n* estación *f*; (*period*) temporada *f*. ● *vt* (*culin*) sazonar; secar ‹*wood*›. ~able *a* propio de la estación. ~al *a* estacional. ~ed /'si:znd/ *a* (*fig*) experto. ~ing *n* condimento *m*. ~ticket *n* billete *m* de abono

seat /si:t/ *n* asiento *m*; (*place*) lugar *m*; (*of trousers*) fondillos *mpl*; (*bottom*) trasero *m*. take a ~ sentarse. ● *vt* sentar; (*have seats for*) tener asientos para. ~belt *n* cinturón *m* de seguridad

sea: ~urchin *n* erizo *m* de mar. ~weed /'si:wi:d/ *n* alga *f*. ~worthy /'si:wɜ:ðɪ/ *a* en estado de navegar

secateurs /'sekətə:z/ *npl* tijeras *fpl* de podar

sece|de /sɪ'si:d/ *vi* separase. ~ssion /-eʃn/ *n* secesión *f*

seclu|de /sɪ'klu:d/ *vt* aislar. ~ded *a* aislado. ~sion /-ʒn/ *n* aislamiento *m*

second¹ /'sekənd/ *a* & *n* segundo (*m*). on ~ thoughts pensándolo bien. ● *adv* (*in race etc*) en segundo lugar. ● *vt* apoyar. ~s *npl* (*goods*) artículos *mpl* de segunda calidad; (*more food, fam*) otra porción *f*

second² /sɪ'kɒnd/ *vt* (*transfer*) trasladar temporalmente

secondary /'sekəndrɪ/ *a* secundario. ~ school *n* instituto *m*

second: ~best *a* segundo. ~class *a* de segunda clase. ~hand *a* de segunda mano. ~ly *adv* en segundo lugar. ~rate *a* mediocre

secre|cy /'si:krəsɪ/ *n* secreto *m*. ~t /'si:krɪt/ *a* & *n* secreto (*m*). in ~t en secreto

secretar|ial /sekrə'teərɪəl/ *a* de secretario. ~iat /sekrə'teərɪət/ *n* secretaría *f*. ~y /'sekrətrɪ/ *n* secretario *m*. S~y of State ministro *m*: (*Amer*) Ministro *m* de Asuntos Exteriores

secret|e /sɪ'kri:t/ *vt* (*med*) secretar. ~ion /-ʃn/ *n* secreción *f*

secretive /'si:krɪtɪv/ *a* reservado

secretly /'si:krɪtlɪ/ *adv* en secreto

sect /sekt/ *n* secta *f*. ~arian /-'teərɪən/ *a* sectario

section /'sekʃn/ *n* sección *f*; (*part*) parte *f*

sector /'sektə(r)/ *n* sector *m*

secular /'sekjʊlə(r)/ *a* seglar

secur|e /sɪ'kjʊə(r)/ *a* seguro; (*fixed*) fijo. ● *vt* asegurar; (*obtain*) obtener. ~ely *adv* seguramente. ~ity /sɪ'kjʊərətɪ/ *n* seguridad *f*; (*for loan*) garantía *f*, fianza *f*

sedate /sɪ'deɪt/ *a* sosegado

sedat|ion /sɪ'deɪʃn/ *n* sedación *f*. ~ive /'sedətɪv/ *a* & *n* sedante (*m*)

sedentary /'sedəntrɪ/ *a* sedentario

sediment /'sedɪmənt/ *n* sedimento *m*

seduc|e /sɪ'dju:s/ *vt* seducir. ~er /-ə(r)/ *n* seductor *m*. ~tion /sɪ'dʌkʃn/ *n* seducción *f*. ~tive /-tɪv/ *a* seductor

see¹ /si:/ ● *vt* (*pt* saw, *pp* seen) ver; (*understand*) comprender; (*notice*) notar; (*escort*) acompañar. ~ing that visto que. ~ you later! ¡hasta luego! ● *vi* ver; (*understand*) comprender. ~ about ocuparse de. ~ off despedirse de. ~ through llevar a cabo; descubrir el juego de ‹*person*›. ~ to ocuparse de

see² /si:/ *n* diócesis *f*

seed /si:d/ *n* semilla *f*; (*fig*) germen *m*; (*tennis*) preseleccionado *m*. ~ling *n* plantón *m*. go to ~ granar; (*fig*) echarse a perder. ~y /'si:dɪ/ *a* (-ier, -iest) sórdido

seek /si:k/ *vt* (*pt* sought) buscar. ~ out buscar

seem /si:m/ *vi* parecer. ~ingly *adv* aparentemente

seemly /'si:mlɪ/ *a* (-ier, -iest) correcto

seen /si:n/ *see* **see**[1]

seep /si:p/ *vi* filtrarse. **~age** *n* filtración *f*

see-saw /'si:sɔ:/ *n* balancín *m*

seethe /si:ð/ *vi* (*fig*) hervir. **be seething with anger** estar furioso

see-through /'si:θru:/ *a* transparente

segment /'segmənt/ *n* segmento *m*; (*of orange*) gajo *m*

segregat|e /'segrigeit/ *vt* segregar. **~ion** /-'geiʃn/ *n* segregación *f*

seiz|e /si:z/ *vt* agarrar; (*jurid*) incautarse de. **~e on** *vi* valerse de. **~e up** *vi* (*tec*) agarrotarse. **~ure** /'si:ʒə(r)/ *n* incautación *f*; (*med*) ataque *m*

seldom /'seldəm/ *adv* raramente

select /si'lekt/ *vt* escoger; (*sport*) seleccionar. **●** *a* selecto; (*exclusive*) exclusivo. **~ion** /-ʃn/ *n* selección *f*. **~ive** *a* selectivo

self /self/ *n* (*pl* **selves**) sí mismo. **~-addressed** *a* con su propia dirección. **~-assurance** *n* confianza *f* en sí mismo. **~-assured** *a* seguro de sí mismo. **~-catering** *a* con facilidades para cocinar. **~-centred** *a* egocéntrico. **~-confidence** *n* confianza *f* en sí mismo. **~-confident** *a* seguro de sí mismo. **~-conscious** *a* cohibido. **~-contained** *a* independiente. **~-control** *n* dominio *m* de sí mismo. **~-defence** *n* defensa *f* propia. **~-denial** *n* abnegación *f*. **~-employed** *a* que trabaja por cuenta propia. **~-esteem** *n* amor *m* propio. **~-evident** *a* evidente. **~-government** *n* autonomía *f*. **~-important** *a* presumido. **~-indulgent** *a* inmoderado. **~-interest** *n* interés *m* propio. **~-ish** /'selfiʃ/ *a* egoísta. **~-ishness** *n* egoísmo *m*. **~-less** /'selflis/ *a* desinteresado. **~-made** *a* rico por su propio esfuerzo. **~-opinionated** *a* intransigente; (*arrogant*) engreído. **~-pity** *n* compasión *f* de sí mismo. **~-portrait** *n* autorretrato *m*. **~-possessed** *a* dueño de sí mismo. **~-reliant** *a* independiente. **~-respect** *n* amor *m* propio. **~-righteous** *a* santurrón. **~-sacrifice** *n* abnegación *f*. **~-satisfied** *a* satisfecho de sí mismo. **~-seeking** *a* egoísta. **~-service** *a* & *n* autoservicio (*m*). **~-styled** *a* sedicente, llamado. **~-sufficient** *a* independiente. **~-willed** *a* terco

sell /sel/ *vt* (*pt* **sold**) vender. **be sold on** (*fam*) entusiasmarse por. **be sold out** estar agotado. **●** *vi* venderse. **~-by date** *n* fecha *f* de caducidad. **~ off** *vt* liquidar. **~ up** *vt* vender todo. **~er** *n* vendedor *m*

Sellotape /'seləteip/ *n* (*P*) (papel *m*) celo *m*, cinta *f* adhesiva

sell-out /'selaʊt/ *n* (*betrayal*, *fam*) traición *f*

semantic /si'mæntik/ *a* semántico. **~s** *n* semántica *f*

semaphore /'seməfɔ:(r)/ *n* semáforo *m*

semblance /'semblans/ *n* apariencia *f*

semen /'si:mən/ *n* semen *m*

semester /si'mestə(r)/ *n* (*Amer*) semestre *m*

semi... /'semi/ *pref* semi...

semi|breve /'semibri:v/ *n* semibreve *f*, redonda *f*. **~circle** /'semisɜ:kl/ *n* semicírculo *m*. **~circular** /-'sɜ:kjʊlə(r)/ *a* semicircular. **~colon** /semi'kəʊlən/ *n* punto *m* y coma. **~detached** /semidi'tætʃt/ *a* ‹house› adosado. **~final** /semi'fainl/ *n* semifinal *f*

seminar /'semina:(r)/ *n* seminario *m*

seminary /'seminəri/ *n* (*college*) seminario *m*

semiquaver /'semikweivə(r)/ *n* (*mus*) semicorchea *f*

Semit|e /'si:mait/ *n* semita *m* & *f*. **~ic** /si'mitik/ *a* semítico

semolina /semə'li:nə/ *n* sémola *f*

senat|e /'senit/ *n* senado *m*. **~or** /-ətə(r)/ *n* senador *m*

send /send/ *vt/i* (*pt* **sent**) enviar. **~ away** despedir. **~ away for** pedir (por correo). **~ for** enviar a buscar. **~ off for** pedir (por correo). **~ up** (*fam*) parodiar. **~er** *n* remitente *m*. **~-off** *n* despedida *f*

senil|e /'si:nail/ *a* senil. **~ity** /si'niləti/ *n* senilidad *f*

senior /'si:niə(r)/ *a* mayor; (*in rank*) superior; ‹partner etc› principal. **●** *n* mayor *m* & *f*. **~ citizen** *n* jubilado *m*. **~ity** /-'orəti/ *n* antigüedad *f*

sensation /sen'seiʃn/ *n* sensación *f*. **~al** *a* sensacional

sense /sens/ *n* sentido *m*; (*common sense*) juicio *m*; (*feeling*) sensación *f*. **make ~** *vt* tener sentido. **make ~ of** comprender. **~less** *a* insensato; (*med*) sin sentido

sensibilities /sensi'bilətiz/ *npl* susceptibilidad *f*. **~ibility** /sensi'biləti/ *n* sensibilidad *f*

sensible /'sensəbl/ a sensato; ‹clothing› práctico

sensitiv|e /'sensɪtɪv/ a sensible; (touchy) susceptible. ~ity /-'tɪvətɪ/ n sensibilidad f

sensory /'sensərɪ/ a sensorio

sensual /'senʃʊəl/ a sensual. ~ity /-'ælətɪ/ n sensualidad f

sensuous /'sensʊəs/ a sensual

sent /sent/ see **send**

sentence /'sentəns/ n frase f; (jurid) sentencia f; (punishment) condena f. ● vt. ~ **to** condenar a

sentiment /'sentɪmənt/ n sentimiento m; (opinion) opinión f. ~al /sentɪ'mentl/ a sentimental. ~ality /-'tælətɪ/ n sentimentalismo m

sentry /'sentrɪ/ n centinela f

separable /'sepərəbl/ a separable

separate[1] /'sepərət/ a separado; (independent) independiente. ~ly adv por separado. ~s npl coordinados mpl

separat|e[2] /'sepəreɪt/ vt separar. ● vi separarse. ~ion n separación f. ~ist /'sepərətɪst/ n separatista m & f

September /sep'tembə(r)/ n se(p)tiembre m

septic /'septɪk/ a séptico. ~ **tank** n fosa f séptica

sequel /'siːkwəl/ n continuación f; (consequence) consecuencia f

sequence /'siːkwəns/ n sucesión f; (of film) secuencia f

sequin /'siːkwɪn/ n lentejuela f

serenade /serə'neɪd/ n serenata f. ● vt dar serenata a

seren|e /sɪ'riːn/ a sereno. ~ity /-'enətɪ/ n serenidad f

sergeant /'sɑːdʒənt/ n sargento m

serial /'sɪərɪəl/ n serial m. ● a de serie. ~ize vt publicar por entregas

series /'sɪəriːz/ n serie f

serious /'sɪərɪəs/ a serio. ~ly adv seriamente; (ill) gravemente. **take ~ly** tomar en serio. ~ness n seriedad f

sermon /'sɜːmən/ n sermón m

serpent /'sɜːpənt/ n serpiente f

serrated /sɪ'reɪtɪd/ a serrado

serum /'sɪərəm/ n (pl -a) suero m

servant /'sɜːvənt/ n criado m; (fig) servidor m

serve /sɜːv/ vt servir; (in the army etc) prestar servicio; cumplir ‹sentence›. ~ **as** servir de. ~ **its purpose** servir para el caso. **it ~s you right** ¡bien te lo mereces! ¡te está bien merecido! ● vi servir. ● n (in tennis) saque m

service /'sɜːvɪs/ n servicio m; (maintenance) revisión f. **of ~ to** útil a. ● vt revisar ‹car etc›. ~able /'sɜːvɪsəbl/ a práctico; (durable) duradero. ~ **charge** n servicio m. ~man /'sɜːvɪsmən/ n (pl -men) militar m. ~s npl (mil) fuerzas fpl armadas. ~ **station** n estación f de servicio

serviette /sɜːvɪ'et/ n servilleta f

servile /'sɜːvaɪl/ a servil

session /'seʃn/ n sesión f; (univ) curso m

set /set/ vt (pt set, pres p setting) poner; poner en hora ‹clock etc›; fijar ‹limit etc›; (typ) componer. ~ **fire to** pegar fuego a. ~ **free** vt poner en libertad. ● vi ‹sun› ponerse; ‹jelly› cuajarse. ● n serie f; (of cutlery etc) juego m; (tennis) set m; (TV, radio) aparato m; (of hair) marcado m; (in theatre) decorado m; (of people) círculo m. ● a fijo. **be ~ on** estar resuelto a. ~ **about** vi empezar a. ~ **back** vt (delay) retardar; (cost, sl) costar. ~ **off** vi salir. ● vt (make start) poner en marcha; hacer estallar ‹bomb›. ~ **out** vi (declare) declarar; (leave) salir. ~ **sail** salir. ~ **the table** poner la mesa. ~ **up** vt establecer. ~back n revés m. ~ **square** n escuadra f de dibujar

settee /se'tiː/ n sofá m

setting /'setɪŋ/ n (of sun) puesta f; (of jewel) engaste m; (in theatre) escenario m; (typ) composición f. ~lotion n fijador m

settle /'setl/ vt (arrange) arreglar; (pay) pagar; fijar ‹date›; calmar ‹nerves›. ● vi (come to rest) posarse; (live) instalarse. ~ **down** calmarse; (become orderly) sentar la cabeza. ~ **for** aceptar. ~ **up** ajustar cuentas. ~ment /'setlmənt/ n establecimiento m; (agreement) acuerdo m; (com) liquidación f; (place) colonia f. ~r /-ə(r)/ n colonizador m

set: ~to n pelea f. ~up n (fam) sistema m

seven /'sevn/ a & n siete (m). ~teen /sevn'tiːn/ a & n diecisiete (m). ~teenth a & n decimoséptimo (m). ~th a & n séptimo (m). ~tieth a & n setenta (m), septuagésimo (m). ~ty /'sevntɪ/ a & n setenta (m)

sever /'sevə(r)/ vt cortar; (fig) romper

several /'sevrəl/ a & pron varios

severance /'sevərəns/ n (breaking off) ruptura f

sever|e /sɪ'vɪə(r)/ a (-er, -est) severo; (violent) violento; (serious) grave; ⟨weather⟩ riguroso. **~ely** adv severamente; (seriously) gravemente. **~ity** /-'verətɪ/ n severidad f; (violence) violencia f; (seriousness) gravedad f

sew /səʊ/ vt/i (pt sewed, pp sewn, or sewed) coser

sew|age /'su:ɪdʒ/ n aguas fpl residuales. **~er** /'su:ə(r)/ n cloaca f

sewing /'səʊɪŋ/ n costura f. **~-machine** n máquina f de coser

sewn /səʊn/ see **sew**

sex /seks/ n sexo m. **have ~** tener relaciones sexuales. ● a sexual. **~ist** /'seksɪst/ a & n sexista (m & f)

sextet /seks'tet/ n sexteto m

sexual /'seksʊəl/ a sexual. **~ intercourse** n relaciones fpl sexuales. **~ity** /-'ælətɪ/ n sexualidad f

sexy /'seksɪ/ a (-ier, -iest) excitante, sexy, provocativo

shabb|ily /'ʃæbɪlɪ/ adv pobremente; (act) mezquinamente. **~iness** n pobreza f; (meanness) mezquindad f. **~y** /'ʃæbɪ/ a (-ier, -iest) ⟨clothes⟩ gastado; ⟨person⟩ pobremente vestido; (mean) mezquino

shack /ʃæk/ n choza f

shackles /'ʃæklz/ npl grillos mpl, grilletes mpl

shade /ʃeɪd/ n sombra f; (of colour) matiz m; (for lamp) pantalla f. **a ~ better** un poquito mejor. ● vt dar sombra a

shadow /'ʃædəʊ/ n sombra f. **S~ Cabinet** n gobierno m en la sombra. ● vt (follow) seguir. **~y** a (fig) vago

shady /'ʃeɪdɪ/ a (-ier, -iest) sombreado; (fig) dudoso

shaft /ʃɑːft/ n (of arrow) astil m; (mec) eje m; (of light) rayo m; (of lift, mine) pozo m

shaggy /'ʃægɪ/ a (-ier, -iest) peludo

shak|e /ʃeɪk/ vt (pt shook, pp shaken) sacudir; agitar ⟨bottle⟩; (shock) desconcertar. **~e hands with** estrechar la mano a. ● vi temblar. **~e off** vi deshacerse de. ● n sacudida f. **~e-up** n reorganización f. **~y** /'ʃeɪkɪ/ a (-ier, -iest) tembloroso; ⟨table etc⟩ inestable; (unreliable) incierto

shall /ʃæl/ v, aux (first person in future tense). **I ~ go** iré. **we ~ see** veremos

shallot /ʃə'lɒt/ n chalote m

shallow /'ʃæləʊ/ a (-er, -est) poco profundo; (fig) superficial

sham /ʃæm/ n farsa f; (person) impostor m. ● a falso; (affected) fingido. ● vt (pt shammed) fingir

shambles /'ʃæmblz/ npl (mess, fam) desorden m total

shame /ʃeɪm/ n vergüenza f. **what a ~!** ¡qué lástima! ● vt avergonzar. **~faced** /'ʃeɪmfeɪst/ a avergonzado. **~ful** a vergonzoso. **~fully** adv vergonzosamente. **~less** a desvergonzado

shampoo /ʃæm'pu:/ n champú m. ● vt lavar

shamrock /'ʃæmrɒk/ n trébol m

shandy /'ʃændɪ/ n cerveza f con gaseosa, clara f

shan't /ʃɑːnt/ = **shall not**

shanty /'ʃæntɪ/ n chabola f. **~ town** n chabolas fpl

shape /ʃeɪp/ n forma f. ● vt formar; determinar ⟨future⟩. ● vi formarse. **~ up** prometer. **~less** a informe. **~ly** /'ʃeɪplɪ/ a (-ier, -iest) bien proporcionado

share /ʃeə(r)/ n porción f; (com) acción f. **go ~s** compartir. ● vt compartir; (divide) dividir. ● vi participar. **~ in** participar en. **~holder** /'ʃeəhəʊldə(r)/ n accionista m & f. **~out** n reparto m

shark /ʃɑːk/ n tiburón m; (fig) estafador m

sharp /ʃɑːp/ a (-er, -est) ⟨knife etc⟩ afilado; ⟨pin etc⟩ puntiagudo; ⟨pain, sound⟩ agudo; ⟨taste⟩ acre; (sudden, harsh) brusco; (well defined) marcado; (dishonest) poco escrupuloso; (clever) listo. ● adv en punto. **at seven o'clock ~** a las siete en punto. ● n (mus) sostenido m. **~en** /'ʃɑːpn/ vt afilar; sacar punta a ⟨pencil⟩. **~ener** n (mec) afilador m; (for pencils) sacapuntas m invar. **~ly** adv bruscamente

shatter /'ʃætə(r)/ vt hacer añicos; (upset) perturbar. ● vi hacerse añicos. **~ed** a (exhausted) agotado

shav|e /ʃeɪv/ vt afeitar. ● vi afeitarse. ● n afeitado m. **have a ~e** afeitarse. **~en** a ⟨face⟩ afeitado; ⟨head⟩ rapado. **~er** n maquinilla f de afeitar). **~ing-brush** n brocha f de

afietar. **~ing-cream** *n* crema *f* de afeitar

shawl /ʃɔːl/ *n* chal *m*

she /ʃiː/ *pron* ella. ● *n* hembra *f*

sheaf /ʃiːf/ *n* (*pl* **sheaves**) gavilla *f*

shear /ʃɪə(r)/ *vt* (*pp* **shorn**, *or* **sheared**) esquilar. **~s** /ʃɪəz/ *npl* tijeras *fpl* grandes

sheath /ʃiːθ/ *n* (*pl* **-s** /ʃiːðz/) vaina *f*; (*contraceptive*) condón *m*. **~e** /ʃiːð/ *vt* envainar

shed[1] /ʃed/ *n* cobertizo *m*

shed[2] /ʃed/ *vt* (*pt* **shed**, *pres p* **shedding**) perder; derramar ⟨*tears*⟩; despojarse de ⟨*clothes*⟩. **~ light on** aclarar

sheen /ʃiːn/ *n* lustre *m*

sheep /ʃiːp/ *n invar* oveja *f*. **~-dog** *n* perro *m* pastor. **~ish** /ʃiːpɪʃ/ *a* vergonzoso. **~ishly** *adv* tímidamente. **~skin** /ʃiːpskɪn/ *n* piel *f* de carnero, zamarra *f*

sheer /ʃɪə(r)/ *a* puro; (*steep*) perpendicular; ⟨*fabric*⟩ muy fino. ● *adv* a pico

sheet /ʃiːt/ *n* sábana *f*; (*of paper*) hoja *f*; (*of glass*) lámina *f*; (*of ice*) capa *f*

sheikh /ʃeɪk/ *n* jeque *m*

shelf /ʃelf/ *n* (*pl* **shelves**) estante *m*. **be on the ~** quedarse para vestir santos

shell /ʃel/ *n* concha *f*; (*of egg*) cáscara *f*; (*of building*) casco *m*; (*explosive*) proyectil *m*. ● *vt* desgranar ⟨*peas etc*⟩; (*mil*) bombardear. **~fish** /ʃelfɪʃ/ *n invar* (*crustacean*) crustáceo *m*; (*mollusc*) marisco *m*

shelter /ʃeltə(r)/ *n* refugio *m*, abrigo *m*. ● *vt* abrigar; (*protect*) proteger; (*give lodging to*) dar asilo a. ● *vi* abrigarse. **~ed** *a* ⟨*spot*⟩ abrigado; ⟨*life etc*⟩ protegido

shelv|e /ʃelv/ *vt* (*fig*) dar carpetazo a. **~ing** /ʃelvɪŋ/ *n* estantería *f*

shepherd /ʃepəd/ *n* pastor *m*. ● *vt* guiar. **~ess** /-ˈdes/ *n* pastora *f*. **~'s pie** *n* carne *f* picada con puré de patatas

sherbet /ʃɜːbət/ *n* (*Amer, water-ice*) sorbete *m*

sheriff /ʃerɪf/ *n* alguacil *m*, sheriff *m*

sherry /ʃerɪ/ *n* (vino *m* de) jerez *m*

shield /ʃiːld/ *n* escudo *m*. ● *vt* proteger

shift /ʃɪft/ *vt* cambiar; cambiar de sitio ⟨*furniture etc*⟩; echar ⟨*blame etc*⟩. ● *n* cambio *m*; (*work*) turno *m*;

⟨*workers*⟩ tanda *f*. **make ~** arreglárselas. **~less** /ʃɪftlɪs/ *a* holgazán

shifty /ʃɪftɪ/ *a* (**-ier, -iest**) taimado

shilling /ʃɪlɪŋ/ *n* chelín *m*

shilly-shally /ʃɪlɪʃælɪ/ *vi* titubear

shimmer /ʃɪmə(r)/ *vi* rielar, relucir. ● *n* luz *f* trémula

shin /ʃɪn/ *n* espinilla *f*

shine /ʃaɪn/ *vi* (*pt* **shone**) brillar. ● *vt* sacar brillo a. **~ on** dirigir ⟨*torch*⟩. ● *n* brillo *m*

shingle /ʃɪŋgl/ *n* (*pebbles*) guijarros *mpl*

shingles /ʃɪŋglz/ *npl* (*med*) herpes *mpl* & *fpl*

shiny /ʃaɪnɪ/ *a* (**-ier, -iest**) brillante

ship /ʃɪp/ *n* buque *m*, barco *m*. ● *vt* (*pt* **shipped**) transportar; (*send*) enviar; (*load*) embarcar. **~building** /ʃɪpbɪldɪŋ/ *n* construcción *f* naval. **~ment** *n* envío *m*. **~per** *n* expedidor *m*. **~ping** *n* envío *m*; (*ships*) barcos *mpl*. **~shape** /ʃɪpʃeɪp/ *adv* & *a* en buen orden, en regla. **~wreck** /ʃɪprek/ *n* naufragio *m*. **~wrecked** *a* naufragado. **be ~wrecked** naufragar. **~yard** /ʃɪpjɑːd/ *n* astillero *m*

shirk /ʃɜːk/ *vt* esquivar. **~er** *n* gandul *m*

shirt /ʃɜːt/ *n* camisa *f*. **in ~sleeves** en mangas de camisa. **~y** /ʃɜːtɪ/ *a* (*sl*) enfadado

shiver /ʃɪvə(r)/ *vi* temblar. ● *n* escalofrío *m*

shoal /ʃəʊl/ *n* banco *m*

shock /ʃɒk/ *n* sacudida *f*; (*fig*) susto *m*; (*elec*) descarga *f*; (*med*) choque *m*. ● *vt* escandalizar. **~ing** *a* escandaloso; (*fam*) espantoso. **~ingly** *adv* terriblemente

shod /ʃɒd/ *see* **shoe**

shodd|ily /ʃɒdɪlɪ/ *adv* mal. **~y** /ʃɒdɪ/ *a* (**-ier, -iest**) mal hecho, de pacotilla

shoe /ʃuː/ *n* zapato *m*; (*of horse*) herradura *f*. ● *vt* (*pt* **shod**, *pres p* **shoeing**) herrar ⟨*horse*⟩. **be well shod** estar bien calzado. **~horn** /ʃuːhɔːn/ *n* calzador *m*. **~lace** *n* cordón *m* de zapato. **~maker** /ʃuːmeɪkə(r)/ *n* zapatero *m*. **~ polish** *n* betún *m*. **~string** *n*. **on a ~string** con poco dinero. **~tree** *n* horma *f*

shone /ʃɒn/ *see* **shine**

shoo /ʃuː/ *vt* ahuyentar

shook /ʃʊk/ *see* **shake**

shoot /ʃuːt/ *vt* (*pt* **shot**) disparar; rodar ⟨*film*⟩. ● *vi* (*hunt*) cazar. ● *n*

(*bot*) retoño *m*; (*hunt*) cacería *f*. ∼
down *vt* derribar. ∼ **out** *vi* (*rush*)
salir disparado. ∼ **up** ⟨*prices*⟩ subir
de repente; (*grow*) crecer. ∼**ing-
range** *n* campo *m* de tiro

shop /ʃɒp/ *n* tienda *f*; (*work-shop*)
taller *m*. **talk** ∼ hablar de su
trabajo. ● *vi* (*pt* **shopping**) hacer
compras. ∼ **around** buscar el mejor
precio. **go** ∼**ping** ir de compras. ∼
assistant *n* dependiente *m*.
∼**keeper** /ˈʃɒpkiːpə(r)/ *n* tendero *m*.
∼**lifter** *n* ratero *m* (de tiendas).
∼**lifting** *n* ratería *f* (de tiendas).
∼**per** *n* comprador *m*. ∼**ping**
/ˈʃɒpɪŋ/ *n* compras *fpl*. ∼**ping bag** *n*
bolsa *f* de la compra. ∼**ping centre**
n centro *m* comercial. ∼ **steward** *n*
enlace *m* sindical. ∼**window** *n*
escaparate *m*

shore /ʃɔː(r)/ *n* orilla *f*

shorn /ʃɔːn/ *see* **shear**

short /ʃɔːt/ *a* (**-er, -est**) corto; (*not
lasting*) breve; (*person*) bajo; (*curt*)
brusco. **a ∼ time ago** hace poco. **be
∼ of** necesitar. **Mick is ∼ for Michael** Mick es el diminutivo de
Michael. ● *adv* (*stop*) en seco. ∼ **of
doing** a menos que no hagamos.
● *n*. **in ∼** en resumen. ∼**age** /ˈʃɔː-
tɪdʒ/ *n* escasez *f*. ∼**bread** /ˈʃɔːtbred/
n galleta *f* de mantequilla.
∼**change** *vt* estafar, engañar. ∼
circuit *n* cortocircuito *m*. ∼**coming**
/ˈʃɔːtkʌmɪŋ/ *n* deficiencia *f*. ∼ **cut** *n*
atajo *m*. ∼**en** /ˈʃɔːtn/ *vt* acortar.
∼**hand** /ˈʃɔːthænd/ *n* taquigrafía *f*.
∼**hand typist** *n* taquimecanógrafo
m, taquimeca *f* (*fam*). ∼**lived** *a* efímero. ∼**ly** /ˈʃɔːtlɪ/ *adv* dentro de
poco. ∼**s** *npl* pantalón *m* corto.
∼**sighted** *a* miope. ∼**tempered** *a*
de mal genio

shot /ʃɒt/ *see* **shoot**. ● *n* tiro *m*; (*person*) tirador *m*; (*photo*) foto *f*; (*injection*) inyección *f*. **like a ∼** como una
bala; (*willingly*) de buena gana.
∼**gun** *n* escopeta *f*

should /ʃʊd, ʃəd/ *v, aux*. **I ∼ go** debería ir. **I ∼ have seen him** debiera
haberlo visto. **I ∼ like** me gustaría.
if he ∼ come si viniese

shoulder /ˈʃəʊldə(r)/ *n* hombro *m*.
● *vt* cargar con ⟨*responsibility*⟩; llevar a hombros ⟨*burden*⟩. ∼**blade** *n*
omóplato *m*. ∼**strap** *n* correa *f* del
hombro; (*of bra etc*) tirante *m*

shout /ʃaʊt/ *n*. ● *vt/i* gritar.
∼ **at s.o.** gritarle a uno. ∼ **down**
hacer callar a gritos

shove /ʃʌv/ *n* empujón *m*. ● *vt*
empujar; (*put, fam*) poner. ● *vi*
empujar. ∼ **off** *vi* (*fam*) largarse

shovel /ˈʃʌvl/ *n* pala *f*. ● *vt* (*pt* **shov-
elled**) mover con la pala

show /ʃəʊ/ *vt* (*pt* **showed**, *pp* **shown**)
mostrar; (*put on display*) exponer;
poner ⟨*film*⟩. ● *vi* (*be visible*) verse.
● *n* demostración *f*; (*exhibition*)
exposición *f*; (*ostentation*) pompa *f*;
(*in theatre*) espectáculo *m*; (*in cinema*) sesión *f*. **on ∼** expuesto. ∼ **off**
vt lucir; (*pej*) ostentar. ● *vi* presu-
mir. ∼ **up** *vi* destacar; (*be present*)
presentarse. ● *vt* (*unmask*) desenmascarar. ∼**case** *n* vitrina *f*.
∼**down** *n* confrontación *f*

shower /ˈʃaʊə(r)/ *n* chaparrón *m*; (*of
blows etc*) lluvia *f*; (*for washing*)
ducha *f*. **have a ∼** ducharse. ● *vi*
ducharse. ● *vt*. ∼ **with** colmar de.
∼**proof** /ˈʃaʊəpruːf/ *a* impermeable. ∼**y** *a* lluvioso

show: ∼**jumping** *n* concurso *m* hípico. ∼**manship** /ˈʃəʊmənʃɪp/ *n*
teatralidad *f*, arte *f* de presentar
espectáculos

shown /ʃəʊn/ *see* **show**

show: ∼**off** *n* fanfarrón *m*. ∼**place**
n lugar *m* de interés turístico.
∼**room** /ˈʃəʊruːm/ *n* sala *f* de exposición *f*

showy /ˈʃəʊɪ/ *a* (**-ier, -iest**) llamativo;
⟨*person*⟩ ostentoso

shrank /ʃræŋk/ *see* **shrink**

shrapnel /ˈʃræpnəl/ *n* metralla *f*

shred /ʃred/ *n* pedazo *m*; (*fig*) pizca *f*.
● *vt* (*pt* **shredded**) hacer tiras;
(*culin*) cortar en tiras. ∼**der** *n*
desfibradora *f*, trituradora *f*

shrew /ʃruː/ *n* musaraña *f*; (*woman*)
arpía *f*

shrewd /ʃruːd/ *a* (**-er, -est**) astuto.
∼**ness** *n* astucia *f*

shriek /ʃriːk/ *n* chillido *m*. ● *vt/i*
chillar

shrift /ʃrɪft/ *n*. **give s.o. short ∼**
despachar a uno con brusquedad

shrill /ʃrɪl/ *a* agudo

shrimp /ʃrɪmp/ *n* camarón *m*

shrine /ʃraɪn/ *n* (*place*) lugar *m*
santo; (*tomb*) sepulcro *m*

shrink /ʃrɪŋk/ *vt* (*pt* **shrank**, *pp*
shrunk) encoger. ● *vi* encogerse;
(*draw back*) retirarse; (*lessen*) disminuir. ∼**age** *n* encogimiento *m*

shrivel /ˈʃrɪvl/ *vi* (*pt* **shrivelled**) (*dry
up*) secarse; (*become wrinkled*)
arrugarse

shroud /ʃraʊd/ n sudario m; (fig) velo m. ● vt (veil) velar

Shrove /ʃrəʊv/ n. ~ **Tuesday** n martes m de carnaval

shrub /ʃrʌb/ n arbusto m

shrug /ʃrʌg/ vt (pt **shrugged**) encogerse de hombros. ● n encogimiento m de hombros

shrunk /ʃrʌŋk/ see **shrink**

shrunken /ʃrʌŋkən/ a encogido

shudder /ʃʌdə(r)/ vi estremecerse. ● n estremecimiento m

shuffle /ʃʌfl/ vi arrastrar los pies. ● vt barajar ‹cards›. ● n arrastramiento m de los pies; (of cards) barajadura f

shun /ʃʌn/ vt (pt **shunned**) evitar

shunt /ʃʌnt/ vt apartar, desviar

shush /ʃʊʃ/ int ¡chitón!

shut /ʃʌt/ vt (pt **shut**, pres p **shutting**) cerrar. ● vi cerrarse. ~ **down** cerrar. ~ **up** vt cerrar; (fam) hacer callar. ● vi callarse. ~**down** n cierre m. ~**ter** /ʃʌtə(r)/ n contraventana f; (photo) obturador m

shuttle /ʃʌtl/ n lanzadera f; (train) tren m de enlace. ● vt transportar. ● vi ir y venir. ~**cock** /ʃʌtlkɒk/ n volante m. ~ **service** n servicio m de enlace

shy /ʃaɪ/ a (-er, -est) tímido. ● vi (pt **shied**) asustarse. ~ **away from** huir. ~**ness** n timidez f

Siamese /saɪəˈmiːz/ a siamés

sibling /ˈsɪblɪŋ/ n hermano m, hermana f

Sicil|ian /sɪˈsɪljən/ a & n siciliano (m). ~**y** /ˈsɪsɪlɪ/ n Sicilia f

sick /sɪk/ a enfermo; ‹humour› negro; (fed up, fam) harto. **be** ~ (vomit) vomitar. **be** ~ **of** (fig) estar harto de. **feel** ~ sentir náuseas. ~**en** /ˈsɪkən/ vt dar asco. ● vi caer enfermo. **be** ~**ening for** incubar

sickle /ˈsɪkl/ n hoz f

sick: ~**ly** /ˈsɪklɪ/ a (-ier, -iest) enfermizo; ‹taste, smell etc› nauseabundo. ~**ness** /ˈsɪknɪs/ n enfermedad f. ~**room** n cuarto m del enfermo

side /saɪd/ n lado m; (of river) orilla f; (of hill) ladera f; (team) equipo m; (fig) parte f. ~ **by** ~ uno al lado del otro. **on the** ~ (sideline) como actividad secundaria; (secretly) a escondidas. ● a lateral. ● vi. ~ **with** tomar el partido de. ~**board** /ˈsaɪdbɔːd/ n aparador m. ~**boards** npl, ~**burns** npl (sl) patillas fpl.

~**car** n sidecar m. ~**effect** n efecto m secundario. ~**light** /ˈsaɪdlaɪt/ n luz f de posición. ~**line** /ˈsaɪdlaɪn/ n actividad f secundaria. ~**long** /-lɒŋ/ a & adv de soslayo. ~**road** n calle f secundaria. ~**saddle** n silla f de mujer. **ride** ~**saddle** adv a mujeriegas. ~**show** n atracción f secundaria. ~**step** vt evitar. ~**track** vt desviar del asunto. ~**walk** /ˈsaɪdwɔːk/ n (Amer) acera f, vereda f (LAm). ~**ways** /ˈsaɪdweɪz/ a & adv de lado. ~**whiskers** npl patillas fpl

siding /ˈsaɪdɪŋ/ n apartadero m

sidle /ˈsaɪdl/ vi avanzar furtivamente. ~ **up to** acercarse furtivamente

siege /siːdʒ/ n sitio m, cerco m

siesta /sɪˈestə/ n siesta f

sieve /sɪv/ n cernedor m. ● vt cerner

sift /sɪft/ vt cerner. ● vi. ~ **through** examinar

sigh /saɪ/ n suspiro. ● vi suspirar

sight /saɪt/ n vista f; (spectacle) espectáculo m; (on gun) mira f. **at (first)** ~ a primera vista. **catch** ~ **of** vislumbrar. **lose** ~ **of** perder de vista. **on** ~ a primera vista. **within** ~ **of** (near) cerca de. ● vt ver, divisar. ~**seeing** /ˈsaɪtsiːɪŋ/ n visita f turística. ~**seer** /-ə(r)/ n turista m & f

sign /saɪn/ n señal f. ● vt firmar. ~ **on**, ~ **up** vt inscribir. ● vi inscribirse

signal /ˈsɪgnəl/ n señal f. ● vt (pt **signalled**) comunicar; hacer señas a ‹person›. ~**box** n casilla f del guardavía. ~**man** /ˈsɪgnəlmən/ n (pl -**men**) guardavía f

signatory /ˈsɪgnətrɪ/ n firmante m & f

signature /ˈsɪgnətʃə(r)/ n firma f. ~ **tune** n sintonía f

signet-ring /ˈsɪgnɪtrɪŋ/ n anillo m de sello

significan|ce /sɪgˈnɪfɪkəns/ n significado m. ~**t** /sɪgˈnɪfɪkənt/ a significativo; (important) importante. ~**tly** adv significativamente

signify /ˈsɪgnɪfaɪ/ vt significar. ● vi (matter) importar, tener importancia

signpost /ˈsaɪnpəʊst/ n poste m indicador

silen|ce /ˈsaɪləns/ n silencio m. ● vt hacer callar. ~**cer** /-ə(r)/ n silenciador m. ~**t** /ˈsaɪlənt/ a silencioso;

⟨*film*⟩ mudo. **∼tly** *adv* silencio-samente

silhouette /sɪluː'et/ *n* silueta *f*. ● *vt.* **be ∼d** perfilarse, destacarse (**against** contra)

silicon /'sɪlɪkən/ *n* silicio *m*. **∼ chip** *n* pastilla *f* de silicio

silk /sɪlk/ *n* seda *f*. **∼en** *a*, **∼y** *a* (*of silk*) de seda; (*like silk*) sedoso. **∼worm** *n* gusano *m* de seda

sill /sɪl/ *n* antepecho *m*; (*of window*) alféizar *m*; (*of door*) umbral *m*

silly /'sɪlɪ/ *a* (**-ier, -iest**) tonto. ● *n*. **∼billy** (*fam*) tonto *m*

silo /'saɪləʊ/ *n* (*pl* **-os**) silo *m*

silt /sɪlt/ *n* sedimento *m*

silver /'sɪlvə(r)/ *n* plata *f*. ● *a* de plata. **∼ plated** *a* bañado en plata, plateado. **∼side** /'sɪlvəsaɪd/ *n* (*culin*) contra *f*. **∼smith** /'sɪlvəsmɪθ/ *n* platero *m*. **∼ware** /'sɪlvəweə(r)/ *n* plata *f*. **∼ wedding** *n* bodas *fpl* de plata. **∼y** *a* plateado; ⟨*sound*⟩ argentino

simil|ar /'sɪmɪlə(r)/ *a* parecido. **∼arity** /-ɪ'lærətɪ/ *n* parecido *m*. **∼arly** *adv* de igual manera

simile /'sɪmɪlɪ/ *n* símil *m*

simmer /'sɪmə(r)/ *vt/i* hervir a fuego lento; (*fig*) hervir. **∼ down** calmarse

simpl|e /'sɪmpl/ *a* (**-er, -est**) sencillo; ⟨*person*⟩ ingenuo. **∼e-minded** *a* ingenuo. **∼eton** /'sɪmpltən/ *n* simplón *m*. **∼icity** /-'plɪsetɪ/ *n* sencillez *f*. **∼ification** /-ɪ'keɪʃn/ *n* simplificación *f*. **∼ify** /'sɪmplɪfaɪ/ *vt* simplificar. **∼y** *adv* sencillamente; (*absolutely*) absolutamente

simulat|e /'sɪmjʊleɪt/ *vt* simular. **∼ion** /-'leɪʃn/ *n* simulación *f*

simultaneous /sɪml'teɪnɪəs/ *a* simultáneo. **∼ly** *adv* simultáneamente

sin /sɪn/ *n* pecado *m*. ● *vi* (*pt* **sinned**) pecar

since /sɪns/ *prep* desde. ● *adv* desde entonces. ● *conj* desde que; (*because*) ya que

sincer|e /sɪn'sɪə(r)/ *a* sincero. **∼ely** *adv* sinceramente. **∼ity** /-'serətɪ/ *n* sinceridad *f*

sinew /'sɪnjuː/ *n* tendón *m*. **∼s** *npl* músculos *mpl*

sinful /'sɪnfl/ *a* pecaminoso; (*shocking*) escandaloso

sing /sɪŋ/ *vt/i* (*pt* **sang**, *pp* **sung**) cantar

singe /sɪndʒ/ *vt* (*pres p* **singeing**) chamuscar

singer /'sɪŋə(r)/ *n* cantante *m* & *f*

singl|e /'sɪŋgl/ *a* único; (*not double*) sencillo; (*unmarried*) soltero; ⟨*bed, room*⟩ individual. ● *n* (*tennis*) juego *m* individual; (*ticket*) billete *m* sencillo. ● *vt.* **∼e out** escoger; (*distinguish*) distinguir. **∼e-handed** *a* & *adv* sin ayuda. **∼e-minded** *a* resuelto

singlet /'sɪŋglɪt/ *n* camiseta *f*

singly /'sɪŋglɪ/ *adv* uno a uno

singsong /'sɪŋsɒŋ/ *a* monótono. ● *n*. **have a ∼** cantar juntos

singular /'sɪŋgjʊlə(r)/ *n* singular *f*. ● *a* singular; (*uncommon*) raro; ⟨*noun*⟩ en singular. **∼ly** *adv* singularmente

sinister /'sɪnɪstə(r)/ *a* siniestro

sink /sɪŋk/ *vt* (*pt* **sank**, *pp* **sunk**) hundir; perforar ⟨*well*⟩; invertir ⟨*money*⟩. ● *vi* hundirse; ⟨*patient*⟩ debilitarse. ● *n* fregadero *m*. **∼ in** *vi* penetrar

sinner /'sɪnə(r)/ *n* pecador *m*

sinuous /'sɪnjʊəs/ *a* sinuoso

sinus /'saɪnəs/ *n* (*pl* **-uses**) seno *m*

sip /sɪp/ *n* sorbo *m*. ● *vt* (*pt* **sipped**) sorber

siphon /'saɪfən/ *n* sifón *m*. *vt.* **∼ out** sacar con sifón

sir /sɜː(r)/ *n* señor *m*. **S∼** *n* (*title*) sir *m*

siren /'saɪərən/ *n* sirena *f*

sirloin /'sɜːlɔɪn/ *n* solomillo *m*, lomo *m* bajo

sirocco /sɪ'rɒkəʊ/ *n* siroco *m*

sissy /'sɪsɪ/ *n* hombre *m* afeminado, marica *m*, mariquita *m*; (*coward*) gallina *m* & *f*

sister /'sɪstə(r)/ *n* hermana *f*; (*nurse*) enfermera *f* jefe. **S∼ Mary** Sor María. **∼-in-law** *n* (*pl* **∼s-in-law**) cuñada *f*. **∼ly** *a* de hermana; (*like sister*) como hermana

sit /sɪt/ *vt* (*pt* **sat**, *pres p* **sitting**) sentar. ● *vi* sentarse; ⟨*committee etc*⟩ reunirse. **be ∼ting** estar sentado. **∼ back** *vi* (*fig*) relajarse. **∼ down** *vi* sentarse. **∼ for** *vi* presentarse a ⟨*exam*⟩; posar para ⟨*portrait*⟩. **∼ up** *vi* enderezarse; (*stay awake*) velar. **∼-in** *n* ocupación *f*

site /saɪt/ *n* sitio *m*. **building ∼** *n* solar *m*. ● *vt* situar

sit|ting *n* sesión *f*; (*in restaurant*) turno *m*. **∼ting-room** *n* cuarto *m* de estar

situat|e /'sɪtjʊeɪt/ vt situar. ∼**ed** a situado. ∼**ion** /-'eɪʃn/ n situación f; (job) puesto m

six /sɪks/ a & n seis (m). ∼**teen** /sɪk'sti:n/ a & n dieciséis (m). ∼**teenth** a & n decimosexto (m). ∼**th** a & n sexto (m). ∼**tieth** a & n sesenta (m), sexagésimo (m). ∼**ty** /'sɪkstɪ/ a & n sesenta (m)

size /saɪz/ n tamaño m; (of clothes) talla f; (of shoes) número m; (extent) magnitud f. ● vt. ∼ **up** (fam) juzgar. ∼**able** a bastante grande

sizzle /'sɪzl/ vi crepitar

skate[1] /skeɪt/ n patín m. ● vi patinar. ∼**board** /'skeɪtbɔːd/ n monopatín m. ∼**r** n patinador m

skate[2] /skeɪt/ n invar (fish) raya f

skating /'skeɪtɪŋ/ n patinaje m. ∼**-rink** n pista f de patinaje

skein /skeɪn/ n madeja f

skelet|al /'skelɪtl/ a esquelético. ∼**on** /'skelɪtn/ n esqueleto m. ∼**on staff** n personal m reducido

sketch /sketʃ/ n esbozo m; (drawing) dibujo m; (in theatre) pieza f corta y divertida. ● vt esbozar. ● vi dibujar. ∼**y** /'sketʃɪ/ a (-ier, -iest) incompleto

skew /skju:/ n. **on the** ∼ sesgado

skewer /'skju:ə(r)/ n broqueta f

ski /ski:/ n (pl skis) esquí m. ● vi (pt skied, pres p skiing) esquiar. **go** ∼**ing** ir a esquiar

skid /skɪd/ vi (pt skidded) patinar. ● n patinazo m

ski: ∼**er** n esquiador m. ∼**ing** n esquí m

skilful /'skɪlfl/ a diestro

ski-lift /'ski:lɪft/ n telesquí m

skill /skɪl/ n destreza f, habilidad f. ∼**ed** a hábil; (worker) cualificado

skim /skɪm/ vt (pt skimmed) espumar; desnatar (milk); (glide over) rozar. ∼ **over** vt rasar. ∼ **through** vi hojear

skimp /skɪmp/ vt escatimar. ∼**y** /'skɪmpɪ/ a (-ier, -iest) insuficiente; (skirt, dress) corto

skin /skɪn/ n piel f. ● vt (pt skinned) despellejar; pelar (fruit). ∼**deep** a superficial. ∼**diving** n natación f submarina. ∼**flint** /'skɪnflɪnt/ n tacaño m. ∼**ny** /'skɪnɪ/ a (-ier, -iest) flaco

skint /skɪnt/ a (sl) sin una perra

skip[1] /skɪp/ vi (pt skipped) vi saltar; (with rope) saltar a la comba. ● vt saltarse. ● n salto m

skip[2] /skɪp/ n (container) cuba f

skipper /'skɪpə(r)/ n capitán m

skipping-rope /'skɪpɪŋrəʊp/ n comba f

skirmish /'skɜːmɪʃ/ n escaramuza f

skirt /skɜːt/ n falda f. ● vt rodear; (go round) ladear

skirting-board /'skɜːtɪŋbɔːd/ n rodapié m, zócalo m

skit /skɪt/ n pieza f satírica

skittish /'skɪtɪʃ/ a juguetón; (horse) nervioso

skittle /'skɪtl/ n bolo m

skive /skaɪv/ vi (sl) gandulear

skivvy /'skɪvɪ/ n (fam) criada f

skulk /skʌlk/ vi avanzar furtivamente; (hide) esconderse

skull /skʌl/ n cráneo m; (remains) calavera f. ∼**cap** n casquete m

skunk /skʌŋk/ n mofeta f; (person) canalla f

sky /skaɪ/ n cielo m. ∼**blue** a & n azul (m) celeste. ∼**jack** /'skaɪdʒæk/ vt secuestrar. ∼**jacker** n secuestrador m. ∼**light** /'skaɪlaɪt/ n tragaluz m. ∼**scraper** /'skaɪskreɪpə(r)/ n rascacielos m invar

slab /slæb/ n bloque m; (of stone) losa f; (of chocolate) tableta f

slack /slæk/ a (-er, -est) flojo; (person) negligente; (period) de poca actividad. ● n (of rope) parte f floja. ● vt aflojar. ● vi aflojarse; (person) descansar. ∼**en** /'slækən/ vt aflojar. ● vi aflojarse; (person) descansar. ∼**en (off)** vt aflojar. ∼ **off** (fam) aflojar

slacks /slæks/ npl pantalones mpl

slag /slæg/ n escoria f

slain /sleɪn/ see **slay**

slake /sleɪk/ vt apagar

slam /slæm/ vt (pt slammed) golpear; (throw) arrojar; (criticize, sl) criticar. ∼ **the door** dar un portazo. ● vi cerrarse de golpe. ● n golpe m; (of door) portazo m

slander /'slɑːndə(r)/ n calumnia f. ● vt difamar. ∼**ous** a calumnioso

slang /slæŋ/ n jerga f, argot m. ∼**y** a vulgar

slant /slɑːnt/ vt inclinar; presentar con parcialidad (news). ● n inclinación f; (point of view) punto m de vista

slap /slæp/ vt (pt slapped) abofetear; (on the back) dar una palmada; (put) arrojar. ● n bofetada f; (on back) palmada f. ● adv de lleno. ∼**dash**

/'slæpdæʃ/ a descuidado. ∼**happy** a (*fam*) despreocupado; (*dazed*, *fam*) aturdido. ∼**stick** /'slæpstɪk/ n payasada f. ∼**up** a (*sl*) de primera categoría

slash /slæʃ/ vt acuchillar; (*fig*) reducir radicalmente. ● n cuchillada f

slat /slæt/ n tablilla f

slate /sleɪt/ n pizarra f. ● vt (*fam*) criticar

slaughter /'slɔːtə(r)/ vt masacrar; matar ⟨animal⟩. ● n carnicería f; (*of animals*) matanza f. ∼**house** /'slɔːtəhaʊs/ n matadero m

Slav /slɑːv/ a & n eslavo (m)

slav|e /sleɪv/ n esclavo m. ● vi trabajar como un negro. ∼**e-driver** n negrero m. ∼**ery** /-ərɪ/ n esclavitud f. ∼**ish** /'sleɪvɪʃ/ a servil

Slavonic /slə'vɒnɪk/ a eslavo

slay /sleɪ/ vt (*pt* slew, *pp* slain) matar

sleazy /'sliːzɪ/ a (-ier, -iest) (*fam*) sórdido

sledge /sledʒ/ n trineo m. ∼**hammer** n almádena f

sleek /sliːk/ a (-er, -est) liso, brillante; (*elegant*) elegante

sleep /sliːp/ n sueño m. **go to** ∼ dormirse. ● vi (*pt* slept) dormir. ∼ vt poder alojar. ∼**er** n durmiente m & f; (*on track*) traviesa f; (*berth*) coche-cama m. ∼**ily** adv soñolientamente. ∼**ing-bag** n saco m de dormir. ∼**ing-pill** n somnífero m. ∼**less** a insomne. ∼**lessness** n insomnio m. ∼**walker** n sonámbulo m. ∼**y** /'sliːpɪ/ a (-ier, -iest) soñoliento. **be** ∼**y** tener sueño

sleet /sliːt/ n aguanieve f. ● vi caer aguanieve

sleeve /sliːv/ n manga f; (*for record*) funda f. **up one's** ∼ en reserva. ∼**less** a sin mangas

sleigh /sleɪ/ n trineo m

sleight /slaɪt/ n. ∼ **of hand** prestidigitación f

slender /'slendə(r)/ a delgado; (*fig*) escaso

slept /slept/ *see* sleep

sleuth /sluːθ/ n investigador m

slew[1] /sluː/ *see* slay

slew[2] /sluː/ vi (*turn*) girar

slice /slaɪs/ n lonja f; (*of bread*) rebanada f; (*of sth round*) rodaja f; (*implement*) paleta f. ● vt cortar; rebanar ⟨bread⟩

slick /slɪk/ a liso; (*cunning*) astuto. ● n. **(oil)**∼ capa f de aceite

slid|e /slaɪd/ vt (*pt* slid) deslizar. ● vi resbalar. ∼**e over** pasar por alto de. ● n resbalón m; (*in playground*) tobogán m; (*for hair*) pasador m; (*photo*) diapositiva f; (*fig*, *fall*) baja f. ∼**e-rule** n regla f de cálculo. ∼**ing** a corredizo. ∼**ing scale** n escala f móvil

slight /slaɪt/ a (-er, -est) ligero; (*slender*) delgado. ● vt ofender. ● n desaire m. ∼**est** a mínimo. **not in the** ∼**est** en absoluto. ∼**ly** adv un poco

slim /slɪm/ a (**slimmer**, **slimmest**) delgado. ● vi (*pt* **slimmed**) adelgazar

slime /slaɪm/ n légamo m, lodo m, fango m

sliminess /'slɪmnɪs/ n delgadez f

slimy /'slaɪmɪ/ a legamoso, fangoso, viscoso; (*fig*) rastrero

sling /slɪŋ/ n honda f; (*toy*) tirador; (*med*) cabestrillo m. ● vt (*pt* slung) lanzar

slip /slɪp/ vt (*pt* slipped) deslizar. ∼ **s.o.'s mind** olvidársele a uno. ● vi deslizarse. ● n resbalón m; (*mistake*) error m; (*petticoat*) combinación f; (*paper*) trozo m. ∼ **of the tongue** n lapsus m linguae. **give the** ∼ **to** zafarse de, dar esquinazo a. ∼ **away** vi escabullirse. ∼ **into** vi ponerse ⟨clothes⟩. ∼ **up** vi (*fam*) equivocarse

slipper /'slɪpə(r)/ n zapatilla f

slippery /'slɪpərɪ/ a resbaladizo

slip: ∼**road** n rampa f de acceso. ∼**shod** /'slɪpʃɒd/ a descuidado. ∼**up** n (*fam*) error m

slit /slɪt/ n raja f; (*cut*) corte m. ● vt (*pt* slit, *pres p* slitting) rajar; (*cut*) cortar

slither /'slɪðə(r)/ vi deslizarse

sliver /'slɪvə(r)/ n trocito m; (*splinter*) astilla f

slobber /'slɒbə(r)/ vi babear

slog /slɒg/ vt (*pt* slogged) golpear. ● vi trabajar como un negro. ● n golpetazo m; (*hard work*) trabajo m penoso

slogan /'sləʊgən/ n eslogan m

slop /slɒp/ vt (*pt* slopped) derramar. ● vi derramarse. ∼**s** npl (*fam*) agua f sucia

slop|e /sləʊp/ vi inclinarse. ● vt inclinar. ● n declive m, pendiente m. ∼**ing** a inclinado

sloppy /'slɒpɪ/ a (-ier, -iest) (*wet*) mojado; ⟨food⟩ líquido; ⟨work⟩

descuidado; ⟨person⟩ desaliñado; (fig) sentimental

slosh /slɒʃ/ *vi* (fam) chapotear. ● *vt* (hit, sl) pegar

slot /slɒt/ *n* ranura *f*. ● *vt* (*pt* **slotted**) encajar

sloth /sləʊθ/ *n* pereza *f*

slot-machine /'slɒtməʃiːn/ *n* distribuidor *m* automático; (for gambling) máquina *f* tragaperras

slouch /slaʊtʃ/ *vi* andar cargado de espaldas; (in chair) repanchigarse

Slovak /'sləʊvæk/ *a* & *n* eslovaco (*m*). **~ia** /sləʊ'vækɪə/ *n* Eslovaquia *f*

sloven|liness /'slʌvnlɪnɪs/ *n* despreocupación *f*. **~y** /'slʌvnlɪ/ *a* descuidado

slow /sləʊ/ *a* (-er, -est) lento. be ~ ⟨clock⟩ estar atrasado. in ~ motion a cámara lenta. ● *adv* despacio. ● *vt* retardar. ● *vi* ir más despacio. ~ down, ~ up *vt* retardar. ● *vi* ir más despacio. **~coach** /'sləʊkəʊtʃ/ *n* tardón *m*. **~ly** *adv* despacio. **~ness** *n* lentitud *f*

sludge /slʌdʒ/ *n* fango *m*; (sediment) sedimento *m*

slug /slʌg/ *n* babosa *f*; (bullet) posta *f*. **~gish** /'slʌgɪʃ/ *a* lento

sluice /sluːs/ *n* (gate) compuerta *f*; (channel) canal *m*

slum /slʌm/ *n* tugurio *m*

slumber /'slʌmbə(r)/ *n* sueño *m*. ● *vi* dormir

slump /slʌmp/ *n* baja *f* repentina; (in business) depresión *f*. ● *vi* bajar repentinamente; (flop down) dejarse caer pesadamente; (collapse) desplomarse

slung /slʌŋ/ *see* **sling**

slur /slɜː(r)/ *vt/i* (*pt* **slurred**) articular mal. ● *n* dicción *f* defectuosa; (discredit) calumnia *f*

slush /slʌʃ/ *n* nieve *f* medio derretida; (fig) sentimentalismo *m*. ~ fund *n* fondos *mpl* secretos para fines deshonestos. **~y** *a* ⟨road⟩ cubierto de nieve medio derretida

slut /slʌt/ *n* mujer *f* desaseada

sly /slaɪ/ *a* (slyer, slyest) (crafty) astuto; (secretive) furtivo. ● *n*. on the ~ a escondidas. **~ly** *adv* astutamente

smack[1] /smæk/ *n* golpe *m*; (on face) bofetada *f*. ● *adv* (fam) de lleno. ● *vt* pegar

smack[2] /smæk/ *vi*. ~ of saber a; (fig) oler a

small /smɔːl/ *a* (-er, -est) pequeño. ● *n*. the ~ of the back la región *f* lumbar. ~ ads *npl* anuncios *mpl* por palabras. ~ change *n* cambio *m*. **~holding** /'smɔːlhəʊldɪŋ/ *n* parcela *f*. **~pox** /'smɔːlpɒks/ *n* viruela *f*. ~ talk *n* charla *f*. **~time** *a* (fam) de poca monta

smarmy /'smɑːmɪ/ *a* (-ier, -iest) (fam) zalamero

smart /smɑːt/ *a* (-er, -est) elegante; (clever) inteligente; (brisk) rápido. ● *vi* escocer. **~en** /'smɑːtn/ *vt* arreglar. ● *vi* arreglarse. **~en up** *vi* arreglarse. **~ly** *adv* elegantemente; (quickly) rápidamente. **~ness** *n* elegancia *f*

smash /smæʃ/ *vt* romper; (into little pieces) hacer pedazos; batir ⟨record⟩. ● *vi* romperse; (collide) chocar (into con). ● *n* (noise) estruendo *m*; (collision) choque *m*; (com) quiebra *f*. **~ing** /'smæʃɪŋ/ *a* (fam) estupendo

smattering /'smætərɪŋ/ *n* conocimientos *mpl* superficiales

smear /smɪə(r)/ *vt* untar (with de); (stain) manchar (with de); (fig) difamar. ● *n* mancha *f*; (med) frotis *m*

smell /smel/ *n* olor *m*; (sense) olfato *m*. ● *vt/i* (*pt* **smelt**) oler. **~y** *a* maloliente

smelt[1] /smelt/ *see* **smell**

smelt[2] /smelt/ *vt* fundir

smile /smaɪl/ *n* sonrisa *f*. ● *vi* sonreír(se)

smirk /smɜːk/ *n* sonrisa *f* afectada

smite /smaɪt/ *vt* (*pt* **smote**, *pp* **smitten**) golpear

smith /smɪθ/ *n* herrero *m*

smithereens /smɪðə'riːnz/ *npl* añicos *mpl*. smash to ~ hacer añicos

smitten /'smɪtn/ *see* **smite**. ● *a* encaprichado (with por)

smock /smɒk/ *n* blusa *f*, bata *f*

smog /smɒg/ *n* niebla *f* con humo

smok|e /sməʊk/ *n* humo *m*. ● *vt/i* fumar. **~eless** *a* sin humo. **~er** /-ə(r)/ *n* fumador *m*. **~e-screen** *n* cortina *f* de humo. **~y** *a* ⟨room⟩ lleno de humo

smooth /smuːð/ *a* (-er, -est) liso; ⟨sound, movement⟩ suave; ⟨sea⟩ tranquilo; ⟨manners⟩ zalamero. ● *vt* alisar; (fig) allanar. **~ly** *adv* suavemente

smote /sməʊt/ *see* **smite**

smother /'smʌðə(r)/ *vt* sofocar; (*cover*) cubrir

smoulder /'sməʊldə(r)/ *vi* arder sin llama; (*fig*) arder

smudge /smʌdʒ/ *n* borrón *m*, mancha *f*. ● *vt* tiznar. ● *vi* tiznarse

smug /smʌg/ *a* (**smugger, smuggest**) satisfecho de sí mismo

smuggl|e /'smʌgl/ *vt* pasar de contrabando. **~er** *n* contrabandista *m* & *f*. **~ing** *n* contrabando *m*

smug: **~ly** *adv* con suficiencia. **~ness** *n* suficiencia *f*

smut /smʌt/ *n* tizne *m*; (*mark*) tiznajo *m*. **~ty** *a* (**-ier, -iest**) tiznado; (*fig*) obsceno

snack /snæk/ *n* tentempié *m*. **~-bar** *n* cafetería *f*

snag /snæg/ *n* problema *m*; (*in cloth*) rasgón *m*

snail /sneɪl/ *n* caracol *m*. **~'s pace** *n* paso *m* de tortuga

snake /sneɪk/ *n* serpiente *f*

snap /snæp/ *vt* (*pt* **snapped**) (*break*) romper; castañetear ⟨*fingers*⟩. ● *vi* romperse; ⟨*dog*⟩ intentar morder; (*say*) contestar bruscamente; ⟨*whip*⟩ chasquear. **~ at** ⟨*dog*⟩ intentar morder; (*say*) contestar bruscamente. ● *n* chasquido *m*; (*photo*) foto *f*. ● *a* instantáneo. **~ up** *vt* agarrar. **~py** /'snæpɪ/ *a* (**-ier, -iest**) (*fam*) rápido. **make it ~py!** (*fam*) ¡date prisa! **~shot** /'snæpʃɒt/ *n* foto *f*

snare /sneə(r)/ *n* trampa *f*

snarl /snɑːl/ *vi* gruñir. ● *n* gruñido *m*

snatch /snætʃ/ *vt* agarrar; (*steal*) robar. ● *n* arrebatamiento *m*; (*short part*) trocito *m*; (*theft*) robo *m*

sneak /sniːk/ ● *n* soplón *m*. ● *vi*. **~ in** entrar furtivamente **~ out** salir furtivamente

sneakers /'sniːkəz/ *npl* zapatillas *fpl* de lona

sneak|ing /'sniːkɪŋ/ *a* furtivo. **~y** *a* furtivo

sneer /snɪə(r)/ *n* sonrisa *f* de desprecio. ● *vi* sonreír con desprecio. **~ at** hablar con desprecio a

sneeze /sniːz/ *n* estornudo *m*. ● *vi* estornudar

snide /snaɪd/ *a* (*fam*) despreciativo

sniff /snɪf/ *vt* oler. ● *vi* aspirar por la nariz. ● *n* aspiración *f*

snigger /'snɪgə(r)/ *n* risa *f* disimulada. ● *vi* reír disimuladamente

snip /snɪp/ *vt* (*pt* **snipped**) tijeretear. ● *n* tijeretada *f*; (*bargain, sl*) ganga *f*

snipe /snaɪp/ *vi* disparar desde un escondite. **~r** /ə(r)/ *n* tirador *m* emboscado, francotirador *m*

snippet /'snɪpɪt/ *n* retazo *m*

snivel /'snɪvl/ *vi* (*pt* **snivelled**) lloriquear. **~ling** *a* llorón

snob /snɒb/ *n* esnob *m*. **~bery** *n* esnobismo *m*. **~bish** *a* esnob

snooker /'snuːkə(r)/ *n* billar *m*

snoop /snuːp/ *vi* (*fam*) curiosear

snooty /'snuːtɪ/ *a* (*fam*) desdeñoso

snooze /snuːz/ *n* sueñecito *m*. ● *vi* echarse un sueñecito

snore /snɔː(r)/ *n* ronquido *m*. ● *vi* roncar

snorkel /'snɔːkl/ *n* tubo *m* respiratorio

snort /snɔːt/ *n* bufido *m*. ● *vi* bufar

snout /snaʊt/ *n* hocico *m*

snow /snəʊ/ *n* nieve *f*. ● *vi* nevar. **be ~ed under with** estar inundado por. **~ball** /'snəʊbɔːl/ *n* bola *f* de nieve. **~drift** *n* nieve amontonada. **~drop** /'snəʊdrɒp/ *n* campanilla *f* de invierno. **~fall** /'snəʊfɔːl/ *n* nevada *f*. **~flake** /'snəʊfleɪk/ *n* copo *m* de nieve. **~man** /'snəʊmæn/ *n* (*pl* **-men**) muñeco *m* de nieve. **~plough** *n* quitanieves *m invar*. **~storm** /'snəʊstɔːm/ *n* nevasca *f*. **~y** *a* ⟨*place*⟩ de nieves abundantes; ⟨*weather*⟩ con nevadas seguidas

snub /snʌb/ *vt* (*pt* **snubbed**) desairar. ● *n* desaire *m*. **~-nosed** /'snʌbnəʊzd/ *a* chato

snuff /snʌf/ *n* rapé *m*. ● *vt* despabilar ⟨*candle*⟩. **~ out** apagar ⟨*candle*⟩

snuffle /'snʌfl/ *vi* respirar ruidosamente

snug /snʌg/ *a* (**snugger, snuggest**) cómodo; (*tight*) ajustado

snuggle /'snʌgl/ *vi* acomodarse

so /səʊ/ *adv* (*before a or adv*) tan; (*thus*) así. ● *conj* así que. **~ am I** yo tambien. **~ as to** para. **~ far** *adv* (*time*) hasta ahora; (*place*) hasta aquí. **~ far as I know** que yo sepa. **~ long!** (*fam*) ¡hasta luego! **~ much** tanto. **~ that** *conj* para que. **and ~ forth, and ~ on** y así sucesivamente. **if ~** si es así. **I think ~** creo que sí. **or ~** más o menos

soak /səʊk/ *vt* remojar. ● *vi* remojarse. **~ in** penetrar. **~ up** absorber. **~ing** *a* empapado. ● *n* remojón *m*

so-and-so /'səʊənsəʊ/ *n* fulano *m*

soap /səʊp/ n jabón m. ● vt enjabonar. **~ powder** n jabón en polvo. **~y** a jabonoso

soar /sɔː(r)/ vi elevarse; ⟨price etc⟩ ponerse por las nubes

sob /sɒb/ n sollozo m. ● vi (pt **sobbed**) sollozar

sober /'səʊbə(r)/ a sobrio; ⟨colour⟩ discreto

so-called /'səʊkɔːld/ a llamado, supuesto

soccer /'sɒkə(r)/ n (fam) fútbol m

sociable /'səʊʃəbl/ a sociable

social /'səʊʃl/ a social; (sociable) sociable. ● n reunión f. **~ism** /-zəm/ n socialismo m. **~ist** /'səʊʃəlɪst/ a & n socialista m & f. **~ize** /'səʊʃəlaɪz/ vt socializar. **~ly** adv socialmente. **~ security** n seguridad f social. **~ worker** n asistente m social

society /sə'saɪətɪ/ n sociedad f

sociolog|ical /səʊsɪə'lɒdʒɪkl/ a sociológico. **~ist** n sociólogo m. **~y** /səʊsɪ'ɒlədʒɪ/ n sociología f

sock[1] /sɒk/ n calcetín m

sock[2] /sɒk/ vt (sl) pegar

socket /'sɒkɪt/ n hueco m; (of eye) cuenca f; (wall plug) enchufe m; (for bulb) portalámparas m invar, casquillo m

soda /'səʊdə/ n sosa f; (water) soda f. **~-water** n soda f

sodden /'sɒdn/ a empapado

sodium /'səʊdɪəm/ n sodio m

sofa /'səʊfə/ n sofá m

soft /sɒft/ a (-er, -est) blando; ⟨sound, colour⟩ suave; (gentle) dulce, tierno; (silly) estúpido. **~ drink** n bebida f no alcohólica. **~ spot** n debilidad f. **~en** /'sɒfn/ vt ablandar; (fig) suavizar. ● vi ablandarse; (fig) suavizarse. **~ly** adv dulcemente. **~ness** n blandura f; (fig) dulzura f. **~ware** /'sɒftweə(r)/ n programación f, software m

soggy /'sɒgɪ/ a (-ier, -iest) empapado

soh /səʊ/ n (mus, fifth note of any musical scale) sol m

soil[1] /sɔɪl/ n suelo m

soil[2] /sɔɪl/ vt ensuciar. ● vi ensuciarse

solace /'sɒləs/ n consuelo m

solar /'səʊlə(r)/ a solar. **~ium** /sə'leərɪəm/ n (pl -a) solario m

sold /səʊld/ see **sell**

solder /'sɒldə(r)/ n soldadura f. ● vt soldar

soldier /'səʊldʒə(r)/ n soldado m. ● vi. **~ on** (fam) perseverar

sole[1] /səʊl/ n (of foot) planta f; (of shoe) suela f

sole[2] /səʊl/ (fish) lenguado m

sole[3] /səʊl/ a único, solo. **~ly** adv únicamente

solemn /'sɒləm/ a solemne. **~ity** /sə'lemnətɪ/ n solemnidad f. **~ly** adv solemnemente

solicit /sə'lɪsɪt/ vt solicitar. ● vi importunar

solicitor /sə'lɪsɪtə(r)/ n abogado m; (notary) notario m

solicitous /sə'lɪsɪtəs/ a solícito

solid /'sɒlɪd/ a sólido; ⟨gold etc⟩ macizo; (unanimous) unánime; ⟨meal⟩ sustancioso. ● n sólido m. **~arity** /sɒlɪ'dærətɪ/ n solidaridad f. **~ify** /sə'lɪdɪfaɪ/ vt solidificar. ● vi solidificarse. **~ity** /sə'lɪdətɪ/ n solidez f. **~ly** adv sólidamente. **~s** npl alimentos mpl sólidos

soliloquy /sə'lɪləkwɪ/ n soliloquio m

solitaire /sɒlɪ'teə(r)/ n solitario m

solitary /'sɒlɪtrɪ/ a solitario

solitude /'sɒlɪtjuːd/ n soledad f

solo /'səʊləʊ/ n (pl -os) (mus) solo m. **~ist** n solista m & f

solstice /'sɒlstɪs/ n solsticio m

soluble /'sɒljʊbl/ a soluble

solution /sə'luːʃn/ n solución f

solvable a soluble

solve /sɒlv/ vt resolver

solvent /'sɒlvənt/ a & n solvente (m)

sombre /'sɒmbə(r)/ a sombrío

some /sʌm/ a alguno; (a little) un poco de. **~ day** algún día. **~ two hours** unas dos horas. **will you have ~ wine?** ¿quieres vino? ● pron algunos; (a little) un poco. **~ of us** algunos de nosotros. **I want ~** quiero un poco. ● adv (approximately) unos. **~body** /'sʌmbədɪ/ pron alguien. ● n personaje m. **~how** /'sʌmhaʊ/ adv de algún modo. **~how or other** de una manera u otra. **~one** /'sʌmwʌn/ pron alguien. ● n personaje m

somersault /'sʌməsɔːlt/ n salto m mortal. ● vi dar un salto mortal

some: ~thing /'sʌmθɪŋ/ pron algo m. **~thing like** algo como; (approximately) cerca de. **~time** /'sʌmtaɪm/ a ex. ● adv algún día; (in past) durante. **~time last summer** a (durante) el verano pasado. **~times** /'sʌmtaɪmz/ adv de vez en cuando, a veces. **~what** /'sʌmwɒt/ adv algo, un poco. **~where** /'sʌmweə(r)/ adv en alguna parte

son /sʌn/ n hijo m
sonata /sə'nɑ:tə/ n sonata f
song /sɒŋ/ n canción f. **sell for a ~**
vender muy barato. **~book** n can-
cionero m
sonic /'sɒnɪk/ a sónico
son-in-law /'sʌnɪnlɔ:/ n (pl **sons-
in-law**) yerno m
sonnet /'sɒnɪt/ n soneto m
sonny /'sʌnɪ/ n (fam) hijo m
soon /su:n/ adv (-er, -est) pronto; (in
a short time) dentro de poco; (early)
temprano. **~ after** poco después.
~er or later tarde o temprano. **as
~ as** en cuanto; **as ~ as possible** lo
antes posible. **I would ~er not go**
prefiero no ir
soot /sʊt/ n hollín m
soothe /su:ð/ vt calmar. **~ing** a
calmante
sooty /'sʊtɪ/ a cubierto de hollín
sophisticated /sə'fɪstɪkeɪtɪd/ a sofis-
ticado; (complex) complejo
soporific /sɒpə'rɪfɪk/ a soporífero
sopping /'sɒpɪŋ/ a. **~ (wet)**
empapado
soppy /'sɒpɪ/ a (-ier, -iest) (fam) sentimental; (silly, fam) tonto
soprano /sə'prɑ:nəʊ/ n (pl -os) (voice)
soprano m; (singer) soprano f
sorcerer /'sɔ:sərə(r)/ n hechicero m
sordid /'sɔ:dɪd/ a sórdido
sore /sɔ:(r)/ a (-er, -est) que duele,
dolorido; (distressed) penoso;
(vexed) enojado. ● n llaga f. **~ly** /'sɔ:
lɪ/ adv gravemente. **~ throat** n
dolor m de garganta. **I've got a ~
throat** me duele la garganta
sorrow /'sɒrəʊ/ n pena f, tristeza f.
~ful a triste
sorry /'sɒrɪ/ a (-ier, -ier) arrepentido;
(wretched) lamentable; (sad) triste.
be ~ sentirlo; (repent) arrepentirse. **be ~ for s.o.** (pity) compadecerse de uno. **~!** ¡perdón!,
¡perdone!
sort /sɔ:t/ n clase f; (person, fam) tipo
m. **be out of ~s** estar indispuesto;
(irritable) estar de mal humor. ● vt
clasificar. **~ out** (choose) escoger;
(separate) separar; resolver (problem)
so-so /'səʊsəʊ/ a & adv regular
soufflé /'su:fleɪ/ n suflé m
sought /sɔ:t/ see **seek**
soul /səʊl/ n alma f. **~ful** /'səʊlfl/ a
sentimental
sound¹ /saʊnd/ n sonido m; ruido m.
● vt sonar; (test) sondar. ● vi sonar;
(seem) parecer (**as if** que)

sound² /saʊnd/ a (-er, -est) sano; (argument etc) lógico; (secure) seguro.
~ asleep profundamente dormido
sound³ /saʊnd/ (strait) estrecho m
sound barrier /'saʊndbærɪə(r)/ n
barrera f del sonido
soundly /'saʊndlɪ/ adv sólidamente;
(asleep) profundamente
sound: **~proof** a insonorizado.
~track n banda f sonora
soup /su:p/ n sopa f. **in the ~** (sl) en
apuros
sour /'saʊə(r)/ a (-er, -est) agrio;
(cream, milk) cortado. ● vt agriar.
● vi agriarse
source /sɔ:s/ n fuente f
south /saʊθ/ n sur m. ● a del sur.
● adv hacia el sur. **S~ Africa** n
Africa f del Sur. **S~ America** n
América f (del Sur), Sudamérica f.
S~ American a & n sudamericano
(m). **~east** n sudeste m. **~erly**
/'sʌðəlɪ/ a sur; (wind) del sur. **~ern**
/'sʌðən/ a del sur, meridional.
~erner n meridional m. **~ward** a
sur; ● adv hacia el sur. **~wards** adv
hacia el sur. **~west** n sudoeste m
souvenir /su:və'nɪə(r)/ n recuerdo m
sovereign /'sɒvrɪn/ n & a soberano
(m). **~ty** n soberanía f
Soviet /'səʊvɪət/ a (history) soviético. **the ~ Union** n la Unión f
Soviética
sow¹ /səʊ/ vt (pt sowed, pp sowed or
sown) sembrar
sow² /saʊ/ n cerda f
soya /'sɔɪə/ n. **~ bean** n soja f
spa /spɑ:/ n balneario m
space /speɪs/ n espacio m; (room)
sitio m; (period) período m. ● a (research etc) espacial. ● vt espaciar. **~
out**. **~craft** /'speɪskrɑ:ft/ n,
~ship n nave f espacial. **~suit** n
traje m espacial
spacious /'speɪʃəs/ a espacioso
spade /speɪd/ n pala f. **~s** npl (cards)
picos mpl, picas fpl; (in Spanish
pack) espadas fpl. **~work** /'speɪdwɜ:
k/ n trabajo m preparatorio
spaghetti /spə'getɪ/ n espaguetis
mpl
Spain /speɪn/ n España f
span¹ /spæn/ n (of arch) luz f; (of
time) espacio m; (of wings) envergadura f. ● vt (pt spanned) extenderse sobre
span² /spæn/ see **spick**
Spaniard /'spænjəd/ n español m

spaniel /'spænjəl/ n perro m de aguas

Spanish /'spænɪʃ/ a & n español (m)

spank /spæŋk/ vt dar un azote a. ~ing n azote m

spanner /'spænə(r)/ n llave f

spar /spɑ:(r)/ vi (pt sparred) entrenarse en el boxeo; (argue) disputar

spare /speə(r)/ vt salvar; (do without) prescindir de; (afford to give) dar; (use with restraint) escatimar. ● a de reserva; (surplus) sobrante; ⟨person⟩ enjuto; ⟨meal etc⟩ frugal. ~ **(part)** n repuesto m. ~ **time** n tiempo m libre. ~ **tyre** n neumático m de repuesto

sparing /'speərɪŋ/ a frugal. ~ly adv frugalmente

spark /spɑ:k/ n chispa f. ● vt. ~ **off** (initiate) provocar. ~ing-plug n (auto) bujía f

sparkl|e /'spɑ:kl/ vi centellear. ● n centelleo m. ~ing a centelleante; ⟨wine⟩ espumoso

sparrow /'spærəʊ/ n gorrión m

sparse /spɑ:s/ a escaso; ⟨population⟩ poco denso. ~ly adv escasamente

spartan /'spɑ:tn/ a espartano

spasm /'spæzəm/ n espasmo m; (of cough) acceso m. ~odic /spæz'mɒdɪk/ a espasmódico

spastic /'spæstɪk/ n víctima f de parálisis cerebral

spat /spæt/ see **spit**

spate /speɪt/ n avalancha f

spatial /'speɪʃl/ a espacial

spatter /'spætə(r)/ vt salpicar (with de)

spatula /'spætjʊlə/ n espátula f

spawn /spɔ:n/ n hueva f. ● vt engendrar. ● vi desovar

speak /spi:k/ vt/i (pt **spoke**, pp **spoken**) hablar. ~ **for** vi hablar en nombre de. ~ **up** vi hablar más fuerte. ~er /'spi:kə(r)/ n (in public) orador m; (loudspeaker) altavoz m. **be a Spanish ~er** hablar español

spear /spɪə(r)/ n lanza f. ~head /'spɪəhed/ n punta f de lanza. ● vt (lead) encabezar. ~mint /'spɪəmɪnt/ n menta f verde

spec /spek/ n. **on ~** (fam) por si acaso

special /'speʃl/ a especial. ~ist /'speʃəlɪst/ n especialista m & f. ~ity /-ɪ'ælətɪ/ n especialidad f. ~ization /-'zeɪʃn/ n especialización f. ~ize /'speʃəlaɪz/ vi especializarse.

~ized a especializado. ~ty n especialidad f. ~ly adv especialmente

species /'spi:ʃi:z/ n especie f

specif|ic /spə'sɪfɪk/ a específico. ~ically adv específicamente. ~ication /-ɪ'keɪʃn/ n especificación f; (details) descripción f. ~y /'spesɪfaɪ/ vt especificar

specimen /'spesɪmɪn/ n muestra f

speck /spek/ n manchita f; (particle) partícula f

speckled /'spekld/ a moteado

specs /speks/ npl (fam) gafas fpl, anteojos mpl (LAm)

spectac|le /'spektəkl/ n espectáculo m. ~les npl gafas fpl, anteojos mpl (LAm). ~ular /spek'tækjʊlə(r)/ a espectacular

spectator /spek'teɪtə(r)/ n espectador m

spectre /'spektə(r)/ n espectro m

spectrum /'spektrəm/ n (pl -tra) espectro m; (of ideas) gama f

speculat|e /'spekjʊleɪt/ vi especular. ~ion /-ʃn/ n especulación f. ~ive /-lətɪv/ a especulativo. ~or n especulador m

sped /sped/ see **speed**

speech /spi:tʃ/ n (faculty) habla f; (address) discurso m. ~less a mudo

speed /spi:d/ n velocidad f; (rapidity) rapidez f; (haste) prisa f. ● vi (pt **sped**) apresurarse. (pt **speeded**) (drive too fast) ir a una velocidad excesiva. ~ **up** vt acelerar. ● vi acelerarse. ~**boat** /'spi:dbəʊt/ n lancha f motora. ~ily adv rápidamente. ~ing n exceso m de velocidad. ~ometer /spi:'dɒmɪtə(r)/ n velocímetro m. ~way /'spi:dweɪ/ n pista f; (Amer) autopista f. ~y /'spi:dɪ/ a (-ier, -iest) rápido

spell[1] /spel/ n (magic) hechizo m

spell[2] /spel/ vt/i (pt **spelled** or **spelt**) escribir; (mean) significar. ~ **out** vt deletrear; (fig) explicar. ~ing n ortografía f

spell[3] /spel/ (period) período m

spellbound /'spelbaʊnd/ a hechizado

spelt /spelt/ see **spell**[2]

spend /spend/ vt (pt **spent**) gastar; pasar ⟨time etc⟩; dedicar ⟨care etc⟩. ● vi gastar dinero. ~thrift /'spendθrɪft/ n derrochador m

spent /spent/ see **spend**

sperm /spɜ:m/ n (pl **sperms** or **sperm**) esperma f

spew /spju:/ vt/i vomitar

spher|e /sfɪə(r)/ *n* esfera *f*. **~ical** /'sferɪkl/ *a* esférico

sphinx /sfɪŋks/ *n* esfinge *f*

spice /spaɪs/ *n* especia *f*; *(fig)* sabor *m*

spick /spɪk/ *a*. **~ and span** impecable

spicy /'spaɪsɪ/ *a* picante

spider /'spaɪdə(r)/ *n* araña *f*

spik|e /spaɪk/ *n (of metal etc)* punta *f*. **~y** *a* puntiagudo; *(person)* quisquilloso

spill /spɪl/ *vt (pt spilled or spilt)* derramar. ● *vi* derramarse. **~ over** desbordarse

spin /spɪn/ *vt (pt spun, pres p spinning)* hacer girar; hilar *(wool etc)*. ● *vi* girar. ● *n* vuelta *f*; *(short drive)* paseo *m*

spinach /'spɪnɪdʒ/ *n* espinacas *fpl*

spinal /'spaɪnl/ *a* espinal. **~ cord** *n* médula *f* espinal

spindl|e /'spɪndl/ *n (for spinning)* huso *m*. **~y** *a* larguirucho

spin-drier /spɪn'draɪə(r)/ *n* secador *m* centrífugo

spine /spaɪn/ *n* columna *f* vertebral; *(of book)* lomo *m*. **~less** *a (fig)* sin carácter

spinning /'spɪnɪŋ/ *n* hilado *m*. **~-top** *n* trompa *f*, peonza *f*. **~-wheel** *n* rueca *f*

spin-off /'spɪnɒf/ *n* beneficio *m* incidental; *(by-product)* subproducto *m*

spinster /'spɪnstə(r)/ *n* soltera *f*; *(old maid, fam)* solterona *f*

spiral /'spaɪərəl/ *a* espiral, helicoidal. ● *n* hélice *f*. ● *vi (pt spiralled)* moverse en espiral. **~ staircase** *n* escalera *f* de caracol

spire /'spaɪə(r)/ *n (archit)* aguja *f*

spirit /'spɪrɪt/ *n* espíritu *m*; *(boldness)* valor *m*. **in low ~s** abatido. ● *vt*. **~ away** hacer desaparecer. **~ed** /'spɪrɪtɪd/ *a* animado, fogoso. **~-lamp** *n* lamparilla *f* de alcohol. **~-level** *n* nivel *m* de aire. **~s** *npl (drinks)* bebidas *fpl* alcohólicas

spiritual /'spɪrɪtjʊəl/ *a* espiritual. ● *n* canción *f* religiosa de los negros. **~ualism** /-zəm/ *n* espiritismo *m*. **~ualist** /'spɪrɪtjʊəlɪst/ *n* espiritista *m & f*

spit¹ /spɪt/ *vt (pt spat or spit, pres p spitting)* escupir. ● *vi* escupir; *(rain)* lloviznar. ● *n* esputo *m*; *(spittle)* saliva *f*

spit² /spɪt/ *(for roasting)* asador *m*

spite /spaɪt/ *n* rencor *m*. **in ~ of** a pesar de. ● *vt* fastidiar. **~ful** *a* rencoroso. **~fully** *adv* con rencor

spitting image /spɪtɪŋ'ɪmɪdʒ/ *n* vivo retrato *m*

spittle /'spɪtl/ *n* saliva *f*

splash /splæʃ/ *vt* salpicar. ● *vi* esparcirse; *(person)* chapotear. ● *n* salpicadura *f*; *(sound)* chapoteo *m*; *(of colour)* mancha *f*; *(drop, fam)* gota *f*. **~ about** *vi* chapotear. **~ down** *vi (spacecraft)* amerizar

spleen /spliːn/ *n* bazo *m*; *(fig)* esplín *m*

splendid /'splendɪd/ *a* espléndido

splendour /'splendə(r)/ *n* esplendor *m*

splint /splɪnt/ *n* tablilla *f*

splinter /'splɪntə(r)/ *n* astilla *f*. ● *vi* astillarse. **~ group** *n* grupo *m* disidente

split /splɪt/ *vt (pt split, pres p splitting)* hender, rajar; *(tear)* rajar; *(divide)* dividir; *(share)* repartir. **~ one's sides** caerse de risa. ● *vi* partirse; *(divide)* dividirse. **~ on s.o.** *(sl)* traicionar. ● *n* hendidura *f*; *(tear)* desgarrón *m*; *(quarrel)* ruptura *f*; *(pol)* escisión *f*. **~ up** *vi* separarse. **~ second** *n* fracción *f* de segundo

splurge /splɜːdʒ/ *vi (fam)* derrochar

splutter /'splʌtə(r)/ *vi* chisporrotear; *(person)* farfullar. ● *n* chisporroteo *m*; *(speech)* farfulla *f*

spoil /spɔɪl/ *vt (pt spoilt or spoiled)* estropear, echar a perder; *(ruin)* arruinar; *(indulge)* mimar. ● *n* botín *m*. **~s** *npl* botín *m*. **~-sport** *n* aguafiestas *m invar*

spoke¹ /spəʊk/ *see* **speak**

spoke² /spəʊk/ *n (of wheel)* radio *m*

spoken /spəʊkən/ *see* **speak**

spokesman /'spəʊksmən/ *n (pl -men)* portavoz *m*

spong|e /spʌndʒ/ *n* esponja *f*. ● *vt* limpiar con una esponja. ● *vi*. **~e on** vivir a costa de. **~e-cake** *n* bizcocho *m*. **~er** /-ə(r)/ *n* gorrón *m*. **~y** *a* esponjoso

sponsor /'spɒnsə(r)/ *n* patrocinador *m*; *(surety)* garante *m*. ● *vt* patrocinar. **~ship** *n* patrocinio *m*

spontane|ity /spɒntə'neɪtɪ/ *n* espontaneidad *f*. **~ous** /spɒn'teɪnjəs/ *a* espontáneo. **~ously** *adv* espontáneamente

spoof /spuːf/ *n (sl)* parodia *f*

spooky /'spuːkɪ/ *a* (-ier, -iest) *(fam)* escalofriante

spool /spuːl/ *n* carrete *m*; (*of sewing-machine*) canilla *f*

spoon /spuːn/ *n* cuchara *f*. **~fed** *a* (*fig*) mimado. **~feed** *vt* (*pt* **-fed**) dar de comer con cuchara. **~ful** *n* (*pl* **-fuls**) cucharada *f*

sporadic /spəˈrædɪk/ *a* esporádico

sport /spɔːt/ *n* deporte *m*; (*amusement*) pasatiempo *m*; (*person, fam*) persona *f* alegre, buen chico *m*, buena chica *f*. **be a good ~** ser buen perdedor. ● *vt* lucir. **~ing** *a* deportivo. **~ing chance** *n* probabilidad *f* de éxito. **~s car** *n* coche *m* deportivo. **~s coat** *n* chaqueta *f* de sport. **~sman** /ˈspɔːtsmən/ *n*, (*pl* **-men**), **~swoman** /ˈspɔːtswʊmən/ *n* (*pl* **-women**) deportista *m & f*

spot /spɒt/ *n* mancha *f*; (*pimple*) grano *m*; (*place*) lugar *m*; (*in pattern*) punto *m*; (*drop*) gota *f*; (*a little, fam*) poquito *m*. **in a ~** (*fam*) en un apuro. **on the ~** en el lugar; (*without delay*) en el acto. ● *vt* (*pt* **spotted**) manchar; (*notice, fam*) observar, ver. **~ check** *n* control *m* hecho al azar. **~less** *a* inmaculado. **~light** /ˈspɒtlaɪt/ *n* reflector *m*. **~ted** *a* moteado; ‹*cloth*› a puntos. **~ty** *a* (**-ier, -iest**) manchado; ‹*skin*› con granos

spouse /spaʊz/ *n* cónyuge *m & f*

spout /spaʊt/ *n* pico *m*; (*jet*) chorro *m*. **up the ~** (*ruined, sl*) perdido. ● *vi* chorrear

sprain /spreɪn/ *vt* torcer. ● *n* torcedura *f*

sprang /spræŋ/ *see* **spring**

sprat /spræt/ *n* espadín *m*

sprawl /sprɔːl/ *vi* ‹*person*› repanchigarse; ‹*city etc*› extenderse

spray /spreɪ/ *n* (*of flowers*) ramo *m*; (*water*) rociada *f*; (*from sea*) espuma *f*; (*device*) pulverizador *m*. ● *vt* rociar. **~gun** *n* pistola *f* pulverizadora

spread /spred/ *vt* (*pt* **spread**) (*stretch, extend*) extender; untar ‹*jam etc*›; difundir ‹*idea, news*›. ● *vi* extenderse; ‹*disease*› propagarse; ‹*idea, news*› difundirse. ● *n* extensión *f*; (*paste*) pasta *f*; (*of disease*) propagación *f*; (*feast, fam*) comilona *f*. **~eagled** *a* con los brazos y piernas extendidos

spree /spriː/ *n*. **go on a ~** (*have fun, fam*) ir de juerga

sprig /sprɪg/ *n* ramito *m*

sprightly /ˈspraɪtlɪ/ *a* (**-ier, -iest**) vivo

spring /sprɪŋ/ *n* (*season*) primavera *f*; (*device*) muelle *m*; (*elasticity*) elasticidad *f*; (*water*) manantial *m*. ● *a* de primavera. ● *vt* (*pt* **sprang**, *pp* **sprung**) hacer inesperadamente. ● *vi* saltar; (*issue*) brotar. **~ from** *vi* provenir de. **~ up** *vi* surgir. **~board** *n* trampolín *m*. **~time** *n* primavera *f*. **~y** *a* (**-ier, -iest**) elástico

sprinkl|e /ˈsprɪŋkl/ *vt* salpicar; (*with liquid*) rociar. ● *n* salpicadura *f*; (*of liquid*) rociada *f*. **~ed with** salpicado de. **~er** /-ə(r)/ *n* regadera *f*. **~ing** /ˈsprɪŋklɪŋ/ *n* (*fig, amount*) poco *m*

sprint /sprɪnt/ *n* carrera *f*. ● *vi* correr. **~er** *n* corredor *m*

sprite /spraɪt/ *n* duende *m*, hada *f*

sprout /spraʊt/ *vi* brotar. ● *n* brote *m*. **(Brussels) ~s** *npl* coles *fpl* de Bruselas

spruce /spruːs/ *a* elegante

sprung /sprʌŋ/ *see* **spring**. ● *a* de muelles

spry /spraɪ/ *a* (**spryer, spryest**) vivo

spud /spʌd/ *n* (*sl*) patata *f*, papa *f* (*LAm*)

spun /spʌn/ *see* **spin**

spur /spɜː(r)/ *n* espuela *f*; (*stimulus*) estímulo *m*. **on the ~ of the moment** impulsivamente. ● *vt* (*pt* **spurred**). **~ (on)** espolear; (*fig*) estimular

spurious /ˈspjʊərɪəs/ *a* falso. **~ly** *adv* falsamente

spurn /spɜːn/ *vt* despreciar; (*reject*) rechazar

spurt /spɜːt/ *vi* chorrear; (*make sudden effort*) hacer un esfuerzo repentino. ● *n* chorro *m*; (*effort*) esfuerzo *m* repentino

spy /spaɪ/ *n* espía *m & f*. ● *vt* divisar. ● *vi* espiar. **~ out** *vt* reconocer. **~ing** *n* espionaje *m*

squabble /ˈskwɒbl/ *n* riña *f*. ● *vi* reñir

squad /skwɒd/ *n* (*mil*) pelotón *m*; (*of police*) brigada *f*; (*sport*) equipo *m*

squadron /ˈskwɒdrən/ *n* (*mil*) escuadrón *m*; (*naut, aviat*) escuadrilla *f*

squalid /ˈskwɒlɪd/ *a* asqueroso; (*wretched*) miserable

squall /skwɔːl/ *n* turbión *m*. ● *vi* chillar. **~y** *a* borrascoso

squalor /ˈskwɒlə(r)/ *n* miseria *f*

squander /ˈskwɒndə(r)/ *vt* derrochar

square /skweə(r)/ *n* cuadrado *m*; (*open space in town*) plaza *f*; (*for drawing*) escuadra *f*. ● *a* cuadrado; (*not owing*) sin deudas, iguales; (*honest*) honrado; ⟨*meal*⟩ satisfactorio; (*old-fashioned*, *sl*) chapado a la antigua. **all** ~ iguales. ● *vt* (*settle*) arreglar; (*math*) cuadrar. ● *vi* (*agree*) cuadrar. ~ **up to** enfrentarse con. ~**ly** *adv* directamente

squash /skwɒʃ/ *vt* aplastar; (*suppress*) suprimir. ● *n* apiñamiento *m*; (*drink*) zumo *m*; (*sport*) squash *m*. ~**y** *a* blando

squat /skwɒt/ *vi* (*pt* **squatted**) ponerse en cuclillas; (*occupy illegally*) ocupar sin derecho. ● *n* casa *f* ocupada sin derecho. ● *a* (*dumpy*) achaparrado. ~**ter** /-ə(r)/ *n* ocupante *m* & *f* ilegal

squawk /skwɔːk/ *n* graznido *m*. ● *vi* graznar

squeak /skwiːk/ *n* chillido *m*; (*of door etc*) chirrido *m*. ● *vi* chillar; ⟨*door etc*⟩ chirriar. ~**y** *a* chirriador

squeal /skwiːl/ *n* chillido *m*. ● *vi* chillar. ~ **on** (*inform on*, *sl*) denunciar

squeamish /ˈskwiːmɪʃ/ *a* delicado; (*scrupulous*) escrupuloso. **be** ~ **about snakes** tener horror a las serpientes

squeeze /skwiːz/ *vt* apretar; exprimir ⟨*lemon etc*⟩; (*extort*) extorsionar (**from** de). ● *vi* (*force one's way*) abrirse paso. ● *n* estrujón *m*; (*of hand*) apretón *m*. **credit** ~ *n* restricción *f* de crédito

squelch /skweltʃ/ *vi* chapotear. ● *n* chapoteo *m*

squib /skwɪb/ *n* (*firework*) buscapiés *m invar*

squid /skwɪd/ *n* calamar *m*

squiggle /ˈskwɪɡl/ *n* garabato *m*

squint /skwɪnt/ *vi* ser bizco; (*look sideways*) mirar de soslayo. ● *n* estrabismo *m*

squire /ˈskwaɪə(r)/ *n* terrateniente *m*

squirm /skwɜːm/ *vi* retorcerse

squirrel /ˈskwɪrəl/ *n* ardilla *f*

squirt /skwɜːt/ *vt* arrojar a chorros. ● *vi* salir a chorros. ● *n* chorro *m*

St *abbr* (*saint*) /sənt/ S, San(to); (*street*) C/, Calle *f*

stab /stæb/ *vt* (*pt* **stabbed**) apuñalar. ● *n* puñalada *f*; (*pain*) punzada *f*; (*attempt*, *fam*) tentativa *f*

stabili|ty /stəˈbɪlətɪ/ *n* estabilidad *f*. ~**ze** /ˈsteɪbɪlaɪz/ *vt* estabilizar. ~**zer** /-ə(r)/ *n* estabilizador *m*

stable[1] /ˈsteɪbl/ *a* (**-er**, **-est**) estable

stable[2] /ˈsteɪbl/ *n* cuadra *f*. ● *vt* poner en una cuadra. ~**-boy** *n* mozo *m* de cuadra

stack /stæk/ *n* montón *m*. ● *vt* amontonar

stadium /ˈsteɪdjəm/ *n* estadio *m*

staff /stɑːf/ *n* (*stick*) palo *m*; (*employees*) personal *m*; (*mil*) estado *m* mayor; (*in school*) profesorado *m*. ● *vt* proveer de personal

stag /stæɡ/ *n* ciervo *m*. ~**-party** *n* reunión *f* de hombres, fiesta *f* de despedida de soltero

stage /steɪdʒ/ *n* (*in theatre*) escena *f*; (*phase*) etapa *f*; (*platform*) plataforma *f*. **go on the** ~ hacerse actor. ● *vt* representar; (*arrange*) organizar. ~**-coach** *n* (*hist*) diligencia *f*. ~ **fright** *n* miedo *m* al público. ~**-manager** *n* director *m* de escena. ~ **whisper** *n* aparte *m*

stagger /ˈstæɡə(r)/ *vi* tambalearse. ● *vt* asombrar; escalonar ⟨*holidays etc*⟩. ● *n* tambaleo *m*. ~**ing** *a* asombroso

stagna|nt /ˈstæɡnənt/ *a* estancado. ~**te** /stæɡˈneɪt/ *vi* estancarse. ~**tion** /-ʃn/ *n* estancamiento *m*

staid /steɪd/ *a* serio, formal

stain /steɪn/ *vt* manchar; (*colour*) teñir. ● *n* mancha *f*; (*liquid*) tinte *m*. ~**ed glass window** *n* vidriera *f* de colores. ~**less** /ˈsteɪnlɪs/ *a* inmaculado. ~**less steel** *n* acero *m* inoxidable. ~ **remover** *n* quitamanchas *m invar*

stair /steə(r)/ *n* escalón *m*. ~**s** *npl* escalera *f*. **flight of** ~**s** tramo *m* de escalera. ~**case** /ˈsteəkeɪs/ *n*, ~**way** *n* escalera *f*

stake /steɪk/ *n* estaca *f*; (*for execution*) hoguera *f*; (*wager*) apuesta *f*; (*com*) intereses *mpl*. **at** ~ en juego. ● *vt* estacar; (*wager*) apostar. ~ **a claim** reclamar

stalactite /ˈstæləktaɪt/ *n* estalactita *f*

stalagmite /ˈstæləɡmaɪt/ *n* estalagmita *f*

stale /steɪl/ *a* (**-er**, **-est**) no fresco; ⟨*bread*⟩ duro; ⟨*smell*⟩ viciado; ⟨*news*⟩ viejo; (*uninteresting*) gastado. ~**mate** /ˈsteɪlmeɪt/ *n* (*chess*) ahogado *m*; (*deadlock*) punto *m* muerto

stalk[1] /stɔːk/ *n* tallo *m*

stalk[2] /stɔːk/ *vi* andar majestuosamente. ● *vt* seguir; ⟨*animal*⟩ acechar

stall[1] /stɔːl/ *n* (*stable*) cuadra *f*; (*in stable*) casilla *f*; (*in theatre*) butaca *f*; (*in market*) puesto *m*; (*kiosk*) quiosco *m*

stall[2] /stɔːl/ *vt* parar ⟨*engine*⟩. ● *vi* ⟨*engine*⟩ pararse; (*fig*) andar con rodeos

stallion /'stæljən/ *n* semental *m*

stalwart /'stɔːlwət/ *n* partidario *m* leal

stamina /'stæmɪnə/ *n* resistencia *f*

stammer /'stæmə(r)/ *vi* tartamudear. ● *n* tartamudeo *m*

stamp /stæmp/ *vt* (*with feet*) patear; (*press*) estampar; poner un sello en ⟨*envelope*⟩; (*with rubber stamp*) sellar; (*fig*) señalar. ● *vi* patear. ● *n* sello *m*; (*with foot*) patada *f*; (*mark*) marca *f*, señal *f*. ∼ **out** (*fig*) acabar con

stampede /stæm'piːd/ *n* desbandada *f*; (*fam*) pánico *m*. ● *vi* huir en desorden

stance /stɑːns/ *n* postura *f*

stand /stænd/ *vi* (*pt* **stood**) estar de pie; (*rise*) ponerse de pie; (*be*) encontrarse; (*stay firm*) permanecer; (*pol*) presentarse como candidato (**for** en). ∼ **to reason** ser lógico. ● *vt* (*endure*) soportar; (*place*) poner; (*offer*) ofrecer. ∼ **a chance** tener una posibilidad. ∼ **one's ground** mantenerse firme. **I'll** ∼ **you a drink** te invito a una copa.● *n* posición *f*, postura *f*; (*mil*) resistencia *f*; (*for lamp etc*) pie *m*, sostén *m*; (*at market*) puesto *m*; (*booth*) quiosco *m*; (*sport*) tribuna *f*. ∼ **around** no hacer nada. ∼ **back** retroceder. ∼ **by** *vi* estar preparado. ● *vt* (*support*) apoyar. ∼ **down** *vi* retirarse. ∼ **for** *vt* representar. ∼ **in for** suplir a. ∼ **out** destacarse. ∼ **up** *vi* ponerse de pie. ∼ **up for** defender. ∼ **up to** *vt* resistir a

standard /'stændəd/ *n* norma *f*; (*level*) nivel *m*; (*flag*) estandarte *m*. ● *a* normal, corriente. ∼**ize** *vt* uniformar. ∼ **lamp** *n* lámpara *f* de pie. ∼**s** *npl* valores *mpl*

stand: ∼**-by** *n* (*person*) reserva *f*; (*at airport*) lista *f* de espera. ∼**-in** *n* suplente *m* & *f*. ∼**ing** /'stændɪŋ/ *a* de pie; (*upright*) derecho. ● *n* posición *f*; (*duration*) duración *f*. ∼**-offish** *a* (*fam*) frío. ∼**point** /'stændpɔɪnt/ *n*

punto *m* de vista. ∼**still** /'stændstɪl/ *n*. **at a** ∼**still** parado. **come to a** ∼**still** pararse

stank /stæŋk/ *see* **stink**

staple[1] /'steɪpl/ *a* principal

staple[2] /'steɪpl/ *n* grapa *f*. ● *vt* sujetar con una grapa. ∼**r** /-ə(r)/ *n* grapadora *f*

star /stɑː/ *n* (*incl cinema, theatre*) estrella *f*; (*asterisk*) asterisco *m*. ● *vi* (*pt* **starred**) ser el protagonista

starboard /'stɑːbəd/ *n* estribor *m*

starch /stɑːtʃ/ *n* almidón *m*; (*in food*) fécula *f*. ● *vt* almidonar. ∼**y** *a* almidonado; ⟨*food*⟩ feculento; (*fig*) formal

stardom /'stɑːdəm/ *n* estrellato *m*

stare /steə(r)/ *n* mirada *f* fija. ● *vi*. ∼ **at** mirar fijamente

starfish /'stɑːfɪʃ/ *n* estrella *f* de mar

stark /stɑːk/ *a* (**-er, -est**) rígido; (*utter*) completo. ● *adv* completamente

starlight /'stɑːlaɪt/ *n* luz *f* de las estrellas

starling /'stɑːlɪŋ/ *n* estornino *m*

starry /'stɑːrɪ/ *a* estrellado. ∼**-eyed** *a* (*fam*) ingenuo, idealista

start /stɑːt/ *vt* empezar; poner en marcha ⟨*machine*⟩; (*cause*) provocar. ● *vi* empezar; (*jump*) sobresaltarse; (*leave*) partir; ⟨*car etc*⟩ arrancar. ● *n* principio *m*; (*leaving*) salida *f*; (*sport*) ventaja *f*; (*jump*) susto *m*. ∼**er** *n* (*sport*) participante *m* & *f*; (*auto*) motor *m* de arranque; (*culin*) primer plato *m*. ∼**ing-point** *n* punto *m* de partida

startle /'stɑːtl/ *vt* asustar

starv|ation /stɑː'veɪʃn/ *n* hambre *f*. ∼**e** /stɑːv/ *vt* hacer morir de hambre; (*deprive*) privar. ● *vi* morir de hambre

stash /stæʃ/ *vt* (*sl*) esconder

state /steɪt/ *n* estado *m*; (*grand style*) pompa *f*. **S**∼ *n* Estado *m*. **be in a** ∼ estar agitado. ● *vt* declarar; expresar ⟨*views*⟩; (*fix*) fijar. ● *a* del Estado; (*schol*) público; (*with ceremony*) de gala. ∼**less** *a* sin patria

stately /'steɪtlɪ/ *a* (**-ier, -iest**) majestuoso

statement /'steɪtmənt/ *n* declaración *f*; (*account*) informe *m*. **bank** ∼ *n* estado *m* de cuenta

stateroom /'steɪtrʊm/ *n* (*on ship*) camarote *m*

statesman /'steɪtsmən/ *n* (*pl* **-men**) estadista *m*

static /'stætɪk/ a inmóvil. **~s** n estática f; (rad, TV) parásitos mpl atmosféricos, interferencias fpl

station /'steɪʃn/ n estación f; (status) posición f social. ● vt colocar; (mil) estacionar

stationary /'steɪʃənərɪ/ a estacionario

stationer /'steɪʃənə(r)/ n papelero m. **~'s (shop)** n papelería f. **~y** n artículos mpl de escritorio

station-wagon /'steɪʃnwægən/ n furgoneta f

statistic /stə'tɪstɪk/ n estadística f. **~al** /stə'tɪstɪkl/ a estadístico. **~s** /stə'tɪstɪks/ n (science) estadística f

statue /'stætʃuː/ n estatua f. **~sque** /-ʊ'esk/ a escultural. **~tte** /-ʊ'et/ n figurilla f

stature /'stætʃə(r)/ n talla f, estatura f

status /'steɪtəs/ n posición f social; (prestige) categoría f; (jurid) estado m

statut|e /'stætʃuːt/ n estatuto m. **~ory** /-ʊtrɪ/ a estatutario

staunch /stɔːnʃ/ a (-er, -est) leal. **~ly** adv lealmente

stave /'steɪv/ n (mus) pentagrama m. ● vt. **~ off** evitar

stay /steɪ/ n soporte m, sostén m; (of time) estancia f; (jurid) suspensión f. ● vi quedar; (spend time) detenerse; (reside) alojarse. ● vt matar ⟨hunger⟩. **~ the course** terminar. **~ in** quedar en casa. **~ put** mantenerse firme. **~ up** no acostarse. **~ing-power** n resistencia f

stays /steɪz/ npl (old use) corsé m

stead /sted/ n. **in s.o.'s ~** en lugar de uno. **stand s.o. in good ~** ser útil a uno

steadfast /'stedfɑːst/ a firme

stead|ily /'stedɪlɪ/ adv firmemente; (regularly) regularmente. **~y** /'stedɪ/ a (-ier, -iest) firme; (regular) regular; (dependable) serio

steak /steɪk/ n filete m

steal /stiːl/ vt (pt stole, pp stolen) robar. **~ the show** llevarse los aplausos. **~ in** vi entrar a hurtadillas. **~ out** vi salir a hurtadillas

stealth /stelθ/ n. **by ~** sigilosamente. **~y** a sigiloso

steam /stiːm/ n vapor m; (energy) energía f. ● vt (cook) cocer al vapor; empañar ⟨window⟩. ● vi echar vapor. **~ ahead** (fam) hacer progresos. **~ up** vi ⟨glass⟩ empañar.

~engine n máquina f de vapor. **~er** /'stiːmə(r)/ n (ship) barco m de vapor. **~roller** /'stiːmrəʊlə(r)/ n apisonadora f. **~y** a húmedo

steel /stiːl/ n acero m. ● vt. **~ o.s.** fortalecerse. **~ industry** n industria f siderúrgica. **~ wool** n estropajo m de acero. **~y** a acerado; (fig) duro, inflexible

steep /stiːp/ ● a (-er, -est) escarpado; ⟨price⟩ (fam) exorbitante. ● vt (soak) remojar. **~ed in** (fig) empapado de

steeple /'stiːpl/ n aguja f, campanario m. **~chase** /'stiːpltʃeɪs/ n carrera f de obstáculos

steep: ~ly adv de modo empinado. **~ness** n lo escarpado

steer /stɪə(r)/ vt guiar; gobernar ⟨ship⟩. ● vi (in ship) gobernar. **~ clear of** evitar. **~ing** n (auto) dirección f. **~ing-wheel** n volante m

stem /stem/ n tallo m; (of glass) pie m; (of word) raíz f; (of ship) roda f. ● vt (pt stemmed) detener. ● vi. **~ from** provenir de

stench /stentʃ/ n hedor m

stencil /'stensl/ n plantilla f; (for typing) cliché m. ● vt (pt stencilled) estarcir

stenographer /ste'nɒgrəfə(r)/ n (Amer) estenógrafo m

step /step/ vi (pt stepped) ir. **~ down** retirarse. **~ in** entrar; (fig) intervenir. **~ up** vt aumentar. ● n paso m; (surface) escalón m; (fig) medida f. **in ~** (fig) de acuerdo con. **out of ~** (fig) en desacuerdo con. **~brother** /'stepbrʌðə(r)/ n hermanastro m. **~daughter** n hijastra f. **~father** n padrastro m. **~ladder** n escalera f de tijeras. **~mother** n madrastra f. **~ping-stone** /'stepɪŋstəʊn/ n pasadera f; (fig) escalón m. **~sister** n hermanastra f. **~son** n hijastro m

stereo /'sterɪəʊ/ n (pl -os) cadena f estereofónica. ● a estereofónico. **~phonic** /sterɪəʊ'fɒnɪk/ a estereofónico. **~type** /'sterɪəʊtaɪp/ n estereotipo m. **~typed** a estereotipado

steril|e /'steraɪl/ a estéril. **~ity** /stə'rɪlətɪ/ n esterilidad f. **~ization** /-'zeɪʃn/ n esterilización f. **~ize** /'sterɪlaɪz/ vt esterilizar

sterling /'stɜːlɪŋ/ n libras fpl esterlinas. ● a ⟨pound⟩ esterlina; (fig) excelente. **~ silver** n plata f de ley

stern[1] /stɜːn/ n (of boat) popa f

stern[2] /stɜːn/ a (-er, -est) severo. ~ly adv severamente

stethoscope /'steθəskəʊp/ n estetoscopio m

stew /stjuː/ vt/i guisar. ● n guisado m. **in a** ~ (fam) en un apuro

steward /stjʊəd/ n administrador m; (on ship, aircraft) camarero m. ~ess /-'des/ n camarera f; (on aircraft) azafata f

stick /stɪk/ n palo m; (for walking) bastón m; (of celery etc) tallo m. ● vt (pt stuck) (glue) pegar; (put, fam) poner; (thrust) clavar; (endure, sl) soportar. ● vi pegarse; (remain, fam) quedarse; (jam) bloquearse. ~ **at** (fam) perseverar en. ~ **out** sobresalir; (catch the eye, fam) resaltar. ~ **to** aferrarse a; cumplir (promise). ~ **up for** (fam) defender. ~**er** /'stɪkə(r)/ n pegatina f. ~**ing-plaster** n esparadrapo m. ~**in-the-mud** n persona f chapada a la antigua

stickler /'stɪklə(r)/ n. **be a** ~ **for** insistir en

sticky /'stɪkɪ/ a (-ier, -iest) pegajoso; (label) engomado; (sl) difícil

stiff /stɪf/ a (-er, -est) rígido; (difficult) difícil; (manner) estirado; (drink) fuerte; (price) subido; (joint) tieso; (muscle) con agujetas. ~**en** /'stɪfn/ vt poner tieso. ~**ly** adv rígidamente. ~ **neck** n tortícolis f. ~**ness** n rigidez f

stifl|e /'staɪfl/ vt sofocar. ~**ing** a sofocante

stigma /'stɪgmə/ n (pl -as) estigma m. (pl stigmata /'stɪgmətə/) (relig) estigma m. ~**tize** vt estigmatizar

stile /staɪl/ n portillo m con escalones

stiletto /stɪ'letəʊ/ n (pl -os) estilete m. ~ **heels** npl tacones mpl aguja

still[1] /stɪl/ a inmóvil; (peaceful) tranquilo; (drink) sin gas. ● n silencio m. ● adv todavía; (nevertheless) sin embargo

still[2] /stɪl/ (apparatus) alambique m

still: ~**born** a nacido muerto. ~ **life** n (pl -s) bodegón m. ~**ness** n tranquilidad f

stilted /'stɪltɪd/ a artificial

stilts /stɪlts/ npl zancos mpl

stimul|ant /'stɪmjʊlənt/ n estimulante m. ~**ate** /'stɪmjʊleɪt/ vt estimular. ~**ation** /-'leɪʃn/ n estímulo m. ~**us** /'stɪmjʊləs/ n (pl -li /-laɪ/) estímulo m

sting /stɪŋ/ n picadura f; (organ) aguijón m. ● vt/i (pt stung) picar

sting|iness /'stɪndʒɪnɪs/ n tacañería f. ~**y** /'stɪndʒɪ/ a (-ier, -iest) tacaño

stink /stɪŋk/ n hedor m. ● vi (pt stank or stunk, pp stunk) oler mal. ● vt. ~ **out** apestar (room); ahuyentar (person). ~**er** /-ə(r)/ n (sl) problema m difícil; (person) mal bicho m

stint /stɪnt/ n (work) trabajo m. ● vi. ~ **on** escatimar

stipple /'stɪpl/ vt puntear

stipulat|e /'stɪpjʊleɪt/ vt/i estipular. ~**ion** /-'leɪʃn/ n estipulación f

stir /stɜː(r)/ vt (pt stirred) remover, agitar; (mix) mezclar; (stimulate) estimular. ● vi moverse. ● n agitación f; (commotion) conmoción f

stirrup /'stɪrəp/ n estribo m

stitch /stɪtʃ/ n (in sewing) puntada f; (in knitting) punto m; (pain) dolor m de costado; (med) punto m de sutura. **be in** ~**es** (fam) desternillarse de risa. ● vt coser

stoat /stəʊt/ n armiño m

stock /stɒk/ n (com, supplies) existencias fpl; (com, variety) surtido m; (livestock) ganado m; (lineage) linaje m; (finance) acciones fpl; (culin) caldo m; (plant) alhelí m. **out of** ~ agotado. **take** ~ (fig) evaluar. ● a corriente; (fig) trillado. ● vt abastecer (with de). ● vi. ~ **up** abastecerse (with de). ~**broker** /'stɒkbrəʊkə(r)/ n corredor m de bolsa. **S**~ **Exchange** n bolsa f. **well-**~**ed** a bien provisto

stocking /'stɒkɪŋ/ n media f

stock: ~**-in-trade** /'stɒkɪntreɪd/ n existencias fpl. ~**ist** /'stɒkɪst/ n distribuidor m. ~**pile** /'stɒkpaɪl/ n reservas fpl. ● vt acumular. ~**still** a inmóvil. ~**taking** n (com) inventario m

stocky /'stɒkɪ/ a (-ier, -iest) achaparrado

stodg|e /stɒdʒ/ n (fam) comida f pesada. ~**y** a pesado

stoic /'stəʊɪk/ n estoico. ~**al** a estoico. ~**ally** adv estoicamente. ~**ism** /-sɪzəm/ n estoicismo m

stoke /stəʊk/ vt alimentar. ~**r** /'stəʊkə(r)/ n fogonero m

stole[1] /stəʊl/ see **steal**

stole[2] /stəʊl/ n estola f

stolen /'stəʊlən/ see **steal**

stolid /'stɒlɪd/ a impasible. ~**ly** adv impasiblemente

stomach /'stʌmək/ *n* estómago *m*.
● *vt* soportar. **~ache** *n* dolor *m* de estómago

ston|e /stəʊn/ *n* piedra *f*; (*med*) cálculo *m*; (*in fruit*) hueso *m*; (*weight, pl* **stone**) peso *m* de 14 libras (= *6,348 kg*). ● *a* de piedra. ● *vt* apedrear; deshuesar ⟨*fruit*⟩. **~e-deaf** *a* sordo como una tapia. **~emason** /'stəʊnmeɪsn/ *n* albañil *m*. **~ework** /'stəʊnwɜːk/ *n* cantería *f*. **~y** *a* pedregoso; (*like stone*) pétreo

stood /stʊd/ *see* **stand**

stooge /stuːdʒ/ *n* (*in theatre*) compañero *m*; (*underling*) lacayo *m*

stool /stuːl/ *n* taburete *m*

stoop /stuːp/ *vi* inclinarse; (*fig*) rebajarse. ● *n.* **have a ~** ser cargado de espaldas

stop /stɒp/ *vt* (*pt* **stopped**) parar; (*cease*) terminar; tapar ⟨*a leak etc*⟩; (*prevent*) impedir; (*interrupt*) interrumpir. ● *vi* pararse; (*stay, fam*) quedarse. ● *n* (*bus etc*) parada *f*; (*gram*) punto *m*; (*mec*) tope *m*. **~ dead** *vi* pararse en seco. **~cock** /'stɒpkɒk/ *n* llave *f* de paso. **~gap** /'stɒpgæp/ *n* remedio *m* provisional. **~(-over)** *n* escala *f*. **~page** /'stɒpɪdʒ/ *n* parada *f*; (*of work*) paro *m*; (*interruption*) interrupción *f*. **~per** /'stɒpə(r)/ *n* tapón *m*. **~press** *n* noticias *fpl* de última hora. **~light** *n* luz *f* de freno. **~watch** *n* cronómetro *m*

storage /'stɔːrɪdʒ/ *n* almacenamiento *m*. **~ heater** *n* acumulador *m*. **in cold ~** almacenaje *m* frigorífico

store /stɔː(r)/ *n* provisión *f*; (*shop, depot*) almacén *m*; (*fig*) reserva *f*. **in ~** en reserva. **set ~ by** dar importancia a. ● *vt* (*for future*) poner en reserva; (*in warehouse*) almacenar. **~ up** *vt* acumular

storeroom /'stɔːruːm/ *n* despensa *f*

storey /'stɔːrɪ/ *n* (*pl* **-eys**) piso *m*

stork /stɔːk/ *n* cigüeña *f*

storm /stɔːm/ *n* tempestad *f*; (*mil*) asalto *m*. ● *vi* rabiar. ● *vt* (*mil*) asaltar. **~y** *a* tempestuoso

story /'stɔːrɪ/ *n* historia *f*; (*in newspaper*) artículo *m*; (*fam*) mentira *f*, cuento *m*. **~teller** *n* cuentista *m* & *f*

stout /staʊt/ *a* (**-er, -est**) (*fat*) gordo; (*brave*) valiente. ● *n* cerveza *f* negra. **~ness** *n* corpulencia *f*

stove /stəʊv/ *n* estufa *f*

stow /stəʊ/ *vt* guardar; (*hide*) esconder. ● *vi.* **~ away** viajar de polizón. **~away** /'stəʊəweɪ/ *n* polizón *m*

straddle /'strædl/ *vt* estar a horcajadas

straggl|e /'strægl/ *vi* rezagarse. **~y** *a* desordenado

straight /streɪt/ *a* (**-er, -est**) derecho, recto; (*tidy*) en orden; (*frank*) franco; ⟨*drink*⟩ solo, puro; ⟨*hair*⟩ lacio. ● *adv* derecho; (*direct*) directamente; (*without delay*) inmediatamente. **~ on** todo recto. **~ out** sin vacilar. **go ~** enmendarse. ● *n* recta *f*. **~ away** inmediatamente. **~en** /'streɪtn/ *vt* enderezar. ● *vi* enderezarse. **~forward** /streɪt'fɔːwəd/ *a* franco; (*easy*) sencillo. **~forwardly** *adv* francamente. **~ness** *n* rectitud *f*

strain¹ /streɪn/ *n* (*tension*) tensión *f*; (*injury*) torcedura *f*. ● *vt* estirar; (*tire*) cansar; (*injure*) torcer; (*sieve*) colar

strain² /streɪn/ *n* (*lineage*) linaje *m*; (*streak*) tendencia *f*

strained /streɪnd/ *a* forzado; ⟨*relations*⟩ tirante

strainer /-ə(r)/ *n* colador *m*

strains /streɪnz/ *npl* (*mus*) acordes *mpl*

strait /streɪt/ *n* estrecho *m*. **~jacket** *n* camisa *f* de fuerza. **~laced** *a* remilgado, gazmoño. **~s** *npl* apuro *m*

strand /strænd/ *n* (*thread*) hebra *f*; (*sand*) playa *f*. ● *vi* ⟨*ship*⟩ varar. **be ~ed** quedarse sin recursos

strange /streɪndʒ/ *a* (**-er, -est**) extraño, raro; (*not known*) desconocido; (*unaccustomed*) nuevo. **~ly** *adv* extrañamente. **~ness** *n* extrañeza *f*. **~r** /'streɪndʒə(r)/ *n* desconocido *m*

strangl|e /'stræŋgl/ *vt* estrangular; (*fig*) ahogar. **~lehold** /'stræŋglhəʊld/ *n* (*fig*) dominio *m* completo. **~ler** /-ə(r)/ *n* estrangulador *m*. **~ulation** /stræŋgjʊ'leɪʃn/ *n* estrangulación *f*

strap /stræp/ *n* correa *f*; (*of garment*) tirante *m*. ● *vt* (*pt* **strapped**) atar con correa; (*flog*) azotar

strapping /'stræpɪŋ/ *a* robusto

strata /'strɑːtə/ *see* **stratum**

strat|agem /'strætədʒəm/ *n* estratagema *f*. **~egic** /strə'tiːdʒɪk/ *a* estratégico. **~egically** *adv* estratégicamente. **~egist** *n* estratega *m & f*. **~egy** /'strætədʒɪ/ *n* estrategia *f*

stratum /'strɑːtəm/ *n* (*pl* **strata**) estrato *m*

straw /strɔː/ *n* paja *f*. **the last ~** el colmo

strawberry /'strɔːbərɪ/ *n* fresa *f*

stray /streɪ/ *vi* vagar; (*deviate*) desviarse (**from** de). ● *a* ⟨*animal*⟩ extraviado, callejero; (*isolated*) aislado. ● *n* animal *m* extraviado, animal *m* callejero

streak /striːk/ *n* raya *f*; (*of madness*) vena *f*. ● *vt* rayar. ● *vi* moverse como un rayo. **~y** *a* (**-ier, -iest**) rayado; ⟨*bacon*⟩ entreverado

stream /striːm/ *n* arroyo *m*; (*current*) corriente *f*; (*of people*) desfile *m*; (*schol*) grupo *m*. ● *vi* correr. **~ out** *vi* ⟨*people*⟩ salir en tropel

streamer /'striːmə(r)/ *n* (*paper*) serpentina *f*; (*flag*) gallardete *m*

streamline /'striːmlaɪn/ *vt* dar línea aerodinámica a; (*simplify*) simplificar. **~d** *a* aerodinámico

street /striːt/ *n* calle *f*. **~car** /'striːtkɑː/ *n* (*Amer*) tranvía *m*. **~ lamp** *n* farol *m*. **~ map** *n*, **~ plan** *n* plano *m*

strength /streŋθ/ *n* fuerza *f*; (*of wall etc*) solidez *f*. **on the ~ of** a base de. **~en** /'streŋθn/ *vt* reforzar

strenuous /'strenjʊəs/ *a* enérgico; (*arduous*) arduo; (*tiring*) fatigoso. **~ly** *adv* enérgicamente

stress /stres/ *n* énfasis *f*; (*gram*) acento *m*; (*mec, med, tension*) tensión *f*. ● *vt* insistir en

stretch /stretʃ/ *vt* estirar; (*extend*) extender; (*exaggerate*) forzar. **~ a point** hacer una excepción. ● *vi* estirarse; (*extend*) extenderse. ● *n* estirón *m*; (*period*) período *m*; (*of road*) tramo *m*. **at a ~** a seguido; (*in one go*) de un tirón. **~er** /'stretʃə(r)/ *n* camilla *f*

strew /struː/ *vt* (*pt* **strewed**, *pp* **strewn** *or* **strewed**) esparcir; (*cover*) cubrir

stricken /'strɪkən/ *a*. **~ with** afectado de

strict /strɪkt/ *a* (**-er, -est**) severo; (*precise*) estricto, preciso. **~ly** *adv* estrictamente. **~ly speaking** en rigor

stricture /'strɪktʃə(r)/ *n* crítica *f*; (*constriction*) constricción *f*

stride /straɪd/ *vi* (*pt* **strode**, *pp* **stridden**) andar a zancadas. ● *n* zancada

f. **take sth in one's ~** hacer algo con facilidad, tomarse las cosas con calma

strident /'straɪdnt/ *a* estridente

strife /straɪf/ *n* conflicto *m*

strike /straɪk/ *vt* (*pt* **struck**) golpear; encender ⟨*match*⟩; encontrar ⟨*gold etc*⟩; ⟨*clock*⟩ dar. ● *vi* golpear; (*go on strike*) declararse en huelga; (*be on strike*) estar en huelga; (*attack*) atacar; ⟨*clock*⟩ dar la hora. ● *n* (*of workers*) huelga *f*; (*attack*) ataque *m*; (*find*) descubrimiento *m*. **on ~** en huelga. **~ off, ~ out** tachar. **~ up a friendship** trabar amistad. **~r** /'straɪkə(r)/ *n* huelguista *m & f*

striking /'straɪkɪŋ/ *a* impresionante

string /strɪŋ/ *n* cuerda *f*; (*of lies, pearls*) sarta *f*. **pull ~s** tocar todos los resortes. ● *vt* (*pt* **strung**) (*thread*) ensartar. **~ along** (*fam*) engañar. **~ out** extender(se). **~ed** *a* (*mus*) de cuerda

stringen|cy /'strɪndʒənsɪ/ *n* rigor *m*. **~t** /'strɪndʒənt/ *a* riguroso

stringy /'strɪŋɪ/ *a* fibroso

strip /strɪp/ *vt* (*pt* **stripped**) desnudar; (*tear away, deprive*) quitar; desmontar ⟨*machine*⟩. ● *vi* desnudarse. ● *n* tira *f*. **~ cartoon** *n* historieta *f*

stripe /straɪp/ *n* raya *f*; (*mil*) galón *m*. **~d** *a* a rayas, rayado

strip: **~ light** *n* tubo *m* fluorescente. **~per** /-ə(r)/ *n* artista *m & f* de striptease. **~tease** *n* número *m* del desnudo, striptease *m*

strive /straɪv/ *vi* (*pt* **strove**, *pp* **striven**). **~ to** esforzarse por

strode /strəʊd/ *see* **stride**

stroke /strəʊk/ *n* golpe *m*; (*in swimming*) brazada *f*; (*med*) apoplejía *f*; (*of pen etc*) rasgo *m*; (*of clock*) campanada *f*; (*caress*) caricia *f*. ● *vt* acariciar

stroll /strəʊl/ *vi* pasearse. ● *n* paseo *m*

strong /strɒŋ/ *a* (**-er, -est**) fuerte. **~box** *n* caja *f* fuerte. **~hold** /'strɒŋhəʊld/ *n* fortaleza *f*; (*fig*) baluarte *m*. **~ language** *n* palabras *fpl* fuertes, palabras *fpl* subidas de tono. **~ly** *adv* (*greatly*) fuertemente; (*with energy*) enérgicamente; (*deeply*) profundamente. **~ measures** *npl* medidas *fpl* enérgicas. **~minded** *a* resuelto. **~room** *n* cámara *f* acorazada

stroppy /'strɒpɪ/ *a* (*sl*) irascible

strove /strəʊv/ *see* strive

struck /strʌk/ *see* strike. ∼ on (*sl*) entusiasta de

structur|al /'strʌktʃərəl/ *a* estructural. ∼e /'strʌktʃə(r)/ *n* estructura *f*

struggle /'strʌgl/ *vi* luchar. ∼ to one's feet levantarse con dificultad. ● *n* lucha *f*

strum /strʌm/ *vt/i* (*pt* strummed) rasguear

strung /strʌŋ/ *see* string. ● *a*. ∼ up (*tense*) nervioso

strut /strʌt/ *n* puntal *m*; (*walk*) pavoneo *m*. ● *vi* (*pt* strutted) pavonearse

stub /stʌb/ *n* cabo *m*; (*counterfoil*) talón *m*; (*of cigarette*) colilla *f*; (*of tree*) tocón *m*. ● *vt* (*pt* stubbed). ∼ out apagar

stubble /'stʌbl/ *n* rastrojo *m*; (*beard*) barba *f* de varios días

stubborn /'stʌbən/ *a* terco. ∼ly *adv* tercamente. ∼ness *n* terquedad *f*

stubby /'stʌbɪ/ *a* (-ier, -iest) achaparrado

stucco /'stʌkəʊ/ *n* (*pl* -oes) estuco *m*

stuck /stʌk/ *see* stick. ● *a* (*jammed*) bloqueado; (*in difficulties*) en un apuro. ∼ on (*sl*) encantado con. ∼-up *a* (*sl*) presumido

stud[1] /stʌd/ *n* tachón *m*; (*for collar*) botón *m*. ● *vt* (*pt* studded) tachonar. ∼ded with sembrado de

stud[2] /stʌd/ *n* (*of horses*) caballeriza *f*

student /'stju:dənt/ *n* estudiante *m* & *f*

studied /'stʌdɪd/ *a* deliberado

studio /'stju:dɪəʊ/ *n* (*pl* -os) estudio *m*. ∼ couch *n* sofá *m* cama. ∼ flat *n* estudio *m* de artista

studious /'stju:dɪəs/ *a* estudioso; (*studied*) deliberado. ∼ly *adv* estudiosamente; (*carefully*) cuidadosamente

study /'stʌdɪ/ *n* estudio *m*; (*office*) despacho *m*. ● *vt/i* estudiar

stuff /stʌf/ *n* materia *f*, sustancia *f*; (*sl*) cosas *fpl*. ● *vt* rellenar; disecar ⟨*animal*⟩; (*cram*) atiborrar; (*block up*) tapar; (*put*) meter de prisa. ∼ing *n* relleno *m*

stuffy /'stʌfɪ/ *a* (-ier, -iest) mal ventilado; (*old-fashioned*) chapado a la antigua

stumbl|e /'stʌmbl/ *vi* tropezar. ∼e across, ∼e on tropezar con. ● *n*

tropezón *m*. ∼ing-block *n* tropiezo *m*, impedimento *m*

stump /stʌmp/ *n* cabo *m*; (*of limb*) muñón *m*; (*of tree*) tocón *m*. ∼ed /stʌmpt/ *a* (*fam*) perplejo. ∼y /'stʌmpɪ/ *a* (-ier, -iest) achaparrado

stun /stʌn/ *vt* (*pt* stunned) aturdir; (*bewilder*) pasmar. ∼ning *a* (*fabulous*, *fam*) estupendo

stung /stʌŋ/ *see* sting

stunk /stʌŋk/ *see* stink

stunt[1] /stʌnt/ *n* (*fam*) truco *m* publicitario

stunt[2] /stʌnt/ *vt* impedir el desarrollo de. ∼ed *a* enano

stupefy /'stju:pɪfaɪ/ *vt* dejar estupefacto

stupendous /stju:'pendəs/ *a* estupendo. ∼ly *adv* estupendamente

stupid /'stju:pɪd/ *a* estúpido. ∼ity /-'pɪdətɪ/ *n* estupidez *f*. ∼ly *adv* estúpidamente

stupor /'stju:pə(r)/ *n* estupor *m*

sturd|iness /'stɜ:dɪnɪs/ *n* robustez *f*. ∼y /'stɜ:dɪ/ *a* (-ier, -iest) robusto

sturgeon /'stɜ:dʒən/ *n* (*pl* sturgeon) esturión *m*

stutter /'stʌtə(r)/ *vi* tartamudear. ● *n* tartamudeo *m*

sty[1] /staɪ/ *n* (*pl* sties) pocilga *f*

sty[2] /staɪ/ *n* (*pl* sties) (*med*) orzuelo *m*

styl|e /staɪl/ *n* estilo *m*; (*fashion*) moda *f*. in ∼ con todo lujo. ● *vt* diseñar. ∼ish /'staɪlɪʃ/ *a* elegante. ∼ishly *adv* elegantemente. ∼ist /'staɪlɪst/ *n* estilista *m* & *f*. hair ∼ist *n* peluquero *m*. ∼ized /'staɪlaɪzd/ *a* estilizado

stylus /'staɪləs/ *n* (*pl* -uses) aguja *f* (de tocadiscos)

suave /swɑ:v/ *a* (*pej*) zalamero

sub... /sʌb/ *pref* sub...

subaquatic /sʌbə'kwætɪk/ *a* subacuático

subconscious /sʌb'kɒnʃəs/ *a* & *n* subconsciente (*m*). ∼ly *adv* de modo subconsciente

subcontinent /sʌb'kɒntɪnənt/ *n* subcontinente *m*

subcontract /sʌbkən'trækt/ *vt* subcontratar. ∼or /-ə(r)/ *n* subcontratista *m* & *f*

subdivide /sʌbdɪ'vaɪd/ *vt* subdividir

subdue /səb'dju:/ *vt* dominar ⟨*feelings*⟩; sojuzgar ⟨*country*⟩. ∼d *a* (*depressed*) abatido; ⟨*light*⟩ suave

subhuman /sʌb'hju:mən/ *a* infrahumano

subject /'sʌbdʒɪkt/ a sometido. ~ **to** sujeto a. ● n súbdito m; (theme) asunto m; (schol) asignatura f; (gram) sujeto m; (of painting, play, book etc) tema m. /səb'dʒekt/ vt sojuzgar; (submit) someter. ~**ion** /-ʃn/ n sometimiento m

subjective /səb'dʒektɪv/ a subjetivo. ~**ly** adv subjetivamente

subjugate /'sʌbdʒʊgeɪt/ vt subyugar

subjunctive /səb'dʒʌŋktɪv/ a & n subjuntivo (m)

sublet /sʌb'let/ vt (pt **sublet**, pres p **subletting**) subarrendar

sublimat|e /'sʌblɪmeɪt/ vt sublimar. ~**ion** /-'meɪʃn/ n sublimación f

sublime /sə'blaɪm/ a sublime. ~**ly** adv sublimemente

submarine /sʌbmə'riːn/ n submarino m

submerge /səb'mɜːdʒ/ vt sumergir. ● vi sumergirse

submi|ssion /səb'mɪʃn/ n sumisión f. ~**ssive** /-sɪv/ a sumiso. ~**t** /səb'mɪt/ vt (pt **submitted**) someter. ● vi someterse

subordinat|e /sə'bɔːdɪnət/ a & n subordinado (m). /sə'bɔːdɪneɪt/ vt subordinar. ~**ion** /-'neɪʃn/ n subordinación f

subscri|be /səb'skraɪb/ vi suscribir. ~**be to** suscribir (fund); (agree) estar de acuerdo con; abonarse a (newspaper). ~**ber** /-ə(r)/ n abonado m. ~**ption** /-rɪpʃn/ n suscripción f

subsequent /'sʌbsɪkwənt/ a subsiguiente. ~**ly** adv posteriormente

subservient /səb'sɜːvjənt/ a servil

subside /səb'saɪd/ vi (land) hundirse; (flood) bajar; (storm, wind) amainar. ~**nce** n hundimiento m

subsidiary /səb'sɪdɪərɪ/ a subsidiario. ● n (com) sucursal m

subsid|ize /'sʌbsɪdaɪz/ vt subvencionar. ~**y** /'sʌbsədɪ/ n subvención f

subsist /səb'sɪst/ vi subsistir. ~**ence** n subsistencia f

subsoil /'sʌbsɔɪl/ n subsuelo m

subsonic /sʌb'sɒnɪk/ a subsónico

substance /'sʌbstəns/ n substancia f

substandard /sʌb'stændəd/ a inferior

substantial /səb'stænʃl/ a sólido; (meal) substancial; (considerable) considerable. ~**ly** adv considerablemente

substantiate /səb'stænʃɪeɪt/ vt justificar

substitut|e /'sʌbstɪtjuːt/ n substituto m. ● vt/i substituir. ~**ion** /-'tjuːʃn/ n substitución f

subterfuge /'sʌbtəfjuːdʒ/ n subterfugio m

subterranean /sʌbtə'reɪnjən/ a subterráneo

subtitle /'sʌbtaɪtl/ n subtítulo m

subtle /'sʌtl/ a (-er, -est) sutil. ~**ty** n sutileza f

subtract /səb'trækt/ vt restar. ~**ion** /-ʃn/ n resta f

suburb /'sʌbɜːb/ n barrio m. **the** ~**s** las afueras fpl. ~**an** /sə'bɜːbən/ a suburbano. ~**ia** /sə'bɜːbɪə/ n las afueras fpl

subvention /səb'venʃn/ n subvención f

subver|sion /səb'vɜːʃn/ n subversión f. ~**sive** /səb'vɜːsɪv/ a subversivo. ~**t** /səb'vɜːt/ vt subvertir

subway /'sʌbweɪ/ n paso m subterráneo; (Amer) metro m

succeed /sək'siːd/ vi tener éxito. ● vt suceder a. ~ **in doing** lograr hacer. ~**ing** a sucesivo

success /sək'ses/ n éxito m. ~**ful** a que tiene éxito; (chosen) elegido

succession /sək'seʃn/ n sucesión f. **in** ~ sucesivamente, seguidos

successive /sək'sesɪv/ a sucesivo. ~**ly** adv sucesivamente

successor /sək'sesə(r)/ n sucesor m

succinct /sək'sɪŋkt/ a sucinto

succour /'sʌkə(r)/ vt socorrer. ● n socorro m

succulent /'sʌkjʊlənt/ a suculento

succumb /sə'kʌm/ vi sucumbir

such /sʌtʃ/ a tal. ● pron los que, las que; (so much) tanto. **and** ~ y tal. ● adv tan. ~ **a big house** una casa tan grande. ~ **and** ~ tal o cual. ~ **as it is** tal como es. ~**like** a (fam) semejante, de ese tipo

suck /sʌk/ vt chupar; sorber (liquid). ~ **up** absorber. ~ **up to** (sl) dar coba a. ~**er** /'sʌkə(r)/ n (plant) chupón m; (person, fam) primo m

suckle /sʌkl/ vt amamantar

suction /'sʌkʃn/ n succión f

sudden /'sʌdn/ a repentino. **all of a** ~ de repente. ~**ly** adv de repente. ~**ness** n lo repentino

suds /sʌds/ npl espuma f (de jabón)

sue /suː/ vt (pres p **suing**) demandar (**for** por)

suede /sweɪd/ n ante m

suet /'suːɪt/ n sebo m

suffer /'sʌfə(r)/ vt sufrir; (tolerate) tolerar. ● vi sufrir. ~ance /'sʌfərəns/ n. on ~ance por tolerancia. ~ing n sufrimiento m

suffic|e /sə'faɪs/ vi bastar. ~iency /sə'fɪʃənsɪ/ n suficiencia f. ~ient /sə'fɪʃnt/ a suficiente; (enough) bastante. ~iently adv suficientemente, bastante

suffix /'sʌfɪks/ n (pl -ixes) sufijo m

suffocat|e /'sʌfəkeɪt/ vt ahogar. ● vi ahogarse. ~ion /-'keɪʃn/ n asfixia f

sugar /'ʃʊgə(r)/ n azúcar m & f. ● vt azucarar. ~bowl n azucarero m. ~ lump n terrón m de azúcar. ~y a azucarado.

suggest /sə'dʒest/ vt sugerir. ~ible /sə'dʒestɪbl/ a sugestionable. ~ion /-tʃən/ n sugerencia f; (trace) traza f. ~ive /sə'dʒestɪv/ a sugestivo. be ~ive of evocar, recordar. ~ively adv sugestivamente

suicid|al /suː'saɪdl/ a suicida. ~e /'suːɪsaɪd/ n suicidio m; (person) suicida m & f. commit ~e suicidarse

suit /suːt/ n traje m; (woman's) traje m de chaqueta; (cards) palo m; (jurid) pleito m. ● vt convenir; (clothes) sentar bien a; (adapt) adaptar. be ~ed for ser apto para. ~ability n conveniencia f. ~able a adecuado. ~ably adv convenientemente. ~case /'suːtkeɪs/ n maleta f, valija f (LAm)

suite /swiːt/ n (of furniture) juego m; (of rooms) apartamento m; (retinue) séquito m

suitor /'suːtə(r)/ n pretendiente m

sulk /sʌlk/ vi enfurruñarse. ~s npl enfurruñamiento m. ~y a enfurruñado

sullen /'sʌlən/ a resentido. ~ly adv con resentimiento

sully /'sʌlɪ/ vt manchar

sulphur /'sʌlfə(r)/ n azufre m. ~ic /-'fjʊərɪk/ a sulfúrico. ~ic acid n ácido m sulfúrico

sultan /'sʌltən/ n sultán m

sultana /sʌl'tɑːnə/ n pasa f gorrona

sultry /'sʌltrɪ/ a (-ier, -iest) (weather) bochornoso; (fig) sensual

sum /sʌm/ n suma f. ● vt (pt summed). ~ up resumir (situation); (assess) evaluar

summar|ily /'sʌmərɪlɪ/ adv sumariamente. ~ize vt resumir. ~y /'sʌmərɪ/ a sumario. ● n resumen m

summer /'sʌmə(r)/ n verano m. ~house n glorieta f, cenador m. ~time n verano m. ~ time n hora f de verano. ~y a veraniego

summit /'sʌmɪt/ n cumbre f. ~ conference n conferencia f cumbre

summon /'sʌmən/ vt llamar; convocar (meeting, s.o. to meeting); (jurid) citar. ~ up armarse de. ~s /'sʌmənz/ n llamada f; (jurid) citación f. ● vt citar

sump /sʌmp/ n (mec) cárter m

sumptuous /'sʌmptjʊəs/ a suntuoso. ~ly adv suntuosamente

sun /sʌn/ n sol m. ● vt (pt sunned). ~ o.s. tomar el sol. ~bathe /'sʌnbeɪð/ vi tomar el sol. ~beam /'sʌnbiːm/ n rayo m de sol. ~burn /'sʌnbɜːn/ n quemadura f de sol. ~burnt a quemado por el sol

sundae /'sʌndeɪ/ n helado m con frutas y nueces

Sunday /'sʌndeɪ/ n domingo m. ~ school n catequesis f

sun: ~dial /'sʌndaɪl/ n reloj m de sol. ~down /'sʌndaʊn/ n puesta f del sol

sundry /'sʌndrɪ/ a diversos. all and ~ todo el mundo. sundries npl artículos mpl diversos

sunflower /'sʌnflaʊə(r)/ n girasol m

sung /sʌŋ/ see sing

sun-glasses /'sʌnglɑːsɪz/ npl gafas fpl de sol

sunk /sʌŋk/ see sink. ~en /'sʌŋkən/ ● a hundido

sunlight /'sʌnlaɪt/ n luz f del sol

sunny /'sʌnɪ/ a (-ier, -iest) (day) de sol; (place) soleado. it is ~ hace sol

sun: ~rise /'sʌnraɪz/ n amanecer m, salida f del sol. ~roof n techo m corredizo. ~set /'sʌnset/ n puesta f del sol. ~shade /'sʌnʃeɪd/ n quitasol m, sombrilla f; (awning) toldo m. ~shine /'sʌnʃaɪn/ n sol m. ~spot /'sʌnspɒt/ n mancha f solar. ~stroke /'sʌnstrəʊk/ n insolación f. ~tan n bronceado m. ~tanned a bronceado. ~tan lotion n bronceador m

sup /sʌp/ vt (pt supped) sorber

super /'suːpə(r)/ a (fam) estupendo

superannuation /suːpərænjʊ'eɪʃn/ n jubilación f

superb /suː'pɜːb/ a espléndido. ~ly adv espléndidamente

supercilious /suːpə'sɪlɪəs/ a desdeñoso

superficial /suːpə'fɪʃl/ a superficial. ~ity /-ɪ'ælətɪ/ n superficialidad f. ~ly adv superficialmente

superfluous /suːˈpɜːfluəs/ a superfluo

superhuman /suːpəˈhjuːmən/ a sobrehumano

superimpose /suːpərɪmˈpəʊz/ vt sobreponer

superintend /suːpərɪnˈtend/ vt vigilar. ~ence n dirección f. ~ent n director m; (of police) comisario m

superior /suːˈpɪərɪə(r)/ a & n superior (m). ~ity /-ˈɒrətɪ/ n superioridad f

superlative /suːˈpɜːlətɪv/ a & n superlativo (m)

superman /ˈsuːpəmæn/ n (pl -men) superhombre m

supermarket /ˈsuːpəmɑːkɪt/ n supermercado m

supernatural /suːpəˈnætʃrəl/ a sobrenatural

superpower /ˈsuːpəpaʊə(r)/ n superpotencia f

supersede /suːpəˈsiːd/ vt reemplazar, suplantar

supersonic /suːpəˈsɒnɪk/ a supersónico

superstitio|n /suːpəˈstɪʃn/ n superstición f. ~us a supersticioso

superstructure /ˈsuːpəstrʌktʃə(r)/ n superestructura f

supertanker /ˈsuːpətæŋkə(r)/ n petrolero m gigante

supervene /suːpəˈviːn/ vi sobrevenir

supervis|e /ˈsuːpəvaɪz/ vt supervisar. ~ion /-ˈvɪʒn/ n supervisión f. ~or /-zə(r)/ n supervisor m. ~ory a de supervisión

supper /ˈsʌpə(r)/ n cena f

supplant /səˈplɑːnt/ vt suplantar

supple /ˈsʌpl/ a flexible. ~ness n flexibilidad f

supplement /ˈsʌplɪmənt/ n suplemento m. ● vt completar; (increase) aumentar. ~ary /-ˈmentərɪ/ a suplementario

suppl|ier /səˈplaɪə(r)/ n suministrador m; (com) proveedor m. ~y /səˈplaɪ/ vt proveer; (feed) alimentar; satisfacer ⟨a need⟩. ~y with abastecer de. ● n provisión f, suministro m. ~y and demand oferta f y demanda

support /səˈpɔːt/ vt sostener; (endure) soportar, aguantar; (fig) apoyar. ● n apoyo m; (tec) soporte m. ~er /-ə(r)/ n soporte m; (sport) seguidor m, hincha m & f. ~ive a alentador

suppos|e /səˈpəʊz/ vt suponer; (think) creer. **be** ~**ed to** deber. **not be** ~**ed to** (fam) no tener permiso para, no tener derecho a. ~**edly** adv según cabe suponer; (before adjective) presuntamente. ~**ition** /sʌpəˈzɪʃn/ n suposición f

suppository /səˈpɒzɪtərɪ/ n supositorio m

suppress /səˈpres/ vt suprimir. ~**ion** n supresión f. ~**or** /-ə(r)/ n supresor m

suprem|acy /suːˈpreməsɪ/ n supremacía f. ~**e** /suːˈpriːm/ a supremo

surcharge /ˈsɜːtʃɑːdʒ/ n sobreprecio m; (tax) recargo m

sure /ʃʊə(r)/ a (-er, -est) seguro, cierto. **make** ~ asegurarse. ● adv (Amer, fam) ¡claro! ~ **enough** efectivamente. ~**footed** a de pie firme. ~**ly** adv seguramente

surety /ˈʃʊərətɪ/ n garantía f

surf /sɜːf/ n oleaje m; (foam) espuma f

surface /ˈsɜːfɪs/ n superficie f. ● a superficial, de la superficie. ● vt (smoothe) alisar; (cover) recubrir (with de). ● vi salir a la superficie; (emerge) emerger. ~ **mail** n por vía marítima

surfboard /ˈsɜːfbɔːd/ n tabla f de surf

surfeit /ˈsɜːfɪt/ n exceso m

surfing /ˈsɜːfɪŋ/ n, **surf-riding** /ˈsɜːfraɪdɪŋ/ n surf m

surge /sɜːdʒ/ vi ⟨crowd⟩ moverse en tropel; ⟨waves⟩ encresparse. ● n oleada f; (elec) sobretensión f

surgeon /ˈsɜːdʒən/ n cirujano m

surgery /ˈsɜːdʒərɪ/ n cirugía f; (consulting room) consultorio m; (consulting hours) horas fpl de consulta

surgical /ˈsɜːdʒɪkl/ a quirúrgico

surl|iness /ˈsɜːlɪnɪs/ n aspereza f. ~**y** /ˈsɜːlɪ/ a (-ier, -iest) áspero

surmise /səˈmaɪz/ vt conjeturar

surmount /səˈmaʊnt/ vt superar

surname /ˈsɜːneɪm/ n apellido m

surpass /səˈpɑːs/ vt sobrepasar, exceder

surplus /ˈsɜːpləs/ a & n excedente (m)

surpris|e /səˈpraɪz/ n sorpresa f. ● vt sorprender. ~**ing** a sorprendente. ~**ingly** adv asombrosamente

surrealis|m /səˈrɪəlɪzəm/ n surrealismo m. ~**t** n surrealista m & f

surrender /səˈrendə(r)/ vt entregar. ● vi entregarse. ● n entrega f; (mil) rendición f

surreptitious /sʌrəp'tɪʃəs/ a clandestino

surrogate /'sʌrəgət/ n substituto m

surround /sə'raʊnd/ vt rodear; (mil) cercar. ● n borde m. **~ing** a circundante. **~ings** npl alrededores mpl

surveillance /sɜː'veɪləns/ n vigilancia f

survey /'sɜːveɪ/ n inspección f; (report) informe m; (general view) vista f de conjunto. /sə'veɪ/ vt examinar, inspeccionar; (inquire into) hacer una encuesta de. **~or** n topógrafo m, agrimensor

surviv|al /sə'vaɪvl/ n supervivencia f. **~e** /sə'vaɪv/ vt/i sobrevivir. **~or** /-ə(r)/ n superviviente m & f

susceptib|ility /səseptə'bɪlətɪ/ n susceptibilidad f. **~le** /sə'septəbl/ a susceptible. **~le to** propenso a

suspect /sə'spekt/ vt sospechar. /'sʌspekt/ a & n sospechoso (m)

suspend /sə'spend/ vt suspender. **~er** /səs'pendə(r)/ n liga f. **~er belt** n liguero m. **~ers** npl (Amer) tirantes mpl

suspense /sə'spens/ n incertidumbre f; (in film etc) suspense m

suspension /sə'spenʃn/ n suspensión f. **~ bridge** n puente m colgante

suspicion /sə'spɪʃn/ n sospecha f; (trace) pizca f

suspicious /sə'spɪʃəs/ a desconfiado; (causing suspicion) sospechoso

sustain /sə'steɪn/ vt sostener; (suffer) sufrir

sustenance /'sʌstɪnəns/ n sustento m

svelte /svelt/ a esbelto

SW abbr (south-west) sudoeste m

swab /swɒb/ n (med) tapón m

swagger /'swægə(r)/ vi pavonearse

swallow[1] /'swɒləʊ/ vt/i tragar. ● n trago m. **~ up** tragar; consumir (savings etc)

swallow[2] /'swɒləʊ/ n (bird) golondrina f

swam /swæm/ see **swim**

swamp /swɒmp/ n pantano m. ● vt inundar; (with work) agobiar. **~y** a pantanoso

swan /swɒn/ n cisne m

swank /swæŋk/ n (fam) ostentación f. ● vi (fam) fanfarronear

swap /swɒp/ vt/i (pt swapped) (fam) (inter)cambiar. ● n (fam) (inter)cambio m

swarm /swɔːm/ n enjambre m. ● vi ⟨bees⟩ enjambrar; (fig) hormiguear

swarthy /'swɔːðɪ/ a (-ier, -iest) moreno

swastika /'swɒstɪkə/ n cruz f gamada

swat /swɒt/ vt (pt swatted) aplastar

sway /sweɪ/ vi balancearse. ● vt (influence) influir en. ● n balanceo m; (rule) imperio m

swear /sweə(r)/ vt/i (pt swore, pp sworn) jurar. **~ by** (fam) creer ciegamente en. **~-word** n palabrota f

sweat /swet/ n sudor m. ● vi sudar

sweat|er /'swetə(r)/ n jersey m. **~shirt** n sudadera f

swede /swiːd/ n naba f

Swede /swiːd/ n sueco m

Sweden /'swiːdn/ n Suecia f

Swedish /'swiːdɪʃ/ a & n sueco (m)

sweep /swiːp/ vt (pt swept) barrer; deshollinar ⟨chimney⟩. **~ the board** ganar todo. ● vi barrer; ⟨road⟩ extenderse; (go majestically) moverse majestuosamente. ● n barrido m; (curve) curva f; (movement) movimiento m; (person) deshollinador m. **~ away** vt barrer. **~ing** a (gesture) amplio; ⟨changes etc⟩ radical; ⟨statement⟩ demasiado general. **~stake** /'swiːpsteɪk/ n lotería f

sweet /swiːt/ a (-er, -est) dulce; (fragrant) fragante; (pleasant) agradable. **have a ~ tooth** ser dulcero. ● n caramelo m; (dish) postre m. **~bread** /'swiːtbred/ n lechecillas fpl. **~en** /'swiːtn/ vt endulzar. **~ener** /-ə(r)/ n dulcificante m. **~heart** /'swiːthɑːt/ n amor m. **~ly** adv dulcemente. **~ness** n dulzura f. **~ pea** n guisante m de olor

swell /swel/ vt (pt swelled, pp swollen or swelled) hinchar; (increase) aumentar. ● vi hincharse; (increase) aumentarse; ⟨river⟩ crecer. ● a (fam) estupendo. ● n (of sea) oleaje m. **~ing** n hinchazón m

swelter /'sweltə(r)/ vi sofocarse de calor

swept /swept/ see **sweep**

swerve /swɜːv/ vi desviarse

swift /swɪft/ a (-er, -est) rápido. ● n (bird) vencejo m. **~ly** adv rápidamente. **~ness** n rapidez f

swig /swɪg/ vt (pt swigged) (fam) beber a grandes tragos. ● n (fam) trago m

swill /swɪl/ vt enjuagar; (drink) beber a grandes tragos. ● n (food for pigs) bazofia f

swim /swɪm/ vi (pt swam, pp swum) nadar; ⟨room, head⟩ dar vueltas. ● n baño m. **~mer** n nadador m. **~ming-bath** n piscina f. **~mingly** /'swɪmɪŋlɪ/ adv a las mil maravillas. **~ming-pool** n piscina f. **~ming-trunks** npl bañador m. **~suit** n traje m de baño

swindle /'swɪndl/ vt estafar. ● n estafa f. **~r** /-ə(r)/ n estafador m

swine /swaɪn/ npl cerdos mpl. ● n (pl swine) (person, fam) canalla m

swing /swɪŋ/ vt (pt swung) balancear. ● vi oscilar; ⟨person⟩ balancearse; (turn round) girar. ● n balanceo m, vaivén m; (seat) columpio m; (mus) ritmo m. in full ~ en plena actividad. ~ bridge n puente m giratorio

swingeing /'swɪndʒɪŋ/ a enorme

swipe /swaɪp/ vt golpear; (snatch, sl) birlar. ● n (fam) golpe m

swirl /swɜːl/ vi arremolinarse. ● n remolino m

swish /swɪʃ/ vt silbar. ● a (fam) elegante

Swiss /swɪs/ a & n suizo (m). ~ roll n bizcocho m enrollado

switch /swɪtʃ/ n (elec) interruptor m; (change) cambio m. ● vt cambiar; (deviate) desviar. ~ off (elec) desconectar; apagar ⟨light⟩. ~ on (elec) encender; arrancar ⟨engine⟩. **~back** /'swɪtʃbæk/ n montaña f rusa. **~board** /'swɪtʃbɔːd/ n centralita f

Switzerland /'swɪtsələnd/ n Suiza f

swivel /'swɪvl/ ● vi (pt swivelled) girar

swollen /'swəʊlən/ see swell. ● a hinchado

swoon /swuːn/ vi desmayarse

swoop /swuːp/ vi ⟨bird⟩ calarse; ⟨plane⟩ bajar en picado. ● n calada f; (by police) redada f

sword /sɔːd/ n espada f. **~fish** /'sɔːdfɪʃ/ n pez m espada

swore /swɔː(r)/ see swear

sworn /swɔːn/ see swear. ● a ⟨enemy⟩ jurado; ⟨friend⟩ leal

swot /swɒt/ vt/i (pt swotted) (schol, sl) empollar. ● n (schol, sl) empollón m

swum /swʌm/ see swim

swung /swʌŋ/ see swing

sycamore /'sɪkəmɔː(r)/ n plátano m falso

syllable /'sɪləbl/ n sílaba f

syllabus /'sɪləbəs/ n (pl -buses) programa m (de estudios)

symbol /'sɪmbl/ n símbolo m. **~ic(al)** /-'bɒlɪk(l)/ a simbólico. **~ism** n simbolismo m. **~ize** vt simbolizar

symmetr|ical /sɪ'metrɪkl/ a simétrico. **~y** /'sɪmətrɪ/ n simetría f

sympath|etic /sɪmpə'θetɪk/ a comprensivo; (showing pity) compasivo. **~ize** /-aɪz/ vi comprender; (pity) compadecerse (with de). **~izer** n (pol) simpatizante m & f. **~y** /'sɪmpəθɪ/ n comprensión f; (pity) compasión f; (condolences) pésame m. be in **~y with** estar de acuerdo con

symphon|ic /sɪm'fɒnɪk/ a sinfónico. **~y** /'sɪmfənɪ/ n sinfonía f

symposium /sɪm'pəʊzɪəm/ n (pl -ia) simposio m

symptom /'sɪmptəm/ n síntoma m. **~atic** /-'mætɪk/ a sintomático

synagogue /'sɪnəgɒg/ n sinagoga f

synchroniz|ation /sɪŋkrənaɪ'zeɪʃn/ n sincronización f. **~e** /'sɪŋkrənaɪz/ vt sincronizar

syncopat|e /'sɪŋkəpeɪt/ vt sincopar. **~ion** /-'peɪʃn/ n síncopa f

syndicate /'sɪndɪkət/ n sindicato m

syndrome /'sɪndrəʊm/ n síndrome m

synod /'sɪnəd/ n sínodo m

synonym /'sɪnənɪm/ n sinónimo m. **~ous** /-'nɒnɪməs/ a sinónimo

synopsis /sɪ'nɒpsɪs/ n (pl -opses /-siːz/) sinopsis f, resumen m

syntax /'sɪntæks/ n sintaxis f invar

synthesi|s /'sɪnθəsɪs/ n (pl -theses /-siːz/) síntesis f. **~ze** vt sintetizar

synthetic /sɪn'θetɪk/ a sintético

syphilis /'sɪfɪlɪs/ n sífilis f

Syria /'sɪrɪə/ n Siria f. **~n** a & n sirio (m)

syringe /'sɪrɪndʒ/ n jeringa f. ● vt jeringar

syrup /'sɪrəp/ n jarabe m, almíbar m; (treacle) melaza f. **~y** a almibarado

system /'sɪstəm/ n sistema m; (body) organismo m; (order) método m. **~atic** /-ə'mætɪk/ a sistemático. **~atically** /-ə'mætɪklɪ/ adv sistemáticamente. **~s analyst** n analista m & f de sistemas

T

tab /tæb/ n (flap) lengüeta f; (label) etiqueta f. **keep ~s on** (fam) vigilar
tabby /'tæbɪ/ n gato m atigrado
tabernacle /'tæbənækl/ n tabernáculo m
table /'teɪbl/ n mesa f; (list) tabla f. **~ of contents** índice m. ● vt presentar; (postpone) aplazar. **~cloth** n mantel m. **~mat** n salvamanteles m invar. **~spoon** /'teɪblspuːn/ n cucharón m, cuchara f sopera. **~spoonful** n (pl **-fuls**) cucharada f
tablet /'tæblɪt/ n (of stone) lápida f; (pill) tableta f; (of soap etc) pastilla f
table tennis /'teɪbltenɪs/ n tenis m de mesa, ping-pong m
tabloid /'tæblɔɪd/ n tabloide m
taboo /tə'buː/ a & n tabú (m)
tabulator /'tæbjʊleɪtə(r)/ n tabulador m
tacit /'tæsɪt/ a tácito
taciturn /'tæsɪtɜːn/ a taciturno
tack /tæk/ n tachuela f; (stitch) hilván m; (naut) virada f; (fig) línea f de conducta. ● vt sujetar con tachuelas; (sew) hilvanar. **~ on** añadir. ● vi virar
tackle /'tækl/ n (equipment) equipo m; (football) placaje m. ● vt abordar (problem etc); (in rugby) hacer un placaje a
tacky /'tækɪ/ a pegajoso; (in poor taste) vulgar, de pacotilla
tact /tækt/ n tacto m. **~ful** a discreto. **~fully** adv discretamente
tactic|al /'tæktɪkl/ a táctico. **~s** /'tæktɪks/ npl táctica f
tactile /'tæktaɪl/ a táctil
tact: ~less a indiscreto. **~lessly** adv indiscretamente
tadpole /'tædpəʊl/ n renacuajo m
tag /tæg/ n (on shoe-lace) herrete m; (label) etiqueta f. ● vt (pt **tagged**) poner etiqueta a; (trail) seguir. ● vi. **~ along** (fam) seguir
tail /teɪl/ n cola f. **~s** npl (tailcoat) frac m; (of coin) cruz f. ● vt (sl) seguir. ● vi. **~ off** disminuir. **~-end** n extremo m final, cola f
tailor /'teɪlə(r)/ n sastre m. ● vt confeccionar. **~-made** n hecho a la medida. **~-made for** (fig) hecho para
tailplane /'teɪlpleɪn/ n plano m de cola

taint /teɪnt/ n mancha f. ● vt contaminar
take /teɪk/ vt (pt **took**, pp **taken**) tomar, coger (not LAm), agarrar (esp LAm); (contain) contener; (capture) capturar; (endure) aguantar; (require) requerir; tomar (bath); dar (walk); (carry) llevar; (accompany) acompañar; presentarse para (exam); sacar (photo); ganar (prize). **~ advantage of** aprovechar. **~ after** parecerse a. **~ away** quitar. **~ back** retirar (statement etc). **~ in** achicar (garment); (understand) comprender; (deceive) engañar. **~ off** quitarse (clothes); (mimic) imitar; (aviat) despegar. **~ o.s. off** marcharse. **~ on** (undertake) emprender; contratar (employee). **~ out** (remove) sacar. **~ over** tomar posesión de; (assume control) tomar el poder. **~ part** participar. **~ place** tener lugar. **~ sides** tomar partido. **~ to** dedicarse a; (like) tomar simpatía a (person); (like) aficionarse a (thing). **~ up** dedicarse a (hobby); (occupy) ocupar; (resume) reanudar. **~ up with** trabar amistad con. **be ~n ill** ponerse enfermo. ● n presa f; (photo, cinema, TV) toma f
takings /'teɪkɪŋz/ npl ingresos mpl
take: ~-off n despegue m. **~-over** n toma f de posesión.
talcum /'tælkəm/ n. **~ powder** n (polvos mpl de) talco (m)
tale /teɪl/ n cuento m
talent /'tælənt/ n talento m. **~ed** a talentoso
talisman /'tælɪzmən/ n talismán m
talk /tɔːk/ vt/i hablar. **~ about** hablar de. **~ over** discutir. ● n conversación f; (lecture) conferencia f. **small ~** charla f. **~ative** a hablador. **~er** n hablador m; (chatterbox) parlanchín m. **~ing-to** n represión f
tall /tɔːl/ a (**-er, -est**) alto. **~ story** n (fam) historia f inverosímil. **that's a ~ order** n (fam) eso es pedir mucho
tallboy /'tɔːlbɔɪ/ n cómoda f alta
tally /'tælɪ/ n tarja f; (total) total m. ● vi corresponder (**with** a)
talon /'tælən/ n garra f
tambourine /tæmbə'riːn/ n pandereta f
tame /teɪm/ a (**-er, -est**) (animal) doméstico; (person) dócil; (dull) insípido. ● vt domesticar; domar

⟨*wild animal*⟩. ~**ly** *adv* dócilmente.
~**r** /-ə(r)/ *n* domador *m*

tamper /'tæmpə(r)/ *vi.* ~ **with** manosear; (*alter*) alterar, falsificar

tampon /'tæmpən/ *n* tampón *m*

tan /tæn/ *vt* (*pt* **tanned**) curtir ⟨*hide*⟩; ⟨*sun*⟩ broncear. ● *vi* ponerse moreno. ● *n* bronceado *m*. ● *a* (*colour*) de color canela

tandem /'tændəm/ *n* tándem *m*

tang /tæŋ/ *n* sabor *m* fuerte; (*smell*) olor *m* fuerte

tangent /'tændʒənt/ *n* tangente *f*

tangerine /tændʒə'ri:n/ *n* mandarina *f*

tangibl|e /'tændʒəbl/ *a* tangible. ~**y** *adv* perceptiblemente

tangle /'tæŋgl/ *vt* enredar. ● *vi* enredarse. ● *n* enredo *m*

tango /'tæŋgəʊ/ *n* (*pl* -**os**) tango *m*

tank /tæŋk/ *n* depósito *m*; (*mil*) tanque *m*

tankard /'tæŋkəd/ *n* jarra *f*, bock *m*

tanker /'tæŋkə(r)/ *n* petrolero *m*; (*truck*) camión *m* cisterna

tantaliz|e /'tæntəlaɪz/ *vt* atormentar. ~**ing** *a* atormentador; (*tempting*) tentador

tantamount /'tæntəmaʊnt/ *a.* ~ **to** equivalente a

tantrum /'tæntrəm/ *n* rabieta *f*

tap¹ /tæp/ *n* grifo *m*. **on** ~ disponible. ● *vt* explotar ⟨*resources*⟩; interceptar ⟨*phone*⟩

tap² /tæp/ *n* (*knock*) golpe *m* ligero. ● *vt* (*pt* **tapped**) golpear ligeramente. ~**dance** *n* zapateado *m*

tape /teɪp/ *n* cinta *f*. ● *vt* atar con cinta; (*record*) grabar. **have sth** ~**d** (*sl*) comprender perfectamente. ~**measure** *n* cinta *f* métrica

taper /'teɪpə(r)/ *n* bujía *f*. ● *vt* ahusar. ● *vi* ahusarse. ~ **off** disminuir

tape: ~ **recorder** *n* magnetofón *m*, magnetófono *m*. ~ **recording** *n* grabación *f*

tapestry /'tæpɪstrɪ/ *n* tapicería *f*; (*product*) tapiz *m*

tapioca /tæpɪ'əʊkə/ *n* tapioca *f*

tar /tɑː(r)/ *n* alquitrán *m*. ● *vt* (*pt* **tarred**) alquitranar

tard|ily /'tɑːdɪlɪ/ *adv* lentamente; (*late*) tardíamente. ~**y** /'tɑːdɪ/ *a* (-**ier**, -**iest**) (*slow*) lento; (*late*) tardío

target /'tɑːgɪt/ *n* blanco *m*; (*fig*) objetivo *m*

tariff /'tærɪf/ *n* tarifa *f*

tarmac /'tɑːmæk/ *n* pista *f* de aterrizaje. **T**~ *n* (*P*) macadán *m*

tarnish /'tɑːnɪʃ/ *vt* deslustrar. ● *vi* deslustrarse

tarpaulin /tɑː'pɔːlɪn/ *n* alquitranado *m*

tarragon /'tærəgən/ *n* estragón *m*

tart¹ /tɑːt/ *n* pastel *m*; (*individual*) pastelillo *m*

tart² /tɑːt/ *n* (*sl, woman*) prostituta *f*, fulana *f* (*fam*). ● *vt.* ~ **o.s. up** (*fam*) engalanarse

tart³ /tɑːt/ *a* (-**er**, -**est**) ácido; (*fig*) áspero

tartan /'tɑːtn/ *n* tartán *m*, tela *f* escocesa

tartar /'tɑːtə(r)/ *n* tártaro *m*. ~ **sauce** *n* salsa *f* tártara

task /tɑːsk/ *n* tarea *f*. **take to** ~ reprender. ~ **force** *n* destacamiento *m* especial

tassel /'tæsl/ *n* borla *f*

tast|e /teɪst/ *n* sabor *m*, gusto *m*; (*small quantity*) poquito *m*. ● *vt* probar. ● *vi.* ~**e of** saber a. ~**eful** *a* de buen gusto. ~**eless** *a* soso; (*fig*) de mal gusto. ~**y** *a* (-**ier**, -**iest**) sabroso

tat /tæt/ *see* **tit²**

tatter|ed /'tætəd/ *a* hecho jirones. ~**s** /'tætəz/ *npl* andrajos *mpl*

tattle /'tætl/ *vi* charlar. ● *n* charla *f*

tattoo¹ /tə'tu:/ (*mil*) espectáculo *m* militar

tattoo² /tə'tu:/ *vt* tatuar. ● *n* tatuaje *m*

tatty /'tætɪ/ *a* (-**ier**, -**iest**) gastado, en mal estado

taught /tɔːt/ *see* **teach**

taunt /tɔːnt/ *vt* mofarse de. ~ **s.o. with sth** echar algo en cara a uno. ● *n* mofa *f*

Taurus /'tɔːrəs/ *n* (*astr*) Tauro *m*

taut /tɔːt/ *a* tenso

tavern /'tævən/ *n* taberna *f*

tawdry /'tɔːdrɪ/ *a* (-**ier**, -**iest**) charro

tawny /'tɔːnɪ/ *a* bronceado

tax /tæks/ *n* impuesto *m*. ● *vt* imponer contribuciones a ⟨*person*⟩; gravar con un impuesto ⟨*thing*⟩; (*fig*) poner a prueba. ~**able** *a* imponible. ~**ation** /-'seɪʃn/ *n* impuestos *mpl*. ~**collector** *n* recaudador *m* de contribuciones. ~**free** *a* libre de impuestos

taxi /'tæksɪ/ *n* (*pl* -**is**) taxi *m*. ● *vi* (*pt* **taxied**, *pres p* **taxiing**) ⟨*aircraft*⟩ rodar por la pista. ~ **rank** *n* parada *f* de taxis

taxpayer /'tækspeɪə(r)/ n contribuyente m & f

te /ti:/ n (mus, seventh note of any musical scale) si m

tea /ti:/ n té m. ~**bag** n bolsita f de té. ~**break** n descanso m para el té

teach /ti:tʃ/ vt/i (pt taught) enseñar. ~**er** n profesor m; (primary) maestro m. ~**in** n seminario m. ~**ing** n enseñanza f. ● a docente. ~**ing staff** n profesorado m

teacup /'ti:kʌp/ n taza f de té

teak /ti:k/ n teca f

tea-leaf /'ti:li:f/ n hoja f de té

team /ti:m/ n equipo m; (of horses) tiro m. ● vi. ~ **up** unirse. ~**work** n trabajo m en equipo

teapot /'ti:pɒt/ n tetera f

tear[1] /teə(r)/ vt (pt tore, pp torn) rasgar. ● vi rasgarse; (run) precipitarse. ● n rasgón m. ~ **apart** desgarrar. ~ **o.s. away** separarse

tear[2] /tɪə(r)/ n lágrima f. **in** ~**s** llorando

tearaway /'teərəweɪ/ n gamberro m

tear /tɪə(r)/: ~**ful** a lloroso. ~**gas** n gas m lacrimógeno

tease /ti:z/ vt tomar el pelo a; cardar ‹cloth etc›. ● n guasón m. ~**r** /-ə(r)/ n (fam) problema m difícil

tea: ~**set** n juego m de té. ~**spoon** /'ti:spu:n/ n cucharilla f. ~**spoonful** n (pl -**fuls**) (amount) cucharadita f

teat /ti:t/ n (of animal) teta f; (for bottle) tetilla f

tea-towel /'ti:taʊəl/ n paño m de cocina

technical /'teknɪkl/ a técnico. ~**ity** n /-'kælətɪ/ n detalle m técnico. ~**ly** adv técnicamente

technician /tek'nɪʃn/ n técnico m

technique /tek'ni:k/ n técnica f

technolog|ist /tek'nɒlədʒɪst/ n tecnólogo m. ~**y** /tek'nɒlədʒɪ/ n tecnología f

teddy bear /'tedɪbeə(r)/ n osito m de felpa, osito m de peluche

tedious /'ti:dɪəs/ a pesado. ~**ly** adv pesadamente

tedium /'ti:dɪəm/ n aburrimiento m

tee /ti:/ n (golf) tee m

teem /ti:m/ vi abundar; (rain) llover a cántaros

teen|age /'ti:neɪdʒ/ a adolescente; (for teenagers) para jóvenes. ~**ager** /-ə(r)/ n adolescente m & f, joven m & f. ~**s** /ti:nz/ npl. **the** ~**s** la adolescencia f

teeny /'ti:nɪ/ a (-ier, -iest) (fam) chiquito

teeter /'ti:tə(r)/ vi balancearse

teeth /ti:θ/ see **tooth**. ~**e** /ti:ð/ vi echar los dientes. ~**ing troubles** npl (fig) dificultades fpl iniciales

teetotaller /ti:'təʊtələ(r)/ n abstemio m

telecommunications /telɪkəmju:nɪ'keɪʃnz/ npl telecomunicaciones fpl

telegram /'telɪgræm/ n telegrama m

telegraph /'telɪgrɑ:f/ n telégrafo m. ● vt telegrafiar. ~**ic** /-'græfɪk/ a telegráfico

telepath|ic /telɪ'pæθɪk/ a telepático. ~**y** /tɪ'lepəθɪ/ n telepatía f

telephon|e /'telɪfəʊn/ n teléfono m. ● vt llamar por teléfono. ~**e booth** n cabina f telefónica. ~**e directory** n guía f telefónica. ~**e exchange** n central f telefónica. ~**ic** /-'fɒnɪk/ a telefónico. ~**ist** /tɪ'lefənɪst/ n telefonista m & f

telephoto /telɪ'fəʊtəʊ/ a. ~ **lens** n teleobjetivo m

teleprinter /'telɪprɪntə(r)/ n teleimpresor m

telescop|e /'telɪskəʊp/ n telescopio m. ~**ic** /-'kɒpɪk/ a telescópico

televis|e /'telɪvaɪz/ vt televisar. ~**ion** /'telɪvɪʒn/ n televisión f. ~**ion set** n televisor m

telex /'teleks/ n télex m. ● vt enviar por télex

tell /tel/ vt (pt told) decir; contar ‹story›; (distinguish) distinguir. ● vi (produce an effect) tener efecto; (know) saber. ~ **off** vt reprender. ~**er** /'telə(r)/ n (in bank) cajero m

telling /'telɪŋ/ a eficaz

tell-tale /'telteɪl/ n soplón m. ● a revelador

telly /'telɪ/ n (fam) televisión f, tele f (fam)

temerity /tɪ'merətɪ/ n temeridad f

temp /temp/ n (fam) empleado m temporal

temper /'tempə(r)/ n (disposition) disposición f; (mood) humor m; (fit of anger) cólera f; (of metal) temple m. **be in a** ~ estar de mal humor. **keep one's** ~ contenerse. **lose one's** ~ enfadarse, perder la paciencia. ● vt templar ‹metal›

temperament /'temprəmənt/ n temperamento m. ~**al** /-'mentl/ a caprichoso

temperance /'tempərəns/ *n* moderación *f*

temperate /'tempərət/ *a* moderado; ‹*climate*› templado

temperature /'temprɪtʃə(r)/ *n* temperatura *f*. **have a ~** tener fiebre

tempest /'tempɪst/ *n* tempestad *f*. **~uous** /-'pestjʊəs/ *a* tempestuoso

temple[1] /'templ/ *n* templo *m*

temple[2] /'templ/ (*anat*) sien *f*

tempo /'tempəʊ/ *n* (*pl* **-os** *or* **tempi**) ritmo *m*

temporar|ily /'tempərərəlɪ/ *adv* temporalmente. **~y** /'tempərərɪ/ *a* temporal, provisional

tempt /tempt/ *vt* tentar. **~ s.o. to** inducir a uno a. **~ation** /-'teɪʃn/ *n* tentación *f*. **~ing** *a* tentador

ten /ten/ *a* & *n* diez (*m*)

tenable /'tenəbl/ *a* sostenible

tenaci|ous /tɪ'neɪʃəs/ *a* tenaz. **~ty** /-'æsətɪ/ *n* tenacidad *f*

tenan|cy /'tenənsɪ/ *n* alquiler *m*. **~t** /'tenənt/ *n* inquilino *m*

tend[1] /tend/ *vi*. **~ to** tener tendencia a

tend[2] /tend/ *vt* cuidar

tendency /'tendənsɪ/ *n* tendencia *f*

tender[1] /'tendə(r)/ *a* tierno; (*painful*) dolorido

tender[2] /'tendə(r)/ *n* (*com*) oferta *f*. **legal ~** *n* curso *m* legal. ● *vt* ofrecer, presentar

tender: ~ly *adv* tiernamente. **~ness** *n* ternura *f*

tendon /'tendən/ *n* tendón *m*

tenet /'tenɪt/ *n* principio *m*

tenement /'tenəmənt/ *n* vivienda *f*

tenfold /'tenfəʊld/ *a* diez veces mayor, décuplo. ● *adv* diez veces

tenner /'tenə(r)/ *n* (*fam*) billete *m* de diez libras

tennis /'tenɪs/ *n* tenis *m*

tenor /'tenə(r)/ *n* tenor *m*

tens|e /tens/ *a* (**-er, -est**) tieso; (*fig*) tenso. ● *n* (*gram*) tiempo *m*. ● *vi*. **~ up** tensarse. **~eness** *n*, **~ion** /'tenʃn/ *n* tensión *f*

tent /tent/ *n* tienda *f*, carpa *f* (*LAm*)

tentacle /'tentəkl/ *n* tentáculo *m*

tentative /'tentətɪv/ *a* provisional; (*hesitant*) indeciso. **~ly** *adv* provisionalmente; (*timidly*) tímidamente

tenterhooks /'tentəhʊks/ *npl*. **on ~** en ascuas

tenth /tenθ/ *a* & *n* décimo (*m*)

tenuous /'tenjʊəs/ *a* tenue

tenure /'tenjʊə(r)/ *n* posesión *f*

tepid /'tepɪd/ *a* tibio

term /tɜːm/ *n* (*of time*) período *m*; (*schol*) trimestre *m*; (*word etc*) término *m*. ● *vt* llamar. **~s** *npl* condiciones *fpl*; (*com*) precio *m*. **on bad ~s** en malas relaciones. **on good ~s** en buenas relaciones

terminal /'tɜːmɪnl/ *a* terminal, final. ● *n* (*rail*) estación *f* terminal; (*elec*) borne *m*. (**air**) **~** *n* término *m*, terminal *m*

terminat|e /'tɜːmɪneɪt/ *vt* terminar. ● *vi* terminarse. **~tion** /-'neɪʃn/ *n* terminación *f*

terminology /tɜːmɪ'nɒlədʒɪ/ *n* terminología *f*

terrace /'terəs/ *n* terraza *f*; (*houses*) hilera *f* de casas. **the ~s** *npl* (*sport*) las gradas *fpl*

terrain /tə'reɪn/ *n* terreno *m*

terrestrial /tɪ'restrɪəl/ *a* terrestre

terribl|e /'terəbl/ *a* terrible. **~y** *adv* terriblemente

terrier /'terɪə(r)/ *n* terrier *m*

terrific /tə'rɪfɪk/ *a* (*excellent, fam*) estupendo; (*huge, fam*) enorme. **~ally** *adv* (*fam*) terriblemente; (*very well*) muy bien

terrify /'terɪfaɪ/ *vt* aterrorizar. **~ing** *a* espantoso

territor|ial /terɪ'tɔːrɪəl/ *a* territorial. **~y** /'terɪtrɪ/ *n* territorio *m*

terror /'terə(r)/ *n* terror *m*. **~ism** /-zəm/ *n* terrorismo *m*. **~ist** /'terərɪst/ *n* terrorista *m* & *f*. **~ize** /'terəraɪz/ *vt* aterrorizar

terse /tɜːs/ *a* conciso; (*abrupt*) brusco

test /test/ *n* prueba *f*; (*exam*) examen *m*. ● *vt* probar; (*examine*) examinar

testament /'testəmənt/ *n* testamento *m*. **New T~** Nuevo Testamento. **Old T~** Antiguo Testamento

testicle /'testɪkl/ *n* testículo *m*

testify /'testɪfaɪ/ *vt* atestiguar. ● *vi* declarar

testimon|ial /testɪ'məʊnɪəl/ *n* certificado *m*; (*of character*) recomendación *f*. **~y** /'testɪmənɪ/ *n* testimonio *m*

test: ~ match *n* partido *m* internacional. **~tube** *n* tubo *m* de ensayo, probeta *f*

testy /'testɪ/ *a* irritable

tetanus /'tetənəs/ *n* tétanos *m invar*

tetchy /'tetʃɪ/ *a* irritable

tether /'teðə(r)/ *vt* atar. ● *n.* **be at the end of one's ~** no poder más

text /tekst/ *n* texto *m*. **~book** *n* libro *m* de texto

textile /'tekstaɪl/ *a & n* textil (*m*)

texture /'tekstʃə(r)/ *n* textura *f*

Thai /taɪ/ *a & n* tailandés (*m*). **~land** *n* Tailandia *f*

Thames /temz/ *n* Támesis *m*

than /ðæn, ðən/ *conj* que; (*with numbers*) de

thank /θæŋk/ *vt* dar las gracias a, agradecer. **~ you** gracias. **~ful** /'θæŋkfl/ *a* agradecido. **~fully** *adv* con gratitud; (*happily*) afortunadamente. **~less** /'θæŋklɪs/ *a* ingrato. **~s** *npl* gracias *fpl*. **~s!** (*fam*) ¡gracias! **~s to** gracias a

that /ðæt, ðət/ *a* (*pl* **those**) ese, aquel, esa, aquella. ● *pron* (*pl* **those**) ése, aquél, ésa, aquélla. **~ is** es decir. **~'s it!** ¡eso es! **~ is why** por eso. **is ~ you?** ¿eres tú? **like ~** así. ● *adv* tan. ● *rel pron* que; (*with prep*) el que, la que, el cual, la cual. ● *conj* que

thatch /θætʃ/ *n* techo *m* de paja. **~ed** *a* con techo de paja

thaw /θɔ:/ *vt* deshelar. ● *vi* deshelarse; ⟨*snow*⟩ derretirse. ● *n* deshielo *m*

the /ðə, ði:/ *def art* el, la, los, las. **at ~** al, a la, a los, a las. **from ~** del, de la, de los, de las. **to ~** al, a la, a los, a las. ● *adv*. **all ~ better** tanto mejor

theatr|e /'θɪətə(r)/ *n* teatro *m*. **~ical** /-'ætrɪkl/ *a* teatral

theft /θeft/ *n* hurto *m*

their /ðeə(r)/ *a* su, sus

theirs /ðeəz/ *poss pron* (el) suyo, (la) suya, (los) suyos, (las) suyas

them /ðem, ðəm/ *pron* (*accusative*) los, las; (*dative*) les; (*after prep*) ellos, ellas

theme /θi:m/ *n* tema *m*. **~ song** *n* motivo *m* principal

themselves /ðəm'selvz/ *pron* ellos mismos, ellas mismas, (*reflexive*) se; (*after prep*) sí mismos, sí mismas

then /ðen/ *adv* entonces; (*next*) luego, después. **by ~** para entonces. **now and ~** de vez en cuando. **since ~** desde entonces. ● *a* de entonces

theolog|ian /θɪə'ləʊdʒən/ *n* teólogo *m*. **~y** /θɪ'ɒlədʒɪ/ *n* teología *f*

theorem /'θɪərəm/ *n* teorema *m*

theor|etical /θɪə'retɪkl/ *a* teórico. **~y** /'θɪərɪ/ *n* teoría *f*

therap|eutic /θerə'pju:tɪk/ *a* terapéutico. **~ist** *n* terapeuta *m & f*. **~y** /'θerəpɪ/ *n* terapia *f*

there /ðeə(r)/ *adv* ahí, allí. **~ are** hay. **~ he is** ahí está. **~ is** hay. **~ it is** ahí está. **down ~** ahí abajo. **up ~** ahí arriba. ● *int* ¡vaya! **~, ~!** ¡ya, ya! **~abouts** *adv* por ahí. **~after** *adv* después. **~by** *adv* por eso. **~fore** /'ðeəfɔ:(r)/ *adv* por lo tanto.

thermal /'θɜ:ml/ *a* termal

thermometer /θə'mɒmɪtə(r)/ *n* termómetro *m*

thermonuclear /θɜ:məʊ'nju:klɪə(r)/ *a* termonuclear

Thermos /'θɜ:məs/ *n* (*P*) termo *m*

thermostat /'θɜ:məstæt/ *n* termostato *m*

thesaurus /θɪ'sɔ:rəs/ *n* (*pl* -**ri** /-raɪ/) diccionario *m* de sinónimos

these /ði:z/ *a* estos, estas. ● *pron* éstos, éstas

thesis /'θi:sɪs/ *n* (*pl* **theses** /-si:z/) tesis *f*

they /ðeɪ/ *pron* ellos, ellas. **~ say that** se dice que

thick /θɪk/ *a* (-**er, -est**) espeso; (*dense*) denso; (*stupid, fam*) torpe; (*close, fam*) íntimo. ● *adv* espesamente, densamente. ● *n.* **in the ~ of** en medio de. **~en** /'θɪkən/ *vt* espesar. ● *vi* espesarse

thicket /'θɪkɪt/ *n* matorral *m*

thick: ~ly *adv* espesamente, densamente. **~ness** *n* espesor *m*

thickset /θɪk'set/ *a* fornido

thick-skinned /θɪk'skɪnd/ *a* insensible

thief /θi:f/ *n* (*pl* **thieves**) ladrón *m*

thiev|e /θi:v/ *vt/i* robar. **~ing** *a* ladrón

thigh /θaɪ/ *n* muslo *m*

thimble /'θɪmbl/ *n* dedal *m*

thin /θɪn/ *a* (**thinner, thinnest**) delgado; ⟨*person*⟩ flaco; (*weak*) débil; (*fine*) fino; (*sparse*) escaso. ● *adv* ligeramente. ● *vt* (*pt* **thinned**) adelgazar; (*dilute*) diluir. **~ out** hacer menos denso. ● *vi* adelgazarse; (*diminish*) disminuir

thing /θɪŋ/ *n* cosa *f*. **for one ~** en primer lugar. **just the ~** exactamente lo que se necesita. **poor ~!** ¡pobrecito! **~s** *npl* (*belongings*) efectos *mpl*; (*clothing*) ropa *f*

think /θɪŋk/ *vt* (*pt* **thought**) pensar, creer. ● *vi* pensar (**about, of** en); (*carefully*) reflexionar; (*imagine*) imaginarse. **~ better of it** cambiar de idea. **I ~ so** creo que sí. **~ over** *vt* pensar bien. **~ up** *vt* idear, inventar. **~er** n pensador m. **~tank** n grupo m de expertos

thin: **~ly** adv ligeramente. **~ness** n delgadez f; (of person) flaqueza f

third /θɜːd/ a tercero. ● n tercio m, tercera parte f. **~rate** a muy inferior. **T~ World** n Tercer Mundo m

thirst /θɜːst/ n sed f. **~y** a sediento. **be ~y** tener sed

thirteen /θɜːˈtiːn/ a & n trece (m). **~th** a & n decimotercero (m)

thirt|ieth /ˈθɜːtɪəθ/ a & n trigésimo (m). **~y** /ˈθɜːtɪ/ a & n treinta (m)

this /ðɪs/ a (pl these) este, esta. **~ one** éste, ésta. ● pron (pl these) éste, ésta, esto. **like ~** así

thistle /ˈθɪsl/ n cardo m

thong /θɒŋ/ n correa f

thorn /θɔːn/ n espina f. **~y** a espinoso

thorough /ˈθʌrə/ a completo; (deep) profundo; ‹cleaning etc› a fondo; ‹person› concienzudo

thoroughbred /ˈθʌrəbred/ a de pura sangre

thoroughfare /ˈθʌrəfeə(r)/ n calle f. **no ~** prohibido el paso

thoroughly /ˈθʌrəlɪ/ adv completamente

those /ðəʊz/ a esos, aquellos, esas, aquellas. ● pron ésos, aquéllos, ésas, aquéllas

though /ðəʊ/ conj aunque. ● adv sin embargo. **as ~** como si

thought /θɔːt/ see **think**. ● n pensamiento m; (idea) idea f. **~ful** /ˈθɔːtfl/ a pensativo; (considerate) atento. **~fully** adv pensativamente; (considerately) atentamente. **~less** /ˈθɔːtlɪs/ a irreflexivo; (inconsiderate) desconsiderado

thousand /ˈθaʊznd/ a & n mil (m). **~th** a & n milésimo (m)

thrash /θræʃ/ vt azotar; (defeat) derrotar. **~ out** discutir a fondo

thread /θred/ n hilo m; (of screw) rosca f. ● vt ensartar. **~ one's way** abrirse paso. **~bare** /ˈθredbeə(r)/ a raído

threat /θret/ n amenaza f. **~en** /ˈθretn/ vt/i amenazar. **~ening** a amenazador. **~eningly** adv de modo amenazador

three /θriː/ a & n tres (m). **~fold** a triple. ● adv tres veces. **~some** /ˈθriːsəm/ n conjunto m de tres personas

thresh /θreʃ/ vt trillar

threshold /ˈθreʃhəʊld/ n umbral m

threw /θruː/ see **throw**

thrift /θrɪft/ n economía f, ahorro m. **~y** a frugal

thrill /θrɪl/ n emoción f. ● vt emocionar. ● vi emocionarse; (quiver) estremecerse. **be ~ed with** estar encantado de. **~er** /ˈθrɪlə(r)/ n (book) libro m de suspense; (film) película f de suspense. **~ing** a emocionante

thriv|e /θraɪv/ vi prosperar. **~ing** a próspero

throat /θrəʊt/ n garganta f. **have a sore ~** dolerle la garganta

throb /θrɒb/ vi (pt **throbbed**) palpitar; (with pain) dar punzadas; (fig) vibrar. ● n palpitación f; (pain) punzada f; (fig) vibración f. **~bing** a ‹pain› punzante

throes /θrəʊz/ npl. **in the ~ of** en medio de

thrombosis /θrɒmˈbəʊsɪs/ n trombosis f

throne /θrəʊn/ n trono m

throng /θrɒŋ/ n multitud f

throttle /ˈθrɒtl/ n (auto) acelerador m. ● vt ahogar

through /θruː/ prep por, a través de; (during) durante; (by means of) por medio de; (thanks to) gracias a. ● adv de parte a parte, de un lado a otro; (entirely) completamente; (to the end) hasta el final. **be ~** (finished) haber terminado. ● a ‹train etc› directo

throughout /θruːˈaʊt/ prep por todo; (time) en todo. ● adv en todas partes; (all the time) todo el tiempo

throve /θrəʊv/ see **thrive**

throw /θrəʊ/ vt (pt **threw**, pp **thrown**) arrojar; (baffle etc) desconcertar. **~ a party** (fam) dar una fiesta. ● n tiro m; (of dice) lance m. **~ away** vt tirar. **~ over** vt abandonar. **~ up** vi (vomit) vomitar. **~-away** a desechable

thrush /θrʌʃ/ n tordo m

thrust /θrʌst/ vt (pt **thrust**) empujar; (push in) meter. ● n empuje m. **~ (up)on** imponer a

thud /θʌd/ n ruido m sordo

thug /θʌg/ n bruto m

thumb /θʌm/ n pulgar m. **under the ~ of** dominado por. ● vt hojear ‹book›. **~ a lift** hacer autostop. **~-index** n uñeros mpl

thump /θʌmp/ vt golpear. ● vi ‹heart› latir fuertemente. ● n porrazo m; (noise) ruido m sordo

thunder /'θʌndə(r)/ n trueno m. ● vi
tronar. ~ **past** pasar con estruendo.
~**bolt** /'θʌndəbəʊlt/ n rayo m.
~**clap** /'θʌndəklæp/ n trueno m.
~**storm** /'θʌndəstɔːm/ n tronada f.
~**y** a con truenos
Thursday /'θɜːzdeɪ/ n jueves m
thus /ðʌs/ adv así
thwart /θwɔːt/ vt frustrar
thyme /taɪm/ n tomillo m
thyroid /'θaɪrɔɪd/ n tiroides m invar
tiara /tɪ'ɑːrə/ n diadema f
tic /tɪk/ n tic m
tick[1] /tɪk/ n tictac m; (mark) señal f,
marca f, (instant, fam) momentito
m. ● vi hacer tictac. ● vt. ~ (**off**)
marcar. ~ **off** vt (sl) reprender. ~
over vi (of engine) marchar en vacío
tick[2] /tɪk/ n (insect) garrapata f
tick[3] /tɪk/ n. **on** ~ (fam) a crédito
ticket /'tɪkɪt/ n billete m, boleto m
(LAm); (label) etiqueta f; (fine)
multa f. ~**collector** n revisor m.
~**office** n taquilla f
tickl|e /'tɪkl/ vt hacer cosquillas a;
(amuse) divertir. ● n cosquilleo m.
~**ish** /'tɪklɪʃ/ a cosquilloso; (problem) delicado. **be** ~**ish** tener
cosquillas
tidal /'taɪdl/ a de marea. ~ **wave** n
maremoto m
tiddly-winks /'tɪdlɪwɪŋks/ n juego m
de pulgas
tide /taɪd/ n marea f; (of events)
curso m. ● vt. ~ **over** ayudar a salir
de un apuro
tidings /'taɪdɪŋz/ npl noticias fpl
tid|ily /'taɪdɪlɪ/ adv en orden; (well)
bien. ~**iness** n orden m. ~**y** /'taɪdɪ/
a (-ier, -iest) ordenado; (amount,
fam) considerable. ● vt/i. ~**y** (**up**)
ordenar. ~**y o.s. up** arreglarse
tie /taɪ/ vt (pres p **tying**) atar; hacer
(a knot); (link) vincular. ● vi (sport)
empatar. ● n atadura f; (necktie)
corbata f; (link) lazo m; (sport)
empate m. ~ **in with** relacionar con.
~ **up** atar; (com) inmovilizar. **be** ~**d
up** (busy) estar ocupado
tier /tɪə(r)/ n fila f; (in stadium etc)
grada f; (of cake) piso m
tie-up /'taɪʌp/ n enlace m
tiff /tɪf/ n riña f
tiger /'taɪgə(r)/ n tigre m
tight /taɪt/ a (-er, -est) (clothes) ce-
ñido; (taut) tieso; (control etc) ri-
guroso; (knot, nut) apretado; (drunk,
fam) borracho. ● adv bien; (shut)
herméticamente. ~ **corner** n (fig)

apuro m. ~**en** /'taɪtn/ vt apretar.
● vi apretarse. ~**fisted** a tacaño.
~**ly** adv bien; (shut) herméticamente. ~**ness** n estrechez f.
~**rope** /'taɪtrəʊp/ n cuerda f floja.
~**s** /taɪts/ npl leotardos mpl
tile /taɪl/ n (decorative) azulejo m;
(on roof) teja f; (on floor) baldosa f.
● vt azulejar; tejar (roof); embaldosar (floor)
till[1] /tɪl/ prep hasta. ● conj hasta que
till[2] /tɪl/ n caja f
till[3] /tɪl/ vt cultivar
tilt /tɪlt/ vt inclinar. ● vi inclinarse.
● n inclinación f. **at full** ~ a toda
velocidad
timber /'tɪmbə(r)/ n madera f (de
construcción); (trees) árboles mpl
time /taɪm/ n tiempo m; (moment)
momento m; (occasion) ocasión f;
(by clock) hora f; (epoch) época f;
(rhythm) compás m. ~ **off** tiempo
libre. **at** ~**s** a veces. **behind the** ~**s**
anticuado. **behind** ~ atrasado. **for
the** ~ **being** por ahora. **from** ~ **to**
~ de vez en cuando. **have a good** ~
divertirse, pasarlo bien. **in a year's**
~ dentro de un año. **in no** ~ en un
abrir y cerrar de ojos. **in** ~ a tiempo;
(eventually) con el tiempo. **on** ~ a la
hora, puntual. ● vt elegir el
momento; cronometrar (race). ~
bomb n bomba f de tiempo. ~**honoured** a consagrado. ~**lag** n intervalo m
timeless /'taɪmlɪs/ a eterno
timely /'taɪmlɪ/ a oportuno
timer /'taɪmə(r)/ n cronómetro m;
(culin) avisador m; (with sand) reloj
m de arena; (elec) interruptor m de
reloj
timetable /'taɪmteɪbl/ n horario m
time zone /'taɪmzəʊn/ n huso m
horario
timid /'tɪmɪd/ a tímido; (fearful) miedoso. ~**ly** adv tímidamente
timing /'taɪmɪŋ/ n medida f del
tiempo; (moment) momento m;
(sport) cronometraje m
timorous /'tɪmərəs/ a tímido; (fearful) miedoso. ~**ly** adv tímidamente
tin /tɪn/ n estaño m; (container) lata
f. ~ **foil** n papel m de estaño. ● vt (pt
tinned) conservar en lata, enlatar
tinge /tɪndʒ/ vt teñir (**with** de); (fig)
matizar (**with** de). ● n matiz m
tingle /'tɪŋgl/ vi sentir hormigueo;
(with excitement) estremecerse

tinker /'tɪŋkə(r)/ n hojalatero m.
● vi. ~ **(with)** jugar con; (repair) arreglar

tinkle /'tɪŋkl/ n retintín m; (phone call, fam) llamada f

tin: ~**ned** a en lata. ~**ny** a metálico. ~**-opener** n abrelatas m invar. ~ **plate** n hojalata f

tinpot /'tɪnpɒt/ a (pej) inferior

tinsel /'tɪnsl/ n oropel m

tint /tɪnt/ n matiz m

tiny /'taɪnɪ/ a (-ier, -iest) diminuto

tip[1] /tɪp/ n punta f

tip[2] /tɪp/ vt (pt tipped) (tilt) inclinar; (overturn) volcar; (pour) verter● vi inclinarse; (overturn) volcarse. ● n (for rubbish) vertedero m. ~ **out** verter

tip[3] /tɪp/ vt (reward) dar una propina a. ~ **off** advertir. ● n (reward) propina f; (advice) consejo m

tip-off /'tɪpɒf/ n advertencia f

tipped /tɪpt/ a ‹cigarette› con filtro

tipple /'tɪpl/ vi beborrotear. ● n bebida f alcohólica. **have a** ~ tomar una copa

tipsy /'tɪpsɪ/ a achispado

tiptoe /'tɪptəʊ/ n. **on** ~ de puntillas

tiptop /'tɪptɒp/ a (fam) de primera

tirade /tar'reɪd/ n diatriba f

tire /'taɪə(r)/ vt cansar. ● vi cansarse. ~**d** /'taɪəd/ a cansado. ~**d of** harto de. ~**d out** agotado. ~**less** a incansable

tiresome /'taɪəsəm/ a (annoying) fastidioso; (boring) pesado

tiring /'taɪərɪŋ/ a cansado

tissue /'tɪʃuː/ n tisú m; (handkerchief) pañuelo m de papel. ~**paper** n papel m de seda

tit[1] /tɪt/ n (bird) paro m

tit[2] /tɪt/ n. ~ **for tat** golpe por golpe

titbit /'tɪtbɪt/ n golosina f

titillate /'tɪtɪleɪt/ vt excitar

title /'taɪtl/ n título m. ~**d** a con título nobiliario. ~**deed** n título m de propiedad. ~**role** n papel m principal

tittle-tattle /'tɪtltætl/ n cháchara f

titular /'tɪtjʊlə(r)/ a nominal

tizzy /'tɪzɪ/ n (sl). **get in a** ~ ponerse nervioso

to /tuː, tə/ prep a; (towards) hacia; (in order to) para; (according to) según; (as far as) hasta; (with times) menos; (of) de. **give it** ~ **me** dámelo. **I don't want to** no quiero. **twenty** ~ **seven** (by clock) las siete menos veinte. ● adv. **push** ~, **pull** ~

cerrar. ~ **and fro** adv de aquí para allá

toad /təʊd/ n sapo m

toadstool /'təʊdstuːl/ n seta f venenosa

toast /təʊst/ n pan m tostado, tostada f; (drink) brindis m. **drink a** ~ **to** brindar por. ● vt brindar por. ~**er** n tostador m de pan

tobacco /tə'bækəʊ/ n tabaco m. ~**nist** n estanquero m. ~**nist's shop** n estanco m

to-be /tə'biː/ a futuro

toboggan /tə'bɒgən/ n tobogán m

today /tə'deɪ/ n & adv hoy (m). ~ **week** dentro de una semana

toddler /'tɒdlə(r)/ n niño m que empieza a andar

toddy /'tɒdɪ/ n ponche m

to-do /tə'duː/ n lío m

toe /təʊ/ n dedo m del pie; (of shoe) punta f. **big** ~ dedo m gordo (del pie). **on one's** ~**s** (fig) alerta. ● vt. ~ **the line** conformarse. ~**hold** n punto m de apoyo

toff /tɒf/ n (sl) petimetre m

toffee /'tɒfɪ/ n caramelo m

together /tə'geðə(r)/ adv junto, juntos; (at same time) a la vez. ~ **with** junto con. ~**ness** n compañerismo m

toil /tɔɪl/ vi afanarse. ● n trabajo m

toilet /'tɔɪlɪt/ n servicio m, retrete m; (grooming) arreglo m, tocado m. ~**paper** n papel m higiénico. ~**ries** /'tɔɪlɪtrɪz/ npl artículos mpl de tocador. ~ **water** n agua f de Colonia

token /'təʊkən/ n señal f; (voucher) vale m; (coin) ficha f. ● a simbólico

told /təʊld/ see **tell**. ● a. **all** ~ con todo

tolerabl|e /'tɒlərəbl/ a tolerable; (not bad) regular. ~**y** adv pasablemente

toleran|ce /'tɒlərəns/ n tolerancia f. ~**t** /'tɒlərənt/ a tolerante. ~**tly** adv con tolerancia

tolerate /'tɒləreɪt/ vt tolerar

toll[1] /təʊl/ n peaje m. **death** ~ número m de muertos. **take a heavy** ~ dejar muchas víctimas

toll[2] /təʊl/ vi doblar, tocar a muerto

tom /tɒm/ n gato m (macho)

tomato /tə'mɑːtəʊ/ n (pl ~**oes**) tomate m

tomb /tuːm/ n tumba f, sepulcro m

tomboy /'tɒmbɔɪ/ n marimacho m

tombstone /'tuːmstəʊn/ n lápida f sepulcral

tom-cat /'tɒmkæt/ *n* gato *m* (macho)

tome /təʊm/ *n* librote *m*

tomfoolery /tɒm'fu:lərɪ/ *n* payasadas *fpl*, tonterías *fpl*

tomorrow /tə'mɒrəʊ/ *n & adv* mañana (*f*). **see you ∼!** ¡hasta mañana!

ton /tʌn/ *n* tonelada *f* (= 1,016 kg). **∼s of** (*fam*) montones de. **metric ∼** tonelada *f* (métrica) (= 1,000 kg)

tone /təʊn/ *n* tono *m*. ● *vt*. **∼ down** atenuar. **∼ up** tonificar ‹*muscles*›. ● *vi*. **∼ in** armonizar. **∼deaf** *a* que no tiene buen oído

tongs /tɒŋz/ *npl* tenazas *fpl*; (*for hair, sugar*) tenacillas *fpl*

tongue /tʌŋ/ *n* lengua *f*. **∼ in cheek** *adv* irónicamente. **∼tied** *a* mudo. **get ∼tied** trabársele la lengua. **∼twister** *n* trabalenguas *m invar*

tonic /'tɒnɪk/ *a* tónico. ● *n* (*tonic water*) tónica *f*; (*med, fig*) tónico *m*. **∼ water** *n* tónica *f*

tonight /tə'naɪt/ *adv & n* esta noche (*f*); (*evening*) esta tarde (*f*)

tonne /tʌn/ *n* tonelada *f* (métrica)

tonsil /'tɒnsl/ *n* amígdala *f*. **∼litis** /-'laɪtɪs/ *n* amigdalitis *f*

too /tu:/ *adv* demasiado; (*also*) también. **∼ many** *a* demasiados. **∼ much** *a & adv* demasiado

took /tʊk/ *see* **take**

tool /tu:l/ *n* herramienta *f*. **∼bag** *n* bolsa *f* de herramientas

toot /tu:t/ *n* bocinazo *m*. ● *vi* tocar la bocina

tooth /tu:θ/ *n* (*pl* **teeth**) diente *m*; (*molar*) muela *f*. **∼ache** /'tu:θeɪk/ *n* dolor *m* de muelas. **∼brush** /'tu:θbrʌʃ/ *n* cepillo *m* de dientes. **∼comb** /'tu:θkəʊm/ *n* peine *m* de púa fina. **∼less** *a* desdentado, sin dientes. **∼paste** /'tu:θpeɪst/ *n* pasta *f* dentífrica. **∼pick** /'tu:θpɪk/ *n* palillo *m* de dientes

top[1] /tɒp/ *n* cima *f*; (*upper part*) parte *f* de arriba; (*upper surface*) superficie *f*; (*lid, of bottle*) tapa *f*; (*of list*) cabeza *f*. **from ∼ to bottom** de arriba abajo. **on ∼ (of)** encima de; (*besides*) además. ● *a* más alto; (*in rank*) superior, principal; (*maximum*) máximo. **∼ floor** *n* último piso *m*. ● *vt* (*pt* **topped**) cubrir; (*exceed*) exceder. **∼ up** *vt* llenar

top[2] /tɒp/ *n* (*toy*) trompa *f*, peonza *f*

top: **∼ hat** *n* chistera *f*. **∼heavy** *a* más pesado arriba que abajo

topic /'tɒpɪk/ *n* tema *m*. **∼al** /'tɒpɪkl/ *a* de actualidad

top: **∼less** /'tɒplɪs/ *a* ‹*bather*› con los senos desnudos. **∼most** /'tɒpməʊst/ *a* (el) más alto. **∼notch** *a* (*fam*) excelente

topography /tə'pɒgrəfɪ/ *n* topografía *f*

topple /'tɒpl/ *vi* derribar; (*overturn*) volcar

top secret /tɒp'si:krɪt/ *a* sumamente secreto

topsy-turvy /tɒpsɪ'tɜ:vɪ/ *adv & a* patas arriba

torch /tɔ:tʃ/ *n* lámpara *f* de bolsillo; (*flaming*) antorcha *f*

tore /tɔ:(r)/ *see* **tear**[1]

toreador /'tɒrɪədɔ:(r)/ *n* torero *m*

torment /'tɔ:ment/ *n* tormento *m*. /tɔ:'ment/ *vt* atormentar

torn /tɔ:n/ *see* **tear**[1]

tornado /tɔ:'neɪdəʊ/ *n* (*pl* **-oes**) tornado *m*

torpedo /tɔ:'pi:dəʊ/ *n* (*pl* **-oes**) torpedo *m*. ● *vt* torpedear

torpor /'tɔ:pə(r)/ *n* apatía *f*

torrent /'tɒrənt/ *n* torrente *m*. **∼ial** /tə'renʃl/ *a* torrencial

torrid /'tɒrɪd/ *a* tórrido

torso /'tɔ:səʊ/ *n* (*pl* **-os**) torso *m*

tortoise /'tɔ:təs/ *n* tortuga *f*. **∼shell** *n* carey *m*

tortuous /'tɔ:tjʊəs/ *a* tortuoso

torture /'tɔ:tʃə(r)/ *n* tortura *f*, tormento *m*. ● *vt* atormentar. **∼r** /-ə(r)/ *n* atormentador *m*, verdugo *m*

Tory /'tɔ:rɪ/ *a & n* (*fam*) conservador (*m*)

toss /tɒs/ *vt* echar; (*shake*) sacudir. ● *vi* agitarse. **∼ and turn** (*in bed*) revolverse. **∼ up** echar a cara o cruz

tot[1] /tɒt/ *n* nene *m*; (*of liquor, fam*) trago *m*

tot[2] /tɒt/ *vt* (*pt* **totted**). **∼ up** (*fam*) sumar

total /'təʊtl/ *a & n* total (*m*). ● *vt* (*pt* **totalled**) sumar

totalitarian /təʊtælɪ'teərɪən/ *a* totalitario

total: **∼ity** /təʊ'tælətɪ/ *n* totalidad *f*. **∼ly** *adv* totalmente

totter /'tɒtə(r)/ *vi* tambalearse. **∼y** *a* inseguro

touch /tʌtʃ/ *vt* tocar; (*reach*) alcanzar; (*move*) conmover. ● *vi* tocarse. ● *n* toque *m*; (*sense*) tacto *m*; (*contact*) contacto *m*; (*trace*) pizca *f*. **get in ∼ with** ponerse en contacto con. **∼ down** ‹*aircraft*› aterrizar. **∼ off**

disparar ⟨gun⟩; (fig) desencadenar. ~ **on** tratar levemente. ~ **up** retocar. ~**-and-go** a incierto, dudoso

touching /'tʌtʃɪŋ/ a conmovedor

touchstone /'tʌtʃstəʊn/ n (fig) piedra f de toque

touchy /'tʌtʃɪ/ a quisquilloso

tough /tʌf/ a (-er, -est) duro; (strong) fuerte, resistente. ~**en** /'tʌfn/ vt endurecer. ~**ness** n dureza f; (strength) resistencia f

toupee /'tu:peɪ/ n postizo m, tupé m

tour /tʊə(r)/ n viaje m; (visit) visita f; (excursion) excursión f; (by team etc) gira f. ● vt recorrer; (visit) visitar

touris|m /'tʊərɪzəm/ n turismo m. ~**t** /'tʊərɪst/ n turista m & f. ● a turístico. ~**t office** n oficina f de turismo

tournament /'tɔ:nəmənt/ n torneo m

tousle /'taʊzl/ vt despeinar

tout /taʊt/ vi. ~ **(for)** solicitar. ● n solicitador m

tow /təʊ/ vt remolcar. ● n remolque m. **on** ~ a remolque. **with his family in** ~ (fam) acompañado por su familia

toward(s) /tə'wɔ:d(z)/ prep hacia

towel /'taʊəl/ n toalla f. ~**ling** n (fabric) toalla f

tower /'taʊə(r)/ n torre f. ● vi. ~ **above** dominar. ~ **block** n edificio m alto. ~**ing** a altísimo; ⟨rage⟩ violento

town /taʊn/ n ciudad f, pueblo m. **go to** ~ (fam) no escatimar dinero. ~ **hall** n ayuntamiento m. ~ **planning** n urbanismo m

tow-path /'təʊpɑ:θ/ n camino m de sirga

toxi|c /'tɒksɪk/ a tóxico. ~**n** /'tɒksɪn/ n toxina f

toy /tɔɪ/ n juguete m. ● vi. ~ **with** jugar con ⟨object⟩; acariciar ⟨idea⟩. ~**shop** n juguetería f

trac|e /treɪs/ n huella f; (small amount) pizca f. ● vt seguir la pista de; (draw) dibujar; (with tracing-paper) calcar; (track down) encontrar. ~**ing** /'treɪsɪŋ/ n calco m. ~**ing-paper** n papel m de calcar

track /træk/ n huella f; (path) sendero m; (sport) pista f; (of rocket etc) trayectoria f; (rail) vía f. **keep** ~ **of** vigilar. **make** ~**s** (sl) marcharse. ● vt seguir la pista de. ~ **down** vt localizar. ~ **suit** n traje m de deporte, chandal m

tract[1] /trækt/ n (land) extensión f; (anat) aparato m

tract[2] /trækt/ n (pamphlet) opúsculo m

traction /'trækʃn/ n tracción f

tractor /'træktə(r)/ n tractor m

trade /treɪd/ n comercio m; (occupation) oficio m; (exchange) cambio m; (industry) industria f. ● vt cambiar. ● vi comerciar. ~ **in** (give in part-exchange) dar como parte del pago. ~ **on** aprovecharse de. ~ **mark** n marca f registrada. ~**r** /-ə(r)/ n comerciante m & f. ~**sman** /'treɪdzmən/ n (pl -men) (shopkeeper) tendero m. ~ **union** n sindicato m. ~ **unionist** n sindicalista m & f. ~ **wind** n viento m alisio

trading /'treɪdɪŋ/ n comercio m. ~ **estate** n zona f industrial

tradition /trə'dɪʃn/ n tradición f. ~**al** a tradicional. ~**alist** n tradicionalista m & f. ~**ally** adv tradicionalmente

traffic /'træfɪk/ n tráfico m. ● vi (pt trafficked) comerciar (**in** en). ~**lights** npl semáforo m. ~ **warden** n guardia m, controlador m de tráfico

trag|edy /'trædʒɪdɪ/ n tragedia f. ~**ic** /'trædʒɪk/ a trágico. ~**ically** adv trágicamente

trail /treɪl/ vi arrastrarse; (lag) rezagarse. ● vt (track) seguir la pista de. ● n estela f; (track) pista f. (path) sendero m. ~**er** /'treɪlə(r)/ n remolque m; (film) avance m

train /treɪn/ n tren m; (of dress) cola f; (series) sucesión f; (retinue) séquito m. ● vt adiestrar; (sport) entrenar; educar ⟨child⟩; guiar ⟨plant⟩; domar ⟨animal⟩. ● vi adiestrarse; (sport) entrenarse. ~**ed** a (skilled) cualificado; ⟨doctor⟩ diplomado. ~**ee** n aprendiz m. ~**er** n (sport) entrenador m; (of animals) domador m. ~**ers** mpl zapatillas fpl de deporte. ~**ing** n instrucción f; (sport) entrenamiento m

traipse /treɪps/ vi (fam) vagar

trait /treɪ(t)/ n característica f, rasgo m

traitor /'treɪtə(r)/ n traidor m

tram /træm/ n tranvía m

tramp /træmp/ vt recorrer a pie. ● vi andar con pasos pesados. ● n (vagrant) vagabundo m; (sound) ruido m de pasos; (hike) paseo m largo

trample /'træmpl/ *vt/i* pisotear. **~ (on)** pisotear

trampoline /'træmpəli:n/ *n* trampolín *m*

trance /trɑ:ns/ *n* trance *m*

tranquil /'træŋkwɪl/ *a* tranquilo. **~lity** /-'kwɪlətɪ/ *n* tranquilidad *f*

tranquillize /'træŋkwɪlaɪz/ *vt* tranquilizar. **~r** /-ə(r)/ *n* tranquilizante *m*

transact /træn'zækt/ *vt* negociar. **~ion** /-ʃn/ *n* transacción *f*

transatlantic /trænzət'læntɪk/ *a* transatlántico

transcend /træn'send/ *vt* exceder. **~ent** *a* sobresaliente

transcendental /trænsen'dentl/ *a* trascendental

transcribe /træns'kraɪb/ *vt* transcribir; grabar ⟨recorded sound⟩

transcript /'trænskrɪpt/ *n* copia *f*. **~ion** /-ɪpʃn/ *n* transcripción *f*

transfer /træns'fɜ:(r)/ *vt* (*pt* **transferred**) trasladar; calcar ⟨drawing⟩. ● *vi* trasladarse. **~ the charges** (on telephone) llamar a cobro revertido. /'trænsfɜ:(r)/ *n* traslado *m*; (paper) calcomanía *f*. **~able** *a* transferible

transfigur|ation /trænsfɪgjʊ'reɪʃn/ *n* transfiguración *f*. **~e** /træns'fɪgə(r)/ *vt* transfigurar

transfix /træns'fɪks/ *vt* traspasar; (fig) paralizar

transform /træns'fɔ:m/ *vt* transformar. **~ation** /-ə'meɪʃn/ *n* transformación *f*. **~er** /-ə(r)/ *n* transformador *m*

transfusion /træns'fju:ʒn/ *n* transfusión *f*

transgress /træns'gres/ *vt* traspasar, infringir. **~ion** /-ʃn/ *n* transgresión *f*; (sin) pecado *m*

transient /'trænzɪənt/ *a* pasajero

transistor /træn'zɪstə(r)/ *n* transistor *m*

transit /'trænsɪt/ *n* tránsito *m*

transition /træn'zɪʒn/ *n* transición *f*

transitive /'trænsɪtɪv/ *a* transitivo

transitory /'trænsɪtrɪ/ *a* transitorio

translat|e /trænz'leɪt/ *vt* traducir. **~ion** /-ʃn/ *n* traducción *f*. **~or** /-ə(r)/ *n* traductor *m*

translucen|ce /trænz'lu:sns/ *n* traslucidez *f*. **~t** /trænz'lu:snt/ *a* traslúcido

transmission /trænz'mɪʃn/ *n* transmisión *f*

transmit /trænz'mɪt/ *vt* (*pt* **transmitted**) transmitir. **~ter** /-ə(r)/ *n*

transmisor *m*; (TV, radio) emisora *f*

transparen|cy /træns'pærənsɪ/ *n* transparencia *f*; (photo) diapositiva *f*. **~t** /træns'pærənt/ *a* transparente

transpire /træn'spaɪə(r)/ *vi* transpirar; (happen, fam) suceder, revelarse

transplant /træns'plɑ:nt/ *vt* trasplantar. /'trænsplɑ:nt/ *n* trasplante *m*

transport /træns'spɔ:t/ *vt* transportar. /'trænspɔ:t/ *n* transporte *m*. **~ation** /-'teɪʃn/ *n* transporte *m*

transpos|e /træn'spəʊz/ *vt* transponer; (mus) transportar. **~ition** /-pə'zɪʃn/ *n* transposición *f*; (mus) transporte *m*

transverse /'trænzvɜ:s/ *a* transverso

transvestite /trænz'vestaɪt/ *n* travestido *m*

trap /træp/ *n* trampa *f*. ● *vt* (*pt* **trapped**) atrapar; (jam) atascar; (cut off) bloquear. **~door** /'træpdɔ:(r)/ *n* trampa *f*; (in theatre) escotillón *m*

trapeze /trə'pi:z/ *n* trapecio *m*

trappings /'træpɪŋz/ *npl* (fig) atavíos *mpl*

trash /træʃ/ *n* pacotilla *f*; (refuse) basura *f*; (nonsense) tonterías *fpl*. **~can** *n* (Amer) cubo *m* de la basura. **~y** *a* de baja calidad

trauma /'trɔ:mə/ *n* trauma *m*. **~tic** /-'mætɪk/ *a* traumático

travel /'trævl/ *vi* (*pt* **travelled**) viajar. ● *vt* recorrer. ● *n* viajar *m*. **~ler** /-ə(r)/ *n* viajero *m*. **~ler's cheque** *n* cheque *m* de viaje. **~ling** *n* viajar *m*

traverse /træ'vɜ:s/ *vt* atravesar, recorrer

travesty /'trævɪstɪ/ *n* parodia *f*

trawler /'trɔ:lə(r)/ *n* pesquero *m* de arrastre

tray /treɪ/ *n* bandeja *f*

treacher|ous *a* traidor; (deceptive) engañoso. **~ously** *adv* traidoramente. **~y** /'tretʃərɪ/ *n* traición *f*

treacle /'tri:kl/ *n* melaza *f*

tread /tred/ *vi* (*pt* **trod**, *pp* **trodden**) andar. **~ on** pisar. ● *vt* pisar. ● *n* (step) paso *m*; (of tyre) banda *f* de rodadura. **~le** /'tredl/ *n* pedal *m*. **~mill** /'tredmɪl/ *n* rueda *f* de molino; (fig) rutina *f*

treason /'tri:zn/ *n* traición *f*

treasure /'treʒə(r)/ *n* tesoro *m*. ● *vt* apreciar mucho; (store) guardar

treasur|er /'treʒərə(r)/ n tesorero m.
~y /'treʒərɪ/ n tesorería f. **the T~y**
n el Ministerio m de Hacienda

treat /tri:t/ vt tratar; (consider) considerar. **~ s.o.** invitar a uno. ● n
placer m; (present) regalo m

treatise /'tri:tɪz/ n tratado m

treatment /'tri:tmənt/ n tratamiento m

treaty /'tri:tɪ/ n tratado m

treble /'trebl/ a triple; ⟨clef⟩ de sol;
⟨voice⟩ de tiple. ● vt triplicar. ● vi
triplicarse. ● n tiple m & f

tree /tri:/ n árbol m

trek /trek/ n viaje m arduo, caminata f. ● vi (pt **trekked**) hacer un
viaje arduo

trellis /'trelɪs/ n enrejado m

tremble /'trembl/ vi temblar

tremendous /trɪ'mendəs/ a tremendo; (huge, fam) enorme. **~ly**
adv tremendamente

tremor /'tremə(r)/ n temblor m

tremulous /'tremjʊləs/ a
tembloroso

trench /trentʃ/ n foso m, zanja f;
(mil) trinchera f. **~ coat** n trinchera
f

trend /trend/ n tendencia f; (fashion) moda f. **~-setter** n persona f
que lanza la moda. **~y** a (-ier, -iest)
(fam) a la última

trepidation /trepɪ'deɪʃn/ n
inquietud f

trespass /'trespəs/ vi. **~ on** entrar
sin derecho; (fig) abusar de. **~er**
/-ə(r)/ n intruso m

tress /tres/ n trenza f

trestle /'tresl/ n caballete m. **~-table**
n mesa f de caballete

trews /tru:z/ npl pantalón m

trial /'traɪəl/ n prueba f; (jurid) proceso m; (ordeal) prueba f dura. **~
and error** tanteo m. **be on ~** estar a
prueba; (jurid) ser procesado

triang|le /'traɪæŋgl/ n triángulo m.
~ular /-'æŋgjʊlə(r)/ a triangular

trib|al /'traɪbl/ a tribal. **~e** /traɪb/ n
tribu f

tribulation /trɪbjʊ'leɪʃn/ n tribulación f

tribunal /traɪ'bju:nl/ n tribunal m

tributary /'trɪbjʊtrɪ/ n (stream)
afluente m

tribute /'trɪbju:t/ n tributo m. **pay ~
to** rendir homenaje a

trice /traɪs/ n. **in a ~** en un abrir y
cerrar de ojos

trick /trɪk/ n trampa f; engaño m;
(joke) broma f; (at cards) baza f;
(habit) manía f. **do the ~** servir.
play a ~ on gastar una broma a.
● vt engañar. **~ery** /'trɪkərɪ/ n
engaño m

trickle /'trɪkl/ vi gotear. **~ in** (fig)
entrar poco a poco. **~ out** (fig) salir
poco a poco

trickster /'trɪkstə(r)/ n estafador m

tricky /'trɪkɪ/ a delicado, difícil

tricolour /'trɪkələ(r)/ n bandera f
tricolor

tricycle /'traɪsɪkl/ n triciclo m

trident /'traɪdənt/ n tridente m

tried /traɪd/ see **try**

trifl|e /'traɪfl/ n bagatela f; (culin)
bizcocho m con natillas, jalea,
frutas y nata. ● vi. **~e with** jugar
con. **~ing** a insignificante

trigger /'trɪgə(r)/ n (of gun) gatillo
m. ● vt. **~ (off)** desencadenar

trigonometry /trɪgə'nɒmɪtrɪ/ n trigonometría f

trilby /'trɪlbɪ/ n sombrero m de
fieltro

trilogy /'trɪlədʒɪ/ n trilogía f

trim /trɪm/ a (**trimmer, trimmest**)
arreglado. ● vt (pt **trimmed**) cortar;
recortar ⟨hair etc⟩; (adorn)
adornar. ● n (cut) recorte m; (decoration) adorno m; (state) estado m.
in ~ en buen estado; (fit) en forma.
~ming n adorno m. **~mings** npl
recortes mpl; (decorations) adornos
mpl; (culin) guarnición f

trinity /'trɪnɪtɪ/ n trinidad f. **the T~**
la Trinidad

trinket /'trɪŋkɪt/ n chuchería f

trio /'tri:əʊ/ n (pl **-os**) trío m

trip /trɪp/ vt (pt **tripped**) hacer tropezar. ● vi tropezar; (go lightly) andar
con paso ligero. ● n (journey) viaje
m; (outing) excursión f; (stumble)
traspié m. **~ up** vi tropezar. ● vt
hacer tropezar

tripe /traɪp/ n callos mpl; (nonsense,
sl) tonterías fpl

triple /'trɪpl/ a triple. ● vt triplicar.
● vi triplicarse. **~ts** /'trɪplɪts/ npl
trillizos mpl

triplicate /'trɪplɪkət/ a triplicado. **in
~** por triplicado

tripod /'traɪpɒd/ n trípode m

tripper /'trɪpə(r)/ n (on day trip etc)
excursionista m & f

triptych /'trɪptɪk/ n tríptico m

trite /traɪt/ a trillado

triumph /'traɪʌmf/ n triunfo m. ● vi trinufar (**over** sobre). ~**al** /-'ʌmfl/ a triunfal. ~**ant** /-'ʌmfnt/ a triunfante

trivial /'trɪvɪəl/ a insignificante. ~**ity** /-'ælətɪ/ n insignificancia f

trod, trodden /trɒd, trɒdn/ see **tread**

trolley /'trɒlɪ/ n (pl **-eys**) carretón m. **tea** ~ n mesita f de ruedas. ~**bus** n trolebús m

trombone /trɒm'bəʊn/ n trombón m

troop /truːp/ n grupo m. ● vi. ~ **in** entrar en tropel. ~ **out** salir en tropel. ● vt. ~**ing the colour** saludo m a la bandera. ~**er** n soldado m de caballería. ~**s** npl (mil) tropas fpl

trophy /'trəʊfɪ/ n trofeo m

tropic /'trɒpɪk/ n trópico m. ~**al** a tropical. ~**s** npl trópicos mpl

trot /trɒt/ n trote m. **on the** ~ (fam) seguidos. ● vi (pt **trotted**) trotar. ~ **out** (produce, fam) producir

trotter /'trɒtə(r)/ n (culin) pie m de cerdo

trouble /'trʌbl/ n problema m; (awkward situation) apuro m; (inconvenience) molestia f; (conflict) conflicto m; (med) enfermedad f; (mec) avería f. **be in** ~ estar en un apuro. **make** ~ armar un lío. **take** ~ tomarse la molestia. ● vt (bother) molestar; (worry) preocupar. ● vi molestarse; (worry) preocuparse. **be** ~**d about** preocuparse por. ~**-maker** n alborotador m. ~**some** a molesto

trough /trɒf/ n (for drinking) abrevadero m; (for feeding) pesebre m; (of wave) seno m; (atmospheric) mínimo m de presión

trounce /traʊns/ vt (defeat) derrotar; (thrash) pegar

troupe /truːp/ n compañía f

trousers /'traʊzəz/ npl pantalón m; pantalones mpl

trousseau /'truːsəʊ/ n (pl **-s** /-əʊz/) ajuar m

trout /traʊt/ n (pl **trout**) trucha f

trowel /'traʊəl/ n (garden) desplantador m; (for mortar) paleta f

truant /'truːənt/ n. **play** ~ hacer novillos

truce /truːs/ n tregua f

truck[1] /trʌk/ n carro m; (rail) vagón m; (lorry) camión m

truck[2] /trʌk/ n (dealings) trato m

truculent /'trʌkjʊlənt/ a agresivo

trudge /trʌdʒ/ vi andar penosamente. ● n caminata f penosa

true /truː/ a (**-er, -est**) verdadero; (loyal) leal; (genuine) auténtico; (accurate) exacto. **come** ~ realizarse

truffle /'trʌfl/ n trufa f; (chocolate) trufa f de chocolate

truism /'truːɪzəm/ n perogrullada f

truly /'truːlɪ/ adv verdaderamente; (sincerely) sinceramente; (faithfully) fielmente. **yours** ~ (in letters) le saluda atentamente

trump /trʌmp/ n (cards) triunfo m. ● vt fallar. ~ **up** inventar

trumpet /'trʌmpɪt/ n trompeta f. ~**er** /-ə(r)/ n trompetero m, trompeta m & f

truncated /trʌŋ'keɪtɪd/ a truncado

truncheon /'trʌntʃən/ n porra f

trundle /'trʌndl/ vt hacer rodar. ● vi rodar

trunk /trʌŋk/ n tronco m; (box) baúl m; (of elephant) trompa f. ~**call** n conferencia f. ~**road** n carretera f (nacional). ~**s** npl bañador m

truss /trʌs/ n (med) braguero m. ~ **up** vt (culin) espetar

trust /trʌst/ n confianza f; (association) trust m. **on** ~ a ojos cerrados; (com) al fiado. ● vi confiar. ~ **to** confiar en. ● vt confiar en; (hope) esperar. ~**ed** a leal

trustee /trʌ'stiː/ n administrador m

trust: ~**ful** a confiado. ~**fully** adv confiadamente. ~**worthy** a, ~**y** a digno de confianza

truth /truːθ/ n (pl **-s** /truːðz/) verdad f. ~**ful** a veraz; (true) verídico. ~**fully** adv sinceramente

try /traɪ/ vt (pt **tried**) probar; (be a strain on) poner a prueba; (jurid) procesar. ~ **on** vt probarse (garment). ~ **out** vt probar. ● vi probar. ~ **for** vi intentar conseguir. ● n tentativa f, prueba f; (rugby) ensayo m. ~**ing** a difícil; (annoying) molesto. ~**-out** n prueba f

tryst /trɪst/ n cita f

T-shirt /'tiːʃɜːt/ n camiseta f

tub /tʌb/ n tina f; (bath, fam) baño m

tuba /'tjuːbə/ n tuba f

tubby /'tʌbɪ/ a (**-ier, -iest**) rechoncho

tube /tjuːb/ n tubo m; (rail, fam) metro m. **inner** ~ n cámara f de aire

tuber /'tjuːbə(r)/ n tubérculo m

tuberculosis /tjuːbɜːkjʊ'ləʊsɪs/ n tuberculosis f

tub|ing /'tjuːbɪŋ/ *n* tubería *f*, tubos *mpl*. **~ular** *a* tubular

tuck /tʌk/ *n* pliegue *m*. ● *vt* plegar; (*put*) meter; (*put away*) remeter; (*hide*) esconder. **~ up** *vt* arropar ‹*child*›. ● *vi*. **~ in(to)** (*eat, sl*) comer con buen apetito. **~shop** *n* confitería *f*

Tuesday /'tjuːzdeɪ/ *n* martes *m*

tuft /tʌft/ *n* (*of hair*) mechón *m*; (*of feathers*) penacho *m*; (*of grass*) manojo *m*

tug /tʌg/ *vt* (*pt* **tugged**) tirar de; (*tow*) remolcar. ● *vi* tirar fuerte. ● *n* tirón *m*; (*naut*) remolcador *m*. **~of-war** *n* lucha *f* de la cuerda; (*fig*) tira *m* y afloja

tuition /tjuːˈɪʃn/ *n* enseñanza *f*

tulip /'tjuːlɪp/ *n* tulipán *m*

tumble /'tʌmbl/ *vi* caerse. **~ to** (*fam*) comprender. ● *n* caída *f*

tumbledown /'tʌmbldaʊn/ *a* ruinoso

tumble-drier /tʌmbl'draɪə(r)/ *n* secadora *f* (eléctrica con aire de salida)

tumbler /'tʌmblə(r)/ *n* (*glass*) vaso *m*

tummy /'tʌmɪ/ *n* (*fam*) estómago *m*

tumour /'tjuːmə(r)/ *n* tumor *m*

tumult /'tjuːmʌlt/ *n* tumulto *m*. **~uous** /-ˈmʌltjʊəs/ *a* tumultuoso

tuna /'tjuːnə/ *n* (*pl* **tuna**) atún *m*

tune /tjuːn/ *n* aire *m*. **be in ~** estar afinado. **be out of ~** estar desafinado. ● *vt* afinar; sintonizar ‹*radio, TV*›; (*mec*) poner a punto. ● *vi*. **~ in (to)** ‹*radio, TV*› sintonizarse. **~ up** afinar. **~ful** *a* melodioso. **~r** /-ə(r)/ *n* afinador *m*; (*radio, TV*) sintonizador *m*

tunic /'tjuːnɪk/ *n* túnica *f*

tuning-fork /'tjuːnɪŋfɔːk/ *n* diapasón *m*

Tunisia /tjuːˈnɪzɪə/ *n* Túnez *m*. **~n** *a* & *n* tunecino (*m*)

tunnel /'tʌnl/ *n* túnel *m*. ● *vi* (*pt* **tunnelled**) construir un túnel en

turban /'tɜːbən/ *n* turbante *m*

turbid /'tɜːbɪd/ *a* túrbido

turbine /'tɜːbaɪn/ *n* turbina *f*

turbo-jet /'tɜːbəʊdʒet/ *n* turborreactor *m*

turbot /'tɜːbət/ *n* rodaballo *m*

turbulen|ce /'tɜːbjʊləns/ *n* turbulencia *f*. **~t** /'tɜːbjʊlənt/ *a* turbulento

tureen /tjʊˈriːn/ *n* sopera *f*

turf /tɜːf/ *n* (*pl* **turfs** *or* **turves**) césped *m*; (*segment*) tepe *m*. **the ~** *n* las carreras *fpl* de caballos. ● *vt*. **~ out** (*sl*) echar

turgid /'tɜːdʒɪd/ *a* ‹*language*› pomposo

Turk /tɜːk/ *n* turco *m*

turkey /'tɜːkɪ/ *n* (*pl* **-eys**) pavo *m*

Turk|ey /'tɜːkɪ/ *f* Turquía *f*. **T~ish** *a* & *n* turco (*m*)

turmoil /'tɜːmɔɪl/ *n* confusión *f*

turn /tɜːn/ *vt* hacer girar, dar vueltas a; volver ‹*direction, page, etc*›; cumplir ‹*age*›; dar ‹*hour*›; doblar ‹*corner*›; (*change*) cambiar; (*deflect*) desviar. **~ the tables** volver las tornas. ● *vi* girar, dar vueltas; (*become*) hacerse; (*change*) cambiar. ● *n* vuelta *f*; (*in road*) curva *f*; (*change*) cambio *m*; (*sequence*) turno *m*; (*of mind*) disposición *f*; (*in theatre*) número *m*; (*fright*) susto *m*; (*of illness, fam*) ataque *m*. **bad ~** mala jugada *f*. **good ~** favor *m*. **in ~** a su vez. **out of ~** fuera de lugar. **to a ~** (*culin*) en su punto. **~ against** *vt* volverse en contra de. **~ down** *vt* (*fold*) doblar; (*reduce*) bajar; (*reject*) rechazar. **~ in** *vt* entregar. ● *vi* (*go to bed, fam*) acostarse. **~ off** *vt* cerrar ‹*tap*›; apagar ‹*light, TV, etc*›. ● *vi* desviarse. **~ on** *vt* abrir ‹*tap*›; encender ‹*light etc*›; (*attack*) atacar; (*attract, fam*) excitar. **~ out** *vt* expulsar; apagar ‹*light etc*›; (*produce*) producir; (*empty*) vaciar. ● *vi* (*result*) resultar. **~ round** *vi* dar la vuelta. **~ up** *vi* aparecer. ● *vt* (*find*) encontrar; levantar ‹*collar*›; poner más fuerte ‹*gas*›. **~ed-up** *a* ‹*nose*› respingona. **~ing** /'tɜːnɪŋ/ *n* vuelta *f*; (*road*) bocacalle *f*. **~ing-point** *n* punto *m* decisivo.

turnip /'tɜːnɪp/ *n* nabo *m*

turn: ~out *n* (*of people*) concurrencia *f*; (*of goods*) producción *f*. **~over** /'tɜːnəʊvə(r)/ *n* (*culin*) empanada *f*; (*com*) volumen *m* de negocios; (*of staff*) rotación *f*. **~pike** /'tɜːnpaɪk/ *n* (*Amer*) autopista *f* de peaje. **~stile** /'tɜːnstaɪl/ *n* torniquete *m*. **~table** /'tɜːnteɪbl/ *n* plataforma *f* giratoria; (*on record-player*) plato *m* giratorio. **~up** *n* (*of trousers*) vuelta *f*

turpentine /'tɜːpəntaɪn/ *n* trementina *f*

turquoise /'tɜːkwɔɪz/ *a* & *n* turquesa (*f*)

turret /'tʌrɪt/ n torrecilla f; (mil) torreta f

turtle /'tɜ:tl/ n tortuga f de mar. ~**neck** n cuello m alto

tusk /tʌsk/ n colmillo m

tussle /'tʌsl/ vi pelearse. ● n pelea f

tussock /'tʌsək/ n montecillo m de hierbas

tutor /'tju:tə(r)/ n preceptor m; (univ) director m de estudios, profesor m. ~**ial** /tju:'tɔ:rɪəl/ n clase f particular

tuxedo /tʌk'si:dəʊ/ n (pl -os) (Amer) esmoquin m

TV /ti:'vi:/ n televisión f

twaddle /'twɒdl/ n tonterías fpl

twang /twæŋ/ n tañido m; (in voice) gangueo m. ● vt hacer vibrar. ● vi vibrar

tweed /twi:d/ n tela f gruesa de lana

tweet /twi:t/ n piada f. ● vi piar

tweezers /'twi:zəz/ npl pinzas fpl

twel|fth /twelfθ/ a & n duodécimo (m). ~**ve** /twelv/ a & n doce (m)

twent|ieth /'twentɪəθ/ a & n vigésimo (m). /'twentɪ/ a & n veinte (m)

twerp /twɜ:p/ n (sl) imbécil m

twice /twaɪs/ adv dos veces

twiddle /'twɪdl/ vt hacer girar. ~ one's thumbs (fig) no tener nada que hacer. ~ with jugar con

twig[1] /twɪg/ n ramita f

twig[2] /twɪg/ vt/i (pt twigged) (fam) comprender

twilight /'twaɪlaɪt/ n crepúsculo m

twin /twɪn/ a & n gemelo (m)

twine /twaɪn/ n bramante m. ● vt torcer. ● vi enroscarse

twinge /twɪndʒ/ n punzada f; (fig) remordimiento m (de conciencia)

twinkle /'twɪŋkl/ vi centellear. ● n centelleo m

twirl /twɜ:l/ vt dar vueltas a. ● vi dar vueltas. ● n vuelta f

twist /twɪst/ vt torcer; (roll) enrollar; (distort) deformar. ● vi torcerse; (coil) enroscarse; ⟨road⟩ serpentear. ● n torsión f; (curve) vuelta f; (of character) peculiaridad f

twit[1] /twɪt/ n (sl) imbécil m

twit[2] /twɪt/ vt (pt twitted) tomar el pelo a

twitch /twɪtʃ/ vt crispar. ● vi crisparse. ● n tic m; (jerk) tirón m

twitter /'twɪtə(r)/ vi gorjear. ● n gorjeo m

two /tu:/ a & n dos (m). in ~ minds indeciso. ~**faced** a falso, insincero. ~**piece** (suit) n traje m (de dos piezas). ~**some** /'tu:səm/ n pareja f. ~**way** a ⟨traffic⟩ de doble sentido

tycoon /taɪ'ku:n/ n magnate m

tying /'taɪɪŋ/ see **tie**

type /taɪp/ n tipo m. ● vt/i escribir a máquina. ~**cast** a ⟨actor⟩ encasillado. ~**script** /'taɪpskrɪpt/ n texto m escrito a máquina. ~**writer** /'taɪpraɪtə(r)/ n máquina f de escribir. ~**written** /-ɪtn/ a escrito a máquina, mecanografiado

typhoid /'taɪfɔɪd/ n. ~ (fever) fiebre f tifoidea

typhoon /taɪ'fu:n/ n tifón m

typical /'tɪpɪkl/ a típico. ~**ly** adv típicamente

typify /'tɪpɪfaɪ/ vt tipificar

typi|ng /'taɪpɪŋ/ n mecanografía f. ~**st** n mecanógrafo m

typography /taɪ'pɒgrəfɪ/ n tipografía f

tyran|nical /tɪ'rænɪkl/ a tiránico. ~**nize** vi tiranizar. ~**ny** /'tɪrənɪ/ n tiranía f. ~**t** /'taɪərənt/ n tirano m

tyre /'taɪə(r)/ n neumático m, llanta f (Amer)

U

ubiquitous /ju:'bɪkwɪtəs/ a omnipresente, ubicuo

udder /'ʌdə(r)/ n ubre f

UFO /'ju:fəʊ/ abbr (unidentified flying object) OVNI m, objeto m volante no identificado

ugl|iness /ʌglɪnɪs/ n fealdad f. ~**y** /'ʌglɪ/ a (-ier, -iest) feo

UK /ju:'keɪ/ abbr (United Kingdom) Reino m Unido

ulcer /'ʌlsə(r)/ n úlcera f. ~**ous** a ulceroso

ulterior /ʌl'tɪərɪə(r)/ a ulterior. ~ motive n segunda intención f

ultimate /'ʌltɪmət/ a último; (definitive) definitivo; (fundamental) fundamental. ~**ly** adv al final; (basically) en el fondo

ultimatum /ʌltɪ'meɪtəm/ n (pl -ums) ultimátum m invar

ultra... /'ʌltrə/ pref ultra...

ultramarine /ʌltrəmə'ri:n/ n azul m marino

ultrasonic /ʌltrə'sɒnɪk/ a ultrasónico

ultraviolet /ˌʌltrəˈvaɪələt/ a ultravioleta a invar

umbilical /ʌmˈbɪlɪkl/ a umbilical. ~ **cord** n cordón m umbilical

umbrage /ˈʌmbrɪdʒ/ n resentimiento m. **take** ~ ofenderse (**at** por)

umbrella /ʌmˈbrelə/ n paraguas m invar

umpire /ˈʌmpaɪə(r)/ n árbitro m. • vt arbitrar

umpteen /ˈʌmptiːn/ a (sl) muchísimos. ~**th** a (sl) enésimo

UN /juːˈen/ abbr (United Nations) ONU f, Organización f de las Naciones Unidas

un... /ʌn/ pref in..., des..., no, poco, sin

unabated /ʌnəˈbeɪtɪd/ a no disminuido

unable /ʌnˈeɪbl/ a incapaz (**to** de). be ~ **to** no poder

unabridged /ʌnəˈbrɪdʒd/ a íntegro

unacceptable /ʌnəkˈseptəbl/ a inaceptable

unaccountabl|e /ʌnəˈkaʊntəbl/ a inexplicable. ~**y** adv inexplicablemente

unaccustomed /ʌnəˈkʌstəmd/ a insólito. be ~ **to** a no estar acostumbrado a

unadopted /ʌnəˈdɒptɪd/ a ⟨of road⟩ privado

unadulterated /ʌnəˈdʌltəreɪtɪd/ a puro

unaffected /ʌnəˈfektɪd/ a sin afectación, natural

unaided /ʌnˈeɪdɪd/ a sin ayuda

unalloyed /ʌnəˈlɔɪd/ a puro

unanimous /juːˈnænɪməs/ a unánime. ~**ly** adv unánimemente

unannounced /ʌnəˈnaʊnst/ a sin previo aviso; (unexpected) inesperado

unarmed /ʌnˈɑːmd/ a desarmado

unassuming /ʌnəˈsjuːmɪŋ/ a modesto, sin pretensiones

unattached /ʌnəˈtætʃt/ a suelto; (unmarried) soltero

unattended /ʌnəˈtendɪd/ a sin vigilar

unattractive /ʌnəˈtræktɪv/ a poco atractivo

unavoidabl|e /ʌnəˈvɔɪdəbl/ a inevitable. ~**y** adv inevitablemente

unaware /ʌnəˈweə(r)/ a ignorante (**of** de). be ~ **of** ignorar. ~**s** /-eəz/ adv desprevenido

unbalanced /ʌnˈbælənst/ a desequilibrado

unbearabl|e /ʌnˈbeərəbl/ a inaguantable. ~**y** adv inaguantablemente

unbeat|able /ʌnˈbiːtəbl/ a insuperable. ~**en** a no vencido

unbeknown /ʌnbɪˈnəʊn/ a desconocido. ~ **to me** (fam) sin saberlo yo

unbelievable /ʌnbɪˈliːvəbl/ a increíble

unbend /ʌnˈbend/ vt (pt unbent) enderezar. • vi (relax) relajarse. ~**ing** a inflexible

unbiased /ʌnˈbaɪəst/ a imparcial

unbidden /ʌnˈbɪdn/ a espontáneo; (without invitation) sin ser invitado

unblock /ʌnˈblɒk/ vt desatascar

unbolt /ʌnˈbəʊlt/ vt desatrancar

unborn /ʌnˈbɔːn/ a no nacido todavía

unbounded /ʌnˈbaʊndɪd/ a ilimitado

unbreakable /ʌnˈbreɪkəbl/ a irrompible

unbridled /ʌnˈbraɪdld/ a desenfrenado

unbroken /ʌnˈbrəʊkən/ a (intact) intacto; (continuous) continuo

unburden /ʌnˈbɜːdn/ vt. ~ **o.s.** desahogarse

unbutton /ʌnˈbʌtn/ vt desabotonar, desabrochar

uncalled-for /ʌnˈkɔːldfɔː(r)/ a fuera de lugar; (unjustified) injustificado

uncanny /ʌnˈkænɪ/ a (-ier, -iest) misterioso

unceasing /ʌnˈsiːsɪŋ/ a incesante

unceremonious /ʌnserɪˈməʊnɪəs/ a informal; (abrupt) brusco

uncertain /ʌnˈsɜːtn/ a incierto; (changeable) variable. **be** ~ **whether** no saber exactamente si. ~**ty** n incertidumbre f

unchang|ed /ʌnˈtʃeɪndʒd/ a igual. ~**ing** a inmutable

uncharitable /ʌnˈtʃærɪtəbl/ a severo

uncivilized /ʌnˈsɪvɪlaɪzd/ a incivilizado

uncle /ˈʌŋkl/ n tío m

unclean /ʌnˈkliːn/ a sucio

unclear /ʌnˈklɪə(r)/ a poco claro

uncomfortable /ʌnˈkʌmfətəbl/ a incómodo; (unpleasant) desagradable. **feel** ~ no estar a gusto

uncommon /ʌnˈkɒmən/ a raro. ~**ly** adv extraordinariamente

uncompromising /ʌnˈkɒmprəmaɪzɪŋ/ a intransigente

unconcerned /ʌnkənˈsɜːnd/ a indiferente

unconditional /ʌnkən'dɪʃənl/ a incondicional. **~ly** adv incondicionalmente

unconscious /ʌn'kɒnʃəs/ a inconsciente; (med) sin sentido. **~ly** adv inconscientemente

unconventional /ʌnkən'venʃənl/ a poco convencional

uncooperative /ʌnkəʊ'ɒpərətɪv/ a poco servicial

uncork /ʌn'kɔːk/ vt descorchar, destapar

uncouth /ʌn'kuːθ/ a grosero

uncover /ʌn'kʌvə(r)/ vt descubrir

unctuous /'ʌŋktjʊəs/ a untuoso; (fig) empalagoso

undecided /ʌndɪ'saɪdɪd/ a indeciso

undeniabl|e /ʌndɪ'naɪəbl/ a innegable. **~y** adv indiscutiblemente

under /'ʌndə(r)/ prep debajo de; (less than) menos de; (in the course of) bajo, en. ● adv debajo, abajo. **~ age** a menor de edad. **~ way** adv en curso; (on the way) en marcha

under... pref sub...

undercarriage /'ʌndəkærɪdʒ/ n (aviat) tren m de aterrizaje

underclothes /'ʌndəkləʊðz/ npl ropa f interior

undercoat /'ʌndəkəʊt/ n (of paint) primera mano f

undercover /ʌndə'kʌvə(r)/ a secreto

undercurrent /'ʌndəkʌrənt/ n corriente f submarina; (fig) tendencia f oculta

undercut /'ʌndəkʌt/ vt (pt undercut) (com) vender más barato que

underdeveloped /ʌndədɪ'veləpt/ a subdesarrollado

underdog /'ʌndədɒg/ n perdedor m. **the ~s** npl los de abajo

underdone /ʌndə'dʌn/ a ⟨meat⟩ poco hecho

underestimate /ʌndər'estɪmeɪt/ vt subestimar

underfed /ʌndə'fed/ a desnutrido

underfoot /ʌndə'fʊt/ adv bajo los pies

undergo /'ʌndəgəʊ/ vt (pt -went, pp -gone) sufrir

undergraduate /ʌndə'grædjʊət/ n estudiante m & f universitario (no licenciado)

underground /ʌndə'graʊnd/ adv bajo tierra; (in secret) clandestinamente. /'ʌndəgraʊnd/ a subterráneo; (secret) clandestino. ● n metro m

undergrowth /'ʌndəgrəʊθ/ n maleza f

underhand /'ʌndəhænd/ a (secret) clandestino; (deceptive) fraudulento

underlie /ʌndə'laɪ/ vt (pt -lay, pp -lain, pres p -lying) estar debajo de; (fig) estar a la base de

underline /ʌndə'laɪn/ vt subrayar

underling /'ʌndəlɪŋ/ n subalterno m

underlying /ʌndə'laɪŋ/ a fundamental

undermine /ʌndə'maɪn/ vt socavar

underneath /ʌndə'niːθ/ prep debajo de. ● adv por debajo

underpaid /ʌndə'peɪd/ a mal pagado

underpants /'ʌndəpænts/ npl calzoncillos mpl

underpass /'ʌndəpaːs/ n paso m subterráneo

underprivileged /ʌndə'prɪvɪlɪdʒd/ a desvalido

underrate /ʌndə'reɪt/ vt subestimar

undersell /ʌndə'sel/ vt (pt -sold) vender más barato que

undersigned /'ʌndəsaɪnd/ a abajo firmante

undersized /ʌndə'saɪzd/ a pequeño

understand /ʌndə'stænd/ vt/i (pt -stood) entender, comprender. **~able** a comprensible. **~ing** /ʌndə'stændɪŋ/ a comprensivo. ● n comprensión f; (agreement) acuerdo m

understatement /ʌndə'steɪtmənt/ n subestimación f

understudy /'ʌndəstʌdɪ/ n sobresaliente m & f (en el teatro)

undertake /ʌndə'teɪk/ vt (pt -took, pp -taken) emprender; (assume responsibility) encargarse de

undertaker /'ʌndəteɪkə(r)/ n empresario m de pompas fúnebres

undertaking /ʌndə'teɪkɪŋ/ n empresa f; (promise) promesa f

undertone /'ʌndətəʊn/ n. **in an ~** en voz baja

undertow /'ʌndətəʊ/ n resaca f

undervalue /ʌndə'væljuː/ vt subvalorar

underwater /ʌndə'wɔːtə(r)/ a submarino. ● adv bajo el agua

underwear /'ʌndəweə(r)/ n ropa f interior

underweight /'ʌndəweɪt/ a de peso insuficiente. **be ~** estar flaco

underwent /ʌndə'went/ see **undergo**

underworld /'ʌndəwɜ:ld/ n (*criminals*) hampa f

underwrite /ʌndə'raɪt/ vt (*pt* **-wrote**, *pp* **-written**) (*com*) asegurar. **~r** /-ə(r)/ n asegurador m

undeserved /ʌndɪ'zɜ:vd/ a inmerecido

undesirable /ʌndɪ'zaɪərəbl/ a indeseable

undeveloped /ʌndɪ'veləpt/ a sin desarrollar

undies /'ʌndɪz/ npl (*fam*) ropa f interior

undignified /ʌn'dɪgnɪfaɪd/ a indecoroso

undisputed /ʌndɪs'pju:tɪd/ a incontestable

undistinguished /ʌndɪs'tɪŋgwɪʃt/ a mediocre

undo /ʌn'du:/ vt (*pt* **-did**, *pp* **-done**) deshacer; (*ruin*) arruinar; reparar ⟨*wrong*⟩. **leave ~ne** dejar sin hacer

undoubted /ʌn'daʊtɪd/ a indudable. **~ly** adv indudablemente

undress /ʌn'dres/ vt desnudar. ● vi desnudarse

undue /ʌn'dju:/ a excesivo

undulat|e /'ʌndjʊleɪt/ vi ondular. **~ion** /-'leɪʃn/ n ondulación f

unduly /ʌn'dju:lɪ/ adv excesivamente

undying /ʌn'daɪɪŋ/ a eterno

unearth /ʌn'ɜ:θ/ vt desenterrar

unearthly /ʌn'ɜ:θlɪ/ a sobrenatural; (*impossible*, *fam*) absurdo. **~ hour** n hora intempestiva

uneas|ily /ʌn'i:zɪlɪ/ adv inquietamente. **~y** /ʌn'i:zɪ/ a incómodo; (*worrying*) inquieto

uneconomic /ʌni:kə'nɒmɪk/ a poco rentable

uneducated /ʌn'edjʊkeɪtɪd/ a inculto

unemploy|ed /ʌnɪm'plɔɪd/ a parado, desempleado; (*not in use*) inutilizado. **~ment** n paro m, desempleo m

unending /ʌn'endɪŋ/ a interminable, sin fin

unequal /ʌn'i:kwəl/ a desigual

unequivocal /ʌnɪ'kwɪvəkl/ a inequívoco

unerring /ʌn'ɜ:rɪŋ/ a infalible

unethical /ʌn'eθɪkl/ a sin ética, inmoral

uneven /ʌn'i:vn/ a desigual

unexceptional /ʌnɪk'sepʃənl/ a corriente

unexpected /ʌnɪk'spektɪd/ a inesperado

unfailing /ʌn'feɪlɪŋ/ a inagotable; (*constant*) constante; (*loyal*) leal

unfair /ʌn'feə(r)/ a injusto. **~ly** adv injustamente. **~ness** n injusticia f

unfaithful /ʌn'feɪθfl/ a infiel. **~ness** n infidelidad f

unfamiliar /ʌnfə'mɪlɪə(r)/ a desconocido. **be ~ with** desconocer

unfasten /ʌn'fɑ:sn/ vt desabrochar ⟨*clothes*⟩; (*untie*) desatar

unfavourable /ʌn'feɪvərəbl/ a desfavorable

unfeeling /ʌn'fi:lɪŋ/ a insensible

unfit /ʌn'fɪt/ a inadecuado, no apto; (*unwell*) en mal estado físico; (*incapable*) incapaz

unflinching /ʌn'flɪntʃɪŋ/ a resuelto

unfold /ʌn'fəʊld/ vt desdoblar; (*fig*) revelar. ● vi ⟨*view etc*⟩ extenderse

unforeseen /ʌnfɔ:'si:n/ a imprevisto

unforgettable /ʌnfə'getəbl/ a inolvidable

unforgivable /ʌnfə'gɪvəbl/ a imperdonable

unfortunate /ʌn'fɔ:tʃənət/ a desgraciado; (*regrettable*) lamentable. **~ly** adv desgraciadamente

unfounded /ʌn'faʊndɪd/ a infundado

unfriendly /ʌn'frendlɪ/ a poco amistoso, frío

unfurl /ʌn'fɜ:l/ vt desplegar

ungainly /ʌn'geɪnlɪ/ a desgarbado

ungodly /ʌn'gɒdlɪ/ a impío. **~ hour** n (*fam*) hora f intempestiva

ungrateful /ʌn'greɪtfl/ a desagradecido

unguarded /ʌn'gɑ:dɪd/ a indefenso; (*incautious*) imprudente, incauto

unhapp|ily /ʌn'hapɪlɪ/ adv infelizmente; (*unfortunately*) desgraciadamente. **~iness** n tristeza f. **~y** /ʌn'hæpɪ/ a (**-ier**, **-iest**) infeliz, triste; (*unsuitable*) inoportuno. **~y with** insatisfecho de ⟨*plans etc*⟩

unharmed /ʌn'hɑ:md/ a ileso, sano y salvo

unhealthy /ʌn'helθɪ/ a (**-ier**, **-iest**) enfermizo; (*insanitary*) malsano

unhinge /ʌn'hɪndʒ/ vt desquiciar

unholy /ʌn'həʊlɪ/ a (**-ier**, **-iest**) impío; (*terrible*, *fam*) terrible

unhook /ʌn'hʊk/ vt desenganchar

unhoped /ʌn'həʊpt/ a. **~ for** inesperado

unhurt /ʌn'hɜ:t/ a ileso

unicorn /'ju:nɪkɔ:n/ n unicornio m

unification /juːnɪfɪˈkeɪʃn/ *n* unificación *f*

uniform /ˈjuːnɪfɔːm/ *a & n* uniforme (*m*). **~ity** /-ˈfɔːmətɪ/ *n* uniformidad *f*. **~ly** *adv* uniformemente

unify /ˈjuːnɪfaɪ/ *vt* unificar

unilateral /juːnɪˈlætərəl/ *a* unilateral

unimaginable /ʌnɪˈmædʒɪnəbl/ *a* inconcebible

unimpeachable /ʌnɪmˈpiːtʃəbl/ *a* irreprensible

unimportant /ʌnɪmˈpɔːtnt/ *a* insignificante

uninhabited /ʌnɪnˈhæbɪtɪd/ *a* inhabitado; (*abandoned*) despoblado

unintentional /ʌnɪnˈtenʃənl/ *a* involuntario

union /ˈjuːnjən/ *n* unión *f*; (*trade union*) sindicato *m*. **~ist** *n* sindicalista *m & f*. **U~ Jack** *n* bandera *f* del Reino Unido

unique /juːˈniːk/ *a* único. **~ly** *adv* extraordinariamente

unisex /ˈjuːnɪseks/ *a* unisex(o)

unison /ˈjuːnɪsn/ *n*. **in ~** al unísono

unit /ˈjuːnɪt/ *n* unidad *f*; (*of furniture etc*) elemento *m*

unite /juːˈnaɪt/ *vt* unir. ● *vi* unirse. **U~d Kingdom (UK)** *n* Reino *m* Unido. **U~d Nations (UN)** *n* Organización *f* de las Naciones Unidas (ONU). **U~d States (of America) (USA)** *n* Estados *mpl* Unidos (de América) (EE.UU.)

unity /ˈjuːnɪtɪ/ *n* unidad *f*; (*fig*) acuerdo *m*

univers|al /juːnɪˈvɜːsl/ *a* universal. **~e** /ˈjuːnɪvɜːs/ *n* universo *m*

university /juːnɪˈvɜːsətɪ/ *n* universidad *f*. ● *a* universitario

unjust /ʌnˈdʒʌst/ *a* injusto

unkempt /ʌnˈkempt/ *a* desaseado

unkind /ʌnˈkaɪnd/ *a* poco amable; (*cruel*) cruel. **~ly** *adv* poco amablemente. **~ness** *n* falta *f* de amabilidad; (*cruelty*) crueldad *f*

unknown /ʌnˈnəʊn/ *a* desconocido

unlawful /ʌnˈlɔːfl/ *a* ilegal

unleash /ʌnˈliːʃ/ *vt* soltar; (*fig*) desencadenar

unless /ʌnˈles, ənˈles/ *conj* a menos que, a no ser que

unlike /ʌnˈlaɪk/ *a* diferente; (*not typical*) impropio de. ● *prep* a diferencia de. **~lihood** *n* improbabilidad *f*. **~ly** /ʌnˈlaɪklɪ/ *a* improbable

unlimited /ʌnˈlɪmɪtɪd/ *a* ilimitado

unload /ʌnˈləʊd/ *vt* descargar

unlock /ʌnˈlɒk/ *vt* abrir (con llave)

unluck|ily /ʌnˈlʌkɪlɪ/ *adv* desgraciadamente. **~y** /ʌnˈlʌkɪ/ *a* (**-ier, -iest**) desgraciado; ⟨*number*⟩ de mala suerte

unmanly /ʌnˈmænlɪ/ *a* poco viril

unmanned /ʌnˈmænd/ *a* no tripulado

unmarried /ʌnˈmærɪd/ *a* soltero. **~ mother** *n* madre *f* soltera

unmask /ʌnˈmɑːsk/ *vt* desenmascarar. ● *vi* quitarse la máscara

unmentionable /ʌnˈmenʃənəbl/ *a* a que no se debe aludir

unmistakabl|e /ʌnmɪˈsteɪkəbl/ *a* inconfundible. **~y** *adv* claramente

unmitigated /ʌnˈmɪtɪɡeɪtɪd/ *a* (*absolute*) absoluto

unmoved /ʌnˈmuːvd/ *a* (*fig*) indiferente (**by** a), insensible (**by** a)

unnatural /ʌnˈnætʃərəl/ *a* no natural; (*not normal*) anormal

unnecessar|ily /ʌnˈnesəsərɪlɪ/ *adv* innecesariamente. **~y** /ʌnˈnesəsərɪ/ *a* innecesario

unnerve /ʌnˈnɜːv/ *vt* desconcertar

unnoticed /ʌnˈnəʊtɪst/ *a* inadvertido

unobtainable /ʌnəbˈteɪnəbl/ *a* inaseguible; (*fig*) inalcanzable

unobtrusive /ʌnəbˈtruːsɪv/ *a* discreto

unofficial /ʌnəˈfɪʃl/ *a* no oficial. **~ly** *adv* extraoficialmente

unpack /ʌnˈpæk/ *vt* desempaquetar ⟨*parcel*⟩; deshacer ⟨*suitcase*⟩. ● *vi* deshacer la maleta

unpalatable /ʌnˈpælətəbl/ *a* desagradable

unparalleled /ʌnˈpærəleld/ *a* sin par

unpick /ʌnˈpɪk/ *vt* descoser

unpleasant /ʌnˈpleznt/ *a* desagradable. **~ness** *n* lo desagradable

unplug /ʌnˈplʌɡ/ *vt* (*elec*) desenchufar

unpopular /ʌnˈpɒpjʊlə(r)/ *a* impopular

unprecedented /ʌnˈpresɪdentɪd/ *a* sin precedente

unpredictable /ʌnprɪˈdɪktəbl/ *a* imprevisible

unpremeditated /ʌnprɪˈmedɪteɪtɪd/ *a* impremeditado

unprepared /ʌnprɪˈpeəd/ *a* no preparado; (*unready*) desprevenido

unprepossessing /ʌnpriːpəˈzesɪŋ/ *a* poco atractivo

unpretentious /ʌnprɪˈtenʃəs/ *a* sin pretensiones, modesto

unprincipled /ʌnˈprɪnsɪpld/ a sin principios

unprofessional /ʌnprəˈfeʃənəl/ a contrario a la ética profesional

unpublished /ʌnˈpʌblɪʃt/ a inédito

unqualified /ʌnˈkwɒlɪfaɪd/ a sin título; (*fig*) absoluto

unquestionabl|e /ʌnˈkwestʃənəbl/ a indiscutible. **~y** adv indiscutible-mente

unquote /ʌnˈkwəʊt/ vi cerrar comillas

unravel /ʌnˈrævl/ vt (*pt* **unravelled**) desenredar; deshacer ⟨*knitting etc*⟩. ● vi desenredarse

unreal /ʌnˈrɪəl/ a irreal. **~istic** a poco realista

unreasonable /ʌnˈriːzənəbl/ a irrazonable

unrecognizable /ʌnrekəgˈnaɪzəbl/ a irreconocible

unrelated /ʌnrɪˈleɪtɪd/ a ⟨*facts*⟩ inconexo, sin relación; ⟨*people*⟩ no emparentado

unreliable /ʌnrɪˈlaɪəbl/ a ⟨*person*⟩ poco formal; ⟨*machine*⟩ poco fiable

unrelieved /ʌnrɪˈliːvd/ a no aliviado

unremitting /ʌnrɪˈmɪtɪŋ/ a in-cesante

unrepentant /ʌnrɪˈpentənt/ a im-penitente

unrequited /ʌnrɪˈkwaɪtɪd/ a no correspondido

unreservedly /ʌnrɪˈzɜːvɪdlɪ/ adv sin reserva

unrest /ʌnˈrest/ n inquietud f; (*pol*) agitación f

unrivalled /ʌnˈraɪvld/ a sin par

unroll /ʌnˈrəʊl/ vt desenrollar. ● vi desenrollarse

unruffled /ʌnˈrʌfld/ ⟨*person*⟩ imperturbable

unruly /ʌnˈruːlɪ/ a indisciplinado

unsafe /ʌnˈseɪf/ a peligroso; ⟨*per-son*⟩ en peligro

unsaid /ʌnˈsed/ a sin decir

unsatisfactory /ʌnsætɪsˈfæktərɪ/ a insatisfactorio

unsavoury /ʌnˈseɪvərɪ/ a desagradable

unscathed /ʌnˈskeɪðd/ a ileso

unscramble /ʌnˈskræmbl/ vt descifrar

unscrew /ʌnˈskruː/ vt destornillar

unscrupulous /ʌnˈskruːpjʊləs/ a sin escrúpulos

unseat /ʌnˈsiːt/ vt (*pol*) quitar el escaño a

unseemly /ʌnˈsiːmlɪ/ a indecoroso

unseen /ʌnˈsiːn/ a inadvertido. ● n (*translation*) traducción f a primera vista

unselfish /ʌnˈselfɪʃ/ a desinteresado

unsettle /ʌnˈsetl/ vt perturbar. **~d** a perturbado; ⟨*weather*⟩ variable; ⟨*bill*⟩ por pagar

unshakeable /ʌnˈʃeɪkəbl/ a firme

unshaven /ʌnˈʃeɪvn/ a sin afeitar

unsightly /ʌnˈsaɪtlɪ/ a feo

unskilled /ʌnˈskɪld/ a inexperto. **~ worker** n obrero m no cualificado

unsociable /ʌnˈsəʊʃəbl/ a insociable

unsolicited /ʌnsəˈlɪsɪtɪd/ a no solicitado

unsophisticated /ʌnsəˈfɪstɪkeɪtɪd/ a sencillo

unsound /ʌnˈsaʊnd/ a defectuoso, erróneo. **of ~ mind** demente

unsparing /ʌnˈspeərɪŋ/ a pródigo; (*cruel*) cruel

unspeakable /ʌnˈspiːkəbl/ a indecible

unspecified /ʌnˈspesɪfaɪd/ a no especificado

unstable /ʌnˈsteɪbl/ a inestable

unsteady /ʌnˈstedɪ/ a inestable; ⟨*hand*⟩ poco firme; ⟨*step*⟩ inseguro

unstinted /ʌnˈstɪntɪd/ a abundante

unstuck /ʌnˈstʌk/ a suelto. **come ~** despegarse; (*fail*, *fam*) fracasar

unstudied /ʌnˈstʌdɪd/ a natural

unsuccessful /ʌnsəkˈsesfʊl/ a fraca-sado. **be ~** no tener éxito, fracasar

unsuitable /ʌnˈsuːtəbl/ a in-adecuado; (*inconvenient*) incon-veniente

unsure /ʌnˈʃʊə(r)/ a inseguro

unsuspecting /ʌnsəˈspektɪŋ/ a confiado

unthinkable /ʌnˈθɪŋkəbl/ a inconcebible

untid|ily /ʌnˈtaɪdɪlɪ/ adv desor-denadamente. **~iness** n desorden m. **~y** /ʌnˈtaɪdɪ/ a (**-ier**, **-iest**) desor-denado; ⟨*person*⟩ desaseado

untie /ʌnˈtaɪ/ vt desatar

until /ənˈtɪl, ʌnˈtɪl/ prep hasta. ● conj hasta que

untimely /ʌnˈtaɪmlɪ/ a inoportuno; (*premature*) prematuro

untiring /ʌnˈtaɪərɪŋ/ a incansable

untold /ʌnˈtəʊld/ a incalculable

untoward /ʌntəˈwɔːd/ a (*incon-venient*) inconveniente

untried /ʌnˈtraɪd/ a no probado

untrue /ʌnˈtruː/ a falso

unused /ʌnˈjuːzd/ a nuevo. /ʌnˈjuːst/ a. **~ to** no acostumbrado a

unusual /ʌnˈjuːʒʊəl/ *a* insólito; (*exceptional*) excepcional. **~ly** *adv* excepcionalmente

unutterable /ʌnˈʌtərəbl/ *a* indecible

unveil /ʌnˈveɪl/ *vt* descubrir; (*disclose*) revelar

unwanted /ʌnˈwɒntɪd/ *a* superfluo; ⟨*child*⟩ no deseado

unwarranted /ʌnˈwɒrəntɪd/ *a* injustificado

unwelcome /ʌnˈwelkəm/ *a* desagradable; ⟨*guest*⟩ inoportuno

unwell /ʌnˈwel/ *a* indispuesto

unwieldy /ʌnˈwiːldɪ/ *a* difícil de manejar

unwilling /ʌnˈwɪlɪŋ/ *a* no dispuesto. **be ~** no querer. **~ly** *adv* de mala gana

unwind /ʌnˈwaɪnd/ *vt* (*pt* **unwound**) desenvolver. ● *vi* desenvolverse; (*relax, fam*) relajarse

unwise /ʌnˈwaɪz/ *a* imprudente

unwitting /ʌnˈwɪtɪŋ/ *a* inconsciente; (*involuntary*) involuntario. **~ly** *adv* involuntariamente

unworthy /ʌnˈwɜːðɪ/ *a* indigno

unwrap /ʌnˈræp/ *vt* (*pt* **unwrapped**) desenvolver, deshacer

unwritten /ʌnˈrɪtn/ *a* no escrito; ⟨*agreement*⟩ tácito

up /ʌp/ *adv* arriba; (*upwards*) hacia arriba; (*higher*) más arriba; (*out of bed*) levantado; (*finished*) terminado. **~ here** aquí arriba. **~ in** (*fam*) versado en, fuerte en. **~ there** allí arriba. **~ to** hasta. **be one ~** llevar la ventaja a. **be ~ against** enfrentarse con. **be ~ to** tramar ⟨*plot*⟩; (*one's turn*) tocar a; a la altura de ⟨*task*⟩; (*reach*) llegar a. **come ~** subir. **feel ~ to it** sentirse capaz. **go ~** subir. **it's ~ to you** depende de tí. **what is ~?** ¿qué pasa? ● *prep* arriba; (*on top of*) en lo alto de. ● *vt* (*pt* **upped**) aumentar. ● *n*. **~s and downs** *npl* altibajos *mpl*

upbraid /ʌpˈbreɪd/ *vt* reprender

upbringing /ˈʌpbrɪŋɪŋ/ *n* educación *f*

update /ʌpˈdeɪt/ *vt* poner al día

upgrade /ʌpˈɡreɪd/ *vt* ascender ⟨*person*⟩; mejorar ⟨*equipment*⟩

upheaval /ʌpˈhiːvl/ *n* trastorno *m*

uphill /ˈʌphɪl/ *a* ascendente; (*fig*) arduo. ● *adv* /ʌpˈhɪl/ cuesta arriba. **go ~** subir

uphold /ʌpˈhəʊld/ *vt* (*pt* **upheld**) sostener

upholster /ʌpˈhəʊlstə(r)/ *vt* tapizar. **~er** /-rə(r)/ *n* tapicero *m*. **~y** *n* tapicería *f*

upkeep /ˈʌpkiːp/ *n* mantenimiento *m*

up-market /ʌpˈmɑːkɪt/ *a* superior

upon /əˈpɒn/ *prep* en; (*on top of*) encima de. **once ~ a time** érase una vez

upper /ˈʌpə(r)/ *a* superior. **~ class** *n* clases *fpl* altas. **~ hand** *n* dominio *m*, ventaja *f*. **~most** *a* (el) más alto. ● *n* (*of shoe*) pala *f*

uppish /ˈʌpɪʃ/ *a* engreído

upright /ˈʌpraɪt/ *a* derecho; ⟨*piano*⟩ vertical. ● *n* montante *m*

uprising /ˈʌpraɪzɪŋ/ *n* sublevación *f*

uproar /ˈʌprɔː(r)/ *n* tumulto *m*. **~ious** /-ˈrɔːrɪəs/ *a* tumultuoso

uproot /ʌpˈruːt/ *vt* desarraigar

upset /ʌpˈset/ *vt* (*pt* **upset**, *presp* **upsetting**) trastornar; desbaratar ⟨*plan etc*⟩; (*distress*) alterar. /ˈʌpset/ *n* trastorno *m*

upshot /ˈʌpʃɒt/ *n* resultado *m*

upside-down /ʌpsaɪdˈdaʊn/ *adv* al revés; (*in disorder*) patas arriba. **turn ~** volver

upstairs /ʌpˈsteəz/ *adv* arriba. /ˈʌpsteəz/ *a* de arriba

upstart /ˈʌpstɑːt/ *n* arribista *m & f*

upstream /ˈʌpstriːm/ *adv* río arriba; (*against the current*) contra la corriente

upsurge /ˈʌpsɜːdʒ/ *n* aumento *m*; (*of anger etc*) arrebato *m*

uptake /ˈʌpteɪk/ *n*. **quick on the ~** muy listo

uptight /ˈʌptaɪt/ *a* (*fam*) nervioso

up-to-date /ʌptəˈdeɪt/ *a* al día; ⟨*news*⟩ de última hora; (*modern*) moderno

upturn /ˈʌptɜːn/ *n* aumento *m*; (*improvement*) mejora *f*

upward /ˈʌpwəd/ *a* ascendente. ● *adv* hacia arriba. **~s** *adv* hacia arriba

uranium /jʊˈreɪnɪəm/ *n* uranio *m*

urban /ˈɜːbən/ *a* urbano

urbane /ɜːˈbeɪn/ *a* cortés

urbanize /ˈɜːbənaɪz/ *vt* urbanizar

urchin /ˈɜːtʃɪn/ *n* pilluelo *m*

urge /ɜːdʒ/ *vt* incitar, animar. ● *n* impulso *m*. **~ on** animar

urgen|cy /ˈɜːdʒənsɪ/ *n* urgencia *f*. **~t** /ˈɜːdʒənt/ *a* urgente. **~tly** *adv* urgentemente

urin|ate /ˈjʊərɪneɪt/ *vi* orinar. **~e** /ˈjʊərɪn/ *n* orina *f*

urn /ɜːn/ n urna f

Uruguay /juərəgwaɪ/ n el Uruguay m. ∼an a & n uruguayo (m)

us /ʌs, əs/ pron nos; (after prep) nosotros, nosotras

US(A) /juːesˈeɪ/ abbr (United States (of America)) EE.UU., Estados mpl Unidos

usage /ˈjuːzɪdʒ/ n uso m

use /juːz/ vt emplear. /juːs/ n uso m, empleo m. **be of** ∼ servir. **it is no** ∼ es inútil, no sirve para nada. **make** ∼ **of** servirse de. ∼ **up** agotar, consumir. ∼**d** /juːzd/ a ‹clothes› gastado. /juːst/ pt. **he** ∼**d to say** decía, solía decir. ● a. ∼**d to** acostumbrado a. ∼**ful** /ˈjuːsfl/ a útil. ∼**fully** adv útilmente. ∼**less** a inútil; ‹person› incompetente. ∼**r** /-zə(r)/ n usuario m

usher /ˈʌʃə(r)/ n ujier m; (in theatre etc) acomodador m. ● vt. ∼ **in** hacer entrar. ∼**ette** n acomodadora f

USSR abbr (history) (Union of Soviet Socialist Republics) URSS

usual /ˈjuːʒəl/ a usual, corriente; (habitual) acostumbrado, habitual. **as** ∼ como de costumbre, como siempre. ∼**ly** adv normalmente. **he** ∼**ly wakes up early** suele despertarse temprano

usurer /ˈjuːʒərə(r)/ n usurero m

usurp /juːˈzɜːp/ vt usurpar. ∼**er** /-ə(r)/ n usurpador m

usury /ˈjuːʒərɪ/ n usura f

utensil /juːˈtensl/ n utensilio m

uterus /ˈjuːtərəs/ n útero m

utilitarian /juːtɪlɪˈteərɪən/ a utilitario

utility /juːˈtɪlətɪ/ n utilidad f. **public** ∼ n servicio m público. ● a utilitario

utilize /ˈjuːtɪlaɪz/ vt utilizar

utmost /ˈʌtməʊst/ a extremo. ● n. **one's** ∼ todo lo posible

utter[1] /ˈʌtə(r)/ a completo

utter[2] /ˈʌtə(r)/ vt (speak) pronunciar; dar ‹sigh›; emitir ‹sound›. ∼**ance** n expresión f

utterly /ˈʌtəlɪ/ adv totalmente

U-turn /ˈjuːtɜːn/ n vuelta f

V

vacan|cy /ˈveɪkənsɪ/ n (job) vacante f; (room) habitación f libre. ∼**t** a libre; (empty) vacío; ‹look› vago

vacate /vəˈkeɪt/ vt dejar

vacation /vəˈkeɪʃn/ n (Amer) vacaciones fpl

vaccin|ate /ˈvæksɪneɪt/ vt vacunar. ∼**ation** /-ˈneɪʃn/ n vacunación f. ∼**e** /ˈvæksiːn/ n vacuna f

vacuum /ˈvækjʊəm/ n (pl -cuums or -cua) vacío m. ∼ **cleaner** n aspiradora f. ∼ **flask** n termo m

vagabond /ˈvægəbɒnd/ n vagabundo m

vagary /ˈveɪgərɪ/ n capricho m

vagina /vəˈdʒaɪnə/ n vagina f

vagrant /ˈveɪgrənt/ n vagabundo m

vague /veɪg/ a (-er, -est) vago; ‹outline› indistinto. **be** ∼ **about** no precisar. ∼**ly** adv vagamente

vain /veɪn/ a (-er, -est) vanidoso; (useless) vano, inútil. **in** ∼ en vano. ∼**ly** adv vanamente

valance /ˈvæləns/ n cenefa f

vale /veɪl/ n valle m

valentine /ˈvæləntaɪn/ n (card) tarjeta f del día de San Valentín

valet /ˈvælɪt, ˈvæleɪ/ n ayuda m de cámara

valiant /ˈvælɪənt/ a valeroso

valid /ˈvælɪd/ a válido; ‹ticket› valedero. ∼**ate** vt dar validez a; (confirm) convalidar. ∼**ity** /-ˈɪdətɪ/ n validez f

valley /ˈvælɪ/ n (pl -eys) valle m

valour /ˈvælə(r)/ n valor m

valuable /ˈvæljʊəbl/ a valioso. ∼**s** npl objetos mpl de valor

valuation /væljʊˈeɪʃn/ n valoración f

value /ˈvæljuː/ n valor m; (usefulness) utilidad f. **face** ∼ n valor m nominal; (fig) significado m literal. ● vt valorar; (cherish) apreciar. ∼ **added tax (VAT)** n impuesto m sobre el valor añadido (IVA). ∼**d** a (appreciated) apreciado, estimado. ∼**r** /-ə(r)/ n tasador m

valve /vælv/ n válvula f

vampire /ˈvæmpaɪə(r)/ n vampiro m

van /væn/ n furgoneta f; (rail) furgón m

vandal /ˈvændl/ n vándalo m. ∼**ism** /-əlɪzəm/ n vandalismo m. ∼**ize** vt destruir

vane /veɪn/ n (weathercock) veleta f; (naut, aviat) paleta f

vanguard /ˈvængɑːd/ n vanguardia f

vanilla /vəˈnɪlə/ n vainilla f

vanish /ˈvænɪʃ/ vi desaparecer

vanity /ˈvænɪtɪ/ n vanidad f. ∼ **case** n neceser m

vantage /'vɑːntɪdʒ/ n ventaja f. ~ **point** n posición f ventajosa

vapour /'veɪpə(r)/ n vapor m

variable /'veərɪəbl/ a variable

varian|ce /'veərɪəns/ n. **at** ~**ce** en desacuerdo. ~**t** /'veərɪənt/ a diferente. ● n variante m

variation /veərɪ'eɪʃn/ n variación f

varicoloured /'veərɪkʌləd/ a multicolor

varied /'veərɪd/ a variado

varicose /'værɪkəʊs/ a varicoso. ~ **veins** npl varices fpl

variety /və'raɪətɪ/ n variedad f. ~ **show** n espectáculo m de variedades

various /'veərɪəs/ a diverso. ~**ly** adv diversamente

varnish /'vɑːnɪʃ/ n barniz m; (for nails) esmalte m. ● vt barnizar

vary /'veərɪ/ vt/i variar. ~**ing** a diverso

vase /vɑːz, Amer veɪs/ n jarrón m

vasectomy /və'sektəmɪ/ n vasectomía f

vast /vɑːst/ a vasto, enorme. ~**ly** adv enormemente. ~**ness** n inmensidad f

vat /væt/ n tina f

VAT /viːeɪ'tiː/ abbr (value added tax) IVA m, impuesto m sobre el valor añadido

vault /vɔːlt/ n (roof) bóveda f; (in bank) cámara f acorazada; (tomb) cripta f; (cellar) sótano m; (jump) salto m. ● vt/i saltar

vaunt /vɔːnt/ vt jactarse de

veal /viːl/ n ternera f

veer /vɪə(r)/ vi cambiar de dirección; (naut) virar

vegetable /'vedʒɪtəbl/ a vegetal. ● n legumbre m; (greens) verduras fpl

vegetarian /vedʒɪ'teərɪən/ a & n vegetariano (m)

vegetate /'vedʒɪteɪt/ vi vegetar

vegetation /vedʒɪ'teɪʃn/ n vegetación f

vehemen|ce /'viːəməns/ n vehemencia f. ~**t** /'viːəmənt/ a vehemente. ~**tly** adv con vehemencia

vehicle /'viːɪkl/ n vehículo m

veil /veɪl/ n velo m. **take the** ~ hacerse monja. ● vt velar

vein /veɪn/ n vena f; (mood) humor m. ~**ed** a veteado

velocity /vɪ'lɒsɪtɪ/ n velocidad f

velvet /'velvɪt/ n terciopelo m. ~**y** a aterciopelado

venal /'viːnl/ a venal. ~**ity** /-'nælətɪ/ n venalidad f

vendetta /ven'detə/ n enemistad f prolongada

vending-machine /'vendɪŋ məʃiːn/ n distribuidor m automático

vendor /'vendə(r)/ n vendedor m

veneer /və'nɪə(r)/ n chapa f; (fig) barniz m, apariencia f

venerable /'venərəbl/ a venerable

venereal /və'nɪərɪəl/ a venéreo

Venetian /və'niːʃn/ a & n veneciano (m). **v~ blind** n persiana f veneciana

vengeance /'vendʒəns/ n venganza f. **with a** ~ (fig) con creces

venison /'venɪzn/ n carne f de venado

venom /'venəm/ n veneno m. ~**ous** a venenoso

vent /vent/ n abertura f; (for air) respiradero m. **give** ~ **to** dar salida a. ● vt hacer un agujero en; (fig) desahogar

ventilat|e /'ventɪleɪt/ vt ventilar. ~**ion** /-'leɪʃn/ n ventilación f. ~**or** /-ə(r)/ n ventilador m

ventriloquist /ven'trɪləkwɪst/ n ventrílocuo m

venture /'ventʃə(r)/ n empresa f (arriesgada). **at a** ~ a la ventura. ● vt arriesgar. ● vi atreverse

venue /'venjuː/ n lugar m (de reunión)

veranda /və'rændə/ n terraza f

verb /vɜːb/ n verbo m

verbal /'vɜːbl/ a verbal. ~**ly** adv verbalmente

verbatim /vɜː'beɪtɪm/ adv palabra por palabra, al pie de la letra

verbose /vɜː'bəʊs/ a prolijo

verdant /'vɜːdənt/ a verde

verdict /'vɜːdɪkt/ n veredicto m; (opinion) opinión f

verge /vɜːdʒ/ n borde m. ● vt. ~ **on** acercarse a

verger /'vɜːdʒə(r)/ n sacristán m

verif|ication /verɪfɪ'keɪʃn/ n verificación f. ~**y** /'verɪfaɪ/ vt verificar

veritable /'verɪtəbl/ a verdadero

vermicelli /vɜːmɪ'tʃelɪ/ n fideos mpl

vermin /'vɜːmɪn/ n sabandijas fpl

vermouth /'vɜːməθ/ n vermut m

vernacular /və'nækjʊlə(r)/ n lengua f; (regional) dialecto m

versatil|e /'vɜːsətaɪl/ a versátil. ~**ity** /-'tɪlətɪ/ n versatilidad f

verse /vɜːs/ n estrofa f; (poetry) poesías fpl; (of Bible) versículo m

versed /vɜːst/ a. ~ **in** versado en

version /ˈvɜːʃn/ n versión f

versus /ˈvɜːsəs/ prep contra

vertebra /ˈvɜːtɪbrə/ n (pl **-brae** /-briː/) vértebra f

vertical /ˈvɜːtɪkl/ a & n vertical (f). ~**ly** adv verticalmente

vertigo /ˈvɜːtɪgəʊ/ n vértigo m

verve /vɜːv/ n entusiasmo m, vigor m

very /ˈverɪ/ adv muy. ~ **much** muchísimo. ~ **well** muy bien. **the** ~ **first** el primero de todos. ● a mismo. **the** ~ **thing** exactamente lo que hace falta

vespers /ˈvespəz/ npl vísperas fpl

vessel /ˈvesl/ n (receptacle) recipiente m; (ship) buque m; (anat) vaso m

vest /vest/ n camiseta f, (Amer) chaleco m. ● vt conferir. ~**ed interest** n interés m personal; (jurid) derecho m adquirido

vestige /ˈvestɪdʒ/ n vestigio m

vestment /ˈvestmənt/ n vestidura f

vestry /ˈvestrɪ/ n sacristía f

vet /vet/ n (fam) veterinario m. ● vt (pt vetted) examinar

veteran /ˈvetərən/ n veterano m

veterinary /ˈvetərɪnərɪ/ a veterinario. ~ **surgeon** n veterinario m

veto /ˈviːtəʊ/ n (pl **-oes**) veto m. ● vt poner el veto a

vex /veks/ vt fastidiar. ~**ation** /-ˈseɪʃn/ n fastidio m. ~**ed question** n cuestión f controvertida. ~**ing** a fastidioso

via /ˈvaɪə/ prep por, por vía de

viab|ility /vaɪəˈbɪlətɪ/ n viabilidad f. ~**le** /ˈvaɪəbl/ a viable

viaduct /ˈvaɪədʌkt/ n viaducto m

vibrant /ˈvaɪbrənt/ a vibrante

vibrat|e /vaɪˈbreɪt/ vt/i vibrar. ~**ion** /-ʃn/ n vibración f

vicar /ˈvɪkə(r)/ n párroco m. ~**age** /-rɪdʒ/ n casa f del párroco

vicarious /vɪˈkeərɪəs/ a indirecto

vice[1] /vaɪs/ n vicio m

vice[2] /vaɪs/ n (tec) torno m de banco

vice... /vaɪs/ pref vice...

vice versa /vaɪsɪˈvɜːsə/ adv viceversa

vicinity /vɪˈsɪnɪtɪ/ n vecindad f. **in the** ~ **of** cerca de

vicious /ˈvɪʃəs/ a (spiteful) malicioso; (violent) atroz. ~ **circle** n círculo m vicioso. ~**ly** adv cruelmente

vicissitudes /vɪˈsɪsɪtjuːdz/ npl vicisitudes fpl

victim /ˈvɪktɪm/ n víctima f. ~**ization** /-aɪˈzeɪʃn/ n persecución f. ~**ize** vt victimizar

victor /ˈvɪktə(r)/ n vencedor m

Victorian /vɪkˈtɔːrɪən/ a victoriano

victor|ious /vɪkˈtɔːrɪəs/ a victorioso. ~**y** /ˈvɪktərɪ/ n victoria f

video /ˈvɪdɪəʊ/ a video. ● n (fam) magnetoscopio m. ~ **recorder** n magnetoscopio m. ~**tape** n videocassette f

vie /vaɪ/ vi (pres p **vying**) rivalizar

view /vjuː/ n vista f; (mental survey) visión f de conjunto; (opinion) opinión f. **in my** ~ a mi juicio. **in** ~ **of** en vista de. ● vt expuesto. **with a** ~ **to** con miras a. ● vt ver; (visit) visitar; (consider) considerar. ~**er** /-ə(r)/ n espectador m; (TV) televidente m & f. ~**finder** /ˈvjuːfaɪndə(r)/ n visor m. ~**point** /ˈvjuːpɔɪnt/ n punto m de vista

vigil /ˈvɪdʒɪl/ n vigilia f. ~**ance** n vigilancia f. ~**ant** a vigilante. **keep** ~ velar

vigo|rous /ˈvɪgərəs/ a vigoroso. ~**ur** /ˈvɪgə(r)/ n vigor m

vile /vaɪl/ a (base) vil; (bad) horrible; ⟨weather, temper⟩ de perros

vilif|ication /vɪlɪfɪˈkeɪʃn/ n difamación f. ~**y** /ˈvɪlɪfaɪ/ vt difamar

village /ˈvɪlɪdʒ/ n aldea f. ~**r** /-ə(r)/ n aldeano m

villain /ˈvɪlən/ n malvado m; (in story etc) malo m. ~**ous** a infame. ~**y** n infamia f

vim /vɪm/ n (fam) energía f

vinaigrette /vɪnɪˈgret/ n. ~ **sauce** n vinagreta f

vindicat|e /ˈvɪndɪkeɪt/ vt vindicar. ~**ion** /-ˈkeɪʃn/ n vindicación f

vindictive /vɪnˈdɪktɪv/ a vengativo. ~**ness** n carácter m vengativo

vine /vaɪn/ n vid f

vinegar /ˈvɪnɪgə(r)/ n vinagre m. ~**y** a ⟨person⟩ avinagrado

vineyard /ˈvɪnjəd/ n viña f

vintage /ˈvɪntɪdʒ/ n (year) cosecha f. ● a (wine) añejo; (car) de época

vinyl /ˈvaɪnɪl/ n vinilo m

viola /vɪˈəʊlə/ n viola f

violat|e /ˈvaɪəleɪt/ vt violar. ~**ion** /-ˈleɪʃn/ n violación f

violen|ce /ˈvaɪələns/ n violencia f. ~**t** /ˈvaɪələnt/ a violento. ~**tly** adv violentamente

violet /ˈvaɪələt/ a & n violeta (f)

violin /ˈvaɪəlɪn/ n violín m. ~**ist** n violinista m & f

VIP /viːaɪˈpiː/ *abbr* (*very important person*) personaje *m*

viper /ˈvaɪpə(r)/ *n* víbora *f*

virgin /ˈvɜːdʒɪn/ *a & n* virgen (*f*). ∼**al** *a* virginal. ∼**ity** /vəˈdʒɪnətɪ/ *n* virginidad *f*

Virgo /ˈvɜːgəʊ/ *n* (*astr*) Virgo *f*

viril|e /ˈvɪraɪl/ *a* viril. ∼**ity** /-ˈrɪlətɪ/ *n* virilidad *f*

virtual /ˈvɜːtʃʊəl/ *a* verdadero. **a** ∼ **failure** prácticamente un fracaso. ∼**ly** *adv* prácticamente

virtue /ˈvɜːtʃuː/ *n* virtud *f*. **by** ∼ **of**, **in** ∼ **of** en virtud de

virtuoso /vɜːtjʊˈəʊzəʊ/ *n* (*pl* **-si** /-ziː/) virtuoso *m*

virtuous /ˈvɜːtʃʊəs/ *a* virtuoso

virulent /ˈvɪrʊlənt/ *a* virulento

virus /ˈvaɪərəs/ *n* (*pl* **-uses**) virus *m*

visa /ˈviːzə/ *n* visado *m*, visa *f* (*LAm*)

vis-a-vis /viːzɑːˈviː/ *adv* frente a frente. ● *prep* respecto a; (*opposite*) en frente de

viscount /ˈvaɪkaʊnt/ *n* vizconde *m*. ∼**ess** *n* vizcondesa *f*

viscous /ˈvɪskəs/ *a* viscoso

visib|ility /vɪzɪˈbɪlətɪ/ *n* visibilidad *f*. ∼**le** /ˈvɪzɪbl/ *a* visible. ∼**ly** *adv* visiblemente

vision /ˈvɪʒn/ *n* visión *f*; (*sight*) vista *f*. ∼**ary** /ˈvɪʒənərɪ/ *a & n* visionario (*m*)

visit /ˈvɪzɪt/ *vt* visitar; hacer una visita a ⟨*person*⟩. ● *vi* hacer visitas. ● *n* visita *f*. ∼**or** *n* visitante *m & f*; (*guest*) visita *f*; (*in hotel*) cliente *m & f*

visor /ˈvaɪzə(r)/ *n* visera *f*

vista /ˈvɪstə/ *n* perspectiva *f*

visual /ˈvɪʒʊəl/ *a* visual. ∼**ize** /ˈvɪʒʊəlaɪz/ *vt* imaginar(se); (*foresee*) prever. ∼**ly** *adv* visualmente

vital /ˈvaɪtl/ *a* vital; (*essential*) esencial

vitality /vaɪˈtælətɪ/ *n* vitalidad *f*

vital: ∼**ly** /ˈvaɪtəlɪ/ *adv* extremadamente. ∼**s** *npl* órganos *mpl* vitales. ∼ **statistics** *npl* (*fam*) medidas *fpl*

vitamin /ˈvɪtəmɪn/ *n* vitamina *f*

vitiate /ˈvɪʃɪeɪt/ *vt* viciar

vitreous /ˈvɪtrɪəs/ *a* vítreo

vituperat|e /vɪˈtjuːpəreɪt/ *vt* vituperar. ∼**ion** /-ˈreɪʃn/ *n* vituperación *f*

vivaci|ous /vɪˈveɪʃəs/ *a* animado, vivo. ∼**ously** *adv* animadamente. ∼**ty** /-ˈvæsətɪ/ *n* viveza *f*

vivid /ˈvɪvɪd/ *a* vivo. ∼**ly** *adv* intensamente; (*describe*) gráficamente. ∼**ness** *n* viveza *f*

vivisection /vɪvɪˈsekʃn/ *n* vivisección *f*

vixen /ˈvɪksn/ *n* zorra *f*

vocabulary /vəˈkæbjʊlərɪ/ *n* vocabulario *m*

vocal /ˈvəʊkl/ *a* vocal; (*fig*) franco. ∼**ist** *n* cantante *m & f*

vocation /vəʊˈkeɪʃn/ *n* vocación *f*. ∼**al** *a* profesional

vociferate /vəˈsɪfəreɪt/ *vt/i* vociferar. ∼**ous** *a* vociferador

vogue /vəʊg/ *n* boga *f*. **in** ∼ de moda

voice /vɔɪs/ *n* voz *f*. ● *vt* expresar

void /vɔɪd/ *a* vacío; (*not valid*) nulo. ∼ **of** desprovisto de. ● *n* vacío *m*. ● *vt* anular

volatile /ˈvɒlətaɪl/ *a* volátil; ⟨*person*⟩ voluble

volcan|ic /vɒlˈkænɪk/ *a* volcánico. ∼**o** /vɒlˈkeɪnəʊ/ *n* (*pl* **-oes**) volcán *m*

volition /vəˈlɪʃn/ *n*. **of one's own** ∼ de su propia voluntad

volley /ˈvɒlɪ/ *n* (*pl* **-eys**) (*of blows*) lluvia *f*; (*of gunfire*) descarga *f* cerrada

volt /vəʊlt/ *n* voltio *m*. ∼**age** *n* voltaje *m*

voluble /ˈvɒljʊbl/ *a* locuaz

volume /ˈvɒljuːm/ *n* volumen *m*; (*book*) tomo *m*

voluminous /vəˈljuːmɪnəs/ *a* voluminoso

voluntar|ily /ˈvɒləntərəlɪ/ *adv* voluntariamente. ∼**y** /ˈvɒləntərɪ/ *a* voluntario

volunteer /vɒlənˈtɪə(r)/ *n* voluntario *m*. ● *vt* ofrecer. ● *vi* ofrecerse voluntariamente; (*mil*) alistarse como voluntario

voluptuous /vəˈlʌptjʊəs/ *a* voluptuoso

vomit /ˈvɒmɪt/ *vt/i* vomitar. ● *n* vómito *m*

voracious /vəˈreɪʃəs/ *a* voraz

vot|e /vəʊt/ *n* voto *m*; (*right*) derecho *m* de votar. ● *vi* votar. ∼**er** /-ə(r)/ *n* votante *m & f*. ∼**ing** *n* votación *f*

vouch /vaʊtʃ/ *vi*. ∼ **for** garantizar

voucher /ˈvaʊtʃə(r)/ *n* vale *m*

vow /vaʊ/ *n* voto *m*. ● *vi* jurar

vowel /ˈvaʊəl/ *n* vocal *f*

voyage /ˈvɔɪɪdʒ/ *n* viaje *m* (en barco)

vulgar /ˈvʌlgə(r)/ *a* vulgar. ∼**ity** /-ˈgærətɪ/ *n* vulgaridad *f*. ∼**ize** *vt* vulgarizar

vulnerab|ility /vʌlnərəˈbɪləti/ *n* vulnerabilidad *f*. **~le** /ˈvʌlnərəbl/ *a* vulnerable

vulture /ˈvʌltʃə(r)/ *n* buitre *m*

vying /ˈvaɪɪŋ/ *see* **vie**

W

wad /wɒd/ *n* (*pad*) tapón *m*; (*bundle*) lío *m*; (*of notes*) fajo *m*; (*of cotton wool etc*) bolita *f*

wadding /ˈwɒdɪŋ/ *n* relleno *m*

waddle /ˈwɒdl/ *vi* contonearse

wade /weɪd/ *vt* vadear. ● *vi*. **~ through** abrirse paso entre; leer con dificultad ⟨*book*⟩

wafer /ˈweɪfə(r)/ *n* barquillo *m*; (*relig*) hostia *f*

waffle[1] /ˈwɒfl/ *n* (*fam*) palabrería *f*. ● *vi* (*fam*) divagar

waffle[2] /ˈwɒfl/ *n* (*culin*) gofre *m*

waft /wɒft/ *vt* llevar por el aire. ● *vi* flotar

wag /wæg/ *vt* (*pt* **wagged**) menear. ● *vi* menearse

wage /weɪdʒ/ *n*. **~s** *npl* salario *m*. ● *vt*. **~ war** hacer la guerra. **~r** /ˈweɪdʒə(r)/ *n* apuesta *f*. ● *vt* apostar

waggle /ˈwægl/ *vt* menear. ● *vi* menearse

wagon /ˈwægən/ *n* carro *m*; (*rail*) vagón *m*. **be on the ~** (*sl*) no beber

waif /weɪf/ *n* niño *m* abandonado

wail /weɪl/ *vi* lamentarse. ● *n* lamento *m*

wainscot /ˈweɪnskət/ *n* revestimiento *m*, zócalo *m*

waist /weɪst/ *n* cintura *f*. **~band** *n* cinturón *m*

waistcoat /ˈweɪstkəʊt/ *n* chaleco *m*

waistline /ˈweɪstleɪn/ *n* cintura *f*

wait /weɪt/ *vt/i* esperar; (*at table*) servir. **~ for** esperar. **~ on** servir. ● *n* espera *f*. **lie in ~** acechar

waiter /ˈweɪtə(r)/ *n* camarero *m*

wait: ~ing-list *n* lista *f* de espera. **~ing-room** *n* sala *f* de espera

waitress /ˈweɪtrɪs/ *n* camarera *f*

waive /weɪv/ *vt* renunciar a

wake[1] /weɪk/ *vt* (*pt* **woke**, *pp* **woken**) despertar. ● *vi* despertarse. ● *n* velatorio *m*. **~ up** *vt* despertar. ● *vi* despertarse

wake[2] /weɪk/ *n* (*naut*) estela *f*. **in the ~ of** como resultado de, tras

waken /ˈweɪkən/ *vt* despertar. ● *vi* despertarse

wakeful /ˈweɪkfl/ *a* insomne

Wales /weɪlz/ *n* País *m* de Gales

walk /wɔːk/ *vi* andar; (*not ride*) ir a pie; (*stroll*) pasearse. **~ out** salir; ⟨*workers*⟩ declararse en huelga. **~ out on** abandonar. ● *vt* andar por ⟨*streets*⟩; llevar de paseo ⟨*dog*⟩. ● *n* paseo *m*; (*gait*) modo *m* de andar; (*path*) sendero *m*. **~ of life** clase *f* social. **~about** /ˈwɔːkəbaʊt/ *n* (*of royalty*) encuentro *m* con el público. **~er** /-ə(r)/ *n* paseante *m* & *f*

walkie-talkie /wɔːkɪˈtɔːkɪ/ *n* transmisor-receptor *m* portátil

walking /ˈwɔːkɪŋ/ *n* paseo *m*. **~-stick** *n* bastón *m*

Walkman /ˈwɔːkmən/ *n* (*P*) estéreo *m* personal, Walkman *m* (*P*), magnetófono *m* de bolsillo

walk: ~-out *n* huelga *f*. **~-over** *n* victoria *f* fácil

wall /wɔːl/ *n* (*interior*) pared *f*; (*exterior*) muro *m*; (*in garden*) tapia *f*; (*of city*) muralla *f*. **go to the ~** fracasar. **up the ~** (*fam*) loco. ● *vt* amurallar ⟨*city*⟩

wallet /ˈwɒlɪt/ *n* cartera *f*, billetera *f* (*LAm*)

wallflower /ˈwɔːlflaʊə(r)/ *n* alhelí *m*

wallop /ˈwɒləp/ *vt* (*pt* **walloped**) (*sl*) golpear con fuerza. ● *n* (*sl*) golpe *m* fuerte

wallow /ˈwɒləʊ/ *vi* revolcarse

wallpaper /ˈwɔːlpeɪpə(r)/ *n* papel *m* pintado

walnut /ˈwɔːlnʌt/ *n* nuez *f*; (*tree*) nogal *m*

walrus /ˈwɔːlrəs/ *n* morsa *f*

waltz /wɔːls/ *n* vals *m*. ● *vi* valsar

wan /wɒn/ *a* pálido

wand /wɒnd/ *n* varita *f*

wander /ˈwɒndə(r)/ *vi* vagar; (*stroll*) pasearse; (*digress*) divagar; ⟨*road, river*⟩ serpentear. ● *n* paseo *m*. **~er** /-ə(r)/ *n* vagabundo *m*. **~lust** /ˈwɒndəlʌst/ *n* pasión *f* por los viajes

wane /weɪn/ *vi* menguar. ● *n*. **on the ~** disminuyendo

wangle /ˈwæŋgl/ *vt* (*sl*) agenciarse

want /wɒnt/ *vt* querer; (*need*) necesitar; (*require*) exigir. ● *vi*. **~ for** carecer de. ● *n* necesidad *f*; (*lack*) falta *f*; (*desire*) deseo *m*. **~ed** *a* ⟨*criminal*⟩ buscado. **~ing** *a* (*lacking*) falto de. **be ~ing** carecer de

wanton /ˈwɒntən/ *a* (*licentious*) lascivo; (*motiveless*) sin motivo

war /wɔː(r)/ *n* guerra *f*. **at ~** en guerra

warble /'wɔ:bl/ vt cantar trinando.
● vi gorjear. ● n gorjeo m. **~r** /-ə(r)/
n curruca f

ward /wɔ:d/ n (in hospital) sala f; (of
town) barrio m; (child) pupilo m.
● vt. **~ off** parar

warden /'wɔ:dn/ n guarda m

warder /'wɔ:də(r)/ n carcelero m

wardrobe /'wɔ:drəub/ n armario m;
(clothes) vestuario m

warehouse /'weəhaus/ n almacén m

wares /weəz/ npl mercancías fpl

war: **~fare** /'wɔ:feə(r)/ n guerra f.
~head /'wɔ:hed/ n cabeza f
explosiva

warily /'weərɪlɪ/ adv cautelosamente

warlike /'wɔ:laɪk/ a belicoso

warm /wɔ:m/ a (-er, -est) caliente;
(hearty) caluroso. **be ~** ⟨person⟩
tener calor. **it is ~** hace calor. ● vt.
~ (up) calentar; recalentar ⟨food⟩;
(fig) animar. ● vi. **~ (up)** calentarse; (fig) animarse. **~ to** tomar
simpatía a ⟨person⟩; ir entu-
siasmándose por ⟨idea etc⟩.
~-blooded a de sangre caliente.
~-hearted a simpático. **~ly** adv
(heartily) calurosamente

warmonger /'wɔ:mʌŋɡə(r)/ n beli-
cista m & f

warmth /wɔ:mθ/ n calor m

warn /wɔ:n/ vt avisar, advertir.
~ing n advertencia f; (notice) aviso
m. **~ off** (advise against) aconsejar
en contra de; (forbid) impedir

warp /wɔ:p/ vt deformar; (fig) per-
vertir. ● vi deformarse

warpath /'wɔ:pɑ:θ/ n. **be on the ~**
buscar camorra

warrant /'wɒrənt/ n autorización f;
(for arrest) orden f. ● vt justificar.
~officer n suboficial m

warranty /'wɒrəntɪ/ n garantía f

warring /'wɔ:rɪŋ/ a en guerra

warrior /'wɒrɪə(r)/ n guerrero m

warship /'wɔ:ʃɪp/ n buque m de
guerra

wart /wɔ:t/ n verruga f

wartime /'wɔ:taɪm/ n tiempo m de
guerra

wary /'weərɪ/ a (-ier, -iest) cauteloso

was /wəz, wɒz/ see **be**

wash /wɒʃ/ vt lavar; (flow over)
bañar. ● vi lavarse. ● n lavado m;
(dirty clothes) ropa f sucia; (wet
clothes) colada f; (of ship) estela f.
have a ~ lavarse. **~ out** vt enjuagar; (fig) cancelar. **~ up** vi fregar

los platos. **~able** a lavable. **~-basin**
n lavabo m. **~ed-out** a (pale) pálido;
(tired) rendido. **~er** /'wɒʃə(r)/ n
arandela f; (washing-machine) lavadora f. **~ing** /'wɒʃɪŋ/ n lavado m;
(dirty clothes) ropa f sucia; (wet
clothes) colada f. **~ing-machine** n
lavadora f. **~ing-powder** n jabón m
en polvo. **~ing-up** n fregado m;
(dirty plates etc) platos mpl para fregar. **~out** n (sl) desastre m.
~room n (Amer) servicios mpl.
~stand n lavabo m. **~tub** n tina f
de lavar

wasp /wɒsp/ n avispa f

wastage /'weɪstɪdʒ/ n desperdicios
mpl

waste /weɪst/ ● a de desecho; ⟨land⟩
yermo. ● n derroche m; (rubbish)
desperdicio m; (of time) pérdida f.
● vt derrochar; (not use) desperdiciar; perder ⟨time⟩. ● vi. **~ away**
consumirse. **~-disposal unit** n trituradora f de basuras. **~ful** a dis-
pendioso; ⟨person⟩ derrochador.
~-paper basket n papelera f. **~s** npl
tierras fpl baldías

watch /wɒtʃ/ vt mirar; (keep an eye
on) vigilar; (take heed) tener cuidado con; ver ⟨TV⟩. ● vi mirar; (keep
an eye on) vigilar. ● n vigilancia f;
(period of duty) guardia f; (time-
piece) reloj m. **on the ~** alerta. **~
out** vi tener cuidado. **~-dog** n perro
m guardián; (fig) guardián m. **~ful**
a vigilante. **~-maker**
/'wɒtʃmeɪkə(r)/ n relojero m. **~-man**
/'wɒtʃmən/ n (pl -men) vigilante m.
~-tower n atalaya f. **~-word**
/'wɒtʃwɜ:d/ n santo m y seña

water /'wɔ:tə(r)/ n agua f. **by ~** (of
travel) por mar. **in hot ~** (fam) en
un apuro. ● vt regar ⟨plants etc⟩;
(dilute) aguar, diluir. ● vi ⟨eyes⟩ llorar. **make s.o.'s mouth ~** hacérsele
la boca agua. **~ down** vt diluir; (fig)
suavizar. **~-closet** n wáter m. **~-col-
our** n acuarela f. **~-course** /'wɔ:təkɔ:
s/ n arroyo m; (artificial) canal m.
~-cress /'wɔ:təkres/ n berro m. **~-fall**
/'wɔ:təfɔ:l/ n cascada f. **~-ice** n sorbete m. **~ing-can** /'wɔ:tərɪŋkæn/ n
regadera f. **~-lily** n nenúfar m.
~-line n línea f de flotación. **~-log-
ged** /'wɔ:təlɒgd/ a saturado de agua,
empapado. **~ main** n cañería f principal. **~ melon** n sandía f. **~-mill** n
molino m de agua. **~ polo** n polo m

acuático. **~power** n energía f hidráulica. **~proof** /'wɔːtəpruːf/ a & n impermeable (m); ⟨watch⟩ sumergible. **~shed** /'wɔːtəʃed/ n punto m decisivo. **~skiing** n esquí m acuático. **~softener** n ablandador m de agua. **~tight** /'wɔːtətaɪt/ a hermético, estanco; (fig) irrecusable. **~way** n canal m navegable. **~wheel** n rueda f hidráulica. **~wings** npl flotadores mpl. **~works** /'wɔːtəwɜːks/ n sistema m de abastecimiento de agua. **~y** /'wɔːtəri/ a acuoso; ⟨colour⟩ pálido; ⟨eyes⟩ lloroso

watt /wɒt/ n vatio m

wave /weɪv/ n onda f; (of hand) señal f; (fig) oleada f. ● vt agitar; ondular ⟨hair⟩. ● vi (signal) hacer señales con la mano; ⟨flag⟩ flotar. **~band** /'weɪvbænd/ n banda f de ondas. **~length** /'weɪvleŋθ/ n longitud f de onda

waver /'weɪvə(r)/ vi vacilar

wavy /'weɪvɪ/ a (-ier, -iest) ondulado

wax¹ /wæks/ n cera f. ● vt encerar

wax² /wæks/ vi ⟨moon⟩ crecer

wax: **~en** a céreo. **~work** /'wækswɜːk/ n figura f de cera. **~y** a céreo

way /weɪ/ n camino m; (distance) distancia f; (manner) manera f, modo m; (direction) dirección f; (means) medio m; (habit) costumbre f. **be in the ~** estorbar. **by the ~** a propósito. **by ~ of** a título de, por. **either ~** de cualquier modo. **in a ~** en cierta manera. **in some ~s** en ciertos modos. **lead the ~** mostrar el camino. **make ~** dejar paso a. **on the ~** en camino. **out of the ~** remoto; (extraordinary) fuera de lo común. **that ~** por allí. **this ~** por aquí. **under ~** en curso. **~bill** n hoja f de ruta. **~farer** /'weɪfeərə(r)/ n viajero m. **~ in** n entrada f

waylay /weɪ'leɪ/ vt (pt -laid) acechar; (detain) detener

way: **~ out** n salida f. **~-out** a ultramoderno, original. **~s** npl costumbres fpl. **~side** /'weɪsaɪd/ n borde m del camino

wayward /'weɪwəd/ a caprichoso

we /wiː/ pron nosotros, nosotras

weak /wiːk/ a (-er, -est) débil; ⟨liquid⟩ aguado, acuoso; (fig) flojo. **~en** vt debilitar. **~kneed** a irresoluto. **~ling** /'wiːklɪŋ/ n persona f débil. **~ly** adv débilmente. ● a enfermizo. **~ness** n debilidad f

weal /wiːl/ n verdugón m

wealth /welθ/ n riqueza f. **~y** a (-ier, -iest) rico

wean /wiːn/ vt destetar

weapon /'wepən/ n arma f

wear /weə(r)/ vt (pt wore, pp worn) llevar; (put on) ponerse; tener ⟨expression etc⟩; (damage) desgastar. ● vi desgastarse; (last) durar. ● n uso m; (damage) desgaste m; (clothing) ropa f. **~ down** vt desgastar; agotar ⟨opposition etc⟩. **~ off** vi desaparecer. **~ on** vi ⟨time⟩ pasar. **~ out** vt desgastar; (tire) agotar. **~able** a que se puede llevar. **~ and tear** desgaste m

wear|ily /'wɪərɪlɪ/ adv cansadamente. **~iness** n cansancio m. **~isome** /'wɪərɪsəm/ a cansado. **~y** /'wɪərɪ/ a (-ier, -iest) cansado. ● vt cansar. ● vi cansarse. **~y of** cansarse de

weasel /'wiːzl/ n comadreja f

weather /'weðə(r)/ n tiempo m. **under the ~** (fam) indispuesto. ● a meteorológico. ● vt curar ⟨wood⟩; (survive) superar. **~beaten** a curtido. **~cock** /'weðəkɒk/ n, **~vane** n veleta f

weave /wiːv/ vt (pt wove, pp woven) tejer; entretejer ⟨story etc⟩; entrelazar ⟨flowers etc⟩. **~ one's way** abrirse paso. ● n tejido m. **~r** /-ə(r)/ n tejedor m

web /web/ n tela f; (of spider) telaraña f; (on foot) membrana f. **~bing** n cincha f

wed /wed/ vt (pt wedded) casarse con; ⟨priest etc⟩ casar. ● vi casarse. **~ded to** (fig) unido a

wedding /'wedɪŋ/ n boda f. **~cake** n pastel m de boda. **~ring** n anillo m de boda

wedge /wedʒ/ n cuña f; (space filler) calce m. ● vt acuñar; (push) apretar

wedlock /'wedlɒk/ n matrimonio m

Wednesday /'wenzdeɪ/ n miércoles m

wee /wiː/ a (fam) pequeñito

weed /wiːd/ n mala hierba f. ● vt desherbar. **~killer** n herbicida m. **~ out** eliminar. **~y** a ⟨person⟩ débil

week /wiːk/ n semana f. **~day** /'wiːkdeɪ/ n día m laborable. **~end** n fin m de semana. **~ly** /'wiːklɪ/ a semanal. ● n semanario m. ● adv semanalmente

weep /wiːp/ vi (pt wept) llorar. **~ing willow** n sauce m llorón

weevil /'wiːvɪl/ n gorgojo m

weigh /weɪ/ vt/i pesar. ~ **anchor** levar anclas. ~ **down** vt (fig) oprimir. ~ **up** vt pesar; (fig) considerar

weight /weɪt/ n peso m. ~**less** a ingrávido. ~**lessness** n ingravidez f. ~**lifting** n halterofilia f, levantamiento m de pesos. ~**y** a (-**ier**, -**iest**) pesado; (influential) influyente

weir /wɪə(r)/ n presa f

weird /wɪəd/ a (-**er**, -**est**) misterioso; (bizarre) extraño

welcome /'welkəm/ a bienvenido. ~ **to do** libre de hacer. **you're** ~**e!** (after thank you) ¡de nada! ● n bienvenida f; (reception) acogida f. ● vt dar la bienvenida a; (appreciate) alegrarse de

welcoming /'welkəmɪŋ/ a acogedor

weld /weld/ vt soldar. ● n soldadura f. ~**er** n soldador m

welfare /'welfeə(r)/ n bienestar m; (aid) asistencia f social. **W~ State** n estado m benefactor. ~ **work** n asistencia f social

well[1] /wel/ adv (**better**, **best**) bien. ~ **done!** ¡bravo! **as** ~ también. **as** ~ **as** tanto... como. **be** ~ estar bien. **do** ~ (succeed) tener éxito. **very** ~ muy bien. ● a bien. ● int bueno; (surprise) ¡vaya! ~ **I never!** ¡no me digas!

well[2] /wel/ n pozo m; (of staircase) caja f

well: ~**appointed** a bien equipado. ~**behaved** a bien educado. ~**being** n bienestar m. ~**bred** a bien educado. ~**disposed** a benévolo. ~**groomed** a bien aseado. ~**heeled** a (fam) rico

wellington /'welɪŋtən/ n bota f de agua

well: ~**knit** a robusto. ~**known** a conocido. ~**meaning** a, ~ **meant** a bienintencionado. ~ **off** a acomodado. ~**read** a culto. ~**spoken** a bienhablado. ~**to-do** a rico. ~**wisher** n bienqueriente m & f

Welsh /welʃ/ a & n galés (m). ~ **rabbit** n pan m tostado con queso

welsh /welʃ/ vi. ~ **on** no cumplir con

wench /wentʃ/ n (old use) muchacha f

wend /wend/ vt. ~ **one's way** encaminarse

went /went/ see **go**

wept /wept/ see **weep**

were /wɜː(r), wə(r)/ see **be**

west /west/ n oeste m. **the** ~ el Occidente m. ● a del oeste. ● adv hacia el oeste, al oeste. **go** ~ (sl) morir. **W~ Germany** n Alemania f Occidental. ~**erly** a del oeste. ~**ern** a occidental. ● n (film) película f del Oeste. ~**erner** /-ənə(r)/ n occidental m & f. **W~ Indian** a & n antillano (m). **W~ Indies** npl Antillas fpl. ~**ward** a, ~**ward(s)** adv hacia el oeste

wet /wet/ a (**wetter**, **wettest**) mojado; (rainy) lluvioso, de lluvia; (person, sl) soso. ~ **paint** recién pintado. **get** ~ mojarse. ● vt (pt **wetted**) mojar, humedecer. ~ **blanket** n aguafiestas m & f invar. ~ **suit** n traje m de buzo

whack /wæk/ vt (fam) golpear. ● n (fam) golpe m. ~**ed** /wækt/ a (fam) agotado. ~**ing** a (huge, sl) enorme. ● n paliza f

whale /weɪl/ n ballena f. **a** ~ **of a** (fam) maravilloso, enorme

wham /wæm/ int ¡zas!

wharf /wɔːf/ n (pl **wharves** or **wharfs**) muelle m

what /wɒt/ a el que, la que, lo que, los que, las que; (in questions & exclamations) qué. ● pron lo que; (interrogative) qué. ~ **about going?** ¿si fuésemos? ~ **about me?** ¿y yo? ~ **for?** ¿para qué? ~ **if?** ¿y si? ~ **is it?** ¿qué es? ~ **you need** lo que te haga falta. ● int ¡cómo! ~ **a fool!** ¡qué tonto!

whatever /wɒt'evə(r)/ a cualquiera. ● pron (todo) lo que, cualquier cosa que

whatnot /'wɒtnɒt/ n chisme m

whatsoever /wɒtsəʊ'evə(r)/ a & pron = **whatever**

wheat /wiːt/ n trigo m. ~**en** a de trigo

wheedle /'wiːdl/ vt engatusar

wheel /wiːl/ n rueda f. **at the** ~ al volante. **steering-**~ n volante m. ● vt empujar ⟨bicycle etc⟩. ● vi girar. ~ **round** girar. ~**barrow** /'wiːlbærəʊ/ n carretilla f. ~**chair** /'wiːltʃeə(r)/ n silla f de ruedas

wheeze /wiːz/ vi resollar. ● n resuello m

when /wen/ adv cuándo. ● conj cuando

whence /wens/ adv de dónde

whenever /wen'evə(r)/ adv en cualquier momento; (every time that) cada vez que

where /weə(r)/ adv & conj donde; (interrogative) dónde. ~ **are you going?** ¿adónde vas? ~ **are you from?** ¿de dónde eres?

whereabouts /'weərəbauts/ adv dónde. ● n paradero m

whereas /weər'æz/ conj por cuanto; (in contrast) mientras (que)

whereby /weə'baɪ/ adv por lo cual

whereupon /weərə'pɒn/ adv después de lo cual

wherever /weər'evə(r)/ adv (in whatever place) dónde (diablos). ● conj dondequiera que

whet /wet/ vt (pt whetted) afilar; (fig) aguzar

whether /'weðə(r)/ conj si. ~ **you like it or not** que te guste o no te guste. **I don't know** ~ **she will like it** no sé si le gustará

which /wɪtʃ/ a (in questions) qué. ~ **one** cuál. ~ **one of you** cuál de vosotros. ● pron (in questions) cuál; (relative) que; (object) el cual, la cual, lo cual, los cuales, las cuales

whichever /wɪtʃ'evə(r)/ a cualquier. ● pron cualquiera que, el que, la que

whiff /wɪf/ n soplo m; (of smoke) bocanada f; (smell) olorcillo m

while /waɪl/ n rato m. ● conj mientras; (although) aunque ● vt. ~ **away** pasar (time)

whilst /waɪlst/ conj = **while**

whim /wɪm/ n capricho m

whimper /'wɪmpə(r)/ vi lloriquear. ● n lloriqueo m

whimsical /'wɪmzɪkl/ a caprichoso; (odd) extraño

whine /waɪn/ vi gimotear. ● n gimoteo m

whip /wɪp/ n látigo m; (pol) oficial m disciplinario. ● vt (pt whipped) azotar; (culin) batir; (seize) agarrar. ~**cord** n tralla f. ~**ped cream** n nata f batida. ~**ping-boy** /'wɪpɪŋbɔɪ/ n cabeza f de turco. ~**round** n colecta f. ~ **up** (incite) estimular

whirl /wɜːl/ vt hacer girar rápidamente. ● vi girar rápidamente; (swirl) arremolinarse. ● n giro m; (swirl) remolino m. ~**pool** /'wɜːlpuːl/ n remolino m. ~**wind** /'wɜːlwɪnd/ n torbellino m

whirr /wɜː(r)/ n zumbido m. ● vi zumbar

whisk /wɪsk/ vt (culin) batir. ● n (culin) batidor m. ~ **away** llevarse

whisker /'wɪskə(r)/ n pelo m. ~**s** npl (of man) patillas fpl; (of cat etc) bigotes mpl

whisky /'wɪskɪ/ n güisqui m

whisper /'wɪspə(r)/ vt decir en voz baja. ● vi cuchichear; (leaves etc) susurrar. ● n cuchicheo m; (of leaves) susurro m; (rumour) rumor m

whistle /'wɪsl/ n silbido m; (instrument) silbato m. ● vi silbar. ~**stop** n (pol) breve parada f (en gira electoral)

white /waɪt/ a (-er, -est) blanco. **go** ~ ponerse pálido. ● n blanco; (of egg) clara f. ~**bait** /'waɪtbeɪt/ n (pl ~bait) chanquetes mpl. ~ **coffee** n café m con leche. ~**collar worker** n empleado m de oficina. ~ **elephant** n objeto m inútil y costoso

Whitehall /'waɪthɔːl/ n el gobierno m británico

white: ~ **horses** n cabrillas fpl. ~**hot** a (metal) candente. ~ **lie** n mentirijilla f. ~**n** vt/i blanquear. ~**ness** n blancura f. **W**~ **Paper** n libro m blanco. ~**wash** /'waɪtwɒʃ/ n jalbegue m; (fig) encubrimiento m. ● vt enjalbegar; (fig) encubrir

whiting /'waɪtɪŋ/ n (pl whiting) (fish) pescadilla f

whitlow /'wɪtləʊ/ n panadizo m

Whitsun /'wɪtsn/ n Pentecostés m

whittle /'wɪtl/ vt. ~ (**down**) tallar; (fig) reducir

whiz /wɪz/ vi (pt whizzed) silbar; (rush) ir a gran velocidad. ~ **past** pasar como un rayo. ~**kid** n (fam) joven m prometedor, promesa f

who /huː/ pron que, quien; (interrogative) quién; (particular person) el que, la que, los que, las que

whodunit /huː'dʌnɪt/ n (fam) novela f policíaca

whoever /huː'evə(r)/ pron quienquera que; (interrogative) quién (diablos)

whole /həʊl/ a entero; (not broken) intacto. ● n todo m, conjunto m; (total) total m. **as a** ~ en conjunto. **on the** ~ por regla general. ~**hearted** a sincero. ~**meal** a integral

wholesale /'həʊlseɪl/ n venta f al por mayor. ● a & adv al por mayor. ~**r** /-ə(r)/ n comerciante m & f al por mayor

wholesome /'həʊlsəm/ a saludable

wholly /'həʊlɪ/ adv completamente

whom /huːm/ *pron* que, a quien; (*interrogative*) a quién

whooping cough /'huːpɪŋkɒf/ *n* tos *f* ferina

whore /hɔː(r)/ *n* puta *f*

whose /huːz/ *pron* de quién. ● *a* de quién; (*relative*) cuyo

why /waɪ/ *adv* por qué. ● *int* ¡toma!

wick /wɪk/ *n* mecha *f*

wicked /'wɪkɪd/ *a* malo; (*mischievous*) travieso; (*very bad, fam*) malísimo. ∼**ness** *n* maldad *f*

wicker /'wɪkə(r)/ *n* mimbre *m* & *f*. ● *a* de mimbre. ∼**work** *n* artículos *mpl* de mimbre

wicket /'wɪkɪt/ *n* (*cricket*) rastrillo *m*

wide /waɪd/ *a* (**-er, -est**) ancho; (*fully opened*) de par en par; (*far from target*) lejano; ⟨*knowledge etc*⟩ amplio. ● *adv* lejos. **far and** ∼ por todas partes. ∼ **awake** *a* completamente despierto; (*fig*) despabilado. ∼**ly** *adv* extensamente; (*believed*) generalmente; (*different*) muy. ∼**n** *vt* ensanchar

widespread /'waɪdspred/ *a* extendido; (*fig*) difundido

widow /'wɪdəʊ/ *n* viuda *f*. ∼**ed** *a* viudo. ∼**er** *n* viudo *m*. ∼**hood** *n* viudez *f*

width /wɪdθ/ *n* anchura *f*. **in** ∼ de ancho

wield /wiːld/ *vt* manejar; ejercer ⟨*power*⟩

wife /waɪf/ *n* (*pl* **wives**) mujer *f*, esposa *f*

wig /wɪg/ *n* peluca *f*

wiggle /'wɪgl/ *vt* menear. ● *vi* menearse

wild /waɪld/ *a* (**-er, -est**) salvaje; (*enraged*) furioso; ⟨*idea*⟩ extravagante; (*with joy*) loco; (*random*) al azar. ● *adv* en estado salvaje. **run** ∼ crecer en estado salvaje. ∼**s** *npl* regiones *fpl* salvajes

wildcat /'waɪldkæt/ *a*. ∼ **strike** *n* huelga *f* salvaje

wilderness /'wɪldənɪs/ *n* desierto *m*

wild: ∼**fire** /'waɪldfaɪl(r)/ *n*. **spread like** ∼**fire** correr como un reguero de pólvora. ∼**goose chase** *n* empresa *f* inútil. ∼**life** /'waɪldlaɪf/ *n* fauna *f*. ∼**ly** *adv* violentamente; (*fig*) locamente

wilful /'wɪlfʊl/ *a* intencionado; (*self-willed*) terco. ∼**ly** *adv* intencionadamente; (*obstinately*) obstinadamente

will¹ /wɪl/ *v aux.* ∼ **you have some wine?** ¿quieres vino? **he** ∼ **be** será. **you** ∼ **be back soon, won't you?** volverás pronto, ¿no?

will² /wɪl/ *n* voluntad *f*; (*document*) testamento *m*

willing /'wɪlɪŋ/ *a* complaciente. ∼ **to** dispuesto a. ∼**ly** *adv* de buena gana. ∼**ness** *n* buena voluntad *f*

willow /'wɪləʊ/ *n* sauce *m*

will-power /'wɪlpaʊə(r)/ *n* fuerza *f* de voluntad

willy-nilly /wɪlɪ'nɪlɪ/ *adv* quieras que no

wilt /wɪlt/ *vi* marchitarse

wily /'waɪlɪ/ *a* (**-ier, -iest**) astuto

win /wɪn/ *vt* (*pt* **won**, *pres p* **winning**) ganar; (*achieve, obtain*) conseguir. ● *vi* ganar. ● *n* victoria *f*. ∼ **back** *vi* reconquistar. ∼ **over** *vt* convencer

wince /wɪns/ *vi* hacer una mueca de dolor. **without wincing** sin pestañear. ● *n* mueca *f* de dolor

winch /wɪntʃ/ *n* cabrestante *m*. ● *vt* levantar con el cabrestante

wind¹ /wɪnd/ *n* viento *m*; (*in stomach*) flatulencia *f*. **get the** ∼ **up** (*sl*) asustarse. **get** ∼ **of** enterarse de. **in the** ∼ en el aire. ● *vt* dejar sin aliento.

wind² /waɪnd/ *vt* (*pt* **wound**) (*wrap around*) enrollar; dar cuerda a ⟨*clock etc*⟩. ● *vi* ⟨*road etc*⟩ serpentear. ∼ **up** *vt* dar cuerda a ⟨*watch, clock*⟩; (*provoke*) agitar, poner nervioso; (*fig*) terminar, concluir

wind /wɪnd/: ∼**bag** *n* charlatán *m*. ∼**cheater** *n* cazadora *f*

winder /'waɪndə(r)/ *n* devanador *m*; (*of clock, watch*) llave *f*

windfall /'wɪndfɔːl/ *n* fruta *f* caída; (*fig*) suerte *f* inesperada

winding /'waɪndɪŋ/ *a* tortuoso

wind instrument /'wɪndɪnstrəmənt/ *n* instrumento *m* de viento

windmill /'wɪndmɪl/ *n* molino *m* (de viento)

window /'wɪndəʊ/ *n* ventana *f*; (*in shop*) escaparate *m*; (*of vehicle, booking-office*) ventanilla *f*. ∼**box** *n* jardinera *f*. ∼**dresser** *n* escaparatista *m* & *f*. ∼**shop** *vi* mirar los escaparates

windpipe /'wɪndpaɪp/ *n* tráquea *f*

windscreen /'wɪndskriːn/ *n*, **windshield** *n* (*Amer*) parabrisas *m invar*. ∼ **wiper** *n* limpiaparabrisas *m invar*

wind /wɪnd/: ~**swept** a barrido por el viento. ~**y** a (**-ier, -iest**) ventoso, de mucho viento. **it is** ~**y** hace viento

wine /waɪn/ n vino m. ~**cellar** n bodega f. ~**glass** n copa f. ~**grower** n vinicultor m. ~**growing** n vinicultura f. ● a vinícola. ~ **list** n lista f de vinos. ~**tasting** n cata f de vinos

wing /wɪŋ/ n ala f; (*auto*) aleta f. **under one's** ~ bajo la protección de uno. ~**ed** a alado. ~**er** /-ə(r)/ n (*sport*) ala m & f. ~**s** npl (*in theatre*) bastidores mpl

wink /wɪŋk/ vi guiñar el ojo; ⟨*light etc*⟩ centellear. ● n guiño m. **not to sleep a** ~ no pegar ojo

winkle /'wɪŋkl/ n bígaro m

win: ~**ner** /-ə(r)/ n ganador m. ~**ning-post** n poste m de llegada. ~**ning smile** n sonrisa f a encantadora. ~**nings** npl ganancias fpl

winsome /'wɪnsəm/ a atractivo

wint|er /'wɪntə(r)/ n invierno m. ● vi invernar. ~**ry** a invernal

wipe /waɪp/ vt limpiar; (*dry*) secar. ● n limpión m. **give sth a** ~ limpiar algo. ~ **out** (*cancel*) cancelar; (*destroy*) destruir; (*obliterate*) borrar. ~ **up** limpiar; (*dry*) secar

wire /'waɪə(r)/ n alambre m; (*elec*) cable m; (*telegram, fam*) telegrama m

wireless /'waɪəlɪs/ n radio f

wire **netting** /waɪə'netɪŋ/ n alambrera f, tela f metálica

wiring n instalación f eléctrica

wiry /'waɪərɪ/ a (**-ier, -iest**) ⟨*person*⟩ delgado

wisdom /'wɪzdəm/ n sabiduría f. ~ **tooth** n muela f del juicio

wise /waɪz/ a (**-er, -est**) sabio; (*sensible*) prudente. ~**crack** /'waɪzkræk/ n (*fam*) salida f. ~**ly** adv sabiamente; (*sensibly*) prudentemente

wish /wɪʃ/ n deseo m; (*greeting*) saludo m. **with best** ~**es** (*in letters*) un fuerte abrazo. ● vt desear. ~ **on** (*fam*) encajar a. ~ **s.o. well** desear buena suerte a uno. ~**bone** n espoleta f (de las aves). ~**ful** a deseoso. ~**ful thinking** n ilusiones fpl

wishy-washy /'wɪʃɪwɒʃɪ/ a soso; ⟨*person*⟩ sin convicciones, falto de entereza

wisp /wɪsp/ n manojito m; (*of smoke*) voluta f; (*of hair*) mechón m

wisteria /wɪs'tɪərɪə/ n glicina f

wistful /'wɪstfl/ a melancólico

wit /wɪt/ n gracia f; (*person*) persona f chistosa; (*intelligence*) ingenio m. **be at one's** ~**s' end** no saber qué hacer. **live by one's** ~**s** vivir de expedientes, vivir del cuento

witch /wɪtʃ/ n bruja f. ~**craft** n brujería f. ~**doctor** n hechicero m

with /wɪð/ prep con; (*cause, having*) de. **be** ~ **it** (*fam*) estar al día, estar al tanto. **the man** ~ **the beard** el hombre de la barba

withdraw /wɪð'drɔ:/ vt (*pt* **withdrew**, *pp* **withdrawn**) retirar. ● vi apartarse. ~**al** n retirada f. ~**n** a ⟨*person*⟩ introvertido

wither /'wɪðə(r)/ vi marchitarse. ● vt (*fig*) fulminar

withhold /wɪð'həʊld/ vt (*pt* **withheld**) retener; (*conceal*) ocultar (**from** a)

within /wɪð'ɪn/ prep dentro de. ● adv dentro. ~ **sight** a la vista

without /wɪð'aʊt/ prep sin

withstand /wɪð'stænd/ vt (*pt* ~**stood**) resistir a

witness /'wɪtnɪs/ n testigo m; (*proof*) testimonio m. ● vt presenciar; firmar como testigo ⟨*document*⟩. ~**box** n tribuna f de los testigos

witticism /'wɪtɪsɪzəm/ n ocurrencia f

wittingly /'wɪtɪŋlɪ/ adv a sabiendas

witty /'wɪtɪ/ a (**-ier, -iest**) gracioso

wives /waɪvz/ *see* **wife**

wizard /'wɪzəd/ n hechicero m. ~**ry** n hechicería f

wizened /'wɪznd/ a arrugado

wobbl|e /'wɒbl/ vi tambalearse; ⟨*voice, jelly, hand*⟩ temblar; ⟨*chair etc*⟩ balancearse. ~**y** a ⟨*chair etc*⟩ cojo

woe /wəʊ/ n aflicción f. ~**ful** a triste. ~**begone** /'wəʊbɪɡɒn/ a desconsolado

woke, woken /wəʊk, 'wəʊkən/ *see* **wake**[1]

wolf /wʊlf/ n (*pl* **wolves**) lobo m. **cry** ~ gritar al lobo. ● vt zamparse. ~**whistle** n silbido m de admiración

woman /'wʊmən/ n (*pl* **women**) mujer f. **single** ~ soltera f. ~**ize** /'wʊmənaɪz/ vi ser mujeriego. ~**ly** a femenino

womb /wu:m/ n matriz f

women /'wɪmɪn/ npl *see* **woman**. ~**folk** /'wɪmɪnfəʊk/ npl mujeres fpl.

~**'s lib** n movimiento m de liberación de la mujer

won /wʌn/ see **win**

wonder /'wʌndə(r)/ n maravilla f; (*bewilderment*) asombro m. **no** ~ no es de extrañarse (**that** que). ● vi admirarse; (*reflect*) preguntarse

wonderful /'wʌndəfl/ a maravilloso. ~**ly** adv maravillosamente

won't /wəʊnt/ = **will not**

woo /wuː/ vt cortejar

wood /wʊd/ n madera f; (*for burning*) leña f; (*area*) bosque m; (*in bowls*) bola f. **out of the** ~ (*fig*) fuera de peligro. ~**cutter** /'wʊdkʌtə(r)/ n leñador m. ~**ed** a poblado de árboles, boscoso. ~**en** a de madera. ~**land** n bosque m

woodlouse /'wʊdlaʊs/ n (*pl* -**lice**) cochinilla f

woodpecker /'wʊdpekə(r)/ n pájaro m carpintero

woodwind /'wʊdwɪnd/ n instrumentos mpl de viento de madera

woodwork /'wʊdwɜːk/ n carpintería f (*in room etc*) maderaje m

woodworm /'wʊdwɜːm/ n carcoma f

woody /'wʊdɪ/ a leñoso

wool /wʊl/ n lana f. **pull the** ~ **over s.o.'s eyes** engañar a uno. ~**len** a de lana. ~**lens** npl ropa f de lana. ~**ly** a (-**ier**, -**iest**) de lana; (*fig*) confuso. ● n jersey m

word /wɜːd/ n palabra f; (*news*) noticia f. **by** ~ **of mouth** de palabra. **have** ~**s with** reñir con. **in one** ~ en una palabra. **in other** ~**s** es decir. ● vt expresar. ~**ing** n expresión f, términos mpl. ~**perfect** a. **be** ~**perfect** saber de memoria. ~ **processor** n procesador m de textos. ~**y** a prolijo

wore /wɔː(r)/ see **wear**

work /wɜːk/ n trabajo m; (*arts*) obra f. ● vt hacer trabajar; manejar ⟨*machine*⟩. ● vi trabajar; ⟨*machine*⟩ funcionar; ⟨*student*⟩ estudiar; ⟨*drug etc*⟩ tener efecto; (*be successful*) tener éxito. ~ **in** introducir(se). ~ **off** desahogar. ~ **out** vt resolver; (*calculate*) calcular; elaborar ⟨*plan*⟩. ● vi (*succeed*) salir bien; (*sport*) entrenarse. ~ **up** vt desarrollar. ● vi excitarse. ~**able** /'wɜː kəbl/ a ⟨*project*⟩ factible. ~**aholic** /wɜːkə'hɒlɪk/ n trabajador m obsesivo. ~**ed up** a agitado. ~**er** /'wɜː-

kə(r)/ n trabajador m; (*manual*) obrero m

workhouse /'wɜːkhaʊs/ n asilo m de pobres

work: ~**ing** /'wɜːkɪŋ/ a ⟨*day*⟩ laborable; ⟨*clothes etc*⟩ de trabajo. n (*mec*) funcionamiento m. **in** ~**ing order** en estado de funcionamiento. ~**ing class** n clase f obrera. ~**ing-class** a de la clase obrera. ~**man** /'wɜːkmən/ n (*pl* -**men**) obrero m. ~**manlike** /'wɜːkmənlaɪk/ a concienzudo. ~**manship** n destreza f. ~**s** npl (*building*) fábrica f; (*mec*) mecanismo m. ~**shop** /'wɜːkʃɒp/ n taller m. ~**to-rule** n huelga f de celo

world /wɜːld/ n mundo m. **a** ~ **of** enorme. **out of this** ~ maravilloso. ● a mundial. ~**ly** a mundano. ~**wide** a universal

worm /wɜːm/ n lombriz f; (*grub*) gusano m. ● vi. ~ **one's way** insinuarse. ~**eaten** a carcomido

worn /wɔːn/ see **wear**. ● a gastado. ~**out** a gastado; ⟨*person*⟩ rendido

worr|ied /'wʌrɪd/ a preocupado. ~**ier** /-ə(r)/ n aprensivo m. ~**y** /'wʌrɪ/ vt preocupar; (*annoy*) molestar. ● vi preocuparse. ● n preocupación f. ~**ying** a inquietante

worse /wɜːs/ a peor. ● adv peor; (*more*) más. ● n lo peor. ~**n** vt/i empeorar

worship /'wɜːʃɪp/ n culto m; (*title*) señor, su señoría. ● vt (*pt* **worshipped**) adorar

worst /wɜːst/ a (el) peor. ● adv peor. ● n lo peor. **get the** ~ **of it** llevar la peor parte

worsted /'wʊstɪd/ n estambre m

worth /wɜːθ/ n valor m. ● a. **be** ~ valer. **it is** ~ **trying** vale la pena probarlo. **it was** ~ **my while** (me) valió la pena. ~**less** a sin valor. ~**while** /'wɜːθwaɪl/ a que vale la pena

worthy /'wɜːðɪ/ a meritorio; (*respectable*) respetable; (*laudable*) loable

would /wʊd/ v aux. ~ **you come here please?** ¿quieres venir aquí? ~ **you go?** ¿irías tú? **he** ~ **come if he could** vendría si pudiese. **I** ~ **come every day** (*used to*) venía todos los días. **I** ~ **do it** lo haría yo. ~**be** a supuesto

wound[1] /wuːnd/ n herida f. ● vt herir

wound[2] /waʊnd/ see **wind**[2]

wove, woven /wəʊv, 'wəʊvn/ *see* **weave**

wow /waʊ/ *int* ¡caramba!

wrangle /'ræŋgl/ *vi* reñir. ● *n* riña *f*

wrap /ræp/ *vt* (*pt* **wrapped**) envolver. **be ~ped up in** (*fig*) estar absorto en. ● *n* bata *f*; (*shawl*) chal *m*. **~per** /-ə(r)/ *n*, **~ping** *n* envoltura *f*

wrath /rɒθ/ *n* ira *f*. **~ful** *a* iracundo

wreath /ri:θ/ *n* (*pl* **-ths** /-ðz/) guirnalda *f*; (*for funeral*) corona *f*

wreck /rek/ *n* ruina *f*; (*sinking*) naufragio *m*; (*remains of ship*) buque *m* naufragado. **be a nervous ~** tener los nervios destrozados. ● *vt* hacer naufragar; (*fig*) arruinar. **~age** *n* restos *mpl*; (*of building*) escombros *mpl*

wren /ren/ *n* troglodito *m*

wrench /rentʃ/ *vt* arrancar; (*twist*) torcer. ● *n* arranque *m*; (*tool*) llave *f* inglesa

wrest /rest/ *vt* arrancar (**from** a)

wrestl|e /'resl/ *vi* luchar. **~er** /-ə(r)/ *n* luchador *m*. **~ing** *n* lucha *f*

wretch /retʃ/ *n* desgraciado *m*; (*rascal*) tunante *m* & *f*. **~ed** *a* miserable; (*weather*) horrible, de perros; (*dog etc*) maldito

wriggle /'rɪgl/ *vi* culebrear. **~ out of** escaparse de. **~ through** deslizarse por. ● *n* serpenteo *m*

wring /rɪŋ/ *vt* (*pt* **wrung**) retorcer. **~ out of** (*obtain from*) arrancar. **~ing wet** empapado

wrinkle /'rɪŋkl/ *n* arruga *f*. ● *vt* arrugar. ● *vi* arrugarse

wrist /rɪst/ *n* muñeca *f*. **~-watch** *n* reloj *m* de pulsera

writ /rɪt/ *n* decreto *m* judicial

write /raɪt/ *vt/i* (*pt* **wrote**, *pp* **written**, *pres p* **writing**) escribir. **~ down** *vt* anotar. **~ off** *vt* cancelar; (*fig*) dar por perdido. **~ up** *vt* hacer un reportaje de; (*keep up to date*) poner al día. **~-off** *n* pérdida *f* total. **~r** /-ə(r)/ *n* escritor *m*; (*author*) autor *m*. **~-up** *n* reportaje *m*; (*review*) crítica *f*

writhe /raɪð/ *vi* retorcerse

writing /'raɪtɪŋ/ *n* escribir *m*; (*handwriting*) letra *f*. **in ~** por escrito. **~s** *npl* obras *fpl*. **~-paper** *n* papel *m* de escribir

written /'rɪtn/ *see* **write**

wrong /rɒŋ/ *a* incorrecto; (*not just*) injusto; (*mistaken*) equivocado. **be ~** no tener razón; (*be mistaken*) equivocarse. ● *adv* mal. **go ~** equivocarse; (*plan*) salir mal; (*car etc*) estropearse. ● *n* injusticia *f*; (*evil*) mal *m*. **in the ~** equivocado. ● *vt* ser injusto con. **~ful** *a* injusto. **~ly** *adv* mal; (*unfairly*) injustamente

wrote /rəʊt/ *see* **write**

wrought /rɔːt/ *a*. **~ iron** *n* hierro *m* forjado

wrung /rʌŋ/ *see* **wring**

wry /raɪ/ *a* (**wryer, wryest**) torcido. (*smile*) forzado. **~ face** *n* mueca *f*

X

xenophobia /zenə'fəʊbɪə/ *n* xenofobia *f*

Xerox /'zɪərɒks/ *n* (*P*) fotocopiadora *f*. **xerox** *n* fotocopia *f*

Xmas /'krɪsməs/ *n abbr* (*Christmas*) Navidad *f*, Navidades *fpl*

X-ray /'eksreɪ/ *n* radiografía *f*. **~s** *npl* rayos *mpl* X. ● *vt* radiografiar

xylophone /'zaɪləfəʊn/ *n* xilófono *m*

Y

yacht /jɒt/ *n* yate *m*. **~ing** *n* navegación *f* a vela

yam /jæm/ *n* ñame *m*, batata *f*

yank /jæŋk/ *vt* (*fam*) arrancar violentamente

Yankee /'jæŋkɪ/ *n* (*fam*) yanqui *m* & *f*

yap /jæp/ *vi* (*pt* **yapped**) (*dog*) ladrar

yard[1] /jɑːd/ *n* (*measurement*) yarda *f* (= *0.9144 metre*)

yard[2] /jɑːd/ *n* patio *m*; (*Amer, garden*) jardín *m*

yardage /'jɑːdɪdʒ/ *n* metraje *m*

yardstick /'jɑːdstɪk/ *n* (*fig*) criterio *m*

yarn /jɑːn/ *n* hilo *m*; (*tale, fam*) cuento *m*

yashmak /'jæʃmæk/ *n* velo *m*

yawn /jɔːn/ *vi* bostezar. ● *n* bostezo *m*

year /jɪə(r)/ *n* año *m*. **be three ~s old** tener tres años. **~-book** *n* anuario *m*. **~ling** /'jɜːlɪŋ/ *n* primal *m*. **~ly** *a* anual. ● *adv* anualmente

yearn /jɜːn/ *vi*. **~ for** anhelar. **~ing** *n* ansia *f*

yeast /jiːst/ *n* levadura *f*

yell /jel/ *vi* gritar. ● *n* grito *m*

yellow /'jeləʊ/ a & n amarillo (m).
~**ish** a amarillento

yelp /jelp/ n gañido m. ● vi gañir

yen /jen/ n muchas ganas fpl

yeoman /'jəʊmən/ n (pl -men). **Y~ of the Guard** alabardero m de la Casa Real

yes /jes/ adv & n sí (m)

yesterday /'jestədeɪ/ adv & n ayer (m). **the day before** ~ anteayer m

yet /jet/ adv todavía, aún; (already) ya. **as** ~ hasta ahora. ● conj sin embargo

yew /ju:/ n tejo m

Yiddish /'jɪdɪʃ/ n judeoalemán m

yield /ji:ld/ vt producir. ● vi ceder.
● n producción f; (com) rendimiento m

yoga /'jəʊgə/ n yoga m

yoghurt /'jɒgət/ n yogur m

yoke /jəʊk/ n yugo m; (of garment) canesú m

yokel /'jəʊkl/ n patán m, palurdo m

yolk /jəʊk/ n yema f (de huevo)

yonder /'jɒndə(r)/ adv a lo lejos

you /ju:/ pron (familiar form) tú, vos (Arg), (pl) vosotros, vosotras, ustedes (LAm); (polite form) usted, (pl) ustedes; (familiar, object) te, (pl) os, les (LAm); (polite, object) le, la, (pl) les; (familiar, after prep) ti, (pl) vosotros, vosotras, ustedes (LAm); (polite, after prep) usted, (pl) ustedes. **with** ~ (familiar) contigo, (pl) con vosotros, con vosotras, con ustedes (LAm); (polite) con usted, (pl) con ustedes; (polite reflexive) consigo. **I know** ~ te conozco, le conozco a usted. **you can't smoke here** aquí no se puede fumar

young /jʌŋ/ a (-er, -est) joven. ~ **lady** n señorita f. ~ **man** n joven m. **her** ~ **man** (boyfriend) su novio m. **the** ~ npl los jóvenes mpl; (of animals) la cría f. ~**ster** /'jʌŋstə(r)/ n joven m

your /jɔ:(r)/ a (familiar) tu, (pl) vuestro; (polite) su

yours /jɔ:z/ poss pron (el) tuyo, (pl) (el) vuestro, el de ustedes (LAm); (polite) el suyo. **a book of** ~s un libro tuyo, un libro suyo. **Y~s faithfully**, **Y~s sincerely** le saluda atentamente

yourself /jɔ:'self/ pron (pl yourselves) (familiar, subject) tú mismo, tú misma, (pl) vosotros mismos, vosotras mismas, ustedes mismos (LAm), ustedes mismas (LAm);

(polite, subject) usted mismo, usted misma, (pl) ustedes mismos, ustedes mismas; (familiar, object) te, (pl) os, se (LAm); (polite, object) se; (familiar, after prep) ti, (pl) vosotros, vosotras, ustedes (LAm); (polite, after prep) sí

youth /ju:θ/ n (pl youths /ju:ðz/) juventud f; (boy) joven m; (young people) jóvenes mpl. ~**ful** a joven, juvenil. ~**hostel** n albergue m para jóvenes

yowl /jaʊl/ vi aullar. ● n aullido m

Yugoslav /'ju:gəslɑ:v/ a & n yugoslavo (m). ~**ia** /-'slɑ:vɪə/ n Yugoslavia f

yule /ju:l/ n, **yule-tide** /'ju:ltaɪd/ n (old use) Navidades fpl

Z

zany /'zeɪnɪ/ a (-ier, -iest) estrafalario

zeal /zi:l/ n celo m

zealot /'zelət/ n fanático m

zealous /'zeləs/ a entusiasta. ~**ly** /'zeləslɪ/ adv con entusiasmo

zebra /'zebrə/ n cebra f. ~ **crossing** n paso m de cebra

zenith /'zenɪθ/ n cenit m

zero /'zɪərəʊ/ n (pl -os) cero m

zest /zest/ n gusto m; (peel) cáscara f

zigzag /'zɪgzæg/ n zigzag m. ● vi (pt **zigzagged**) zigzaguear

zinc /zɪŋk/ n cinc m

Zionis|m /'zaɪənɪzəm/ n sionismo m. ~**t** n sionista m & f

zip /zɪp/ n cremallera f. ● vt. ~ **(up)** cerrar (la cremallera)

Zip code /'zɪpkəʊd/ n (Amer) código m postal

zip fastener /zɪp'fɑ:snə(r)/ n cremallera f

zircon /'zɜ:kən/ n circón m

zither /'zɪðə(r)/ n cítara f

zodiac /'zəʊdɪæk/ n zodiaco m

zombie /'zɒmbɪ/ n (fam) autómata m & f

zone /zəʊn/ n zona f

zoo /zu:/ n (fam) zoo m, jardín m zoológico. ~**logical** /zəʊə'lɒdʒɪkl/ a zoológico

zoolog|ist /zəʊ'ɒlədʒɪst/ n zoólogo m. ~**y** /zəʊ'ɒlədʒɪ/ n zoología f

zoom /zu:m/ vi ir a gran velocidad. ~ **in** (photo) acercarse rápidamente. ~ **past** pasar zumbando. ~ **lens** n zoom m

Zulu /'zu:lu:/ n zulú m & f

Numbers · Números

zero	0	cero
one (first)	1	uno (primero)
two (second)	2	dos (segundo)
three (third)	3	tres (tercero)
four (fourth)	4	cuatro (cuarto)
five (fifth)	5	cinco (quinto)
six (sixth)	6	seis (sexto)
seven (seventh)	7	siete (séptimo)
eight (eighth)	8	ocho (octavo)
nine (ninth)	9	nueve (noveno)
ten (tenth)	10	diez (décimo)
eleven (eleventh)	11	once (undécimo)
twelve (twelfth)	12	doce (duodécimo)
thirteen (thirteenth)	13	trece (decimotercero)
fourteen (fourteenth)	14	catorce (decimocuarto)
fifteen (fifteenth)	15	quince (decimoquinto)
sixteen (sixteenth)	16	dieciséis (decimosexto)
seventeen (seventeenth)	17	diecisiete (decimoséptimo)
eighteen (eighteenth)	18	dieciocho (decimoctavo)
nineteen (nineteenth)	19	diecinueve (decimonoveno)
twenty (twentieth)	20	veinte (vigésimo)
twenty-one (twenty-first)	21	veintiuno (vigésimo primero)
twenty-two (twenty-second)	22	veintidós (vigésimo segundo)
twenty-three (twenty-third)	23	veintitrés (vigésimo tercero)
twenty-four (twenty-fourth)	24	veinticuatro (vigésimo cuarto)
twenty-five (twenty-fifth)	25	veinticinco (vigésimo quinto)
twenty-six (twenty-sixth)	26	veintiséis (vigésimo sexto)
thirty (thirtieth)	30	treinta (trigésimo)
thirty-one (thirty-first)	31	treinta y uno (trigésimo primero)
forty (fortieth)	40	cuarenta (cuadragésimo)
fifty (fiftieth)	50	cincuenta (quincuagésimo)
sixty (sixtieth)	60	sesenta (sexagésimo)
seventy (seventieth)	70	setenta (septuagésimo)
eighty (eightieth)	80	ochenta

		(octogésimo)
ninety (ninetieth)	90	noventa
		(nonagésimo)
a/one hundred (hundredth)	100	cien (centésimo)
a/one hundred and one (hundred and first)	101	ciento uno (centésimo primero)
two hundred (two hundredth)	200	doscientos (ducentésimo)
three hundred (three hundredth)	300	trescientos (tricentésimo)
four hundred (four hundredth)	400	cuatrocientos (cuadringentésimo)
five hundred (five hundredth)	500	quinientos (quingentésimo)
six hundred (six hundredth)	600	seiscientos (sexcentésimo)
seven hundred (seven hundredth)	700	setecientos (septingentésimo)
eight hundred (eight hundredth)	800	ochocientos (octingentésimo)
nine hundred (nine hundredth)	900	novecientos (noningentésimo)
a/one thousand (thousandth)	1000	mil (milésimo)
two thousand (two thousandth)	2000	dos mil (dos milésimo)
a/one million (millionth)	1,000,000	un millón (millonésimo)

Spanish Verbs · Verbos españoles

Regular verbs:
in -ar (*e.g.* **comprar**)
Present: compr|o, ~as, ~a, ~amos,
~áis, ~an
Future: comprar|é, ~ás, ~á,
~emos, ~éis, ~án
Imperfect: compr|aba, ~abas, ~aba,
~ábamos, ~abais, ~aban
Preterite: compr|é, ~aste, ~ó,
~amos, ~asteis, ~aron
Present subjunctive: compr|e, ~es,
~e, ~emos, ~éis, ~en
Imperfect subjunctive: compr|ara,
~aras ~ara, ~áramos, ~arais,
~aran
compr|ase, ~ases, ~ase,
~ásemos, ~aseis, ~asen
Conditional: comprar|ía, ~ías, ~ía,
~íamos, ~íais, ~ían
Present participle: comprando
Past participle: comprado
Imperative: compra, comprad

in -er (*e.g.* **beber**)
Present: beb|o, ~es, ~e, ~emos,
~éis, ~en
Future: beber|é, ~ás, ~á, ~emos,
~éis, ~án
Imperfect: beb|ía, ~ías, ~ía,
~íamos, ~íais, ~ían
Preterite: beb|í, ~iste, ~ió, ~imos,
~isteis, ~ieron
Present subjunctive: beb|a, ~as, ~a,
~amos, ~áis, ~an
Imperfect subjunctive: beb|iera,
~ieras, ~iera, ~iéramos, ~ierais,
~ieran
beb|iese, ~ieses, ~iese,
~iésemos, ~ieseis, ~iesen
Conditional: beber|ía, ~ías, ~ía,
~íamos, ~íais, ~ían
Present participle: bebiendo
Past participle: bebido
Imperative: bebe, bebed

in -ir (*e.g.* **vivir**)
Present: viv|o, ~es, ~e, ~imos, ~ís,
~en
Future: vivir|é, ~ás, ~á, ~emos,
~éis, ~án
Imperfect: viv|ía, ~ías, ~ía, ~íamos,
~íais, ~ían
Preterite: viv|í, ~iste, ~ió, ~imos,
~isteis, ~ieron

Present subjunctive: viv|a, ~as, ~a,
~amos, ~áis, ~an
Imperfect subjunctive: viv|iera,
~ieras, ~iera, ~iéramos, ~ierais,
~ieran
viv|iese, ~ieses, ~iese,
~iésemos, ~ieseis, ~iesen
Conditional: vivir|ía, ~ías, ~ía,
~íamos, ~íais, ~ían
Present participle: viviendo
Past participle: vivido
Imperative: vive, vivid

Irregular verbs:
[1] cerrar
Present: cierro, cierras, cierra,
cerramos, cerráis, cierran
Present subjunctive: cierre, cierres,
cierre, cerremos, cerréis, cierren
Imperative: cierra, cerrad

[2] contar, mover
Present: cuento, cuentas, cuenta,
contamos, contáis, cuentan
muevo, mueves, mueve,
movemos, movéis, mueven
Present subjunctive: cuente, cuentes,
cuente, contemos, contéis,
cuenten
mueva, muevas mueva,
movamos, mováis, muevan
Imperative: cuenta, contad mueve,
moved

[3] jugar
Present: juego, juegas, juega,
jugamos, jugáis, juegan
Preterite: jug|ué, jugaste, jugó,
jugamos, jugasteis, jugaron
Present subjunctive: juegue, juegues,
juegue, juguemos, juguéis,
jueguen

[4] sentir
Present: siento, sientes, siente,
sentimos, sentís, sienten
Preterite: sentí, sentiste, sintió,
sentimos, sentisteis, sintieron
Present subjunctive: sienta, sientas,
sienta, sintamos, sintáis, sientan
Imperfect subjunctive: sint|iera,
~ieras, ~iera, ~iéramos, ~ierais,
~ieran

sint|iese, ~ieses, ~iese,
~iésemos, ~ieseis, ~iesen
Present participle: sintiendo
Imperative: siente, sentid

[5] pedir
Present: pido, pides, pide, pedimos,
pedís, piden
Preterite: pedí, pediste, pidió,
pedimos, pedisteis, pidieron
Present subjunctive: pid|a, ~as, ~a,
~amos, ~áis, ~an
Imperfect subjunctive: pid|iera,
~ieras, ~iera, ~iéramos, ~ierais,
~ieran
pid|iese, ~ieses, ~iese,
~iésemos, ~ieseis, ~iesen
Present participle: pidiendo
Imperative: pide, pedid

[6] dormir
Present: duermo, duermes, duerme,
dormimos, dormís, duermen
Preterite: dormí, dormiste, durmió,
dormimos, dormisteis, durmieron
Present subjunctive: duerma,
duermas, duerma, durmamos,
durmáis, duerman
Imperfect subjunctive: durm|iera,
~ieras, ~iera, ~iéramos, ~ierais,
~ieran
durm|iese, ~ieses, ~iese,
~iésemos, ~ieseis, ~iesen
Present participle: durmiendo
Imperative: duerme, dormid

[7] dedicar
Preterite: dediqué, dedicaste, dedicó,
dedicamos, dedicasteis, dedicaron
Present subjunctive: dediqu|e, ~ues,
~e, ~emos, ~éis, ~en

[8] delinquir
Present: delinco, delinques,
delinque, delinquimos, delinquís,
delinquen
Present subjunctive: delinc|a, ~as,
~a, ~amos, ~áis, ~an

[9] vencer, esparcir
Present: venzo, vences, vence,
vencemos, vencéis, vencen
esparzo, esparces, esparce,
esparcimos, esparcís, esparcen
Present subjunctive: venz|a, ~as,
~a, ~amos, ~áis, ~an esparz|a,
~as, ~a, ~amos, ~áis, ~an

[10] rechazar
Preterite: rechacé, rechazaste,
rechazó, rechazamos,
rechazasteis, rechazaron
Present subjunctive: rechac|e, ~es,
~e, ~emos, ~éis, ~en

[11] conocer, lucir
Present: conozco, conoces, conoce,
conocemos, conocéis, conocen
luzco, luces, luce, lucimos, lucís,
lucen
Present subjunctive: conozc|a, ~as,
~a, ~amos, ~áis, ~an luzc|a,
~as, ~a, ~amos, ~áis, ~an

[12] pagar
Preterite: pagué, pagaste, pagó,
pagamos, pagasteis, pagaron
Present subjunctive: pagu|e, ~es,
~e, ~emos, ~éis, ~en

[13] distinguir
Present: distingo, distingues,
distingue, distinguimos,
distinguís, distinguen
Present subjunctive: disting|a, ~as,
~a, ~amos, ~áis, ~an

[14] acoger, afligir
Present: acojo, acoges, acoge,
acogemos, acogéis, acogen
aflijo, afliges, aflige, afligimos,
afligís, afligen
Present subjunctive: acoj|a, ~as, ~a,
~amos, ~áis, ~an
aflij|a, ~as, ~a, ~amos, ~áis,
~an

[15] averiguar
Preterite: averigüé, averiguaste,
averiguó, averiguamos,
averiguasteis, averiguaron
Present subjunctive: averigü|e, ~es,
~e, ~emos, ~éis, ~en

[16] agorar
Present: agüero, agüeras, agüera,
agoramos, agoráis, agüeran
Present subjunctive: agüere,
agüeres, agüere, agoremos,
agoréis, agüeren
Imperative: agüera, agorad

[17] huir
Present: huyo, huyes, huye, huimos,
huís, huyen

Preterite: huí, huiste, huyó, huimos,
huisteis, huyeron
Present subjunctive: huy|a, ~as, ~a,
~amos, ~áis, ~an
Imperfect subjunctive: huy|era,
~eras, ~era, ~éramos, ~erais,
~eran
huy|ese, ~eses, ~ese, ~ésemos,
~eseis, ~esen
Present participle: huyendo

[18] **creer**
Preterite: creí, creíste, creyó,
creímos, creísteis, creyeron
Imperfect subjunctive: crey|era,
~eras, ~era, ~éramos, ~erais,
~eran
crey|ese, ~eses, ~ese, ~ésemos,
~eseis, ~esen
Present participle: creyendo
Past participle: creído

[19] **argüir**
Present: arguyo, arguyes, arguye,
argüimos, argüís, arguyen
Preterite: argüí, argüiste, arguyó,
argüimos, argüisteis, arguyeron
Present subjunctive: arguy|a, ~as,
~a, ~amos, ~áis, ~an
Imperfect subjunctive: arguy|era,
~eras, ~era, ~éramos, ~erais,
~eran
arguy|ese, ~eses, ~ese,
~ésemos, ~eseis, ~esen
Present participle: arguyendo
Imperative: arguye, argüid

[20] **vaciar**
Present: vacío, vacías, vacía,
vaciamos, vaciáis, vacían
Present subjunctive: vacíe, vacíes,
vacíe, vaciemos, vaciéis, vacíen
Imperative: vacía, vaciad

[21] **acentuar**
Present: acentúo, acentúas, acentúa,
acentuamos, acentuáis, acentúan
Present subjunctive: acentúe,
acentúes, acentúe, acentuemos,
acentuéis, acentúen
Imperative: acentúa, acentuad

[22] **ateñer, engullir**
Preterite: atañ|í, ~aste, ~ó, ~amos,
~asteis, ~eron engull|í ~iste,
~ó, ~imos, ~isteis, ~eron
Imperfect subjunctive: atañ|era,
~eras, ~era, ~éramos, ~erais,

~eran
atañ|ese, ~eses, ~ese, ~ésemos,
~eseis, ~esen
engull|era, ~eras, ~era,
~éramos, ~erais, ~eran
engull|ese, ~eses, ~ese,
~ésemos, ~eseis, ~esen
Present participle: atañendo
engullendo

[23] **aislar, aullar**
Present: aíslo, aíslas, aísla, aislamos,
aisláis, aíslan
aúllo, aúllas, aúlla, aullamos,
aulláis, aúllan
Present subjunctive: aísle, aísles,
aísle, aislemos, aisléis, aíslen
aúlle, aúlles, aúlle, aullemos,
aulléis, aúllen
Imperative: aísla, aislad
aúlla, aullad

[24] **abolir, garantir**
Present: abolimos, abolís
garantimos, garantís
Present subjunctive: not used
Imperative: abolid
garantid

[25] **andar**
Preterite: anduv|e, ~iste, ~o,
~imos, ~isteis, ~ieron
Imperfect subjunctive: anduv|iera,
~ieras, ~iera, ~iéramos, ~ierais,
~ieran
anduv|iese, ~ieses, ~iese,
~iésemos, ~ieseis, ~iesen

[26] **dar**
Present: doy, das, da, damos, dais,
dan
Preterite: di, diste, dio, dimos,
disteis, dieron
Present subjunctive: dé, des, dé,
demos, deis, den
Imperfect subjunctive: diera, dieras,
diera, diéramos, dierais, dieran
diese, dieses, diese, diésemos,
dieseis, diesen

[27] **estar**
Present: estoy, estás, está, estamos,
estáis, están
Preterite: estuv|e, ~iste, ~o, ~imos,
~isteis, ~ieron
Present subjunctive: esté, estés, esté,
estemos, estéis, estén

Imperfect subjunctive: estuv|iera, ~ieras, ~iera, ~iéramos, ~ierais, ~ieran
estuv|iese, ~ieses, ~iese, ~iésemos, ~ieseis, ~iesen
Imperative: está, estad

[28] caber
Present: quepo, cabes, cabe, cabemos, cabéis, caben
Future: cabr|é, ~ás, ~á, ~emos, ~éis, ~án
Preterite: cup|e, ~iste, ~o, ~imos, ~isteis, ~ieron
Present subjunctive: quep|a, ~as, ~a, ~amos, ~áis, ~an
Imperfect subjunctive: cup|iera, ~ieras, ~iera, ~iéramos, ~ierais, ~ieran
cup|iese, ~ieses, ~iese, ~iésemos, ~ieseis, ~iesen
Conditional: cabr|ía, ~ías, ~ía, ~íamos, ~íais, ~ían

[29] caer
Present: caigo, caes, cae, caemos, caéis, caen
Preterite: caí, caiste, cayó, caímos, caísteis, cayeron
Present subjunctive: caig|a, ~as, ~a, ~amos, ~áis, ~an
Imperfect subjunctive: cay|era, ~eras, ~era, ~éramos, ~erais, ~eran
cay|ese, ~eses, ~ese, ~ésemos, ~eseis, ~esen
Present participle: cayendo
Past participle: caído

[30] haber
Present: he, has, ha, hemos, habéis, han
Future: habr|é ~ás, ~á, ~emos, ~éis, ~án
Preterite: hub|e, ~iste, ~o, ~imos, ~isteis, ~ieron
Present subjunctive: hay|a, ~as, ~a, ~amos, ~áis, ~an
Imperfect subjunctive: hub|iera, ~ieras, ~iera, ~iéramos, ~ierais, ~ieran
hub|iese, ~ieses, ~iese, ~iésemos, ~ieseis, ~iesen
Conditional: habr|ía, ~ías, ~ía, ~íamos, ~íais, ~ían
Imperative: habe, habed

[31] hacer

Present: hago, haces, hace, hacemos, hacéis, hacen
Future: har|é, ~ás, ~á, ~emos, ~éis, ~án
Preterite: hice, hiciste, hizo, hicimos, hicisteis, hicieron
Present subjunctive: hag|a, ~as, ~a, ~amos, ~áis, ~an
Imperfect subjunctive: hic|iera, ~ieras, ~iera, ~iéramos, ~ierais, ~ieran
hic|iese, ~ieses, ~iese, ~iésemos, ~ieseis, ~iesen
Conditional: har|ía, ~ías, ~ía, ~íamos, ~íais, ~ían
Past participle: hecho
Imperative: haz, haced

[32] placer
Preterite: plació/plugo
Present subjunctive: plazca
Imperfect subjunctive: placiera/pluguiera
placiese/pluguiese

[33] poder
Present: puedo, puedes, puede, podemos, podéis, pueden
Future: podr|é, ~ás, ~á, ~emos, ~éis, ~án
Preterite: pud|e, ~iste, ~o, ~imos, ~isteis, ~ieron
Present subjunctive: pueda, puedas, pueda, podamos, podáis, puedan
Imperfect subjunctive: pud|iera, ~ieras, ~iera, ~iéramos, ~ierais, ~ieran
pud|iese, ~ieses, ~iese, ~iésemos, ~ieseis, ~iesen
Conditional: podr|ía, ~ías, ~ía, ~íamos, ~íais, ~ían
Past participle: pudiendo

[34] poner
Present: pongo, pones, pone, ponemos, ponéis, ponen
Future: pondr|é, ~ás, ~á, ~emos, ~éis, ~án
Preterite: pus|e, ~iste, ~o, ~imos, ~isteis, ~ieron
Present subjunctive: pong|a, ~as, ~a, ~amos, ~áis, ~an
Imperfect subjunctive: pus|iera, ~ieras, ~iera, ~iéramos, ~ierais, ~ieran
pus|iese, ~ieses, ~iese, ~iésemos, ~ieseis, ~iesen

Conditional: pondr|ía, ~ías, ~ía,
~íamos, ~íais, ~ían
Past participle: puesto
Imperative: pon, poned

[35] querer
Present: quiero, quieres, quiere,
queremos, queréis, quieren
Future: querr|é, ~ás, ~á, ~emos,
~éis, ~án
Preterite: quis|e, ~iste, ~o, ~imos,
~isteis, ~ieron
Present subjunctive: quiera, quieras,
quiera, queramos, queráis,
quieran
Imperfect subjunctive: quis|iera,
~ieras, ~iera, ~iéramos, ~ierais,
~ieran
quis|iese, ~ieses, ~iese,
~iésemos, ~ieseis, ~iesen
Conditional: querr|ía, ~ías, ~ía,
~íamos, ~íais, ~ían
Imperative: quiere, quered

[36] raer
Present: raigo/rayo, raes, rae,
raemos, raéis, raen
Preterite: raí, raíste, rayó, raímos,
raísteis, rayeron
Present subjunctive: raig|a, ~as, ~a,
~amos, ~áis, ~an
ray|a, ~as, ~a, ~amos, ~áis, ~an
Imperfect subjunctive: ray|era,
~eras, ~era, ~éramos, ~erais,
~eran
ray|ese, ~eses, ~ese, ~ésemos,
~eseis, ~esen
Present participle: rayendo
Past participle: raído

[37] roer
Present: roo/roigo/royo, roes, roe,
roemos, roéis, roen
Preterite: roí, roíste, royó, roímos,
roísteis, royeron
Present subjunctive: roa/roiga/roya,
roas, roa, roamos, roáis, roan
Imperfect subjunctive: roy|era,
~eras, ~era, ~éramos, ~erais,
~eran
roy|ese, ~eses, ~ese, ~ésemos,
~eseis, ~esen
Present participle: royendo
Past participle: roído

[38] saber
Present: sé, sabes, sabe, sabemos,
sabéis, saben

Future: sabr|é, ~ás, ~á, ~emos,
~éis, ~án
Preterite: sup|e, ~iste, ~o, ~imos,
~isteis, ~ieron
Present subjunctive: sep|a, ~as, ~a,
~amos, ~áis, ~an
Imperfect subjunctive: sup|iera,
~ieras, ~iera, ~iéramos, ~ierais,
~ieran
sup|iese, ~ieses, ~iese,
~iésemos, ~ieseis, ~iesen
Conditional: sabr|ía, ~ías, ~ía,
~íamos, ~íais, ~ían

[39] ser
Present: soy, eres, es, somos, sois,
son
Imperfect: era, eras, era, éramos,
erais, eran
Preterite: fui, fuiste, fue, fuimos,
fuisteis, fueron
Present subjunctive: se|a, ~as, ~a,
~amos, ~áis, ~an
Imperfect subjunctive: fu|era, ~eras,
~era, ~éramos, ~erais, ~eran
fu|ese, ~eses, ~ese, ~ésemos,
~eseis, ~esen
Imperative: sé, sed

[40] tener
Present: tengo, tienes, tiene,
tenemos, tenéis, tienen
Future: tendr|é, ~ás, ~á, ~emos,
~éis, ~án
Preterite: tuv|e, ~iste, ~o, ~imos,
~isteis, ~ieron
Present subjunctive: teng|a, ~as, ~a,
~amos, ~áis, ~an
Imperfect subjunctive: tuv|iera,
~ieras, ~iera, ~iéramos, ~ierais,
~ieran
tuv|iese, ~ieses, ~iese,
~iésemos, ~ieseis, ~iesen
Conditional: tendr|ía, ~ías, ~ía,
~íamos, ~íais, ~ían
Imperative: ten, tened

[41] traer
Present: traigo, traes, trae, traemos,
traéis, traen
Preterite: traj|e, ~iste, ~o, ~imos,
~isteis, ~eron
Present subjunctive: traig|a, ~as,
~a, ~amos, ~áis, ~an
Imperfect subjunctive: traj|era,
~eras, ~era, ~éramos, ~erais,
~eran

traj|ese, ~eses, ~ese, ~ésemos,
~eseis, ~esen
Present participle: trayendo
Past participle: traído

[42] valer
Present: valgo, vales, vale, valemos,
valéis, valen
Future: vald|ré, ~ás, ~á, ~emos,
~éis, ~án
Present subjunctive: valg|a, ~as, ~a,
~amos ~áis, ~an
Conditional: vald|ría, ~ías, ~ía,
~íamos, ~íais, ~ían
Imperative: val/vale, valed

[43] ver
Present: veo, ves, ve, vemos, véis,
ven
Imperfect: ve|ía, ~ías, ~ía, ~íamos,
~íais, ~ían
Preterite: vi, viste, vio, vimos,
visteis, vieron
Present subjunctive: ve|a, ~as, ~a,
~amos, ~áis, ~an
Past participle: visto

[44] yacer
Present: yazco/yazgo/yago, yaces,
yace, yacemos, yacéis, yacen
Present   subjunctive:
yazca/yazga/yaga, yazcas,
yazca, yazcamos, yazcáis, yazcan
Imperative: yace/yaz, yaced

[45] asir
Present: asgo, ases, ase, asimos, asís,
asen
Present subjunctive: asg|a, ~as, ~a,
~amos, ~áis, ~an

[46] decir
Present: digo, dices, dice, decimos,
decís, dicen
Future: dir|é, ~ás, ~á, ~emos,
~éis, ~án
Preterite: dij|e, ~iste, ~o, ~imos,
~isteis, ~eron
Present subjunctive: dig|a, ~as, ~a,
~amos, ~áis, ~an
Imperfect subjunctive: dij|era,
~eras, ~era, ~éramos, ~erais,
~eran
dij|ese, ~eses, ~ese, ~ésemos,
~eseis, ~esen
Conditional: dir|ía, ~ías, ~ía,
~íamos, ~íais, ~ían
Present participle: dicho

Imperative: di, decid

[47] reducir
Present: reduzco, reduces, reduce,
reducimos, reducís, reducen
Preterite: reduj|e, ~iste, ~o, ~imos,
~isteis, ~eron
Present subjunctive: reduzc|a, ~as,
~a, ~amos, ~áis, ~an
Imperfect subjunctive: reduj|era,
~eras, ~era, ~éramos, ~erais,
~eran
reduj|ese, ~eses, ~ese, ~ésemos,
~eseis, ~esen

[48] erguir
Present: irgo, irgues, irgue,
erguimos, erguís, irguen
yergo, yergues, yergue, erguimos,
erguís, yerguen
Preterite: erguí, erguiste, irguió,
erguimos, erguisteis, irguieron
Present subjunctive: irg|a, ~as, ~a,
~amos, ~áis, ~an
yerg|a, ~as, ~a, ~amos, ~áis,
~an
Imperfect subjunctive: irgu|iera,
~ieras, ~iera, ~iéramos, ~ierais,
~ieran
irgu|iese, ~ieses, ~iese,
~iésemos, ~ieseis, ~iesen
Present participle: irguiendo
Imperative: irgue/yergue, erguid

[49] ir
Present: voy, vas, va, vamos, vais,
van
Imperfect: iba, ibas, iba, íbamos,
ibais, iban
Preterite: fui, fuiste, fue, fuimos,
fuisteis, fueron
Present subjunctive: vay|a, ~as, ~a,
~amos, ~áis, ~an
Imperfect subjunctive: fu|era, ~eras,
~era, ~éramos, ~erais, ~eran
fu|ese, ~eses, ~ese, ~ésemos,
~eseis, ~esen
Present participle: yendo
Imperative: ve, id

[50] oír
Present: oigo, oyes, oye, oímos, oís,
oyen
Preterite: oí, oíste, oyó, oímos, oísteis,
oyeron
Present subjunctive: oig|a, ~as, ~a,
~amos, ~áis, ~an

Imperfect subjunctive: oy|era, ~eras,
~era, ~éramos, ~erais, ~eran
oy|ese, ~eses, ~ese, ~ésemos,
~eseis, ~esen
Present participle: oyendo
Past participle: oído
Imperative: oye, oíd

[51] reír
Present: río, ríes, ríe, reímos, reís,
ríen
Preterite: reí, reíste, rió, reímos,
reísteis, rieron
Present subjunctive: ría, rías, ría,
riamos, riáis, rían
Present participle: riendo
Past participle: reído
Imperative: ríe, reíd

[52] salir
Present: salgo, sales, sale, salimos,
salís, salen
Future: saldr|é, ~ás, ~á, ~emos,
~éis, ~án

Present subjunctive: salg|a, ~as, ~a,
~amos, ~áis, ~an
Conditional: saldr|ía, ~ías, ~ía,
~íamos, ~íais, ~ían
Imperative: sal, salid

[53] venir
Present: vengo, vienes, viene,
venimos, venís, vienen
Future: vendr|é, ~ás, ~á, ~emos,
~éis, ~án
Preterite: vin|e, ~iste, ~o, ~imos,
~isteis, ~ieron
Present subjunctive: veng|a, ~as,
~a, ~amos, ~áis, ~an
Imperfect subjunctive: vin|iera,
~ieras, ~iera, ~iéramos, ~ierais,
~ieran
vin|iese, ~ieses, ~iese,
~iésemos, ~ieseis, ~iesen
Conditional: vendr|ía, ~ías, ~ía,
~íamos, ~íais, ~ían
Present participle: viniendo
Imperative: ven, venid

Verbos Irregulares Ingleses

Infinitivo	Pretérito	Participio pasado
arise	arose	arisen
awake	awoke	awoken
be	was	been
bear	bore	borne
beat	beat	beaten
become	became	become
befall	befell	befallen
beget	begot	begotten
begin	began	begun
behold	beheld	beheld
bend	bent	bent
beset	beset	beset
bet	bet, betted	bet, betted
bid	bade, bid	bidden, bid
bind	bound	bound
bite	bit	bitten
bleed	bled	bled
blow	blew	blown
break	broke	broken
breed	bred	bred
bring	brought	brought
broadcast	broadcast(ed)	broadcast
build	built	built
burn	burnt, burned	burnt, burned
burst	burst	burst
buy	bought	bought
cast	cast	cast
catch	caught	caught
choose	chose	chosen
cleave	clove, cleft, cleaved	cloven, cleft, cleaved
cling	clung	clung
clothe	clothed, clad	clothed, clad
come	came	come
cost	cost	cost
creep	crept	crept
crow	crowed, crew	crowed
cut	cut	cut
deal	dealt	dealt
dig	dug	dug
do	did	done
draw	drew	drawn
dream	dreamt, dreamed	dreamt, dreamed
drink	drank	drunk
drive	drove	driven
dwell	dwelt	dwelt
eat	ate	eaten
fall	fell	fallen
feed	fed	fed
feel	felt	felt
fight	fought	fought
find	found	found

Infinitivo	Pretérito	Participio pasado
flee	fled	fled
fling	flung	flung
fly	flew	flown
forbear	forbore	forborne
forbid	forbad(e)	forbidden
forecast	forecast(ed)	forecast(ed)
foresee	foresaw	foreseen
foretell	foretold	foretold
forget	forgot	forgotten
forgive	forgave	forgiven
forsake	forsook	forsaken
freeze	froze	frozen
gainsay	gainsaid	gainsaid
get	got	got
give	gave	given
go	went	gone
grind	ground	ground
grow	grew	grown
hang	hung, hanged	hung, hanged
have	had	had
hear	heard	heard
hew	hewed	hewn, hewed
hide	hid	hidden
hit	hit	hit
hold	held	held
hurt	hurt	hurt
inlay	inlaid	inlaid
keep	kept	kept
kneel	knelt	knelt
knit	knitted, knit	knitted, knit
know	knew	known
lay	laid	laid
lead	led	led
lean	leaned, leant	leaned, leant
leap	leaped, leapt	leaped, leapt
learn	learned, learnt	learned, learnt
leave	left	left
lend	lent	lent
let	let	let
lie	lay	lain
light	lit, lighted	lit, lighted
lose	lost	lost
make	made	made
mean	meant	meant
meet	met	met
mislay	mislaid	mislaid
mislead	misled	misled
misspell	misspelt	misspelt
mistake	mistook	mistaken
misunderstand	misunderstood	misunderstood
mow	mowed	mown
outbid	outbid	outbid
outdo	outdid	outdone
outgrow	outgrew	outgrown
overcome	overcame	overcome

Infinitivo	*Pretérito*	*Participio pasado*
overdo	overdid	overdone
overhang	overhung	overhung
overhear	overheard	overheard
override	overrode	overridden
overrun	overran	overrun
oversee	oversaw	overseen
overshoot	overshot	overshot
oversleep	overslept	overslept
overtake	overtook	overtaken
overthrow	overthrew	overthrown
partake	partook	partaken
pay	paid	paid
prove	proved	proved, proven
put	put	put
quit	quitted, quit	quitted, quit
read /ri:d/	read /red/	read /red/
rebuild	rebuilt	rebuilt
redo	redid	redone
rend	rent	rent
repay	repaid	repaid
rewrite	rewrote	rewritten
rid	rid	rid
ride	rode	ridden
ring	rang	rung
rise	rose	risen
run	ran	run
saw	sawed	sawn, sawed
say	said	said
see	saw	seen
seek	sought	sought
sell	sold	sold
send	sent	sent
set	set	set
sew	sewed	sewn, sewed
shake	shook	shaken
shear	sheared	shorn, sheared
shed	shed	shed
shine	shone	shone
shoe	shod	shod
shoot	shot	shot
show	showed	shown, showed
shrink	shrank	shrunk
shut	shut	shut
sing	sang	sung
sink	sank	sunk
sit	sat	sat
slay	slew	slain
sleep	slept	slept
slide	slid	slid
sling	slung	slung
slit	slit	slit
smell	smelt, smelled	smelt, smelled
smite	smote	smitten
sow	sowed	sown, sowed
speak	spoke	spoken

Infinitivo	*Pretérito*	*Participio pasado*
speed	speeded, sped	speeded, sped
spell	spelt, spelled	spelt, spelled
spend	spent	spent
spill	spilt, spilled	spilt, spilled
spin	spun	spun
spit	spat	spat
split	split	split
spoil	spoilt, spoiled	spoilt, spoiled
spread	spread	spread
spring	sprang	sprung
stand	stood	stood
steal	stole	stolen
stick	stuck	stuck
sting	stung	stung
stink	stank, stunk	stunk
strew	strewed	strewn, strewed
stride	strode	stridden
strike	struck	struck
string	strung	strung
strive	strove	striven
swear	swore	sworn
sweep	swept	swept
swell	swelled	swollen, swelled
swim	swam	swum
swing	swung	swung
take	took	taken
teach	taught	taught
tear	tore	torn
tell	told	told
think	thought	thought
thrive	thrived, throve	thrived, thriven
throw	threw	thrown
thrust	thrust	thrust
tread	trod	trodden, trod
unbend	unbent	unbent
undergo	underwent	undergone
understand	understood	understood
undertake	undertook	undertaken
undo	undid	undone
upset	upset	upset
wake	woke, waked	woken, waked
waylay	waylaid	waylaid
wear	wore	worn
weave	wove	woven
weep	wept	wept
win	won	won
wind	wound	wound
withdraw	withdrew	withdrawn
withhold	withheld	withheld
withstand	withstood	withstood
wring	wrung	wrung
write	wrote	written